P9-BJU-350

Twentieth-Century
Literary Criticism

Topics Volume

Guide to Gale Literary Criticism Series

For criticism on	Consult these Gale series
Authors now living or who died after December 31, 1959	*CONTEMPORARY LITERARY CRITICISM (CLC)*
Authors who died between 1900 and 1959	*TWENTIETH-CENTURY LITERARY CRITICISM (TCLC)*
Authors who died between 1800 and 1899	*NINETEENTH-CENTURY LITERATURE CRITICISM (NCLC)*
Authors who died between 1400 and 1799	*LITERATURE CRITICISM FROM 1400 TO 1800 (LC)* *SHAKESPEAREAN CRITICISM (SC)*
Authors who died before 1400	*CLASSICAL AND MEDIEVAL LITERATURE CRITICISM (CMLC)*
Authors of books for children and young adults	*CHILDREN'S LITERATURE REVIEW (CLR)*
Dramatists	*DRAMA CRITICISM (DC)*
Poets	*POETRY CRITICISM (PC)*
Short story writers	*SHORT STORY CRITICISM (SSC)*
Black writers of the past two hundred years	*BLACK LITERATURE CRITICISM (BLC)*
Hispanic writers of the late nineteenth and twentieth centuries	*HISPANIC LITERATURE CRITICISM (HLC)*
Native North American writers and orators of the eighteenth, nineteenth, and twentieth centuries	*NATIVE NORTH AMERICAN LITERATURE (NNAL)*
Major authors from the Renaissance to the present	*WORLD LITERATURE CRITICISM, 1500 TO THE PRESENT (WLC)*

ISSN 0276-8178

Volume 82

Twentieth-Century Literary Criticism

Topics Volume

**Excerpts from Criticism of Various Topics
in Twentieth-Century Literature, including Literary
and Critical Movements, Prominent Themes and
Genres, Anniversary Celebrations, and Surveys
of National Literatures**

Jennifer Baise
Editor

Thomas Ligotti
Associate Editor

The Gale Group

DETROIT • SAN FRANCISCO • LONDON • BOSTON • WOODBRIDGE, CT

STAFF

Jennifer Baise, *Editor*

Thomas Ligotti, *Associate Editor*

Maria Franklin, *Interim Permissions Manager*
Kimberly F. Smilay, *Permissions Specialist*
Kelly A. Quin, *Permissions Associates*
Sandy Gore, *Permissions Assistant*

Victoria B. Cariappa, *Research Manager*
Michele P. LaMeau, Andrew Guy Malonis, Barbara McNeil, Gary J. Oudersluys, Maureen Richards, *Research Specialists*
Tamara C. Nott, Tracie A. Richardson, Cheryl L. Warnock, *Research Associates*
Corrine Stocker, *Research Assistant*

Mary Beth Trimper, *Production Director*
Deborah L. Milliken, *Production Assistant*

Christine O'Bryan, *Desktop Publisher*
Randy Bassett, *Image Database Supervisor*
Robert Duncan, Michael Logusz, *Imaging Specialists*
Pamela Reed, *Imaging Coordinator*

Library of Congress Catalog Card Number 76-46132
ISBN 0-7876-2746-1
ISSN 0276-8178

Printed in the United States of America
10 9 8 7 6 5 4 3 2 1

Contents

Preface   vii

Acknowledgments   xi

Preface

Since its inception more than fifteen years ago, *Twentieth-Century Literary Criticism* has been purchased and used by nearly 10,000 school, public, and college or university libraries. *TCLC* has covered more than 500 authors, representing 58 nationalities, and over 25,000 titles. No other reference source has surveyed the critical response to twentieth-century authors and literature as thoroughly as *TCLC*. In the words of one reviewer, "there is nothing comparable available." *TCLC* "is a gold mine of information—dates, pseudonyms, biographical information, and criticism from books and periodicals—which many libraries would have difficulty assembling on their own."

Scope of the Series

TCLC is designed to serve as an introduction to authors who died between 1900 and 1960 and to the most significant interpretations of these author's works. The great poets, novelists, short story writers, playwrights, and philosophers of this period are frequently studied in high school and college literature courses. In organizing and excerpting the vast amount of critical material written on these authors, *TCLC* helps students develop valuable insight into literary history, promotes a better understanding of the texts, and sparks ideas for papers and assignments. Each entry in *TCLC* presents a comprehensive survey of an author's career or an individual work of literature and provides the user with a multiplicity of interpretations and assessments. Such variety allows students to pursue their own interests; furthermore, it fosters an awareness that literature is dynamic and responsive to many different opinions.

Every fourth volume of *TCLC* is devoted to literary topics. These topic entries widen the focus of the series from individual authors to such broader subjects as literary movements, prominent themes in twentieth-century literature, literary reaction to political and historical events, significant eras in literary history, prominent literary anniversaries, and the literatures of cultures that are often overlooked by English-speaking readers.

TCLC is designed as a companion series to Gale's *Contemporary Literary Criticism*, which reprints commentary on authors now living or who have died since 1960. Because of the different periods under consideration, there is no duplication of material between *CLC* and *TCLC*. For additional information about *CLC* and Gale's other criticism titles, users should consult the Guide to Gale Literary Criticism Series preceding the title page in this volume.

Coverage

Each volume of *TCLC* is carefully compiled to present:

- criticism of authors, or literary topics, representing a variety of genres and nationalities

- both major and lesser-known writers and literary works of the period

- 6-12 authors or 3-6 topics per volume

- individual entries that survey critical response to each author's work or each topic in literary history, including early criticism to reflect initial reactions; later criticism to represent any rise or decline in reputation; and current retrospective analyses.

Organization of This Book

An author entry consists of the following elements: author heading, biographical and critical introduction, list of principal works, excerpts of criticism (each preceded by an annotation and a bibliographic citation), and a bibliography of further reading.

- The **Author Heading** consists of the name under which the author most commonly wrote, followed by birth and death dates. If an author wrote consistently under a pseudonym, the pseudonym will be listed in the author heading and the real name given in parentheses on the first line of the biographical and critical introduction. Also located at the beginning of the introduction to the author entry are any name variations under which an author wrote, including transliterated forms for authors whose languages use nonroman alphabets.

- The **Biographical and Critical Introduction** outlines the author's life and career, as well as the critical issues surrounding his or her work. References to past volumes of *TCLC* are provided at the beginning of the introduction. Additional sources of information in other biographical and critical reference series published by Gale, including *Short Story Criticism, Children's Literature Review, Contemporary Authors, Dictionary of Literary Biography,* and *Something about the Author,* are listed in a box at the end of the entry.

- Some *TCLC* entries include **Portraits** of the author. Entries also may contain reproductions of materials pertinent to an author's career, including manuscript pages, title pages, dust jackets, letters, and drawings, as well as photographs of important people, places, and events in an author's life.

- The **List of Principal Works** is chronological by date of first book publication and identifies the genre of each work. In the case of foreign authors with both foreign-language publications and English translations, the title and date of the first English-language edition are given in brackets. Unless otherwise indicated, dramas are dated by first performance, not first publication.

- Critical excerpts are prefaced by **Annotations** providing the reader with information about both the critic and the criticism that follows. Included are the critic's reputation, individual approach to literary criticism, and particular expertise in an author's works. Also noted are the relative importance of a work of criticism, the scope of the excerpt, and the growth of critical controversy or changes in critical trends regarding an author. In some cases, these annotations cross-reference excerpts by critics who discuss each other's commentary.

- A complete **Bibliographic Citation** designed to facilitate location of the original essay or book precedes each piece of criticism.

- Criticism is arranged chronologically in each author entry to provide a perspective on changes in critical evaluation over the years. All titles of works by the author featured in the entry are printed in boldface type to enable the user to easily locate discussion of particular works. Also for purposes of easier identification, the critic's name and the publication date of the essay are given at the beginning of each piece of criticism. Unsigned criticism is preceded by the title of the journal in which it appeared. Some of the excerpts in *TCLC* also contain translated material. Unless otherwise noted, translations in brackets are by the editors; translations in parentheses or continuous with the text are by the critic. Publication information (such as footnotes or page and line references to specific editions of works) have been deleted at the editor's discretion to provide smoother reading of the text.

- An annotated list of **Further Reading** appearing at the end of each author entry suggests secondary sources on the author. In some cases it includes essays for which the editors could not obtain reprint rights.

Cumulative Indexes

- Each volume of *TCLC* contains a cumulative **Author Index** listing all authors who have appeared in Gale's Literary Criticism Series, along with cross references to such biographical series as *Contemporary Authors* and *Dictionary of Literary Biography*. For readers' convenience, a complete list of Gale titles included appears on the first page of the author index. Useful for locating authors within the various series, this index is particularly valuable for those authors who are identified by a certain period but who, because of their death dates, are placed in another, or for those authors whose careers span two periods. For example, F. Scott Fitzgerald is found in *TCLC,* yet a writer often associated with him, Ernest Hemingway, is found in *CLC.*

- Each *TCLC* volume includes a cumulative **Nationality Index** which lists all authors who have appeared in *TCLC* volumes, arranged alphabetically under their respective nationalities, as well as Topics volume entries devoted to particular national literatures.

- Each new volume in Gale's Literary Criticism Series includes a cumulative **Topic Index,** which lists all literary topics treated in *NCLC, TCLC, LC 1400-1800,* and the *CLC* yearbook.

- Each new volume of *TCLC*, with the exception of the Topics volumes, includes a **Title Index** listing the titles of all literary works discussed in the volume. In response to numerous suggestions from librarians, Gale has also produced a **Special Paperbound Edition** of the *TCLC* title index. This annual cumulation lists all titles discussed in the series since its inception and is issued with the first volume of *TCLC* published each year. Additional copies of the index are available on request. Librarians and patrons will welcome this separate index; it saves shelf space, is easy to use, and is recyclable upon receipt of the following year's cumulation. Titles discussed in the Topics volume entries are not included *TCLC* cumulative index.

Citing Twentieth-Century Literary Criticism

When writing papers, students who quote directly from any volume in Gale's literary Criticism Series may use the following general forms to footnote reprinted criticism. The first example pertains to materials drawn from periodicals, the second to material reprinted from books.

[1]William H. Slavick, "Going to School to DuBose Heyward," *The Harlem Renaissance Reexamined,* (AMS Press, 1987); excerpted and reprinted in *Twentieth-Century Literary Criticism,* Vol. 59, ed. Jennifer Gariepy (Detroit: Gale Research, 1995), pp. 94-105.

[2]George Orwell, "Reflections on Gandhi," *Partisan Review,* 6 (Winter 1949), pp. 85-92; excerpted and reprinted in *Twentieth-Century Literary Criticism,* Vol. 59, ed. Jennifer Gariepy (Detroit: Gale Research, 1995), pp. 40-3.

Suggestions Are Welcome

In response to suggestions, several features have been added to *TCLC* since the series began, including annotations to excerpted criticism, a cumulative index to authors in all Gale literary criticism series, entries devoted to criticism on a single work by a major author, more extensive illustrations, and a title index listing all literary works discussed in the series since its inception.

Readers who wish to suggest authors or topics to appear in future volumes, or who have other suggestions, are cordially invited to write the editors.

Acknowledgments

The editors wish to thank the copyright holders of the excerpted criticism included in this volume and the permissions managers of many book and magazine publishing companies for assisting us in securing reproduction rights. We are also grateful to the staffs of the Detroit Public Library, the Library of Congress, the University of Detroit Mercy Library, Wayne State University Purdy/Kresge Library Complex, and the University of Michigan Libraries for making their resources available to us. Following is a list of the copyright holders who have granted us permission to reproduce material in this volume of *TCLC*. Every effort has been made to trace copyright, but if omissions have been made, please let us know.

COPYRIGHTED EXCERPTS IN *TCLC,* VOLUME 82, WERE REPRODUCED FROM THE FOLLOWING PERIODICALS:

American Drama, v. 5, Fall, 1995. Copyright © 1995, American Drama Institute. Reproduced by permission.—*American Poetry Review*, v. 20, May-June, 1991. Copyright © 1991 by World Poetry, Inc. Reproduced by permission of the author.—*Arizona Quarterly*, v. 30, Summer, 1974, for "The Word Out of the Sea: A View of Crane's 'The Open Boat'" by Max L. Autrey. Copyright © 1974 by the Regents of the University of Arizona. Reproduced by permission of the publisher and the author.—*Ball State University Forum*, v. XIV, Summer, 1973. Copyright © 1973 by Ball State University.—*College Literature*, v. 22, June, 1995. Copyright © 1995 by West Chester University. Reproduced by permission.—*Comparative Drama*, v. 14, Spring, 1980; v. 15, Spring, 1981. © copyright 1980, 1981 by the Editors of *Comparative Drama*. Both reproduced by permission.—*Conradiana*, v. VI, 1974. Reproduced by permission.—*Contemporary Literature*, v. 27, Winter, 1986. © 1986 by the Board of Regents of the University of Wisconsin System. Reprinted by permission of The University of Wisconsin Press.—*Critical Quarterly*, v. 38, Autumn, 1996. © 1996. Reproduced by permission of Blackwell Publishers.—*Critique: Studies in Modern Fiction*, v. XXVI, Spring, 1985. Copyright © 1985 Helen Dwight Reid Educational Foundation. Reproduced with permission of the Helen Dwight Reid Educational Foundation, published by Heldref Publications, 1319 18th Street, NW, Washington, DC 20036-1802.—*English Studies*, v. 66, February, 1985. Reproduced by permission.—*Essays in Criticism*, v. XLVI, 1996. © 1996. Reproduced by permission of Oxford University Press.—*Forum for Modern Language Studies*, v. IX, July, 1973. Reproduced by permission.—*Journal of American Culture*, v. 10, Summer, 1987. Copyright © 1987 by Ray B. Browne. All rights reserved. Reproduced by permission.—*Living Blues*, Autumn, 1970 for "If Blues Was Reefers" by Paul Garon. Reproduced by permission of the author.—*MELUS*, v. 10, Spring, 1983; v. 12, 1985. Copyright, *MELUS*, The Society for the Study of Multi-Ethnic Literature of the United States, 1983, 1985. Both reproduced by permission.—*Modern Drama*, v. XXV, December, 1982; v. XXIX, September, 1986; v. XXXVI, December, 1993. © 1982, 1986, 1993 University of Toronto, Graduate Centre for Study of Drama. All reproduced by permission.—*Modern Fiction Studies*, v. 23, Winter, 1977-78. Copyright © 1977 Helen Dwight Reid Educational Foundation. Reproduced with permission of the Helen Dwight Reid Educational Foundation, published by Heldref Publications, 1319 18th Street, NW, Washington, DC 20036-1802.—*Modern Poetry Studies*, v. 6, Autumn, 1975. Copyright 1975, by Media Study, Inc. Reproduced by permission.—*New England Review*, v. 18, Summer, 1997 for "Petrarch, Shakespeare, and the Blues" by Carol Frost. Copyright © 1997 by Middlebury College. Reproduced by permission of the author.—*Novel: A Forum on Fiction*, v. 8, Winter, 1975. Copyright NOVEL Corp. © 1975. Reproduced with permission.—*Partisan Review*, v. XXXIV, Fall, 1967. Copyright © 1967 by *Partisan Review*. Reproduced by permission.—*Philological Quarterly*, v. 69, Winter, 1990 for "The Marine Metaphor, Henry James, and the Moral Center of 'The Awkward Age'" by Greg W. Zacharias. Copyright © 1990 by The University of Iowa. Reproduced by permission of the author.—*Science Fiction Studies*, v. 19, July, 1992. Copyright © 1992 by SFS Publications. Reproduced by permission.—*South Dakota Review*, v. 20, Autumn, 1982. © 1982, University of South Dakota. Reproduced by permission.— *Studies in American Fiction*, v 2, Autumn, 1974; v. 16, Autumn, 1988. Copyright © 1974, 1988 Northeastern University. Both reproduced by permission.—*Studies in Black Literature*, v. 6, Fall, 1975. Copyright ©1975 by the editor. Reproduced by permission.—*Studies in Short Fiction*, v. 30, Fall, 1993. Copyright © 1993 by Newberry College. Reproduced by permission.—*Studies in the Novel*, v. 11, Spring, 1970; v. XVIII, Spring, 1986; v. XXII, Spring, 1990. Copyright © 1970, 1986, 1990 by North Texas State University. All reproduced by permission.—*T. S. Eliot Review*, v. 3, 1976 for "Eliot and 'Huck Finn': River and Sea in 'The Dry Salvages'" by Lois A. Cuddy. Reproduced by permission of the author.— *Texas Studies in Literature and Language*, v. X, Spring, 1968; v. 28, Fall, 1986. © 1968, 1986. Both reproduced by permission of the University of Texas Press.—*The Hemingway Review*, v. 12, Fall, 1992. Copyright ©1992 by The Ernest Hemingway Foundation. All rights reserved. Reproduced by permission.—*The Hopkins Quarterly*, v. 11, January, 1976. Reproduced by permission.—*The Literary Half-Yearly*, v. XXIII, July, 1982. © 1982 *The Literary Half-Yearly*. Reproduced by permission.—*The Literary Review*, v. 26, Summer, 1983. for "Kafka's Traffic in Women: Gender, Power, and Sexuality" by Evelyn Torton Beck. Copyright © 1983 by Evelyn Torton Beck. Fairleigh Dickinson University. Reproduced by permission of the author.—*The Massachusetts Review*, 1967. Copyright © 1967. Reproduced from *The Massachusetts Review*, The Massachusetts Review, Inc. by permission.—*The Midwest Quarterly*, v.

The Blues in Literature

INTRODUCTION

Blues music is generally regarded as having derived from African music and African-American "field hollers," improvised songs that were used by slaves to communicate their whereabouts to overseers, to set the pace for manual labor, and to communicate in code with other slaves. Field hollers developed into work songs and spirituals that were sung by black farmers and laborers in the rural South, particularly in the Mississippi Delta region. Early blues musicians carried the form throughout the South; during the Industrial Revolution, African-Americans moved north to cities to seek jobs, bringing blues music with them. Cornet player W. C. Handy is often credited as the first person to expose the blues to audiences outside the Deep South. According to Handy, he heard street musicians in the South playing a song entitled "East St. Louis Blues" as early as 1892. His own adoption of blues techniques came after he heard a musician in Tutweiler, Mississippi, playing a six-string guitar and maneuvering a knife across the strings to create a slide-guitar effect. As a result of its spread, the blues developed many stylistic variations. Linking these different styles were lyrics that emphasized the hardships of everyday life, as well as musical and lyrical improvisation within a firmly established set of conventions. Collections of lyrics made by such white scholars as Charles Peabody provide much of the early written commentary on blues music. Peabody and others such as Howard W. Odum regarded the blues as primitive and coarse form of artistic expression, and their scholarship reflects the prevalent racist views of their era. Commentators writing in the later twentieth century approach the blues as a form of lyric poetry or folk song that has had a profound influence on music and literature in the United States and elsewhere.

REPRESENTATIVE WORKS

Louis Armstrong
  Louis Armstrong Plays the Blues (songs) 1953
Edward Albee
  The Death of Bessie Smith (drama) 1961
Big Bill Broonzy
  Good Time Tonight (songs) 1940
Sterling A. Brown
  Southern Road (poetry) 1932
Blind John Davis
  1938 (songs) 1938
Champion Jack Dupree
  The Blues of Champion Jack Dupree (songs) 1994

Ralph Ellison
  Invisible Man (novel) 1952
  Shadow and Act (essays) 1964
T. S. Eliot
  The Waste Land (poetry) 1922
William Faulkner
  Sartoris (novel) 1929
  The Sound and the Fury (novel) 1929
F. Scott Fitzgerald
  The Great Gatsby (novel) 1925
Peter Guralnick
  Night-Hawk Blues (novel) 1980
W. C. Handy
  "The Memphis Blues" (song) 1909
  W. C. Handy's Memphis Blues Band (songs) 1923
Howlin' Wolf
  Howlin' Wolf Sings the Blues (songs) 1962
Langston Hughes
  Ask Your Mama: 12 Moods for Jazz (poetry) 1961
Zora Neale Hurston
  Their Eyes Were Watching God (novel) 1937
Blind Lemon Jefferson
  The Classic Folk Blues of Blind Lemon Jefferson (songs) 1957
Robert Johnson
  The Complete Recordings (songs) 1990
B. B. King
  The Definitive B. B. King Collection (songs) 1992
Huddie "Leadbelly" Ledbetter
  Convict Blues (songs) 1935
  Leadbelly: Huddie Ledbetter's Best (songs) 1962
Memphis Minnie
  Hoodoo Lady (songs) 1937
Muddy Waters
  At Newport (songs) 1960
Howard Odum
  Rainbow round My Shoulder: The Blue Trail of Black Ulysses (novel) 1928
Oliver Pitcher
  Dust of Silence (poetry) 1958
Gertrude "Ma" Rainey
  Ma Rainey, 2 vols. (songs) 1953
Bessie Smith
  Collection (songs) 1933
Mamie Smith
  Complete Recorded Works, 1920-1922, 4 vols. (songs) 1995
Sonny Terry
  Folkways Years, 1944-1963 (songs) 1963
Nathanael West
  The Day of the Locust (novel) 1939
Bukka White
  The Complete Sessions, 1930-1940 (songs) 1976

Richard Wright
   Native Son (novel) 1940
   Black Boy (novel) 1945
   The Long Dream (novel) 1959
   Lawd Today (novel) 1963

CRITICISM

Charles Peabody

SOURCE: "Notes on Negro Music," in *The Journal of American Folk-Lore,* Vol. XVI, No. LXII, 1903, pp. 255-94.

[*In the following excerpt, the author analyzes the music sung by the African-American men hired to help at an archeological excavation in Mississippi.*]

During May and June of 1901 and 1902 I was engaged in excavating for the Peabody Museum of Harvard University a mound in Coahoma County, northern Mississippi. At these times we had some opportunity of observing the Negroes and their ways at close range, as we lived in tent or cabin very much as do the rest of the small farmers and laborers, white and black, of the district. Busy archaeologically, we had not very much time left for folk-lore, in itself of not easy excavation, but willy-nilly our ears were beset with an abundance of ethnological material in song,—words and music. In spite of faulty memory and musical incompetency, what follows, collected by Mr. Farabee and myself, may perhaps be accepted as notes, suggestions for future study in classification, and incidents of interest in the recollecting, possibly in the telling.

The music of the Negroes which we listened to may be put under three heads: the songs sung by our men when at work digging or wheeling on the mound, unaccompanied; the songs of the same men at quarters or on the march, with guitar accompaniment; and the songs, unaccompanied, of the indigenous Negroes,—indigenous opposed to our men imported from Clarksdale, fifteen miles distant.

Most of the human noise of the township was caused by our men, nine to fifteen in number, at their work. On their beginning a trench at the surface the woods for a day would echo their yelling with faithfulness. The next day or two these artists being, like the Bayreuth orchestra, sunk out of sight, there would arise from behind the dump heap a not unwholesome μυγμός as of the quiescent Furies. Of course this singing assisted the physical labor in the same way as that of sailors tugging ropes or of soldiers invited to march by drum and band. They tell, in fact, of a famous singer besought by his co-workers not to sing a particular song, for it made them work too hard, and a singer of good voice and endur-

ance is sometimes hired for the very purpose of arousing and keeping up the energy of labor.

This singing in the trenches may be subdivided into melodic and rhythmic; the melodic into sacred and profane, the rhythmic into general and apposite.

Our men had equal penchants for hymns and "ragtime." The Methodist hymns sung on Sundays were repeated in unhappy strains, often lead by one as choragus, with a refrain in "tutti," hymns of the most doleful import. Rapid changes were made from these to "ragtime" melodies of which "Molly Brown" and "Googoo Eyes" were great favorites. Undoubtedly picked up from passing theatrical troupes, the "ragtime" sung for us quite inverted the supposed theory of its origin. These syncopated melodies, sung or whistled, generally in strict tempo, kept up hour after hour a not ineffective rhythm, which we decidedly should have missed had it been absent.

More interesting humanly were the distichs and improvisations in rhythm more or less phrased sung to an intoning more or less approaching melody. These ditties and distichs were either of a general application referring to manners, customs, and events of Negro life or of special appositeness improvised on the spur of the moment on a topic then interesting. Improvising sometimes occurred in the general class, but it was more likely to be merely a variation of some one sentiment.

The burden of the songs of the former class were "hard luck" tales (very often), love themes, suggestions anticipative and reminiscent of favorite occupations and amusements. Some examples of the words and some of the music are:—

> They had me arrested for murder
> And I never harmed a man.

(A Negro and the law courts are not for long parted.) Other songs had a refrain of "going down the river" (possibly a suggestion of the old slave market at New Orleans), or a continuous wail on "The time ain't long," or hopes for "next pay-day."

Referring to occupations or amusements:—

> Some folks say preachers won't steal;
> But I found two in my cornfield.
> One with a shovel and t'other with a hoe,
> A-diggin' up my taters row by row.
>
> Old Brudder Jones setten on de log,
> His hand on de trigger and his eyes on de hog.
>
> Old Dan Tucker he got drunk,
> Fell in de fire and kicked up a chunk.
>
> I don't gamble but I don't see
> How my money gets away from me.
>
> When I look up over my head

> Makes me think of my corn and bread.
>> (Possibly meteorological.)

If one would complain of the heat, another would sing out:—

> Don't bother me.
> The hotter the sun shines the better I feel.

Love ditties:—

> The reason I loves my baby so,
> 'Case when she gets five dollars she give me fo'.

> Say, Sal, don't you powder so
> We'll be too late for de party, oh.

> Oh we'll live on pork and kisses
> If you'll only be my missus. . . .

Some pronunciations were noted. Murder came out plainly as "muddo" and baby as "bébé;" the latter may be from Creole influence, but I am at a loss to explain the former. No preference otherwise for "o" sounds was evinced.

Coming to more apposite ditties, the cover of this quasi-music was used to convey hints to us up above. One Saturday, a half-holiday, a sing-song came out of the trench,

> Mighty long half day, Capta-i-n,

and one evening when my companion and I were playing a game of mumble-the-peg, our final occupation before closing work, our choragus shouted for us to hear.

> I'm so tired I'm most dead,
> Sittin' up there playing mumblely-peg.

These are only a few. It is impossible to remember and it was impossible to put down all. The men were not good on parade. Asked to sing for my wife while she was with us on a visit, they suddenly found it too hot, and as a whole a request performance got no further than very poor "ragtime," "Goo-goo Eyes" with any number of encores, and "Nigger Bully" and others quite as original probably with Miss May Irwin as with them. Their rhymes were not necessarily more than assonance. Consonants, as seen above, were of little importance.

There was some jealousy among them as to leadership. A handsome fellow named Ike Antoine had been undisputed leader for three months and enjoyed besides a county-wide reputation as a dancer; we imported a burley jail-bird for the last few weeks; he was a capital worker with a voice comparable to the Bashan Bull and Tamagno. He out-bawled Antoine, not altogether to the improvement of the music.

As regards execution, the men's voices, with the exception of Antoine's, were mediocre, but their tempo was singularly accurate. In their refrains ending on the tonic, they sometimes sang the last note somewhat sharp. So frequent was this that it seemed intentional or unavoidable, not merely a mistake in pitch. Otherwise their pitch was fairly true.

Their singing at quarters and on the march with the guitar accompaniment was naturally mostly "ragtime" with the instrument seldom venturing beyond the inversions of the three chords of a few major and minor keys. At their cabin the vocal exercise was of a Polyphemic nature, causing congratulations at its distance. Occasionally we would get them to sing to us with the guitar, but the spontaneity was lacking and the repertoire was limited. They have, however, the primitive characteristic of patience under repetition, and both in the trench and out of it kept up hours-long ululation of little variety.

As to the third division, the autochthonous music, unaccompanied, it is hard to give an exact account. Our best model for the study of this was a diligent Negro living near called by our men "Five Dollars" (suggestive of craps), and by us "Haman's Man," from his persistent following from sunrise to sunset of the mule of that name. These fifteen hours he filled with words and music. Hymns alternated with quite fearful oaths addressed to Haman. Other directions intoned to him melted into strains of apparently genuine African music, sometimes with words, sometimes without. Long phrases there were without apparent measured rhythm, singularly hard to copy in notes. When such sung by him and by others could be reduced to form, a few motives were made to appear, and these copied out were usually quite simple, based for the most part on the major or minor triad. . . .

The long, lonely sing-song of the fields was quite distinct from anything else, though the singer was skilful in gliding from hymn-motives to those of the native chant. The best single recollection I have of this music is one evening when a negress was singing her baby to sleep in her cabin just above our tents. She was of quite a notable Negro family and had a good voice. Her song was to me quite impossible to copy, weird in interval and strange in rhythm; peculiarly beautiful. It bore some likeness to the modern Greek native singing but was better done. I only heard her once in a lullaby, but she used sometimes to walk the fields at evening singing fortissimo, awakening the echoes with song extremely effective. I should not omit mention of a very old negro employed on the plantation of Mr. John Stovall of Stovall, Mississippi. He was asked to sing to us one very dark night as we sat on the gallery. His voice as he sang had a timbre resembling a bagpipe played pianissimo or a Jew's-harp played legato, and to some indistinguishable words he hummed a rhythm of no regularity and notes apparently not more than three or more in number at intervals within a semi-tone. The effect again was monotonous but weird, not far from Japanese. I have not heard that kind again nor of it.

The volume of song is seen to be large and its variety not spare; they are in sharp contrast to the lack of music among the white dwellers of the district; their life is as hard as the Negroes', with some added responsibility; they take it infinitely harder and for one thing seem not to be able to throw off their sorrows in song as are the true sons of the torrid zone, the Negroes.

Howard W. Odum

SOURCE: "Folk-Song and Folk-Poetry as Found in The Secular Songs of the Southern Negroes," in *The Journal of American Folk-Lore,* Vol. XXIV, No. XCIII, July-September, 1911, pp. 255-94, 351-92.

[*In the following excerpt, Odum identifies and categorizes the various types of African-American music, dividing the between the spiritual and secular, the latter of which displayed the style and subject matter for early blues songs.*]

An examination of the first twenty volumes of the *Journal of American Folk-Lore,* and a study of the published folk-songs of the Southern negroes, reveal a large amount of valuable material for the student of folk-songs and ballads. Investigation of the field indicates a still larger supply of songs as yet not collected or published. Unfortunately the collection of these songs has been permitted to lapse within recent years, although there is no indication that even a majority have been collected. In fact, the supply seems almost inexhaustible, and the present-day negro folk-songs appear to be no less distinctive than formerly. It is hoped that special efforts will be made by as many persons as possible to contribute to the negro department of American folklore as many of the songs of the Southern negroes as can be obtained. That they are most valuable to the student of sociology and anthropology, as well as to the student of literature and the ballad, will scarcely be doubted.

Two distinct classes of folk-songs have been, and are, current among the Southern negroes,—the religious songs, or "spirituals;" and the social or secular songs. An examination of the principal collections of negro songs, a list of which is appended at the end of this paper, shows that emphasis has been placed heretofore upon the religious songs, although the secular songs appear to be equally as interesting and valuable. My study of negro folk-songs included originally the religious and secular songs of the Southern negroes; analysis of their content; a discussion of the mental imagery, style and habit, reflected in them; and the word-vocabulary of the collection of songs. The religious songs have already been published in the *American Journal of Religious Psychology and Education* (vol. iii, pp. 265-365). In order to bring this paper within the scope and limits of the *Journal of American Folk-Lore,* it has been necessary to omit the introductory discussion of the songs, for the most part, and to omit entirely the vocabulary and discussion of the mental imagery, style and habits, of the negro singers. In this paper, therefore, only the secular songs are given, which in turn are divided into two classes,—the general social songs, and work songs and phrases.

To understand to the best advantage the songs which follow, it is necessary to define the usage of the word "folk-song" as applied in this paper, to show how current negro songs arise and become common property, to note their variations, and to observe some of the occasions upon which they are sung. Each of these aspects of the Southern negro's songs is interdependent upon the others; the meaning of the folk-songs is emphasized by the explanations of their origin and variations; the singing of the songs by many individuals on many occasions emphasizes the difficulty of confining any song to a given locality or to a single form; and the value of the song is increased as it passes through the several stages.

The songs in this collection are "negro folk-songs," in that they have had their origin and growth among the negroes, or have been adapted so completely that they have become the common songs of the negroes. They are "folk-poetry which, from whatever source and for whatever reason, has passed into the possession of the folk, the common people, so completely that each singer or reciter feels the piece to be his own."[1] Each singer alters or sings the song according to his own thoughts and feelings. How exactly this applies to the negro songs may be seen from the explanations which follow, and from the study and comparison of the different songs. It is not necessary, therefore, in order to classify the songs as negro songs, to attempt to trace each song to its origin or to attempt to determine how much is original and how much borrowed. Clearly many of the songs are adapted forms of well-known songs or ballads; others, which in all probability had their origin among the negroes, resemble very strongly the songs of other people; while still others combine in a striking way original features with the borrowed. In any case, the song, when it has become the common distinctive property of the negroes, must be classed with negro folksongs. Variations of negro folk-songs among themselves may be cited as an illustration of this fact. Likewise there is abundant material for comparing with well-known folk-songs or ballads of other origins. One may note, for instance, the striking similarity between the mountain-song—

"She broke the heart of many poor fellows,
But she won't break this of mine"—

and the negro song "Kelly's Love," the chorus of which is,

"You broke de heart o' many a girl,
But you never will break dis heart o' mine."

Or, again, compare the version of the Western ballad, "Casey Jones,"—which begins,

"Come, all you rounders, for I want you to hear
The story told of an engineer.
Casey Jones was the rounder's name,

A heavy right-wheeler of mighty fame,"—

with the negro song, "Casey Jones," which begins,

"Casey Jones was an engineer,
Told his fireman not to fear,
All he wanted was boiler hot,
Run into Canton 'bout four 'clock,"

and, having recited in a single stanza the story of his death, passes on to love affairs, and ends,

"Wimmins in Kansas all dressed in red,
Got de news dat Casey was dead;
De wimmins in Jackson all dressed in black,
Said, in fact, he was a cracker-jack."

Thus Canton and Jackson, Mississippi, are localized; in "Joseph Mica" similar versions are found, and localized in Atlanta and other cities,—

"All he want is water 'n coal,
Poke his head out, see drivers roll;"

and the entire story of the engineer's death is told in the verse,

"Good ole engineer, but daid an' gone."

In the same way comparisons may be made with "Jesse James," "Eddy Jones," "Joe Turner," "Brady," "Stagolee," of the hero-songs; "Won't you marry me?" "Miss Lizzie, won't you marry me?" "The Angel Band," and others similar to some of the short Scottish ballads and song-games of American children; and "I got mine," "When she roll dem Two White Eyes," "Ain't goin' be no Rine," and many others adapted from the popular "coon-songs;" together with scores of rhymes, riddles, and conundrums. In any case, the songs with the accompanying music have become the property of the negroes, in their present rendition, regardless of their sources or usage elsewhere.

In the same way that it is not possible to learn the exact origin of the folk-songs, or to determine how much is original and how much traditional, it is not possible to classify negro songs according to the exact locality or localities from which they come. The extent to which they become common property, and the scope of their circulation, will be explained in subsequent discussions of the songs. The best that can be done, therefore, is to classify the songs according to the locality *from which they were collected,* . . . and to give the different versions of the same song as they are found in different localities. The majority of the songs collected from Lafayette County, Mississippi, were also heard in Newton County, Georgia; and a large number of the songs heard in Mississippi and Georgia were also heard in Tennessee (Sumner County). From many inquiries the conclusion seems warranted that the majority of the one hundred and ten songs or fragments here reported are current in southern Georgia, southern Mississippi, parts of Tennessee, and the Carolinas and Virginia. It may

well be hoped that other collections of negro songs will be made, and that similarities and differences in these songs may be pointed out in other localities, as well as new songs collected. The large number of "one-verse songs" and "heave-a-hora's" were collected with the other songs, and are representative of the negro song in the making.

In studying the negro's songs, three important aids to their interpretation should be kept in mind,—first, facts relating to the manner of singing, and the occasions upon which they are sung; second, the general classes of negro songs, and the kinds of songs within each class; and, third, the subject-matter, methods of composition, and the processes through which the songs commonly pass in their growth and development. The majority of songs current among the negroes are often sung without the accompaniment of an instrument. The usual songs of the day, songs of laborers, of children, and many general care-free songs, together with some of the songs of the evening, are not accompanied. In general, the majority of the songs of the evening are accompanied by the "box" or fiddle when large or small groups are gathered together for gayety; when a lonely negro sits on his doorstep or by the fireside, playing and singing; when couples stay late at night with their love-songs and jollity; when groups gather after church to sing the lighter melodies; when the "musicianers," "music physicianers," and "songsters" gather to render music for special occasions, such as church and private "socials," dances, and other forms of social gatherings. Special instances in which a few negroes play and sing for the whites serve to bring out the combined features of restrained song and the music of the instrument. The old-time negro with his "box" (a fiddle or guitar), ever ready to entertain the "white folks" and thus be entertained himself, is less often observed than formerly. The majority of younger negroes must be well paid for their music. In the smaller towns, such negroes not infrequently organize a small "ochestra," and learn to play and sing the new songs. They often render acceptable music, and are engaged by the whites for serenades or for occasions of minor importance. They do not, however, sing the negro folk-songs.

Of special importance as makers and mediums for negro folk-songs are the "music physicianers," "musicianers," and "songsters." These terms may be synonymous, or they may denote persons of different habits. In general, "songster" is used to denote any negro who regularly sings or makes songs; "musicianer" applies often to the individual who claims to be expert with the banjo or fiddle; while "music physicianer" is used to denote more nearly a person who is accustomed to travel from place to place, and who possesses a combination of these qualities; or each or all of the terms may be applied loosely to any person who sings or plays an instrument. A group of small boys or young men, when gathered together and wrought up to a high degree of abandon, appear to be able to sing an unlimited number of common songs. Perhaps the "music physicianer" knows the "moest songs." With a prized "box," perhaps his only property, such a negro may wander from town to town, from section to section, loafing in general, and working only when compelled to do so, gathering new songs and singing the old ones. Negroes of this type may be called professionals, since their life of wandering is facilitated by the practice of singing. Through their influence, songs are easily carried from place to place. There are other "music physicianers" whose fields of activity are only local. In almost every community such individuals may be found, and from them many songs can be obtained. From them and from promiscuous individuals, a "musicianer" may be influenced to obtain songs new to himself, which he, in turn, will render to the collector. Finally, a group of young negroes, treated to a "bait" of watermelons or to a hearty meal, make excellent "songsters" in the rendering of the folk-songs. In addition to these special cases, it is a constant source of surprise to the observer to learn how many songs the average negro knows; and they may be heard during work hours, or, in some cases, by request.

The great mass of negro songs may be divided into three general classes, the last of which constitutes the folk-songs as commonly used,—first, the modern "coon-songs" and the newest popular songs of the day; second, such songs greatly modified and adapted partially by the negroes; and, third, songs originating with the negroes or adapted so completely as to become common folk-songs. The first class of songs is heard more frequently by the whites. All manner of "ragtimes," "coon-songs," and the latest "hits," replace the simpler negro melodies. Young negroes pride themselves on the number of such songs they can sing, at the same time that they resent a request to sing the older melodies. Very small boys and girls sing the difficult airs of the new songs with surprising skill, until one wonders when and how they learned so many words and tunes. The second class of songs easily arises from the singing of popular songs, varied through constant singing or through misunderstanding of the original versions. These songs appear to be typical of the process of song-making, and indicate the facility of the negroes in producing their own songs from material of any sort. The third class of negro songs is made up of the "folk-songs" proper; and while the variations of the songs of the first and second classes would constitute an interesting study, they are in reality not negro songs. Accordingly, only those that have become completely adapted are given in this collection. In all of these the characteristic music and manner prevail, and the principal characteristics may be enumerated simply. The music may be reduced to a few combinations. The harmonies are made up mostly of minor keys, without reference to studied combinations or movement toward related keys. There is much repetition in both words and music. The song and chorus are adapted to an apparent mood or feeling. Verses are sung in the order in which they occur to the singer, or as they please the fancy. The great majority of the songs are made up of repetitions, but they do not tire the singers or the hearers. The negro song often begins with one conception of a theme, and ends with another entirely foreign to the first, after passing through various other themes. This may be explained by the fact that when the negro begins to sing, he loves to continue, and often passes from one song to another without pausing. In time he mingles the two or more songs. Most of the groups and "socials," and especially the dance, require continuous music for a longer period of time than the average song will last. It thus happens that the negro could sing the great majority of his songs to a single tune, if the necessity called for it; although it is likely that the last part of his melody would scarcely be recognizable as that with which he began. In words, as in music, variation seems unlimited. As is pointed out subsequently, and as was true in the case of the religious songs, there is no consistency in the use of dialect. Perhaps there is less consistency in the social songs than elsewhere. It is common for the negro to mingle every kind of song into one, or to transpose the one from its usual place or origin to any other position. Thus "coon-songs," "ragtimes," "knife-songs," "devil-songs," "corn-songs," "work-songs,"—all alike may become love-songs or dancing "breakdowns." The original names given to such songs serve to distinguish them in the mind of the negro, rather than to indicate their separateness. However, the distinctions are often made clearly enough for a definition of what the negro means to be made.

The "musicianer" will play many "rag-times," which he carefully names, and calls off with pride. Usually they are not accompanied by words, but are represented on the fiddle or guitar. When he is through with these, he will offer to play and sing "some song." This he does to precisely the same music as the "rag-time." With the words, it is a song; without the words, it is a "rag-time," in which case the negro puts more life into the music. Likewise the "knife-song" is by origin instrumental only, but it is regularly associated with several songs of many verses. Its name is derived from the act of running the back of a knife along the strings of the instrument, thus making it "sing" and "talk" with skill. Instead of the knife, negroes often carry a piece of bone, polished and smooth, which they slip over a finger, and alternate between picking the strings and rubbing them. This gives a combination of fiddle and guitar. The bone may also serve as a good-luck omen. The knife, however, is more commonly used. The "musicianer" places his knife by the side of the instrument while he picks the strings and sings. He can easily take it up and use it at the proper time without interrupting the harmony. In this way the instrument can be made to "sing," "talk," "cuss," and supplement in general the voice and the ringing of the fiddle or the tinkling of the guitar. It is undoubtedly one of the negro's best productions, and defies musical notation to give it full expression.

The "train-song" derives its name from its imitation of the running train. The most popular name for it is "The Fast Train." The negro's fondness for trains and railroad life has been observed. In the railroad-songs that follow, the extent to which the train appeals to the negro may be seen. In no way is this spirit better portrayed than in the train-songs, which picture to the vivid imagination the rapidly-moving train. This imitation is done by the rapid running of the fingers along the strings, and by the playing of successive chords with a regularity that makes a sound similar to that of the moving train. The train is made to whistle by a prolonged and consecutive striking of the strings, while the bell rings with the striking of a single string. As the negroes imagine themselves observing the train, or riding, the fervor of the occasion is increased; and when "she blows for the station," the exclamations may be heard, "Lawd, God, she's a-runnin' now!" or, "Sho' God railroadin'!" with others of a similar nature. The train "pulls out" from the station, passes the road-crossings, goes up grade, down grade, blows for the crossing, blows for smaller stations, blows for the operators at the stations, rings the bell for crossings and for stopping the train; this train meets the "express" and the mail-train, blows for the side-track, rings the bell; the mail-train in turn whistles, rings the bell, passes; both bells ring, and they continue on their run; the wheels are heard rolling on the track and crossing the joints in the rails. If the song is instrumental only, the man at the guitar announces the several stages of the run. If the song is one of words, such as the railroad-songs cited subsequently, the words are made to heighten the imagination, and between the stanzas there is ample time to picture the train and its occupants.

I. GENERAL SOCIAL SONGS

A study of the social songs current among the Southern negroes shows that they have arisen from every-day life, and that they portray many of the common traits and social tendencies. The majority may be said to have sprung up within comparatively recent years. For the subject-matter of his songs, the negro has drawn freely upon his favorite themes; and the growth and development of his songs have been spontaneous and natural. The singers are often conscious that they are singing folk-songs, and they attempt to pose as the authors; others give interesting stories to show how they learned the songs; while many negroes are averse to singing or collecting such songs for those desiring them. The accounts given by negroes concerning the origin and authorship of their songs, while most interesting, are quite misleading, for the most part. One negro affirmed that he had heard a song "played by a white lady in New York," and that, from hearing it there, he had learned to reproduce the music on his guitar and sing the song to accompany it. Another affirmed that he got the same song from a neighboring town, and that he had been forced to pay dearly for it (therefore he should be rewarded accordingly). The song was one of the widest known of the negro songs. So, too, negro singers may often purposely mislead the investigator by misquoting the song, or by giving verses which they have got from books or papers, or heard from "coon-songs." Many negroes maintain that they are the original authors of the songs they sing, and they are able to give apparent

good evidence to substantiate the statement. Even if one were inclined to accept such testimony, it would be a difficult matter to select the author from a number who thus claim to have composed the song. This is well illustrated by the young negro who wished to call out his name before each song which he was singing into the graphophone. "Song composed by Will Smith of Chattanooga, Tennessee," he would cry out, then begin his song; for, he maintained, these songs would be sung all over the world, and he deserved the credit for them. His varied song furnished excellent material for getting the characteristic notation of the music. Once or twice he hesitated before giving his name as the author, and several times said that he guessed that the song was composed by some other person whose name he wished to give. This person was a "partner rounder" of his acquaintance; and when told that the origin of a song which he was singing was not that which he gave, but was well known, he begged to have his name taken away, adding that he only meant to say, "Song sung by Will Smith." This may be cited as an illustration of the difficulty of getting at the origin of a song through the negroes. In no case could the general testimony be accepted for any purpose other than to give an insight into the negro's own conception of the possible origin of songs.

The negroes have many songs which they call "one-verse songs." By this they mean a single line, repeated again and again, constituting the entire song. Usually the line is repeated with regularity, so that it makes a stanza of two, four, or six lines, sometimes three and five. In such cases the last repetition adds some word or exclamation, as "oh," "my," "yes," "well," "and," "so," and others. The great majority of negro songs which are current now are "one-verse songs," and almost all have arisen and developed along the one-verse method. A close examination of the songs that follow in subsequent pages will show the processes. In this way the origin of song is simple and natural. Any word may lead to a phrase which itself becomes a one-verse song, and naturally calls for a rhyme and additional verses. A negro is driving a delivery-wagon; the weather is cold, and the wind is blowing with a drizzling rain. He pulls his coat around him, and says, "The wind sho' do blow." Not having any special song which he wishes to sing at the moment, he sings these words and others: "Sho' God is cold dis mornin'," "Ain't goin' to rain no mo'," "Goin' where chilly win' don't blow." In the same way he sings whatever happens to be foremost in his mind. Perhaps it is, "I bin workin' so long—hungry as I kin be;" "Where in de worl' you bin?" "I'm goin' 'way some day;" "Jus' keep a knockin' at yo' do';" "Had a mighty good time las' night;" or as many others as there are common scenes in the negro's life. The examples given in the list of one-verse songs will serve to illustrate further this common origin of many of the negro songs. In the same general way the prose or monotone songs have arisen. The negro often talks to himself; his singing is simply a musical "thinking out loud." His monologues uttered in a monotone manner lead to song. Perhaps he will talk to himself a while, then sing the same words that he has been uttering. Pleased with this effect, he may then introduce his chant into a group. Such a song is given farther on.

I. DONY GOT A HOLE IN DE WALL

"A girl was luvin' a coon," so the story goes, "an' she thought he did not go to see any other girl; she found out he did, an' she made a hole in the wall of her house so she could watch an' see did her lover go to see any other coon. Her luvin' man found this out an' it made him laugh; an' he wus sorry, too." Thus is given the origin of a bit of song. The lover makes a song, and says,—

> "Dony got a hole in de wall,
> Dony got a hole in de wall,
> Dony got a hole in de wall,
> Oh, my Dony got a hole in de wall.
> "Baby weahs a number fo' shoe,
> Baby weahs a number fo' shoe,
> Baby weahs a number fo' shoe,
> Oh, my baby weahs a number fo' shoe."

In this way the negro makes a story back of the song. If it is a lover's song, he tells of a particular man and his woman. If it is Railroad Bill, he tells when and where he lived and what he did, then sings the song. If it is another "bully boy," the same is true. If the song be that of the wanderer, he tells of the adventures; if it is of a murder, he narrates the story of arrest and trial. A study of the songs reveals the immense possibilities for stories back of the song. No song is enjoyed so much as when the singer has told his story before singing it. In theory at least, then, the negro song is based on incident; in practice it develops through the common events of negro life. Indeed, one may accept the statement that many of their songs are actually derived from story; but there may be as many variations to the song and story as there are negroes who sing it.

Individuals among the negroes take pride in making secular songs, as they do in claiming the composition of religious songs. Enough has been said to indicate this habit. But undoubtedly the negro has a consciousness of power or ability to create new songs when he wishes to do so. This very feeling enables him to make his boasts true. Most negroes are bright in composing songs of some kind. Besides being led to it by their own assertions, they enjoy it. It matters little what the theme is, the song will be forthcoming and the tune applied. Nor would one suspect that the song was a new one, were it not for its unfinished lines and the lack of characteristic folk-song qualities. In the examples here given it will be seen that the lines do not have the finished form of the older songs. In time they too may become good folk-songs.

2. MULE-SONG

The negroes have much to say about the mule in their work, and have much to do with him in actual life. Their songs also contain references to him. A mixture of parts of song added to experience and imagination produced the following "mule-song:"

> "I went up Zion Hill this mornin' on a wagon,
> I went on a wagon up Zion's Hill this mornin',
> The durn ole mule stop right still this mornin',
>   this mornin', so soon.
>
> "I got out an' went 'round to his head this
>   mornin',
> I got out an' went 'round to his head this
>   mornin',
> The durn ole mule was standin' there dead, this
>   mornin', so soon.
>
> "Yes, I hollow at the mule, an' the mule would
>   not gee, this mornin',
> Yes, I hollow at the mule, an' the mule would not
>   gee,
> An' I hit him across the head with the single-tree,
>   so soon."

The negro expected that his song would be a humorous one, as indeed it is. Such songs lack the rhyme and more regular measures, and employ words at random to fill out the lines.

3. THE NEGRO AND HIS MULE

In the following song the same characteristics may be observed:

> "Say, look here, Jane!
> Don't you want to take a ride?"—
> "Well, I doan care if I do."
> So he hitch up his mule an' started out.
>
> *Well, it's whoa, mule, git up an' down,*
> *Till I say whoa-er, mule.*
>
> Well it's git up an' down
>   Jus' fas' as you can,
> Fer I goin' to buy you
>   All of de oats an' bran.
>
> *An' it's whoa-er mule, git up an' down,*
> *Till I say whoa-er mule:*
> *Ain't he a mule, Miss Jane—'m—huh.*

4. POOR JOHN

In the next song may be observed a peculiarly mixed imagery: Quite a number of phrases are borrowed from other songs, but the arrangement is new. "Poor John" is a common character with the negro; stabbing and running are common accomplishments with the criminal. The other scenes, losing his hat, falling down the steps, the cry of murder, and the policemen, all appeal to the imagery of the negro. He sings, with a combination of vaudeville rhyme,—

> "Yes, he caught poor John with his hawk-tail
>   coat,
>   An' he stab him to the fat;
> He ran the race an' he run so fas',
>   Till he bust his beaver hat.

"Poor John fell down them winding steps,
   Till he could not fall no further;
      An' the girls all holler murder;
Go tell all policemen on this beat to see,
   Can't they catch that coon.

"'What coon am you talkin' about?'
   'The coon that stab po' John;
I'm goin', I'm goin', to the shuckin' o' de corn,
   I'm goin' jus' sho's you born.'"

5. AT THE BALL

An adopted form of an old song, "Won't you marry me," but equally as true in its representative features, is the song "At the Ball." Here the rhyming effort is clearly felt, and the picture is definitely portrayed. The negro's idea of courtship may here be hinted at, as it has been in many of the songs that follow.

Yes, there's going to be a ball,
   At the negro hall;
      Ain't you goin'?
Lizzie will be there,
   Yes, with all her airs;
      Don't you want to see the strolling?

Ha, ha, Miss Lizzie, don't you want to marry
   me—marry me?
I will be as good to you as anybody—anybod-e-e,
   If you'll only marry me.

Yes, I goin' to the negro hall,
   Have a good time, that's all,
      For they tell me Miss Lizzie will be there:
An' you bet yo' life,
   I goin' win her for my wife,
      An' take her home to-night.

Well, Miss Lizzie could not consent,
   She didn't know what he meant,
      By askin' her to marry him;
Well, Miss Lizzie couldn't consent,
   She didn't know what he meant,
      By askin' her to marry him.

So he got down on his knees,
   "O Miss Lizzie, if you please,
      Say that you will marry me;
An' I'll give you every cent,
   If I git you to consent,
      If you'll only marry me."

6. WHEN HE GITS OLD—OLD AN' GRAY

There are apparently a good many sayings current among the negroes about the whites. Few of these, however, are heard by any save the negroes themselves. Likewise the songs of this nature would scarcely be sung where the whites could hear them. Two of these are here given. The first is a reply to the accusation that the negroes are nothing more than apes or monkeys. As the story goes, it is likely that the song originated with a bright negro's

retort behind the back of a white who had called him an ape. "That's all right," said the negro in the proverbial phrase; but

When he gits old,
      old and gray,
When he gits old,
      old and gray,
Then white folks looks like monkeys,
When dey gits old, old an' gray.

It is needless to say that the song struck a responsive note as well as appealed to the negro as a very bright song for the occasion. In fact, it must be admitted to be a good rejoinder. The subtle and sulky manner in which it is sung is a powerful comment on the negro's growing sense of race feeling. Whether there are other verses to this comment on the aged whites has not been ascertained.

7. AIN'T IT HARD TO BE A NIGGER

The second song which is now well known is composed of two popular rhymes about the negro and the white man, together with other verses composed to make an agreeable song and to make suitable rhymes and combinations. The effort to make a complete song is easily felt as one reads the words. The tune may be one that the singer happens to think of; it matters little which he chooses. The theme "Ain't it Hard?" is one that is common in negro life and song. He sings,—

"Ain't it hard, ain't it hard,
Ain't it hard to be a nigger, nigger, nigger?
Ain't it hard, ain't it hard,
For you can't git yo' money when it's due.

"Well, it make no difference,
   How you make out yo' time;
White man sho' bring a
   Nigger out behin'.

"Nigger an' white man
   Playin' seven-ups;
Nigger win de money—
   Skeered to pick 'em up.

"If a nigger git 'rested,
   An' can't pay his fine,
They sho' send him out
   To the county gang.

"A nigger went to a white man,
   An' asked him for work;
White man told nigger,
   'Yes, git out o' yo' shirt.'

"Nigger got out o' his shirt
   An' went to work;
When pay-day come,
   White man say he ain't work 'nuf.

"If you work all the week,
   An' work all the time,
White man sho' to bring
   Nigger out behin'."

The above song illustrates the method of making song out of rhymes, fragments, sayings, and improvised rhymes. The song as heard in its present form was collected in Newton County, Georgia. In a negro school in Mississippi, at a Friday afternoon "speaking," one of the children recited for a "speech" the stanza "Nigger an' white man playin' seven-ups," etc., exactly as it occurs in the song. The stanza ending "white man sho' bring nigger out behin'" incorporates the exact sentiment of an old ex-slave who maintained that in slavery and out of slavery the white man always brought the nigger out behind. So also it is a most common saying among the negroes that "if nigger git 'rested, he sho' be sent to gang." The other two stanzas are clearly made to order in the effort to make song and rhyme. However, this mixed assortment of verses and sentiments made a most attractive song when sung to a common tune.

Just as in the religious songs many verses are composed with the avowed intention of contributing a song, so in the secular songs original "poems" are turned into songs. One thrifty teacher wrote verses on the sinking of the "Maine," to be sung to the tune of "John Brown's Body," etc.; another, called "Hog-killin' Time," to be sung to the tune of "The Old Oaken Bucket." While such songs do not ordinarily become standard folk-songs, they illustrate the ease with which any sort of song may arise and become current. Thus the "songster" closes his description of a day's ploughing in the hot month of June:

> "Dem skeeters dey callin' me cousin,
>   Dem gnats dey calls me frien',
> Dem stingin' flies is buzzin',
>   Dis nigger done gone in."

Enough has been pointed out to show something of the environment of the negro songs. Further explanations and analysis must be made in connection with the songs themselves. It was pointed out that the negro's religious songs did not lend themselves to exact classification. The social songs can be classified with no more exactness than can the spirituals. The best that can be done is to arrange the songs according to a partial analysis of the subject-matter; but any such classification must be considered entirely flexible, just as, for instance, work-songs may be sung on occasions where no work is done, and just as any popular song may be adapted to become a work-song. Themes are freely mingled; verses, disjointed and inconsequential, are sung to many tunes and variations. Repetition of words and thought is thus most common. Each song may consist of a number of themes, which in turn are sung to other songs of other subject-matter. Thus it happens that it matters little what the song is called, provided it is given its proper setting. In the songs that follow, not infrequently a song is reported as having only three or four stanzas, whereas stanzas already reported are included by the singer until his song is as long as desired. The effort is made to avoid as much repetition as possible, and at the same time to report the songs in such a way as to do justice to the characteristic qualities of the song. Hence stanzas that

have been given in one song will generally be omitted in others in which they are found. The dialect is that of the average singing; for the negro, in his social and secular songs, even more than in his religious songs, uses no consistent speech. The language is neither that of the whites nor that of the blacks, but a freely mingled and varied usage of dialect and common speech. Colloquialisms are frequent. The omission of pronouns and connectives, assyndeton in its freest usage, mark many negro verses, while the insertion of interjections and senseless phrases go to the other extreme. Such peculiarities may be best noted when the songs are studied. In the songs that follow, the words of the chorus are italicized. It should be remembered that in addition to beginning and ending the song with the regular chorus, each stanza is followed by the same chorus, thus doubling the length of the song.

Perhaps no person is sung more among the negroes than the homeless and friendless wanderer, with his disappointments in love and adventure; but here the negro sings of woman, and the desire for pity and love, as the accompanying feelings of the wanderer: These references must be added to those songs of the next division which tell of woman, sweetheart, and love. In no phases of negro life do the negro's self-feeling and self-pity manifest themselves more than in the plaintive appeals of the wandering negro. With his characteristic manner, he appeals to both whites and blacks for pity and assistance. As the tramp invents many ingenuous stories in order to arouse the pity of those whom he meets; as the cook tells of many misfortunes in the family, thinking thus to secure more provisions,—so these songs portray the feelings of the negro vagrant. He especially appeals to his women friends, and thus moves them to pity him. His appeals to their sympathy are usually effective; and the negro thus gets shelter, food, and attention. The wandering "songster" takes great pride in thus singing with skill some of his favorite songs; then he can boast of his achievements as "a bad man" with his "box." As he wanders from negro community to community, he finds lodging and solace. So the negroes at home take up the songs, and sing them to their companions, this constituting perhaps the most effective method of courtship. In these songs the roving, rambling thoughts of the negro are well brought out by the quick shifting of scenes; so his rambling and unsteady habits are depicted with unerring though unconscious skill.

8. PO' BOY LONG WAY FROM HOME

In the following song, which is sometimes sung with the knife instrumental music described elsewhere, each stanza consists of a single line repeated three times.

> I'm po' boy 'long way from home,
> Oh, I'm po' boy 'long boy way from home.
>
> I wish a 'scushion train would run,
> Carry me back where I cum frum.
>
> Come here, babe, an' sit on yo' papa's knee.

You brought me here an' let 'em throw me down.

I ain't got a frien' in dis town.

I'm out in de wide worl' alone.

If you mistreat me, you sho' will see it again.

My mother daid an' my father gone astray,
You never miss yo' mother till she done gone
    away.

Come 'way to Georgia, babe, to git in a' home.

No need, O babe! try to throw me down,
A po' little boy jus' come to town.

I wish that ole engeneer wus dead,
Brought me 'way from my home.

Central gi' me long-distance phone,
Talk to my babe all night long.

If I die in State of Alabam',
Send my papa great long telegram.

In the same way the following "one-verse" songs are added:

Shake hands an' tell yo' babe good-by.

Bad luck in de family sho' God fell on me.
Have you got lucky, babe, an' then got broke?
I'm goin' 'way, comin' back some day.
Good ole boy, jus' ain't treated right.
I'm Tennessee raise, Georgia bohn.
I'm Georgia bohn, Alabama rais'.

9. ON A HOG

Very much like the above song is "On a Hog," which means the condition of a "broke ho-bo" or tramp. By "broke" he means the usual state of being without money, or place to sleep, or food to eat. The song, like the above one, consists of lines repeated, without a chorus. There is little sense or connection in the words and verses. It represents the characteristic blending of all kinds of words to make some sort of song. At the same time its verses are classics in negro song.

Come 'way to Georgia to git on a hog, *(three times)*
Lord, come 'way to Georgia to git on a hog.

If you will go, babe, please don't go now,

But heave-a-hora heave-a-hora, babe, heave!

I didn't come here to be nobody's dog.

I jest come here to stay a little while.

Well, I ain't goin' in Georgia long.

And with characteristic rhyme-making, a negro, after he had finished the few verses that he knew, began adding others. Said he,

I didn't come here to be nobody's dog,
Jes' come here to git off'n dat hog.

10. FRISCO RAG-TIME

Even more disjointed and senseless is the song called, for convenience at the moment, "Frisco Rag-Time," "K. C.," or any other railroad name that happens to be desired. The song may be sung by man or woman or by both. It is expected that the viewpoint of man be indicated in the use of woman as the object, and woman's viewpoint be indicated in the reference to man. Such is sometimes the case; but usually the negro sings the song through, shifting from time to time from man to woman without so much as noticing the incongruity of meaning. In the verses which follow the scenes will be portrayed with clear vision by the negro singer.

Got up in the mornin', couldn't keep from cryin',
    (three times)
Thinkin' 'bout that brown-skin man o' mine.

Yonder comes that lovin' man o' mine, *(three times)*
Comin' to pay his baby's fine.

Well, I begged the jedge to low' my baby's fine,
    (three times)
Said de jedge done fine her, clerk done wrote it
    down.

Couldn't pay dat fine, so taken her to de jail.
    (three times)

So she laid in jail back to de wall, *(three times)*
Dis brown-skin man cause of it all.

No need babe tryin' to throw me down, *(three times)*
Cause I'm po' boy jus' come to town.

But if you don't want me, please don't dog me
    'round, *(three times)*
Give me this money, sho' will leave this town.

Ain't no use tryin' to send me 'roun', *(three times)*
I got plenty money to pay my fine.

It will be observed that the last-named verses are practically the same as those given in other songs, and have no connection with the theme with which the song was begun; yet they formed an integral part of the song. In the same way single lines repeated four times are sung at length, although one would need to search diligently for the connection of meaning.

If you don't find me here, come to Larkey's
    dance.
If you don't find me there, come to ole
    Birmingham.
Ain't goin' to be in jungles long.
Yonder comes that easy-goin' man o' mine.
Ain't Jedge Briles a hard ole man!

"Jedge Briles" is only a local name given to Judge Broyles of Atlanta. His reputation is widely known among the negroes of Georgia. Instead of this name are often inserted the names of local characters, which serve to add concreteness to the song. So instead of Birmingham, the negro may sing Atlanta, Chattanooga, or any other city that ranks as a favorite among the negroes. Besides the feeling of the wayward wanderer, the scenes of court and jail are here pictured. Another division of song will group these scenes together. The difficulty of any sort of accurate classification of such a song is apparent. In addition to the words of the wandering man, this song gives also an insight into the reckless traits of the negro woman, which are clearly pictured in many of the negro love-songs.

11. LOOK'D DOWN DE ROAD

Mixed in just the same way, and covering a number of themes, utterly without sense-connection, the following song might well be a continuation of those just given. It is sung, however, to a different tune, and should be ranked as a separate song. Its form is not unlike that already cited,—repetition of a single line twice, or, in rare instances, a rhymed couplet.

> Look'd down de road jes' far as I could see,
> Well, the band did play "Nearer, my God, to
>   Thee."
>
> I got the blues, but too damn mean to cry.
>
> Now when you git a dollar, you got a frien'
> Will stick to you through thick an' thin.
>
> I didn't come here fer to steal nobody's find.
> I didn't jes' come here to serve my time.
>
> I ask jailer, "Captain, how can I sleep?"
> All 'round my bedside Police S. creeps.
>
> The jailer said, "Let me tell you what's best:
> Go 'way back in yo' dark cell an' take yo' rest."
>
> If my kind man quit me, my main man throw me
>   down;
> I goin' run to de river, jump overboard 'n' drown.

Here, again, the local policeman is always spoken of as creeping around the bedside. It makes an interesting comparison to note the contrast between the police and the angels of the old wish-rhyme. Various versions of the above stanzas are given, some of which are far from elegant. So in the last stanza the negroes sing, "If my *good* man quit me, my *main* man throw me down." Profanity is inserted in the songs in proportion as the singer is accustomed to use it, or as the occasion demands or permits its use.

12. IF I DIE IN ARKANSAS

Ridiculous and amusing in its pathos, "If I die in Arkansas" is typical and representative. It is quite impres-

sive when sung with feeling. The negro gets a kind of satisfaction in believing that he is utterly forlorn, yet begs to be delivered from such a condition. He sings,—

> If I die in Arkansa',
> Oh, if I die in Arkansa',
> If I die in Arkansa',
> Des ship my body to my mother-in-law.
>
> "If my mother refuse me, ship it to my pa.
>
> "If my papa refuse me, ship it to my girl.
>
> "If my girl refuse me, shove me into de sea,
> Where de fishes an' de whales make a fuss over
>   me.

And then, after this wonderful rhyme and sentiment, the singer merges into plaintive appeal, and sings further,—

> "Pore ole boy, long ways from home,
> Out in dis wide worl' alone."

Suppose he should die! Suppose he has no friends! How he pities himself! Indeed, he is a forlorn being, and his emotions might well be wrought up.

13. GOT NO WHERE TO LAY MY WEARY HEAD

Another song, also called "Po' Boy 'way from Home," repeats much the same sentiment; and besides many verses of other songs, the singer adds,—

> I want to see do my baby know right from wrong,
>   O babe!
>
> Well, I got no where to lay my weary head, O
>   babe!
>
> Well, a rock was my pillar las' night, O girl!

Thus repetition makes a long song of a short one.

14. BABY, YOU SHO' LOOKIN' WARM

So in the next song, "Baby, You sho' lookin' Warm," three lines are alike, while the fourth varies only by an exclamation. This, too, is an appeal to the "baby" or sweetheart for pity and admission into the house.

> Baby, you sho' lookin' warm, *(three times)*
> O my babe! you sho' lookin' warm.
>
> Baby, I'm feelin' so tired, *(three times)*
> O my babe! I'm feelin' so tired.
>
> Got no whar' to lay my weary head, *(three times)*
> O my babe! got no whar' to lay my weary head.
>
> Sometimes I'm fallin' to my face, *(three times)*
> O my babe! sometimes I'm fallin' to my face.
>
> I'm goin' whar' de water drinks like wine. *(as
>   before)*

Gwine whar' I never been befo'. *(as before)*

Baby, I love the clothes you wear. *(as before)*

Whar' in de worl' my baby gone? *(as before)*

Gone away never come back no more. *(as before)*

15. TAKE YOUR TIME

"Take your Time" represents the negro in a more tranquil and independent state of mind. It matters little what the circumstances may be, he does not care: there's no hurry, so "take your time." And these circumstances are varied enough: from the home to the court he is rambling aimlessly about.

> Baby, baby, didn't you say,
> You'd work for me both night and day?
> *Take your time, take your time.*
>
> Baby, baby, don't you know
> I can git a girl anywhere I go?
> *Take yo' time, take yo' time.*
>
> Baby, baby, can't you see
> How my girl git away from me?
> *Take yo' time, take yo' time.*
>
> Went down country see my frien',
> In come yaller dog burnin' the win',
> *Take yo' time, take yo' time.*
>
> 'Tain't but the one thing grieve my mind:
> Goin' 'way, babe, an' leave you behin',
> *Take yo' time, take yo' time.*
>
> Carried me 'roun' to de court-house do',
> Place wher' I never had been befo',
> *Take yo' time, take yo' time.*
>
> Jedge an' jury all in de stan',
> Great big law-books in dere han',
> *Take yo' time, take yo' time.*
>
> Went up town 'bout four o'clock,
> Rapt on door, an' door was locked,
> *Take yo' time, take yo' time.*
>
> I'm goin' back to de sunny South,
> Where sun shines on my honey's house,
> *Take yo' time, take yo' time.*

16. 'TAIN'T NOBODY'S BIZNESS BUT MY OWN

Jingling rhymes are sought at the sacrifice of meaning and the sense of the song. Rhymes are thus more easily remembered. If the sentiment of the subject of the song appeals to a negro, he may take it and make his own rhymes, departing from the original version. The frequent omission of words, and the mixing of dialect and modern slang, usually result. "'Tain't Nobody's Bizness but my Own" represents the more reckless temperament of the wanderer.

> Baby, you ought-a tole me,
> Six months before you roll me,
> I'd had some other place to go,
> *'Tain't nobody's bizness but my own.*
>
> Sometimes my baby gets boozy,
> An' foolish 'bout her head,
> An' I can't rule her,
> *'Tain't nobody's bizness but my own.*
>
> I'm goin' to happy Hollow,
> Where I can make a dollar,
> *'Tain't nobody's bizness but my own.*
>
> I want to see my Hanner
> Turn tricks in my manner,
> *'Tain't nobody's bizness but my own.*
>
> Don't care if I don't make a dollar,
> So I wear my shirt an' collar,
> *'Tain't nobody's bizness but my own.*

17. I'M GOING 'WAY

The swaggering tramp decides to leave the town, as indeed he is often doing; but he expects to come back again. He looks forward to the adventures of the trip with pleasure, not with fear, although he knows he must ride the rods, go without victuals, and sleep where he may. He sings,—

> I'm goin' 'way, comin' back some day,
> I'm goin' 'way, comin' back some day,
> I'm just from the country, come to town—
> A Zoo-loo-shaker from my head on down.
> If I git drunk, who's goin' ter carry me home?
> Brown-skin woman, she's chocolate to de bone.

18. O BABE!

Thus he visualizes and grows boisterous. He begins again the life of the "rounder," whose adventures are sung in other songs. In anticipation of his future adventures, the negro continues,—

> Late every evenin' 'bout half pas' three,
> I hire smart coon to read the news to me.
> *O babe, O my babe, O my babe!*
>
> O babe, O babe, O my babe! take a one on me,
> An' my padhna', too, that's the way sports do,
> *O babe, O my babe, O my babe!*
>
> Well you talk 'bout one thing, you talk 'bout
>   another,
> But 'f you talk 'bout me, gwine talk 'bout yo'
>   mother.
> *O babe, O my babe, O my babe!*

19. SWEET TENNESSEE

But this is not all the easy times he is going to have. To be sure, he will not work: he will have his own way, where the "water drinks like wine," and where the "wimmins" are "stuck" on him. He bids farewell.

> Come an' go to sweet Tennessee,
> Where de money grows on trees,
> Where the rounders do as they please, babe!
> Come an' go to sweet Tennessee.
>
> Come an' go to sweet Tennessee,
> Where the wimmins all live at ease,
> Where the rounders do as they please, babe!
> Come an' go to sweet Tennessee.
>
> Come an' go to sweet Tennessee,
> Where the wimmins do as they please,
> Where the money grows on trees, babe!
> Come an' go to sweet Tennessee.

As woman occupies a prominent place in the songs of the wanderer, so woman and sweetheart occupy the most prominent part in the majority of negro social songs. The negro's conception of woman as seen in his songs has been observed. There are few exalted opinions of woman, little permanent love for sweetheart, or strong and pure love emotions. Woman and sensual love, physical characteristics and actions and jealousy, are predominant. The singer is not different from the wanderer who figured as the hero in the class of songs just given. Woman here is not unlike woman there. The negro sings,—

20. I AIN'T BOTHER YET

> I got a woman an' sweetheart, too,
> If woman don't love me, sweetheart do,
> *Yet, I ain't bother yet, I ain't bother yet.*
>
> Honey babe, I can't see
> How my money got away from me,
> *Yet I ain't bother yet, ain't bother yet.*

Or the woman sings in retort to the husband who thus sings, and who does not support her properly, or has failed to please her in some trifle,

> I got a husband, a sweetheart, too,
> *Ain't goin' to rain no mo',*
> Husband don't love me, sweetheart do,
> *Ain't goin' to rain no mo'.*

21. I'M ON MY LAST GO-ROUND

But the negro lover sometimes gets more or less despondent, after which he assures himself that he does not care. The theme of rejected love is strong, but the sorrow lasts only a short time. While this feeling lasts, however, the lover, in his jealousy, will do many things for his sweetheart, and often is unwilling to be out of her presence. Sometimes he is determined.

> It's no use you sendin' no word,
> It's no use you sendin' or writin' no letter,

I'm comin' home pay-day.

> I'm on my last go-round, *(three times)*
> God knows Albirdie won't write to me.
>
> There's mo' pretty girls 'an one,
> Swing an' clang an' don't git lost,
> There's mo' pretty girls 'an one.

22. LEARN ME TO LET ALL WOMEN ALONE

The negro is constantly singing that woman will get him into trouble; and such is the case. In a large per cent of his quarrels and fights the cause of the trouble is the "woman in the case." It is she who gets his money and makes him do all manner of trifling things to please her fancy. He then claims that she will turn from him as soon as she has got all he has. Such is, in fact, true. It is not surprising to hear the song "Learn me to let all Women alone" as the expression of a disgruntled laborer.

> One was a boy, an' one was a girl;
> If I ever specs to see 'em again,
> I'll see 'em in de other worl':
> *Learn me to let all women alone.*
>
> All I hope in this bright worl',
> If I love anybody, don't let it be a girl:
> *Learn me to let all women alone.*
>
> Firs' girl I love, she gi' me her right han',
> She's quit me in de wrong fer anoder man:
> *Learn me to let all women alone.*
>
> Woman is a good thing, an' a bad thing too,
> They quit in the wrong an' start out bran'-new:
> *Learn me to let all women alone.*
>
> I got up early nex' mornin', to meet fo' day train,
> Goin' up the railroad to find me a man:
> *Learn me to let all women alone.*

23. O MY BABE! WON'T YOU COME HOME

The negro sings, "I don't know what I'll do! Oh, I don't know what I'll do!" "Oh, I'll take time to bundle up my clothes! Oh, I'll take time to bundle up my clothes," and he is off; but he is soon involved again, and sings his promiscuous allegiance.

> I love my babe and wouldn't put her out of doors,
> I'd love to see her kill a kid wid fohty-dollar suit
>   o' clothes,
> *O my babe! won't you come home?*
>
> Some people give you nickel, some give you
>   dime;
> I ain't goin' give you frazzlin' thing, you ain't no
>   girl o' mine.
> *O my babe! won't you come home?*

Remember, babe, remember givin' me yo' han';
When you come to marry, I may be yo' man.
O my babe! won't you come home?

Went to the sea, sea look so wide,
Thought about my babe, hung my head an' cried.
O my babe! won't you come home?

24. MAKE ME A PALAT ON DE FLO'

Perhaps the lover is again turned out of doors, and pines
around the house. He studies up various means to regain
the affections of his lady-love, but finds it difficult.
"That's all right, treat me mean, treat me wrong, babe.
Fare you well forever mo', how would you like to have a
luvin' girl turn you out o' doors?" he sings, and pretends
to leave. But true to the negro proverb, "Nigger ain't gone
ever time he say good-by:" he returns again to sing,—

Make me a palat on de flo',
Make it in de kitchen behin' de do'.

Oh, don't turn good man from yo' do',
May be a frien', babe, you don't know.

Oh, look down dat lonesome lan',
Made me a palat on de flo'.

Oh, de reason I love Sarah Jane,
Made me a palat on de flo'.

In another strain the lover sings promiscuously,—

O Jane! love me lak you useter,
O Jane! chew me lak you useter,
Ev'y time I figger, my heart gits bigger,
Sorry, sorry, can't be yo' piper any mo'.

So, too, he sings "Ev'y time I dodge her, my heart gits
larger."

25. CAN'T BE YOUR TURTLE ANY MO'

Somewhat like it is the song "Can't be your Turtle any
mo'," localized to apply to Atlanta, Memphis, or other
specific places.

Goin' to Atlanta, goin' to ride de rod,
Goin' to leave my babe in de hands o' God,
Sorry, sorry, can't be your turtle any mo'.

Goin' up town, goin' hurry right back,
Honey got sumpin' I certainly lak',
Sorry, sorry, can't be yo' warbler any mo'.

26. NO MORE GOOD TIME

While there is much repetition in thought in the songs
of woman and sweetheart, they are very true to actual
life, and depict with accuracy the common scenes and
speeches of the negroes. The morals of the negro are
also reflected. Some of his ideals of love and "a good
time" are indicated. "No More Good Time" tells of a
common scene.

No more good time, woman, like we used to
  have,
Police knockin' woman at my back do'.

Meet me at the depot, bring my dirty clothes,
Meet me at depot, woman, when the train comes
  down;

For I goin' back to leave you, ain't comin' back
  no mo';
You treated me so dirty, ain't comin' back no
  mo'.

I got a little black woman, honey, an' her name's
  Mary Lou,
She treat me better, baby, heap better than you.

The negro adds much zest and fun to his song when he
introduces local characters. In the above line it is "Police Johnson, woman, knockin' at de do'," or in other
localities it is the name of the most dreaded officer. The
negroes sing these and laugh heartily, boasting now and
then of fortunate escapes.

27. DIAMON' JOE

Very much like the above in general tone, but sung by
a woman, "Diamon' Joe" typifies the usual custom common in every negro community. It is a love-song.

Diamon' Joe, you better come an' git me:
Don't you see my man done quit?
Diamon' Joe com'n git me.

Diamon' Joe he had a wife, they parted every
  night;
When the weather it got cool,
Ole Joe he come back to that black gal.

But time come to pass,
When old Joe quit his last,
An' he never went to see her any mo'.

28. BABY, WHAT HAVE I DONE?

"Baby, what have I done?" introduces the various scenes
of negro love-life. The same wail of "knockin' at de
do'" is heard again and again,—a hint at infidelity,
which is so often sung in the next few songs. The simple
life and simple thought appear primitive. What if this
poetry means as much to him as any other? No other
ideals would satisfy him, or even appeal to him.

Late las' night an' night befo',
Heard such a knockin' at my do',
Jumped up in stockin' feet, skipped across the
  flo',
Baby, don't never knock at my do' no mo'.

Oh me, oh my! baby, what have I done?

Where were you las' Saturday night,
When I lay sick in my bed?
You down town wid some other ole girl,
Wasn't here to hold my head.

Ain't it hard to love an' not be loved? *(four
    times)*

Other verses of one long line are divided into two short lines or repeated each four times to make the stanza. The art of negro singing is brought out best in his repetition.

It's ninety-six miles from Birmingham
I tramped it day by day.

It's fifteen cents' wuth o' morphine,
A dollar's all I crave.

I didn't bring nuthin' in this bright worl',
Nuthin' I'll carry away.

I laid my head in bar-room do',
Ain't goin' to get drunk no mo'.

Han' me down my grip-sack,
An' all my ole dirty clothes.

If my baby ask for me,
Tell her I boun' to go.

29. THINGS AIN'T SAME, BABE, SINCE I WENT 'WAY

Both men and women appear changeable in their affections. A husband and wife may quarrel the first of the week, separate, vow that they will never speak again; the latter part of the week may find them as loving as ever. This does not happen one week, but many times. A negro man will often give his entire week's or month's wages in order to pacify his wife who has threatened to go live with some other man. She in turn spends the money, and begins to quarrel again. In the same way the wife may often beg to be received back after she has left him; she is often received, sometimes with a beating, sometimes not at all. A typical appeal of these characters is sung:

Things ain't same, babe, since I went 'way,
Now I return, please let me stay;
I'm sorry I lef' you in this worl' alone,
I'm on my way, babe, I'm comin' home.

30. BABY, LET ME BRING MY CLOTHES BACK HOME

Another appeal of the husband to his wife is a little more forceful. It is the present moment that counts with the average negro: he will easily promise to do anything to get out of an emergency or to get into favor. So the negro often makes promises of fidelity, if only he will be given another chance. The picture of the big, brawny

negro thus whining before his "woman's" door is an amusing one. It is, however, characteristic in its adaptation of the "coon" song into a negro song:

The burly coon, you know,
He packed his clothes to go,
Well, he come back las' night,
His wife said, "Honey, I'm tired o' coon,
I goin' to pass for white."

But the coon got mad,
He's 'bliged to play bad,
Because his color was black;
O my lovin' baby! don't you make me go;
I git a job, if you let me, sho'.

I'll wuk both night an' day,
An' let you draw my pay;
Baby, let me bring my clothes back home!
When you kill chicken, save me the bone;
When you bag beer, give me the foam.

I'll work both night an' day,
An' let you draw the pay;
Baby, let me bring my clothes back home;
When she make them strange remarks,
He look surprise—goin' roll them white eyes,
Goin' cry, baby, don't make me go!

31. LONG AND TALL AN' CHOCOLATE TO THE BONE

One of the most common descriptions, and one of the most complimentary to the negro woman, as found in negro songs, is "chocolate to the bone." The negro often makes trouble for the meddler in his home. Here arises many of the capital crimes of the negroes. Jealousy runs riot among both men and women. In the following song a hint is given of the boasting spirit of the negro:

Well, I'm goin' to buy me a little railroad of my
    own,
Ain't goin' to let nobody ride but the chocolate to
    the bone.

Well, I goin' to buy me a hotel of my own,
Ain't goin' to let nobody eat but the chocolate to
    the bone.

She's long an' tall an' chocolate to the bone,

Well, I goin' to start a little *graveyard* of my
    own,
If you don't, ole nigger, let my woman alone.

She's long an' tall an' chocolate to the bone,
She make you married man, then leave yo' home.

32. GOIN' BACK TO SWEET MEMPHIS, TENNESSEE

In much the same way, now the woman, now the man, sings back at each other. In the first stanza of the song "Yo' Man," the woman is supposed to be talking; the man often sings the song, however, as he does all of them. It is also interpreted to be the words of one man to his wife, and also of one woman to another. The song is well mixed.

> Well, if that's yo' man, you'd better buy a lock
> 　an' key, O babe!
> An' stop yo' man from runnin' after me-e-e.
>
> *Well, I goin' back to sweet Memphis, Tennessee,*
> 　*O babe!*
> *Where de good-lookin' wimmins take on over*
> 　*me—make a fuss over me.*
>
> Now, a good-lookin' man can gift a home
> 　anywaher' he go,
> The reason why is, the wimmins tell me so.
>
> She change a dollar an' give me a lovin' dime,
> I'll see her when her trouble like mine.

33. STARTED TO LEAVE

The sense of humor is very marked in many of the verses sung by the negroes. The commonplace, matter-of-fact statement in the following song is noticeable. Says the negro, "Yes,"

> I'm goin' 'way, goin' 'way,
> Goin' sleep under the trees till weather gits
> 　warmer,
> Well, me an' my baby can't agree,
> Oh, that's the reason I'm goin' to leave.

But, as in other cases, the negro does not stay long. Perhaps it is too cold under the trees for him; perhaps the song has it all wrong, anyway. But the negro again sings,—

> Well, I started to leave, an' got 'way down the
> 　track,
> Got to thinkin' 'bout my woman, come runnin'
> 　back, O babe!
>
> She have got a bad man, an' he's as bad as hell, I
> 　know,
> For ev'body, sho' God, tell me so.
>
> I thought I'd tell you what yo' nigger woman'll
> 　do,
> She have another man an' play sick on you.

34. I COULDN'T GIT IN

Thus, although the singer begins, as he often does, with the better thoughts of the woman, he ends with the usual abuse and distrust. This spirit of infidelity is unfortunately common among the negroes. With some it is a matter of no concern, for what does it matter to them? with others it is a matter of anger and revenge; while still others are jealously troubled about it. What has already been touched upon in the songs given may be shown further in "I couldn't git in."

> Lawd, went to my woman's do',
> Jus' lak I bin goin' befo':
> "I got my all-night trick, baby,
> An' you can't git in."
>
> "Come back 'bout half pas' fo',
> If I'm done, I'll open de do', (or let you know)
> Got my all-night trick, baby,
> An' you can't git in."
>
> I keep a rappin' on my woman's do',
> Lak I never had been dere befo';
> She got a midnight creeper dere,
> An' I couldn't git in.
>
> "Buddy, you oughter to do lak me,
> Git a good woman, let the cheap ones be,
> Fur dey always got a midnight creeper,
> An' you can't come in.
>
> "Buddy, stop an' let me tell you
> What yo' woman'll do;
> She have 'nurther man in, play sick on you,
> She got all-night creeper, Buddy,
> An' you can't git in.
>
> "You go home; well, she layin' in bed,
> With red rag tied all 'round her head;
> She done had fo'-day creeper in here,
> Dat's de reason you couldn't git in."

In the same way other verses are sung: "Keep a knockin', can't come in, I got company an' you can't come in," or "You can't come in dis do'."

35. WHAT, STIRRIN', BABE

The singer uses the common slang "fallin' den" for his bed. As he has sung of his love and jealousies, so he sings of varied affection and infidelity, but with little serious regret.

> Went up town 'bout four o'clock,
> *What, stirrin' babe, stirrin' babe?*
> When I got there, door was locked:
> *What stir'd babe, what stir'd babe?*
>
> Went to de window an' den peeped in:
> *What, stirrin' babe, stirrin' babe?*
> Somebody in my fallin' den—
> *What, stirrin' babe, stirrin' babe?*

The woman tells the "creeper" that he had best be watchful while he is about her house. At the same time, besides his general rowdyism, he is perhaps eating all the provisions in the house. She sings,—

> Don't you let my honey catch you here—*(three*
> 　*times)*
> He'll kill you dead jus' sho's you born.

36. HOP RIGHT

It will thus be seen that the songs of the most characteristic type are far from elegant. Nor are they dignified in theme or expression. They will appear to the cultured reader a bit repulsive, to say the least. They go beyond the interesting point to the trite and repulsive themes. Nor can a great many of the common songs that are too inelegant to include be given at all. But these are folk-songs current among the negroes, and as such are powerful comment upon the special characteristics of the group. A few of the shorter themes thus sung will illustrate further.

> Hop right, goin' to see my baby Lou,
> Goin' to walk an' talk wid my honey,
> Goin' to hug an' kiss my honey,
>   *Hop right, my baby!*

The negro does not mind that his comment may not be undignified, or that it may be injurious to personal feelings or race opinion. Sings he,—

> I wouldn't have yellow gal,
>   Tell you de reason why:
> Her neck so long, 'fraid she never die.
> I wouldn't have a black gal,
>   Tell you de reason why:
> Her hair so kinky, she break every comb I buy.

37. IF YOU WANT TO GO A COURTIN'

More original and satisfying in sentiment and rhyme and sensuous pictures is the following:

> If you want to go a courtin', I sho' you where to
>   go,
> Right down yonder in de house below.
>
> Clothes all dirty an' ain't got no broom,
> Ole dirty clothes all hangin' in de room.
>
> Ask'd me to table, thought I'd take a seat,
> First thing I saw was big chunk o' meat.
>
> Big as my head, hard as a maul,
> Ash-cake, corn-bread, bran an' all.

38. IF YOU WANT TO MARRY

Another that sounds like some of the songs used in children's games in the Colonial days is "Marry Me." The song has come to be thought a negro song, but is apparently a form of the old rhymes, "If you will marry, marry, marry; If you will marry me," or "For I want to marry, marry, marry, you;" "Soldier, will you marry me?" The negro sings,—

> If you want to marry, come an' marry me-e-e,
> Silk an' satin you shall wear, but trouble you
>   shall see-e-e.
>
> If you want to marry, marry the sailor's daughter,
> Put her in a coffee-pot and sen' her 'cross the
>   water.

> I marry black gal, she was black, you know,
> For when I went to see her, she look like a crow-
>   ow,
>   She look like a crow-ow-ow.

39. HONEY, TAKE A ONE ON ME

A variation of the well-known little song, "Honey, take a One on Me," has a great number of verses that have become popular, and are undoubtedly negro verses. Most of these, however, are not suitable for publication. An idea may be given of the song.

> Comin' down State Street, comin' down Main,
> Lookin' for de woman dat use cocaine,
> *Honey, take a one on me!*
>
> Goin' down Peter Street, comin' down Main,
> Lookin' for de woman ain't got no man,
> *Honey, take a one on me!*

40. DON'T HIT THAT WOMAN

One other illustration may be given, to show this mental attitude toward a woman:

> Don't hit that woman, I tell you why:
> Well, she got heart-trouble an' I scared she die.
>
> That shot got her, how do you know?
> For my woman she told me so.
>
> Now, if you hit that woman, I tell you fine,
> She will give you trouble all the time.

41. I LOVE THAT MAN

More serious and of much better sentiment is the lover's song, ordinarily sung as the appeal of a woman.

> I love that man, O God! I do,
> I love him till the day he die;
>
> If I thought that he didn't love me,
> I'd eat morphine an' die.
>
> If I had listened to what mamma said,
> I wouldn't a been here to-day;
>
> But bein' so young, I throwed
> That young body o' mine away.
>
> Look down po' lonesome road,
> Hacks all dead in line.
>
> Some give nickel, some give dime,
> To bury dis po' body o' mine.

42. KELLY'S LOVE

In "Kelly's Love" the note of disappointed love is sounded:

Love, Kelly's love, (three times)
You broke de heart o' many a girl,
You never break dis heart o' mine.

When I wo' my aprons low, *(three times)*
Couldn't keep you from my do'.

Now I weahs my aprons high, *(three times)*
Sca'cely ever see you passin' by.

Now I weahs my aprons to my chin, *(three times)*
You pass my do', but can't come in.

See what Kelly's love have done. *(three times)*
See what Kelly's love have done.

If I had listened to what my mamma said; *(three times)*
I would a been at home in mamma's bed.

43. MY LOVE FOR YOU IS ALL I KNEW

Nearer the simple longing of a sincere affection is the chorus "Farewell." This conception has been found in the common mixed song that is current:

My love for you is all I knew, *(three times).*
Hope I will see you again.

Farewell, my darling, farewell! *(three times)*
Hope I will see you again.

44. THOUGHT I HEARD THAT K. C.

The negro grows imaginative when he thinks of things absent. In his religious song it is Heaven and the angels that bring forth his best expressions. He is an idealist, and utopianism is perhaps only the childlike imagery of fairy fancies. So in his social songs he tells of the good times he has had and is going to have. He does not sing so much of the present: he sings of dangers he has escaped. In the same way he longs to see his sweetheart while he is away from her. Says he, "My honey might be far from home; ask central to gi' me long-distance phone."

Thought I heard that K. C. whistle blow,
Blow lak she never blow befo'.

How long has Frisco train been gone?
Dat's train carried my baby home.

Look down de Southern road an' cry,
Babe, look down de Southern road an' cry.

45. SWEET, FORGET ME NOT

The negro looks longingly for the train and the time when he will have money enough to go back "home." Pay-day will come, and for a time he will be happy.

Sometimes he thinks of all good times in the future. Sometimes, however, he sings plaintively that they are gone.

O girl, O girl! what have I done?
Sweet, forget me not. (three times)

I've got a girl dat's on de way,
Sweet, forget me not.

Times ain't like dey use ter be,
Sweet, forget me not.

Times have been, won't be no more,
Sweet, forget me not.

Nowhere is the negro more characteristic than in his wanton and reckless moods. Nothing pleases this type of negro fancy more than deeds of bravado and notoriety. He loves to tell of them and hear them recited. He is apparently at his best on such occasions. His self-feeling in its positive state is given gratification, and his vivid imagination easily makes him the hero of the hour. The feeling of rowdyism is thus encouraged. The notorious character is thus sung as the hero of the race: his deeds are marvelled at. Perhaps he is the most interesting figure within the whole field of activities. Certainly he is a distinct character, and has a tremendous influence upon the conduct of his people. He is admired by young and old; and those who do not approve of his deeds or example marvel at his powers.

46. STAGOLEE

"Stagolee" must have been a wonderful fellow! though not so much dreaded as "Railroad Bill" and some others. Here the negro sings in his best vein.

Stagolee, Stagolee, what's dat in yo' grip?
Nothin' but my Sunday clothes, I'm goin' to take
   a trip,
O dat man, bad man, Stagolee done come.

Stagolee, Stagolee, where you been so long?
I been out on de battle fiel' shootin' an' havin'
   fun,
O dat man, bad man, Stagolee done come.

Stagolee was a bully man, an' ev'y body knowed,
When dey seed Stagolee comin', to give Stagolee
   de road,
O dat man, bad man, Stagolee done come.

The refrain "*O dat man, bad man, Stagolee done come*" is sung at the end of each stanza, and adds much to the charm of the song, giving characteristic thought to the words, and rhythmical swing to the music. The singer continues his narration, adding the refrain to each stanza,—

Stagolee started out, he give his wife his han',
"Good-by, darlin', I'm goin' to kill a man."

Stagolee killed a man an' laid him on de flo',

What's dat he kill him wid? Dat same ole fohty-fo'.

Stagolee killed a man an' laid him on his side,
What's dat he kill him wid? Dat same ole fohty-
  five.

Out of house an' down de street Stagolee did run,
In his hand he held a great big smokin' gun.

Stagolee, Stagolee, I'll tell you what I'll do,
If you'll git me out'n dis trouble I'll do as much
  for you.

Ain't it a pity, ain't it a shame?
Stagolee was shot, but he don't want no name.

Stagolee, Stagolee, look what you done done,
Killed de best ole citerzen; now you'll hav' to be
  hung.

Stagolee cried to de jury an' to de judge: Please
  don't take my life,
I have only three little children an' one little
  lovin' wife,
O dat man, bad man, Stagolee done come.

47. STAGOLEE

The above version is more usually sung in Mississippi, Louisiana, and Tennessee, though it is known in Alabama and Georgia, besides being sung by the negro vagrants all over the country. Another version more common in Georgia celebrates Stagolee as a somewhat different character, and the song is sung to different music. The negro sings,—

I got up one mornin' jes' 'bout four o'clock;
Stagolee an' big bully done have one finish'
  fight:
What 'bout? All 'bout? dat raw-hide Stetson hat.

Stagolee shot Bully; Bully fell down on de flo',
Bully cry out: "Dat fohty-fo' hurts me so."
Stagolee done killed dat Bully now.

Sent for de wagon, wagon didn't come,
Loaded down wid pistols an' all dat gatlin' gun,
Stagolee done kill dat Bully now.

Some giv' a nickel, some giv' a dime,
I didn't give a red copper cent, 'cause he's no
  friend o' mine,
Stagolee done kill dat Bully now.

Carried po' Bully to cemetary, people standin'
  'round,
When preacher say Amen, lay po' body down,
Stagolee done kill dat Bully now.

Fohty dollah coffin, eighty dollah hack,
Carried po' man to cemetary but failed to bring
  him back,
Ev'y body been dodgin' Stagolee.

The scenes of Stagolee's activities are representative of this type of negro life. From the home to the cemetery he has gone the road of many a negro. Sometimes the man killed is at a picnic or public gathering, sometimes elsewhere. The scenes of the burial, with its customs, are but a part of the life: hence they are portrayed with equal diligence.

48. RAILROAD BILL

But Stagolee has his equal, if not his superior, in the admiration of the negro. "Railroad Bill" has had a wonderful career in song and story. The negro adds his part, and surpasses any other in his portrayal of this hero of the track. One must take all the versions of the song in order to appreciate fully the ideal of such a character. In the first song that follows, the reader will note that after the theme is once in the mouth of the singer, it matters little what the song is. The effort is to sing something about "Bill," and to make this conform to the general idea; and at the same time it must rhyme. Here is the song, and a wonderful picture it is:

Some one went home an' tole my wife
All about—well, my pas' life,
It was that bad Railroad Bill.

Railroad Bill, Railroad Bill,
He never work, an' he never will,
Well, it's that bad Railroad Bill.

Railroad Bill so mean an' so bad,
Till he tuk ev'ything that farmer had,
It's that bad Railroad Bill.

I'm goin' home an' tell my wife,
Railroad Bill try to take my life,
It's that bad Railroad Bill.

Railroad Bill so desp'rate an' so bad,
He take ev'ything po' womens had,
An' it's that bad Railroad Bill.

49. IT'S THAT BAD RAILROAD BILL

With all these crimes to his credit, it is high time that some one was going after Railroad Bill. The singer starts on his journey as quickly as he can, but has to make many trips.

I went down on Number One,
Railroad Bill had jus' begun.
It's lookin' for Railroad Bill.

I come up on Number Two,
Railroad Bill had jus' got through,
It's that bad Railroad Bill.

I caught Number Three and went back down the
  road,
Railroad Bill was marchin' to an' fro.
It's that bad Railroad Bill.

An' jus' as I caught that Number Fo',

Somebody shot at me wid a fohty-fo'.
It's that bad Railroad Bill.

I went back on Number Five,
Goin' to bring him back, dead or alive.
Lookin' for Railroad Bill.

When I come up on Number Six,
All the peoples had done got sick,
Lookin' for Railroad Bill.

When I went down on Number Seven,
All the peoples wish'd they's in heaven,
A-lookin' for Railroad Bill.

I come back on Number Eight,
The folks say I was a minit too late,
It's lookin' for Railroad Bill.

When I come back on Number Nine,
Folks say, "You're just in time
To catch that Railroad Bill."

When I got my men, they amounted to ten,
An' that's when I run po' Railroad Bill in,
An' that was last of po' Railroad Bill.

50. IT'S LOOKIN' FOR RAILROAD BILL

But that was *not* the last of Railroad Bill; for the singer had only imagined that he was the hero to "down him." Railroad Bill soon appears again, and now he is worse than before. The next version differs only slightly from the foregoing one. One must remember that the chorus line follows each couplet, and the contrast in meaning makes a most interesting song.

Railroad Bill mighty bad man,
Shoot dem lights out o' de brakeman's han',
It's lookin' fer Railroad Bill.

Railroad Bill mighty bad man,
Shoot the lamps all off the stan',
An' it's lookin' for Railroad Bill.

First on table, nex' on wall,
Ole corn whiskey cause of it all,
It's lookin' fer Railroad Bill.

Ole McMillan had a special train,
When he got there wus a shower of rain,
Wus lookin' fer Railroad Bill.

Ev'ybody tole him he better turn back,
Railroad Bill wus goin' down track,
An' it's lookin' fer Railroad Bill.

Well, the policemen all dressed in blue,
Comin' down sidewalk two by two,
Wus lookin' fer Railroad Bill.

Railroad Bill had no wife,
Always lookin' fer somebody's life,
An' it's lookin' fer Railroad Bill.

Railroad Bill was the worst ole coon,

Killed McMillan by de light o' de moon,
It's lookin' fer Railroad Bill.

Ole Culpepper went up on Number Five,
Goin' bring him back, dead or alive,
Wus lookin' fer Railroad Bill.

Standin' on corner didn't mean no harm,
Policeman grab me by my arm,
Wus lookin' fer Railroad Bill.

The negroes sing different forms of these verses, as they are suggested at the moment; so they add others or omit parts. Also are sung:

MacMillan had a special train,
When he got there, it was spring.

Two policemen all dressed in blue
Come down street in two an' two.

Railroad Bill led a mighty bad life,
Always after some other man's wife.

Railroad Bill went out Wes',
Thought he had dem cowboys bes'.

Railroad Bill mighty bad man,
Kill McGruder by de light o' the moon.

51. RIGHT ON DESPERADO BILL

It is not surprising that a song so popular as "Railroad Bill" should find its way into others of similar type. Another version of the same song has a separate chorus, to be sung after each stanza. This chorus, of which there are two forms, adds recklessness to the theme. Another achievement is given the desperado; and he combines gambling, criminal tendencies, and his general immorality, in one. The following version is somewhat mixed, but is known as "Railroad Bill:"

Railroad Bill was mighty sport,
Shot all buttons off high sheriff's coat,
Den hollered, *"Right on desperado Bill!"*
Lose, lose—I don't keer,
If I win, let me win lak' a man,
If I lose all my money,
I'll be gamblin' for my honey,
Ev'y man ought to know when he lose.

Lose, lose, I don't keer,
If I win, let me win lak' a man,
Lost fohty-one dollars tryin' to win a dime,
Ev'y man plays in tough luck some time.

Honey babe, honey babe, where have you been so
    long?
I ain't been happy since you been gone,
Dat's all right, dat's all right, honey babe.

Honey babe, honey babe, bring me de broom,
De lices an' chinches 'bout to take my room,
O my baby, baby, honey, chile!

Honey babe, honey babe, what in de worl' is dat?

Got on tan shoes an' black silk hat,
Honey babe, give it all to me.

Talk 'bout yo' five an' ten dollar bill,
Ain't no Bill like ole desperado Bill,
Says, Right on desperado Bill.

Railroad Bill went out west,
Met ole Jesse James, thought he had him best,
But Jesse laid ole Railroad Bill.

Honey babe, honey babe, can't you never hear?
I wants a nuther nickel to git a glass o' beer,
Dat's all right, honey babe, dat's all right.

Some of the verses just given are far from elegant; others still less elegant must be omitted. Some conception of popular standards of conduct and dress, social life and the home, may be gained from the song, in addition to the now familiar character of "Railroad Bill."

52. LOOKIN' FOR THAT BULLY OF THIS TOWN

In most communities there is one or more notorious characters among the negroes. Often these are widely known throughout the State, and they are familiar names to the police. Sometimes they are known for the most part to the negroes. Such characters, noted for their rowdyism and recklessness, sometimes with a criminal record, are usually called "bullies." To be sure, "Stagolee," "Railroad Bill," "Eddy Jones," and the others, were "bullies," but they were special cases. The song "I'm lookin' for the Bully of this Town" represents a more general condition. It is rich in portrayals of negro life and thought.

Monday I was 'rested, Tuesday I was fined,
Sent to chain gang, done serve my time,
Still I'm lookin' for that bully of this town.

The bully, the bully, the bully can't be found,
If I fin' that bully, goin' to lay his body down,
I'm lookin' for that bully of this town.

The police up town they're all scared,
But if I fin' that bully, I goin' to lay his body
   'way,
For I'm lookin' for that bully of this town.

I'm goin' down on Peter Street;
If I fin' that bully, will be bloody meet,
For I'm lookin' for that bully of this town.

I went down town the other day,
I ask ev'ybody did that bully come this way,
I wus lookin' fer that bully of this town.

Oh, the gov'ner of this State offer'd one hundred
   dollars reward,
To any body's arrested that bully boy,
I sho' lookin' for dat bully of this town.

Well, I found that bully on a Friday night,
I told that bully I's gwine to take his life,

I found dat bully of this town.

I pull out my gun an' begin to fire,
I shot that bully right through the eye,
An' I kill that bully of this town.

Now all the wimmins come to town all dressed in
   red,
When they heard that bully boy was dead,
An' it was the last of that bully of this town.

What a picture the song gives of the bully and his pursuer! The boasting braggart sees himself the hero of the whole community, but chiefly among the women. He is better than the police: they will even thank him for his valor. The governor will give him his reward. Everybody he meets he asks about the bully boy, and takes on a new swagger. What satisfaction he gets from it! Perhaps he too will be a bully. The scene of the shooting, the reaching for the pistol, and the "laying-down" of the bully's body,—these offer unalloyed satisfaction to the singer. Every word becomes pregnant with new meaning and feeling; and invariably he must remember that his deeds are lauded, and he is the hero among the "wimmins" from the country round about. His picture would never be complete without this. Altogether it is a great song, and defies a superior picture.

53. EDDY JONES

Other notorious characters are sung with the same satisfaction. The characteristic pleasure and oblivion of time accompany the singing. While at work, one may sing the words, whistle the tunes, and visualize the picture, thus getting a richer field of vision. When alone, the negro gets much satisfaction out of songs like those here given. Likewise such songs are sung in groups, at which times the singers talk and laugh, jeer one another, and retort, thus varying the song. "Eddy Jones" seems very similar in character to "Stagolee."

Slow train run thru' Arkansas,
   Carryin' Eddy Jones.

Eddy died with a special in his hand,
   Eddy Jones, Eddy Jones.

Eddy Jones call for the coolin'-board,
   Lawdy, lawdy, lawd!

Eddy Jones look'd 'round an' said,
"Man that kill'd me won't have no luck."

Ain't it sad 'bout po' Eddy bein' dead?
Eddy Jones was let down in his grave.

What did Eddy say before he died?
He said, "Nearer, my God, to Thee."

Eddy's mother she weeped a day,
Lawdy, Eddy Jones, Eddy Jones!

The singer turns to the "ladies," if they be present, and sings,—

You want me to do like Eddy Jones?
You mus' want me to lay down an' die for you.

54. JOE TURNER

The "special" is a well-known term for the negro's "gun," which is usually a pistol; the "44" is always the favorite. The "coolin'-board is the death-bed, and is a common expression used to signify that one's time is at an end; that is, when he is to be on the "coolin'-board." The negro criminal almost invariably dies at peace with God. The conception commonly found among the negroes, and one which they cultivate, is that the criminal will always be reconciled before his death. So in this case Eddy Jones dies singing "Nearer, my God, to Thee." In much the same way the man who has been to the chain gang or prison is looked upon with some sort of admiration at the same time that he is feared. In "Joe Turner" an ideal is hinted at. Each line is sung three times to make a stanza.

> Dey tell me Joe Turner he done come,
> Dey tell me Joe Turner he done come,
> Oh, dey tell me Joe Turner he done come.
>
> Come like he ain't never come befo'. *(three times)*
>
> Come with that fohty links o' chain. *(three times)*
>
> Tell a me Joe Turner is my man. *(three times)*

55. CASEY JONES

A hero of less criminal intents and habits was "Casey Jones." He is the hero of the engine and train. As will be noted, the negro is fascinated by the train-song. He would like to be an engineer all his days. Negroes often discuss among themselves the possibility of their occupying positions on the trains; they take almost as much pride in being brakemen and subordinates. It is interesting to hear them boasting of what they would do in emergencies, or whether or not they would be frightened. The song that follows gives a favorite version of the ballad.

> Casey Jones was engineer,
> Told his fireman not to fear,
> All he wanted was boiler hot,
> Run in Canton 'bout four o'clock.
>
> One Sunday mornin' it wus drizzlin' rain,
> Looked down road an' saw a train,
> Fireman says, "Let's make a jump,
> Two locomotives an' dey bound to bump."
>
> Casey Jones, I know him well,
> Tole de fireman to ring de bell;
> Fireman jump an' say good-by,
> Casey Jones, you're bound to die.
>
> Went on down to de depot track,

Beggin' my honey to take me back,
She turn 'roun some two or three times,
"Take you back when you learn to grind:"

> Womens in Kansas all dressed in red,
> Got de news dat Casey was dead;
> De womens in Jackson all dressed in black,
> Said, in fact, he was a cracker-jack.

The verse about "begging his honey" is intended to give the scene after the wreck, when the fireman, who did not stay on the engine with Casey, was out of a job. "Canton" and "Jackson" are regularly sung in Mississippi, while "Memphis" is more often sung in Tennessee.

56. JOSEPH MICA

Another version of the song as found in Georgia and Alabama is sung in honor of "Joseph Mica." Atlanta or Birmingham are the local places.

> Joseph Mica was good engineer,
> Told his fireman not to fear,
> All he want is water'n coal,
> Poke his head out, see drivers roll.
>
> Early one mornin' look like rain,
> 'Round de curve come passenger train,
> On powers lie ole Jim Jones,
> Good ole engineer, but daid an' gone.
>
> Left Atlanta hour behin',
> Tole his fireman to make up the time,
> All he want is boiler hot,
> Run in there 'bout four o'clock.

The picture of the man looking out of the locomotive window and watching the "drivers" roll is a good one. The negroes love to watch the trains; and no more complete happiness could be imagined than to be an engineer, with nothing to do but watch the scenes and the engine.

57. BRADY

A more mixed scene is pictured in "Brady." Here, too, the women hear of the news, as, indeed, they always do; but this time they are glad of his death. Why this is, the song does not tell. Brady, however, must have been a pretty bad fellow, for he did not stay long in hell.

> Brady went to hell, but he didn't go to stay,
> Devil say, "Brady, step 'roun' dis way,
> I'm lookin' for you mos' every day."
>
> Brady, Brady, you know you done wrong,
> You come in when game was goin' on,
> An' dey laid po' Brady down.
>
> Up wid de crowbar, bus' open de do',
> Lef' him lyin' dead on pool-room flo',
> An' they laid his po' body down.
>
> Womens in Iowy dey heard de news,

Wrote it down on ole red shoes,
Dat dey glad po' Brady wus dead.

The scene is one of a killing in a game of poker or craps. "They laid his po' body down" is the common way of saying they killed him. The expression has been met in a number of verses previously given. Just what the conclusion of the scene with the devil was, the negro singer does not seem to know.

58. THE NEGRO BUM

More personal and less conspicuous are the boasts of individuals. Here the negro's wit appears again, and he refuses to be interrupted with anything serious, unless it be fear of some officer. The "Negro Bum" is the name of a short song that is a good exposition of his feelings.

 I wus goin' down the railroad, hungry an' wanted
  to eat,
 I ask white lady for some bread an' meat,
 She giv' me bread an' coffee, an' treated me
  mighty kin',
 If I could git them good handouts, I'd quit work,
  bum all the time.

 Well, the railroad completed, the cars upon the
  track,
 Yonder comes two dirty hobos with grip-sacks on
  dere backs,
 One look like my brother, the other my brother-
  in-law,
 They walk all the way from Mississippi to the
  State of Arkansas.

59. ONE MO' ROUNDER GONE

The term "rounder" is applied not only to men, but to women also. In general, the interpretation is that of a worthless and wandering person, who prides himself on being idle, and thus on the acquirement of as many passing accomplishments as possible. It is also a term of fellowship. In songs that follow, the chorus "One mo' Rounder gone" will be found to express fitting sentiment to the accompanying scenes. The song by that name gives a repetition of the burial-scenes and general feeling which was caused by the death of a girl. Its unusual feature lies in the fact that the song applies to a girl.

 Rubber-tired buggy, double-seated hack,
 Well, it carried po' Delia to graveyard, failed to
  bring her back,
  Lawdy, one mo' rounder gone.

 Delia's mother weep, Delia's mother mourn,
 She wouldn't have taken it so hard if po' girl had
  died at home,
  Well, one mo' ole rounder gone.

 Yes, some give a nickel, some give a dime,
 I didn't give nary red cent, fo' she was no friend
  o' mine,
  Well, it's one mo' rounder gone.

60. EASTMAN

The negroes have appropriate names for many of their typical characters, the meaning of which is difficult to explain. "Eastman," "rounder," "creeper," and other characters, have their own peculiar characteristics. The "rounder" is more than the idle character. He becomes the meddler in the home. The "Eastman" is kept fat by the women among whom he is universally a favorite. The "creeper" watches his chance to get admittance into a home, unknown to the husband. The "Natu'al-bohn Eastman" gives a view of his opinion of himself, with adopted forms of burlesque.

 I went down to New Orleans
 To buy my wife a sewin'-machine,
 The needle broke an' she couldn't sew,
 I'm a natu'al-bohn Eastman, for she tole me so.

 I'm a Eastman, how do you know?
 I'm a natu'al-bohn Eastman, for she tole me so.

 Well, they call me a Eastman if I walk around,
 They call me a Eastman if I leave the town,
 I got it writ on the tail o' my shirt,
 I'm a natu'al-bohn Eastman, don't have to work.

 Oh, I'm a Eastman on the road again,
 For I'm an Eastman on the road again.

 Wake-up, ole rounder, it's time to go,
 I think I heard dat whistle blow,
 You step out, let work-ox step in,
 You're a natu'al-bohn Eastman, you k'n come
  agin.

 Carry me down to the station-house do',
 Find nuther Eastman an' let me know.

 Wake up, ole rounder, you sleep too late,
 Money-makin' man done pass yo' gate,
 You step out, let money-makin' man step in,
 You a natu'al-bohn Eastman, you can come agin.

61. BAD-LAN' STONE

The negro loves to boast of being a "bad man." "I bin a *bad man* in my day," says the older fellow to the boys about him. Much the same sentiment is here sung as that in the songs just given. He sings,—

 I was bohn in a mighty bad lan',
 For my name is Bad-Lan' Stone.

 Well, I want all you coons fer to understan',
 I am dangerous wid my licker on.

 You may bring all yo' guns from de battle-ship,
 I make a coon climb a tree.

 Don't you never dare to slight my repertation,
 Or I'll break up this jamberee.

 Well, well, I wus bohn in a mighty bad lan',
 For my name—my name—is *Bad-Man Stone.*

62. YOU MAY LEAVE, BUT THIS WILL BRING YOU BACK

It will be seen that the negro loves to sing of trials in court, arrests, idleness, crime, and bravado. The tramp and the "rounder," the "Eastman" and the "creeper," are but typical extremes. The notorious characters sung are the objective specimens of the common spirit of self-feeling. Now comes the song with the personal boast and the reckless brag. Mixed with it all is the happy-go-lucky sense of don't-care and humor. It is a great philosophy of life the negro has.

> Satisfied, tickled to death,
> Got a bottle o' whiskey on my shelf,
> *You may leave, but this will bring you back.*

> Satisfied, satisfied,
> Got my honey by my side,
> *You may leave, but this will bring you back.*

> An' I'm jus' frum the country-come to town,
> A too-loo-shaker from my head on down,
> *You may leave, but this will bring you back.*

63. THIS MORNIN', THIS EVENIN', SO SOON

What does it matter to him if he has been in serious trouble? Is not the jail about as good as home, the chain gang as good as his every-day life? He will get enough to eat and a place to sleep. The negro sings with characteristic humor "This mornin', this evenin'," and mingles his scenes in such a way that the singer enjoys them all. Says he,—

> Went up town wid my hat in my han' dis
>   mo'nin',
> Went up town wid my hat in my han',
> "Good mornin', jedge, done killed my man,"
>   *This mornin', this evenin', so soon.*

> I didn't quite kill him, but I fixed him so, this
>   mornin',
> I didn't quite kill him, but I fixed him so,
> He won't boder wid me no mo',
>   *This mornin', this evenin', so soon.*

> All I want is my strong hand-out, this mornin',
> All I want is my strong hand-out,
> It will make me strong and stout,
>   *This mornin', this evenin', so soon.*

In the same way other couplets are sung,—the first line repeated twice with "this mornin';" the third time without it, and rhymed with the second line of the couplet, after which follows the refrain *This mornin', this evenin', so soon."* The effect is striking.

> When you kill a chicken, save me the feet,
> When you think I'm workin', I'm walkin' the
>   street.

> When you kill a chicken, save me the whang,
> When you think I'm workin', I ain't doin' a thing.

'Tain't no use a me workin' so,
'Cause I ain't goin' ter work no mo'.

I'm goin' back to Tennessee,
Where dem wimmins git stuck on me,
This mornin', this evenin', so soon.

64. BRER RABBIT

With the same song the negroes of the Carolinas sing some verses about Brer Rabbit. While they are not the purely original creation of negro song, they are very appropriate, and easily please the negro's fancy. These verses consist, as above, of various repetitions, two of which follow.

> O Brer Rabbit! you look mighty good this
>   mornin',
> O Brer Rabbit! you look mighty good,
> Yes, by God! you better take to de wood,
>   *This mornin', this evenin', so soon.*

> O Brer Rabbit! yo' ears mighty long, this
>   mornin',
> O Brer Rabbit! yo' ears mighty long,
> Yes, by God! dey's put in wrong,
>   *This mornin', this evenin', so soon.*

> O Brer Rabbit! yo' tail mighty white, this
>   mornin',
> O Brer Rabbit! yo' tail mighty white,
> Yes, by God! yer better take to flight,
>   *This mornin', this evenin' so soon.*

65. EV'YBODY BIN DOWN ON ME

Doleful and gruesome verses are very much in vogue among the negroes. Repetition of such lines makes a peculiar effect. The following song, which represents another phase of the wantonness and simplicity of the negro, is sung at length. Each stanza is made to contain six lines by repeating each line of the stanza three times.

> Ev'y since I lef' dat county farm,
>   Ev'ybody bin down on me.

> I killed a man, killed a man,
>   Nobody to pay my fine.

> I went on down to de railroad,
>   Could not find a frien'.

> When I git up de road,
>   Wonder who'll pay my fine!

> Long as I make my nine a week,
>   'Round yo' bedside I goin' to creep.

66. NOBODY'S BIZNESS BUT MINE

Repeated much in the same way is the song "Nobody's Bizness but Mine." The sentiment is somewhat similar to the song "'Tain't Nobody's Bizness but my Own," but is more careless and care-free. The chorus is repeated after each stanza or omitted at will.

> *Georgia Luke, how do you do?*
> *Do lak' I use ter, God knows!*
> *Do lak' I use ter, God knows!*

And in the stanzas the first two lines are sung, with the second or the chorus line repeated four times, or the second sung once with the chorus line three times, either of which makes a good impression.

> Goin' to my shack,
> Ain't comin' back,
> Nobody's bizness but mine. *(four times)*

> Git upon my bunk,
> Look into my trunk,
> Count my silver an' my gold.

> If you don't believe I'm fine,
> Git me behin' a pine,
> Treat you lak' a lady, God knows!

> Goin' back up North,
> Goin' pull my britches off,
> Goin' sleep in my long shirt-tail.

> Goin' to my shack,
> Goin' have hump on my back,
> Nobody's bizness but mine.

> Goin' be hump on my back—
> So many chickens in de sack,
> Nobody's bizness but mine.

> Chickens in my sack—
> Big hounds on my track,
> Nobody's bizness but mine.

> Hounds on my track, boys,
> Never did look back,
> Nobody's bizness but mine.

67. I'M GOIN' BACK

The above song perhaps reaches a climax of the happy and careless disposition of the vaudeville negro. Such pictures as he paints there, he sees vividly, and enjoys them. There are many other verses which are sung to the song, but which will not permit reproducing. In much the same spirit, but with perhaps a little more recklessness, the negro man sings,—

> My name is Uncle Sam,
> An' I do not give a damn,
> I takes a little toddy now an' then,
> *I'm goin' back.*

> Well, some folks do say
> Dat it is not a sin
> If I takes a little toddy now an' then,
> *I goin' back.*

> I was born in sweet ole Alabam',
> An' I do not give a damn,
> *Where* I takes a little toddy now an' then,
> *Well, I'm goin' back.*

68. DAT FORTUNE-TELLER MAN

Again he sings of his prowess. This time he is the "fortune-teller man," which term has a hidden meaning, to which the other verses are adapted.

> I'm dat fortune-teller man,
> Can read yo' future by lookin' in yo' han',
> Can tell yo' fortune by lookin' in yo' han',
> Oh, I'm dat fortune-teller man.

69. COCAINE HABIT

The negro singer pays his respects to the cocaine habit and whiskey. The majority of these songs are indecent in their suggestion. An example of the better verses will illustrate.

> Well, the cocaine habit is might' bad,
> It kill ev'ybody I know it to have had,
> *O my babe!*

> Well, I wake in de mornin' by the city-clock bell,
> An' the niggers up town givin' cocaine hell,
> *O my babe, O my babe!*

> I went to the drug-store, I went in a lope,
> Sign on the door, "There's no mo' coke,"
> *O my babe, O my babe, O my babe!*

70. ROLLIN'-MILL.

So in the "Rollin'-Mill" the singer says there's no more iron to ship to town. Sometimes he means he won't have to work because the material is exhausted, sometimes he means there will be no more chains for him, but it is most likely that he symbolizes liquor by the iron. He sings of local whiskey-houses in the same manner, and urges getting a full supply.

> *Rollin'-mill done shut down,*
> *Ain't shippin' no mo' iron to town.*

> If you don't believe Jumbagot's dead,
> Jus' look at crepe on 'Liza's head,
> *O babe, O babe!*

> Carried him off in hoo-doo wagon,
> Brought him back wid his feet a-draggin',
> *O babe, O babe!*

> Carried him off on smoky road,
> Brought him back on his coolin'-board,
> *O babe, O babe!*

> Well, cocaine womens oughter be like me,
> Drink corn whiskey, let cocaine be,

O babe, O babe!

If you don't believe I'm right,
Let me come to see you jus' one night,
　O babe, O my babe!

Murder, conviction, courts, and fines are thus seen to be
common themes along with the general results that
would be expected to follow the use of whiskey and
weapons; and just as the knife, razor, and "special" are
common companions with the negro, and indicate much
of his criminal nature, so his songs boast of crimes
which he thinks of and sometimes commits. But the
negro is often a coward, and loves to boast of things he
is *going to do.* The fellow who sang of asking everybody
if the bully boy had been that way, was pretty certain
that he had not; and the appearance of the bully would
have meant a hasty retreat of the pursuer. He boasts of
his brave acts and "strong nerve." However, this boasting attitude itself leads to actual crime. The negro who
places himself in such a position often is compelled to
commit the crime; he often fights because he has an
advantage, and makes a suitable occasion to give vent to
his feelings. This tendency has been noted in many of
his songs. He says, "Well, I goin' to kill you, but dat's
all right," and sings,—

　I tell you once, an' I tell you twice,
　Nex' time I tell you, gwine take yo' life.

So he laughs at his predicament when, he is out of it:

　Went up town one Friday night,
　Went to kill a kid,
　Reach my-han' in my pocket.
　Nothin' to kill him wid.

71. JULIA WATERS

In the same mood he tells of his escape from the county
gang while he was supposed to be working in the rocks.
His song is almost as varied as his experiences. He sings
in a monotone-like chant.

　O Julia Waters! do you remember the day,
　When we wus drivin' steel in ole rock querry,
　　I tried to git away?

　Round de mountain I went skippin';
　Thru' de weeds I went flyin',
　Out-run lightening fas' mail on Georgia line.

　Well, I walked up to conductor for to give him
　　game o' talk,
　"If you got money or ticket, I take you to New
　　York;
　If you have no money or ticket"—

　"Pity me, sir, for I am po',
　Yonder come brakeman on outside,
　Goin' shut up box-car do'."

　I was boun' down to Louisville,

Got stuck on Louisville girl,
You bet yo' life she's out o'sight,
She wore the Louisville curl.

72. THOUGHT I HEARD THAT K. C. WHISTLE BLOW

Much has already been said of the negro's attitude toward the railroad and train. His songs abound in references to the train as an agent for his desires. From
"ridin' the rods" to a long-desired trip back to see his
sweetheart, the negro is the frequent patron of the train.
Some years ago the agents for some of the Western
business concerns offered attractive inducements to the
negroes to migrate for permanent work. These agents
went throughout the South, securing large numbers of
laborers. Many a family disposed of their goods for a
trifle in order to accept the flattering terms offered, for
they thought that in the new environment they would
soon become wealthy and prosperous. The history of
their experience is well known. They were carried out,
given poor treatment, with no money and often not
enough to eat. It is needless to say that all who could
obtain the money, and escape, came back to their old
homes. Some of the most interesting and pathetic stories
told by the negroes are those of adventure and privation
incurred in their effort to return home. Many of them
are humorous. The following song represents one of
these laborers, a man or a woman, waiting at the station
for the train to carry her back "where she come frum."
The song is pathetic in its appeal. Each line is repeated
three times; or, if the stanza consists of a rhyming couplet, the first is repeated twice with the second once.
The woman waits.

　Thought I heard that K.C. whistle blow,
　Oh, I thought I heard that K.C. whistle blow!

　Blow lak' she never blow befo',
　Lawd, she blow lak' she never blow befo'.

　Wish to God some ole train would run,
　Carry me back where I come frum.

　Out in the wide worl' alone.

　Take me back to sweet ole Birmingham.

　Baby-honey, come an' go with me.

　Ev'ybody down on us.

　　(Whistle blows)

　Thought I heard whistle when it blow,
　Blow lak' she ain't goin' blow no mo'.

　　(Train has come, now moves away)

　Good by, baby, call it gone.

　Fireman, put in a little mo' coal.

　Fireman, well, we're livin' high.

Yonder comes that easy-goin' man o' mine.

Ain't no use you tryin' send me roun',
I got 'nuf money to pay my fine.

Out in this wide worl' to roam,
Ain't got no place to call my home.

73. K. C.

Still another version of the song represents a lone laborer working near the railroad, and watching the trains
go by. He has not the money, nor can he get away, but
he longs to go home. As he works, he pictures these
scenes; imagines himself on board the train, and happy
in going back to the "sunny South, where sun shines on
his baby's house." Or as a train comes from his home,
he imagines that some of his friends have come to see
him. He sings,—

Well, I thought I heard that K.C. whistle blow,
Blow lak' she never blow befo'.

I believe my woman's on that train,
O babe! I b'lieve my woman's on that train.

She comin' back from sweet ole Alabam',
She comin' to see her lovin' man.

Fireman, put in a little mo' coal,
Run dat train in some lonesome hole.

74. L. & N.

A song of the same origin, and very much like the "K.
C.," is another called "L. & N." Instead of "L. & N.,"
other roads may be designated. This negro man labors
with the hope that he will soon go home again. By
"home" he means the community where he knows the
most people. It is a song of the wanderer, and repeats
much the same sentiment as that found in many of the
songs under that class. This song and the one just given
are sung to the "Frisco Rag-Time" music or train-song.
The train is heard running; the wheels distinctly roar as
they cross the joints of rail; the whistle blows between
each verse, and the bell rings anon for the crossing. A
more vivid picture than this is not portrayed with the
aid of words and music. The negro sees, and sees vividly, every scene here portrayed. Indeed, one forgets
himself, and unconsciously visualizes the train with its
passengers. The song with the music is described elsewhere. The lonely laborer sings,—

Just as sho' as train run thru' L. & N. yard,
I'm boun' do go home if I have to ride de rod.

So good-by, little girl! I'm scared to call yo'
name;
Good-by, little girl! I'm scared to call yo' name.

Now, my mamma's dead, an' my sweet ole
popper, too,

An' I got no one fer to carry my trouble to.

An' if I wus to die, little girl, so far 'way from
home,
The folks, honey, for miles 'round would mourn.

Now, kiss yo' man, an' tell yo' man good-by;
Please kiss yo' man, an' tell yo' man good-by!

I'm goin' tell my mommer, whenever I git home,
How people treated me way off from home.

75. KNIFE-SONG

Very much like the railroad-song is the knife-song,
which has also been described previously. Sometimes
the two are combined; and with the blowing of the
whistle, the ringing of the bell, and the "talkin'" of the
knife as it goes back and forth over the strings, the
"music physicianer" has a wonderful production. Many
songs are sung to this music. One version of the well-
known knife-song has been given. Another, which is
sung more generally in the Southern States, follows.
The verses consist of either a single line repeated, or a
rhyming couplet. Two lines are sung in harmony with
the running of the knife over the strings of the negro's
guitar; while the refrain, "*Lawd, lawd, lawd!*" wherever
found, is sung to the "talking" of the knife. The other
two lines are sung to the picking of the guitar, as in
ordinary cases. The sentiment of the song is much the
same as that in those of the first two divisions,—the
wanderer and his love-affairs. The stanzas given in full
repetition will illustrate the song. The lines sung with
the knife are italicized; other verses are then given in
their simple form.

'Fo' long, honey, 'fo' long, honey,
'Fo' long, honey, 'fo' long, honey,
    Law-d, l-a-w-d, l-a-w-d!

'Fo' long, honey, 'fo' long, honey,
'Fo' long, honey, 'fo' long, honey,
    L-a-w-d, la-w-d, la-w-d!

Don't never git one woman on yo' min',
Keep you in trouble all yo' time,
    L-a-w-d, l-a-w-d, l-a-w-d!

Don't never git one woman on yo' min',
Keep you in trouble all yo' time,
    L-a-w-d, l-a-w-d, l-a-w-d!

In the same manner the song continues, couplets being
sung like the one just given. They give a general review
of negro life as seen in his songs. He sings,—

Don't never let yo' baby have her way,
Keep you in trouble all yo' day,
    L-a-w-d, l-a-w-d, l-a-w-d!

Don't never take one woman for yo' frien',
When you out 'nuther man in,
    L-a-w-d, l-a-w-d, l-a-w-d!

I hate to hear my honey call my name,
Call me so lonesome an' so sad.
    Etc.

I got de blues an' can't be satisfied,
Brown-skin woman cause of it all.
    Etc.

That woman will be the death o' me,
Some girl will be the death o' me.
    Etc.

Honey, come an' go with me,
When I'm gone what yer gwine ter say?
    Etc.

Sung like the first stanza given, are many "one-verse" songs. Nor are they less attractive. The insertion of the chorus line takes away any monotony; besides, the knife adds zest.

I'm goin' 'way, won't be long,
I'm goin' 'way, won't be long,
    L-a-w-d, l-a-w-d, l-a-w-d!

Went up town to give my troubles away,
Went up town to give my troubles away,
    L-a-w-d, l-a-w-d, l-a-w-d!

Too good a man to be slighted down.

Slide me down—I'll slow-slide up again.

Baby, you always on my min'.

The girl I love's the girl I crave to see.

Baby, do you ever think of me?

Baby, what have I done to you?

Wonder whar' my honey stay las' night!

Got a baby, don't care wher' she goes.

I goin' pack my grip—git further down de road.

Gwine to leave if I haf' ter ride de rod.

Ridin' de rod ain't no easy job.

76. BREAK-DOWN SONG.

The "break-down" or dancing songs have been described in relation to their repetition and use. The instrument is more incentive to the dance than the song, but would be far less effective without the singing. These examples give an insight, again, into the simple life of the negro. It is one of his happy traits to combine his entertainment with scenes appropriate to the occasion: however, his themes are often very irrelevant *per se.*

Give me a little buttermilk, ma'am, *(three times)*
Please give me a little buttermilk, ma'am.

Ain't had none so long, so long, *(three times)*
Oh, I ain't had none so long!

The repetition not only is not unpleasant, but adds whatever of charm there is to the line. The singer continues,—

Cows in de bottom done gone dry

Sister got so she won't churn.

Goin' to tell auntie fo' long.

77. GREASY GREENS

But buttermilk is not more attractive than "greasy greens." In this remarkable song the negroes dance with merriment, each final line being suitable to the "s-w-i-n-g c-o-r-n-e-r" of the dance. The picture, while not exactly elegant, is at least a strong one.

Mamma goin' to cook some,
Mamma goin' to cook some,
Mamma goin' to cook some—
    Greasy greens.

How I love them,
How I love them,
How I love them—
    Greasy greens.

Mamma goin' ter boil them—*(three times)*
    Greasy greens.

Sister goin' pick them—*(three times)*
    Greasy greens.

I goin' eat them—*(three times)*
    Greasy greens.

78. LOST JOHN

Still others are composed of single lines repeated without variation. The single song often has only three or four verses; these are repeated as long as that particular song is wanted for the dance. Another will then be taken up. The negroes enjoy variety.

Lost John, lost John, lost John,
Lost John, lost John, lost John,

Lost John, lost John, lost John,
Help me to look for lost John.

Lost John done gone away,
Help me to look for lost John.

Still I ain't bother yet,
Still I ain't bother none.

Sun is goin' down,
Sun is goin' down.

I goin' 'way some day.
Yes, I goin' way some day.

I'm goin' 'way to stay,
Still I'm goin' 'way to stay.

Come an' go with me—
Oh, yes! come an' go with me.

I got a honey here,
Yes, I got a honey here.

Goin' away to leave you,
Well, I goin' 'way to leave you

79. AIN'T YOU SORRY

With more humor than those just given the negro sings
the following verses. Sorry for what? Anything.

Ain't you sorry,
Ain't you sorry,
Ain't you sorry,
Ain't you sorry, sorry-y?

Let us marry, marry, *(three times)*
Let us marry Miss Carrie.

Marry Miss Carrie—*(as above)*
Yes, marry, marry Miss Carrie.

80. LILLY

The next song gives much insight into negro life, at the
same time that it gives the negro's interpretation of the
scenes. In the song that follows, the varied events from
the home to the grave are told; and here is found again
a review and summary of the negro's social life. The
song, sometimes called respectively "Pauly," "Frankie,"
"Lilly," is the story of the murder committed, and of the
conviction of the murderess. The pathos is typical, and
re-echoes the sentiment of other negro songs. The scene
is Atlanta, one singer says; another says Memphis. The
reader will recognize verses common to negro songs in
general. The combination and scene make a new setting.
The song is an unusually strong portrayal of negro life
and thought.

Lilly was a good girl—ev'ybody knows,
Spent a hundred dollars to buy her father suit o'
   clothes,
Her man certainly got to treat her right.

She went to Bell Street—bought a bottle of beer;
"Good-mornin', bar-keeper, has my lovin' man
   been here?"
My man certainly got to treat me right.

It is Sunday an' I ain't goin' to tell you no lie,
He was standin' over there jus' an hour ago,
My man certainly got to treat me right.

She went down to First Avenue, to pawn-broker.
"Good-mornin', kind lady, what will you
   have?"—
"I want to git a fohty-fo' gun, for
All I got's done gone."

He say to the lady, "It's against my law
To rent any woman '44' smokin gun,
For all you got'll be daid an' gone."

She went to the alley,—dogs begin to bark.—
Saw her lovin' man standin' in de dark,
Laid his po' body down.

"Turn me over Lilly, turn me over slow,
May be las' time, I don't know,
All you got's daid an' gone."

She sent for the doctors—doctors all did come;
Sometimes they walk, sometimes they run;
An' it's one mo' rounder gone.

They picked up Pauly, carried him to infirmiary,
He told the doctors he a's a gamblin' man,
An' it's one mo' rounder gone.

Newsboys come runnin'—to tell de mother de
   news.
She said to the lads, "That can't be true,
I seed my son 'bout an hour ago."

Come here, John, an' git yo' hat;
Go down the street an' see where my son is at,
Is he gone, is he gone?

The policemen all dressed in blue,
Dey come down de street by two an' two,
One mo' rounder gone.

Lucy, git yo' bonnet! Johnnie, git yo' hat!
Go down on Bell Street an' see where my son is
   at,
Is he gone, is he gone?

Sunday she got 'rested, Tuesday she was fined,
Wednesday she pleaded for all-life trial,
An' it's all she's got done gone.

Lilly said to jailer, "How can it be?
Feed all prisoners, won't feed me.
Lawd, have mercy on yo' soul!"

Jailer said to Lilly, "I tell you what to do,—
Go back in yo' dark cell an' take a good sleep!"
An' it's all she's got done gone.

She said to the jailer, "How can I sleep?
All 'round my bedside lovin' Paul do creep,
It's all I got's gone."

The wimmins in Atlanta, dey heard de news,
Run excursion with new red shoes,
An' it's one mo' rounder gone.

Some give a nickel, some give a dime,
Some didn't give nary red copper cent,
An' it's one mo' rounder gone.

Well, it's fohty-dollar hearse an' rubber-tire
   hack,
Carry po' Paul to cemetary, but fail to bring him
   back,
An' it's one mo' rounder gone.

Well, they pick up Pauly, an' laid him to rest;
Preacher said de ceremony, sayin',
"Well, it's all dat you got's daid an' gone."

81. BABY LET THE DEAL GO DOWN

The negro has portrayed some pictures of his adventures
in crime and rowdyism. He has told of shooting and
killing, of his arrests and conviction, and of his day in
jail. The judges and jury make permanent impressions
upon him. He is yet to tell something of his gambling
pleasures. The negro's propensities for "shootin' craps"
and gambling in general are well known. He boasts of
his good and bad luck. In "Let the Deal go Down" he
gives a characteristic picture:

Baby, let the deal go down (three times)

I gamble all over Kentucky,
Part of Georgia, too,
Everywhere I hang my hat,
Home, sweet home, to me.

I lose my watch an' lose my chain,
Lose ev'y thing but my diamon' ring.—
Come here, all you Birmingham scouts!
Set down yo' money on Number Six.

When I left Kansas City, Missouri, had three
    hundred dollars;
Soon as I struck Birmingham, put cup on me.

82. GET THAT MONEY

The song continues in a monotone, the singer often
chanting the words to the accompaniment of the guitar.
The concrete suggestion makes the song more fascinating to the negro. The negro woman talks to her "man,"
and tells him to go and get the money from that "nigger
up-stairs." He asks her what he must do if the fellow
offers trouble. To be sure of his safety, she asks him the
same question; and when assured, she tells him to go
and get the money, she will then give him the "slip."
This song also reflects the vaudeville adaptation.

Nigger up-stairs got hundred dollars:
Some matches lyin' on mantelpiece,
Lamp standin' right side of 'em,
Now I want you to be sho' an' git dat money.

When you git dat money,
I'll be down in big skin game,
Baby, let the deal go down.

"Suppose dat nigger start sumpin'?"
"I got my pistol in my right pocket."
"Be sho' an' git dat money; an' when you git it,
    give me the wink,
Baby, let the deal go down."

Ev'y since I bin a gam'lin' man,
I bin a skippin' an' a-dodgin' in the lan'.

83. ODD-FELLOWS HALL

Says a negro, "I went up to Odd-Fellows Hall—Cards
and dices scattered all over flo';" and if he had a good
time, perhaps he does not mind a little fight or losing
his money. Odd-Fellows Hall, in most communities, is a
general meeting-place. So it happens often that informal
meetings like the one here mentioned are held. The
"brago" spirit is here seen again in the burlesque—

I went up to Odd-Fellows Hall,
Had a good time, dat was all:
Hats an' cuffs all lyin' on de flo',
I bet six bits—all I had—
Nigger bet seven—made me mad.
To dat coon I could not help but say,—

"Git off my money—don't you hit my honey—
'Cause I'm a nigger—don't cuts no figger—
I'm gamblin' for my Sady—she's a lady—
I'm a hustlin' coon, that's what I am."

84. I GOT MINE

A version of the popular song "I got Mine" has been
arranged and adapted, and is sung with hilarity.

I got mine, boys, I got mine;
Some o' them got six long months;
Some o' them paid their fine;
With balls and chains all 'round my legs,
    I got mine.

I went down to a nigger crap game,
Really was against my will;
Lose ev'thing I had but bran new dollar bill.
Well, a five-dollar bet was lyin' on de flo',
An' the nigger's point was nine,
When the cops come in—
    Well, I got mine.

When they brought them chains 'round,
How them niggers' eyes did shine—
With balls and chains all 'round their legs—
    Like I got mine.

85. GAMBLIN' STORY

Very much like the above is a scene given in a colloquy
which may have been between two negroes, but more
likely between four. They are playing a game; and, being in constant fear of being apprehended, they hear
sounds that do not exist. They picture it with humor.

Quit, stop, I say! Don't you hear?
Some one's at that do'.
O Lord, have mercy! They've got us at las'.

Why don't you niggers stop all that fuss?
If you wusn't shootin' craps, they'd think so—
Now you done giv' ev'ything away.

Why don't you open that do'?
Well, if you want it open, yo'd better

Come an' open it yo'self.

Say, you niggers, you better stop jumpin' out.
Guess I better go out that window myself—
An' there was nobody at the door.

86. YOU SHALL BE FREE

No one appreciates more than himself the ridiculous predicaments in which the negro often gets. His wit is quick, his repartee is effective. He makes funny puns, and sings of remarkable scenes in which a negro takes part. His pictures are extremes, his sentiment trifling, his rhymes fastidious. What a description he gives of the negro and his environment, mingled with absurdities, in the following song!

> Nigger be a nigger, whatever he do:
> Tie red ribbon 'round toe of his shoe,
> Jerk his vest on over his coat,
> Snatch his britches up 'round his throat,
> *Singin' high-stepper, Lawd, you shall be free.*

> Great big nigger, settin' on log,
> One eye on trigger, one eye on hog,
> Gun said "blop!" hog said "sip!"
> An' he jumped on de hog wid-all his grip,
> *Singin' high-stepper, Lawd, you shall be free.*

> *Shout to glory, Lawd, you shall be free,*
> *Shout to glory, Lord, you shall be free,*
> *Shout, mourner, Lord, you shall be free,*
> *Shout when de good Lord set you free!*

> I went down to hog-eye town,
> Dey sot me down to table;
> I et so much dat hog-eye grease,
> Till de grease run out my nabel.
> Run 'long home, Miss Hog-eye,
> *Singin' high-stepper, Lord, you shall be free.*

> Nigger an' rooster had a fight,
> Rooster knowk nigger clean out o' sight,
> Nigger say, "Rooster, dat's all right,
> Meet you at hen-house do' to-morrow night,
> *Singin', high-stepper, Lord, you shall be free."*

> Two barrels apples, three barrels cheese,
> When I git to heaven, goin' shout on my knees,
> Shout to glory, Lord, you shall be free,
> Shout to glory, mourner, you shall be free.

> With the crokus sack you shall be free,
> With the crokus sack you shall be free,
> Shout to glory, Lord, you shall be free,
> *When de good Lord set you free!*

> A nigger went up town actin' a hoss,
> De jedge he found him ten an' cost,
> Shout, mourner, you shall be free,
> *When de good Lord shall set you free!*

87. PANS O' BISCUIT

Here is another delightful picture which he paints of himself. It is perhaps much simpler than the one just

given, which was originally adapted from a religious song, "Mourner, you shall be Free." For simplicity and exuberance of expression combined, one ought to see a crowd of small negroes singing the following verses. With mouths open and teeth shining, bodies swaying, they make a most incomparable scene.

> Settin' in de wily woods—
> Settin' on a seven—
> Throwed 'im in a feather bed—
> Swore he'd gone to heaven.

> *Pans o' biscuit, bowls o' gravy,*
> *Slice-pertater pie*
> *Kill a nigger dead.*

> Had a sweet pertater
> Roastin' in de san',
> Saw my mother comin'—
> How I burnt my hand!

88. WHEN THE BAND BEGINS TO PLAY

Much has been said of the negro's love of music. It is needless to repeat that a musical band in the community is enough to thoroughly "demoralize" every negro within hearing distance. The song "When the Band begins to Play" shows much of the complexity of feeling possible. Here, again, the negro is at his best in clownish portrayal of unusual scenes. His memory carries him back; his feeling idealizes the present. The chorus, always sung after each stanza, serves to unify the song; while the two-line refrain gives hilarity to the singing.

> *When de ban' begins to play, (three times as*
> *chorus)*

> See dat mule a-comin', ain't got half a load,
> If you think he unruly mule, give him all de road,
> *Whoa, mule, whoa! Whoa dere, I say!*
> *Keep yo' seat, Miss 'Liza Jane! Hold on to the*
> *sleigh!*

> Musketer fly high, musketer fly low;
> If I git my foot on him, he won't fly no mo';
> *Well, it's whoa, mule, whoa! Whoa dere, I say!*
> *Keep yo' seat, Miss Liza Jane! Hold on to the*
> *sleigh!*

> Had ole banjo one time, strings made out o'
> twine;
> All song I could sing was "Wish dat Gal was
> Mine!"
> *An' it's whoa, mule, whoa! Whoa dere, I say, etc.*

Sung like the above, each of the following stanzas of two long lines, but sung with emphasis and pause as if four short lines, is followed by the two lines as refrain, *"whoa, mule,"* etc., with the original chorus, *"When the band begins to play,"* following each stanza. This, too, is the negro's vaudeville song:

> If you want to see dat mule kick,
> If you want to hear him hollar,

Tie a knot in his tail,
  An' poke his head through a collar,
Den you kin hollow, "Whoa, mule," etc.

Went runnin' down to turkey-roost,
  Fell down on his knees,
Liked to kill'd hisself laughin',
  'Cause he heard a turkey sneeze.

Ole Massa bought a yaller gal,
  Brought her from de South;
He wrapped her hair so mazen tight,
  She could not shut her mouth.

He taken her down to blacksmith shop,
  To have her mouth cut smaller,
She made a whoop, she made a squall,
  Den swallowed shop an' all.

On Sat'day night he stole a sheep,
  On Sunday he was taken,
Monday was his trial day,
  Tuesday he hung like bac'n.

Keep yo' seat, Miss Liza Jane!
  Don't act jes' lak a fool.
Ain't got time to kiss you,
  'Cause I'm tendin' to dis mule.

Ole marster he raise a cow,
  He knowed de day when she wus bohn,
Hit took a jay-bird seventeen years
  To fly from ho'n to ho'n.

Ole marster raised ole gray mule,
  He knowed de day he wus born,
Ev'y tooth in his head
  Would hold a barrel o' corn.

Ole master had little ole mule,
  Name was Simon Slick,
Dey tied a knot in his tail,
  Oh, how dat thing did kick!

Ole Mistus raised a little black hen,
  Black as any crow;
She laid three eggs ev'y day,
  On Sunday she laid fo'.

An' it's whoa, mule, whoa! Whoa dere, I say!
Keep yo' seat, Miss Liza Jane! Hold on to the
  sleigh,
When de ban' begins to play.

89. "ONE-VERSE" SONGS

What has been called the "one-verse" song was described in the previous section. These songs are practically without number. Parts of every song known by the negro may be sung line by line, or a single line that is especially pleasing may be sung for an hour at a time. Further examples, other than those already given, will illustrate the complexity of the subjects and the irregularity of the metres. Fragments of song are always interesting; and one wonders to which song, if to any, they

originally belonged, or how they may ultimately be combined.

Carried my woman to the world's fair;
Would a won a fortune, but she had bad hair.

I goin' to ride that Cincinnati Southern 'fore
  long, little girl.
If I miss you, God intended it, Baby mine.

How in worl' can I miss you,
When I'm good dead, Amy, true girl?

Up on the hillside to see who I could see;
There was no boat runnin' but the "Cherokee,"
  little girl,

An' she won't go.

Time ain't long like use to be.

I'm on my way, babe, I'm comin' home.

Shame on you, can't treat me right.

Don't you love no other coon.

Baby, won't you hold my head,
While I go to bed.

I bin' in the bin so long,
With rough an' rowdy men.

Goin' whar' ain't never bin befo'.

My woman did sumpin' never did befo'.

Swear, by God, never goin' dere no mo'.

Creeper, won't you step in?

Ain't goin' to rain no mo'.

Goin' whar de sun don't never shine.

Goin' whar chily win' don't blow.

Goin' whar de water drink like wine,
Watermelon smilin' on de vine.

Chicken don't roos' too high for me.

90. SHE ROLL DEM TWO WHITE EYES

As in the religious songs of the negro, so in his social folk-songs, he quickly adapts new songs to his own environment. Mention has been made of the negro's fondness for the new and popular coon-songs; but these songs often lose their original words, and take on words of negro origin. The music does not change so much as in the case of the spirituals. The song itself often becomes amusing because of its paraphrases. "Goo-goo Eyes" was sung much among the negroes, as among the whites. The negroes have improvised more than a score of verses, some of which may be given.

Nex' day when show wus gone,
  His baby threw him down;
She say to him, "I'll have you inched
If you lay 'round dis town.
Now, let me tell my tale of woe.

"Well, de fust time I seed my brother-in-law,
  He had some chickens for sale;
De nex' time I seed my brother-in-law,
  He wus laid up in Collin's jail.
Den he rolled dem two white eyes."

Jus' because he had them thirty days,
He thought he had to lay in jail de res' of his
  days,
He's de bes' dey is, an' dey need him in dey biz,
Well, jes' because he had them thirty days.

Of all de beastes in de woods,
  I'd rather be a tick;
I'd climb up 'roun' my true love's neck,
  An' there I'd stick,
Jes' to see her roll dem snow-white eyes.

Let me tell you 'bout a cheap sport—
  Was on a Sunday morn,
Put five cents in missionary box,
  Took out fo' cents for change,
Well, won't he cheap! well, won't he cheap!

Well, I would not marry black gal;
  Tell you de reason why;
Ev'y time she comb her head,
  She make dem goo-goo eyes;
Well, she roll dem two white eyes.

91. HONEY, TAKE A ONE ON ME (SECOND VERSION)

Another version of "Honey, take a One on Me" differs from the one already given, being more like the original; but the ordinary person would scarcely recognize the verse that the negroes sing.

A yellow girl I do despise,
But a jut black girl I can't denies,
  O honey! take a whiff on me.

A jut black nigger, jus' black as tar,
Tryin' to git to heaven on eligater car,
  O honey! take a whiff on me.

Hattie don't love me, Esther do,
Because I wear my Sunday clothes,
  Honey, take a whiff on me.

92. DON'T YOU HEAR THEM BELLS A-RINGIN'?

A probable variation of "In the Evening by the Moonlight" is scarcely recognizable. The song is thoroughly mixed with the old spiritual; the result is a song without individuality.

Don't you hear them bells a-ringin'?
  How sweet, I do declare!

Don't you hear them darkies singin',
  Climbin' up the golden stairs?

Oh, Peter was so wicked,
  Climbin' up the golden stairs,
When I asked him for a ticket,
  Climbin' up the golden stairs.

If you think he is a fool,
  Climbin' up the golden stairs,
He will treat you mighty rude,
  Climbin' up the golden stairs.

93. CARVE 'IM TO DE HEART

For a long time the 'possum and the 'tater, the chicken and the watermelon, have been considered the requisites of the negro's happiness. He himself admits that this would make a good heaven. Formerly he sung of two seasons when "the good Lord fed the nigger;" namely, in blackberry time and when the watermelons were ripe. He is much the same to-day, and the 'possum is still proverbial. "Carve dat 'Possum" smacks with good times for the negro. His recipe is quite appetizing. This is a well-known song, and much quoted.[3]

Well, 'possum meat's so nice an' sweet,
  Carve 'im to de heart;
You'll always find hit good ter eat,
  Carve 'im to de heart.

Carve dat 'possum,
Carve dat 'possum, chillun,
Carve dat 'possum,
Oh, carve 'im to de heart.

My ole dog treed, I went to see,
  Carve 'im to de heart;
Dar wus a 'possum in dat tree,
  Carve 'im to de heart.

I went up dar to fetch 'im down,
  Carve 'im to de heart.
I bus' 'im open agin de groun,
  Carve 'im to de heart.

De way ter cook de 'possum nice,
  Carve 'im to de heart;
Fust parbile 'im, stir 'im twice,
  Carve 'im to de heart.

Den lay sweet 'taters in de pan,
  Carve 'im to de heart;
Nuthin' beats dat in de lan',
  Carve 'im to de heart.

94. CROSS-EYED SALLIE

The negro's ready wit and marked propensities for making song have been noted. Songs thus composed, and sung in whatever manner the occasion demands, give the negro a wide range of song service. His tendency to put everything into song is well illustrated in the following monotone song. One would scarcely believe this to be a song. The negro appeared to be making it as he sang, all the while picking his guitar in the regular way; but he repeated the song in the exact words except for the usual variation of dialect. This he could do as often as required. The song is one of many stories which the negroes devise to tell of their adventures. It tells of varied life and custom; it hints at undercurrents of negro thought; it tells again of woman in her relations to man; it gives splendid insight into negro characteristics in the rôle of the clown, who has mixed his thoughts, wits, bits of song and burlesque, with the crude jokes he has heard. The rendering of the song is perhaps its chief value.

Had ole one time, name was Cross-eyed Sally,

She was the blackest girl in Paradise Alley.—

She had liver lips an' kidney feet.—Didn't know she was so black till I took a fire-coal one mornin' an' made a white mark on her face.—An' I didn't know she was so cross-eyed till one mornin' she come up to me an' say, "Look here, boy, I want to eat!"—I tole her if she had anything, she had better go to eatin' it—I never had nuthin.—It hurt my girl so bad when I tole her this, that she cried; an' in cryin' she so cross-eyed till the tears run down her back.—Thought I felt sorry for my girl an' I taken her up to ole massa's home dat day—an' we seen a heap o' chickens—all sorts an' all sizes—an' I tole her to hold quiet till dat night when we go up an' see what we could do to dem chickens.—So we looked all 'round de house, an' we couldn't find nuthin'.—We looked in de trees an' yard, an' couldn't find nuthin'.—We looked in hen-house, wher' chickens oughter bin, an' never found nuthin'.—We looked under de house, an' couldn't find nuthin'.—So my girl got oneasy—thought dere was no chickens 'round dere.—Long 'bout 'leven or twelve o'clock dat night, I heard ole rooster crow in hollow back of de hen-house.—I says, "Look here, girl! Dey's chickens here."—He couldn't set up an' not crow for midnight nor mornin' neither: so me'n her goes down, an' chickens wus settin; way up in cedar-tree.—She say to me, "How in worl' you goin' git dem chickens out'n dat high tree?" I tole her I can clam jes' good as they can fly—I can clam jes' as good as they can fly.—So up de tree I went like anything else wid sharp claws—cat or squirrel—clam jes fas' as please.—So I seen all sorts o' chickens,—boot-legs, Shanghais, Plymouth Rock,—an' found some ole freezlins.—She say to me, "I doan know how in de worl' de freezlin git up dere." An' I say, "Nor me, neither. He ain't got 'nuf feathers to fly over a rail, much less up in a tree."—I say he mus' clam' tree lak' I did.—I reached 'roun' an' got every kind o' rock but flint rock—But dem ole Plymouth Rock hens kind er rocks I'm talkin' 'bout—I got ever kind er eyes I seen but buckeye; an' reason I didn't git dat wus a cedar-tree—But Shanghai (eye) pullets kind o' eye I talkin' 'bout—I got ever kind o' freeze I seen but de weather, an' it wus hot when I went up dere.—But freezlin chicken what I'm talkin' about.—An' I got ever kind o' leg I seen but de thousand leg, an' dey tells me dat's a worm, an' I didn't need him.—Boot-legged roosters dem's de kind o' legs I got.—My girl say, "You better make haste an' come down 'way from up'n dat tree."—I say, "Why?"—She say, "I'm gittin' oneasy down here."—I say, "'Bout what?" She say, "Somebody may come an' ketch you up dat tree: if they do, times sho' will be hard wid you."—I says, "Wait a minit! Here's sumpin'! I don't know whether it's a chicken or a bird. I say he mighty little, but he's got feathers on him. I ketchin' everything what's got feathers on it."—Come to find out, it wus little ole banter rooster.—I grabbed him, an jobbed him into my sack. I says, "Look out, girl! Here dey comes!" She say, "Naw, don't throw them chickens down here! You may break or bruise or kill some uv them." She say, "How in de worl' you gwine git down dat tree wid all dem chickens?"—I wus settin' out on big lim': I goes out to de body of de tree.—Then I slap my sack in my mouth—you oughter seen me slidin' down dat tree—you oughter seen me slidin' down dat tree.—We struck right out thru' de woods fer home.—I had chickens enuf to las' a whole week.—But let me tell you what a jet black gal will do, especially if she's cross-eyed, lak' mine.—When de chickens give out, de gal give out too.—She quit me nex' mornin'.—I got up, lookin' fer my gal: she's done gone.—Her name was Lulu, but we called her Cross-eyed Sally.—So I looked fer Lulu all that day, but could not find her nowhere.—So I found her de nex' evenin'.—You know I tole you she was so black till I could take a fire-coal an' make a white mark on her face.—She wus settin' up courtin' a great big nigger twice as black as she wus.—He look jes' precise lak' black calf lookin' thru crack of whitewashed fence.—Reason he look dat way was, he had on one o' dese deep turn-down collars; but when he put it on, he didn't turn it down, he turn it up—settin' 'way up to his years—look lak' hoss wid blin' bridle on.—So I goes in an' says, "Good-evenin', Lulu!"—She wouldn't say a word.—I says, "How are you, mister?" He wouldn't say a word, neither.—I goes out-doors an' gits me a brick.—"Say, how you do, mister?" He wouldn't say a word.—I drawed back wid my brick.—I knocked him in de head, an' 'bout dat time I thought I killed him dead.—I reach'd up an' got my hat an' hollered, "Good-by, Miss Lulu, I'm gone—I'm gone."

II. WORK-SONGS

It has been observed that the negro sings on all occasions. This has been especially true of the laborer. The tendency of the negro workers to sing is well known; and it matters little what the work is, the negro will have a song which he may sing while working. Those who have ample opportunity for continued observation maintain that the negro is fast losing his cheerfulness and gayety, his love of song and practice of singing. They affirm that the laborers work in silence; and instead of singing as of yore, the negroes are becoming perhaps each year more morose. The solitary workman, too, sings less continually than in former days. Undoubtedly this is the prevailing tendency; but the negro still retains much of his disposition to sing while at work. Whoever has seen in the spring-time a score of negroes with hoes, chopping in the fields to a chant, making rhythm, motion, and clink of hoe harmonize; whoever has heard in the autumn a company of cotton-pickers singing the morning challenge to the day, and uniting in song and chorus at the setting of the sun and "weighing-time,"—will not soon forget the scene. The negroes still work and sing. They sing while going to and coming from the fields, while driving their teams and performing their sundry tasks; and the ploughman has been known to repeat his song until his mule waited for the accustomed voice before swinging into the steady walk for the day. So in town and country, in the city and at the camps, every class of workers finds song a good supplement to work. The railroad and section gangs, the contractor's "hands," the mining groups and convict camps,—all re-echo with the sound of shovel, pick, and song. The more efficient the song-leader is, the better work will the company do: hence the singer is valued as a good workman. As motion and music with the negro go hand in hand, so the motion of work calls forth the song; while the song, in turn, strengthens the movements of the workers. The roustabout is willing to do almost any kind of work of short duration: he is likely to sing through his work. With song and jest these laborers rush through great feats of labor, and enjoy it. Sometimes the singers seem to set the ship in motion by the rhythm of their work and song,—songs of the moment, perhaps. From the woman at the wash-tub to the leader of a group, from the child to the older darkies, song is a natural accompaniment to work.

The negro songs are, for the most part, easily suited to common work, and therefore the number of work-songs is not limited. The stateliness of the religious song assists the workman as it does the shouters in the church; the common secular songs are easily adapted to any occasion. Indeed, there is no song which the negro knows, that he may not sing at any time. However, as a rule, certain songs are judged to be more naturally suited for work-songs, and are so designated. They are thus sung more frequently as work-songs. Their rhythm and metre must be more regular; their words must be adapted to slow and successive motions of the body. The kind of song is often determined by the nature of the work and the number of workmen. Songs are improvised at will, under the influence of work. The themes vary with the thoughts of the workmen or with the suggestions of the occasion. In general, however, work-songs are not unlike the average negro song, and are taken at random from the experiences of every-day life. The negro sings his flowing consciousness into expression. Like the other songs, the work-songs give a keen insight into the negro's real self.

NOTES

[1] Dr. John Meier, quoted by Professor H. M. Belden, *Journal of American Folk-Lore,* vol. xxiv, p. 3.

. . .

[3] This song is sung with as much zest and enjoyment by the negro girls in a Pennsylvania institution of correction as by the darkies of southern Mississippi.

Paul Garon

SOURCE: "If Blues Was Reefers," in *Living Blues,* Autumn, 1970, pp. 13-18.

[*In the following essay, Garon traces the use of drugs as related in the lyrics of blues songs.*]

What follows is intended only as a short and incomplete survey of references to drugs that occur in the blues. Although the lyrics can be revealing, care must be taken not to misconstrue what exactly is being revealed. One must presuppose the various singers' familiarity with drugs and the drug scene of the time, but it would be erroneous to assume that all singers who mentioned drugs in their songs were habitual drug users. Contrary to the opinion of some, it is probably true that there are some singers who sang songs about drugs without ever having used drugs at all.

All of this is not to suggest that a study of such lyrics is useless. Rather, much can be learned of the culture of which the blues-singer was a part, and the lyrics themselves, taken as a whole, are as intriguing a group of compositions as can be found in the blues.

As one might guess, the majority of drug references pertain to marihuana. There are some cocaine songs, but songs that refer unequivocally to heroin are a great rarity. At times, it would seem that the blues singer Champion Jack Dupree had a monopoly on heroin blues—he recorded at least two different songs referring to the drug, and no other singer has ever dealt with the subject so openly. He first recorded "Junker Blues" in 1941:

> They call, they call me a junker 'cause I'm
> loaded all the time. (2)
> I don't use no reefers, I be knocked out with that
> angel wine.
>
> Six months, six months ain't no sentence, and
> one year ain't no time. (2)
> They got boys in penetentiary doing from nine to
> ninety-nine.
>
> I was standing, I was standing on the corner with
> my reefers in my hand. (2)
> Up step the sergeant, took my reefers out my
> hand.
>
> My brother, my brother used the needle, and my
> sister sniffed cocaine. (2)
> I don't use no junk, I'm the nicest boy you ever
> seen.
>
> My mother, my mother she told me, and my
> father told me, too. (2)
> That "That junk is a bad habit, why don't you
> leave it, too?"

My sister, she even told me, and my grandma told
    me, too, (2)
"That using junk, pardner, was gonna be the
    death of you."

This song was recorded in an only slightly altered form
by Fats Domino—it was titled "The Fat Man". Dupree's
1958 version of "Junker's Blues" is, if anything, even
more cheerful and optimistic than his earlier one:

Spoken: My, my, my; sick as I can be.

Some people call me a junker 'cause I'm loaded
    all the time. (2)
I just feel happy, and I feel good all the time.

Some people say I use the needle, and some say I
    sniff cocaine, (2)
But that's the best of feeling in the world that
    I've ever seen.

Say goodbye, goodbye to whiskey, Lord, and so
    long to gin. (2)
I just want my reefers, I just want to feel high
    again.

Spoken: Oh, yes, I'm a junker—I feel all right.

Some people, some people crave for chicken and
    some people for porterhouse steak.
But when I get loaded, Lord, I want my milk and
    cake.

Spoken: Oh; yeah, that's all I want now. They
    call me a junker 'cause I'm loaded all the
    time;
        But that ain't nothing if I feel good all the
    time.

At the same 1958 session, Dupree recorded the more
somber "Can't Kick The Habit". A remarkably moving
song, the pessimistic attitude is kept nearly unbroken
until the very last line where the mood is stunningly
shattered with Champion Jack's hopeful and incontest-
ably good advice:

Well, I can't kick this habit, and this junk is
    killing me. (2)
Ever since I started this habit, everything's been
    down on me.

I hung around my friends and smoked reefers,
    and I thought I was doing all right. (2)
Now I've done lost a good woman, and I have no
    place to sleep at night.

Well, I went to the doctor, see could he cure this
    habit for me. (2)
He looked at me and shook his head, and said
    that dope is killing me.

Spoken: Yes, I know it's killing me. But I feel
    good anyhow. I wish I had listened to what my
    mother said. She told me that dope wasn't no
    good—I didn't pay it no mind; I thought I was
    doing (all right?). Now I'm just sick as I can be!

I don't pay nobody just to live their life so fast.
    (2)
If you just take it slow and easy, just as long as
    this habit lasts.

It should be remembered that although heroin had been
illegal at least since 1914, marihuana did not become so
until 1937. Marihuana was not only the subject of most
of the drug songs—it also proved to be the theme around
which were woven some of the more intricately composed and richly poetic songs. Perhaps the best known
of these songs is "If You're a Viper", quoted here as
sung by Rosetta Howard in 1937:

Dreamed about a reefer five feet long, mighty
    mezz, but not too strong,
You'll be high but not for long, if you're a viper.

I'm the queen of everything, I've got to be high
    before I can swing.
Light a tea and let it be, if you're a viper.

When your throat gets dry, you know you're high,
    everything is dandy.
Truck on down to the candy store, bust your conk
    on peppermint candy.

Then you'll know your body's sent, you don't
    care if you don't pay rent.
The sky is high, and so am I, if you're a viper.

"If You're a Viper" was well known enough to be
quoted in 1939 by Nathaniel West in his novel *The Day
of the Locust*. The origin of the word "mezz" in the song
was revealed by Milton "Mezz" Mezzrow in his 1946
autobiography, *Really the Blues*. During the years that
Mezzrow was a dealer, he consistently sold such a high-
grade product that the word "mezz", for Mezzrow, came
to mean "the best"!

The popular Lil Green wrote "Knocking Myself Out"
and recorded it in early 1941. It was recorded only two
or three months later by two other women singers, Jean
Brady and Yack Taylor. Here is Yack Taylor's version:

Listen girls and boys, I've got one stick,
Give me a match and let me take a whiff quick.
I'm gonna knock myself out; I'm gonna kill
    myself.
I'm gonna knock myself out, gradually, by
    degrees.

I started blowing my gage, and I was having my
    fun,
Spied the police, and I started to run.
I was knocking myself out, etc.

But the very moment I looked around,
(My) mind said, "Yack, throw that gage on the
    ground."
The policeman said, "Just kill yourself."
The policeman said, "Just kill yourself."
He said, "Knock yourself out, Yack, gradually, by
    degrees."

I used to didn't blow gage, did nothing of the
          kind,
But my man quit me and I changed my mind.
That's why I'm knocking myself out, etc.

I'm gonna blow this jive, it's a sin and a shame,
But it's the only thing that ease my heart off of
          my man.
When I knock myself out, when I kill myself.
I just knock myself smack out, gradually, by
          degrees.

Jazz Gillum recorded his "Reefer Head Woman" in 1938:

I can't see why my baby sleeps so sound. (2)
She must have smoked a reefer, and it's 'bout to
          carry her down.

When I left her this morning, I left her sleeping
          sound. (2)
The only way you could catch me was to run like
          a full-blood hound.

She said she was gonna leave me, going to some
          no-good town. (2)
She was a rug-cutting woman, she did like to
          break 'em down.

If you got a good woman, men, please don't take
          her round. (2)
She will get full of reefers and raise sand all over
          this town.

The obscure Texas musician, Will Rowland, recorded a "Reefer Blues" for Gold Star in the late 40s. It was a jazz/R&B instrumental, featuring tenor sax; with one verse and a spoken introduction:

Spoken: Well, where's that reefer man?
          I want to flip my cookies this morning.
          That's right.

If the blues was reefers, I'd stay high all the
          time. (2)
I'd stay high and crazy until I wear you off my
          mind.

Spoken: Well, let's light up a stick.

As the song ends, Rowland says, somewhat overemphatically: "The connection man!"

Also in the late forties, Buster Bennett recorded "Mellow Pot Blues" which contained this verse:

Then you smoke some pot, you feel gay, and
          everything seems to go your way.
So come on baby, let's get in the groove, and
          once you're in the groove,
You sure don't want to move.

"Viper Man," recorded in 1938 by Noble Sissle's Swingsters, with a vocal by O'Neil Spencer, is even more in the jazz idiom than Rosetta Howard's song, but it's worth quoting:

Just viper mad, must have my fun, I never 'clared
          it can't be done.
The people are talking, but I don't care, I'm
          twenty-one, far from done, I've just begun.

Wrap your chops around a stick of tea blow this
          gage and get high with me.
Good tea is my weakness, I know it's bad, it
          sends me (?), and I can't (quit?), I'm viper mad.

There were a number of blues that could not be considered "drug songs" that do, nevertheless, refer to some drug, at least in passing. Among these are Dr. Clayton's 1941 version of "Gotta Find My Baby," which contains this verse:

When my head starts aching, I grab my hat and go,
'Cause cocaine and reefers can't reach my case
          no more.
I gotta find my baby, I declare I wouldn't lie.
I ain't had no real good loving since that gal said
          good-bye.

Sonny Boy Williamson (1st) sang this verse in his 1947 "Mellow Chick Swing:"

I got her way, been blowing gage,
Don't know what to say, can't have my way,
I know she's kind of slick, but I'm hip to this
          mellow chick.

And Red Nelson included this gem in his "Working Man Blues" (1937):

Cocaine is made for horses, weeds is made for
          Georgia mules. (2)
Whiskey is made for whiskey-headed people,
          reefers made for doggone fools.

In addition to the above minor references to cocaine, there were several cocaine blues recorded, although, interestingly enough, they were made nearly a decade earlier than the other material already quoted. The Memphis Jug Band recorded "Cocaine Habit Blues" in 1930; the vocalist was the powerful Hattie Hart. The first line in the third verse was one of the few possible references to heroin use, other than Jack Dupree's:

Cocaine habit's mighty bad, it's the worst ol'
          habit that I ever had.
Hey, hey, honey take a whiff on me.
I went to Mr. Leeman's in a lope, saw a sign on
          the window, there's no more dope.
Hey, etc.

If you don't believe cocaine is good, ask Alma
          Rose and Eva Wood.
Hey, etc.
I love my whiskey and I love my gin, but the way
          I love my coke is a doggone sin.
Hey, etc.

Since cocaine went out of style, you can catch
          'em shooting needles all the while.
Hey, etc.
It takes a little coke to give me ease, strut your
          stuff long as you please.
Hey, etc.

Spoken: Let's all take a whiff on Hattie now.

Hey, hey, hey, hey, hey.

The East Coast songster Luke Jordan recorded "Cocaine Blues" in 1927—it was recorded,nearly verbatim, by the white country singer Dick Justice in 1929 as "Cocaine," and one year later, the black singer Lil McClintock recorded a related song called "Furniture Man." All three versions leaned heavily on white and traditional folk material. McClintock's version doesn't mention cocaine at all, and it is often difficult to see what relation the verses have to the refrain, for it is in the refrain alone that cocaine is mentioned. The song is too long to quote in its entirety, so only the refrain and its variant are given here:

> I call my Cora, hey, hey.
> She come on sniffing with her nose all sore.
> The doctor swore he wouldn't sell no more.
> Say run doctor, ring the bell, the women in the
>   alley. . . .
> I'm simply wild about my good cocaine.
>
> Coke's for horses, not for women or men,
> The doctor said it'd kill you, but he didn't say
>   when.
> I'm simply wild about my good cocaine.

As I was collecting these lyrics, it occurred to me that a disproportionately large number of the songs that referred favorably to marihuana and cocaine were sung by women. As I found more material, this one-sidedness began to diminish somewhat, but it did not disappear. It's difficult to draw any concrete conclusions from such scanty evidence, although it would seem possible that many male blues singers found it difficult to associate marihuana and cocaine use with the sort of self-image they wanted to project in their songs. Also, women have always been the victims of more repression and oppression than men in this society (the ability to obtain domestic work notwithstanding). It would be no surprise if drug use were found to be more frequent among women than men in this group, even if available statistics indicate otherwise. It could also be said that the level of sophistication reached by the jazz musician would result in his or her having a different attitude than the blues singer. But this may not be the case. In "Hear Me Talkin' To Ya" (Shapiro and Hentoff, Dover Publications), Clarence Williams, a figure who was certainly familiar with the early jazz scene, is quoted as saying, "But I never knew hardly any musicians that took dope. It was mostly the girls. . . ."!

The number of references we have seen does at least show that many blues singers, a large number of them women, were familiar with various aspects of the drug scene of their time. How much they indulged in drug use can hardly be told from the songs. The association between the drug sub-culture and jazz musicians has been developed into a stereotype of legendary proportions, augmented by the publicity given to heroin use among certain jazz stars. And examining the recordings leads to even more surprises. In 1933, a Benny Goodman group, with Jack Teagarden as vocalist, recorded a drug song called "Texas Tea Party"—so drug songs were being done 37 years ago by groups that most readers would associate more with their parents than with jazz!

To add to the confusion, it is difficult to establish a line that separates jazz from blues, especially with a performer like Rosetta Howard (who was accompanied by a jazz group, the Harlem Hamfats). Still, it would be worth comparing jazz and blues musicians, city and country musicians, singers from the 20s, 30s and 40s, as well as men and women performers, regarding their familiarity with the drug scene of their time. Perhaps someone will come across a song as splendid as Victoria Spivey's "Dope Head Blues," recorded in 1927—the drug referred to here would almost certainly be cocaine:

> Just give me one more sniffle, another sniffle of
>   that dope. (2)
> I'll catch a cow like a cowboy, throw a bull
>   without a rope.
>
> Doggone, I got more money than Henry Ford or
>   John D. ever had. (2)
> I bit a dog last Monday, and forty doggone dogs
>   went mad.
>
> Feel like a fighting rooster, feeling better than I
>   ever felt. (2)
> (I could have) pneumonia and still I feel I've got
>   the best health.
>
> Say, Sam, go get my airplane and drive it up to
>   my door. (2)
> I think I'll fly to London, these monkey men
>   make mama sore.
>
> The President sent for me, the Prince of Wales is
>   on my trail. (2)
> They worry me so much, I'll take another sniff
>   and put them both in jail.

Gene Bluestein

SOURCE: "The Blues as Literary Theme," in *The Voice of the Folk: Folklore and American Literary Theory,* The University of Massachusetts Press, 1970, pp. 117-40.

[In the following essay, Bluestein examines the use of blues and jazz as motifs in the literary works of F. Scott Fitzgerald, William Faulkner, and Ralph Ellison.]

The use of folklore by American writers is a subject that has been discussed only briefly. Daniel Hoffman's *Form and Fable in American Fiction* (1961) is the most successful attempt to understand the impact on our early writers of themes and techniques related to folk tradition, and he has gone far toward correcting the view that folklore has counted for little in our literary developments. My concern here will be with the use of Negro folklore and folksong in more recent works which reflect both the ideological and technical implications of folklore as a basis for literary expression. One area of special interest is jazz and themes related to its origin and development.

It has been widely noted that there is a special relationship between the Negro and the American experience in general. For one thing, it is important to recall that of all the diverse groups who came to this country only the blacks came in large numbers against their will and under conditions of chattel slavery. David Brion Davis has pointed out that while slavery posed a general moral problem for all of Western culture, it had special relevance in the New World. His major conclusion in *The Problem of Slavery in Western Culture* (1966) is that the central patterns of slavery in all cultures have been more like than unlike, yet there is a sense in which slavery came close to defining the very meaning of the "American mission." He observes that "Americans have often been embarrassed when reminded that the Declaration of Independence was written by a slaveholder and that Negro slavery was a legal institution in all thirteen colonies at the beginning of the revolution." Critics of America's national aspirations have made the most of what is an obvious contradiction and inconsistency in our equalitarian ideology, and Davis shows in his study how widely spread were the rationalizations used to justify the existence of slavery within the context of a democratic society such as the United States claimed to be. His explorations stop short of the abolitionist period in this country, concluding with the prophecy of Quaker John Woolman that "if Americans continued to be unfaithful to their high destiny, their descendants would face the awful retribution of God's justice." In general, and to the present day, Americans have relied on standard rationalizations to justify either slavery or the separation of blacks from the mainstream of American life. Several of our major folklorists (Constance Rourke and the Lomaxes), on the other hand, have attempted to find a central position for the Negro and his accomplishments within the framework of American civilization, emphasizing the seminal influence of Negro folk materials. Most academic folklorists, however, tended to place black tradition outside the main lines of American development, identifying it either as African or as mere imitation of white traditions.

Our formal writers have often taken a rather different approach. Mark Twain, for example, used Jim in *Huckleberry Finn* as a way of expressing strong opposition to the hypocrisy of middle-class American society. Hoffman has pointed out that Jim rises above the stereotyped notion of the fearful slave to become "a source of moral energy," though he also recognizes that "Mark Twain's triumph here is incomplete: despite the skillful gradation of folk beliefs and other indications of Jim's emergent stature, what does come through for many readers is, as Mr. Ellison remarks, Jim's boy-to-boy relationship with Huck, 'a violation of our conception of adult maleness.' We remember that Mark Twain himself admired Uncle Remus extravagantly, and much as he means for

us to admire Jim—much as he admires Jim himself—the portrait, though drawn in deepest sympathy, is yet seen from the outside." I shall return later to Ralph Ellison's comments about Negro folklore and American literature. But it is interesting to see what that outsider's view of the Negro has meant not only for the characterization of blacks in our literature, but also for the uses of Negro folklore as well. Curiously, one of the main purposes of employing Negro materials by many of our writers has been ideological—as a way of establishing some sense of the world view of non-Negro characters in fiction.

Some obvious examples from the period after the First World War come to mind, and they illustrate the general approach. Most of them take place in the context of the "jazz age," and they provide a good contrast between white writers who know little about the history or meaning of jazz and those later writers whose knowledge of jazz and its folk sources are more sophisticated. F. Scott Fitzgerald limns a scene early in *The Great Gatsby* (1925) which is calculated to dramatize the opulence and emptiness of American society in the twenties. At one of Gatsby's wild parties the orchestra leader announces: "'At the request of Mr. Gatsby we are going to play for you Mr. Vladimir Tostoff's latest work which attracted so much attention at Carnegie Hall last May. If you read the papers, you know there was a big sensation.' He smiled with jovial condescension, and added: 'Some sensation!' Whereupon everybody laughed. 'The piece is known,' he concluded lustily, 'as Vladimir Tostoff's *Jazz History of the World.*'" Fitzgerald's narrator comments that when it was over "girls were putting their heads on men's shoulders in a puppyish, convivial way, girls were swooning over backward playfully into men's arms, even into groups, knowing that some one would arrest their falls . . . ," though Gatsby himself remains aloof from the activities. Despite the fact that we get no description of the work, it is easy to piece together the nuances of the passage. The performance of the work was a sensation—apparently a scandalous occasion in the major hall associated with symphonic music and recitals. The composer's name suggests why: it is a piece simply tossed off, which is a close approximation of the main criticism of jazz, namely that it is not carefully or consciously composed but simply a kind of musical fling. (The less pejorative term would be *improvised,* which is an accurate way of defining one of the essential elements in jazz performances.) *A Jazz History of the World* would have been an assault on the very idea of history itself, expressing the lack of order with an equally shocking disregard of conventional musical sound—cacophonous, perhaps polyrhythmic, and above all sensual in its appeal, as the orchestra leader's "lusty" introduction and the following aphrodisiacal effects reveal. (Fitzgerald may have been referring to one of Igor Stravinsky's early works which were received with great hostility in the first part of this century precisely because they contained innumerable innovations, including techniques borrowed from jazz.) The important point is that jazz is defined in essentially negative terms as a way of identifying the chaos and libertinism of Gatsby's world, and although the composer is obviously a Russian, the controlling elements of his work depend on their relationship to jazz, a Negro music.

Fitzgerald's interest in what he calls jazz as well as in popular music reminds us how rarely American writers use music thematically in their work, unlike European writers (Mann, for example) who often derive major elements of their form and content through conscious analogies with music. (Whitman, as has been widely noted, is an exception, and so is Eliot.) There are, however, a great number of references to popular songs in *The Great Gatsby* and they generally reflect the uncommitted, lackadaisical attitudes of Fitzgerald's characters—other than Gatsby, of course, who pays little attention to the surface atmosphere which he has caused to be created. The tunes include "The Sheik of Araby," "Ain't We Got Fun," "Three O'Clock in the Morning," and "The Love Nest," several of these performed by Gatsby's boarder, Mr. Klipspringer. In a flashback which details Gatsby's early involvement with Daisy in Louisville, Fitzgerald wrote: "For Daisy was young and her artificial world was redolent of orchids and pleasant, cheerful snobbery and orchestras which set the rhythm of the year, summing up the madness and suggestiveness of life in new tunes. All night long the saxophones wailed the hopeless comment of the *Beale Street Blues* while a hundred pairs of golden slippers shuffled the shining dust." Shortly thereafter Fitzgerald announces Daisy's decision to marry Tom Buchanan. Again it is apparent that the music reflects the hollowness of Daisy's environment and although Fitzgerald identifies the pop tunes with sadness as well as the possibilities of new life, the clinching reference is to the "hopeless comment" of the blues. All of these statements amount to an ideological position which appears regularly in American literature thereafter, probably through the influence of Fitzgerald, though he was familiar with Eliot's similar approach in *The Waste Land* (1922): "When lovely woman stoops to folly and / Paces about her room again, alone, / She smoothes her hair with automatic hand, / And puts a record on the gramophone." On the one hand, we might define this position as the use of popular songs to provide incidental music for the decline of man's vitality and sensibility in the modern world. The pop tune works marvelously in this manner, for it is technically slight (a simple formula defines almost all the compositions) and its diction illustrates perfectly a cloying, sentimental tone that contrasts obviously with the achievements of "serious" poetry.

But even as we identify these elements of commercial, popular music, it is apparent that it contributes something else to the values asserted by writers such as Fitzgerald—and we might add Hemingway, Dos Passos, and Faulkner, among others. However trite and barbaric the music appears to be, it functions nevertheless as a lever against the cultural pretensions of conventional middle-class society. And it does so, I would suggest,

not so much for its own sake as for its association with a tradition of which it is a heavily watered down version—namely, Negro jazz and its folk sources. Despite their limited awareness of the nature and sources of American music, some sense of what underlay the popular songs leaked through in the work of writers like Fitzgerald. Jazz carried clear associations with a level of culture decidedly outside the stream of middle-class white morality and rooted essentially in the attitudes and expression of the Negro. For the writers of the twenties and thirties jazz carried strong connotations and was associated with stereotypes of the Negro as fantastically virile and barbarously effective in his sexual life. Attempts to pinpoint the etymology of the word have failed to produce a clear explanation, but all discover a primary use of jazz (sometimes *jass*) as a verb meaning to fornicate.

The Jazz Age (the coinage seems in fact to have been Fitzgerald's) picked up all these nuances: the disillusionment with the Great War, the reaction to Prohibition and associated "puritanical" restrictions of the period, the wide open life of the speakeasies with their flow of bootleg liquor and promiscuous women—though the latter are always underplayed in our nostalgic recreations of the period, in films particularly. Although Negroes appear occasionally (as musicians) the Jazz Age is presented to us in literature from the disaffected white's point of view; what it suggests to us about the Negro himself is a form of sentimental primitivism: jazz is his music and the white listener uses it as a way of making some small contact with the jungle madness which its beat suggests. The sense of distance is important, for while jazz is conceived to be a threat to the values of the sick world in the period after the First World War, it is also the fitting accompaniment for its impending demise. Tostoff's composition is ironically only the other side of Tom Buchanan's assertion: "'Civilization's going to pieces. . . . I've gotten to be a terrible pessimist about things. Have you read "The Rise of the Colored Empires" by this man Goddard? . . . Well it's a fine book, and everybody ought to read it. The idea is if we don't look out the white race will be—will be utterly submerged. It's all scientific stuff; it's been proved.'" *The Jazz History of the World* is the finale for the last act.

William Faulkner's response to music is in general very much like Fitzgerald's. But occasionally he gives us a view of Negro music (and folklore) which is much less patronizing than that of his contemporaries, and at times he comes close to folkloristic precision. Ralph Ellison has noted in *Shadow and Act* (1964) that, despite his ambivalence and his willingness to accept major stereotypes of the Negro, Faulkner "has explored perhaps more successfully than anyone else, either white or black, certain forms of Negro humanity." In part this is due to his remarkably prolific exploration of the South in general, but Ellison observes that Faulkner's central quest is for human truth rather than regional or racial insights. Because the social order of the South "harms whites no less than blacks, the sensitive Southerner, the artist, is apt to feel its effects acutely—and within the deepest levels of his personality. For not only is the social division forced upon the Negro by the ritualized ethic of discrimination, but upon the white man by the strictly enforced set of anti-Negro taboos. The conflict is always within him. Indeed, so rigidly has the recognition of Negro humanity been tabooed that the white Southerner is apt to associate any form of personal rebellion with the Negro. So that for the Southern artist the Negro becomes a symbol of his personal rebellion, his guilt and his repression of it. The Negro is thus a compelling object of fascination, and this we see very clearly in Faulkner." Since Faulkner has also recognized how inextricably the Negro is involved in the meaning of America itself, he has often taken an approach somewhat different from Fitzgerald's. At the same time, like many of our Southern writers, he is closer to the roots of Negro folk tradition and often reproduces elements from it with great accuracy, as we can see from some descriptions of black music in his novels. *Sartoris* (1929) was Faulkner's third novel but the first in which he found his distinctive voice and most of his major themes. It abounds in Negro stereotypes—"his race's fine feeling for potential theatrics," "the grave and simple pleasure of his race." But it also contains some prime examples of the quality, style, and range of black music. Elnora, the house servant, sings snatches of spirituals "as she soused her mop into the pail and thumped it on the floor again."

> Sinner riz fum de moaner's bench,
> Sinner jump to de penance bench;
> When de preacher ax 'im whut de reason why,
> Say, "Preacher got de women jes' de same ez I."
>   Oh, Lawd, oh, Lawd!
> Dat's whut de matter wid de church today.

On other occasions Elnora's voice floats "in meaningless minor suspense" or wells "in mellow falling suspense"—a description which catches nicely the melismatic quality of Negro singing as it moves from tone to tone, rarely stopping squarely on a given pitch.

In another section young Bayard puts together a Negro trio to provide an evening serenade: "They stopped here, in shadow. The Negroes descended and lifted the bass viol out, and a guitar. The third one held a slender tube frosted over the keys upon which the intermittent moon glinted in pale points, and they stood with their heads together, murmuring among themselves and touching plaintive muted chords from the strings. . . . The tunes were old tunes. Some of them were sophisticated tunes and formally intricate, but in the rendition this was lost and all of them were imbued instead with a plaintive similarity, a slurred and rhythmic simplicity; fading, dying in minor reiterations along the treacherous vistas of the moon." The performance ends with "Home, Sweet Home" and a rendition of "Good Night, Ladies," sung in the "true, oversweet tenor" of one of the white men who accompany the Negroes. (Faulkner refers to the rich *minor* of "Home, Sweet Home" although it is actually in a major key. Yet the rendition of this standard senti-

mental tune by a black group could easily give it a minor tonality.) But as in much of his work, Faulkner is perhaps more accurate than he knew, because the description of Negroes appropriating materials from the general culture into their own style is a precise illustration of that hybridization of diverse materials which defines the quality of American folksong. (It recalls Alan Lomax's observation that the major elements in American folksong derive from West African and British sources combined uniquely in the United States.)

Finally there is Bayard's response to the movements of country Negroes through the town at noon: "—Negroes slow and aimless as figures of a dark placid dream, with an animal odor, murmuring and laughing among themselves; there was in their consonantless murmuring something ready with mirth, in their laughter something grave and sad. . . ." Bayard continues to watch: "Against the wall, squatting, a blind Negro beggar, with a guitar and a wire frame holding a mouth-organ to his lips, patterned the background of smells and sounds with a plaintive reiteration of rich, monotonous chords, rhythmic as a mathematical formula, but without music. He was a man of at least forty and his was that patient resignation of many sightless years. . . ." Bayard groped for a coin in his pocket "and the beggar sensed his approach and his tune became a single repeated chord, but without a break in the rhythm, until the coin rang into the cup, and still without a break in the rhythm and the meaningless strains of the mouth-organ, his left hand dropped groping a little to the cup and read the coin in a single motion; then once more guitar and mouth-organ resumed their monotonous pattern." What Faulkner had caught here is the central tradition of Negro folksong—the blues. In fact, one of the main sources of its dispersion through the South was the blind street singer such as the one described in the passage, and Faulkner is exceptionally accurate in his description of what the music sounded like; it is indeed a heavily rhythmic, formulaic repetition of standard motifs, though more complex than Faulkner suggests. The combination of guitar and mouth-organ is a traditional one—in the South the harmonica is more likely to be called a French harp, I think because it is tongued and hence by analogy from French kiss. In any case, the style associated with blues harmonica is a major innovation of Southern blacks. It is accomplished by playing the instrument in a key different from the one in which it is tuned, which results in a striking blues tonality ordinarily not possible on the instrument, which is nonchromatic and has a very limited range. As in some of his other comments about black music and singing Faulkner refers to meaningless strains, and of course, having omitted any reference to the singing which would accompany the blues, he misses the verbal comment as well as the complex relationship between instrumental and vocal styles that is inherent in the country blues. In other words, Faulkner is still far from understanding fully the meaning or the function of blues in black tradition, and he uses the music to underscore the disaffection of his lost-generation protagonist, Bayard Sartoris. Yet he comes closer to the materials than any writer up to his time, just as in *The Sound and the Fury* (1929) he gives us one of the best descriptions of a Negro singing sermon which has ever been presented in American literature. The Reverend Shegog begins in the standard speech of educated Southerners and then suddenly breaks into a country dialect: "'Breddren en sistuhn!' His voice rang again, with the horns. He removed his arm and stood erect and raised his hands. 'I got de ricklickshun en de blood of de lamb!' They did not mark just when his intonation, his pronunciation became negroid, they just sat swaying a little in their seats as the voice took them into itself." It is a perceptive insight into the pluralistic pattern of American Negro life, and when the disguise is lifted Shegog fits immediately into the pattern of call and response which is basic to Negro folksong and folk sermons, the preacher half-speaking and half-singing, in response to the occasional cries and melodic intonations of the congregation.

But while Faulkner's is a significant accomplishment, it yet falls short of fulfilling the possibilities of Negro materials for their own sake as well as for what they can tell us of American life in general. We can see this best by looking closely at Ralph Ellison's *Invisible Man* (1952), which defines the ideological and technical possibilities of American Negro materials more accurately and effectively than any work in our literary history. Ellison is valuable also because he is one of those writers whose criticism is as carefully crafted as his fiction—it is a virtue we often associate with poets (from Dryden to Eliot) but which, with the major exception of Henry James, seems less prevalent among fiction writers.

To begin with, it is important to recognize that Ellison does not conceive the book as a "Negro novel" in any sense of the term. What he has learned from Faulkner is that the relationships between black and white are central to the meaning of *American* development. That does not prevent him from understanding the unique qualities of Negro life and culture, but it does mark him from the tendency discernible in some Negro writers to associate themselves with separatism or Black Nationalism. Ellison explains his position partly from the fact that his roots are in the Southwest rather than in the deep South, though it seems to me he could have arrived at a similar conclusion even if he had been brought up in the Black Belt. Still it is important for him to recall (in *Shadow and Act*) that as a boy he and his companions felt little of the pressure to move inwardly toward the ghetto and away from the possibilities of American life: "Contrary to the notion currently projected by certain specialists in the 'Negro problem' which characterizes the Negro American as self-hating and defensive, we did not so regard ourselves. We felt, among ourselves at least, that we were supposed to be whoever we would and could be and do anything and everything which other boys did, and do it better. Not defensively, because we were ordered to do so; not because it was held in the society at large that we were naturally, as Negroes, limited—but because we demanded it of ourselves. Because to mea-

sure up to our own standards was the only way of affirming our notion of manhood." This is in line with Ellison's general conception of the meaning of American life which, as I think can be made clearer from the novel, is closest to the ideas of Emerson. Consequently, he points out, it was perfectly logical for him and his companions to think of themselves as Renaissance men, just as white Southerners viewed themselves as ancient Greeks or Cavaliers: "Surely our fantasies have caused far less damage to the nation's sense of reality, if for no other reason than that ours were expressions of a more democratic ideal. Remember, too, as William Faulkner made us so vividly aware, that the slaves often took the essence of the aristocratic ideal (as they took Christianity) with far more seriousness than their masters, and that we, thanks to the tight telescoping of American history, were but two generations from that previous condition." Ellison's point is that the Negro has never really been out of the mainstream of American experience, despite continuing assertions that the Negro is best understood as a man without a past: his African inheritance stripped away, this argument insists, there was nothing capable of replacing it in a society which consciously kept him hermetically sealed in the ghetto. Ellison's formulation is familiar—indeed it is another version of the frontier hypothesis: "One thing is certain, ours was a chaotic community, still characterized by frontier attitudes and by that strange mixture of the naive and sophisticated, the benign and malignant, which makes the American past so puzzling and its present so confusing; that mixture which often affords the minds of the young who grow up in the far provinces such wide and unstructured latitude, and which encourages the individual's imagination—up to the moment 'reality' closes in upon him—to range widely and, sometimes, even to soar." Like pioneer Americans, the Negro lost elements of his inherited background but assimilated others from the materials available to him in this country.

Ellison uses just these circumstances to point out how closely the Negro's experience reproduces that of the American's. In response to a critic's attempt to define the Negro as a primitive "trickster," Ellison argues that the Negro uses the mask precisely as all Americans have, in the context of "the old American problem of identity." For the American, as Constance Rourke pointed out, was always defined as a "barbarian" who had left his claim to culture in the Old World. The idea of the smart man playing dumb is a strategy hardly limited to Negroes. "Actually," Ellison notes, "it is a role which Negroes share with other Americans, and it might be more 'Yankee' than anything else. It is a strategy common to the culture. . . . The white American has charged the Negro American with being without a past or tradition (something which strikes him with nameless horror), just as he himself has been so charged by European and American critics with a nostalgia for the stability of European cultures; and the Negro knows that both were 'mammy-made' right here at home. What's more, each secretly believes that he alone knows what is valid in the American experience, and the other knows he knows, but will not admit it, and each suspects the other of being at bottom a phony."[2] This is a version of what I called "The Arkansas Traveler" strategy of humor, in which the American faces his critic by pretending to be even dumber than he is expected to be, all the while undercutting his opponent by a play of witty *double-entendre*.

But Ellison goes even farther along folkloristic lines. As he has suggested, one of his essential interests is in the revelation of the peculiarly American problem of identity. Many of our writers and critics have turned to folklore as a way of answering some of the questions that problem raises; and Ellison takes the same tack, though here we are in a position to see how the strategy will work in the context of black folk tradition. The general approach, however, is the same one that I have traced to Herder. It uses folk tradition as the basis for an understanding of the national character, and in this case it becomes possible to examine closely the roots of Negro folklore in order to discern the elements that have formed major segments of American Negro expression. (At the same time, Ellison understands the Negro to represent some essential qualities of the American himself—as Constance Rourke and the Lomaxes had already argued in their own versions of Herderian folk ideology.) Yet another major connection is apparent when Ellison notes that his major interest is literary and he explains that his concern with folklore is primarily for what it will allow him to do as a writer: "I use folklore in my work not because I am Negro, but because writers like Eliot and Joyce made me conscious of the literary value of my folk inheritance. My cultural background, like that of most Americans, is dual (my middle name, sadly enough, is Waldo). . . . My point is that the Negro American writer is also an heir of the human experience which is literature, and this might well be more important to him than his living folk tradition. For me, at least, in the discontinuous, swiftly changing and diverse American culture, the stability of the Negro American folk tradition became precious as a result of an act of literary discovery." Ralph Waldo Ellison is a lot closer politically and esthetically to his namesake than he has admitted. More importantly, and despite his valid objection to being construed as a folk writer, he has given us a major illustration of how the American writer uses folk materials to create a distinctly national expression which yet speaks in broadly human rather than racial or regional terms. . . . Ellison not only brings us up to date; he is an effective and impressive heir to what has gone before, filling in outlines of crucial areas that had only been sketched earlier.

Ellison's central concern in *Invisible Man* is to provide a portrait of the American and his focusing on a black hero raises at once that peculiarly American formulation which we have encountered earlier. The American is conceived to be a man without a past or anterior folklore which will serve to define his national values and literary expression. If this is true for the American in general, it is especially true for the Negro—and Ellison's

point is that his situation is the same as his white counterpart's. But the circumstances of his attempt to define his identity will be framed by his relationships to the white world, which functions in relation to the Negro as the European world operated in regard to the white American. The hero, in short, is *peau rouge* whatever the actual color of his skin. And he is also the American barbarian, although the source of barbarism in this case is not the frontier but the jungle heritage of Africa. In the face of this collection of stereotypes, the hero assumes the mask as a means of undercutting the assumptions of his adversaries. The next step is predictable: as the American in general needs to show that his tradition is rich and meaningful, so the American Negro needs to convince himself and his critics that black folk tradition is more than the mumbo-jumbo or the cacophony that jazz is usually taken to be. The dynamic of the novel stems from the hero's struggle with himself to acknowledge the legitimacy of his heritage in the face of constant attacks by the white community or its allies in the society of Negroes. Nothing is simple and the virtue of Ellison's comic strategy is that it cuts both ways, undermining the stereotypes of the whites and exposing the insecurities of the Negroes. But the progression of values is clear: in order to acknowledge his existence as a man, the hero must first accept the folk legacy of his people; having attained this position, he will discover his identity as an American; but then he must move to the next stage, which expresses the universal values of humanity. The progression is from folk to national and finally international values.

But everything depends on the identification of the folk culture as rich and sufficiently sophisticated to pass the test of the self-appointed culture which judges it to be innately inferior. In order to satisfy these demands, Ellison must first establish the legitimacy of black folk tradition, and his argument runs along lines already familiar to us. The anterior folklore of the Negro (like all folklore) is not simpleminded or barbaric but operates on a level very close to that of formal art. The central question can be resolved in terms of the richness of folk diction, and Ellison gives us several scenes which make the point well. After the narrator arrives in New York he encounters a junk man one morning singing a blues as he pushes his cart along: "She's got feet like a monkey / Legs like a frog—Lawd, Lawd! / But when she starts to loving me / I holler Whoooo, God-dog! / Cause I loves my baabay, / Better than I do myself. . . ." The junk man asks the narrator if he's "got the dog," and the narrator plays "The Arkansas Traveler," pretending he doesn't understand the reference:

> I laughed nervously and stepped back. He watched me out of shrewd eyes. "Oh, goddog, daddy-o," he said with a sudden bluster, "who got the damn dog? Now I know you from down home, how come you trying to act like you never heard that before! Hell, ain't nobody out here this morning but us colored—why you trying to deny me?"

The narrator is uncomfortable in the face of this attempt to make him acknowledge his country background, but he cannot resist the junk man's spiel and his relish for language:

> "Well, daddy-o, it's been good talking with a youngster from the old country but I got to leave you now. This here's one of them good ole downhill streets. I can coast a while and won't be worn out at the end of the day. . . . I thought you was trying to deny me at first, but now I be pretty glad to see you . . ."

> "I hope so," I said. "And you take it easy."

> "Oh, I'll do that. All it takes to get along in this here man's town is a little shit, grit, and mother-wit. And man, I was bawn with all three. In fact, I'maseventhsonofaseventhsonbawnwithacauloverboth eyesandraisedonblackcatboneshighjohntheconquerorand-greasygreens—" he spieled with twinkling eyes, his lips working rapidly. "You dig me, daddy?"

> "You're going too fast," I said, beginning to laugh.

> "Okay, I'm slowing down. I'll verse you but I won't curse you—my name is Peter Wheatstraw, I'm the Devil's only son-in-law, so roll 'em. You a southern boy, ain't you?" he said, with his head to one side like a bear's.

> "Yes," I said.

> "Well, git with it! My name's Blue and I'm coming at you with a pitchfork. Fe Fi Fo Fum. Who wants to shoot the devil one, Lord God Stingeroy!"

> He had me grinning despite myself. I liked his words though I didn't know the answer. I'd known the stuff from childhood, but had forgotten it; had learned it back of school. . . .

This is only one of several scenes in which the issues of identity, name, and black tradition are brought together. (Joyce has a similar motif in *A Portrait of the Artist* in which a play of language is associated with Stephen's name and relationship to Ireland.) Ellison's nameless narrator is prodded by the junk man to acknowledge his roots as a Southern Negro and though he has been trained to look down his nose at the country people and their culture, he has nevertheless intimations that there is something rich and valuable in their expression. The combination of blues and folk speech appears in several other sequences where the same point is made.

The Jim Trueblood episode, which is one of the best drawn scenes (and to judge from the critics, one of the most problematical) moves along similar lines. The narrator is ordered by one of the white trustees to show him the countryside, and by mistake they arrive at Trueblood's. Mr. Norton is a New Englander who represents the legacy of abolitionism and there are several pointed references to Emerson—"I am a New Englander," Mr. Norton says, "like Emerson. You must learn about him, for he was important to your people. He had a hand in your destiny." Ellison is reacting against the white liberal's patronizing attitude toward the Negro and, as in a later scene involving a young man actually named Emerson, the tone is ironic and pejorative. At the same time, Mr. Norton becomes nostalgic over the memory of his dead daughter, for whom he had an unnatural affection. All this is foreshadowing for the interview with Trueblood, a sharecropper "who told the old stories with a sense of humor and magic that made them come alive. He was also a good tenor singer, and sometimes when special guests visited the school he was brought up along with members of a country quartet to sing what the officials called 'their primitive spirituals' when we assembled in the chapel on Sunday evenings." Ellison's handling of this situation reveals how well he can utilize the materials of folk tradition to expose the full range of their ideological and technical meaning. To begin with, it gives him a chance to undercut the conventional image of the Negro folk character whose major reference for most readers is the kindly Uncle Remus. Norton is ready to receive the impression of a fascinating spinner of tales in the quaint and curious diction of the country folk. What he gets is Trueblood's devastatingly effective recital of incest. Norton reveals the basis for his own interest in the story when he comments, "'You did and are unharmed!' . . . his blue eyes blazing into the black face with something like envy and indignation." This leads into a little dialogue that employs the strategy of "The Arkansas Traveler":

> "You have looked upon chaos and are not destroyed!"

> "No suh! I feels all right."

> "You do? You feel no inner turmoil, no need to cast out the offending eye?"

> "Suh?"

> "Answer me!"

> "I'm all right suh," Trueblood said uneasily. "My eyes is all right too. And when I feels po'ly in my gut I takes a little soda and it goes away."

The contrast between Norton's stilted diction and Trueblood's folk speech (which is one of the technical achievements of "The Arkansas Traveler" motif) works as well as ever. Ellison has pointed out that the "Negro stereotype is really an image of the unorganized, irrational forces of American life, forces through which, by projecting them in forms of an easily dominated minority, the white individual seeks to be at home in the vast unknown world of America. Perhaps the object of the stereotype is not so much to crush the Negro as to console the white man." It is just this kind of psychological projection that the Trueblood incident illustrates, and it accounts for the compulsion Norton has to hear the tale to the end, relishing every tabooed nuance that Trueblood narrates.

Having punctured the stereotype of the kindly folk character, Ellison pursues the implications of the scene. Like many of Ellison's characters, Trueblood's name carries much of the meaning. Incest is literally being true to one's blood and though Trueblood does not know it, the practice is an ancient and often honorable one, reserved indeed for the aristocracy. It is, in short, an old folkway and Ellison can thereby indicate his rejection of the sentimental notion that folklore will reveal the naiveté and innocence of the common people. The white trustee anticipates a version of pastoral innocence and agrarian antisepsis, quite unaware that for the Negro, pastoral would carry major associations with the horror and brutality of slavery. (Ellison clearly identifies Emerson with just such a simpleminded optimism, although as I have noted earlier, Emerson occasionally recognized that the reliance on folk diction might dredge up some materials that would shock genteel society.) In another more fundamental sense, however, Jim is true to his blood as a man, that is, he experiences the possibility of sin which inheres in the human condition. (Trueblood's dream in the midst of his sexual relations with his daughter invokes images suggesting the fires of hell.) What counts most heavily is Trueblood's reaction after his sin—and after he barely manages to escape the wrath of his wife. (It is true that sex figures prominently in certain areas of Negro folklore, but that should not lead to the dangerous and erroneous conception that Negroes are generally promiscuous—a point made by Trueblood's wife with an axblade!) The old man is rejected by his family, his preacher, and the Negro community but the whites take a great interest in him, encouraging him to tell the story over and over again. Finally, he is forced back on his own resources:

> I leaves tryin' to pray, but I can't. I thinks and thinks until I thinks my brain go'n bust, 'bout how I'm guilty and how I ain't guilty. I don't eat nothin' and I don't drink nothin' and cain't sleep at night. Finally, one night, way early in the mornin', I looks up and sees the stars and starts singin'. I don't know what it was, some kinda church song, I guess. All I know is I *ends up* singin' the blues. I sings me some blues that night ain't never been sang before, and while I'm singin' them blues I makes up my mind that I ain't nobody but myself and ain't nothin' I can do but let whatever is gonna happen happen. I made up my mind that I was goin' back home and face Kate; yeah, and face Matty Lou too.

It will take the rest of the book for Ellison's hero to learn the lesson, but ultimately he comes to the same understanding that "a man ain't nothin' but a man." Unlike Norton, who represses the knowledge of his deep instinct, Trueblood owns up to his sin—it is another sense in which his name is symbolic. But it is important to emphasize that the catharsis occurs through a creative act which Ellison accurately relates to a black folk tradition, the blues. As much as the spirituals, the blues is susceptible of ideological interpretation, though its definition was much later in coming. Yet the form easily takes on esthetic, political, and historical meanings. As one of the major forms of black music, the blues has defined a central tradition in American music at large.

The tonality comes from an indeterminacy in several crucial intervals of the scale, the third, fifth, or seventh degrees, which are the so-called blues notes. But actually something more complicated is involved and this is compounded by the fact that one of the characteristics of Negro folk music is that in performance it sounds very different from what any notation can describe. (This is true of all music, but it seems unusually so in black styles which depend on highly complex vocal effects and extensive ornamentation.) The sources of these effects are still not entirely known; some are clearly African, but the "blue notes" themselves do not seem to have African sources.

Although the form is often described as three lines in a twelve bar framework, there is in fact almost an unlimited number of variations possible, with a strong tendency toward improvisation in most authentic performances. But blues suggests sadness, an awareness of trouble or a general lament, and that meaning of the term goes back to Elizabethan usage. The poetry of the blues reveals the ability of the folk to create striking and impressive imagery and in this case it exposes the remarkable range of black folk expression. The themes are often love, death, the sense of loss and at the same time a hope for release and fulfillment. The imagery is often frankly sexual but in highly metaphorical terms which contribute a joy in language and the possibility for a witty humor based on *double-entendre*. Ellison's definition of the blues expresses succinctly and effectively the ideological implications of the form: "the blues is an impulse to keep the painful details and episodes of a brutal experience alive in one's aching consciousness, to finger its jagged grain, and to transcend it, not by the consolation of philosophy but by squeezing from it a near-tragic, near-comic lyricism. As a form the blues is an autobiographical chronicle of personal catastrophe expressed lyrically." We can see how far this is from earlier conceptions of black music as an expression of hopelessness and chaos. What emerges is an artistic form that makes possible the catharsis we usually associate with tragedy. Ellison pointedly emphasizes that the blues does not skirt the painful facts of human experience, but works through them to an artistic transcendence. We have already seen that this is the formula of Emerson's prescription for achieving the epiphanic moment—to work through the natural fact in order to express the spiritual truth that underlies it. But this similarity is less important than the fact that Ellison recognizes both the force of folk tradition and its close relationship to a sophisticated literary expression. Inevitably such an approach will move against the idea of isolated literary genres (such as tragedy) and in the direction of those mixed modes which seem to define American literary tendencies. The blues is not the "power of positive thinking" but a transformation of catastrophe through the agency of art. This esthetic, like Emerson's, will not allow a poetry of abstract generalization, for the "jagged grain" is valued in its own terms—it is roughly comparable to Emerson's natural facts which make it possible for the low but vital levels of diction to make themselves felt. And because of its close association with black folk culture, it is an esthetic which will also resist a movement toward expression for its own sake. There is, in short, that same balance of natural facts and spiritual truths which pervades a good deal of the literature in America that has been influenced by the Emerson-Whitman tradition.

This is precisely what Trueblood accomplishes with his blues. But Ellison extends this possibility to jazz as well, for if, on the one hand, the blues is a stage forward from earlier black musical expression (work songs, field cries, and spirituals) it is also a major link with jazz; and Ellison's use of jazz as a literary theme is one of his most impressive accomplishments. He raises the issue first in the Prologue, after a reference that comes close to reproducing Emerson's transparent eyeball image: "Nor is my invisibility exactly a matter of a bio-chemical accident to my epidermis. That invisibility to which I refer occurs because of a peculiar disposition of the eyes of those with whom I come in contact. A matter of the construction of their *inner* eyes, those eyes with which they look through their physical eyes upon reality." The mass of men are blind to the spiritual truths, and Ellison's narrator explains that "without light I am not only invisible, but formless as well; and to be unaware of one's form is to live a death." To be free is a function of the awareness of form, that is to say, it is closely related to the creative act, and the analogue of that combination is best defined by jazz: "I'd like to hear five recordings of Louis Armstrong playing and singing 'What Did I Do to Be so Black and Blue'— all at the same time. . . . Perhaps I like Louis because he's made poetry out of being invisible. I think it must be because he's unaware that he is invisible. And my own grasp of invisibility aids me to understand his music. . . . Invisibility, let me explain, gives one a slightly different sense of time, you're never quite on the beat. Sometimes you're ahead and sometimes behind. Instead of the swift imperceptible flowing of time, you are aware of its nodes, those points where time stands still or from which it leaps ahead. And you slip into the breaks and look around. That's what you hear vaguely in Louis' music." Appropriately it is a jazz performance of a blues that the narrator responds to and it is not accidental that the selection has strong social overtones. Ellison's knowledge of the sources of jazz helps him to pinpoint the meaning of Armstrong's music. He knows, for example, that Louis plays cornet (later trumpet), an instrument associated with military bands and that the marching band was one of the musical traditions absorbed and adapted by early New Orleans jazz groups. What Armstrong does with the military tradition is related to what he makes of his invisibility: he bends the inflexible lockstep militarism into a lyrical sound as he turns the condition of invisibility into poetry. It is an affirmation of the ability to overcome oppression through the creation of art and it is another example of Ellison's tendency to associate the idea of freedom with the awareness of form.

In more positive terms, jazz provides one with a new sense of time; again it is not the rhythm of a military march in which everyone must be in step; for despite the regular pulsing beat of a jazz band, there is always the offbeat, or offbeats, which are characteristic of jazz style. Even the drummer, who establishes the fundamental beat, will be more valued if he pushes it a bit, and the instrumentalists will take their solos either slightly behind or ahead of the other musicians. (The ultimate source of this is in black folk tradition where the leader and chorus patterns are strong, but overlapping of the relationship between the two is a standard device—it is what one critic has called "overlapping antiphony.") Instead of a mechanical rhythm, then, jazz demands an awareness of the nodes, those moments within the heart of pulsation which are static or which provide the occasion for a leap to another level of rhythmic awareness. This is an effective description of those essential qualities of jazz syncopation which are difficult to notate but which we recognize as fundamental to the jazz performance. But the rhythmic awareness that Ellison is concerned with also provides an analogy to the recognition of spiritual truths, the opening of the inner eye. The musician slips into the breaks and looks around; he enters into the center of meaning and creates his own statement, which is precisely what the jazz soloist must do. Ellison puts this also in terms of "The Arkansas Traveler" motif. The narrator describes a prize fight between a professional boxer and a yokel: "The fighter was swift and amazingly scientific. His body was one violent flow of rapid rhythmic action. He hit the yokel a hundred times while the yokel, rolling about in the gale of boxing gloves, struck one blow and knocked science, speed and footwork as cold as the well-digger's posterior. The smart money hit the canvas. The long shot got the nod. The yokel had simply stepped inside of his opponent's sense of time." This is precisely what the Squatter does, and in both cases, the opponent never knows what hit him.

The difference between Armstrong and the narrator is important. Louis is not aware of his invisibility because he is positively and deeply associated with the cultural sources of his art. For if jazz provides an outlet for individual expression it also demands an allegiance to the group as well, and Ellison employs this circumstance thematically as a way of defining the relationship of the individual to his society, thus raising the issue from a purely esthetic to a political level as well. It seems to me the best explanation for the denouement of the book in which the narrator affirms his resolve to emerge from underground: "I'm shaking off the old skin, and I'll leave it here in the hole. I'm coming out, no less invisible without it, but coming out nevertheless. And I suppose it's damn well time. Even hibernation can be overdone, come to think of it. Perhaps that's my greatest social crime, I've overstayed my hibernation, since there's a possibility that even an invisible man has a socially responsible role to play." Louis Armstrong figures prominently in the final decision: "With Louis Armstrong one half of me says, 'Open the window and let the foul air out,' while the other says, 'It was good green corn before the harvest.' Of course Louis was kidding, *he* wouldn't have thrown old Bad Air out, because it would have broken up the music and the dance, when it was the good music that came from the bell of old Bad Air's horn that counted." This is another formulation of Ellison's definition of blues, that transformation of brutal experience into the language of art—the bad air transmitted through Louis' horn becomes the remarkable achievement that we call jazz. And if one part of it is foul, another reflects the green corn, the folk roots of jazz itself. (Foul air is reminiscent of a Jelly Roll Morton tune, "Buddy Bolden's Blues," which is based on the theme of expelling ugly and obnoxious characters; the green corn reference may be to any number of Southern folksongs which use the expression, in dance or play-party tunes, as an image of vitality.)

Ellison reveals his relationship to the folk ideology that I have considered earlier in his awareness that the individual talent draws on the well of tradition from which the art form is derived. This is handled indirectly in the novel, though it counts heavily in the narrator's sense of social responsibility. Ellison develops the idea, however, in one of his essays in *Shadow and Act* where he explains what jazz has meant to him as an artist: "Now, I had learned from the jazz musicians I had known as a boy in Oklahoma City something of the discipline and devotion to his art required of the artist. . . . These jazzmen, many of them now world famous, lived for and with music intensely. Their driving motivation was neither money or fame, but the will to achieve the most eloquent expression of idea-emotions through the technical mastery of their instruments (which, incidentally, some of them wore as a priest wears the cross) and the give and take, the subtle rhythmical shaping and blending of idea, tone and imagination demanded of group improvisation. The delicate balance struck between strong individual personality and the group during those early jam sessions was a marvel of social organization. I had learned too that the end of all this discipline and technical mastery was the desire to express an affirmative way of life through its musical tradition and this tradition insisted that each artist achieve his creativity within its frame. He must learn the best of the past, and add it to his personal vision. Life could be harsh, loud and wrong if it wished, but they lived it fully, and when they expressed their attitude toward the world it was with a fluid style that reduced the chaos of living to form." This is the antithesis of the earlier attitude toward jazz as the very apex of confusion, but it is also important to note that Ellison's affirmation enables him to solve problems usually considered insoluble by the American writer. In black folklore and the music which issued from it, Ellison finds his sense of the past, and also the basis for his commitment to technical and artistic competence. But the technical accomplishment of the jazz musician is never strictly an individual phenomenon, however much improvisation and personal vision are valued. For underlying it is the folk tradition from which it emerged and hence, as Herder had pointed out,

there is a communal base which the folk themselves provided as a legacy to the individual artist. That delicate balance which Ellison describes between the individual and the group in a jam session becomes as well a description of what the society as a whole might be. The political implications of Ellison's folk ideology begin to emerge as inevitably as in the approaches of the writers I have discussed earlier. For jazz is a uniquely American expression and when we understand it as Ellison does, it encompasses just that sense of individualism directed toward communal concerns which we have already encountered in Emerson and Whitman. The metaphor of the jazzman illustrates the relationship better than any analogy we have seen to this point. Jazz values improvisation, personal vision, an assault on the conventional modes of musical expression, but it will not allow the individual to forget what he owes to tradition—not the tradition of a great man, but the legacy shaped by a whole people. It is precisely what folk ideologues have always argued: the authentic sources of a nation's culture lie in the lower levels and if they are developed sensitively, not only the poet speaks but his nation also finds its expression.

Hence the narrator of *Invisible Man* is finally able to unravel the meaning of his grandfather's advice: "I want you to overcome 'em with yeses, undermine 'em with grins, agree 'em to death and destruction, let 'em swoller you till they vomit or bust open." At first he takes this to mean accepting the values of the white world, playing the good Negro, all the while making the most of his opportunities for himself. But ultimately he understands that the grandfather's plea for affirmation was toward something else: "Could he have meant—hell he *must* have meant the principle, that we were to affirm the principle on which the country was built and not the men, or at least not the men who did the violence. Did he mean say 'yes' because he knew that the principle was greater than the men, greater than the numbers and the vicious power and all the methods used to corrupt its name? Did he mean to affirm the principle, which they themselves dreamed into being out of the chaos and darkness of the feudal past, and which they had violated and compromised to the point of absurdity even in their own corrupt minds? Or did he mean that we had to take the responsibility for all of it, for the men as well as the principle because no other fitted our needs? Not for the power or for vindication, but because we, with the given circumstances of our origin, could only thus find transcendence?" For all his awareness of evil and his contempt for an easy optimism, the narrator reveals himself to be essentially an Emersonian "yea sayer." He has tried all the versions of the American dream, beginning with the tradition that hard work and prudence will lead to material success. "Though invisible, I am in the great American tradition of tinkers," the narrator explains at the outset. "That makes me kin to Ford, Edison and Franklin. Call me, since I have a theory and a concept, a 'thinker-tinker.'" But what he finally learns is to accept his humanity (as his grandfather and Louis Armstrong always have) and the idea of self-reliance: "But my world has become one of infinite possibilities. What a phrase—still it's a good phrase and a good view of life, and a man shouldn't accept any other; that much I've learned underground. Until some gang succeeds in putting the world in a strait jacket, its definition is possibility. Step outside the narrow borders of what men call reality and you step into chaos—ask Rinehart, he's a master of it—or imagination. That too I've learned in the cellar, and not by deadening my sense of perception; I'm invisible, not blind." This is essentially what one strand of Emerson's thought has come to suggest—that the reality of our life needs to be held constantly to the demands of the American dream; and when it fails to measure up to the standard, it is the individual's responsibility to say so. But Emerson's individualism was balanced by an awareness of national requirements, which would be best expressed esthetically in the creation of a truly American art. The principle that Ellison's narrator affirms is best defined as nonconformity, but it contains also a commitment to that balance between individualism and communal responsibility which we noted in Whitman's concern with both the "I and the en-masse"; the danger is still that the balance will be tilted in the extreme of either direction: "Now I know that men are different and all life is divided and that only in division is there true health. . . . Whence all this passion toward conformity anyway?—diversity is the word. Let man keep his many parts and you'll have no tyrant states. Why if they follow this conformity business they'll end up forcing me to become white, which is not a color but the lack of one. Must I strive toward colorlessness? But seriously, and without snobbery, think of what the world would lose if that should happen. America is woven of many strands; I would recognize them and let it so remain. It's winner take nothing that is the great truth of our country or of any country. Life is to be lived, not controlled; and humanity is won by continuing to play in face of certain defeat. Our fate is to become one, yet many—This is not prophecy but description."

The character who symbolizes the idea of possibilities as a way of life is Rinehart, ideologically the most important figure in the book, though dramatically just a sketch. In response to a question about Rinehart, Ellison recalled that the name appeared in one of blues singer Jimmy Rushing's songs and was not a conscious play on Django Rhinehardt, the great jazz guitarist. The line from the blues was haunting, "and as I was thinking of a character who was a master of disguise, of coincidence, this name with its suggestion of inner and outer came to mind. Later I learned that it was a call used by Harvard students when they prepared to riot, a call to chaos. Which is very interesting, because it is not long after Rinehart appears in my novel that the riot breaks out in Harlem. Rinehart is my name for the personification of chaos. He is also intended to represent America and change. He has lived so long with chaos that he knows how to manipulate it. It is the old theme of *The Confidence Man*. He is a figure in a country with no solid or stable past or stable class lines; therefore he is able to move about easily from one to the other." The

reference to Melville is interesting because it seems to me that stylistically Ellison is closer to him than any other source, and this seems the more evident if we recall Melville's use of Emerson's esthetic and his insistence on seeing the darker implications of Emerson's political philosophy. But Rinehart's ability to manipulate chaos also suggests that he is a symbol of the artist. He is a Proteus and Ellison himself has made this analogy with the artist: "For the novelist, Proteus stands for both America and the inheritance of illusion through which all men must fight to achieve reality. . . . " Encountering Rinehart in an evangelical mission, the narrator finally understands his function: "I had heard it before but I'd never come so close. Still, could he be all of them: Rine the runner and Rine the gambler and Rine the briber and Rine the lover and Rinehart the Reverend? Could he himself be both rind and heart? What is real anyway? But how could I doubt it? He was a broad man, a man of parts who got around. Rinehart the rounder. It was true as I was true. His world was possibility and he knew it. He was years ahead of me and I was a fool. I must have been crazy and blind. The world in which we lived was without boundaries. A vast seething, hot world of fluidity, and Rine the rascal was at home in it. It was unbelievable, but perhaps only the unbelievable could be believed. Perhaps the truth was always a lie." Yet although Rine-hart is closest to the truth he has a major fault; he is in danger of tipping the scales too far in the direction of selfish exploitation of the world's possibilities. He is irresponsible in not acknowledging the communal sources of that artistic power which enables him to master illusion. (It is the analogue of art for art's sake and Ellison is as uncomfortable as Emerson at the prospect.) Rinehart, to recall Cotton Mather's metaphor of the sinner rowing toward heaven, is like a man pulling only one oar; he has forgotten his social responsibilities.

Hence, although Rinehart is attractive, he cannot provide the narrator with a complete world view. And Ellison has resented inferences that his narrator will remain an antihero, simply a version of Dostoievsky's underground man: "The final act of *Invisible Man*," he notes, "is not that of a concealment in darkness in the Anglo-Saxon connotation of the word, but that of a voice issuing its little wisdom out of the substance of its own inwardness—after having undergone a transformation from ranter to writer. . . . And in keeping with the reverse English of the plot, and with the Negro American conception of blackness, his movement vertically downward (not into a 'sewer,' Freud notwithstanding, but into a coal cellar, a source of heat, light, power and through association with the character's motivation, self-perception) is a process of *rising* to an understanding of his human condition." That underground suggests as well the substratum of folk culture upon which an American art can be built, and Ellison's hero plays a variation on the Marxist dictum: "All boundaries down, freedom was not only the recognition of necessity, it was the recognition of possibility."

The narrator will not give up his color because that would mean rejecting as well the heritage of black culture which, as Ellison has argued, is a major contribution to America as well. But the force of black culture (in folklore and jazz) is to remind us of the principle especially appropriate for American development—that the roots of high culture lie in the expression of the common people. Ellison modifies the optimism of Emerson's ideology with his blues formulation; it is what he means by "continuing to play in face of certain defeat"—play refers not just to the game, but also to Louis Armstrong playing his music, though conscious that he is black and blue. What Ellison has in mind in his formulation of equality recalls Herder's conception of the equal validity of incommensurable cultures. The aim is not to make the Negro white, or the white Negro, but to allow for the fullest development of each strand which will ultimately contribute to the definition of a black *and* white America. It is not black nationalism Ellison is after, but American nationalism as the Emerson-Whitman tradition had defined it. For the Negro it means first accepting his folk heritage in order to be an American; then he can acknowledge his status as a man. (Ellison knows that "in the United States when traditions are juxtaposed they tend, regardless of what we do to prevent it, irresistibly to merge," and he adds: "Those who know their native culture and love it unchauvinistically are never lost when encountering the unfamiliar.") Meanwhile the familiar strategy continues to work. It is the seeming barbarian whose level of culture defines the highest values of our civilization, while his language revitalizes our literary expression.

This has been the central motif of this study and Ellison has defined even more accurately what it has meant for his own career as an artist. The Negro's experience, he noted, "is that of America and the West, and is as rich a body of experience as one can find anywhere. We can view it narrowly as something exotic, folksy, or 'lowdown,' or we may identify ourselves with it and recognize it as an important segment of the larger American experience—not lying at the bottom of it, but intertwined, diffused in its very texture." The irony is that Americans at large still need to be convinced that it is so.

Paul Oliver

SOURCE: "Can't Even Write: The Blues and Ethnic Literature," in *Melus,* Vol. 10, No. 1, Spring, 1983, pp. 7-14.

[*In the following essay, Oliver argues that blues music is a legitimate extension of the African-American folk experience, but it is a limited genre as a source for a true ethnic literature.*]

Lord, the reason why baby, I been so long writin'
   to you
I say, the reason why baby, I been so long writin'
   to you,

Because I been studyin' so hard, Lord how to
   sing these blues.[1]

Sleepy John Estes' verse may not summarize the whole issue of the relationship between ethnic song and literature, but it does give us a hint of where the folk composer's priorities lie. Estes was a blues singer from Brownsville, Tennessee, one of the hundreds of such singers whose recordings have constituted one of the largest reserves of a folk literature among any ethnic group. He was Black, he was a poor farmer, and he was nearly blind; if he had sent a letter to his woman, it would have been very probably through the hand of a friend.

"Got me accused of forgery, I cain't even write my name . . ." sang another blues singer, Eddie Boyd—sang several other blues singers, in fact, for blues has its traditional stanzas and phrases which express succinctly ideas that can be drawn into new compositions. Though he lived in Chicago and eventually settled in Sweden, and though he was more sophisticated a blues singer than some, Eddie Boyd wrote with great difficulty; even as famous a blues singer as Muddy Waters, with numerous international tours behind him and many a college appearance in his yearly calendar—even he signs his name with a rubber stamp. Literacy is not unknown among blues singers: Whistling Alex Moore, who drove a junk cart and horse around the streets of Dallas for decades, had a flowing "copperplate" hand when he wrote his pencilled letters on pages of an exercise book, filling in the loops with indelible pencil to improve their decorative appearance. But he was an exception. When Garfield Akers sang his "Cottonfield Blues,"

I'm gon' write me a letter ooh, I'm gon' mail it in
   the air . . .
Said, I' know you'll catch it, mama in the world
   somewhere . . . [2]

he probably was referring to his own singing.

Blues is for singing. It is not a form of folk song that stands up particularly well when written down. Sometimes the poetic qualities of a blues verse survive the transfer to the printed page and the stark economy of the words, the occasional touches of sardonic humor or the bleakness of a despairing stanza stabs home:

They sentenced me to ten years on Big Brazos,
   picking cotton and corn
   and listening to the big bell tone (twice)
Now every time I hear a street light jingle, I start
   aching all in my bone . . . [3]

sang Mercy Dee Walton in a long blues, "Mercy's Troubles."

Baby next time you go out, carry your black suit
   along (twice)
Coffin gonna be your present; Hell gonna be your
   brand new home . . . [4]

—the words of King Solomon Hill in "Whoopie Blues" are no more and no less poetic, laconic or ironic than those in countless other recordings.

The elusive poetry of the blues has been the subject of separate studies by Samuel Charters and Paul Garon, anthologized by Eric Sackheim, analyzed for their formulaic structure related to meaning by Jeff Todd Titon, and as binary systems of expression by myself.[5] But they stand as what they are: stanzas that are sometimes new, sometimes traditional, composed in forms that are predetermined, most frequently to a three-line, twelve-bar structure, sung to a solo accompaniment of guitar or piano or to the playing of a small group of instrumentalists. Blues can be analyzed on the printed page, but they do not exist there; blues are essentially performed—they exist in the singing and the playing. The music of the blues is inseparable from the words when considered as a totality, even though the words considered in isolation from the complement of the instrumental accompaniment may still have powerful messages to convey.

So where does this leave blues in relation to an ethnic literature? The question begs others, and though they have doubtless been discussed in these pages often before, some comments on them must be made. In the first place, there is the considerable problem of whether there is such an entity as an ethnic literature, or indeed an ethnic art form at all, if by ethnic is meant "racially identifiable." Culture is not a quality of race, and races do not automatically produce identifiable cultural traits. Racial groups, by their need to retain their identity, or sometimes because of their visible separation from others of different races (by skin pigmentation or hair type), may keep together as a discrete group and in so doing evolve as cultures. In the process, an "ethnic culture" might be identified both by the group itself and by those outside it, a product of its separate life within the larger society. Whether that culture is made evident by the food it eats, the clothes it wears, the argot it speaks, the rhythms it beats or the songs it sings, it gains its strength from the reinforcement of its own identity which the cultural expression manifests. But it is not inherently racial in origin, but cultural.

Cultural here may mean, however, not merely the mores and material artifacts of a racial group, but of a part of it—of a culture within the culture. Blues is not the music of all Black Americans, many of whom consider it of low class and status, lewd, irreverent and unsophisticated. All of which it is, as a folk culture or as a popular culture, from which many middle-class Blacks are, or choose to be, alienated. Blues is an expression of a working-class subculture, or rather, of several. For the blues in the cities is different from that of the rural regions; and the blues of the 1950s is different from the blues of the 1920s. The latter issue is complex, but there is a substantial literature available for those who wish to study the regional and temporal distinctions further.[6] Moreover, blues is not representative of the whole of Black culture in the lower economic brackets: it is re-

garded as the music of the Devil by the members of churches of all denominations. Even the relationship of the blues singer to his (the majority of blues singers in the folk tradition are male) group is itself ambivalent. He is often regarded as dissolute, irresponsible, and something of a clown while being admired for his music making and his capacity to speak through his blues songs for the community. And, it must be said that such opinions are often justified even though many blues singers in no way fit such stereotypical descriptions.

Because blues singers have been drawn generally from among the poorest in the Black communities, in an ethnic minority which is itself largely disadvantaged, they have frequently been illiterate, educated only in the experience of a hard life. Whatever ideas may be in the literature of middle-class Black Americans, whatever poems may have been written under the inspiration of blues of one kind or another, remains entirely unknown to them. If the issue of "inter-relationship of ethnic music and literature" is the one that concerns us here then it must be accepted that any such relationship is not "inter-" but one-sided. There is no inter-relationship in the sense that the blues singer and creator of this form of ethnic music has any awareness of, or seeks any inspiration from, Black literature.

So, the position is one of the educated, literary poets and writers within the Black community looking to the blues for a source of ideas, and perhaps for a means of identification with what they may perceive as the roots of their culture. Such a perception may be romantic and insecurely based, but it is one that several Black writers have believed in. In passing, it should be mentioned that such a romantic identification is no less evident among white writers, and that literary narratives of the life of fictitious blues singers from Howard Odum's *Rainbow Round My Shoulder: The Blue Trail of Black Ulysses* (1928) to Peter Guralnick's *Night-hawk Blues* (1980)[7] have been by authors who could claim no ethnic links with their subjects. But, that is another (in some ways, more fascinating) issue.

Blues-related poetry appeared first in the 1920s "Negro Renaissance" when the experience of blues by Black poets was mainly through recordings or the stage presentations of Harlem shows and the vaudeville performances of Bessie Smith and Clara Smith. Langston Hughes (born 1902) and Sterling Brown (born 1901) were the most sensitive to the idiom and Hughes, in particular, closely followed it:

> I'm gonna walk to de graveyard
> 'Hind my friend, Miss Cora Lee,
> Gonna walk to de graveyard
> 'Hind ma dear friend, Cora Lee,
> Cause when I'm dead some
> Body'll have to walk with me.[8]

Brown also essayed the three-line blues form with "Tornado Blues":

Black wind came aspeedin' down de river from
   de Kansas plains,
Black wind came aspeedin' down de river from
   de Kansas plains,
Black wind came aroarin' like a flock of giant
   aeroplanes.

Destruction was adrivin' it and close behind was
   Fear,
Destruction drivin', pa'dner at his side was Fear,
Grinnin' Death and skinny Sorrow was abringin'
   up de rear. . . .

Both Hughes and Brown seem to have felt their detachment from the folk community while working in the idiom and sprinkled their verses with "ma" and "de" as liberally as any plantation memories of the 1890s. The long lines of the blues form were divided by Hughes, and in "Memphis Blues," Sterling Brown shattered it:

Was another Memphis
'Mongst de olden days,
Dome been destroyed
In many ways . . .
Dis here Memphis
It may go.
Floods may drown it,
Tornado blow
Mississippi wash it
Down to sea—
Like de other Memphis in
History.

As poets, both were developing concepts that would not occur in blues. Personification of Death, Sorrow and Fear are alien to its imagery, though possibly because personification of "the Blues" embraces them all in the traditional idiom. Both poets wrote longer works like Brown's "Long Gone" in *Southern Road,* or Hughes's *Ask Your Mama* which has "the traditional folk melody of the 'Hesitation Blues' (as) the leitmotif for this poem," but Hughes's rightly termed it "Twelve Moods for Jazz"; poems to be read between or against jazz improvisation and not poems that simulated blues form or expression.[9] Like Sterling Brown's "Ma Rainey," which was a poem about and to the singer, not an attempt at recreating her song composition, it was far more effective as poetry.

Myron O'Higgins (born 1918), a student of Sterling Brown, also wrote of one of the great figures in vaudeville blues, Bessie Smith, keeping approximately to the blues form:

Bessie lef' Chicago
   in a bran' new Cad'lac Eight
Yes, Bessie lef' Chicago
   in a gret big Cad'lac Eight
But dey shipped po' Bessie back (Lawd)
   on dat lonesome midnight freight.
Lawd, let de peoples know
   what dey did in dat Southern Town,
Yes, let de peoples know
   what dey did in dat Southern Town
Well, dey lef' po'. Bessie dyin'
   wid de blood (Lawd) a-streamin' down.[10]

Like Edward Albee in his play *The Death of Bessie Smith,* O'Higgins was making both a political and poetic point. Blues singer Booker T. Washington merely mourned her passing with the curious specific details that often occur in blues, but without the background of "de thunder rolled an' de lightnin' broke de sky," which O'Higgins felt necessary to his poem. Sang Booker T. Washington:

Bessie Smith went out ridin', went out ridin' in a
   limousine (twice)
Well that poor girl died suddenly, it was the
   worst I ever seen.
Well they took poor Miss Bessie way down some
   lonesome road (twice)
Well that poor girl gone this morning, yessir, she
   ain't gonna sing no more.

Bessie Smith wore pearls, and she wore
   diamonds, gold (twice)
Well that poor girl gone, Bessie Smith won't
   wear no more.[11]

It is arguable whether Myron O'Higgins makes a more effective comment—or poem—than does Washington with his reflection on wealth and mortality. Another poet who also wrote of Bessie Smith's death, or rather, the popularly believed version of it, was Oliver Pitcher (born 1923) in his bitter poem "Salute." He, too, has been drawn to the blues as in "Harlem: Sidewalk Icons."

Man, in some lan
I hear tell, tears wep
in orange baloons will
bus wide open with
laughter
Aw, cry them blues Man![12]

—but the last line strikes a false note. Other poets have felt the challenge of the blues and have—like James C. Morris (born 1920) tried to describe them:

These are the blues:
a longing beyond control
left on an unwelcome doorstep,
slipping in when the door is opened.

These are the blues:
a lonely woman crouched at a bar,
gulping a blaze of Scotch and rye,
using a tear for a chaser.

The blues are fears that
blossom like ragweeds
in a well-kept bed of roses.

(Nobody knows how tired I am.
And there ain't a soul who gives a damn.)[13]

In 1924, before James Morris had started school at Talladega, Alabama, blues singer Ida Cox had recorded her own definition:

Oh the blues ain't nothin' but a slow achin'-heart
   disease (twice)

Just like consumption it kills you by degrees.

Oh papa, papa, mama done gone mad (twice)
Oh the blues ain't nothin' but a good woman
    feelin' bad.[14]

Few Black poets have tested their work by having it sung by a blues singer. One that did was Richard Wright who made the mistake of getting Paul Robeson to sing "King Joe" with the Count Basie Band. Robeson was too much of a concert singer to sing blues and Wright too much of a poet to write them. Its folksiness struck the wrong note when Joe Louis was the theme:

Black-eyed pea said "Cornbread, what makes you
    so strong?" (twice)
Cornbread say, 'I come from where Joe Louis was
    born.'

Bull-frog told boll-weevil, "Joe's done quit the
    ring," (twice)
Boll-weevil say, "He ain't gone and he is still the
    king."[15]

Among Black poets, Wright was unusual in having been born on a plantation (1908) and having educated himself. His contact with blues was far closer than most, but he rarely essayed the form. His great poems like "I Have Seen Black Hands" or "Between the World and Me" are all the more impressive because they do not affect an artificial naivete. All the other poets quoted here had a good education; several went to universities and one or two have university appointments: very appropriate for poetry and literature, but far removed from the milieu of the blues. Poets are trained to structure their compositions, to understand the rhythms and the resonances of words; they develop critical ears and write with fastidious hands. But the ears of blues singers are atuned to the sounds of freight trains and Martin guitars, and their hands are calloused by hoes, ice-picks and metal guitar strings.

There is little point in making further comparisons between the poets' use of blues form or the blues singers' language, and those of the blues singers themselves. Ethnically, they may well be related, but in terms of literacy, world-view and cultural milieu, they are separated by a gulf which may perhaps be bridged, but will not be closed. Of course, this is not an argument for rejecting the blues, nor is it a way of saying that poets should not turn to blues, or anything else, for inspiration: the poet should have the creative freedom to draw his resources from where he chooses. All the same, it is worth emphasizing that this kind of choice is seldom the luxury of the blues singer.

Is there a future for an ethnic poetry of Black writers inspired by the blues? Maybe, but just as there seems little to look forward to in blues with literary pretensions, so there is little to be said for a literature with pretensions to being folk composition. The beauty of the blues resides so often in the relationship of the vocal and the words expressed to the music that is a part of it. As folk art in its origins and popular art today, it is remarkable, but, to date, it has not been a convincing source for an ethnic literature.

NOTES

[1] Sleepy John Estes, "Street Car Blues," Victor, V-38614, 1930.

[2] Garfield Akers, "Cottonfield Blues," Vocalion, 1442, 1929.

[3] Mercy Dee Walton, "Mercy's Troubles," Arhoolie, F1007, 1961.

[4] King Solomon Hill, "Whoopie Blues," Paramount, 13116, 1932.

[5] Samuel Charters, *The Poetry of the Blues* (New York: Oak Publications, 1963).

Paul Garon, *Blues and the Poetic Spirit* (London: Eddison, 1975).

Eric Sackheim, *The Blues Line* (New York: Schirmer Books, 1975).

Jeff Todd Titon, *Early Down Home Blues* (Urbana: University of Illinois, 1979).

Paul Oliver "Blues and the Binary Principle," in *Popular Music* 2, eds. Middleton and Hom (Cambridge: Cambridge University Press, 1982).

[6] Further reading is suggested in these books:

Paul Oliver *The Story of the Blues* (New York: Chilton Books, 1969).

Giles Oakley, *The Devil's Music* (New York: Taplinger, 1977).

Samuel Charters, *The Bluesmen Vol. 1* (New York: Oak Publications, 1967).

The Bluesmen Vol. 2 (New York: Oak Publications, 1977).

[7] Howard Odum, *Rainbow Round My Shoulder* (New York: Grosset and Dunlap, 1928).

Peter Guralnick, *Nighthawk Blues* (Chicago: Seaview Books, 1981).

[8] Examples quoted by Alain Locke in "The Negro in American Culture," in *Anthology of American Negro Literature*, ed. V. F. Calverton (New York: Modern Library, 1929), pp. 256-58. Following two quotations are from the same source.

[9] Sterling A. Brown, *Southern Road* (New York: Harcourt Brace and Co., 1932).

Langston Hughes, *Ask Your Mama: 12 Moods For Jazz* (New York: Knopf, 1969).

[10] Myron O'Higgins, "Blues For Bessie," in *The Poetry of the Negro,* eds. Langston Hughes and Arna Bontemps (New York: Doubleday and Co., 1949), p. 194.

Booker T. Washington, "Death of Bessie Smith," Bluebird, B8352, 1939.

[12] Oliver Pitcher, "Harlem: Sidewalk Icons," in *Dust of Silence* (New York: Troubador Press, 1958).

Oliver Pitcher, "Salute" in *Dust of Silence* (New York: Troubador Press, 1958).

[13] James C. Morris, "The Blues," in *Cleopatra* (New York: Exposition Press, 1955).

[14] Ida Cox, "The Blues Ain't Nothin' Else But . . . ," Paramount, 12212, 1924.

[15] Paul Robeson with Count Basie and His Orchestra, "King Joe," Okeh, 6475, 1941.

See Paul Oliver, "Joe Louis and John Henry," *Screening the Blues* (London: Cassell and Co., 1968) for fuller discussion of this item.

Steven C. Tracy

SOURCE: A review of 'Blues, Ideology, and Afro-American Literature', in *Melus,* Vol. 12, No. 2, 1985, pp. 97-102.

[*In the following review of* Blues, Ideology, and Afro-American Literature: A Vernacular Study, *Tracy takes exception to author Houston A. Baker's assertion that the blues exist solely as an anthropological record of African-American experiences.*]

In *The Journey Back: Issues in Black Literature and Criticism,* Houston A. Baker, Jr. applied what Leonard B. Meyer termed the "anthropology of art"—"methods and models drawn from a number of intellectual disciplines"—as a corrective to the nationalist idealism of the writers of the Black Aesthetic. He wished to demonstrate that Blacks imposed a linguistic order on the upheaval and chaotic experience precipitated by their confrontation with the network of Western values, both retaining and expressing culturally unique meanings. In his new volume, *Blues, Ideology, and Afro-American Literature: A Vernacular Study,* Baker departs from his tactics of focusing on a "speaking subject" who creates a language (code) to be deciphered; here language (the code) speaks the subject. The language is the vernacular and the subject is the "economics of slavery," a system that exploited and dehumanized African labor while it created and sustained a mythology of a patriarchal and paternal ruling class. However, this "economics of sla-

very" also occasioned an Afro-American response to the system, one which both exploits and transcends that system by combining economic pragmatism with what Baker calls "the rhythms of Afro-American blues" to form a matrix or womb or network—a vernacular life that helps explain not only Afro-American expressive culture but the essential spirit of the existing America straining to become its ideal (AMERICA).

Baker fleshes out his vernacular theory in four sections: an introduction and three chapters, portions of which have appeared previously in print. Baker might have done better to revise and restructure his ideas more extensively than he has here. Rather than starting out with his excellent survey of the Afro-American critical theory as it has shifted over the past three decades (a logical starting point for demonstrating both his continuities with and departures from previous theoretical stances) Baker introduces his own theory set against a backdrop of economics, history, anthropology, Marxist criticism, semiotics and deconstruction. His overview of the shift from Integrationist poetics to the Black Aesthetic to reconstructionism would have provided an excellent backdrop itself for his own shift, which draws upon the cultural-anthropological approach found in Stephen Henderson's work but qualifies it in the emphasis upon the anthropology of art and on the need for a critic with "a tropologically active imagination—that ceaselessly compels the analyst to introduce tropes that effectively disrupt familiar conceptual determinations. By calling attention to this frame of reference at the outset, Baker would have much more forcefully established his assertion that the *critic* is a creator and a catalyst like the poet and novelist (and blues singer), and that he needs to draw on a common matrix that activates not only African-American literature but American history and literature as well. At that point, then, his assertions about the blues and the need to subject the canon of American literary history to a scrutiny relative to the hierarchal importance it has placed on material generated outside the coterie of the Boston Brahmins and their heirs could fit much better. This is a minor point given the comprehensiveness and intellectual vigor that characterize Baker's discussion, but this rearrangement would allow the theoretical ground to be cleared and reestablished as a prerequisite to his discussions of particular literary works, which could then be done contiguously. Baker's justification for the structure is his assertion that "the disappearance of traditional American literary history leads to Afro-American literary history," which in turn sets the stage for more insightful Afro-American practical criticism. However, it seems much more likely that the slow process of acceptance of Afro-American literature as "legitimate" started America's process of discovering itself and led to the disappearance of "traditional" American literary history as well as the further exploration of Afro-American literature and practical criticism.

In his discussion of integrationist poetics in Chapter Two, Baker seems to go a bit too far in interpreting the introductory statements made by Arthur P. Davis, Sterling Brown, and Ulysses Lee in *The Negro Caravan*. When they reject the expression "Negro literature," they are not rejecting the "Negro" but the idea that the adjective implies simply structural peculiarities or a monotomy of expression. They prefer "literature by American Negroes" because they recognize, as Baker does, the peculiar combination of both African and American sources that provide for a diversity of expression. And when the editors call for a "single standard of criticism" they do not mean to accept white aims or methods, but seek to convince white non-believers that their own aims and methods can be applied *with the same level of excellence*—the demand is for discerning and sympathetic critics who can recognize the excellence of poetry like Brown's. After all, though Brown did do some conventional European versifying, his best work did not abandon the oral literature of his people. Indeed, it drew on it for both style and soul, recognizing its validity as literature: as he said in "The Blues as Folk Poetry," "These blues belong, with all their distinctive differences, to the best of folk literature. And to some lovers of poetry that is not at all a negligible best"; he cites a slave's depiction of Calvary, asserting that it "belongs with the greatest Christian poetry." No doubt some intergrationist poets sought to enter the mainstream by imitating European poetic standards; poets like Brown, though, sought to draw attention to strong currents that coexisted with those that were already charted.

Central to Baker's theory is his depiction of the blues and its role as a matrix, a "point of ceaseless input and output." Baker feels that the blues are not a "rigidly personalized form," but a "phylogenetic recapitulation—a non-linear, freely associative, nonsequential meditation—of species experience." That is certainly one of the most clinical definitions of blues on record, one that seems to assume that all blues are the same—that there are no linear, sequential, and non-meditative blues that are rigidly personalized and singer specific. Of course, we know that some blues may be as Baker describes them, but we know just as surely that there are blues that do not fully fit Baker's description.

In *Big Road Blues,* for example, David Evans traces the changes in the types of songs recorded by Blind Lemon Jefferson, from his early traditional, non-thematic compositions to his later original thematic blues that can be both linear and sequential. The commercialization of folk blues singers by the record companies often influenced them to write blues of this type, blues that developed a single story or theme in a recognizable sequence. Indeed, the vaudeville blues of the professional female blues singer might do this as well—blues often written either by professional tunesmiths or the vaudeville singers themselves. Perhaps Baker deliberately wishes to exclude such blues from his definition, but he should certainly do so specifically. Baker also insists that the "blues singer's signatory coda is always *atopic,* placeless" and that what emerges from the blues is "an

anonymous (nameless) voice." Surely this disembodying and uprooting of the blues by Baker is an overstatement, a removal of the blues to a highly symbolic level that it does not have to occupy. The stereotype of the constantly wandering blues singer can be counterbalanced by those blues singers like Mississippi John Hurt, who lived in the same location all of his life, venturing forth to record his blues for record companies, or by other blues singers who were rooted in a particular place and who sang about that place regularly. Baker is correct in asserting that the blues reflect a restlessness, but his identity is not disconnected from a particular place, but from a position—from the type of life owed him as opposed to the life he leads.

Finally, though Baker is probably right in invoking a blues matrix as the network or "always ready" present for the Afro-American writer, he does not explain why spirituals, jubilees, hollers, work songs, or any other type of Afro-American folk song, or jazz, do *not* fulfill the same function as the blues here. We might infer the reasons, but Baker should have at least briefly explored the blues in the context of these other kinds of songs to demonstrate their comparative worth. After all, in the early decades of the twentieth century, the spirituals were considered the important Afro-American songs; Baker now infers that the secular blues have been the "always ready." Some elaboration on this point would have been welcome.

When in Chapter One, Baker begins discussing changing the contours of American literature and switches his focus to three slave narratives—*The Life of Olaudah Equiano, Written By Himself; Narrative of the Life of Frederick Douglas, An American Slave, Written By Himself; and Incidents in the Life of a Slave Girl, Mrs. Harriet Brent Jacobs, Written By Herself*—his writing and ideas become distinctly clearer, providing a model for the intelligent discussion of the genre. Baker finds that their "transformation of property [themselves] by property [themselves] into humanity [themselves]" demonstrates their coming to terms with the "economics of slavery," which Baker argues persuasively is "the basic subtext . . . that necessarily informs any genuinely Afro-American narrative text." In other words, Baker feels that the protagonists arrive at commercial views of their lives as opposed to Christian moral views. In doing so, they gain their freedom. His close examinations of the texts support his view for both male and female protagonists. Additionally, Baker's discussion of Dunbar, Wright, and Ellison, the latter two in relation to his trope of a black hole, are intriguing. Baker posits the black hole "as an invisible, attractive force—a massive concentration of energy that draws all objects to its center. It reduces matter that passes its event horizon to zero sum." At this point it becomes fuel for "a black blues life's pressing desire." In this system, a "normal" state is disrupted by a rite of separation, at which time the protagonist withdraws from society to a marginal state until his appropriate reintegration can be effected. This idea works quite well with Wright's work, and it is quite nice to see a positive reevaluation of Wright, who is called "undisputed master of Black wholeness." However, Baker's depiction of Ellison's Trueblood as a man "who sells his own expressive product—a carefully constructed narrative, framed to fit market demands" somehow rings false. It is difficult to afford a man who has committed incest with his daughter the status of a man who has successfully negotiated the economics of slavery—that almost seems to legitimize his act, and his Freudian rationalizations seem more ridiculous than carefully constructed. No one in the story seems to want to recognize Trueblood for what he is. He is not a disgrace to his race, as Bledsoe felt, or representative of his race, as the whites felt, but a man who had committed incest with his daughter, who had figured out how to exploit the situation, as he had exploited his daughter, for material gain. That is a peculiarly negative way of going about negotiating the economics of slavery.

Ultimately, *Blues, Ideology and Afro-American Literature* is a stimulating foray into the origins of Afro-American literature and a discerning look at their implications for American history and literature. There are some troubling points in the book, but overall it is an elucidating endeavor. There is one other thing about the book that is bothersome, although perhaps it shouldn't be. In discussing Zora Neale Hurston's *Their Eyes Were Watching God,* Baker asserts that "Nanny, Janie's grandmother, is resoundingly correct in her conclusion that the pulpit (a propertied position on high ground) is a prerequisite for a stirring sermon." Beyond the implication that artistic production is tied to high social status, the statement might well serve as a metaphor for Baker's writing style. Although, of course, one need not write in the vernacular to write about the vernacular, still Baker's language is often so elevated, so erudite, that the vernacular and the blues seem very far away. Howlin' Wolf would not have sung, "The blues ain't nothin' but a *phylogenetic recapitulation,*" and, though it is perfectly acceptable for Baker to do so, it seems a bit remote.

Bruce Dick

SOURCE: "Richard Wright and the Blues Connection," in *Mississippi Quarterly,* Vol. 42, No. 4, Fall, 1989, pp. 393-408.

[*In the following essay, Dick links the influence of blues music on the works of Richard Wright with that of his contemporaries Zora Neale Hurston and Ralph Ellison.*]

Of the major twentieth-century African-American writers, Zora Neale Hurston and Ralph Ellison are famous for celebrating their forebears' folk roots. Hurston secured a permanent place among eminent American folklorists after the release of *Mules and Men* (1935), her monumental study of black American folk beliefs. Ellison also joined the first rank of American writers with the publication of *Invisible Man* (1952), which

traced a young black man's coming to terms with his folk past. Although critics rarely say so, the same folk interests that kindled the writings of Hurston and Ellison also inspired the works of Richard Wright, their contemporary.

Wright recognized the important value of African-American folk culture, particularly a form that received but scant critical attention during his lifetime, the blues. In fact, considering his numerous writings on the blues, which included a long article extolling Huddie Ledbetter, an essay comparing the blues to surrealism, several record reviews, and the foreword to blues critic Paul Oliver's first important book, *Blues Fell This Morning* (1960), Wright easily stands as one of the forerunners of interpretive blues criticism. That he tried his own hand some ten times at writing the blues makes him both a participant in and an interpreter of the blues, and certainly ranks him beside Hurston and Ellison in overall contribution to this particular facet of African-American folk culture.

It is possible that Wright's first contact with the blues, or at least with some of the folk ditties which closely resembled them, came as early as his fourth year, in 1911, on the *Kate Adams,* a tattered riverboat mentioned in early blues lore.[1] In *Black Boy,* the autobiography of his Southern youth, Wright describes a typical blues setting as he "wandered about the boat and gazed at Negroes throwing dice, drinking whiskey, playing cards, lolling on boxes, eating, talking, and singing."[2] If he was too young to savor this experience completely, he definitely absorbed the blues during his first stay in Memphis. Blues music thrived, not only in the vaudeville halls lining Beale Street, the major thoroughfare cutting through the heart of the city, but in pool halls, poker dens, and taverns.[3] Wright claimed these places as his territory, especially since he "found [them] irresistible to roam during the day" (*Black Boy,* p. 26). As he writes in *Black Boy,* "Every happening in the neighborhood, no matter how trivial, became my business" (p. 27): "With a gang of children, I roamed the streets, begging pennies from passerby, haunting the doors of saloons, wandering farther and farther away from home each day. I saw more than I could understand and heard more than I could remember" (p. 29).

After leaving Memphis in 1916, Wright lived with his grandmother and various relatives around the South, from Elaine and West Helena, Arkansas (both of them Delta towns, just across the river from Charley Patton's celebrated Lula), to Jackson, Mississippi. Like Memphis, these towns served as vital links in the blues hinterland. Thus Wright's exposure to the blues continued. A humorous quip taken from an unpublished essay called "Memories of My Grandmother" confirms this exposure. It also shows the consequences when Wright pushed his contact with the blues too far. "If my grandmother heard me so much as humming a blues song," he writes, "she would have struck me with whatever she happened to hold in her hand, be it a broom or an eight-pound skillet."[4] A 1943 letter to his good friend Joe Brown in Oxford, Mississippi, further supports Wright's early awareness of the blues and reveals the importance he had come to place on African-American folklore:

> I heard a record recently called "The Dirty Dozens." It consisted of a recital of the little jingles which you and I heard in our childhood set to boogie woogie music; the dumb folks around New York are eating it up. Boy, why don't you take pencil and paper and hang around the black boys and put on paper what they say, their tall tales, their words, their songs, their jokes? That stuff is some of the . . . best stuff this country has produced.[5]

When the seventeen-year-old Wright returned to Memphis in 1925, the town was jumping with the blues. Although Handy Park had not yet blossomed into a musician's paradise, blues acts poured in from as far south as Louisiana and Texas. For the next two years Wright lived on or close to Beale Street. And because he wandered "aimlessly about the streets of Memphis, gaping . . . at the crowds" and "killing time" (*Black Boy*, p. 224), it is safe to assume that once again he absorbed the blues. In fact in "Memories of My Grandmother," Wright states that one of his favorite pastimes was to venture each Saturday night to the Palace Theatre, the hottest nightspot in Memphis, just to hear blues singer Gertrude Saunders sing the blues.

Thus, before he was twenty, Wright had developed an appreciation of vaudeville blues and the downhome Delta blues characteristic of much of the Deep South. He began cultivating a more thorough understanding of the blues, particularly the urban blues, after his move to Chicago, where he stayed from 1927 until 1937. By the 1930's Chicago had become the major recording center for blue artists like Memphis Minnie and Big Bill Broonzy, whom Wright eulogized in a 1960 review for Barclay Disques called "So Long, Big Bill Broonzy." These musicians and others frequented taverns up and down Maxwell Street, the equivalent to Memphis' Beale Street and the center for Chicago blues acts. Wright reveals his knowledge of such clubs in his early fiction, particularly in *Native Son* (1940) and the posthumously published *Lawd Today* (1963), when he depicts raucous nights punctuated with violence, drink, and music. He also reveals his familiarity with juke joints in *12 Million Black Voices* (1941), his photo-journalistic history of his race. In this important folk study, Wright describes an assortment of makeshift music halls, where "black folk . . . play guitars, trumpets, and pianos, beating out rough and infectious rhythms that create an instant appeal among all classes of people."[6] He aptly calls the blues "the spirituals of the city" because they capture the longing for freedom and opportunity, especially for those who are caught in the "paradoxical cleavage" (p. 127) of laboring in the factories and mills of Western Civilization, only to be denied entry into that civilization.

By the time Wright moved to New York in 1937, he was well equipped to write about the blues. In fact, because his past had coincided almost simultaneously with their development, he had experienced the same hardships, heartaches, and frustrations as had the early blues singers. The restless moving and family quarrels that plagued his youth also defined the early bluesmen, as Wright himself points out in his writings. "The locale of the [blues] shifts continuously," he states in his foreword to Oliver's book, "and very seldom is a home site hymned or celebrated."[7] In an earlier piece called "The Literature of the Negro in the United States" (1945), Wright quoted Bessie Smith's "Backwater Blues" to show how impulse and dissatisfaction prodded millions of blacks, blues singers included, to abandon the rural South for the industrial cities of the North:

> Then I went an' stood up on some high ol' lonesome hill
> I went and stood up on some high ol' lonesome hill
> And looked down on the house where I used to live
> Backwater blues done cause me to pack mah things and go
> Backwater blues done cause me to pack mah things and go
> Cause mah house fell down an' I cain' live there no mo'.[8]

Although Wright recognized that a constant reference to loved ones was a noticeable feature of the blues, he also pointed out that "little or no mention [was] made of the family as such."[9] He attributed this neglect to the fact that the blues singer had no real family life to celebrate. According to Wright, the family institution in African-American society had remained ineffectual until the 1950's. The early blues singer, like Wright, was born sometime between the end of Reconstruction and the beginning of the First World War, at a time when the black family was only beginning to take root.

Wright pointed out that the bluesman extolled other items akin to his immediate surroundings, such as "sawmills, cotton-gins, lumber-camps, levee-banks, floods, swamps, jails, highways, trains, buses, tools, depressed states of mind, voyages, accidents, and various forms of violence."[10] As his autobiography and early fiction reveal, these environmental influences were constant in his own life and thus reason for him naturally to turn to the blues as a form of artistic expression. Indeed, by his thirtieth birthday, Wright was not only ready to write about the blues but also seriously prepared to attempt writing them himself.

Wright's earliest publication on the blues was a 1937 article for the *Daily Worker* called "Huddie Ledbetter, Famous Negro Folk Artist, Sings the Songs of Scottsboro and His People." Wright praised the barrel-chested baritone Leadbelly, whose endless repertoire of blues, spirituals, and folk songs "poured forth in such profusion that it [seemed] he knew every song his race [had] ever written."[11] For Wright, Leadbelly embodied "the entire folk culture of the American Negro" (p. 7), and his uncharacteristic rise to fame reflected the blues singer's strong will in the fact of adversity, especially the racism of white America.

As an ardent Marxist, however, Wright promoted the line of the Communist tabloid as much as Leadbelly's musical achievements. He called special attention to Leadbelly's political songs like "Bourgeois Blues" and "Scotsboro Boys" and contended that only after joining the Workers' Alliance did Leadbelly find "relief." "The folks in the Workers' Alliance are the finest I've known," Wright quotes Leadbelly. "I feel happy when I'm with the boys here in the Workers' Alliance. They are different from those Southern white men" (p. 7). Although he eventually renounced his Communist ties, Wright continued using Marxist parlance to define the blues aesthetic. In his introduction to blues/folk singer Josh White's three-record album collection, *Southern Exposure* (1940), Wright states that "there also exist blues which indict the social system. . . . Their very titles indicate the mood and state of mind in which they were written."[12] Even as late as 1959, a year before his death, Wright speaks of "dialectical redemption" in relation to the blues.[13] Wright's political vocabulary here contrasts with the orthodox position of many blues critics.[14] The powerlessness of performers within the intolerable context of sharecropping and post-reconstruction racism ensured that the lyrics of blues songs would develop codes of covert protest while they remained overtly bland. At the same time, Wright's 1959 remark anticipated the recent desire to lever up the political subtext in blues lyrics.

In the same article Wright exposes what he considered one of the biggest "cultural swindles in American history." According to Wright, John A. Lomax, the famous collector of American folklore for the Library of Congress, heard of Leadbelly and went to visit him in a Louisiana prison. Convinced Leadbelly could help him in uncovering heretofore hidden prison folklore, Lomax asked Leadbelly to join him in a tour of Southern prisons. After winning a pardon from the Louisiana governor, Leadbelly accepted Lomax's offer, but only under the gentleman's agreement that Lomax use his influence to help Leadbelly establish his music career. The twosome traveled through Texas, Arkansas, Alabama, and Louisiana, gathering scores of folk songs, which later were compiled into Lomax's famous book, *American Ballads and Folk Songs* (1934). Wright claims that the only credit Leadbelly received for his work was "the 'high honor' of seeing his name in print"(p. 7).[15]

Wright also argues that when Lomax tried promoting Leadbelly's concerts, "in order to make engagements and more profit, [he] gave out a vicious tirade of publicity" to radio stations, *Time Magazine,* and other publications that generally billed Leadbelly, in Wright's words, as a "half sex-mad, knifetoting, black buck from Texas" (p. 7). Disillusioned with what Wright considered Lomax's shifty dealings, Leadbelly approached Lomax about a legal contract and demanded the money

owed him from several Northern concert tours. Lomax told Leadbelly he simply had been saving his earnings for him. When Leadbelly continued to press his demands, Lomax, according to Leadbelly, responded with a curt reply: "If I gave you your money you'd throw it away in Harlem" (p. 7).[16] Some twenty years later when Wright wrote for Barclay Disques in Paris, he still held an antipathy for what he considered self-interested music moguls like Lomax.

One of Wright's favorite New York nightclubs was the Cafe Society Downtown, a popular gathering spot for musicians and record producers like Columbia's John Hammond, who had helped launch the career of the great jazz pianist and band leader Count Basie. Partly because of Hammond's influence, the club attracted some of the biggest names in popular music, including Basie, Billie Holiday, Lena Horne, Buck Clayton, and Teddy Wilson and his combo. It also became the center for boogie-woogie, a craze popularized in the 1940's by the important band leader, saxophonist, and singer Louis Jordan, whom Wright exalted in a 1960 record review for Barclay Disques.

Wright occasionally visited the cafe with Joe Louis, whom he had interviewed twice, once following the Max Baer-Louis fight in 1935, the second time three years later after Louis's world championship bout with the German boxer Max Schmeling. Louis's triumph over the white Schmeling, who was in the American public's mind linked to Fascism, symbolized a moral victory for blacks. In an article titled "How He Did It, and Oh!—Where Were Hitler's Pagan Gods?" Wright details a giant Harlem demonstration following Louis's knockout of Schmeling, in which thousands of blacks "hurled slogans of defiance at Hitler's pretensions of Aryan superiority."[17] In one short round Joe Louis had elevated his heroic status, and thunderous shouts of "Heil Louis!" echoed in "mocking taunt" throughout the city.

One night at the Cafe, Hammond, who had become Wright's good friend, suggested making a record dedicated to Louis.[18] Wright would compose the lyrics for a twelve-bar blues tune to be played by the Count Basie Orchestra and sung by Paul Robeson. Considering Wright's reputation as an established writer as well as his continuing interest in the blues, which guitar lessons in the past year had enhanced, Hammond planted his suggestion in firm ground. In less than three weeks Wright took Hammond thirty-nine lines praising Louis. Count Basie's jazz influence on the subsequent arrangement embellished the song. In 1941 Okeh Records released "Joe Louis Blues." With an advanced order numbering in the thousands, the record met with a more than average commercial success.[19]

As in his early journalism, Wright elevates Joe Louis's status to that of king. He accomplishes this task with the aid of black folk characters, including the boll weevil, the subject of many blues songs. Unlike the pest lamented in the boll weevil blues of Bessie Smith and

Leadbelly, Wright's boll weevil, along with other popular folk animals portrayed in traditional blues, engages in dialogue to help set the conversational tone of the song. Some of the less conventional folk characters, not all of them animals, call attention to Louis's humble roots:

> Black-eyed peas ask cornbread: What make you
> so strong?
> Black-eyed peas ask cornbread: What make you
> so strong?
> Cornbread say: I come from Alabam where Joe
> Louis was born.

Others praise the "big black bearcat's" physical and sexual strengths:

> Jack Rabbit say to Bumble-bee: What make you
> sting so deep?
> Jack Rabbit say to Bumble-bee: What make you
> sting so deep?
> Bumble-bee say: I sting like Joe Louis and rock
> 'em all to sleep.

Wright also compares Louis to the Ford engine to highlight the boxer's prowess, as well as to accentuate the urban origin of certain blues. He points out that it is in American cities, especially ones with the greatest concentration of blacks, that the great boxer finds his most appreciative and loyal support. The following lines echo Wright's newspaper piece on Hitler's "pagan Gods":

> Been in Cleveland, St. Louis, Washington, and
> Chicago too,
> Been in Cleveland, St. Louis, Washington, and
> Chicago too,
> But the best is Harlem when a Joe Louis fight is
> through.

Wright's first incursion into the field of music raises some interesting questions. In an essay called "Can't Even Write: The Blues and Ethnic Literature," Paul Oliver argues that the blues "is not a form of folk song that stands up particularly well when written down. . . . Blues can be analyzed on the printed page," he contends," but they do not exist there: blues are essentially performed—they exist in the singing and playing" (Oliver, p. 8). Oliver also points out that Wright was too much of a trained poet to write the blues. Like Langston Hughes and Sterling Brown before him, he was conditioned to "develop critical ears" and "write with fastidious hands." For Oliver "Joe Louis Blues" affected an "artificial naivete" because, unlike the songs of most blues singers, it relied too heavily on structured composition, on the "rhythms and the resonances of words" (p. 8).

On Oliver's first point, Wright would have agreed. "The meaning is not in the bald, literal words," he writes in "Memories of My Grandmother." "The meaning is in the music, in the mood and interpretation that Bessie Smith brings to the verses." That is, according to Wright, the outstanding trait of the blues lies in its "sustained dynamics," or the moving forces that unite audience, singer, words, and sound. Wright would also have difficulty refuting Oliver's other charge of "fastidious hands." Some of the rhymes in "Joe Louis Blues" do appear forced and the "folksiness" of the song as a whole, despite Wright's good intentions, strikes "the wrong note" (Oliver, p. 13).[20]

Wright returned to America only once after his departure for Paris in 1947—to shoot Chicago slum scenes for the 1950/51 film version of *Native Son*. In order to adapt the book to the screen, he added several new scenes, including one in a black cabaret with Bessie Spears, Bigger Thomas's girl friend, crooning a bluesy, melancholy love tune. This song, prepared by John Elert and the Katherine Dunham Quartet, stands as Wright's only other formal venture into music. It is conventional and uninspiring and, like his "Deadbeat Blues" and "Blue-Black Blues," written outside the classical AAB blues mode. The following lines highlight the song's overt sentimentalism:

> I'll follow you anywhere
> Just tell me what to do
> I'll suffer with you there
> And break this heart for you
>
> I'll fight for you to the end
> I'll never give you up
> I'll throw my life to the wind
> I'll drink the bitter cup

It is difficult to place exact dates on Wright's later blues pieces. None were published during his lifetime, and he left few marginal comments on his original drafts to help locate the poems chronologically. It is also difficult to determine if the motivation that produced "Joe Louis Blues" also prompted these later writings. Wright had experimented with the blues form as early as 1936 when he published "Hearst Headline Blues," a satirical poem scorning the wealthy press baron William Randolph Hearst. There is little evidence suggesting that Wright intended this poem as a blues song. On the other hand, Wright co-wrote a blues piece in 1939 with Langston Hughes called "Red Clay Blues," a poem about a migrant's longing for his Georgia homeland. Both writers approached the singer Josh White about possibly recording the poem. Considering that Wright's blues criticism coincided with his own attempts at writing the blues, it stands to reason that one kind of writing helped inspire the other.

Not surprisingly, Wright's blues reflect the salient characteristics he applied to others' blues tunes. They cover a wide range of topics, from the politically oppressed to the homeless wanderer, from the helpless drunk victim to the downtrodden and broken-hearted lover. Most of them explore threads common in both rural and urban blues: police, devils, promiscuity and deceit, unrequited love, movement, violence, nightfall, dreams, and various kinds of animals. Others examine unusual or more esoteric themes, like the draftsmen, lathehands, and riveters in "Machine Shop Blues."

Considering that racial hatred was the determining factor in shaping his often grim vision, it was natural for Wright to condemn oppression in his blues. Like some of the protest songs of Josh White, Wright's blues frequently indicted the society in which he lived. In "Joe Louis Blues" he had already hinted at the racial theme that dominated his famous fiction:

> Wonder what Joe Louis thinks when he's fighting
> a white man.
> Say wonder what Joe Louis thinks when he's
> fighting a white man.
> Bet he thinks what I'm thinking cause he wears a
> dead pan.

In "The F. B. Eye Blues," a poem comparable to Casey Bill Weldon's "W. P. A. Blues," Wright launches a satirical attack on this clandestine agency of his white-run government:

> That old mean FB Eye
> Tied a bell to my bed stall
> Say that old mean FB Eye
> Tied a bell to my bed stall
> And every time I loved my baby the government
> knew it all
>
> Woke up this morning
> FB Eye under my bed
> Say I woke up this morning
> And FB Eye was under my bed
> Told me what I dreamed last night, every word I
> said.

This poem depicts the prevailing mood among American dissidents during the McCarthy era and foreshadows the mistreatment leveled against M. L. King and other black activists by the F. B. I. during the civil rights movement of the 1960's. "The FB Eye Blues" also condemns the harassment Wright himself received while living in Paris in the 1950's. Although he managed to acclimate himself to French society and gain entrance into various cultural and political circles, Wright still felt threatened by the American and French secret police who moved freely among Parisian intellectual communities. "I'm sick and tired of dodging government spies," Wright wails near the end of his poem. Such a cry typified the frustration he felt near the end of his life, especially considering his belief that government agents were plotting to discredit his literary reputation as well as his stands on certain controversial political issues.[21]

As he had done in "Joe Louis Blues," Wright reverts to characters from black folklore, including cats, rats, snakes, and insects, to assist his assault. The courageous grasshopper in the following stanza mirrors society's oppressed and reflects Wright's own bitter feelings toward police surveillance:

> Grasshopper sure like to
> Spit in bloodhound's eye
> Say grasshopper really like to

> Spit in bloodhound's eye
> And that's what I'm gonna do one day to the FB
> Eye.

Two of Wright's blues fall under the rubric of travel blues. Like Bessie Smith's "Backwater Blues," "I Been North and East" speaks of agitated displacement:

> I been North and East
> Rambling South and West—
> I have rambled North and East
> Rambled the South and in the West—
> But Lawd Lawd there just ain't no place
> Where a black man can get some rest . . .

This poem echoes the longing for freedom that Wright felt played such a dominant role in the blues. It also complements the flight motif that characterized so much of his fiction and, like *Native Son,* attempts to dispel the myth that racism was confined only to the Deep South. "Today" expresses similar concerns, casting the blues singer as the "lonesome wanderer"[22], struggling with a "bruised tongue" and "aching eyes":

> Like a man who's lost his way
> I stare at streets and houses
> Like a man losing his way
> I search streets and houses
> I stare lost
> Looking for the land whose horizons were in my
> heart.

Although both poems follow the AAB blues formula, the diction in "Today" is awkward and reads as if Wright were forcing his lines to fit the standard blues mode. Such strained writing resembles the artificiality Oliver points out in "Joe Louis Blues." Each poem also voices the oppression and alienation proclaimed in "The FB Eye Blues," further supporting Wright's own use of the blues form as an indictment of the social system.

Some of Wright's blues were exceedingly long, like the nineteen-stanza "Blue Snow Blues," an anti-drug poem in which Wright uses snow as a metaphor for heroin. That Wright had certain jazz and blues musicians in mind when writing this ambitious piece is highly likely, especially considering it was written in Paris in the late fifties when heroin had claimed several established performers who were playing there. In this poem Wright borrows words, pharases, and verses from traditional blues tunes—the "stanza storehouse"—and relies on the familiar blues device of warning others of impending trouble:

> This falling curtain of snow
> Paints my soul a deep blue
> Said this falling curtain of snow
> Paints my soul a deep blue
> You'd better be careful
> It'll do the same to you.

The poem examines addiction, escapism, and isolation, common themes in drug-and alcohol-related blues songs, and paints a gloomy picture of the desperate and forlorn victim:

Slowly falling snowflakes
Pinching at the skin on my back
Said slowly falling snowflakes
Clawing at the skin on my back
My old eyes become bloodshot
And my stomach becomes a sack.

Of course not all of Wright's blues were so melancholy. In fact several of them reveal the writer's livelier, less political side. "Nightmare Blues" tells the story of a man making love to his best friend's wife. And once again, Wright intersperses black folk characters to enliven his tale:

I got to have my best friend's gal
Or I feel I'm going to die.
Say I got to have my best friend's gal
Or I feel I'm going to die.
I know what I'm craving is wrong
But I can't help but try.

A devil and a great big baboon
A standing at my bedside
A devil and a great big baboon
A standing at my bedside
And I feel like a cold slab of ice,
Like I had gone and died.

All right, I confess I had her,
Took her one night on the sly.
Yes, I confess I slipped and had her,
Took her one night on the sly.
And now I'm oh, too ashamed
To look my friend in the eye.

Wright exposes a similar side in "Cat Blues," a tale of the lustful rambler celebrated in numerous traditional blues songs. In nine stanzas he writes how

I had me nine good loves
Like a cat's got nine good lives
Said I had nine good loves
Like a cat's got nine good lives.
But I'd much rather have
Nine good loves than nine good lives.

Both poems show how Wright was able to transcend overt social and political statement and highlight the personal or more self-centered themes of so many traditional blues. The sexual desire in "Nightmare Blues" haunts the speaker and shows the result when a man breaks a code of friendship. The common blues thread of guilt overwhelms him and the sexual gratification he receives does nothing to soothe his troubled mind: his actions turn into a nightmare. The blatant chauvinism in "Cat Blues" belittles women and points out yet another theme Wright carries in his blues canon.

Wright's blues are not great blues. On the whole they are too erudite, elaborate and contrived and do not measure up to the simplicity and tone of the blues of a poet like Langston Hughes. At the same time they anchor him firmly in the blues tradition. Wright's blues are replete with imagery, symbolism and personification

and cover the full gamut of standard blues themes. In "Joe Louis Blues" Wright proved that with the proper music connections he could blend words, tone, and form to produce a popular blues tune. Perhaps if his other blues had been set to music, they too would have met with a similar commercial success.

One of Wright's most compelling contributions to the blues appears in "Memories of My Grandmother," written shortly after "Joe Louis Blues." In this roughly 70-page manuscript, originally intended as an analysis of "The Man Who Lived Underground," the Wright novella that influenced Ellison's *Invisible Man,* Wright outlines his theory comparing the blues to surrealism. For years Wright had been fascinated by what he considered a vital function of a "certain phase" in the creative process: "the ability to take seemingly unrelated images and symbols and link them together into a meaningful whole" ("Memories of My Grandmother"). He believed such a function applied specifically to a reactionary group like the surrealists, especially to a painter like Dali. In his "wild canvasses" the rational merged with the irrational, the conscious with the unconscious, to create a new view of life, or surreality.

Wright felt this idea of using partial concepts to communicate an overall whole also operated in the blues. After studying the lyrics to numerous blues songs, he concluded that isolated verses had no meaning or relationship to one another, that the verses rarely told a straightforward, comprehensible narrative, that one tercet could be substituted for another and still produce the same overall effect. In "Memories of My Grandmother" Wright states, "The meaning does not reside in the verses but in what is brought to bear upon them." He goes on to explain:

> A black woman, singing the blues, will describe a rainy day, then suddenly, to the same tune and tempo of the music, she will croon of a red pair of shoes; then, without any logical or causal connection, she will sing about how blue and lowdown she feels: the next verse may deal with a horrible murder, the next with theft, the next with tender love, and so on.

Thus, according to Wright, blues lyrics are not always progressive or sequential. They are associational in their improvisation; they are guided by "the urge to express something deeply felt" ("Memories of My Grandmother").

Wright realized that discussing surrealism in relation to a particular facet of African-American culture would strike most people like mixing "oil and water." He also doubted that Louis Armstrong or Duke Ellington had ever discussed surrealism, and felt that if he mentioned the blues to them in relation to Freud's theory of dream analysis, which influenced the surrealists considerably, they would call him "crazy." But Wright remained convinced of what he considered obvious links. According to him, the structure and function of both art forms are strikingly similar: a song like "Yellow Dog Blues" and a painting like Dali's "Battle of Tetuan" employ similar manners of looking at the world.

Wright's interest in the blues continued long after his self-imposed exile to Paris. The respect French audiences showed blues musicians like Big Bill Broonzy and Blind John Davis, who first toured Paris in the early 1950's, encouraged Wright to keep his concern for the form. Unlike most Americans, Parisians had held black music, particularly jazz, in high esteem. In fact as early as the 1930's they considered jazz a "high" art form and flocked to jazz musicians wherever they performed. This enthusiasm carried over to the blues, and by the end of the fifties Paris ranked second only to London as a favorite European stage for black blues singers.

Although Wright's literary ventures varied throughout the fifties, he maintained an ongoing interest in the blues. In *Blues Off the Road* Paul Oliver details how Wright took him to the "dark cellar clubs of the Rue de la Huchette" (p. 11) to hear Bill Coleman, Lil Armstrong, Sam Price, and others play their tunes. Oliver also acknowledges that he and Wright sat in Parisian cafes for hours discussing the blues. Wright continued writing and rewriting his own blues as well as reviewing those of established blues performers. One of his last blues publications was the jacket notes of *The Blues of Big Bill Broonzy* (Mercury 7198 Standard) titled "So Long, Big Bill Broonzy." This piece not only praises the late Broonzy, whom Wright considered a "daringly truthful and universal" poet, but recapitulates the blues aesthetic that Wright had been formulating for almost twenty-five years. "That's the blues," Wright writes in his review: "Despair transmuted into sensuality, sorrow and rhythms, defeat measured in the jumping cadences of triumph." Such a synthesis is the same one he develops in his foreword to Oliver's book: "Yet the most astonishing aspect of the blues is that, though replete with a sense of defeat and down-heartedness, [the blues] are not intrinsically pessimistic; their burden of woe and melancholy is . . . redeemed through sheer force of sensuality, into an almost exultant affirmation of life, of love, of sex, of movement, of hope." (p. ix).

For Wright, Broonzy and bluesmen like him epitomized the freedom "to do what you like . . . and say what you please" ("So Long"). Their "not belongingness" was a "strange and dubious wealth," for unlike the senator or Wall Street stock broker, they yielded to no public opinion. Through melancholic but joyful, humble songs, they were free to tell what life meant to them. Wright cites one line from Broonzy's album to show that on the whole, life had been a just reward:

> Lord, I ain't got no money, but I'm the happiest
>   man in town!

As did Hurston's and Ellison's folk pieces, Wright's blues ventures inspired some of his other writings. Much of the action in *The Long Dream* (1959), his last novel, centers around the Grove, a blues juke joint nestled deep in the rural blackbelt of Clintonville, Mississippi. There are several incidents in his other fiction in which characters croon melancholy folk tunes to wile away their blues. Wright's blues writings stimulated writings in other music areas as well, particularly jazz. In fact, near the end of his life, Wright was working for Nicole Barclay of Barclay Disques, the leading French jazz production company. Although he was motivated partly by financial concerns, Wright believed his new music venture worthwhile. "I'm not doing any serious writing at the moment," he states in a letter to his friend, M. de Sablonière, "but the writing I'm doing for the records does say something" (Fabre, p. 623). Indeed, in an unpublished essay called "Another Heroic Beginning," Wright prophesied the career of Quincy Jones, the talented young musician who was living in Paris at the time, as "something worth watching."

Wright's blues connection is of more significance than most commentators have previously acknowledged. Exposed to a variety of folk music since his childhood, Wright was motivated from the beginning of his literary career by a pronounced feeling for the blues, and was either studying them or working on his own until just a few days before he died. That his major literary contribution rests in his autobiographies and famous fiction is unquestionable. To limit Wright's achievements to two or three books, however, is a grave disservice to academic scholarship as well as to Wright and African-American folk culture. We must re-examine Wright's blues writings as well as his own blues if we are to gain a complete understanding of such a complex and fascinating writer.

NOTES

[1] See "Dink's Blues," Alan Lomax, *American Ballads and Folksongs* (New York: Macmillan, 1934), pp. 193-194.

[2] Richard Wright, *Black Boy: A Record of Childhood and Youth* (New York: Harper, 1945), p. 16.

[3] Robert Palmer, *Deep Blues* (New York: Penguin, 1982), pp. 225-227.

[4] Richard Wright, "Memories of My Grandmother," Typescript (Original) JWJ Wright Misc 473, Beinecke Library, Yale University, New Haven. I wish to thank Mrs. Ellen Wright for permission to quote this and other previously unpublished material in my article. I also thank the Beinecke Library for permission to quote unpublished Wright material housed there.

[5] Richard Wright, "Letter to Joe Brown," 4 June 1943, Kent State University Library, Kent, Ohio.

[6] Richard Wright, *12 Million Black Voices: A Folk History of the Negro in the United States* (New York: Viking Press, 1941), p. 128.

[7] Richard Wright, "Foreword," to Paul Oliver, *Blues Fell This Morning* (London: Horizon Press, 1960), p. ix.

[8] Richard Wright, *White Man, Listen!* (New York: Doubleday, 1957), p. 88.

[9] "Foreword," p. ix.

[10] "Foreword," p. ix.

[11] Richard Wright, "Huddie Ledbetter, Famous Negro Folk Artist," *Daily Worker,* August 12, 1937, p. 7.

[12] Michel Fabre, *Unfinished Quest of Richard Wright* (New York: William Morrow & Co., 1973), p. 237.

[13] "Foreword," p. ix.

[14] Several leading blues critics have argued that blues songs are self-centered and individualistic, and that only the most special cases of the blues are dogmatic and sectarian in lyrics. The blues hope for amelioration, they argue, but rarely even state that. Mostly they are about continuing to cope within intolerable situations. See Samuel Charters, *The Poetry of the Blues* (New York: Oak Publications, 1963), for a lengthy discussion of blues lyrics; William Ferris, *Blues From the Delta* (New York: Anchor, 1978); Oliver's *Blues Fell This Morning;* Giles Oakley, *The Devil's Music; A History of the Blues* (London: British Broadcasting Corporation, 1976); Albert Murray, *The Hero and the Blues;* Paul Garon, *Blues and the Poetic Spirit* (New York: De Capo Press, 1975); and Jeff Titon, Early *Downhome Blues: A Musical and Cultural Analysis* (Urbana: University of Illinois Press, 1977), who asks, "And who can imagine that Leadbelly did not have some help composing 'Bourgeois Blues'?" (p. 191).

[15] It should be pointed out that Lomax had released a long book commemorating Leadbelly the year before Wright's article, called *Negro Folk Songs As Sung by Leadbelly* (New York: Macmillan, 1936). The book includes a lengthy biographical sketch, told mostly in Leadbelly's own words, as well as forty-nine songs representative of Leadbelly's repertoire.

[16] Regarding Lomax's budgeting of Leadbelly's earnings, Lomax in *Sung by* quotes from a letter Leadbelly had written him:

> . . . the peoples are after me to play at the Strain theater so I told them i would right you about it so if you want me to play i will Do so But i want you there to take care of the money i Dont want no white man in the world outside of you and Mr. Allen [sic]. (p. 64)

Lomax also includes a biographical "Chronology" at the beginning of his book on Leadbelly. In a footnote Lomax writes: "These statements are not consistent. Neither was Lead Belly, at least not always" (p. 2).

[17] *Daily Worker,* June 24, 1938, p. 1.

[18] Wright's song was one of several celebrating the great boxer. Memphis Minnie's hit, "He's in the Ring," was recorded in 1935 in Chicago, while Wright was still living there.

[19] See Fabre, *Unfinished Quest,* p. 237.

[20] Oliver's respect for Wright as a friend and critic never faltered, however. When recalling his early trips to Paris in *Blues Off the Road* (1984), Oliver states that Wright's "support for [*Blues Fell This Morning*] I valued then, as I do now, more than I can say" (p. 11). Oliver also mentions that he "felt a deep loss" after Wright's sudden death in 1960.

[21] See Fabre, *The Unfinished Quest,* p. 622.

[22] Garon, *Blues and the Poetic Spirit,* p. 90.

Carol Frost

SOURCE: "Petrarch, Shakespeare, and the Blues," in *New England Review,* Vol. 18, No. 3, Summer, 1997, pp. 118-131.

[*In the following essay, Frost compares the evolution of the sonnet form with that of the blues song.*]

I

Art, as we know, concerns form: symmetry and surprise. And in poetry, no less in modern times than in antiquity, an important distinction is made between the poets who look for new forms and those who borrow existing forms. The attention paid to poets relates to this distinction. An audience may ask, Does the poet go on his nerve, or is he careful? In this matter general taste, rather than particular aesthetic considerations, seems to determine poetic value for people—for reader and writer both. People know what they like and what they don't like. If they like a good story, they like narrative poetry, and they read or write narrative poetry. If they value the familiar, then poetry that looks or sounds like that remembered from *A Child's Garden of Verses* will be appreciated and approved of. So it is for the other arts. In Henry Cowell's music as in Beethoven's, certain notes—until they became familiar—and the structure familiar—were unpleasant to the ear of an audience (including the artist's peers) whose taste for the tried and true could not be made subordinate to the experience of the new music.

For me, back of the idea that artists either invent or borrow is the more interesting concept of performance—how well the work performs *in its design.* Where and when the design was invented may not be quite exterior to the work—when attention is drawn to its historical features, or when and where the ultimate newness becomes a feature of the expression—but it isn't of primary importance. During the performance that a poem is, language and image, eye and ear, content and form, passion and intellect interrelate subtly and vividly; the mark of the poem's excellence is not in my sense of how the poem ought to look or sound or what it should say, but in the superior forms of energy and expression that are created.

Poets are inventors and interpreters of form, form being, in art, a revelation of content. Form may be other things—it may have its history, an intrinsic beauty, even rightness—but when any of these matter more than revelation, the poetry becomes merely verse. This is not to say that a feasible paraphrase of the poem is equal to the poem. The kind of disclosure that a poem is is not thematic, nor is it arrived at by adding together the several features of the poet's style or technique (lineation, image pattern, tone, assonance, etc.). Rather, while rising out of the combination of its parts, including its statement about the human condition, poetry lays open to view something both natural (as a field of flowers is natural) and artificial (the field transformed by speech). When William Wordsworth read his sister's diary entry about their walk in 1804, he remembered the daffodils they saw, and he had before him a sufficiency of emotion already brought to words together with his own feelings, his knowledge of the countryside, and some ideas of his own—all qualifying each other—to make an experience like the one they both had and also unlike it enough to be poetry.

Verse, where form is all, is even less like life than poetry is. Does form affect the performance of poetry? It does, but the effect isn't absolute as in verse. In poetry the form, whether traditional or free, isolates from measure to measure the relationship between what is being said and how it is said. But the relationship changes because of artistic temperament and intuition. Suppose a poet were to try to imitate absolutely an experience, as an artist might try to articulate with points of color the light on the face of a church at 3:00 P.M. An hour later, dust, shadow, air, and light would require that he paint it again. A different palette would make its own requirements. So, too, for the poet. Invention, without the adaptations and flexibilities of temperament, is no better than the dusty models of the past. The new, without attention to the subtleties of art (past and present), will not, to remember Ezra Pound's phrase, *stay* new.

. . . . .

The sonnet (from the Italian *sonnetto,* a little sound or song[1]) is the longest-lived of all poetic forms, and its well-established, unfamiliar history offers insights into the changing relationship between form and the poetic imagination. Petrarch (1304-1374), for the purposes of English poetry, invented the sonnet, which is to say that his sequence of 317 fourteen-line poems in praise of his love for one woman, his Laura, were the model that Thomas Wyatt (1503-1542) brought back from his travels in Italy. In reality, the sonnet was invented one hundred years earlier, as a variant of another Italian pattern, by Giacomo Da Lentini (1210-1240), the legal deputy to the king of Sicily. Of his two dozen poems in

this mode—all of them on the theme of Love and spoken in the first person—little is known beyond the evidence they provide and their similarities to other forms of the time. There are no drafts or critical comments by the author to establish how he envisioned the space of the poem as he saw it. The construction of the stanzas in the *canzone,* a long poem made up of identical stanzas, offers one model. Each stanza fell into two not necessarily equal parts, the *fronte* and *sirma* (often six lines), each with its own musical phrase. Marking the break between the parts was the *volta* or *diesis* (turn). While the lengths of the *canzone* stanza and the sonnet and their rhyme schemes were dissimilar, the essential proportioning of space (sound and thought) were similar. But no one can say for certain whether Da Lentini deliberately adapted the *canzone* (a form he also wrote in) for his new lyric, or if—as some scholars suggest—he decided to add a six-line *sirma* to the popular verse form sung by Sicilian peasants called the *strambotto,* with its two quatrains, rhyming *abab abab.*

What Da Lentini managed, however, was a frame: fourteen lines of eleven syllables, breaking eight and six. While the structure appears to be binary, a further requirement of the form places atop the two parts a tripartite structure of discourse: to announce a theme, to change it, and to close it. This is the essence of the design of the poem. And in all the adaptations of the sonnet form that follow, Shakespeare's being perhaps the best known, its turn occurring after line twelve, every part of the form has been susceptible to change. The most conspicuous variant in English poetry can be found in George Meredith's sonnet sequence *Modern Love,* where the sonnets are sixteen lines long *(abba cddc effe ghhg).*

Da Lentini's sonnet *"Lo basilico a lo speclo lucente"* is representative of the necessary rhetorical (and syntactic) quality of the sonnet:

> Lo basilisco a lo speclo lucente
> traggi a morire con isbaldimento;
> lo cesne canta plu gioiosamente
> quand'e plu presso a lo suo finimento;
>   lo paon turba, istando plu gaudente.
> poi c'a suoi piedi fa riguadimento;
> l'augel fenise s'arde veramente
> per ritornare i' novo nasciemento.
>   In ta' nature eo sentom' abenuto,
> ch'allegro vado a morte, a le bellezze,
> e 'nforzo il canto presso a lo fibire;
>   estando gaio torno dismaruto,
> ardendo in foco inovo in allegreze,
> per voi, plu gente, a cui spero redire.

(The basilisk is drawn rejoicing to its death in the polished mirror; the swan sings most joyfully when nearest to its death; the peacock is disturbed just at the moment of its greatest joy when it sees its feet; the phoenix burns gratefully so that it can be reborn. 1-8

In these natures I feel my own self, for I joyfully go to my death, toward beauty, and I press my

song when I am near my end; being joyful, I turn
to being unhappy; burning in fire, I am reborn in
joy because of you, dear lady, to whom I hope to
return. 9-14)

This is a well-designed sonnet, partially in that its form
and content are interdependent and partially because the
poem's tensions are significant enough so that their reconciliation matters. For it isn't enough only to *unify a* poem;
in poetry harmony and *discord* exist together. The poem
starts in one rhetorical position and changes to another,
change, even contradiction, is an essential element in lyric
structure. The rhyme scheme *(abab abab cde cde)* supports
the change in the rhetorical stance, which begins with an
impersonal voice describing in the octave the paradoxical
behavior of animals and ending with the voice of the
lower, the *eo* (1) introduced in line 9. As the voice shifts
after line 8, the rhyme scheme alters, and so does the
argument of the poem. The imagery in the octave, one
image from medieval lore for each distich, disappears in
the sestet, and the basilisk, swan, peacock, and phoenix are
only referred to generally as Da Lentini uses their behavior
as points of reference for his own. Then in the last line we
are given the motivation for this natural/unnatural behavior ("*per voi, plu gente*")—he is in love. The paradoxes
throughout the poem, the struggles of opposites in such
phrases as "*estando gaio torno dismaruto*" (being joyful, I turn to being unhappy), are in a sense resolved by
this admission, though they do not entirely go away;
were they to be utterly resolved—too insignificant, perhaps, in wording or sentiment—the unity of the poem
would seem superficial. Da Lentini's sonnet argues and
asserts in a voice that deeply understands the bitter
passion of worldly experience. The control of the voice
is proportional to the depth of feeling expressed—herein
lies the poem's great eloquence.

A well-designed sonnet does more than meet its formal
requirements of length and lineation; it synchronizes those
requirements with the other elements of language that the
poet has brought into the poem, and it turns. Its structure
becomes of importance when considering how well it
manages to be a sonnet—instead of merely looking like
one. Structure relates to form in *effect* in approximately the
same way a performance relates to jazz notation or the way
fiction relates to anecdote. What is structure? Put most
generally, it is the element in art that exposes art to the
contradictions and complexities of immediate experience.
In poetry it is what binds a heterogeneous mixture of formal and linguistic elements (including tone, imagery,
rhetoric) and creates room for emotional change. An example of a beautifully structured sonnet is "Sonnet 73" by
Shakespeare.[2] The poem presents its argument fairly
straightforwardly in three quatrains and a concluding
rhyming couplet. The formal features of the poem are
neither arbitrary to the poem, nor of primary interest, but
serve to clarify, modify, and develop the poem's meaning.
In this sense, the poem's words and sentences give the
rhyming, etc., another potential, just as a well-structured
jazz solo or house makes its material—the notes or the
stone lintels—expressive.

That time of year thou mayst in me behold
When yellow leaves, or none, or few do hang
Upon those boughs which shake against the cold,
Bare ruined choirs where late the sweet birds sang.
In me thou see'st the twilight of such day
As after sunset fadeth in the west,
Which by and by black night doth take away,
Death's second self, that seals up all in rest.
In me thou see'st the glowing of such fire
That on the ashes of his youth doth lie,
As the death bed whereon it must expire,
Consumed with that which it was nourished by.
This thou perceivest, which makes thy love more
     strong
To love that well which thou must leave ere long.

Each quatrain with its alternating rhyme pattern *(abab)*
presents an image of conclusion: autumn, twilight, a
dying fire. The last two lines offer the denouement of
the implied argument and a clear change in the language of the poem. The rhetorical shift lends its force to
what the poem says, as does the new scheme of rhyming—the couplet. In paraphrase, the poem, addressing
the beloved as "you," says that the beloved's seeing the
weakening of summer, the loss of daylight, and the self-
consuming strength of fire in the poet makes love "more
strong." The logic of the poem's argument is clear, even
if the position flirts with paradox. Does death lead to
love? Does the waning of life necessarily make love
wax? Passion, after all, as implied by the image of fire
in the third quatrain, is nearly used up ("Consumed with
that which it was nourished by"). Seen in this light, the
logical conclusion to the poem takes on the quality of
plea. As corollary, consider this: If the lover loves more
strongly, won't sentimentality—or, worse, pity—be the
reasons why? Iron-clad and beautifully presented in four
simple parts, the logic of the poem is ambivalent—in
part ironic—with Shakespeare presenting the state of
mind of the lover who must rue his own losses so
strongly that he anticipates the pity of a lover and contrary to our notions of simple dignity asks for pity.[3]

The several ideas of this sonnet or any other are not
really detachable from its progress; neither is the emotion. The sonnet absorbs the emotional and intellectual
materials into its two-part structure, which in turn
frames them and the proposition (or theme) of the poem.
The form of the sonnet is part of its structuring, helping
to create the room for a dramatic process to unfold. A
sonnet does not merely eventuate in the fourteenth line.
The conclusion of any poem is the working through of
various tensions set up in however many lines there
are—in this sonnet by the three sad conceits in the first
twelve lines. When the poem turns, a logic isn't concluded so much as a variety of dramatic forces and of
attitudes is brought into equilibrium, which is to say
that the second part of a sonnet—here the rhyming couplet—is true in relation to the lines that came before.

Over the course of the one hundred years after Da
Lentini various poets improvised on the basic form, altering the rhyme scheme, introducing a variety of tones,

subjects, and styles. Dante, the first writer to notice the sonnet theoretically, in his treatise *De vulgari cloquentia (Pop Eloquence)*, praised its use of the vernacular. The sonnet could be comic, sublime in its rhetorical flights, exhoratory, dramatic, or quite simply vulgar. Where, for instance, the traditional Sicilian love-sonnet created an "I" who worships beauty and pleads for grace, Cecco Angiolieri's speaker in *"L'altrier si mi ferio un tal ticca"* (cxx) brags about being able to buy his lady's affections with cash. He finishes the poem with a pun on his purse *("la borsa queta"),* with its resemblance to a codpiece.

The Italian sonnet stabilized during the latter part of the thirteenth century, and in Petrarch's sequence, including *canzoni,* and a number of *ballate* and madrigals at irregular intervals, 303 out of 317 sonnets use the octave associated with the Italian sonnet *abba abba.* He favors nearly equally two rhyme patterns for the sestet: *cdecde* (115) and *cdcdcd* (118). The sixty-six others are arranged *cdedce.* His sonnets aren't memorable and praiseworthy because of his strict adherence to a rhyme scheme; they are remarkable in sequence and individually for their fluency, their versatility in style and crafting, their sensitive rendering of the engagement with beauty (that of a woman, or that of art or of God) at its most intense, and also in their dissidence, where the usual equilibrium of style and statement are often more than tipped slightly toward antithesis.

The clear musicality of sonnet 90, for instance, presents more than a moment of intense feeling:

> *Erano i capei d'oro a l'aura sparsi,*
> *che'n mille dolci modi gli avolgea,*
> *e 'l vago lume oltra misura ardea*
> *di quei begli occhi, ch'or ne son si scarsi;*
> *e 'l viso di pietosi color farsi*
> *(non so se vero o falso) me parea:*
> *i' che l'esca amorosa al petto avea,*
> *qual meraviglia se di subito arsi?*
>   *Non era l'andar suo cosa mortale,*
> *ma d'angelica forma, et le parole*
> *sonavan altro che pur voce umana:*
>   *uno spirto celeste, un vivo sole*
> *fu quel ch'i'vidi; e se non fosse or tale,*
> *piaga per allentar d'arco non sana.*

(The breezes spread her golden hair, twisting it into a thousand sweet curls, her fair eyes, which now are reluctant to give it, were once filled with light, and her face seemed, truly or falsely, to take on the color of pity toward me: What wonder if I, for whom love was a glowing ember in my chest, had burst into flame? 1-8

She walked unlike a mortal being, but like an angel in disguise, and her words sounded to me much more than human: I beheld a celestial spirit, a living sun; and should she not be such now, the wound is not healed by the unstringing of a bow. 9-14)

The sonnet flexes a little under a new pressure introduced in the phrases *"ch'or ne son si scarsi"* (which now are so reluctant to give it), *"non so se vero o falso"* (truly or falsely, I don't know), and *"e se non fosse or tale"* (and should she not be such now). The poem speaks of the beautiful golden tresses of the beloved and the golden light in her eyes, which caused the speaker to burn suddenly with desire. To him she was a heavenly creature, an angel, *"un vivo sole"* (a living sun), but as the last lines reveal most beautifully—and not for the first time—she may not still be just as she was before. The lexis of light in the first quatrain, love blazing up in the lover in lines 5-8, the recognition of a spiritual experience—all these are lovely; but a counter movement plays against the familiar joys involved with intense love, from line 4, when we notice the two verb tenses in the poem—past and present. The ideal of romance is under the threat of being over or perhaps never having occurred at all *("non so se vero o falso").* The concluding line is especially strong in its implication that the lucid and happy memories of the past and of oneself are in question. The poem is not, then, about love's joys, but about its mutability. The equilibrium in the poem is also tipped. One barely notices the two early warnings, which are presented almost as afterthoughts, at the end of the first clause (line 4) and then in parentheses two lines later in the octave, the immediacy of the description of the beloved taking precedence. Their full significance is likewise withheld in the sestet until the second-to-last line, where the meaning of the vision is revealed and fully comprehended as being either a cause for lasting joy, if she is the same as before, or the source of undiminished pain, if that which was may no longer be.

Arguably the most thrilling part of the sonnet is the last line, for which there is no metaphoric precedent in the poem—the unexpected image of the bow, perhaps still aquiver after releasing the arrow. On the other hand, those readers whose idea of unity presupposes homogeneity rather than variety may be hard-pressed to comprehend this bold stroke. How does the poet, one may ask, get from golden hair and sweet curls to an intense image for danger and even death? How does Petrarch *get away* with it? The answer has to do with lyric structure, which can hold the most intense and the most banal statements and images together in suspension while the dramatic situation or the conclusion of the argument in the poem produces a reconciliation of these and other opposites; one needn't look for smoothness in poetry (good poetry). The last image is a surprise, but its figuring forth completes the poem's argument. (The rhyme *umana/sana* (human/heal) also supports the line to some extent, and the tradition of the sonnet, especially as that tradition relates to experiment, also prepares us for it.) Clearly, counterpoint is the style of this sonnet, a counterpoint so brilliantly executed that the poem becomes nothing less than a self-conceived demonstration of how to write poetry, at least lyric poetry.

The changes in the sonnet are by no means unique in the history of changes in given forms, which, rather than being absolutely circumscribed by the inventor, are susceptible to the moldings and shadings of those who come afterwards. In the evolution of a form, an artist's individual and often quite small alteration of the received form because of its effectiveness is imitated by others until it, too, becomes a standard, duly from which another artist feels he must eventually depart. Petrarch's and Sir Thomas Wyatt's changes (the alteration in the sestet from 3 + 3 to 4 + 2 as seen in poems of Wyatt's published in *Tottel's Miscellany* in 1557[4]) in the sonnet's rhyme scheme, no less than explicitly noted trills in baroque music and Mozart's variations on a theme during public performances, may therefore be understood as forms of improvisation.[5] Improvisation in general is a vital aspect of art; in certain quarters it is considered inferior to the initiating form, for being either facile or ignorant, tradition (history) tells us otherwise.

. . . . .

Similar to the sonnet in its evolution is the blues, whose stellar early performer Bessie Smith inherited a form that derived from field hollers and spirituals, what W. E. B. DuBois called "sorrow songs," as well as from European musical structures. The first blues record ("Crazy Blues") was recorded in February 1920, and the following lyrics are a fair transcription of those in the recording:

> I can't sleep at night
> I can't eat a bite
> 'Cause the man I love, he done don't treat me
>   right.
>
> He make me feel so blue,
> I don't know what to do.
> Sometimes I sit and sigh and then begin to cry
> 'Cause my best friend, then he's left. Goodbye.
>
> There's a change in the orchard, change in the
>   deep blue sky, my baby,
> I'll tell you something, ain't no change in me.
> My love for that man will always be.
>
> Now I've got the crazy blues. . . .
>
>   *Mamie Smith*

But the recording artist Mamie Smith didn't invent the blues. Instead of being invented, the blues *developed* over several decades into the distinct musical form and idiom that emerged in the 1920s. Its roots are in the slave music of the eighteenth century, during a time when the "master" or "overseer" could be fined for permitting his slaves to beat drums or blow horns, and slaves were denied the use of their language and the worship of their gods. The little religious freedom that they had resulted in services and songs that preserved and passed on some aspects of African music. The hand clapping and foot stomping that substituted for drumming produced a mixture of meters both reminiscent of African music and a strong part of the blues idiom. The call and response typical of African music became the verse and chorus in the spiritual and was imitated in the blues by an instrumental response to a vocal line of melody. Sung within earshot of owners and overseers and needing to be a private means of communication, in a situation that was by all standards untenable, the songs became coded, so that a verse in a song that expressed a desire to be at peace (where death could offer more than this life) might also well be a message about plans to run away: "I'll meet you in the morning/Safe in the promised land;/on the other side of Jordan/I'm bound for the promised land." Blues lyrics also use double entendre and often, though not always, express the personal (and collective) yearnings and feelings of someone in a state of melancholy.

The holler started as a practical way for the masters of different plantations to keep tabs on the muleskinners' and teamsters' whereabouts. In order to let the overseer know where he was, the teamster would sing or holler, with each teamster initiating and developing his own particular melodies, phrasing, and style—in part to distinguish him from other teamsters from plantation to plantation and, no doubt, too, as a small act of personal identification, using trills, slurs, vibrato, cries, and falsetto. This is felt to be the origin of the blue note, a bending or flattening of the voice to color a pitch in relation to a particular vowel or word. Later when the notes to the music that evolved from these early examples of Negro music were put into musical notation, mere notes and signs did not express their character. The rich tonal possibilities of even a single note became part of the developing idiom, with individual artists performing as close to or far away from the given form as their intuition and skill allowed.

The sung speech—a linking together in irregular, freely improvised patterns—became the blues at the turn of the century, when the use of musical accompaniment required a prearranged pattern. W. C. Handy published the first blues composition, "The Memphis Blues," in 1912, though the song was originally written in 1909. Handy popularized the form, and Ma Rainey claimed to have given the blues its name after specializing in a kind of song she said she heard a girl in Missouri sing plaintively and poignantly, a song about a man who had deserted her. Many people asked her the name of the music she performed, and in a moment of inspiration she said it was the blues.

The form that Bessie Smith inherited typically has a three-line stanza, or chorus, of which the second line is a restatement of the first, and the third is a contrasting statement. The musical form parallels the poetic form, generally with an *a a b* arrangement, each phrase consisting of four measures and the entire chorus of twelve measures. Since the melody for each line may be condensed, there is room for the singer or an instrument to improvise, or for the singer to interject spoken asides ("Yeah, man," "Play it," "My baby," etc.) at the end of the line while the instrumentalist improvises. The beauty in the *form* is in its room for improvisation and expression—in the repetition or variation of the line, for instance, and in the coloring of the notes, in rhythmic variations and phrasing—and in its simplicity. The inventors of the form may have felt this was so, but Bessie Smith was the first great interpreter of the form. Whereas the earliest blues singers sang and played a music that wavered little from the prescribed form, memorizing the form and repeating identical vocal lines regardless of the subject matter or emotional content in a song, Bessie Smith was able to liberate the vocal lines rhythmically and melodically in ways that dramatized the text. She sang phrases that could begin with a fierce pleading, pain-racked quality and end with a sound of bittersweet resignation. She would break a line or melodic pattern in unexpected and asymmetrical ways, even in the middle of a word, to create tension, and then release it in the next line with more standard phrasing. With whatever combination of musicality, intuition, emotional sophistication, and instinct she possessed, she was able to express in the space of a very few prescribed measures, and in a prescribed form, something of personal and universal truthfulness, enlivening the blues form in much the same way that Petrarch and Shakespeare, with their particular skills, enlivened the sonnet.

For people who don't like jazz, a Bessie Smith or a Billie Holiday may not seem a genuinely terrific singer. One's appreciation and disapproval seem related less to systematic judgment than to overall taste, after all. Knowing less about jazz than poetry, I am more easily pleased and less able to articulate the reasons for my pleasure. I think I know when something is good but I suspect my knowing (feeling) is less related to details of the actual performance than to my predilections. I prefer Billie Holiday, for instance, to Mildred Bailey, who is an expert musician by all accounts, but whose voice doesn't appeal to me. I like, for instance, the undulations on the words *strange, Southern, bitter,* and *drop* and *crop,* in the final rhyme in Holiday's singing of "Strange Fruit":

> Southern trees bear a strange fruit,
> Blood on the leaf and blood at the root—
> Black bodies swinging in the Southern breeze,
> Strange fruit hanging from the poplar trees.
>
> Pastoral scene of the gallant South—
> The bulging eyes and the twisted mouth,
> Scent of magnolias sweet and fresh,
> Then the sudden smell of burning flesh.
>
> Here is the fruit for the crows to pluck,
> For the rain to gather, for the wind to suck,
> For the sun to rot, for the trees to drop.
> Here is a strange and bitter crop.

When her voice veers—as a sultry breeze in full day might—I like that. The notes are still familiar and graceful, but an element of turmoil has been introduced by those little turnings. The turmoil seems apt here and, moreover, I like turmoil. Mildred Bailey, on the other hand, sounds too girlish to me, and I don't approve of grown women sounding girlish. This shouldn't matter in my judgment of a performance, but if I rely on first

responses, I can find logic and reasons easily enough to confirm my taste and call it into judgment. I might say that she has sacrificed her emotional depth for technique or that her voice is wanting in natural feeling and expression—unfairly, I suspect. Unless I learn more about how jazz is designed, what other recourse is there but to rely on my intuition and my biases? In what I recognize as the four stages of appreciation (*predilection, familiarity, knowledge,* and *imitation*), at present I fall in the second with regard to jazz. In this stage I can do little more than guess about whether something I like is really good.

Everyone has taste. My argument isn't against it absolutely in proportion to the elements of art which when known also compel. The point is not that when we listen to music or read a poem we put to sleep our various interests as individuals. The point in listening or reading well is to be willing to suppress our prejudices enough to keep from altering the piece by concentrating on its parts or partial meanings or bringing to it ideologies, feelings and valuations of a particular age or preference. In short, the unfamiliar no less than the familiar needs our full attention to be properly appreciated—attention which is both subjective and objective, exterior and deeply interior. We may well start outside the work of art and with our predilections, but we must dare, or make, ourselves enter it. Only then can we know the power of its tensions and reconciliations, the modulations and interludes of the design, the nuances of style, motion, and tone, the *voice,* as it were, of the piece.

Whimsical as a comparison of the sonnet and the blues form may seem, their makers have much in common—to give voice to an essentially private, or individual, experience in a way that makes it universal and lasting. With the blues as with the sonnet, a discussion of it is no substitute for the performance; the discussion can only return us to the experience or the encounter. And as with the sonnet, the blues is not to be conceived of as a statement (of sorrow), a feeling, or of some truth imposed upon the music from without; it has its characteristic design, variable and lasting, that the performer, according to temperament, intuition, and skill, performs in. In the blues as well as in a sonnet the confinements of meter and rhythm can provide a doorway to nudge open when a singer like Bessie Smith phrases the music. In "Jailhouse Blues" the colloquial language is rendered with syncopations and embellishments, the voice occasionally keening, as introduced on the first syllable, the spoken word *Oh.* The notes corresponding to end words (*wall, jar, long, gone, chin, in, do, choose*) are always held, but the rhyming end words are treated rhythmically differently in every case. In the second verse, for instance, the accents in the first phrasing of the refrain line fall on *jail, stay, long,* and *long.* In the second instance the rhythmic stress changes for emphasis and, even more, one might argue, for simple variation, falling on the words *jail, so,* and *so.* Perhaps the most striking example of Bessie Smith's style of variation in beat comes in the last verse, which can be scanned as follows:

Good morning blues, blues how do you do?—how
   do you do?

Good morning blues, blues how do you do?

Her voice is small with its insistence coming largely
from the rhythmic changes, and the effect on this listener is of hearing someone feeling the sound of her
aloneness: trying it out in more than one way as one
might close the eyes in a dark room to test the quality
of darkness already in the room.

Jailhouse Blues

[spoken] Oh, this house is gonna get raided, yes
   sir.

Thirty days in jail with my back turned to the
   wall—turned to the wall.
Thirty days in jail with my back turned to the
   wall.
Tell Mr. Jailkeeper put another (?) in my jar.

I don't mind being in jail, but I got to stay there
   so long—so long.
I don't mind being in jail, but I got to stay there
   so long—so long.
And every friend I had is done shook hands and
   gone.

You better stop your man from tickling me under
   my chin—under my chin.
You better stop your man from tickling me under
   my chin,
'Cause if he keeps on tickling, I'm sure gonna
   kick him on in.

Good morning blues, blues how do you do?—how
   do you do?
Good morning, blues, blues how do you do?
Did I get from here to ever choose what we
   choose?

Bessie Smith

Successive takes of her recordings often show that she
knew eloquently and clearly what she was going to do
during her improvisations. The air of improvisation is
there (in the final take: September 21, 1923), but so too
is the preparation. In improvisation lies the greatness of
the blues singer and the sonneteer[6]—the ability to take
the known framework, to absorb what has come before,
and to alter it.

II

Today, as ever, in the arts, much emphasis is put on the
new, with individual musicians and writers practicing
their art as if what they are doing does not reflect an
overriding artistic evolution working itself out according to its own logic and momentum. There will always
be writers and musicians who suppose that originality
means setting one's clothes on fire, pretending that
clothing never had its uses. I obviously don't mean that
invention is impossible or that the audience is unrespon-

sive to original work; the poetry of the age (and here I'd
better return to development in the medium I am most
familiar with) is full of premonitions. The tendencies of
the poetry of the past sixty years—a great emphasis on
the suggestive and on sensation, lack of restraint, an
extremely personal style, quite a lot of obscurity, deeply,
deeply felt emotion, innovations in language, high lyricism—some feel have been forced to their limits. Unable
or unwilling to go any further, some poets are returning
to models of the past, writing once again in traditional
meters—cultural conservationists, they might be termed.

If one considers contemporary poetry as a part of the
historical process, one wonders why this didn't happen
sooner; sixty years in the twentieth century is a long
time. And of course it did. I mean that there have always been poets who practiced a more formal kind of
poetry, even as they seemed to be doing something more
original and more disquieting. Berryman and Hart
Crane are two cases in point. Both poets wanted to write
something new, and both were much influenced by the
whole of the literature that had come before. And their
admirers are split between those who care for the modernist tendencies and those who care for the traditional
affinities, not always the two together. The poets I
myself admire are the ones more cognizant of the
whole of the tradition—in meter *and* in free verse—
and responsive to the subtle, complicated relationship
between literary momentum and the audience, an audience which tires equally from parlor tricks (fire)
and the disguised past.

If a poet's tendency toward formlessness and disorgani-
zation is overcome by writing in the received forms (and
one knows when one has a sonnet done by reading again
its description), a good poem won't necessarily be the
end product. Neither will the invention of a new form
necessarily lead to quality. The new and the old both
exert their attractions because of the poet's and audience's
hope that something good will necessarily result; now
enough mediocre poetry has been written to show that
neither affinity (or strategy) will work absolutely. How can
the poet go any further? How can poems be written that
are any more organized? disorganized? violent? pretty?
narrative? lyric? fresh? reminiscent? Hasn't it all been
done? And how does one write a genuinely good poem
in one's specialization (rhyme, free verse) or out of it?
The poet may be the last to know, just as the jazz singer
may be the last to recognize definitely the degree of his
of her success. But it seems obvious that a more than
passing knowledge of what has come before—the continuum—can give the artist at least some means to
measure greatness. After that, temperament, character,
and talent will make their indelible contributions to the
work. Will it be truly original? Originality is a rare
commodity, and it comes where it is least expected. Da
Lentini and W. C. Handy may have been the originators
of their art forms, but it is Petrarch, Shakespeare,
Sydney, Meredith, Cummings, and Berryman whose
interpretations of the sonnet mattered more and whose
poems we don't forget—and singers, too, like Bessie

Smith, Joe Williams, and Billie Holiday, their art transcending the particular expectations of the form that shaped their art.

NOTES

[1] George Gascoigne was the first British writer to define the sonnet as we understand it: "Then you have Sonnets: some think that all Poemes (being short) may be called Sonets, as in deede it is a diminutive worde derived of Sonare, but yet I can beste allow to call those Sonnets which are of fourtene lynes, every line conteyning tenne syllables. The first twelve do rhyme in staves of foure lines by cross meetre, and the last two ryming together do conclude the whole." "Certayne Notes of Instruction," 1579.

[2] It seems worth noting that Shakespeare's contributions to the sonnet form are not in experiments with its shape. But for the exceptions provided by one fifteen-line sonnet (99), one twelve-liner (126) written in couplets, one in tetrameter (145), and his double sonnets (73 & 74 and 89 & 90 are examples), the sonnets—154 of them—are quite conventional, with their 4 + 4 + 4 + 2 scheme made even more distinct by Shakespeare's habit of matching his syntax to the rhyming units (and the sense). But if the shape is conventional, the movement imparted to it is not. The poems very often start melodiously and deceptively simply, then become more and more complex, accelerating, if you will—aurally, metaphorically, and in paradox—then concluding with an epigrammatic braking of the argument. If a sonnet were a car, a Shakespearean sonnet would be a Lamborghini on a short street.

[3] Reading sonnets 73 and 74 as one poem, the meaning quite changes, with the speaker reminding the beloved, and himself, of the more valuable part than the body, the spirit ("Mine spirit is thine the better part of me"). The poem offers a kindly but firm rebuke to anyone who would lavish love upon the mortal part ("Too base . . . to be remembered") or pity a dying man. This reading gives new meaning to the very first line: "That time of year thou mayst in me behold"—not a sad, "You probably see me as elderly," but, "Though I may look old to you, remember that even after the wreckage of time, the greater part of me . . ."

[4] Wyatt likely was introduced to the Petrarchan (Italian) sonnet, from which he derived and adapted seventeen of his thirty-two sonnets, as early as 1527 during a visit to the Italian court.

[5] Improvisation indicates an activity which occurs in real time—for the jazz musician, for instance, variations and embellishments in performance of a known tune. The activity of the poet is similar to the improvising musician's in that the poet may during composition take a known form and change it at the spur of the moment. In poetry the printed poem offers evidence of the extemporizing, whereas in music the sheet music will be different from the musical performance and composition.

In both cases there is an important element of motion, a mind or sensibility in process, rather than stasis.

[6] The free verse poet is not excluded from this notion of improvisation—whenever instead of what has been said, the quality of the assertion and expression is foremost, and this involves the motion and tempo, the play of imagery, the aura of words, the short and long sequences of phrases and clauses, the abiding rhythms, rhythmic shifts, and the abiding notion of natural speech transformed into something else (varied, augmented, diminished, regrouped into new variants), then improvisation is to some degree at work. Further, there is now a significant body of work in free verse which constitutes a tradition that the contemporary poet must absorb or be in peril of making old choices.

FURTHER READING

Secondary Sources

Baker, Houston A., Jr. *Blues, Ideology, and Afro-American Literature: A Vernacular Theory.* Chicago: University of Chicago Press, 1984, 227 p.
    Constructs a linguistic matrix for African-American literature derived from the patterns of American blues music.

Garon, Paul. *Blues & The Poetic Spirit.* New York: Da Capo Press, 1978, 178 p.
    Examines the literary merits of the blues as an outgrowth of a repressed society, and draws comparisons between the supernatural images within the genre and twentieth-century surrealism.

Guralnick, Peter. *Feel Like Going Home: Portraits in Blues and Rock'n'Roll.* New York: Vintage Books, 1981, 260 p.
    Originally published in 1971, Guralnick's book contains chapters dedicated to a brief history of the blues, Muddy Waters, Skip James, Johnny Shines, Robert Pete Williams, and Howlin' Wolf.

------. *Sweet Soul Music: Rhythm and Blues and the Southern Dream of Freedom.* New York: Harper & Row, 1986, 438 p.
    Picks up where *Feel Like Going Home* ended by examining the continuation of African-American soul music in the 1960s as evolving from the blues idiom.

Jones, LeRoi. *Blues People: The Negro Experience in White America and the Music that Developed from It.* New York: Morrell Quill Paperbacks, 1963, 244 p.
    Discusses themes of isolation and helplessness in blues music, and concludes that the recognition that this isolation is society's fault and not the individual African-American's exacerbates this isolation.

Oliver, Paul. *Blues Fell This Morning.* New York: Cambridge University Press, 1990, 348 p.

First published in 1960, Oliver's book contains personal observations from Big Bill Broonzy, Jimmy Rushing, Sonny Terry, and Brownie McGhee, as well as extensive transcriptions of little-known and popular blues songs.

------. *The Story of the Blues.* Boston: Northeastern University Press, 1998, 288 p.

Documents the evolution of blues music from Mississippi Delta plantations to contemporary Chicago, and contains many photographs of prominent and obscure blues performers.

Palmer, Robert. *Deep Blues.* New York: The Viking Press, 1981, 310 p.

Traces the history of the blues from Mississippi to Memphis and Chicago, presenting biographical and critical information on such formative influences as Charley Patton, Robert Johnson, Muddy Waters, Sonny Boy Williamson, B.B. King, and Little Walter.

Rowe, Mike. *Chicago Blues: The City & the Music.* New York: Da Capo Press, 1975, 226 p.

Originally published in 1973, Rowe's book explores the social and economic factors impacting the relocation of many Mississippi Delta musicians to Chicago, and the music that evolved following their arrival.

Russell, Tony. *The Blues: From Robert Johnson to Robert Cray.* New York: Schirmer Books, 1998, 224 p.

Traces the development of the blues from W. C. Handy and Hart Wand in 1912 to 1992, including profiles of twenty-four blues performers from Leadbelly to Blind Lemon Jefferson, and a discography of fifty-five influential blues recordings.

The Sea in Literature

INTRODUCTION

Tracing their origins in part to classical antiquity and the Homeric epic poem *The Odyssey*, modern literary representations of the sea continue to evoke the limitless power and elemental mystery of the ocean as supreme adversary. By the nineteenth century, however, sea imagery and maritime settings had become common tropes of the English and American literary traditions, with writers such as James Fenimore Cooper, Herman Melville, and Joseph Conrad skillfully evoking the sea as a symbolic site of conflict, both external and internal. The appearance of Melville's *Moby-Dick; or, The Whale* in 1851 proved the defining work of sea literature in the American tradition, eclipsing the swashbuckling, high-seas adventure stories of Cooper, such as *The Red Rover* (1827), and inaugurating the era of the serious sea novel. At the turn of the century, Conrad again invoked the majesty of the sea in his *The Nigger of the "Narcissus"* (1897), a subject he continued to exploit in many of his later writings. With Ernest Hemingway's *The Old Man and the Sea* (1952) the Homeric struggle between man and the seemingly indomitable sea had been taken up again. In more recent times, the sea remains a topic of considerable importance. Perhaps unsurpassed by any other sea novel of the contemporary era, Peter Matthiessen's *Far Tortuga* (1975) is acknowledged by critics as a work that carries on the maritime tradition of Melville and Conrad. Like Hemingway's work, *Far Tortuga* is also said to emphasize the sea as an important site of struggle and self-discovery, and additionally to dramatize humanity's often tenuous relationship with nature.

In poetry, as in fiction, the sea is frequently figured as a primal, unforgiving, or inscrutable force. Critics have observed this symbolism in a range of poets, from Basil Bunting to T. S. Eliot. Among them, the Imagist H. D., in the poetry of her *Sea Garden* (1916), pays homage to the sensual power of the sea with her elemental imagery and erotic lyricism. Gerard Manley Hopkins, in his ode "The Wreck of the Deutschland" (1918) invokes a disastrous shipwreck in order to dramatize his theme of everlasting life. Other common poetic themes associated with the sea include those of loss, destruction, time, and love. Several of these are taken up by the Modernist poet Hart Crane in his poetic sequence "Voyages," which, according to critics, meditates upon the intertwined subjects of desire, separation, and death.

REPRESENTATIVE WORKS

Elizabeth Bishop
  "At the Fishhouses" (poetry) 1955
Basil Bunting
  Briggflatts (poetry) 1966
Joseph Conrad
  The Nigger of the "Narcissus" (novel) 1897
  "The Secret Sharer" (short story) 1912
James Fenimore Cooper
  The Pilot (novel) 1824
  The Red Rover (novel) 1827
  The Sea-Lions (novel) 1849
Hart Crane
  "Voyages" (poetry) 1926
Stephen Crane
  "The Open Boat" (short story) 1898
H. D.
  Sea Garden (poetry) 1916
T. S. Eliot
  "The Dry Salvages" (poetry) 1941
Ernest Hemingway
  The Old Man and the Sea (novel) 1952
Gerard Manley Hopkins
  "The Wreck of the Deutschland" (poetry) 1918
Mary Johnston
  The Slave Ship (novel) 1924
D. H. Lawrence
  Kangaroo (novel) 1923
Stanislaw Lem
  Solaris (novel) 1975
Malcolm Lowry
  Ultramarine (novel) 1933
Peter Matthiessen
  Far Tortuga (novel) 1975
Herman Melville
  Moby-Dick; or, The Whale (novel) 1851
  Billy Budd (novella) 1924
Marianne Moore
  "A Grave" (poetry) 1924
Mary Oliver
  "Sunday Morning, High Tide" (poetry) 1979
  "The Waves" (poetry) 1986
Eugene O'Neill
  Ile (drama) 1917
  The Long Voyage Home (drama) 1917
Ole Rölvaag
  Længselens baat [*The Boat of Longing*] (novel) 1921
Derek Walcott
  "The Schooner *Flight*" (poetry) 1979

DRAMA

Johan Callens

SOURCE: "Memories of The Sea in Shepard's Illinois," in *Modern Drama*, Vol. XXIX, No. 3, September, 1986, pp. 403-15.

[*In the following essay, Callens assesses the underlying "mythic-symbolic dimension" of Sam Shepard's drama* Buried Child, *focusing on the complex and ambivalent water symbolism in the play.*]

> Truly landlocked people know they are. Know the occasional Bitter Creek or Powder River that runs through Wyoming; that the large tidy Salt Lake of Utah is all they have of the sea and that they must content themselves with *bank, shore,* and *beach* because they cannot claim a coast. And having none, seldom dream of flight. But the people living in the Great Lakes region are confused by their place on the country's edge—an edge that is border but not coast. They seem to be able to live a long time believing, as coastal people do, that they are at the frontier where final exit and total escape are the only journeys left. But those five Great Lakes which the St. Lawrence feeds with memories of the sea are themselves landlocked, in spite of the wandering river that connects them to the Atlantic. Once the people of the lake region discover this, the longing to leave becomes acute, and a break from the area, therefore, is necessarily dream-bitten, but necessary nonetheless. (Toni Morrison, *Song of Solomon*)

Buried Child is often described, together with *Curse of the Starving Class* and *True West,* as belonging to Shepard's "realistic family plays." This critical simplification fails to take into account the play's underlying symbolism. The misfortunes of Shepard's midwestern family proclaim the demise as well as the endurance of the American Dream, which entailed both independence of mind and action and, what is usually forgotten, an organic bond with nature.

The Dream's rich and ambivalent contents were well apprehended and expressed by Emerson. His famous essay, "Self-Reliance," has often been equated with an outright defense of untrammelled individualism and of the spirit behind the conquest of the North American continent. The self-reliant soul is indeed, in Emerson's view, active and full of potential. "Life only avails," he says, "not the having lived. Power ceases in the instant of repose; it resides in the moment of transition from a past to a new state, in the shooting of the gulf, in the darting to an aim. . . . Inasmuch as the soul is present, there will be power not confident but agent."[1] But Emerson did not advocate territorial possessiveness nor did he excuse an excessive dependence upon private property.[2] And there was no need to, because the self-reliant man "takes place of the whole creation,"[3] he is an independent world, sharing in the larger cosmos.

Whoever trusts his Intuition, his aboriginal self, is at one with himself and the universe: "In that deep force, the last fact behind which analysis cannot go, all things find their common origin. For, the sense of being which in calm hours rises, we know not how, in the soul, is not diverse from things, from space, from light, from time, from man, but one with them, and proceeds obviously from the same source whence their life and being also proceed. We first share the life by which things exist, and afterwards see them as appearances in nature, and forget that we have shared their cause."[4] This cause, this timeless and spaceless Whole, Emerson called the Over-Soul. Whenever man is in touch with it, there is "an ebb of the individual rivulet before the flowing surges of the sea of life"[5] which "new date and new create the whole."[6]

Buried Child reminds us of this original, mythical state of One-ness, a feminine and organic bond between man and nature, through water and fertility symbols. The play also illustrates the ideal's deterioration in the course of colonization, through incest, infanticide, and regression of the male characters into irresponsible, childish behaviour, all connected with the underlying water symbolism. Nevertheless, incest also represents an attempt, however misguided, to make the holistic Dream come true by re-establishing the union between mother and child. Moreover, the ritualistic revelation of the family's crimes functions as exorcism and guarantees survival and continuity. Commentators have so far neglected this mythic-symbolic dimension of *Buried Child,* thus also overlooking the positive part of Shepard's female characters in it.

In 1979 Shepard received the Pulitzer Prize for *Buried Child,* written one year earlier. In his plays for the decade and a half that preceded this award, critics have distinguished three periods for which they have devised various labels. Borrowing Michael McClure's term, Ross Wetzsteon calls the plays written between 1963 and the mid-seventies "vibrations," those of the late seventies parables or "visions," and the recent offerings beginning with *Curse of the Starving Class* (1976) the "family plays."[7] Ruby Cohn dubs the plays of these three periods respectively collages, fantasies and realistic pieces.[8] In *Tongues and Savage/Love,* Shepard tried his hand at a more experimental mode, though with his latest play, *Fool for Love,* he seems to have returned to his "apparent" realism.

Taken together, Wetzsteon's and Cohn's characterizations would lead us to consider *Buried Child* a "realistic family play." Though family relationships featured already in his first published play, *The Rock Garden* (1964), a decade later Shepard wanted:

> to try a whole different way of writing now, which is very stark and not so flashy and not full of a lot of mythic figures and everything, and try to scrape it down to the bone as much as possible . . . it could be called realism, but not the kind of realism where husbands and wives squabble and that kind of stuff.[9]

Buried Child indeed lacks any central stage property that is both visually fascinating and metaphorically powerful such as the bath-tub of *Chicago*, the giant bookcase of *Fourteen Hundred Thousand*, the snake/computer of *Operation Sidewinder* or the battered American car of *The Unseen Hand*. Like *True West*, it contains comparatively few of the monologues that were Shepard's earlier trademark; the idiom is rich but realistic and colloquial. The characters are consistent and fairly "round" which warrants psychological interpretation of them. The action develops in a straight line, and the setting is easily recognizable as a realistic living room with an outside porch, backdoor and stairway.[10]

Appearances are deceiving, however. In *Buried Child* Shepard does not give up his writer's quest "to penetrate into another world. A world behind the form."[11] Like the American Indian, Shepard is aware of the sacredness and mystery of daily life; this sense of mystery is precisely what he means by myth, and in this respect *Buried Child* does not differ from the early plays. However, Shepard no longer confronts those mysterious forces head-on. In the past, it has been said, he used a "'collision' technique" to create character and action, "une dynamique de rupture."[12] The surreal mystery almost always erupted and pulverized ordinary reality. In *Buried Child* it gradually emanates from the quotidian and suffuses it, without causing a break. For this reason, Thomas Nash may justly call Shepard's mode "ironic"; in Northrop Frye's words, it "begins in realism and dispassionate observation" and "moves steadily towards myth."[13]

Critics now feel that Shepard strikes a "balance between naturalistic detail and the wilder, more secret landscapes of being . . . between the banal and the strange. . . .He makes us believe in the unexpected because he conjures it out of very ordinary things."[14] This balance is more precisely a tension which would be lost in experimental productions of the play. What director Michael Smith, the first to mention Shepard's surrealism, said about *Icarus's Mother*, applies even more to *Buried Child*: it "needs reality in order to transcend reality."[15] Thus, when Tilden is heaping corn husks on Dodge while he is sleeping on the sofa, the surreal should emerge naturally, as in *Curse*, when a drunken Weston falls asleep, spread-eagled on the kitchen table amidst a pile of dirty laundry, or in *True West*, when the suburban kitchen and den slowly deteriorate as electric toasters accumulate. The qualitative change from the realistic to the overtly mythic is the result of a manipulation of everyday objects—the cornhusks, the laundry, the toasters—which is justified in the plays' context and which does not disrupt the stage picture through the intrusion of foreign elements.

Shepard's ironic mode provides the key to the deeper meaning of *Buried Child*. Some commentators begrudge the play's narrow focus of interest. Thus Bonnie Marranca finds that *Buried Child* "lacks a strong social reference point. The family depicted represents a private, closed, highly individualistic universe that exists beyond the conventions of society."[16] But despite the apparent narrowing of society to the family circle, the need for and the memory of a larger community lingers on. It is a memory exacerbated by the irresistible urge to dissent, to strike out a course for one's self, so that growing sons leave their home on a quest, until disillusion, traces of their childhood, of the past drive them back.[17] Dissidence and communality: both have upheld the encompassing American Dream from the crossing of the Atlantic and the innocent beginnings of the first settlements to the conquest of the West and the race to the Pacific, with its promise of new beginnings.

Buried Child thus touches upon hopes and disillusions, departures and homecomings. The fate of its midwestern family mirrors the simultaneous disintegration and tenacity of the Dream; the double offense of incest and infanticide reveals as much its power as its defilement. For on the mythic-symbolic level the incest betrays man's longing for an organic relationship with his surroundings, with Mother Earth, which Shepard conveys through the water and fertility symbolism. Thus, he fuses a family's struggle against its own guilt with the nation's soiled Dream and, by vivisecting this family's subconscious, he explores the nation's collective, mythical past.

Dodge, Shepard's founding father, still recalls the "Faith and hope" (p. 52) that urged pioneers like him and the "Persistence, fortitude and determination" (pp. 42-43) it took to succeed. That conquest also entailed mobility, speed, power and adventure—all properties that emerge from Tilden's fascination with car-driving (pp. 46-47). It required "independence" and "forging ahead" (p. 25) to stake a claim in this unexplored country. But despite the hardships, the rewards were often abundant: Dodge's farm used to produce a "Bumper crop" (p. 22) and milk enough to "fill Lake Michigan twice over" (p. 64). Dodge here summons up a vision of some "paradise" (p. 72), the lost Garden of Eden itself.

For years now, the farm-lands, like those of Thebes in *Oedipus the King,* have lain fallow, and Dodge, his wife, Halie, and their remaining sons, Bradley and Tilden, have shared a monotonous still-life from which there seems to be no escape. Immobility or death threatens the men: Dodge, racked by a bad cough, is confined to his sofa; Ansel, the star athlete, is dead; Bradley has cut off his leg with a chain saw; and Tilden no longer drives. The rashness and cynicism with which Dodge is willing to torment the members of his family, reminds us that the West was not won without cruelty: "There's nothing a man can't do. You dream it up and he can do it. Anything" (p. 53). In Tilden's case, going West meant creating trouble and ultimately failing (p. 55). Historically, attempts to start a new life frequently did end in failure, and for some the pioneering past turned out to be, in Jack Richardson's words, a "history of drift and disconnection."[18] Settlements quickly turned into prisons, freedom soured into homelessness. The discrepancy between the settlers' ideals and the reality of frontier life prompts Pierre-Yves Petillon to comment that:

sous le cadastre de la conquête telle qu'elle s'est faite à partir des enclos puritains de la Nouvelle-Angleterre, droit vers l'Ouest, une autre carte transparaît, une carte enfouie, une topographie fantôme et rêveuse de l'Amérique telle qu'elle aurait pu être . . . un autre mode de l'occupation du sol qui ne se ferait plus, ne serait pas faite, dans la direction Est-Ouest de l'effraction et de la conquête . . . mais aurait été une pénétration rêveuse, voluptueuse . . . du Nord au Sud, suivant le fil de l'eau, depuis l'origine (la fourche) jusqu'à la haute mer et le delta.[19]

In Petillon's alternative, movement through the landscape would have resembled the drowsy floating and surrender to the Mississippi's current which the French critic calls "le sommeil" as opposed to "la cavale," a term which captures Dodge's pioneering and Tilden's car-rides. The sexual overtones in Petillon's different mode of possessing the land cannot be overlooked. In fact, the land here corresponds to the "landscape of the female body" which, Marranca complains, "has yet to appear" in Shepard's plays because he "conceives of space—emotional, intellectual, physical—as a male domain, a territorial imperative, as it were."[20] In *Buried Child* Shepard nevertheless gets close to evoking such a female landscape through the incest on the one hand and water and fertility symbolism on the other.[21] This discovery in turn implies a re-evaluation of Shepard's female characters.

In psychoanalytic terms Tilden's incest reveals the longing for a reunion with the mother-figure, for the comfort of a prenatal condition. It betrays his primary narcissism and love for his mother which coincide during early childhood. This stage in a child's development is characterized by a sense of identification with the environment, including the mother. Significantly, it is Halie and Tilden who are most sensitive to their surroundings, to the crops and the rain. They exemplify the transcendental trait of Shepard's vision, his holistic Dream.

Shepard's unpublished *Little Ocean* (1974), a series of sketches in which three women talk about pregnancy and childbirth, is said to end with "the idea of the mother turning into a 'little ocean' at the moment of bearing the child" and briefly feeling at one with the world.[22] In *Red Cross*, too, Shepard associates water with the amniotic fluid; in her swimming fantasy, the Maid moves "through the water like you were born in that very same place and never even knew what land was like." Earlier Jim suggested that "When it rains" is "the best time for swimming. . . . That way you get completely wet." When you are swimming, the rain creates "A constant wetness" which joins earth and sky.[23] Elsewhere one gets the impression that Shepard considers the sea to be the element that precedes everything (earth, man, civilization, . . .) and will outlast it all. "Snake Tide" conveys the desire for a reunion between earth and sea as the tide "soaks the dry/Thirsty earth's/ Cracked cry/Of longing to be out there/Moving/With the sea green sea."[24] "Back in the 1970's," a story about the

invasion and corruption by Americans of a boring Canadian village, ends with the apocalyptic image: "And far off you could hear the sound of America cracking open and crashing into the sea."[25] Finally, in "Sea Sleep," a story strongly reminiscent of Kafka's "Die Verwandlung," a man's bed turns into an ocean which floods the surroundings of his house and in the end relentlessly brings it down.[26]

Seen in this broader context, the rain in *Buried Child* can be interpreted as releasing in Tilden memories of the sea, of the (incestuous) union with his mother and a feeling of One-ness in a primal world. Halie and Tilden both like the rain. Halie loves the smell after the rain has stopped (p. 24), and Tilden enjoys himself in the yard, "Especially in the rain." He likes the feeling of it, "Feels like it always did" (p. 26). The rain here suggests familiarity, the positive unity of mother and child, a beneficent continuity with nature. At the end of the play (p. 72), moreover, the rain proves to be instrumental in the resurrection of the buried child (in Vince's person) and in securing a miraculous crop.

Nature, however, can also be hostile to man. The rain forces Vince and Shelly to look for shelter. Dodge triumphantly debunks the American Dream and its sunny philosophy of life ("L.A. is stupid! So is Florida! All those Sunshine States. They're all stupid!" p. 35); his ironical insistence that Illinois is "the only place it's raining. All over the rest of the world it's bright golden sunshine" (p. 22) suggests that the farm may be an infernal place—the "Black spot from the Midwest"[27]— where sins (America's or this family's) are expiated, and that water, like the biblical Flood, is a retributive element. Quite appropriately, the water symbol links the mysterious and threatening exterior world with the characters' guilt-ridden souls. In his drunken stupor, Vince warns against "Beasts from the deep;" "Tentacles animals!" (p. 67), possibly pointing to the unsettling feelings repressed below the threshold of the conscious. In visions of drowning in the backyard, the garden and water symbols finally acquire an unambiguous, negative meaning.[28] Dodge doubts that Vince can get him a bottle of whiskey because he would "Probably drown himself if he went out the back. Fall right into a hole" (p. 44). In psychoanalytical terms, one may argue, Dodge experiences the incest as "the threat of 'maternal engulfment' by the overpowering womb," as an emasculation.[29] He fittingly retaliates by drowning Halie's and Tilden's child and burying it in the backyard. Over this garden brood "awe and terror," as Emerson once said about the vastness of the American West.[30]

The holism and ambiguity of the water symbol also exist in the elegy by Pablo Neruda, "Alberto Rojas Giménez viene volando,"[31] from which Shepard borrowed his epigraph: "While the rain of your fingertips falls,/ while the rain of your bones falls,/ and your laughter and marrow fall down,/ you come flying" (p. 9). To Neruda the loss of Alberto Rojas Giménez must have been a watershed ("las últimas aguas terrestres") similar to the symbolic watershed, the outpouring of repressed feelings in *Buried Child*. The rain in the epigraph is said to fertilize the burial grounds and to guarantee the reincarnation of Neruda's friend into nature. Earth, sea and sky are fused in Neruda's poetic vision of after-life (Giménez's after his death and Neruda's after his friend's death). Though there is a strong sense of being submerged and buried, of darkness, blindness and oppression, the poem conveys an equally strong positive sense of light and colour, weightlessness and flight, a sense absent from *Buried Child,* except for its end.

Shepard carefully prepares for this cathartic end and the revelation of the family crime. In order to prevent sacrilege, this can only take place in a "sacred space and time."[32] In other words, the family's desecration is subtly balanced by a ritualization of the event.

Vince, the family's prodigal son, arrives unexpectedly at his grandparents' house in an attempt to revisit his childhood and "to pick up from where he left off' (p. 60). He can be seen as a belated incarnation of the "back to the roots" movement of the late 60s and early 70s (a manifestation of the universal longing for a community), since he is naive enough to believe that he can get to know his family again, "After all this time" (p. 32). To Shelly Vince's "home" at first looks like a "Norman Rockwell cover or something" and she expects to encounter the milkman and a dog named Spot (p. 30), "turkey dinners and apple pie and all that kinda stuff' (p. 36). The representativeness of this farm and its inhabitants is at once established, though the facade of happiness will later be pierced. In fact, through her mother-goose story about the cat that ate too much licorice, Shelly unwittingly depicts a house full of excrement. Later, Halie, complaining about "the stench of sin in this house" (p. 58), identifies the girl with a prostitute who turns the house into a brothel. Finally, instead of receiving a warm welcome and immediately being allowed into the family circle, Vince is not even recognized and Shelly is totally ignored.

The stage is nevertheless set for Vince's ritualistic initiation into the family. Halie's early reference to horse racing on Sundays (p. 13) anticipates the breaking of taboos, which in primitive tribes is tolerated only under special circumstances. The second act takes place at night; it is raining so badly that the bridge is almost flooded. In other words, Vince and Shelly are stranded for the night, cut off from the outer world. Somehow they have stumbled into the past, through some "time warp" (p. 41), and then got stuck there, "frozen in time" (p. 70). The stronger the confinement and immobility, the more acute the desire to escape. So Vince clears out and in a drunken fit drives all the way to the Iowa border. But during this ride he has a visionary experience which convinces him that "You can't escape, that's the whole thing, you can't."[33] Vince, the artist-visionary who appears so often in Shepard's plays, feels at first estranged, a separate person (p. 70). Gradually, however, he merges with his ancestors. The merging of

identities effects a merging of past and present into a mythical, eternal present[34] in which Vince can be at the same time the buried child (p. 44), Tilden (p. 33) and Dodge (p. 72). This intermingling expands the incest-theme and the associative range of the American Dream again to an aboriginal state of One-ness.

Upon his return, Vince finally confirms our premonitions of a sacred space and time. The porch (and by extension his entire inheritance) is "Off limits! Verboten! This is taboo territory. No man or woman has ever crossed the line and lived to tell the tale!" (p. 68). The porch functions in this case as the liminal zone between inside and outside, between sacred and profane. It is screened-in for practical purposes, to prevent glass slivers from spilling onto the acting area (when Vince smashes some empty bottles against the porch's sidewall), but it is also an area of physical violence bridging to the verbal and symbolic violence occurring inside.

The importance of the porch as a liminal zone can further be derived from the relevance of the themes brought up by the characters crossing it. Halie refers to the "back lot" where she does not want Tilden to hang around, especially not in the rain, because he is still a child who needs to be watched (p. 24). Thus, Shepard expertly joins earth, rain, Tilden and the buried child into a significant associative cluster. Further evidence comes from Vince and Shelly talking about the "heritage" and alluding to excrement and idiocy (p. 30). In this sacred space and time, a kind of madness threatens everywhere. It is circumstantial and temporary, accompanying the revelation of the family secret and the succession ritual. The characters and events are best described as "unsane," in keeping with the sexual perversions (the incest, Shelly's indentification with a prostitute, her symbolic rape, the sexual innuendoes) and in order to stress the difficulty in clearly separating "sane" from "insane." People constantly accuse others of being mad so as to make them inoffensive, to marginalize them. Vince reproaches Shelly for acting like an idiot (p. 30); he does not want his family to "think that I've suddenly arrived out of the middle of nowhere completely deranged" (p. 31). He is thus identified with his father who returned from New Mexico in a state of confusion, and Dodge appropriately mistakes his grandson for his son. Both Vince and Shelly fear that Dodge may be deranged (p. 33), and Halie explicitly says so (p. 59).

Final proof of the particular meaning of the porch can be found in Halie's and the Reverend's discussion of punishment while crossing it. The family's early confession of its crime would have entailed a punishment administered by the outside world but that might have been better than becoming one's own judge and executioner. Like Ansel's Italians Shepard's characters are "busy punishing each other" (p. 56). The play is in a way a crime and punishment story. As in Sartre's vision of afterlife, *Huis clos,* justice is no longer allotted by God but by one's fellows. Shelly plays the role of public prosecutor so well that Dodge feels he is in a court of justice (p. 53) and Bradley feels he is in a police-station. She is assisted by Tilden who has set his mind on un-earthing the truth and who initially even cross-questions Shelly herself (p. 45). Similarly, Halie's intimidation and manipulation of Shelly, forcing her to admit that she took the liberty of making herself some bouillon (p. 58), exhibits all the characteristics of a police-interrogation.

The many indications that the characters behave like children reveal that in its effects the punishment is tailored to the crime: a child was killed and the male characters seem to have regressed into childish behaviour. Shepard thus exemplifies and at the same time parodies the longing for an ideal childlike state at the heart of *Buried Child* and its incest. Tilden likes to drive but suspects it is childish (p. 47); he immediately falls for Shelly's fur coat and wants it (p. 46). Dodge hides his head like a child in terror (p. 57) and holds on to his milk stool as though it were a teddy bear. Bradley yells for his artificial leg and for Dodge's blanket with a child's possessiveness (pp. 57, 62); when Vince is playing soldier in his fit of drunkenness (p. 66), Bradley childishly wants to pull his ear, if only he could lay his hands on him (p. 67). Even Shelly's rape, in what is another instance of Shepard's unobtrusive, reality-grounded symbolism, gets reduced to a child's prank, as Halie exclaims: "Bradley! Did you put your hand in her mouth?" (p. 61) and chides him for it. In other words, the buried child of the title, Shepard suggests, is the child in each of the men. It is never completely outgrown and keeps hiding in some dark corner of the self. It need not be the cherubic child radiating happiness and innocence; greed and possessiveness characterize it, too.

Buried Child, like *Curse* and *True West,* can be related to the fact that in its "first phase" the West is said psychologically to have been occupied by "boys without fathers"[35] or by irresponsible fathers. So Dodge refuses to consider Bradley his son (p. 23) or a son he can talk to (p. 15); he does not want to be called "grandpa" (p. 36); and he even claims to be invisible (p. 16). The men on the whole cut a rather poor figure in *Buried Child:* they are crippled (physically, like Bradley and Dodge, or psychically, like Tilden), dead (Ansel) or drunken (Vince). The women, on the other hand, whom Shepard usually dramatizes negatively, turn out much better in this play.

To begin with Shelly: though originally depicted as a flashy, silly girl, she shows more courage than Vince; at least she stands firm whereas Vince flees with the excuse that he has to go and get Dodge a bottle of whiskey. As the outsider looking in on this crazy family but ultimately leaving it—i.e. judging it upon moral grounds— Shelly achieves dignity even though she first has to bear humiliations. But this is, as Florence Falk has argued, a survival strategy in which Shelly acts the obedient child to protect herself from male abuse, nothing comparable to the childish behaviour of the men. Shelly's original passivity, Falk maintains, hides "inner resourcefulness and resilience of more positive merit . . . Shelly submits

to molestation by Tilden (who symbolically strokes her rabbit coat) and rape by Bradley (who symbolically thrusts his fingers into her mouth), but she retaliates by hiding Bradley's dismantled wooden leg (obviously a symbolic castration);"[36] she also stands up against Halie and smashes a cup and saucer in protest against being ignored.

What prevents critics from impartially assessing Halie herself is their initial revulsion from incest. Once its connotations of an organic (feminine) relationship with the surroundings are understood, however, the complexity of Halie's character stands out more clearly. A brief comparison between Dodge and Halie, on the basis of how they cope with their guilt, should corroborate this.

Dodge and Halie illustrate respectively total and selective repression of feelings. When the bastard child was born they had not slept together for six years because they "had enough boys already" (p. 64). Ever since, Dodge may have been deprived of sex. So he not only had to bury his murderer's guilt, his anger, shame and disgust over his wife and son, but also his own sexual frustrations. That is why he yearns for a "little massage. A little contact" with Shelly (p. 52). He has attempted a total repression of his feelings. He tells Vince that "It's much better not to know anything. Much, much better" (p. 34), and as far as he is concerned "the past never happened" (p. 54). Because Dodge thrusts back any thought concerning his illegitimate grandson, he rejects his role of grandfather unconditionally and at first obstinately refuses to recognize Vince, his other grandson. But Tilden's reminiscence of his anguish at temporarily having lost his voice provides a telling gloss on the need to abreact inner pressures in order to conquer them: "You gotta talk," he says, "or you'll die" (p. 25). However, it is too late now: Dodge's suppression, his self-denial, has sapped his health for too long and his death can no longer be delayed. On the contrary, his confession only speeds it up because hiding the secret had become Dodge's only reason for living. The will he makes—an ironical paean to the lost American craftsmanship—is also a desperate attempt to hold on to reality by conjuring it up in words, to assert his identity by enumerating his possessions.

Halie is more a victim of selective repression. American society forbids incest, but she gave birth to a child, after all, whereas Dodge killed one. As a life-giver she stands a better chance to survive than her husband, a murderer. Halie never told any stranger about the incestuous relationship to save all appearances of respectability. But in her bedroom, a sacred space decorated with photographs from the past, she nurtured the memory of it. (The possibility that she, the guardian of the past, may also falsify it, is symptomatic of her power: Halie is in practical charge of this family.) Her flirtations with Father Dewis furnish an outlet for her sexual longings, though at the same time they lead critics to call her a "whore-wife-mother."[37] Such negative reviews, together with her neurotic character, may be the price she has to pay for her survival. Nevertheless, the conflation of different roles into one character hints at Halie's mythic-symbolic identity as a monistic, primal force associated with the water symbol (the sea, the rain, . . .) and which, like this symbol, possesses ambivalent meanings, both negative and positive.

Halie's change of clothes provides a case in point. To negotiate with the Reverend about a statue in Ansel's honour, she is dressed in black; after she has conquered she returns dressed in yellow. On the one hand, this example theatrically expresses her extroversion (as opposed to Dodge's interiorization) as well as her hypocrisy and manipulation. On the other hand, in accordance with the fertility symbols (the corn, the carrots, the rain), the change also marks the shift from winter to spring. Stasio finds in *Buried Child* elements of the ancient fertility legend of the impotent Fisher King whose deposition makes the wasteland bear fruits again. Nash calls the play a "modern version of the central theme of Western mythology, the death and rebirth of the Corn King."[38] Both critics focus on the male King and obfuscate the part played in the rebirth by feminine forces. Shelly is a catalyst in the ritual revelation of the double offense of incest and infanticide. Of these two, murder is the worse evil; and though love, as in Ansel's "Liebestod" (p. 21), often proves a destructive power, on the mythic-symbolic level the incest carries positive connotations.

To conclude: one needs to acknowledge fully the mythic-symbolic dimension of *Buried Child* to become aware of its complexity. Labelling it a "realistic family play" hardly does it justice. Underneath the play's realistic concerns throbs a holistic (feminine) longing which animated the American Dream but was thwarted in the practical process of colonizing a new continent. The offensive incest betokens this fall, but in mythic terms it still echoes a vision of childhood and primal innocence, a union with the mother and the world. The water symbol confirms the ambivalent significance of the incest; and within the crime and punishment story that *Buried Child* also is, childhood comes to stand for greed, possessiveness and immaturity. Shepard's ambivalence ultimately rubs off on the female characters, too. Our discovery that, on a deeper level, feminine forces play a positive role in safeguarding "continuity," redresses the one-sided negative view of women in Shepard's play.[39]

NOTES

[1] Ralph Waldo Emerson, "Self-Reliance," in *Essays and Lectures* (New York, 1983), pp. 271-72.

[2] Ibid., p. 281.

[3] Ibid., p. 267.

[4] Ibid., p. 269.

[5] Ibid., p. 392.

[6] Ibid., p. 270.

[7] Ross Wetzsteon, "Sam Shepard: Escape Artist," *Partisan Review/2*, 49, No. 2 (1982), 253-54.

[8] Ruby Cohn, *New American Dramatists: 1960-1980* (New York, 1982), pp. 171-86.

[9] Sam Shepard, "Metaphors, Mad Dogs and Old Time Cowboys," *Theatre Quarterly*, 4, No. 15 (Aug.-Oct. 1974), 16.

[10] When a drunken Vince smashes bottles against the porch's sidewall upon returning from his nighttime escapade, the script insists that "This should be the actual smashing of bottles and not tape sound" (p. 66 in Sam Shepard, *Buried Child, Seduced, Suicide in B*ᵇ [New York, 1979]. All quotations are from this text; references to it will be cited parenthetically in the text). In *True West* Shepard's insistence upon a realistic staging requires a full separate "Note on set and costume" preceding the play.

[11] Sam Shepard, "Language, Visualization and the Inner Library," in *American Dreams. The Imagination of Sam Shepard*, ed. Bonnie Marranca (New York, 1981), p. 217.

[12] Bonnie Marranca and Guatam Dasgupta, *American Playwrights. A Critical Survey* (New York, 1981), I, 87; Liliane Kerjan, "Sam Shepard et l'invisible espace," *Revue Française d'Etudes Américaines*, No. 10 (Oct. 1980), 277.

[13] Thomas Nash, "Sam Shepard's *Buried Child*: The Ironic Use of Folklore," *Modern Drama*, 26 (Dec. 1983), 486. Nash quotes from Frye's *Anatomy of Criticism* (New York, 1967), p. 42.

[14] Jack Richardson, Introduction to *Buried Child*, p. II.

[15] Michael Smith, Notes on *Icarus's Mother*; Sam Shepard, *Chicago and Other Plays* (London, 1982), p. 28.

[16] Marranca, *American Playwrights*, p. 109.

[17] Gerald Rabkin, "La communauté perdue et retrouvée: deux auteurs dramatiques américains," *Alternatives Théâtrales*, 10 (Jan. 1982), 28-39; Marilyn Stasio, "An Outlaw Comes Home," *After Dark*, Jan. 1980, pp. 58-63.

[18] Richardson, Introduction to *Buried Child*, p. III.

[19] Pierre-Yves Petillon, *La grand-route. Espace et écriture en Amérique* (Paris, 1979), pp. 123-24: "through the land registry of the conquest as it originated from the puritan settlements of New England, straight to the West, another map shines, a submerged map, a ghostly and dreamy topography of America as it might have

been . . . another mode of occupying the land which would no longer follow, would not have followed the East-West direction of exploration and conquest . . . but would have been a dreamy, voluptuous penetration . . . from North to South, following the water's course, from the origin (the cross-roads) to the open sea and the delta" (my translation).

[20] Marranca, "Alphabetical Shepard. The Play of Words," *Performing Arts Journal,* 5, No. 2 (1981), 24.

[21] In *Buried Child* Shepard uses symbols rather than images. Though the meaning of, e.g., the rain is not fixed, univocal, or literal, it unifies rather than fragments reality, is psychological rather than non-psychological, literary rather than theatrical. See Marranca, "Imagery vs. symbol" in "Alphabetical Shepard," 74-75.

[22] David Engel, "Sam Shepard," in *Twentieth Century Dramatists,* ed. John MacNicholas (Detroit, 1981), p. 237. The poetic association of the sea with mothers and love is a staple in Western culture. Hesiod, to take one of the earliest examples, tells us in his *Theogony* that Aphrodite, who presides over sexual union and marriage, was born out of the sea when one of Ouranos's testicles fell in it after Chronos had castrated him. The French language makes the association simply through a pun: "la mèr(e)" signifies both the sea and the mother.

[23] Shepard, *Chicago,* p. 122; p. 115.

[24] Sam Shepard, *Hawk Moon. A Book of Short Stories, Poems, and Monologues.* (New York, 1981), p. 80.

[25] Ibid., p. 12.

[26] Ibid., p. 78.

[27] Ibid., p. 45.

[28] In *Chicago,* too, "water" carries negative overtones. Stu dreams he is stuck in a tiny boat on a lake or ocean surrounded by rapacious barracuda. His made-up story of a decaying civilization ends in some kind of collective suicide through drowning. In the end Stu imagines himself on the beach, trapped (even though he seems to be moving: a recurring paradox in the play) between the water and the hills.

[29] Herbert Marcuse, *Eros and Civilization. A Philosophical Inquiry into Freud* (New York, 1955), p. 210.

[30] Quoted by R. W. B. Lewis in "The Man Behind the Sage," *The New Republic,* 21 October 1981, p. 26.

[31] The complete (Spanish) text of the poem can be found in *Pablo Neruda. A Basic Anthology,* ed. Robert Pring-Mill (Oxford, 1975), pp. 27-29.

[32] Mircea Eliade, *Le sacré et le profane* (Paris, 1965 [1957]).

[33] Sam Shepard, "Metaphors, Mad Dogs," 16.

[34] Mircea Eliade, *Le mythe de l'éternel retour* (Paris, 1969).

[35] William Kleb, "Sam Shepard's *True West,*" *Theater,* 12, No. I (Fall/Winter 1980), 71. To support his case, Kleb relies on Gary Snyder's *The Old Ways.*

[36] Florence Falk, "Men Without Women: The Shepard Landscape," in *American Dreams,* pp. 99-100. See also Marranca's "the zero gravity of women" in "Alphabetical Shepard," 23-24, and Stasio, p. 59, for a further assessment of Shepard's treatment of women.

[37] Falk, p. 100.

[38] Stasio, p. 60; Nash, 486.

[39] This article was read, in a different version, at the Annual Conference of the Belgian Association of Anglicists in Higher Education, held November 12, 1983 at the Free University of Brussels.

POETRY

Anthony Suter

SOURCE: "The Sea in the Poetry of Basil Bunting," in *Forum for Modern Language Studies,* Vol. IX, No. 3, July, 1973, pp. 293-7.

[*In the following essay, Suter discusses Basil Bunting's poetic representation of the sea as a primal, hostile force.*]

In an article on Bunting in *Stony Brook,* Kenneth Cox talks of the presence of "the indistinguishable inexpressible mass or void" beneath the poetry. "The timeless sea re-enters towards the end of *Villon,* as it re-enters towards the end of *Briggflatts* and *The Spoils.*"[1] It would be a mistake, however, to interpret Bunting's use of the sea simply as a reference to something primal, the traditional use of the sea by the Romantic poets, Baudelaire, Rimbaud and Yeats, although this aspect does exist in his work. Nor is the sea in Bunting merely part of his extensive nature imagery, as could be expected of a poet who has spent part of his life as a sailor. Sea imagery forms a pattern of symbolism in his work. Bunting's use of the sea symbol is not referential in a facile way. It is definitely post-"Symboliste." (This is where Kenneth Cox's words, "indistinguishable inexpressible" are appropriate.) Bunting insists too much on the sea—from its appearance in *Villon* as an expression of the eternal movement of time, to the Coda of *Briggflatts* where everything is thrown back to its dark force—for it not to have a significance personal to him.

Bunting begins by referring to the sea as something primal. It is against its background of infinite indifference—

> The sea has no renewal, no forgetting,
> no variety of death,
> is silent with the silence of a single note.
>
> (p. 17)[2]

—that Bunting's immature poet-narrator raises his voice in *Villon*. This is a hint of a nuance to come in the later poetry: we sense the protagonist keyed to fight against the impersonal force.

Man's weariness of the eternal repetition of the cosmic cycle is expressed by sea imagery in a poem Bunting wrote shortly before *Villon*:

> Weary on the sea
> for sight of land
> gazing past the coming wave we
> see the same wave;
> drift on merciless reiteration of years;
> descry no death; but spring
> is everlasting
> resurrection.
>
> (*Odes I,* 1 [1924], p. 87)

The last proposition is ironic: spring cannot bring new life in a system where there is no death. (This preoccupation with Man's horror of unbroken eternity is echoed much later in Eliot's *Four Quartets*:

> Where is there an end of it, the soundless
>   wailing,
> The silent withering of autumn flowers
> Dropping their petals and remaining motionless . . .)[3]

Similarly, in *Attis: or, Something Missing* (1931), the flow of the tide is the perpetual wash of past reacting with present, and expressive of despair:

> . . . reluctant ebb:
>   salt from all beaches:
> disrupt Atlantis, days forgotten,
> extinct peoples, silted harbours.
> He regrets that brackish
>   train of the huntress
> driven into slackening fresh,
> expelled when the
>   estuary resumes
> colourless potability;
>   wreckage that drifted
> in drifts out
>
> (p. 19)

Also, the sea can simply be associated with the passage of time humanity wishes to arrest, as in the image of the submerged island in *Odes I,* 17 (1930) ("Now that sea's over that island . . ."), transformed into that of a woman who has aged:

> some trick of refraction,
> a film of light in the water crumpled and spread
> like a luminous frock on a woman walking
> alone in her garden.

> Oval face, thin eyebrows wide of the eyes,
> a premonition in the gait
> of this subaqueous persistence
> of a particular year—
>
> (p. 103)

More often, the sea is neither neutral nor indifferent. If one fits together all the references in Bunting's middle and late poems, it is obvious that the sea represents forces hostile to Bunting's protagonists and in particular to the poet. That Bunting felt embittered at the impossibility of making any headway in the face of an effete literary establishment is obvious from *Attis, or: Something Missing* and *The Well of Lycopolis* (1935). In the former, he viciously attacks T. S. Eliot, satirising what he considers to be his artistic infertility after *The Waste Land* by picturing him as the eunuch, Attis. *The Well of Lycopolis* lashes out as much at the Bloomsbury Group as at "committed" writers. In the same poem and in *Aus dem zweiten Reich* (1931), literary sterility is shown to be connected with a deeper, social malaise. Bunting attacks an age that is unfavourable to poets. The sea represents the whole of the philistine, easy-going society in which Bunting found himself.

After a passage attacking the Bloomsbury Group, sea imagery shows the true poet's hard struggle:

> Neither *(aequora pontis)*
> on the sea's bulge
> would the "proud, full sail"
> avail
> us, stubborn against the trades,
> closehauled,
> stiff, flat canvas;
> our fingers bleed
> under the nail
> when we reef.
>
> (*The Well of Lycopolis,* p. 32)

Venus smiles on some: the Latin tag "aequora pontis" (actually a misquotation of "aequora ponti") directs us to the opening address of Lucretius to the goddess in *De Rerum Natura,* a passage which Bunting himself translated in 1927.[4] However, trying to be a poet and to flaunt one's talent, even if one has real genius (the "proud, full sail" is Shakespeare's tribute in Sonnet LXXXVI to George Chapman's "great verse") is impossible in modern society. Bunting's poet nonetheless continues his unrelenting fight.

Similar imagery is employed in *Briggflatts*, Part II, where the spiritual autobiography of the "poet appointed" is at the same stage as the state of mind of the protagonist in *The Well of Lycopolis*:

> Under his right oxter the loom of his sweep
> the pilot turns from the wake.
> Thole-pins shred where the oar leans,
> grommets renewed, tallowed;
> halliards frapped to the shrouds.
> Crew grunt and gasp.
>
> (pp. 55-56)

The young poet of *Briggflatts,* Part II, is shown surrounded by cheap tricksters, against whom he must fight to preserve the integrity of his art. The sea is at this point specifically linked with the theme of literature:

> Who cares to remember a name cut in ice
> or be remembered?
> Wind writes in foam on the sea.
>
> (p. 56)

The poet is the seer and the hated outsider:

> Nothing he sees
> they see, but hate and serve.
>
> (p. 56)

Seen in this context, *Odes I,* 22 (1932) ("Mesh cast for mackerel . . .", originally called *The Fishermen*) is symbolic of the lonely life of poets who exercise a difficult, dangerous technique and have

> the sea to stare at,
> its treason, copiousness, tedium.
>
> (p. 109)

Of course, the temptation is to join the vulgar crowd, for recognition and for the comfort of being with the others, but the poet's vision, his superior thought and craft separate him from the rest of humanity, hence his paradoxical position and his tragedy:

> the sea
> trembling with alteration must perfect
> our loneliness by its hostility.
> The dear companionship of its elect
> deepens our envy. Its indifference
> haunts us to suicide.
>
> (*Odes I,* 3 (1926), p. 89)

The "dear" is ambiguous: it refers to the great value of human relations, but also to the too great price—dullness and conformity—the poet would have to pay to achieve integration in society. The sea represents the spiritual death of the artist here. One can compare these lines with "the dear unintelligible ocean" Bunting talks about towards the end of *The Spoils.*

Here is not just the resurgence of the primal view as Kenneth Cox would seem to suggest, but a symbol of a rare moment of union between poet and society:

> In watch below
> meditative heard elsewhere
> surf shout, pound shores seldom silent
> from which heart naked swam
> out to the dear unintelligible ocean.
>
> (p. 47)

For the third part of *The Spoils* depicts a temporary regeneration of philistine society through the effects of a war that brings men together in death and nearer the essence of life where "the spoils" should be "for God". This shows the extent of humanity's and the poet's spiritual refinement after the testing battle with the el-

ements. Before the shock of such a war, only the poet was capable of the struggle. The sea's new association with a kind of redemption is a measure of Bunting's ability to develop his symbolism.

The sea as a primal force comes to the fore again in the conclusion of *Briggflatts.* At the end of Part V, it is one of the elements which the poet transmutes and binds into his completed "oeuvre", but it is the element that has the last laugh. Everything is thrown back to the uncertainty of the sea again in the Coda:

> A strong song tows
> us, long carsick.
> Blind, we follow
> rain slant, spray flick
> to fields we do not know.
>
> Night, float us.
> Offshore wind, shout,
> ask the sea
> what's lost, what's left,
> what horn sunk,
> what crown adrift.
>
> Where we are who knows
> of kings who sup
> while day fails? Who,
> swinging his axe
> to fell kings, guesses
> where we go?
>
> (p. 71)

But by giving the last word to the sea in this way, Bunting assumes its multiple identity in his art. The tension between its force and the formal artefact is basic to the fight for poetic creation. If one fits this passage together with Bunting's other references to the sea, one has the complete spiritual symbol of Bunting's poet, who is the lone visionary, traveller across uncharted wastes, a traveller who learns snatches of language in the ports where he passes, even forms attachments, but is forced by his fascination with the very forces he strives to conquer, to journey on, his only protection the integrity of his art.

NOTES

[1] *Stony Brook Poetry Journal,* New York, 1969, Nos. 3-4, pp. 59-69. "A Commentary on Basil Bunting's *Villon*." Quotation, p. 69.

[2] Page references in brackets after the quotations are to the 1968 Fulcrum Press edition of the *Collected Poems.*

[3] *The Dry Salvages,* II, *Four Quartets,* Faber & Faber, 1954, p. 37.

[4] *Overdrafts, Collected Poems,* p. 135.

Suzanne Ferguson

SOURCE: "Fishing the Deep Sea: Archetypal Patterns in Thomas' 'Ballad of the Long-legged Bait'," in *Modern Poetry Studies,* Vol. 6, No. 2, Autumn, 1975, pp. 102-14.

[*In the following essay, Ferguson contends that Dylan Thomas's sea voyage poem "Ballad of the Long-legged Bait" relates a "quest for [the] integration of personality" and features a selection of Jungian archetypes.*]

According to William York Tindall, Dylan Thomas once offered the basis for interpreting his "Ballad of the Long-legged Bait" as a poem of quest: "a young man goes out to fish for sexual experience, but he catches a family, the church, and the village green. Indeed, he himself is caught by his bait."[1] Other readings have been advanced by the critics. Fixing upon the physical suffering and death of the bait, Elder Olson saw the theme as "mortification of the flesh," while Clark Emery, allegorizing, called the "Ballad" a "creation poem." Richard Condon, closest to Thomas' summary, saw the poem as describing the act of sex and its consequences, while Elsie Leach, farthest from Thomas' précis but not from the language of the poem, thought it was about man's relation to Christ. Tindall, bringing together a number of plausible interpretations, noted that the fisherman-hero, a surrogate for Thomas himself, "grows up, faces reality, becomes a poet."[2] While all of these interpretations deserve serious consideration as possible meanings legitimately observed in the poem, they do not in my view deal satisfactorily with its literal level, the concrete particulars in which the meaning must inhere.

This poem, like all poems, "lives along the line," and there are a lot of queer things for the would-be explicator to ponder in these lines. Why, if the young man "goes out to fish for sexual experience," does he not—as a number of Thomas' protagonists do—engage in sexual activity? What does he expect to catch using a girl for bait? Where did she come from? Why does he treat her as he does, and why doesn't she resist? How can the rape and destruction of the bait by sea-creatures be productive of a new Eden which turns out to be the fisherman's home town? If the poem is coherent and significant, and I think it is, these questions should be answerable in a way that convinces us of psychological validity. Because the happenings of this poem taken literally do not make sense, we know we must read them symbolically; but how can we begin to interpret such bewildering images and actions? Tindall and Jacob Korg have both noted that the bait is in part at least a version of the archetypal figure Jung called the Anima.[3] I should like to go much farther, inquiring whether not only the bait but all the human figures of the poem may be embodiments of anthropomorphic archetypal figures identified by Jung—Anima and Mother, Shadow and Wise Old Man; whether the voyage which forms the plot of the poem may represent the archetypal Voyage of Rebirth; and consequently, whether on a level of mean-

ing even more fundamental than the "search for sexual experience," the poem concerns the quest for integration of personality (individuation), a quest both personal and, as Jung would have it, universal.

My reading springs from a key passage of Jung's 1934 essay, "Archetypes of the Collective Unconscious," in which the psychologist utilized an extended metaphor that contains close parallels to the characters and actions of Thomas' "Ballad." Having stated that *water* is the commonest symbolic representation of the unconscious, Jung developed his idea as follows:

> Our concern with the unconscious has become a vital question for us—a question of spiritual being or non-being. All those who have had an experience [of searching in the unconscious] know that the treasure lies in the depths of the water and will try to salvage it. As they must never forget who they are, they must on no account imperil their consciousness. They will keep their standpoint firmly anchored to the earth, and will thus—to preserve the metaphor—become fishers who catch with hook and net what swims in the water. There may be consummate fools who do not understand what fishermen do, but the latter will not mistake the timeless meaning of their action, for the symbol of their craft is many centuries older than the still unfaded story of the Grail. . . . Whoever looks into the water sees his own image, but behind it living creatures soon loom up; fishes, presumably, harmless dwellers of the deep—harmless, if only the lake were not haunted. They are water beings of a peculiar sort. Sometimes a nixie gets into the fisherman's net, a female half-human fish. . . . The nixie is an even more instinctive version of a magical feminine being whom I call the anima. . . . An alluring nixie from the dim bygone is today called an "erotic fantasy," and she may complicate our psychic life in a most painful way.[4]

Images analogous to those of the "Ballad" are immediately apparent. Thomas' fisherman seeks an unknown "treasure" in the depths of the ocean. His journey is recognizable in the first stanzas as a quest of some sort, though no object is discernable. The sea on which he sails is palpably "haunted" by strange, ambiguous images, the most prominent of which is the creature at the hook end of his line: not a mermaid, but a real girl brutally though seemingly willingly given to the sea. Her predicament implies that she has complicated the fisherman's psychic life "in a most painful way," for the only immediately plausible explanations of her situation are that she is being sacrificed or punished or perhaps both.

As Jung describes the process of individuation in "Archetypes of the Collective Unconscious," when a man begins to explore his unconscious in the attempt to know himself, he first encounters a mirror image, the reflection in water; it is the Shadow, or dark side of his personality, in which are contained desires and other emotions suppressed by the outer self, or persona. If we are to read the "Ballad" as a narrative of self-discovery, we will see the protagonist, with his "thrashing hair and whale-blue eye"[5] not as the total personality but as the Shadow, this rebellious, sexually aggressive part of the whole man. The narrator of the poem who maintains a safe, though intensely interested, distance from the violent action may be identified as the conscious, ego-dominated persona, the public self or mask, watching as his Shadow is whipped out to sea on the mad voyage. Within the narrative, however, the fisherman is the clear and single protagonist; through secret, vicarious identification with his Shadow, the persona is able to achieve an authenticity of being otherwise denied him. The narrator's refusal to present or even speculate on the fisherman's feelings is part of this attempt to deny his relationship with this Shadow, a relationship that threatens the very existence of the persona through the Shadow's "sinful," anti-social behavior.

A curious aspect of the poem is the reluctance of the narrator to express openly his own attitudes toward his material, although numerous "characters" continually address the fisherman and the reader with praises, laments, and commands. The sand, quay, bell-buoys, and the boat, nightingale, hyena, the ancestors, the sea, all "strike and sing" their highly emotive commentary. It would appear that the narrator is taking full advantage of the ballad convention in which the speaker remains non-committal as he allows the action and the internal observers to speak for themselves. Psychologically, he takes the best course, for the dramatic action of individuation should play itself out uncensored for its resolution to be valid. While the ballad form very likely suggested itself to Thomas through the work of his friend Vernon Watkins, Thomas used it only once, seizing upon the convention of impersonal narration—rare in his poetry—because it was peculiarly appropriate to the psychic events of the plot. That Thomas here recognized and wished formally to emphasize the primal nature of his subject, that he perceived only gradually that ballad form would best accommodate the wild, detailed, but ritualistic narrative, shows through the revisions of the worksheets, which only gradually assume the ballad stanza.

In the same way as the bait takes the role of antagonist to the fisherman in the poem, confronting the Shadow in the collective unconscious is its sexual opposite: the Anima, in Jung's metaphor a nixie who may play dreadful tricks on the persona. Here the bait seems to betray the persona's dark self, the fisherman, with all the denizens of the ocean.[6] The narrator is as reticent about the bait's feelings as he was about the fisherman's because on the surface her behavior is incomprehensible, and its symbolism can only be known through the outcome of her actions. Thomas' bait, "a girl alive with . . . hooks through her lips," is no mermaid or nixie (so much the worse!), but closely identified with the water and the fish as she is, such association is proximate, especially in the context of her role as a lure to sexual activity. She is the "seductive young witch" of Erich Neumann's schema of the forms of the Archetypal Feminine.[7] The fisherman's attitude toward her is mysterious; although

she is sexually attractive and apparently willing, as she "stalk[s] out of the sack," he does not make love to her but throws her "to the swift flood," a certain death. This anomalous situation is not untypical of the relationship between a man and his Anima, who according to Jung will ordinarily be suppressed if she is not projected upon some real woman who can be an appropriate love object.

It is worth emphasizing that in life, all of the archetypes have both inner and outer manifestations; that is, while they are aspects of the unconscious part of a man's personality, they are also projected in symbolic fantasies that may fasten upon other people. When this psychic activity of projection is transformed into art, the Shadow appears in literature of the "Double" or "Secret Sharer," and the Anima in that of the *femme fatale*. In the final scene of Offenbach's opera, *Tales of Hoffmann,* for example, we find the resolution of all Hoffmann's loves into the Muse of Poetry, his inner voice: a female image. The wonderful doll, the pure maiden, the dangerous courtesan, and the actress are thus seen as blanks upon which the poet has imprinted or "found" his Anima in her manifold aspects. In the stanzas of Thomas' "Ballad" in which the bait is identified first with the women of the fisherman's dream, "mast-high, moon-white . . . naked / Walking in wishes and lovely for shame," and then with traditional female figure both innocent and experienced—Sheba, Susannah, Venus, Anadyomene, and implicitly, Eve—her archetypal nature is strongly underscored.[8] That she is a fragment of the fisherman's self, as Hoffmann's loves are of his self, is suggested overtly in stanza 49 ("his long-legged flesh") and made explicit in the final stanza, where the bait has become "his long-legged heart"; the whole action makes a good deal more sense, however, when we see her as the feminine element of a masculine personality, the sustaining, regenerating complement to the aggressive male.

The process by which the fisherman comes to accept his relationship with the bait is arduous and complicated. She is the lure with which he hopes to "make a catch," but a catch of what? Clearly it is not fish which he seeks with such bait, and what he finally does haul in proves unusual in the extreme:

> . . . through the sundered water crawls
> A garden holding to her hand
> With birds and animals
>
> With men and women and waterfalls
> Trees cool and dry in the whirlpool of ships
> And stunned and still on the green, laid veil
> Sand with legends in its virgin laps
>
> And prophets loud on the burned dunes;
> Insects and valleys hold her thighs hard,
> Time and places grip her breast bone,
> She is breaking with seasons and clouds[.]

For eight quatrains the catalogue of the world born through the bait's death accumulates, finally leading the fisherman "home to his terror, / The furious ox-killing house of love." As the agent of the fisherman's understanding that he cannot escape the outer world, the bait again resembles Jung's Anima. Another passage from "Archetypes of the Collective Unconscious" is pertinent, for here Jung describes a psychic event that parallels the rebirth of the land in the "Ballad."

> Although [the Anima] may be the chaotic urge to life, something strangely meaningful clings to her, a secret knowledge or hidden wisdom, . . . [though] the first encounter with her usually leads one to infer anything rather than wisdom. This aspect appears only to the person who gets to grips with her seriously. Only then, . . . does he come to realize more and more that behind all her cruel sporting with human fate there lies something like a hidden purpose which seems to reflect a superior knowledge of life's laws. . . . And the more this meaning is recognized, the more the anima loses her impetuous and compulsive character. Gradually breakwaters are built against the surging chaos, and the meaningful divides itself from the meaningless. When sense and nonsense are no longer identical, the force of chaos is weakened by their subtraction; sense is then endued with the force of meanings, and nonsense with the force of meaninglessness. In this way a new cosmos arises.[9]

The turbulence and confusion of the first part of the "Ballad" correspond to Jung's metaphoric "chaos": the state of the unintegrated or partially integrated personality. The sea, the fisherman, the fish, the bait, octopus and eagle, nightingale and hyena are all caught up in chaos—objectified in the furious storm—and for some time no destination or real object is discernible in the voyage. But when the bait is destroyed in her own amours, thus losing her "impetuous and compulsive character," the fisherman comes to perceive her true significance. Coherence and knowledge, personified by the "fathers," "cling to [her] hand . . . / And the dead hand leads the past." The "force of chaos is weakened," in Jung's phrase, and the storm passes into the measured calm of the closing quatrains. The rising of the new cosmos is quite literal in the poem, as we have seen in the lines quoted above.

Jung continues his explication of the Anima archetype in yet another statement that helps us to understand the climax of Thomas' "Ballad."

> Only when all props and crutches are broken, and no cover from the rear offers even the slightest hope of security, does it become possible for us to experience an archetype that up till then had lain hidden behind the meaningful nonsense played out by the anima. This is the archetype of meaning just as the anima is the archetype of life itself.[10]

Through the death of the Anima, who was earlier identified by the narrator as "all the wanting flesh his enemy," the fisherman's own character changes. In the first half of the poem he was a masterful figure who achieved godlike proportions and power. In keeping with his Shadow aspect, however, he was a dark god,

presiding over storm and destruction; with his numinous rod he carried out the sacrifice of the bait. At her death, he, too, loses his energy: "the fisherman winds his reel / with no more desire than a ghost." Beyond retreat, the fisherman confronts the meaning that lay behind the bait's sexual "nonsense": the sense of human existence in a social context, in which sexuality is never independent from the "family, the church, and the village green."

The above analysis further suggests the meaning embodied in the ocean creatures of the poem. Although in Jung's parable the "dwellers of the deep" are not assigned a specific meaning, here they must be seen as projections of the self who, though he longs for sexual fulfillment, would like to free himself from social disapprobation by assigning his lust to the amoral beasts of the sea, which so brutally and freely make love to the hapless bait. Insofar as she is an aspect of himself, tricky, feminine, incomprehensible, he would like to destroy her, and thus simplify his existence; at the same time he wishes to find a suitable object for his masculine sexual impulses and to gratify his subliminal longing for union with this female part of himself.

The "archetype of meaning" appears in the wisdom of which the fisherman partakes following the bait's demise. It is delivered to him not by the girl herself, but by his "fathers," old men led from the depths by the dead bait. Being his ancestors, they can be regarded as earlier avatars of himself, but they have a specific function among the many things brought to the surface by the bait. By virtue of their prophetic song, these sages represent still another of the archetypal figures identified by Jung: the Wise Old Man, a tutor of the emerging self. This figure Jung said, "symbolizes the pre-existent meaning hidden in the chaos of life. He is the father of the soul [the Anima], and yet the soul, in some miraculous manner, is also his virgin mother."[11] The old men are the fathers of the self whose Shadow is represented by the fisherman; and the feminine aspect of the self, the bait, is indeed their "Mother," for in the poem she literally accomplishes their rebirth.

> One by one in dust and shawl,
> Dry as echoes and insect-faced,
> His fathers cling to the hand of the girl
> And the dead hand leads the past,
>
> Leads them as children and as air
> On to the blindly tossing tops;
> The centuries throw back their hair
> And the old men sing from newborn lips. . . .

The emergence of the fathers and the transformation of Anima into Mother require further comment. With the latter process, Erich Neumann is more helpful than Jung, explaining schematically this interesting metamorphosis.[12] Both female figures are avatars of what Neumann calls the primordial Feminine Archetype; he designates the Mother as the "elementary," the Anima as the "transformative" aspect of the Feminine. "While the elementary character of the Feminine tends to dissolve the ego and consciousness in the unconscious, the transformative character of the anima fascinates but does not obliterate; it sets the personality in motion, produces change and ultimately transformation."[13] In the dynamic interchange of the bait as temptress with bait as mother in stanzas 22-50, we may see the negative, threatening, transformational aspect of the feminine itself transformed into the Good Mother in order that the "rebirth" of the soul may take place. As for the fathers, they may readily be seen as "elementary" characters of the masculine, complementing the "transformational" Shadow. Jung's explanation of the symbolic entelechy of the seemingly distinct figures of Anima, Mother, and Wise Old Man, in the passage quoted earlier, helps us to understand why Thomas has the broken bait not only bringing new birth to past generations and resurrecting Eden from its sunken refuge, but directing the fisherman into new life after his epiphany. This peculiar maternity is an especially striking adaptation of the archetypal relationships, for the strange and incestuous family so created resolves itself, by the end of the poem, into the polymorphous equilibrium of the one: the individuated self, the transformed fisherman with his long-legged heart.

The precise nature of the knowledge bestowed upon the fisherman by his fathers is, like the voyage itself, far from unique: it is after all Thomas' major theme, the "human predicament" with which the archetypes of the collective unconscious enable us to cope. When the "old men sing with newborn lips" that

> Time is bearing another son.
> Kill Time! She turns in her pain!
> The oak is felled in the acorn
> And the hawk in the egg kills the wren[,]

they are producing a variation on, perhaps a parody of, "The force that through the green fuse drives the flower / Drives my green age; that blasts the roots of trees / Is my destroyer." Their pronouncement abstracts and translates into conventional apothegms the meaning of the poem's action. Newborn, they foretell destruction, and along with all the natural world, they themselves are born out of the dissolution of the bait:

> Venus lies star-struck in her wound
> And the sensual ruins make
> Seasons over the liquid world,
> White springs in the dark.

For the fisherman—and the man whose Shadow he represents—there is neither exemption nor escape from this process in nature. He must go "home to his terror, / The furious, ox-killing house of love" where his search began, there himself to die begetting. If ever a man were "caught in that sensual music" Yeats wished to leave behind, Thomas' fisherman is he.

The wisdom of the "fathers" is thus both truism and prophecy. The vital "meaning" they reveal in the "chaos" of sexual impulses that have destroyed the long-legged bait provides a paradigm for the union of bait and fisherman in the continuous cycle of life and death. Knowledge of the nature of all life is the same knowledge that is necessary for recognition of the self; out of the experience of death and rebirth comes the articulated "wisdom."

In this climactic section of the poem we may perceive the crisis of the actual process of self-discovery, called by Jung the "archetype of transformation." The fishing trip has turned out to be Thomas' version of what Jung and others designate the Voyage of Rebirth, ubiquitous in world mythologies and literature.[14] To Jung the stories of the death and rebirth of a hero embody more than the simple wish of man to transcend physical death; they reflect the need to know and accept the wisdom of the unconscious, to recognize the primordial impulses, to be born into consciousness as an individuated personality. The fact that the bait, an apparent antagonist in the poem, rather than the protagonist, is the one to be literally sacrificed, and that she is resurrected only as "his long-legged heart," does not alter the significance of the event, for as we have seen both fisherman and bait are complementary aspects of the whole man, who is symbolically born anew as the result of his journey to "fish for sexual experience." Although in stanza 50 he was led "home to his terror," when in the last stanza the fisherman stands "at the door of his home / With his long-legged heart in his hand," he exhibits not fear but quiet acquiescence. This culminating image represents the assimilation of the opposing forces which constitute the psyche. The bait has lost her threat, is no longer an enemy; and the aggressive contentious nature of the fisherman is similarly subdued. Anima and Shadow, subsuming Mother and Father, are reconciled.

In its main action and in much of its imagery, the "Ballad of the Long-legged Bait" has frequently been compared to "The Rime of the Ancient Mariner," "Le Bateau ivre," "The Wreck of the Deutschland" and even to *Moby Dick* and *The Tempest*. All five of these analogues utilize the sea voyage, with its familiar features of storm, destruction, and ultimate resurrection, as a metaphor for the process of self-discovery and discovery of the nature of the universe. Whether or not any of them influenced Thomas is probably less important than the fact that all, including Thomas' "Ballad," dramatize the process defined in Jung's "archetype of transformation."

Thomas' reaching out to the archetypal figures and the transformational quest, in a number of poems and in the early prose,[15] may indicate to the psychologist a crisis in Thomas' own individuation, but to the critic it will provide only a key to discovering the most profound and valid meanings of the works themselves. In their miraculous reconciliation at the end of the "Ballad," Thomas' fisherman and his family—the separate, sometimes warring aspects of a total self—present a symbolic vision of the integration of personality which indeed springs from the unconscious, but is made viable for his audience by the poet's conscious, shaping art.

NOTES

[1] William York Tindall, *The Literary Symbol* (New York, 1955), p. 155. See also John Malcolm Brinnin, *Dylan Thomas in America* (London, 1956), p. 12: "His one sentence explication of the central meaning of his 'Ballad of the Long-Legged Bait' was so lewd and searing as to stop conversation altogether."

[2] Elder Olson, *The Poetry of Dylan Thomas* (Chicago, 1954), p. 24; Clark Emery, *The World of Dylan Thomas* (Coral Gables, Florida, 1962), p. 123; R. A. Condon, "Thomas' 'Ballad of the Long-Legged Bait,'" *Explicator,* XVI (March, 1958), Item 37; Elsie Leach, "Dylan Thomas' 'Ballad of the Long-Legged Bait,'" *MLN,* LXXVI (Dec., 1961), 724-28; William York Tindall, *A Reader's Guide to Dylan Thomas* (New York, 1962), p. 250.

[3] Tindall, *A Reader's Guide to Dylan Thomas,* p. 250; Jacob Korg, *Dylan Thomas* (New York, 1965), p. 148. Korg's identification of the bait as "an idealized projection" of the poet is not in keeping with Jung's anima concept.

[4] *The Archetypes and the Collective Unconscious.* Vol. IX, pt. 1 of *The Collected Works of C. G. Jung* (London, 1959), pp. 24-25.

[5] All quotations from the poetry are taken from Dylan Thomas, *Collected Poems 1934-1952* (London, 1952).

[6] In the almost contemporaneous poem, "Into her lying down head," the imagined lovemaking of the beloved with whales and an "oceanic lover"—among others— more openly shows the narrator's jealousy, a submerged motif in the "Ballad." In this poem, we may perceive the psychological dynamics of projection as the anima-lover both lures and repels the persona.

[7] Erich Neumann, *The Great Mother* (Princeton, 1955), Schema III, facing p. 82.

[8] Compare Neumann, pp. 80-81.

[9] Jung, pp. 30-31. See also Neumann, p. 33.

[10] Jung, p. 32.

[11] *Ibid.* p. 35.

[12] See Neumann, pp. 64-83. In "Archetypes of the Collective Unconscious," the Mother is not designated as a distinct archetype of the individual personality, but as a form of the Anima. The Mother archetype per se is described in Chapters V-VII of Part II in Jung's *Symbols of Transformation (Collected Works,* Vol. V [London, 1956]), and in Chapter II of *The Archetypes and the Collective Unconscious.* See also Neumann, pp. 18-38.

[13] Neumann, pp. 33-34.

[14] See "Symbols of the Mother and of Rebirth," Chapter V of Part II in *Symbols of Transformation,* especially pp. 209-11, 234-43. The latter passage analyzes in detail the story of Isis and Osiris.

[15] For example the poems, "I in my intricate image," "Do you not father me," "Then was my neophyte," "A Winters Tale"; and the stories, "The Map of Love," "A Prospect of the Sea," "In the Direction of the Beginning," and, closest to the "Ballad," "An Adventure from a Work in Progress." See also Annis Pratt, *Dylan Thomas' Early Prose: A Study in Creative Mythology* (Pittsburgh, 1970), pp. 72, 193.

Sister Marcella M. Holloway

SOURCE: "An Immortalized Shipwreck: One Century Later," in *The Hopkins Quarterly,* Vol. 11, No. 4, January, 1976, pp. 153-61.

[*In the following essay, Holloway discusses Gerard Manley Hopkins's shipwreck ode "The Wreck of the Deutschland" as a poem concerned with life and resurrection.*]

In St. Patrick's cemetery in Laytonstone just outside London stands a modest headstone bearing this inscription: "Pray for the Souls of / Barbara Hultenschmidt / Henrica Fassbender (not found) / Norberta Reinkober / Aurea Badziura / Brigitta Damhorst / Franciscan nuns from Germany, / who were drowned near Harwich in the wreck / of the Deutschland, Decr. 7th, 1875 / Four of whom were interred here, Dec. 13th / R.I.P.

To the casual visitor of cemeteries the death by drowning of five Franciscan nuns in a shipwreck one hundred years ago raises perhaps but a few ripples of curiosity. Why should German nuns be buried out here near London? The ship was, after all, wrecked off Harwich. Why were these nuns on the ship? And Sister Henrica Fassbender's fate—her body was not recovered. Who was she in real life?

Five German nuns wrecked in a German ship called "The Deutschland" off the English coast a century ago would actually have little or no significance beyond this teasing curiosity if one of England's greatest poets, Gerard Manley Hopkins, had not responded to the tragedy in an Ode, which in the long view of literature will rank with Wordsworth's "Ode on the Intimations of Immortality." I refer, of course, to the magnificent "The Wreck of the Deutschland," written one hundred years ago this past December.

About fifty passengers out of a total of 220 were drowned in that wreck. Not an earth-shaking tragedy when planes explode on run-ways and strew hundreds of bodies about. But if a poet is touched by the tragedy and can single out meaning in the suffering, then there is cause célèbre even one hundred years after the dark night.

Hopkins' Ode, "The Wreck of the Deutschland," was not printed during his lifetime. Not until his friend Robert Bridges published his poetry in 1918 did England know there was such a poet. The story behind the Ode needs to be pieced together, and that story as it affected the poet is in great part the story of the five nuns who died, but especially of one nun identified in the poem as "the lioness" who amid the storm "arose breasting the babble," the "prophetess" who "towered in the tumult."

In real life these nuns were exiles being sent to North America to escape persecution under the Falck Law. This law, sometimes referred to as the May Law, was issued in May of 1873 by Adalbert Falck, appointed by Bismarck to the office of Minister of Public Worship. It was directed against Catholic education and all religious institutes in Prussia.

The Order to which the Sisters belonged bears the lengthy title of Franciscan Sisters, daughters of the Sacred Hearts of Jesus and Mary. It is a religious congregation of the Third Order of St. Francis whose rule was approved October 30, 1860. The foundress of the group was Mother Mary Clara Pfaender. In the history of her Order entitled *The Burning Seal,* Mother Brunhild Probst gives a brief account of these five nuns of the Deutschland. She tells us that on Dec. 3, 1875, Mother Mary Clara again gave her farewell blessing to five sisters for their journey to America. She chose Sister Henrica Fassbender, the nun whose body was not recovered from the sea, as superior. These were all young women. Sister Henrica was 28 and undoubtedly the oldest of the group, for early on the day of their departure one sister made her temporary vows and the others pronounced their final vows.

It was from small beginnings that this Order had grown. Mother Clara had been a Sister of Christian Charity for nine years when she founded her own Order. She and two companions acquired a house, garden, and barn at Salzhotten. After that the growth was phenomenal. By March 19, 1863, there were 14 sisters and 15 postulants (see *The Burning Seal,* p. 14).

But under the shadow of the Kulturkampf, elementary schools were being closed. The only task left these sisters in Germany was nursing the sick. Because of this Mother Clara answered the call from America. The pastor of St. Boniface Church in Carondelet, St. Louis, was the first to ask for their services. A group of nurses left in December of 1873. Then followed a second and a third group, each consisting of eight sisters. And on December 3, 1875, Mother Clara gave her farewell blessing to these five nuns whose heroic death is enshrined in Hopkins' Ode.

The Sisters in the Mother House, we are told in *The Burning Seal,* kept hours of adoration before the Blessed Sacrament to plead for their safe journey out on the wintry sea. Sister Henrica left a letter on the desk of her superior which was found after the group had departed. In it she expressed her anguish at leaving her country, her community, and her superior. She asked the superior to beg for her "the courage, the strength, and the power that holy zeal for His honor within me may burn." She concluded with a series of farewells to her Sisters, "to the hallowed spot where she knelt so often in the convent chapel," and "the hallowed room where she lived so happily without pain" (*The Burning Seal,* p. 79).

The Deutschland left Bremen haven, destined for New York with an intended stop for more passengers and mail at Southampton, on Saturday, December 5. Because of a haze it dropped anchor for the night and started out on Sunday. Hopkins describes in simple narrative style the departure:

> On Saturday sailed from Bremen,
> American-outward-bound,
> Take settler and seamen, tell men with women,
> Two hundred souls in the round—

And no one, the nuns keeping their vigils in Germany, Captain Berkenstein commanding the ship, or the two hundred passengers aboard, could have anticipated the agony ahead. As Hopkins says, "The goal was a shoal, of a fourth the doom to be drowned." Nor could anyone at that time have dreamed that a century later the wreck of that ship would be indelibly written into the history of English literature.

In the night between Sunday and Monday, because of particularly bad weather, the Captain lost his reckoning, and the Deutschland struck a sandbank known as "The Kentish Knock":

> She drove in the dark to leeward,
> She struck—not a reef or a rock
> But the combs of a smother of sand: night drew her
> Dead to the Kentish Knock;

For twenty-eight hours the vessel was grounded before help arrived. A vivid account of the last hours of suffering was carried in *The Times,* December 11, 1875. The scene at 2 a.m. on Tuesday climaxed hours of anxiety. It was the vigil of the feast of the Immaculate Conception.

The Captain, so the news account runs, ordered all passengers to come on deck. Most obeyed, but others lingered below determined to meet death without further struggle. Most of the crew and many of the passengers went into the rigging where they were safe as long as they could hold on. One brave sailor, we are told in *The Times* account, "who was safe in the rigging, went down to try to save a child or woman who was drowning on deck. He was secured by a rope to the rigging, but a wave dashed him against the bulwarks, and when daylight dawned his headless body, detained by the rope, was seen swaying to and fro with the waves." His heroic act is embodied in Hopkins' Ode:

One stirred from the rigging to save
The wild woman-kind below;
With a rope's end round the man, handy and
brave—
He was pitched to his death at a blow,

The wreck of this ship was no ordinary shipwreck. And as we re-read the accounts published in the current newspapers, we can understand why the English were stirred by the reports of those hours and hours of suffering off their coast. But we can also understand why this wreck had the particular impact it did on Hopkins, who at the time was a young Jesuit scholastic at St. Beuno's College in Wales. It was the response of the nuns to their suffering that particularly touched him and sparked his creative genius. It was their willingness from the depth of suffering to say "Yes" that gives to Hopkins' Ode its vital insight into the mystery of love and sacrifice.

His dedication of the Ode bears testimony to the part they played in his masterpiece: "To the / happy memory of five Franciscan nuns / exiles by the Falck Laws / drowned between midnight and morning of / Dec. 7th, 1875." But it was the death of one nun in particular, Sister Henrica, that sparked the poet's creative imagination and gives a depth of meaning to the Ode beyond the mere narrative of a shipwreck.

The factual materials Hopkins had to work from were the various news accounts of the wreck. The detailed *Times* account of December 11 (from Harwich) describes the nuns thus: "Five German nuns whose bodies are now in the dead-house here, clasped hands and were drowned together, the chief sister, a gaunt woman 6 ft. high, calling out loudly and often 'O Christ, come quickly!' till the end came." (That tall nun's body, as we know, was not recovered.)

In real life Sister Henrica Fassbender submitted in the midst of the storm to the will of God, crying out into the darkness for Christ to come quickly. In the Ode, she takes on the stature of a heroine. In her cry she is identified with Mary, the Mother of God, who by her fiat gave birth to Christ. Sister Henrica too gives birth through uttering Christ. Hers was "heart-throe, birth of a brain, / Word, that heard and kept thee and uttered thee outright." And then the poet plumbed the depths for all the symbolism that he could uncover in the Number Five: the five Franciscan Nuns, followers of St. Francis of Assisi who bore in his body the marks of the five wounds of the crucified Christ. In the Ode the poet calls out:

> Joy fall to thee, father Francis,
> Drawn to the Life that died;
> With the gnarls of the nails in thee, niche of
> the lance,
> his
> Lovescape crucified
> And seal of his seraph-arrival! and these thy
> daughters
> And five-livèd and leavèd favour and pride,

Are sisterly sealed in wild waters,
To bathe in his fall-gold mercies, to breathe in
his all-fire
glances.

Certainly the nun's cry, her recognition of Christ in the depth of her anguish, awakened something very special in Hopkins. And it took no more than a hint from his Rector that someone should write a poem on this wreck for Hopkins to break a seven-year period of silence. After his conversion to the Catholic Church (he was received into the Church by Newman in 1866), and his entry into the Jesuit Order in 1868, Hopkins burned the poetry of his youth and Oxford days as a kind of symbolic holocaust. But during these years, he told his friend Canon Dixon, he had haunting his ears the echo of a new rhythm. The physical event of the shipwreck, the tall nun's cry of recognition of Christ, and his own life of external peace in Wales coupled with his internal spiritual battles all took form and united themselves into an integral patterning of this new rhythm, "sprung rhythm," as the poet called it. In fact, the poem was so new and strange that Father Coleridge, editor of the Jesuit publication, *The Month,* would not print it. Today we are conditioned to the heightened speech and can respond to this Ode without too much difficulty.

But I think there was another reason why this particular shipwreck affected the poet so deeply. And that takes us back to the burial of the nuns. Four, we know, were rescued from the waters. As soon as the report reached the small town of Stratford, Essex, that these nuns were Franciscans, Father Francis, superior of the Franciscans there, had the bodies brought from Harwich to Stratford for burial. It was here at Stratford that Hopkins was born on July 28, 1844. He was baptised in the Anglican Church of St. John. And so as he followed the various accounts of the wreck, he also read the accounts of the funeral ritual of these nuns. He lived at Stratford for the first six years of his life. St. Francis' Church was just a matter of minutes away from St. John's where his baptism is recorded. And St. Patrick's cemetery is not too far from the city. Perhaps he had as a very small boy walked out Leytonstone way.

The funeral ritual was, according to newspaper accounts, an impressive one. In the December 18, 1875, *Universe* account we are told about the solemn Requiem which took place on Monday, December 13. His eminence Cardinal Manning, Archbishop of Westminster, gave the eulogy. The sanctuary was draped in black, and just in front of the altar outside the communion railings, the bier was erected on which four elm coffins were laid. After Cardinal Manning entered the sanctuary, the lids of the coffins were lifted and he gazed for several minutes upon the lifeless forms before him. All the current news releases stress the fact there was no disfigurement of these nuns, clothed in their Franciscan habits and dressed for this final resting by the Sisters at Stratford.

The ceremony of burial did not find a place in Hopkins' Ode. Yet, as a convert and an Englishman he must have rejoiced that his birthplace responded so magnificently to make of this final burial ritual an occasion long to remember. Catholics and Protestants alike joined in the ceremony. Thousands who could not get into the Church stood outside. Fifty priests were present at the Mass. Wreaths, crosses of flowers, and other mementoes of affection testified to the genuine sorrow of these people. The nuns of the Sacred Hearts of Jesus and Mary gave to their Sisters from Germany the final testimony of royalty. Long trains of boy acolytes wearing white surplices and girls with white sashes manifested that sense of innocence and joy so appropriate for the occasion.

But Hopkins' Ode is not about death and burial. It is about life and resurrection, eternal life as it triumphs over suffering. It is especially about renewal, about union with the crucified Christ. For Christ in the Ode is called "Our passion-plunged giant risen." And it is the feast that followed the night of suffering on which the poet concentrates, the "Feast of the one woman without stain," the Feast of the Immaculate Conception.

Cardinal Manning's eulogy had as its center of meaning the same mystery that is at the heart of Hopkins' poem, that mystery of love and suffering. For he asked in his eulogy this significant question: "Why should we mourn over those whose whole life was given to service of their heavenly Father?"

Simply on the natural level the death of the nuns was heroic, but it was the kind of heroism that would not have survived a century. The nuns in Sulzhotten, those who had kept vigil for the safety of their American-bound fellow religious, were given a kind of consolation in the account sent to them by a survivor of the wreck. Their sisters, they were told, strengthened their despairing fellow passengers up to the last moment to recognize God's Will. And in their self-sacrifice they rejected lifeboats so that mothers, fathers, and children could be saved.

Hopkins' Ode is divided into two parts. The first part portrays the private battle of the poet with his God, a battle in which he submitted: "I did say yes / O at lightning and lashed rod." The second part of the Ode depicts the public suffering of those on the Deutschland, especially of the tall nun who also said her "Yes" and with the poet was made one through suffering with Christ: "Sister, a sister calling / A master, her master and mine!—"

The Ode ends with a prayer to the tall nun, a prayer for renewal, both for the individual and the country where the nuns died. The last stanza deserves to be quoted in full:

> Dame, at our door
> Drowned, and among our shoals,
> Remember us in the roads, the heaven-
> haven of the
> reward:

> Our King back, Oh, upon English souls!
> Let him easter in us, be a dayspring to the
> dimness of us,
>   be a crimson-cresseted east,
> More brightening her, rare-dear Britain, as his
> reign rolls,
>   Pride, rose, prince, hero of us, high-priest,
> Our hearts' charity's hearth's fire, our thoughts'
> chivalry's
>   throng's Lord.

A hundred years after the wreck of this ship bound for America, carrying five exiled nuns, the event is still remembered. Because a young priest-poet out in Wales responded with his rare genius we have cause to celebrate. His great Ode, "The Wreck of the Deutschland," is as meaningful today in our age of renewal as it was in December, 1875. The mystery of love and suffering, the daring to say "Yes" to God's touch even in the height of storm is at the center of the mystery of being.

Lois A. Cuddy

SOURCE: "Eliot and 'Huck Finn': River and Sea in 'The Dry Salvages'," in *T. S. Eliot Review,* Vol. 3, Nos. 1 & 2, 1976, pp. 3-12.

[*In the following essay, Cuddy asserts that the sea and river imagery in "Dry Salvages" points to "the unifying theme of peregrination" in T. S. Eliot's poetry.*]

Whether we speak of his criticism, his lectures, or the prefaces which grace other authors' books, it is hardly a critical revelation to state that each prose piece written by T. S. Eliot is a clarification of his other work. Until now, however, little has been said of the prefaces and introductions, yet they reveal a great deal, not only about Eliot's preferences and motives in choosing to single out those authors as meriting his special recognition, but also about his own poetry, its meaning and direction. One prefatory essay, in particular, explicates Part I of "The Dry Salvages"[1] and, in so doing, directs us to a central concept of Eliot's poetry, the unifying theme of peregrination.[2]

In the "Introduction" to Mark Twain's *The Adventures of Huckleberry Finn,*[3] Eliot provides the context for the literal river of his poem, defines the metaphoric river god, and presents his own conception of the sea as symbol. The paradoxical juxtaposition of man's life as internal, existential river and external, conditional sea is precisely rendered in Eliot's observations about Twain's novel. Eliot further identifies Huck Finn, the "detached"[4] solitary figure, who, like his book and Eliot's poetry, has "no beginning and no end" (*Finn,* p. xvi), with the mythic peregrine personae uniting all ages of literature[5] generally and all Eliot's lyric poetry specifically.

Eliot begins the third Quartet with these words:

> I do not know much about gods; but I think that
> the river

Is a strong brown god—sullen, untamed and
   intractable,
Patient to some degree, at first recognised as a
   frontier;
Useful, untrustworthy, as a conveyor of
   commerce;
Then only a problem confronting the builder of
   bridges.
The problem once solved, the brown god is
   almost forgotten
By the dwellers in cities—ever, however,
   implacable,
Keeping his seasons and rages, destroyer,
   reminder
Of what men choose to forget.

                                        (*DS,* I, 1-9)

This description of the river recreates, through memory
fragments, the poet's origin; for on the literal level,
Eliot is speaking of the Mississippi River of his childhood. He personalizes this apparently objective, philosophical poem in his discussion of *Huck Finn:*

> But the river with its strong, swift current is the
> dictator to the raft or to the steamboat. It is a
> treacherous and capricious dictator. At one season,
> it may move sluggishly in a channel so narrow
> that, encountering it for the first time at that point,
> one can hardly believe that it has travelled already
> for hundreds of miles, and has yet many hundreds
> of miles to go; at another season, it may obliterate
> the low Illinois shore to a horizon of water, while
> in its bed it runs with a speed such that no man
> or beast can survive in it. At such times, it carries
> down human bodies, cattle and houses. At least
> twice, at St. Louis, the western and eastern shores
> have been separated by the fall of bridges, until
> the designer of the great Eads Bridge devised a
> structure which could resist the floods. In my own
> childhood, it was not unusual for the spring freshet
> to interrupt railway travel; (*Finn,* xiii)

Thus, "what men choose to forget" (*DS,* I, 9) is both
death and the impotence of man confronting natural
forces. The river, with its spring floods, is certainly
"sullen, untamed and intractable" (*DS,* 2) and, however
"useful," remains seasonally "untrustworthy, as a conveyor of commerce" (*DS,* 4). When in its "rages" (*DS,*
8) the Mississippi "runs with a speed such that no man
or beast can survive in it," the river may well be called
a "destroyer" (*DS,* 8). Eliot also refers in his essay to the
"builder of bridges" (*DS,* 5) who, in fact, designed the
"Eads Bridge" which "could resist the floods." Twain's
book, then, offers the poet an occasion for suggesting
the biographical context of the poem while commenting
on the symbolic function of his river.

And the river is infinitely more to Eliot than simply a
geographical feature, as this excerpt from *Huck Finn*
indicates:

> Like Huckleberry Finn, the River itself has no
> beginning or end. In its beginning, it is not yet
> the River; in its end, it is no longer the River.
> What we call its headwaters is only a selection

from among the innumerable sources which flow
together to compose it. At what point in its course
does the Mississippi become what the Mississippi
means?

It is in Eliot's metaphor of the river as "god" and its
personified "rhythm" of linear time[6] that Eliot's river
becomes what it "means." The literal river image is
transformed into a symbol of individual human life, that
unfathomable unknown which we constantly seek to
find and hope to understand when it is once found. It
may be called identity, that spirit within each of us that
is different from yet identified with all other men, or the
Bradleyan "finite centre."[7] Whatever name one gives to
it, this river god is the idea of ourselves, the spirit
within each of us.

From its sources and origin, then, the river "becomes"
itself, its own significance; and the "meaning" of this life,
this god, emerges in Eliot's discussion of *Huck Finn:*

> Thus the River makes the book a great book. As
> with Conrad, we are continually reminded of the
> power and terror of Nature, and the isolation and
> feebleness of Man. Conrad remains always the
> European observer of the tropics, the white man's
> eye contemplating the Congo and its black gods.
> But Mark Twain is a native, and the River God
> is his God. It is as a native that he accepts the
> River God, and it is the subjection of Man that
> gives to Man his dignity. For without some kind
> of God, Man is not even very interesting. (*Huck
> Finn,* p. xv)

The river god is the shape one man gives to the process
of life as he sees it. Whatever that form is to each man,
this river is a "god" to Twain (according to Eliot) in
providing the allegorical structure for his work and life.
Always concerned with a larger "Order"[8] and the place
of the individual in this system, Eliot sees Twain's
River God as an element in that scheme which is larger
than yet part of the novelist. Not *The* God, or a Bradleyan Absolute incorporating all reality, yet the river becomes a "god" in offering a shape to his novel, a structure to his view of life. The river concretizes Twain's
(and Eliot's) concept of life as the spirit of movement
and adventure which provides the opportunity for experience and self-knowledge. As the immutable form determining the pattern of life, the River God becomes the
evocation of that part of each man which reaches toward
something beyond himself in order to find himself.

Eliot says in the last stanza of "Burnt Norton," "The
detail of the pattern [of life and his poetry] is movement."[9] And variations of the related phrase, "Fare
forward," are found several times in "The Dry Salvages." The ceaseless movement of the water, or man's
life from beginning to end, is indeed a detail in the
pattern determined by the boundaries of a River whose
essence speaks for the form of existence. To call that
form "god" is to give it a verbal reality, or "presentation,"[10] concretized by the image of a river. This "brown
god," then, in its connotations and denotation, actual-

izes the concept of life as movement and thereby offers man reference outside himself. The word "god" becomes a symbol incorporating and transcending each finite being.

The River as God now assumes, through its "rhythm," the physicality and the internal spirit of man, the predetermined shape of a human life from source, origin, or birth, to its conclusion:

> His rhythm was present in the nursery bedroom,
> In the rank ailanthus of the April dooryard,
> In the smell of grapes on the autumn table,
> And the evening circle in the winter gaslight.
>
> (*DS,* I, 11-14)

Through all the seasons of life, the movement of the river, its shape and course, control the journey. Although each man gives the shape of human existence some uniqueness, or "style," the "form" of life is still defined and circumscribed by the polarities of physical birth and death: "It is Huck who gives the book style. The River gives the book its form" (*Finn,* xii). Indeed, one must never forget the power of this "brown god" demanding obeisance.

It is significant that there can be no actual end of a river, for it flows into the sea. Therefore, Part I of "The Dry Salvages" recreates the "movement" of existence as the river in the first stanza merges with the sea in the second stanza. The life of the individual man slowly passes into the universal experience of mankind.

Certainly when Eliot equates this River God with the Mississippi River, he alludes to his own past which is indeed one kind of "frontier" (*DS,* I, 3) beyond which each man must travel. But, more than that, in considering Huck to be "the spirit of the River" (*Finn,* p. xiv), the poet identifies the River with the ego, or Self, for he notes that "The river is within us, the sea is all about us" (*DS,* I, 15). And when the river god is recognized as the spirit of Self—imagination, identity, intellect, memory, the senses, and all else encompassed by that term—Eliot's River of Life is elevated far above the anticipated symbol of linear time that it initially seems to be.

> The brown god, Eliot says, is
> . . . at first recognised as a frontier;
> Useful, untrustworthy, as a conveyor of
>   commerce;
> Then only a problem confronting the builder of
>   bridges
>
> (*DS,* I, 3-6)

Like the shadow which falls between the idea and the reality in "The Hollow Men," the river is any god or belief, concept or ego which must first be understood and then framed into the context of reconciliation. To the builder of bridges, to the poet or philosopher—or saint—who would unite all disparates, this river god always moves between opposite banks, always keeps

them apart. The builder of bridges is like the "builder of the system" discussed by Eliot in his dissertation.[11] Any philosophical system attempting to explicate and incorporate all reality into a higher Order or Absolute ultimately requires an "act of faith,"[12] a bridge which ideationally links, but cannot merge, opposite banks. Yet, despite our impotence to overcome the river and unite its two sides, one can find joy in bridging it even as we delight in creating a "system" in which we can believe.[13]

Through poetry, Eliot attempted to designate the shapes of experience and existence and, out of those shapes, to create a new Order requiring the discarding and incorporation of older systems. In *Ash-Wednesday* (Part I) Eliot says, "Consequently I rejoice, having to construct something / Upon which to rejoice." The poet of "The Dry Salvages" again reminds us of the

> Years of living among the breakage
> Of what was believed in as the most reliable—
> And therefore the fittest for renunciation.
>
> (*DS,* II, 10-12)

The river, seen as god, is part of the form "constructed[ed]" out of the "breakage," out of the "fragments . . . shored against [his] ruins" in *The Waste Land* of the world. Thus, the river's movement and form contribute to a greater understanding of the Order of existence.

The two river banks also represent Earthly Life and Death, or the Hereafter in mythology. Thus, as Charon ferries souls across the River Styx, from the times of Homer and Virgil through Dante and even to contemporary literature, this river god continues to be a "reminder / Of what men choose to forget" (*DS,* I, 8-9). There is irony in this line, for another important river to which Eliot often alludes in his verse is the Dantesque Purgatorial River, Lethe, which wipes away the memory of man's sins but recalls the good deeds and happiness of a lifetime. But Lethe is a river in the next world and consequently has its own unique function; while the Mississippi is of this world and is therefore a "reminder" of painful things, the "reenactment / Of all that you have done, and been" ("Little Gidding," II). No matter how much man would wish to forget his past misdeeds and the consequent reality of death, his river god awakens the memory and thus remains "unhonoured, unpropitiated" by materialists of every age, "but waiting, watching and waiting." As the spirit of individual life, each man's "finite centre,"[14] and the substance of temporal life, the brown god of the river is unavoidable.

The river, then, is the reality of oneself and, as such, can never be predictable in spite of its certain course from source to sea:

> The river is never wholly chartable; it changes its
> pace, it shifts its channel, unaccountably; it may
> suddenly efface a sandbar, and throw up another

bar where before was navigable water. (*Finn,* xiii)

By seeing any River as unchartable, because of what is hidden beneath its surface or what is waiting ahead, the poet acknowledges the uncontrollable power of those aspects of a man which present the impediments to a self-knowledge that might grant fulfillment. In man's river passage, the hindrances created by his senses and unconscious—and whatever else is in the nature of man—resemble the buffetings of the sea which often seems to determine the passage of one's life. But Eliot makes the distinction in this essay between the River as the spirit and nature of man and the sea as the non-human experiential life force.

It is in the concept of movement, or peregrination, as it relates to experience and knowledge that the contrast between and paradoxical unification of the River and the sea are most significant. In Eliot's comments on *Huck Finn,* the river and sea are conceptualized:

> A river, a very big and powerful river, is the only natural force that can wholly determine the course of human peregrination. At sea, the wanderer may sail or be carried by winds and currents in one direction or another; a change of wind or tide may determine fortune. In the prairie, the direction of movement is more or less at the choice of the caravan; among mountains there will often be an alternative, a guess at the most likely pass. But the river with its strong, swift current is the dictator to the raft or to the steamboat. . . . (*Finn,* xii-xiii)

Each geographical aspect of the Earth's surface assumes symbolic significations. While Eliot depicts the prairie as societal pressures that control the will, and the mountains become a metaphor for personal choice, the river and sea have much larger dimensions that go far beyond the implication of momentary experiences, or temporary states of existence. The river determines the form of man's wandering by limiting the direction to a birth-death process, as noted previously, and to the shape of his own individual spirit (the path a particular river must take). The sea, however, is seen as Fate or Fortune, offering almost limitless alternatives during the journey through life. The course of a man's life, then, seems controlled by forces outside of himself on this Sea, the symbol of historical, traditional, therefore universal, experiences of all men traveling over the world in search of the knowledge which must ultimately be found within himself, in his own river god. And so a human life is metaphorically both temporal, subjective river and universal, timeless sea.

When Eliot says that a "river . . . is the only natural force that can wholly determine the course of human peregrination" (*Finn,* xii), he points to the primary theme of his poetry, the thematic journey for the experience that will grant knowledge found, even as it is feared, by searching internally and externally:

> So we come to see Huck himself in the end as one of the permanent symbolic figures of fiction; not unworthy to take a place with Ulysses, Faust, Don Quixote, Don Juan, Hamlet and other great discoveries that man has made about himself. (*Finn,* ix)

Thus, the course of a man's life must be understood by the progress down the river of emotional, intellectual, spiritual, and physical development, and simultaneously by his wanderings over the sea of all time and worlds. Unable to predict, or even see, the exact course of the unchartable river at any given time in life, nevertheless, at the moment of any experience the peregrine poet is ever determined to understand the under-currents of the river (and the sea) and its overall pattern. Preoccupied with the struggle to know—from his first Prufrockian encounter with the mermaid-Sirens who had tantalized Ulysses with a promise of greater knowledge, to his dissertation on Bradley's epistemology, to the last stanza of the *Four Quartets*—Eliot continues his quest. The poet finally sees himself, like Huck, as one of the many "Who are only undefeated / Because we have gone on trying" (*DS,* V, 45-6). As meditations[15] on life, Eliot's lyrics are attempts to actualize and thus order the observations and experiences which lead, in the time of the river, to understanding of himself, of his own gods and those of other men. The unification of all reality awaits another world.[16]

By identifying Huck with Ulysses, the symbol of the "pure poetic imagination,"[17] the poet links his river (Huck's spirit and Twain's God, which are the same things) with the sea, the Odyssean source of experiences in search of knowledge. The sea then becomes the perfect symbol for the poet's own quest. The "many voices" of the sea, the "losses," "broken oar," "gear of foreign dead men," and so on, recreate the world of the *Odyssey* which even provides new meaning to the following lines about Penelope (or any woman excluded from such a journey):

> . . . time counted by anxious worried women
> Lying awake, calculating the future,
> Trying to unweave, unwind, unravel
> And piece together the past and the future,
> Between midnight and dawn, when the past is all
>   deception,
> The future futureless . . .
>
> (*DS,* I, 39-44)

The sea images in Part I of "The Dry Salvages" suggest the development, or Odyssey, of Eliot's poetry even as they recapture the experiences of the supreme peregrination hero, Ulysses. Thus, the "hints of earlier and other creation" (*DS,* I, 18) are both personal and universal in alluding to literary as well as biological and historical origins: the sea, voices, fog, and time recall "Prufrock"; the crab and broken objects tossed upon the beach, "Rhapsody on a Windy Night"; the winds, seagulls, the salt of marsh and tears, "Gerontion"; April, foreign dead men, and other images, *The Waste Land;* and so on, to the last stanza of the *Four Quartets* when the river ("At the source of the longest river") and the sea ("Between two waves of the sea") express the evolution that strives for the union of intrinsic nature and external, eternal moments of experience,[18] the finite and the infinite.

In the River and the Sea of "The Dry Salvages," then, Eliot captured the essence of human life as he perceived it and recreated it in the form and content of his lyric poems. And his Introduction to Twain's novel provided yet another opportunity to elaborate on his poetic and metaphysical vision.

NOTES

[1] T. S. Eliot, "The Dry Salvages," *Four Quartets, The Complete Poems and Plays, 1909-1950* (New York: Harcourt, Brace & World, Inc., 1952), 130-31. Hereafter cited in the text as *DS* with section and line numbers.

[2] It is not suggested here that the poet wrote "The Dry Salvages" with *Huck Finn* in mind; rather, that Eliot used the Introduction to Twain's novel, like his other criticism, as a vehicle for illuminating his own poetic ideas. George Williamson, "Epilogue," *A Reader's Guide to T. S. Eliot,* 2nd ed. (New York: The Noonday Press, 1966), introduces the relationship of the "Dry Salvages" and Eliot's Introduction to *Huckleberry Finn,* which, he notes, offers "the kind of background that explains the power of *The Dry Salvages,* that brings understanding to 'the course of human peregrination' in *Four Quartets*" (p. 257).

[3] (London: The Cresset Press, 1950). Hereafter cited in the text of the paper.

[4] In his observations on Huck, "the passive observer of men and events" (*Finn,* xi), and his relation to Jim, "the submissive sufferer from them," Eliot sheds some light on several concepts intrinsic to his metaphysics and poetry: point of view; objectivity and subjectivity; and the "attachment," "detachment," and "indifference" in Part III of "Little Gidding."

[5] See T. S. Eliot, *Dante* (London: Faber & Faber, 1929), 62.

[6] Peter F. Dzwonkoski, Jr., "Time and the River, Time and the Sea: A Study of T. S. Eliot's 'Dry Salvages'," *Cimarron Review* (January 1976), pp. 48-57.

[7] See T. S. Eliot, *Knowledge and Experience in the Philosophy of F. H. Bradley* (London: Faber & Faber, 1964).

[8] T. S. Eliot, "Virgil and the Christian World," *From the Third Programme (BBC),* John Morris, ed. (London: Nonesuch Press, 1956), 243-58.

[9] Eliot, *Complete Poems,* 122.

[10] Eliot, *Knowledge and Experience,* 100.

[11] Eliot, *Knowledge and Experience,* 167.

[12] Eliot, *Knowledge and Experience,* 167.

[13] Eliot, *Dante,* 43.

[14] Eliot, "Leibniz' Monads and Bradley's Finite Centres," reprinted in *Knowledge and Experience,* 205.

[15] T. S. Eliot, *The Three Voices of Poetry* (New York: Cambridge University Press, 1954), 27, prefers to call poems written in the first voice "meditative verse" rather than lyrics.

[16] The future tense of the last four lines of "Little Gidding" indicates that the unification of the fire and the rose will come in another time.

[17] Eliot, *Dante,* 29.

[18] The concept of "immediate experience" and its relation to the moment out of time is an essential part of Bradley's and Eliot's metaphysics, an idea captured perfectly in the imagistic phrase, "Between two waves of the sea."

E. J. Ekambaram

SOURCE: "Sea Imagery in American Poetry," in *The Literary Half-Yearly,* edited by Anniah Gowda, Vol. XXIII, No. 2, July, 1982, pp. 115-22.

[*In the following essay, Ekambaram examines traditional images of the sea in American poetry, viewing it as symbolic of love and death, loss, destruction, or cosmic order/disorder.*]

One way of responding to the recurrent theme of loss and death in American poetry is to notice the use of "sea as a spatial metaphor for the positive as well as negative principles of life. [W. H. Auden, *The Enchanted Flood*]. There is, more or less, a continuous tradition of its use in American poetry from the early nineteenth century. To a number of "colonial" writers, the marine frontier was the principal focus of poetic interest, and they were fascinated by the wilderness of the sea as much as the virgin continent. A great deal of sea fiction deals with these ideas, but I wish to confine my attention to the study of sea imagery as it is reflected in the samples of American verse.

Philip Freaneu, a pioneering poet in the early American tradition, chose the sea as the major interest of his verse. Poems like "The Hurricane" and "The Argonaut," while capturing the appearance and mood of the sea in different situations, project the sea as a sinister force capable of destroying its own children. There are striking images of death in "Dread Neptune's wild, unsocial sea:"

Though now this vast expanse appear
With glassy surface, calm and clear,
Be not deceived—it's but a show
For many a corpse is laid below.

The sailor, whether he likes it or not, will have to reckon with the sea which is presented as a mighty force. The sailors who "sink in storms" will ultimately sleep on "coral beds" and "mingle with the deep." So, in Freaneu's verse, man is pitted against the cruel sea and found wanting in his might. This simple and somewhat undistinguished attitude to sea is reflected in the poetry of other writers too. For instance, William Cullen Bryant and Oliver Wendell Holmes gave vivid pictures of the violent sea but what troubles the reader of their verse is the pronounced moral tone which subdues the narrative content of their composition. Perhaps, less didactic or sentimental in purpose is Longfellow who shows a significant understanding of the sea in "The Tide Rises and the Tide Falls." But, Longfellow is a simple craftsman and his verse has none of the explosive encounters between man and the sea that is so persuasively portrayed by the major poets of the nineteenth century.

Melville's poems, like his *Moby Dick,* present the basic antagonism between man and the sea as the only relation possible between the two. The sea is an inimical, impersonal force against which man pits his courage and strength. Nevertheless, the typical Melville character, fascinated by the "inhuman sea," evolves a highly defined attitude to sea:

Thou lumpish thou, a lumbering one,
A lumbering lubb and loitering slow
Impingers rue thee and go down
Sounding thy precipice below
Nor stir the slimy slug that sprawls
Along thy dead indifference of walls.

The deceptive iceberg is, no doubt, a menace to man but its very immensity evokes his tragic admiration for it. To Melville, sea is an enchanting savage and his "Pebbles" and "The Maldive Shark" which give us sensitive portrayals of sea-sailor relationship, show their obvious connection with Whitman's treatment of the sea.

Whitman's persistent use of the sea permits a range of value attached to the image in his verse. In several sections of *Leaves of Grass* sea, as a major symbol, connotes the paradoxical principle of life and death. In "Out of the Cradle Endlessly Rocking" there is, at the level of simple perception, an intimate view of the sea which is described in terms of physical love:

Hissing melodious, neither like the bird
            nor like my aroused child's heart,
But edging near as privately for me rustling at
            my feet,
Creeping thence steadily upto my ears and loving
  me
                        softly all over,
Death, death, death, death, death.

Notwithstanding the erotic undertones of the passage, we may notice that the sea is associated with mystery, and most importantly with the creative process. The surging of the sea merges with the song of the bird which evokes "the thousand responsive songs at random." The sea assumes sinister significance in "As I ebbed with ocean of life" which presents a scene of total annihilation, reminding man of his utter helplessness before the mystery of the majestic sea. The sea is no longer a gentle mother of the cradle poem, but a destructive force which "swells and rolls, fills the onlooker with fear and despair." A somewhat different attitude is suggested in the minor poems of the sea-Group in which the poet strikes an elegiac note, coupled of course with a feeling of comfort or solace. The central situation in "Tears" is built around an angry old mother who cries uncontrollably on a stormy night—"the moist tears from the eyes of a muffled head." When "all is dark and desolate," the sea, strange to note, assures the old woman of "calm countenance, of stoical strength." In another poem of similar situation—"On the Beach at Night"—a father comforts his small daughter who is weeping at the thought of death:

Weep not, child,
Weep not, my darling,
With these hisses let me remove your tears,
The ravening clouds shall not long be victorious.

The poet's voice merges with the whispering voice of the sea which assuages the feeling of fear and uncertainty, and assures the child that there is something more immortal than the stars, something that shall endure longer than the lustrous Jupiter.

Closely related to the image, there are references to sailing in Whitman's verse. In some poems, the voyage is unending; in others, it terminates with "other shores." For instance, "Aboard at a ship's Helm" presents a symbolic voyage to death and the voyaging ship flows back into the mystical ocean where all will be assimilated in due course. The sea is the origin and destination of all life, or as Whitman put it in another poem, it is "a boundless aggregate, a vast similitude that interlocks all." In his concept of the sea and the aspects it images, Whitman invites a comparison with Poe's attitude and treatment. "The World Below the Brine" and "The City in the Sea" present a seemingly similar situation but Poe's city, in its details, somewhat resembles death's dream-kingdom. The Sea, in Poe's verse, is generally a scene of nightmarish suffering and pain and he specifically offers "visions of shipwreck and famine," "of a lifetime dragged out in sorrow and tears." Sea, in Poe's poem, has a destructive potential and images like "seas without shores" and "scoriae rivers" point to this significance. But Whitman sees a different vision in the same situation, his world below the brine teems with life, it resembles ours in its passion and violence, in its flora and fauna. He views the sea as a bridge between nations, an idea paralleled in Emerson's "Terminus." The sailing imagery in Emerson's poem embodies a metaphysical view. That is, the port and seashore representing active life on the land, will have to be renounced in order to set sail for the mystic sea. Emerson's image, used in the traditional sense, acquires subsequently a great deal of variety and complexity of suggestion at the hands of Emily Dickinson.

Emily Dickinson expresses her extraordinary awareness of the fundamental realities of life through the sea imagery. In a number of poems, sea figures as a major symbol for love-hate relationship. For instance, a little known poem "I started early, took my dog," at its literal level, gives an account of Emily's walk by the seaside along with her dog. While she is standing on the sands, the mermaids and the frigates come up to greet her:

> I started early, took my dog,
> And visited the sea;
> The mermaids in the basement
> Came out to look at me.

The poet is obviously unmoved by their presence. Sea personified first as Tide and then as He reaches her and tries to overtake the poet in slow degrees—simple shoes, apron, belt, bodice and so on. Again, the lady is unmoved at the dramatic development of the scene. Only when it is too late, she turns back with fear and realises that she is like a dew upon a "Dandelion's sleeve." She retreats from the sea but He follows her as if trying to court her. She resists his advances and yet regards his action as cherishable:

> And then I started too—
> And He followed, close behind.

The verb 'started' is deliberately ambiguous. Perhaps, it means her withdrawal from stimulation because such an interpretation links this poem with other poems in which Emily presents her acute awareness of death. In a poem that describes a dialogue between the sea and the Brook, sea is treated as an image for the final absolute, as the be-all and end-all of life. This attitude reminds us of Poe's vision of nothingness, but Emily goes far beyond it and discovers the sea as a place of Quest.

Poems in the first half of this century display a most diversified motif of the sea, ranging from the conventional usage to the characteristic complexity of a contemporary writer, Stephen Crane, who made a clean break with the past in his selection of material and craftsmanship, gives a pictorial image of a sailor caught in the cruelty of the sea. The sea in "A Man Adrift on a Slingpar" is a wrecker of a lifetime's efforts but is, paradoxically, likened to God's creative intention. Stephen's vision of a hostile sea finds a parallel in the poetry of Robinson Jeffers who depicts the Atlantic in "The Eye" as an elemental force that raids on the beauty of the coast. More significant than these two perspectives is the evocative picture of "an ungoverned ocean" in "The Yachts" by William Carlos Williams. The yachts, "moth-like" and "youthful," pass over the striking waves that "fail completely." What strikes me as

significant in the poem is the unusual presentation of the sea as something "broken, beaten and desolate," and the grim association of youthful beauty with premature death in the manner of Edgar Allan Poe.

Although, it is said, the influence of Poe is generally traceable in Hart Crane's verse, the vision of "Voyages" is Whitmanesque because both Whitman and Hart Crane, in their final understanding of the sea, associate it with the creative principle of life. "Voyage II" depicts the sea's gigantic surface, of "rimless floods" and "sheeted samite" whereas "Voyage I" begins with a warning to children:

> O brilliant kids, frisk with your dog
> Fondle your shells and sticks, bleached,
> By time and the elements; but there is a line
> you must not cross nor even trust beyond it
> Spry cordage of your bodies to caresses
> Too licken—faithful from too wide a breast;
> The bottom of the sea is cruel.

The image changes in the next section where the sea resembles a sleeping woman and the waves billow like her belly shaking in laughter. In fact, the sea is consistently presented in the poem as a woman and the underlying action is obviously a "voyage." The sea-image gathers further significance when it is equated with a mighty Queen who reflects on "this great wink of eternity," on "the unbetrayable reply whose accent no farewell can know." What the sea finally means to Hart Crane is man's mystic communion with it when "sleep, death and desire" close round one instant in one floating flower."

If it is desirable to group contemporary poets according to their attitude to the most diversified motif of the sea, then Wallace Stevens, Allen Tate and Robert Lowell belong to a group of poets who notice in the sea image the ordering power of poetic imagination. A poet of exceptional originality and power, Robert Lowell searched for a heritage of his ancestors in "The Quaker graveyard at Nantucket" which is, in fact, dedicated to his cousin killed in the sea. Sea, in Lowell's verse, stands for the historical sense, the vision of past interpenetrated by the present and future. As a Symbol of antiquity, sea brings to mind, rather peripherally, certain associations of death and music. Music figures centrally in Wallace Stevens's concept of reality and imagination. Sea is a formless chaotic reality, and every encounter with it enlarges man's awareness of himself and his world. The girl in "The Idea of Order in Key West" is singing and dancing by the sea and the poet who observed her artistic efforts, reflect on the relationship of the singer to the sea:

> For she was the maker of the song she sang.
> The ever-hooded, tragic-gestured sea
> Was merely a place by which she walked to sing.

The shaping spirit of her song and the dark voice of the sea are juxtaposed in such a way that the interpenetration of imagination and reality is possible only in the consciousness of the artist. The sea assumes an order only for the duration of the song, whereas:

> There will never be an end
> To this drawing of the surf.

The sea is both the external and the internal chaos that man hopes to subdue or shape. In another poem, an artist, Hoon, while meditating on the dark voice of the sea, resolves that his creative mind is what gives shape to the sea of reality—"I was myself the compass of that sea." It is interesting to note that outside the tradition of American poetry, one poet who used extensively the imagery of music and sea for presenting the vision of discord and harmony, is the Shakespeare of the final plays.

What is discussed so far is an attempt to trace a more or less continuous tradition of American poets who handled the sea image with a surprising depth and range of interest. Their interest ranges from depicting the sea as a simple, scenic background to treating it as a sophisticated symbol for cosmic order or disorder. The sea figures variously as a destructive principle, as an impersonal force and as a terminus situation. The idea has also given rise to other symbolic suggestivity of shipwreck and sailing motif. Such is the relevance and growing significance of the sea in objectifying the two major preoccupations of mankind, love and death, and in also conveying the experiential sense of loss in American poetry of death.

Eileen Gregory

SOURCE: "Rose Cut in Rock: Sappho and H.D.'s 'Sea Garden'," in *Contemporary Literature*, Vol. 27, No. 4, Winter, 1986, pp. 525-52.

[*In the following essay, Gregory reveals how H.D. evokes the erotic lyricism of Sappho and the elemental power and imagery of the sea in the poems of her* Sea Garden.]

A familiar shade has haunted the female lyricist and the perception of her work throughout this century—the specter of the Poetess. Within recent tradition the Poetess is identified with the prolific, sentimental "songbird" of nineteenth-century romanticism. Engraved in popular iconography through imaginary and legendary figures such as Emile Grangerford and Elizabeth Barrett Browning, this woman appears as pale and withdrawn, sensitive to the point of neurosis and hysteria, passionate, ecstatic, and morbid. Such a cultural image, surviving into the twentieth century, has negatively affected the critical assessment of women poets. The female lyricist, Theodore Roethke said, is generally considered to suffer from certain "aesthetic and moral shortcomings": limitation of range, triviality, superficiality, vapid repetition of themes, moral cowardice and inauthenticity, misplaced eroticism, and "lyric or religious posturing" (133-34). The Poetess has received ample enough scorn

from female poets and critics as well. A modern woman writer must shun this specter, fearing that she be seen as a love poet, "a reincarnation of Edna St. Vincent" (Sexton 80, 40), or a poet of "bland ladylike archness or slightness" (Plath 172); and she must distance herself from the company of other "female songbirds" (Bogan, *What the Woman Lived* 86). If the Poetess is a figure of disdain to male poets and of shame to women poets, she represents oppressive limitation to some feminist commentators, who see her poetic postures and themes as somewhat neurotic strategies of response to a male culture with a reductive view of female destiny.[1]

The rejection of the Poetess, then, has some historical justification. But the consistent distaste for this figure goes beyond such a clear critical ground. Moreover, the dismissal of the female lyricist cannot be entirely explained as an ambivalent response to a woman's assuming a male role.[2] The antipathy is more fundamental—a suspicion of the latent power of the Poetess, and of the woman poet's access to a potent lyric voice. The capacity for "perfect and poignant song," Louise Bogan claims, is the special province of the woman poet; and "when this song comes through in its high and rare form, the result has always been regarded not only with delight but with a kind of awe" ("Heart and Lyre" 429). Though Bogan herself, having great ambivalence toward the role of woman poet, suffered from the shame attending such a poetic voice, her remarks here show distinct insight into a lyric mode that she knew intimately and consistently honored. She here names the awesomeness of the Poetess that lies beyond the diminished images we inherit.

Much of the ambivalent response to H.D.'s poetry has come from the presence of this cultural figure. Critics have continued to admire the early imagist poems and ignore subsequent work because, as Susan Stanford Friedman says, the "short, passionate lyric has conventionally been thought appropriate for women poets if they insist on writing, while the longer, more philosophic epic belongs to the real (male) poet" ("Who Buried H.D.?" 807). Thus to point exclusively to the excellence of the Poetess is already to condemn with faint praise, to admire, as Ezra Pound said of H.D., the "refined, charming, and utterly narrow minded shebard" (157). In the past few years critics have rightly attempted to redress the exaggerated emphasis on representative "imagist" poems of H.D. with studies of her fiction and of the long poems of her middle and late life. But this recovery of her stature is made in part out of aversion to the specter of the Poetess, the limited lyricist. In this approach the early lyrics are understood in terms of a developmental reading of H.D.'s career, so that they necessarily appear to demonstrate limitation she would later transcend, incipient vision that would gain scope and substance.[3] Recent remarks take this reversal in the valuation of H.D.'s work almost to the point of putting away the early achievement as relatively "trivial" (Grahn 27, 101). A recent study of the "nightingale" tradition among American women poets consistently views H.D.'s poems, especially the early lyrics, as continuous with the self-limiting postures of her predecessors (Walker 142ff.).

Thus the early poems have been admired in the past for the same reason that they have lately been ignored: they point to the limitation of the Poetess. From the beginning of her career, H.D. indeed takes the Poetess as a guide. As a presence in her poetry, however, this figure suggests not limitation but scope, not shallowness but depth of erotic experience, not shamefulness and cowardice but deliberate courage. I attempt here to recover something of the complexity of vision informing H.D.'s first book of poems, *Sea Garden* (1916). In reading this work I am not primarily interested in H.D.'s place within modern poetic movements, or with the way in which these poems encode private or social history. I approach her as a great lyricist, a great love poet, at once in the mainstream and at the margins of lyric traditions in Western poetry. In her early poems, as much as in the explicitly mythical and occult work of her middle and late career, H.D. establishes herself within an archaic lyric tradition in which the voice of the woman poet has distinct potency.

Just as feminists have reclaimed such marginal figures as the Spinster and the Witch, so we need now to recover proper awe for the Poetess. In this attempt I follow Robert Duncan in his "H.D. Book," who, in fidelity to H.D.'s poetic achievement, reverses the accepted reading of this figure.[4] The Poetess, he claims, the woman in whom daimonic genius resides, is "an enormous persona like the hieratic figures of women in the major arcana of the Tarot." The general disdain for the woman poet, Duncan implies, is a response to the ambivalent power she carries, "the genius of a woman that men would propitiate or exorcise" (39). When the Poetess, the daimonic psychic woman, is present in a male poet, she is highly suspect, and the poet, especially the modern poet, often feels shame at his own "feminine" gift (79-80). But when this Poetess *is* a woman, then the defense against the disturbing authority of her voice is more virulent: "Aroused to battle by the claims of genius wherever they are made—for *genius* is itself of the old titanic order—male guardians of the literary Olympus have been the more aroused when the titaness appears, with the sense that 'it is unseemly that a woman / appear disordered, dishevelled'" (55).

The reclamation of this figure of the Poetess has great implications. It pertains to the question of the "Muse" of the woman poet, which some are beginning to explore (Rich 162-66; Diehl; DuPlessis). Duncan would agree with Mary J. Carruthers, who suggests that women poets gain unusual power when they accept the Muse, the imagined source or inspiration of their work, as a female figure. When the woman takes the Muse as female, Carruthers says, "she is not Other but Familiar, maternal and sororal, a well-known face in the poet's immediate community." This myth of the female Muse "seeks to recreate and remember wholeness . . . through a

meeting of familiars which recalls a completeness that is present but forgotten or suppressed by history" (295-96). She sees the power arising from this "familiarization of the muse" in "Lesbian" poets, taking that term in the large sense that Adrienne Rich defines. Rich says that *lesbian* was for her not a simple sexual identification but an "elusive configuration" that she always sought: "It was a sense of desiring oneself; above all, of choosing oneself; it was also a primary intensity between women, an intensity which in the world at large was trivialized, caricatured, or invested with evil" (200). Such an awareness on the part of the poet, Carruthers asserts, means an affirmation of women's community and of erotic connections between women past and present, and an acceptance of an essentially marginal place in relation to culture at large, with a view to the psychic regeneration of that world in terms of a "metaethic" of personal integrity (294-95, 321-22).

H.D. always imagined herself as Poetess in the sense that Duncan describes and that Carruthers suggests in speaking of the woman's Muse. Her early work is continuous with the later explicitly visionary poems in seeking a recovery of "the Sceptre, / the rod of power" of the poet-goddess (*CP* 512), in proposing an hieratic role for the poet, and in affirming the healing power of poetry. In *Sea Garden* in particular she attempts to recover the imagination of goddess-centered Lesbos. The sea-washed landscape she renders here is, as Rich has described the lesbian "configuration," the place where the virginity of the soul is achieved, an integrity born of "choosing oneself." Though it does not explicitly affirm bonds between women in a community set apart, it is nevertheless in conversation with such a world. In *Sea Garden* the poet has "familiarized" the Muse, has fully acknowledged a female source of poetic potency, insisting on a radical valuation of the world within the intense clairvoyance and vulnerability of erotic feeling.

In the polytheistic world of the sea garden there is no one figure of god or goddess who represents a Muse. But beyond the figures within the poems there is a latent mythic presence: Sappho herself, the first love-possessed lyricist, who carries for H.D. an authority for her own marginal explorations, for her sustained spiritualized eroticism.[5] While many women poets have avoided the Sapphic inheritance, seeing it as representing narrow "feminine" lyricism (Gubar 59), H.D. takes this Poetess as a crucial source of lyric power. From the very beginning of her career she possessed a keen instinct leading her toward the "maternal and sororal" image at the origin of her poetic gift. With the restraint of one who knows her familiar spirit intimately, H.D. recovers the memory of Lesbos obliquely, through radical austerity. Faithful to her guide, she understands that this intimate landscape is communicable only as it is interiorized and recreated in spirit.

If we accept Sappho as a great erotic poet, Paul Friedrich suggests, "then her body becomes an icon for a myth of the inner life" (113). What are the contours of the myth seen through this female "body" of language? What is that interior landscape of Lesbos, and how is it present in H.D.'s *Sea Garden*? I would like to evoke Sappho herself, as her poetry—in translation—can render her presence, and to evoke as well H.D.'s Sappho. H.D.'s specific meditation on the Greek poet, recently published as "The Wise Sappho," has great resonance in the world of *Sea Garden*.[6] Here H.D. shows keen awareness of Sappho's poetry, and at the same time sees the Greek poet through the lens of her own alienation from the island and her longing as lover and poet for such a place.

Perhaps the most remarkable quality of Sappho's imagined Lesbos is the "liminality," the threshold quality, of its central mysteries, all of which reflect the goddess Aphrodite whom Sappho both serves and embodies in song.[7] Aphrodite's theophany occurs within mood, in the state of *aphrodite,* an interiorized quality of feeling indistinguishable from the numinous presence of the goddess herself (Friedrich 97, 124). Aphrodite dissolves boundaries between inner and outer, between self and other. In the same way the central values of Sappho's world are at once deeply subjective and radically impersonal (god-given); they represent a deep interiority infusing an outward shape or motion, making it vibrant and golden. The quality of grace, or *charis,* which the goddess and the poet cultivate, is a refined excellence at the center of life, a revelation, through one's whole presence—in movement, speech, action—that one shares in the life of the gods (Friedrich 106-7). A similar quality of exquisiteness *(habrosune)* is the very texture of aphroditic/sapphic vision (Friedrich 122-23). Sappho says in one fragment (Lobel and Page no. 58), "But I love [the exquisite], . . . this, and yearning for the sun has won me Brightness and Beauty" (trans. Nagy 176). This delicacy and refinement, like the quality of grace, is present both in the outward richness of the other and in the vision that endows it with beauty. Aphrodite stands within and between seer and seen, speaker and spoken, giver and given. And the poet through the liminal rite of the poem makes the moment of her theophany a communal event.

One Sapphic fragment especially points to the nature of Aphrodite and to some of the images surrounding her. In fragment LP 2, Sappho summons Aphrodite to come to a sacred grove and participate in ritual festivities in her honor:[8]

> You know the place: then
>
> Leave Crete and come to us
> waiting where the grove is
> pleasantest, by precincts
>
> sacred to you; incense
> smokes on the altar, cold
> streams murmur through the
>
> apple branches, a young
> rose thicket shades the ground
> and quivering leaves pour

down deep sleep; in meadows
where horses have grown sleek
among spring flowers, dill

scents the air. Queen! Cyprian!
Fill our gold cups with love
stirred into clear nectar

Sappho invokes the goddess to leave her island and come to this intimate place; but the sensuous, incantatory poem itself manifests her presence. For both Aphrodite and poetry have each the power of *thelxis,* enchantment, manifest in bodily response (Segal 144). In the erotic charm of the poet's language, Aphrodite enters the body and soul, awakening the motions of desire. The rich and dense fragrance of frankincense mingles with the delicate odors of flowers, and the murmur of cold water through graceful trees blends with the exquisite shadowing of roses. This complex heightening of senses is climaxed, when from quivering leaves—kindled and alive, as are body and vision too—a *koma,* an enchanted sleep, descends. The spell complete, the entranced eyes open to the larger animation of burgeoning spring, to feeding horses, to a meadow of blossoms, through which move refreshing breezes. When Sappho calls, finally, "Queen! Cyprian! / Fill our gold cups with love / stirred into clear nectar," the goddess is with these words no longer latent but suddenly manifest. Having already awakened the suppliant to the fresh yet erotically charged life within her presence, she crowns the moment as Divine Queen. As if among the imperishable gods, she pours out into gold cups immortal nectar mingled with the lucid joy of this consummated mortal rite.

What is this rite, and where does it take place? An altar has been prepared, and perhaps a feast as well, but no one is present; nothing is present except the longing voice of Sappho and the images by which she gives body to longing. This sacred place where the goddess enters is intimate and interior: it is, Thomas McEvilley suggests, "the imagination of the poet, the grove of transformations in which visions are seen and the breaches in reality are healed." Moreover, the "sacred grove" is the poem itself, creating in the reader through the speech of the poet "the trance of paradise" in which the goddess is entertained ("Fragment Two" 332-33).

This poem also suggests a set of images that are central to Sappho's world. One of these is the spatial image of a "private space." Lesbos itself—or Sappho's *thiasos* or group of young girls—is such an insular space, a liminal "island" set apart from ordinary life, within which a ritual passage is experienced.[9] But there are still other distinct spaces within the daily life of the *thiasos,* Eva Stehle Stigers says, such as the "invisible bond or . . . single enclosure, impenetrable by others" wherein two women are united in intimacy. The private space in Sappho's poetry "is a metaphor for emotional openness in a psychological setting apart . . . from everything experienced by a woman in the ordinary course of life" ("Private World" 56-57). These spaces often enclose one another within imagination and memory, as in LP 96, when Sappho in an intimate moment with Atthis comforts her for the loss of a friend, creating the space of the remembered *thiasos* as well as the imagined solitary moment when her separated friend in Lydia now longs for her. Likewise in LP 2, the space of the grove is interiorized to become the space of the longing body and the innermost shrine of the goddess. Through the poems, however, this private space is communal space, the very matter of intimacy celebrated within the *thiasos*.

This "emotional openness" so necessary to the growth of the young woman is also at the basis of two other mysteries: the figure of the bride or *nymphe*, and the image of the flower. These recurring presences point to the paradoxical, threshold quality of Sapphic eroticism, both virginal (cold streams through apple branches, the meadow of spring flowers, fresh breezes) and sensually charged (smoking incense, shadows of roses, quivering leaves, the gold cup waiting to be filled).

The young women on Lesbos are virgins being prepared for marriage. The nuptial moment is a threshold state, and the bride is a figure of passage. For the Greeks, the bride or *nymphe* denotes a woman at the moment of transition from maiden to wife and mother. Aphrodite, who is herself a Bride, guides these women in the refinement of their grace and in the cultivation of desire. The threshold of the bridal moment, sacred to the goddess, represents then a moment of fullness in beauty, of openness to the demands of Eros. That very openness carries intense potency; mythically the bride or nymph is associated with an ambiguous, aphroditic state of delicate yet awesome erotic potential.[10] The name of nymph is also given to the goddesses who inhabit the wild regions of nature. They too are elusive and liminal figures, being, like aspects of elemental nature itself, both inviolate and erotically suggestive.

The flower is a natural image for the young girls of Sappho's Lesbos, for the delicacy and beauty of youth coming to distinct perfection at the moment of opening. The brief time of the opened flower is another liminal moment; and it is the major image attending descriptions of the community of girls surrounding the poet. But in Sappho's poetry—contrasting markedly, as Stigers shows, with a male poet's use of the image—the flower does not represent an incomplete process of development, but rather a specific kind of fullness possible in the *thiasos*, wherein a "maiden's delicate charm" and her "youthful, self-celebrating erotic drive could find expression without compromise of . . . her emotional freshness" ("Retreat from the Male" 92).

That flower and maiden are at the center of Sappho's world points to an obvious lyric preoccupation: loving and witnessing to the ephemeral. These two images represent "that brief moment when the beautiful shines out brilliantly and assumes, for all its perishability, the stature of an eternal condition in the spirit if not in the body" (McEvilley, "Sapphic Imagery" 269). Because

they represent the gracious time of the union of souls in beauty, flowers carry the remembrance of the bonds within the *thiasos* of maidens. In one fragment (LP 94) Sappho recalls her parting words to a woman: "'If you forget me, think / of our gifts to Aphrodite / and all the loveliness that we shared / all the violet tiaras, / braided rosebuds'" (trans. Barnard no. 42). The garlands of flowers are woven times of the animated body, woven graces. Sappho's poems, recalling that unfading beauty in the heart, are themselves such moments, such woven roses (McEvilley, "Sapphic Imagery" 269).

Though H.D. understands fully her distance from this religious and mythic world of Lesbos, she nevertheless claims it in her way. She drew at least as much guidance from her study of Greek lyric poetry as from any contemporary influence or immediate tradition. That she absorbed aspects of craft and conception from these sources seems evident in her early poetry, in the choric voice, in rhythms associated with dance and erotic enchantment; in the figure of the nymph and the image of the flower; and in the image of the marginal space of erotic intimacy. Furthermore, like Sappho's lyrics, the early poems are forcefully ritualistic and liminal, demanding that the reader surrender ordinary orientation and participate in the erotic ordering of the poem. Jean Kammer has seen H.D.'s early poems as resting in a certain poetic mode which, unlike other forms of metaphor, does not move from concrete to abstract, but which rests in juxtaposition and suspension of concrete poetic elements in a configuration. Kammer says that the "absence of a named feeling . . . force[s] us to search for other, less rational entries into the poem." This form of speech turns the metaphoric activity inward, so that "the reader is forced *through* the singular experience of the poem" (158).

H.D.'s poetic affinities with Sappho, however, are more fundamental than any external influences. They rest ultimately, one might say, in the kind of "goddess" they each imagine serving, and in the kind of lyric necessities that service entails. Sappho has Aphrodite at the center, and H.D. a more complex, syncretic figure drawing together qualities of Aphrodite, Artemis, and Athene. It is not so important to name this figure as to recognize her powerful, shaping presence. She insists upon the primacy of Eros as a ground of value and vision, and thus upon the worth of the animated mortal body. She promises within the experience of passion not only suffering but grace and loveliness, and a certain kind of purity and wisdom. This figure compels an ever deepening interiority as the matter of poetic exploration, so that a moment of mood comes to reveal its lucid truth, and the ephemeral becomes the god-given, oracular substance upon which the poetess works. Finally, this goddess by her liminal nature, her movement under and between cultural fixities, bequeaths to the lyricist her paradoxical role as a threshold figure, pointing inward to the truth of intimacy and suggesting withdrawal, while at the same time inviting public celebration.

H.D. in her essay "The Wise Sappho" might be describing this veiled and complex figure who gives sanction and potency to her lyric song. She calls upon the memory of Sappho's creation in a meditation upon the question of poetic and psychic survival. H.D. opens her reflection with the remark of Meleager of Gadara about the poems of Sappho that he gathered in his *Garland:* "'Little, but all roses'" (*Notes* 57). Her whole meditation plays upon this phrase. H.D. at first negates, then qualifies and turns, then finally returns at the end of the essay to affirm his statement. But what accounts for her continuous metamorphic word play? *Not* roses, not *all* roses, not roses *at all;* not flowers—but rocks, island, country, spirit, song (*Notes* 57-58). This rhetorical process is necessary in order for H.D. to articulate the network of association defining for her the nature of Sappho's immortality. In this essay the Greek poet serves as a guide to her in working through what is essentially her own puzzle: what is the durable matter of fragile lyric song, what is the principle of durability within one's openness to the suffering of Eros? In other words, how does the rose survive, how is the rose a rock? One thing is certain: upon Sappho's endurance as the image of woman/poet/lover somehow depends her own.

In "The Wise Sappho" H.D. places herself implicitly in the position of Hellenistic Meleager, who lived, like the modern poet, in a mongrel and graceless age. In the proem to his *Garland,* Meleager says that he has gathered "flowers" from the ancient poets, adding his own, to weave a "garland" for his friends, though "the sweet-speaking garland of the Muses is common possession of all the initiated" (*Palantine Anthology* 4.1 [Paton 1]; my translation). In her work H.D., too, in a sense, gathers those flowers, the woven roses of Sappho and others, transmuted into her own severe poems; and they too are for an implied audience of friends and *mystai,* those within the mysteries of Eros.

But H.D. in this essay seems also to identify herself with Sappho—like the ancient poet she fashions roses with stubborn endurance in time. In that transmission/transmutation of Sappho into a new time, H.D. would not choose roses as the sign of Sapphic power and beauty: "I would bring orange blossoms, implacable flowerings made to seduce the sense when every other means has failed, poignard that glints, fresh sharpened steel: after the red heart, red lilies, impassioned roses are dead" (*Notes* 57). H.D. here reveals her literary place in relation to Sappho: after the "impassioned roses" are dead—after the living poems are lost, after the passionate life they represent is inaccessible—she would offer through her poetry what Sappho's fragments also seem to offer—other "implacable flowerings" that would "seduce the sense," almost through violence, within the extreme numbness of modern life.

Though little remains of Sappho's work, H.D. reflects, it is durable matter: her fragmentary, "broken" poems are not lush roses, not flowers of any color, but rocks, within which "flowers by some chance may grow but

which endure when the staunch blossoms have perished." The fragments, in other words, are a ground, an enduring subtext, for imagination. More durable than individual poems is this rock-world: "Not roses, but an island, a country, a continent, a planet, a world of emotion, differing entirely from any present day imaginable world of emotion" (*Notes* 58).

What are the qualities of Sappho's Lesbos that flourish in imagination? H.D. remembers it in terms of its grace, its ample loveliness. Yet more than this she emphasizes the deep bitterness, "the bitterness of the sweat of Eros," within which Sappho suffered (*Notes* 59-62). That suffering is essential to Sappho's "wisdom"—which H.D. understands not as an abstract, Platonic wisdom, not Greek *sophrosyne* or Christian constancy, but one gained within the nets of devastating feeling (*Notes* 63-64). The wisdom of Sappho's poetry, H.D. suggests, came from "the wind from Asia, heavy with ardent myrrh," but tempered with a Western wind, "bearing in its strength and salt sting" the image of Athene (*Notes* 63). It is, in other words, characterized by its sensuous immediacy, but also by its questing spirit, its penetrating consciousness, its clarity and control. Sappho was "emotionally wise," capable in her simplicity of seeing within the momentary awkward gesture of a girl "the undying spirit of goddess, muse or sacred being." Sappho's wisdom is a concrete, human love which merges "muse and goddess and . . . human woman" in the perception of grace and beauty (*Notes* 64-65).

"Sappho has become for us a name." As a cultural and artistic figure, H.D. finally implies, she is one with her poems and one with the power of her poems: she is "a pseudonym for poignant human feeling, she is indeed rocks set in a blue sea, she is the sea itself, breaking and tortured and torturing, but never broken." She is an island "where the lover of ancient beauty (shipwrecked in the modern world) may yet find foothold and take breath and gain courage" (*Notes* 67). For this reason the puzzle of Sappho's mortal durability is significant—her poetry, rose/rock/island/sea, is the timeless *matter* of ephemeral feeling and ephemeral speech at the basis of lyric expression. In this sense—that Sappho *is* feeling, *is* a rocky island retreat for the lover of beauty—she *is,* I suggest, H.D.'s "sea garden." She is the mythic figure at the ground of H.D.'s world of fragile sea- and rock-roses. She is the goddess who guards it, the sea that washes it, and the spirit informing the poet who suffers her ecstasies within it.

I suggest that *Sea Garden* is a consciously crafted whole, with studied consistency in landscape, voice, and theme. The landscape is a sufficiently constant feature among the poems that we get the sense of a finite place: desolate sandy beach strewn with broken shells, large promontories and rocky headlands; inland, a barren stretch of sparse but hardy vegetation beyond the beach, and low wooded hills nearby; deeper inland, the marshes and places of luxuriant or cultivated growth. The voice in these poems also possesses consistency. All the speakers have a similar tone and intensity, even in poems dealing with specific dramatic situations and appearing to have sometimes male and sometimes female speakers.[11] This voice is similar to that in H.D.'s translations of Euripidean choruses. Though few of the poems speak of "we," the collective voice is suggested; the "I" dissolves within the pervasive sense of generalized suffering and exaltation, like the single voice in the chorus of tragedy. The poems are often addressed to another person or to a god, and, in a few instances, they are simple meditations. But the most representative address, occurring in more than a third of the poems, is the apostrophe, the vocative voice. It seems in part to function as prayer or supplication, summoning presences, as do some of the poems in the *Greek Anthology*. More than this, the apostrophe, as Jonathan Culler points out, serves to create "a detemporalized immediacy, an immediacy of fiction." The "apostrophic" force is central to lyric power, creating "a fictional time in which nothing happens but which is the essence of happening" (152). The voice of these poems, then, is hermaphroditic, collective, and atemporal. The poem is, in a sense, a liminal state without ordinary determinations of gender, person, or tense.[12]

The poems of *Sea Garden* appear to have been selected and arranged quite deliberately. The separate lyrics are not presented in chronological order, though their order is clearly not random. Furthermore, the volume does not represent merely a gathering of H.D.'s already published poems, for many of the best of these—for instance "Oread," "Sitalkas," and "The Pool"—do not appear until her third collection, *Heliodora and Other Poems*. The unity of *Sea Garden* is not immediately apparent; nevertheless the work gives a singleness of affect. It is this affective coherence that first led me to contemplate the possibility of hidden authorial motives.[13]

I find evidence of self-conscious crafting not only in the consistency of landscape and mood but in several details of structuring as well. Similar poems, such as the encounters with gods, the intense dramatic monologues, and especially the five sea-flower poems, are spaced evenly throughout the work, giving the impression of rhythmic or cyclic recurrence of moods and images. Furthermore, there is slight but deliberate progression in the poems depicting times of day (midday, evening, and night), and another, more subtle, progression in the placement of the precincts of the chief gods (the "shrine" at the beginning, the "temple" in the center, the "herm" as a boundary marker at the end). But to perceive the most significant instances of artistic choice in arrangement requires that one grasp the ritual intent of the whole volume: that one enter the sea garden, a world ritually set apart, as an initiate in its mysteries. Seen in this light the volume has a group of three initiatory poems that move us immediately and deeply into the mysteries of the sea garden, and three poems of closure that allow reflection upon the marginal nature of that world and the cultivation of the soul's beauty it allows. Considering first the governing images and themes of the book as a whole, I wish to treat the initiatory poems, others that suggest the character of the sea garden experience, and finally the poems of closure.

The title of the collection points to the governing experience in all its poems. The *garden* is traditionally the place of consummation of love. In H.D.'s poems the garden is still the place of love, but love washed with salt. It is a *sea* garden, inimical to all but the most enduring. The sea represents here the harsh power of elemental life, to which the soul must open itself, and by which it must be transformed or die. H.D. need not have known, but probably did, that sea/salt is the arcane alchemical substance linked to the mysterious bitterness and wisdom essential to spiritual life. "Without salt," it is said, "the work [the alchemical *opus* of transformation] has no success" (Jung par. 329). To experience sea/salt is to be within the visceral elements of bodily life, the "common salts" (Hillman, "Salt" 117). It is to feel open wounds, to suffer desire without fulfillment, to be made aware of vulnerability and fear. More importantly, the psychological experience of salt *specifies* and *clarifies* pain: "No salt, no experiencing—merely a running on and running through of events without psychic body. Thus salt makes events sensed and felt, giving us each a sense of the personal—my tears, my sweat and blood, my taste and value" (Hillman, "Salt" 117). It gives ground and substance to subjectivity, to feeling and desire.

This salt experience and the wisdom and beauty born of it are the central mysteries to which H.D.'s *Sea Garden* allows access. C. G. Jung associates alchemical salt with the sea, thus with Luna and with the "feminine," with Eros and feeling (par. 330). One need not fix its mysterious character in Jung's terms. But nevertheless it is clear that for H.D. these associations—marah ("bitter"), mar, mer, mater, Maia, Mary—to some degree pertain. Indeed, they are at the heart of the network of imagery informing her longer works and centering in the Goddess, who is both hetaira and mother, who is "sea, brine, breaker, seducer, / giver of life, giver of tears" (*CP* 552). Working the mystery of salt, H.D. in *Sea Garden* explores in a deeply interiorized and careful way the very matter of subjectivity.

In the opening three poems we move from an intense, static focus upon a mysterious icon ("Sea Rose"), to a choice for movement and engagement with the sea ("The Helmsman"), and, finally, to a ritual passage of entrance into the sacred mysteries of the sea garden ("The Shrine").

H.D.'s flowers, like Sappho's, represent a moment when a certain poignant beauty takes on "the stature of an eternal condition in the spirit" (McEvilley, "Sapphic Imagery" 269). "Sea Rose" (*CP* 5) immediately reveals to the reader the necessity to *look through* the image to read that eternal condition. The initiate's work begins with learning *clairvoyance*. This "harsh" rose, "marred and with stint of petals, / meagre . . . thin, / sparse of leaf," has no conventional worth, but, marked by the inimical elements, is altogether poor. Yet it is "more precious / than a wet rose / single on a stem." Here the typical standards of beauty are reversed, and in the last stanza the "spice-rose" is deficient for not possessing the "acrid fragrance" of this harsh flower. The relentless elements in action are annihilating ("you are caught in the drift . . . you are flung on the sand"); yet they exalt ("you are lifted / in the crisp sand / that drives in the wind"). The beauty is in the mark of sea-torture.

This movement in the wash of waves, in the near annihilation of elemental power, is repeated in many poems, especially in "Storm" and in the flower poems, which end frequently, as this one does, with an exalted moment, a movement upward—you are caught, flung, *lifted.* In "Sea Lily," too, the flower is "lifted up," though the wind hisses "to cover [it] with froth" (*CP* 14). And in "Storm" a leaf is "broken off . . . hurled out, / *whirls up* and sinks" (*CP* 36; emphasis added). The ecstatic image at the end of "Sea Violet" is even clearer: "Violet / your grasp is frail . . . but you catch the light— / frost, a star edges with its fire" (*CP* 26). This exaltation belongs to a "virginal" ecstasy of salt, to the "fervor of salt" associated, James Hillman suggests, with a psychological desire for purification *through* the impure element of salt, through the intensity of subjective experience ("Salt" 130-36). "Sea Rose" and these other poems reveal the spiritual potency residing in a surrender to the process of "sea-change." The flowers represent, like those of Sappho, a pure openness to life; however, rather than the fresh, natural virgin threshold of the young girls in Lesbos, these show a virginity, an integrity, *achieved* within desire. Moreover, in these key recurring poems the voice itself reveals its radical openness, its own movement in the wash of feeling. The dominant voice in *Sea Garden* comes from within the sea-washed flower.

This first poem in *Sea Garden* gives an image of the soul's sea-torture and the second (*CP* 5-7) calls upon the sea-guide, the steersman, within it: "O be swift— / we have always known you wanted us." The "we" of this poem is one of only a few in the volume, but here as elsewhere it is ambiguous. The intensity of the voice suggests that if it is not a single person speaking as many, it is a group of initiates speaking as one: it is a choric voice. The mystery of "The Helmsman" is in its opening cry. With this we know we are in an ominous yet exuberant territory where knowledge ("we have always known") and desire ("you wanted us") work in inevitable, reciprocal concert. The Helmsman seems to have initiated desire, and the initiate seems to have avoided that call. She has gone inland, "cut off from the wind / and the salt track of the marsh," as she has been enchanted with the tangles, brambles, knotted roots of earth, "the feel of the clefts in the bark, / and the slope between tree and tree" leading her further on. Indeed the greatest part of the poem is the joyous recollection of the adverse path: "we loved all this." But she has returned, for the love of inland places, though rich,

leaves the soul in suspension, a static, becalmed state, while the sea love is connected with motion and impetus:

> But now, our boat climbs—hesitates—drops—
> climbs—hesitates—crawls back—
> climbs—hesitates—
> O be swift—
> we have always known you wanted us.

To the initiate, one who knows she is called to it, the choice for sea experience comes with a mysterious inevitability. For there is never any question that the Helmsman, whom she has always known to want her, will have her. It is only a question of time, until the rich openness to life which his love initiates has run its course, through her growing awareness, back to him. The initiate, caught in desire and knowledge, has no choice. The Helmsman is in a sense like the Greek figure of the personal daimon who is connected with one's character and fate, the invisible presence who steers one toward a destined end.[14] She cannot leave the sea behind, for her experience, even on land, is one of passionate immersion—"we parted green from green . . . we dipped our ankles"—and sharp tactile rhythmic apprehension. Fleeing the sea brings her to it—since the sea that brought her in motion informs her every movement.

If the initial poem opens vision, and the second awakens desire for destined motion, then the third brings holy dread. "The Shrine" (*CP* 7-10) imitates a rite of passage into the sacred place of the goddess. It does not seem to matter precisely who this figure is, whether Artemis or Aphrodite,[15] for to H.D. the two were often fused. The goddess is simply "She [who] watches over the sea," the primary power within this cosmos. Whoever approaches must overcome inward and outward voices of resistance and accept what is then given.

Just as in Sappho's poems, H.D.'s shrine of the goddess is both inside and outside, and the goddess' presence is manifest as the desire for her is more evident. The initiate at first resists the claim of the goddess, assuming the skepticism of the landsmen. Even as she resists, she is drawn inexorably forward, and as she comes nearer her desire increases, even as her awareness of danger grows. Addressing the goddess (present in her shrine on a promontory), the speaker demands for her to reveal herself: is she, or is she not, evil? "Quiet men" seek a secure headland, yet she treacherously gives no shelter from wind and tide, exposing the staggering ships to tumult. The goddess does not answer such profane questions. Still in turmoil, the initiate suddenly remembers the goddess, as though she were indeed intimate with her, and only now after long exile were returning to her:

> You are not forgot,
> O plunder of lilies,
> honey is not more sweet
> than the salt stretch of your beach.

The goddess embodies the sweetness of salt, the sensual ecstasy (plunder) of the inviolate (lilies). These qualities, uniting bodily and spiritual desire, are essential within the sea garden. That desire *is* the goddess, and *is* the ritual experience of her power.

Approaching the shrine, the initiate feels the goddess' paradoxically destructive and creative brilliance, both "sparks that unknot the flesh" and "splendour athwart our eyes." After this terrible ascent of the initiate to her precincts, however, the goddess reveals herself in her deep sympathy and tenderness. For all her terribleness, she has "touched us":

> your eyes have pardoned our faults,
> your hands have touched us—
> you have leaned forward a little
> and the waves can never thrust us back
> from the splendour of your ragged coast.

Opened to the initiate as she enters the sacred space of the shrine is the revelation of the goddess as only those know who have seen her. It is the image of a mother, intimate and tender, who leans to join herself with her suppliant. The speaker's choice to serve the "splendour of [the] ragged coast" embodies the desire within the whole of this volume; it is analogous to the poet's resolution to write *Sea Garden,* to serve her austere and dangerous calling. This passage to the shrine represents in other terms the longing of the soul to meet the familiar "maternal or sororal" face at its center, to join oneself to oneself.

The quest underlying the poems of *Sea Garden* entails acceptance of one's given destiny and responsiveness to the sacred presences that appear to shape and guide. For the initiate who speaks in these poems, a governing destiny compels the endurance of distinct intensities. We might speak of different aspects of erotic suffering within *Sea Garden* in terms of distinct figures, all of which converge in the choric voice of the initiate: the lover, in ecstasy within the suffering of external bondage or necessity; the nymph, in her experience of wild spirits; the poet, in her endurance of the process of creation; and the seer, in her surrender to her clairvoyant gift.

The three poems speaking through the figure of the lover—"Acon," "Prisoners," and "Loss"—are alike in one respect: they each show human desire as it becomes transmuted within the experience of death; and the clear image of the beloved crystallizes within the suffering of harsh necessity. In "Acon" the lover, with the image of his dying Hyella, "whom no god pities," gathers flowers and calls upon nymphs to bear them to her, for "The light of her face falls from its flower, / as a hyacinth . . . perishes upon burnt grass" (*CP* 32). In "Loss" the lover, himself about to die, remembers his perished comrade and imagines the beauty of his cleansed, sea-washed body: "your white flesh covered with salt / as with myrrh and burnt iris" (*CP* 22). And in "Prisoners" the lovers incarcerated, crushed by fate, have distilled their desire; the speaker at the moment of going to his death recalls how his lover once picked up a flower: "and it flamed, the leaf and shoot / and the threads, yellow,

yellow— / sheer till they burnt / to red-purple" (*CP* 35). These are extreme instances of love, yet they share the same essential code as "Sea Rose"—the torture and transfiguration of the soul within the suffering of elemental salt.

The group of poems exploring the figure of the nymph—"Pursuit," "The Wind Sleepers," "Huntress," and "Sea Gods"—are remarkable in sharing a certain puzzling ambiguity: for in them it is difficult to distinguish the god from natural effects. These poems ask for our participation in a moment in which wildness dissolves the boundaries between human and nonhuman, or in which a wild domain is reinhabited by its gods through the summoning of the poem. "Pursuit" and "Huntress" share the same landscape of woodlands, the same action of the hunt. In the first a frenzied lover pursues someone through the land, someone, however, who is never visible except in the signs of violence, the crushing of flowers and snapping of branches, left in his/her track. The lover reads in these signs evidence of desperate flight, but when the trail simply ends he/she imagines that a "wood-daemon" has saved the fleeing figure (*CP* 12). The drama here is simply the speaker's merging with the wildness of another creature, who, whether human, animal, or spirit, is absorbed into the element of nature, like a dryad into a tree. The "Huntress" too, whether god or human, is the very spirit of wind, of animal instinct and abandon; and the speaker here is one of a band like Artemisian nymphs or Dionysian Maenads, merged with the nature of their god (*CP* 24).

In the other two poems of the nymph—"The Wind Sleepers" and "Sea Gods"—the nature of our participation is more complex. Here the sea-presences in wind and wave have lost their power: the wind sleepers, unable to endure the wind, have retreated into the city walls; the sea gods, now mangled and broken by the sea, are "no stronger than the strips of sand / along your ragged beach" (*CP* 30). This is to say that the gods are overwhelmed by their own elements: gods of wind and sea succumb to the *mere* (literal) wind and sea. The recovery of the elemental gods from this naturalistic oblivion is through a conjuration, a summoning of song. For the wind sleepers one must "pour meted words / of sea-hawks and gulls / and sea-birds that cry / discords" (*CP* 15): one must imitate the animated life of the sea air. For the sea gods, however, the nymph conjures through the offering of masses of violets, hoping that "you will answer our taut hearts, / you will break the lie of men's thoughts, / and cherish and shelter us" (*CP* 31). The violets serve in this summoning because their brilliant and lovely colors return to the sea its delicate animation, and because they show the "taut hearts" of those open to the presence of the gods.

The figure of the poet, too, has distinct encounters, which take place in the "private space" of imagination, the cultivated garden or orchard. Within the "sea garden" itself are two other gardens, both of which taken together define clearly the exigencies of creation in this marginal world. In "Sheltered Garden" (*CP* 19-21), the speaker is within a place containing masses of perfect fragrant flowers (pure "essences"); it is enclosed and tranquil. Yet this kind of beauty inspires, in the speaker, the panic of suffocation ("I have had enough. / I gasp for breath"), and entrapment ("Every way ends, every road, / every foot-path leads at last / to the hill-crest"). She desires a sharp astringent aroma, a "scent of resin" or a "taste of bark," and exposure to wind and cold: "For this beauty, / beauty without strength, / chokes out life." Finally she wishes to destroy the garden ("I want wind to break, / scatter . . . snap off . . . fling . . . leave half-trees, torn, twisted"). A strange instinct conceives of the need for extreme change:

> O to blot out this garden
> to forget, to find a new beauty
> in some terrible
> wind-tortured place.

The soul needs terribleness (awe, intensity, excess) and torture (tension, strife) in order to possess vitality or to achieve its distinctive beauty. Where these are not present, as in a sheltered garden, the soul is threatened with death and responds desperately with a desire for violence.

"Garden" (*CP* 24-25), a poem in two parts, does not describe a place antithetical to life and creation but one essential to it. In a sense it defines the "aesthetic" of creative apprehension and suffering within the sea garden. In the first part of the poem, a rose is again an image of beauty, but here it carries a sense of power as the untouchable, inaccessible thing that the poet desires, like the adamantine "rock roses" in H.D.'s essay on Sappho: "You are clear / O rose, cut in rock, / hard as the descent of hail." The rose "cut in rock" (growing in the crevice of a rock, or made precise by the background of rock) is clear and "hard as the descent of hail" (sharp, cold, relentless). The austerity and clarity of the image is compelling, and the speaker is drawn to its force. She imagines what she "could" do, what her power could be before this image, with increasingly conditional claims, until she admits her powerlessness before it. She "could scrape the colour / from the petals," seize the image directly and violently, but to do so would destroy and denature the rose; to do so would be to have it only as "spilt dye from a rock." The speaker cannot possess the rose, and cannot break its crystal, because this would involve superhuman strength ("If I could break you / I could break a tree"). She ends with the strange conditional statement: "If I could stir / I could break a tree— / I could break you." Before the image of the rose she cannot even stir; so much less can she break a tree, or, indeed, assert her mastery at all.

In this poem the rose is *image,* the object of the poet's desire; yet she cannot touch or possess it, cannot shatter its ice, but only witness to its radiance. Thus the poem dramatizes the aesthetic of H.D.'s early work: poetry is the evocation and reenactment of the experienced power

of the image. The knowledge of her weakness before the image is a refined salt experience—the consciousness of longing in the presence of a beautiful but unyielding object. A similar though more satisfying longing is shown in "The Contest" (*CP* 12), where the human athlete also represents the image—but here one that is humanly crafted. As image, the male figure is highly liminal; his aspects of grace and power, as experienced by the poet, reside between nature and human artifice. This image has the "rare silver" of a resolved epiphany.

The second part of "Garden" is the familiar poem "Heat." It is tied to the first enigmatic part by the common theme of longing within the process of creation, and by the sense of stasis and need for release. In both poems, too, the endurance of the moment is part of the necessary process of insight and making. The speaker asks the wind to "rend open the heat," cut it, plough through it, so that ripe fruit can drop. The heat is a palpable force that "presses up and blunts / the points of pears." In this imagined oppression of unbearable pregnancy she prays for a deliverance from the process of gestation and ripening, though even her own metaphor acknowledges that without the force of heat the growing and ripening fruit would not assume its proper shape. Thus in this essential garden both poems speak of salt suffering in terms of creative process, within which it is hard to bear attention to the potency of specific image and to be patient in the heated forging of the destined shape. The poem "Orchard," too, extends the image of the cultivated place of creation. It seems, in a sense, to continue the agony of creation: the pears are ripe, the bees are animated, but the poet cannot bear "the beauty / of fruit trees" (*CP* 28). They signify a fruition difficult to embrace, unless she acknowledge the elemental power who governs the process of natural growth.

The voice of the seer in the sea garden has a different agony than that of others. She must endure the revelations that the strange light of the sea garden gives, and these are not always without their terror and danger. A group of poems, "Mid-day," "Evening," and "Night," shows a procession in the light of the day, and the seer's intense awareness makes these passages difficult. The too-brilliant noon exacerbates the mind and dissipates the body, and the speaker longs for the deep-rooted, shady poplar on the hill (*CP* 10). In the more liminal light of evening body and soul are awake and clairvoyant. Yet in "Evening" that intense consciousness brings a vision of the obliteration of identity, as gradually when night comes the shadows fold flower and bud and grass stem in upon themselves until everything is lost, moving inward to obscurity (*CP* 18-19). The intensity of clairvoyance, strangely, brings one close to death. In "Night" (*CP* 33) the relentless darkness that takes apart, undoes, the petals is the inexorable force of dissolution leading to death, connected with the mechanism of linear time. After the rose is finally disintegrated by night, the "stark core" is left to perish—an image not only of mortality but of the loneliness of a being held in a dead absence within time.

Two other poems deal with the seer's clairvoyance in a particular way: one of these, "The Gift," shows a woman coming to understand the necessities that her visionary "gift" demands; another, "The Cliff Temple," shows the longing of a woman for the god of light. The woman in "The Gift" (*CP* 15-18) suffers from her clairvoyance, finding that like a curse it brings isolation and confusion to her attempt to love another. In this intensely rendered address, the seer/poet, shaken by an intimate encounter with a woman she loves, offers her the "gift" of this poem. This gift honors the woman, yet while doing so it shows the necessity of the seer's withdrawal. Just as in "Sheltered Garden," so here too the beauty of the woman, her luxuriant garden, her rich loving, are too much to bear: "The house, too, was like this, / over painted, over lovely." Yet the unendurable quality of the woman's beauty, it is important to notice, comes from her unreflective and careless regard for it: having so much, her beauty means too little. She is innocent: "The world is yet unspoiled for you, / you wait, expectant," as children wait for random, insignificant favors to fall to them.

To the seer, however, beauty is so potent and portentous that it puts her in danger. "Sleepless nights, / I remember the initiates, / their gesture, their calm glance," she explains, but though she lives as these *mystai,* she lives without the containment of a ritual. She yearns for another life, where beauty does not "crowd / madness upon madness," where "a still place," the barren seascape, would allow peace. The seer intuits that in that "still place" "some hideousness" is necessary in order "to stamp beauty, / a mark . . . on our hearts." Beauty, visionary beauty, must be brought to the body and felt by its deep impression. The speaker's gift to the woman expresses the nature of her pain; it lies in her "gift" of vision, which demands retreat, austerity, and care.

"The Cliff Temple" (*CP* 26-28) renders the sometimes precipitous passion within the seer's dedication to the god of light. The god of the temple seems to be both Apollo, who had a cliff shrine on the Greek island Leukas, and the sun god Helios. Just as H.D. conflates Aphrodite and Artemis, so she sees these gods as one. As in "The Shrine," here too the supplicant summons the god through her own desire, invoking first the distant heights themselves—the high rock pillar—which somehow *is* the god; and, doing so, she is suddenly *with* the god. In this poem the god's temple, the "Great, bright portal, / shelf of rock . . . clean cut, white against white," has about it that clarity and perfection of form (as in "O rose, cut in rock") associated with Apollo. At this height "next to the sky" one experiences the sense of sublimity, distance, removal from strife ("the terrible breakers are silent / from this place"), aspects of Apollo's nature. Yet the place carries its own tumult—the wind "booms" and "thunders," as though one with the violent breath of the god. The aspiration for the sanctum of Apollo is for lucid vision, oracular power, and, aesthetically, for measure and formal control.

But the sky temple seems an image as well of the Gate of the Sun—"you lift, you are the world-edge, / pillar for the sky-arch"—through which Helios passes. Helios, as distinct from Apollo, has an erotic aspect, as well as vibrancy and immediacy. The seer, while sensing the peace of the place, is also frenzied in pursuit of the elusive god—"for ever and for ever, must I follow you / through the stones? . . . I wondered at you . . . dear—mysterious—beautiful." The madness of loving the sun was known to Aphrodite, who threw herself from the White Rock of Leukas for love of Phaethon, son of Helios; and also to Sappho, who jumped from the same rock in a related story, and who says of herself that "yearning for the sun has won me Brightness and Beauty."[16] The speaker of this poem, like Aphrodite and Sappho, so longs for the unattainable lover that she also asks, "Shall I hurl myself from here, / shall I leap and be nearer you?" But unlike the goddess of "The Shrine," this power never welcomes, but only beckons, ever beyond and upward. The experience of the ascent to the heights, then, is clear vision, sublimity, and quiet, yet also an agonized erotic possession. The allusion here to the fall from the White Rock of Leukas points to the hidden danger within clairvoyant ecstasy, in part explaining the sinister quality that may accompany the seer's gift: the visionary and erotic intoxication has a deathly counterpoint—the plunge into salty depths.

The closing poems of *Sea Garden* establish a complex passage out of this marginal world, marking its boundaries ("Hermes of the Ways"), affirming its splendid illusion ("Pear Tree"), and framing it in relation to the modern world ("Cities"). This passage of closure brings us again, as with "The Shrine," to a god who can lead one at this threshold; and to a clairvoyant image, like that in "Sea Rose," iconic of the soul's state. It adds, however, as a way to define the necessity for the garden, a vision of a world in which spirit and beauty can live only as they are marginal and sequestered.

"Hermes of the Ways" (*CP* 37-39) speaks of the god of the crossroads, who stands at boundaries. His power is important in seeing the "marginal" nature of the "sea garden." Hermes marks the boundary to this world, standing in the place of the "sea garden" itself, the place of severe exposure between the sea and land where wind, water, and sand buffet and score the "sea" flowers. At this very edge one meets "him / of the triple path-ways, / Hermes, / who awaits." This god attends souls at such thresholds, "Dubious, / facing three ways, / welcoming wayfarers." He stands with the sea orchard to the west, the sea wind approaching from the east, and the great dunes before him. This is the *cosmos* of *Sea Garden* in miniature, the place between the terrible sea and the "poplar-shaded hill." There the twisted trees produce hard and small fruit, "too late ripened / by a desperate sun / that struggles through sea-mist." Here Hermes waits to welcome those who enter this place "where sea-grass tangles with / shore-grass." Only to those journeying, in process of change, he allows his power, giving not certainty but only steadiness and patience.

"Pear Tree" (*CP* 39) follows "Hermes of the Ways" and precedes the last poem, "Cities." If I am justified in seeing the selection and placement of the poems as deliberate, reflecting a ritual awareness on the poet's part, then "Pear Tree" is somewhat puzzling. In the whole of the volume there is no other such unqualified beauty or such unqualified ecstasy as we find here. This image seems in some sense outside the ordeal of the sea garden. And indeed it is outside—past the boundaries marked by the god of thresholds. I suggest that in terms of *Sea Garden* the pear tree becomes an image of the soul's completion or fullness, an image of the transformed soul, as well as an image of the poetic illusion, the transforming artifice, of *Sea Garden* itself.

Some of these possible meanings reside in part in the white/silver images of the poem. The tree is "Silver dust / lifted from the earth." Its white flowers open, parting "silver / from . . . rare silver." It floats like a body of air, or like the bright moon; yet it is air with substance: "you front us with great mass." In the alchemical language of transformation, silver represents a high moment of fulfillment: it is the recovery of the "second whiteness," of innocence and virginity, at the culmination of a tortuous and intense process; it is the full light of the moon, wherein soul and imagination are solidly realized; and finally white/silver is a state-between, a liminal state, often referred to as bride, dawn, or dove (Hillman, "Silver [One]" 22-24; "Silver [Two]" 21). These occult senses seem coincident with the images and themes of *Sea Garden* and appropriate to the joyous moment rendered in the poem. As a spiritual image, the blossoms of the pear, like other flowers in the sea garden, carry the paradox of virginity: white and inviolate, yet with purple at the heart. Moreover, this brilliant flowering of white and silver has issue as part of a generative process: the flowers "bring summer and ripe fruits / in their purple hearts." The blossoming pear tree is a new beginning after the arduous process of fertility and growth shown in the sea garden.

In another occult sense white/silver is essentially associated with the imagination: silver is the moon's "subtle air body," nourishing the soul with the "continual generation of images" (Hillman, "Silver [One]" 24). The pear tree, like the moon's air body, is the poetic illusion itself. It is a seeming that is real: it is dust, yet it is a "great mass"; it hardly occupies space, yet it fills space brilliantly. On another level the tree, like the rose cut in rock, represents the awesomeness, the otherness, belonging to the *image*; yet here that power seems miraculous, rather than inexorable. This poem serves to mark the completion of the ritual of the sea garden with pleasure, aspiration, and hope.

The last work, "Cities" (*CP* 39-42), breaks dramatically with the preceding ones in subject and tone. Its placement at the end of the volume is deliberate, serving as a kind of epilogue to speak of the nature of the poetic work that it completes. It recalls the context of the disfigured modern city in terms of which the marginal world of the "sea garden" takes on vital significance. The city *necessitates* the sea garden, a place of seclusion where intense desire is felt; and its hideousness focuses the value, the "rare gold," of recollected beauty. We are told that those who serve the old splendor of cities in the context of the swarming squalor of the new city are given their animation through the still vital "*spirits, not ghosts*" that people the city: "*their breath was your gift, / their beauty, your life.*" This concluding poem of the book tells us what we have experienced in the sea garden, a place distinct from, yet within, the city—like old cells of honey in a new hive—where beauty is remembered. It also presents explicitly the figure of a guardian and speaker—the voice in the poems of *Sea Garden*—who is given the gift of utterance through the breath of spirits, ancient *daimones*. In this context the sea garden is a sacred place where the ever-present voices are entertained, where the work of spirit, marginal yet essential to life, can continue.

Sappho's "emotional wisdom," as H.D. saw it, rested in her capacity to love and to transfigure the mortal gesture within the lucid, uncompromising light of imagination. Such wisdom, too, H.D. possesses. In *Sea Garden* Sappho is "She [who] watches over the sea," moving one inward to her severe salt domain. H.D., serving this mortal Muse, makes of the ephemeral rose the durable substance of rock. Like Meleager she shapes and gives a "sweet-speaking garland" to initiates who wish experience of the common mysteries.

NOTES

[1] See, for example, the discussion of Dickinson in Gilbert and Gubar 582-86ff. An extended treatment of the self-limiting postures of female poets is that of Walker.

[2] Gilbert and Gubar (539-49ff.) persuasively argue such a position.

[3] Two thoughtful developmental readings of the early poetry are those of Friedman in *Psyche Reborn* 3-10; and Ostriker 30-33.

[4] The essay of Duncan from which I here draw is a rich meditation on the nature of the genius and the muse; I have attempted not to distort his thought in converting it into linear argument.

[5] Two critics, Gubar (46-47, 53) and Grahn (5-8), make this point in their studies of Sappho as a source of poetic and religious authority for H.D. and other women—especially lesbian—writers.

[6] The manuscript from which "The Wise Sappho" was taken is not precisely dated. I do not claim, then, that H.D.'s essay directly informs *Sea Garden*—the case may indeed be the reverse—but that both come from the same imagination of the island experience, of which Lesbos was a configuration.

[7] My understanding of Aphrodite and of the liminal qualities of Sappho's world has been greatly shaped by Friedrich, especially chs. 5 and 6.

[8] In the major points of my interpretation of this poem I am indebted to McEvilley, "Sappho, Fragment Two."

Because of its grace, and not because of its literal accuracy, I quote here the version of Barnard. Here is my own literal rendering of the fragment: Come from Crete, for my sake, to this holy temple, where is the lovely grove of apple-trees, and where altars are smoking with frankincense; therein cold water murmurs through apple branches, and the space is all shaded over with roses, and from quivering leaves an enchanted sleep descends; therein a meadow where horses feed has blossomed with spring flowers, and soothing breezes blow . . . there. . . . Cypris, pour gracefully in golden cups nectar mingled with these festivities.

[9] For a discussion of rites of passage see Turner 94ff.

[10] Two important elaborations of the significance of the *nymphe* are those of Winkler 77-78; and Detienne 102-3.

[11] Ostriker (30) notes the androgyny of the speaker.

[12] See Turner (96, 102-3, 106) for discussion of timelessness, anonymity, and sexlessness in liminal states.

[13] Fraistat (4-21) discusses the dynamics of reading a collection as a single work. See as well Rosenthal and Gall, who, in making a case for the "poetic sequence" as a modern genre, give brief notice to *Sea Garden* (477-78).

[14] See Dodds (42ff.) for a discussion of the individual daimon.

[15] Swann (30) claims that the poem refers to the shrine of Artemis at Leukas. But Aphrodite too was known as guardian of seafarers, and H.D. would have known a poem in the *Palantine Anthology* by Anyte (9.144 [Paton 3]) speaking of a sea shrine of Aphrodite.

[16] See Nagy's essay exploring the connection of Sappho and Aphrodite with the sun-god and the White Rock of Leukas. This is his translation of Sappho's fragment (176).

WORKS CITED

Bogan, Louise. "The Heart and the Lyre." *A Poet's Alphabet: Reflections on the Literary Art and Vocation.* Ed. Robert Phelps and Ruth Limmer. New York: McGraw, 1970. 424-29.

———. *What the Woman Lived: Selected Letters of Louise Bogan 1920-1970.* Ed. Ruth Limmer. New York: Harcourt, 1973.

Carruthers, Mary J. "The Re-Vision of the Muse: Adrienne Rich, Audre Lorde, Judy Grahn, Olga Broumas." *Hudson Review* 36 (1983): 293-322.

Culler, Jonathan. "Apostrophe." *The Pursuit of Signs: Semiotics, Literature, Deconstruction.* Ithaca, N.Y.: Cornell UP, 1981. 135-54.

Detienne, Marcel. "The Myth of 'Honeyed Orpheus.'" *Myth, Religion and Society: Structuralist Essays by M. Detienne, L. Gernet, J. P. Vernant and P. Vidal-Naquet.* Ed. R. L. Gordon. Cambridge: Cambridge UP; Paris: Editions de la maison des sciences de l'homme, 1981. 95-109.

Diehl, Joanne Feit. "'Come Slowly—Eden': An Exploration of Women Poets and Their Muse." *Signs* 3 (1978): 572-87.

Dodds, E. R. *The Greeks and the Irrational.* Berkeley: U of California P, 1951.

Doolittle, Hilda (H.D.). *H.D.: Collected Poems 1912-1944.* Ed. Louis L. Martz. New York: New Directions, 1983.

———. *Notes on Thought and Vision & The Wise Sappho.* San Francisco: City Lights Books, 1982.

Duncan, Robert. "The H.D. Book Part Two: Nights and Days Chapter 9." *Chicago Review* 30.3 (1979): 37-88.

DuPlessis, Rachel Blau. "Family, Sexes, Psyche: An Essay on H.D. and the Muse of the Woman Writer." *Montemora* 6 (1979): 137-56.

Fraistat, Neil. *The Poem and the Book: Interpreting Collections of Romantic Poetry.* Chapel Hill: U of North Carolina P, 1985.

Friedman, Susan Stanford. *Psyche Reborn: The Emergence of H.D.* Bloomington: Indiana UP, 1981.

———. "Who Buried H.D.? A Poet, Her Critics, and Her Place in 'The Literary Tradition.'" *College English* 36 (1975): 801-14.

Friedrich, Paul. *The Meaning of Aphrodite.* Chicago: U of Chicago P, 1978.

Gilbert, Sandra M., and Susan Gubar. *The Madwoman in the Attic: The Woman Writer and the Nineteenth-Century Literary Imagination.* New Haven: Yale UP, 1979.

Grahn, Judy. *The Highest Apple: Sappho and the Lesbian Poetic Tradition.* San Francisco: Spinsters, Ink, 1985.

Gubar, Susan. "Sapphistries." *Signs* 10 (1984): 43-62.

Hillman, James. "Salt: A Chapter in Alchemical Psychology." *Images of the Untouched: Virginity in Psyche, Myth and Community.* Ed. Joanne Stroud and Gail Thomas. Dallas: Spring, 1982. 111-37.

———. "Silver and the White Earth (Part One)," *Spring: An Annual of Archetypal Psychology and Jungian Thought* (1980): 21-48.

———. "Silver and the White Earth (Part Two)," *Spring: An Annual of Archetypal Psychology and Jungian Thought* (1981): 21-66.

Jung, C. G. *Mysterium Coniunctionis: An Inquiry into the Separation and Synthesis of Psychic Opposites in Alchemy.* Trans. R. F. C. Hull. 2nd ed. New York: Princeton UP, 1970. Vol. 14 of *The Collected Works of C. G. Jung.* Ed. William McGuire, et al. Bollingen Series 20. 20 vols. 1953-1979.

Kammer, Jean. "The Art of Silence and the Forms of Women's Poetry." *Shakespeare's Sisters: Feminist Essays on Women Poets.* Ed. Sandra M. Gilbert and Susan Gubar. Bloomington: Indiana UP, 1979. 153-64.

Lobel, Edgar, and Denys Page, eds. *Poetarum Lesbiorum Fragmenta.* 1955. Oxford: Clarendon-Oxford UP, 1968.

McEvilley, Thomas. "Sapphic Imagery and Fragment 96." *Hermes* 101 (1973): 257-78.

———. "Sappho, Fragment Two." *Phoenix* 26 (1972): 323-33.

Nagy, Gregory. "Phaethon, Sappho's Phaon, and the White Rock of Leukas." *Harvard Studies in Classical Philology* 77 (1973): 137-77.

Ostriker, Alicia. "The Poet as Heroine: Learning to Read H.D." *American Poetry Review* 12.2 (1983): 29-38.

Paton, W. R., ed. *The Greek Anthology.* 5 vols. 1916. Loeb Classical Library. Cambridge, Mass.: Harvard UP; London: William Heinemann, 1969.

Plath, Sylvia. *The Journals of Sylvia Plath.* Ed. Frances McCullough and Ted Hughes. New York: Dial, 1982.

Pound, Ezra. *The Letters of Ezra Pound 1907-1941.* Ed. D. D. Paige. New York: Harcourt, 1950.

Rich, Adrienne. *On Lies, Secrets, and Silence: Selected Prose 1966-1978.* New York: Norton, 1979.

Roethke, Theodore. "The Poetry of Louise Bogan." *On the Poet and His Craft: Selected Prose of Theodore Roethke,* ed. Ralph J. Mills, Jr. Seattle: U of Washington P, 1965. 133-48.

Rosenthal, M. L., and Sally M. Gall. *The Modern Poetic Sequence: The Genius of Modern Poetry.* Oxford: Oxford UP, 1983.

Sappho. Trans. Mary Barnard. Berkeley: U of California P, 1958.

Segal, Charles. "Eros and Incantation: Sappho and Oral Poetry." *Arethusa* 7.2 (1974): 139-60.

Sexton, Anne. *Anne Sexton: A Self-Portrait in Letters.* Ed. Linda Gray Sexton and Lois Ames. Boston: Houghton, 1977.

Stigers, Eva Stehle. "Retreat from the Male: Catullus 62 and Sappho's Erotic Flowers." *Ramus* 6.2 (1977): 83-102.

———. "Sappho's Private World." *Reflections of Women in Antiquity.* Ed. Helene P. Foley. New York: Gordon and Breach Science, 1981. 45-61.

Swann, Thomas Burnett. *The Classical World of H.D.* Lincoln: U of Nebraska P, 1962.

Turner, Victor. *The Ritual Process: Structure and Anti-Structure.* 1969. Symbol, Myth, and Ritual Series. Ithaca, N.Y.: Cornell Paperbacks-Cornell UP, 1977.

Walker, Cheryl. *The Nightingale's Burden: Women Poets and American Culture before 1900.* Bloomington: Indiana UP, 1982.

Winkler, Jack. "Gardens of Nymphs: Public and Private in Sappho's Lyrics." *Reflections of Women in Antiquity.* Ed. Helene P. Foley. New York: Gordon and Breach Science, 1981. 63-89.

Robin Riley Fast

SOURCE: "Moore, Bishop, and Oliver: Thinking Back, Re-Seeing the Sea," in *Twentieth Century Literature,* Vol. 39, No. 3, Fall, 1993, pp. 364-79.

[*In the following essay, Fast uses images of the sea offered in the poems of Marianne Moore, Elizabeth Bishop, and Mary Oliver to demonstrate that the literary influence of women writers upon one another differs from that of their male counterparts.*]

Several poems by Marianne Moore, Elizabeth Bishop, and Mary Oliver offer an extended and illuminating example of what it might mean, in Virginia Woolf's phrase, for women writers to "think back through our mothers" (79), or, in Alicia Ostriker's terms, to "re-think ourselves by re-thinking them" (475). The friendship of Moore and Bishop is well documented.[1] Although there exists to date no definitive, explicit evidence of connection between Oliver and either Bishop or Moore, a deep responsiveness to Bishop's work, and through it, to Moore's, resonates from many of Oliver's poems. Thus "Mussels" and "The Fish," from *Twelve Moons,* and "The Fish," from *American Primitive,* recall Bishop's "The Fish"; "Postcard from Flamingo," from *American Primitive,* and "At Loxahatchie," in *Dream Work,* recall Bishop's "Florida." Further, the recurring, clear indications in her poetry that Oliver conceives of her own poetic voice as a woman's voice invite us to look at her work in relation to that of other women writers.[2]

Questioning the appropriateness to women of the Bloomian model of influence as the son's struggle against his poetic fathers, some feminist critics have proposed an alternative paradigm as describing the relationships more common between women writers and their female predecessors. This paradigm essentially thinks back through Woolf's observation that "we think back through our mothers": it describes the younger writer as seeking out her poetic mothers, whose example and works nurture and support her, and whom she affirms in her own work. Betsy Erkkila, while acknowledging the presence of ambivalence in such relationships, argues that "there is a primary sense of identification and mutuality between women poets that sets them apart from the more agonistic relationship between precursor and ephebe in the Bloomian model" (335). Erkkila uses this paradigm to examine, in Bishop's poetry, a pattern of seeking a powerful woman figure and a "matrilineal heritage," both associated for Bishop with Marianne Moore. In the poems by Moore, Bishop, and Oliver that I have chosen to discuss we can see the poet answering her forebears or inviting her successors. Including Oliver in this family of women allows us to consider how a poet of a new generation might enter (adopt herself into?) and hence enlarge the circle of influence.

Two of the poems I will consider here, Moore's "A Grave" and Bishop's "At the Fishhouses," have received much critical comment but have not been considered in relation to each other. The absence of such a discussion is surprising. "A Grave" is often thought of as uncharacteristic of Moore's poetry; it is also a poem that Bishop identified late in her career as one of her favorites.[3] These facts, together with Moore's unquestioned influence on Bishop, and the equally unquestioned and important differences between the two poets' work, demand that we inquire where Bishop's high regard for her friend's atypical poem might be evident in her own poetry. Once we inquire, "At the Fishhouses" reveals parallels and differences that suggest the poem is a meditation on and a response to Moore's. Similarly, through parallels and divergences, and in the context of an apparent responsiveness to Bishop's work, Oliver's "Sunday Morning, High Tide," "The Sea," "The Swimmer," and "The Waves" seem to carry on a familiar conversation with "At the Fishhouses" and, through Bishop's poem, to think back to "A Grave." In the process Oliver deepens her conception of the self's relation to nature and suggests new perceptions of Moore's and Bishop's seas.

One could think of these poems as representing two parallel movements—from Moore's apparently genderless to Oliver's overtly gendered response to nature, with Bishop, between them, more or less covertly identifying her voice as a woman's, and from Moore's depiction of the sea as genderless to Oliver's identification of it as

female, with Bishop again playing somewhat ambivalently upon a middle ground. Though one might wish to define such movements as constituting a progression, such a reading seems to be at odds with the tones and effects of Oliver's and Bishop's "thinking back." For as Bishop looks back to Moore, and Oliver to Bishop and Moore, each writer, meditating on the meanings of immersion, contests and re-imagines both her predecessor's sea and her own. Thus the processes of the poets' and their poems' interactions are better thought of not as linear and progressive, but rather as circular and recursive, a "shape" or conception that seems consistent, too, with the paradigm of relationships among women writers proposed by Ostriker, Erkkila, and others.[4]

In "At the Fishhouses" Bishop draws attention to a powerful ambivalence of desire and dread that Moore, at most, may subtly adumbrate under the surfaces of "A Grave," a poem more given to indignation at human failing and assertions of nature's complicity in our mortality. Oliver's poems, moved by a daring born of dynamic autonomy, adopt and revise Bishop's and Moore's perceptions. But Oliver's role in this conversation is not to displace or drown out her predecessors' voices; rather it is deeply to engage Moore's and Bishop's perceptions, to illuminate their depths with her clarity, and to immerse herself in all the possibilities that their poems—and the sea—offer.

Moore's "A Grave" (*Complete Poems* 49; first published in *Observations*, 1924) addresses a man who has blocked the speaker's view of the sea; the poem punishes his presumptuousness with the certainty that, far from being subject to his appropriation, the sea will eventually overwhelm him, in death. We are never shown the view the man has blocked and the speaker has lost. Instead the sea is characterized as deceptive, perhaps malevolently so, inexorably advancing, unmoved by the lives that sink within it. The speaker is aggrieved, perhaps vindictive; she attempts to wrest "ownership" of the sea from him by insisting upon her superior knowledge. But the facts that she understands will doom him will ultimately overwhelm her too, so, ironically, she must implicitly admit the limits of her own will and knowledge ("volition" and "consciousness"), her own inclusion in the universal certainties she proclaims.

The poem's emphasis on our inevitable immersion in death is reinforced by its impersonal quality and the nature of its actions. Though a speaking presence is evident in the poem's insistent denials, it admits no personal identity: the man's presumption affronts not "me" but "those who have as much right"; never does a first-person pronoun even appear. Further, the offending man's presence is grammatically effaced, as "you" disappears after the tenth line and the sea takes over, semantically as well as thematically. Correspondingly, human actions—looking, taking, and fleeing—are undermined by denials of all kinds (for example, "you cannot stand," "whose expression is no longer a protest," "unconscious"), and all evidence of human presence, let alone volition or consciousness, is submerged as the sea collects, progresses and fades, rustles, and "advances as usual." This sea absolutely negates human energy, integrity, and creativity; its occasional charm—the "phalanx" of wrinkles, "beautiful under networks of foam"—intensifies its horror. Yet Moore may subtly invite re-vision, by intimating that alternative meanings are possible. Such an invitation is implied by Bonnie Costello's reading of "A Grave": "Moore uses an image to explore . . . a subject. . . . The experience of the poem is constant revision and ambiguity, suggesting that human observation is never definitive" (56-57). More persuasively, Taffy Martin observes that "Moore has placed her readers in the uncomfortable position of facing not just the insufficiency and the error of their perceptions, but their inability—because of the scene's very attraction—to abandon hope in it" (90). Both readings propose a latent ambiguity that careful reading of other poems by Moore could conceivably draw to the surface of "A Grave." Thus the delight in chaos, danger, and multiplicity that abounds in other poems Moore published in close proximity to "A Grave," while heightening this poem's stark effect, might also call it into question. I am thinking of poems like "The Steeple-Jack" and "An Octopus," the latter of which Martin accurately characterizes as arguing that "the fear itself can become a positive adventure," that "survival and even genuine enjoyment result from complete and unquestioning immersion in the chaos" (21, 26). Especially given its distinctiveness, a perception of such hints and possibilities in "A Grave" or in other nearby poems could well have contributed to Bishop's (or Oliver's) inclination to think back through it, or enter into conversation with it.

Bishop's "At the Fishhouses" (*Complete* 64; first published in *A Cold Spring,* 1955) meditates on and in a sense revises "A Grave," which Bishop would have read in Moore's *Observations* early in her own career. Though of course by the time Bishop wrote "At the Fishhouses" she was no longer a young poet seeking a mentor's advice, Moore's recommendation of risk-taking, early in the two poets' relationship, might also be thought of as opening the door to this kind of response. Moore had written in 1938, "I can't help wishing you would sometime in some way risk some unprotected profundity of experience. . . . I do feel that tentativeness and interiorizing are your danger as well as your strength" (Kalstone 58-59).

Bishop's poem enacts a sustained effort to approach the sea, to engage with nature, rather than exposing the futility of such an effort. In this endeavor Bishop risks "unprotected profundity" from beginning to end, as she breaks from the dominant convictions of Moore's poem, that immersion is both inevitable and dreadful, to posit a kind of immersion that is not inevitable but both frightening and desirable. Like Moore's, Bishop's poem includes a man, but rather than intruding upon and attempting to appropriate the scene, Bishop's old fisherman, covered with fish scales, mending his nets, and waiting for the fishing boats to return, is almost part of

it, and the speaker chats with him familiarly. Her old man represents an alternative to the men Moore dismisses by remarking that they "lower [their] nets" and "row quickly away . . . as if there were no such thing as death." Like Moore, Bishop confronts the sea's power to erode and destroy, but her acknowledgment does not turn her away from the beauty wrought by erosion or lead her to dismiss the small but appealing human activities she describes. Her first verse paragraph moves back and forth between reminders of the sea's annihilating power and the homely pleasure she nonetheless enjoys, while the second is suspended in a tension between looking and physically moving down to the water and up to the shore. In this way Bishop's structure, at least provisionally, contests the inexorable progress of Moore's sea.

Only in the third and final section of "At the Fishhouses" does the sea's cold power become ascendant and render palpable the poem's qualifying first clause, "Although it is a cold evening." The effect is gradually to efface the image of the old man, who has been sitting "in the gloaming almost invisible" despite the cold, rather as the "man looking into the sea" was effaced in "A Grave." Here, in this final section, Bishop most closely parallels "A Grave," and here she reaches a modified agreement with her predecessor. She begins by acknowledging the sea's inhuman, inhospitable cold and depth, in a phrase she will repeat; "Cold dark deep and absolutely clear." The seal she attempts to befriend, like the fish Moore mentions, proves uninterested. Its lack of interest also undermines the impulse toward belief in spiritual transcendence implicit in the hymns she hears. This is the only place where Bishop even obliquely dallies with the kind of arrogance embodied in Moore's man. Bishop humorously derails that inclination, even as she undercuts literal (baptismal) total immersion in the sea by describing its effects on the flesh. This double subversion, though, may serve as an invitation for Mary Oliver's later re-vision of "total immersion." Bishop's hymn, "A Mighty Fortress Is Our God," like Moore's "pulsation of lighthouses and the noise of bell buoys," ultimately makes no difference, provides no shelter against the sea's power. Moore's "reserved" firs standing "in a procession" become Bishop's "million Christmas trees . . . waiting for Christmas"; both gestures toward anthropomorphizing the landscape are dwarfed by the sea's insistent, indifferent presence.

But Bishop, nonetheless, does not seem entirely to have joined Moore. The crucial fact is that her speaker is attracted to the sea, as Oliver's will be and as Moore's is not. Like Moore's man, she wants some kind of proximity and relationship, but, unlike Moore's intruder, she isn't "rapacious," and her approach is more complex: she combines a self-conscious desire for familiarity with an understanding very like that of Moore's speaker. As the poem nears its end she warns us, but in a tone that suggests she shares, despite her sobering knowledge, the desire to put her hand into the sea's burning cold. As a consequence of these differences, Bishop's speaker is not chastised, not condemned, by her poem, as, in Moore's poem, the man and ultimately the speaker are.

While Bishop clearly knows the sea's power to overwhelm her, unlike Moore she never uses the words "grave" or "death" here. Her sea is not the ultimate fact: "utterly free," it is yet "drawn" by some other force, "derived from the rocky breasts" of the world, and like our knowledge, it is "flowing, and flown." Thus, though it remains both dangerous and elusive, its powerful finality is diminished. Both burning and cold, its paradoxical nature enables and invites us to approach it, for it is not all unequivocally one reality that we must name "a grave" or "death." It is unquestionably at once ominous and a source of beauty. That is why "It is like what we imagine knowledge to be," and if our knowledge, too, is temporary and incomplete, recognizing that need not imply annihilation. If it doesn't invite simple celebration, it does allow a considered ambivalence, and that makes more room for the personal and individual than does Moore's poem. The personal element is apparent in the figure of the old man, the speaker's familiarity with him, and their conversation. It is evident, too, in the speaker's humorous self-depiction as a singer of hymns and a curiosity to a seal. Finally, even as she evokes the sea's power most sternly, she brings the reader directly into the poem: "If you should dip your hand in . . . ," making the moment individual and immediate.

Bishop concedes Moore's point and modifies it, by reclaiming the personal, the particular, the immediate, and the at least temporarily knowable. For Moore, in "A Grave," meditation on the sea becomes meditation on the limits of human power and human language, and immersion, literal or figurative, threatens dissolution. "At the Fishhouses" hardly denies the realities of erosion, burning, or drowning, or the limits of our knowledge. Bishop's speaker, however, maintains her equanimity not on the strength of the superior knowledge claimed by Moore's (knowledge that must finally undo that speaker's claims, as she seems to know), but by holding tenaciously to volition ("*If* you should dip your hand in," "*If* you tasted it"—emphasis added) and consciousness, by recognizing and recreating the engaging particulars of her surroundings. As a result, Bishop can find the sea, as she says in the wonderful last line of another poem from *A Cold Spring,* "The Bight," "awful but cheerful." She will have it both ways.

Bishop's tone takes on a note of argument, as well as humorous concession, when paired in this way with "A Grave." At the same time, Bishop's re-visions of elements from "A Grave" cast into relief, by a kind of back- or under-lighting, the possibilities that Moore suppresses. Bishop, I think, might here be inviting (almost teasing?) Moore to reconsider the kind of skeptical, provisional stance that is typical of Bishop's poetry and that could be thought of as a middle ground between Moore's most characteristic stance and that which she takes in "A Grave."

Mary Oliver seems to carry on a conversation about the sea with Moore and Bishop both, in "Sunday Morning, High Tide" (*Twelve* 54), "The Sea" (*American* 69), "The Swimmer" (*Dream* 63), and "The Waves" (*Dream* 66). Taken together these poems demonstrate an understanding and acceptance of immersion based on a sense of relationship to nature and the sea that is analogous to what, in human relationships, Evelyn Fox Keller calls "dynamic autonomy." Keller emphasizes that "dynamic autonomy is a product at least as much of relatedness as it is of delineation"; as such, it "enables the very real indeterminacy in the distinction between subject and object to function as a resource rather than as a source of confusion and threat."[5] Dynamic autonomy "presupposes that the fears of merging, the loss of boundaries, on the one hand, and the fears of loneliness and disconnection, on the other, *can* be balanced. It also presupposes the compatibility of one's contrasting desires for intimacy and independence" (99, 100). From this perspective, immersion can be seen as desirable.

"Sunday Morning, High Tide" partially shares the visions of Bishop and Moore, but finally claims different connotations for similar imagery. The sea is dark, powerful, "a cold slate," "booming under the wharf," "smashing" with "gray fists / among the pilings." It shakes the foundations of human life, interrupting "the Sunday gossip" and "the flameless, vague / philosophies mournful / as our own hearts." The juxtaposition of "cold" sea and "flameless" philosophies (in contrast to the presumably not flameless sea) recalls the sea's burning cold in "At the Fishhouses," while the violence is more reminiscent of "A Grave." But Oliver imaginatively welcomes the tide's assault. Unlike Bishop, but perhaps in accord with Moore's speaker, she sees the human behavior she depicts as trivial, solipsistic, even despicable. She differs from Moore, though, in seeing the sea's action as cleansing, and she goes beyond the figurative practice of both "A Grave" and "At the Fishhouses" when she animates the sea, giving it "desire" and "appetite," making it responsive to our "mournful," "wasteful" lives, and imagining the aftermath of the wishful tide's sweep through

> the fallen gardens, the empty house:
> room after room peaceful, its beautiful
> boards washed clean.

On the one hand, Oliver's evocation of the sea's "desire" might suggest a sense of relatedness, of affinity with nature, that promises an openness to engagement with the other; on the other, the pathetic fallacy belies the acknowledgment of otherness, of alien if wondrous power, that initially gives the poem its impact. The sea's harshness is acknowledged only while it is under the wharf; when Oliver imagines it washing away the inhabitants but leaving the house intact and "peaceful," she makes it oddly benign. The poem thus illustrates the conceptual danger of too easily opting for immersion. She negotiates the attractions and risks of literal and figurative immersion more successfully in "The Sea," "The Swimmer," and "The Waves."

"The Sea" can be read as embracing wholeheartedly the "total immersion" that Bishop finally advocates only figuratively in "At the Fishhouses," as Oliver remembers and yearns for the embrace of "that mother lap . . . that dreamhouse," the sea. In fact the whole poem can be read as a response to Bishop's poem. From the beginning the fact that this speaker is swimming ("Stroke by / stroke my / body remembers that life") belies and even rebukes Bishop's warnings about the danger of physical contact with the sea. Oliver does Bishop and her fishscale-encrusted old man one better when she swears she knows "just what the blue-gray scales / shingling / the rest of me would / feel like! / paradise!" Instead of warily watching Bishop's "heavy surface of the sea, / swelling slowly as if considering spilling over," Oliver delights in the "spillage of nostalgia" that "pleads" from her "very bones"; she longs to become "again a flaming body . . . in the luminous roughage of the sea's body."

The desire that pulses through Oliver's poem is not simply for physical pleasure, but also for knowledge. Oliver imagines turning away from "the long trek / inland, the brittle / beauty of understanding"—the kind of knowledge afforded by separating the self from nature. Moore and Bishop glance toward this kind of knowledge when they turn momentarily inland and note the "procession" of firs, "reserved . . . saying nothing," and the "million Christmas trees . . . waiting for Christmas," but in neither case, as each would agree, does the turn inland offer a way of knowing the sea. Bishop finally sees the sea as "like what we imagine knowledge to be," but she appears to have no closer access to the sea itself at the end than at the beginning of her poem. Indeed, the shock of touching and tasting the sea—even conjecturally—may, paradoxically, have distanced her further than she was when she first contemplated the beautifully scale-encrusted and eroded scene. Oliver seems to take up the pleasure implicit in Bishop's initial emotional responsiveness and, trusting to "that mother lap," dive in. If she did so, she would be "vanished / like victory inside that / insucking genesis, that . . . perfect / beginning and / conclusion of our own." The unexplained conflations and juxtapositions of these final lines indicate that what she yearns for is visionary knowledge, attained through a dissolution of boundaries between self and other, self and nature, that enables a larger, more dynamic, more empowering knowledge of self and other, in relationship.[6] Thus, unlike Bishop, in "At the Fishhouses," she doesn't pull back. Yet it is important to recognize that in going beyond Bishop's provisional alternative to Moore's inexorable assertions, Oliver takes a risk for which Bishop's poem may have prepared the way. For as Bishop humorously undercut her own pretensions to spiritual transcendence of nature, she indirectly opened the possibility of deeper knowledge in and of nature. And in yet another way Oliver replays, even while going beyond, Bishop's (and Moore's) poems: Oliver emphasizes her longing for the imagined experience of immersion so consistently and sensuously that she draws us into her desire and tempts (or enables) us to forget that in the poem itself she

swims and wishes, but does not finally give herself up to that vanishing that would be at once vision and death. Her risk, too, is a risk of language and desire, of conjecture, just as was the case at the end of Bishop's poem. Thus Oliver imagines diving more deeply, empowered, I suggest, by the example of precursors whose desires *and* whose knowledge of limits she implicitly affirms.

"The Swimmer" also voices desire for immersion, now projected onto the reader, "you," in a way similar to Bishop's address to "you" in "At the Fishhouses." Though Bishop was warning her listener, in both poems the implication is that speaker and listener share a desire to enter and be immersed in the sea. But Oliver's description of immersion here is more soberingly suggestive than was "The Sea," and closer in tone to Bishop's ambivalence. Now, a brief swim in the wintry water leaves one "gasping," struggling to find the way "through the blue ribs back / to the sun." As the swimmer emerges, the experience becomes a recollection—at once of evolution and of gestation and birth—that is tinged with ambivalence: swimming "toward the world" that first time, the swimmer trailed "a mossy darkness— / a dream that would never breathe air / and was hinged to your wildest joy / like a shadow." The longing for origins is now more explicitly shadowed by the knowledge that return would be death. (Moore's man, with his desire to "stand in the middle," arouses an even sharper assertion of the power of death because his immobility is such a contradiction of the sea's fluidity.)

Oliver negotiates her ambivalence in this poem through the figure of a dream:

> . . . you dream
> of lingering
>
> in the luminous undertow
> but can't; you splash
> through the bursting
> white blossoms
>
> the silk sheets—gasping,
> you rise and struggle
> lightward . . .

Her language doesn't settle on a single tenor and vehicle; her swimmer dreams and her dreamer swims, and in this way both desire and knowledge can be granted. Oliver's version of this ambivalence, then, in contrast to Bishop's, permits a momentary experience of joyful immersion, even while she acknowledges the same sorrowful recognition of mortality with all its limits.

"The Waves" represents Oliver's closest engagement yet with Moore's and Bishop's meditations on the sea and our relationship to it. With its emphasis on the sea's mystery and constant motion, its fishermen and screaming gulls, its understated nervousness and its recognition of death, the poem seems to carry Oliver and us back through Bishop's evocation of the sea and our desire for contact, to Moore's insistent vision of "a grave." But like Bishop before her, she both shares and modifies her predecessors' visions.

The poem begins with a flat statement reminiscent of Moore's beginning:

> The sea
>   isn't a place
>   but a fact, and
>   a mystery
>   under its green and black
>   cobbled coat that never
>   stops moving.

Moore states "the sea has nothing to give but a well excavated grave," and this is the final admission of Oliver's poem, too. But Moore's blunt statements aim to undo mystery—the sea's beautiful surfaces are simply deceptive. Affirming mystery and paying attention to the fishermen, Oliver also links herself to Bishop. Oliver's use of personal pronouns here, too, places her between her two predecessors. She uses first-person pronouns twice, but in plural, generic forms—"we" and "our," thus speaking more personally than Moore allows her speaker to do, but less intimately than does Bishop, with her "I" and "you."

Oliver manages to tell us of shipwreck without saying the words: "After the storm / the other boats didn't / hesitate—they spun out / from the rickety pier." This repression, contrasted to the overt curiosity she has just expressed about death on land, implies an emotional response unacknowledged in Moore's poem (though, ironically, Oliver uses the Moore-like strategy of omission to convey it) and rendered, in Bishop's, through direct physical sensations. The suppressed emotional response is deepened by contrast to "Sunday Morning, High Tide," where Oliver never concedes that the cleansing wash of the tide would drown the speaker who longingly imagines it. "The Waves" continues,

> Surely the sea
>
> is the most beautiful fact
>   in our universe, but
>   you won't find a fisherman
>   who will say so;
>
> what they say is,
> *See you later.*

The affirmation of beauty again recalls Bishop, the direct assertion Moore, the colloquial expression both. These are hardly the fishermen Moore criticized, "unconscious of the fact that they are desecrating a grave," nor are they Bishop's scale-spangled old man. "Gulls white as angels scream / as they float in the sun"; the scream reminds us of the birds' "catcalls" in Moore's poem; "white as angels" recalls the brightness of Bishop's "silver" benches and "creamy iridescent" herring scales; yet "angels," too, suggests the angel of death, hovering, in Oliver's poem, "just off the sterns." Oliver thus starkly, yet indirectly, reminds us that death is the busi-

ness of Bishop's fisheries and the tenor of her images of erosion and rust, as it is the burden of Moore's birds' mocking catcalls.

The last lines of the poem combine Moore's finality ("neither with volition nor consciousness") and Bishop's old man, mending and remending his nets:

> everything is here
>   that you could ever imagine.
>   And the bones
> of the drowned fisherman
>   are returned, half a year later,
>   in the glittering,
>   laden nets.

Could we or could we not imagine those bones, those nets? At the end, we are given a powerful image of finality, and a claim that recalls mystery and reinstates ambivalence. Oliver is not dreaming of immersion here; she is clearly a separate observer, but as such she is capable both of emotional response and of cool statement. In this doubleness, as in the question implied in "everything . . . you could ever imagine," she intertwines both Moore's and Bishop's perceptions and responses.

The ways in which each writer, contemplating the sea, revises her predecessor's vision demonstrate a simultaneous continuity and change, a circling back as part of moving into one's own vision and words, that coincides with Ostriker's reading of "think[ing] back through our mothers" as a way of moving forward. This dynamic of relationship is consistent, as well, with a model of influence that is based on a relationship of nurture and mutual support.

On the one hand, we can see, in Oliver's poems, a kind of progress beyond the realities and possibilities imagined by Moore and Bishop. In "A Grave" and even in "At the Fishhouses" the possible human responses to nature are severely limited by the speakers' conceptions of the meanings of the sea's power and presence, and its effects on human beings. Bishop's cultivation of paradox and her corollary ambivalence open the door to other conceptions of nature and our relationship to it, but it is not a door through which in this, or most of her poems, she passes.[7] Oliver, so to speak, walks through the door, joyously but carefully: far from turning her back on her forebears, she takes their insights with her. Another way of defining the process evident here is in terms of Merrin's observation that Moore and Bishop acknowledge nature's separate integrity by not subsuming it to their own appropriative imaginations, and by (as she says specifically of Moore) instead honoring "the world's independence from the human compulsion to order" (78-79). Oliver, we might say, goes a step further: while, in these poems, Moore's and Bishop's separate nature *is* fundamentally other than human, Oliver's sea, the "mother lap" from which we have come, is not absolutely and always separate.

Yet progress is not an adequate name for what happens when we look at these poems together. Bishop's "Cold dark deep and absolutely clear, / Element bearable to no mortal" makes the inhuman coldness of Moore's sea palpable. Moore's descriptions are almost entirely visual—Bishop makes us feel the nullifying horror, even as she complicates it with the inquisitive seal, the "emerald moss," the "creamy iridescent coats of mail" and the Lucky Strike. Similarly, Oliver's "Sunday Morning, High Tide" recalls and recasts the indignation of Moore's speaker at the man who, presuming to take the view, assumes his own central importance. Oliver's evocation of the cleansing force of the sea opens the question whether Moore's speaker (and Moore, too) might feel a secret (unconscious?) satisfaction in her certain knowledge of the sea's ultimate power. At the same time, the harshness of Moore's and Bishop's sea is not contradicted, but thrown into relief, intensified both by Oliver's evasion (in "Sunday Morning") of the desired flood's human meaning, and by her yearnings for return to primordial immersion in "The Sea" and "The Swimmer." Together, the nullifying sea of "A Grave" and the seductive, "luminous," paradisal "dreamhouse" of "The Sea" and "The Swimmer" intensify the ambivalences of "At the Fishhouses," pulling tighter the thread on which Bishop's speaker (and reader) must balance, narrowing that ambiguous edge between land and sea where we may stand and consider all that surrounds—or *would* surround—us.

"The Waves," perhaps, makes clearest the conversational quality of the relationship among these three poets. Moore's and Bishop's poems have clearly offered Oliver an opportunity for speech, for exchange, which Oliver accepts, as she adopts her predecessors' images and insights and remakes them, not agonistically, yet with her own insights (and her own sea-evoking form: what Bishop accomplishes with long lines and repetitions, Oliver does through short, symmetrically cresting stanzas). Oliver's fishermen are courageous though she doesn't say as much: they will not "stand in the middle," as Moore knew they couldn't; rather they spin "out / from the rickety pier," no safer, though less presumptuous, in their action than was Moore's man in his stolidity. Oliver's gulls, screaming while they float in the sun, and her "glittering / laden nets" ("glittering" both more brightly and more harshly than Bishop's silver sea and benches) capture the ways she has found to honor, answer, and think through her predecessors' works to perceptions that both include and add to their own with the promise of ongoing conversation.

NOTES

[1] David Kalstone, Lynn Keller, Jeredith Merrin, Bonnie Costello, and Lorrie Goldensohn are some of those who have offered perceptive analyses of the relationship.

[2] This is not, of course, to dismiss the evident significance for Oliver of James Wright and other male writers and artists such as Thoreau, Whitman, and those to whom she dedicates poems in *Dream Work.* Janet McNew and Patricia Yeager have discussed some of the woman-defined qualities of Oliver's poetry.

[3] Among those who have found "A Grave" uncharacteristic are Lynn Keller, who says, "'A Grave' provides one notable exception" to Moore's "faith in the world's . . . fixed moral order that includes humankind and which humankind can, for the most part, both apprehend and describe" (109; 180, note 2), and Donald Hall, who remarks on the poem's unusual "overstatement" (42). Bishop expresses her affection for the poem in "Influences" (14).

[4] Leigh Gilmore's discussion of how the "other woman" inspires women poets suggests a parallel to Erkkila's argument and to Ostriker's claim that women poets want poetic mothers. Alice Walker's affirmation of Zora Neale Hurston's enabling influence (and her own reciprocal efforts to restore Hurston's fame and potential as a literary mother for others) demonstrates the centrality, for Walker, of such a relationship. Sandra Gilbert and Susan Gubar remind us that while it may offer empowerment and choice, twentieth-century women's experience of the "affiliation complex" can involve anxiety about relationships with maternal as well as with paternal predecessors. Nonetheless, "even in the unprecedented presence of female literary history, [most feminist modernists and their successors] . . . do not engage in the kind of purely agonistic struggle that Bloom describes" (199).

[5] This positive view of the blurring of distinctions, or of the merging of "subject" and "object," is to a considerable extent what Susan Griffin claims and promotes for women's relationship to nature. Janet McNew, who identifies Oliver's receptivity to immersion as one of the major traits distinguishing her from the poets of the Romantic tradition, also suggests affinities between Griffin's and Oliver's approaches to nature. For a compelling discussion of the positive potential of merging in women's lives and creativity, see Jean Wyatt.

[6] This is strikingly similar to the process of discovery and the relationship between researcher and nature that Evelyn Fox Keller describes in her discussion of Nobel laureate Barbara McClintock's work on plant genetics (158-76). Though she pointedly does not claim that dynamic autonomy or its correlative, "dynamic objectivity," is more characteristic of either men or women, Keller does argue that the core of McClintock's stance can be found in gender. See Janet McNew for a fuller discussion of Oliver's visionary impulse in the context of gender, and of "immersion . . . [as] revelation of a mystical consciousness and an experience of renewal" (65).

[7] Lynn Keller argues that the late poem "Santarem" demonstrates an attraction to flux, figured in the "conflux" of two rivers and the vibrant and varied life of land and water (135). Her discussion of this poem is the closest

she comes to developing her claim that by the end of her life Bishop was committed to a preference for immersion. See Fast for a full discussion of Bishop's response to nature in terms of immersion and relationship.

WORKS CITED

Bishop, Elizabeth. *The Complete Poems 1927-1979.* New York: Farrar, 1983.

———. "Influences." *American Poetry Review.* Jan./Feb. 1985, 11-14.

Costello, Bonnie. *Marianne Moore, Imaginary Possessions.* Cambridge: Harvard UP, 1981.

———. "Marianne Moore and Elizabeth Bishop: Friendship and Influence." *Twentieth Century Literature* 28 (1984): 130-49. Rpt. in *Marianne Moore.* Ed. Harold Bloom. New York: Chelsea, 1987. 119-37.

Erkkila, Betsy. "Elizabeth Bishop and Marianne Moore: The Dynamics of Female Influence." *Marianne Moore: Woman and Poet.* Ed. Patricia C. Willis. Orono, Me.: National Poetry Foundation, 1990. 335-50.

Fast, Robin Riley. "A Daughter's Response: Elizabeth Bishop and Nature." *Journal of the Midwest Modern Language Association* 21.2 (1988): 16-33.

Gilbert, Sandra, and Susan Gubar. "'Forward into the Past': The Female Affiliation Complex," Ch. 4 in *No Man's Land: The Place of the Woman Writer in the Twentieth Century.* Vol. I. New Haven: Yale UP, 1988.

Gilmore, Leigh. "The Gaze of the Other Woman: Beholding and Begetting in Dickinson, Moore, and Rich." In Temma F. Berg, et al., eds. *Engendering the Word: Feminist Essays in Psychosexual Poetics.* Urbana: U of Illinois P, 1989: 81-102.

Goldensohn, Lorrie. *Elizabeth Bishop: The Biography of a Poetry.* New York: Columbia UP, 1992.

Griffin, Susan. *Woman and Nature. The Roaring Inside Her.* New York: Harper, 1978.

Hall, Donald. *Marianne Moore: The Cage and the Animal.* New York: Pegasus, 1970.

Kalstone, David. *Becoming a Poet: Elizabeth Bishop with Marianne Moore and Robert Lowell.* Ed. Robert Hemenway. New York: Farrar, 1989.

Keller, Evelyn Fox. *Reflections on Gender and Science.* New Haven: Yale UP, 1985.

Keller, Lynn. *Re-making It New: Contemporary American Poetry and the Modernist Tradition.* New York: Cambridge UP, 1987.

Martin, Taffy. *Marianne Moore, Subversive Modernist.* Austin: U of Texas P, 1986.

McNew, Janet. "Mary Oliver and the Tradition of Romantic Nature Poetry." *Contemporary Literature* 30.1 (1989): 59-77.

Merrin, Jeredith. *An Enabling Humility: Marianne Moore, Elizabeth Bishop, and the Uses of Tradition.* New Brunswick: Rutgers UP, 1990.

Moore, Marianne. *The Complete Poems of Marianne Moore.* New York: Macmillan/Penguin, 1982.

Oliver, Mary. *American Primitive.* Boston: Little, 1983.

———. *Dream Work.* Boston: Atlantic, 1986.

———. *Twelve Moons.* Boston: Little, 1979.

Ostriker, Alicia. "What Do Women (Poets) Want?: H.D. and Marianne Moore as Poetic Ancestresses." *Contemporary Literature* 27.4 (1986): 475-92.

Walker, Alice. "Zora Neale Hurston: A Cautionary Tale and a Partisan View," Foreword to Robert Hemenway, *Zora Neale Hurston, A Literary Biography.* Urbana: U of Illinois P, 1977. Rpt. in *In Search of Our Mothers' Gardens.* New York: Harcourt, 1983.

Woolf, Virginia. *A Room of One's Own.* 1928. New York: Harcourt, 1957.

Wyatt, Jean. "Avoiding Self-Definition: In Defense of Women's Right to Merge (Julia Kristeva and *Mrs. Dalloway*)" *Women's Studies* 13 (1986): 115-26.

Yeager, Patricia. *Honey-Mad Women: Emancipatory Strategies in Women's Writing.* New York: Columbia UP, 1988.

William Empson, Bernard Heringman, and John Unterecker

SOURCE: "Three Critics on One Poem: Hart Crane's 'Voyages III'," in *Essays in Criticism,* Vol. XLVI, No. 1, 1996, pp. 16-27.

[*In the following commentary, which was written in 1948 but not published until 1996, Empson, Heringman, and Unterecker analyze the "consanguinity" of the narrator's lover and the sea in Hart Crane's poem "Voyages III."*]

Infinite consanguinity it bears—
This tendered theme of you that light
Retrieves from sea plains where the sky
Resigns a breast that every wave enthrones;
While ribboned water lanes I wind
Are laved and scattered with no stroke
Wide from your side, whereto this hour
The sea lifts, also, reliquary hands.

And so, admitted through black swollen gates
That must arrest all distance otherwise,—
Past whirling pillars and lithe pediments,
Light wrestling there incessantly with light,
Star kissing star through wave on wave unto
Your body rocking!
                    and where death, if shed,
Presumes no carnage, but this single change,—
Upon the steep floor flung from dawn to dawn
The silken skilled transmemberment of song;

Permit me voyage, love, into your hands . . .

At Kenyon College Summer School, where Empson first taught in 1948, the students amply repaid his efforts, as he acknowledged: 'the boys have made a variety of points which if I can remember them ought to be put in the book [Complex Words] before it is posted off'. Also notably, he had a direct hand in stimulating the work of another scholar. When he asked the students to produce a close reading of a poem of their own choice, Bernard Heringman tackled Hart Crane's 'Voyages III'; in turn, Empson felt challenged by Heringman's essay to produce his own explication of the poem, running to three pages, though modestly beginning 'Just a few minor points'. Subsequently, Heringman took both pieces back to Columbia University in New York (where he was working on an MA), and showed them to his contemporary John Unterecker, who added further pages to this chance collaborative paper. All three critics came to consider their exchange eminently publishable, and so Heringman undertook to test the market; but every periodical he tried—including Sewanee Review, Partisan Review, Hudson Review, Yale Review *and* Furioso—*turned down the unique offering. John Crowe Ransom, editor of* Kenyon Review, *even told Heringman, among other things, 'I hate to celebrate a homosexual poem' (quoted in a letter from Heringman to Empson, 9 August 1949). Nevertheless, their joint effort bore good long-term fruit, as Unterecker recalled in a letter to John Haffenden of 25 September 1987: 'It has a particular interest for me since it represented my first reading, so far as I can remember, of anything by Hart Crane—certainly the first time I ever wrote anything on him, nearly 15 years before I was to start work on the biography. . . . I think it's a very solid piece of work—a good example of three minds working on a difficult poem, each in turn learning from and transforming what the earlier commentator had to say.'*

                              JOHN HAFFENDEN

NOTE BY BERNARD HERINGMAN

This is the kind of poem that carries to an extreme MacLeish's statement that a poem must not mean but be. Perhaps it also validates Crane's own conception, given in 'General Aims and Theories', an essay relating to the poems in *White Buildings*, which includes the 'Voyages'. He says:

the motivation of the poem must be derived from the implicit emotional dynamics of the materials used, and the terms of expression employed are often selected less for their logical (literal) significance than for their associational meanings. Via this and their metaphorical inter-relationships, the entire construction of the poem is raised on the organic principle of a 'logic of metaphor,' which antedates our so-called pure logic, and which is the genetic basis of all speech, hence consciousness and thought-extension. (*The Complete Poems and Selected Letters and Prose of Hart Crane,* ed. Brom Weber, 1968, p. 221).

'Voyages III' is one of the considerable group of Crane's poems which is largely unavailable to normal methods of direct textual analysis. The prose passage throws some light on the poem but does not explain it. Material external to the actual text thus becomes necessary to rational analysis of the poem.

In April, 1924, Crane wrote a letter to Waldo Frank from his room overlooking the harbor in New York, where he was engaged in an intensely happy love affair with a young man who lived with him there between trips to sea. One passage from it is particularly *a propos*: 'I think the sea has thrown itself upon me and been answered, at least in part, and I believe I am a little changed—not essentially, but changed and transubstantiated as anyone is who has asked a question and been answered'. With the letter he enclosed a 'Sonnet' which was to function soon as a sort of rough draft for 'Voyages III'.

It seems reasonable to interpret the poem in the light of the situation, the letter describing it, and the particular passage. In other words, the poem is addressed to Crane's lover at sea; it is a *creation* of a vision of unity, conveyed in a 'logic of metaphor' something like that used by Donne in the 'Valediction: Forbidding Mourning', though the earlier poem works chiefly with similes and has a clear logical structure, and the later one is conceived in terms of a single, over-all metaphor with some subsidiary figures. A relationship now appears between the word *transubstantiated* in the letter and the words *consanguinity* and *transmemberment* in the poem. The fact that neither of these was in the 'Sonnet' and *transmemberment* is a coinage indicates that Crane was intent on realizing and extending the idea of *transubstantiation* suggested in his letter.

The over-all metaphor is similar in effect to Donne's simile of the beaten gold, stating that the lovers, though separated, are essentially together because they are essentially one. *Consanguinity* carries the full weight of the Latin derivation (a frequent trick of Crane's vocabulary), with the sense of 'sharing blood', a suggestion of intimacy which has nothing to do, in this context, with matters of lineage. Lines 5 to 7 carry out the metaphor with the idea that poet and lover are really in the same place; that is, the track the poet makes (in his vision) in the sea is the same as that his lover makes. Lines 9 to

14 suggest that the poet joins his lover on the sea by means of a mystical vision, projecting his spirit in a death-like ecstasy perhaps, and then, in lines 15 to 17, in the immortal communion of song.

The transforming sea of the letter is now, in the poem, a vehicle for the poet's projection of himself, because it is also the actual vehicle of his beloved. In the first lines the I, poet or speaker, merges with sea, sky and light into a sort of continuum which contains and supports the *you*. This feeling is summed up in the word *tendered,* for which there is no specified agent and only an implied recipient, the poet and/or the sea. The verb has the idea of something held out or proffered, as by the collective hand of the universe, and it puns on *tender* to include the sense of *you* as a precious object. This theme of praise may be extended in the following lines, reading *breast* as synecdoche for *you:* thus, '"Your body rocking" on the sea is like that of a god coming down from heaven and being enthroned, raised up again, by the waves.' Line 8 continues the theme with *reliquary,* indicating that *you* is a jewel tenderly encased and guarded by the sea, as *also* by the poet.

Line 11 is difficult, probably to be read as a description of the waves, but carrying the idea of the sea as a temple, dedicated to *your body.* Lines 12 to 13 seem primarily a picturesque description of the seascape, but they reinforce the reader's sense of the universal continuum, as well. The sensuality of the metaphors, converging on body, works in two directions, making the continuum sensual and the sensuality cosmic. The shedding of death, whether it means death as transcended or death as suffered, becomes the assumption of immortality, requiring no fleshy destruction but only something like Yeats' 'artifice of eternity,' to be realized, however, in an ecstasy which starts with the flesh. Love is somehow equated with death, in what may well be an extension of the Elizabethan pun and the 'metaphysical shudder'.

But this interpretation by means of the passage in Crane's letter and the biographical facts to which it relates can only be tentative and hardly explain everything about the poem. There is the 'organic impact on the imagination' implied in the passage quoted from Crane's essay and mentioned specifically elsewhere in the essay. The impact is richly emotive, and largely unexplainable. It may be founded, as he says, on a basic 'logic of metaphor', on a kind of associational meaning which is basic because it stems from the very texture of consciousness.

This kind of meaning must be closely related to the music of the poem, but again, rational discourse can only touch on the objective facts and hardly defines the important organic effect. The surprisingly regular iambic verse is rich, the sonorities of the blank verse lines like those of Marlowe and Shakespeare, the tense compactness of the tetrameters like Donne's and Marvell's. The various internal echoes are effectively close to the repetitive patterns of thought (Retrieves-resigns, Wide-side,

must-arrest, silken-skilled, While-wind-Wide-whereto, lithe-light, and some simpler alliterations). The chief effect of the music probably comes from its share in the 'associational meaning', but this is indefinable.

Perhaps the music seems rich and strange because the words are rich and strange, because of the logically startling juxtapositions and the syntax, which is desperate without seeming strained, like the syntax of emotional thought. The vagueness of reference of some of the words, particularly of verbs like *tendered, wind, shed, flung,* helps the 'organic impact', I think, because it helps to realize the fusion of *light, sea, sky, you* and *I.* The startling diction acts largely to personify or concretize the otherwise impersonal vastness of light, sea and sky, the monotony of waves, the abstractness of *song.* The archaic flavor of the last line helps make what might be a merely sentimental tag-line into a rounded summary comment on the poem, on the experience which is the poem. It is a comment which might have been a first line for many other poems. Here it seems to set this poem off in time and space, to sharpen and focus it in a very particular experience, and thus, somehow, to make it available to the reader after all.

NOTE BY WILLIAM EMPSON

Just a few minor points. I assumed that *consanguinity* (when one gets hold of the poem) is not between the lovers only but states their harmony with Nature as well; the theme—the love—gives them the common life-blood of Nature and mankind. (It is an idea that crops up in the metaphysicals and even Wordsworth 'along his infant veins are interfused / The gravitation' etc., [*The Prelude,* Book II (1850), ll. 242-43] and easily arrived at from the blood of Christ.) You may well be right about the *breast,* but I assumed that the sky was making love to the sea, chiefly by making it blue perhaps, and thus *resigning its breast* to it by lying on it. Thus the light is literally 'collecting evidence' of love in inorganic nature parallel to the theme of the human love affair. (The *use* of the apparently self-conscious term *theme,* 'about' the poem, is to help in generalizing the theme.)

The *picture* needed all through, I think, is a common experience in looking at sea water which does actually make you dazzled. The sun catches the small waves at random points (so as to make *stars* from where your eye is) and these points are always changing. But the eye tries to connect random sparks; you can connect near ones, giving the surface a sort of lazy crackle, or after watching for a bit and getting hypnotized you can connect more and more distant ones so that the sparks seem to be leaping violently and endlessly in a way which is exhausting but very exhilarating to follow. That is what he is actually looking at, on the sea surface, when *star kisses star through wave on wave, wrestling incessantly with light,* and the lines of light (the apparent lines) cross each other to make a sort of textile—that is why the theme of love, turned into the love of the sun to the sea, becomes a *silken . . . transmemberment* of the *song* (of the theme of love); it is turned from a solid body into something which is present all over the surface of the water, though its network still has these visible though very impalpable *members*. The *steep floor* I imagine then takes the jumps as going so far that the roundness of the world can be noticed; some of the jumps go right round, past areas where from his point of view the sea is on edge. The whole world is therefore drawn into the same ecstasy. In short, if you see what he is seeing I think that all the words fit in, and the 'associational meaning' is not 'indefinable' at all.

No doubt you are right in supposing that his voyage was imaginary. I in my literal minded way thought that he and the sailor took two little shore pleasure boats, and I still think that idea is in view. Crane's boat is leaving a wake of ripples which extend to the sailor's boat but are thrown back from it without disturbing him—their mutual feelings are dissolved into the continuum of nature. (The whole movement of thought is like regarding the unit of matter as a collection of waves in the ether.) The *whirling pillars,* to start with, are of course water-spouts; he would take his silly little boat through any destructive sea to reach the other boat. These pillars are like a building in their strength but based on shifting water only—the whole construct of the poem is based on something impalpable. The *black swollen gates* are no doubt great waves but here for once I should fancy an obscure Freudian parallel with the human body is coming in. 'Not *carnage* but *change*' says that when they die in ecstasy they are (or will be) reabsorbed into the love of Nature, in the regular Shelleyan (pantheist) manner; there is no need to wince away from this quite coherent philosophical opinion, and if you admitted it there would be no need I think even to suspect that the splendid last line is sentimental.

However I think a basic feeling, a human situation, is required to make all this philosophical stuff relevant; so one needs to pile on another point of view not to make the thing more complicated but to make it relevant and obvious. He is obviously pretty frightened of his sailor, I think, who is liable to jeer at him and beat him up at any moment; that is why the storms (and the waterspouts which seem deliberately designed by the sea to sink boats) are brought in, also it is why the building envisaged has no base—the whole love affair provides a basis for ecstasy but is liable to go horribly wrong the next moment; and the thrill of *permit me voyage* into these enormous hands (in his boat) is that at any moment the hands will get sick of him and smash him down and drown him. That is what ties all the imagery together and makes the poem so extremely powerful and moving.

Reliquary brings in death too; normally the object is expensive and jewelled and takes care of bones of saints; the sea though glittering will hide forever the bones of the lovers. The movement of the line gives a wonderful evocation I think of the lazy rise and fall of the adoring

water around the boat of the sailor it is likely to drown—the whole point of *also* is that the sea loves him as much as Crane does. *Reliquary* introduces *and so,* the sentence about how Crane will follow his lover through the sea even though it is murderous—and indeed will be able to get through.

So I don't think any of your phrases which in effect apologize for the meaninglessness of the poem are needed; I think your analysis is right as far as it goes but if completed leaves no word which is at all meaningless.

NOTE BY JOHN UNTERECKER

Perhaps one of the values of textual analysis is the demand it makes for further textual analysis. In any event, both of your clarifications of and insights into 'Voyages III' invite me to append a few notes of my own.

In general I am in accord with Empson's enlargement of Heringman, but I feel both of you have allowed yourselves to build rather complicated images that leave difficult passages almost as difficult as when one first sees them. I have particularly in mind your comments on the *reliquary hands,* the *breast,* the *black swollen gates,* the *whirling pillars* and the *lithe pediments.* All of these are made even more difficult to sort out because of Empson's suggestion that the poem is built on a structure of sunlight on sea surface.

I want, therefore, to try a slightly different reading that will help point up the *infinite consanguinity* of all the images in the poem if we make the *reliquary hands* central and the rest of the imagery supportive.

In order to look at the poem in this fashion it is necessary to reconsider Empson's view of the light on the sea surface. Empson assumed that the sky was 'making love to the sea, chiefly by making it blue perhaps,' and then went on to build that impressive image of sun glittering like starlight on the little waves.

But what if the stars really are stars—and the light not the broken up light of the sun but the reflected light of the stars themselves? And the sky, which does make love to the sea (both of you have commented on the richness of the interrelationship of the words *love* and *death*), the sky then would not make love to the sea by making it *blue,* but *black,* the funeral black of the black swollen gates of the sea, the *reliquary* starlight-jewelled black hands which the sea lifts. If one rereads the text one more time, there is little suggestion of a sun, and there is considerable evidence to suggest a night scene. The you *retrieved* (recovered—a suggestion not only of death but of the dark of night when things are most easily lost) from the sea by light is retrieved not by the big light of the sun (which would make the loss difficult if not impossible) but by the little searching light of the moon and the stars. If the scene is a night scene, the transition also becomes easier to the night of death, becomes easier to the sea's and the speaker's *reliquary hands* that in the next line transform into *black swollen gates.* The sea / lover's hands / gates are reliquary not merely because they are jewelled (by starlight) but because they contain the true relique, the real jewel, the saintly corpse: you. So the reliquary hands not only suggest the worship of a sacred person, they remind us that the sacred person is dead. The double love, which Empson points out, of the sea and Crane for the sailor is a love that hugs closely on death. We have only to glance at the end of 'Voyages II', a passage beginning six lines from the opening of 'Voyages III', to see Crane anticipating this poem in another (the same?) night death in which love figures largely: ' . . . sleep, death, desire, / Close round one instant in one floating flower.'

The passionate love of death not so much at the hands of the lover as in the embrace of the lover (who does become equated to the sea through the poem's last line) informs the whole poem and ties it together. Consider again what happens if the scene is a night seascape: the sailor is pictured at sea (his image—the *theme* of him— retrieved by the starlight) but wrapped in the reliquary hands (the glittering black waves) of the sea. These reliquary hands open out into black swollen gates. But gates admit one to something. Black, swollen, they admit one to death—death at sea. Heringman finds the whirling pillars a troublesome image, and Empson sees them in terms of waterspouts. Empson's seems to me a logical reading but—in terms of the action of the poem—an inverted one. For couldn't they just as well be whirlpools—pillars sinking into the sea and leading to death? Again, a glance back to 'Voyages II' provides us what seems to me fairly clear verification: 'Bequeath us to no earthly shore until / Is answered in the *vortex of our grave* / The seal's wide spindrift gaze toward paradise' (my italics). If the imagery of the second stanza of 'Voyages III' does suggest an undersea scene, then the *rocking body* is a dead body, and the lithe pediments are the shifting wave-tops supported by the *whirling pillars* of the vortex itself. Undersea, light does wrestle incessantly with light—in a much richer fashion than on the sea surface. This interwoven light, twisting, comes literally *through* wave on wave to the rocking body. If the black swollen gates (the reliquary hands) are the waves as well as the gates, black and swollen, to death, as well as the hands of the sea, then the star can kiss the star (in Empson's sea-surface manner) but now really through wave on wave until it reaches, embraces, the rocking body of the dead sailor.

To recapitulate: Light retrieves *the tendered theme of you* from the sea plains. (It seems clear that the light must be above the wave, the sailor beneath it, since he must be retrieved.) The *ribboned water lanes* the speaker floats on are *laved and scattered with no stroke / Wide from* the sailor's side precisely because Crane, as speaker, is—in imagination, at least—*over* the body and cannot be *wide from* it. (It is also worth noting here how the death-at-sea imagery carries through *laved* and *scattered.* Bodies are washed before their ashes are scattered. Here, though, it is the water itself which is laved

and scattered since the sailor has become one with the sea.) As the speaker lifts *reliquary hands* (worshipping hands which hold sacred a precious corpse), so the black waves, the literally reliquary hands, the hands which have created the relique, are raised. But they are not murdering hands; they are the hands of a lover. (The love of the sea and the sky has been pointed out. It might be worth adding that the breast image is of both sky and sea—the wave itself a breast shape and the sky filling the trough between waves a parallel inverted breast shape.) The wave's reliquary hands are also gates, black and swollen, and through them light is admitted (this seems the most obvious syntax for the stanza) to penetrate downward to the floating body of the sailor—to penetrate downward past the whirling pillars of the vortex that supports the shifting lithe pediments of the slippery gates, the waves, to penetrate and wrestle with itself, twisted by the underwater, so that star kisses star (how tempting it is to read into that second star the sailor himself!)—penetrating unto the sailor's body rocking above the steep floor of the ocean. This is where death may presume no carnage (no great destruction of life or mass slaughter) but rather a single sea change (the beautiful change of one life, through a love, into death). Here, in the dark, star-flecked underwater, flung by the reliquary hands of the sea through the black swollen gates of the waves, here, rocking above the steep floor of the sea, is the discovered lost sailor's tendered (carried) theme—a musical theme, a *silken skilled transmemberment of song.* The sailor has completed the ultimate voyage.

But it is a voyage that Crane, as the speaker, would attempt too. The voyage *down,* not across, the voyage into the reliquary hands of the sea. The sea and the lover have the same hands, after all; sea and lover share one identity. This consanguinity of lover and sea is genuinely infinite and can extend, if they permit it, to Crane himself. He can become consanguineous with his lover, with the sea, and with the cosmos through this final fatal act of love.

FICTION

Bernadette Wild

SOURCE: "Malcolm Lowry: A Study of the Sea Metaphor in 'Under the Volcano'," in *The University of Windsor Review,* Vol. IV, No. 1, Fall, 1968, pp. 46-60.

[*In the following essay, Wild investigates Malcolm Lowry's complex use of the sea—primarily as a symbolic place of healing—in his novel* Under the Volcano.]

On the surface it would seem that *Under the Volcano* would not have anything at all to do with the sea in plot, or have an obvious sea metaphor. The very title suggests desert rather than ocean. Nevertheless, the ocean metaphor does play a very important role in this novel, and in a much more complex way than in Malcolm Lowry's first novel, *Ultramarine.*

In *Ultramarine* the sea metaphor is used in the traditional way established by writers like Joseph Conrad in *Lord Jim,* Herman Melville in *Redburn, Billy Budd* and *Moby Dick,* Conrad Aiken in *Blue Voyage,* Nordahl Grieg in *The Ship Sails On,* and, to quote Malcolm Lowry, Rudyard Kipling in *Captains Courageous.* The ship becomes a society, a world in itself, a microcosm of universal life and of the emotions that actuate humanity at large. Here the ocean functions as the ground for the exploration of the nature and condition of man.

In *Under the Volcano,* Malcolm Lowry uses the sea metaphor in multiple and complex ways. The romantic is juxtaposed to a sense of evil. Actually in this novel, neither the fire under the volcano, nor the possibility of its disastrous eruption are ever far from the reader's consciousness. This suggests some difficulty as far as having "much needed ozone blow in with the sea air."[1] However, both the Consul and Hugh have spent much of their lives at sea, and both have been involved in wars in which ships and navies have exercised significant roles. This gives the novelist a biographical point of departure for the use of the sea metaphor.[2]

For Hugh and Yvonne the sea is a panacea offering regeneration and escape from the nightmare of the present; for the Consul it is much more in the nature of a nemesis, offering only death and disgrace to this man already sufficiently haunted by his own private hell, and suffering from a compulsive alienation from the world and from those who love him.

Malcolm Lowry considered Chapter VI of *Under the Volcano* as the heart of the book. (SL, 65, 67) It begins with the slightly misquoted opening lines of Dante's *Divine Comedy:* "Nel mezzo del bloody camin di nostra vita me ritrovai in . . ." Although this suggests the *Inferno* theme, I will use this chapter as my starting point in discussing the significance of the sea metaphor as Malcolm Lowry uses it to reveal Hugh's character and to add substance to the novel. Then I will consider its relevance in the case of the Consul and Yvonne, and something of the sea metaphor's interlocking with the central theme of the need for love, and Lowry's preoccupation with alcohol and death.

At this point a brief summary of the narrative surface action is relevant. The overt action is slight, but, on the metaphorical level, it is gripping, very intense and of deep spiritual significance.

While Chapter 1 of *Under the Volcano* is concerned with the thoughts of Jacques Laruelle on the first anniversary of the deaths of Yvonne and Geoffrey Firmin, essentially, *Under the Volcano* tells the story of a single day, beginning at seven in the morning, and ending,

with the death of Geoffrey, at seven o'clock on the evening of the same day, the Day of the Dead, November 2, 1938. Geoffrey, former British Consul, then living in the town of Quauhnahuac in Mexico has spent the night in hard, unbroken drinking. Yvonne Firmin, divorced from the Consul but still loved and loving, has come back, after a year's separation, in a brave attempt to rescue Geoffrey from inevitable disaster, and to salvage what she can of their disrupted lives. Yvonne's return is the answer to Geoffrey's prayers and yearnings. Nevertheless he is also plagued with the desire to be left at peace with his bottle, and is pursued with a sense of the utter futility of anything he might attempt. Eventually this overcomes his passing desire to leave with Yvonne and start life anew in the dream cabin by the sea. He decides not to accept "offers of a sober and non-alcoholic Paradise."[3]

From the Bella Vista bar where Yvonne finds Geoffrey, the two wander back to their old home, where the Consul's half-brother, Hugh, a young radical journalist, is the Consul's guest. He is on his way to Spain to help the Loyalists, now losing the Civil War. All day long the intricate relationships of the three continue to develop while the Consul continues to drink. In the course of the morning Hugh and Yvonne take a walk, which ends in a ride through the sunlit Mexican countryside. They rejoin Geoffrey, who asks Hugh to help him shave. Hugh's presence, as later that of Laruelle, French movie producer and former lover of Yvonne, only adds to the dilemma, and awakens the unreasoning resentment of Geoffrey, for he knows that Hugh also has had an affair with Yvonne. However, at this point, there is no doubt that Yvonne is wholly devoted to Geoffrey, and wholly occupied with the problem of reclaiming her husband.

Out of a blue haze of alcohol, Geoffrey suggests that they go to a bull-throwing at Tomalin. On the way there, the bus stops near a dying Indian, assassinated by one of his own race. Yvonne turns away from the wounded man because she "cannot stand the sight of blood." (UtV, 272) They leave again without anyone having done anything for the man, who literally and metaphorically has fallen among thieves. This is part of the important Samaritan theme that runs through the story as one phase of the love motif, which is the central theme of the novel.[4]

At Tomalin the three attend the bull-throwing. They are bored, the performers are drunk, and, to the disgust of the Consul, at one point, Hugh himself enters the arena and rides the bull,—not to show off as Yvonne tells Geoffrey: "No, he was simply submitting to the absurd necessity he felt for action, so wildly exacerbated by the dawdling inhuman day." (UtV, 306) This moment of action brings Yvonne and the Consul closer together than they have been all day, and almost leads to the reconciliation and the escape from México, which they both desire.

Later Geoffrey, who has been constantly getting separated from Hugh and Yvonne, accuses and abuses them both, and turns most bitterly on Yvonne. Then, his jealousy, which at this point, is as ill-founded as Othello's, precipitates him into his final flight, which ends in his death and that of Yvonne, just as the devilish insinuations of Iago, whose words he paraphrases, (UtV, 344) led Othello to murder Desdemona.

Yvonne and Hugh search for Geoffrey, and get lost in the jungle, where Yvonne is trampled to death by a panic-stricken horse, which Geoffrey has drunkenly released during the storm, which reverberates through the last hours of that day. The separate deaths of Yvonne and Geoffrey are in keeping with their broken lives, but each thinks of the other to the end, and there is a haunting note of loneliness and love in these thoughts of each other. Separated tragically in life, it is ironic that, unwittingly, Geoffrey drags Yvonne down with him in death. Almost his last conscious thought is that "No se puede vivir sin amar" would somehow explain everything. (UtV, 405)

Around this sequence of events, Lowry creates a web of interlocking metaphors. One of the most crucial of these is the sea metaphor.

The theme of man's guilt, "vague images of grief and tragedy," at one point become symbolized in the mind of Geoffrey as a "butterfly flying out to sea" and becoming lost out there with his frustrations at the whole "queer dumbshow of incommunicable tendernesses and loyalties and eternal hopes of their marriage." (UtV, 114) It is as if at this moment even the Consul regards the sea as that vast expanse of endless waters, where new hopes can blossom—only to be lost as the butterfly will be lost—as his own best memories of the sea will turn to bitter gall.

There is a keen sense of loss in Hugh's mind also as he muses on how quickly life has sped by him, and he recognizes his own immaturity at twenty-nine. (UtV, 179) He muses on the problem of aging and recalls A. E. Housman, whose *Shropshire Lad* has much to say on human relations and death, a thought quite in keeping with Hugh's despondency at this time, and a significant aspect of the sea metaphor as used here. His Spanish project makes the sea loom large as a possible death-trap.

On this turbulent day, Hugh admits he is going back to sea—"going back to sea for a while," and he admits that he sees the sea as the panacea for assuaging his guilt feelings. Between actual speech and stream of consciousness, the reader learns some of the intricate details of Hugh's plan to run the blockade, using the *S.S. Noemijolea*. This ship, the beautiful Noemi, has as ironic a name as did the *Samaritan*, Geoffrey's ship. It is named for a woman for love of whom Ruth could be "homesick amid the alien corn."[5] Now the *Beautiful Noemi* is bringing TNT so that brother can kill brother in Spain. Even while Yvonne stares fascinated into the Malebolge,[6] the horrible barranca, that meets them at every turn during their morning ride, Hugh sees himself standing at the wheel of his ship, "Columbus in *reverse*";

Hugh's heart was lifting with the ship, he was aware that the officer on duty had changed from white to blue for winter but at the same time of exhilaration, the limitless purification of the sea. . . . (UtV, 131)

But if one part of his dreaming makes the five feet eleven man stretch to his "full mental height of six feet two," (UtV, 131) it is only too clear that the "limitless purification of the sea" for which he yearns brings him little comfort at this time.

It is ironic here that Hugh's ship is also a disguised ship ostensibly on a peaceful mission, but also bound for a war where brother is fighting brother. It is another link between him and his alter-ego, his half-brother, Geoffrey.

In a way Hugh is as frustrated as Geoffrey—but he has not taken the latter's way out. On the other hand for him too the sea is beginning to fail as a panacea. His romantic notions are being pared down to the core of reality. He visualizes himself as a martyr going to sea, as he has once rationalized himself into a hero, when, as a young boy, the sea became alluring as a place offering him a refuge and a cleansing from guilt. Later in the shaving scene he decides to accept himself as he is, with all his contradictions,—"an Englishman, in short, unable to follow out his own metaphors," (UtV, 211) including the sea metaphor as he envisions it on this occasion.

During his ambivalent self-appraisal, he recalls the seagull which seems to him an emblem of liberation, a something out of the past which might spell "aid against the future." (UtV, 180)

In his long letter to Jonathan Cape analyzing *Under the Volcano*, Malcolm Lowry says Hugh may "be a bit of a fool but he none the less typifies the sort of person who makes or breaks our future. . . . He is Everyman tightened a screw. . . . And he is the youth of Everyman." (SL, 75) He goes on to say that Hugh's desire to go to sea is really everyone's desire, conscious or unconscious, to be a part of the brotherhood of man. It is this very thing, this need to go to sea, to a world where all men are brothers, where guilt can be washed away, that makes Hugh's frustrations with music, with the sea, his "desire to be good and decent, his very self-deceptions, triumphs, defeats and dishonesties" (SL, 75) part of that much needed ozone that only the seascape and the sea-escape can give. This also helps to clarify what Lowry himself wanted to include in his interpretation of the sea metaphor.

In *Ultramarine*, Lowry's *Oedipus Tyrannus* carries Dana Hilliot within sight of the *Oxenstjerna* on various occasions, and there is something of "-stjerna"—of starlight about her for Hilliot each time he sees her. The communication is meaningful to him. This communication, or lack of it, of one world with another is a significant facet in any major sea story. In *Under the Volcano*, two ships have special significance for Hugh other than the *S.S. Noemijolea*: the *S.S. Philoctetes* and the *Oedipus Tyrannus*,[7] the latter being "another Greek in trouble." It is suggested in Chapter One of *Under the Volcano* that the sea metaphor has taken on a more significant meaning for Hugh after the tragic deaths of Yvonne and Geoffrey. To some extent the sea remains a panacea for him, but there is also the suggestion that the sea is the mother, fostering maturity.

It is particularly in his treatment of Hugh's reminiscences of his experiences on the *S.S. Philoctetes* and the *Oedipus Tyrannus* that Malcolm Lowry gives rein to his extravagant comic sense. He makes this humorous interlude of sea air serve a twofold purpose. On the one hand it spells out various facets of Hugh's personality. On the other hand, Hugh's sea story and its metaphorical significance are as valuable here as is the hell-porter scene in *Macbeth*. In the course of the intense psychological drama of the Consul's last encounter with himself, Geoffrey himself evokes this "knocking at the Gate scene" when he pursues his bottle hidden in the shrubbery of his neglected garden. Quincey, who shares with the sunflower the unique role of being something like the eye of God watching Geoffrey's every move, also brings to the Consul's well-stocked mind the memory of DeQuincey—"That mere dope addict—and his "Knocking at the Gate." (UtV, 164)

Pre-occupied with his Spanish expedition, Hugh also wonders whether, having been born in India, he should not be considered "a piece of driftwood on the Indian Ocean." (UtV, 182) Certainly there is accuracy in the metaphor. Later, in the same chapter, during the shaving scene, Geoffrey recalls taking care of the sea-sick three-year-old on the old *Cocanada,* the "P and O boat, coming back from India," (UtV, 204) paralleling his action with Hugh's return service now. Unfortunately Geoffrey's present "seasickness" is a sickness unto death.

It is significant that Hugh instinctively sees the sea as a panacea for the solution of whatever problem faces him, but his view takes on increasing shades of complexity. His first voyage is undertaken to escape from conditions that have become psychologically insufferable at home—a journey that will wipe Hugh's slate clean, take him to sea where all men are brothers, and where regeneration will give him a new start in a life of independence. In this particular instance, Hugh expects to come back to the glamorous existence of a much-acclaimed new song-writer.

However, even Hugh's first going to sea suffers an undercutting. He mysteriously imagines himself running away to sea, but he gets every assistance from the very people he thinks he is running away from. Moreover the world of his ship is a deep disappointment. The world of brotherhood he expects to find on board ship dissolves into the same kind of a world he has left behind,—the same kind of profit-hunting, the same type of ugly and petty meannesses. In this microcosm of the world, many of the men at first seem kind, but it turns out they have ulterior motives. The sea becomes his University of Life, but learning in depth remains his big problem.

Part of Hugh's guilt complex longs for martyrdom to expiate that very guilt. For that reason the petty persecutions and misunderstandings of his life on board ship vaguely compensate for what is to him one of the most serious deficiencies in his new life. He finds that life too "soft." In a particularly humorous passage Lowry now depicts picayune odds and ends which Hugh recalls as the "little inconceivable things," he objected to on the ship. Busied with petty criticisms, he gets no more out of his sea voyage than he did when he passed the same points going in the opposite direction as a child of three.

However, something of importance does happen to Hugh, thanks to the isolation of the sea: the ship's library becomes his preparation for Cambridge. Moreover a dose of homesickness makes the sea the vehicle whereby he learns to appreciate what once was his.

After a month on the *Oedipus Tyrannus,* Hugh is back on the *Philoctetes* a bit wiser, a bit more cynical, a little clearer about himself, and horribly ashamed that he has ever exploited the romance of the sea with a senseless publicity stunt. Miserable and sick, he is man enough to recognize the real stature of the men who are tough enough to take the life of a sailor and its "years of crashing dullness, of exposure, to every kind of peril and disease." (UtV, 197)

At this point, life on board the *Oedipus Tyrannus* becomes Lowry's vehicle to theorize about what it is that makes seamen distrust and fear members of the monied classes, and why greenhorns from that social stratum—greenhorns like Dana Hilliot and Hugh Firmin—are made to undergo such trying initiation experiences. Perhaps even more important is the underscoring that the sea, as Hugh's University of Life, brings him back to reality whenever he is inclined to dream himself into an ivory tower.

Despite the long sea-story involving Hugh, Geoffrey is the centre of interest in *Under the Volcano.* Hugh's story gives us the traditional panorama of sea-stories, but it also gives us Hugh's special view of the sea as a place where all men are brothers, one angle of the Samaritan theme of brotherhood which plays such a vital part in the novel. On board the Consul's old ship, the *Samaritan,* we meet the contrasting picture of the brotherhood of man becoming a hellish mockery, and the name of the ship an ironic deception.

There is another reason for dwelling at such length on Hugh's story. Hugh thinks of Geoffrey as his "ghostly other self." Since these memories are significantly revelatory of Hugh's personality and character, they also reveal the basic pattern with which Geoffrey started out. Yet somewhere along the way, their development took slightly different turns. Hugh remains the romantic dream-spinner, viewing the sea as a panacea offering refuge and renewal. On the other hand, Geoffrey flees to the sea of alcohol and its dazzling disintegration.[8] Both Hugh and Geoffrey are haunted by feelings of guilt.

Hugh grasps at straws in an optimism that springs eternal: the sea, the sea in a "cold, clean scourge" would give him another chance. In contrast, the Consul grasps his bottle.

In the course of this last fatal day, Hugh analyzes the situation, describing his half-brother's condition as if his objective self "had at last withdrawn from him altogether, like a ship secretly leaving harbor." (UtV, 213) Indeed this is the perfect image of what the Consul is doing progressively on this his last Day of the Dead. His life is a ship secretly leaving harbor. All through the shaving episode, Hugh's stream of consciousness pursues his thoughts about the sea, and what his experiences on it have done to him. Malcolm Lowry uses this fact to give a sort of unity to his sea metaphor. Hugh reminisces that the harsh reality of his first voyage somehow recalls the farm that Yvonne was talking about earlier in the morning—the farm, somewhere on the sea shore where she and Geoffrey can start their lives over again. Then, suddenly, all three and their relation to the sea are brought together in one focus when Hugh recognizes that his persistent sea-dreaming at this time is doubtless subconsciously brought on by the photograph on the wall—the photograph that both Geoffrey and Hugh find themselves studying. It is the picture of a small camouflaged freighter, everything about it suggesting the *Sea Devil*'s ship of World War 1,[9] including the fact that the picture comes from a German magazine which also carries the picture of the Emden. (UtV, 214) This recalls Geoffrey's earlier stream of consciousness evoking this episode:

> Liverpool whence sailed so often during the war under sealed orders those mysterious submarine catchers Q-boats, fake freighters turning into turreted men-of-war at a moment's notice, obsolete peril of submarines, the snouted voyagers of the sea's unconscious . . . (UtV, 159)

Like so much that is fake about Hugh, everything about the *Samaritan* is a ruse. At this point Geoffrey is enthusiastic about the cleverness that went into making the *Samaritan* such a menace to the German submarine. (UtV, 214) However, just as the audience knows that Duncan is dead when the bell-porter opens his gates, so readers remember in this case that Laruelle's back-flashing in Chapter I of *Under the Volcano* has dwelled on the unsavory details of this incident. The story seems to be that the German officers from the captured submarine found a fiery death in the furnaces of the *Samaritan*. This is one of the secret griefs and torments of the Consul, though the courts declared him innocent. This adds a sobering note of reality to the sea metaphor. The sea may be a refuge for Hugh, and a haven for Yvonne. But the Consul knows it is also the home of evil, and therein lies part of his problem.

When Laruelle tries to interpret the Consul's guilt complex, he recalls that "unlike 'Jim' Geoffrey has grown careless of his honor and the German officers were merely an excuse to buy another bottle of mescal." (UtV, 60)

The evocation of *Lord Jim* is significant from another point of view: There is a similar, almost passive acceptance of death in each of the two men, Jim and Geoffrey. Moreover, Geoffrey's immediate confrontation with death gives the sea metaphor greater complexity because of his pre-occupation with the Samaritan theme at this time. For Geoffrey, as for Jim, the sea becomes the teacher preparing him for a manly acceptance of death. But it also encompasses the spiritual vision of the true brotherhood of man. Thus it holds some hint of future vision—something that Lowry refined and crystallized in "The Forest Path to the Spring."

Malcolm Lowry uses the Samaritan theme suggested by the ship called the *Samaritan* to link the sea experience of Geoffrey's life with the major theme of the story of the Paradise lost because of the loss of love. Thus the sea metaphor is inextricably interwoven with the very heart of the story. The Samaritan theme goes with Geoffrey to his death, and in his journey to the Volcano, there is an analogy to Ahab's quest, both in the futility and in its final horror—another quest that has ended in a question mark.

At this point it might be well to repeat that Geoffrey is the main concern of the novel. While Hugh is a perfect foil to Geoffrey, the latter wins the full sympathy of the reader. Stuck away in his own particular lost paradise, his mind staggering through "horripilating hangovers thunderclapping about his skull, and accompanied by a protective screen of demons gnattering in his ears," (UtV, 154) his "agenbite of inwit"[10] gives him little peace as he slips into a consuming sea of alcohol.

Since a passage to India has often been on his agenda, and since the disastrous expedition of his *Samaritan,* rightly or wrongly, haunts him, it is appropriate that Geoffrey's thoughts are often expressed in terms of a sea metaphor. When Yvonne comes back to him after that harrowing year of separation, he feels a subtle change in her, "Much as the demoted skipper's lost command seen through the barroom window lying out in the harbor is changed." (UtV, 99) With this vision of the ship's world, Geoffrey becomes engrossed with the sea. The sea becomes all waters. In his mind "the swimming pool ticked on," and the message it conveys is "Might a soul bathe there and be cleansed and slake its drought?" (UtV, 100) The same message does a repeat hammering at his brain somewhat later when he imagines he sees a fountain as the source of the cleansing and revivifying waters. What with this persistent image of water, and Geoffrey's need for it for cleansing his conscience and slaking his thirst, "his thoughts crashed like cannon balls through his brain," (UtV, 102) and evoke Melville. Geoffrey watches while Popocatepetl "like a gigantic surfacing whale shouldered out of the clouds again." (UtV, 103) This sight brings a queer foreboding to Geoffrey's heart, and it is significant that as the day progresses the need for climbing Popocatepetl becomes an obsession. Like Ahab, pursuing Moby Dick, the Consul finally heads for his white whale, his promise of an elusive paradise, and his Moby Dick destroys him in the process. Even the "frightful extremity" in which he finds himself on this last day of his life finally strikes the Consul "as something almost beautiful,"—as something of oceanic proportions. "It was a hangover like a dark ocean swell finally rolled up against a foundering steamer, by countless gales to windward that have long since blown themselves out." (UtV, 323)

It is significant that Malcolm Lowry uses Yvonne to bring a ray of hope into the story at various points but particularly during Chapter XI. Of course, this makes the final denouement of Chapter XII all the more climactic. Towards the end of their early morning ride, just before Hugh and Yvonne stop at another ruined paradise, the ruined palace of Maximillian and Carlotta, Yvonne finally gets it across to Hugh that she is serious about getting Geoffrey away from Mexico and going to Canada where the healing powers of the sea would save Geoffrey. Then it is the poet in Hugh that sees the possibility of having "a shack slap spang on the sea," the forest on one side, the pier going down to the water on the other. As he dreams for the two, somehow this vision of a redeeming sea, shared with Yvonne, makes him feel a sense of change, "the keen elemental pleasure one experiences on board a ship which, leaving the choppy waters of the estuary, gives way to the pitch and swing of the open sea." (UtV, 149) He feels that somehow his betrayal of his brother has been redeemed. Judas has not forgotten: "nay, Judas had been, somehow, redeemed." (UtV, 150) The sea metaphor assumes an iridescent gleam of hope.

During the bull-throwing at Tomalin, Yvonne continues to dream again and again of that cabin by the sea where salvation beckons for her and the man she loves. But it will not be a shack—"it is a home." In this way her vision of hope and of a new life with Geoffrey takes shape. The sight of the sea spells salvation to her. She dreams of Geoffrey working happily on his book, which she types for him. (UtV, 302) Almost echoing her thoughts of the ocean as a vista of hope for them, the Consul does a clever misquote of Keats' "On First Looking into Chapman's Homer," with Cortes gazing on the Pacific with a wild surmise, "Silent on a peak in Quauhnahuac." (UtV, 304)

Despite the ominous awareness on Yvonne's part that a man seems to have been shadowing the Consul all day, the estranged couple come closer to each other at Tomalin than they have been at any other time that day, and the little house across the water seems within reach of both of them. "She saw it from the beach rising above her, and she saw it, tiny, in the distance, a haven and a beacon against the trees, from the sea." (UtV, 309) Even as the beacon of hope and safety beckons encouragingly, part of her mind recognizes the very fragile tenuousness of the metaphor that has captured her imagination. Their very conversation is "A little boat . . . moored precariously; she could hear it banging against the rocks; later she would drag it up further where it would be safe." (UtV, 309-310) There is

a haunting moment of deep significance—almost an epiphany underscoring the ultimate futility of Yvonne's dream—not only in her mental picture of "a woman having hysterics, jerking like a puppet and banging her fists upon the ground," but also in the ageless drama of life enacted before them, as Geoffrey, Hugh and Yvonne watch an old Indian "carrying on his back . . . another poor Indian, yet older and more decrepit than himself." (UtV, 310)

To hammer home the relevance of this moment of truth, Chapter X begins with the word "Mescal" as does Chapter XII somewhat later. "Oozing alcohol from every pore," (UtV, 314) Geoffrey quickly reaches the stage, where, in his misery and deep unhappiness, he turns on Hugh and Yvonne. Lines from *Hamlet, Othello* and *Doctor Faustus* tease his tortured mind, and become as real as the hallucinations of his delirium tremens. "Was this the face that launched five hundred ships?" (UtV, 317) preludes his ugly, unjustified attack, first on Hugh and Yvonne, then scathingly on Yvonne. Inevitably he ends by rejecting what he calls "their offer of a non-alcoholic paradise," (UtV, 344) hurls defiance at them with "I love hell" (UtV, 345) and rushes out into the night, on towards the volcanoes which "seemed to draw nearer." (UtV, 345)

As Hugh and Yvonne follow Geoffrey out into the darkening world, hope eternal goes with them. At one point there is a parallel to Hugh's sea-gull episode. To her as his sea-gull was to Hugh, there is something of the phoenix-symbol in this caged bird in which she sees herself. Like Hugh, she frees the creature, and it soars "with a sudden cleaving of pinions into the dark blue pure sky above, in which at that moment appeared one star." (UtV, 350) It becomes a beacon of hope. From her star, Yvonne's thoughts move on to other stars and to the universe where sea and stars melt into one meaningful whole for her. (UtV, 353)

As in desperate yearning, Yvonne reaches out for rebirth, loving thoughts once more envelop her visions of life with the Consul. In spirit she sees "their house by the sea" on fire.

> She stretched out her hand for the other mescal, Hugh's mescal and the fire went out, was overwhelmed by a sudden wave through her whole being of desperate love and tenderness for the Consul.
>
> —VERY DARK AND CLEAR WITH AN ON-SHORE WIND, AND THE SOUND OF THE SURF YOU COULDN'T SEE, DEEP IN THE SPRING NIGHT THE SUMMER STARS WERE OVERHEAD, PRESAGE OF SUMMER, AND THE STARS BRIGHT, CLEAR AND DARK, AND THE MOON HAD NOT YET RISEN; A BEAUTIFUL STRONG CLEAN ONSHORE WIND, AND THEN THE WANING MOON RISING OVER THE WATER, AND LATER, INSIDE THE HOUSE THE ROAR OF UNSEEN SURF BEATING IN THE NIGHT— (UtV, 356-357)

Yvonne's faith in the all-healing power of the sea is fighting a losing battle. However, the obsession with the sea continues into the final hours of the day. As they search for the Consul, the real or imagined sound of the surf goes with them and helps them cling to their dream of making the sea the haven that will save Geoffrey at this hour.

Both Yvonne and the Consul have been represented as thinking of "immense and gorgeous butterflies swooping seaward." (UtV, 71) Now, when Yvonne is hurt to death by the riderless horse set loose when the Consul is shot, when her mind is completely occupied with her yearning over Geoffrey, the stars above her somehow change to myriads of butterflies,

> zigzagging overhead and endlessly vanishing astern over the sea, the sea rough and pure, the long dawn rollers advancing, rising, crashing down to glide in colorless ellipses over the sand. (UtV, 365)

—Then she hears someone calling her; she knows they are in a dark wood, and she knows she must escape to "their little home by the sea." But the house is burning—she and Geoffrey are involved in a terrible conflagration, and then Yvonne imagines herself being swept up through the stars, "through eddies of stars scattering aloft with ever widening circlings like rings on water" right up to the Pleiades. Later it becomes clear that it is at this moment that the Consul hurtles down into the abyss under the Volcano. Goethe's *Faust* and his Gretchen have found another parallel.

In conclusion, it is apparent that in *Under the Volcano* Mexico gives the protagonists an isolation from society that parallels isolation on shipboard. Moreover, despite the setting, Lowry uses the sea metaphor on many levels, and achieves a many-faceted world, a true microcosm within the macrocosm and within the cosmos. Geoffrey, Yvonne and Hugh frequently think and speak in terms of sea experience because the sea metaphor in its many shades of meaning has such significance for each of them. Hugh lives on the memory of wrecked romantic enterprises, but still expects to unravel the complexities of life by turning to the sea as the regenerating and purifying element in his life. In his personal involvement the sea becomes a compelling force to which he turns in every major crisis. Yvonne turns to the sea, essentially as a haven of rest and a beacon of hope for herself and for the man she loves. Geoffrey's attitude to the sea reveals a peculiar ambivalence: on the one hand, he treats the sea as the home of brave men, of brothers, an opinion natural to the man who has learned to love the sea in all its moods; on the other hand, he thinks of the sea as the place where evil may happen. Therein lies the stark realism which underlies his real or imagined guilt.

In a word, the ocean becomes a factor that shapes and symbolizes human destiny in a complex world, where death, alcohol and the loss of love also play significant roles. The struggle against the elements in the isolation of the ocean and against the human condition in that world shows man's inner worth, not only to others but to himself. It is a test that ultimately brings self-knowledge as perhaps the greatest gift from the sea.

In *Under the Volcano* the romantic is juxtaposed to a sense of evil but, amid growing darkness, Lowry also places a vision of hope. Yvonne carries her dream of salvation and a new life with the Consul into death, but the novelist himself carries the vision of happiness and fulfillment into the intriguing human story, "The Forest Path to the Spring." This, too, evokes Goethe's *Faust,* where Faust ultimately finds elevation to higher spheres through the power of love. There is a similar intense, tragic and emotional atmosphere in *Faust,* Part 1, and the final hours of *Under the Volcano.*

Malcolm Lowry hoped that when the reader has read the book carefully, he may once again go to the beginning where his "eye might alight once more upon Sophocles' *Wonders are many and none is more wonderful than man.*" (SL, 88) Indeed few men are more wonderful than the creative artist. In *Under the Volcano,* Lowry achieves a difficult feat. He creates a web of interlocking metaphors dealing with the ocean, with death, with alcohol, with love and the meaning of life. Against the unlikely background of Mexico, he offers a plausible and fascinating panorama of the sea not merely as a place of romance, but as a realm where man comes to grips with reality—a reality that can be shockingly grim.

NOTES

[1] Malcolm Lowry, Letter to Jonathan Cape, January 2, 1946 in *Selected Letters By Malcolm Lowry* (New York: Lippincott, 1965), ed. Harvey Breit and Margerie Bonner Lowry, p. 58. Subsequent references to this text will be indicated by: (SL and the appropriate page number).

[2] David Markson mentions this biographical point of departure for the sea analogy in "Myth in Under the Volcano" in *Prairie Schooner,* XXXVI, p. 342.

[3] Malcolm Lowry, *Under the Volcano* (Signet Books, 1966), p. 344. This is the text copyrighted in 1947. Subsequent references to this text will be indicated by: (UtV and the appropriate page number).

[4] Malcolm Lowry himself indicated this in his critical analysis of his novel, *Under the Volcano.* (SL, 74)

[5] John Keats, "Ode to the Nightingale."

[6] In Dante, the Malebolge is the eighth circle, a name derived from the ten ditches in the circle, each ditch called a "bolgia." Those punished in the Malebolge include panders and seducers, flatterers, simonists, soothsayers, grafters, hypocrites, thieves, sowers of discord, and those who practised frauds of a similar nature.

[7] It is interesting to note that in his thesis, Anthony Kilgallin says: "Both *Philoctetes* and *Oedipus Tyrannus* are plays by Sophocles. In the former play the relationship of Philoctetes and the older Neoptolemus is psychologically parallel to that of Hugh and Geoffrey. Therefore it is noteworthy that the book's first epigraph is from yet another Sophoclean play: *Antigone:*" *The Use of Literary Sources for Theme and Style in Under the Volcano,* Unpublished Thesis, Toronto, 1965, p. 63.

[8] John Woodburn used "Dazzling Disintegration" as his title for his book review of *Under the Volcano* in *Saturday Review of Literature,* February 22, 1947, p. 9-10.

[9] Thomas Lowell, *Count Luckner, The Sea-Devil* (Garden City, N.Y., 1927). This is the story of a German War-raider of World War 1, the story of a camouflaged "windjammer" that did much damage to allied shipping during the latter part of the war.

[10] James Joyce, *Ulysses* (New York: The Modern Library, 1961), p. 206, one of many references.

Marilyn Schauer Samuels

SOURCE: "Water, Ships, and the Sea: Unifying Symbols in Lawrence's 'Kangaroo'," in *The University Review,* Vol. XXXVII, No. 1 October, 1970, pp. 46-57.

[*In the following essay, Samuels surveys the maritime symbolism of D. H. Lawrence's novel* Kangaroo, *seeing in the work's sea imagery the irresistible forces of nature, society, and the unconscious.*]

There is running through *Kangaroo,* a sustained symbolic language, other than that used simply to describe the Australian landscape, which connects artistically the various elements of its central theme—the relationship of the individual to his inner self, to other individuals, and to his world. All of these relationships, both in Somers' present and in his past, are represented symbolically and allegorically through descriptions of water, ships, and the sea.

Richard Lovat Somers' first reaction to Australia is negative. Spanning the wide Pacific which separates him from his native land is a "long navel string fastening him to Europe."[1] All that keeps him going is the knowledge that in three months time he will be boarding a "steamer" that will take him back across the Pacific and home. As an Englishman he feels in his blood a fundamental distinction between the "responsible" and the "irresponsible" members of society. But in the democratic system of Australia such distinctions are obliterated. Sydney is "like a full river of life, made up of drops of water all alike" (p. 16). Somers finds himself "immersed" in this river of Democracy with the result that, on the one hand, his sense of order is threatened, and, on the other, his individualism.

Australia too has a navel string connecting her to the mother country and, according to Richard, providing her with her only protection against chaos: "Was it just the hollow word 'Authority,' sounding across seven thousand miles of sea, that kept Australia from Anarchy?" (p. 17). In Manly, a bathing suburb of Sydney, he and Harriet find an overwhelming sense of freedom. Once again, however, it is freedom based on lack of responsibility, "inner meaning," and consciousness: "Great swarming, teeming Sydney flowing out into these myriads of bungalows, like shallow waters spreading undyked" (p. 22). At the same time, while the disorder frightens him, he cannot help being attracted by the "sense of release from old pressure and old tight control, from the old world of watertight compartments" (p. 22).

As the narrator comments, this view of the problem of "new countries" is Somers' externalization of a conflict going on inside himself. What is really compatible with his "nature?" (p. 31). Is it as he claims "the gulf between the native servants and the whites" which he encountered in India, or is it the "silent, involuntary" communication among common people, where "the give and take flows like waves from person to person" (p. 31) without speech? This instinctive flow between people which he encounters in the Australians takes Lovat back to his boyhood in the English midlands. He seems to wish to escape this connection, again because it threatens his sense of self.

Illustrating his initial avoidance of any real contact or involvement with the Australians is the incident on the ferry-boat:

> One day the ferry steamer bumped into a collier that was heading for the harbour outlet—or rather, their ferry-boat headed across the nose of the collier, so the collier bumped into them and had his nose put out of joint. There was a considerable amount of yelling, but the ferry-boat slid flatly away towards Manly, and Harriet's excitement subsided. (p. 19)

The significance of this incident is best expressed by Jack Calcott, when he says to Somers: ". . . you don't take to the Aussie at first sight. Bit of collision between their aura and yours . . ." (p. 25).

Somers does not take to his neighbor Jack, at first, either. But gradually, as a result of forced proximity, the hedge which separates their houses and them becomes less of a barrier. One evening, Somers feels "waves of friendliness coming across" from Jack's wife, Victoria, and he responds. On that same evening, playing checkers with Calcott, he becomes almost suddenly aware of an unexpected relationship between them: "Somers wondered at it, the rich, full peace that there seemed to be between him and the other man. It was something he was not used to. As if one blood ran warm and rich between them. 'Then shall thy peace be as a river.'" The river of democracy Richard rebelled against because it threatened to submerge him in anonymity. To this rich-blooded river of peace that "seemed" to connect him with Jack, he responds more favorably. The quotation is a paraphrase of Isaiah 48:18, in which God through his prophet admonishes the "house of Jacob" for their disobedience: "O that thou hadst harkened to my commandments! then had thy peace been as a river, and thy righteousness as the waves of the sea." The peace which Richard seeks, however, is to be found neither in adherence to the "absolute" laws of the God of Israel (see pp. 272-3), nor in a communion with Jack.

In spite of all his talk about friends dying for one another, Calcott appears incapable of sustaining a friendship as peaceful and ever-flowing as a river. In observing his behavior with other men, Somers notes: "Like so many Flying Dutchmen the Australian's acquaintances seemed to steer slap through his consciousness, and were gone on the wind. What was the consecutive thread in the man's feelings? . . . His friends, even his loves, were just a series of disconnected, isolated moments in his life" (p. 55). While Somers begins to see Jack as a body of water in which no ship may anchor, Jack's wife, Victoria, views him as a "piece of driftwood, drifting on the strange unknown currents in an unexplored nowhere, without any place to arrive at" (p. 72). Consequently, despite his manliness, she feels insecure with him, and finds in Harriet a much firmer support against the turbulent waters of life: ". . . at last she could come to perfect rest in her, like a bird in a tree that remains still firm when the floods are washing everything else about" (p. 72). Somers, too, feels in Harriet a "rooted" centre, and eventually turns back to her, away from his unfulfilling relationship with Jack.

When he first goes with Calcott to meet William James, however, Somers is just beginning to think that it is Jack who will lead him to his ultimate goal: "to move with men and get them to move with me" (p. 64).

Before, he had thought of England's voice of authority sounding across the Pacific as the only thing separating Australia from chaos. Now, in a very confident manner he suggests to Jack and Jaz that England "has really kept the world steady so far" but is not keeping it so steady any more: ". . . the world's sick of being bossed. . . . Seems to me you may as well sink or swim on your own resources." And when Jaz objects, "perhaps, we're too likely to find ourselves sinking," he counters: "Then you'll come to your senses, after you've sunk for the third time" (p. 58). Nevertheless, he shows a reluctance to be "gulfed" (flowed over and enclosed) in "politics and social stuff" (p. 59). And when he is asked by Jack, "soft as a drop of water falling into water," what he does care about, he hastily puts an end to their prying. His privacy threatened, Somers grows cold toward Jack. A "gulf" develops between them over which Jack flings a "flimsy rope of intimacy, . . . embracing . . . his neighbors in mid-air . . . without a grain of common foothold" (p. 62). The wave of friendliness is replaced by a mutual "wave of revulsion" (p. 63).

During this period of coolness between the neighbors, Jaz comes to warn Harriet not to let her husband become involved with Jack and his associates, because they will use him for their own ends and pull him down to their level: "I've got another set of eyes inside me . . . that can tell real differences. . . . That's what these people don't seem to have at all. They've only got the outside eyes" (p. 69). Jack expresses the fundamental difference between him and Jaz in two descriptions using images of water. When Kangaroo (Ben Cooley) says that he would not like to see Jack turn discreet, the latter teasingly replies: "Even a crystal-gazer can't gaze to the bottom of a deep well, eh? Never mind, I'm as shallow as a pie-dish and proud of it . . ." (p. 106). Whereas, of Jaz he comments: "He's as deep as a five-hundred-feet boring, and I've never got down to sweet water in him yet" (p. 71).

Between Jaz and Somers, however, there develops "a bond of sympathy" which is "hardly sympathy at all, but an ancient sort of root knowledge" (p. 129). Even Somers cannot get to the very bottom of Jaz, but at least he believes there is one. At Somers' second meeting with Kangaroo, the leader of the Diggers' Movement insists that the Australians are not empty because they contain the "seeds of fire," while the spirit of the Europeans is too "damp" to ignite (p. 131). Jaz, on the other hand, very readily admits to a characteristic that Somers is discovering to be equally true of himself: "Warm isn't my way" (p. 127). When Kangaroo calls Jaz a traitor, Somers defends him as a Celt who remembers "older gods," as someone "nearer to the magic of the animal world" (pp. 209-210). And it is the deep-watered Jaz, who, in his unobtrusive way, helps Somers to recognize the "dark god" at the source of his own deep body of water—his soul.

The Calcotts and the Somers resume their relationship when they go on a pre-arranged weekend trip to the Australian South Shore. On the morning of his first day at Coo-ee, Somers observes a tramp-steamer being turned away from the jetty to which it has come in search of coal. The dramatic incident that Somers makes out of this commonplace occurrence seems to indicate that he is relating the ship's dilemma to his own. He describes it as a "lost mongrel" and the place where it desires to land as a jetty with red coal trucks behind which is a strip of land with a row of what appear to him as "ragged Noah's Ark trees" (p. 79). The steamer watches the jetty "yearningly, like a dog outside a shut door," and after the red flag is hung out, turns "slowly" and "fearfully" back into the "waves." The incident seems to foreshadow the Somers' attempt and failure to anchor in Australia. It parallels Lovat's eventual disillusionment with the political movements to which he has been momentarily attracted, and his eventual departure on an unquiet sea.

If Somers fears immersion in Democracy because of its threat to his individualism, he fears immersion in the Diggers' Movement for similar reasons. Lovat's reaction to his first dip in the Pacific is a forecast of these fears. Up until his visit to Mullumbimby, Somers had merely viewed the Pacific from a safe distance. Consequently, he was able to be quite flip about her dual nature, as when at Manly he observed: "There was a heavy swell on, so the Pacific belied its name and crushed the earth with its rollers. Perhaps the heavy, earth-despising swell is part of its pacific nature" (p. 19). Now, however, he himself experiences that swell: ". . . Somers had never known that he weighed so little, that he was such a scrap of unimportance. And he still dared not quite imagine the whole of the blind, invisible force of the water. It was so different being in it, even on the edge of it, from looking at it from the outside" (p. 82).

Similarly, when Jack tells Somers about the philosophy of the diggers and asks him to join in, Somers is tempted, but apprehensive of making the plunge. Their discussion takes place by the sea, where like "two mariners," two "pilots," they stand right at the tip of the "low rocks" shouting theories of power against the "roar of the waves" (p. 86). The sea's interference in their conversation serves at least two purposes. First, its loud roaring, almost drowning out their voices, mocks their assertion of power, their sea-worthy stance, just as Harriet will later mock it. For Richard to set his sails with Jack, she realizes, would be to set off "on a trip that led to nowhere": "if he was to excurse ahead, it must be ahead, and her instinct must be convinced as the needle of a mariner's compass is convinced" (p. 99). Second, Lovat's glance at the "dark sea" just at the moment when Calcott embraces him reminds him of his "own everlasting gods" and of still another and deeper reason for him not to collaborate. Finally, he shies away from commitment, promising Jack that he will give him an answer in Sydney: "You wouldn't want me to jump in and then squirm because I didn't like it" (p. 92).

Up until the time Somers meets Kangaroo, water functions in the novel primarily as a symbol of the various threats to individualism and the deceptive representatives of peace that confront the main character. With the introduction of Ben Cooley's "fire of love" as still another choice open to Somers, water takes on a third, more positive significance. It is now a means of escape, a means of preserving one's individuality against the "cloying warmth" of humanity. ". . . he wished as he had never wished before that he could be cold, as sea things are cold. . . . To be an isolated swift fish in the big seas . . . fierce with cold, cold life, in the watery twilight before sympathy was created to clog us . . . to get away . . . into that icily self-sufficient vigour of a fish" (p. 124).

Richard senses that there is another force of inspiration which is superior to warm human love, a dark god which unlike the Holy Spirit of Christianity enters us from below, from the "phallic self" (p. 134). But he cannot convince Kangaroo of the existence of this dark god and of the dark communion among men that is deeper than love. He cannot, because "the communica-

tive soul is like the ass, you can lead him to water, but you can't make him drink" (p. 134). For himself, however, Somers discovers a symbolic representation of the dark communion he is seeking. It is like a gannet's "plunging" into the "invisible underwater," where it "seizes the object of desire," and "then away" (p. 137). What he wants is not to be "clogged down like billions of fish in water" but to "strike at communion out of the unseen underwater" and then "back away into isolation" (p. 138). By Lovat's rejection of an affair with Victoria, Lawrence tries not too effectively to differentiate between the underwater communion he desires and mere conscious sexual desire based on the sight of a desirable object: there was a "vast phallic sacred darkness, where one was enveloped into the greater god. . . . He would meet there or nowhere . . ." (p. 143).

As the pressure on Lovat to either totally commit himself or totally withdraw becomes greater, instances of water as a positive and water as a negative symbol appear side by side. Lovat in one of his brasher moments had told Jack and Jaz that Australia ought to break free from the British Empire and "sink or swim" on her own. He had scoffed at Jaz's reservations. Now, Jack says to Somers that *he* is too cautious: "You've got to sink a few times before you can swim." "You want to have a thing all ready in your hand, know all about it, before you'll try it. And there's some things you can't do that with. You've just got to flop into them, like when you chuck a dog into water." (p. 144).

Instead of flopping immediately into the involving waters of the Digger Movement as a result of Jack's advice, Somers escapes from the "emotional heat" in town by plunging into the cooling waters of the Pacific. He puts off his problems and comes to his wife like a "creature" from the sea. Afterwards, having tea with Harriet in Coo-ee he seems to have achieved, temporarily at least, a perfect balance between undyked waters, democracy, and watertight compartments, the conservatism both of the "old world" and of the fascist Diggers. The sea is "shut out"; but "the room felt as penetrable to the outside influence as if it were a sea-shell lying on the beach, cool with the freshness and insistence of the sea, not a snug, cozy box to be secured inside" (p. 211).

A few days later, having received letters from his friends in Europe that bring once more to the forefront of his mind the "tangle of quibbles" to which his own country has been reduced, Somers flees a third time to the solace of the sea. Now, lulled by the "disintegrative, elemental language" of the water to an "inward peace," instead of identifying himself with the objects flung on the shore, he sees himself in opposition to them. The sea becomes for Lovat an outward manifestation that he, unlike Australia and its inhabitants, is not inwardly empty. While Jack Calcott is at the "centre" a "vast empty 'desert,'" Richard Somers when he is "truly himself" has ". . . a quiet stillness in his soul. . . . Not content, but peace like a river, something flowing and full. A stillness at the very core" (p. 155).

Before, he had thought he could feel peace like a river through his relationship with another man. Now, the waves beating on the shore are an "ever-recurring warning that some men must of their own choice and will listen only to the living life that is a rising tide in their own being" (p. 155). Above all, they "must not let the rush of the world's 'outwardness' sweep them away: or if they are swept away, they must struggle back" (p. 155). Somers half wanted to be swept away, to be "transported" (p. 131) by Kangaroo's enthusiasm, but he has managed to drift back. The sea at Mullumbimby has been for him a means of re-entry into the "sea of his own inward soul" (p. 155). Consequently, he has been more fortunate than the "poor, weird 'ink bubbles',," to which he contrasts himself. They, like the "vast masses of people," have been tossed up on the shore, "left high and dry on the sands." The sea functions almost simultaneously in these passages as both comforter and tormenter.

But contrary to R. P. Draper's belief, its purpose in the book as a whole is not "simply" to represent "the immense natural forces that make up the context of human life."[2] In Lawrence's opinion, it is man who makes up the context of his own life, and his relationship to natural forces (*i.e.* the sea) and to the social forces and institutions of which they are symbols is up to him. Unlike the sea creatures that Somers sees on the shore, the majority of his fellow men are not "swept" out of the sea, they voluntarily "rush" out like "souls with hydrophobia rushing away from the pool of water" (p. 155). If man loses his inner self, it is because he voluntarily turns away from it, and is either left high and dry or is drowned in some other sea.

Whether Richard is being temporarily swept up in the current of Kangaroo's love or retreating to the less turbulent waters of his inner soul, in both instances he is creating the further problem of interrupting the "flow" (p. 164) between him and Harriet. Lawrence presents the resulting marital difficulties in an elaborate allegory in which Mr. and Mrs. Somers are a ship at sea in the troubled waters of perfect love, pulled this way and that by two opposing currents. The current from the "democratic Atlantic" draws them toward the ocean of "perfect companionship," while that of the Pacific draws them toward the "lord and mastership" of Lovat. Granted, the business about ships is a bit overdone, but take away some careless writing and what remains is a useful parallel between Lovat's marriage and all of the other potential relationships with which he is confronted throughout the novel.

Lovat refuses to chart the course of his marriage boat for the democratic Atlantic for the same reason that in the political sphere of his life he refuses to become one of the indistinguishable drops of water in the river of Australian democracy. He refuses because of the same obsessive need to maintain his sense of self which will also make him rebel in horror from the type of love relationship that Kangaroo has in mind: "'He doesn't love *me*,' he thought to himself. 'He just turns a great

general emotion on me, like a tap'" (p. 212). At the same time, his desire to pilot the Pacific, to be Harriet's captain, leading her into "unchartered seas" to a land beyond "where life rose again" reflects the desire to move with men and make men move with him which is the real basis of his interest in both Kangaroo and Struthers in the first place.

Struthers entices Lovat with the prospect of introducing a "new bond" among men—not devotion to an ideology, but the "love of a man for his mate" (p. 200). But while Lovat realizes the potential value in this "new unifying passion," he also sees that under present conditions human love between members of the opposite or of the same sex is a "relative thing not an absolute." When the "fashionable" theory of relativity had been brought up by Kangaroo at his first meeting with Somers, Jack Calcott had his own amusing explanation of its popularity: "It absolutely takes the wind out of anybody's sails who wants to say 'I'm it'" (p. 107). Now, Somers, also using nautical figures, but with a more serious intention, thinks to himself that it is because each and every person is "it," because every person must maintain his sense of self, that every bond among men is relative to the individual integrity of the persons involved in it: " . . . each human being is a ship that must sail its own course, even if it go in company with another ship. Two ships may sail together to the world's end. But lock them together in mid-ocean and try to steer both with one rudder, and they will smash one another to bits" (p. 201).

The human heart, however, "must have an absolute," and this need can only be filled when each individual has rediscovered for himself the "great dark God" who is the "source of all passion and life" and who alone can hold men "separate and yet sustained in accord" (p. 202).

But while he senses that belief in the dark god is not something that can be verbally communicated from one man to another, nevertheless, because of his sincere admiration for Kangaroo and his unwillingness to be misunderstood by him, he cannot resist making one vain attempt. He tries to explain that what he is against is the "whole sticky stream of love" that Kangaroo wants to pour over people "as if one were only a cherry in the syrup" (p. 213). "Let's be hard, separate men," he pleads: "Let's understand one another deeper than love." The result is that Kangaroo does replace the sticky stream of love, not with deeper understanding, however, but with an "intense hatred," which Somers feels "coming at him in cold waves," as he hastily departs (p. 214).

Contrary to the opinion of many Lawrence critics, the supposedly sudden introduction of the long chapter on Somers' experiences in the war is carefully prepared for in the preceding chapters of the book. The first slight hint that the war has some unusual significance for Somers comes in Chapter II. The narrator notes that Harriet in relating her visit with Mrs. Calcott to her husband "very wisely suppressed" from him Victoria's suggestion that he might like to look at a mantlepiece ornament featuring a bullet that had lodged in Jack's jaw when he was a soldier in that war. One of Somers' preliminary objections to joining the Diggers is his doubting what he can possibly have in common with "returned soldiers" (p. 90). And in Chapter X a monument to fallen soldiers which is described in great detail becomes a "bone of contention" between Harriet and Lovat because he refuses to do anything about having it "enclosed." The statue is of a "fawn-coloured soldier standing forever stiff and pathetic," and a little behind it is a German machine-gun, "also looking as if it had been scrapped and forgotten" (p. 194).

Regardless of these subtle but effective preparations, however, it is primarily Lawrence's presentation of "The Nightmare" in figurative language similar to that he has been using throughout the novel that prevents its appearing out of keeping with what has preceded. More important, it is through this extended water metaphor that Lawrence discovers Somers' treatment by the British during the war to be the cause of the unending sea-voyage which the novel portrays. For Somers the greatest horror of the war was the loss by so many of their "inward, isolated, manly integrity" (p. 217): "Practically every man being caught away from himself, as in some horrible flood, and swept away with the ghastly masses of other men . . . delivered over and swirling in the current, suffocated for the time being" (p. 216).

Not only the individual Englishman went under, but the "English soul" itself was "submerged." The "ship of human adventure" became booty for pirates, and Lovat had "nothing to hang on to but his own soul": "he had to grip on so desperately, like a man on a plank in a shipwreck" (p. 226). Because he refuses to be swept out with the tide of ultra-patriotism, he and Harriet are suspected and persecuted, and finally driven from their home in Cornwall. All the invasions of privacy and the humiliating medical examinations that Somers experienced come back to him now in Australia, where once again he is suspect and a stranger: "He was loose again like a single timber of some wrecked ship, drifting over the face of the earth. Without a people, without a land. So be it. He was broken apart, apart he would remain" (p. 265).

F. P. Jarvis has called attention to Somers as an "Odyssean figure," citing among other things his constant attempts to "steer a straight course between Charybdis and Scylla,"[3] *Kangaroo* and Willie Struthers. Certainly the shipwreck figures are reminiscent of Homer's epic. It is also possibly significant that while Ulysses had most of his troubles because he had offended Poseidon, the God of the Sea, Somers' troubles begin when he offends the ruling powers or prevailing opinions of England, the monarch of the sea. It is for different types of assertion of self that both men are set adrift.

Again in the figurative landscape which Somers sets up to describe his predicament there are two bodies of water—the external and the internal, the persecutor and the comforter. There is the sea of society in which he is like a small piece of flotsam heading against the current, and there is the "living unutterable," the "new flood" of "God-darkness" which "surges" into his unconscious and of which his living soul is the "well-head" (p. 271). Resistance to the outer forces of society strengthens the soul in its convictions, whereas resistance to the "sensitive influx of the dark" gradually "withers" it.

All men experience the "throbs and pulses of the God-urge," but only the most exquisitely sensitive soul "listens and struggles to interpret" (pp. 301, 303). The rest like boats trying to pass through the straits perish between the Scylla of the democratic ideal and the Charybdis of the "conservative opposition to that ideal," which are really the head and tail of one monster. The real opposition to this monster is the "unadmitted god-urge." It is the dark, unconscious current, the human vessel's source of power; but as long as it is "unacknowledged" by the daylight or conscious, it is merely a source of unexplainable rage rather than of direction: "There is a gulf between the quivering hurt in the unconscious soul, and the round, flat world of the visible existence" (p. 304).

Since it is only through this unconscious that vertebrates, man included, can truly communicate, the resulting mob is a frenzied group of unrelated individuals. For them the water, the sea of life, is a negative force because they allow themselves to be swept up in its fury. Symbolically this condition is expressed in the article that Somers has read in the Globe: "There can't be much telepathy about bullocks, anyhow. In Gippsland (Vic.) last season a score of them were put into a strange paddock, and the whole 20 were found drowned in a hole next morning. Tracks showed that they had gone each on his own along a path, overbalanced one after the other, and were unable to clamber up the rocky banks" (p. 284).

Opposed to these "mechanical logs of life," are the "great sperm whales" who have attained the perfect balance of isolation and communication of the type which Somers had before represented in the dual life of the gannet: "In the sperm whale, intense is the passion of amorous love, intense is the cold exultance in power, isolate kingship" (p. 306). The whales, unlike the bullocks, are in control of the natural forces that provide the context of their lives. Consequently, the water for them is not destructive, but constructive: it "acts as a most perfect transmitter of vertebral telepathy" (p. 305).

In "The Crown" (1915), an allegorical essay in which Lawrence discusses the real problems created and revealed by World War I, and which treats of many questions confronted again in *Kangaroo,* he gives the following description of the "duality" of man: " . . . while I am temporal and mortal, I am framed in the struggle and embrace of the two opposite waves of darkness and of light" (p. 24).[4] This is a constructive opposition leading to an ultimate consummation in which flesh and spirit become one and man becomes eternal (p. 23). But when in society or in the individual the conscious or light absolutely refuses to recognize the unconscious or dark, neither to struggle with it, nor to embrace it, but merely to crush it, the result is violent rebellion.

The sperm whale for Lawrence, as Robert Hogan has pointed out, is both in *Kangaroo* and in Melville's *Moby Dick* the symbol of this violent rebellion on the part of the unrecognized unconscious in the present world.[5] In his essay on *Moby Dick* in *Studies in Classic American Literature* (New York, 1923), Lawrence describes the great whale as "the last phallic being of the white man . . . our blood-self subjected to our will . . . , sapped by a parasitic mental or ideal consciousness" (p. 237). The whale's sinking of the *Pequod* represents the sinking of the "ship of the Great White Soul" (pp. 239-40). Similarly, in *Kangaroo,* he uses the figure of whales "suddenly charging upon the ship which tortures them" to describe "the dynamic vertebral consciousness in man bursting up and smashing through . . . the superimposed mental consciousness of mankind" (p. 307).

Richard in moments of discouragement has sought in the sea of his inner being, outwardly represented by the soothing voice of the Pacific, a complete detachment from his fellow men. He now acknowledges that man cannot completely isolate himself from the rest of the world: he must attempt a "vertebral correspondence." After Kangaroo is wounded, Richard goes to visit him in the hospital bringing as a gift a box of shells that Harriet has collected for his amusement. Kangaroo comments that he can "smell the sea in them" (p. 329). Later, he tries once more to make Lovat confess belief in his vision of the "full beauty of love." His words come to Richard like a "far-off voice of annunciation." But Richard has too much of the smell of the sea on him, both the turbulent social sea and the inner sea of the dark god, to be at all moved by the dying man's plea: "Yet Richard's face was hard and clear and sea-bitter as one of the worn shells he had brought" (p. 332).

After his visit he is, nevertheless, disturbed by what Cooley has said. He feels it necessary to reaffirm for himself his belief in the "inwelling magnificence, the direct flow from the unknowable God," and its superiority to the "white octopus love" from which he wishes to be free (p. 335). Again, he escapes to the sea, where his soul becomes "a moonlit hollow with the waves striding home" (p. 336). Wandering by the shores, examining the strange sea-creatures he finds on the beach, he forgets not only Kangaroo but also the dark god. It is the old, mysterious emptiness of Australia to which once again he falls prey: "Like a stone that has fallen into the sea, his old life . . . fell, and rippled, and there was a vacancy, with the sea and the Australian shore in it." He is "soul-less and alone, by the Southern Ocean, in Australia" (p. 339).

Reluctantly he goes back for one last visit with the dying leader of the Diggers, but only after assuring himself that he need not care. Australia is a continent, he rationalizes, in which like "snow in aboriginal wine one could float and deliciously melt down, to nothingness, having no choice" (p. 342). Obviously, however, Richard does care, and does have a choice. He exercises it when he refuses the last request of the dying Kangaroo: to tell him he loves him. His choice is a final covenant with the dark god. Now when he returns to the sea, it is not soothing forgetfulness, but a huge "cold passion swinging back and forth" (p. 348). It is the essence of the "radium-rocking, wave-knocking night," the call and the answer, the "living unutterable."

The significance of the description of this "cold passion" as "foam like the hissing open mouths of snakes" is suggested by two related passages, one in "The Crown" and the other in the essay on *Moby Dick.* Lawrence writes in the earlier passage that the "beauty of the swan, the lotus, the snake" is their "cold white salty fire of infinite reduction," and adds that "there was some suggestion of this in the Christ of the early Christians, the Christ who was the Fish" (p. 75). Similarly, in the Melville essay he relates the great whale, also symbolic of the cold phallic passion, to Christ, the Redeemer, who in the "first centuries" was Cetus, Leviathan (p. 240), the Old Testament sea monster who almost always appears as an object of the Hebrew God's wrath. Whether Somers himself is a potential Christ of the new dark religion is unclear. Nevertheless, he is referred to several times as being a snake, or as wanting to be a whale and a fish; and he does refer to Calcott's treatment of him as the "Judas approach."

The cyclone, like a "great bucket of water pouring itself down," is the outward manifestation of the inward break that Lovat has already made with the Australian sea and its offered escape from his responsibilities to the dark god. Being totally isolated during the flood gives Harriet a chance to come to terms with her own reaction to Australia. Her experience is also related through water metaphors and confirms Lovat's decision that it is time for them to go. When they first came, Harriet was intoxicated with the atmosphere of freedom: "In the silvery pure air of this undominated continent she could swim like a fish that is just born, alone in a crystal ocean" (p. 358). Lovat warned her that she could not have this "absolved sort of freedom," that she had to maintain a "deep, dark weight of authority in her own soul." Harriet would not believe it until she herself saw the less pleasant side of their Australian friends, the "hateful revulsions" which she now associates with the "dirty water" of the flood (p. 359).

Even when the flood subsides, the sandy foreshore where Lovat used to wander and lose himself never comes back: the waves "lashed with a venomousness to the cliffs, to cut man off" (p. 361). But although the sea itself now tells him he must go, he knows that "one of his souls would stand for ever out on those rocks beyond the jetty . . . advanced into the sea . . ." (p. 364).

The first time Richard fled to the sea to find there the soothing peace of his own inner soul, the narrator commented that "he was only resting," that "the fight would come again, and only in the fight would his soul burn its way once more to . . . the intense knowledge of his 'dark god'" (p. 156). Before he had to go back, however, Richard saw "beyond the sea" a "rainbow." The rainbow, as he then remembers, has always been a symbol to him of the "pledge of unbroken faith, between the universe and the innermost" (p. 156). He remembers the huge "supernatural rainbow" that he saw spanning Sydney Harbour on the day that he entered it. Now, leaving Sydney Harbour, resuming his journey, like Odysseus, over a "cold, dark, inhospitable sea" (p. 367), he once again sees a rainbow, this time formed by the colored streamers which momentarily connect him with the people he is about to leave behind. But although the streamers flutter and break, the rainbow and the promise it represents are not broken. The sea is cold and dark because it represents the dark god with whom Lovat must struggle to find himself; and it is "inhospitable" because, at the same time, it represents the hostile society against which Lovat must defend that dark god to the end. But beyond that end, beyond that sea, is the unbroken promise—the Rainbow.

Kangaroo is admittedly not one of Lawrence's great novels. Its figurative language, although often effectively applied, is frequently marred by careless or overponderous writing. But in the basic choice of his figures of water, ships, and the sea and particularly, in his ingenious use of the dual nature of water to show both the extreme difference and the dangerous seeming similarity between life and love as it is and life and love as Lawrence thinks it should be, the novel is undeniably impressive. It is not just a successful travel book demonstrating an Englishman's sensitivity to the subtler aspects of a foreign continent, it is also a valuable work of fiction showing a novelist's sensitivity to the subtler aspects of the human condition in general.

NOTES

[1] D. H. Lawrence, *Kangaroo*, p. 15. All subsequent quotations refer to this Viking Press (New York, 1968) edition.

[2] R. P. Draper, *D. H. Lawrence* (New York, 1964), p. 100.

[3] F. P. Jarvis, "A Textual Comparison of the First British and American Editions of D. H. Lawrence's *Kangaroo*," *Papers of the Bibliographical Soc. of Amer.*, LIX (1965), 422.

[4] D. H. Lawrence, "The Crown," *Reflections on the Death of a Porcupine* . . . (Philadelphia, 1925).

[5] Robert Hogan, "The Amorous Whale: A Study in the Symbolism of D. H. Lawrence," *MFS*, V (1959), 41.

William E. Messenger

SOURCE: "Conrad and His 'Sea Stuff'," in *Conradiana*, Vol. VI, No. 1, 1974, pp. 3-18.

[*In the following essay, Messenger recounts Joseph Conrad's conflict between being a writer of popular sea romances and one of serious literature, using his novel* The Nigger of the "Narcissus" *as a test case that signaled Conrad's shift to the latter.*]

> It seems to me that people imagine I sit here and brood over sea stuff. That is quite a mistake.
>
> —Conrad to H. S. Canby, April 7, 1924

In later life, his fame safely established, Joseph Conrad fought against being called a sea writer. Certainly he cannot be blamed for objecting to this oversimplification, but however justified his complaint, it is worth noting that in general his most violent outbursts were reserved for imputations that revealed truths about him that for one reason or another he found uncomfortable. His railing against Dostoevsky and Melville, for example, surely resulted from some inner realization of his affinity with them. The insistence by "the mass of readers and critics" on thinking of him as primarily a writer of "sea stuff"—as he put it in a late letter to Richard Curle—touched him on a similarly sensitive spot.[1] It is clear that he wanted recognition for his artistic achievement; and it is equally clear, I think, that his intense dislike of being thought of as wearing his other hat, that of the "old salt," was a result of his inner knowledge that he had, in however small and temporary a way, abdicated his artistic responsibility in assuming that very role in his early quest for popularity.

It is a commonplace that *The Nigger of the "Narcissus"* represents Conrad's discovery of his real powers, that it is the work in which he found himself as an artist.[2] Less well known, however, are certain of the circumstances contributing to that process of discovery. I believe that it is time for a new look at his attitudes toward himself and his public, and at that period early in his writing career when he turned to sea fiction—first with Part One of *The Rescue* and then with *The Nigger of the "Narcissus."* Such an examination will show that, to a greater degree than has previously been observed, Conrad then saw himself facing a dilemma, a choice between writing for popular success and writing according to the dictates of his artistic conscience. He seems not at that time to have understood the nature of his talent sufficiently well to realize that in effect he could not make such a choice, that however hard he tried to write for the popular ear, he was too much of an artist to succeed at it. Thus *Nigger,* intended as a piece of popular sea fiction, instead achieved its qualified success as an artistic novel. But we must go back to the beginning of his career as a writer in order to understand his confrontation with this artificial dilemma. This exercise will enable us better to appreciate the nature of Conrad's achievement not only in *Nigger* itself but in the master-pieces which he wrote immediately after it, and also in later works, especially those having to do with the sea.

In *A Personal Record* Conrad makes a great deal of how accidental it was that he took up a literary career. A number of facts contradict him, however, as several critics have pointed out. For one thing, his tenacious hold on the manuscript of *Almayer's Folly* over several hectic years, especially through the Congo period, suggests anything but a casual attitude toward it. His claim that he had never made any notes is disproved by the existence of the "Congo Diary."[3] And he may well have made others, for Captain Craig of the *Vidar* told Jean-Aubry that "when he went down to the cabin to talk to his first mate [Conrad], he usually found him writing." Indeed, Jean-Aubry assumes that Conrad must have taken at least some notes, for he says that "it is not likely that he took more notes of what he heard and saw during this period [on the *Vidar*] than he did at any other," and speaks of Conrad as being unable to "resist those secret stirrings toward authorship. . . ."[4] Indeed, according to the memory of one of his childhood friends, he was, as early as 1873, "intellectually well developed" and

> hated the rigors of school, which tired and bored him; he used to say that he had a great talent and would become a great writer. This coupled with a sarcastic smile on his face and frequent critical remarks on everything, provoked surprise in his teachers and ridicule among his colleagues. He liked always to be untrammelled and at school, at home, or on a visit preferred to lounge rather than sit.[5]

There is at least a hint here, and elsewhere, not only of literary ambition, but also of aristocratic arrogance and even *sprezzatura* coloring such ambition. Further, when in later life he began quite systematically to carry out his childhood dream, this seemingly casual attitude could act as a protection against failure. If he had not succeeded—and his letters during his early years suggest strongly that he had moments of despair as well as of confidence—he could always have said that it was only a whim, that after all he had never taken it seriously.

But there is no question that he did take it seriously. He had, in a sense, staked his very self-respect on succeeding as an author, on acquiring a literary reputation; but the casual pose faintly persisted. A number of his letters during these early years help us to understand some of the complexity of his attitudes. To his "Aunt" Marguerite Poradowska, in June of 1895, he crowed over one review of *Almayer's Folly:*

> I . . . have gone back to writing, much encouraged by *seven columns and a half* in the *Weekly Sun*, in which T. P. O'Connor buried me under an avalanche of compliments, admiration, analysis, and quotations, and all with an enthusiasm that caused him to make some quite absurd statements. That, however, sets one up, as the *Sun* specializes in this kind of literary notice—and I am pleased.[6]

It is worth remarking here on the legend that Conrad initiated later, to the effect that Edward Garnett's neatly phrased suggestion—"Why not write another?" rather than "Why not go on writing?"—had been responsible for his writing his second novel, *An Outcast of the Islands.*[7] His letters to Marguerite Poradowska make it quite clear that he had been quite seriously and strenuously engaged upon *Outcast* long before the publication of *Almayer's Folly* was assured, and before this supposed remark during a conversation with Garnett. As Jocelyn Baines puts it:

> The discrepancies between the various versions of the facts and the facts themselves show how easy it is for events in a person's life to become distorted and romanticised. More important still, this provides a further example of Conrad's persistent tendency to play down the strength of his impulse to write. He wished it to be thought that his process of becoming an author was due first to chance and then to the persuasion of Garnett.[8]

In a letter of October 2, 1897, to his Polish friend Janina de Brunnow, Conrad goes into considerable detail about himself as a writer. Here both the serious ambition and the aristocratic attitude come through clearly, as well as a strong confidence coupled with a modesty which is part *sprezzatura* and probably part rationalization for his failure to achieve immediate popular success:

> I married about 18 months ago and since then I have worked without interruption. I have acquired a certain reputation—a literary one—but the future is still uncertain because I am not a popular author and I shall probably never become one. That does not depress me in the least as I have never had any ambition to write for the all-powerful masses. I have no liking for democracy and democracy has no liking for me! I have gained the appreciation of a few chosen spirits and I do not doubt that I shall eventually create my own public—limited of course, but large enough for me to earn my living. I do not dream of making a fortune and anyway it is not something to be found in an ink-well. However, I must confess that I dream of peace, of a little recognition and of devoting to Art the rest of a life that would be free from financial worries. Here you have, chère Madame, the secret of my life.[9]

Conrad's judgment of his talent here is sound, and his prognostication accurate; this letter, however, was written while *Nigger* was appearing in the *New Review*; we must go back again to March of 1896 to discover some of the causes surrounding the writing of that novel, Conrad's first published piece of real sea fiction, which was undertaken in part against Conrad's own better judgment as expressed in this letter.

In a letter to Charles Zagorski, March 10, 1896, Conrad informed his Polish friend of his coming marriage, on the 24th of that month, and his intention of spending his honeymoon "on the wild and picturesque shores of Brittany."

It is there that I shall set about writing my third book since one must write to live. A few days ago I was offered the command of a sailing ship. This idea pleased Jessie (who is fond of the sea) very much, but the conditions were so unsatisfactory that I refused. Only literature remains to me as a means of existence. You understand, my dear friend, that if I have undertaken this thing, it is with the firm resolution to make a name—and I have no doubt that I shall be successful in this connection. I know what I can do. The question is only to earn the money *"qui est une chose tout-à-fait à part du mérite littéraire,"* yet I am not sure of it—but my needs are very moderate and I can wait. I therefore look toward the future rather calmly.[10]

Jean-Aubry quoted this letter again in *The Sea-Dreamer,* where he follows it with this comment: "He was plunging resolutely into this new career, yet at the bottom of his heart he had still not renounced the one he had pursued for twenty years."[11] He had, in fact, been "plunging resolutely" for at least two years already. Clearly he was not desperate to return to the sea, or he would probably have been able to overcome his scruples about the unsatisfactory conditions. What he did feel the need for, as Baines explains, is "some sort of material security," for he was about to get married. As Baines also notes, "it is clear . . . that Conrad felt himself to be committed to writing but could not yet live by his pen . . ." (p. 169). Jean-Aubry, however, in continuing to make his point about Conrad, in March of 1896, resolutely plunging into a new career, quotes from still another letter. "As he had done all his life," says Jean-Aubry, "he was obeying a mental compulsion—obeying it resolutely, and the very evening before his marriage he wrote to his friend and confidant Edward Garnett: ' . . . You have driven home the conviction and I *shall* write the sea-story—. . . .'"[12]

But Jean-Aubry is careless here. This letter to Garnett begins with a long paragraph on general philosophical matters, which may or may not have some application to Conrad's choice of a career. Nevertheless, the second paragraph, from which Jean-Aubry quotes, begins as follows: "So much for trifles. As to that other kind of foolishness: my work, there you have driven home the conviction. . . ."[13] The line and a half at the beginning, which Jean-Aubry omits, makes it quite clear that the meaning he ascribes to Conrad's statement to Garnett is quite other than the one Conrad actually intended. Jean-Aubry makes it like the "Why not write another?" episode with Garnett earlier, with its spurious implication that Garnett was responsible for Conrad going on writing. On the contrary, however, as Conrad's letter to Charles Zagorski and other considerations clearly show, Conrad was by then committed to writing. And his reference to "my work," and Garnett's own note identifying that work as *The Sisters,* both of which Jean-Aubry omits, preclude any possibility that Conrad had in mind any divided loyalty between a sea career and a literary one.

But Garnett *had* "driven home [a] conviction," and this letter does deal with a divided loyalty on Conrad's part. To make clear the nature of the division it will be necessary to quote more extensively from that letter, beginning with the passage already considered:

So much for trifles. As to that other kind of foolishness: my work, there you have driven home the conviction and I *shall* write the sea-story—at once (12 months). It will be on the lines indicated to you. I surrender to the infamous spirit which you have awakened within me and as I want my abasement to be very complete I am looking for a sensational title. You had better help O Gentle and Murderous Spirit! You have killed my cherished aspiration and now must come along and help to bury the corpse decently. I suggest

THE RESCUER.

A Tale of Narrow Waters.

Meditate for a fortnight and by that time you will get my address and will be able to let me know what your natural aptitude for faithlessness and crime has suggested to you.

My dear Garnett you are a perfect nuisance! Here I sit (with ever so many things to do) and what's worse I have no inclination to leave off. (Surrender to impulses—you see). If I was not afraid of your enigmatical (but slightly venomous) smile I would be tempted to say with Lingard: "I am an old fool!" But I don't want to give you an opportunity for one of your beastly hearty approvals. So I won't say that, I will say: "I am a wise old man of the sea"—to you (pp. 46-47).

If we consider this letter in the larger context of Conrad's attitudes toward his art and his public, certain meanings implicit in it will become clear. Indeed, these meanings are all but explicit, but nonetheless have either been overlooked or inadequately dealt with by commentators.

First, Conrad's attitude toward the public. In another letter to Garnett, in 1902, he expressed feelings of acute depression concerning his work:

I am simply afraid to show you my work; and as to writing about it—this I can't do. I have now lost utterly all faith in myself, all sense of style, all belief in my power of telling the simplest fact in a simple way. For no other way do I care now. It is an unattainable way. My expression has become utterly worthless: it is time for the money to come rolling in.

And he goes on to speak of a volume of stories which is to be published soon, "four stories of which Typhoon is first and best. I am ashamed of them all; I don't believe either in their popularity or in their merit" (p. 180). Conrad's contempt for the reading public is well known; in spite of the many statements in his Author's Notes which express his confidence in the acumen of that public—"(. . . it would be outrageous to deny to the general public the possession of a critical mind)"—and in spite of the similarly suspect statements regarding his "belief in the solidarity of all mankind in simple ideas and in sincere emotions,"[14] his contempt for them and his lack of any very deep fellow-feeling toward them are clear from many letters. And it is clear from these remarks to Garnett in 1902 that he equated poor writing—or at least what he then felt to be poor—with public success; when the writing becomes "worthless," then "it is time for the money to come rolling in"; "merit" and "popularity" are not only separable, but almost mutually exclusive.[15] As Albert J. Guerard notes, "as early as 1902" Conrad was convinced of the need to compromise; he wrote to Galsworthy in that year about one of the latter's manuscripts: "I would suggest . . . a certain compromise,—a concession to the need of popularity."[16] What is interesting is that he himself had already made such a compromise, of "merit" for the sake of "popularity," when in 1896 he followed Garnett's advice and took up "the sea-story."[17]

Garnett's advice was good. Sea fiction, of however inferior quality, was then and long had been irrepressibly popular. W. W. Jacobs, William Clark Russell, and others had been doing well, not to mention Stevenson and Kipling. However much he scorned such tales of the sea, Conrad clearly recognized their popular appeal; although *The Rescue* was only partly concerned with the sea, it was clearly thought of by Conrad, and presumably by Garnett as well, as a piece of sea fiction, "the sea-story."

Thomas Moser suggests that during this period Conrad, unable to handle the love material, the "uncongenial subject," of *The Rescue* and *The Sisters*, turned for "relief" to writing "aggressively masculine stories of the sea."[18] But from the evidence it seems rather that, in turning to sea fiction during this crucial period, Conrad was striving for popularity, for something "the man in the street"[19] could understand easily and perhaps like rather than be put off by. There can be no question that Conrad thought of "sea" writing, as such, in connection with his attempt to gain popular success. When *The Mirror of the Sea* failed to gain the popularity and wide sale he had hoped it would bring, he wrote, about two years after its publication: "I don't think of the sea now. No one cares about it really, or I would have had as much success here as Loti in France."[20]

Conrad, then, had two reasons for shifting to fairly straightforward romantic sea fiction. First, he would, as Baines says, be dealing with material that he knew well, thus avoiding at least some of the difficulties he was having with *The Sisters*. But even more important, the new field would offer him what he and Garnett hoped would be a surer path to popular acclaim. It may have been—as Conrad indeed protested—that popular fame meant less to him than critical acclaim from minds he respected; nevertheless, the wider kind of popularity was unfortunately becoming increasingly necessary for him if he was to be able to support his family and get out of debt.

Conrad, then, was courting the very public he scorned. Also, his flippancy in his wedding-eve letter to Garnett reveals a great deal about his attitude toward himself as an artist. Such phrases as "infamous spirit" and "my abasement" indicate his awareness of what it would mean to him to follow Garnett's advice. He wants his "abasement" to the level of crass popularity-seeking to be "complete," he says, half in irony and half in seriousness, and therefore needs a rousing "sensational title." The one chosen is at least sufficiently of that kind to suggest that he was not being altogether ironic—in fact, very few of Conrad's titles depart from that mode, and at least one such, *Outcast*, was already in print. What the "cherished aspiration" was that Conrad accuses the "Gentle and Murderous Spirit" of having killed is not, of course, readily apparent. Jean-Aubry believed that it was Conrad's desire to return to the sea. But the logic of this letter, and of the immediate circumstances, and of this whole aspect of Conrad's life and work, strongly suggest that Conrad saw his "surrender" to Garnett's practical wisdom and advice as a betrayal of his artistic ambitions, his artistic conscience, his artistic integrity; they also strongly suggest that the "cherished aspiration" he referred to was that early dream of becoming a "great writer" and acquiring a "literary reputation." Here he was, directly and designedly about to stoop in search of public approval, the approval by that vast democratic mass that he never ceased to look upon with contempt and scorn, but that yet held the key to his—and his family's—financial well-being. Is it any wonder that he could, however facetiously, accuse Garnett of "faithlessness and crime"?

There is a further complication of attitude here. Very few artists, especially writers, are content, finally—financial matters aside—to win the approval only of themselves and a few close friends and critics, however discerning. Public acceptance is too attractive to most egos for it to be left out of account. I suspect that a good deal of Conrad's scathing comments on the reading public were partly motivated at first by resentment against them for not making him an immediate best seller, and later by resentment against them for making him one. As Dumby in *Lady Windermere's Fan* says, "In this world there are only two tragedies. One is not getting what one wants, and the other is getting it. The last is much the worst, the last is a real tragedy!" Conrad's flippancy in the letter is surely at least partly defensive, a way of trying to hide, perhaps even from himself, just how serious a break with his artistic conscience his "surrender" entailed. The artist in him, as the end of the quoted portion of the letter suggests, felt like saying "I am an old fool!" But the practical and poor man, the writer who had once protested to Garnett: "I *won't* live in an attic!"[21]—this man now says instead, "'I am a wise old man of the sea'—to you." To Garnett, yes, but also to the public, for they too got the message, and once assumed, the mantle of the old salt was impossible to doff; Conrad was stuck with the "infernal tail of ships" until the end of his life.[22]

So Conrad abandoned *The Sisters* and sat down to write *The Rescue*. Upon receipt of the opening of this new work Garnett wrote back: "Excellent, oh Conrad. Excellent. I have read every word of *The Rescuer* and think you have struck a new note."[23] Along with the manuscript, Conrad sent a letter that further indicates the nature of his endeavors at this time:

> I am sending you MS. already—if it's only twenty-four pages. But I must let you see it. I am so afraid of myself, of my likes and dislikes, of my thought and of my expression that I must fly to you for relief—or condemnation—for anything to kill doubt with. . . .
>
> Is the thing tolerable? Is the thing readable? *Am I mindful enough of your teaching—of your expoundings of the ways of the readers?* . . .
>
> Do tell the truth. I do not mind telling you that *I have become such a scoundrel* that all your remarks shall be accepted by me without a kick, without a moan, without the most abject of timid whispers! I am ready to cut, slash, erase, destroy; spit, trample, jump, wipe my feet on that MS. at a word from you. Only say where, how, when. *I have become one of the damned and the lost—I want to get on!* (pp. 49-50; my italics)

The "new note" mentioned by Garnett was almost certainly that of sea fiction with romantic appeal. As Conrad wrote to Garnett shortly after: "I had some hazy idea that in the first part I would present to the reader the impression of the sea—the ship—the seaman" (p. 58). Another reference to this new novel, a month later, corroborates that it was the "sea stuff" that Conrad was most intent upon: "I am now setting Beatrix [later Edith], her husband and Linares [later d'Alcacer] (the Spanish gent) on their feet. . . . I am trying to make all this short and forcible. I am in a hurry to start and raise the devil generally upon the sea" (p. 61).

Moser's argument that Conrad's problems are attributable to his difficulty in handling love situations, "the uncongenial subject," is partly convincing, but still leaves a great deal of room for Conrad to have been plagued by another difficulty as well, that of trying to be a "popular" writer. As Gordan suggests, "The desire to be popular may well have contributed to his difficulty in writing" (p. 200). It is interesting, when one considers Moser's argument, to remark that "woman" had been one of Conrad's counters in his bid for popularity; it is simply that now he was trying a different tack, the "exotic" and the "woman" both having proved poor guarantees of wide sale. His turning to simpler, more "masculine" pieces about the sea was, indeed, for "relief," but importantly for relief in a special sense, namely to appeal to the public in a new way, as he felt the more tractable first part of *The Rescue* would do.

But once the first part was done, there was the second part. And this is when the other kind of difficulty began to plague him. The uncongeniality of love as a subject gave him less trouble than did his attempt to write in a popular vein when he was not, at heart, a "popular" writer. That he was having just such difficulties even with *The Rescue* is attested to by another letter to Garnett:

> Your commendation of part I plunges me simply into despair—because part II *must* be very different in theme if not in treatment and I am afraid this will make the book a strange and repulsive hybrid, fit only to be stoned, jumped upon, defiled and then held up to ridicule as a proof of my ineptitude. You see I must justify—give a motive—to my yacht people the artificial, civilized creatures that are to be brought in contact with the primitive Lingard. I must do that—or have a Clark Russell puppet show which would be worse than starvation (p. 63).

The difficulty is obvious. Part I, a kind of fiction he had not written before, was relatively simple, straightforward romantic sea fiction; in part II, however, his felt need to "justify" the new characters indicates that he was still the old Conrad, unwilling or unable to give up altogether the mode of fiction he had practiced before. As he wrote to his publishers about *The Rescue* when he was just beginning it:

> If the virtues of Lingard please most of the critics, they shall have more of them. The theme of it shall be the rescue of a yacht from some Malay vagabonds and there will be a gentleman and a lady cut out according to the regulation pattern.[24]

Conrad had, in a sense, compromised his compromise; he was trying to have his cake and eat it too. He could not keep to the mode of Part I—the mode he and Garnett had agreed was a desirable one—when he got to Part II and the other characters; he could not leave these characters without "justification," and if he proceeded to "justify" them he would be right back at the old stand. He was making what Guerard has called a "conscious effort to popularize his work without sacrificing his best elements. . . ."[25] The battle with his principles, his artistic conscience, was not to be so easily won as he had hoped, for to stoop to the level of William Clark Russell still appeared "worse than starvation."

Obviously a choice had to be made. Quite literally, he could not go on with *The Rescue*. He turned to writing a few short stories, avowedly for relief: "In desperation I took up another short story."[26] He had already written "The Idiots," on Ile Grande, where this major crisis with *The Rescue* was taking place. In July (1896) he wrote "Outpost of Progress" and in August "The Lagoon." And he probably also began *The Nigger of the "Narcissus"* there in June, before either "Outpost" or "Lagoon."[27] Clearly he first conceived of it as another short story.[28] His first reference to it was apparently in a letter to Unwin, his publisher, in October: "The story will contain 25,000 words *at least* and shall be ready very soon." The wrapper of the manuscript, however, bears the inscription "Begun in 1896—June. Finished in 1897—February."[29]

Although he began *Nigger* as a short story, he may soon have seen that it was going to be more than a simple tale like "Idiots," "Outpost," or "Lagoon," that it was something he wanted to work on more carefully, back in England. Also, he may have realized that some of the material and technique of Part I of *The Rescue* would be useful in it, and for that reason put it aside for more careful handling in the near future.[30] If he began it in June, it must have been after the 19th, when he complains to Garnett that he has "written one page. Just one page" since he sent Part I of *The Rescue* to Garnett, on the 10th or 11th.[31] Up to the end of the first part, "The Man and the Brig," he had had little if any trouble with *The Rescue*. But once finished with the sea-oriented part, and confronting for over a week the recalcitrant second part, what more natural than that he should turn—not for relief so much as in order to perpetuate the relative pleasure of writing about the sea—to a short story of the sea, and also one for which he drew more on his own experience than before? Not only that; by taking up another "sea-story" he would be continuing in the spirit of Garnett's advice.

Garnett's own attitude toward the book, as expressed in his "Introductory Essay" to *Conrad's Prefaces,* published in 1937, makes it very probable that prominent among its aims was the creation of a new image for Conrad. He calls the novel "a new departure in sea literature," and contrasts it with Marryat's merely "externalized breezy and vivacious chronicle." Conrad, unlike Marryat, "fuses the human life on board the sailing ship with sea and wind and weather into an integral whole." He cites certain remarks of Captain Allistoun as "incarnating the tough spirit of the British sailor," which was among the "things Conrad celebrated as no writer had done before him." In spite of possible flaws, he concludes, "*The Nigger* none the less holds its place as a great sea classic."

Clearly, the "Englishness" of the subject matter and, by implication, of the author, is what Garnett sees as principally important: "In his apostrophe to England, as the *Narcissus* is racing up the Channel, Conrad has defined the spiritual tie that bound him for twenty years to the merchant service, a tie that crystallized, later, in his fame and place in English literature. . . ." And again: "the closing description of the paying-off of the crew of the *Narcissus* and their dispersing on Tower Hill is one of the most moving tributes to British sailors ever written."[32] Garnett seems to be trying to reassert, in 1937, Conrad's reputation as a patriotic and popular Britisher, and he does it by citing, particularly, Conrad's handling of "sea stuff." This is probably the strategy Garnett had in mind for Conrad in 1896, as well. As R. L. Mégroz has said, Conrad's "material of seamanship . . . was not only precious intellectual capital, but a cheque drawn

upon the fund of English readers' confidence and a passport to their understanding sympathy."[33]

Conrad's two acknowledged masters in sea fiction were Marryat and Cooper, Marryat for the glory of English sea tradition, and Cooper for the sea itself.[34] The appeal of the sea is virtually universal, but it remains particularly characteristic of England. The opening words of Conrad's "Youth" are a good example of his artistic commitment to and use of this idea:

> This could have occurred nowhere but in England, where men and sea interpenetrate, so to speak— the sea entering into the life of most men, and the men knowing something or everything about the sea, in the way of amusement, of travel, or of breadwinning (p. 3).

Richard Curle, who was a close enough associate of Conrad to know how he felt about these matters—or at least to know what Conrad wanted him to know—emphasizes the connection between England and the sea and Conrad:

> . . . It is fair to say that the sea was one of the great ties that bound Conrad to England. Why Conrad, the child of an inland nation, should have had such a passion for the sea is one of the mysteries of personality, but that, having such a passion, he should turn towards England to fulfil it is in the natural logic of events. Our innermost history hinges upon the sea, and to the young Conrad's burning imagination the sea and England were almost synonymous terms. In Conrad's whole attitude towards the sea there was something symbolic, and in that symbolism England herself plays a part. In the words, for example, with which he closes *A Personal Record* one perceives—not only in the lines but almost more within them, like a spiritual essence—the lofty vision, beheld by Conrad, of England and the sea bound together as one entity.

For Curle, this answers even the question of Conrad's having chosen to write in English:

> To him English was the language of the sea, and it would have appeared fantastic to him to assume English nationality as a seaman and then to record his memories in French.[35]

This of course can scarcely be accepted as an accurate representation of the case. Nevertheless, insofar as Curle was his ideal audience, it is reasonable to assume that what he says about Conrad and the sea fairly represents what Conrad, at least with part of himself, wanted his public to think.

In any event, there seems little room for doubt that *Nigger* was begun as part of the program advised by Garnett; as *The Rescue* became more and more difficult, *Nigger* was begun as a substitute, a "sea-story" with which to appeal to the public and, perhaps equally important, with which he could feel himself at home.[36]

Unlike *The Rescue,* bogged down in its compromises, *Nigger* was a real sea story, one with no "land entanglements" whatsoever.[37] Virtual proof of this whole complex of attitudes is provided by Conrad's remarks in another late letter to Curle:

> This damned sea business keeps off as many people as it gathers in. It may have been otherwise twenty-five years ago. Now the glamour is worn off and even twenty-five years ago the sea glamour did not do much for the *Nigger.*[38]

Here is compound bitterness. Not only had he, as Curle says in a note to this passage, "the greatest dislike of being taken for a mere writer of sea stories," but he is also still disappointed at the failure of *Nigger* to gather people in twenty-five years before, when he surely hoped for the "otherwise" he mentions; the qualifying "may" indicates his awareness that it was his failure, not that of the genre.

We know that Conrad had what was for him an unusually easy time with Part I of *The Rescue* and with *Nigger.* But the job of writing was still difficult, for he was still Joseph Conrad. Although it took him only five months to write *Nigger,* Gordan's examination of the manuscript shows that it involved an almost incredible amount of work, writing, re-writing, revising, editing. His inability to compromise his principles, to choose the way of popularity rather than the way of artistic integrity, made his attempts to write in a popular vein difficult in a particular way. He could understand the techniques and effects of the masters, but the popular mode consistently baffled him. "I remember Conrad, one day," relates Garnett, "when he was depressed at his lack of popular success, throwing down some miserable novel by Guy Bothby [sic], which he vowed he would imitate, saying: 'I can't get the secret of this fellow's manner. It's beyond me, how he does it!'"[39] His inability to give up his old mode for a new and simpler one forced him, even when he was writing—or trying to write—a simple piece of sea fiction, to make it indubitably Conradian. His letters to Garnett during the composition of *Nigger* once more make clear his divided loyalties:

> I am (as the sailors say to express a state of painful destitution) "sitting in the lee scuppers" (p. 72). I am letting myself go with the *Nigger.* He grows and grows. I do not think it's wholly bad though (p. 74). Remains to be seen whether the story is good enough—or effective enough.
>
> That I doubt. I also remember days when I did not doubt. So I sit tight now; like a man with a lottery ticket; and hope for unheard-of fortunes (pp. 78-79).
>
> Of course nothing can alter the course of the "Nigger." Let it be unpopularity it *must* be. But it seems to me that the thing—precious as it is to me—is trivial enough on the surface to have some charm for the man in the street. . . . Till it's over there's no watch below for me. A sorry business this scribbling (p. 80).

And then, when he was almost finished with it:

> I can't eat—I dream—nightmares—and scare my wife. I wish it was over! But I think it will do! It will do—Mind I only think—not sure. But if I didn't think so I would jump overboard. . . .
>
> May the Gods help you. I am all right—have sold myself to the devil. Am proud of it (p. 83).

During this time, when he was finishing *Nigger,* he was also looking at a manuscript by Garnett, a book called *London,* described by Garnett as "a contemplated book on London of a realistic-poetic nature, which the publishers commissioned, and then took fright at. It remains unfinished" (p. 83, note). Characteristically, Conrad heaped praise on Garnett's work, and then, when he learned of its being turned down—at a time when *Nigger* had been approved by Henley and was virtually assured of appearing serially in the *New Review* as well as in book form—he wrote Garnett, with some return of the semi-ironic flippancy noted before:

> I do not know whether I am to be sorry or to rejoice at your publishers shying from your London. It is a damnable thing in one sense and glorious in another. I envy you almost in a way you may imagine a scoundrel envying the serenity of honourable power. But it is obvious that dishonesty (of the right kind) is the best policy: and henceforth my concern shall be to discover and steadfastly pursue a dishonest and profitable course. With characteristic cynicism I inform you that I shall seek illumination in your misfortunes—and advice from your sophisticated mind—which, incapable as it is to serve (and distort) your pure art, can yet direct and mould my deliberate conscienceless villainy. The fate of the Lark—The Bridge—The River—and of many other admirable chapters which I haven't seen shall be a lesson to me—a lesson in the virtues of shallowness, imbecility, hypocrisy—as instruments of success (p. 88).

Obviously Conrad did not pursue the course he here laid out for himself. But he was still thinking in terms of popular appeal *versus* artistic conscience. He may—perhaps with considerable ironic modesty—have felt that he had in writing *Nigger* sold his artistic soul to the commercial devil, but the famous Preface, which he wrote shortly after finishing the novel, attests to the real victor.

Nevertheless, it is these circumstances, the complex of attitudes and loyalties described and documented above, that led to *The Nigger of the "Narcissus"* being what it is, a flawed masterpiece, virtually a compendium of the conventions and clichés of sea fiction—sometimes unintegrated and even contradictory ones—and Conrad's last real training exercise. What he learned from it—about romantic sea fiction and its elements, about handling narrator and point of view, and about himself as an artist simply not cut out to write potboilers—put him in full command of his powers and enabled him to produce, in the peak period of his career which immediately followed, such works as *Lord Jim,* "Heart of Darkness," "Youth," "Typhoon," and "The Secret Sharer," and also most of his other works, including *The Shadow Line,* with greater self-knowledge and confidence, full control of his materials, and perhaps most important, single-mindedness about his job as an artist and his relationship to the public instead of a feeling of being pulled two ways, towards both a popular and an artistic reputation. He finally achieved both, of course, but when the popular reputation did come, ironically enough it came in the form of the reputation as a sea writer that Conrad had once courted so assiduously. And however much he enjoyed both his reputations, he knew which one he deserved the most, and he could never quite forgive the public—who persisted in connecting him with mere "sea stuff"—for failing to appreciate him aright and for thus reminding him of his early breach of artistic integrity.

NOTES

[1] *Conrad to a Friend: 150 Selected Letters from Joseph Conrad to Richard Curle* (Garden City, New York: Doubleday, Doran, 1928), pp. 147-48.

[2] See for example John D. Gordan, *Joseph Conrad: The Making of a Novelist* (1940; rpt. New York: Russell & Russell, 1963), p. 133.

[3] See *A Personal Record,* Canterbury Edition (New York: Doubleday, Page, 1924), p. 68: "I never made a note of a fact, or an impression or of an anecdote in my life." (Unless otherwise noted, subsequent references to Conrad's works will be to this edition.) See also *Last Essays* (Garden City, New York: Doubleday, Page, 1926), p. 93: "Indeed, life is but a dream—especially for those of us who have never kept a diary or possessed a notebook in our lives."

[4] G. Jean-Aubry, *Joseph Conrad: Life and Letters* (Garden City, New York: Doubleday, Page, 1927), I, 98. See also Jocelyn Baines' discussion of the matter, and his speculation that Conrad may have been trying his hand at creative writing this early, in *Joseph Conrad: A Critical Biography* (London: Weidenfeld and Nicolson, 1960), p. 90.

[5] Mrs. Tekla Wojakowska (née Syroczyńska), quoted by Zdzislaw Najder, *Conrad's Polish Background* (London: Oxford Univ. Press, 1964), p. 13. See also Andrzej Busza, *Conrad's Polish Literary Background and Some Illustrations of the Influence of Polish Literature on His Work* (Rome: Institutium Historicum Polonicum; London: Societas Polonica Scientiarum et Litterarum in Exteris, 1966), p. 172.

[6] *Letters of Joseph Conrad to Marguerite Poradowska, 1890-1920,* ed. John A. Gee and Paul A. Sturm (New Haven: Yale Univ. Press, 1940), p. 98. Conrad's underscoring suggests his glee at the very quantity of the review.

[7] "Author's Note" to *An Outcast of the Islands,* p. viii. See also Edward Garnett's partial demurrer in his Introduction to *Letters from Joseph Conrad, 1895-1924* (Indianapolis: Bobbs, Merrill, 1928), p. 4, and p. 3n., where he quotes another of Conrad's accounts of the meeting.

[8] Baines, p. 141; see also pp. 137ff. Edmund A. Bojarski, in "Conrad at the Crossroads: From Navigator to Novelist with Some New Biographical Mysteries," *Texas Quarterly* (Winter 1968), pp. 15-29, notes that it was the very day after Conrad's last official act as a British sea captain that he sent the manuscript of *Almayer's Folly* to Fisher Unwin. "Once that step had been taken," concludes Professor Bojarski, "there was no returning to the serenity of the sea!" (p. 18).

[9] Najder, p. 219. It is perhaps useful to adduce here H. G. Wells' impression of Conrad as one who "had set himself to be a great writer, an artist in words, and to achieve all the recognition and distinction that he imagined should go with that ambition, he had gone literary with a singleness and intensity of purpose that made the kindred concentration of Henry James seem lax and large and pale."—*Experiment in Autobiography* (New York: Macmillan, 1934), p. 526.

[10] *Life and Letters,* I, 185.

[11] *The Sea-Dreamer: A Definitive Biography of Joseph Conrad,* trans. Helen Sebba (Garden City, New York: Doubleday, 1957), p. 215.

[12] Ibid.

[13] Garnett, *Letters,* p. 46.

[14] "Author's Note" to *Chance,* p. xi.

[15] He had made a similar remark to Garnett earlier—significantly, about *The Rescue:* "I am getting on—and it is very very bad. Bad enough I sometimes think to make my fortune" (Garnett, *Letters,* p. 130).

[16] *Life and Letters,* I, 305; Guerard, *Joseph Conrad* (New York: New Directions, 1947), p. 22. In fact, as early as 1894 Conrad had written, during the early stages of writing *Outcast,* or "Two Vagabonds" as he then called it, to Marguerite Poradowska: "Do you think that one can make a thing interesting [read "popular"?] without a woman in it?!" (Gee and Sturm, p. 77). He soon put a woman in it. See also an earlier letter to Galsworthy, *Life and Letters,* I, 301.

[17] See Gordan, p. 200.

[18] "'The Rescuer' Manuscript: A Key to Conrad's Development and Decline," *Harvard Library Bulletin,* 10 (1956), 333-34. See also Gordan, p. 104.

[19] Garnett, *Letters,* p. 80.

[20] *Life and Letters,* II, 70.

[21] Garnett, *Letters,* p. 9. Interestingly, this was a retort to Garnett's "declaration," during the time when Conrad was writing *Outcast,* "about the necessity for a writer to follow his own path and disregard the public's taste." A year later, apparently, they had reversed positions somewhat. Garnett may not have helped matters, on the earlier occasion, by citing such examples as Stevenson, Kipling, and Rider Haggard—"the work of the last-named, I remember, Conrad stigmatized as being 'too horrible for words.'"

[22] The phrase comes from the letter to Curle quoted earlier; *Conrad to a Friend,* p. 147. See also Curle's *The Last Twelve Years of Joseph Conrad* (Garden City, New York: Doubleday, Doran, 1928), pp. 37-38.

[23] Garnett, *Letters,* p. 19 (Introduction). And see Baines, pp. 167, 172-73.

[24] *Life and Letters,* I, 164, note 1. Note the self-mockery again.

[25] Guerard, *Joseph Conrad,* pp. 29-30.

[26] Garnett, *Letters,* p. 64.

[27] The only authority for this is Jean-Aubry, who is not always trustworthy; see his *Life and Letters,* I, 164. However, Garnett (*Letters,* p. 21) accepts the story of "ten pages" on Ile Grande.

[28] See Jean-Aubry, *Sea-Dreamer,* p. 230. As a story, it was meant to fill the place in *Tales of Unrest* finally occupied by "Karain" and "The Return."

[29] Baines, p. 177n. Also, Conrad's letter to Garnett of [25 Oct. 1896], in which he mentions *Nigger,* makes it clear that he and Garnett had talked about it considerably before that time, and before Conrad's letter to Unwin; see Garnett, *Letters,* pp. 71-72.

[30] See René Kerf, "'The Nigger of the "Narcissus"' and the MS. Version of 'The Rescue,'" *English Studies,* 44 (1963), 437-43. As Conrad wrote to William Blackwood, on August 28, 1897: "I began [*The Rescue*] last year but after finishing Part 1st laid it aside to write some short stories—one of which (rather unexpectedly) developed itself into a longer work. . . ."—*Joseph Conrad: Letters to William Blackwood and David S. Meldrum,* ed. William Blackburn (Durham, North Carolina: Duke Univ. Press, 1958), pp. 5-6.

[31] Garnett, *Letters,* pp. 57, 59. Gordan, however, thinks he began it "around June 10" (p. 202). It was a month and a half later that he responded despairingly to Garnett's "commendation" of Part I of *The Rescue;* he had still got nowhere with Part II.

[32] *Conrad's Prefaces* (London: Dent, 1937), pp. 9-12.

[33] *Joseph Conrad's Mind and Method: A Study of Personality in Art* (London: Faber and Faber, 1931), p. 135. A letter to Garnett indicates Conrad's own conscious awareness of this inherent tie between Englishness and things of the sea. Complaining about a journalist who had called him "a man without country and language," Conrad wrote: "I thought that a man who has written the *Nigger, Typhoon, The End of the Tether, Youth,* was safe from that sort of thing" (Garnett, *Letters,* p. 212). To John Galsworthy, complaining of the same "ass," he wrote: "I wonder in what language the *Nigger, Youth,* or the *Mirror* could have been written?" (*Life and Letters,* II, 70). The significance, of course, lies in his here citing exclusively his sea writings.

[34] As Conrad himself said, Marryat "loved his country first, the Service next, the sea perhaps not at all" ("Tales of the Sea," *Notes on Life and Letters,* p. 55). See also Ford Madox Ford, *Joseph Conrad: A Personal Remembrance* (London: Duckworth, 1924), pp. 62-68.

[35] *The Last Twelve Years of Joseph Conrad,* pp. 169-70.

[36] As Gordan points out, "Conrad always associated the novel with Garnett. On August 24, 1897, he wrote to him: 'The Nigger is *your* book'" (p. 234). And of course *Nigger* was dedicated to Garnett. "Garnett," notes Gordan, "did all he could to help the novel to success: some thirty pages of the manuscript bear his marginal comments" (p. 229).

[37] Conrad's phrase, in the letter to Canby from which my epigraph comes (*Life and Letters,* II, 342).

[38] Curle, *Conrad to a Friend,* p. 153.

[39] Garnett, *Letters,* p. 25 (Introduction). Garnett means Guy Newell Boothby (1867-1905), a prolific but decidedly inferior Australian novelist. That Conrad should for a moment have considered emulating such "miserable" stuff is a measure not only of his depression but of his sometimes failing to understand the nature of his own artistic abilities—a measure, then, of his blurring of the distinction between popular success and artistic excellence.

Max L. Autry

SOURCE: "The Word Out of the Sea: A View of Crane's 'The Open Boat'," in *Arizona Quarterly,* Vol. 30, No. 2, Summer, 1974, pp. 101-10.

[In the following essay, Autry examines Stephen Crane's use of the sea in his "The Open Boat" to demonstrate the weakness of man and the futility of human struggle against nature.]

Although presented as an anticlimax and beautifully understated, the death of the oiler holds the key to Stephen Crane's study of mankind in "The Open Boat."

As the most significant single occurrence in a work composed primarily of inner action, Billie's drowning gives meaning to the final periodic comment:

> When it came night, the white waves paced to and fro in the moonlight, and the wind brought the sound of the great sea's voice to the men on shore, and they felt that they could then be interpreters.[1]

His death offers the final lesson for these "interpreters." Paradoxically incorporating the pathos of the human situation as well as the nobility of the individual effort, this lesson teaches the futility of life itself. Similar to the four men desperately seeking the shore which represents much that they repudiate, the lines of intellectual inquiry gravitate to the pronouncement on the frustrating alternatives of either struggle without meaning or knowledge without action.

In the study, Crane presents a microcosm of society and of the life-journey of man. The occupants of the dinghy, who remain unidentified by either origin or destination, represent a cross section of society, and their respective positions are clearly demonstrated through their actions, comments, and musings. Their journey in the open boat is the basic life-movement or life-struggle; Crane draws this parallel by noting that "A singular disadvantage of the sea lies in the fact that after successfully surmounting one wave you discover that there is another behind it just as important and just as nervously anxious to do something effective in the way of swamping boats" (p. 69). This struggle may represent the movement of man toward religion or belief, as symbolized by the church on shore; or toward society, as symbolized by the very occupants of the boat; or toward one of various objectives of life. In any circumstance, it is a desperate search for meaning, hope, and destiny with direction and control minimal, if not nonexistent. Inherent in the total microcosm is the mystery of life itself, expressed in Crane's conclusion that "The manner of her [the boat's] scramble over these walls of water is a mystic thing" (p. 69).

Populating this world at sea are the captain, the correspondent, the cook, and the oiler. From the outset, the captain is symbolic of the loss of control on both a personal and public level and is incapable of providing more than perfunctory leadership:

> The injured captain, lying in the bow, was at this time buried in that profound dejection and indifference which comes, temporarily at least, to even the bravest and most enduring when, willy nilly, the firm fails, the army loses, the ship goes down. (p. 68)

It would seem that the captain has already "seen the elephant" and, as a result, represents experience and sad acceptance. Because he is experienced, he knows the compromises needed to live, as well as the whims of fate for which man must allow.

However, it is not from the captain's viewpoint that the story is told, but basically from the correspondent's. He is the first to develop the "interpretive" power; or, at least, he is the first to evidence such. It is he who, long before the boat is swamped and the final lesson is taught amid the swirls of the unconscious in the savage surf, becomes knowledgeable of man's plight. As a person and as an embodiment of universal sympathy, the correspondent comes to feel sorrow for the dying Legionnaire in Algiers.

In contrast to both the captain and the correspondent, as well as the nondescript cook, the oiler is given a proper name, Billie, and is seen as an individual committing independent actions. As a result, he differs from his comrades at sea in various ways. For example, he is more realistic and less concerned with "appearances"; therefore, he shuns much of the pretense, false hope, and rationalization of the others. He is also endowed with greater personal strength than they and should probably be seen as an outstanding specimen of physical man. In accord with his personal strength, he contributes more to the journey than do the others—at the oars and also at "watch." Not only does he supply the momentum, but he provides direction and control; when the boat is under sail by use of the overcoat, it is the oiler who steers, an assignment which is definitely in keeping with his character and destiny. It is also Billie who rows the final distance into the teeth of the paradoxically savage but indifferent surf, into the incessant rollers. At this time, his individuality is most clearly accentuated, his great physical strength is displayed, and his rebellion is greatest. He knows no subjection of self. In further contrast to the others, the oiler is a naturally good, industrious, and cooperative man, but these qualities seem to be of little consequence as he must eventually be made aware of his true position in relationship to the "controlling force" or fate.

Through the use of this microcosm and its four inhabitants, Crane explores the general state of both man's ignorance and his knowledge. The opening sentence in the tale recognized the former: "None of them knew the color of the sky." As a counterpart, the third sentence of the opening paragraph defines the limits of man's knowledge: " . . . all of the men knew the colors of the sea." As the narrative concludes, the sky, the sea, and the land fuse under the darkness of night, and the wind carries the "great sea's voice" to the rescued men on shore, transforming them into interpreters. The final state is the result of the literal and symbolic journey that dominates the narrative.

The movement made by the four surviving crew members on the open sea is presented as tragic, pathetic, and even humorous. All elements are symbolized by the tableau of the cigar-smoking men:

> . . . the four waifs rode impudently in their little boat, and with an assurance of an impending rescue shining in their eyes, puffed at the big

cigars and judged well and ill of all men. Everybody took a drink of water. (p. 75)

The last act, the drinking, is a sign of supreme impudence as well as courage. It indicates how easily man can convince himself of his importance and how very little basis one's confidence needs, even under the most trying circumstances. Equally effective, the cigar is a fine symbol of the earthly side of man and its many contrivances for pleasure or satisfaction. However, the men seem to have forgotten, for the moment, that they must eventually pay a demanding tribute to the "roller of big cigars."

Implicit in the story is the belief that man cannot hope to win a struggle with nature; instead, he must be willing to accept whatever is offered. He must submit to the "grim water," the "snarling of the crests," and the "terrible grace." He must succumb to the various elements of nature and the passive presence of the "old ninny-woman, Fate." To use one of Crane's analogies, man must become like the gulls that form a natural part of the scene, appearing as "gruesome and ominous" as the sea itself.

Because man unconsciously realizes the futility of his struggle, his resistance to fate is never more than a puny or half-hearted effort. This is effectively demonstrated by the correspondent's simple rebellious act: " . . . he leaned a little way to one side and swore softly into the sea." When he qualifies as an interpreter, man is able to comprehend his true position in the universe. The effect which this self-knowledge has upon the individual is directly stated by Crane:

> When it occurs to a man that nature does not regard him as important, and that she feels she would not maim the universe by disposing of him, he at first wishes to throw bricks at the temple, and he hates deeply the fact that there are no bricks and no temples. Any visible expression of nature would surely be pelleted with his jeers.
>
> Then, if there be no tangible thing to hoot he feels, perhaps, the desire to confront a personification and indulge in pleas, bowed to one knee, and with hands supplicant, saying, "Yes, but I love myself."
>
> A high cold star on a winter's night is the word he feels that she says to him. Thereafter he knows the pathos of his situation. (pp. 84-85)

Knowing his situation does not necessitate that man outwardly surrender to it. Even the potential interpreters do not let their mounting apprehensions show in their actions, thoughts, and countenances because, now that life is seen as the journey of the open boat, the same dictum applies as before—"the ethics of their condition was decidedly against any open suggestion of hopelessness."

Until the concluding sequence of events, the four men refuse (with the possible exception of the correspondent)

to hear the final word, the message out of the sea—"Submit." They feel they still have control over their own destinies and that a final struggle may yet prove worthwhile. This optimism, derived from the pride and ignorance of man, is evidenced by the captain when he explains, "Well, . . . if no help is coming, we might better try a run through the surf right away. If we stay out here much longer we will be too weak to do anything for ourselves at all" (p. 88). At this point, the oiler is not a solitary figure striking out against the elements and against fate; instead, he is at one with his society in its effort. Awaiting all of them, however, is the knowledge that the world laboratory is but the chimerical toy given to man in order that he may while away his time in meaningless activity and thought. The last lesson must be learned; they must recognize the necessity to submit.

The futility of struggle is succinctly summed up in the crew's final effort to reach shore. Their true position is established by the strikingly simple and painfully clear symbol of the water jar: "They passed on, nearer to shore—the oiler, the cook, the captain—and following them went the water-jar, bouncing gayly over the seas" (p. 90). This inanimate object proceeds as well as do the men who are thrashing about in the water. All are flotsam, but man alone is cursed with the intelligence that paradoxically prevents true knowledge and understanding of his position.

When this final struggle for survival begins, a meaningful distinction is soon drawn between the oiler and his three comrades. All but Billie seek out and accept available assistance. They recognize the fact that man has but the strength to tease him into self-destructive action and, therefore, they place themselves at the mercy of fate. As they had earlier scanned the shoreline for possible help (from religion as represented by the church and from fellowman as associated with the rescue station), they now humble themselves to accept any assistance—they submit and thereby pay silent homage to an unknown and indifferent force. The captain remains with the boat: " . . . in the rear the captain was hanging with his one good hand to the keel of the overturned dinghy" (p. 90). The cook makes use of the same lifebelt that he had tied around himself earlier in a futile effort to provide warmth as he slept in the bottom of the boat. Now, "the cook's great white and corked back bulged out of the water" (p. 90). Later, upon instructions from his captain (it is ironic that, in the face of superior commanding forces, the captain still tries to direct his men), the cook gets further assistance: "The cook turned on his back, and, paddling with an oar, went ahead as if he were a canoe" (p. 90). Sharing the life-belt with the cook is the correspondent: "A piece of life-belt had lain in the bottom of the boat, and as the correspondent went overboard he held this to his chest with his left hand" (p. 89). He does not fight the sea but, instead, "the correspondent knew that it was a long journey, and he paddled leisurely. The piece of life-preserver lay under him" (p. 90). He is finally saved by a "true miracle of the sea"—an act over which he has no control and one which is not initiated by him. "A large wave caught him and flung him with ease and supreme speed completely over the boat and far beyond it" (p. 91). Shortly thereafter, the correspondent receives assistance from the naked rescuer. All three—the cook, the captain, and the correspondent—accept help; and, especially if life is the end desired, they are right in accepting this proffered assistance.

In contrast to the others, Billie fights against the unseen forces, the fates, and does not seek, request, or accept assistance in the struggle. As a result, a different fate awaits the oiler:

> The welcome of the land to the men from the sea was warm and generous, but a still and dripping shape was carried slowly up the beach, and the land's welcome for it could only be the different and sinister hospitality of the grave. (p. 92)

Chance or fate, factors beyond man's control, offers help to the crew, and the other three humble themselves in the face of a greater force (one may call it an "old ninny-woman" or whatever he likes) and are saved. Billie does not, and dies.

To heighten the lesson involved, the oiler is permitted to move ahead in the early stages of the fight for survival: "The oiler was ahead in the race. He was swimming strongly and rapidly" (p. 90). However, it is soon reported that "In the shallows, face downward, lay the oiler. His forehead touched sand that was periodically, between each wave, clear of the sea" (p. 92). At this point, he is closer to the safety of the shore than any of the others, and no assistance has been sought or gained. But he lies in the clutches of the fickle "old ninny-woman," and in a gruesome jest she opens and closes her hand with the alternating water and sand surrounding the oiler. He belongs to neither the elemental world of the sea from which he has just emerged nor the rational, structured world of the shore. He has spent his energies, he has made a noble fight of it, he has exercised self-reliance, he has fully utilized the particular powers with which he is endowed. He is dead.

Consciously or unconsciously, probably the latter, Billie chose to test the system, to commit a personal, self-motivated act. As a result, he got the ultimate punishment or ultimate reward (depending on the freedom sought). Billie was unwittingly testing not only himself, but man's power and destiny, and the limitation of choice was obvious—death or pawnship. Billie alone was exercising freedom of choice and action, and only he ended up lying face down.

The oiler's action could be seen as revealing a weakness of man that is often disguised as a strength. In conjunction with this interpretation, Billie would represent the highly individualistic man, the man of strength and independence who thereby proves weak and a failure. He fails to realize man's position as a pawn in the hands

of a controlling force. This lone casualty of the open boat might be viewed as a nonrepentant Samson; he does not prostrate himself but, instead, strikes out as an individual, a puny man versus the might of the unknown force. The fact that this controlling force is not viewed as a highly moralistic or religious one does not enter into the inherent lesson which man learns.

Surviving the experience and returning to society, the three remaining crewmen are now "interpreters," but little satisfaction can be realized from the knowledge gained as it reveals the futility of independent action by man. In contrast, the oiler is not permitted the recognition and reversal (the latter revealing itself in the form of resignation as opposed to struggle) that the other three attain, but only he reaches the "comfortable arrangement, a cessation of hostilities accompanied by a large degree of relief . . ." (p. 91). Although the correspondent can intellectualize upon this sensation, he cannot emotionally accept it; however, this cynical man is aware that he has known "the best experience of his life" (p. 73) in the open boat and that he has observed the restrictions imposed on man's nature, thoughts, and general life-experience. Also in contrast with the oiler, the captain arrives at a state of resignation long before the actual abandoning of the dinghy. He expresses this in his reluctant comment, "I suppose we'll have to make a try for ourselves" (p. 76), and in his comment on the handling of the notification of his death. Now that the captain has "interpretive" powers, the irony of his situation is only increased as he has even greater knowledge of man's situation, but is still totally lacking in the ability to commit a worthwhile action based on this knowledge.

The interpreters have gone through a questioning period and even a rebellious one (both moods well illustrated by the famous statements on the "seven mad gods" and "this old ninny-woman, Fate"); but, at the end, they realize that all struggles, mental and spiritual, as well as physical, are futile. At the end, they are no more to contemplate ham sandwiches and kinds of pie, as did the cook on board the dinghy. They realize that man is not meant to nibble the sacred cheese of life; instead, life is to be either a frustrating experience, a groping, a search—or the resignation of those having reached a state of knowledge.

Although "The Open Boat" obviously concludes on a highly philosophic note, it is certainly a negative one—at best, it can only be seen as an affirmation of a negation. The ability to "interpret" is hardly significant if it reveals but the pawn-like existence of man. To have knowledge and yet to realize that this knowledge dooms man to a life of futility and inaction, to a passive existence, is the ultimate in frustration and the greatest of ironies. Not only has the action of Crane's story negated the idea of the power to act and the concept of the "whole man" who can be the meaningfully productive man, but it does so despite permitting an experience which brings about a state of understanding. A modified

Cassandra's curse is upon man—nothing of value can be derived from his knowledge.

The story negates the concept of a benevolent, justice-conscious, or even a retributive supreme power. Man is emphatically denied the choice of the puppeteer or the chessplayer into whose insensitive hand he falls. Attempts at action lead to inaction—death; but here there is a basis for hope, as death is seen as a state of freedom. Billie achieves this ultimate state—freedom from this earth.

In contrast to the oiler, the interpreters have come to a state of earthly knowledge, but the lesson that has been brutally taught to them is certainly not a new one. And it is still highly debatable as to the good derived from knowledge that can lead to absolutely no action. Man does come to know his true state of existence, his position in relation to other elements; and, if knowledge is unequivocally a "good," then some optimism can be gleaned from the experience. However, it is questionable whether this realization, and the experience from which it is derived, permits life to be conceived as a worthwhile, meaningful process. The author himself is undecided as to the preferred state. He seems to favor the state of knowledge even with its curse of inaction and resignation, yet he definitely finds a degree of nobility, if not a slight hope, in the constant and courageous battle of man as he blindly opposes the forces which appear to be directing his actions and determining his course but are actually totally indifferent to him.

Summarily, four men of highly variant powers, of intellect and physical strength, are spilled into an angry sea—immersed in nature—and constitute a "test case." Both the rational powers and the physical strength of man become insignificant, and both are abandoned, as the symbolic boat is abandoned, before the desired place and the necessary state of mind are reached. Only one member does not resign himself to man's fate, and he, relying on his particular source of strength, his physical prowess, serves as the example needed to complete the lesson. His act and fate give concrete form to the abstract lesson taught by "the great sea's voice" (p. 92). However, the final word need not have been "Death," but, harking back to the translations of previous listeners, it need only have been "Submit."

NOTES

[1] *The University of Virginia Edition of the Works of Stephen Crane,* V (Charlottesville: The University Press of Virginia, 1970), 92. All quotations are from this edition.

Emilio de Grazia

SOURCE: "The Great Plain: Rölvaag's New World Sea," in *South Dakota Review,* Vol. 20, No. 3, Autumn, 1982, pp. 35-49.

[*In the following essay, de Grazia studies the symbolic influence of the sea as a creative force, and the negative effects of the sea's absence, in the novels of Ole Rölvaag.*]

It is but one touch of Melville's genius that he opens *Moby-Dick* by introducing us to a neurotic Ishmael who, with "nothing particular to interest [him] on shore,"[1] decides on the sea as the way of driving off the spleen. That Ishmael's condition is typical—felt if not realized by ordinary folk—Melville's opening paragraphs also make clear. We are introduced there to streets that lead inevitably waterward, to crowds of water-gazers with backs turned to jobs and green fields, to "thousands upon thousands of mortal men fixed in ocean reveries" (M-D, p. 24). In a later chapter Melville extends a metaphor to describe the great whale's forehead. "For you see no one point precisely; not one distinct feature is revealed . . . nothing but that one broad firmament of a forehead, pleated with riddles; dumbly lowering with the doom of boats, and ships, and men" (M-D, pp. 447-448). The whale's forehead is like the sea, we say. Yet a different, more dominant, metaphor runs like a strong silent undertow in this chapter. This chapter is called "The Prairie."

From the time prairie schooners sailed through the open grasslands, to these latter days, when amber waves of grain dominate charted fields, the comparison between prairie and sea has pervaded our language, literature and culture. While the comparison is often explicit, it is more generally cast in metaphorical terms and thus lost to consciousness. That the comparison is so pervasive is important, moreso if we are inclined to think of Ishmael's neurosis as typical. It is perhaps most important to that broad spread of Americans who, unlike Ishmael, have no access to the sea and its healing powers—the prairie peoples themselves. No one speaks at once more parochially and more universally for these peoples than Ole Rölvaag, whose novels of prairie life depict the consequences of leaving the sea, and the way of life dependent on it, forever behind. From *The Third Life of Per Smevik* and *The Boat of Longing,* Rölvaag's early accounts of young Norwegians' emigration to Dakota Territory, to the trilogy (*Giants in the Earth, Peder Victorious* and *Their Father's God*) that concluded his writing career, Rölvaag struggled to balance the "gains and losses" of life on the New World prairie. What emerges from his writings is a sense both of the heroic and the tragic, the heroic born of a vague romantic longing inspired by the sea, and the tragic reflecting a loss of the sense of the sea by landlocked generations inevitably more and more removed from it. If the novels express this loss—most notably frustrated attempts, some of them conscious, to keep the sea metaphorically alive—they also prophetically warn of the negative consequences to American culture of losing a sense of the sea.

Rölvaag's own boyhood experiences around his childhood home on Donna Island just south of the Arctic Circle formed the basis for the vision eventually projected into his six novels. The son of a fisherman, Rölvaag was fifteen when he first went to sea in January of 1892. That he emerged from his experiences with an ambiguous sense of realism and romance is clear. He found himself "in battle with [the sea] in the ordinary and perilous ways men who live by fishing do," and yet he confesses that "about it my dream-life was in part woven."[2] The spectacular mountains visible from Donna— *Hestmanden* (The Horseman), *Syv Sostre* (Seven Sisters) and *Donnmannen* (The Man of Donna, shaped like a man lying dead)—he imagined to be keeping "terrible secrets." The romance of the mountains Rölvaag in turn associated with the legendary Castle of Soria Moria, and himself he imagined as the *askeladd* (ashlad) triumphantly scaling the Glass Mountain to win the princess and gain a vision of what lies beyond the sea, "a wonderland of unknown seas and uncharted lands, all mystery-filled."[3] "By and by," he writes, "there sprang up a great intimacy between me and the mountains. After I got so big that I could handle a boat alone we became good friends."[4] The single act that somehow would satisfy the young Rölvaag's fancy is one worthy of Captain Ahab himself. "My first all-consuming ambition," he admits in an unpublished autobiographical sketch, "was to kill a whale."[5]

Rölvaag explored the New World's effect upon his youthful dream-visions in *The Third Life of Per Smevik* (*America Breve* or "Letters from America"), an epistolary account, first published in 1912, in which he assesses the gains and losses of emigration. Per Smevik's first impressions of America are unfavorable. The North Star, once his guide on the sea, betrays him on the prairie, leaving him alone and disoriented. The work required by the land undermines masculinity, reduces him to chore boy, dairy maid. The landscape, "as flat as the flattest floor in our house,"[6] conceals serpents that render his new Garden a perilous Eden. Before he can make a bundle of money and return home, however, he begins to adjust, sporadically feeling "unfaithful" to his "first love," Norway. Yet with the increasing stability he feels on the land comes a growing unrest, and eventually a struggle to deny his Americanization. "This is a dead world" (PS, p. 54), he concludes, even as he, projection of the young Rölvaag determined to be a writer, learns English and ventures out, unsuccessfully, to be a book salesman.

Pulling him back more forcefully than any influence is the sea. On his first day he transforms the prairie grass into a vision of home, "the bay lying mirror-like before [him]," and when war breaks out in 1898 he dreams of enlisting in the navy to escape the land. At the end when he figures his "losses and gains," he gives America its due—fine houses, well-kept farms, civil and religious freedom, opportunity for individual growth, and "the value of really economical and intensive work" (PS, pp. 120-121). But what has Per Smevik lost? In general terms it is the fatherland, contact with his own people. He, indeed all Norwegian immigrants, are "adopted children," rootless, alienated, incapable of

entering fully into the public life of their new country. But the greatest loss, the one underlying all these, is suggested at the opening of the final chapter when Per Smevik receives word of his mother's death and envisions her waving at him across the bay. Per Smevik climbs the highest hill and "searche[s] and hunt[s] in vain for the sea" (PS, p. 124). In its absence he leaps by poetic logic to another stark conclusion about America's deficiency: "The prairie has not yet produced any really great artist" (PS, p. 124).

But there is a consolation. Asked to preach one day at the local church, Per Smevik lights upon Peter's miraculous draft of fish as a sermon topic. "I saw the sea, I saw the tired old fishermen lying there on the shore after the night's struggle with their nets, I saw the Saviour come down to them in the morning light . . ." (PS, p. 103). The poetry of Per Smevik's vision transcends the standard terms promising salvation, for the poetry resurrects the sea-longing he is losing on American soil. It returns him not to institutional Christianity but to a sense of existential mystery.

These themes repeat themselves in more complicated and symbolic terms in *The Boat of Longing,* Rölvaag's fourth novel (1921, translated in 1933) but in some respects *Per Smevik's* natural predecessor. If Per Smevik looks longingly back to Norway, Nils, youthful Norwegian protagonist, looks out to sea and beyond. The four parts of the novel describe Nils' movement from the insular but stable protection of Norwegian fishing village ("The Cove under the Hill") to a new life in America ("In Foreign Waters") where he finds himself alienated ("Adrift") and, like parents left behind, again longing ("Hearts that Ache"). The novel's central metaphor is the legendary boat of longing, a vessel always expected, sometimes glimpsed but never arriving. The boat is a vehicle for Nils' longing, his desiring for something better somewhere else, an elusive, sometimes illusory, lure that distances itself as he approaches. For Nils the sea is not simply the lure itself, for it lures him beyond itself; the sea is a reflection of himself and of the longing that carries him along. Nils himself is the boat of longing, the lure he himself pursues.

It is not simple narcissism that moves Nils. Rölvaag chides Nils for his youthful foolishness, for dreams, such as his vision of marble houses in Minneapolis, or a "big building in the middle of the city with an enormously high tower on it, reaching clean to the sky,"[7] cast in static terms. He is foolish to imagine he will come to rest in such a heavenly city on earth, even though ashore. But Nils' more serious search is for self-definition and creative fulfillment. In the opening section of the novel we find the boat of longing associated with four basic human desires: the desire for creative work, for beauty as it expresses itself in nature and the arts, for love and sexual fulfillment, and for the preservation of a "long" view that keeps alive existential awe. As fisherman Nils is "seized with a love of battle" that makes him want to shout for joy (BL, p. 41), a joy equalled only by that brought by his violin, "beside the sea . . . really [the] only one other power which had any hold on him" (BL, p. 18). It is "sea-dreams" that Nils tries to express with his playing, a "song of the sea" shared by the dark mysterious Zalma, whose swaying body lures him toward manhood and away from father, mother and the safety of shore. Later, when Nils finds himself on shore, music and the sea become associated with a land animal, the horse. A three-year-old Norwegian boy, coming upon Nils' violin during the trainride inland, exclaims: "Look! Mommy, look! . . . A horse what c'n sing!" (BL, p. 229). Nils intoxicates the Norwegian travellers with his song. The section entitled "Adrift" finds Nils at Wild Horse Lake, a dark vision overwhelming him as he fishes there alone, desperate to revive a past now gone but not dead.

These episodes serve to illustrate that Nils feels the broadly established associations suggested by the etymology linking the horse *(mare)* with the sea *(mare)* and, as we shall see in later variations on the theme, archetypal source of life, the mother *(mer, mere)*, the basic stuff of life *(madre, mater, matter)*, and the procreative process *(mate, marry)*.

As Nils adjusts to the New World his sense of the sea undergoes a conversion. If once the sea expressed a creative urge, in the New World it comes to express his alienation, frustration and despair. He feels city traffic as a "current" bringing no pleasure or sense of control, and his despair he expresses in maelstrom terms. Toward the middle of *The Boat of Longing* Rölvaag begins developing a metaphor that will figure as an important symbol in later work. As Nils heads toward a logging job in the Minnesota northwoods, he finds the train rocking him like a boat. The train—agent of the new industrial order, of a "progress" requiring the expending of creative energy on the development of an ever-expanding (and ever-inflating) Gross National Product—conspicuously, and inauspiciously, will return as a "monster" at the end of *Giants in the Earth,* making its serpentine way through Per Hansa's New World Garden to signal the arrival of a new age of irony and steel. It is little wonder that Rölvaag abandons Nils, at the end of the section entitled "Adrift," in the Great Northern Station in Minneapolis, the only place he feels at home while he awaits another train to take him to another—any—city. Disillusioned but unenlightened, Nils, Rölvaag's twentieth-century Ishmael, is lost in the anonymity of the American wasteland, and his parents, for a time deluded that he will return the proud owner of a steel steamship, try to console themselves with the illusion that he lives happily in a towered city full of marble houses. Only silence answers their letters.

It is worth mentioning that Rölvaag's neighbor and contemporary, F. Scott Fitzgerald, documented the transformation of the train into its slicker child, the automobile. In *The Great Gatsby* the lovely sailboats Tom Buchanen sees off the coast are vehicles of sport, nothing else. His carelessness of vision—moral, aesthetic, and political—typifies the new generation of Americans and is responsible for the accidents, boredom, violence and eventual crash. Gatsby, like Nils, can still look out over water and long, but the longing has no creative dimension to it; it is directed at objects, even Daisy herself, static, undeveloped, fighting the processes of growth. Gatsby's story, Nick Carraway realizes late in the novel, has been a "story of the West," and of "some deficiency" the characters, all midwesterners, share. "So we beat on," Nick nihilistically concludes in words that might have finished Nils' story, "boats against the current, borne back ceaselessly into the past."[8]

In his trilogy Rölvaag explores this theme more broadly through the lives of people who settle for homesteads on the prairie. That a sense of the sea follows the settlers Rölvaag makes clear on the first page, where he describes the track of their wagon as "like the wake of a boat"; that this wake closes in behind the wagon suggests his pessimistic prognosis for the democratic dream. Through two generations and into a third Rölvaag traces the diminuendo of the sea-sense, its further frustration and further transformations by the evolving culture of the New Land.

The prairie wagon and his own storm-tossed body are Per Hansa's boats of longing. Like Nils he can only look "ever onward," the prairie frontier leading inexorably to a promising sunset ever westward. Like Nils, he cannot endure stasis. The prairie grass sounds like the sea only when men move through it; when at rest it is "lifeless," its silence impressing on them their landlocked doom. Per Hansa acts as if the sea is still alive as prairie. He schemes to catch ducks with a fishnet and buys boards to build a "boat" to cradle his new son. During his few moments of leisure he is a man "resting on his oars." Ultimate rest comes for him only on the last page of *Giants in the Earth,* where we find him still facing west, the sea in him finally frozen by the land.

Per Hansa is Rölvaag's most big-hearted character, more ambiguous and less romantic than the Nils who in the end disappears into anonymous American cities. Per Hansa directs to the land the full vigor of manhood once expended on the sea, and from his efforts he too expects to reap creative fulfillment. The sexual longing Nils directs toward Zalma, strange sea-girl, Per Hansa directs to husbandry of the land, and he envisions an ever-expanding horizon of property to inseminate. This is his creative mission. But Nils' vision is fuller and more demanding: it includes beauty as well as sex and work, and a religious sense that existence, typified by mountain and sea, is sublime. Per Hansa, able to lose himself in the flow of work that sublimates his sexual impulses, cannot lose himself in the landscape as Nils once could. And as for art, the best he can manage is a bucket of paint to whitewash the walls of his hut. The deficiency of Per Hansa's cultural legacy is evident: apparently endless squared fields of grain interrupted by stark white houses and by gopher prairie towns that insist on keeping their Carole Kennicotts from influencing their Main Streets.

Rölvaag makes clear what the root of Per Hansa's *hubris* is. If Nils' delusion is that Minneapolis is a city of marble and towers (actually its skyline is made up mainly of random grain elevators), Per Hansa's is that he can build a "royal mansion" on the prairie. The aesthetic pleasure Nils derives from the process of playing his violin, Per Hansa tries objectifying in a fairy tale farm. He is "transported, . . . carried farther and farther away on the wings of a wondrous fairy tale—a romance in which he was both prince and king, the sole possessor of countless treasures. In this, as in all other fairy tales, the story grew ever more fascinating and dear to the heart, the farther it advanced. Per Hansa drank it in; he was like the child who constantly cries: 'More—more.'"[9]

Thus the sense of process that once moved Per Hansa is translated into a desire for quantitative increase. That Per Hansa's vision is cast in Edenic terms suggesting an unfortunate fall is appropriate. On the prairie sea he will erect a white house with "nothing less than a snow-white picket fence around a big, big garden" and apple trees will grow there (GE, p. 109). His first furrow, marking his transformation from seaman to farmer, "comes winding up behind him like a snake" (GE, p. 46). Significantly, the waving grass itself, reminder of the sea, reveals the fatal flaw of his scheme. What the waving grass reveals is what it tried to overwhelm, the Irishmen's stakes, signs of the illigitimacy of Per Hansa's efforts, wrong-minded preoccupation with property, and betrayal of the life-giving grass itself. Little wonder that Per Hansa, his "ardor" lost after he hides the stakes, assumes a Faustian aspect; Rölvaag saw clearly that Per Hansa, as type, is farmer-friend of the technocrat who one day would bring big machines into the New World Garden.

No one in Rölvaag's work denies the sea with such morbid persistence as Beret (a pun on "bear-it"?), and no one endures more stubbornly the disease her denial brings. As fisherman's wife forced to wait storms out for the return of her man, Beret had reason to fear the sea; that Per Hansa was a "reckless" seaman intensifies her fear. This recklessness, which ties Per Hansa in kinship to the sea, is in part what Beret tries to deny, moreso because their mutual recklessness led to a premarital pregnancy and a guilty marriage bond. Thus Beret's rejection of Per Hansa's recklessness is self-denial, her denial of his ardor a denial of the life he loves most, the life of the sea he vicariously and vainly tries to resurrect on the prairie and in her. But Beret is a cold fish. House-bound as husband, Per Hansa turns his erotic energy into husbandry of the land, exhilirated to see the wheat "filling out like a young girl" (GE, p. 325). In turn he comes to see Beret as not fully developed, as "delicate child" whom to "desire physically would be as far from his mind as the crime of incest" (GE, p. 440).

Beret's condition is much like that of Rosie, the cow. Like Rosie she is tethered to the wagon and led grudgingly to her prairie home. Once there she, like Rosie, wanders away, rejects her place and becomes spiritually lost. What terrifies Beret, however, is the power that has led Rosie to wander: "When lust can be so strong in a dumb brute, what mustn't it be in a human being!" (GE, p. 106). While she herself would wander away to reject the prairie and Per Hansa's recklessness, she is bound to stay because she fears going elsewhere, escape impossible. Ironically, however, Rosie is also a projection of the "beast" in her, of her own need for sexual fulfillment, a need she is also bound to confine. Alienated from home where sea and shore interplay, Beret alienates spirit and body. "Man and beast in one building?" she asks when she considers the way of life Per Hansa would impose on her, "How could one live that way?" (GE, p. 53).

Beret's denial of sexuality colors her perception of the prairie landscape. Per Hansa's grassy sea full of endless promise Beret colors in tones that express her own denial of being. Herself she sees as "a chip on the current . . . washed ashore," (GE, p. 221) and the prairie "almost like the ocean . . . [with] no heart, no waves that sang, no soul that could be touched . . . or cared . . ." (GE, p. 37). Yet its healing qualities work on her. As Per Hansa fixes his nets in preparation for the duck-hunt, his cheerful voice sounds like "lapping ocean waves" that bring her restful sleep. Most often, however, she denies or dichotomizes the ocean-prairie connection, seeing the prairie as emblem of the world, flesh and devil. The heart that dares not let in the sun is also one that dares not let the prairie work as sea through her. As her sexual guilt drives her toward increasing self-denial and withdrawal, she visualizes the prairie as "too open and wild," prostitute stretching herself "voluptuously." Even the prairie sunset is to her eyes too full of "wanton" colors.

Her guilty fear of sexuality extends to deepest fear of existence itself. Just as she abandoned herself to Per Hansa's sexual advances, she feels abandoned on the prairie. When Per Hansa leaves her to work the fields, she is cut off, physically and emotionally, from community and vital relationship to the land. The consequence is the deepest existential terror, the terror Melville speaks of in his chapter on the whiteness of the whale. This terror, of course, is most deeply felt when the prairie least resembles the sea, when it becomes a "rigid frozen silence," "a universe of nothing but dead whiteness" (GE, p. 241), metaphor for the Ultima Thule of Norwegian folklore and the ultimate stasis, death.

In desperation Beret shrinks from this terror, covers the windows, curls fetally in her womb-like trunk, reminder of childhood and home. This terror is also the source of her desperate Christianity. With nothing to hide behind on the prairie, she dreams of the stone-walled churches of Norway. A natural religious sense inspired by the sublime aspects of mountain, prairie and sea she affronts with an institution based on dogma, creed and superstition. Her rejection of natural religion—and Rölvaag's rejection of hers—becomes clear when we see her motives for sending Per Hansa, in her eyes a natural fallen man, to certain death at the novel's end.

In rejecting Beret's religious sense as a denial of exist-ence, however, Rölvaag does not abandon her. Beret, like Rosie the cow, is eventually found; both live use-fully on into the novels that complete the trilogy. The redemptive possibility in *Giants in the Earth* is sounded through the minister, who prays that all sins be "cast into the ocean of grace" (GE, p. 349).

Peder Victorious and *Their Father's God,* sequels to *Giants in the Earth,* record the gradual diminuendo and trivialization of a sense of the sea. References to the sea decrease as the new generations, born with no direct sea-experience, grow older on the land. Sea imagery, when used at all, gradually becomes imposed more and more from above by the novels' omniscient narrators rather than growing dramatically out of the characters' consciousness. If the exception to this rule is Beret, in whom the sea is still present generally as a bad memory, the rule is observed in Peder, whose experiences are central to these two rather diffusely structured novels. In them Rölvaag traces not so much the loss of the sense of the sea as its "leavening" and new transformations by the prairie settlers.

> The leaven was working. A people's soul had begun to stir. That which the mind in some hidden cove of a Norwegian fiord, or on some lonely island—far out where the mighty sea booms eternally—through centuries had conceived of religious mysticism, and there shaped so as to fit the conditions of life, now sought a natural expression on the open reaches of the prairies. New forces, forces which they themselves did not understand, were at work here. The lure of the unknown and the restless, roving spirit of the race had torn them loose from their ancient moorings, from home and kindred and fatherland, and from all that hitherto had given them a sense of security and a feeling of safety, and had led them into this strange and faraway land. Now the tide bore back again; their imagination was busily at work, painting enchanting pictures of the old home which they never more could regain; on evenings when the weather was fair, they might stand on the prairie and sense its presence in the gloaming as a sunken Atlantis. With these people the feeling of strangeness in this alien land and the utter impossibility of striking new roots here gave to their testimony the tone of deep, rich spiritual experience.[10]

This rich spiritual experience has to be painfully gained against the backdrop of a landscape still "float[ing] in a sea of sun" and of westward moving bands still follow-ing not sun but railroad "like seagulls." The lure of the west as endless sea persists; just beyond Dakota is Montana, and beyond Montana is Washington. But the lure is a temptation resisted by Peder, who must forge his "victory" out of his place and present. And the vic-tory must be expressed in metaphors that leave the sea as vehicle further and further in the background.

The two novels develop dialectically, with Beret and Peder defining polar values that in the end must come

to some creative synthesis. The conflict is generational but cultural as well, expressing itself as an opposition between Norwegian and Irish tribes, Old and New World, Medieval and modern. On a more elemental level the conflict pits spirit against the flesh and sea against the land, the two novels describing a collective groping toward integrated balance. The most unbal-anced character is still Beret, whose life-denying struggles against the New World and Peder finally work themselves out into a stable if not creative health.

Almost until the very end Beret insists on denying the forces represented by the sea. The prairie to her is still a "flood tide" which in winter becomes a "billowing sea of white." She still sees herself as "on a lone rock far out at sea," beseiged by a bird with designs on her body (PV, p. 195); she is possessed by the need for a solid barn to stand against a sense of being "shipwrecked," afloat on a sea lacking substance. Resisting seculariza-tion and Americanization, she opposes the tide of life manifesting itself in liberal democratic institutions de-signed to free creative energies and marry opposing sexes, nationalities and religions. The new schoolhouse, where drama and dancing take place, symbolizes every-thing she fears. Her attempt to burn it to the ground is thwarted by a downpour that comes in "huge waves" and "singing breakers." For months after she sends Per Hansa to his death she too faces west waiting for his return, and as prairie farm widow she spends a lifetime waiting for her man. When Rosie, aged cow, finally dies, so does Beret, still longing for a safe stasis, a heaven beyond the horizon. She, like Peder, settles for a Pyrrhic victory, one bought mainly by endurance, the stuff of service and sacrifice, yet touched by the forgive-ness and grace that in the end wash away her sins.

It is up to Peder, inheritor of Per Hansa's restless energy and emerging American, to attempt a less self-defeating victory. His initial and continuing battles are sexual as he struggles through shame toward awareness and ful-fillment. Unconscious of the power of sex, he feels the same sexual sea-sense that Nils and Per Hansa feel. But as he comes to sexual consciousness, Peder sees the sunset west as alluring woman, himself as conquering pioneer. Until he comes into vital contact with sensual Norwegian girl Nikoline, the sea distances itself as metaphorical vehicle for sexuality, a paradise lost, unre-membered and therefore available only unconsciously and vicariously in the New World. Significantly, Peder's favorite vehicle (literally) is his horse, whom he rides with obvious sexual joy. That his horse is named Dolly only strengthens the insinuations.

Peder, tossing and turning through the course of these novels, is compelled by a longing greater than himself and by a vision broader than his father's. As the society around Peder becomes more materialistic and as divi-sions persist, a dryness begins to spread. No longer content to splash in a rain barrel, Peder emerges at the beginning of *Their Father's God* as adversary of the swindler hired by the town board to end the Dakota drought. Rölvaag signals that the inchoate longing for sexual fulfillment so pervasive in earlier novels is being converted to a desire for viable community. That Peder denies the ministry, his mother's hope for him, for a political calling makes clear his further distancing from her sense of life; that his first political speech is followed by a drunken spree suggests a new intoxication and unquenched thirst. While he is easily induced to think bigger and bigger as farmer and politician, Peder cannot resist the new pull, the "restless undertow . . . calling him to other things than milking cows and swilling hogs."[11]

Peder finally comes to realize that he must be either ordinary or extraordinary, a "porridge bowl Viking" or one who "must sail the far seas." His deepest inclination is suggested when, rocking with his infant son in a chair reminiscent of the cradle-"boat" which per Hansa made for him, he sings Norwegian songs. His new adversary is Susie, Irish-Catholic wife gradually evincing many of Beret's worst qualities, and his new love is Nikoline, at once freshly Norwegian and pagan, like him a "sea-gull with a broken wing." As Peder's marriage fails, his thoughts turn more and more to Norway via Nikoline, sex and beauty personified, paradise lost. Yet it is she, as woman of strength and sense as well, who tells Peder how self-defeating his romanticism is: "We [Norwegians] know when we see *hilder* [mirage]: we can tell and make allowance. You Americans believe all you see until you run your heads against a stone wall; then you don't believe anything any more" (TFG, p. 235).

Rölvaag abandons us in mid-stream. The disease that brought Beret down threatens Peder's marriage and swells the moral majority that will assure his defeat in the election. Peder's last act is to go on, recover Susie home again where the ongoing struggle must continue and conclude. Thus Rölvaag leaves us where Melville begins: with a neurotic protagonist too bound to the responsibilities of home and shore. The difference is also plain. Ishmael retreats to new adventures leading to illumination: he must "lower, or at least shift, [his] conceit of attainable felicity, not placing it anywhere in the intellect or fancy; but in the wife, the heart, the bed, the table, the saddle, the fireside, the country" (M-D, p. 533). Renewed by the sea, Ishmael has found the strength to go on. Peder, metaphorically and physically divorced from the source of renewal, must plod on, his marriage a dreary duty, his conceit of attainable felicity undiscovered.

The severest consequences of this frustration appear in the lives of Louis and Lizzy Houglum, the pathetic couple of *Pure Gold,* Rolvaag's third novel (1921, English translation, 1931) but the one best fit to serve as simple moral to all his stories. The Houglums, after a brief romance, develop the habit of hoarding money. This irrepressible urge, reminiscent of Per Hansa's quest for more and more land, destroys the couple socially and spiritually, leaving Louis, like Per Hansa, frozen in the end. The novel is remarkable for having

only two references to the sea—one which describes Louis' contentment when he considers giving some money away, the other in reference to the war, "The Great Flood" that threatens the couple's fortune. The moral is clear: the longing for a better life makes a wasteland of lives when the process is not made viable by itself.

It is perhaps not accidental that *Pure Gold* is Rölvaag's weakest novel—that its characters and style are flat, its narrative a swift, dully detailed account of people whose lives pass them by. While aesthetically indefensible, the novel's stylistic deficiencies reflect the flat lives of its principal characters. The critical consensus is that Rölvaag's work as a whole—except for *Giants in the Earth*—is uneven, the unevenness apparent in *The Boat of Longing* but conspicuous in the last two novels. Appropriately, *The Boat of Longing* opens lyrically, rhapsodically, but as it traces Nils' distancing from home its style flattens into realistic narration broken only by lyrical interludes. Similarly, the style flattens through the course of the later trilogy, the powerful prose of *Giants in the Earth* reduced to a dryer plain style emptier of metaphorical and rhythmic innuendo. It is the flatter plain style—a reflection of the Great Plain itself—that in part has led to Rölvaag's being dismissed as a "regional realist," a label that does little justice to the undertow of vital symbolism and myth present in much of his work.

Yet the deficiency in Rölvaag's work perhaps also reflects the deficiency of his own situation as midwesterner. Like his protagonists—and like Melville himself, most creative when fresh from the sea—Rölvaag became more and more removed from his beloved sea. His protagonists, full of creative urges, misspend and lose their best energies on the plains, which drinks the blood of Christian men and women desiring creative work, sexual expression, and community based on tolerant social justice. Most importantly, life in Rölvaag's farms and towns sends the existential self into hiding, inclines individuals to the parochial rather than long view of life, the institutionalized church, itself parochial and antagonistic to the natural, urging them away from creative living.

About the cultural implications of this deficiency we are left to speculate. If Rölvaag's sea-longing protagonists characteristically struggle against and endure their alienation, they do so in a cultural context that, however faintly reminiscent of the motions of the sea, has hardened and trivialized original natural longings.

NOTES

[1] Herman Melville, *Moby-Dick* (Indianapolis, N.Y., Kansas City, 1964), p. 23. Quotations taken from novels are indicated parenthetically in the text after the editions used are initially cited in the notes.

[2] Paul Reigstad, *Rölvaag: His Life and Art* (Lincoln, Neb., 1972), p. 6.

3 Ibid., p. 19.

4 Ibid., p. 3.

5 Ibid., p. 7.

6 Ole Rölvaag, *The Third Life of Per Smevik* (Minneapolis, 1971), p. 10.

7 Ole Rölvaag, *The Boat of Longing* (New York and London, 1933), p. 49.

8 F. Scott Fitzgerald, *The Great Gatsby,* (New York, 1925), p. 182.

9 Ole Rölvaag, *Giants in the Earth* (New York, 1974), p. 107.

10 Ole Rölvaag, *Peder Victorious* (New York and London, 1929), pp. 52-53.

11 Ole Rölvaag, *Their Father's God* (New York and Chicago, 1931), p. 97.

Lynn Veach Sadler

SOURCE: "The Sea in Selected American Novels of Slave Unrest," in *Journal of American Culture*, Vol. 10, No. 2, Summer, 1987, pp. 43-8.

[*In the following essay, Sadler looks at depictions of the sea in several slave novels—as an avenue of escape, a symbol of oppression, or "a metaphor for humans' enslavement of their fellows and themselves."*]

The sea and streams of water in general play an important role in American "novels of slave unrest." Two of the best of the genre—Harriet Beecher Stowe's *Dred; A Tale of the Great Dismal Swamp* (1856) and William Styron's *The Confessions of Nat Turner* (1966), both by White authors—treat the sea extensively, on both literal and figurative levels, and constantly link the swamp-as-temporary-haven theme with ultimate escape by the sea. Perhaps the best of the group by a Black author, Arna Bontemps' *Black Thunder* (1936) merges the forces of Nature, with water one of its most powerful instruments, to suggest an elemental power determined to prevent the rise of the oppressed. Mary Johnston in *The Slave Ship* (1924), on the other hand, conceives the sea in its most universal terms and applies it as a metaphor for humans' enslavement of their fellows and of themselves. Certain others of these novels treating insurrections and insurrectionists remain largely literal in their depiction of the sea; examples are Richard Hildreth's *The Slave: or Memoirs of Archy Moore* (1836), William Wells Brown's *Clotelle* (1864; the first version, 1853), and Martin R. Delany's *Blake; or the Huts of America* (1859-62).

Stowe originally named her two-volume novel *Canema* after the plantation of Nina Gordon, the intended heroine; but political events (Johnston, 300-02) evoked a change in tone and brought the introduction of Dred in Chapter 18 of Volume I. Stowe imbues the title character with a dreamy, nostalgic, seemingly archetypal longing for the sea, quite apart from the prominent swamp-as-haven theme. Indeed, Dred refuses to escape himself to and by the sea and, rather, secures his swamp fortress, in which he lives with a wife and his dog Buck, and helps others, largely slaves and slave sympathizers, make their escapes. He has worked out elaborate relations with the slaves and the poor Whites in the area and is able to trade easily for supplies and to send and receive news. Although he dies from a wound received in a final fight to free the other major characters, they are able to negotiate with the slaves of a lumber camp and escape by a vessel carrying lumber to Norfolk, where they in turn take passage to New York and eventually reach Canada.

Since one of Stowe's aims in *Dred* is to universalize—in order to heighten—the experience of the slaves, she constantly links their fight to free themselves with similar efforts by leaders around the world. The Dismal Swamp, then, has its parallel in world history: "What the mountains of Switzerland were to the persecuted Vaudois, this swampy belt has been to the American slave" (I: 255). Yet the image of the swamp is ambiguous, too, for Stowe links it with "goblin growth" and misuse:

> The wild, dreary belt of swamp-land which girds in those states scathed by the fires of despotism is an apt emblem, in its rampant and . . . delirious exuberance of vegetation, of that darkly struggling, wildly vegetating swamp of human souls, cut off, like it, from the usages and improvements of cultivated life.

> Beneath that fearful pressure, souls whose energy, well-directed, might have blessed mankind, start out in preternatural and fearful developments, whose strength is only a portent of dread.
>
> (II: 274-75)

This dual view of the swamp, shunned by most but sought as a refuge by the slaves, is in consonance with the sea as both life-giving and life-taking. The swamp is healthy (e.g., I: 290-92, II: 289-90), and its "resinous trees" "impart a balsamic property" and cause it "to be an exception to the usual rule of the unhealthiness of swampy land" (I: 291). Similarly, a great storm terrorizes the area and simultaneously deposits a runaway slave at Dred's feet. Moreover, near the end, once those escaping to Canada are on their way to New York, filled with "joyous security" at being "out at sea in a white-winged vessel, flying with all speed toward the distant port of safety" (II: 325), another great storm sends their ship on the rocks and requires the sacrifice of Black Tiff, who is providentially recovered:

> Says I, "Good Lord, you knows I don't car nothing 'bout it on my own 'count; but 'pears like dese chil'en is so young and tender, I couldn't leave dem, no way;" and so I axed him if he wouldn't

jest please to help me, 'cause I knowed he had de power of de winds and de sea. Well, sure 'nough, dat ar big wave toted me clar up right on de sho'. . . .

(II: 329)

Ambiguity is a dominant tone throughout the novel. Dred has taken to the swamp originally only his Bible, and his watery retreat is also heightened by frequent biblical references. His personal "estate," "isolated from the rest of the swamp by some twenty yards of deep morass, in which it was necessary to wade almost to the waist," is called the "strong hold of Engedi" (II: 273), a famous well on the west shore of the Dead Sea mentioned with some frequency in the Bible, and his efforts are repeatedly described in images from Revelation, which also becomes his datum for studying the sea. Like it, he is redeemer and executioner, instrument of salvation and of judgment (Sadler, "The Samson Figure. . . .").

Dred is intensely interested in the literal sea and has learned from its mysteries and in turn endowed it with an apocalyptic cast:

. . . he had wandered along the dreary and perilous belt of sand which skirts the southern Atlantic shores, full of quicksands and of dangers, and there he had mused of the eternal secret of the tides, with whose restless, never-ceasing rise and fall the soul of man has a mysterious sympathy. Destitute of the light of philosophy and science, he had revolved in the twilight of his ardent and struggling thoughts the causes of natural phenomena, and settled these questions for himself by theories of his own.

(II: 291)

He once spent three weeks in the hulk of a ship at "Okerecoke" (Ocracoke, in North Carolina), sent by the Spirit:

. . . and the Lord bade me to go from the habitations of men, and to seek out the desolate places of the sea, and dwell in the wreck of a ship that was forsaken for a sign of desolation unto this people. So I went and dwelt there, and the Lord called me Amraphal, because hidden things of judgment were made known unto me. And the Lord showed unto me that even as a ship which is forsaken of the waters, wherein all flesh have died, so shall it be with the nation of the oppressor.

(II: 292)

What he learns is the message of Revelation—that God has "appointed the tide" (II: 293) of coming judgment:

Because every day is full of labor, but the labor goeth back again into the seas. So that travail of all generations hath gone back, till the desire of all nations shall come, and He shall come with burning and with judgment, and with great shakings; but in the end thereof shall be peace. Wherefore, it is written that in the new heavens and the new earth *there shall be no more sea.*

(II: 293, my italics)

Dred, as the instrument of that judgment, is self-divided; he has no assurance of being among the elect (II: 294), as his compatriots could not be assured that they were saved even after they had boarded the ship bound for New York. In Stowe, the only stability is the God Who wields the tide.

Stowe was influenced by the historical figure of Nat Turner (Sadler, "Dr. Stephen Graham's Narration. . . .") in her depiction of Dred; and one of the principal Turner conspirators was named "Dred," a rather standard slave name for those of great physical force. Still, the similarities between the treatment of the protagonists in her novel and Styron's are striking, and *The Confessions of Nat Turner* contains a minor figure named Dred, though he is a mental deficient harshly treated (299-300). A kindred, though more intense, symbolic investment in the sea is present in Styron's novel, which also employs apocalyptic imagery and has Nat preaching Revelation's time when "the former things are passed away" (frontispiece). It opens with an extended recurrent vision of Nat Turner in which a promontory or cliff, the "last outpost of land," rises hundreds of feet "above the barren, sandy cape where the river joins the sea." He approaches this "almost seasonless" place alone in some kind of boat. The shores have no people and no animals, and the effect is of silence and solitude "as if life here had not so much perished as simply disappeared, leaving all—river shore and estuary and rolling sea—to exist forever unchanged like this beneath the light of a motionless afternoon sun" (3). On the promontory is a building white in the sunlight and like a temple, but one "in which no one worships, or a sarcophagus in which no one lies buried, or a monument to something mysterious, ineffable, and without name." It has no doors; even if it could be opened, it would yield "only a profusion of darker and perhaps more troubling mysteries, as in a maze" (4). Nat believes the dream and its "emotion of a tranquil and abiding mystery" (5) to derive from his childhood recollections of hearing Whites talk of going to the seaside in Norfolk. He never sees the sea, a hope he is still expressing in his written plans for the rebellion (330), but his imagination is "inflamed" "in such a way that my desire to see this sight became a kind of fierce, inward, almost physical hunger, and there were days when my mind seemed filled with nothing but fantasies of the waves and the distant horizon and the groaning seas, the free blue air like an empire above arching eastward to Africa—as if by one single glimpse of this scene I might comprehend all the earth's ancient, oceanic, preposterous splendor" (5). The vision always leaves "the remnant of something frail and unutterably sweet, like a bird call, lingering in my memory" (129). In the final (fourth) section of the book, "It Is Done . . . ," the vision recurs as Nat waits to be hanged.

The facts of the insurrection are equally infused with reliance on the sea. Nat and his men know that the Dismal Swamp, again perceived as "a perfect stronghold" "as wild as the dawn of creation" (335), is not many miles from the Atlantic. Once there, they can rest and gain the strength to get to Norfolk and then slip on a merchant ship for the North. Earlier, he has discovered a sanctuary in the woods and patterned it on Isaiah: "Is not this the fast that I have chosen? To loose the bonds of wickedness, to undo the heavy burdens, and to let the oppressed go free, and that ye break every yoke?" (275). The stream that feeds it becomes in his mind the River Jordan.

Dichotomies similar to those in *Dred* thread *The Confessions of Nat Turner,* too. The temple on the cape, for example, so obviously a positive image for Nat, reverberates for the reader with notes of the "whited sepulchre" (Matthew 23:27). Nat suffers the same doubts as Dred and looks for signs that are never forthcoming. When an evil master is crushed by a cypress in the swamp "just as he was engaged in brandy-befuddled remonstrance with two black timber hands" (166), the tale is current for years, with hints of foul play, but Nat doubts this reasoning and seems to imply, rather, providential intervention.

Nat tends also to employ sea images and similes, yielded up, again, entirely from his imagination. A wagon, which he sees practically daily, looks "like the picture of a sailing ship, foundered now upon the edge of the forest" (213) or heaves and rocks "like a rudderless ship amid a sea of frozen glass" (253). His master's mill, land, and people disintegrate before his eyes "like one of those river islands at flood time which slowly crumbles away at the edges, toppling all of its drenched and huddled ragtag occupants, coons and rabbits and blacksnakes and foxes, into the merciless brown waters" (222). The sea that he has never seen interpenetrates his conscious and his unconscious.

Initially, *Black Thunder,* perhaps the outstanding novel of slave unrest by a Black author, seems to have many parallels with the works of Stowe and Styron. Gabriel, the leader of the slaves, has the same religious bent as Dred and Nat Turner and, at the end, is even more pronouncedly a Christ figure. He and his fellow conspirators (eleven hundred men and one woman) will meet in Brook Swamp and ultimately plan to take Richmond. If they are unsuccessful, they will flee, this time, to the mountains. Like Dred, Gabriel is not afraid to fight but is afraid of signs or their absence. Once he decides that the "stars" are against him, he calls off the rebellion. He is too late, however, since Pharaoh, angry at not being allowed to lead one of the lines of march, has betrayed him. Gabriel eventually makes his way to Richmond; hides out for eleven days on the schooner, *Mary;* and surrenders himself to the men questioning his cousin Mott, declaring again that he "ain't much hand at running. I was in for fighting, me" (256).

Yet *Black Thunder,* though also highly imaginative and symbolic, is quite different from the Stowe and Styron novels in its attitude toward and treatment of the sea (and, by extension, water generally). Even in his intro-

duction to the 1968 edition, for example, Bontemps suggests that difference when he rejects a standard water analogy to declare that "Time is not a river. Time is a pendulum" (vii). The sea here becomes part of a seeming conspiracy of the elements against the oppressed as the area, at precisely the moment of the slaves' uprising, becomes a "sea":

> Nothing like it had happened before in Virginia. The downpour came first in swirls; then followed diagonal blasts that bore down with withering strength. The thirsting earth sucked up as much water as it could but presently spewed little slobbery streams into the wrinkles of the ground. Small gullies took their fill with open mouths and let the rest run out. Rivulets wriggled in the wheel paths, cascaded over small embankments. The creeks grew fat. Water rose in the swamps and in the low fields, and gradually Henrico County *became a sea with islands and bays, reefs and currents and*
> *atolls.*
>
> (108, my italics)

Gabriel, we infer, does not connect Nature's conspiracy against him with God. He, instead, defies the elements:

> "Thunder and lightning ain't nothing neither. If it is, I invites it to try me a barrel." He put out a massive chest, struck it a resounding smack. "Touch me if you's so bad, Big Man." A huge roar filled the sky. The lightning snapped bitterly. Gabriel roared with laughter, slapping his chest again and again. "Sign, hunh! Is y'-all ready to come with me?"
>
> (106)

His defiance persists; at first, he hides under a woodpile, then declares to himself that he has hidden long enough: "I'm going to run them till they tongues hang out, run them till they start going round and round in one place. But I ain't crawling in no hole, peoples. They takes the general standing up, do they take him at all. They takes him with his sword in the air, do he have one then. On'erstand?" (213).

Again, ambiguity reigns. In his vision of his defiance, Gabriel would have his enemies "going round and round in one place." In fact, the image for the failed rebellion becomes Mingo's jack, crazed by the storm, running in circles. Moreover, he has just sounded his defiance when he is seen and fired upon and must run again; this time, water (with the marsh) is a haven:

> Safely out of view, he hastened again. Switches whipped his legs. He went through *puddles* of crisp airy leaves and felt them *foam up* around his knees and settle down again with *a tiny golden splash.* Somewhere, incredibly sweet, there was the voice of a brown thrasher. Gabriel *recalled a marsh of shallow water, a marsh dense with trees and vines. And now, without his taking thought, something was drawing him toward it.*
>
> (216, my italics)

Nat Turner's vision of the sea and the tower leave, we recall, a memory as "unutterably" sweet as a bird's call. The reader has difficulty avoiding the conclusion of an almost diabolical force countering the slaves' every move—or of an almost similar powerful effect by the sea on these writers, who seem to sense that it, in turn, can counter evil.

Where Stowe draws on occasional comparisons with world events and leaders to enhance the efforts of the slaves in the eyes of the reader, Bontemps persistently universalizes the experience of Gabriel and his cohorts. To that end, for example, he brings in a set of secondary characters allied with the tradition of liberty, fraternity, and equality of the French Revolution. In Stowe, the Whites come to exist merely to support the story lines of Dred and of Harry, Nina Gordon's slave half-brother. Styron has no subplot. For Bontemps, the French, the slaves in the West Indies and America, and the Jeffersonians all seek freedom; indeed, a leitmotif in the book is that everything equal to a gray squirrel or a groundhog yearns to be free. While ships and the sea have been responsible for bringing the incendiary news of uprisings from San Domingo, Gabriel, ironically, does not think of trying to get to the West Indies. Rather, Mott tells him, before his capture, that the *Mary* will be going "To some them islands" (254). Yet, if time is a pendulum, Gabriel's story-legend will take its place alongside the accounts of Christophe, Dessalines, and Toussaint and will cross the water to San Domingo to work its own effect (Sadler, "The West Indies as a Symbol of Freedom. . . .").

Curiously, Bontemps allows two momentarily introduced Whites (124-26) to voice the usual romanticism about the sea and travel to exotic places. These ordinary men guarding the arsenal air their longings. One of them participates in the theme of the universal need for freedom when he expresses his feeling of being like a caged thing wanting the open. He is a man whose blood requires adventure, and he desires a year in the "Carribees," where he expects to find, among other things, Spanish galleons and pirates' daughters. Obviously, alongside the crushing of the slaves, Ovid's desires are poor stuff, but Bontemps' point is that the necessity for freedom is universal and will not be denied; he makes it here precisely with the call of the sea.

The novel that most universalizes the human desire for freedom and in specific connections with the sea, however, is *The Slave Ship*,[1] whose title is more figurative than literal. While David Scott, the central figure, becomes the master of a "Guineaman," the real slave ship is the world of man, and his experience culminates in this epiphany: "I saw Earth a slave ship and the wake it made. I saw that the yoke was of self, but not forever" (286). Pro-Stuart, Scott is punished by enslavement in Virginia, where he sees the lot of American slaves and Indians; escapes; and becomes involved despite himself in the slave trade, eventually ending up re-enslaved literally as he has been figuratively throughout. Even the

Africans, however, sell their own kind and create wars to have an excuse to take captives for the barracoons. Thus the great slave center at Daga is described in images evoking the "whited sepulchre" (and, oddly, anticipating the vision of Nat Turner in Styron's novel) and reinforcing the universality of the situation:

> The sun blazed over Daga. The whitened castle and the many palm trees, the river mouth, the village, the factor's hill, the white beach and the ant procession out of castle, out of barracoon— and again there flashed to me Edinburgh. . . .
> (148; see also 291.)

Other novels of slave unrest are much more literal in their use of the sea (of water) as an escape route. In *The Slave,* a group of slaves establishes a commonwealth in the swamp, replete with a system of laws. Throughout, Archy makes his way largely by sea and effects his escape by steamboat to Pittsburgh, through the mountains to Baltimore, and by ship to New York and Liverpool. At one point, when he is sent to the Charleston slave market, a storm frightens the crew into abandoning ship, and he takes charge and saves it. While he is merely thrown into jail for his efforts, he is later able to apply his knowledge of ships and the sea, defeats a ship's bully, is taught by a young sailor, is allowed to enlist on the English side during the War of 1812, leads the defeat of an American privateer and is allowed to become its master, and becomes a captain. He especially likes to sail the American coast, thinking of kidnaping wealthy Southern planters, and his shares in his ship make him wealthy. After over twenty years as a British subject, he returns to America as Captain Archer Moore to look for his slave wife and child.

Clotelle has a runaway who has survived two years in the swamp. Another slave disguises as a woman and escapes by a steamer to Cincinnati. The heroine's mother jumps from Long Bridge into the Potomac rather than be returned to slavery. Jerome escapes to Canada and ultimately gets by ship to Liverpool and makes his fortune. He and Clotelle honeymoon on the Rhine and allow Brown to compare the great rivers of the world (98). The greatest symbolism in the novel, however, derives from the meeting of Clotelle and her White father at Ferney on Lake Leman and their visits to Geneva, where, among other champions of freedom, Voltaire, "the mighty genius, who laid the foundation of the French Revolution" (104), had also been. In the imagery of waters, Brown describes the effect of such individuals:

> Fame is generally the recompense, not of the living, but of the dead,—not always do they reap and gather in the harvest who sow the seed; the flame of its altar is too often kindled from the ashes of the great. A distinguished critic has beautifully said, "The sound which the stream of high thought, carried down to future ages, makes, as it flows—deep, distant, murmuring ever more, like the waters of the mighty ocean." No reputation can be called great that will not endure this test. The distinguished men who had lived in Geneva

transfused their spirit, by their writings, into the spirit of other lovers of literature and everything that treated of great authors.

(104)

Under the tutelage of that spirit, Henry Linwood, who sees "no hatred to [a] man in Europe, on account of his color" (104), at last recognizes the horrors of slavery and vows to return to America, free his slaves and situate them in the North, and then settle in France with his daughter and her family.

Although the ending of *Blake* (first published serially in *The Anglo-African Magazine* and *The Weekly Anglo-African,* 1859-62) is lost, most of the extant novel is set in Cuba; and the leader, who secretly organizes a slave rebellion throughout the Southern states, also plans to lead a take-over of the Cuban government and stop the aim of the Southern expansionists who would annex the island (an intention referred to as well in *Dred,* where Cuba and the Sandwich Islands would become a slave-holding empire, II: 243). Henry Blake, too, is a sailor. Although he is a pure blooded West Indian and the son of a wealthy Cuban tobacco manufacturer, at seventeen, he apprentices on a Spanish man-of-war that is actually a slaver and gets sold as a slave to a planter in Mississippi. Part of the planned rebellion on which the novel centers is to have Blake become the sailing-master of a slaver and then take it over in mid-ocean. Again, however, while most of the focus on the sea is literal, Delany has Blake record the songs of the Mississippi boatmen and comment on their pitiful lot in a larger context:

> Men of sorrow they are in reality; for if there be a class of men anywhere to be found, whose sentiments of song and words of lament are made to reach the sympathies of others, the black slave-boatmen of the Mississippi river is that class. Placed in positions the most favorable to witness the pleasures enjoyed by others, the tendency is only to augment their own wretchedness.

(100)

As Dred learned by observing nature, Blake learns by observing these slaves on the Great River and their backdrop: "Swiftly as the current of the fleeting Mississippi was time passing by, and many states lay in expanse before him, all of which . . . he was compelled to pass over as a messenger of light and destruction" (101). Again, like Dred, Nat Turner, and Gabriel—and like the sea—, he plays the dual role of redeemer and destroyer.

Accounts of slavery have often told of the underground railroad and of following the North Star. Clearly, however, in many of the novels that treat slave unrest, the sea and bodies of water in general have great importance, if merely as escape routes. Even in the simplest treatments in these novels, the sea becomes a classless, raceless medium from which the Black man can be reborn into status and sometimes wealth. Often in the best of the genre, moreover, the sea is an image of mystery and of the seeming fact that answers come in God's time, not in the human's.

NOTES

[1] Mary Johnston had already used ocean voyages and the theme of a ship as a microcosm for the world in *1492* (1923), in which Columbus, seeing the mistreatment of the natives of San Salvador and the subsequent violence, resigns himself to the recognition that the New World is not perfect either.

WORKS CITED

Bontemps, Arna. *Black Thunder.* New York: The Macmillan Company, 1936.

Brown, W[illiam] W[ells]. *Clotelle: A Tale of the Southern States.* Boston: James Redpath, 1864.

Delany, Martin R. *Blake or The Huts of America.* Boston: Beacon Press, 1970 [originally published serially, 1859-62].

Hildreth, Richard. *The Slave: or Memoirs of Archy Moore.* N.p.: John H. Eastburn, 1836.

Johnston, Johanna. *Runaway to Heaven: The Story of Harriet Beecher Stowe.* Garden City, New York: Doubleday, 1963.

Johnston, Mary. *The Slave Ship.* Boston: Little, Brown, and Company, 1924.

Sadler, Lynn Veach. "Dr. Stephen Graham's Narration of the 'Duplin Insurrection': Additional Evidence of the Impact of Nat Turner." *Journal of American Studies* 12 (1978): 359-67.

———. "The Samson Figure in Milton's *Samson Agonistes* and Stowe's Dred." *New England Quarterly* 56 (1983): 440-48.

———. "The West Indies as a Symbol of Freedom in Johnston's *Prisoners of Hope* and *The Slave Ship* and in Bontemps' *Black Thunder.*" *Jack London Newsletter* 15 (1982): 42-48.

Stowe, Harriet Beecher. *Dred: A Tale of the Great Dismal Swamp.* Boston: Phillips, Sampson, and Company, 1856. 2 vols.

Styron, William. *The Confessions of Nat Turner.* New York: Random House, 1966.

Charles H. Adams

SOURCE: "Cooper's Sea Fiction and 'The Red Rover'," in *Studies in American Fiction,* Vol. 16, No. 2, Autumn, 1988, pp. 155-68.

[*In the following essay, Adams contends that the ocean in James Fenimore Cooper's novel* The Red Rover *"represents a place where liberation and law meet, a place where the republican concept of full identity can be nurtured."*]

Cooper's sea novels generally blur the traditional distinction in maritime literature between sea and shore. The dichotomy persists in Cooper's works between the shore as a realm of conflict and the sea as one of resolution between, as W. H. Auden puts it in *The Enchafed Flood,* a state of "disorder" and a world of harmony, where change and turmoil are "not merely at the service of order, but inextricably intertwined, indeed identical with it."[1] But most of the action in a typical Cooper narrative takes place somewhere between these two worlds. In *The Pilot* (1824) the central conflicts and resolutions occur in shallow water. The political struggle is settled among the treacherous rocks and shoals of the "Ripples," while the parallel domestic discord finds a happy ending in Colonel Howard's death scene aboard a ship at anchor in a safe harbor. In *The Red Rover* (1827), similarly, almost half the narrative is devoted to the hero's efforts to get out of Newport harbor, while the events of *The Water-Witch* (1830) and *The Wing-and-Wing* (1842) take place almost exclusively in the harbors of New York and Naples respectively.

Cooper's sea novels are, that is, most often set in a "neutral ground," to adopt the controlling image of *The Spy* (1821). That novel concerns the "neutral ground" between the British and American forces in revolutionary Westchester but evokes more broadly a moral "neutral ground" in which struggle the forces of law and lawlessness, justice and anarchy, principle and brute strength.[2] The metaphor is useful for reading the sea fiction as well, for if Cooper's nautical works are loosely structured by the "classic" dualism of maritime literature, they more pointedly describe the hero's struggle to resolve a conflict existing in the "neutral ground" of his own uncommitted spirit. The middle ground between sea and shore serves as a moral stage on which the central drama of the fiction is enacted: the hero's effort to reconcile the claims of self with the prerogatives of the various structures of authority that condition individual freedom. The most important "neutral ground" in the sea fiction is, in short, the inner arena of conflict between authority and identity.[3]

It is important to note that the resolution of this conflict has most often a neoclassical cast; the novels generally stress a conception of identity in which the private self is meaningful only within the context provided by legitimate authority. The Byronic strain in many of Cooper's captains is strong, and his wavering heroes are often powerfully drawn by—to quote Thomas Philbrick's description of the ocean in the early novels—a "way of life unfettered by artificial restrictions and stripped of the security of an ordered society."[4] But the resolutions of the majority of the sea novels, like the resolutions of the heroes' inner conflicts, most often imply a rejection of the rhetoric of liberation that characterizes *The Corsair.* The emotional energy generated in sea stories by the idea of rebellion accounts for the power of their most effective scenes and characters, but to stress the novels' romantic strain without acknowledging their persistent conservatism is to misrepresent them.

Cooper's sea amply illustrates this point of view. It is often a "free state of nature," a "lawless jungle in which strength and craft are the only sanctions."[5] It inevitably draws rebels who exalt the prerogatives of the liberated self over the claims of legitimate authority. The Red Rover is perhaps the most remarkable of these heroes. But the ocean in Cooper's fiction is indeed a "neutral ground," since immanent in this "lawless" realm, and often obscured by its tempestuous splendor, is a moral order—a world of law—that represents the spiritual conditions imposed on those who sail his ocean. The imperative for a Cooper hero is to properly interpret the world; whether the central symbol is the ocean or the forest, his duty is to find law where others see chaos, to discern order where others see waste, to see harmony where others find only a threatening force to be subdued or destroyed. If the churning foam provides characters like the Red Rover or Admiral Bluewater of *The Two Admirals* (1842) a reflection of their own "romantic celebration of wild freedom"[6] in both public and private spheres, the same ocean offers those who see more clearly a vision of the inner laws that move the world.

The ocean is most evidently a place of law in Cooper's later sea fictions. There, the language of law—which in the novels written in the 1840s is often inseparable from religious rhetoric—dominates the maritime descriptions. As the narrator says in *The Two Admirals,* at sea man lives and works in the "immediate presence of the power of God" and knows first-hand not only "His earthly magnificence" but the divine "laws" embedded in His tempestuous splendor.[7] "Ships and sea have their laws," claims good Admiral Oakes, "just the same as the planets in the heavens" (p. 363). *The Sea-Lions* (1849), with its explicit theological context, provides an especially powerful argument for the presence of order beneath the churning foam. Stephen Stimson, the last in a line of homespun nautical philosophers that begins with Tom Coffin of *The Pilot,* speaks continually of the ocean's sacred architecture. Stimson hovers at Roswell's elbow, pouring into the captain's ear his faith that the "finger of divine Providence" controls the sea and all who sail on it. The success of the Sag Harbor sealers is due not to luck, as Gardiner would have it, but to the "sartain laws" that govern life at sea.

Stephen's simple creed is often advanced by the narrator of *The Sea-Lions* in language that suggests a more complex faith. At several points, the narrative is interrupted by pedagogical explanations of certain natural wonders. For instance, scientific discussions are provided of the physics behind the apparently random movements of icebergs (p. 255), the cause of the terrifying waves that seem to rise of their own will in a calm antarctic sea (p. 310), and the astronomical rationale for the puzzling seasonal fluctuations at the South Pole (pp. 347-49).

The obvious effect is to both retain and rationalize the sublime. The awe and terror inspired by these natural phenomena is strongly felt, but the iron law behind the sea's apparent caprice is even more powerfully understood. Randomness, like luck, is merely an illusion, though one which may blind ignorant seamen.

This frequently repeated idea strongly suggests that the law of the sea is fundamentally a matter of interpretation. The sea presents an appearance that is strictly "incomprehensible," since to understand all of its laws would be to understand God Himself. But the insistence on human "humility" in *The Sea-Lions* does not render this incomprehensibility absolute. The "secret laws" (p. 9) behind the sublime mask may, slowly and by degrees, be more and more clearly perceived by mere mortals. Mankind's ability to read the sea accurately is augmented by any number of epistemological tools: "induction, science, [and] revelation" all provide keys to God's "secret laws." Incomprehension, superstition, and terror represent a failure of vision, a confusion of appearance with reality.

This connection between law and proper interpretation is evident enough in the novels of the 1840s but is equally a concern in earlier novels. Indeed, the theme is handled in the earlier sea stories with much more art and philosophical subtlety than in the dogmatic novels of the final period. Perhaps *The Water-Witch* (1830) offers the most adroit exposition of this theme. In part, *Water-Witch* is about the contrast between superstition and true knowledge. In this sense, the novel anticipates the theme of the rationalized sublime in *The Sea-Lions;* events are described that suggest the operation of the irrational or occult, only to be explained later in terms of firm natural law. The fantastical aspect of the book has been justly condemned from the time of its publication, and even Cooper recognized in the introduction he wrote for the novel in 1850 that the "ideal" element was a failure (p. vi). But the effect of introducing and then rationalizing the "ideal" is, again, to demonstrate the importance of reading the "incomprehensible" universe to get at its laws. The ship's amazing escape from the cove (pp. 220-21), the seeming metamorphosis of the *Water-Witch* into the *Stately Pine,* and the Skimmer's miraculous navigation of Hell-Gate (p. 377) are conscientiously explained in terms of submarine topography, the physics of fog and current, and the conventions of ship navigation. The sailors' failure to perceive the order behind the mystery makes them bewitched followers of the Skimmer's flag but poor masters either of their own lives or of the watery world around them.

The device of the "sea-green lady" explicitly links the theme of reading with the law of the sea. The ship's apparently animated figure-head is the central symbol of the novel, and its most important function is to represent the connection between law and the ocean. The lady is clearly identified with the water: she wears "drapery" of a "sea-green tint, as if it had imbibed a hue from the element beneath," and her hair is like seaweed,

"dishevelled" and "rich" (p. 44). She is just as clearly, though, a symbol of the law the ship sails under. The Skimmer's smuggling operation violates Queen Anne's laws in the name of the higher law of individual liberty and free trade. The codebook of the Skimmer's law is the great tome that the "seagreen lady" holds in her outstretched arms. The book, which the Skimmer consults in times of crisis, contains primarily passages from Shakespeare's plays, the significance of which are interpreted to the crew to give them courage in their dangerous work. The passages, like the ocean, are at first mysterious and even disturbing, opaque to the common seamen and to the landsmen who read them. But the Skimmer is able to see through their obscurity to the truth that warrants their inclusion in the lady's book. When Ludlow, the obtuse English officer, dismisses the lady's law as mere "superstition," saying that he has "read the book, and can make but little of its meaning," the Skimmer gives him a significant hint: "Then read again. 'Tis by many reaches that the leeward vessel gains upon the wind" (p. 177).

This point is emphasized in the song the Skimmer sings to his "sea-green lady" just after his conversation with Ludlow:

> Lady of mine!
> More light and swift than thou, none thread the sea,
> With surer keel, or steadier on its path;
> We brave each waste of ocean-mystery,
> And laugh to hear the howling tempest's wrath;
> For we are thine!
>
> My brigantine!
> Trust to the mystic power that points thy way,
> Trust to the eye that pierces from afar,
> Trust the red meteors that around thee play,
> And fearless trust the green-lady's star;
> Thou bark divine!
>
> (p. 179).

That is, the key to real knowledge is to "trust" both lady and the sea she symbolizes since each conceals behind "ocean-mystery" a "mystic power" as steady as the "stars." The ocean, to "the eye that pierces" the "howling tempest's wrath," is a place of beauty because it is ultimately a place of law.

The hero of such a world must evidently be a man of law or, more precisely, a man who understands the law beneath the waves and can ally the law of the sea with the law of his character. Cooper's nautical heroes are challenged to subdue, both within themselves and in their world, the impulse to lawlessness, to the "wild freedom" that nature and the human spirit offer along with the possibility of submission to the authority of Stimson's "sartain laws." Their allegiance to the principle of legitimate order allows them to survive inner and outer anarchy and establish through their legal authority both a coherent character and a meaningful order in the moral and political world. In the deepest sense, their struggle is to forge an identity through law.

The Red Rover is typical. The action revolves around the relationship between the charming but insidious Rover and the earnest but conflicted Wilder. At its core, this relationship is a struggle between a false legal hero—a man who claims a legal authority for his actions but is in fact ruled by his lawless impulses—and a true man of law. The true hero's task is primarily to "read" correctly the world and thus realize his most profound self. The novel turns on Wilder's effort to fuse law, perception, and identity into a comprehensible moral structure. His struggle does not at all gainsay the emotional and imaginative appeal of rejecting the "artificial restrictions" of an "ordered society." Indeed, Wilder's evident and protracted ambivalence about his allegiance to the Rover emphasizes the seductiveness of the pirate's rebellious spirit. But he must make a deliberate choice in the face of this ambivalence: He must make a reasoned commitment to a structuring context within which a coherent and constructive identity can be maintained.[8]

The reasons for the Rover's strong appeal have been well described by Thomas Philbrick in his landmark study of American sea fiction. Philbrick uses *Red Rover* as a primary case study to elucidate his Byronic interpretation of Cooper's early sea fiction. He says he chose to center his discussion on this book because it is "the best integrated expression of the extreme romanticism which characterizes Cooper's early treatment of maritime life." The Rover is a "noble outcast," the "aloof and inscrutable superman, the passionate guilt-ridden sufferer." His wildness of character "exalts" values of "independence, daring, and honor."[9] There is no doubt that the Rover is a deeply attractive character; the powerful hold he has on Wilder's spirit for most of the novel is felt as well by every reader.[10] But this argument understates the extent to which the Rover's "independence" is mere egotism. The Rover's law originates in, and answers to, the pirate's despotic self. Although he occasionally hints that his career is consecrated to a higher law, and although the novel's conclusion provides a clumsy vindication for this engaging pirate by picturing him a hero of the Revolution, the Rover's law derives principally from its author's whims. A careful reading of the language and imagery describing the Rover indicates that any evocation in this novel of the Byronic hero is ironic. Rather than a celebration of the Rover and his deeds, the novel offers a dark parody of Byron's "noble outcast," a meretricious "superman" whose faith in himself as the sole legitimate lawgiver rests less on his adherence to a private sense of justice than on an imperious egotism.[11]

As John McWilliams has pointed out, the Rover is introduced as a lawyer, but not just any sort of lawyer.[12] The Rover's initial avatar is described in some detail, including his "deep red face," his hair, which falls "about his temples in rich, glossy, and exuberant curls," his "voluptuous" eyes, his green frock, and the "small whip" with which, "he cut[s] the air with . . . the utmost indifference . . ." (p. 40). He is, clearly, a conventional picture of the devil. The introduction of the *Dolphin's* commander as a demonic attorney suggests a theme that Melville would address in rather more grand terms in *Moby-Dick,* the image of the captain as lawgiver, albeit of a false and destructive law.[13] As the pirate tells Wilder early in the action, "there are no courts to protect" men at sea, so he must play King and Court with a power that may seem "a little unlimited" to a newcomer.

In fact, the Rover goes well beyond the disciplinary exigencies of life at sea. His roguish charm in the opening chapters belies the fact that he is a tyrant, and one of the most devilish sort. Though he refers frequently to the ship's "law" by which he governs, he rules the *Dolphin* through a private reign of terror. He employs numerous spies and *agents provocateurs* among his crew (p. 352), augmenting his men's sense of his authority as a malevolent omniscience: "An eye that was not seen was believed to be ever on them, and an invisible hand was thought to be at all times ready to strike or reward" (p. 345). His law is plainly "illegitimate," a "despotic power" (p. 428) held intact by the arsenal of "muskets, blunderbusses, pistols, sabres, half-pikes, etc." that "ornaments" the captain's cabin (pp. 117-18).[14]

This violence is necessary since, as the "Father Neptune" episode makes clear, the ship's order is quite precarious: The "lawless" crewmen that follow the Rover are always on the edge of mutiny and await only a momentary lapse in their Captain's vigilance to rebel (p. 337). But the intrinsic disorder of the ship's political sphere simply reflects the lawlessness of the pirate's soul. If on Cooper's ocean one's perception of the sea is a function of one's identity—if his seagoing men of law invariably "read" for the law beneath the "ocean-mystery"—the Rover's vision of the water indicates an unquiet eye. Where Wilder consistently sees the eternal geometry beneath the ocean's fury (p. 257), the Rover perceives only a "wild and fickle element" (p. 367). When the captain of this lawless vessel looks at the waves, he sees a world "not more unstable than" his violent crew (p. 419). The Rover several times frightens the innocents aboard by the "fearful contrariety of passions that could reveal themselves in the same individual, under so very different and so dangerous forms" (p. 375). He is, indeed, just a little mad.

If the Byronic hero is evoked in this and similar passages, the effect is not to glorify the pirate's rebelliousness but rather to dramatize the "dangerous" element beneath the Rover's alluring exterior. The Rover's cabin clearly illustrates this point. The room is strongly reminiscent of Poe's interiors and similarly "afford[s] no bad illustration of the character of its occupant" (p. 91). The room is a "singular admixture" of articles, including a lamp and mahogany table evidently of European origin, velvet and silk upholstery from Asia, and an odd jumble of other "peculiar" items. In short, "caprice" rather than "propriety" is the principle of the place. Again, if the Rover's Oriental exoticism alludes to Byron's interiors,[15] the language of the description more clearly deprecates the "occupant's" inability to create order. This reading is confirmed by the Rover's conversation with Wilder after he ushers the latter into his "citadel." He draws Wilder's attention first to a pile of forged and otherwise "stretched" commissions, which he uses at will to create false identities for himself and his ship as they pursue their trade. Then he leads the young man to a flag locker containing the emblems of dozens of nations under which he has plundered his victims. He opens and furls flags and commissions with a wicked nonchalance, until it is clear that the Rover is a man without identity, that beneath the successive masks he displays to Wilder there is no coherent self.[16]

The conventional justification of the Rover's lawlessness—that he is a man ahead of his time, and that his crimes will be absolved by the Revolution foreshadowed by his "personal war" against the British[17]—has been questioned by several of Cooper's best readers. As James Grossman says, when "in the end . . . the Rover redeems himself by dying on the American side, . . . it is of course the reader's and not the pirate's morality that is being redeemed. We need some excuse for liking a gentlemanly villain. . . ."[18] McWilliams similarly refuses to take the Revolutionary excuse seriously when he argues that the Rover is not so much a "wronged libertarian" as an example of "excessive individual[ism]."[19] Indeed, the emptiness of the Revolutionary rationale is exposed when the Rover tells Wilder that he began his piratical trade after he killed a man who "dared to couple the name of [America] with an epithet" too vulgar to repeat (p. 355). This is a strange patriotism; an "epithet," vulgar or not, hardly justifies murder and a career of indiscriminate plunder. The Rover's "ghastly smile" as he explains his grotesque sense of justice suggests another of Cooper's false patriots, Ralph in *Lionel Lincoln*. Like Ralph's, the Rover's relationship to the Revolution is that of an evil shade. His resistance is only a rejection of authority, an affirmation of an egotistic lawlessness thinly masked by Revolutionary rhetoric. And, like Ralph's passion, the Rover's cynicism must be purged by the legitimate Revolution, the one that rebels in the name of higher law.

The Rover's lawful foil is, of course, Henry Wilder. Wilder bears the weight of the Revolution's redemption in this novel; his mastery of the Rover in light of his eventual identity as a hero of the American cause reveals that his part in the moral drama of *Red Rover* is to lay the foundation for the Revolution by quelling the anarchic impulses that might threaten its integrity. Wilder is throughout the novel trying to preserve the integrity both of his own character and of the law he represents against the Rover's assault. From their first meeting, it is clear that Wilder and the Rover are doubles and that Wilder's struggle in this book is to subdue the Rover within himself in order to achieve a coherent identity. That is, Wilder, like Lionel, is the moral touchstone of his novel—he is the "one who knows how to distinguish between shadow and substance" (p. 185)—and it is the drama of his contention with the devil within himself and without that is finally the subject of the novel.

The grip of the Rover's lawlessness on Wilder's spirit is in fact portrayed in Mephistophelean images. The scene in which Wilder subscribes to the ship's articles dramatizes this theme effectively. The articles, which each member of the crew must sign as a condition of service, create a rather one-sided "compact" (p. 511) between the captain and his crew. Although none of the specific terms of the law are provided, the code evidently reflects its author's harsh command. Wilder remarks that the *Dolphin's* "regulations" are more than "firm"; he has "never found such rigid rules, even in" the Royal Navy (p. 118). That the "compact" is merely an extension of the Rover's personal "despotism" is clear from the description of Wilder's endorsement of the law. For instance, immediately after Wilder pledges his obedience, the Rover several times refers to his new lieutenant as "mine" or, more pointedly, "my acquisition" (p. 106). Alone in his cabin after Wilder has left, the Rover's response to his purchase is a Satanic mingling of pride and guilt.

> The Rover arrested his step, as the other disappeared, and stood for more than a minute in an attitude of high and self-gratulating triumph. He was exulting in his success. But though his intelligent face betrayed the satisfaction of the inward man, it . . . would not have been difficult for a close observer to detect a shade of regret in the lightings of his seductive smile, or in the momentary flashes of his changeful eye (p. 108).

The law to which Wilder assents is indistinguishable from the Rover's personal control of his spirit. As he tells Wilder later, "I angled for you as the fisherman plays with the trout" (p. 348), and in signing the ship's register the young lieutenant is as surely held captive by the Rover as when the motley lawyer traps him in the Newport tower (p. 73). Significantly, the Rover's ship is first disguised in Newport harbor as a slaver. The Rover's law is a dark oppression, stripping others of their individuality and defining them purely in relation to his imperial will.

As a man of law, Wilder must resist the Rover's "unholy" influence. Wilder's dilemma is illustrated by the clearest use in this novel of the "neutral ground" between sea and shore. A narrative sequence that extends over several chapters describes Wilder's effort to clear Newport harbor, to gain, metaphorically, the lawful order of the sea. As Wilder delicately navigates the *Caroline* past the disguised *Dolphin*, it becomes evident that his situation is delicate in more than a nautical sense. He is supposed to be working for the Rover, sailing the *Caroline* to an unscheduled rendezvous with the pirate on the high seas. As a gentleman, though, he feels compelled to protect Gertrude and Mrs. Wyllis from the possible depredations of the Rover's crew. As he glides past the Rover's exposed guns, he is at once anxious to pass unmolested and attentive for any signal from the "slaver" that he should stop and allow a boarding. Yet the awkwardness of his position in the narrative only reflects his deeper moral conflict. Wilder's effort to tiptoe past the Rover is a test of his authority over his ship, most conspicuously, but, most significantly, over himself:

> As each successive order issued from his own lips, our adventurer turned his eye with increasing interest to ascertain whether he would be permitted to execute it; . . . never did he feel certain that he was left to the sole management of the Caroline . . . (p. 207).

His integrity, as a legal authority and as an individual, is threatened by his new association with the Rover. The danger to which Wilder's submission to the *Dolphin*'s law exposes him is made plain when, even as he maneuvers to pass the slaver, he abruptly dismisses the Newport pilot, ordering his men to tumble the stricken harborman into a boat. This event is strongly emphasized: Wilder's behavior is condemned as "lawless," and the narrative pauses clumsily as the legal consequences of the action are detailed, including the pilot's remedies and Wilder's liability if anything should happen (p. 208).

In this scene and elsewhere, Wilder is exhilarated by his flight from the law. His "eagerness" as he helps the Rover outrun the very British cruiser on which he is (in his true identity) the first officer—the ship which is, significantly, commanded by Captain Bignall, the legitimate figure of authority who rivals the Rover for Wilder's allegiance throughout—stems from the temporary unanimity of spirit Wilder feels between himself, the Rover, and the "lawless" crew. Like Oliver Edwards, when he illegally pursues the deer in the lake with Natty and John in *The Pioneers,* Wilder is filled with a sense of freedom and self-realization. But, as in *The Pioneers,* the realization here is specious. Rather than discovering himself in the Rover's service, Wilder is, as the ocean chase amply illustrates, divided against himself; his private compulsion wrenches him temporarily out of the complex of social and historical relationships by which he is inevitably defined. When he flees from Bignall's vessel, Wilder is evidently fleeing from himself, from the public identity apart from which he is incomprehensible.

The novel's final chapters, featuring Wilder's trial by the Rover's crew, offer a climax of the public and private conflict between the forces of law and lawlessness on which the novel is built. When Wilder's subterfuge is discovered, the *Dolphin*'s crew institutes a hearing to determine the spy's fate. Their tribunal, crude as it is, and vengeful as its justice may be, is provided for under the compact that Wilder signed when he first came aboard. Like everything about the false law that rules the *Dolphin,* the trial is a sinister parody of the forms of civil justice. The "ancient laws" of piratical honor are invoked, and the buccaneers appoint themselves Wilder's rightful judges, the "sole ministers of mercy" aboard (pp. 496-97). Of course, Wilder is found guilty of treason against the ship's law, but before the sentence

of death can be carried out, the Rover experiences a change of heart. Guided by his affection for Wilder, the Rover decides to save the young man's life by exercising his sovereign power to annul the law by which the trial is conducted. Mounting the poop to stand by Wilder, and addressing the assembled crew on the deck below, the Rover makes a speech in language familiar to an American ear:

> "Years have united us by a common fortune," he said: "We have long been submissive to the same laws. . . . But the covenant is now ended. I take back my pledge, and give you your faiths. . . . The compact ceases, and our laws are ended. Such was the condition of the service" (p. 511).

His termination of the compact is a critical event in the novel's thematic structure, for it provides the only context within which the Rover's participation in the Revolution may be said to coherently conclude his story. The pirate's nationalistic professions are, until this point, seriously undercut by their use as rationalizations for a profitable life of plunder. But the revocation of the ship's compact creates a new public and private order that makes his role as a patriot morally credible. This is his first genuine act of law in the narrative. His repeal of his "self-enacted laws" (p. 497) makes possible, symbolically at least, the creation of a new law to replace the old, false covenant. The allusion to Jefferson's Declaration in the Rover's speech is ironic, but only half so, since the pirate's abdication from the poop deck foreshadows the impending repudiation of the legal slavery of the colonial system. The Rover's personal act of nullification provides, figuratively, the *sine qua non* of constitutional government. In this novel, even a democracy of thieves is preferable to a criminal despotism, since it represents an indispensable step toward a legitimate policy. Similarly, the Rover's dissolution of the covenant is the *sine qua non* of his moral salvation. If his honor is redeemed by his participation in the Revolution twenty years later, this redemption is comprehensible only in the context of his repudiation of false law. In order for him to be considered a hero—a man of true law, a man of the new order destined to replace a corrupt authority—he must first turn his back on the lawless world he governs.[20]

But if the dissolution of the compact creates the conditions by which he can ultimately ransom his character, the Rover's first truly legal act more conspicuously permits Wilder to achieve a genuine self-realization. When he journeys at the end of the book from the *Dolphin* to the *Dart,* and resumes his lieutenancy aboard the royal cruiser, Wilder consolidates his identity in several ways. He learns, in one of Cooper's less convincing recognition scenes, that he is in fact Mrs. Wyllis' nephew and thus an appropriate suitor for the hand of the demure Gertrude. Like Edwards at the end of *The Pioneers,* he discovers in a moment his past, present, and future; his incoherent identity is suddenly given a full meaning established by social status and familial bonds. But just as importantly, his farewell to the *Dolphin* also represents his personal liberation from the lawlessness to which he had nearly succumbed in the Rover's service. He returns to his ship a stronger character for his brush with anarchy. When he resumes his legal identity at Bignall's side, his faith in law has matured from a mindless obedience to rules into a commitment founded on a deep knowledge that its alternative is unacceptable. Even more, though, his new awareness of the fundamental lawlessness of despotism has prepared him for his greatest role, his acceptance a quarter-century later of a command in the Continental Navy. After his experience on the *Dolphin,* he is equipped to be a warrior for a law that derives its authority not from force but from its ability to foster, in both the personal and political spheres, full identity.

The hero's names before and after his symbolic rebirth emphasize the link between the personal and legal resolutions. The name "Wilder," it turns out, was only adopted for the time that he was a spy on the Rover's vessel. His name on the *Dart's* register is "Henry Ark." In passing from "Wilder" to "Ark," the young man leaves behind the "wild" element in himself and subscribes with renewed faith to a true covenant, a legitimate "ark" on which to found the future.

The nationalistic strain in the novel's resolution—the intimate connection between the resolution of the personal drama and the development of an American identity—reflects clearly the biographical and historical circumstances of the book's composition. *The Red Rover* is, significantly, the first of Cooper's novels written entirely in Europe. He began the tale in Paris in April, 1827, and finished it that autumn at St. Ouen, where he had installed his family in a thirty-room chateau on the Seine. Since his arrival in Paris the previous year, Cooper had been studying closely European politics, those of the French capital in particular. The Bourbons were back on the throne in 1827, but the conditions for their final removal in the Revolution of 1830 were quickly developing. Cooper, with his characteristic insight into the larger issues informing political events, linked the hardening antagonism in France between the *ancien regime* and the Liberals to the struggle throughout Europe between those trying to consolidate the reforms of the great Revolutions of the previous forty years and those doing their best to return the continent to a pre-Revolutionary state. He put the matter in a letter to Peter Jay:

> The whole of this quarter of the world is divided into two great parties. . . . One side is struggling to reap the advantages of the revolutions, and the other to arrest them. Of course the latter class is composed of all those who are in possession of power and emoluments, as things are at present, aided by those who have lost by the struggle.[21]

The close connection between the French and American revolutions, and Cooper's friendship with Lafayette while in Paris, naturally led him to think of his own nation in light of this European strife. The Bourbons'

reactionism represented an assault on the deepest values of the revolutionary age, and thus the very values on which America in the 1820s and 1830s so self-consciously staked its national identity.[22] Cooper's acute awareness of his role as the preeminent American novelist of his day, and as such his responsibility as a sort of guardian of American values,[23] prompted a return in *Red Rover* to the subject of the American Revolution, and particularly the crucial period leading up to the War, in order to remind his countrymen of the purposes of that strife.

The Revolution had been the subject of three of Cooper's first five books, and the point had been generally the same in each: to establish the conditions of a legitimate national authority, in which the claims of law and self could be balanced to achieve full public and private identity. The point is made again in the Rover's character, which combines two threats to republican identity, each of which France had experienced in the wake of its Revolution. The pirate's oppressive authority on the *Dolphin* alludes to the danger posed by the desperate efforts of the Bourbons and their kind to regain the full power of the monarchy. On the other hand, his charismatic power—seductive, though equally oppressive—raises a spectre that would increasingly haunt Cooper's fiction after his return to America: the danger presented to the integrity of the private self and the public order by the anarchy of excessive individualism. The Rover is, in terms of Cooper's European experience, a sinister blend of the very different threats to rational liberty embodied by Robespierre and Charles X.

Significantly, Cooper turns in this monitory effort to the sea. The ocean in *Rover* represents a place where liberation and law meet, a place where the republican concept of full identity can be nurtured. Wilder's growth into a sense of self as part of a web of rights and obligations within an historical community takes place in a "neutral ground" in which the individual is given shape by the "sartain laws" that Stephen Stimson describes in *The Sea-Lions.* In Cooper's later fiction, of course, this "neutral ground" is effectively closed, and the prerogatives of authority prevail over the claims of identity. In novels like *The Two Admirals* and *The Wing-and-Wing,* Cooper's well-documented anger at the compromise of the republican sense of self by the forces of undisciplined self-interest is manifested by a more sympathetic treatment of the captain's power than in *Rover.*[24] The sea novels of the 1840s offer images of the ship's commander drawn in language that celebrates authority. The captain is typically the ship's "soul," its omnipotent and omniscient "mind" or "master spirit," whose firm law provides the best guarantee of both personal identity and public order. But in 1827, and as a resident of a country the promise of whose Revolution had been compromised by forces thankfully absent from America, Cooper could still believe strongly enough in the American experiment, and in the American self, to hope that the "neutral ground" of his ocean might provide a useful reminder to his countrymen of the conditions for the birth of a just nation.

NOTES

[1] W. H. Auden, *The Enchafed Flood; or, the Romantic Iconography of the Sea* (New York: Random House, Inc., 1950), pp. 8–9.

[2] See John P. McWilliams, *Political Justice in a Republic: James Fenimore Cooper's America* (Berkeley: Univ. of California Press, 1972). The significance of the "neutral ground" in Cooper's political fiction is a central theme in McWilliams' study.

[3] See H. Daniel Peck's discussion of the conflict between "authority and freedom" in relation to the "middle hero" in "A Repossession of America: The Revolution in Cooper's Trilogy of Nautical Romances," *SR*, 15 (1976), 597–98.

[4] Thomas Philbrick, *James Fenimore Cooper and the Development of American Sea Fiction* (Cambridge: Harvard Univ. Press, 1961), p. 71.

[5] Philbrick, p. 71.

[6] Philbrick, p. 71.

[7] James Fenimore Cooper, *The Two Admirals,* in *Cooper's Novels,* 32 vols. (New York: W. A. Townsend and Co., 1859), vol. 27, p. 550. All parenthetical page references to Cooper's novels in this essay are to this, the "Darley," edition.

[8] Peck notes the "balance" in the novel between the Rover's "reckless, lawless power" and Wilder's commitment to "civilization and law," although he does not develop the conflict within Wilder between these forces ("A Repossession of America," p. 598).

[9] Philbrick, pp. ix, 61, 207.

[10] The Rover's powerful personal attractiveness has been discussed more recently in Michael Paul Rogin's introductory essay on Melville and *The Red Rover* in *Subversive Genealogy: The Politics and Art of Herman Melville* (Berkeley: Univ. of California Press, 1985), pp. 3–11.

[11] Peck similarly views the Rover's Byronic element as evidence of the "dangerous" element in the pirate's character, although he does not argue that Cooper's evocation of Byron is ironic. Peck describes the pirate as "a most attractive but highly threatening Byronic hero," a "Satanic" character who "acts out the dark side of his nature fully" ("Repossession," pp. 597–98).

[12] McWilliams, p. 66.

[13] See Herman Melville's faint praise of *The Red Rover* in *Literary World,* 6 (March, 1850), 277.

[14] Philbrick notes the Rover's "extraordinary fortifications" in a similar context, although for a different purpose (p. 71).

[15] Philbrick, p. 62.

[16] See Kay House, *Cooper's Americans* (Columbus: Ohio State Univ. Press, 1965), p. 196. House notes that the *Dolphin* has "no real identity" but does not apply her analysis to the Rover's character.

[17] Thomas Philbrick argues, for instance, that the Rover is only perceived as a criminal because he is a man out of time, a prophet of American nationhood, an "outlawed visionary who alone perceives the drift of history" (p. 56). His lawlessness is thus merely a "private war of Independence," which will be vindicated by the eruption of the Revolution a quarter of a century after the events of the novel.

[18] James Grossman, *James Fenimore Cooper* (Stanford: Stanford Univ. Press, 1949), p. 59.

[19] McWilliams, p. 65.

[20] For a different view of the Rover's renunciation of authority, see Daniel Peck's assertion that despite the Rover's discovery of "a lawful context for his rebellious nature" through his participation in the Revolution, the "power" of the Rover's character insures that "*The Red Rover* remains Cooper's most unqualified celebration of the revolutionary spirit" ("Repossession," pp. 598–99). Parallel to this argument is Peck's description of the novel as a "celebration of the terrible sublime, a region of absolute moral and spatial freedom," in *A World By Itself: The Pastoral Moment in Cooper's Fiction* (New Haven: Yale Univ. Press, 1977), p. 144.

[21] *Letters and Journals of James Fenimore Cooper,* ed. James F. Beard (Cambridge: Harvard Univ. Press, 1960–1968), I, 418.

[22] For excellent discussions of the uses to which Cooper's America put the Revolution in its effort to articulate its identity in the midst of the dramatic changes wrought by industrialization, immigration, and Jacksonian politics, see Michael Kammen, *A Season of Youth: The American Revolution and the Historical Imagination* (New York: Oxford Univ. Press, 1978), and Fred Somkin, *Unquiet Eagle: Memory and Desire in the Idea of American Freedom, 1815–1860* (Ithaca: Cornell Univ. Press, 1967).

[23] See Stephen Railton, *Fenimore Cooper: A Study of His Life and Imagination* (Princeton: Princeton Univ. Press, 1978), pp. 3–4, 63–64. In this context, Lafayette's charge to Cooper when asking him to write what would become the ill-fated "Letter to General Lafayette" during the Finance Controversy is relevant: "It belongs to you," the General told the most famous American writer of his day, to write "in vindication of republican institutions" (quoted in *Letters and Journals,* II, 187).

[24] For Cooper's most cogent description of this tendency of American culture, see *The American Democrat* (1838; rpt. Indianapolis: Liberty Fund, Inc., n.d.), especially

(though not exclusively) the sections entitled "On the Disadvantages of Democracy" (pp. 80–87) and "On Individuality" (pp. 231–33).

Greg W. Zacharias

SOURCE: "The Marine Metaphor, Henry James, and the Moral Center of 'The Awkward Age'," in *Philological Quarterly,* Vol. 69, No. 1, Winter, 1990, pp. 91-105.

[*In the following essay, Zacharias examines the ways in which Henry James uses metaphors of the sea in his correspondence and his novel* The Awkward Age *to illuminate his moral outlook.*]

The meaning that James invests in the marine metaphor is worth discussing because of the prevalence and placement of the trope in James's fiction and non-fiction. Gale's descriptive analysis of James's imagery in the fiction shows that the water image occurs more frequently than any other, accounting for fully one-twelfth of all images.[1] Daniel Mark Fogel writes that in *The Wings of the Dove* the sea "stands for life itself" and suggests that a "profoundly beautiful moral change" occurs.[2] With the importance of the marine metaphor in the fiction having been asserted, there are prior questions that ought to be asked: what does the marine metaphor do for James? Why is it useful? And in what way does the vocabulary of the sea help James achieve his purpose for the fiction? Before addressing these questions, however, it will be helpful to summarize the reason why critics have, for the most part, avoided interpreting James's motive for the marine metaphor. That reason rests in the course of image criticism over the past fifty years or so.

Since shortly after Spurgeon's *Shakespeare's Imagery and What It Tells Us,* Anglo-American criticism in general has not accepted efforts to use a poet's imagery to locate the author in the work. Even though it is not as theoretically complex as are objections from critics today, the reasonable argument of Lillian Herlands Hornstein, Spurgeon's contemporary, describes the long-standing opposition to locating an author in the literature through formal analysis. Hornstein objects to critics who "work on the assumption that imagery . . . always has a direct basis in physical experience and that the percentile tabulation of images will reveal the corresponding proportions of everyday, environmental experiences in the life of the man."[3]

Roger Seamon recently has reached a similar, yet at the same time a farther reaching, conclusion regarding problems of what he broadly defines as "scientific" criticism. Even if the formal critic should only compile a table of images in the most "objective" or "scientific" way, Seamon recognizes that "the models that scientific critics make are now understood not as maps of a field but as productions in their own right, which have no privileged place outside the institution of literature or writing generally."[4] Nevertheless, there exist helpful

ways around the conceptual and methodologic problems raised by Hornstein and Seamon. Strategies advanced by Yeazell, Friedman and Burke prepare the ground for my approach because they involve reading the metaphor as a symbolic expression of the author, not as a literal one. They avoid claims to "scientific" objectivity and focus the interpretation by acknowledging the importance of idiosyncratic associations within the oeuvre of an individual author. I will build on their work by tracing James's pattern of associations with the marine metaphor in the letters in order to ground an interpretation of its symbolic meaning in the fiction.

Ruth Bernard Yeazell discusses the symbolic importance of Jamesian metaphor in general and of the marine metaphor specifically in *The Golden Bowl.*[5] Most important for my discussion, Yeazell probes the relation between art and the artist when she asserts that "speaking in metaphors, like thinking in metaphors, is a way at once of confronting and of avoiding unpleasant facts. . . ."[6] According to Yeazell, metaphors provide James a way of controlling experience.

Yeazell's approach to James's figurative language differs significantly from that of the formal critics to whose work Hornstein and Seamon object. Where formal criticism, as Reuben Brower points out, classifies "images as though they were fixed units of meaning" even though "the completely objective value" that critics "often assign to the patterns is spurious," Yeazell sees metaphor formation as a symbolic confrontation between the artist and human experience.[7] Adding to what I have taken from Yeazell, Norman Friedman writes that recurring metaphors, "when systematically inspected" "in the perspective of . . . [an author's] total achievement, act as a symbolic key to his ultimate vision of life."[8] Along the same line, Kenneth Burke reasons that

> Even if you would write a drama . . . simply for the satisfaction of writing a drama, you must write your drama about *something.* . . . These subjects involve tensions, or problems—and since you can't make a drama without the use of some situation marked by *conflict,* even though you hypothetically began through a sheer love of dramatic exercise, in the course of so exercising you tend to use as your subject matter such tensions or problems as exercise yourself, or your potential audience, or mankind in general.[9]

Thus the language James employs in response to fictional and non-fictional "situations" would indicate in symbolic, not literal, terms James's attitude toward those situations. The point here, as we have learned from Hornstein, Seamon, Brower, Yeazell, Friedman and Burke, is not to speculate in literal terms why James tends to use the marine metaphor rather than another one to express his moral attitude. This we can never know and it is likely that James himself did not know. We can only recognize through a study of his fiction and non-fiction that he uses it in situations that demand moral control and commentary.

Since James draws from the language of the sea consistently throughout his career, we must assume that the marine metaphor helps him in some way to manage tensions and problems both within and outside of the fiction. If this were not the case, he would not return to those figures. As such a tool to manage experience, the marine vocabulary stands as a symbolically revealing element of his style.[10] A survey of James's letters supports this claim.

James uses the marine metaphor in the letters for four broad rhetorical purposes: (1) he figures specific, usually threatening, experiences and the uncertainty of "life" in general as the sea; (2) he uses the marine figure as a central element in the consolation of others who themselves confront difficult and tragic circumstances; (3) he figures a "bath" as a non-threatening experience in which one is immersed; (4) he uses the metaphor of rowing to indicate moving through experience under one's own power, by one's own initiative. All four ways of using the language of the sea help James, in one way or another, to advance points of morality—that is, as James uses the term, points of conduct or of human relations—some rather trivial and others deeply serious.[11] If I can demonstrate the moral utility and force of the trope in the letters where James's meaning is relatively direct and clear, readers of James's fiction would have an interpretive context in which to read the most prevalent trope in the fiction. Although space restricts me to an application of the method in terms of *The Awkward Age* and more briefly in reference to *The Ambassadors,* the strategy should be clear enough to allow an interested reader to test its utility in terms of any other James novel, short story or play. My aim is not to explicate every instance of the metaphor in the Jamesian canon. Instead, I aim to model a specific approach to locating James in the fiction and to suggest a way to locate any author in his or her fiction or poetry when extra-literary writing is available as an interpretive context.[12]

The component of the marine metaphor that dramatizes human conduct and grounds in one way or another James's various uses of the language of the sea in the fiction and letters may be summarized thus: a ship captain, like an individual or an author, controls his vessel—his life and/or his literature—and also is responsible for its operation. Under normal weather and sea conditions—that is, under normal conditions of living—the captain holds the power to determine the ship's course and to govern the crew and passengers, who comprise a floating capsule of civilization. Likewise, the individual or the character at the center of the metaphor, at the helm of the ship of experience, so to speak, exercises a significant measure of control over the conditions of life. Implicit in the metaphor as James uses it in the fiction—and often explicit in the letters—rests James's belief that the one who possesses control over the others also assumes responsibility for the quality of the lives of others who sail, or who live, with him or with her. At the same time, however, that control and

knowledge of life, like a captain's control of his ship and knowledge of the sea, never can be absolute. The power of the sea may wrestle command of the ship from the captain just as the tempests of experience may change radically the course of one's life. An experienced mariner, however, may ride out a storm, regain control, and chart a new course. Under the worst conditions, the captain must simply come to terms with the weather and the sea and sail or drift as well as he can. The marine metaphor almost always contains a didactic element because through it James implies that he knows the best way to live. Thus James could be writing of himself when he says of Sainte-Beuve that "a man's work is in a particular degree the record of a mind."[13] I read such a record in James's marine metaphor.

1

The greatest number of James's marine figures in the letters image specific events or types of life experience as the sea. Consequently, this use of the marine metaphor provides the most help in building a context for interpreting the metaphor in *The Awkward Age* and in James's other fiction. For example, James describes the financial burdens of his later life: "I . . . have taken in a great deal of pecuniary sail. . . . but I shall securely outweather it. . . ."[14] Thus James figures his financial obligations as if they buffeted his own ship of life. But once he formalizes the threat with such familiar and symbolic language, he is better able to contain the threat and to cope with it. He ends the statement with confidence that "I shall securely outweather" the drain on his bank account—and so he did.

When James struggles with the various social demands of the London "season," he manages them as if he were a fisherman coping with recurrent bad weather on his daily fishing runs: "I have for the last six weeks been struggling with the high tide, and the breaking waves, of the London Season" (*HJL,* 2:300-1). While James complains of the taxing social demands of the London season, he still manages a productive literary output. He sails on with his work and endures the tide and the waves because he recognizes his problems and is able to overcome them. In other letters he uses the figure to teach brief lessons on living. James addresses his brother William's complaint for "comparative quiet—I mean immunity from the human deluge which seems to roll over you. But I fear that, with so many nets out and raking the waters, this is the boon that will be ever unattainable to you" (*HJL,* 4:5). James implies in the letter to his brother that if William should take in some of his professional "nets," he would have the "comparative quiet" from "the human deluge," which must hamper the efficiency of William's "fishing" and which Henry apparently has managed to learn to control, since he offers such criticism and advice. To Hugh Walpole James writes that "I gather that you are about to hurl yourself into the deep sea of journalism—the more treacherous currents of which . . . I hope you may safely breast" (*HJL,* 4:507).[15] James uses the marine metaphor to warn Walpole indirectly that Walpole ought to be aware of and ready for the potential difficulties of the newspaper business, which James himself had faced, struggled against and had overcome with some personal and professional anguish.[16]

James employs the language of the sea to cope metaphorically with illness. Having endured over a number of years a long series of physical and mental afflictions, James informs his nephew that he feels better and that "quiet work again unspeakably helps to float me" (*HJL*, 4:654). Although James makes no secret of the fact that sickness has slowed him down, his use of the marine metaphor conveys the message that he is again working and vital, not sick and immobile. The marine metaphor symbolizes James's conduct toward his nephew. In his very last letter, written as he lay dying, James uses the marine metaphor. He informs his niece that with good medical care he would "keep afloat" for some time to come (*HJL*, 4:784). Hours later, however, he suffered a sudden stroke and died soon after. Yet his last use of the marine vocabulary operates similarly to earlier ones because it does public and private work. It helps James do practical, public work by consoling his niece about his illness. It also symbolizes his way of coping with the experience in question, namely that he saw his death near and could accept it, but not immediately. When James employs the rhetoric of the sea in this way he conveys not only a struggle to cope with the potentially overwhelming effects of experience by figuring them with terms such as "sail," "outweather," "high tide," "breaking waves," "deluge," "nets," "waters," "deep sea," "treacherous currents" and "float." He implies through the terms that with effort and a proper moral map, his correspondents may follow an implicit course of living charted by James and sail through the specific tempests in their lives that have blown up.

2

Closely related to the association between the marine metaphor, certain forms of experience, and conduct, James deploys the language of the sea as a rather explicit tool to console others and to show them a way of living better.[17] In a letter that Edel quotes as exemplary of James's long and close friendship with Grace Norton, James comforts his friend: "Sorrow comes in great waves—no one can know that better than you—but it rolls over us, and though it may almost smother us it leaves us on the spot and we know that if it is strong we are stronger, inasmuch as it passes and we remain" (*HJL*, 2:424).[18] Alone in his house on the Channel and lonely on Christmas day, 1897, James reaches across the ocean to America by way of a letter to renew his friendship with Grace Norton, whom James had been neglecting. He satisfies his desire to make contact with a friend as well as his desire to manage their relationship by using the language of the sea. "Existence," he tells Norton,

> is mainly a business in which we are constantly throwing overboard the possible to keep the actual

afloat, and it is only today that the possible really rides the waves. . . . Life is all muffled and hushed and hindered by an intensity of fog, and one has literally a shipboard sense of huddling in the cabin and waiting for some resumption of the course. I am lying-to and feeling as if I were talking to you absolutely *through* the fog-horn; save that that is a warning and that this is a fond solicitation. (*HJL*, 4:67)

These two passages from letters to Norton are typical of the way James uses the marine metaphor to affirm the strength of human relations and to console others. First, in practical terms, James employs the "shipboard" image because it shows the two correspondents together in a situation of mutual dependence and mutual protection and therefore it puts back on course the relationship that James had let drift. The nautical language shows Grace Norton that she and James face similar problems of living even though time, experience, and three thousand miles of the cold North Atlantic separate the pair. The language suggests that in the face of threatening circumstances James and Norton ride together in the same boat, hunker down in the shipboard cabin of experience and wait for the resumption of a calmer course of living. Second, the figure represents a moral truth for James: that while life proceeds by means of difficult choices and distasteful compromises, it nevertheless proceeds. And since both must face such situations and make such compromises, the marine metaphor communicates the message that together they face life by throwing overboard the possible in order to keep afloat the actual, and that together they discover that one only endures life's sorrow by living fully day by day. He implies to Norton that one may learn to make the best choices under the circumstances and in that way human beings captain their own lives. Furthermore, the metaphor helps James to establish a bond with Grace Norton by offering to her his privileged wisdom, which he gives by a "fond solicitation," not by an overt, moralistic warning. As a result, the marine metaphor becomes an experience shared, symbolizes shared values, and forms the basis on which the pair may continue their old friendship.

In a moving letter to his friend of many years, Rhoda Broughton, James speaks to the political tension that soon would lead to World War I and to the loss of the older Victorian world of progress and promise. He and Broughton are "ornaments of our generation," whom it hurts badly to realize that "the tide that bore us along was then all the while moving to *this* as its grand Niagara" (*HJL*, 4:713). It is safe to assume that James knew of Niagara's forceful current and of the virtual impossibility of surviving a fall over that cataract or of surviving in a figurative sense the dissolution of Europe that the deluge of the Great War would bring. Even so, by articulating this fear, James confronts and controls it—if only imaginatively. By writing to Broughton of the fear, James sends the consoling message that she is not alone to face the war and all the great social changes it signals. As James argues in "Is There a Life After Death?" one lives exactly to the degree that one confronts and imaginatively contains all forms of experience through consciousness.[19] The marine metaphor marks James's strategy for such confrontation and containment.

3

Although the sea of experience threatens the well-being of anyone not morally skilful enough to manage human relations, the bath figure conveys the non-threatening side of experience. For in a bath of experience, James implies, one may immerse oneself without much danger of drowning. To Francis Boott James reports that "I have thought of you bathed in the waters of kindness, kinship and hospitality. I hope that Duveneck and the dear little boy float at your side in the same warm moral gulfstream" (*HJL*, 3:246). James works to console Fullerton with the bath figure when he offers his friendship and counsel as a "bath of some rare and fragrant essence," which he hopes will relieve Fullerton of the burdens of his soured love affairs (*HJL*, 4:390).[20] These examples demonstrate that the water metaphor contains the pleasant side of human experience for James as well as the unpleasant one. They also imply his reliance on the figure when he wishes to make special contact with his readers.

4

James indicates by the marine metaphor that he holds the individual responsible, at least in part, for his or her attitude toward life. He conveys this message with an image of the individual sailing or rowing through the sea of experience. These figures suggest that his correspondents ought to take greater responsibility for and control of their lives as a rower controls the speed and direction of the rowboat on the water. The rowing figures also serve as Jamesian signals of approval for the way others conduct themselves, as in the passage above in which Boott, Duveneck and the boy "float."

James employs a rowing image to persuade H. G. Wells to accept James's nomination to join the Academic Committee of the Royal Society of Literature, which James believes will boost Wells's career. James tells Wells that his work for the Committee would be as easy as: "lifting your oar and letting yourself float on the current of acclamation" (*HJL*, 4:609). James finds a strategic way of making personal contact with Wells and also finds a way of coping with two life problems—Wells's problem with the Committee and James's own problem with Wells—by deploying the language of the sea. While Wells's coping would be easy since in this instance he would not be rowing, the association between the oar and one's self-direction still operates. When the novelist writes to his literary agent that he has left the details of negotiating a contract with publishers to Pinker because "I thought it not right to put in my oar," he manages to control his life better through the marine metaphor even when he refuses to row (*HJL*, 4:448). By notifying Pinker that he has decided not to row, James figuratively issues the agent an imperative to pick up the oar and to "Stroke! Stroke!"

James describes literary productivity—so nearly an equivalent for him of living itself—as movement through the sea. When he praises Howells in 1908 for the quality and quantity of Howells's literary output, James comments on his own declining work habits by saying that he "can only drift on with the thicker and darker tide" of a stagnant literary life.[21] The drifting without oar or rudder signals his impression that he has virtually lost control of his literary career—although we may assume that he still copes with it at some level because he has not yet been sunk. This marine figure, like the others, performs two moral tasks at once. It represents James's attitude toward living at the same time it communicates affection for his friend, whose work James elevates by gently deprecating his own.

In a fatherly letter to Fullerton in which James offers through the marine metaphor his own conduct as a model, the novelist figures his accumulated experience as a "port" from which he sets sail to meet the rest of his life as if he were taking the role of Tennyson's Ulysses, who of course sails forth "to strive, to seek, to find, but not to yield" (*HJL*, 4:170). Edel hears in this letter echoes of Strether's famous "live all you can" speech to Little Bilham in *The Ambassadors* (*HJL*, 4:170). The key passage from *The Ambassadors* is itself preceded by the language of the sea and adds to discussions of the marine metaphor in *The Golden Bowl* by Yeazell and in *The Wings of the Dove* by Fogel. And while, perhaps, we could have anticipated the following association, it is worthwhile to pause to survey the passage before moving on to look at the Cheval Blanc scene in *The Ambassadors* and then to a broader survey of James's morality in *The Awkward Age*. The narrator reports that Strether's experience in Paris

> had consciously gathered to a head, but the reservoir had filled sooner than he [Strether] knew, and his companion's touch was to make the waters spread. There were some things that had to come in time if they were to come at all. If they didn't come in time they were lost for ever. It was the general sense of them that had overwhelmed him with its long, slow rush.
>
> "It's not too late for *you*. . . . Live all you can; it's a mistake not to."[22]

As is his habit in the letters, so James clusters moments of moral importance in the fiction with the language of the sea. Equipped with knowledge of what James means by the marine metaphor in his non-fiction, we have a tool that helps us interpret the symbolic moral importance of those fictional characters to which the metaphor is applied but not explained. A brief example from another well-known scene in *The Ambassadors* and an example from an underdiscussed novel, *The Awkward Age,* demonstrate this point.

Rowe and Tintner have discussed Strether's understanding and control of his experience in the famous fourth chapter of Book Eleventh—the scene at the Cheval

Blanc—in terms of painting, not in terms of the marine metaphor.[23] It nearly goes without saying that Strether discovers the actual relation between Chad and Madame de Vionnet as he watches his friends round the bend of the river in a rowboat. It is true, moreover, that this moment occurs in the scenic context of water—the river and the rowboat. But my concern is not with setting. It is with the metaphoric figures James associates with moments of moral understanding in his novels and with the symbolic meaning he includes in those figures. And while it is not my chief purpose here to analyze the language of the sea in *The Ambassadors*, I will note briefly the consistency of James's figurative use of the marine vocabulary with Strether's moral awakening in Book Twelfth because it illustrates the technique I am suggesting for reading James. Thus my reading will show that Strether's moral breakthrough does not occur on the river bank in Book Eleventh but later, in his final meeting with Marie de Vionnet.

James prepares us for Strether's later epiphany by describing him immediately before the fourth chapter as "afloat" but not in control of the "oars" (*A*, 2:255). Clearly, Strether is not yet fully aware or in full control of his experience. Although Strether realizes the actual relation of Chad and Madame de Vionnet soon after they round the bend of the river, it is not until James employs the marine vocabulary as an element of description rather than of setting in chapter two of Book Twelfth, Strether's meeting with Marie, that he reconciles what he feels with what he knows, that he reaches full awareness, full control. James signals the awareness and control with the language of the sea:

> Women were thus endlessly absorbent, and to deal with them was to walk on water. . . . This was not the discomposure of last night; that had quite passed. . . . There it was again—it took women, it took women; if to deal with them was to walk on water what wonder that the water rose? And it had never surely risen higher than round this woman. He presently found himself taking a long look from her, and the next thing he knew he had uttered all his thought. "You're afraid for your life!" (*A*, 2:284-85)

I call this scene, marked as it is by the language of the sea, the high point of Strether's moral development because here he finds himself able to understand and even sympathize with the *motivations* of another. In the Cheval Blanc scene he has progressed only far enough to understand more superficially a *situation*.

I would like to go now to two instances of the marine metaphor in *The Awkward Age*, both at the virtual center of what may be, judging from James's Preface account, his most carefully structured book. The first instance is important in the novel because here James signals the moral responsibility of the novel's heroine, Nanda Brookenham. After having described the Duchess's old-fashioned way of protecting her daughter as if the Duchess were "steer[ing]" Aggie's boat, Cashmore explains to Longdon that the others tend to float together over the corrupt current of modern life in their own "boat."[24] When Mrs. Brookenham, Nanda's mother, correctly reads in the metaphor Cashmore's suggestion that she fails to care for her daughter as well as the Duchess cares for hers, Mrs. Brook defends herself by countering that Nanda takes care of herself quite well: "She is in a boat—but she's an experienced mariner" (*AA*, p. 148). While Mrs. Brook admits her own lack of responsibility in caring for Nanda, she affirms her daughter's moral power (that is, her ability to control conduct) through the marine figure. In addition, Mrs. Brook forecasts Nanda's later control of the novel by describing the girl as if she were a skilled sailor. James employs the metaphor in this significant scene in order to identify Nanda as the moral authority, the regulator of conduct, in the novel. His application of the marine language in such a way to Nanda suggests that Nanda carries James's moral attitude.

James utilizes the same marine figure one chapter later to define the role of Longdon, the novel's supplemental moral center and Nanda's eventual spouse—literally her first mate, when Longdon uses nautical language to describe the wandering course of his life. Since we know by now that James uses the marine metaphor to map the current of moral truth, we listen closely when Longdon echoes James's letter to Grace Norton (quoted above):

> "The point is that in the twilight of time . . . there were too many superstitions [my life] had to get rid of. It has been throwing them overboard one by one, so that now the ship sails uncommonly light. That's the way . . . I come to feel so the lurching and pitching. If I weren't a pretty fair sailor—well, as it is, my dear . . . I show you often enough what grabs I make for support." (*AA*, p. 165)

Just as James advises Grace Norton to make her life better by "throwing overboard the possible to keep the actual afloat," that is, to maintain her concentration on the actual rather than to occupy herself with fantasies of the possible, so Longdon communicates his new understanding of the value of life by explaining that he lives better when he applies his mind to actual experience, not to "superstitions." In addition to implying that the rejection of the superstitions has brought him into closer contact with actual experience ("the lurching and the pitching"), Longdon intimates that he accepts the fact that he will never control his vessel completely. His acceptance of "the lurching and the pitching" *as* experience tells us that he accepts the instability that inheres *in* experience. Longdon concedes, moreover, the instability of life as James concedes such instability to Grace Norton and to H. G. Wells. Finally, Longdon indicates that he will attempt to keep the boat on course as long as the power to guide it remains in his hands when he declares himself "a pretty fair sailor." Even so, we should remember that Nanda, being more skilled, is the novel's "experienced mariner." She exerts influence actively—though quietly—to reorganize the circumstances of her little society. Nanda improves her own life by improving the lives of those around her. Civic renewal spreads outward from her steady wake. This too recalls the way James signals solutions to moral problems in the letters with marine terms. The difference is that in the novel James dramatizes a strategy for living better through characters that he associates with the language of the sea, whereas he uses the terms alone to express an attitude toward living in the letters.

By the end of the novel, with all of the major characters having sought, received and accepted Nanda's advice on the conduct of their lives, we realize that the characters in *The Awkward Age* sail willingly through life on a figurative ship now captained by Nanda. She helps them keep above water analogously to the way James helps Grace Norton, Fullerton, Wells and others keep dry. We realize too that Nanda, like her author, understands that rough seas and high winds are inevitable. Yet we also read that after she rides out the storms of her metaphoric sail, she will regain control of the vessel, will have learned a lesson about sailing, therefore about living, and will continue to govern the passengers so that each will achieve the best relation with the others that the circumstances allow. In this way, Nanda's conduct dramatizes James's morality.

So as James works to advance his moral outlook rather directly through the marine metaphor in the letters, he deploys the marine metaphor in the fiction as a way of charting more indirectly, but no less certainly, his attitude toward living. For, as James describes the purpose of art and the artist, "there's a kind of rudimentary intellectual honour to which we must, in the interest of civilisation, at least pretend. . . . What better example than this of the high and helpful public and, as it were, civic use of the imagination?—a faculty for the possible fine employments of which in the interest of morality my esteem grows every hour I live."[25]

NOTES

[1] Robert L. Gale, *The Caught Image: Figurative Language in the Fiction of Henry James* (U. of North Carolina Press, 1954), p. 16.

[2] Daniel Mark Fogel, *Henry James and the Structure of the Romantic Imagination* (Louisiana State U. Press, 1981), pp. 72, 75. R. W. Short also recognizes James's strategic placement of water images in the late fiction. "Henry James's World of Images," *PMLA* 68 (1953): 957-60.

[3] Lillian Herlands Hornstein, "Analysis of Imagery: A Critique of Literary Method," *PMLA* 57 (1942): 639.

[4] Roger Seamon, "Poetics Against Itself: On the Self-Destruction of Modern Scientific Criticism," *PMLA* 104 (1989): 302. Robert Gale sees the validity of this principle in his study of James's images. While Gale admits that dominant images seem to reveal "a good deal" about the author, he rationalizes his analysis carefully

and resists venturing beyond a count and a categorization (pp. 4, 6-17).

[5] Ruth Bernard Yeazell, *Language and Knowledge in the Late Novels of Henry James* (U. of Chicago Press, 1976), pp. 37-63.

[6] Yeazell, p. 53.

[7] Reuben Arthur Brower, *The Fields of Light* (1951; reprint, Westport, Connecticut: Greenwood Press, 1980), p. 15.

[8] Norman Friedman, "Imagery: From Sensation to Symbol," *Journal of Aesthetics and Art Criticism* 12 (1953): 31.

[9] Kenneth Burke, *Language as Symbolic Action* (1966; reprint, U. of California Press, 1968), p. 29.

[10] See Kenneth Burke, "Literature as Equipment for Living," (*The Philosophy of Literary Form*, 3rd ed. [U. of California Press, 1973], pp. 293-304) for a discussion of this concept.

[11] Writing of the character Saltram, James makes the equation "'morality' i.e. his conduct." This is the only place I have seen in James where he comes close to defining his central term, "moral." No use of the term, however, contradicts this passing definition, common in the nineteenth century (*The Complete Notebooks of Henry James*, ed. Leon Edel and Lyall Powers [New York: Oxford U. Press, 1987], p. 96).

[12] For an application of the method to Milton's poetry see my "Young Milton's Equipment for Living: *L'Allegro and Il Penseroso*," *Milton Studies* 24 (1988): 3-15.

[13] Henry James, "Correspondance de C. A. Sainte-Beuve (1822-69)," in *Literary Criticism: French Writers, Other European Writers, The Prefaces to the New York Edition* (New York: Literary Classics of the United States, 1984), p. 680.

[14] Henry James, *Henry James Letters,* ed. Leon Edel, 4 vols. (Harvard U. Press, 1974-84), 4:74. All subsequent references to Henry James Letters will appear in the text as *HJL.*

[15] For additional examples of the use of the marine metaphor in terms of specific events or experiences see *HJL*, 1:230, 434; 3:36; 4:54, 149, 212, 214, 299, 473, 507, 619, 661, 712, 780; Henry James, *Henry James: Selected Letters,* ed. Leon Edel (Harvard U. Press, 1987), p. 322; Henry James, *The Letters of Henry James,* ed. Percy Lubbock, 2 vols. (London: Macmillan, 1920), 1:261, 406; 2:96, 151, 306, 402, 421.

[16] Concerning James and the newspaper business see *HJL*, 2:8, 13, 45, 63-64, 66, 68, 88; Leon Edel, *The Life of Henry James: The Conquest of London (1870-1881)*

(Philadelphia and New York: J. B. Lippincott, 1962), pp. 237-45; George Monteiro, "Henry James and Whitelaw Reid: Some Additional Documents," *Henry James Review* 8.2 (1987): 139-41.

[17] See also *HJL,* 1:478; 3:52; 4:206, 274, 616; *Letters of Henry James,* 1:259, 369; 2:121, 122, 180, 315 for other examples of the marine metaphor used as a rhetorical tool to console others.

[18] Leon Edel, *The Life of Henry James: The Middle Years (1882-1895)* (Philadelphia and New York: J. B. Lippincott, 1962), pp. 73-74.

[19] Henry James, "Is There a Life After Death?" in *The James Family,* ed. F. O. Matthiessen (New York: Alfred A. Knopf, 1947), p. 610.

[20] *HJL,* 2:276 and *The Letters of Henry James,* 2:141, 372 provide other examples of the bath of experience metaphor.

[21] James, *The Letters of Henry James,* 2:107.

[22] Henry James, *The Ambassadors,* New York Edition, 2 vols. (New York: Charles Scribner's Sons, 1909), 1:217. Subsequent references will be cited in the text as *A.*

[23] John Carlos Rowe, *The Theoretical Dimensions of Henry James* (U. of Wisconsin Press, 1984), pp. 197-99; Adeline R. Tintner, *The Museum World of Henry James* (UMI Research Press, 1986), pp. 111-12.

[24] Henry James, *The Awkward Age* (London: William Heinemann, 1899), p. 148. All subsequent references to *The Awkward Age* will appear in the text as *AA.*

[25] Henry James, *The Art of the Novel,* ed. R. P. Blackmur (New York: Charles Scribner's Sons, 1934), pp. 222-23.

Manfred Geier

SOURCE: "Stanislaw Lem's Fantastic Ocean: Toward a Semantic Interpretation of 'Solaris'," in *Science Fiction Studies,* Vol. 19, No. 2, July, 1992, pp. 192-218.

[*In the following essay, Geier analyzes the mechanisms of meaning offered by the ocean in Stanislaw Lem's science fiction novel* Solaris.]

It is a commonplace that human consciousness can refer to things it does not perceive directly.[1] Merely imagined or conceived objects can exist at varying degrees of distance from immediately perceived reality. Concepts can refer to things which were once capable of being experienced as present and are now *absent* ("Monica no longer lives here, she lives in Hamburg"); or to a reality which exists *elsewhere* and the existence of which I do not doubt, although I have never experienced it as a fact

with my own senses, having knowledge of it only through reports or the daily news ("Two Israeli military aircraft were fired upon while flying over Palestinian refugee camps in the southern part of the Lebanese capital"); or to a *non-existent* world created by a poetic imagination, the world of a novel, for example, whose fictional personae and events I can experience while reading as if they were real ones[2] ("One morning at eight o'clock a young man stood before the door of an isolated, seemingly well-tended house"); or, finally, to a *fantastic* reality like those constructed and imagined in, among other places,[3] SF ("The *Invincible,* a space cruiser of the heavy-weight class, the largest ship at the disposal of the fleet based in the constellation of the Lyre, flew with photon drive through the outermost quadrants of the star group").[4] In all of these cases the object of consciousness is a conceptualized, imaginary reality, which is re-presented or cast in language. Of course, consciousness is intentional in any case; it is conscious of Something. But here its object appears only as the *linguistically meant* object, whose real point of reference is *not present* or non-existent.

In all these cases language plays a preeminent role. It is language that allows consciousness to remain focused upon something, precisely when it has freed itself from connection to a perceptible situation. Only because of this can we have the understanding between people which is produced socially and sustained by separation from an immediate situation.[5] Mutual agreement about what is absent or elsewhere is not problematic here, since the corresponding, indicated phenomena are present as linguistically expressed points of reference. (The fragments and experiences of reality indicated by "Monica," "Hamburg," "Palestinian refugee camps," "Israeli military aircraft," and "flight over the Lebanese capital" are asserted to exist, which is shown by the fact that the corresponding assertion can be true or false). The literary or fantasized text does, however, pose the question of what the indicated phenomena refer to, and indeed of whether or not they are signaling the fact that the supposed reality (the "young man at the door of the well-tended house," the "space cruiser with photon-drive") *does not exist.* We are dealing with fictional utterances which possess the same linguistic form as statements which can be true (Roman Ingarden speaks of "quasi-statements"[6]) but which do not refer to actual objects. The statements do not raise the question of truth, only of semantic correctness or coherence.

We are posing the intentionality question here as a semantic question about how an SF novel makes intelligible sense. Stanislaw Lem's *Solaris* serves as an example, and is, in my opinion, one of the most interesting, best conceived, and most suspenseful novels in all SF. We will focus especially on the fictional description of the *ocean,* the fantasized object which is at the thematic center of the novel, and inquire, in Gottlob Frege's words, what is its "mode of presentation" that makes it comprehensible to us? The following analysis can then be understood as a contribution to the "totality of interpretations" (Lem, *Phantastik und Futurologie* 373),[7] that *Solaris* has evoked, and about which Lem himself has said: "A fantastic work that has not yet been stabilized semantically by its recipients can become a screen on which readers project those meanings they consider important and urgent" (372). Even an interpretation such as "the difficulties in establishing contact between the people and the ocean . . . may represent relations between the individual and society" *(Ibid.)* is possible, although it is not convincing, according to Lem. It "can be felt to be inadequate, but it cannot be considered nonsensical, because *Solaris* has not yet been able to produce a solid, 'closed' crystallization of meanings in the totality of interpretations" (373).

A. The Problem: "And what does all this mean?"

Before attempting to answer the more difficult questions concerning the intelligible sense of the linguistic construction of the ocean, let us examine the problem of *reference* as it presents itself within the novel itself. We will approach it as if we were dealing with an objective fact—and, in terms of the linguistic representation, a realistic statement. Inasmuch as we initially enter the literary fiction in precisely this way by reading it quasi-realistically, we can deal with the same problems that Kris Kelvin and the other Solarists face. For they also, human beings on an alien planet, are pursued constantly—like paranoids—by a question that is central to their existence, their thinking and feeling: "So what does all this mean?" (*Solaris* 143/122)[8]. This question, on which Solaristic research has foundered and from which Kelvin can escape only through the speechless and motionless intensity of an *unio mystica* with the ocean, is posed in the novel from a double perspective: first, as a question *referring to an object,* i.e., about the meaning of the ocean itself; second, as a *semantic* question, about the meaning of the linguistic attempts to describe and explain it.

The allusion to paranoids, who perceive meanings where there aren't any, refers to the tension in which the Solaris cosmonauts find themselves in relation to a reality that confronts them as mere existence. The manifestations of the ocean (with their complicated, confusing multiplicity and supposed causal relationships) exhaust themselves in *being*. But those who want to explore this oceanic being are not satisfied with that. For them the manifestations of the ocean must *mean* something. Experimental attempts to establish contact are undertaken, *"signals"* are registered which should be understood as signs, even if they resist interpretation:

> but what does all that mean? Perhaps they were data about the ocean's state of agitation at the time? Perhaps impulses which its gigantic formations created somewhere thousands of miles away from the researchers? Perhaps reflections of the eternal truths of this ocean, transferred into unfathomable electronic networks? Perhaps its art works? (**28**/21)

The experiments support none of the available hypotheses. Since the ocean does not react regularly, it does not accommodate itself to the repeated experimental attempts at establishing contact. Never does the same stimulus produce the same reactions twice (**28**/21). Inquiry into the "*purposeful intent*" (**30**/24) of the oceanic creativity is also futile. In the end, the question about the meaning of the ocean is good only for an anecdote: on one occasion Kelvin, stimulated by the horrible occurrences at the collapse of symmetriads, remembers that during a school class's visit to the Aden Solaris Institute a "plump, perhaps fourteen-year-old girl in glasses with an energetic, comprehending glance suddenly asked the evocative question: 'And what is the whole thing for?' And during the embarrassed silence which followed, the teacher just looked sternly at her rebellious pupil; none of the accompanying Solarists (I was among them) had an answer" (**143**/122). Ultimately, it is the question of the *purpose* of the oceanic constructions, of their production and dissolution, which cannot be answered and which calls into question whether the ocean can have a meaning for human beings. Purposelessness implies meaninglessness. That is one of the insights that places the Solaris research program fundamentally in question. The materializations of the Phi-creatures also occur without a recognizable purpose:

> It has thus taken the memories that are most clearly etched into us, most intimately, most completely, and most deeply imprinted, you understand? But it must absolutely not have known what that is to us, what meaning that has. It is as if we understood how to create a symmetriad and threw it into the ocean, understanding in the process all about its structure, its technology, and its building materials, without, however, understanding what precisely it is for, what purpose it serves, what it means for the ocean. . . . (**226**/193)

This purpose/meaning for someone cannot be understood because the existence of the ocean *has nothing to do* with human beings. It is outside the realm of human activity with its purposes and motives. "It is Being that exists first for science fiction just as it does for science, and we carry values into this being with us" (*P&F* 115). Searching for purpose then appears to be "anthropomorphism." "Where there are no people, there are also no humanly comprehensible motives" (*Solaris* **157**/134). In view of the ontological alienness of the ocean in relation to human beings, its "meaning" can only be determined negatively: it consists of holding up before human beings a mirror of their own anthropomorphic and geocentric limitedness. If there is any purpose/meaning at all, it lies in the attempt to conquer Solaris, not in Solaris itself. In his important essay on futurology and the fantastic Lem makes the claim this way:

> It remains to be considered whether fantastic worlds—regarded as empirical hypotheses—mean something and, if so, then what. As objects they mean nothing, just as a galaxy means nothing: it *simply exists*. But when human beings conquer it,

they become entangled in processes and phenomena which subject their initial axiology (their morality, their customs and conceptual world) to a powerful pressure, to distortions and alterations, and it is in regard to these that their activity will mean something—as a result of the collision with the uncertain and the unpredictable; as ruins of those firmly rooted judgments and new impulses; and perhaps also as a desperate lamentation over the rubble of a semantic system which is inadequate for the cosmic undertaking and therefore is totally shattered. (*P&F* 116)

Inasmuch as the ocean "means nothing as an object," but simply exists, efforts at naming, describing, and explaining it confront the paradox of expecting meaningful signs to refer to realities which fundamentally escape being designated by language. This is shown instrumentally by the fact, among others, that the ocean does not accomodate itself to any of the Solarists' experimental approaches. No experiment is repeatable, no generalization determinable. Under these conditions the designatable object would have to be understood as something singular in each and every case, which fundamentally contradicts the essence of human language. As a "pure object" without an understandable or experimentally delimitable purpose, the ocean either elicits a kind of epistemological optimism (i.e., the ocean exists and produces phenomena in just the way the Solarists describe and explain it, so that at least one of the descriptions will surely be the right one) or it confirms a pessimism which demolishes the attempts at naming by viewing them as mere projections. Since the Solarists are human beings who can perceive through the lenses of their language only what is known and understood by them through the verbalizable experience of their own world, the ocean is for them an alien, and therefore necessarily incomprehensible existence. "And so one has always moved in the circle of earthly, human conceptions . . ." (*Solaris* 145/123). It must then be pessimistically admitted that "no terminology (can) reproduce what happens on Solaris" (**129**/111). There remains the possibility, albeit one disavowed critically as a form of helpless geocentrism, of a kind of mutilated metaphorical language which indeed shows that the signs mean something other than their literal meaning, but also that this other cannot be designated. The "thing" is designated as if it were an ocean, a brain, a protoplasmic machine, a gelatine, although everyone knows that "it" is none of these. The library of the Solaris station, a rubble heap of semantics, displays in a thousand volumes the shattered attempt to overcome the "impossibility . . . that the reality might be totally alien" (**192**/164).

If language lacks an objective-meaningful point of reference, then the solid meaning of its signs appears to be a fiction also. What do "ocean," "plasma," "mimoid," "slime," "gelatine," "brain" mean in the context of descriptions of Solaris? Logically, communication among the Solarists themselves must become a problem: in the midst of the signifiers of their language, the signified objects begin to flow away, to glide like the "liquid" ocean under the metallic colossus of the station. "Veubeke, who was Director of the Institute back in my student years, asked one day: 'How do you expect to communicate with the ocean when you do not even understand each other?'; there was a good deal of truth in this joke" (**29**/22).

This internal problematic of meaning in the novel, which we have identified as a double question of the meaning of the named reality and of the linguistic naming itself, reads like a literary formulation of the relationship between *objective meaning* and *symbolic meaning* as it has been developed theoretically by Klaus Holzkamp. Kelvin's question about the ocean, "And what does all that mean?", can be reformulated as a question about its "objective meaningfulness";[9] in the same way, the problematic of the meaning of the word "ocean" can be read as a question about the "symbolic meaning" in which the experienced qualities of the ocean in its ideal form are meant and designated. From this critical-psychological perspective we can discern more clearly the aporias which must necessarily result from the SF-reality of an alien world into which human beings come only as curious "visitors."

The meaninglessness of the ocean, to which people vainly want to attach their earthly meanings, points to a fundamental difference: the wish of the Solarists that the ocean should mean something objectively can be traced to the fact that they can experience their own world as "meaningful." In the latter world, questions about purposeful intention and motivation, about usefulness and the satisfaction of needs, have a place, whereas such questions are senseless, mere projections, with regard to the extraterrestrial ocean. With this, Lem's novel treats a phenomenon which is central to Klaus Holzkamp's critical-psychological analysis of human perception: the conditions of perception of the human world are meaningful to human beings (i.e., they are not merely bundles of sensations or constellations of stimuli). Human perception distinguishes itself specifically from the merely organic orientation of animals through precisely this "objective meaningfulness" of perceptible phenomena in the world. In perceiving, human beings orient themselves to *objective meaning,* which objects possess in relation to people's vital activity.

Holzkamp derives this concept from the socio-historically reconstructable circumstance "that the meanings of objects originate through *objectifying* work. By virtue of this quality, locating meanings in objects is exclusively a characteristic of the human world" (Holzkamp 119). Human beings, themselves a physical force in nature, encounter natural materials through work, in which they accomplish their conscious purposes and their values based on need; the exchange of matter between human beings and nature, which is itself mediated, regulated, and monitored by human work, is an objectifying transfer of conscious, ideally anticipated goals, an appropriation of nature for the purpose of satisfying social needs.[10] With this materialist reference to the unique-ness of human work, the meaningfulness of the world's phenomena is explicable insofar as "generalized human purposes appear in objective, perceptible form" in them (Holzkamp 118). The "human world" is meaningful in that it is an objectification of human beings' valuation of usefulness and hence of human power.

Under these circumstances, it is obvious that the ocean of the planet Solaris can have no meaning; the percep-tions of the cosmonauts must consequently also lack orientation, insofar as the ocean possesses no character-istics connected to vital human activity. It confronts human beings as alien in principle, and for this reason the exchange of matter between the ocean and human beings is fatal for the latter; nothing about it originated in objectifying work; its phenomena have nothing to do with generalized human purposes; it thus resists any appropriation for the satisfaction of human social needs.

The general determinations of usefulness, which are objectified as objective meanings, can and must (because of the necessity of an accumulation, evaluation, and independent transmission of social knowledge) be estab-lished *in language*. In *symbolic meanings* (Holzkamp 147ff.) the conscious objective meaningfulness of the human world is symbolically "introduced into a con-cept" (151). Symbolic meaning distinguishes itself from the objective meaning of earthly phenomena in that it is meaningful through its reference to something outside itself, while the meaning of objects is tied by the senses to the facts of perception itself.

However, the fact that the objective point of reference is "external" to language does not mean that it is therefore foreign to it. The differentiation of objective from sym-bolic-linguistic meaning, which is implied by the "refer-ential character" of the linguistic sign, is not a strict separation. On the contrary, the relationship between language and world as such remains comprehensible precisely through the posited assumption that the world's phenomena are meaningful for human beings themselves. In contrast, the assumption of a meaning-less reality outside language would make the referential possibility of linguistic form inexplicable:

> As long as one proceeds from the position that human beings confront a world which has nothing to do with them, one will never understand how human beings can ever reach the world with their symbol.—Actually, the symbol and the subject have an inner connection to each other, even if they are not immediately similar in their natures. The world of human beings is a world they appropriate through objectifying, social work. Meanings lie "in" things, because human beings have objectified meanings in them through a historical process of cooperative production. A meaningful world is by no means first created by symbolic meanings. Instead symbolic meanings are *abstract explications of the meanings of objects created by work.* (Holzkamp 151f.)

This formulation can lead to an explanation of the lin-guistically critical pessimism of Kelvin and the other Solarists. Because the ocean must be regarded as mean-ingless, since it stands in no relationship to vital human activity through work, the linguistic symbols must, so to speak, ricochet off of it. Human beings can never reach this world with their language. Just as meanings do not lie "in" the phenomena of the ocean (since nothing about it is an objectification of the human valuing of usefulness and human power), the ocean cannot be con-stituted as meaningful through human language.

B. Textual coherence, isotopies, practical lexicology.

Nevertheless, the novel is not senseless. It is a *text* which can be *understood*. Even if the ocean and its designations are meaningless from the perspective of the Solarists within the narrative, they are not for the reader, who can read the Solaris reality "from the out-side" as the intended story in an understandable text. This means not only that the individual words, expres-sions, or larger textual units can be understood; it also means that readers are guided by the *references* in the text to a story (albeit a fictional one) of which they can create an image for themselves. They can read the text as a "referral,"[11] i.e., they can be referred by means of it to certain objective happenings in the reality on Solaris. Text and reading are structured paradoxically: the linguistically inexpressible meaninglessness of the ocean is at the same time the subject of a story which can be represented as objective reality by means of meaningful textual references. We can to a certain ex-tent *complete and understand the projections* which the Solarists adopt in capturing their experiences in lan-guage. How is that possible?

That *Solaris* is understandable points, first of all, to a foreknowledge which is shared by readers of the text and the (fictional) Solarists—a foreknowledge that lin-guistic signs (and the reality meant by them) out of which the text is constructed are meaningful. We speak the same kind of language as the first-person narrator, Kris Kelvin, or as Lem, his author. The world of Solaris as it appears to us in the novel is not a fully autonomous world. It is instead a *model of reality*—although a pro-jected one—created by an unusual arrangement of lin-guistic elements about which there exists significant foreknowledge among competent readers. All the ele-ments are understandable words in appropriate syntacti-cal combinations. Even the most extravagant fictional creation remains related to the contents of experience established in its linked signifiers; consequently it is also related to the knowledge of possible reality and story models symbolically articulated in the linguistic expressions and textual connections. Lem has discussed this complicated relationship between fictional and real-istic language, using the SF problem of constructing entirely *autonomous worlds* (*P&F* 392ff.). Such a world would have nothing to do with our world and our mean-ings. As an "autonomous, visionary world" (411) it would have to demonstrate a fully self-sufficient autarchy, which would have to be the result neither of secret borrowing nor of mere modifications of our world. "If one is constructing a reality that is supposed to *replace* the real world and not refer to it semantically at all, then it must be able to stand on its own legs and withstand all the tests of stability to which we expose it" (400). The point is clear: an autonomous world cannot be constructed—either the constructions slide in the direction of "miserably prepared artifacts (that is, the author proves to be an incompetent competitor of the Creator) or they mean something with respect to a real 'zero degree'-world" *(Ibid.)* (i.e., the universes of SF prove to be specific transformations of the author's world [Suvin 93]). If the actual, complete creation of an autonomous world were possible, it would mean nothing and its linguistic representation would be incomprehensible. "Every final conclusion about meanings that the semantics of a work locks in and thus makes into a system which is fully separated from the world is like an illusion. One can almost fully enclose the world in a work; to actually seal it hermetically, however, means to take all meaning from it" (P&F 109). Even the most illusionary SF-writers must rely on the semantic potential of their language, for which a priori meaningfulness must be assumed. A visionary world "which is perfect in its autonomy ceases to be a semantic apparatus" (412). It is, one might say, as unthinkable as a pure object without any significance.

Besides the foreknowledge about the meaning of individual linguistic signifiers, readers also have at their disposal a knowledge of possible *referential* stories to which the text makes reference. Authors must also orient themselves to this knowledge. The fictional reality of SF must, even in the case of a structure very far from the empirical zero-world, be *coherent* to the extent to which it is created by means of textual connectedness. *Solaris* displays a definite semantic coherence (from the basic theme to the individual sentences of dialogue), although this does not refer, as does a semantic order in the sense of a potentially truthful statement-structure, to the connectedness of worldly things and facts. It is rather a coherence which is logical within the text and technically useful for story-telling and which manifests itself in certain possibilities for combining and connecting linguistic signs. It deals with syntactical relationships which are possible in the internal universe of the fantastic work and are perceptible as readable connectedness. The linguistic creation of the ocean modifies and partially injures, it is true, certain "lexical solidarities,"[12] in that, for instance, the protoplasmic machine is constructed as a living, thinking being. Within the framework of the description itself, however, there are limitations and possibilities which are constituent elements of the textual coherence of the novel. Situations are constructed within the framework of the semantically chosen limiting conditions.

It is one of the distinctive characteristics of Lem's prose that it creates coherence through the *purposeful connection of remote meanings* (P&F 381). Its fantastic objects originate through the contamination of linguistic signs which could not be linked unproblematically in "normal" truth-affirming language. One could express this phenomenon graphically by saying that the SF-text is like an opaque mosaic window which possesses, in contrast to the transparent window of speech representing the real world, a self-contained structure belonging to it alone (15f.). "It is not that which is located *behind* the window that determines the coherence of what is perceived, but the specific character of the mosaic window itself" (16). Solaris-reality would disperse into nothingness if the linguistic layer of the novel *Solaris* were destroyed. The question posed at the outset can now finally be put precisely as a semantic problem: How can the semantic coherence of a text like *Solaris* be produced and read, when it consists of newly arranged contaminations of meanings that are drawn from categories remote from each other and which are thus syntactically incompatible in the zero-degree language employed?

To answer this question, it is worthwhile to take an excursion into the area of structural semantics. The concept of *isotopy*, as it has been developed by A. J. Greimas in his *Structural Semantics*, offers an especially useful aid because it refers to just those factors which are relevant for the meaning content of an understandable text.

One of the most important conditions of textual coherence is the availability of *isotopies*, semantic structures which connect meaningful lexical units (lexemes[13]) to form sensible texts. Greimas, as a structural semanticist, tries to establish the cause of this coherence on the basis of *elemental* semantic components which are "smaller" than those manifest in the lexemes joined in the text: it is a question of atomic units, so to speak, of "semantic characteristics," that Greimas calls *sememes* (24ff.), which together, combined into bundles, yield the meaning of the various lexemes and determine their possible uses in the text. The combinability of lexemes into a coherent text is based on a partial commonality (identity, contiguity, equivalence) of their sememes. *Isotopy* can be defined as the repeated (recurrent) appearances of semantic characteristics in a text, i.e., the recurrence of sememes. Through these recurrent sememes (which cannot be perceived directly on the surface of the text, but are effective as hypothetical constructs in the reading) larger meaning units are produced on the syntactic level.

A trivial example for clarification: a sentence like "The fish is bad" appears as well formulated in contrast to something like "The triangle is bad," because "fish" and "bad" are semantically compatible with each other and syntactically combinable as a consequence of certain sememes. "Fish" bundles together such sememes as /concrete/, /organic/, /alive/, /animal/, /preparable as food/ . . . ; for "bad" in the sense of "rotten," "spoiled," sememes like /physical condition/, /result of a process/ . . . can be assumed. The semantic compatibility of the two lexemes results from an isotopy which is supported by a sememic recurrence of /organic/, /physical condition/, /changeable/.

One can clarify the emergence of isotopies especially well with the example of *semantic equivalence* between defined lexemes (Greimas speaks of "denomination") and defining expansion, as it occurs in the case of a *definition*. This equivalence is produced by a bundle of isotopies which repeats and enumerates all the decisive sememes in the defining, expanding syntax (that as a rule is longer than the denomination) (Greimas 63-65). The lexeme "fish," for example, can be defined as "animal being, which is concrete, organic, alive, supplied with gills, lives in water, and . . ." Francois Rastier (158), following Pottier (239) and Greimas, calls such a condensation *metasemy,* showing via the example of crossword puzzles that this (denominative) metasemy need not necessarily be present in the text itself (Rastier 158; Greimas 80f.). The task of the puzzle solver, reversing that of a dictionary user, consists in first finding and inferring the metasemy from the expanded crossword puzzle definition.

If one joins these notions from structural linguistics with the earlier consideration that texts are understood as *referrals* oriented to a referential story as a reality model, then we can form the following hypothesis to guide our semantic interpretation of *Solaris:*

> that the characteristics primarily responsible for the emergence of referrals in the text appear in a majority of lexemes (i.e., they dominate in these and thereby make the emergence possible in the first place) in semantically homogeneous groups. Consequently each referral implies a certain search process on the level of the connection. This recognition can be clothed in a rule of thumb: "If you want to understand a text, first sort its lexemes according to the groups in which a (common) semantic characteristic clearly dominates all other characteristics." (Kallmeyer *et al.* 1:146)

The sememes capable of dominance are, so to speak, conditions for the possibility of coherent texts, which refer to understandable stories.

Complex isotopies make the reading of a text more difficult. This concept also comes from Greimas, who means by it "the presence of several isotopic planes in one and the same utterance" (87). They emerge because the semantic combination of lexemes rests on various semantic characteristics. Structurally they can be analyzed by identifying the sememes whose presence defines the semantic polysemy (multiple-meaningfulness) of the corresponding lexemes. This assumes that the semantic polysemy of the corresponding lexemes is not dissolved and reduced to "monosemy" by the text itself, as is usually the case, but rather flows on into various isotopies. In the example sentence "The fish is bad," a somewhat unusual isotopy could be assumed on the basis of "bad" in the sense of "inactive," "lazy." Thus a complex isotopy is available which is responsible for the multiple meanings of the sentence. The text is thereby, so to speak, open for several possible interpretations. Its reading allows an interpretation through which the various isotopic levels coexisting in the text are exposed.

C. Three Readings of Solaris

(1) Plasmatic reading. We have introduced some of the basic categories we can employ for an initial semantic interpretation of the ocean-text. The attempts to name categorically the "thing" that washes over almost the whole planet appear in certain designations which condense the vivid scientific experiences the Solarists have of the ocean. These designations, which come from diverse symbolic and objective fields and have been contaminated for the purpose of creating the fantastic object, the ocean, are expanded in the novel into ever newer descriptions.

Let us briefly enumerate the main designations and some of their most important expansions. Already at the outset they point to a series of recurrent sememes, which provide the reader with an orientation.

> Ocean: its surface consists of troughs which move, of waves which move rhythmically; foam forms in the pockets between the waves; smoke and fog rise from its surface; it is fluid with shallows, depths and islands, a great sea.
>
> Prebiological formation: an organic formation, a biologically primitive structure, gelatinous, a single, monstrous, overgrown cell, syrupy gelatine, formless mush, expanding like a cancer tissue and growing out beyond the cell walls, slimy and exuding slime.
>
> Plasma: an extraordinarily highly organized physical structure with its own active metabolism, physically comprehensible as a mechanism, capable of goal-oriented activity, generating eruptive new forms out of itself, a plasmatic production-mechanism.
>
> Brain: a protoplasmic brain-sea, which signals huge amounts of information, a source of electrical, magnetic impulses, thinking in the form of an incomprehensible, gigantic monologue, capable of being modeled by means of the most abstract branches of mathematical analysis and measurement, possibly endowed with consciousness, endlessly productive.

This semantic material, which comes from various scientific disciplines and research areas, is drawn together and applied to a single object, whose "fantastic" character is the result of this contamination of categorically remote meanings. At first the contamination appears to be arbitrary. Why precisely this connection and no other? But the arbitrariness is only apparent, for already during this first reading we note a certain linguistic sign which plays a key role for the SF-contamination as a point of intersection: the lexeme *"PLASMA."* Most (if not all) the descriptions which stem from the ocean's semantic potential are compressed into this polyvalent lexeme. The text unfolds the meaning-structure which belongs lexically to the polysemic lexeme "plasma." Ordinarily the relationships in texts are exactly the reverse: a lexeme which in isolation possesses several meanings is made monosemic by the text; i.e., it is limited to a certain textual meaning. In contrast, Lem exploits the lexical polysemy of "plasma" by picking up its various meanings in the text and developing them further. This linguistic polyvalence is used to construct a single object. The "trick" then consists in deducing one possible object from one word which has multiple meanings.

A glance into a dictionary will verify that the lexeme "plasma," etymologically from Greek "plásma" ("constructed, formed, construct"), has various meanings:

1. Biology: living substance, also "protoplasm" (from Greek "protos": "first; earliest; existing at the beginning"; means something like "original material, original substance of life"), the substance of the living cell, surrounded by the cell membrane, in which all processes of life transpire. From a chemical standpoint the plasma is not a uniform material, but an organized colloidal mixture of numerous chemical compounds, especially water, among which more solid and more fluid components can be distinguished. Colloid chemistry provides further clarification. "Colloid": "diffuse construct which, depending on the state of the diffusion medium and the phase of diffusion, is differentiated according to colloidal systems" (*Brockham's Encyc.* 10:356). Such colloid systems include: fog, smoke, foam, emulsion, solid foam, brine. "If the particles are bound to each other in a network by forces working among them so that they have lost their freedom of motion, then a gel exists with gelatinous or slimy consistency. . . . When cooled or on partial withdrawal of the solvent, the fluid brine becomes a gel, which is no longer fluid but still contains much solvent. This transition is reversible" (*Ibid.*). Gelatine is that "tough elastic mass in a solidified fluid state, which colloids acquire when they come into contact with water. . . . It has the capability under certain conditions, e.g., under cooling, to rigidify homogeneously" (*Ibid.* 6:734). (Incidentally, in biology one speaks also of a gelatine or colloid cancer as a cancerlike new construction, "which is characterized by a slimy or gelatinous quality. The gelatine cancer occurs through a slimy change of the cancer cells" [*Ibid.*]). The term "plasma stream" means "the probably autonomously generated flow of plasma within the cell" (*Ibid.* 14:668.)

2. Physiology: fluid, runny components of blood and milk; for example, blood plasma, muscle plasma ("the liquid, containing protein, obtained by pressing upon the living muscle" [*Ibid.* 667]).

3. Mineralogy: leek-green, dense aggregate of microcrystalline silicic acid.

4. Physics: "an ionized gas which contains free ions and electrons besides neutral particles. . . . In plasma, reactions between particles can occur which lead to a release of energy in the form of radiation" (*Ibid.*). In nature one finds plasma "in the highest strata of the atmosphere, in outer space, in the atmospheres of stars and inside stars." Plasma electric waves in interstellar matter are probably a source of the emissions observed by radio astronomy.

These various dictionary readings of the lexeme "plasma" show the *dominant* semantic material with which the writer's fantasy can work. The creation of the fantastic ocean through the polysemy of "plasma" has to be entirely nongraphic. It is a confusing game with semantic units whose combination allows no unified pictorial image. Lem speaks of it in *P&F* in this way: "it is not true that I first perceive the fantastic object with the 'mind's eye' and thereafter describe in language what I imagined. During the writing I see nothing, but I form a situation in my thoughts analogous to the limiting circumstances set up through corresponding decisions" (32). The "decision" to choose the lexeme "plasma" as the semantic focus of the fictional text implies "limiting conditions" which provide a direction for the semantic coherence of the text. Within this framework everything that is offered by the decision to begin from the designation "plasma" can now be expanded and narratively ornamented; in the process, visual vividness develops through the pictorial shaping of the semantic possibilities. The process of oceanic movements, with waves and rhythm, is to be unfolded from the "plasma stream." Even as detailed a picture as "Bits of slimy foam with the color of blood gathered in the troughs between the waves" draws its material from there, adapting the physiological concept of blood plasma and the colloidal state of foam in the process.

In the descriptions of the ocean as a "prebiological formation," the sememes bundled in the conception of biological plasma are unpacked and used in a literary way, each with its particular pictorial content. The colloidal systems (from mist to foam and brine) produce fantastic descriptions of magnificent natural processes. The reversibility of the transition from a solution to a gel manifests itself in the multiple metamorphoses of the ocean. The solidifying of the gelatine or its transition to a solution is described as a planetary event of gigantic proportions. Even the explanation of the ocean as nothing but a huge cancer tissue which formed inside former inhabitants is based on the biological, medical conception of "gelatine or colloid cancer." The convection of the ocean as a muscular mountain of flesh recalls the physiological concept of muscle plasma.

Ultimately, the existence of the ocean as a reality of the planet Solaris is conceived in terms of physical "plasma," which refers to material phenomena in space and the interior of stars. Radiation detectable through radio-astronomy, the electrical waves of interstellar material, are also exploited for literary purposes in the novel: they possess their fictional counterpart in the signals of the ocean, which are to be interpreted as products of its thinking (the ocean consequently appears as a thinking "brain"). And finally the name "Solaris" itself picks up, besides the Latin sol (sun), the chemical concept "sol," which designates a colloidal system that exists in a reversible relationship with the gelatinous consistency of the gel.

Now one might already speak here of a complex isotopy insofar as the sememes of "plasma" belong to various systems—the biological, physical, chemical, physiological. It seems sensible, however, still to speak here of one isotopy, and consequently also of one interpretation, to the extent that the polysememe "plasma," as a natural scientific concept, is fundamental.

(2) Vaginal reading. The plasmatic is not the only possible interpretation. We can also identify other isotopies which refer, in part, to the same recurrent units of the text. Further, many textual elements which appear confusing and chaotic through the lens of a plasmatic reading can be related homogeneously to each other. The plasmatic isotopy is merely the simplest and most obvious because it can be supported by a series of semantic elements of the lexeme "plasma," which are manifest in the text. At the same time it comports well with the preconception that *Solaris* is a scientific SF-novel.

However, the simplest interpretation is not necessarily the most stimulating and most productive one. In the following section we will examine an interpretation which is not the most obvious, but certainly one of the most interesting. This second interpretation involves the same textual units as the first one. However, in contrast to "plasma," their metasemic condensation is not manifest in the text itself. This second reading is thus only possible when, like a crossword puzzle solver, one finds the metasemy which is a "hidden presence" in the text. Some of the relevant lexemes whose recurrent meaning connection also served as a basis for the plasmatic isotopy are: "troughs," "stream," "blood," "slime," "foam," "water," "muscle," "flowing," "life," "cell." Secondly, some additional lexemes and lexeme connections refer to the same metasemy but are not contained in the isotopy produced by "plasma." They turn up especially in Giese's taxonomy of oceanic phenomena: "floods," "a material which has on the surface a gelatinous-foamy consistency," but is in the interior like "a taut muscle," "lips which draw together like living, muscular, closing craters," "abortive mimoid," "umbilical cords," "release of the off-spring creation from the control of the mother-piece," "avalanche of births," "shrinking narrow passages," "fruit of the body," "streams of rosy blood"; André Berton's report mentions "slimy creations," "veined swellings," a "naked infant, as if new born." All these lexemes and syntagms can be coherently related to each other through the adoption of the sememes /corporality/, /sexuality/, /the feminine/. Their referential direction, which implies a definite direction to the search for connections, is supported by the semantic homogeneity of the metasemy *"VAGINA."*

The ocean, which is "meaningless" in its productivity and, as an alien reality, cannot be reduced to a concept in human symbols, can be interpreted as a projected construction, whose dominating semantic potential stems from the area of feminine sexuality summarized in the single lexeme "vagina." "One can, in fact, distinguish the appearance of objects, as well as their condi-

tions of sensibility, only by referring to the sum of actual experiences; the unknown is transposed into partially similar experience," writes Lem (*P&F* 34), thereby describing an act of projection which functions in the construction and reading of an SF novel. Lem's experiences as a former gynecologist doubtless had some influence in the orientation of the fantastic ocean to, as Freud put it, the "complicated topography of the feminine sexual organs," which are symbolized "very often as *landscape*" (Freud *Vorlesungen* 158).

It is not only this topography, however, that forms the basis for the comparison of ocean and vagina. The oceanic events (and the emotions accompanying them) become intelligible through the isotopy of "vagina." André Berton's experience is indeed nothing other than the occurrence of a *birth,* even if it appears as senseless plasmatic creativity. In blood and slime, calling forth disgust in Berton, a child arrives, slippery, shiny, damp, from the agitated waves of the ocean. Other processes can be read as descriptions of coitus: on the flight to the ocean, "which bubbled vehemently, as if driven upward by strong convection currents," Berton tries to stay in the "middle of a "hole"; finally he lets himself down here, "as best I could." The ocean cooperates in establishing contact: "it modified certain elements of apparatus immersed in it so that the recorded rhythms of the discharges changed." These processes turn up repeatedly in Giese's taxonomy also: "the plasma opens the way: it separates before the foreign body"; it behaves "not aggressively" toward the penis-like intruders so that only "he who especially risks it through his own carelessness or thoughtlessness can die" in its eddies.

The emergence of the mimoids reads like a *birth,* prepared by forceful *pains:* "The observer would swear that a violent struggle raged beneath him, for like lips which draw tightly together endless rows of concentric circular waves flow together here from the whole surrounding area like living, muscular, closing craters"; "from the horizons concentric rows of waves rush in, exactly the sort of muscular craters that accompany the birth of the mimoid."

Finally the collapse of a symmetriad appears as a superdimensional *orgasm* of gigantic proportions: the oceanic processes then endure "intense acceleration . . . everything begins to rush. The impression becomes overwhelming that the colossus, in the face of the danger threatening it, presses on by main force toward some fulfillment." Then the oceanic motion collapses "horribly": "forced out as if through gasps of agony, the air rubs against the shrinking, narrowing passages, raising among the collapsing ceilings a gurgling as if from some monstrous throat overgrown with stalactites of slime." The novel itself expressly invokes the orgasm as a possible interpretation—although with defensive and depreciating reservations. Kelvin's diploma thesis in psychology, with which he has made a name for himself in Solaristic research, concentrates on "discharges from oceanic streams" that stand in striking analogy to certain components of the oceanic cortex's processes "which accompany the strongest emotions, despair, pleasure, pain." "This had sufficed to make my name turn up very rapidly in the tabloid press under sensational titles like: 'The despairing gelatine' or 'Planet in orgasm' . . ." (*Solaris* **205**/175).

This reading cannot conceal the debt it owes to Freud's psychoanalysis. The various, partially overlapping isotopic planes that elicit differing interpretations recall Freud's differentiation between *manifest* and *latent* texts, whereby the latent text, in our case the vaginal isotopy, can be seen as "unconscious." A few short allusions must suffice here to clarify this category of the *"unconscious"* in the traditional psychoanalytic sense. They should at the same time help in answering the question of why the vagina is not named in Lem's text, but can only be interpretively revealed as a hidden meaning.

"If one wished to summarize the Freudian discovery in one word, it would be that of the 'unconscious,'" say Laplanche and Pontalis pointedly in their vocabulary of psychoanalysis (536). The therapeutic experiences had, in fact, shown that the conscious mind does not fill up the space of the psyche, that there are psychic contents ("evidence of drives") which are accessible to consciousness only after overcoming resistance; that these contents are ruled by mechanisms (such as fictionalizing, rearranging, and symbolizing) which themselves work unconsciously; and that they are constituted essentially of infantile experiences which are not registered in the consciousness of individuals and their language.

Freud conceived of these contents and mechanisms of the unconscious as *lacking language* and he tried to understand them by means of his early distinction between *fact-imaging* and *word-imaging*. For psychology, as he understood it in his study of aphasia of 1891, the word counts as a unit of the language function. It is defined as a psychic object composed of various associated concepts (sound-, writing-, reading- and motion-images). Associated with this word-imaging as a rule, i.e., in the case of a language used between two subjects, is a fact-image, which is again thought of as a complex, composed of visual, acoustic, tactile elements, although the order of the fact's associative elements is open in principle, in contrast to the word-image (Freud, *Auffassung* 75). In his later writings Freud used this classification to produce the concept of the *unconscious,* when he was stimulated especially by his examination of the utterances of schizophrenics.

> What we might call conscious object-imaging subdivides itself for us now into *word-imaging* and *fact-imaging,* which consists of filling in, if not direct images from memory of the fact, then more remote traces of memories derived from memory of the fact. We now believe that we know what distinguishes a conscious image from an unconscious one. . . . The conscious image embraces the fact-image plus the word-image belonging to it; the unconscious image is the fact-image alone. The system of the *unconscious* contains the attributions of fact to the object, the first and actual appropriation of the object; the system of the *preconscious* originates when the fact-image is further appropriated through association with the corresponding word-image. (Freud, *Das Unbewusste* 300)

Freud's "unconscious" is the conceptualization of the "fact," which cannot be contained in words.[14] It lacks the links with the (corresponding) words through which it can become an object of consciousness. Freud has also shown in his practical work that this unconscious can only be discovered when it is decoded in interpretation and explanation as the *latent meaning* of an assemblage of signs. Especially in the *Interpretation of Dreams* he has elucidated how certain tell-tale marks of the dream-text can be read as traces of the unconscious. Freud understands that dream-language also says something other than what it literally says, and therein lies the difference between *latent* (unconscious) dream-thoughts and *manifest* (conscious) dream-content (Freud, *Die Traumdeutung* 283ff.). On the basis of the narration of manifest dream-content, the analyst, guided by the patients' associations with the individual elements of their dreams, reconstructs the latent thought which, as opposed to the overtly confusing chaos of the content, generally can be read and understood as a coherent and sensible, although unconscious, "text." Paradoxically the interpretation thus first leads to a homogeneous sense, which is understood by Freud to be "normal" and "fits in" as a "fully weighted, equally valued link in the chain of our mental actions" (100). On the other hand, the manifest text, if we try to understand it literally, strikes us immediately as incomprehensible, confused, not of full value. The hidden, latent meaning, the unconscious thought, which is derived from traces of memory not transposed into language, is comprehensible. Its illumination consequently counts as a "translation" of an incomprehensible type of expression "into the normal."

The vaginal interpretation of *Solaris* fits smoothly into this Freudian perspective. The undeniable question about the meaning of the ocean, which can also be posed as a question about the confusing meanings of the manifest "novel content," can be answered by demonstrating the manner in which the unconscious fact-imaging expresses itself in it only in code and emerges only through the detection of close associations. Able to be experienced with all the senses, the "fact-imaging" of the vagina as "primary" expression of the female sex does not attain conscious recognition through connection "with the corresponding word-images." It expresses itself instead in the manifest content of a description which concentrates on an unknown and agnosticized object and tries to name it linguistically in ever new, ever futile attempts. Only the "translation" of this incomprehensible speech about an unimaginable fantastic object into the normality of a "vaginal interpetation" leads to a latent thought which is effective as a "fully weighted" element in human mental experience.

In psychoanalytic theory this latent meaning pattern of the unconscious normal is more precisely identified by its content as the expression of a *wish*. Dream interpretation tries to demonstrate that the dream represents a certain situation just "as I might wish it to be; its content is thus the fulfillment of a wish; its motive is a wish" (Freud, *Psychanalytische Bemerkungen* 269). Wishing, which operates on the basis of a pleasure-pain principle, is a "stream aiming at pleasure in the apparatus" *(Ibid.)* of the psyche, a stream which flows along those memory tracks in which certain experiences—as a rule satisfying ones, but also repressed ones—are unconsciously retained. In dream-thinking the wish finds fulfillment in the hallucinatory reproduction of perceptions that are associated with the indestructible memory track of need creation and satisfaction. It follows logically that the decoded normal would be the uninhibited, unrepressed articulation of the wish in question in its linguistic unambiguousness, an articulation which, because of psychological censoring mechanisms, can only manifest itself encoded and can only be fulfilled scenically on the level of fantasy.

This digression on Freud puts us on the track of why the latent thought about the vagina as the object of wishes (Freud) or the meta-textual isotopy constituted by the metasemy "vagina" (Greimas) does not appear openly, why the "readable," but unusual, "meaningless," partially absurd construction of a fantastic ocean with its countless metamorphoses and frightening phenomena has taken the place of an "unreadable," but comprehensible, clear, and "normal" description of female sexuality. It is certainly not unreasonable to assume that one is dealing here with an example of that repressed masculine fantasy through which feminine sexuality, reduced to an organ, the vagina, is imagined as a forbidden and anxiety-generating object of wishes, which is articulated as a censored thought in the streaming, bleeding, flooding, and slimy metamorphoses of the ocean.

Klaus Theweleit, in his monumental investigation *Male Fantasies,* has traced the linguistic manifestations and causes of these masculine fantasies. He has shown how the fantasized body of woman becomes a fantastic scene of action in which the confrontation of men with feminine sexuality occurs, a site foreign to them and made foreign by them. Using innumerable examples from European and European-influenced literature, Theweleit has discovered that "desire, if it flows at all, flows in a certain sense *through woman*" (272), and is presented in an enormous number of images, of which the ocean is a dominant one. The ocean of Solaris, this sea of movable flesh, whose flowing looks "like the slow tensing of a muscular, naked torso," is also an object of the desire which seeks to be released and fulfilled in the feminine and is expressed in a kind of "oceanic feeling" (Freud, *Das Unbehagen an der Kultur* 422f.; Theweleit 252-54).

But this construction of a feminine territory occupied by wishes is only one aspect of male fantasy. It possesses a complement (and also—as Theweleit has shown—a so-

cial-historical cause) in a development of civilization in which the masculine ego "armors" itself against the woman and from its perspective of self-discipline and muted feelings sees feminine sexuality as a dangerous threat (Theweleit 300ff.).[15] For this civilized ego, which seeks to ground itself not last of all in a language true to reality, the feminine, imagined in the masculine fantasy of the oceanic streaming, flowing, released and releasing, appears as the other, which is to be feared, fought, named, and conquered. The ocean, the phantasmagoric extension of the vagina into the sea of seas (Theweleit 346-48), is an "eternal challenge" (*Solaris* **201**/172), disgusting, horrible, and yet fascinating, marvelous, and fantastic. Protected in the dry order of the metallic station, armored against the influences of the oceanic life, the men hover over it in order to gain control over its production process and to be able to comprehend the unknown territory.

That this feminine principle cannot be linguistically comprehended and designated by name (as all exertions to describe the ocean in language fail miserably in the face of its unworldly strangeness) points finally to a basic cultural structure which plays a central role in the recent discussion of French feminist theorists. Luce Irigaray, Hélène Cixous and Julia Kristeva, to name only the best known, have subjected the sexual imagination of men to a fundamental critique, recognizing in it a phenomenon complementary to women's exclusion from the "symbolic order" determined by men.[16] Insofar as masculine imperialism has excluded woman from the symbolic order, which is also the organization of man's societal power, she is situated as an object of man's wishes in the position of not-knowing, in the position of the unknown and the secret. Within this sexual imaginary realm, founded in the Name of the Father on the armored might of man, woman is nothing other than "a more or less cooperative support for the staging of masculine fantasies" (Irigaray *et al.* 9).

What is the ocean other than precisely such a staging? What tireless exertions are undertaken by the men exploring Solaris in order to recognize, name, and rule that unknown being, the ocean. Even masculine brain waves, "converted into the oscillations of a bundle of beams," are driven into the "depths of this immeasurable, shoreless monster" (*Solaris* **182**/176), the ocean, in order to force an answer there. And behold, after the emission of Kelvin's EEG (which is also a "complete record" of the "unconscious processes" that no one is able to decipher), the ocean halts its production of Phi-creatures and adopts a new virginity ("The black disappeared, covered by little skins that were pale rose at the indentations and a pearly, shimmering brown in the depressions" [**212**/181]). This metamorphosis remains mysterious, however. The ocean withdraws in principle from imperial advances. Only occasionally, in hours of desperation, do the men themselves formulate insights that allow a breach in their imperialism: "We," says Snaut, the man, "need no other worlds. We need mirrors. We do not know what to do with other worlds. . . .

We want to find our own idealized image" (**87**/72). The wish for knowledge runs up against that "other world," to which woman has been sentenced and confined by man's symbolic order.

These feminist considerations have been stimulated and provoked not least of all by a male theorist, the French psychoanalyst Jacques Lacan. The generality of the linguistic (social) order counts for him, in fact, as being possessed by *man*. This order, a condition for the possibility of every meaningful articulation, is conceived from the position of man and his (phallic) representations. "Woman," who, in Lacan's logic, cannot exist "because she is not, in her nature, every woman,"[17] is excluded here. She is repressed into the flowing, agnosticized realm of the unconscious, which, in the name of man, is removed by a clear separation from the symbolic order (of consciousness).

The experiences of women, insofar as they are conceived and formulated by men, have no place within the medium of a generalized linguistic order, according to Lacan. On occasion Lacan's conception can attribute a private pleasure "beyond the phallus" to woman (Lacan 162)—which, as such, is, however, incapable of being articulated. Logically then, when it is a question of woman's particular pleasure, the word is "Let's say nothing!"—and the summary in *Solaris* is no different. What remains is, possibly, mysticism: the *speechless* experience of a pleasure beyond the phallus, excluded from the meaningfulness of language and its meanings. To whoever stands beyond the symbolic on the side of woman (and that can also be *individual* men), there remains only an *experience* about which he or she knows only "when it comes," an experience, however, which is *not utterable* (*Ibid.* 163).[18] It is an experience which, after all the vain attempts at technical and linguistic control of the ocean, nevertheless becomes possible for Kelvin alone in the end as a private wish fulfillment. Prepared through erotic play with a (naively budding and growing) *clitoral* wave of the ocean—not coincidentally, it is typical of the sexual imaginings of the men that they give preference to the clitoris, "which they regard as a trusted and reliable agent that works for them in hostile terrain" (Lyotard 57)—the encounter with the vaginal machinery of the ocean, the masculine occupation of its terrain, ends in Kelvin's speechless feeling "that it comes."

(3) Schizophrenic reading. After this exposition of one of the strongest, although veiled "structures, which are somehow 'personally absent' in the text, yet whose informing qualities are determined on great detours through the text" (*P&F* 387), I would like now to conclude with a third and last interpretation of the text: in terms of the *structure of the productive power* which functions within Lem's novel and manifests itself in its chain of signified meanings. This is the productive power of the unconscious itself.

The interpretive definition of the ocean as a masculine fantasy of feminine sexuality has so far determined only one metasemic content of this unconscious. Just as the original text on a palimpsest can often still be discovered under the new script, the unconscious masculine fantasy had left behind its legible traces in the description of the ocean. It was thus still a question about the interpretation of the intended meaning of an unconscious content, not of the mechanism of the unconscious itself. But the ocean is not only the formulation of a certain representation in the content (which can be decoded interpretively as a possible reading) but of the unconscious as a machine-like process. To find this assumption plausible, we must once more commit ourselves to the internal textual relations of the novel; i.e., we must proceed from an understanding that the *productions* of the ocean are indeed somehow goal-oriented, but are "meaningless" for human beings and beyond their linguistic efforts at signification. For the unconscious as a mechanism is modeled, as shall be shown here, in the meaningless productions and products of the ocean. This unconscious, which is only partially Freudian,[19] is similar to the conception developed by Gilles Deleuze and Félix Guattari in *Anti-Oedipus.*

For the French psychiatrist Guattari and the philosopher Deleuze, the unconscious is a production process. It possesses its productive powers in *"desiring-machines."*[20] Against Freud, in contrast to whose conception of the primary process and its unleashed energies they orient themselves (Freud also, incidentally, repeatedly expressed the functioning of the psyche's "apparatus" in mechanical imagery[21]), they raise the criticism that he restricted and channeled the unconscious production-process socially by applying (oedipal) *meanings and names* to it: "father," "mother," "son," "daughter," "incest wish," "patricidal wish," "castration threat," "guilt feeling," etc.

> The great discovery of psychoanalysis was that of the production of desire, of the productions of the unconscious. But once Oedipus entered the picture, this discovery was soon buried beneath a new brand of idealism: a classical theatre was substituted for the unconscious as factory; representation was substituted for the units of production of the unconscious; and an unconscious that was capable of nothing but expressing itself—in myth, tragedy, dreams—was substituted for the productive unconscious. (Deleuze/Guattari 24)

In contrast, Deleuze/Guattari try to free the unconscious from its oedipalizing meanings once again. As a "mechanical" production process, it precedes its meaningful representations, which, as such, are always already manifestations of a social repression of desire. (They can therefore accuse Freud of having pacified and repressed the explosive productive power of the unconscious). They say pointedly:

> The unconscious poses no problem of meaning, solely problems of use. The question posed by desire is not "What does it mean?" but rather "How does it work?" How do these machines, these desiring-machines, work—yours and mine?

With what sort of breakdowns as a part of their functioning? How do they pass from one body to another? How are they attached to the body without organs? What occurs when their mode of operation confronts the social machines? A tractable gear is greased, or on the contrary an infernal machine is made ready. What are the connections, what are the disjunctions, the conjunctions, what use is made of the syntheses? It represents nothing, but it produces. It means nothing, but it works. Desire makes its entry with the general collapse of the question "What does it mean?" (*Ibid.* 109)

The point of orientation for this notion of the desiring-machines is, just as it was for Freud's, the experiences of the *schizophrenic*—these form the basis on which the production of desire and of the desiring-machines can be demonstrated and analyzed. In the process, Deleuze/Guattari play especially on Daniel Paul Schreber's *Denkwürdigkeiten eines Nervenkranken* [Memoirs of a Nervous Illness]. From this schizophrenic text, which also provided Freud with the material for his theory of paranoia, they cite three syntheses of the desiring-machine's production: (1) connective, (2) disjunctive, and (3) conjunctive.

Lem's novel can serve us as a fantastic example for pursuing these three syntheses of the schizophrenic, non-oedipalized unconscious (the schizo-unconscious does not withdraw from the triad of work, language, and love). Let us read it, then, as an unfolding of the literary from the known reality of schizo-analysis: in each case it is a question of three similarly structured syntheses of the production of the desire-image Harey and of the desiring-machine, the ocean.

The basic pattern of the production of the Phi-creature "Harey" is the binary exchange of presence and absence and renewed presence and renewed absence, an ongoing Gone/Here game (Freud, *Jenseits* 11ff.). She is subject to the law of *connective synthesis:* "and . . . and then . . . ," of an apparently merely mechanical succession without understandable purpose and sense. The productive connections of her being-here and being-gone work in the process like a "paranoid machine." After Kelvin has realized with a shock that Harey is not a dream-image ("Harey," I croaked out, "that can't be . . ." [*Solaris* **68**/56]), he feels he is being persecuted by her ("I no longer told myself: 'That is a dream'; I had long since stopped believing that. Now I thought: 'I must defend myself.'" [**69**/57]) *and* develops a plan to get rid of her. *And then* he locks her into a rocket capsule and shoots her into a Solaris orbit; *and then* Harey comes again, a new Harey of the same production-process, exactly as Snaut had predicted to Kelvin:

"Listen, Snaut, a few questions. You know that . . . for some time. This . . . this . . . what will become of her?"

"You mean, will she come again?"

"Yes."

"She'll come again, but without coming again."

"What does that mean?"

"She'll come again as in the beginning . . . on the first visit. She will simply know nothing." (**83**/69)

And then Harey, after she has learned what she is, wants to kill herself with liquid oxygen and then is regenerated again amid frightful agonies and then resorts finally to a last means of annihilation: she disappears ("A lightning flash. A burst of air. A weak burst of air. Nothing else." [**223**/190]) And then new metamorphoses of the ocean seem to have quieted its guest-producing power.

Into this binary order of productive connections, linked by a repeated "and then," persecuting and threatening in their mere succession, *disjunctive syntheses* have (almost unnoticeably) streamed in: these are efforts to explain and give sense to Harey's existence which refer to the connections and want to lend them meaning. Harey, the product of the ocean, becomes the object of analysis, experimental examinations, and reflections. As the object of the sense-giving, she functions as a "miraculation-machine" (Deleuze/Guattari 10-11), a "wonder-machine." The riddle of her material structure cannot be solved; the scientist can only state his wonder:

Everything is normal, but this is just a disguise, a mask. In a certain sense it is an ultracopy: a reproduction, more perfect than the original. Because at the point where we hit the limit of granularity, the limit of structural divisibility in a human being, the way here leads further because these are constructed out of subatomic material!(. . .) It follows that all the proteins, cells, and cell nuclei are only *masks!* The real structure which generates the functioning of the "guest" is hidden deeper. (**119**/101)

The meaning of her existence remains undeterminable. A confusing profusion of contradictory explanations is possible; none is convincing. *Either* the projective productions that are the Phi-creatures want to hold up to human beings a mirror of their guilt and ugliness, *or* they want playfully, masked, to confuse them, or finally they are only a blind, meaningless process without purpose and motive. "Perhaps your appearance is supposed to be a torture, perhaps a favor, perhaps only a microscopic examination. An expression of friendship, a malicious blow, maybe scorn? Maybe all at once, or, which seems to me most probable, something totally different" (**171**/145). The attempts at explanation are synthesized in the disjunction of "either . . . or. . . . "

The disjunctive attempts seek to explain the production process and to include themselves in it as productions of notations; but they do not exhaust the possibilities of approaching and understanding the Phi-creatures. Kelvin is not only the theoretical head who gets caught up in the disjunctive syntheses of the explanation. He is also a corporeal subject, who is capable of enjoyment and love. There remains the possibility of a third synthesis: that of reconciliation and love, driven by a remnant of consumption-energy which has not depleted itself in the theoretical efforts at explanation. The first appearance of his guest already evokes a kind of mechanical eroticism: "My body committed itself to Harey, wanted her, drew me to her, beyond understanding, beyond the arguments and the fear" (**71**/59). The joys of a bond suggest themselves intensively, an "I feel" which is finally stronger than the love for the original Harey. "'And you are sure that it's not her but me that you . . . ? Me?' 'Yes. You. I don't know. I'm afraid, if you were really she, then I couldn't love you!'" (**171**/146). The possibility of this love, which can and wants to be lived and not explained by arguments, expresses itself as a conjunctive synthesis of the form: "So that is/was that"—without "that" being determinable or representable as a particular meaning. It is a form of mystical reconciliation, which lives entirely through the speechless intensity of an "I feel it."

At first the ocean is also nothing other than a restlessly running production-machine. In an endless succession the metamorphoses of the plasmatic machine develop and pass away; mimoids, symmetriads, and asymmetriads are created, accompanied by strong birth pangs, they stabilize themselves in confusing phenomena and find their "horrible" end, only to originate again by the billions in new formations. In continuously new *connective* syntheses ("and then"), an "inexhaustible multiplicity of Solarian forms" (**129**/111) is produced, production and product at the same time. Here all is mechanical motion, "unceasing formulation, in which the formulation is simultaneously the formulating" (Deleuze/Guattari 141). It is a question of productive connections: and it flows in free, stable conditions and then bodies, swellings, thickenings form and then, after phases of rigidification, everything dissolves again in the mechanical senselessness of the oceanic movements.

Human beings direct their investigatory interest toward this production of production. "Explanations" are applied to the oceanic production process, "myriads of hypotheses are set loose on it" (Solaris **192**/164). The ocean enters the area of designations, explanations, and records, according to the law of disjunctive syntheses and their assignments of meaning. The library is the place where they are kept. Here the experiments are written up to explain the ocean and to name and organize its phenomena in continuously new taxonomies. From the library the ocean appears as an object of wonder: either as a living, or a thinking organism, or as a plasmic machine, as a geological formation, as a syrupy gelatine, a gigantic brain, or a fleshy colossus. That "either . . . or . . . or" characterizes the countless efforts, which, all differing from each other, still lead to the same result: the ocean as an alien world remains an eternal wonder for the human being. The disjunctive synthesis of the significant notations ricochets off this "miraculation machine."

Here too, however, there is still a third possibility. Driven by that remaining energy which is not used up in reading, experiment, and explanation, Kelvin finally draws near to the ocean itself. Landing on the mimoid, he leaves behind him everything which could limit and smother a "feeling" in representational, linguistic forms. Contact with the living waves of the ocean happens as erotic play, as "naive" experience of pure intensity, stripped of every meaning. In the sensuous play of retreating and approaching, a speechless link with this "fluid, blind colossus" reaches realization "in the ever intensifying self-annihilation" (**238**/203). As the expression for this mystical reconciliation, there remains only the conjunctive synthesis: "So that is it." Nothing is now still representational; all is only still felt. "Without the least effort, without words, without a single thought" (**238**/ 203-04), Kelvin can forgive the ocean everything, even if the "time of cruel miracles" (**238**/204) may not yet be past.

This interpretation of the novel has revealed two triads with parallel structures of connective, disjunctive, and conjunctive syntheses. They can be formulated in the three statements:

(1) IT produces/pursues me.

(2) IT makes me wonder.

(3) I feel IT.

This result certainly does not suffice to explain and to make entirely comprehensible the meaning of the quotation from the Anti-Oedipus which has stimulated and provided the orientation for this last reading. But perhaps it has become sufficiently clear what sort of experience Deleuze and Guattari are referring to when they symbolize the schizophrenic unconscious as a production process of desiring-machines that begins its work with the general collapse of the question "What does that mean?" (even if this question, as the disjunctive syntheses show, should catch up with it again repeatedly). "The question posed by desire is not 'What does it mean?' but rather 'How does it work?'" (Deleuze/ Guattari 109), how this nameless and meaningless IT pursues, inspires wonder, and seduces, how IT, expressed in the categories of the *Anti-Oedipus,* synthesizes its connective productions, disjunctive notations, and conjunctive consumptions.

Thus, if it is true that the schizophrenic production of desire and of the desiring-machine is beyond and freed from any meaning (especially the oedipal), and that the schizophrenic unconscious functions and breaks down free from any representation/socialization, then *Solaris* is its literary model: for here indeed nothing is presented other than the production process of a protoplasmic machine, whose functioning evades the social question: "And what does all that mean?" What the schizophrenic experiences is nature, not as nature or as a world of objective meaningfulness, but as a production process:

There is no such thing as either man or nature now, only a process that produces the one within the other and couples the machines together. Producing-machines, desiring-machines everywhere, schizophrenic machines, all species of life: the self and the non-self, outside and inside, no longer have any meaning whatsoever. (Deleuze/Guattari 2).

The ocean/Harey/Kelvin: a molecularly coupled multiplicity—productive, wondrous, erotic—which means nothing; it functions. (The text too functions like a schizophrenic machine.) On Solaris, if it existed, Deleuze/Guattari's schizophrenic would feel at home. For Solaris is an "eternal challenge to the human being" (201/172) only if one looks for meanings or wants to implement one's purposes, only if one wants to keep on living according to the laws of social consciousness even in the "other world" of the schizophrenic.

Instead of arriving at a "solid crystallization of meaning in the totality of interpretations," the path we have travelled—through critical-psychological, structural-semantic, psychoanalytic and schizoanalytic orientations—has led to differing possible coherent semantic structures. We have woven together three different readings—plasmatic, vaginal, and schizoanalytic—which are based on an *interference of mutually overlapping isotopic levels.* *Solaris* does not stand on the rock of a hard and fast meaning, but on complex isotopies, which are responsible for the "capacity for multiple interpretations" of the novel.

NOTES

[1] This essay originally appeared in German as "Stanislaw Lems Phantastischer Ozean: Ein Beitrag zur semantischen Interpretation des Science-Fiction-Romans 'Solaris'," in M. Geier, *Kulturhistorische Sprachanalysen* (Köln, 1979), 67-123. [ICR]

[2] Cf. the essays of Wolfgang Iser, Roman Ingarden, and Felix Vodicka in R. Warning (ed.), *Rezeptionsästhetik* (Munich, 1975). [MG]

[3] Other examples would be, for instance, fairy tales, horror and ghost stories, heroic fantasy. Cf. Tzvetan Todorov, *The Fantastic* (New York, 1973); Roger Callois, *Au coeur du fantastique* (Paris, 1965). [MG]

[4] The differentiation of these various imaginative possibilities draws on Jean-Paul Sartre, *The Psychology of the Imagination* (New York, 1948). (The SF example is taken from the opening sentence of Lem's *The Invincible.*) [MG/ICR]

[5] Cf. especially A. N. Leontjew, *Probleme der Entwicklung des Psychischen* (Berlin, 1971), Pt. II, Ch. II/III. [MG]

[6] Roman Ingarden, *Vom Erkennen des literarischen Kunstwerks* (Tübingen, 1968), 11f. [MG]

[7] References to *Phantastik und Futurologie,* the German translation of Lem's *Fantastyka i Futurologia* (Science Fiction and Futurology), which has not been translated into English, will be abbreviated as *P&F.* [ICR]

[8] Stanislaw Lem, *Solaris,* Frankfurt: Suhrkamp, 1975. The numbers in parentheses following the quotations refer to the page numbers of the quotations in the German edition. Because Geier's argument is based on this translation of Lem's novel we have translated Geier's German quotations directly, without substituting the corresponding English versions from the translation available to English readers. We have, however, added page references to the appropriate passages in the 1987 reprint of *Solaris* by Harcourt Brace Jovanovich; these follow the German references, which are in boldface. We have kept the original Polish text's character names whenever the English text conflicts with them (e.g., Harey for Rheya, Snaut for Snow). [ICR]

[9] Klaus Holzkamp, *Sinnliche Erkenntnis* (Frankfurt, 1973), 25f, 105ff. [MG]

[10] Cf. Karl Marx, *Das Kapital,* Vol. I, *MEW,* 192f. [MG]

[11] Cf. W. Kallmeyer, W. Klein, R. Meyer-Hermann, et al., *Lekturekolleg zur Textlinguistik,* Vol. 1: Einführung (Frankfurt, 1974), 134f. [MG]

[12] Eugenio Coseriu, "Lexikalische Solidaritäten" in *Poetika* 1:293-303, 1967. [MG].

[13] One understands this to mean a lexical unit which, as a "word," is an element in the vocabulary with a relatively independent meaning of its own. Greimas understands the lexeme to be an assemblage of sememes which are linked to each other through hierarchical relationships. [MG]

[14] Jacques Lacan especially has raised objection to this speechless unconscious. Cf. J. Lacan, *Ecrits: A Selection* (New York, 1977). [MG/ICR]

[15] Cf. Theweleit, p. 379ff. Theweleit draws his orientation here especially from Norbert Elias, *The Civilizing Process* (New York, 1978). [MG/ICR]

[16] Cf. Julia Kristeva, "*Une(s) Femme(s),*" in *Essen vom Baum der Erkenntnis* (Berlin, 1977), 37ff.; J. Kristeva, *Revolution in poetic language* (New York, 1984); Luce Irigaray, *This Sex Which Is Not One* (Ithaca, 1985); Luce Irigaray, *Speculum of the Other Woman* (Ithaca, 1985); Hélène Cixous, "The Laugh of the Medusa," *Signs* 1.4 (1975). [MG/ICR]

[17] Jacques Lacan, "La Femme n'existe pas," in *"Das Lächeln der Medusa," Alternative,* 108/109:161. [MG]

[18] *Ibid.,* 163. Directed against this are the attempts at a "feminine writing style and productivity" as they have been developed as a possibility in the works of Irigaray, Cixous, and Kristeva. [MG]

[19] It refers especially to the unconscious insofar as it has been handled thematically by Freud in concepts of strength (and not of sense). On this dialectic, cf. Paul Ricoeur, *The Conflict of Interpretations* (Chicago, 1974). [MG/ICR]

[20] *Anti-Oedipus,* especially Ch. 1. [MG]

[21] In the "draft" from 1895 it is a question of a "neuron-machine"; in *Traumdeutung* of an "optical machine," similar to a telescope; later of a "wonder-block" (1925). [MG]

WORKS CITED

Deleuze, Gilles, and Félix Guattari. *Anti-Oedipus.* Minneapolis, 1983.

Freud, Sigmund. "Jenseits des Lustprinzips." *Gesammelte Werke (G.W.),* Vol. XIII.

————. "Psychoanalytische Bemerkungen über einen autobiographisch beschreibenen Fall von Paranoia (Dementia parnoides)," *G.W.,* Vol. VIII.

————. "Der Realitätsverlust bei Neurose und Psychose," in *G.W.,* Vol. XIII.

————. *Die Traumdeutung, G.W.,* vol. II/III.

————. "Uber den Traum," *G.W.,* Vol. II/III.

————. "Das Unbehagen an der Kultur," *G.W.,* Vol. XIV.

————. "Das Unbewusste," *G.W.,* Vol. XIII.

————. *Vorlesungen, G.W.* Vol. XI.

Greimas, A. J. *Strukturale Semantik.* Brunswick, 1971.

Kallmeyer, W., W. Klein, R. Meyer-Sieber, et al. *Lektürekolleg zur Textlinguistik,* Vol. 2. Frankfurt, 1974.

Laplanche, J., and Pontalis, J.-B., *Das Vokabular der Psychoanalyse.* 2 volumes. Frankfurt, 1973.

Lem, Stanislaw. *Phantastik und Futurologie,* Pt. 1. Frankfurt, 1977.

————. *Solaris.* Frankfurt: Suhrkamp, 1975.

Lyotard, Jean-Francois. *Das Patchwork der Minderheiten.* Berlin, 1977.

Pottier, B. *Présentation de la linguistique.* Paris, 1967.

Rastier, Francois. "Systematik der Isotopien." Kallmeyer, Klein, Meyer-Sieber, et al.

Schreber, Daniel Paul. *Denkwürdigkeiten eines Nervenkranken.* Frankfurt/Berlin/Vienna, 1973.

Suvin, Darko. "Zur Poetik des literarischen Genres Science Fiction." *Science Fiction.* Ed. E. Barmeyer. Munich, 1972.

Theweleit, Klaus. *Male Fantasies.* Vol. 1. Minneapolis, 1987.

Kathleen Morgan and Luis Losada

SOURCE: "Santiago in 'The Old Man and the Sea': A Homeric Hero," in *The Hemingway Review,* Vol. 12, No. 1, Fall, 1992, pp. 35-51.

[*In the following essay, Morgan and Losada trace parallels between Hemingway's fisherman Santiago in* The Old Man and the Sea *and the heroes of the Homeric epics the* Iliad *and the* Odyssey.]

When *The Old Man and the Sea* was published, Malcolm Cowley immediately noted its "classical" qualities (106-7). Within weeks Bernard Berenson, in the blurb he provided for the book, described it thus: "An idyll of the sea as sea, as un-Byronic and un-Melvillian as Homer himself, and communicated in a prose as calm and compelling as Homer's verse" (*SL* 785 n.1). Hemingway was both gratified by and concurred with Berenson's description (Morgan 78-80). Subsequent critics continued to discuss various classical aspects of *OMATS* in terms of both epic and drama, and in a recent work detailing the parallels between Hemingway's narrative art and Homer's, several examples of these parallels in *OMATS* were noted.[1] The object of the present study is to demonstrate the similarities Santiago shares with the heroic figures of the *Iliad* and the *Odyssey.*

Before proceeding, one feature of narrative technique requires elaboration. In the work noted above it was pointed out that in his repetitive use of the adjectives and adjectival phrases, "deep, mile deep, blue, dark blue, deep dark, dark," Hemingway creates the equivalent of Homeric epithets for the sea (Morgan 17). Here it is necessary to add that the characteristics Hemingway chooses to emphasize, depth and dark color, are two commonly highlighted by Homer in his own epithets for the sea, its waves and waters. One can begin with the "sea depths" from which Thetis rises and the "dark wave" that sounds beneath the keel of an Achaean ship (*Il.* 1.358, 482, LLM 11, 15), read through both epics to the "deep sea" that Laertes thinks may hold his dead son (*Od.* 24.291, BL 374), and seldom fail to find within a few pages reference to these two prominent characteristics of the sea; thus Hemingway, who read Homer in translation, in creating his epithets presents Santiago's adventure on a sea that is visibly as well as stylistically Homeric.[2]

The Iliadic Santiago

Hemingway presents his hero, Santiago, in terms that recall Homer's heroes at Troy; in fact, Santiago exhibits three characteristics that are not only specific to, but fundamental in, the definition of the Homeric hero.[3] First, Homeric heroes, as Andromache says of Hector, were "born" (*Il.* 22.477, LLM 414) to their destiny. This is highlighted in Homer by Achilles' statement of his twin destinies (*Il.* 9.412-16, LLM 158), and when he elects to return to the battle to kill Hector, he lays claim to the short, glorious life he was born for (*Il.* 18.79-126, LLM 339-40). Santiago knows, as his thoughts reveal, that he is doing "that which I was born for," that he was "born to be a fisherman" (*OMATS* 40, 105; cf. 50). Achilles' action also underlines another feature of Homeric heroism: "it is not unreflective or unself-conscious" (Griffin 73); it involves choice.[4] Similarly, Santiago has elected his course of action: "My choice was to go there and find him beyond all people" (*OMATS* 50). Finally, basic to the identity of the Homeric heroes is that they are the "best," as Achilles claims he is (*Il.* 1.244, LLM 8), and as others, including Aias, Diomedes, Agamemnon, and Patroklos are described.[5] Santiago is also the "best":

"And the best fisherman is you."

"No, I know others better."

"*Qué va,*" the boy said. "There are many good fishermen and some great ones. But there is only you."

"Thank you. You make me happy. I hope no fish will come along so great that he will prove us wrong." (*OMATS* 23)

In the end the great fish does not prove them wrong, and Santiago's prowess is recognized by the other fishermen who look at the skeleton, one of whom measures it, and by the proprietor of the Terrace who says: "What a fish it was . . . There has never been such a fish."[6]

Hemingway takes great care to show that Santiago is the "best." We may consider, for example, the conversation about baseball that culminates in the passage quoted above (*OMATS* 21-23). Critics have long noted that the evocation of Joe DiMaggio and Santiago's identification with him serve to underline the heroic quality of Santiago himself (Gurko 66; Burhans 76-77; Harada 272). The use of the DiMaggio analogy, however, also serves to emphasize that Santiago, like Homer's great heroes, is perceived as being the "best," a characteristic he does not disavow. As there are "other men on the team," and even other "great" players, there are also other "great" fishermen, but there is "only" Santiago.[7]

This same characteristic is illustrated in another passage in which competitive sport is not an analogue but the reality, the "hand game" that Santiago remembers on the second night at sea; here Santiago himself is a competitor, and as the victor he remains the "champion," certain that "he could beat anyone" (*OMATS* 69-70). Similarly, Homeric heroes vie to be the "best" in athletic contests, as is vividly portrayed in the funeral games Achilles organizes (*Il.* 23.257-895, LLM 423-40). Also Homeric is the reminiscence by an old man of an exploit of his youth, although in the epic such events are recounted in speech. On several occasions Nestor tells of his great deeds as a youth, not only in battle but also, and most relevant here, in athletics (*Il.* 23.629-45, LLM 433-34).

One of Nestor's youthful battle reminiscences is particularly significant for Hemingway's description of Santiago's arm wrestling match. Nestor tells of his victory in combat over the hero of the Arkadians who had come to battle Nestor's own Pylians:

> Then stood up for their champion Ereuthalion, a man the peer of the gods . . . he challenged all our best; but they trembled sore and were afraid . . . But me my hardy spirit aroused to meet him in my confidence; yet I was youngest of all in years. So fought I with him and Athene vouchsafed me glory. Tallest was he and strongest of men that I have slain; as one of huge bulk he lay spread this way and that. (*Il.* 7.136-56, LLM 120)

Like Santiago's contest, Nestor's is a challenge match with an opponent whose great size is emphasized; similarly, the youthful Nestor is, as Santiago, "sure" (*OMATS* 70) of himself, and victorious. In addition, there are several verbal correspondences between the LLM translation and Hemingway's text: "champion," "confidence," "strongest," and "huge" all appear in *OMATS* 69-70. Such correspondences suggest the possibility that Hemingway's scene may have literary antecedents in Homer's.

Santiago's battle with the great marlin and subsequent combat with the sharks are also presented Homerically. First, his contest with the fish is, as many such in the *Iliad,* a duel between two champions, in this case the "best fisherman," and "a great fish," the equal of which "there has never been" (*OMATS* 23, 63, 123). Once Santiago's epic struggle begins, it becomes, as many critics have noted, not only a contest with an equally formidable rival, but also one in which he progressively comes to identify with and feel pity for his opponent.[8]

A similar development is a prominent feature of the presentation of Achilles in the *Iliad.* After he reenters the battle, Achilles comes to identify with and pity the opponents he conquers (Schein 147-63). Before he dispatches Lycaon, he calls him "friend" and tells him that he himself will die also (*Il.* 21.106-13, LLM 380), and after killing Hector, aware that his death is inextricably linked to his fallen opponent's (*Il.* 18.95-126, LLM 339-40), he says, "Die: for my death I will accept it whensoever Zeus and the other immortal gods accomplish it" (*Il.* 22.365-66, LLM 411). Finally, he pities Priam, agrees to return Hector's body, and comments on their common misfortune and fate (*Il.* 24.507-70, LLM 455-57). Then he invites the aged king to eat and afterwards they look at each other:

> But when they had put off the desire of meat and drink, then Priam son of Dardanos marvelled at Achilles to see how great he was and how goodly, for he was like a god to look upon. And Achilles marvelled at Priam son of Dardanos, beholding his noble aspect and hearkening to his words. (*Il.* 24.628-32, LLM 459).

In the development of Santiago's feelings for the great fish there are several specific similarities with the presentation of Achilles' empathy for his Trojan enemies: Santiago begins to "pity" the fish, wishes he "could feed" it, thinks of it as his "brother," and later, he too calls his adversary "friend" (*OMATS* 48, 59, 75). Finally, in the culmination of the struggle he looks admiringly at his opponent and links their mutual vulnerability and mortality:

> You are killing me, fish, the old man thought. But you have a right to. Never have I seen a greater, or more beautiful, or a calmer or more noble thing than you, brother. Come on and kill me. I do not care who kills who. (*OMATS* 92)

Respect for the opponent is another characteristic of Homeric heroism; so Hector and Aias terminate their duel on account of darkness with expressions of mutual esteem:

> Then great Hector of the glancing helm said to him: "Aias, seeing God gave thee stature and might and wisdom, and with the spear thou art excellent above all the Achaians, let us now cease from combat and battle for the day; but hereafter will we fight until God judge between us, giving to one of us the victory." (*Il.* 7.287-92, LLM 124)

Similarly, Santiago has high regard not only for the great marlin, but also for the *dentuso* (*OMATS* 103, 105-6).

In addition, Santiago's actual slaying of the *dentuso,* as well as of the *galanos,* is in the Homeric manner. A hallmark of Homeric battle description is "the detailed account of the moment of death of the warrior" (Griffin 90). Close attention is paid to anatomical particulars:

> And Idomeneus wounded Eryman on the mouth with the pitiless bronze, and the spear of bronze went clean through below, beneath the brain, and shattered his white bones. (*Il.* 16.345-47, LLM 249)

Attention is also paid to the hero's selecting his target on his opponent's body:

> . . . the keen spear Achilles poised in his right hand, devising mischief against noble Hector, eyeing his fair flesh to find the fittest place. Now for the rest of him his flesh was covered by the fair bronze armour . . . but there was an opening where the collar bones coming from the shoulders clasp the neck . . . there Achilles drave at him . . . and right through the tender neck went the point (*Il.* 22.319-27, LLM 409-10)

Similarly, Santiago picks his spot and his dispatch of the *dentuso* is anatomically detailed:

> . . . he rammed the harpoon down onto the shark's head at a spot where the line between his eyes intersected with the line that ran straight back from his nose. There were no such lines. . . . But that was the location of the brain and the old man hit it. (*OMATS* 102)

Later when he battles the *galanos,* he again drives his weapon into the "juncture" of "brain" and "spinal cord," and with the second *galano,* his "blade" severs the "cartilage," as Idomeneus's spear "shattered" Erymas' "white bones" (*OMATS* 108-9).

Santiago's encounter with the sharks recalls another typical scene in the *Iliad,* the battle over the body of the fallen opponent. This occurs after a major hero has been victorious over an important enemy, and the fallen combatant's fellow warriors fight to recover his corpse (Schein 80-82). Prominent among many examples are the battles over the bodies of Sarpedon (*Il.* 16.532-614, LLM 304-8) and Patroklos (*Il.* 17-18.238, LLM 315-43). So when Santiago has defeated the great fish, he must then fight to keep the body (*OMATS* 100-119). Moreover, in the *Iliad* the slain opponent's corpse is always recovered by his side.[9] Thus Santiago, as his Homeric counterparts, cannot retain his prize, save for the stripped skeleton. The great marlin's fellow fish, the sharks, literally recapture his body.

In addition to his battling, Santiago is also prepared for his struggle in the manner of the heroes at Troy. Four times in the *Iliad* Homer describes, in similar language, the ritualistic arming of the hero before battle: first the greaves with ankle clasps of silver, next the corselet or breastplate, then the sword slung round his shoulders, the shield, the horsehair crested helmet, and finally the spear.[10]

Similarly, when Santiago starts out for sea, Hemingway describes the carrying of his equipment for the third time in six pages: "The boy took the rolls of line in the basket and the harpoon and the gaff and the old man carried the mast with the furled sail" (*OMATS* 26; cf. 9, 15). The detailed repetition in a prescribed form of the bringing of the fisherman's gear to the boat endows it with a ceremonial aspect not unlike the arming of the Homeric hero; and as in the Homeric scenes (Griffin 36), the marshalling of the fisherman's weapons foreshadows Santiago's heroic battle with the great marlin.[11]

Santiago also expresses himself in ways reminiscent of the heroes of the *Iliad.* First, in the heat of battle, the Homeric hero prays to the gods; e.g., after Sarpedon has been killed and he himself wounded, Glaukos prays for Apollo to heal him so that he may rouse the Trojans to defend his friend's body (*Il.* 16.513-26, LLM 304).[12] So Santiago turns to prayer, "Hail Marys," after he has seen how great the fish is (*OMATS* 65).[13] In addition, noteworthy here are his vows to perform a service in return for his prayers being answered: "I promise to make a pilgrimage to the Virgin of Cobre if I catch him" (*OMATS* 65; cf. 87). This formula of prayer is also Homeric: Achilles suggests that the Greeks pray and vow sacrifices to Apollo in hope that he will remove the plague at the onset of the *Iliad* (*Il.* 1.99-100, 315-17, LLM 4, 10). The efficacy of such prayer is made explicit in the archery contest where Meriones, who vows a "hecatomb of firstling lambs" to Apollo, defeats Teukros, who "made a vow . . . to the lord of archery" (*Il.* 23.862-83, LLM 440). Santiago, who is "not religious" (*OMATS* 64), prays as Meriones in the *Iliad,* and "not for his own salvation as a Christian would" (Rosenfeld 49).

Second, Homeric heroes constantly address their opponents with challenges, threats, and vows of victory; e.g., when Achilles comes upon Hector, he says: "Come thou near, the sooner thou mayest arrive at the goal of death" (*Il.* 20.429, LLM 380). Santiago similarly addresses the great fish: "But I will kill you dead before this day ends" (*OMATS* 54; cf. 52, 64). Later, when the *galanos* attack, he says: "Come on *galanos*. . . . No? . . . Come on *galano*. . . . Come in again" (*OMATS* 108, 109, 114). Also typical of battle speech is the vaunt over the fallen opponent.[14] So Priam's son Deiphobos boasts over Hypsenor that he has sent him as an "escort" down to Hades for the slain Trojan Asios (*Il.* 13.413-16, LLM 237), and Hector taunts the dying Patroklos by imputing to him failed expectations: "Patroklos, surely thou saidst that thou wouldst sack my town . . . fool!" (*Il.* 16.830-33, LLM 313). Santiago's boasts over the slain *galanos* reflect like sentiments: "Go on, *galano*. Slide down a mile deep. Go see your friend, or maybe it's your mother" (*OMATS* 109); "Eat that, *galanos*. And make a dream you've killed a man" (*OMATS* 119).

Finally, when Santiago sees the first shovel-nosed sharks, his reaction is described thus:

> "Ay," he said aloud. There is no translation for this word and perhaps it is just a noise such as a man might make, involuntarily, feeling the nail go through his hands and into the wood. (*OMATS* 107)

The next word Santiago says, having seen the second shark, is "*galanos*": (*OMATS* 108). Critical attention to this scene has focused on the authorial comment on "*Ay*." The explanation of the Spanish interjection through an allusion to crucifixion is clearly consistent with much of the imagery of the novel, but it has also generated considerable controversy concerning the omniscient narrator's intrusion.[15] What has been overlooked is the Homeric character of Hemingway's presentation.

Such an authorial intrusion is typically Homeric. The poet "often presents his own opinions in the form of explicit comments on the action . . . which may take a number of different forms" (Edwards 35). More significant is the context of Santiago's exclamations, "*Ay . . . galanos.*" After the *dentuso* Santiago became aware that with the renewed bleeding the scent of the great fish could not be kept from the water and, therefore, more sharks would appear; especially important here is the narrator's repeatedly drawing our attention to Santiago's realization: "the bad time is coming . . . a very bad time was coming" (*OMATS* 103, 106). The "very bad time" begins with the appearance of the *galanos*. Santiago's exclamations express his reaction to the inevitable destruction of his fish and the defeat of his hopes. In the *Iliad,* the final pathos begins with the death of Patroklos. As it progresses several characters are presented reacting to its manifestations: Achilles and Antilochos to the death of Patroklos; Thetis to the impending death of Achilles; Hector to his own fate as he awaits the approaching Achilles. In the LLM version they all react with the same exclamation: "Ay me."[16] Thus Santiago's repeated phrase, "*Ay . . . Galanos,*" expressing his profound anguish at the onset of his final agony echoes the phrase repeatedly used in the LLM *Iliad* in comparable contexts as the poem moves toward its tragic conclusion.

Santiago and Odysseus

The Old Man and the Sea begins:

> He was an old man who fished alone in a skiff in the Gulf Stream and he had gone eighty-four days now without taking a fish. In the first forty days a boy had been with him. But after forty days without a fish the boy's parents had told him that the old man was now definitely and finally *salao,* which is the worst form of bad luck, and the boy had gone at their orders in another boat which caught three good fish the first week. (*OMATS* 9)

The *Odyssey* opens with the poet calling on the Muse, "Tell me, Muse, of that man . . ." (*Od.* 1.1, BL 1), and after detailing his request, he begins the story with the hero's present condition:

> Now all the rest, as many as fled from sheer destruction were at home, and had escaped both war and sea, but Odysseus only, craving for his wife and for his homeward path, the lady nymph Calypso held, that fair goddess, in her hollow caves, longing to have him for her lord. (*Od.* 1.11-15, BL 1)

Except for the obvious difference between the initial epic invocation and Hemingway's omniscient narrative beginning, the openings are remarkably similar. In both we are immediately made aware that the subject is to be a "man." In addition, Homer begins his narrative with the happy situation of "all the rest" before introducing Odysseus's plight. The contrast with the successful returns focuses attention on the bad luck of Odysseus; likewise, Hemingway's detail of the boat that caught "three good fish" brings home Santiago's predicament. That the other heroes are all already home also underscores the time Odysseus's bad luck has lasted; similarly, Hemingway's repeated statements of the days impresses upon us the extraordinary length of Santiago's ordeal.[17] Both authors, moreover, continue to emphasize the luckless state of the two heroes (*OMATS* 10, 13, 16, 32; *Od.* 1.49, 55, 219, BL 2, 7). Finally, their bad luck has led to the same result, isolation: Odysseus is a prisoner on a remote island and Santiago must fish alone in his skiff. Thus Santiago's circumstances at the beginning of *The Old Man and the Sea* are strikingly parallel to those of Odysseus at the outset of the *Odyssey*.

Obvious parallels also exist between Hemingway's physical descriptions of Santiago and Homer's descriptions of Odysseus. When Athena disguises Odysseus at the beginning of the second half of the *Odyssey,* she makes him an old man, a beggar:

> His fair flesh she withered on his supple limbs . . .
> over all his limbs she cast the skin of an old man.
> (*Od.* 13.430-32, BL 208)

Although the original description gives no hint of this, we later learn that the "old man" is truly powerful:

> Then Odysseus girt his rags about his loins, and let his thighs be seen, goodly and great, and his broad shoulders and breast and mighty arms were manifest. . . . Then the wooers were exceedingly amazed. (*Od.* 18.66-71, BL 280).

A similar, gradual accretion of knowledge occurs in *The Old Man and the Sea*. The first description Hemingway gives of Santiago is:

> The old man was thin and gaunt with deep wrinkles in the back of his neck. (*OMATS* 9)

Within a few pages, however, Santiago is described again:

> The boy took the old army blanket off the bed and spread it over the back of the chair and over the old man's shoulders. They were strange shoulders, still powerful although very old, and the neck was still strong too and the creases did not show so much when the old man was asleep and his head fallen forward. . . . The boy left him there. (*OMATS* 18-19)

Now it is no longer gauntness but power and strength that are emphasized, a development strongly reminiscent of Homer's descriptions of the "aged" Odysseus.

Moreover, Hemingway's description of the power of Santiago's upper body focuses on the same anatomical details Homer emphasizes in regard to Odysseus: shoulders, neck and back. Homer speaks of Odysseus's "back

and broad shoulders" (*Od.* 6.225, BL 93),[18] with emphasis on his "stalwart neck and mighty strength" (*Od.* 8.225, BL 112). Homer further illustrates the great strength of Odysseus in a memorable episode; after Odysseus kills the stag on Circe's island, he carries the "huge beast" slung across his neck back to his men who "gazed at the mighty quarry" (*Od.* 10.169-80, BL 149).[19] In depicting Santiago's powerful physique, Hemingway follows a similar pattern beginning with the description of the sleeping old man quoted above. This is later followed by an account of a remarkable physical feat, Santiago's struggle with the fish. Santiago's labor lasts a good deal longer than Odysseus's carrying the stag, but throughout it the picture of the old man sustaining the force of the line with his shoulders and back is kept constantly before us.[20]

A second parallel involves the eyes. When Athena tells Odysseus she is going to disguise him as an old man she adds:

> And I will dim thy two eyes, erewhile so fair, in such wise that thou mayest be unseemly in the sight of all the wooers and of thy wife and son, whom thou didst leave in thy halls. (*Od.* 13.401-3, BL 207)

That Athena announces her intention to dim Odysseus's eyes and does so (*Od.* 13.433, BL 208) is not surprising, for on several occasions in the *Odyssey* we are told that the eyes are important in identifying the hero; e.g., at the beginning Athena disguised as Mentes tells Telemachus that his eyes are "beauteous and wondrous like to" his father's (*Od.* 1.208, BL 7).[21] Only after the heroic luster has gone from his eyes can Odysseus move freely about in his disguise as a humble, old beggar. In the same way Hemingway sets Santiago apart from ordinary old men by emphasizing his eyes:

> Everything about him was old except his eyes and they were the same color as the sea and were cheerful and undefeated. (*OMATS* 10)[22]

Not only are both the heroes marked by the extraordinary appearance of their eyes, they also possess excellent vision. The suitors say that Odysseus "has a good eye" (*Od.* 21.397, BL 336) as he handles the bow prior to stringing it, and he soon proves them correct. Similarly, Manolin says Santiago has "good" eyes (*OMATS* 14), a statement both confirmed by the old man himself (*OMATS* 33), and, as in Odysseus's case, subsequently proven in action.

A third point of comparison lies in the description of the hands of the two heroes. Odysseus is famous for his hands, as Telemachus says in the scene in which his father has revealed his true identity:

> Verily, father, I have ever heard of thy great fame, for a warrior hardy of thy hands, and sage in counsel. (*Od.* 16.242, BL 251)

Two points about Odysseus's hands are of significance: first, their strength is emphasized; second, they are prominent in the action. Whether Odysseus is clinging to a rock amidst the waves (*Od.* 5.428, BL 84), kneading a great lump of wax (*Od.* 12.174, BL 186), or driving a sword through an enemy's neck (*Od.* 22.326, BL 348), Homer repeatedly focuses on his hands.[23]

Similarly, Santiago has strong hands. Unlike Homer, Hemingway does not explicitly state the strength of his hero's hands; rather, this is made clear by describing the weight of the fish, the strain of the line, or the hand game at Casablanca (*OMATS* 69-71, 73, 87, 91). As in the *Odyssey,* too, the hands are highlighted in the action. From the moment Santiago takes the line "softly between the thumb and forefinger of his right hand," until his final battle with the *galanos* "holding" the tiller "in both hands and driving it down again and again," one or both of his hands are constantly in view. We see them holding or pulling the line, enduring the cuts, cramping, butchering the dolphin, driving in the harpoon, grasping the oar, and soaking in or lifting sea water (*OMATS* 41-118). Thus while Hemingway's depiction of his hero's hands eclipses the Homeric model in prominence in the narrative,[24] it nonetheless recalls in the strong hands that are repeatedly viewed in action the two salient characteristics of Odysseus's hands in the *Odyssey.*

When Hemingway introduces Santiago's hands, we learn of yet another physical trait he shares with Odysseus:

> . . . and his hands had the deep-creased scars from handling heavy fish on the cords. But none of these scars were fresh. They were as old as erosions in a fishless desert. (*OMATS* 10)

Odysseus is also scarred, on his upper leg. In a well known scene, the old nurse, Eurycleia, discovers by recognizing this scar that the stranger she is bathing is Odysseus (*Od.* 19.386-507, BL 304-7). But Odysseus's scar is more than a device of recognition or revelation;[25] Homer emphasizes its importance by devoting a long digression to how the young Odysseus acquired the scar.[26] Sent to his grandfather's estate to receive gifts in honor of his reaching manhood, Odysseus joins in a boar hunt, is the first to charge the flushed prey and, although gored on the leg, kills the beast with his spear (*Od.* 19.393-466, BL 304-6). The scar remains, a record of both the painful wound suffered and the success of the hunter; moreover, the vanquishing of the boar signals Odysseus's coming of age as a warrior. It is the initial heroic exploit of his career, and the scar, the visible trace of this exploit, marks him as the hero he is.

Santiago's scars are many and were acquired over a long period of time; however, they recall Odysseus's scar in several respects. First, as in the *Odyssey,* they are emphasized. Hemingway calls attention to them by a brief simile that with its epithet of the desert, "fishless,"

is itself Homeric, echoing in its litotes the famous "unharvested" sea (Morgan 17). In addition, they too record not only the pain endured by the hero, but also his success (Wells 58). Finally, as the manifest testament of the execution of his craft, Santiago's scars, as Odysseus's, mark him as what he is and was "born to be", "a fisherman" (*OMATS* 105).

Santiago's resemblances to Odysseus extend beyond the physical. Odysseus is famous as the hero who prevails by his wits as well as his strength. This is frequently stated in the Homeric poems: e.g., by Helen (*Il.* 3.200-202, LLM 50), Nestor (*Od.* 3.120-27, BL 32), and Odysseus himself who first addresses Alcinous's court thus:

> I am Odysseus, son of Laertes, who am in men's minds for all manner of wiles. (*Od.* 9.19-20, BL 126)

Throughout the *Odyssey* we are constantly reminded of this by several of the hero's epithets, such as *polymêtis,* "of many counsels," the most common occurring well over sixty times, and *polymêchanos,* "of many devices."[27] In action, too, Odysseus is consistently presented using his knowledge and intelligence, whether he is building a raft, navigating by the stars, or devising counsel for the destruction of the Cyclops (*Od.* 5.233-75, BL 78-79; 9.316-28, BL 135).

Odysseus is also well known for his ability to withstand adversity. "Many the woes he suffered" announces the poet in his invocation, and several characters including Athena, Circe, Odysseus himself and Telemachus speak both of his pains and unyielding spirit (*Od.* 1.4, BL 1; 5.13, BL 71; 5.222-24, BL 77; 10.458-59, BL 158; 17.142, BL 263). Again several epithets serve to reinforce this aspect of the hero, including *polytlas,* "steadfast," the most prominent occurring close to forty times, and *talasiphronos,* "patient."[28] In action, whether the skin is ripped from his hands as a wave wrenches him from a rock, or he is humiliated by the suitors, Odysseus never succumbs to pain, whether physical or psychological (*Od.* 5.434-35, BL 84; 20.284-302, BL 320).

Santiago is not as versatile as Odysseus; his expertise is in fishing and the sea, but here he too is presented as a hero who prevails by using intelligence and knowledge. Santiago also tenaciously refuses to give in to adversity. His physical pain is more prominently displayed than Odysseus's; indeed, *The Old Man and the Sea* has been called "a study in pain" (Wells 59),[29] but as in the *Odyssey* neither physical pain nor mental anguish deter the hero.

Santiago himself succinctly identifies both these characteristics when he tells the boy, "I know many tricks and I have resolution" (*OMATS* 23); he had already spoken of the "many tricks," and later he thinks about the "snares and traps" and "trickery" by which he prevails (*OMATS* 14, 23, 50, 76, 99). He thinks of his "will" as well as of his "intelligence," of "what a man can do and what a man endures," and that "pain does not matter to a man." Memorable images vivify his "resolution"; e.g., the "hand game" at Casablanca, and always the heavy line across his back (*OMATS* 45, 47, 67, 69-71, 78, 79). His knowledgeable execution of his craft is illustrated by his arrangement and handling of the baits and lines (*OMATS* 30-32, 44, 86-93); he too sails by the stars (*OMATS* 47, 74-78), and, as Odysseus fashions a stake from a piece of olive wood to attack the Cyclops (*Od.* 9.316-28, BL 135), Santiago improvises weaponry, first the knife lashed to the oar, later the tiller, against the sharks (*OMATS* 104, 118). And at the same time the narrator continuously reminds us of his "suffering," "pain," "strain," and "resolution" (*OMATS* 64-65, 74, 82, 93, 101, 102). Thus through dialogue, the old man's soliloquies and thoughts, and narrative, Hemingway emphatically endows Santiago with the same two principal character traits that belong to Homer's Odysseus.

Finally, there are several parallels in vocabulary in the presentations of these traits. That words such as "suffer," "suffering(s)," and "endure" recur in both works may, of course, be a result of the fundamental similarities between the heroes; however, Santiago's exclamation, "God help me endure" (*OMATS* 87) recalls Odysseus's, "Endure, my heart" (*Od.* 20.18, BL 311). Especially noteworthy, moreover, are Santiago's statement that he must "devise" a plan to sleep, with the word "devise" immediately repeated in his thought, and his later remark that his own thought gives him "much good counsel" (*OMATS* 77, 110). These passages specifically echo language commonly used about Odysseus in the Butcher and Lang translation of the *Odyssey*; consequently we must consider the possibility that the several verbal correspondences reflect not merely a coincidence in characterization, but Hemingway's acquaintance with this text.

Conclusion

The similarities between Santiago and the Homeric heroes are extensive and detailed, but it must be remembered that all heroic figures in the western literary tradition are in some sense variants of Homer's heroes. Santiago has been compared to a number of these figures, some more typically heroic than others. His affinities with Captain Beard (Baker 309-11), Sam Fathers (Rosenfeld 42-46, 52), Dante's Ulysses (Lewis 211), or Don Quijote (Capellán 111-12) spring in part from shared heroic qualities, in part from Hemingway's familiarity with the literary tradition he inherited and mastered. Such, no doubt, is also the case with the Homeric heroes.

It is clear, moreover, that in writing *The Old Man and the Sea* Hemingway succeeded in his objective:

> I tried to make a real old man, a real boy, a real sea and real fish and real sharks. But if I made them good and true enough they would mean many things. ("An American Storyteller," *Time*, 13 December 1954)

Certainly Santiago is a strikingly "real old man" and Hemingway's unique creation, but among the "many things" he suggests to the reader is his Homeric dimension, his resemblance to those heroes who sailed their own deep, dark sea to Troy and back home again. Indeed, Santiago's statement that "man is not made for defeat" (*OMATS* 103) recalls Diomedes' characterization of Nestor, a characterization that also applies to Santiago himself: "Thou, old man, art indomitable" (*Il.* 10.167, LLM 172).

NOTES

[1] For the subsequent critics see Morgan, 78 n.19; see also Wylder, 201, 222; Justus, 104; and, a detractor of *OMATS* who faults its "bogus epic solemnity," Way, 165; for the parallels, including onomatopoeia, adjectives of specific detail and of essence (epithets), active verbs and participles, ring composition, descriptions of expertise, objects as images, and descriptions of affective actions, see Morgan, 14-15, 17, 22n, 24n, 29 n.41, 45, 55.

[2] All translations are from the Lang, Leaf and Myers *Iliad*, and the Butcher and Lang *Odyssey*; citations are both to book and line numbers of the poems, and to page numbers of the Modern Library edition of these translations abbreviated LLM and BL respectively. Hemingway read the Lang, Leaf and Myers *Iliad*; see Reynolds, 138; Morgan, 71-75. What translation of the *Odyssey* he left at Key West in 1939 (Reynolds 8, 31, 138; Brasch-Sigman xlix, 179) cannot be stated with certainty; however, it was most probably that of Butcher and Lang. This was the most popular prose version of its day, the companion volume to Lang, Leaf and Myers, and the one recommended in Hemingway's "heavily read" (Reynolds 129) high school text on mythology (Gayley 408). Later, at the Finca Vigía, he owned the Harvard Classics (Brasch-Sigman 167), of which Volume 22 is the Butcher and Lang *Odyssey*. Hemingway's Homeric presentation of the sea has recently been noted by Derek Walcott; see "A Poem in Homage to an Unwanted Man," *New York Times*, 9 October 1990, Section C.

[3] For recent treatments of the Homeric hero, see Edwards, 149-58; Griffin, 70-76, 89-102; Schein, 67-88.

[4] The heroes are often depicted as deciding whether or not to undertake an action. Hector before the final duel with Achilles illustrates this (*Il.* 22.99-130, LLM 403-4).

[5] See: *Il.* 2.768, LLM 41; 5.103, LLM 78; 11.288, LLM 193; 17.689, LLM 384. The word LLM render as "best" here is *aristos*; elsewhere they vary the translation; e.g., "greatest, goodliest, first, and foremost" (*Il.* 1.91, LLM 3; 2.577, 580, LLM 35; 2.761, LLM 40). On heroes and the concept of the "best," see Nagy, 21-41.

[6] *OMATS* 123; even the mistaken tourists "are struck by a sense of the extraordinary" (Gurko 66) as they look at the skeleton. Santiago, however, unlike Homer's heroes, does not seek recognition and reknown.

[7] *OMATS* 21-23; as the one who "makes the difference," DiMaggio is like Achilles in the *Iliad;* moreover, his physical flaw, like Achilles', is his heel. The well known story that Achilles was vulnerable only in his heel is not in Homer; it is, however, in Hemingway's high school mythology text (Gayley 304).

[8] See *OMATS* 43, 59, 75, 92, 95, 99, 110, 115; Gurko, 65; Burhans, 74; Baker, 312; Young, 24.

[9] Edwards, 79; Hector's corpse is recovered not in battle but later by Priam's visit to Achilles.

[10] *Il.* 3.330-8, LLM 54; 11.17-45, LLM 185-86; 16.131-44, LLM 293; 19.369-91, LLM 365. On the arming scene, see Kirk, 313-14.

[11] On early intimations of Santiago's struggle in *OMATS,* see Williams, 175; he also notes the ritual aspect of Santiago's preparation (176).

[12] On Homeric heroes and prayer, see Edwards, 126-27.

[13] Santiago's praying has been the subject of controversial criticism; see, e.g., Gurko, 64-65; Rosenfeld, 51; Baker, 300-301.

[14] On battlefield speeches, see Edwards, 93-94; for a comprehensive account of heroic fliting, see Parks.

[15] See Jobes, 11; Baker, 313-16; Rosenfeld, 51-52; Williams, 180-81; Waldmeir, 162; Backman, 256; Grebstein, 91; Rovit, 74.

[16] *Il.* 18.6, 18, 54, LLM 337-38; 22.99, LLM 403; 23.103, LLM 419. Menelaus and Agenor also use the exclamation, the former as he stands by the body of Patroklos (*Il.* 17.91, LLM 317), the latter as he debates dueling Achilles (*Il.* 21.553, LLM 398). The emotional interjections translated by "Ay me" are: *o moi, o moi ego,* and *o popoi.* The translation is used in the last third of the poem, books 17-24 (contrast, e.g., *Il.* 1.149, LLM 5; 15.286, LLM 274; 16.433, LLM 301). This may be due to Myers having the primary responsibility for the final third, although the translators "deliberated in common" on phrases that recur (LLM: "Prefatory Note"). In any case the result is that *"Ay me"* is associated with the intensifying pathos of books 17-24.

[17] Gurko, 67. Others connect the number of days with Christian symbolism; see Waldmeir, 162; Williams, 183.

[18] Odysseus's broad shoulders are also emphasized in the famous scene in the *Iliad* in which Priam asks Helen to sit by him on the walls of Troy and identify the Greek heroes (*Il.* 3.194, LLM 50).

[19] Cf. the disguised Odysseus who, smashed with a footstool "at the base of the right shoulder by the back . . . stood firm as a rock, nor reeled beneath the blow" (*Od.* 17.462-64, BL 273).

[20] *OMATS* 45-86 passim; 88.

[21] Cf. *Od.* 4.150, BL 49; 19.417, BL 305.

[22] Cf. *OMATS* 13.

[23] Cf. *Od.* 5.434, 454, BL 84; 6.128, BL 90; 8.189, BL 114; 19.448, BL 305.

[24] On the complexity of the presentation of Santiago's hands in terms of Christian symbolism, endurance, and pain, see Williams, 177; Backman, 256-57; Wells, 58-59.

[25] Odysseus confirms his identity to Eumaeus, Philoetius and his father, Laertes, by showing his scar (*Od.* 21.217-21, BL 330; 24.331-35, BL 376); on the recognition scene with Eurycleia, see Austin, 214-27. Harada, 272, connects Odysseus's scar with DiMaggio's bone spur.

[26] On the digression at this dramatic moment, see Stanford, vol. 2, 332.

[27] See, e.g., *Od.* 5.202, 214, BL 77; 11.405, BL 174; 18.14, BL 278. BL occasionally use "wise" for *polymêtis* (e.g., *Od.* 2.173, BL 20); they translate several other epithets by "wise," as well as by "manifold in counsel," and "wise and crafty" (*Od.* 1.48, 83, BL 2, 3; 3.163, BL 34; 7.168, BL 102). On the epithets see Austin, 26-53.

[28] See, e.g., *Od.* 1.88, BL 3; 5.31, BL 72; 7.1, BL 97; 14.148, BL 213. BL also use "of the hardy heart" and, occasionally, "steadfast" for *talasiphronos* (e.g., *Od.* 1.129, BL 31).

[29] See also Backman, 256-57; Williams, 177.

WORKS CITED

Austin, Norman. *Archery at the Dark of the Moon.* Berkeley: U California P, 1975.

Backman, Melvin. "Hemingway: The Matador and the Crucified." In *Hemingway and His Critics: An International Anthology.* Ed. Carlos Baker. New York: Hill and Wang, 1961: 245-58.

Baker, Carlos. *Hemingway: The Writer as Artist.* Princeton: Princeton UP, 1972.

Brasch, James D., and Joseph Sigman. *Hemingway's Library: A Composite Record.* New York: Garland, 1981.

Burhans, Clinton S. "*The Old Man and the Sea:* Hemingway's Tragic Vision of Man." In *Twentieth Century Interpretations of* The Old Man and the Sea. Ed. Katharine T. Jobes. Englewood Cliffs: Prentice Hall, 1968: 72-80.

Capellán, Angel. *Hemingway and the Hispanic World.* Ann Arbor: UMI, 1985.

Cowley, Malcolm. Rev. *The Old Man and the Sea.* In *Twentieth Century Interpretations of* The Old Man and the Sea. Ed. Katharine T. Jobes. Englewood Cliffs: Prentice Hall, 1968: 106-8.

D'Agostino, Nemi. "The Later Hemingway." In *Hemingway: A Collection of Critical Essays.* Ed. Robert P. Weeks. Englewood Cliffs: Prentice Hall, 1962: 152-60.

Edwards, Mark W. *Homer: Poet of the Iliad.* Baltimore: The Johns Hopkins UP, 1987.

Gayley, Charles M. *The Classic Myths in English Literature.* Boston: Ginn, 1913.

Grebstein, Sheldon N. *Hemingway's Craft.* Carbondale: Southern Illinois UP, 1973.

Griffin, Jasper. *Homer on Life and Death.* Oxford: Clarendon, 1980.

Gurko, Leo. "The Heroic Impulse in *The Old Man and the Sea.*" In *Twentieth Century Interpretations of* The Old Man and the Sea. Ed. Katharine T. Jobes. Englewood Cliffs: Prentice Hall, 1968: 64-71.

Harada, Keiichi. "The Marlin and the Shark: A Note on *The Old Man and the Sea.*" In *Hemingway and His Critics: An International Anthology.* Ed. Carlos Baker. New York: Hill and Wang, 1961: 269-76.

Hemingway, Ernest. *Ernest Hemingway: Selected Letters 1917-1961.* Ed. Carlos Baker. New York: Scribner's, 1981.

——. *The Old Man and the Sea.* New York: Scribner's, 1952.

Homer. *The Complete Works of Homer: The Iliad and the Odyssey.* Tr. Andrew Lang, Walter Leaf, Ernest Myers, and S. H. Butcher and Andrew Lang. New York: Modern Library, n.d.

Jobes, Katharine T. Ed. *Twentieth Century Interpretations of* The Old Man and the Sea. Englewood Cliffs: Prentice Hall, 1968.

Justus, James H. "The Later Fiction: Hemingway and the Aesthetics of Failure." In *Ernest Hemingway: New Critical Essays.* Ed. A. Robert Lee. London: Vision, 1983: 103-21.

Kirk, G. S. *The Iliad: A Commentary.* Vol. 1. Books 1-4. Cambridge: Cambridge UP, 1985.

Lewis, Robert W., Jr. *Hemingway on Love.* Austin: U Texas P, 1965.

Morgan, Kathleen. *Tales Plainly Told: The Eyewitness Narratives of Hemingway and Homer.* Studies in English and American Literature, Linguistics and Culture, vol. 7. Columbia, S. C.: Camden House, 1990.

Nagy, Gregory. *The Best of the Achaeans: Concepts of the Hero in Archaic Greek Poetry.* Baltimore: Johns Hopkins UP, 1979.

Parks, Ward. *Verbal Dueling in Heroic Narrative: The Homeric and Old English Traditions.* Princeton: Princeton UP, 1990.

Reynolds, Michael S. *Hemingway's Reading 1910-1940: An Inventory.* Princeton: Princeton UP, 1981.

Rosenfeld, Claire. "New World, Old Myths." In *Twentieth Century Interpretations of* The Old Man and the Sea. Ed. Katharine T. Jobes. Englewood Cliffs: Prentice Hall, 1968: 41-55.

Rovit, Earl and Gerry Brenner. *Ernest Hemingway: Revised Edition.* Boston: Twayne, 1986.

Schein, Seth L. *The Mortal Hero: An Introduction to Homer's* Iliad. Berkeley: U California P, 1984.

Schorer, Mark. "With Grace Under Pressure." In *Ernest Hemingway: Critiques of Four Major Novels.* Ed. Carlos Baker. New York: Scribner's, 1962.

Stanford, W. B. *The Odyssey of Homer.* 2 vols. London: Macmillan, 1959, 1962.

Waldmeir, Joseph. "Confiteor Hominem: Ernest Hemingway's Religion of Man." In *Hemingway: A Collection of Critical Essays.* Ed. Robert P. Weeks. Englewood Cliffs: Prentice Hall, 1962: 161-68.

Way, Brian. "Hemingway the Intellectual: A Version of Modernism." In *Ernest Hemingway: New Critical Essays.* Ed. A. Robert Lee. London: Vision, 1983: 151-71.

Wells, Arvin R. "A Ritual of Transfiguration: *The Old Man and the Sea.*" In *Twentieth Century Interpretations of* The Old Man and the Sea. Ed. Katharine T. Jobes. Englewood Cliffs: Prentice Hall, 1968: 56-63.

Williams, Wirt. *The Tragic Art of Ernest Hemingway.* Baton Rouge: Louisiana State UP, 1981.

Wylder, Delbert E. *Hemingway's Heroes.* Albuquerque: New Mexico UP, 1969.

Young, Philip. "*The Old Man and the Sea:* Vision/Revision." In *Twentieth Century Interpretations of* The Old Man and the Sea. Ed. Katharine T. Jobes. Englewood Cliffs: Prentice Hall, 1968: 18-26.

FURTHER READING

Secondary Sources

Baldwin, Robert. "A Bibliography of the Sea, Shipwreck, and Water in Western Art and Literature." *Bulletin of Bibliography* 48, No. 3 (September 1991): 153-70.
   Bibliography of criticism largely devoted to modern (nineteenth and twentieth century) literature of the sea.

Bender, Bert. *Sea-Brothers: The Tradition of American Sea Fiction from 'Moby-Dick' to the Present.* Philadelphia: University of Pennsylvania Press, 1988, 267 p.
   Finds in American fiction of the sea from Herman Melville and Jack London to Ernest Hemingway, Peter Matthiessen, and others a compelling tradition of "celebrating life" and "affirming . . . democratic values."

Brunvand, Jan Harold. "Sailor's and Cowboys' Folklore in Two Popular Classics." *Southern Folklore Quarterly* XXIX, No. 4 (December 1965): 266-83.
   Comments on the comparison of the American prairie to the sea in R. H. Dana's *Two Years Before the Mast* and Andy Adams's *The Log of a Cowboy.*

Burgess, C. F. *The Fellowship of the Craft: Conrad on Ships and Seamen and the Sea.* Port Washington, N.Y.: Kennikat Press, 1976, 160 p.
   Full-length study of Conrad's perception of the sea and life on it as illuminated in his fiction.

Casarino, Cesare. "The Sublime of the Closet; or, Joseph Conrad's Secret Sharing." *Boundary 2* 24, No. 2 (Summer 1997): 199-243.
   Studies Conrad's maritime story "The Secret Sharer" as a narrative of same-sex desire and betrayal.

Edelman, Lee. "Voyages." In *Modern Critical Views: Hart Crane,* edited by Harold Bloom, pp. 255-91. New York: Chelsea House Publishers, 1986.
   Analyzes Crane's imagery of the sea in the poems of his "Voyages" sequence.

Kleiner, Elaine L. "Conrad's *The Mirror of the Sea.*" *The Explicator* 42, No. 3 (Spring 1984): 33-35.
   Sees Joseph Conrad's *The Mirror of the Sea* as a work of "prophetic autobiography" which suggests "that life at sea offers a pattern of human existence in harmony with eternal order."

Lavery, David L. "'The Genius of the Sea': Wallace Stevens' 'The Idea of Order at Key West,' Stanislaw Lem's *Solaris,* and the Earth as a Muse." *Extrapolation* 21, No. 2 (Summer 1980): 101-105.
   Argues that Lem's science-fiction novel set on a mimetic ocean world tacitly contradicts Stevens's ideal of poetry as a "transcendent analogue" to nature, showing this latter view to be solipsistic and blind to human dependence on the earth.

McCarthy, Shaun. "Home from Sea: Tradition and Innovation in the Novels of Alun Richards." *The Anglo-Welsh Review,* No. 78 (1985): 59-71.
   Assesses the technique of Richards's novels *Ennal's Point* and *Barque Whisper* within the literary tradition of the sea story.

O'Connor, John J. "Saskatchewan Sirens: The Prairie as Sea in Western Canadian Literature." *Journal of Canadian Fiction,* Nos. 28-29 (1980): 157-71.
   Studies the familiar analogy of the prairie and the sea in twentieth-century Canadian literature.

Ross, Ernest C. *The Development of the English Sea Novel from Defoe to Conrad.* Folcroft, Penn.: The Folcroft Press, Inc., 1926, 112 p.
   Traces the rise, decline, and rejuvenation of the sea novel in England over the course of two centuries.

Sex in Literature

INTRODUCTION

Human sexuality in literature has proved the subject of considerable debate and the source of much critical interest, particularly in the latter half of the twentieth century. While literary erotica has enjoyed a sustained following for centuries, the idea of sex as a legitimate topic of literary discourse has had, and continues to have, many detractors. In nineteenth-century England and America, Victorian ideology assured that fictional representations of sexuality would be handled with delicacy, lest authors incite the wrath of censors. Nonetheless, such writers as Thomas Hardy and Henry James confronted the topic, in particular relating it to the role of woman as a sexual being. Hardy's *Tess of the d'Urbervilles* (1891) and James's *The Portrait of a Lady* (1881) approached sexuality from a feminine angle, yet treated it with a level of detachment indicative of the times. On the European continent (where attitudes toward sexuality in literature have been traditionally more relaxed, thanks in part to such figures as the Marquis de Sade) a similar point of view had already emerged, as in Gustave Flaubert's *Madame Bovary* (1857). By the twentieth century, the Modernists had begun to deal frankly with sexuality, at times eliciting the negative reaction of critics and censors. Such was the case with two important works of the period, James Joyce's *Ulysses* (1922) and D. H. Lawrence's *Lady Chatterley's Lover* (1928), which, though relatively tame by contemporary standards, at the time brought the subject of sex to realms hitherto unacceptable in serious literature and incited enough controversy to provoke major censorship cases in court.

Evidence of the dramatic changes in the modern literary treatment of sexuality had become more and more apparent by mid-century. As Vladimir Nabokov's 1947 novel *Lolita* indicated, sex—even that between the middle-aged Humbert Humbert and the adolescent Dolores Haze—could prove to be a permissible subject of literary artistry. Several later writers, including Saul Bellow, Katherine Anne Porter, and others, emphasized the comic component of sexuality and reflected the release of literary sex from the constraining morality of the prior century. The culture of the new sexuality that appeared in the 1960s and 1970s confirmed that even nontraditional sexual experiences and attitudes, ranging from homosexuality to sadomasochism, were no longer taboo as literary subject matter. Accompanying the rise of psychoanalytic theory, which had brought sexuality to the fore in criticism, several French literary theorists—including Michel Foucault and Roland Barthes—began to emphasize sexuality and the mechanics of desire in literature. This process has accompanied the proliferation of literary assays into the sexual in the final decades of the twentieth century, by contemporary artists and critics alike.

REPRESENTATIVE WORKS

Nelson Algren
  A Walk on the Wild Side (novel) 1957
Sherwood Anderson
  Windy McPherson's Son (novel) 1918
  Beyond Desire (novel) 1932
  Kit Brandon (novel) 1936
Djuna Barnes
  Nightwood (novel) 1936
Simone de Beauvoir
  Les Mandarins (novel) 1954
Samuel Beckett
  The Unnamable (novel) 1958
  Happy Days (drama) 1961
Saul Bellow
  The Adventures of Augie March (novel) 1953
  Herzog (novel) 1964
  Mr. Sammler's Planet (novel) 1970
Angela Carter
  Love (novel) 1971
Willa Cather
  My Ántonia (novel) 1918
Louis-Ferdinand Céline
  Journey to the End of the Night (novel) 1932
  Death on the Installment Plan (novel) 1936
James Dickey
  Deliverance (novel) 1970
J. P. Donleavy
  The Ginger Man (novel) 1955
Margaret Drabble
  The Radiant Way (novel) 1987
William Faulkner
  The Wild Palms (novel) 1939
Gustave Flaubert
  Madame Bovary (novel) 1857
Ford Madox Ford
  The Good Soldier: A Tale of Passion (novel) 1915
  Parade's End (novel) 1925
Théophile Gautier
  Mademoiselle de Maupin (novel) 1835
Louise Glück
  The Triumph of Achilles (poetry) 1985
Thomas Hardy
  Tess of the d'Urbervilles (novel) 1891
  Jude the Obscure (novel) 1895

Bret Harte
  "The Judgment of Bolinas Plain" (short story) 1895
John Hawkes
  The Passion Artist (novel) 1978
Ernest Hemingway
  For Whom the Bell Tolls (novel) 1941
William Dean Howells
  Their Wedding Journey (novel) 1872
  The Landlord at Lion's Head (novel) 1897
Aldous Huxley
  Leda (novel) 1920
J. K. Huysmans
  Là-bas (novel) 1891
Eugène Ionesco
  La leçon [*The Lesson*] (drama) 1951
Henry James
  The Portrait of a Lady (novel) 1881
Erica Jong
  Fear of Flying (novel) 1973
James Joyce
  Ulysses (novel) 1922
Oskar Kokoschka
  Mördor, Hoffnung der Frauen [*Murder, Hope of Women*] (drama) 1909
Milan Kundera
  The Book of Laughter and Forgetting (novel) 1980
D. H. Lawrence
  The Rainbow (novel) 1915
  Women in Love (novel) 1920
  Lady Chatterley's Lover (novel) 1928
Doris Lessing
  The Golden Notebook (novel) 1962
Norman Mailer
  The Naked and the Dead (novel) 1949
David Mamet
  Sexual Perversity in Chicago (drama) 1974
  Oleanna (drama) 1992
Larry McMurtry
  The Last Picture Show (novel) 1966
Henry Miller
  The Tropic of Cancer (novel) 1934
  The Rosy Crucifixion—Sexus (novel) 1949
Marianne Moore
  "Marriage" (poem) 1924
Vladimir Nabokov
  Lolita (novel) 1947
Anaïs Nin
  A Spy in the House of Love (novel) 1954
Joe Orton
  What the Butler Saw (drama) 1969
Katherine Anne Porter
  Ship of Fools (novel) 1962
Pauline Réage
  Story of O (novel) 1954
Philip Roth
  Portnoy's Complaint (novel) 1969
Isaac Bashevis Singer
  The Slave (novel) 1962
Charles Algernon Swinburne
  Poems and Ballads, First Series (poetry) 1866

Frank Wedekind
  Frühlings Erwachen [*Spring's Awakening*] (drama) 1891
Virginia Woolf
  Jacob's Room (novel) 1922
  Orlando (novel) 1928
  The Waves (novel) 1931
Emile Zola
  Germinal (novel) 1867

OVERVIEWS

William Phillips

SOURCE: "Writing about Sex," in *Partisan Review*, Vol. XXXIV, No. 4, Fall, 1967, pp. 552-63.

[*In the following essay, Phillips explores the implications of sexual freedom in contemporary literature.*]

Since sex is older than literature, one would think it is entitled to more respect. But the relation has always been just the reverse; literature has always been protected against the encroachments of sex. Even now, when it would seem that almost anything goes, a number of serious critics have been alarmed by the lack of sexual restraint in literature, which they regard as a symptom of moral decline. Most of their fire is directed at figures like Genet, Burroughs and Mailer, though they are generally upset by the moral tone of contemporary writing as a whole.

Now we need hardly be reminded that what goes by the name of the moral question is an old and recurrent one, popping up with almost every new generation, as new sensibilities and new attitudes about the limits of literature come up against old ones. Today the split is wider, though the old values are frequently being defended by more sophisticated people, who themselves were brought up on the idea that art made its own rules. This means only that the confusion is on a higher level. The new values, on the other hand, are supported by people who make a principle of going out of bounds in every possible way—in morals, in sex, in art. Much of the new writing represents not so much a break with an existing tradition as with the very idea of tradition, while those who are holding the line against the so-called new barbarians claim they are defending not some philistine standards but literature itself, and some even go so far as to insist they are protecting the very basis of civilization. Those who feel themselves responsible for the health of art and society have been warning us that what we have is a free-for-all and not the normal kind of experiment and innovation prescribed for progress in the arts.

As things shape up, there seems to be some conflict between the idea of freedom and the idea of civilization—which is nothing new to those who know their Freud and have followed the diversions of Norman O. Brown and his less theoretical cothinkers. Until recently, however, anyone claiming to be advanced had to be for both freedom *and* civilization, though naturally the emphasis varied and there was usually a good deal of vagueness when it came to defining just what one meant and how it applied to art. Now things have changed: freedom literally means going all the way, turning everything on; but civilization today is actually regarded with a certain amount of irony and skepticism, particularly by those who have an adventurous attitude to life and to art, and, of course, by those who think of civilization as a synonym for a corrupt and dying system.

This, I think, is roughly the way the lines are drawn at present. In literature sex is often the issue, though other moral questions are involved. But when we try to examine more exactly what people are for and where certain works stand the picture is not so clear. In some contemporary writing commercial motives have gotten mixed up with what might have been a normal extension of the frontiers of sex and morality. Also different kinds of sex and different uses of them for literary or ideological— or commercial—purposes are not always distinct and they tend to be lumped together under the heading of the new. On the other side of the fence, the guardians of civilized art are hard to pin down, once we get beyond the generalities on which most of us are bound to agree. Often, you can't tell whether they are objecting to violations of current morality, or of current taste, whether there is too much sex, or it is too detailed or too eccentric—in short, whether the objections are literary, or moral, or ideological or just squeamish.

Usually the case against the new sexuality is not made too explicit. But two recent pieces by George P. Elliott (*Harpers*, March, 1965) and George Steiner (*Encounter*, October, 1965) do take fairly clear stands. Both Elliott and Steiner claim to be talking mainly about pornography, though they are really talking about sex and its moral and aesthetic limits in literature, and about moral values in general. At bottom, Elliott's position is that too much sex is bad not only for literature but for society. At first he argues that to keep a safe distance from sex, as from other bodily functions, is simply a matter of good taste, though his argument would seem to have more to do with psychology than with aesthetics.

> We have a certain sense of specialness about these voluntary bodily functions each must perform for himself—bathing, eating, defecating, urinating, copulating, performing the sexual perversions from heavy petting to necrophilia. Take eating, for example. There are few strong taboos around the act of eating; yet most people feel uneasy about being the only one at the table who is, or who is not, eating, and there is an absolute difference between eating a rare steak washed down by plenty of red wine and watching a close-up of a movie of someone doing so. One wishes to draw back when one is actually or imaginatively too close to

the mouth of a man enjoying his dinner; in exactly the same way one wishes to remove oneself from the presence of a man and woman enjoying sexual intercourse. Not to withdraw is to peep, to pervert looking so that it becomes a sexual end in itself. As for a close-up of a private act which is also revolting, a man's vomiting, say, the avoidance-principle is the same as for a close-up of steak-eating, except that the additional unpleasantness makes one wish to keep an even greater distance.

But then he proceeds to connect excessive sexuality with politics and with morality. All the pillars of our existence, according to Elliott—the family, government, society and civilization itself—all are threatened when sex is on the loose. "Indecency," he says, "is put to politically dangerous uses." Furthermore, he says, if one is for civilization, "for even our warped but still possible society in preference to the anarchy that threatens from one side or the other," then one has to sacrifice "some sensuality of the irresponsible." This irresponsible sensuality, Elliott explains, is mostly to be found in "the politically repressed." "This would help to account," he goes on, "for the apparently greater sensuality among American Negroes than among American whites. . . ."

What all this sexual and political irresponsibility adds up to for Elliott is the dread disease of nihilism, which by his definition "would dissolve both the state and the family in the name of unrestricted gratification of natural appetite." The principal carriers are Genet, Burroughs and Henry Miller, though other writers, like Baldwin, are slightly infected. For some reason, however, the most subversive is Miller, whose sexual deviations and social estrangement Elliott regards as a menace to literature and society.

> Again and again he represents the sexual antics of his characters as evidence of desperation, lurking behind the total despair of meaninglessness. He is what he says he is: an enemy not just of the badness of our society, not just of our specific society, but of society as such. To do what he can to get his readers also to become enemies of society, he assaults with persuasive force taboos, especially sexual taboos, which are intrinsic to the social order. . . . As an act against society, to write, publish, and distribute a book like *Tropic of Cancer* is more serious than to write, publish, and distribute a pamphlet which intellectually advocated the forcible overthrow of the government, but less serious than to take arms against the government—about on a par with inciting to rebellion. . . . In other words, the only plausible argument for suppressing *Tropic of Cancer* would be that its publication is a dangerous political act and not that the book is pornographic, even though its pornography is the main instrument of the book's nihilistic force.

Steiner's argument is more sophisticated. He, too, is disturbed by the lack of inhibition in pornography or in any other kind of writing. But his objection to too much sexual exposure is essentially that it makes public something that should remain private and restricts the imagination because sex has a limited repertoire. "Sexual relations are, or should be," says Steiner, "one of the citadels of privacy, the nightplace where we must be allowed to gather the splintered, harried elements of our consciousness to some kind of inviolate order and repose." This sexual homily has little to do with writing for it is really an argument against acts of exhibitionism or voyeurism, though its view of sex as reassuringly serene and relaxing—almost as good as a warm bath—and free of mystery or terror has literary implications. Steiner's seemingly more effective point is that there are only a limited number of sexual variations; hence, for Steiner, the vague and less erotic descriptions of sexual activity, of the kind one finds in writers like Stendhal, George Eliot, Tolstoy or Henry James, are more suggestive, hence more imaginative, than exact or charged descriptions of sexual relations could be. This, it seems to me, is not true, and, anyway, the comparison is unhistorical; but it is at least an arguable position. Like Elliott, however, Steiner introduces moral and political considerations when he claims that "the novels being produced under the new code of total statement . . . leave man less free, less himself, than they found him. . . ." In other words, it is nothing short of human freedom that is at stake when fiction loses its earlier reserve in handling sex and goes in for erotic detail.

There is simply no evidence to indicate that sex is robbed of its power and mystery and the range of feeling or thinking is narrowed when sex is treated as freely as any other kind of experience. On the contrary writers like D. H. Lawrence, Nabokov or Mailer cannot be said to have narrowed our views of sex or interfered with our freedom. It seems to me that Steiner does not like certain kinds of writing, which is his critical right, but what he is really doing is elevating his taste into an intellectual principle.

As for Elliott, I need scarcely point out that his social views are as conservative as his idea of literature. If there is a lesson to be drawn, it is that the two often go together; though recently some political radicals have turned out to be quite conservative in their literary tastes. It is impossible ever to prove such things, but I suspect that one cannot rule out *some* new things without invoking a principle that would rule out *any* new things. If certain kinds of writing or thinking are to be excluded, either because they are immoral or bad for art, it can be done only in the name of some existing norms or values, which are assumed to be fixed, and, therefore, outside of time and history. How else can one justify, for example, saying that Miller's or Genet's or Mailer's treatment of sex is out of bounds, except by appealing to notions of sex and morality of the most conventional kind.

Are we then to conclude that we cannot legitimately set any limits for sexuality—or for anything else—in literature? If by limits we mean arbitrary, *a priori* principles, rules of restraint, it would seem that we cannot impose any such limits without getting into some kind of intel-

lectual if not legal censorship. Even if the taboos are advanced in the name of literature itself, they are in effect an attempt to outlaw a less restricted sensibility.

It might be objected that if no limits can be put on literature, then the role of criticism becomes limited. If anything goes, then there is no basis for literary or intellectual values. However, I am not proposing the abdication of criticism; what I have been suggesting is simply that restraint is an indirect form of criticism, and a very conservative one. Some critics might dismiss such an approach as extraliterary, but in the sense that every judgment, like every new work, is a stand in favor of certain kinds of art and against others—in this sense the literary moralists, in their objections to uninhibited writing, are asserting their preference for another kind of literature. Thus Elliott's remarks about sex and society might be said to be a critical statement, though a fairly conventional one, for his disgust with oversexed writing is actually an endorsement of undersexed, respectable, responsible, unalienated writing that is not too critical of existing society. Similarly, Steiner's distaste for sexual abandon or detail is connected with a nostalgia for the classics. In fact, most moralizing critics rarely propose genuine literary alternatives in the present; hence they are usually scolding contemporary writers in the name of some nonexistent moral or literary purity and responsibility that presumably existed in the past. But this moral Utopia, this myth of propriety and good taste, however vague, arbitrary and illusory, is the ideological equivalent of writing that is not so far out or has already been assimilated.

Editors of popular magazines know very well the distinction between old and new sensibilities, though they find it profitable to treat them as fashions. They are able to trade on the appetite for the new, which is increased by the moral resistance to it, by feeding respectable audiences more and more outrageous writing, so that things that used to be beyond the pale now have become old hat. Of course, this is due partly to a natural loosening up in matters of sex and morals, but it is also because the forbidden has been artificially inseminated into writing. The result is a kind of manufactured chaos, that is numbing the capacity of frivolous people to be shocked, and making it more and more difficult for serious people to think clearly about what is going on. Some writers and critics (like Fiedler) have been rushing to sign up for the future, while others (like Elliott) are busy frantically shoring up the past.

One result of the attempt to merchandize the new sexuality is the confusion between literature and pornography. (I should say I do not believe in any bans on pornography, but if there is a problem, it is legal and social, not literary.)

It has been argued by Susan Sontag that pornography on a certain level, like *Story of O* (and possibly even *Fanny Hill*) is a form of literature. Her argument, which is quite powerful and original, is that the pornographic imagination presents a total vision of sex and experience not unlike other extreme kinds of writing, and that it is not just a recital of sexual acts for purposes of excitation. Still, I think this view might not be incompatible with the idea that there can be good and bad pornography; for I am not sure it completely breaks down the distinction between the genre of pornography and literature.

One aspect of pornography, however, does seem pertinent to the question of sexuality in contemporary fiction, and suggests a link between pornography and literature. The standard form of pornography is usually perverse [I am using the term perverse in its conventional sense, though, obviously, the concept of perversity needs reexamination] and violent in a way that suggests some need to overthrow or transform accepted ideas of the sexual relation. Usually the hero is a victimized woman—or, more frequently, a girl—who is used and abused—rarely used up—and the plot is the story of all the things a man could imagine perpetrating on her. Yet the narrative, which is a male fantasy, is usually told ostensibly from the innocent point of view of the woman who has been violated, as though the author is acting out his fantasies both as a man and as a woman. The obvious example is *Fanny Hill.* And though *Story of O* has been rumored to have been written by a woman, it seems to be the same kind of male fantasy—which might suggest the beginning of a pornographic convention.

One can only guess at the meaning of this kind of sexual conversion. But what is particularly interesting is that a similar kind of converted, mechanized and dispersed sexuality is found in modern writing that cannot be dismissed as pornography. We see it in Burroughs, in Genet; and there is a good deal of perversity and ambiguity in Mailer's willful sexuality (as there was in D. H. Lawrence); in Selby's sadism; in Henry Miller's acting-out of boyish dreams; in Pynchon's bizarre connections; in John Barth's pan-sexuality, which by making everything possible normal, creates a system of comic perversity.

There is clearly a new kind of sexuality in modern fiction: not just more sex, but a different kind of sex, one that is undoubtedly related to the new moods and the new styles of living today. In the past, even in unconventional writers like Joyce or Lawrence or Kafka, the treatment of sex usually was quite straightforward and not very far from the conventions of sex, even though there were occasional perverse implications. The most daring of the earlier novels rarely strayed beyond the heterosexual mold; when they went in for sexual detail it was mostly to describe intense passion or extramarital escapades. One might say they sublimated the more erotic and perverse drives into ambiguities of motive and feeling. Henry James is, of course, a classic instance. An example of how far the traditional novelist permitted himself to go is the story told in Stavrogin's confession in *The Possessed.* But this is an isolated episode, and the psychological underground revealed in it is dispersed in Stavrogin's character and politics, as it probably is in many other of Dostoevsky's obsessive figures and situations.

Of all the writers who have gone in for perversity, Mailer is probably the least perverse. Though his last novel, *An American Dream,* has come in for a good deal of scolding, it seems to me most of the critics have been shocked by only two things, the unconventional sexuality and the attitude toward the murder. If we ask what actually goes on sexually in the novel that might be considered off-limits, I suppose the one thing that stands out is the anal preoccupation. But it is hard to see on what ground this fixation—which Swift and Lawrence also had—could be banned in literature, any more than any other obsessive idea. What is more questionable is the liberating force with which it is endowed by Mailer, as it apparently was, too, by Lawrence, though less explicitly. It is thus the sexual philosophy and not the fantasy or the act that one might be critical of in literary terms. As for other sexual eccentricities in *An American Dream,* the only ones worth noting are the sharing of women in a semi-incestuous way—as Rojack does with his father-in-law—and the heightened sexuality after the murder. But these, too, are obviously matters for literary—or psychological—analysis, not for approval or disapproval.

Some established critics have also charged Mailer with immorality on the grounds that Rojack is neither punished enough nor made to feel guilty enough for the murder of his wife. Now, aside from the primitive notion of the morality of modern literature inherent in such an accusation, whose source is to be found in popular culture, it represents a misreading of the novel. Mailer's novel is obviously a fantasy in which certain sexual obsessions are merged with visions of omnipotence and with fits of frustration. This is not an uncommon fantasy, even though it borders on the psychotic in its utter self-indulgence; but somewhere at the center is the little boy's fear—quite normal—that he might not make it. This fear, one might say, ties the novel to the more acceptable versions of our common experience. If one can talk of the subject of *An American Dream,* it might be said to be a fantasy of abnormal desire grounded by normal fear.

Like Mailer, Henry Miller has had to contend with literary and moral conventions. Yet, despite Miller's wild reputation, his perversity seems to be integrated into a fairly orthodox brand of bohemianism. One notes again and again in works like *Sexus* and *Tropic of Cancer* how Miller slides from sex into observations about literature, or society or existence in general. The elusiveness of sex is entangled in the religion of art. Somehow the footlooseness and the alienation of the young writer is associated with an avant-grade casualness and freedom in bouncing from one woman to another. The perversity, however, is almost always just below the surface, expressing itself in such things as the failure to connect with women, the lack of genuine pleasure, the intimation of voyeurism and exhibitionism in sexual relations involving groups of people and the insatiable appetite for whores, whom Miller is always trying to convert to women in his mind and to machines in bed. If one is to make any kind of judgment, though, it is not that Henry Miller's sexual happenings strain our capacity for novelty. On the contrary, his prowlings and frustrations seem almost commonplace and they succeed only in giving Miller the air of a middle-aged schoolboy. Far from being shocking, Miller's sexual bohemianism appears dated today.

To assimilate Norman Mailer or Henry Miller one simply has to face oneself. To assimilate writers like Genet and Burroughs one might have to redefine one's relation to an alien experience or to an alien idea of experience as well as to oneself. For Genet's hero, in his fiction, is a portrait of the underground man as a homosexual and a criminal; while Burroughs has created a homosexual spaceman who lives in a permanent nightmare of fornication, hallucination and destruction.

Of the two, I think Genet is a much more impressive figure than Burroughs. In my opinion, Genet's plays—particularly *The Balcony* and *The Blacks*—are among the outstanding works of our time. In both plays the morbid sexuality is transformed by a bizarre and perverse system of associations into a sense of wild being, free of moral attitudinizing or social pretense. The novels, however, are narrower: here the perversity exists in its natural habitat and one cannot help see it and judge it in relation to some other system that is not so perverse. I do not mean to take down the novels: on the contrary, I think they are in their own way marvelously conceived and executed; but they are a special genre, probably a limited one, a kind of autobiography of the imagination, though of course Genet appears to be describing real events in his life.

One of the difficulties in relating to the new sexual style is the assumption that the traditional handling of sex in literature is natural and pure and that what we have today is a distortion. The fact is that there is no basic sex—in the way there might be a basic English—except biologically or clinically. Sex in literature has always been ideological: it has always been conceived of in terms of values and attitudes toward other kinds of experience. In this respect, the depiction of sex has been an enactment of an idea of sex. Thus sex has been bawdy, comic, adventurous, immoral, fulfilling, frustrating, mysterious, tragic, open, liberating. In its literary evolution sexuality has reflected various pagan, courtly, pastoral, middle-class and romantic conventions. On the whole, though, the traditional idea of sex has been associated with individual fate, that is, with human realization or destruction, through love and passion. And it is with this sexual tradition that both pornography and the new sexuality might be said to have broken, substituting for it a deflated, polymorphous idea of sex divorced from love and from the institutionalized relations in which sex had in the past been located. It is an idea

of sex that is experimental, unfettered, anarchic; and if, like more traditional views of sex, it is also represented as the expression of true being, it is based on a conception of being entirely fluid and unpredictable, and limited only by one's imagination.

The question, then, of how much perversity can be assimilated into literature has to do with the idea of sex rather than with its reality. If we can talk at all about the "reality" of sex, it would seem that a sense of its willfullness and its inventiveness, partly as an escape from its terrors, is more suggestive of the actual experience than a tasteful and restrained representation. As for one's imagination, it is even less restricted in its pursuit of erotic fantasies. Obviously, normality can no longer be regarded as a meaningful idea for writing, though it would seem that traditional values cannot be entirely disregarded. Frank Kermode recently argued that a commitment to the new, such as Harold Rosenberg advocates, means giving up all critical values, for if novelty creates its own value then the traditional method of judging new works by existing standards can no longer be applied. Kermode, it seems to me, was right in pointing to the danger of a principle that softens us up for any innovation or break with tradition. On the other hand, we run the opposite risk of opposing new styles in the name of old ones, and justifying this by failing to recognize that every new work alters old standards. It is clearly this reciprocal relation that makes for a proper balance of the new and the old, though, admittedly, it is not always easy to keep in mind that one is changing one's tastes in the act of applying them.

In practice, the less eccentric forms of the new sensibility and those which are related if only symbolically to more accepted intellectual conventions are more readily assimilated. John Barth, for example, is a less extreme figure, since sexual and social chaos are represented in his novels as metaphors for each other; as is Pynchon, in whom sexual fluidity appears to be a part of the fluidity of experience; or Susan Sontag, who in most of her writing shows herself to be more an advocate than an exponent of free-wheeling sexuality. Actually, it is the more extreme figures, like Burroughs and Genet (in his novels) who pose the problem and force its definition. And though extremism is one of the means by which literature deals with typical experience, extremist writing has been successful usually when its special vision has been able to generalize the extreme of human behavior. Kafka is perhaps the outstanding example of the invention of a new style of observation by a grotesque—almost psychotic—imagination, that has become a natural style. But I am not at all sure whether it can be said of Burroughs and Genet in his fiction, and particularly of their disciples, that they have succeeded in imposing their style on our experience. Undoubtedly some of the perversity of modern writing has expressed itself in sexual cultism, especially in the less gifted writers, for whom violence, sadism and homosexuality make up a self-inclosed world, sealed off even from other forms of extreme behavior. To some extent, it is a matter of literary quality, as obviously writers like Selby or Rechy exhibit the faults of the genre more than do the larger talents. But this brings us right back to the original problem, for what is lacking in the less talented works is precisely the ability to transcend or to generalize one's sexual obsessions.

In the long run, however, the literary value of this kind of extremism is an historical rather than a theoretical question. One who thinks of himself as a participant in the contemporary scene might even contend that in raising these questions and posing them in this way, one is simply outside the intellectual moods that go into the advanced forms of contemporary writing. Undoubtedly the new sensibility reflects the current emphasis on personal freedom as a way of dissociating from the political establishment. And what is commonly regarded as perversity might be thought of as a symbol of this detachment, as it was, almost explicitly, for example, in Norman O. Brown's *Life Against Death.* To be sure, sexual freedom has gone so far that one wonders what would be out of bounds if the new life style were to take over.

But if one might speculate about the future, perhaps the ideal solution would be to dissociate sex completely from morality and from politics. Who knows whether this will ever happen? But if there were no restrictions on sex, in life or literature, if sexual freedom were not thought of as a paradise for radicals and purgatory for conservatives—if sex were simply taken for granted like other neutral activities, like, say, eating or swimming, then possibly the air might be cleared so that the question of sex in literature could become a purely literary question, not a battlefield for moral and social issues. If sex were free it would have nothing to do with the idea of freedom.

Marilyn Nelson Waniek

SOURCE: "The Space Where Sex Should Be: Toward a Definition of the Black Literary Tradition," in *Studies in Black Literature,* Vol. 6, No. 3, Fall, 1975, pp. 7-13.

[*In the following essay, Waniek discusses the reasons why "the great space where sex ought to be" in novels by African American men is usually filled by violence.*]

Many critics have complained of a scarcity of fulfilling heterosexual relationships in novels by Black American authors. Writes James Baldwin, for example, in an essay about Richard Wright entitled "Alas, Poor Richard": "In most of the novels written by Negroes until today (with the exception of Chester Himes's *If He Hollers Let Him Go*) there is a great space where sex ought to be; and what usually fills this space is violence. This violence, as in so much of Wright's work, is gratuitous and compulsive because the root of the violence is never examined."[1] Certainly even a cursory reading of most of the major novels in the Black American tradition proves at least the first part of this statement to be a fact. James

Weldon Johnson's *Autobiography of an Ex-Colored Man,* Richard Wright's *Native Son,* and Ralph Ellison's *Invisible Man,* which will be discussed here, are only a few examples of novels displaying this dearth; a much longer list could be made, which would include most of the novels written by Black men in this country. However, this fact, while it cannot be denied, is only one-half of a question which must be discussed; the other half is whether this fact is rightfully something worthy of complaint. Baldwin sees it as a problem, something to be remedied, in the Black American literary tradition; one could—and perhaps should—however, examine the roots of the tradition in order to discover the reason for it.

I have mentioned a Black American literary tradition, and one way of getting at the problem is to define that term. We bandy about the phrase "Black literature" all too often without considering what it is that distinguishes that literature from any other American literature—or any other literature, for that matter. This is too easy. There is no reason to suppose that a piece of work written by a man with a dark face should necessarily differ from one written by a man with an any-other-color face just because of the fact of his genetic inheritance. Baldwin questions a second easy definition in his essay, "Princes and Powers," in which he describes the debate at the 1956 Conference of Negro-African Writers and Artists. Perhaps, the debators at the conference posited, it is the fact of oppression that distinguishes this literature from all others. However, one must with this definition face a question similar to the easier one of genetic inheritance: How then is Black American literature different from any other literature of the oppressed? How is it different from the literature of pre-revolutionary Ireland, or of any proletarian movement? Or, if the further distinction of oppression by the white man is made, how is it different from African, East-Indian, South American, or Caribbean literatures?[2] Imamu Amiri Baraka, then LeRoi Jones, wrote several years ago of his awareness of "the hurt the white man has put on the people / any people." ("Jitterbugs") Certainly the history of European expansion in the last three hundred years justifies this. But if Black American literature is not merely a literature of the oppressed, but something even more particular, what *is* it? Let us take a different approach to the definition. Let us, instead of looking for a clear-cut negative definition, try to find a positive one; let us, instead of trying to define Black American literature as a literature of opposition and negation, try to define it as one of construction, creation, the attempt to affirm. Here we may use W. E. B. DuBois as a starting point. DuBois writes of the Negro that he:

> ever feels his twoness,—an American, a Negro; two souls, two thoughts, two unreconciled strivings; two warring ideals in one dark body, whose dogged strength alone keeps it from being torn apart.

> The history of the American Negro is the history of this strife,—this longing to attain self-conscious

manhood, to merge his double self into a better and truer self. In this merging he wishes neither of the older selves to be lost.[3]

Some fifty years after DuBois wrote these words, Baldwin writes of a Black American at the Conference of Negro-African Writers and Artists whom he says he "respected very much, not only because he raised this question, but because he knew what he was doing."[4] This man, says Baldwin, was suggesting:

> . . . a subtle and difficult idea, the idea that part of the great wealth of the Negro experience lay precisely in its double-edgedness. He was suggesting that all Negroes were held in a state of supreme tension between the difficult, dangerous relationship in which they stood to the white world and the relationship, not a whit less painful or dangerous, in which they stood to each other. He was suggesting that in the acceptance of this duality lay their strength, that in this, precisely, lay their means of defining and controlling the world in which they lived.[5]

A quote from a teenager who had been among the first to integrate white schools in the South illustrates this problem: "It's like being two people: when I'm around here I'm me; when I leave and go to school or go downtown, I'm just another person."[6] The "me" and the "other person" this teenager talks about are the Negro and the American DuBois names. The "me" is the self, the individual person, accepting of his individuality and selfhood, while the "other person" is the identity forced upon the Black man by the white world. This situation has been described in almost every piece of literature in the Black American tradition. Countee Cullen's "Incident" is a good example:

> Once riding in old Baltimore,
>   Heart-filled, head-filled with glee,
> I saw a Baltimorean
>   Keep looking straight at me.
>
> Now I was eight and very small,
>   And he was no whit bigger,
> And so I smiled, but he poked out
>   His tongue, and called me, "Nigger."
>
> I saw the whole of Baltimore
>   From May until December;
> Of all the things that happened there
>   That's all that I remember.[7]

Dr. Alvin Poussaint, a Black psychiatrist, describing his own walking with a friend in Jackson, Mississippi says that when a white policeman yelled, "Hey, Boy" to him, he thereby ripped his manhood from him. "In addition," he says, "this had occurred on a public street, for all the local black people to witness, reminding them that *no* black man was as good as *any* white man. All of us—doctor, lawyer, postman, field hand, and shoeshine boy—had been psychologically 'put in our place.'"[8] Poussaint describes this psychological reminder of the Black man's place as castration. "The castration of Negroes, and the resulting problems of

self-image and inner rage, started more than 350 years ago, when black men, women and children were wrenched from their native Africa, stripped bare both psychologically and physically, and placed in an alien land . . . the plantation system implanted a subservience and dependency in the psyche of the Negro that made him dependent upon the goodwill and paternalism of the white man."[9] Thus, the duality of the Black man is a split between the "me"—the adult, potent man, and the "other person"—the castrated, subject child.

Attempting to psychoanalyze the race-sickness of the United States Dr. Joel Kovel writes: "only the theory of the Oedipus Complex—enlarged into a cultural apparatus that defines and binds real roles even as it apportions fantasies amongst the players of these roles—will account for this variety of phenomena . . . Black man, white man, black woman, white woman—each realizes some aspect of the Oedipal situation."[10] Although Kovel's analysis is intended as an exploration of white racial consciousness, his insight into the Oedipal fantasies related to race in America describe the Black racial situation as well. The Black man is a man torn between being the adult he wants to be, who must devote himself to the task of freeing himself from his parents and the child he is forced to be, who lusts after incest and parricide, and who is symbolically castrated again and again by the white father. The social situation of the United States, particularly in the South, is an institutionalization of this enforced Oedipal situation. Thus Kovel writes that: "We know that the archetypal lynching in the old South was for the crime of having a black man rape (= touch, approach, look at, be imagined to have looked at, talk back to, etc.) a white lady. Moreover, the archetypal lynching often included a castration of the black malefactor, and even when it didn't, the idea of castration was immanent in the entire procedure."[11] To explain why this idea of castration was imminent as punishment for a Black man's having dared to approach/look at/speak to/rape/murder a white woman, Kovel says: "Throughout our history, even in these progressive days when the wish to actually punish sexual crimes by castration has been repressed out of the consciousness of all but a few psychotics, sexuality remains a widely acknowledged core of the race problem. Miscegenation is indeed the most forbidden of interracial practices . . . and so sexuality and racism must be indeed intertwined."[12] The fantasy of miscegenation and sexuality is very well presented in LeRoi Jones' play, *The Dutchman*, though Lula is both seductive female and castrating male. In order to deal with the fear that the Black man will seduce the white woman, American society has made the Black man into a child: "Whenever a black man bowed and scraped, whenever a white man called a black man 'boy,' or in other ways infantilized him, just below the surface of the white man's consciousness, a sexual fantasy woul [*sic*] be found yoked to the symbol of power and stature."[13] Kardiner and Ovesey's[14] fine study of abnormal Negro psyche, concentrating primarily on the problems of castration and emasculation of the Black man, serves as additional evidence for this point.

It should be clear now that the problem of duality stems from the peculiar cultural schizophrenia suffered by the Black American. He sees himself through two glasses: when he is at home he sees himself as a man, and when he confronts white America he sees himself as whites see him, as a "boy." The fact of this duality enables us to locate a literary tradition beyond merely political and biological circumstances. The Black American literary tradition, then, is one in which we see writers striving to reconcile these "two warring ideals," to create a viable private identity. Yet the attempt to create a viable private identity is very closely linked to the attempt to create a public one, for the Black American writer strives to demonstrate to white America that his Negro individuality is as much a kind of personhood as any colorless (i.e., white) individuality. Thus the literature of these writers must of necessity be of a more socio-political nature than most other literature. And precisely herein lies the crux of the complaint about the scarcity of heterosexual relationships in novels by Black American authors. It is only ironic that Baldwin, who understands the concerns of his literature so well, criticizes it so unjustly.

How does one go about writing a novel whose concerns are public, while at the same time fulfilling the demand for *belles lettres* instead of a political speech? All of the novelists in the Black American tradition are modern, writing in the late Nineteenth or the Twentieth Centuries, and the modern novel presupposes certain things. In general, it presupposes the realistic tradition: characters, setting, and plot—or at least movement.[15] This obviously presents a problem. If, on the one hand, the novelist wants to explore a public search for a public identity, on the other, he is asked to do this within the boundaries of the realistic novel. One may justly ask whether this is possible at all; certainly if we hold almost any Black American novel up to the measure of "reality" we will find it lacking in many essentials of "real" life. It is from this attempt to measure novels that we get such complaints as, "He doesn't say anything positive about the Black experience," or, "There's too much violence," or, "There's no love." What these authors are attempting, however, is a new kind of literature, in which, under the guise of realism, characters act out complex metaphors for the situation of Black Americans: their duality, their quest to be seen as men, their demand to be freed from the white father and mother. The authors must realize that there *is* something positive in the Black experience; they must enjoy love-making more than they do lynching; they must appreciate the fact that Black men love. But what place do these concerns have in the public arena in which the ritual of trying on mask after mask is performed? Before making the painful transition to Imamu Amiri Baraka, LeRoi Jones wrote,

Cold air batters
the poor (and their minds

turn open
like sores). What kindness
What wealth can I offer? Except
what is for me,
ugliest.

("I Substitute For the Dead Lecturer")

Later, Baraka described what was "ugliest" for him. It was to write war poems, to limit his art to statements of public, not private problems: "Let there be no love poems written / until love can exist freely and / cleanly." ("Black Art") These are the words of one Black American artist, and they describe the situation of the Black artist in general. For the limitations placed upon them are great, because they realize that it is not possible to write of love when one is describing a world in which men are torn, castrated, and searching for identity and manhood.

The Autobiography of an Ex-Colored Man, written by James Weldon Johnson and published in 1927, presents a mulatto boy's transition into manhood. The "tragic mulatto" was a popular theme in the Nineteenth and early Twentieth Centuries, not only in the literature of Black Americans, but also in that of whites. It is easy to see why. If the problem of the Black American is one of duality, of "two warring ideals" in one body, what better battlefield exists than the body of the mulatto? Here is a person whose duality is more than social, for he is torn both biologically and psychologically between the races and cultures of his parents. The protagonist's first awareness of his peculiar racial identity comes from a fight at school, after which he asks his mother whether he is a "nigger." She answers: "No, my darling, you are not a nigger . . . You are as good as anybody; if anybody calls you a nigger, don't notice them . . . No, I am not white, but you—your father is one of the greatest men in the country—the best blood of the South is in you—" (p. 402). As a man, the protagonist looks back on this incident and thinks:

And this is the dwarfing, warping, distorting influence which operates upon each and every coloured man in the United States. He is forced to take his outlook on all things, not from the view-point of a citizen, or a man, or even a human being, but from the view-point of a *coloured* man . . .

This gives to every coloured man, in proportion to his intellectuality, a sort of dual personality. (p. 403)

The problem of the protagonist of *The Autobiography of an Ex-Colored Man* is that he is, indeed, an intellectual, and that he realizes that terms such as "Negro" and "white" cannot serve to define the complexities of any human being. Thus, his education serves to compound his initial impression of the injustice connected to his racial inheritance. What he wants, finally, is to be a man; what America expects of him is that he be a *coloured* man. After the death of his mother, his only real link with the Black race, he is left to find his place alone. He travels, and begins to learn the complex nature of the Black experience in America. He learns that American ideals are held by all Americans, that Negroes are individuals with the same goals as other individuals:

> I think that the white people somehow feel that coloured people who have education and money, who wear good clothes and live in comfortable houses, are "putting on airs," that they do these things for the sole purpose of "spiting the white folks," or are, at best, going through a sort of monkey-like imitation.
>
> It seems that the whites have not yet been able to realize and understand that these people in striving to better their physical and social surroundings in accordance with their financial and intellectual progress are simply obeying an impulse which is common to human nature the world over. (pp. 436-37)

He meets Negro actors who are forced to be comedians though their hearts are full of tragedy, and, in a beautiful scene of symbolic sibling-rivalry, he inadvertently causes another Black man to kill his white mistress because she finds the protagonist attractive. Disgusted by the murder, he flees to Europe.

Europe figures prominently in several Black American novels because here the Black man really discovers that his condition, which he has taken to be inborn, is social, imposed on him by the racist society in which he has been born. This is what Johnson's protagonist discovers in France; and he also experiences something more: he meets his father and his sister. But the racial barriers of American society still prevent him from acknowledging them, and he realizes his infinite isolation from his family. Out of this isolation comes a new dedication to art and to producing art from the roots of Black American culture. He decides to return to America although his bitter white patron-friend (who represents, interestingly enough, a loving father—the counterpart to his white biological father) warns him that he should:

> look at the terrible handicap you are placing on yourself by going home and working as a Negro composer; you can never be able to get the hearing for your work which it might deserve. I doubt that even a white musician of recognized ability could succeed there by working on the theory that American music should be based on Negro themes. Music is a universal art; anybody's music belongs to everybody; you can't limit it to race or country. Now, if you want to become a composer, why not stay right here in Europe? . . . Then if you want to write music on Negro themes, why, go ahead and do it. (pp. 472-73)

He nevertheless separates from his friend, who has been "all in all, the best friend I ever had, except my mother, the man who exerted the greatest influence ever brought into my life, except that exerted by my mother," (p. 475) and returns to the United States. Here, submerged again

in Black American culture, he notes that, "It is remarkable, after all, what an adaptable creature the Negro is. I have seen the black West Indian gentleman in London, and he is in speech and manners a perfect gentleman. I have seen natives of Haiti and Martinique in Paris, and they are more Frenchy than a Frenchman. I have no doubt that the Negro would make a good Chinaman, with the exception of the pigtail" (p. 477). Whether these remarks are true or not, what the protagonist has learned in Europe is that the Negro is a human being whose manners in the United States are the product of culture, not race. And, since the United States places so great a premium on color, "(it is no) sacrifice of self-respect that a black man should give to his children every advantage he can which complexion of the skin carries . . . I once heard a coloured man sum it up in these words: 'It's no disgrace to be black, but it's often very inconvenient'" (p. 479). Though the protagonist has the advantage of a light complexion, because his work is not taken seriously, he soon realizes that a Negro artist in the United States is just as impotent as any other Black man, regardless of his skin tone. Though he explores the South collecting folk material for his new work, he is finally and profoundly brought face to face with the impossibility of making a success of his work when he witnesses a lynching.

It is this lynching which finally drives the protagonist out of the Negro race with a realization of his own emasculation and helplessness, should he choose to remain a Negro. It is literally castration, which reduces the Negro to infancy, to total impotence, which drives the protagonist to forsake his race and identify himself totally with the powerful race of his father. It is as a white man that he achieves fame, as a white man that he is first loved, and as a white man that he becomes a father. Thus his search for a social identity has ended by his becoming a white man, and it is only after he finds this identity that it is possible for him to find love. The novel is about a search for a public, social identity, having little if anything to say about the protagonist's personal life until he finds his social identity. The only personal information we are given about him is information about his public identity, as when he discusses race and music with his white patron-friend. The novel ends properly with his decision to pass for white after the lynching, and it provides only cursory information about his subsequent affairs.

The concerns of Richard Wright's *Native Son* are similar to those of *The Autobiography of an Ex-Colored Man*. *Native Son* is perhaps the most important novel of the Black American tradition, and served as the vanguard of a new rawness and frankness. It is Wright whom Baldwin takes as a starting point in his statement about the lack of sex and the "unexamined root" of violence in Black American literature. According to Baldwin, the root of violence in Wright's work is rage, "almost literally the howl, of a man who is being castrated."[16] But it is dualism, the task of creating himself, which confronts Bigger Thomas in *Native Son*. The novel has suffered from misreading, primarily because of limitations in Wright's plan. It is a naturalistic novel, and one of its most important threads is the thesis of the powerful influence of environment on human beings. However, since Wright devotes much time to the presentation, through Max the lawyer, of the naturalistic argument, the more important story told and lived by Bigger Thomas is often overlooked. Bigger, an inarticulate, ignorant young boy, murders two women. Until the murders are committed, he is a faceless youth, unaware of himself and aware only of a vague uneasiness and yearning which he cannot name, and of the contempt whites show toward him. Afterwards, however, his life is changed:

> *He* had done this. *He* had brought all this about. In all his life these two murders were the most meaningful things that had ever happened to him. He was living, truly and deeply, no matter what others might think, looking at him with their blind eyes. Never had he had the chance to live out the consequences of his actions; never had his will been so free as in this night and day of fear and murder and flight. He had killed twice, but in a true sense it was not the first time he had ever killed. He had killed many times before, but only during the last two days had this impulse assumed the form of actual killing.[17]

Now Bigger is more completely aware of the cause of his uneasiness and yearning, and thinks it was that he wanted "to merge himself with others and be a part of this world, to lose himself in it so he could find himself, to be allowed a chance to live like others, even though he was black" (p. 226). He realizes now that it is impossible for him to find himself in the world of America, and that "he had committed murder twice and had created a new world for himself" (p. 226). Both of the murders are closely akin to rapes, for what Bigger must do to create himself is assert his manhood. He is kissing and fondling the drunk Mary Dalton when her mother enters, and her murder, compelled by Bigger's fear of the consequences of being found in her bedroom (lynching, castration: how he will be seen by whites) actually takes place on her bed. Bigger has possessed the heretofore inaccessible white mother. This rape is symbolic, however, and it is only after the kidnap idea and his literal rape-murder of Bessie, his Black girlfriend, that the creation of Bigger's new world is complete. The two murders become one in his mind and in the press, for they have created a new Bigger, seen by and created by himself. Eldridge Cleaver describes his own and Bigger's rage in *Soul on Ice*: "I became a rapist. . . . Rape was an insurrectionary act. It delighted me that I was defying and trampling upon the white man's law, upon his system of values, and that I was defiling his women . . ."[18]

The last section of the novel deals with the environmental reasons for Bigger's murders and with the world which he has created. In prison he thinks:

> Having been thrown by an accidental murder into a position where he had sensed a possible order and meaning in his relations with the people about him; having accepted the moral guilt and responsibility for that murder because it had made him feel free for the first time in his life; having felt in his heart some obscure need to be at home with people and having demanded ransom money to enable him to do it—having done all this and failed, he chose not to struggle any more. (p. 255)

With his acceptance of moral guilt Bigger Thomas grows from impotent infancy to responsible adulthood, but because his feeling of order and identity is the cause of his being in prison, he thinks it has failed, and resolves to "kill that wayward yearning within him that had led to this end" (p. 255). But that yearning, for selfhood and human community, cannot be killed. It lives through the trial, although he places a wall of apathy between himself and the white court. After he is declared guilty and condemned to die, Bigger makes one final effort to communicate his anguished humanity to another person: "He summoned his energies and lifted his head and struck out desperately, determined to rise from the grave, resolved to force upon Max the reality of his living. 'I'm glad I got to know you before I go!' he said with almost a shout; then was silent, for that was not what he had wanted to say" (p. 386). He then tries to explain his feelings to Max, who fails to understand because he, like the other whites, is blind to Bigger's humanity. "Mr. Max, I sort of saw myself after that night. And I sort of saw other people, too . . . I was always wanting something and I was feeling that nobody would let me have it" (p. 388). So, in committing a murder—the only potent action possible to him because of the limitations placed on him by society—Bigger has seen himself. He has discovered his selfhood and created the only potent identity possible to him: that of a murderer. Bigger's final words to Max are a desperate attempt to explain what and who he is.

> I didn't want to kill! . . . But what I killed for, I *am*! It must've been pretty deep in me to make me kill! I must have felt it awful hard to murder . . .
>
> What I killed for must've been good! . . . It must have been good! When a man kills, it's for something. I didn't know I was really alive in this world until I felt things hard enough to kill for 'em. (p. 392)

But Max is terrified of Bigger's words; he cannot understand that Bigger is telling him that he has created himself out of this rage, frustration and violence. He does not recognize Bigger's manhood. Though Bigger has turned to Max as to a father for recognition, Max turns "like a blind man" and leaves Bigger to die alone. Bigger has created a social identity through murder, but, as the protagonist of *The Autobiography of an Ex-Colored Man*, created his social identity at the expense of membership in part of the human community, Bigger has done so at the expense of membership in the total human community.

The "Battle Royal" scene of *Invisible Man* is the portrayal in miniature of the primary concern of every novel in the Black American literary tradition, and it appears at the beginning of the novel just as DuBois' *Souls of Black Folk* stands at the beginning of the tradition, to present in brief its total concern.

The very first lines of *Invisible Man* proper are: "It goes a long way back, some twenty years. All my life I had been looking for something, and everywhere I turned someone tried to tell me what it was. I accepted their answers too, though they were often in contradiction and even self-contradictory. I was naive. I was looking for myself and asking everyone except myself questions which I, and only I, could answer."[19] The protagonist's first experience in the world is the "smoker" before his high school graduation, which introduces him to the America through which he must wander in search of himself. There he and a handful of other Black boys are stripped naked and forced to watch the gyrations of a nude blonde with an American flag tattooed on her belly. They must not show any signs of arousal. There are obvious parallels between this Great White American Mother and Eldridge Cleaver's description of The Ogre: "As I pranced about, club in hand, seeking new idols to smash, I encountered really for the first time in my life, with any seriousness, The Ogre, rising up before me in a mist. I discovered, with alarm, that The Ogre possessed a tremendous and dreadful power over me, and I didn't understand this power or why I was at its mercy . . . The Ogre had its claws buried in the core of my being and refused to let go . . . I, a black man, confronted The Ogre—the white woman."[20] Immediately after this discovery, Cleaver saw a psychiatrist, who told him that he hated his mother. Cleaver says demeaningly, "How he arrived at this conclusion I'll never know, because he knew nothing about my mother."[21] Yet the psychiatrist was correct. It was not his biological mother whom Cleaver hated, but the symbolic inaccessible mother: the white woman. This is the Black man's initiation into the brotherhood of America.

Ralph Ellison's strange and powerful novel features a protagonist as nameless and faceless as that of *The Autobiography*. The novel takes him through a nightmarish ritual of trying on identities which fail to fit. Each identity is tied to a symbolic white father: the master-father of the prologue, the school superintendent, Norton, Emerson, the white doctor, Brother Jack. And the identities given to the Black protagonist by these white fathers do not fit him because each of them, in one way or another, is a subtle attack on his manhood. At the end of the novel proper, the protagonist burns the symbols of all of his previous "selves" and says, "I couldn't return to Mary's, or to the campus, or to the Brotherhood, or home. I could only move ahead or stay here, underground. So I would stay here until I was chased out. Here, at least, I could try to think things out in peace . . ." (p. 494). In the epilogue, after he has thought things out, he tells us that he has learned how to explain to himself his grandfather's deathbed advice

which he has not understood until this point. "Agree 'em to death and destruction," his grandfather had said; and now the protagonist understands "they (were) their own death and their own destruction except as the principle (on which the country was built) lived in them and in us" (p. 497). This is the discovery made in the dream he has at the end of the novel, in which the group of his symbolic fathers castrates him and throws his testicles over a bridge, where they hang, dripping blood into the water. The protagonist tells the fathers in his dream, "there hang not only my generations wasting upon the water, but your sun, and your moon; your world. There's your universe, and that drip-drop upon the water is all the history you've made, all you're going to make." (p. 493) Men must acknowledge their brotherhood, their equality, their oneness, or they will die. In the epilogue the protagonist adds another discovery: "Weren't we *part of them* as well as apart from them and subject to die when they died?" (p. 497) Weren't we part of them, he asks; he might well have asked, aren't they part of us? What the invisible man has discovered is a central theme in the Black American literary tradition: that we are a part of each other. We must accept each other and our differences, for "our fate is to become one, and yet many" (p. 499). And, just as we must accept the paradoxical oneness and difference of our national situation, so we must learn to accept our inner oneness and duality.

> So it is that now I denounce and defend, or feel prepared to defend. I condemn and affirm, say no and say yes, say yes and say no. I denounce because though implicated and partially responsible, I have been hurt to the point of abysmal pain, hurt to the point of invisibility. And I defend because in spite of all I find that I love . . . I'm a desperate man—but too much of your life will be lost, its meaning lost, unless you approach it as much through love as through hate. So I approach it through division. (pp. 501-2)

The protagonist of *Invisible Man* thus acknowledges and accepts his own duality, the ambivalent nature of the relationship between the Black man and the white man, the love that can and must exist between the symbolically castrated son and his powerful father if the son is to grow to potency without being psychologically maimed. At the end of the epilogue the invisible man is still living underground in retreat from the world. But he is preparing to come out, to accept the painful responsibility of creating, living with, and creating from his social identity. While it is still undefined, he has at least at this point learned that it must be created from his duality. He has not yet created a self-conscious self, but he has accepted the materials from which to create one. The last lines of the novel leave us with a poignant rhetorical question which restates the thesis of the entire book: "Who knows but that, on the lower frequencies, I speak for you?" (p. 503)

In none of these three novels is there a lasting sexual relationship between the Black protagonist and a woman. The protagonist of *The Autobiography of an Ex-Colored*

Man does not find love until he gives up his duality and recreates himself as a white man. Bigger Thomas has used and been used by Bessie, but he is incapable of fulfilled love because he does not discover his humanity until he murders Bessie and Mary Dalton. The protagonist of *Invisible Man* lives in an almost sexless world in which his only sexual experiences are the Golden Day scene (Black whores and madmen) and the scene with the white Sybil, who wants to be raped by a Black man. Indeed, one might say there is no lasting relationship in these novels at all. The protagonist of *The Autobiography* is failed by his father, leaves his white patron-friend forever, and is cut off thereafter from friendships with Blacks because of his decision to live as a white man; Bigger Thomas is failed by Max; the invisible man loses Tod to death and Jack to white hypocrisy. It is interesting to note that the most completely developed relationships are those between the Black protagonists and their white male friends, who tend to be older than the protagonists. All of the protagonists are finally alone, left to build their own identities out of the division within their psyches and in America. And in the space where sex should be is instead the awful confrontation of Black self with white self, and Black self with white society.

NOTES

[1] James Baldwin, *Nobody Knows My Name* (New York, 1963), p. 151.

[2] *Ibid.*, pp. 24-54. Apparently one of the problems of the conference was that the participants failed to make the necessary distinction between Native Africans and Negro-Africans as minority groups in white cultures.

[3] W. E. B. DuBois, *The Souls of Black Folk* (New York, 1961), p. 17.

[4] Baldwin, p. 45.

[5] *Ibid.*

[6] Robert Coles, "It's the Same, but It's Different," *Daedalus*, Fall, 1965, p. 114.

[7] Dudley Randall, ed., *The Black Poets* (New York, 1971), p. 98.

[8] Alvin Poussaint, "A Negro Psychiatrist Explains the Negro Psyche," *Majority & Minority*, Norman R. Yetman and C. Hoy Steele, eds. (Boston, 1971), p. 350.

[9] *Ibid.*

[10] Joel Kovel, *White Racism: A Psychohistory* (New York, 1971), p. 71.

[11] *Ibid.*, p. 67.

[12] *Ibid.*, pp. 67-68.

[13] *Ibid.*, p. 68.

[14] Abram Kardiner and Lionel Ovesey, *The Mark of Oppression: Explorations in the Personality of the American Negro* (New York, 1962).

[15] See Wayne Booth, *The Rhetoric of Fiction* (Chicago, 1961). I am ignoring avant-garde developments in the novel here only because no Black American novelist that has dispensed with these elements. Even William Melvin Kelley, who is in my opinion the most progressive of the group, has not been influenced by post-Joycean fiction.

[16] Baldwin, p. 151.

[17] Richard Wright, *Native Son* (New York, 1966), p. 225.

[18] Eldridge Cleaver, *Soul on Ice* (New York, 1968), p. 14.

[19] Ralph Ellison, *Invisible Man* (New York, 1947), p. 19.

[20] Cleaver, p. 6.

[21] *Ibid.*, p. 11.

Judith A. Spector

SOURCE: "On Defining a Sexual Aesthetic: A Portrait of the Artist as Sexual Antagonist," in *The Midwest Quarterly,* Vol. XXVI, No. 1, Autumn, 1984, pp. 81-94.

[*In the following essay, Spector uses the writings of James Joyce and Virginia Woolf to probe the relationship between literary and sexual creativity.*]

Annette Kolodny made the statement some time ago that "A good feminist criticism . . . must first acknowledge that men's and women's writing in our culture will inevitably share some common ground." More important, if feminist criticism is to flourish, it must become a versatile literary critical approach to literature by men and women. There have been recent indications from feminist scholars that it is time to include the study of male authors once again within an expanding definition of what feminist criticism ought to be and do.

Since no feminist scholar from Woolf to Kolodny has yet managed to define a feminine mode or aesthetic, it might seem unlikely that feminist criticism would be capable of enlightening anyone on the matter of a masculine aesthetic as well. However, it is precisely the inclusion of literature by men within the feminist focus which clarifies those elements which typify a masculine or feminine aesthetic. These two categories, the masculine and feminine, are clearly relative to one another; each is perceived, in some respects, only in a relationship with its opposite. After merging the opposites, in working with the concept of androgyny some years ago, many scholars found it implausible and sexist to classify characteristics as masculine or feminine; in a real sense, there is no such thing as masculine or feminine except within an artificial, consciously contrived opposition between the sexes. It is within such an opposition that one finds a masculine or feminine aesthetic within a work of art or an artist's philosophy.

An author who cultivates a sexual aesthetic to begin with, creates what seems to her or him to be a feminine or masculine perspective. Such perspectives are characterized by common elements whether the artist is male or female. The most basic common element, however, is the psychological association of gender with creativity. Mary Ellmann calls this imaginative and erroneous association "sexual analogy," and Nina Auerbach points out that the alliance of artists and mothers is a false one. Both critics are correct, if we are dealing with reality—one's sexual procreativity has little or nothing to do with one's intellectual creativity. But we are dealing with authors' subjective systems of belief rather than with objective truths. The fact is that competitive feelings about sexual procreative potency and gender are irrevocably linked to the notion of creativity in a similar way for artists of both sexes.

If we begin by looking at the aesthetic systems of two writers of the same period—James Joyce and Virginia Woolf, for example—we will be able to define very clearly those elements which constitute a sexual aesthetic. For Joyce, one aspect of the contest for sexual superiority is more difficult, since male authors are at an apparent disadvantage in relation to the potential for motherhood per se. The issue is further complicated for the male artist in that he must somehow overcome the fact that, in a physical sense, his mother created him. Joyce solves both problems; he has his male protagonist/artist figure in *A Portrait* and *Ulysses* reject his biological mother as well as "Mother Church," and he creates a "mental womb" for the male artist. Thus, Stephen in *A Portrait* announces his authorship of a villanelle in characteristically pompous fashion, "O! In the virgin womb of the imagination the word was made flesh." Joyce has Stephen's statement establish the virginity of the womb as well, thus completing his own parody of an immaculate conception. The joke also serves to indicate a rebellion against "Mother Church" and to declare the superiority of art as a religious/spiritual/sexual endeavor as well as the superiority of the male artist as creator. The message is clear; since women have physical wombs, they must be relegated to the realm of the physical. The female characters in *Dubliners, A Portrait,* and *Ulysses* are limited to their physicality and preoccupied with their sexuality; they are assuredly not intellectuals or artists. The polarization between the sexes in Joyce's work is yet another obvious indicator of a sexual—in his case, masculine—aesthetic. Characters like Molly in *Ulysses* who are really caricatures of the artist's idea of women are clearly the product of sexual polarization.

But to return briefly to an aspect of that polarization discussed earlier, the matter of mothers and mother-

hood, we can see a great deal of hostility toward the mother (the parent of the opposite sex) for even her limited physical creativity. *A Portrait* closes with Stephen's refusal of his mother's request for him to make his Easter duty (*A Portrait,* 239) and *Ulysses* opens after Stephen has refused his mother's dying request to pray for her. The death of the mother removes her "authorship" of the artist. He turns to the sea as a symbolic, amniotic "mother," only as an indicator of his embryonic state, and sets about creating himself through the novel and its representative organs of the body for each chapter. Thus, the metaphor of the creation of the artist becomes incorporated into the form of the book.

There are two major remaining elements of the masculine sexual aesthetic beyond "mental motherhood." They are the matters of fatherhood and of the role of the muse. Both of these sexually based concepts are perverted in the realm of artistic procreation, since that procreation is to remain exclusively intellectual. The effect of this exclusion of the literally physical is to produce what John Irwin has called "a kind of creative onanism." Joyce himself, in a letter to Stanislaus in 1906, refers to the male's "extraordinary cerebral sexualism." The issue is discussed in *Ulysses* in relation to the father/artist figure Shakespeare. When John Eglinton declares, "After God Shakespeare has created most," Stephen responds, "Man delights him not nor woman, neither" (*Ulysses,* 209). What delights the creator who has created everything (including women) is, of course, only himself. Stephen refers back to God:

> The playwright who wrote the folio of this world and wrote it badly (He gave us light first and the sun two days later), the lord of things as they are whom the most Roman of catholics call *dio boia,* hangman god, is doubtless all in all of us, ostler and butcher, and would be bawd and cuckold too but that in the economy of heaven, foretold by Hamlet, there are no more marriages, glorified man, an androgynous angel, being a wife unto himself (209-10).

Although sexual aesthetics involve a good deal of talk about androgyny (and we will see this to be the case with Woolf as well), the matter is, mostly, talk. Two considerations are involved here. The first is that the artist really is so much in love with himself and his mental creation that he feels sexually complete—intellectually, that is. The second is that he fears actual physical sexual involvement with the opposite sex (an issue we shall also see in relation to Woolf). In *Ulysses,* after Stephen announces the "playwright's" self-sufficiency, Buck Mulligan crudely responds, "Being afraid to marry on earth, They masturbated for all they were worth" (213). What Joyce is saying is that the artist does fear the opposite sex because she threatens his safe, separate, intellectual creative power. He wishes to define the male as an artist with a central creative impulse which is exclusively intellectual, as opposed to what he perceives as woman's physically creative drive. His fear of her is in relation to her physical potential "use" of his artistic potency, which he prefers to exercise in the intellectual realm. (Yet again, we shall see this clash between the intellectual and the physical in Woolf's female artist figures.)

The exclusion of physical involvement and the relegation of sex to the intellectual plane is reflected in Joyce's "muses." The wading girl in *A Portrait* is a modified image of the Virgin in blue and white. She is "cerebrally" sexually exciting in that she is a human female with "white fringes of her drawers . . . like featherings of soft white down" (171). Even though she purportedly represents "profane joy," she is still remote, "a wild angel" with whom Stephen has only visual (cerebral) contact.

Bloom, who is a debased artist figure because he does not create art, but is a sort of "life-artist," presents a crude parody of Stephen and the wading girl. In his encounter with Gerty MacDowell on the beach, he observes the spectacle she makes of her stockings and underdrawers in a physical onanistic indulgence (*Ulysses*, 339-76). Bloom's muse in residence, Molly, is significantly an embodiment of woman as the opposite sex perceived by the male artist as continuously engaged in or thinking about physical sexual activity. Yet even Bloom, according to the grapevine in *Ulysses*, has not had "complete" physical sexual contact with Molly for ten years (720). The muse, by definition, must remain physically remote and intellectually close, in order to free the artist to practice intellectual procreativity. The fact that Joyce himself actually married should not alter our perception and assessment of his serio-comic aesthetic as presented in *A Portrait* and *Ulysses*. That aesthetic represents fears and reservations about the opposite sex that, in real life, he managed in part to overcome. Joyce does write to his brother that he avoided sex with Nora in order to avoid having children. He came home as late as possible and took care when sharing a double bed to sleep "lying opposed in opposite directions" (*James Joyce*, 237). Molly and Bloom in *Ulysses* follow the same practice (*Ulysses*, 720-21). The object of the artist's life is to produce literature rather than offspring, and Joyce took great pains to separate intellectual and physical activity. Parenthood becomes a part of the sexual aesthetic by becoming a metaphorical proposition. Bloom and Molly are metaphorical "parents" for Stephen by providing him a sense of connection with other human beings. Intellectually, Stephen must create himself.

The problem of sexuality and parenthood is far less easy to overcome for women who wish to be artists, since biology can make intellectual versus physical procreation an either/or proposition. During the last decade, so many perceptive studies of women writers have been done that it is hardly necessary to mention this obvious fact. Virginia Woolf, in *A Room of One's Own*, remarks that the assembled imaginary company of women artists consisting of George Eliot, the Brontës, and Jane Austen seem incongruous "save for the possibly relevant fact

that not one of them had a child." That they did not, and that Woolf did not choose to have one, suggests, in the words of Nina Auerbach, that for "woman artists made inescapably aware of the social assumptions equating womanhood with motherhood, art is a liberation from that demand." We will see that Woolf feared the demands a man might make for attention that would leave her no space of her own for her art; Woolf's father made such demands. How much more might a child, and how much more justifiably, ask of her.

Woolf is ambivalent about the subject often enough to be confusing. However, she does observe in *A Writer's Diary*, "I don't like the physicalness of having children of one's own," and adds "I can dramatise myself as a parent, it is true." In these two statements which come so close to one another, we can see a great deal of similarity to Joyce's distinctions between the mental and the physical. Physical motherhood would tie Woolf to the milieu which, in Joyce's system, does not allow intellectual creativity. Woolf would be a mother, not an artist. Within Woolf's own system, the artist is an artist precisely because she makes mutually exclusive choices which permit her to do what she wants to do. The character of Lily Briscoe in *To the Lighthouse* demonstrates this very clearly. Commitment to a marriage, let alone motherhood, would place overwhelming demands upon a creative spirit wishing to remain in the artistic sphere as one which requires a separation of attention from others.

Lest we think Lily or Woolf exceptionally limited, we need to look at a brief statement by a contemporary woman writer, Kate Wilhelm, who has discussed the matter in a way that Woolf could not:

> After my second marriage, within months, there were so many pressures to force me into giving up writing again, to become mother-housewife, etc., that I had to go away just to think. . . . Unless a woman knows she is another Virginia Woolf or Jane Austen, how can she say no to the world? It is generally expected that the children, the house, school functions, husband's needs, yard, etc. all come first, and the time left over is hers to use as she chooses. A woman who is determined to write has to reverse that order, and it is hard. Nothing in our background has prepared us for this role; each of us who has done this has had to find the way alone and in the face of criticism, not always explicit, but there (75).

Virginia Woolf, we must assume, knew she was a Virginia Woolf sufficiently to say no to the world. If not, her husband was kind enough to say it for her. By all accounts he made no objection to her preference not to be sexually involved with him, not to be a physical parent.

Parenthood is related in yet another way to Woolf's (and Joyce's) aesthetic. Both *Ulysses* and *To the Lighthouse* contain portraits of "life-artists"—Bloom and Mrs. Ramsay. They are in some respects like parents for the artist figures of the same sex, Stephen and Lily. A life-artist, so far as one can tell, is more closely anchored in the physical mundane world than is the artist. Both Bloom ("There's a touch of the artist about old Bloom," *Ulysses,* 231) and Mrs. Ramsay serve their protégés by demonstrating principles of productivity or connection. Bloom and Molly weave relationships which bring Stephen to them and give him a metaphorical home. Mrs. Ramsay inspires Lily Briscoe and gives her a sense of a home on the physical plane which is Lily's ideal in art. We are told that Lily

> had much ado to control her impulse to fling herself (thank Heaven she had always resisted so far) at Mrs. Ramsay's knee, and say to her—but what could one say to her? "I'm in love with you?" No, that was not true. "I'm in love with this all," waving her hand at the hedge, at the house, at the children (*Lighthouse*, 32).

Lily wants "intimacy itself, which is knowledge" (79), that sense of connection which is vital to the artist. Mrs. Ramsay, a physical mother to children, is in her way a spiritual mother to Lily. If Mrs. Ramsay is a muse, she is one who represents a kind of beauty which Lily admires, but must not choose for herself, as we shall see in our discussion of the "angel in the house."

In *Ulysses,* Stephen derives a sense of belonging and relationship from Bloom, and his shared cup of evening cocoa is a touching ritual; however, Stephen's longing for connection is directed within the formal structure of the novel always toward a suitably heterosexual muse. (Molly is merely a scandalously lascivious "parent" who directs heterosexual longing of an abstract, almost impersonal kind toward Stephen.) One of Stephen's reflections upon a possible muse illustrates the point:

> Touch me. Soft eyes. Soft soft soft hand. I am lonely here. O, touch me soon, now. What is that word known to all men? (48)

Stephen's word—love—may be the same as Lily's, but the style is definitely different. Although Lily mentions being in love with Mrs. Ramsay, eroticism, if flinging oneself at someone's knee qualifies for that, is "not true." It will have to do, though, whatever sort of love it is, since no heterosexual muse is available to Lily. The young man opposite her at the dinner table has told her, "Women can't write, women can't paint—" (*Lighthouse,* 130). Lily can find no sense of belonging in that. There is nothing erotic, for the female artist here, in a union with a hostile selfish creature struggling to fulfill only his own needs. Lily's reaction to Charles Tansley is similar to her reaction to Mr. Ramsay's demands for pity and attention near the end of the novel:

> Look at him, he seemed to be saying, look at me; and indeed, all the time he was feeling, Think of me, think of me. . . . A woman, she had provoked this horror; a woman, she should have known how to deal with it. It was immensely to her discredit, sexually, to stand there dumb. One said—what did one say?—Oh, Mr. Ramsay! Dear Mr. Ramsay! . . . But, no. They stood there, isolated from

the rest of the world. His immense self-pity, his demand for sympathy poured and spread itself in pools at her feet, and all she did, miserable sinner that she was, was to draw her skirts a little closer round her ankles, lest she should get wet. In complete silence she stood there, grasping her paint brush (227-28).

Lily must choose between her sexual role and her artistic one. There is no having both of them. If the young Charles Tansley is a muse, he is a negative one who causes her to retreat from sexuality to her art, to solace herself in relation to his sexism, "There's the sprig on the table-cloth; there's my painting; I must move the tree to the middle; that matters—nothing else" (130).

Lily, in moving away from Mr. Tansley, also moves away from becoming physically like Mrs. Ramsay, who is "tired" and "worn" (127) by virtue of living her socially approved sexual role of life-artist and mother. Mrs. Ramsay creates relationships at the dinner party by overcoming, at the cost of great strain to herself, the forces of isolation operant in individual egos. Beginning to ladle out soup, she reflects,

> And the whole of the effort of merging and flowing and creating rested on her. Again she felt, as a fact without hostility, the sterility of men, for if she did not do it nobody would do it, and so, giving herself the little shake that one gives a watch that has stopped, the old familiar pulse began beating . . . (126).

Mrs. Ramsay rises to the task of creating the party; having begun with serving the soup, she ends by serving the *Boeuf en Daube.* By this time, all is coherence and stability:

> It partook, she felt, carefully helping Mr. Bankes to a specially tender piece, of eternity; as she had already felt about something different once before that afternoon; there is a coherence in things, a stability; something, she meant, is immune from change. . . . Of such moments, she thought, the thing is made that endures (158).

In spite of Mrs. Ramsay's satisfaction with her artistry, Lily paints in a different medium. Lily reflects upon Mrs. Ramsay's death, "Mrs. Ramsay had given. Giving, giving, giving, she had died— . . ." (223). Virginia Woolf, like Lily, regarded Mrs. Ramsay as a typification of "the angel in the house," the ideal of Victorian womanhood which would have a woman sacrifice herself to the needs of others. Woolf writes that had she not killed her, the angel would have "plucked the heart out of my writing."

Woolf's feelings about her mother and her mother's death are the biographical substructure for this aspect of her aesthetic. Nevertheless, both Woolf and Lily, we must assume, do find a sense of connection in Mrs. Ramsay. She gives to them an example of a female artist working in a destructive medium—life. One may give unselfishly to one's art, provided one's art is not the art of self-sacrifice. Woolf felt that the production of her art required a sense of unviolated selfhood, a sort of "self of one's own," apart from the demands of sexual roles. Although she denies the practice of her sexuality in order to retain that sense of self, her artist figure still retains her female gender identification. In her art, she orchestrates unities in the fashion of a woman conducting relationships and lives. It is Lily who completes the action of *To the Lighthouse,* finishing her painting and seeing through to completion Mr. Ramsay's expedition begun and abandoned at about the time of Mrs. Ramsay's dinner party.

Woolf's aesthetic is, after all, sexual, and it is feminine. The artist is a woman all the more for her polarization away from her male antagonist. Woolf characterizes Lily in such a way as to demonstrate that what the female artist requires is to be left free of men's overwhelming demands related to the male ego and to his view of woman as the all-sufficient, all-giving mother. Both Mr. Ramsay and Charles Tansley are characterized as childish, pitiable—incapable, by the way, of being artists. Even the life-artist, Mrs. Ramsay, is said to have "pitied men always as if they lacked something—women never, as if they had something" (129). Mrs. Ramsay may devote herself to giving men what they lack, but Lily must not, if she is to create art. She will do without the reverential treatment Mrs. Ramsay receives from the male sex, and without all the bother she'd have to go to, to obtain it. Lily can withstand the lack, since hers is the stronger sex.

One exceptionally clear glimpse of this is given in Mr. Ramsay's musings on the way to the lighthouse. He:

> staged for himself as he sat in the boat, a little drama; which required of him decrepitude and exhaustion and sorrow (he raised his hands and looked at the thinness of them, to confirm his dream) and then there was given him in abundance women's sympathy, and he imagined how they would soothe him and sympathise with him, and so getting in his dream some reflection of the exquisite pleasure women's sympathy was to him, he sighed and said gently and mournfully,
>
> But I beneath a rougher sea
>
> Was whelmed in deeper gulfs than he,
>
> so that the mournful words were heard quite clearly by them all (248).

Mr. Ramsay wants sympathy from women to compensate for his lack of greatness in the world. Men and children are inexorably related in their helplessness and the demands which they place on women.

Like Stephen Daedalus, Woolf must refuse the demands as well, of the parent of the opposite sex in order to survive. If Mr. Ramsay is in one sense representative of her own father, then it is enlightening that Woolf in *A Writer's Diary,* says of him that had he lived, "His life

would have entirely ended mine. What would have happened? No writing, no books;—inconceivable" (135). The opposite sex in general are merely an extension of those demands which one cannot fulfill without some sort of self-extinction.

In Joyce's aesthetic, which is more concerned with erotic sexuality *per se,* the demands of the opposite sex are embodied in Molly—insatiable in her desire for lovers, ego gratification, and presents ("if I only had a ring with the stone for my month a nice aquamarine I'll stick him for one and a gold bracelet" [*Ulysses,* 729]). Bloom would not be free to bring Stephen in from outside, to be at work in creating relationships, were Molly not otherwise engaged in an affair with Blazes Boylan. As a character, Molly is negative stereotype. She is tolerated, ostensibly "celebrated" (so Joyce hollowly claims), because she is a fertility principle, necessary to man in order to create life. The assumption is that without life, there can be no art; hence, the male artist is stuck with her. When Bloom dresses up in women's clothes in the Nighttown episode, far from his partaking of a similar "celebration" of androgyny, he is reminded of the popping of his trouser button (538) that he has debased himself, and that he ought to be wearing the trousers and managing the female principle. He resolves to change his relationship with Molly and to take charge of her. The closest positive affinity in *Ulysses* is actually the relationship between Bloom and Stephen (the life-artist and the art-artist). Similarly, in *To the Lighthouse,* Lily's love of Mrs. Ramsay is of the sort which would not have killed her by wearing her out.

The fact of the matter is that artists who employ a sexual aesthetic don't much care for the opposite sex. Ironically, the emotions concerning their opposites within the opposing sexual aesthetics for Joyce and Woolf, emotions which range from pity to distaste, from hostility to hatred, create a common bond between the two authors—and among countless other men and women as well. The similarity of these opposites is an area which remains to be studied in depth, and which has only been partially explored by those engaged in "women's studies." It may well be that feminist critics are more skillful at this type of study—which ought to be called "gender study"—because of years of developing a sexual perspective. But the field is relatively open to everyone, and it seems a pity to exclude critics from sharing in the sexual antagonism which affects authors and critics alike.

BIBLIOGRAPHY

Auerbach, Nina. "Artists and Mothers: A False Alliance." *Women and Literature* (Spring, 1978).

———. *Communities of Women: An Idea in Fiction.* Cambridge, Mass., 1978.

Ellman, Mary. *Thinking About Women.* New York, 1968.

Ellman, Richard. *James Joyce.* New York, 1959.

Fetterley, Judith. *The Resisting Reader: A Feminist Approach to American Literature.* Bloomington, 1978.

Gilbert, Sandra. "Life Studies, or Speech After Long Silence: Feminist Critics Today." *College English,* 40 (April, 1979).

————, and Susan Gubar. *The Madwoman in the Attic.* New Haven, 1979.

Gilbert, Stuart. *James Joyce's Ulysses.* New York, 1955.

Harris, Daniel A. "Androgyny: The Sexist Myth in Disguise." *Women's Studies,* 2 (1974).

Heilbrun, Carolyn. *Toward a Recognition of Androgyny.* New York, 1973.

Irwin, John T. *Doubling and Incest, Repetition and Revenge.* Baltimore, 1975.

Joyce, James. *A Portrait of the Artist as a Young Man.* New York, 1968.

————. *Ulysses.* New York, 1934.

Kolodny, Annette, "Some Notes on Defining a 'Feminist Literary Criticism.'" *Critical Inquiry,* 2 (Autumn, 1975).

Rose, Phyllis. *Woman of Letters: A Life of Virginia Woolf.* New York, 1978.

Wilhelm, Kate. "To Women Writers." *Frontiers: A Journal of Women's Studies,* 2 (Fall, 1977).

Woolf, Virginia. *A Room of One's Own.* New York, 1957.

————. *To the Lighthouse.* New York, 1927.

————. *A Writer's Diary.* New York, 1954.

L. R. Leavis

SOURCE: "The Late Nineteenth Century Novel and The Change Towards The Sexual--Gissing, Hardy and Lawrence," in *English Studies,* Vol. 65, No. 1, February, 1985, pp. 36-47.

[*In the following essay, Leavis traces changes in the literary representation of sexuality through the works of George Gissing, Thomas Hardy, and D. H. Lawrence.*]

Ever since the real beginnings of the English novel in the eighteenth century, and the evolution of the form as a work of art in the nineteenth, it has been intrinsically involved with the relationships between the sexes in society. This of course has been often enough put forward by critics in the past, with emphases ranging from the balanced and flexible to the purely sociological and the crudely sexual—or more recently, the sexist. Certainly, from the outset where the novelist has been preoccupied with the social, the novel has demonstrated an unrivalled grasp of social reality in dramatic terms. This we can see as early as the interests dramatised in the art of Richardson (with his feminine sensibility), in his study of the female predicament and his keen understanding of (for instance) the destructive intelligence of a purely female gathering in tearing to pieces for their entertainment male stupidity and affectation—for the purposes of this brief survey I leave out of consideration the more superficial and extrovertly masculine Fielding and the picaresque novel of the eighteenth century.

Jane Austen took up Richardson's discoveries for her satire, while achieving in her best art a subtle balance of scrupulosity of evaluative judgement and understanding of the predicaments of both sexes. Jane Austen is justly famous for her destructive portraits of both sexes—be they within an eighteenth century satirical tradition or of an intensity peculiar to her—but with few exceptions the reader always senses her clarity of vision and her objectiveness in exploring her own deeply-felt standards in the body of the works. Not in any way sex-centred, Jane Austen's maturity about sexual relations is manifest, and may well be connected with the healthiness of Regency society.

In the Victorian novel one often finds a lack of this balance and healthiness; Mrs. Oliphant, a not untalented writer, and a highly intelligent and formidable woman, displays an attitude to her characters that while apparently rooted in compassion seems in fact to be allied to contempt and, through the writer's sense of superiority, belittlement. From a male standpoint, one would rather be a Mr. Collins, heartily despised by Jane Austen, than one of Mrs. Oliphant's male weaklings so contemptuously stroked by her pitying irony. An explanation for the cause of this distinction between the two writers depends not only on the fact that the later one was surrounded by weak men, and struggling to earn a living, but also on the changed nature of Victorian society, which is bound up with cultural attitudes in the relationship between men and women.

Charlotte Brontë in her Romantic novels was fighting against this very phenomenon, the Victorian attitude towards the sexes, but one might conclude that the influence on the novel of her most striking innovations was delayed until the end of the century. This is not to say that her *Jane Eyre* didn't importantly affect Dickens in his composition of *David Copperfield,* or influence the minor novelist Mrs. Gaskell. However, if one lays *David Copperfield* next to *Jane Eyre,* one can see that with regard to the Victorian novel's coverage of its society Charlotte Brontë was artistically a 'freak'. Whatever Dickens learned from her novel, his is written distinctly in his own terms and focuses solidly on the world of the practical, while Charlotte Brontë's heroine drifts painfully as an outside observer of social reality. For all their great originality neither *Jane Eyre* nor *Villette* contain an adequate equivalent of Betsey Trotwood, a character who insists that Dickens's protagonist should be entrenched in the practical—though we realise that Charlotte Brontë's heroines are deprived of a man's possibilities in the world, and appreciate their frantic efforts to survive and keep a self-respect, while driven on by a puritan refusal to shirk any hostile odds. A less blunt formulation would be that Jane Eyre's adult experience of the world is circumscribed, the book moving on from one enclosed set of circumstances to another. In *Villette* the temporary protector of Lucy Snowe, Miss Marchmont, is herself a refugee from life, and her history proves to set a pattern for the heroine's. One suspects that despite the attempted detachment of the diary-form of her novels. Charlotte Brontë's heroines are close to their author; and Dickens's employment of the same form is more meaningful and functional, not allowing the same suspicion. That Charlotte Brontë's heroines are observers on the fringe of life is the source of her main creative perceptions, and in exploring their situations her novels show a strange blend of the puritan and the ultra-Romantic, two conflicting qualities which at times hang together uneasily. Despite her puritan temperament Charlotte Brontë was a pioneer of the explicitly sexual in intense psychological poetry, and she came to decisively influence the novel in this way much later, even as late as the time of D. H. Lawrence.

Dickens and George Eliot, the major and most influential novelists of the Victorian period, naturally stand on their own both in their relationships to their societies and in their psychological investigation. Both achieve a dramatic intensity in portraying character, George Eliot intellectually and through realism, Dickens through poetic exaggeration and 'psychological realism'. George Eliot's inward description of Dorothea Brooke's confused emotions during her honeymoon in Rome (Chap. XX, *Middlemarch*) or Dickens's study of Miss Wade in *Little Dorrit* are two clear examples from a profusion of psychological drama encompassing the sexual, being all the more effective for not having an explicitly sexual emphasis.

The stirrings of the late nineteenth and early twentieth century writers of lesser talent in adapting the novel to a new consciousness of life and of society is intriguing. Kingsley had been early with a radical view of aspects of his society in *Alton Locke* (1850) and *Yeast* (1851), both social tracts, but it is when we come to Gissing in the Nineties that we find the beginning of a wave of novelists portraying society with different emphases from the great Victorian novelists. Gissing was influenced profoundly by Dickens and George Eliot, with the rider that like all distinguished minor artists, this influence in his best work was used with individuality and transformed to his own tastes and interests. Once Gissing had got over his early Naturalistic mode it

seemed that he was searching for a means to express his particular sensibility without being overwhelmed by the two major Victorian novelists. *New Grub Street* (1891) contains debates among more than one set of characters about the possibility of the novel adapting to new social conditions. One infers that Gissing was through them exploring his position as novelist. Biffen, a novelist of realism, in conversation with Reardon, a failing writer, puts forward his theory of a new objective treatment of low-class life, an anti-heroic realism about what he terms 'the ignobly decent'. Though Gissing (unlike Biffen) no longer endorses 'realism for realism's sake', treating Biffen with a certain amount of irony, one is sure in the light of Gissing's mature writing and of his study of Dickens, that he has great sympathy with that figure's observations:

> As I came along by Regent's Park half an hour ago a man and a girl were walking close in front of me, love-making; I passed them slowly, and heard a good deal of their talk . . . Now, such a love-scene as that has absolutely never been written down; it was entirely decent, yet vulgar to the nth power. Dickens would have made it ludicrous—a gross injustice. Other men who deal with low-class life would perhaps have preferred idealising it—an absurdity . . .

The same character concludes shortly afterwards:

> I shall never write anything like a dramatic scene. Such things do happen in life, but so very rarely that they are nothing to my purpose. Even when they happen, by-the-by, it is in a shape that would be useless to the ordinary novelist; he would have to cut away this circumstance, and add that. Why? I should like to know. Such conventionalism results from stage necessities. Fiction hasn't yet outgrown the influence of the stage on which it originated. Whatever a man writes *for effect* is wrong and bad.

Gissing continued to be interested in 'dramatic scenes', but of a low-key unrhetorical nature in his best work. Within *New Grub Street* the shabby tragedy of the Alfred Yule family is an admirable instance of Gissing's originality in this field. We see a fastidious and pedantic book-worm humiliating his illiterate lower-class wife, while his only child, the sensitive and intelligent Marian looks on in silence. His daughter's subsequent sufferings stem from the pain of her upbringing and her lack of emotional outlet. Several Gissing-experts would see the Yule parents as direct transposition of Gissing's relationship with at least one of his wives. Gissing lived through certain experiences that take a central place in his best novels, but one cannot at least here accept an undiluted 'autobiography embodied in fiction' approach. If one considers the literary influences on Gissing in such scenes, one must appreciate how intelligently yet spontaneously Gissing has employed them. Plainly he has understood the domestic drama (mostly with a comic emphasis, but sometimes as in *Dombey and Son*, tending to melodrama) of Dickens's novels. At the same time George Eliot's *Middlemarch,* with its insistent authorial definition of tragedy which is too common to be called tragic in the accepted sense (especially applied to Casaubon and Dorothea Brooke) must have helped him find a corrective to what he felt was alien to his sensibility in Dickens. Gissing clearly valued her psychological character-studies; as several critics have remarked (to take one instance), Amy Reardon, the villain of *New Grub Street* bears traces of Rosamond Vincy.

While Gissing could be parasitic in his reliance on George Eliot, reducing her to the level of a pot-boiler in *The Whirlpool* (1897), he was acutely aware of the danger of being too much under her spell. As John Halperin shows in his *Gissing, A Life in Books* (New York, 1982) he expressed in his letters a strong reaction against the rationalistic art of George Eliot by turning violently to Charlotte Brontë. We know that he particularly admired *Villette,* re-reading it in 1887. As Halperin suggests, he could see her position as a social-outsider as comparable with his own, and found her poetic treatment of passion congenial. Charlotte Brontë's work may reveal a curious composition of the puritan and Romantic, but Gissing's character appears even more confused and contradictory. He comes across as a mixture of Radical and die-hard conservative, his private frustrations turning him against women, yet his decency and non-conformist scrupulosity combined with an acute sensitivity making him understand feminine suffering in feminine terms. Charlotte Brontë's novels must have helped him in *New Grub Street* with his opening portraits of the Milvain sisters (before he disappoints the reader by making them their brother's puppets) and with Marian Yule's love-affair.

The book's sexual outspokenness may have been inspired by Charlotte Brontë's example, but is idiosyncratically expressed. Gissing delineates in his own way the sufferings of the struggling artist and his restricted possibilities with women, pursuing an anti-Romantic path in stressing that for such a person any sexual relation will lead to disaster. Reardon and Biffen turn to classical learning and landscape to compensate for their sexual starvation. Jasper Milvain and Whelpdale provide a new kind of commentary on the state of feeling, typical of the end of the century:

> 'I object to the word "love" altogether. It has been vulgarised. Let us talk about compatibility. Now, I should say that, no doubt, and speaking scientifically, there *is* one particular woman supremely fitted to each man . . . If there were any means of discovering this woman in each case, then I have no doubt it would be worth a man's utmost effort to do so, and any amount of erotic jubilation would be reasonable when the discovery was made. But the thing is impossible, and, what's more, we know what ridiculous fallibility people display when they imagine they have found out the best substitute for that indiscoverable. This is what makes me impatient with sentimental talk about marriage. An educated man mustn't play so into the hands of an ironic destiny. Let him think he *wants* to marry a woman; but don't let him

exaggerate his feelings or idealise their nature.'

> 'There's a good deal in all that,' admitted Whelpdale, though discontentedly.

> 'There's more than a good deal; there's the last word on the subject. The days of romantic love are gone by. The scientific spirit has put an end to that kind of self-deception. Romantic love was inextricably blended with all sorts of superstitions—belief in personal immortality, in superior beings, in—all the rest of it. What we think of now is moral, and intellectual and physical compatibility; I mean, we are reasonable people . . .'

While the main talker here is a selfish cynic who knows that he himself has no moral integrity, Gissing's irony does not disguise the fact that this post-Darwinian position on sexual relations is in keeping with the novel's fatalism.

Born in Exile (1892) continues Gissing's period when he impressively attempted to turn the unhappiness and frustrations of his life into art which novelistically explores the human condition on a level beyond the narrowly personal, however much he asserted to a friend that the book's hero was a phase of himself.

Godwin Peak through temperament and chance becomes cut off from any possibility of fulfilling his talents and ambition in society, even though his brilliant scholastic career promised so much. Bitterly disillusioned with society and himself, he discovers that he is also out of sympathy with the Radical reaction against his times. The novel takes up a theme thrown out in *New Grub Street* of the individualist and déclassé man of talent who gradually finds any position in his society impossible. Peak's desperate attempt at a solution in trying to get into the Church of England (a Church destroyed by loss of faith from the New Science) makes us think of one of the phases of Hardy's *Jude the Obscure* (1895). However Peak lacks Jude's mediæval idealism, and is not dominated by a Sue Bridehead. His woman is a sweet and well-bred upperclass girl, conventional and unintellectual; Peak finds intellectual Radical females sexually repulsive.

The novel ends with the collapse of Peak's ambitions through the hostility of the conventional towards his social position and his hardly-to-be-disguised unconventionality of intellect. He is driven into exile from his own country and dies from emotional starvation. After reading this, one can feel that Dickens could have devoted a whole novel to Pip's predicament after the termination of all his hopes and ambitions (whichever ending one chooses of *Great Expectations*) though of course the emphasis of Dickens's novel does not need to entail such a study. One admires the originality of Gissing's treatment of extreme social isolation—one quite different from Arthur Clennam's position in *Little Dorrit.*

The third novel of this successful period [ignoring the sensational *Denzil Quarrier* (1892)] is the more limited

The Odd Women (1893). Gissing in his earlier work was interested in the position of late-Victorian women, but now devotes a whole novel to the subject. He continues the frank and open discussion of sexual attitudes seen in the previous two books. In *Born in Exile* we encountered Marcella Moxey, an emancipated Radical who was rigidly 'enlightened' and manifestly 'unfeminine'. Rhoda Nunn is a sympathetic study of an intelligent 'new' feminist with a sense of humour and feminine attractiveness below the surface:

> It was a face that invited, that compelled study.

> Self-confidence, intellectual keenness, a bright humour, frank courage, were traits legible enough; and when the lips parted to show their warmth, their fullness, when the eyelids drooped a little in meditation, one became aware of a suggestiveness directed not solely to the intellect, of something like an unfamiliar sexual type, remote indeed from the voluptuous, but hinting a possibility of subtle feminine forces that might be released by circumstance . . .

Certainly Gissing has been affected by Charlotte Brontë's Lucy Snowe, but despite his bent in private life of detesting free-thinking women so often cited by his biographers, we see that in *The Odd Women* he could reconsider his judgements.

One reason for qualifying one's estimate of the novel relates to the simplicity of its plot, where the contrast between the story of a conventional woman marrying a jealous and overbearing older man with the attempts of a 'male-chauvinist' philanderer in subduing Miss Nunn is ultimately too schematic. Another is that Gissing has been too markedly affected both by Charlotte Brontë's full-blown Romantic language and by Dickens's theatrical confrontation-scenes to be himself. The would-be seducer of the novel, Everard Barfoot, is an interesting variant of a villain in the Steerforth mould, but rhetorical confrontation-scenes and passionate outbursts do not fit in to the generally realistic mode of the book. The novel's merit lies in the more muted psychological treatment of the main women's situations, done with an admirable disinterest and understanding.

Hardy's *Jude the Obscure* (1895) is often taken as an important and original novel expressing the new pessimism of its time. However, unlike Gissing, on Hardy's part there seems to be an uncreative or 'journalistic' use of literary influences, which must indicate the work's real stature. One instance is the obtrusiveness of Hardy's emphasis on general 'cosmic pessimism', which has probably originated from *Middlemarch* and its tragedy of the ordinary human condition. Hardy has taken this source and added his own kind of references to Greek Tragedy, backed up by a blatant reliance on coincidence. Gissing himself rejected (and was too much a novelist to affect the same pose in his best writing) the asserted pessimism that characters in *Jude* are made to voice:

> And then he again uneasily saw, as he had latterly seen with more and more frequency, the scorn of Nature for man's finer emotions, and her lack of interest in his aspirations . . .

This position (while obviously derivative from) is a long way from George Eliot's:

> But anyone watching keenly the stealthy convergence of human lots, sees a slow preparation of effects from one life on another, which tells like a calculated irony on the indifference or the frozen state with which we look at our unintroduced neighbour. Destiny stands by sarcastic with our *dramatis personae* folded in her hand . . . (*Middlemarch,* Chap. XI)

Similar employment of influences is to be met in Hardy's other 'adaptations'; the figure of the boy 'Father Time' is certainly taken from little Paul of *Dombey and Son,* with the subtle delicacy of Dickens's art changed into an insertion, a topical perspective relying on the ramming home of the theme of a typical modern child too old for his years. Indeed, if one compares Dickens's treatment of childhood in his maturity with the childhood of Jude and Father Time, one may feel that in taking over the nineteenth century novel's discovery of childhood from Romantic poetry, Hardy has sensationalised and parodied a tradition, adding nothing original. Again we must surely exempt Gissing from this charge, as he has creatively transformed material in his best work to suit a refined and original sensibility. If this conclusion about Hardy seems too harsh, or unsupported, I can only invite the reader to compare the scene in *Jude* concerning the bohemian support of Phillotson against 'respectable society' (Section VI, 'At Shaston') with Dickens's circus people in *Hard Times.* That a writer can lift material in such a way from other novelists is the mark of a literary vulgariser.

As a social novel, despite its reputation of sweeper-away of conventions, *Jude* is similarly unsatisfactory. Unlike Gissing's best works, the terms which should establish a concrete sense of reality only exist through the bitter observations Jude and Sue make on the social system. When a social reality is offered outside these characters' sense of persecution, the few scenes we get such as of the interior of a Christminster tavern ('real Christminster life') hardly provide a substantial picture. One is left with Hardy's cynicism about marriage, and the attitudes of the main characters, which surely are often mere attitudes, such as Sue's horror of legal wedlock (note that Rhoda Nunn had similar reactions towards marriage), an 'outrageous' challenging of conformity and the Ten Commandments, a questioning of a literal reading of the Bible, and other equally disconnected fragments.

On religious belief in late Victorian England *Born in Exile* has much more to say than *Jude,* and Margaret Maison in her *Search Your Soul, Eustace* (London, 1961) is surely not overstating the case when she remarks:

Jude's orthodoxy is almost entirely non-combatant—it is a mere Aunt Sally to be knocked down, not by the scientists or the biblical critics, but by the forces of social setbacks and unrestrained fleshly lusts . . .

Nevertheless a fascinating and most important aspect of Hardy's novel remains to be mentioned, one which D. H. Lawrence expounded in his *Study of Thomas Hardy;* the relationship between Sue and Jude. Margaret Maison (among others) has pointed out that in the minor Victorian novel there were many 'stories of young women whose scepticism was part of their emancipation, and who proved totally unable to control passion by principle', and cites Olive Schreiner's *The Story of an African Farm* (1883) and Mrs. W. D. Humphrey's *Sheba* (1889) as two such popular novels which were near-contemporaries of *Jude.* To these one could add Gissing's *The Odd Women,* especially as it may help to explain certain discrepancies within the character of Sue herself. Lawrence's most interesting study of Hardy's abstract conceptions of women in society has perhaps made of *Jude* a more coherent novel than the one Hardy actually wrote. It is difficult to reconcile the extremes in Hardy's picture of a female militant, who is sexless, even a man-killer as heartless as Amy Reardon in *New Grub Street,* yet is highly impulsive and feminine (a distinctly Hardian emphasis), who has children of her own, who is a relentless Radical crusader, yet ends up in a masochistic conservatism of an insanely puritan nature. *The Odd Women* in contrast intelligently used current interest in the 'new woman' to produce a coherent study. Gissing for this employs two varieties of woman, two friends, one of which is a radical and the other a conventional woman who is in danger of becoming an 'old maid'. While the execution of the novel is too limited, making one wish for more flesh in the book, the ideas behind it are convincing enough. The older man whom the conventional woman (Monica Madden) marries is called Widdowson, a name suspiciously close to Phillotson in *Jude.* The wife comes to rebel against her husband's irrational jealousy, which in the end forces her into the arms of a lover. Monica Madden finds her husband physically repulsive, as Sue does Phillotson. It is this relationship between the Maddens that ends in tragedy.

One suspects that Hardy in drawing on the novelistic convention of the sceptical woman has been affected by Gissing's treatment of sexual relations. Sue Bridehead reads like a curious amalgam of the uncompromising feminist Rhoda Nunn, and her unemancipated man-needing friend Monica Madden, an amalgam that involves too many conflicting elements to be contained in one character. Sue starts off as a Rhoda Nunn and by the end of the novel is thoroughly 'Maddened'. In the process of this transformation Phillotson is rather implausibly made to abandon his movingly described understanding of his young wife's plight and to practise an unnaturally ruthless cruelty upon her, this being 'explained' by his having learned from experience. Widdowson in comparison seems while less sympathetic

at least 'all of a piece'. One's sense of Hardy's indebtedness to Gissing is supported by the fact that the two men knew each other and sent each other their novels, Gissing sending Hardy copies of two of his novels as early as 1886. Gissing in fact visited Hardy when he was working on his final version of *Jude,* but little comes out of Gissing's record of that meeting (or indeed of Gissing's note in his diary on first reading *Jude).*

Hardy's importance as a source for D. H. Lawrence's creative innovations has already been well-established in criticism; the unassimilated influence on Lawrence's early work is well-known, and the relationship between his *Study of Thomas Hardy* and the marriage of Will and Anna in *The Rainbow* is a striking example of a great novelist's creative use of material. Perhaps too Hardy's example is distantly behind *Women in Love.* Another sort of novel than *The Rainbow, Women in Love* is restricted in its number of characters and relies for its sense of reality on vivid and dramatic conversations. The characters are carefully grouped to make a controlled pattern through the plan of the chapters, while the social implications of Lawrence's investigation are wide-ranging and ambitious. The apparent result is the range of the social study of a major novel with the poetry of the 'moral fable'. In fact life in England as a background to the main groups of characters is limited to a few brief concrete examples (outside the representative nature of the conversations); the 'A Chair' chapter with its picture of city life seems a sudden switch on Lawrence's part to illustrate a thesis on the state of modern English society. Impossible as it is to come up with a nineteenth century work of a similar nature, one could suggest *Jude* as a possible inspiration—hardly a model—for it (at least) offers to give a study of a whole society through specified encounters and conversations.

In the consideration of literary influences on Lawrence's mature art severe problems arise. On the one hand Lawrence is an original genius who revolutionised the novel, so that in the *execution* of his art he is beyond all simple questions of influence. On the other hand he can be seen as an inheritor of the developments in the novel of the late nineteenth and early twentieth centuries. One can even go as far back as Charlotte Brontë and conclude that her psychological and intensely poetic studies of sexual relations were waiting for a modern and less openly Romantic treatment to enforce the truth of their insights. The strikingly original study of St. John Rivers in *Jane Eyre* is a case in point, and a more specific instance could be seen in a comparison between 'The Cleopatra', a chapter of *Villette* dealing with English and Continental sexual attitudes through the symbolic use of a painting, and Lawrence's treatment of the same area in *The Captain's Doll.* Such a comparison is instructive, despite Lawrence's hostility to Charlotte Brontë when writing on her.

On a lesser level H. G. Well's overtly sexual interest in *Tono Bungay* (1909) and *The New Machiavelli* (1911), while inimical in feeling, must have helped Lawrence in his interest in exploring sexual relationships in the novel—indeed in his comments on Wells in various places he clearly valued him. Wells is directly linked with Gissing, not only because he was an unreliable friend and a reviewer of Gissing's novels, but also because he took the cue from him in dealing with 'the new woman' and in presenting a partially un-Romantic view of sexual relations. Lawrence (a voracious reader) clearly knew his Gissing, and in his letters expressed respect for him while qualifying his admiration with:

> Gissing hasn't enough energy, enough sanguinity, to capture me. But I esteem him a good deal . . . (to Edward Garnett, 21 Jan. 1912)

and 'I've no sympathy with starvers . . .' (to same, 12 Jan. 1913). He seems to have read *The Odd Women* in 1909, praising the book in a letter of July 24, 1910 to Louie Burrows. *Sons and Lovers* (1913) bears the influence of the nineteenth century, most obviously Thomas Hardy's, but perhaps the schematic presence of Clara Dawes owes not only to Hardy's thesis of woman's conventionality in the face of a rigid social code, but also comes from reading Rhoda Nunn's physical and intellectual challenge to Barfoot, who like Paul wishes to assert his masculinity by conquering the emancipated woman.

It would be fascinating to know if Lawrence had read *Born in Exile,* which stands in interesting contrast to *Women in Love.* Gissing's novel is indeed a pessimistic story of a 'starver', who can find no place in his home-country, and drifts to a death lost abroad in exile. *Women in Love* is permeated by a rejection of English society and its way of life. Parallelling Lawrence's own rejection of England, Birkin and Ursula throw up their jobs to leave England, perhaps for ever. Social conditions are quite different in Gissing's novel, of course. Godwin Peak's classlessness is a drawback in his society, Birkin having a financial independence and being in a society that does not socially stigmatise him and hinder him from finding a suitable mate. Lawrence's novel, while containing a tragic sub-plot, works towards a cautious but defiant optimism in which the individual seems able to exist transplanted from his society. The emphasis is quite unlike the hopeless pessimism of the end of *Born in Exile.*[1]

We come now to consider the revolutionary effect on our time of Lawrence's novels. His art works here in uneasy harness with the Bloomsbury drive against the inhibitions of the Victorian ethos. Lawrence was violently anti-Bloomsbury, but curiously, though not surprisingly, it seems that in our time there is little awareness of a distinction between the two forces; the *Lady Chatterley* trial has helped to establish Lawrence as a debunker of prudish inhibitions. The dangers of being a pioneer of the treatment of relationships with an explicitly sexual emphasis were apparent even in Lawrence's own lifetime, and his reception by admirers of his books as 'the high-priest of sex' seems to have affected Lawrence

himself. Unfair and beside the point as it is to blame Lawrence for the present over-awareness and cynically mechanical nature of sex in the contemporary novel, one can't help appreciating the dangers of his historical position. Lawrence is *the* great 'sexual pioneer' of the novel, and the sanest; Gissing (a minor artist) in his sexual emphasis manifestly suffered from his own perverse views arising from his role as a déclassé; Wells's sexual studies only give us the erotic egotism of Wells himself. Lawrence's life is not tainted in *such* a way, nor is his best art (*pace* the cries of 'sexual fascism' levelled at Lawrence). However, when uprooted from England his treatment of relationships went wrong—if all novels after *Women in Love* are not affected in this way, at least *The Plumed Serpent* and *Lady Chatterley's Lover* (written when he was seriously ill) are examples. *Women in Love* is a turning-point in his art and life. It can be read intelligently with widely varying responses. The novel is a puzzling one, exploring in an open and honest way, expressing some of Lawrence's extreme feelings through Birkin, and criticising for its author the limitations and excesses of their nature (Gissing was doing much the same for his position and outlook in minor art in *Born in Exile*). The pattern the novel takes, of the individual voluntarily isolating himself from his society—as Birkin eventually does despite his apparent involvement—has disturbed many readers, not all of them Marxists. Defenders may state that *Women in Love* was analysing the effects of modern society on the individual, taking the analysis further than *The Rainbow,* and providing a prophecy of the state of modern society and the individual. That this is true, does not alleviate one's unease with the novel that alienation from society is too easily achieved and taken too far, especially with the traditional English novel in mind. Lawrence is certainly honest when he shows us Birkin's interview with Will, Ursula's father, in 'Moony', and exhibits the superior arrogance with which Birkin treats the older man. However this honesty does not affect Lawrence's treatment of Birkin's position, nor provide an understanding of Ursula's 'outmoded' family-life. In fact in 'Flitting' Ursula's rupture with her parents is cursorily treated, and she leaves her old home for ever without effort, even with disgust. Lawrence's flight from England with Frieda is colouring the issue here.

To return to the truth inherent in the suggested defence of *Women in Love;* one tends to distrust a 'general truth', here that 'the modern individual is cut off from a strong sense of social unity', particularly as in contemporary fiction it has been repeated so often that it has become a truism. The very function of the novel (if the form is to have any meaning) is never to rest upon one point, but to move on to other positions by challenging generally accepted assumptions. Lawrence can hardly be blamed for modern errors, but with regard to *Women in Love* the duty and stature of a great novelist (which Lawrence is in that novel) demand that he triumph through his art over the conditions of his environment, and his personal history. This last definition is derived from observing the art of Dickens and George Eliot, and relies on the artist achieving an objective realism through personal experience which rejects both utopianism and defeatism. Lawrence was the one who correctly called Gissing 'a starver', perceiving that his art sadly reflected the misery of his life. But one might feel that ultimately *Women in Love* places such an emphasis on the individual that the dazzlingly original exploration of feeling becomes cut off from social responsibility.

One last point in connection with Lawrence is concerned with the issues involved with a fundamental concentration on the sexual. In *The Rainbow* the interrelated changes in society and sexual relationships are unfolded before our eyes, as we follow the development from the marriage of Tom and Lydia to the relationship of Ursula and Skrebensky. Objection has been made that Skrebensky is an unsatisfactory vehicle for the onus placed upon him, even in the novel's terms, where he is an intentionally unsatisfactory figure. He is unsatisfactory as a character and in general conversation, and he often only 'exists' in the highly-charged language describing love-making, scenes which refer back to previous scenes with other characters. 'Lawrence in *Women in Love* succeeds where he fails in *The Rainbow* with the Skrebensky-Ursula relationship' is a shrewd judgement; however in *The Rainbow* the intensity of the love-making scenes stands out disturbingly in their use of Ursula and Skrebensky, in that Lawrence creates an assertive poetry out of a non-living, puppet-figure. This is an indication that the sexual interest carried on from the bulk of the novel has become divorced from its perspective in the human and the real. Later Lawrence was to make a more unbalanced concentration on the sexual divorced from the social and even at times the human, illustrating the difficulties facing a major artist in working on such a level of emphasis. Even in the core of *The Rainbow* lie the seeds of a subsequent abuse of Lawrence's emphases. One is aware of how the later love-making of Will and Anna relates back to their early relationship, and a comparison of their whole marriage with that of Lydia and Tom involves a moral judgement of which the sexual is only one important element. Making the sexual the *only* index to moral and social values is quite another thing, but in an age where sex is no longer regarded with reverence, estimations of characters have become defined solely in terms of the sexual. Even minor writers of integrity, it could be suggested, must be entangled in vulgarities and dishonesties when employing a mode of writing geared to an expression of feeling through highly-charged poetry of physical relationships. All modes of writing are open to exploitation and abuse, some more than others.

History seems to have shifted strangely with regard to the sexual in literature. From the early ponderings of Kingsley over the sexually-repressed adolescence of the sensitive, we have seen a sexual emphasis which would have appalled Lawrence become paramount, self-consciously obsessed by sensation for its own sake, as the thrill of going further in shocking has burnt itself out to end in the mechanical. The act of excreting bodily liquids and solids is not a creative one, but in the modern novel the sexual act has become debased to such a process; and it would be a most dubious and sophistical interpretation to insist on a criticising intention with this emphasis. Meanwhile writers who are less obviously bent on cynical exploitation offer us embarrassing and wooden parodies of Lawrence's revolution in the novel. It is hard to believe that the following passage is not indeed at least half-facetious in its gestures towards Lawrence, but so ponderous is the novel from which it comes (Malamud's *Dubin's Lives* [1979]) that one concludes that the writer hopes to get away with being serious, as do so many prominent writers on both sides of the Atlantic:

> Dubin set the glass down and began to unbraid Fanny's warm hair. She took it out, heavy full. Her shoulders, breasts, youthful legs, were splendid. He loved her glowing flesh. Fanny removed her heart-shaped locket and his bracelet, placing them on the bookcase near the dripping red candle. She kept the ruby ring on. Forcefully she pulled his undershirt over his head; he drew down her black underpants. Fanny kissed his live cock. What they were doing they did as though the experience were new. It was a new experience. He was, in her arms, a youthful figure. On his knees he embraced her legs, kissed her between them.
>
> So geh herein zu mir.
>
> Du mir erwälte Braut! [A Bach cantata is playing on the hi-fi.]
>
> She led him to bed, flipped aside the blanket. He drew it over their hips . . .
>
> They wrestled in the narrow bed, she with her youth; he with his wiles. At her climax Fanny's mouth slackened; she shut her eyes as though in disbelief and came in silence.
>
> Mit harfen und mit zimbeln schön.
>
> Dubin slept with his arms around her; she with her hand cupping his balls . . .

NOTES

[1] Many original creative writers have to struggle against a hostile reality and must resist the pressures to succumb to the hopelessness of a 'starver' (see Wordsworth's *Resolution and Independence*) often for most of their lives. Lawrence was a particularly heroic resister in this respect, though it did lead him into dreams of a model community and to New Mexico.

DRAMA

Lois S. Josephs

SOURCE: "The Women of Eugene O'Neill: Sex Role Stereotypes," in *Ball State University Forum*, Vol. XIV, No. 3, Summer, 1973, pp. 3-8.

[*In the following essay, Josephs confronts Eugene O'Neill's failure to treat the women in his dramas in any but traditional, sexually-stereotyped ways.*]

Although Ibsen voiced a prophecy of doom for the sexual double standard in *A Doll's House* nearly a century ago, Western playwrights have begun only recently to approach the radicalism of his remedy. Harold Pinter's Ruth in *The Homecoming* provides both a searing criticism of exploitation inherent in the unconscious sexual drives of men and a destructive resolution for the characters involved. She abandons her role as wife and mother to serve the varied lusts and fantasies of her husband's father and brothers. Edward Albee's Jenny in *Everything in the Garden* solves her husband's need for both more money and her presence at home for his convenience by turning to high-priced prostitution. Her spouse learns of her choice with initial shock but eventually accepts it with grace and enlarged respect. David Hare's three women, playing their roles in the microcosmic setting of a girl's boarding school in the play *Slag,* illustrate by the complexities of their interrelationships the dramatic force of satire in women's liberation paralleled with a sympathetic view of the female within the role stereotype. By conventional social standards the three playwrights'[1] resolutions are bizarre and unrealistic, yet they transcend simple complaints about male hypocrisy by suggesting the power of women to alter or resist their conventional sexual roles while retaining private integrity. Perhaps neither story shocks its hearers as much as Nora's rebellion did in its day.

Earlier attempts to deal with the vision of Ibsen must be classed as halfway measures. Shaw regards his Major Barbara with sympathy but with amusement; she simply uses the social order as a new toy upon which to apply her life force. His Mrs. Warren tears aside the exploitative pretensions of her lovers, but Shaw wishes they were better men so she could become a proper wife and mother. The various Joans of Arc, from Brecht to Shaw, act in man's war with society rather than as symbols of sexuality; in a sense they serve as Virgins to a secular world. The women in Williams and in most of Albee live in constant frustration, their tragedies imposed by God or Fate or Freud; there is no way out for them or for their men. Arthur Miller fails to extend his concern for women to suggestions that they alter roles, their tragedies always growing out of male inadequacy, while Thornton Wilder's idealism frequently includes the traditional concept of self-sacrificing wife and mother, especially in *Our Town.* Sartre's Lesbian, Inez, in *No Exit,* acts more deviously than does her male rival. To all these playwrights and characters, the social order deserves to be changed, perhaps overthrown, but hardly through a revolution in sexual roles.

No better example than Eugene O'Neill can be found of the failure of Ibsen's successors to attack the sexual double standard as a central social problem. Why single out O'Neill? Probably because for one thing he concerned himself so intensely with social issues, and for another his plots depend repeatedly on exposing the dilemmas of women in their relationships with men.

O'Neill's early plays, the one acts, deal essentially with men. This is true even in the more sophisticated *Emperor Jones* and *The Hairy Ape.* But a traditional view of women soon emerged in other plays, such as *Ile* where the tragedy lies not in the passivity of a woman who follows her man unthinkingly but in the stubbornness of the man she follows. In O'Neill's first long play, *Beyond the Horizon,* Ruth also follows the man she chooses; and her choice, the crucial issue of her life, determines the manner of her life. Her tragedy follows her error in choice rather than her obvious inability to act independently.

In subsequent plays, whether experimental in form like *The Great God Brown* and *The Iceman Cometh* or more realistic like *Desire Under the Elms* and *Anna Christie,* O'Neill's women play roles within a closely defined, stereotyped sex culture. Cybel, the Earth-Mother prostitute of *The Great God Brown,* feeds both Dion and Brown despite their change of roles. Her purpose is to give sustenance and her life is molded to that purpose. O'Neill applauds her sacrifice; one imagines her always in her room, always ready to give metaphorical breast-feeding, never having a life of her own. The prostitutes in *The Iceman Cometh* play their maternal roles; they speak of their clients as stepchildren, of Rocky, the pimp, as the true child, the mischievous but lovable boy who requires maternal care. Pearl and Margie can hate only when sober and even then their hatred focuses, not on their humiliating roles as women, but on their despair and defeat in a cruel world. While in these plays O'Neill's prostitutes are generally supportive, his good women may be destructive; he never regards them as victims of a male-dominated society in which their sex roles have been defined beyond their control. Socially moral women, Bessie and Evelyn in *The Iceman Cometh* and Margaret in *The Great God Brown,* have infinite but destructive patience in marriages to men who, consumed by restraint, fail to reform.

A stereotyped tragedy also shapes the life of O'Neill's heroine Anna Christie, whose past as a prostitute keeps her from loving Mat Burke freely. She confesses, hoping for forgiveness, but he rejects her despite her valid reasons for having turned to prostitution. While Anna has O'Neill's sympathy, he never suggests that Mat, shaped by society, could do other than he does. It is not the double sexual standard that attracts O'Neill's interest, but rather the tragic implications inherent in the situation.

Abbie, in *Desire Under the Elms,* like Cybel, assumes roles as sexual temptress (for an old and lustful man) and as Earth Mother (for his childish, petulant son). O'Neill manifests concern for a woman beaten down by a Puritan male unable to provide warmth or tenderness; Abbie, like Eben's mother, is totally unfulfilled by Cabot. But even here, tragedy relates to stereotyped female needs. Abbie has no sense of independence. O'Neill extends his moral judgments to all of the characters in the play and does raise Abbie to heroic stature; yet his vision never encompasses the basic sickness in the male-female relationships dictated by society. O'Neill emphasizes lust, guilt, the tragedy written into the cold New England earth as driving forces, but never questions Abbie's assumption that she must be totally owned by Eben, an assumption so deeply ingrained in her culturally-assumed role that she kills her son to prove that she belongs to Eben alone.

O'Neill fails to question traditional sex roles even when he deals so prophetically and perceptively with the effects of racial injustice in *All God's Chillun Got Wings.* Ella cannot love Jim because her culturally-instilled hatred of blackness overcomes her sense of his worth and her love for him as a man; and at a time when the idea of black-white marriage was far from the minds of most writers, O'Neill explored with great insight the social problems of miscegenation. Here his force equals that of Delaney in *A Taste of Honey* or Jones in *Dutchman.* The conflicts of the play expose the insipid qualities of interracial plots in recent dramas such as that of the film *Guess Who's Coming to Dinner.* Yet Ella's failure with Jim, attributed by O'Neill to deep-rooted racial prejudice, seems in a more fundamental sense to be the result of her inability to function as a self-determined, independent human being. Moreover, while one can easily imagine O'Neill portraying a black woman caught in a similar double bind of hopeless prejudice and helpless dependence as in the drama of Ella's self-destruction, one cannot picture an O'Neill male—white or black—yielding up his life for prejudice-crossed love. Thus the root of the matter is sexual rather than racial. Ironically, and perhaps prophetically for those who see relationships between black militancy and women's liberation, Hattie sees the submissive, dependent role as one for white women only, when she tells Jim that he should have married a strong, black woman, a woman of his own kind.

Strange Interlude, Mourning Becomes Electra, and *A Long Day's Journey into Night* illustrate most forcefully of all how O'Neill fails to treat his women in any but traditional ways. Despite his insistence to the contrary,[2] their sex roles stem from O'Neill's Freudian view of the female psyche, and these roles largely determine the dramatic conflicts of the plays. O'Neill is sympathetic, understanding, and compassionate, but his insights extend only to the uniquely feminine needs of his women. Nina Leeds, Christine and Lavinia, Mary Tyrone, all stand in dramatically pivotal positions, but the pulling and straining of their men's lives, careers, neuroses

determine their behavior: Darrell functions as a doctor outside of his relationship with Nina; Ezra Mannon and Orin go off to fight and Adam Brant works as a sailor; James Tyrone has been a successful actor, while his sons either try to write or deplore their inability to act.

In *Strange Interlude* Professor Leeds uses Nina as a wife-substitute, advising her not to marry Gordon until after the war. But if O'Neill explores the destructive, selfish, quality of a father's possessive love of his daughter, he fails to perceive that Nina, as human being, need not belong to anyone: to lover, to father, to son. All the men in the play perceive Nina as an owned object whose favors may or may not be bestowed at will but whose needs require that she bestow those favors in one direction or another. Since she listens to her father, she fails Gordon. Her hatred then descends on her father whose motives she begins to comprehend. Instead of attempting independence, she mitigates her guilt by bestowing favors again, this time to any number of soldiers who have returned from the war. Her role is that of nurse and Earth Mother.

Nina enjoys none of these illicit relationships, though it is always clear that the men with whom she sleeps are nourished by her body given in atonement. Purged of guilt, Nina can return home ready to assume a mother's role—one that O'Neill views as essential to her being as a woman—with a dull husband and a son whom she names, predictably, after her dead lover. O'Neill does provide her with a lover, but the contrived reasons for her affair are suspect. Her affair in the past, her son to be married, she retreats to Marsden, father figure and womb. She has come full cycle, fulfilled only once in her life, never by anything within herself, but for a short time when surrounded by Father Charlie, Son Gordon, Husband Sam, and Lover Darrell.

Christine and Lavinia, mother and daughter, are replicas of each other, especially in their confused needs for brother, father, and lover—their motives and behavior constituting a Freudian package in *Mourning Becomes Electra* which O'Neill parallels with the Oresteia. Fate and the unconscious, Greek tradition and Freudian assumptions fuse in one of O'Neill's most ambitious if cumbersome plays. Christine, though her children are grown, somehow finds it less difficult to poison her husband than to leave him. Does one simply not leave a Mannon? Yet Christine's money and position never seem important to her, and she slips easily into a plan to run away by ship with Adam Brant when the discovery of Ezra's murder brings the realization that she can never bring Adam home. Is it that she hates to relinquish Orin and that Brant, as lover and future husband, cannot fulfill her? Yet faced with a choice when her plans are frustrated, she chooses to give up Orin for Brant. It is difficult to understand Christine's motives for murder in the light of her apparent rationality; she never appears to be mad, and her hatred of Ezra Mannon seems always to be under control. To O'Neill, her husband's death offers the only possible release from her role as his wife, but to the reader, less enamored of simplistic Freudianism, this determinism appears contrived.

Given Christine's behavior as accomplished fact, however, that of Lavinia is more convincing because it seems a logical consequence of her mother's actions. While Lavinia never breaks through the traditional female sex role—her passionate attachment to the beautiful, strong, uneducated native is no more than an exotic stereotype—she has logical motives for wanting revenge on her father's killers and then for refusing marriage in order to care for Orin. She does, after all, instigate her mother's death through Orin's murder of Brant.

The life of the unconscious is less crucial to the conflicts of *A Long Day's Journey into Night,* where problems stem from the unfortunate marriage of a young, inexperienced girl to a selfish, egotistical actor. Mary Tyrone, reared in the seclusion and protection of a convent, innocent and in love, leaves her convent to marry the debonaire actor, James Tyrone, who refuses to sacrifice even a small part of his career to marriage. Their married life exists in a succession of strange hotel rooms, where Mary waits alone. Even less convincing is Tyrone's stinginess; he hires an incompetent physician who uses drugs indiscriminately so that Mary's illness ends in drug addiction. Between cures, she retreats into a fantasy life—a tragic figure she is and one that symbolizes the gradual disintegration of a family. But ironically when she dreams of her simple life in the convent, O'Neill speaks nostalgically through her fantasies for the simplicity and innocence of that virgin life. Never condemning the limitations of a protected childhood, he sees them as romantically suited to a woman's nature.

O'Neill's vision of women's role is reinforced by the picture he offers of Essie Miller in *Ah, Wilderness.* Wife and mother, made happy and good by circumstances obviously compatible with her nature, she epitomizes the best in traditional motherhood—loving, giving, not overprotective nor too possessive but always at home where she belongs in O'Neill's one happy play about family life. Her raison d'être and her peace of mind parallel her acceptance of a traditional role as wife and mother. The pleasures in *Ah, Wilderness* of family life, each member in his proper place, approximate those of Whittier in *Snowbound,* except that in O'Neill's play, the maiden aunt, content in Whittier's poem, suffers because she can never marry her alcoholic suitor.

O'Neill's stage, a center for experiments in dramatic form, consistently reflected concern and involvement with social and cultural issues. O'Neill spoke of social change in a variety of areas at a time when suffragettes were chaining themselves to lamp posts; yet he failed to mention the feminist movement in any of his plays. Whatever experimental form O'Neill uses for drama, whatever his sympathy for his heroine, and however prophetic his social vision, as with Hattie's black chauvinism in *All God's Chillun Got Wings,* he never

reached beyond traditional sex roles as defined by Western culture. Women in O'Neill's plays exist in the home, and alternatives to a stereotyped way of life are never considered. His failure symbolizes the failure of American playwrights expecially—most of them male and most of them concerned about social issues—to grasp this particular nettle. Willy Loman, victim of empty American materialistic values, stands as an ordinary man who achieves heroic stature; he has no female counterpart. Even Lillian Hellman regards her women in traditional ways—the subtly grand view of Regina's manipulations, evil but acceptably female in nature, in *The Little Foxes.* In the newest American theatre of all, every institution except male dominance comes under attack. LeRoi Jones' *Dutchman* places Eve in her traditional role as temptress, one she also assumes in Van Itallie's *The Serpent.* In a different but equally traditional form, Leonard Cohen's plain heroine in *The New Step* finds great joy in the revelation that her beautiful roommate has been rejected by a man who prefers an ugly, deformed but Earth-Mother type. Somehow Nora never crossed the Atlantic.

NOTES

[1] It is interesting to note that the plots of all three plays are British since Albee's play is an adaptation of a British plot.

[2] O'Neill has repeatedly denied the influence of Freud on his works, but most critics agree that O'Neill may not wish to recognize openly that influence, because it is second hand.

Albert Bermel

SOURCE: "Wedekind's Frosty Spring," in *Yale/Theatre,* Vol. 6, No. 2, Winter, 1975, pp. 53-70.

[*In the following essay, Bermel analyzes Frank Wedekind's drama of adolescent life and sexuality in late nineteenth-century Germany,* Spring's Awakening.]

> To Dr. Waldemar Zozo: You, Sir, were the Navy psychiatrist who examined me in Norfolk, Va., about 1942, and told me I was unusually immature. I knew that, but professional confirmation caused me deep anguish. In anguish I was not immature.
>
> --Saul Bellow, *Herzog*

If most criticism of *Spring's Awakening* is on the right track, Wedekind's first play has gone hopelessly out of date. He is said to have deplored the prudishness of German and Swiss-German burghers; to have shown how it inhibited children when they reached puberty; and to have found the inhibitions tragic.[1]

Since 1891, when the play was written, sex-education has advanced tidally. Recent news reports out of West Germany tell of a *Sexwelle,* a sex-wave, which, according to an official of the Federal Ministry of Family and Youth, makes "Germans want to put their bedrooms on the street." It seems that

> some social scientists say the phenomenon represents an overreaction against old German taboos and the stresses of the Nazi period. One suggested that it could be a sublimation of now-outlawed militarism . . .
>
> While it is undoubtedly part of a wider trend sweeping Western civilization, the wave is said to reflect aspects of German history and culture as interpreted by the Western part of the divided nation. There is a preoccupation with technique—with becoming "an efficient sex machine," as some have put it. . . .

Nazi authoritarianism is supposed to have "deprived a German generation of exposure to the work of the Austrian Jew Sigmund Freud." As a result, instructional films on love-making and documentaries on the incidence of prostitution now command wide audiences. Mail-order houses specialize in "erotic literature and stimulants." A columnist who proffered sex-advice in the family weekly *Neue Illustrierte* became known as "the sexual pope."

As though to give posthumous consolation to the generation that Wedekind grew up in, an experiment in West Berlin collected "schoolchildren ranging in age from eight to fourteen." They "were encouraged by scientists of the city's Free University to undress and enact scenes of sexual intercourse," the activity being under the auspices of the University's Institute of Psychology.

> The participants were apparently found on nearby playgrounds. . . . Five to fifteen children participated each day, with some fifty youngsters believed to have been involved. . . .
>
> Two psychologists took the children swimming and they returned "voluptuously tired." Everyone lay on cushions and mattresses arranged on the floor to imitate a giant bed.
>
> "The psychologists provoked insinuations of sexual activity that were then played out in pantomime by Thomas and Koksie," the reports said, referring to otherwise unidentified children.
>
> "At first we wanted them to enact or intimate coitus, but that did not come to pass because Koksie, giggling shamefully, turned the other way on the floor."
>
> Later. . . . the group played at forfeits, in which everyone eventually got undressed.[2]

In America books on "human sexual response" (evoked under controlled and hygienic laboratory conditions) skate to the top of the best-seller list if the publishers give them enough advertising muscle. But the Germans, it appears, are a little ahead (not for long, probably) with their pre-teenagers rounded up like calves from

"nearby playgrounds." Has West Germany turned into an open sex arena? Not yet. The news of the experiment with Thomas and Koksie and other youngsters, who may or may not have been strangers to one another, "shocked the public and the city administration." The sex-wave, the shock and the experiment conducted by lipsmacking "scientists" supply evidence that the sort of warped mentalities Wedekind wrote about persist: prurience is another face of prudery.

Spring's Awakening contains scenes of flagellation, lovemaking between two fourteen-year-olds, masturbation, and an idyllic homosexual affair between two boys. These scenes are the reason why it was not professionally performed for fifteen years. But the sexual escapades are part of a wryly poetic, tragic, and comic study of a group of characters. The three principals are children. Wendla Bergmann, who has just reached her fourteenth birthday, is smitten with Melchior Gabor, a boy of the same age. Melchior has read up scholarly material on making love and reproduction. He knows what to do and does it. Wendla becomes pregnant and dies at the hands of an abortionist. The third child, Moritz Stiefel, a girlish boy of fifteen, is baffled and tormented by the "awakening" of erotic impulses. Unable to cope with them and with the standards that have been prescribed for him at home and at school, unable to escape from his misery, Moritz commits suicide.

Summarized thus, the action sounds Teutonically morbid. But Wedekind splashes comedy into every scene and the dialogue darts about from grisliness to satire, from lyrical sweetness to farce. Wedekind's astringent humor is most overt in his treatment of the adults in the play, the parents and the schoolteachers, most of whom he ridicules unmercifully. But he also makes fun of the youngsters, gracefully but perseveringly, as he counterpoints their own tragic view of their plight with his comic view. His notes on the play, written some twenty years after he had finished it, are worth considering as an antidote to the conventional critical views:

> Since about 1901, above all since Max Reinhardt put it on the stage [in 1906 and in a denatured version], it has been regarded as an angry, deadly, earnest tragedy, as a thesis play, as a polemic in the service of sexual enlightenment—or whatever the current slogans of the fussy, pedantic lower middle class may be. It makes me wonder if I shall live to see the book [sic] taken for what, twenty years ago, I wrote it as—a sunny image of life in every scene of which I tried to exploit an unburdened humor for all it was worth. . . . [3]

One of Wedekind's early translators nevertheless believes that Wedekind has a "thesis," namely, "that it is a fatal error to bring up children. . . . in ignorance of their sexual nature," an explosive remark for the American public in 1912, but an unsatisfactory one as criticism. And one of the few critics in English who has dealt with Wedekind's work at any length, H. F. Garten, suggests that

Wedekind lays the blame on the narrow-mindedness of the schoolmasters and the moral cowardice of the parents who shrink from enlightening their children on the facts of life.[4]

This sort of talk about Wedekind's laying blame or setting down a thesis or promoting enlightenment misses the point that the parents and schoolteachers in the play have muddled through the same sort of upbringing as the children's. It is not so much that they are cowards as that they know no way of speaking to the children about sex. If they tried, they would blunder horribly. Sensing this, they turn evasive. Cowardice is one thing; ineptitude something else. The grownups might have made life easier for the youngsters if they had been able to think back to their own adolescent years, but if they did, Wedekind would have been writing a modern German (or American) sex-advice column and, with any luck, have become known as the sexual pope. The parents cannot speak to the children about anything. In itself, this is material for comedy. What gives the play its tragic cast is the self-destructive impulses (which are related to the erotic ones) in the three principals.

The play begins on Wendla's fourteenth birthday, her entry into womanhood. Frau Bergmann, her mother, has made her a long dress—Wendla calls it a "penitential robe"—and justifies the length by claiming that Wendla would be cold in a shorter garment, as though growth means merely more square inches of skin exposed to the elements. But we see what is in her mind when she says:

> Other girls are gawky and gangling at your age. You're just the opposite.—Who knows what you'll be like when the others are fully developed?

She worries that her daughter may look more tempting in a short hemline. Wendla replies strangely, "Who knows? Maybe I won't be around." This is the first of her premonitions that she will die young.

The premonitions, casually voiced, soon make it clear that Wendla is a character of some size and one of the few rewarding young girl's roles in the drama—not quite a Juliet or an Iphigenia but far more substantial than the run of insipidly naive heroines who have never had a dirty thought. With the instinct of a blossoming woman she rejects the "penitential robe" and decides to go on wearing her short, little girl's dress which will do more for her.

Wendla's home life is not a bad one. It contrasts favorably with that of her schoolfriend, Martha, whom we meet two scenes later.[5] When Martha threaded a blue ribbon through the yoke of her nightdress, as some of her friends had done, her mother pulled her out of bed by the hair:

> I lay on the floor and shrieked and yelled. Enter Papa. Rip! Off comes my nightdress! I head for the door. "So that's it," he shouts, "you'd like to go out like that, wouldn't you?". . . . It was

freezing. I went back in. I had to spend the whole night on the floor in a sack.

What is interesting in this part of the scene is not so much Martha's being treated by her parents as an incipient whore because she wears a blue ribbon in her nightdress, nor her father's behavior in ripping the nightdress off, nor even her punishment, sleeping in a sack, but Wendla's seriocomic reply: "I'd be glad to sleep in your sack for you." There speaks the modern, guilt-charged temperament. Wendla wants to suffer, even to do penance, for others.

As they talk the girls walk through an outdoor scene. The spring wind along the street feels blustery; it makes their hearts beat faster. Melchior goes by, Martha and a third girl admire his "marvelous head" and compare him with "the young Alexander when he was a pupil of Aristotle's." Wendla speaks less committally about Melchior. She mentions that at a recent party he told her that "he didn't believe in anything: God, an afterlife, or anything at all." His remarks seem to have provoked and, at the same time, appealed to her.

Her next scene, the climax of the first act, brings her and Melchior together on a sunny afternoon in a forest. She has been out to gather woodruff for making May wine. She lay for a while in the moss, dreaming. Melchior has been roaming through the forest and almost took her for "a dryad fallen from the branches." It seems that Wendla periodically visits the poor to take them food, clothes, and money. She enjoys these trips; perhaps they lighten her middle-class conscience: she is doing something. Melchior ascribes her pleasure to the local pastor's preachings about the joy of self-sacrifice. This seems unlikely. Wendla does not really sacrifice anything she takes to the poor, only a little time. The charity looks like a substitute for a more drastic kind of giving. We are reminded of how she thought earlier of taking Martha's place in the coal sack when she tells Melchior that she lay in the moss a few minutes before and dreamed that

> I was a poor, poor beggar girl. I was sent into the streets at five in the morning. I had to beg all day, in rain and storm, among rough hard-hearted people, and if I came home in the evening, shivering with hunger and cold, and didn't bring as much as my father expected, I'd get beaten. . . .

The mention of being beaten turns her thoughts back to Martha, who is

> beaten night after night. Next day you can see the welts. What she must have to suffer!. . . . I pity her so, I often cry into my pillow in the middle of the night. . . . I'd gladly take her place for a week or so. . . .
>
> I've tried beating myself to find out how it feels inside.

But beating oneself is not the same as being beaten. She suddenly picks up a switch from the ground and asks Melchior, "Wouldn't you like to hit me with it once?"

He would not. What, and draw blood? Is she mad?

The climax of this scene (and of the act) disqualifies all criticism that tells us that if only parents and children had sat down together and bartered grievances and information—had, in the jargon of our time, thrown down barriers and eliminated a communications gap—this particular spring would have come in tranquilly to the chirping of birds and the unfolding of petals. Wendla pleads with Melchior to flay her. He tries a few tentative strokes with the switch. She cannot feel a thing, she says, and urges him to hit her on the legs. He still cannot strike hard enough to hurt her. He throws away the stick and begins to punch her with his fists. Then she feels the pain and cries out. But he cannot stop his arms from working nor his eyes from pouring tears. By now Wendla is screaming. Melchior lets up, and runs away, still sobbing. He is ashamed of his lack of self-control or the misdirection of his lack of self-control.

In the next act Wendla's older sister, Ina, has just given birth for the third time in two-and-a-half years. Frau Bergmann announces, "Just think, Wendla, the stork paid Ina a visit last night. Brought her a little boy." Wendla retorts, "That explains the never-ending influenza." She inquires whether her mother was there when the stork visited. Frau Bergmann says "it had just flown away," after leaving a brooch as a consolation gift for Wendla. After more of this fencing Wendla responds with some choice syncretism. Outside the house she can see

> a man three times the size of an ox. With feet like steamboats. He's holding a bedstead under his chin and fiddling "The Watch on the Rhine" on it.

But she still has to ask her mother straight out, "How does it happen?—You can't seriously expect me to believe in the stork—at fourteen." Frau Bergmann prevaricates. She cannot say. She would deserve to be—and breaks off the sentence. She will tell Wendla "everything. . . . But not today. . . . tomorrow, next week." Finally, under more pressure from Wendla and after saying that she deserves to go to prison, and to have Wendla taken away from here, she euphemizes.

> To have a child—one must love the man—to whom one is married—love him as only a husband can be loved. One must love him so much, one must love him, Wendla, as you at your age are incapable of loving. . . . Now you know.

She rushes her daughter away to Ina's for chocolate and cakes, as if the girl were four, not fourteen. Wendla's dress, she observes, looks shorter than ever.

A couple of scenes later Wendla is up in a hayloft with Melchior, about to lose her girlhood once and for all. He

tells her to get away from him or he will throw her down, which is exactly the way to tempt Wendla Bergmann to stay. Then she is asking him not to kiss her, and saying, "Don't, don't!" Here the scene has broken lines in place of text.[6] Not that explicit stage instructions are necessary in this ancestor of bucolic movie-seduction episodes. But what, above all else, distinguishes this scene from its thousands of bastard descendants is a brief speech by Melchior:

> There is no such thing as love! That's a fact.— It's all just selfishness and self-seeking.—I love you as little as you love me.

Wedekind avoids romantic slosh. He shows us two children attracted to one another and using one another.

Wendla is now in love with love. She walks in the garden to keep out of her mother's watchful eye, saying she will look for violets. She feels ecstatic, and yet sufficiently outside herself to be awed by her feelings. If she stayed in the house she might say something to her mother.

When Wendla reappears, a great deal later in the action, she is in bed with palpitations, headaches, giddiness, shivering. The family doctor prescribes exercises and a weird intake of pills: "Begin with three or four a day and increase the dose as rapidly as you can stand it." Ina, the mother of three, has no advice for her sister, but does speak one beautiful line that is an unconscious metaphor for Wendla at fourteen-and-a-half:

> Your plane tree is changing color again already.— Can you see it from your bed? A short-lived splendor, hardly worth the joy we feel to see it come and go.

Frau Bergmann tells Wendla she has anemia. Wendla can get the truth out of her only by saying she is sure she has dropsy and will soon die. If this is not a life-and-death disease, why does her mother keep crying? Frau Bergmann at last tells what she knows, but cannot resist adding an accusation:

> You're going to have a baby, Wendla! A baby! Why have you done this to me?

Wendla says it is impossible for her to have a baby; she is not married. Besides—a line that corresponds to Melchior's earlier one: "I never loved anyone but you, Mother." The words have a comic innocence about them, and yet are pathetic. Wendla has not loved, and is not loved. She surrendered to a hunger.

She then wants to know why her mother did not tell her "everything." Frau Bergmann replies with a question:

> How could I have told such things to a fourteen-year-old girl? It would have been the end of the world. I've treated you no different than my mother treated me.

Her counsel now is: Trust in God, hope for the best, be brave. The dialogue is interrupted and the scene concluded by the arrival of a neighbor called Mother Schmidt who does not enter the room or the action. Later we are told that Mother Schmidt was an amateur abortionist and that, as a result of her ministrations, Wendla died.

In one sense we could indeed say that Wendla's death is due to her mother's failure to tell her "everything" and to provide her with contraception. But it is equally due to the absence of a Peace Corps or a VISTA or social work on which this counterpart of a modern suburban teenager could expend some of her missionary energies. Wendla has the soul of a martyr but her goodness gets squandered on daydreams of suffering. Yet it seems to me that Wedekind is writing to a broader theme: the bittersweet agonies of puberty and adolescence. In retrospect we look back on these years fondly and use terms like "calf love." But they are a testing time and not every youngster surmounts them.

Wendla's opposite number in the play, Moritz, is as much a glutton for punishment as she is. And his life is almost as closely linked as hers is with Melchior. Moritz is a year older than his friend, but less self-dependent, less informed; and so Melchior serves as his protector and mentor. On a warm Sunday evening out of doors they talk about the mysterious "stirrings of manhood." But Moritz cannot stop fretting about his homework (Central America, Louis XV, sixty verses of Homer, seven equations, a Latin exercise), due the following morning. Next year's classroom has space for only sixty boys; unless his grades improve he is one of the seven who will flunk. What will his parents do then? He feels terrified, especially when he thinks that they "could have had a hundred better children than me."[7] In his quaintly formal school boy lingo, he asks:

> Don't you agree, Melchior, that the sense of shame
> is simply a product of a person's upbringing?

He can speak of this "sense of shame," just about, but he cannot do anything to overcome it or reconcile himself to it.

> I can remember even as a child of five feeling
> embarrassed if anyone turned up the queen of
> hearts: she wore a décolleté.

He thinks of the queen of hearts because "I hear Mama carried me under her heart." That, and the fact that hens lay eggs, constitute his knowledge of reproduction. Melchior promises to undertake "quite an interesting assignment"—to write up a clear, brief explanation of sex. Moritz asks him to add illustrations in the margin. Melchior suddenly says, "You're like a girl," and then lets the subject drop. Moritz does not take it up nor challenge the statement.

For Moritz, with his feminine tendencies, the queen of hearts may represent a sort of bosom-envy. But his

sexual yearnings not only flutter between masculine and feminine desires; they are tainted by his fear of school. He hesitantly mentions his first sexual dream, of legs in blue tights climbing over a lectern. In this scene Wedekind again feeds humor into nearly every speech without playing down Moritz's anguish.

To most of the older children Moritz is a comic butt. One of the girls says:

> He embarrasses you when you meet him. At the
> children's party. . . . he offered me some
> chocolates. . . . They were soft and warm! . . . .
> He said he'd had them too long in his trouser pocket!

Moritz as the source of warm, flowing chocolate from a pants pocket: it is a devastating comment, especially from a girl. The boys jeer at his anxiety over grades. One day he steals into the classroom to look at the register and find out whether he has been promoted. He has. But only provisionally. Still, he is all "happiness—bliss—jubilation" for the time being. He adds, "If I didn't get my promotion I was going to shoot myself." The boys take this remark as crude bravado, all of them except Melchior.

Moritz continues to drive himself. He sits up until three in the morning contending with verb conjugations and the like; next day he falls asleep in class. But, he says,

> You feel so good when you've won a victory over
> yourself. . . . I mean to work and work till my
> eyes pop out of my head. . . .
>
> If I don't get through, Papa will have a stroke and
> Mama will go to the madhouse.

The irony in Moritz's situation is that the best he can hope for is to stay in the class. He is competing with another boy for the bottom position. The other boy has had six failures during the term, Moritz five. Failure still looms; he lives on the edge of the abyss.

Melchior invites him home to drink tea, relax, and to chat about the essay he wrote for Moritz about reproduction. The house is pleasant; Melchior's mother, Frau Gabor, is the most approachable of the adults in the play; and, warmed by the tea and friendship and the temporary absence of school pressure, Moritz turns garrulous. He tells Melchior a story related by his grandmother about a queen who was "fabulously beautiful," but could not see, hear, eat, drink, laugh, or kiss because she unfortunately lacked a head. But along came a king with two heads. A magician transplanted one of the heads on to her shoulders—really advanced surgery—and they lived happily ever after. Moritz says,

> I can't get the headless queen out of my mind. If
> I see a beautiful girl, I see her without a head,
> then suddenly I myself seem to be a headless
> queen.

Moritz's fellow-feeling for the headless queen, the most potent symbol in the play for his femininity, has a variation rung on it by the author when the two boys come around to talking about Melchior's sex essay. Moritz says,

> I was the most strongly affected by what you wrote about girls. . . . To have to suffer wrong is sweeter than to do wrong. . . . [It] seems to me the essence of all earthly bliss. . . . A girl keeps herself free of everything bitter till the last moment, and then has the pleasure of seeing all heaven break over her. . . . By comparison, a man's satisfaction seems to me shallow, stagnant.

Moritz flunks at school. He turns to the only adult he knows who might assist him, Melchior's mother, and asks her to lend him the fare to America; if she cannot, he may have to put an end to himself. Wedekind encapsulates this part of the story in Frau Gabor's letter of reply. She wants to soothe Moritz, but "frankly, your veiled threats to take your own life. . . . have slightly alienated my sympathies." Like Wendla's mother, she can offer only useless exhortation:

> Chin up!. . . . Such crises of one kind or another confront each of us and must be overcome. If everyone had recourse to poison or the dagger there would soon be no human beings left in the world.[8]

With this avenue closed to him, Moritz sees no escape. He wanders out of the town and toward some marshes. He does not "belong."

> I've signed no contract with the Almighty. . . . I don't hold my parents responsible.

Even into the dusk of this scene, reminiscent of many German films of the 1920s with their underlit, tortured faces and acres of bosky shadow, Wedekind keeps injecting comedy. The plight of Moritz is to be simultaneously laughed and wept at:

> I was an infant when I came into the world, or no doubt I'd have been smart enough to become someone else.

He is going to die, but the thought that he has never had sex with a woman holds him back; he is still talking to himself:

> There's something to be ashamed of [shame again!] in having been human without getting to know the most human thing of all.—You were in Egypt, dear sir, and did not see the Pyramids?[9]

The memory of a certain voluptuous Fraülein Snandulia with whom he danced at a party tempts him to stay alive. Another décolleté:

> Her silk dress was cut low back and front. . . . In front, so low you could almost pass out. She couldn't have been wearing a slip.

A broken line interrupts the dialogue again, presumably to show that, as a pitiful gesture to life, Moritz is masturbating.

From the low-cut Snandulia his thoughts edge away to the "many happy evenings" he has spent with Melchior, from a male role to a female one; and then to the grave and beyond the grave to faces that beckon, "the headless queen, the headless queen—sympathy awaiting me with soft arms." A girl comes up behind him and seizes him by the shoulder. Her name is Ilse; she models for artists and sleeps with them. A girl—an available, older girl—a reprieve! She talks of having been mistreated by an artist, hit and then kissed, brutal love of the sort the masochistic Moritz is bound to envy. Then she exacerbates his masculine longings: she invites him to go home with her and drink warm goat's milk; she will curl his hair, give him a rocking horse, baby him.

Ilse has been away from home for four nights. She has just come from the "priapia," a fraternal organization that sounds like a phallic, avant-garde collection of young Rotarians or Jaycees. When she invites Moritz to go with her he remembers that he has left some of his homework undone: the Sassanids, the Sermon on the Mount, and the parallelepipedon. Ilse is cold; she takes off, saying, "By the time any of you [the schoolboys] are ready, I'll be on the rubbish heap."

Moritz has missed his chance, thinking about his homework when "a single word would have done it." Like the General in *The Balcony* he pictures Ilse for an instant as "an unruly filly" wearing black silk stockings, on his bed with "great crystal mirrors" over it, and there he would love to strangle her. He wants, no matter how, to be a man before he dies.

Or to be a woman. "To be you, Ilse!" Brutalized, manhandled, but kissed. He masturbates again (two broken lines this time) among the willows of the marshes and the reeds, the *Königskerzen* which Eric Bentley has translated literally and suggestively as "king's tapers." Moritz burns the discouraging letter from Frau Gabor. In its sparks he sees "shooting stars." Darkness has settled over the marshes. The expiring flame of the letter marks the transition from twilight to night and the end of Moritz's life.

We do not see him die; nor do we know how he died when his funeral begins in a later scene. The local pastor (the one who believes in self-sacrifice) has come to bury Moritz, not to praise him. Attacked by a Christian impulse, he consigns the boy to hell everlasting for having taken his own life. Moritz's father, in his only appearance in the play, says, "The boy was no son of mine. I never liked him—from the beginning." The school principal remarks that a suicide "saves the moral order the necessity of passing judgment." But judgment has been passed. Not one of the grownups has a generous word to speak in memory of Moritz. Two citizens commiserate with his father, not for having lost a son, but for having had a bad son.

Only the children—some of them—pay tribute to Moritz. Two girls, Ilse and Martha, throw flowers on his grave, ivy and anemones. Ilse, the last person to see Moritz, reveals that he shot himself. She heard the shot as she was leaving, and returned next morning to take the pistol out of his hand. It appears that he blew his head off, ending his life as a headless queen. The last word he spoke that Ilse remembers is parallelepipedon, a reference to some unfinished math. A parallelepipedon is a solid figure bounded by six parallelograms. An example would be a coffin.

Moritz's end, like Wendla's, is potently symbolic. She evokes the image of the plane tree and its short burst of color. She has premonitions before dying of a "monster" flying into her, and of the old man outside the window playing that once-popular song by Max Schneckenburger "The Watch on the Rhine"—an Old Man Death. Moritz dies, a "headless queen" among the "king's tapers", an unmourned flame. Both children are claimed by the frosts and rigors of spring.

The epic structure of *Spring's Awakening* allows Wedekind to devote some of its nineteen scenes to secondary characters and subplots without losing the impetus of the double main plot. We see into the lives of some of Wendla's girl friends, such as Martha and Ilse. Among the boys are two who, like Moritz, are afraid of these girls. The relationship between them develops into a far more explicit homosexual love than that between Moritz and Melchior.

Hänschen Rilow and Ernst Röbel have a scene together in a vineyard that corresponds to the lovemaking between Melchior and Wendla in the hayloft. Ernst is the boy who competed with Moritz for the lowest position in the class; now that Moritz is dead he will get it. Hänschen's earlier appearances have included a solo scene in which he studied a reproduction of Palma Vecchio's Venus and sent himself into masturbatory frenzies and terrors ("You suck the marrow from my bones, you crook my back, you steal the light from my young eyes. . . . My heart! I'm having convulsions!"), after which he dropped the picture into the toilet bowl. Hänschen is the only boy who speaks about Moritz at the funeral with affectionate reverence. He drops a spadeful of earth into the grave and remembers Moritz's "angelic simplicity."

In their love scene Ernst and Hänschen lie down together in the vineyard during the grape harvest, sated with the fruit; they talk about themselves and the autumn evening. Near the end, Hänschen leans over and kisses Ernst on the mouth. For many years the scene went unperformed, and has been omitted from some translations. Yet it is charming and fragile throughout, as candid as any of Gide's and less apologetic; and it has none of the affectation, bitchiness, and groaning ardor of commercial homosexual theatre. Ernst pleads, "I love you, Hänschen, as I have never loved a living soul," and the passion rings true. Hänschen seems to feel it belongs only to this interregnum between boyhood

and manhood. "When we think back in thirty years," he says, "maybe we'll just make a joke of it."

The lynch-pin of the main plot, Melchior, may well be the author's self-portrait, although it hardly matters whether he corresponds to the Frank Wedekind his schoolfellows knew. Melchior claims that behavior—his, at any rate—springs from selfishness. He may say this as a reaction to the self-sacrifice preached by the pastor, the schoolmasters, and his parents. He is capable of a neurotic blow-up, as when he flays Wendla on the legs and then punches her, an attack predicted in the "worst dream" he ever had in which he found himself "flogging our dog Lolo so long he couldn't move his legs." The children, boys and girls, like him; he is a favorite among the teachers, and seeing him with Moritz, one teacher says,

> That my best student should feel himself attracted to my worst is quite incomprehensible to me.

For all his talk of the inevitability of selfishness, Melchior is troubled when he comes across examples of it, for instance, Faust's abandonment of Gretchen. He and Moritz have read the play at school, and he says of Faust's faithlessness:

> Suppose Faust just promised to marry the girl and then left her; as I see it, he wouldn't be a bit less to blame. . . . Gretchen would die of a broken heart.

Later he will see himself as a junior Faust and Wendla his Gretchen after he learns that she died; he will feel despicable, not so much for not having kept faith with her as for not having loved her.

After Moritz's death the essay of "explanation" Melchior wrote for him is discovered, and the teachers, practiced graphologists all, trace it back to Melchior. These teachers are a farcical bunch whom Wedekind cannot begin to take seriously. He gives them names like Zungenschlag (Tonguethump) and Sonnenstich (Sunstroke). They summon Melchior to a faculty meeting. After a great deal of preliminary talk about whether the windows should be kept open or shut, and about the possibilities of Moritz's death setting off "a suicide epidemic such as has already broken out in various other schools," they accuse Melchior of being the author of

> a treatise twenty pages long in dialogue form, entitled *Copulation,* equipped with life-size illustrations and teeming with shameless indecencies, a document that would meet the most extravagant demands of an abandoned libertine, a connoisseur in pornographic literature. . . .

Melchior does not deny the charge, does not have much chance to say anything at all, but he manages to mention that what he wrote

> is fact, no more, no less. . . . Please show me one offense against morals in the document.

This might be Wedekind speaking about *Spring's Awakening* to people who later called him a pornographer. Like the play, the "treatise" is written "in dialogue form." We can assume that it was modeled on Socratic argumentation.

The teachers have no respect for their pupils, as they have none for each other. Buffoons or no, they are cruel disciplinarians. Melchior is expelled.

His father then determines to send him to reform school. Frau Gabor opposes this move bitterly and eloquently, even threatening to leave her husband if he goes through with it. If anybody is to blame, she says, it is she; but she cannot believe her son is anything worse than artless, childlike, and innocent. Her speeches in this scene show the adult world during some of its few fine moments in the play. But Herr Gabor argues:

> Anyone who could write what Melchior wrote must be rotten to the core; the very marrow is infected. . . . This was no unintentional lapse, but the documentation, with horrifying clarity, of. . . . a natural drive toward immorality for its own sake. This piece of writing is evidence of that extreme degree of spiritual corruption which we lawyers describe as "moral depravity."

These forensics do not impress Frau Gabor. A reform school will wreck Melchior with its "crudity" and "filth."

At this point Wedekind twists the situation inside out with stinging efficiency. Herr Gabor reveals that Wendla's mother came to see him that morning (not long before Wendla's death), bringing a letter from Melchior, in which the boy admits that "he has sinned against her, et cetera, et cetera, but that naturally he'll answer for everything." He asks his wife what he should do with Melchior now. With the hurt pride of a more-than-usually affectionate mother, she does not hesitate. Her toleration and sympathy crumble, as they did before when she wrote to Moritz. Melchior must go to the reform school.

The brief scene in the reform school—another one omitted from some earlier translations—shows us the conditions Frau Gabor had feared her son would be exposed to, although that sheltered lady would hardly have imagined the game the young inmates have devised. They stand in a circle, place a coin on the floor, masturbate, and the boy who ejaculates on to the coin wins it. Melchior is invited to join in, and politely declines. He worries about staying out, being different; yet he is more afraid of taking part because "they're killing themselves, that's what prison's done for them." Some of the other youngsters in the play are just as terrified of the consequences of masturbation.[10] Sage though he is, Melchior believes as much as the other boys do in old wives' (or old husbands') tales.

But the reform school will not have time to dirty him. He climbs through a skylight, wraps a handkerchief around the lightning conductor, and slides down it sixty feet to the ground. The last boy who tried this trick had to be picked up in pieces. Melchior is either luckier or more agile.

In the last scene of the play he has taken refuge in a graveyard. His coat is in rags, his pockets are empty, his conscience is playing him up. He is being pursued by the rest of the play. He thinks of Wendla's pregnancy and worries because the girl always takes the brunt of an affair. Perhaps he should follow Moritz's example, suicide: "No mortal ever wandered among graves so full of envy." Yet he does not have the courage to die voluntarily, and he cannot believe he has sinned. He longs for release: "If only madness would overtake me."

And this is what happens, although the "madness" is more like a dream. He comes in turn upon the grave of Wendla, the ghost of Moritz, and an apparition called the Man in the Mask. In this sepulchral evening, with leaves ominously rustling and "ragged clouds" that "race across the moon," the action dissolves into nightmarish coincidences, a dramatic heightening of the afflictions of his conscience. He knocks over the cross on Moritz's grave without noticing. Then, among the hundreds of tombstones, he chances on Wendla's, and is stunned to find she is dead. The inscription coyly says that she "died of anemia" and adds, "Blessed are the pure in heart." He concludes that she died from the pregnancy and that "I am her murderer!"

The ghost of Moritz "comes stomping over the graves," with his shattered head under his arm, like Anne Boleyn in the old music hall song. As a headless queen, perhaps he can be saved by Melchior, who would somehow have to play a two-headed king. He repeatedly asks Melchior to give him his hand, and professes to be pleased with his present existence, if it can be called an existence. He is "above it all." He keeps mentioning how much he laughs these days; he never did when he was alive. He even smiled when he attended his own funeral and watched the proceedings. He is trying to lure Melchior into death, offering him "peace, contentment." Melchior replies:

> If I agree, it will be from self-contempt. I see myself as a pariah. . . . I can't conceive of anything that could stand between me and doom. To myself I am the most ·execrable creature on earth.

Moritz is asking why he still hesitates, when the "thing" that could stand between Melchior and doom appears.

The Man in the Mask refuses to identify himself. He is a function, not a person. He has come to save Melchior from his conscience and from Moritz's dead clasp. First, he reassures Melchior about Wendla:

> That little girl would have given birth splendidly. She was superbly built. It was Mother Schmidt's abortion pills that did for her.

And then he will take Melchior away, "among men," and acquaint him "with everything of interest the world has to offer." He would, he says, "give your survival my best attention." He chastises Moritz for having committed suicide. It came about through morality,

> The real product of two imaginary factors. . . . "I ought to" and "I want to". . . . Your parents would no more have died of [the disgrace] than you need have done.

Thus the Man in the Mask persuades Melchior to live, grow up, and become the author of *Spring's Awakening*.

Critics usually assume that the Man in the Mask is also a limited self-portrait, Melchior grown up, partly because Wedekind himself played the role more than once, partly because the work is "dedicated by the author to the Man in the Mask." If these critics are right, the dedication is a joke, and a feeble one, a pointless stab at some self-aggrandizement. We cannot assign an unmistakable meaning or identity to this character, but his dramatic function during Melchior's stay in the graveyard is unmistakable. He brings Melchior out of his peripeteia and then steers him away from a tragic ending (Melchior's suicide). He is a life force debating with a death force, Moritz, for a claim on Melchior's soul. He confirms this by saying to Moritz that he appeared to him, too:

> You don't remember me? Even at the last moment you were hesitating between death and . . . life.

During the debate Melchior listens and tells himself that "they can't both be the Devil." But Wedekind shows that one of them is. Moritz. Since his translation from life to death he has become a personification of Mephistopheles, the Tempter, who promises the Faustian Melchior amusement and detachment, the cool pleasures of remaining "above it all." As his opponent, Life, the Man in the Mask happens to be the only wholly sympathetic adult in the play the only one who can say, "I would give your survival my best attention." He saves Melchior from the fate of Moritz and Wendla, pulls him past the "spring" and into the later seasons of adulthood. He will take him "among men."

It is characteristic of Wedekind's irony that he did not think such an adult existed. The Man in the Mask is an unfulfilled wish, a smudged hope in the author's imagination. And in Melchior's. For if the scene is a dream— as Moritz's headless ghost tells us it must be—then both the ghost of Moritz and the Man in the Mask are Melchior. He has reached the crisis in his life the combat with his private "morality" between those "two imaginary factors," the I-ought-to (I ought to punish myself for what I have done) and the I-want-to (I want to go on living).

The Man in the Mask wins the debate. Melchior goes off with him. The ghost of Moritz remains, alone, to deliver the last lines which are both comic and agonized:

> So here I sit with my head on my arm. . . . I shall go back to my little plot, set up my cross that that madcap trampled down, and when everything is in order, I shall lie on my back again, warm myself with the putrefaction, and smile . . .

Wedekind, we can recall, said he wrote the play as "a sunny image of life." The "sunny image" may be stretching matters. But of life? Undoubtedly. Life as a stirred-up amalgam of Schiller's joyous ode and the misgivings of a rejuvenated Faust. That is the meaning of the dedication to the Man in the Mask. The play is finally dedicated to Life.

NOTES

[1] To be fair about the criticism: some of it does revere the play, but for reasons that turn it into a relic, a lifeless transition in the history of the drama. It is seen as a "precursor" of Symbolism or Expressionism or as an "example of raw Naturalism," depending on which textbook you read.

[2] These quotations are taken from the New York *Times*. Those relating to the "sex-wave" from a story filed by Ralph Blumenthal, Dec. 22, 1968; the ones about the juvenile sex experiment from an unsigned story published on April 13, 1970.

[3] Translated by Eric Bentley in his Notes to *The Modern Theatre*, Vol. 6, pp. 286-288. The quotations from the play, too, are Dr. Bentley's translation, from the same book.

[4] The "thesis" quotation comes from Francis J. Ziegler's introduction to his translation, *The Awakening of Spring* (Philadelphia: 1912). For H. F. Garten's commentary on the play, see his *Modern German Drama* (New York: 1962).

The "thesis" view of the play persists. In his comments on the National Theatre's revival of *Spring's Awakening* at the Old Vic last June, Benedict Nightingale wrote: "There's a side of me that was depressed to see the National bravely fighting a battle long since won. You could, I imagine, ransack stalls, circle, and gallery without finding one pale and skulking figure who would admit to finding anything controversial, let alone shocking, in the idea that adolescents shouldn't be fobbed off with stories of the stork or threats of retributive blindness. If there is still a conspiracy of parents, clergy and teachers to institutionalise shame and guilt, it does not usually convene at the Old Vic. . . ." (*New Statesman*, 7 June 1974.)

[5] Wedekind's apparently arbitrary plotting, with its broken-off scenes, is worked out with care. There are five scenes in Act 1. Wendla appears in Scenes 1 and 3; Melchior in Scenes 2 and 4. Scene 5 is an encounter between the two of them. This pattern is all the more elegant for not being obtrusive.

In synopsizing the action here, I am following each of the three main characters through their scenes in order, one character at a time. The plotting in the play gets complex. The main plot is a double one, Wendla-Melchior and Moritz-Melchior. But Wendla and Moritz are involved in their own secondary plots, their relationships with their families, schoolfellows, and other people.

[6] I have not been able to discover whether the broken lines were inserted through caution on Wedekind's part or, more likely, owing to the reticence of his original publisher. This is the only enacted coition in the play, but the broken lines break in at subsequent places when there is masturbation on stage.

[7] Most of the children in the play feel unworthy of their parents. In another scene Martha says her father and mother "would feel something was missing if they didn't have a little mess like me for a daughter."

[8] The cold comfort of Frau Gabor's if-everybody argument is another sign of how little Wedekind's play has dated. During the youthful uprisings in this country in the late 1960s sober warnings of the if-everybody stripe poured out of the middle-aged, especially from those Roebuck Ramsdens who were once liberals or socialists. If everybody, they said and wrote, practiced violence or threw bombs or undermined society in some other way, there would be no society left to undermine. The tautology seemed particularly egregious since "everybody" was certainly not thinking of doing any such things. These messengers of "reason" and "commonsense" were bent on protecting themselves, not on offering sincere advice to the young people or putting themselves out to try to understand them.

[9] Wedekind must have felt pleased with this line about the Pyramids. He used it again in a later play *King Nicolo.*

[10] Hänschen, inflamed by his Palma Vecchio print, thinks of developing a crooked back, lackluster eyes, and marrowless bones. Moritz, brooding about Fraülein Snandulia the seductress and Ilse the plaything of artists, cries, "It saps my strength." We laugh at such sentiments today, the supposed "dangers of self-pollution" and so on, yet they pervade our own society. In the introduction to a 1961 edition of Wilhelm Stekel's *Auto-Erotism* Fredric Wertham mentions that "a pamphlet addressed to boys and issued by the U.S. Public Health Service says auto-erotism (which it terms 'self abuse') 'may seriously hinder a boy's progress toward vigorous manhood.'" In this department, too, Wedekind is our contemporary. Spring still awakens in the young to the clatter of accompanying prohibitions.

Kristin Morrison

SOURCE: "Defeated Sexuality in the Plays and Novels of Samuel Beckett," in *Comparative Drama*, Vol. 14, No. 1, Spring, 1980, pp. 18-34.

[*In the following essay, Morrison studies the prevalent motifs of sterility, abortion, sexual disability, deprivation, and futility in Beckett's dramas and novels.*]

"I summoned up my remaining strength and said, Abort, abort. . . ."[1] This cry of the reluctant father in the short novel *First Love* suggests an element which is prevalent throughout Samuel Beckett's work: concern with the physical details of reproduction, its success or lack of success, and specifically the impotence, sterility, and decay of the sexual organs, repulsive copulation and the destruction of progeny. The earlier novels abound with scenes of grotesque and defeated sexual activity (e.g., Watt's laborious and futile fondling of Mrs. Gorman[2]) but in the plays such lengthy scenes are usually replaced by a single word, phrase, or allusion, often oblique and obscure but as important in its context as are the more elaborate fictional passages in theirs. It is these varied and elusive sexual references in the plays which I will discuss, showing them to be not random and incidental details, but rather, as in the fiction, significant metaphors for the misery of human life itself.

Throughout Beckett's career, the fiction with its greater explicitness has provided an important context for words and phrases which appear in the plays. In the increasing condensation which has marked his later work, there is no diminution of sexual references, but their meaning is not always immediately apparent. It is thus very helpful to keep the earlier novels in mind while looking at the later plays. *The Unnamable* (1949) provides a representative and particularly repulsive reference to copulation: "the two cunts . . . the one for ever accursed that ejected me into this world and the other, infundibuliform, in which, pumping my likes, I tried to take my revenge."[3] This passage provides the most explicit statement of motive for the hatred which permeates the story of "Mahood's" return home, where he stamps "underfoot the unrecognizable remains of [his] family, here a face, there a stomach. . . ." Birth—and the sexuality that leads to it—is the great enemy. The only triumph over this enemy is death, a death which *precedes* birth, an annihilation which *precedes* existence, as the narrator makes clear later in this novel when he states, "I'm looking for my mother to kill her, I should have thought of that a bit earlier, before being born" (p. 391).

Copious references of this kind in the fiction alert the reader to the importance of similar, but quite elliptical, references in the plays: that very important "panhysterectomy" in *Embers,* Minnie's menopause in *All That Fall,* the negligent fathers in *Endgame,* Winnie's sexless non-existent legs and breasts in *Happy Days.* These references present a striking coherence from novel to novel, from play to play: over and over again abortion or some kind of sterilization is presented as the term of human existence.[4]

The radio drama *Embers* (1959) provides a useful place to begin this discussion of defeated sexuality because as an early play it is relatively detailed and explicit, and the sexual references (though brief and for the most part unobtrusive) fit together quite neatly. Because the play is directed entirely to the ear and not to the eye, words and their interrelationships have even more importance than they do in a stage play where gestures affect meaning: when Holloway states, "I have a panhysterectomy at nine,"[5] his listeners cannot miss the word and find themselves wondering what a panhysterectomy has to do with the action, the meaning of this play. The answer is, everything.

The main voice in *Embers* is that of Henry, a lonely, tormented man who speaks to himself and conjures up the voices of others in order to cover the sound of the sea, which he constantly hears and hates. The dramatic situation is thus a kind of monologue; and although there is another voice heard at length, that of Anna, his wife, it is clear her voice exists "in" his mind; she is not physically present there on the beach with him (stage directions indicate his movements make noise on the shingles, hers do not). These imaginary conversations include his father (who now will not answer him, will not "appear") and some brief anecdotes concerning his daughter, Addie, with her Music Master and with her Riding Master. Interspersed with these voices are the sounds of galloping hooves and clashing stones summoned by Henry to "drown out" the sucking sound of the sea (heard constantly throughout the play, sometimes softer, sometimes louder). In addition to creating these imaginary sounds and voices, Henry also tells himself a story about an old man named Bolton and a doctor named Holloway. These, then, are the pieces of the structure of the drama: fragments of narrative, snatches of sound, memories worked into imaginary conversations, various characters who relate to Henry in terms of his feelings about them. Among these relationships the most important is that of Henry (as son) to his father and mother, and Henry (as father) to his daughter; of lesser importance is the relationship of Henry (as husband) to his wife. Less clear (but tantalizingly important) is the relationship between Bolton and Holloway and their joint relation to Henry. What ties all these elements together are a few references to methods of preventing or destroying the results of copulation: sterilization and abortion.

The first reference to abortion comes a third of the way through the play. Henry has just been speaking about his own hatred of the sea, his attempts to get away from it, his father's love of the sea and apparent suicide by drowning; he has digressed at length on his Bolton-Holloway story then switches back suddenly to memories of his father:

> Father! *(Pause.)* You wouldn't know me now, you'd be sorry you ever had me, but you were that already, a washout, that's the last I heard from you, a washout. *(Pause. Imitating father's voice.)* "Are you coming for a dip?" "No." "Come on, come on." "No." Glare, stump to door, turn, glare. "A washout, that's all you are, a washout!" *(Violent slam of door. Pause.)* Again! *(Slam. Pause.)*

> Slam life shut like that! *(Pause.)* Washout. *(Pause.)* Wish to Christ she had. (pp. 101f)

In this flow of memory with its psychological rather than logical organization, the phrase "Wish to Christ she had" is elliptical but explicable: wish to Christ she had washed (me) out. This man who feels so keenly his father's disappointment, shares his father's sorrow that he was ever born: he should have been aborted (or perhaps prevented by douche). This wish is Henry's own ineffectual equivalent of his father's suicide. But Henry's wish for death, to have been washed from the womb and never to have lived, extends not only to his own relationship with his parents but also to his relationship with his child. Immediately after the line "Wish to Christ she had. *(Pause.)*" the monologue continues with memories about his wife and daughter:

> Never met Ada, did you, or did you, I can't remember, no matter, no one'd know her now. *(Pause.)* What turned her against me do you think, the child I suppose, horrid little creature, wish to God we'd never had her. . . . (p. 102)

He, as father, duplicates his own father's disappointment; he, too, would prefer a child never to have been born; both important women in his life, mother and wife, should have aborted rather than delivered: "better off dead, better off dead" (p. 103).

Even the copulation which led to these unfortunate births is described with words which suggest a certain displeasure in the act: "It took us a long time to have her. *(Pause.)* Years we kept hammering away at it" (p. 114). In Henry's mind copulation is associated with the sea—"Where we did it at last for the first time" (p. 113)—and the sea is the antithesis of life. (The clashing sounds of stones and horses' hooves he describes as preferable to the sound of the sea: "That's life! . . . Not this . . . *(pause)* . . . sucking!" pp. 112f.)

The fact that reproduction—its act and its result—is connected with death, not life, is further indicated by the Bolton-Holloway story. Bolton is, according to Henry's story, "an old man in great trouble" (p. 98) who has called his doctor on a cold wintry night and begged a special service, something the doctor has repeatedly refused despite Bolton's desperate pleas. The most that Holloway is willing to do for Bolton is give him an injection. Nothing more explicit is stated, but the details of the scene—the deteriorated old man, his tearful pleas, the candle "guttering all over the place" (p. 120), the cold embers—all suggest that Bolton is begging to be put out of his misery, to be given something more permanent than a standard painkilling injection. This association with voluntary death is reinforced by the fact that Henry has resumed his story at this point immediately after reflecting on his father's suicide and his speculation that Ada may have witnessed it (pp. 118f); the story seems, in fact, to be an escape from that memory, a more acceptable distraction, or perhaps a disguised way of thinking about his father's death (both Bolton and his father have "eyes drowned," p. 121).

In his impatience to get away, to avoid any involvement in Bolton's death, Holloway indicates he has other work to do: "If it's an injection you want, Bolton, let down your trousers and I'll give you one. I have a panhysterectomy at nine" (p. 119). After all the colloquial vagueness and imprecision of Henry's language—"washout," "hammering away," "did it"—and his reliance on imagery and mystery in the Bolton-Holloway story, this sudden intrusion of a technical term is startling: the audience notices "panhysterectomy" and is meant to notice it. Somehow the play deals with radical sterilization—not only with frustrated copulation, abortion, and suicide, but with the destruction of the possibility of any existence at all, the utimate state of preannihilation for those "better off dead."

But, of course, Beckett's technical terms, allusions, erudite references are not explicated by an audience while the play is in process; they have their effect almost unconsciously. So, too, with this single technical term; "panhysterectomy" is spoken and the play moves swiftly on. The final lines of the play, however, achieve their impact through whatever meaning "panhysterectomy" has managed to register with the audience. Henry moves toward the sea, continuing his monologue, looking at his appointment book:

> This evening . . . (*Pause.*) Nothing this evening. (*Pause.*) Tomorrow . . . tomorrow . . . plumber at nine, then nothing. (*Pause. Puzzled.*) Plumber at nine? (*Pause.*) Ah yes, the waste. (*Pause.*) Words. (*Pause.*) Saturday . . . nothing. Sunday . . . Sunday . . . nothing all day. (*Pause.*) Nothing, all day nothing. (*Pause.*) All day all night nothing. (*Pause.*) Not a sound. (p. 121)

"Plumber at nine" echoes "panhysterectomy at nine," and both plumber and doctor deal with the "waste." As is so often the case, Beckett turns a simple ordinary word into a complex pun: the waste is the drain through which the washing out occurs (whether of sink or womb), but it also refers to that which is drained off, that which is discarded because it is waste, refuse; even further, the word "waste" serves as a commentary, "the waste" meaning "such loss, what a pity!" When all is drained, when all is discarded, when all is lost, nothing remains. And this, in fact, is Henry's ideal state: "All day all night nothing. Not a sound." Parents, wives, children, all those causes and effects of reproduction, all that pervasive sucking sea is a torment for him: being a father, a lover, a child are equally intolerable. He prefers imaginary relationships, conjured sounds rather than actual ones. He wants a panhysterectomy for his life.

This concern with impaired reproductive powers is found in other early plays. In *All That Fall* (radio drama first broadcast in 1957), Mrs. Rooney, "a lady in her seventies," laments the loss of "little Minnie" (her daughter, it seems, who died long ago) and chooses to speculate about Minnie's menopause: "In her forties now she'd be, I don't know, fifty, girding up her lovely little loins, getting ready for the change. . . ."[6] As she continues her laborious progress to the train station to meet her blind husband, Mrs. Rooney continually inquires about the wives, daughters, mothers of those she meets (there is an occasional father mentioned, but women relatives predominate); she receives answers such as Mr. Tyler's reply that his daughter is "Fair, fair. They removed everything, you know, the whole . . . er . . . bag of tricks. Now I am grandchildless" (p. 38). Even some of the animals heard along the way are described as sexually impaired: the play opens with references to Christie's hinny and later Mrs. Rooney speculates whether hinnies can procreate. (There are also sounds of maternity, a wooly little lamb and its mother, and references to a "true" donkey, all of which serves to emphasize the sterility of the hinny.)

The natural barrenness of women after menopause or hysterectomy is accompanied, in this play as it is in *Embers,* by suggestions of man's hatred for children. Mr. Tyler curses the "wet Saturday afternoon" of his own conception (p. 39) and Mr. Rooney raises the question, "Did you ever wish to kill a child?" (p. 74). In the context of the children's howling and jeering (pp. 74, 79), this is a question any adult might ask, but there is some indication Mr. Rooney may have acted on his impulse. He pretends not to know why the train has been delayed; he tries to prevent Jerry from telling Mrs. Rooney that "a little child fell out of the carriage, On to the line, Ma'am. (*Pause.*) Under the wheels, Ma'am" (pp. 90f). These final words provide an unusually shocking climax to the play, not only as ironic contrast to the lines from Scripture which Mrs. Rooney had sardonically quoted earlier—"The Lord upholdeth all that fall and raiseth up all those that be bowed down" (p. 88)—but also as an implied revelation about Mr. Rooney. What was he doing with the ball Jerry said he left behind on the train; had he used it to lure the child; had he taken it away from the child; did he push the child?

In this play, too, birth and death are closely related, not only by the metaphors of impaired sexuality and child murder but by even more explicit statements. Mrs. Rooney recalls the "mind doctor" whom she consulted—"hoping he might shed a little light on my lifelong preoccupation with horses' buttocks" (p. 83)—and from whom she heard the "story of a little girl, very strange and unhappy in her ways, and how he treated her unsuccessfully over a period of years and was finally obliged to give up the case. He could find nothing wrong with her, he said. The only thing wrong with her as far as he could see was that she was dying. And she did in fact die, shortly after he washed his hands of her" (p. 83). What has haunted Mrs. Rooney about this story is the Doctor's comment "as if he had had a revelation. The trouble with her was she had never been really born!" (p. 84). Rarely is Beckett as direct and obvious as he is in these early plays: "The only thing wrong with her as far as he could see was that she was dying" is a clear statement about "the human condition," as timeless as any *memento mori* of medieval devotion; "The trouble with her was she had never been really born" capsulates the state of every Beckettian character, whose partial life is a living death. Mrs. Rooney's concern with forms of sterility and frustrated procreation and Mr. Rooney's desires to "nip some young doom in the bud" (p. 74) fit into the larger context of the fact that all living beings must die and thus their lives are never fully alive because of this shadow of death. This fact, in turn, has its larger, "cosmic" context in the premise of a benevolent God who watches over all life protectively, a premise Mr. and Mrs. Rooney find laughable. Thus they, too, are "all alone in that great empty house" (p. 87) of their world, "destroyed [as Mrs. Rooney says of herself] with sorrow and pining and gentility and church-going and fat and rheumatism and childlessness" (p. 37). They are not themselves children of a heavenly father nor are they parents of a solacing child: "It's like the sparrows, than many of which we are of more value, they weren't sparrows at all" (p. 86). This play, too, ends with Henry's comforting and tormenting "nothing."

In *Endgame* (1957), a long one-act for the stage, there is no mention of abortion, hysterectomy, sterilization, or similar impairment; instead, the play, like the fictional piece *First Love,* emphasizes the fear that procreation will succeed and an ancillary disgust with the consequent burden of life. Clov, for example, says he has been trying "to be off," to die, ever since he was "whelped";[7] Hamm calls his father "accursed progenitor" (p. 9) and later asks angrily why Nagg engendered him (p. 49). Both Hamm and Clov are grotesquely concerned lest further procreation occur: they want to kill the flea so that humanity won't start all over again (p. 33); and at the end of the play they worry that the small boy on the horizon is "a potential procreator" (p. 78).

This desire to "end"—not only Hamm's individual existence but that of all living things—is not merely an expression of generalized *Angst* but has more specific connection with the parent-child relationships in the play: a missing, negligent father stands at the center of Hamm's experience of loss and constitutes a mutilation of his life equivalent to the physical excisions mentioned in *Embers* and *All That Fall*. The importance of the absent father is established throughout the play by the contrast between the story Hamm tells and his own actual relationship with his father. Hamm's "chronicle" deals with a wasted world in which there are, apparently, only a few people still alive. A man comes crawling out of the devastation to beg food for his dying son; Hamm tries to persuade this man to abandon his son, then to enter Hamm's service (where, presumably, there will be food and shelter); in both versions of the story (pp. 52-54, 59-60) the man asks instead to bring his son with him to share these benefits. This refusal of father to abandon son haunts Hamm; it is one of the last things he talks about before achieving his own end:

> You don't want to abandon him? You want him

to bloom while you are withering? Be there to solace your last million last moments?

> *(Pause.)*

> He doesn't realize, all he knows is hunger, and cold, and death to crown it all. But you! You ought to know what the earth is like, nowadays. Oh I put him before his responsibilities! (p. 83)

Hamm's "beneficent" argument tries to establish that it would be better for the child to die since life in the world is miserable, but his terms "bloom" and "withering" betray the real envy age has of youth. As a deteriorating adult, Hamm resents the vigor and potential of childhood. But even more he resents and envies the devotion of this father to this son because it represents a loving care Hamm himself never experienced yet still yearns for. In an attempt to establish his independence, Hamm boasts not having had a father (p. 38), but later in the play he acknowledges Nagg and even tells him the story of devoted father and needy son (pp. 48ff). At the end of this narration Hamm insists they pray: Nagg begins, "Our Father, which art" but after several intervening lines Hamm comments, "The bastard! He doesn't exist!" (p. 55). And, indeed, for Hamm a powerful and loving father never has existed, and that is why his life appears a wasteland which no amount of fantasy can alter.

Nagg's memories indicate the extent of Hamm's paternal deprivation: "Whom did you call when you were a tiny boy, and were frightened, in the dark? Your mother? No. Me. We let you cry. Then we moved you out of earshot, so that we might sleep in peace" (p. 56). Nagg goes on to criticize the way Hamm treats him now when their roles of dependency are reversed: "I was asleep, as happy as a king, and you woke me up to have me listen to you. It wasn't indispensable, you didn't really need to have me listen to you" (p. 56). But, of course, that is exactly what Hamm needs. He has never gotten over being a frightened child in the dark, with Nagg his "only hope." So now, when he wants to feel powerful, he plays the role of tyrant father, withholding comfort from all his "sons" (dependent Nagg, adopted Clov, suppliant beggars and dogs). And when he wants to end, to die, he simply imagines that frightening double role, the weak child neglected by his powerful father, the aged father neglected by his adult son (p. 69). Hamm calls to them both, father and son, and they do not answer. Thus he is once more, at the end of his life, "a solitary child" afraid, in the dark (p. 70), the dark which is death. By terminating himself, Hamm kills both the negligent father (whom he hates and has become) and the helpless child (whom he once was and now resents). Here, too, as in *Embers,* both parent and child are "better off dead." The play ends as it began, with Hamm's reference to the "old stancher," a final ironic play on words: the primary loyalty of blood relationships is destroyed; parents and children have cut each other out of their lives. Only the rag that binds the wound remains.

In *Happy Days* (1961), one of Beckett's few full-length dramas, physical action is almost entirely absent; and as a result the single strenuous bodily movement which finally occurs constitutes a release of tension, a welcome climax in an otherwise rigid and stifling day. Appropriately enough, this climactic event is a parody of sexual intercourse and as such serves to connect elements in the play which otherwise seem to be unrelated. Here, too, as in *Embers, All That Fall,* and *Endgame,* Beckett is concerned with impaired sexuality. Yes, it is certainly true that—as Hugh Kenner has commented—*Happy Days* presents "an emptiness filled by indomitable energy"[8] and that in some general way the play has to do with a perhaps futile attempt to find, or make, meaning in an absurd world; but more than that, the play deals quite specifically with sexual disability, its cause and its result.

The principal image of sexual disability is Winnie's physical immobilization. For the whole of Act I she is "imbedded up to above her waist" in earth, which she calls that "old extinguisher."[9] That it is sexuality which has been extinguished is indicated by the anecdote about Mr. and Mrs. Shower, by her comments on the dirty postcard, and by her repeated references to hog setae. As she chatters to herself she recounts the remarks made by the last people to see her, Mr. and Mrs. Shower: "What's the idea? he says—stuck up to her diddies in the bleeding ground—coarse fellow—What does it mean? he says—What's it meant to mean?" (p. 43). This question finds the beginning of an answer in his further suggestion: "Why doesn't he get her out? he says—referring to you [Willie] my dear—What good is she to him like that?—What good is he to her like that?—and so on—usual tosh." When this "coarse fellow" asserts that he would dig her out even with his bare hands, Winnie assumes the couple are man and wife. This connection indicates that what is lost by Winnie's burial is not merely physical mobility (for that, a friend or relative might dig one out), but access to sexual organs: Winnie is no good, as a wife, to Willie, nor is Willie any good as a husband while she is buried up to her waist; a real man, a coarse fellow, would dig her out even with his bare hands.

That Willie leaves her where she is because of his own sexual disability is suggested by the incident of the postcard and the hog setae. Throughout the first part of Act I Winnie has, with great comic difficulty, been struggling to read the words inscribed on her hairbrush; her eventual triumph—"fully guaranteed genuine pure hog's setae"—occurs while Willie relishes a postcard which Winnie judges to be "genuine pure filth" (p. 19). She rejects the pornographic picture and returns to her intellectual pursuits, wondering for the rest of the act about the meaning of the word "hog" (and not, as one might expect, about the presumably more obscure word "setae"). A climax for these apparently unrelated details occurs at the end of Act I when Willie finally speaks to her, announcing the definition of "hog" to be "castrated male swine" (p. 47); thus the one thing he chooses to say makes explicit yet another image of sexual impair-

ment. Whether from some actual physical incapacity of his own or simply from Winnie's rejection of "filth," Willie, too, is associated with sexual deprivation.

Winnie remains buried, refusing to notice her loss. The mechanism of denial by which she copes with sexual deprivation is indicated by a remark she makes in Act I: "And should one day the earth cover my breasts, then I shall never have seen my breasts, no one ever have seen my breasts" (p. 38). Thus because they cannot now be seen, her nether regions have in effect never existed. When in Act II the earth indeed covers her breasts as she stands buried up to her neck, all her sexuality is lost except for fantasy and memory, all her physical fire extinguished.

As is usual in Beckett's drama, fantasy and memory (anecdotes and stories the characters recount) are crucial elements in establishing the coherence of the play as a whole. In addition to the anecdote about Mr. and Mrs. Shower (or Cooker, Winnie isn't sure of the name) who comment on her useless buried state, Winnie also enlivens her daily monologue with a series of literary allusions, with memories of her first love, her first kiss, her courtship by Willie, but most important, with her story, "when all else fails" (p. 54). The literary allusions serve as ironic counterpoint to Winnie's reliance on language as a substitute for "life" and her determined optimism in the presence of ultimate disaster (her comic pleasure in quotations containing the word "woe"; her eager association with the blighted loves of Ophelia and Juliet). The various memories also serve a similar ironic function. Most revealing, however, is the story Winnie tells herself, which, like the Holloway-Bolton story in *Embers,* serves to focus the various sexual references in the play on death, not life, establishing once again Beckett's repeated emphasis on impaired reproductivity. The story concerns a little girl, Milly, who gets up early and begins to undress her doll (Milly, it would seem, herself sleeps naked since one of Winnie's corrections in her narrative involves backtracking to add that Milly "slipped on her nightgown," p. 55). As Winnie gets to the description of undressing the doll, with its associations of surreptitiousness and wickedness ("crept under the table," "scolding her") she mentions a mouse and for some reason begins to feel uneasy, leaving the narrative and calling on Willie for attention. He, as usual, ignores her, so she begins a long digression, including reference to sadness after song (less explicable to her than sadness after intimate sexual intercourse, which she takes for granted), and another reference to Mr. Shower and her own buried legs; then, after it becomes apparent Willie is not going to reply to her repeated call for help, she suddenly plunges back into her narrative at the point where she had abandoned it, describes the mouse running up Mildred's thigh, imitates her piercing screams, and lists all the family members who came running to see "what on earth could possibly be the matter." But they arrive "Too late. *(Pause.)* Too late" (p. 59). The story itself is innocent enough, quite general in its description of a childhood terror; what makes it seem fraught with special meaning is its association with the various sexual references in the digression and the concern with nakedness and surreptitiousness in the narrative itself. Whatever "up her little thigh" means to Winnie (whose legs are fully protected), it is clear that something terrible has happened, something irrevocable. Winnie's only solace after this ritualistic reliving of an intense and climactic moment, is to comment that "it can't be long now, until the bell for sleep. *(Pause.)* Then you may close your eyes, then you *must* close your eyes—and keep them closed. *(Pause.)* Why say that again?" (p. 59). Why, indeed, except that a return to buried sleep is the only refuge from the dangers to which little Milly's thigh so fatally awoke. Sexual disability is safer than sexual activity.

In real life, outside her story, Winnie has avoided sexual activity by immobility and by choosing a man who she knows will fail. This fact, and its association of sexuality with death, is most explicit in the final, culminating scene. Immediately after Winnie ends her narrative and begins a coda of miscellaneous memories, Willie finally emerges from behind the mound and begins to advance toward her on all fours. After so much visual tedium, this physical action shocks the audience: something, at last, is about to "happen." According to Beckett's stage directions, Willie is "dressed to kill" (p. 61): dressed up in "top hat, morning coat, striped trousers, etc." but also ready for physical violence. After taunting him ("Reminds me of the day you came whining for my hand") and encouraging him ("Come on dear"), Winnie asks an important question: "Is it a kiss you're after, Willie . . . or is it something else?" (p. 63). The "something else" is, of course, that "revolver conspicuous to her right on mound" (p. 49). Is it murder or love he is after? The question is never answered because Willie does not complete his climb; the play ends with a tableau of the two of them looking at each other. What is important dramatically is not the actual answer but the charge of emotion this potential violence (either murderous or erotic) gives to the climax of the play. Once again Willie has come courting, once again he approaches her mound, her *mons veneris;* in surprised excitement she gleefully urges him to "put a bit of jizz"[10] into his efforts, but now, as in the past, he fails: "There was a time when I could have given you a hand. *(Pause.)* And then a time before that again when I did give you a hand. *(Pause.)* You were always in dire need of a hand, Willie" (p. 63). Her psychological/sexual put-down sends him slithering "back to foot of mound," and once again sexuality is rendered impotent and grotesque, the man grovelling, the woman buried. Winnie's fear of the mouse running up her thigh and Willie's lack of "jizz" constitute mutual sexual disability which results in that barren mound in which Winnie lives, rigid and extinguished, a state even more fatal than the death, the revolver Willie cannot reach.

Although Beckett's later plays have gotten progressively briefer and more elusive, even they contain specific references to impaired sexuality or to birth as a particularly damaging and disgusting event.[11] In *Theatre II* there are the "five or six miscarriages which clouded . . . the early days of our union" and the resultant avoidance of "anything remotely resembling the work of love" (pp. 86f) and later in that same piece the anecdote of the man who accidentally shot off his own genitals (p. 98). *Radio I* concludes with elliptical reference to difficult birth: "a confinement? . . . *(long pause)* . . . two confinements? . . . *(long pause)* . . . one what? . . . what? . . . breech? . . . what? . . ." (p. 112). *Radio II* contains repeated reference to Caesarean delivery, but in this piece the pregnant person is a man who feels he carries his brother inside him, his twin: "Have yourself opened, Maud would say, opened up, it's nothing, I'll give him suck if he's still alive . . ." (p. 121). Another character interprets and justifies this bizarre situation of the pregnant male: "No, no, such things happen, such things happen. Nature, you know . . . *(Faint laugh.)* Fortunately. A world without monsters, just imagine! *(Pause for imagining.)*" (p. 123). The most disgusting image of birth in Beckett's later plays occurs in *That Time* when the central male character talks to himself about various stages in his life and remembers his most important turning point as his birth itself: "that time curled up worm in slime when they lugged you out and wiped you off and straightened you up . . ." (pp. 31f). Here, however, birth has not led to personal identity; in this same passage the character berates himself: "for God's sake did you ever say I to yourself in your life . . ." (p. 31). The question is a crucial one because it connects the failure of life with the failure of birth (as Beckett had earlier done in Mrs. Rooney's story of the little girl who "had never been really born" and, in fact, as he has been doing in all his work since *Proust* [1931], where it is suggested that gravesheets ought to serve as swaddling-clothes[12]).

In *That Time* the question is answered only implicitly, but in a related play, *Not I,* Beckett shows dramatically what happens to a person who never says "I" to himself or herself, and he makes clear that such failure is a function of impaired or deficient birth, of the child's coming "out . . . into this world . . . before its time . . ." (p. 14). In this short monologue a seventy-year-old woman, who has probably had a stroke but whose brain and mouth continue to function, remembers her loveless life. The significant stage direction for this female character is her "vehement refusal to relinquish third person" (p. 14). As she repetitively recounts her miserable existence, abandoned by her parents, reared in an orphanage, cynical of benevolence, haunted by guilt, silent and shamed by her few attempts to communicate—a woman utterly bereft—it is apparent to the audience that hers is a life deserving tears; yet she boasts of not crying since birth. As she struggles to understand her life, to find what it is in her present unchecked flow of language that she must tell, it is clear that her real tragedy is her own refusal to say "I," that is, her insistence on keeping herself remote, not letting herself feel, seeing herself as "she": "tiny little thing . . . out before its time . . . godforesaken hole . . . no love" (p. 22). Who is this, calling for attention and release, who is this whose only cry was a birth cry and who has not allowed herself further expression since emerging from that godforesaken hole, the womb of her damaging mother: "who? . . . no! . . . she! . . . SHE! . . ." And so the evasion continues, "Not I," the ultimate assertion of self-annihilation.

In the play *That Time* love is described as something "just made up," a contrivance to keep the shroud of death away (p. 31), but there, too, as in so many other plays, the real remedy for the damage of birth is "never having been" (p. 33). Similar ideas are advanced in Beckett's later fictional pieces. In *The Lost Ones,* for example, sexuality is shown as merely a futile attempt at "making unmakable love."[13] It is significant that the only extended description of human interaction in this fairly recent "story" involves grotesque attempts at copulation; the event occurs in a passage describing "the effect of this climate" upon the skin:

> This desiccation of the envelope robs nudity of much of its charm as pink turns grey and transforms into a rustling of nettles the natural succulence of flesh against flesh. The mucous membrane itself is affected which would not greatly matter were it not for its hampering effect on the work of love. But even from this point of view no great harm is done so rare is erection in the cylinder. It does occur none the less followed by more or less happy penetration in the nearest tube. Even man and wife may sometimes be seen in virtue of the law of probabilities to come together again in this way without their knowledge. The spectacle then is one to be remembered of frenzies prolonged in pain and hopelessness long beyond what even the most gifted lovers can achieve in camera. For male or female all are acutely aware how rare the occasion is and how unlikely to recur. But here too the desisting and deathly still in attitudes verging at times on the obscene whenever the vibrations cease and for as long as this crisis lasts. Stranger still at such times all the questing eyes that suddenly go still and fix their stare on the void or on some old abomination as for instance other eyes and then the long looks exchanged by those fain to look away. Irregular intervals of such length separate these lulls that for forgetters the likes of these each is the first. Whence invariably the same vivacity of reaction as to the end of a world and the same brief amaze when the twofold storm resumes and they start to search again neither glad nor even sorry. (pp. 53-55)

The very length of this passage is significant in showing how even in his later highly-condensed fiction Beckett's reference to grotesque and futile sexual activity is described much more elaborately than in the plays. But the meaning is the same. In the Dantean hell of *The Lost Ones,* the way out to "the sun and other stars" (p. 18) is only available "prior to never having been" (p. 19)— yet another of those neat temporal impossibilities that so abound in Beckett's work. Here, in recent fiction, as well as in the recent plays, death *before* life provides the only effective deliverance from pain. And here, too, the

metaphor that best expresses this pain and its futility is grotesque, impaired sexuality with its occasional unhappy result of damaging birth.

Character after character in Beckett's plays and fiction finds himself or herself pursued through life by the terrible cry of birth, and—like the reluctant father in *First Love*—feels "all that matters is that it should cease."[14] But unfortunately that cry persists; the slime of birth clings. The only real solution is "panhysterectomy," forestalling the cry, defeating sexuality altogether by removing beforehand those reproductive organs which one embarrassed character has called "the whole . . . er . . . bag of tricks." And if that fails, then "abort, abort."

NOTES

[1] Samuel Beckett, *First Love and Other Shorts* (New York: Grove Press, 1974), p. 34.

[2] Samuel Beckett, *Watt* (New York: Grove Press, 1959), pp. 139-42.

[3] Samuel Beckett, *Molloy, Malone Dies, The Unnamable* (New York: Grove Press, 1965), p. 323.

[4] See also the many abortion references throughout the trilogy identified in the previous note, especially that in *Molloy,* p. 18.

[5] Samuel Beckett, *Krapp's Last Tape and Other Dramatic Pieces* (New York: Grove Press, 1960), p. 119.

[6] Ibid., p. 42.

[7] Samuel Beckett, *Endgame* (New York: Grove Press, 1958), p. 14.

[8] *A Reader's Guide to Samuel Beckett* (New York: Farrar, Straus, and Giroux, 1973), p. 152.

[9] Samuel Beckett, *Happy Days* (New York: Grove Press, 1961), p. 37.

[10] As well as meaning "vigor; speed; animation; excitement" (as in the sentence "put a little jism into it"); "jism" also has the taboo meaning, semen. See Harold Wentworth and Stuart Berg Flexner, *Dictionary of American Slang* (New York: Thomas Y. Crowell, 1960), p. 292.

[11] Samuel Beckett, *Ends and Odds* (New York: Grove Press, 1976); all quotations in the next two paragraphs are from this volume.

[12] Samuel Beckett, *Proust* (New York: Grove Press, 1957), p. 8.

[13] Samuel Beckett, *The Lost Ones* (New York: Grove Press, 1972), p. 37.

[14] Beckett, *First Love,* p. 36.

Thomas Postlewait

SOURCE: "Pinter's 'The Homecoming: Displacing and Repeating Ibsen," in *Comparative Drama*, Vol. 15, No. 3, Fall, 1981, pp. 195-212.

[*In the following essay, Postlewait examines Harold Pinter's* The Homecoming *as a transformation of the drama of Henrik Ibsen, which explores "the sexual politics of bourgeois family life."*]

> Henrik Ibsen: "A woman cannot be herself in the society of the present day, which is an exclusively masculine society. . . .
>
>   --Notes for *A Doll's House*
>
> Teddy (to Ruth): "They're my family. They're not ogres."
>
>   --Harold Pinter, *The Homecoming*

I

What is a home? In drama it is often not a safe place to visit or return to. The homecoming theme, which is so central to the history of drama, reveals that the home is haunted by past crimes, usually concerning sexual matters and the misuse of power. *Oresteia, Oedipus the King, Hamlet, Ghosts*—here is the main line of the dramatic tradition. In this homecoming story two themes are brought together: (1) the sexual definition of woman as either good wife and abiding mother or adulterer and unworthy mother and (2) the struggle of sons against fathers, of young men against false father figures, of children against parents. The corruption of the blood ties these two themes together. Pollution, contamination, disease—metaphors of sickness run through these plays.

In modern plays as different from one another as *The Ghost Sonata, Mourning Becomes Electra, A Streetcar Named Desire,* and even *Six Characters in Search of an Author* the themes of sexual intrigue, sexual guilt, family ghosts, corrupted power, and revenge are brought together by the homecoming situation. The past makes its claims on the present. It takes its revenge. In a sense the revenge play since the *Oresteia* has been the primary dramatic action, going through many variations.

Harold Pinter's *The Homecoming* is within this tradition, but from an ironic perspective. Almost all of the aspects of the homecoming story are present in some form: the double identity of woman, a son's return home, a ghostly presence hovering over the action, the false power of a father figure, the imagery of blood and pollution, the violation of sexual taboos, confusion or controversy over conception, family violence, breakdown of moral codes, revenge of or against the mother, and the call or impulse for vengeance. The central action of this play, even though suffused with Pinter's ironic tone, is directly within this primal story of drama. The conflict thus operates at two levels: (1) between the characters as they struggle with one another within this Ur-text; and (2) between the tradition of the dramatic action, as we know it, and the reworking of it that Pinter presents. Pinter uses comic irony to displace the tradition and key images and motifs to condense the tradition, thus setting up for us an interpretative function of reading these displacements and condensations in the manner of metaphors and metonymies. We have to read the action both for its double perspective (that of the play itself and that of the tradition it plays against) and for its two tones (serious and comic). By reformulating the homecoming story, its structure and its basic conflicts, by means of comic turns and displaced motifs, Pinter provides us with an up-ended *Oresteia,* a comic *Hamlet.*

And yet, while a distant and ironic echo of the major tragedies by the Greek dramatists and by Shakespeare can be heard in Pinter's play, such distance makes his ironic engagement with the tradition often inexplicit and sometimes cryptic. He empties the traditional action of its normal moral register, so that the reversals and recognitions seem more profane than profound, more predatory than philosophic. Unlike Tom Stoppard's *Rosencrantz and Guildenstern Are Dead* or Friedrich Dürrenmatt's *Play Strindberg* or Brecht's various reworkings of plays by earlier playwrights, Pinter's use of the tradition is quite disguised. Just as his characters transform their identities in order to snare, feign, circumvent, mock, and delude, so he teases us with suggestions of the past without giving certain connections. The causal lines are masked. Plays such as the *Oresteia* stand behind Pinter's play, but not in any direct way. Pinter is not specifically reworking the *Oresteia* as Brecht reworks *Antigone* or Gay's *The Beggar's Opera*. It remains a general heritage, comprehensive yet oblique (like his Jewishness), not an exclusive or specific predicate for dramatic action. He draws upon it, but does not mention it; he uses its motifs and themes, but does not parallel it; he writes in terms of it, but not about it.

With Ibsen, however, the distance is not so great and the similarities are greater. Again, there is no immediate correspondence, no *Play Ibsen*. But the modern tradition that Ibsen shaped in turn shapes Pinter's drama, and *The Homecoming* gains much of its significance, both thematically and ironically, when it is seen within that tradition. *A Doll's House, Ghosts,* and *Hedda Gabler* haunt its action. And possibly the best way to show this closeness is to examine the trait of Pinter's drama that is so often noted as "Pinteresque": those rooms and their invaders.

The catalog is easy: Riley invades Rose's room, Stanley is carried out of his retreat, Davies is unsuccessful in establishing his haven, Ruth makes a new home, Anna enters Deeley's and Kate's country retreat and seems to drive a wedge between them, Spooner enters and remains in Hirst's home, Jerry seduces his best friend's wife, Emma, in their bedroom, and the son in *Family Voices* lives in a roominghouse after apparently escaping his own home. Home is the common stage for action. But why? According to Christopher Lasch, the sociologist, the instability of modern bourgeois life has put undue pressure upon the private life of the home, which is supposed to be, according to some theorists, a haven in a heartless world. Unfortunately, the home and family life cannot meet these demands of compensation. Lasch comments:

> the bourgeois family system, which had its heyday in the nineteenth century and now seems to be slowly crumbling, was founded on what sociologists have called companionate marriage, on the child-centered household, on the emancipation or quasi-emancipation of women, and on the structural isolation of the nuclear family from the kinship system and from society in general. The family found ideological support and justification in the conception of the family as an emotional refuge in a cold and competitive society.... At bottom, the glorification of private life and the family represented the other side of the bourgeois perception of society as something alien, impersonal, remote, and abstract—a world from which pity and tenderness had been effectively banished. Deprivations experienced in the public world had to be compensated in the realm of privacy. Yet the very conditions that gave rise to the need to view privacy and the family as a refuge from the larger world made it more and more difficult for the family to serve in that capacity.[1]

While Pinter is not dramatizing the Marxist theory of history nor the bourgeois sins of family life, he does show us the emotional and social consequences of such a retreat into protective rooms, the inadequacy of such private life, and the conflicts that occur when such barriers are invaded. His characters are products of the modern world. Even his loners and tramps such as Stanley and Davies, unlike Beckett's tramps, are in retreat from a modern social and economic world that we recognize as an aspect of our own contemporary lives.

In other words, this dramatic action is not so exclusively "Pinteresque" as we sometimes suggest. The home as an inadequate haven in a heartless world is a topic of which Pinter hardly has the sole market. His talents of invention and imitation derive in part from an accurate reading of the world around him and in part from the Ibsenite tradition. So, let us turn to Ibsen.

II

What is a home? A castle in the sky? A cave for trolls? Ibsen's plays repeatedly probe the meaning of homelife as his characters leave home, return home, destroy home, create home. Peer Gynt abandons one home, creates a new one with his troll wife and brat, abandons this, creates a mountain home with Solveig, who leaves her family home against her parents' wishes. Then Peer must flee this home for a roundabout life of empty achievements and pleasures, only to return belatedly to what he has lost: his home with the waiting Solveig.

Brand tries to turn the home into the kingdom of God, but instead he makes it a deadly ideal. Nora Helmer discovers that her doll house, which her husband calls our "snug and nice home," has been "nothing but a play-pen" without love or honor for a doll-wife. Mrs. Alving, trying to break free from what Pastor Manders calls the "pure morals of home," reveals to her "homecoming son" that her dutiful homelife had been a lie, a corruption that infects all of the characters, including Engstrand who wants Regina "back home with me" at an inn (whorehouse) that he wants to run for sailors. Her answer is emphatic: "Back home with you? Never." Hedda Gabler, returning from a honeymoon to her new home, the Falk mansion, tells Judge Brack that she could not care less about the place but yet finds herself imprisoned within it and the "responsibilities" of married life for a woman. Doctor Stockman is driven out of his home by his neighbors. John Rosmer and Rebecca West destroy the family traditions and life of Rosmersholm as they struggle with their guilty desires. Ellida Wangel tries to decide whether to leave or stay in a home in which she is an outsider. Halvard Solness, whose previous home burned, killing his children, and whose present home is a gloomy workshop and a loveless house, wants to build "homes for human beings," but dies in an attempt to transform this desire into a castle in the sky. Alfred and Rita Allmers, after almost destroying their homelife, decide out of guilt to open their home to poor, mistreated children. And John Gabriel Borkman prowls his one room in the large house, a prisoner cut off from family life in a home so miserable and depressing that his son must escape.

For Ibsen who spent twenty-seven years away from his homeland, returning from self-exile only after he had made himself the father of modern drama, the values and difficulties of homelife are the heart of judgment—for his characters and for himself. Staying home, leaving home, coming back home—each has its dangers and difficulties. In 1897, after returning to Norway, he wrote to George Brandes: "Up here by the fjords is my native land. But—but—but—where am I to find my *home-land?*"[2] Homecomings seldom work out—especially for the homecoming son. Ibsen was welcomed back, but that did not suffice. People read his plays about the problems of home but did not fully understand what he was saying. So, in spite of his return and the import of the plays, he felt that "all the channels of communication are blocked,"[3] as he wrote to Brandes.

Such a statement is probably too pessimistic, but without doubt Ibsen's drama does reveal the alien quality of life in those middle-class homes, those living rooms in which family members are often the intruders. Nora lives in "a comfortable room, tastefully but not expensively furnished,"[4] that she believes is properly her place, only to learn that she is as much a stranger there as she would be in Helmer's private study. The home is the heart of intimacy, but such closeness produces betrayals—of self and others—rather than trusting and open communication. This E. M. Forster noted when he came to describe Ibsen's plays (in terms that also fit Pinter's plays): "Sooner or later his characters draw their little knives, they rip up the present and the past, and the closer their intimacy the better their opportunity for exchanging pain."[5] This dramatic action, with its various perspectives on homelife, locates pain in the nature of intimacy, and intimacy in the desire for relationships that can somehow accommodate the conflicting needs for self-definition and community, for freedom and responsibility, for self-love and the love of others. Withdraw or approach is the basic action. Control or be controlled is the consequence.

Ibsen's critique of desire and power is placed within a framework of false social values, confining homelife, and hypocrisy. Pinter's critique maintains this central concern with desire and power, but removes many of the middle-class values that shape conscience and social action in Ibsen's world. The threatening life in the rooms, the role playing, the uses of memory, the invasion by outsiders (who are aspects of oneself), the need for concealment or disguise—these concerns the two playwrights share, but Pinter's plays have a quality that Ibsen's do not have—that is, the presence of Ibsen's drama as an influence and as a factor in the minds of the audience. Pinter's drama thus necessarily engages with Ibsen's because of these similarities, and he uses his irony and his talent for circumvention to effect his aims.

Pinter's drama is a transformation of Ibsen's drama—a redistribution of elements—that gives us most of the same concerns, yet from a different view. *The Homecoming*, like several of Ibsen's plays, deals with the woman's place in the home, motherhood, female cunning, male manipulative powers, a son's return to a troubled home, a father's questionable authority. Pinter is drawing upon this drama of private life, a drama of self-control and being controlled in terms of family conflicts (as did Strindberg, Chekhov, and Pirandello from their own perspectives), in order to present the interrelated connections between power and desire. His drama is private and intimate. Introspection and retrospection organize action and characterization. He is not writing a political or social drama (which Ibsen did in addition to his psychological drama of private life). Pinter is not examining power in terms of historical and public action in the manner of Shaw, Brecht, Dürrenmatt, Bond, and even Genet (as in *The Balcony*). Politics and government, even public life, have little meaning for his characters. Nevertheless, the uses and abuses of power concern Pinter as much as they do any contemporary playwright, but he locates them in the intrigues of private life—the living rooms and the bedrooms rather than the shops, courtrooms, and streets.

The key question about Pinter's drama here, in comparison to Ibsen's, is what happens when dramatic conflict in a family drama centers on sex and the uses of power, but sex lacks its moral (and immoral) meanings for guiding the attitudes of the characters and the audience. What happens if sex is detached from the traditional meanings it has had—in society and drama?

Women in drama have been characterized in rather conventional ways, with sexual categories providing much of the definition. This does not mean that women characters have been mere types, simple and without depth, for drama has given us some amazing women: Clytaemnestra, Medea, Cassandra, Antigone, Lady Macbeth, Cleopatra, Beatrice, Rosalind, Nora, Mrs. Alving, Hedda, Hilde. But most often their courage, weaknesses, uses of power, desires, needs, and conflicts have taken meaning through their sexual identities. And usually such an identity is a confining one defined in great part in relationship to and by the male characters. The reverse is not nearly as true for the men in drama, whose courage, weaknesses, desires, uses of power, and conflicts are usually only secondarily defined in terms of women. Even Shakespeare's Antony is struggling with issues that go far beyond the sexual characterization.

These conventions are strong and functional. They help define conflict quickly and emotionally. Part of Ibsen's genius is in how extensively and complexly he developed his characterization of women in terms of sexual identity, so much so that even today he is admired by feminists for his insights into these issues. He seems to be such a master of psychological and social identity that we sometimes forget that he is also carefully using a convention of drama just as a musical composer might use the sonata form or the techniques of harmony. To define quickly the conflict of a woman character in terms of motherly anguish over her children, jealousy, dedication to husband, search for husband, or sexual promiscuity is not merely a convention, but it is in part conventional and traditional. The "rules" of characterization are not absolute, but in their conventional ways they have authority—for dramatists and audiences. Just as harmony in music sets up and fulfills expectations, so characterization of women by means of sexual categories sets up and fulfills expectations. And that's not all bad.

What interests us is how various dramatists work variations on the conventions. Some like Ibsen seem to expand the whole vocabulary. Others then work within and against this expansion. Ibsen's women—Nora walking out on her husband and three children, Mrs. Alving caught in her anguish, Hedda struggling against her sexual fears, Ellida drawn to the stranger from the sea, Hilde coming to collect her dream, Irene stalking Rubek with murder in her heart—are the feminine prototypes for modern realistic characterization in terms of sexuality. In part he created our consciousness of such women, of such conflicts, of such sexual identity. Of course to say this implies, as Wilde said, that life imitates art. And to an extent it does, but drama also imitates reality then and now, so that both art and life mutually contribute to our consciousness, as they mutually contribute to one another. Characterization in drama depends in part on conventions, but then so does identity in real life. We quite often tend to think of ourselves and others in conventional terms. We act out of conventions in life as well as art.

This Pinter knows and repeatedly dramatizes. The conventional, often clichéd language that his characters use is one way that he illustrates this. They think in conventional terms, understanding themselves and others within such limits, such traps. And the men usually have the conventional attitude toward women—pure wife and mother versus impure whore. Pinter uses this convention in almost all of his plays—at first, apparently, without much thematic insight or ironic distance from what the male characters themselves thought. But with *The Collection, The Lover,* and *The Homecoming* the convention becomes unconventional—not in his abandonment of it (for he has maintained it throughout his plays) but in the ironic perspective he establishes towards it.

Traditionally, within terms of the convention, the female character in drama usually struggles with the moral meanings of her sexual identity, moral meanings defined in great part by the male characters (and the playwrights). This struggle is at the heart of Ibsen's drama, both conventionally and profoundly. Pinter's trick, as it were, is to remove the moral meanings of a woman's identity in the drama. This immediately gives her a freedom and power that the convention had denied her. For one hundred years the convention of the fallen woman has been prevalent in drama (e.g., Pinero's Mrs. Tanqueray, Tennessee Williams's Blanche DuBois). Pinter, following a possible lead of Shaw's in *Mrs. Warren's Profession* (and other plays of seemingly amoral or unconventional women with strong will powers), has simply gotten rid of the fallen woman in moral terms but kept the conventional dichotomy of woman, as men understand it, so that the woman character can play either role for her own purposes, usually to confound the men.

III

The Homecoming calls for one female role, but the dramatic action actually has two: Teddy's wife Ruth, who comes to visit and decides to stay in Max's home, and Max's wife Jessie, who is dead but still remains lodged in the men's minds. Jessie is the much maligned ghost from the past and Ruth is the avenging spirit of the future. Both women are talked about and perceived as either the dutiful good mother and wife or the whore. Max is, of course, the main character who thinks in these categories, but all the men do to some extent. Their conventional attitudes open up the opportunity for Ruth's unconventional behavior.

At first, in any comparison to Ibsen's women, Ruth must seem a most unlikely and unrelated character. Surely none of Ibsen's women would make a bargain to become a whore after abandoning her husband and her three children? But Ruth has much in common with them. It is not just that Nora in *A Doll's House* gives up her marriage and leaves her three children, nor that Regina in *Ghosts* also walks out of a repressive home and the proper role it requires, into a world in which

she seeks "joy" by means of whoring if necessary, but that Ibsen, for all his Victorian decorum about sex, also shows us women making sexual bargains for independence and power. Several of Ibsen's women, including Maja and Irene in *When We Dead Awaken,* Rebecca in *Rosmersholm,* and Hilde in *The Master Builder,* desire power or passion—or both—and are willing to go after it, social proprieties be damned. And even in marriage, as in the case of Rita in *Little Eyolf* and Ellida in *The Lady from the Sea,* passion and power are linked dangerously, threatening the stability of family life. This convention of characterization (while not necessarily the truest image of women) suggests that passionate desires, deeply incarnate and hidden from view, drive women to seek power over men by means of sexual allurements. Men beware.

Hedda Gabler, with her will to power and her lack of conscience, is the prototype of the clever vixen with a daemonic passion. Like Hedda, Ruth desires power and dislikes shackles, but unlike Hedda she asserts herself instead of trying to live vicariously through others. Hedda must conceal her desires, even finally from herself, and this traps her in a web of deceptions. In contrast, Ruth conceals little or nothing sexually, taking on with cunning the role of the whore, the male persona of desire. The proper respectability that imprisons Hedda, comparable to the life Ruth had in America with her own academic husband, represents prohibitions (and inhibitions) in the form of social conventions. These taboos take the place of moral understanding and self-knowledge for Hedda, so her actions are obsessively proscribed by them. She cannot overstep them because she has accepted their right to define certain actions as forbidden. She is afraid even to step out of a train compartment at a station because someone "looks at your legs."[6] Ruth, in contrast, invites the men to watch her legs. She is not imprisoned by social codes that pass for moral ones.

False moral codes turn Hedda into a "coward," as she describes herself. Such sexual cowardice entraps her in a home that is neither a haven for private sex nor a place to escape sex. She hates the pieties of home life, but unlike Ruth who ignores the moralism in male categories of sexual behavior, she fears the social power of these pieties. When Judge Brack suggests to her that she will be happier once she fulfills her "responsibility" as a mother, he defines the proper role for her. When he warns her against desiring familiar knowledge of a woman like Mademoiselle Diana, whose "home" the men visit, he defines the improper role for her. Such categories divide her against herself, social power against private desire.

Ruth also confronts men who divide women into two categories—good wife or slutbitch—but she uses the stereotypes of desire for the socialization of power. Hedda, however, sees no way to use these roles for her own benefit. She recoils from sensual life except as a voyeur. Sex remains a male prerogative that disfranchises Hedda from both self-control and openness. She has cunning instead of valor, discretion instead of comprehension. Because of her own self-deception, she must deceive others. Trapped this way, she must punish or be punished, becoming finally her own victim. While Judge Brack, using these sexual codes, is able to control Hedda, the same tactic used by Lenny fails to control Ruth. The situation, in fact, between Lenny and Ruth is the counterpart of that between Brack and Hedda. Power and sex are the purpose of these encounters. Lenny tells his two stories of beating up women in order to make Ruth acquiesce in the intent, if not the content, of these calculated self-projections. Dominance is the meaning of authority for him. His story telling, like the series of boxing motifs that run through the play, establishes aggression as the manifest identity of a latent anxiety. What this anxiety is we cannot know for sure, but his feelings about his "dear mother" probably are relevant. Both Pinter and Ibsen, like Freud, have taught us to seek motivations in the past.

Whatever the causes for Lenny's behavior, he is no lady killer in Ruth's eyes. Like Hedda, he is a voyeur, turning hate into the will to power—as best he can. Needing no pistol to threaten him, as Hedda does Brack, Ruth uses the two reductive roles for women, whore and mother, to beat Lenny at his own game of sexual politics. First offering to take him, apparently sexually, she throws him on the defensive in their mock battle in the glass of water scene. Then shifting from this implied passion, she takes on the role of mother: "Sit on my lap. Take a long cool sip. . . . Put your head back and open your mouth."[7] Like a baby he is helpless. Ruth laughs, drinks the water, and walks confidently out of the room—complete mistress of the situation. He is now trapped in the very categories that he—and the other men—have used to trap women.

Ruth enters the all-male home, left womanless since Jessie's death, and takes over the male domain. She collaborates with a ghost, a specter in the minds of the men, replacing Jessie the wife-mother with Ruth the whore. She is in full control of her own inner space as well as the rather empty-headed images that the men project onto her. And she does what Jessie apparently did not do, if we are to believe Sam's story. That is, she has asserted her sexual power openly. In the shady past, Jessie allowed herself to be used by Max, by her lover, MacGregor, and even by Sam. In carrying on a secret affair with MacGregor, Jessie permitted all three men to hold power over her. She was dependent on Sam and MacGregor for their silence and on Max for his ignorance. To this extent, despite the triumph of making Max a cuckold, she allowed the sexual definitions to guide her actions in secrecy. Max may not have controlled her body, but his sexual codes made her acquiesce apparently in a conspiracy of silence. (In *Betrayal* Pinter returns to the interrelated issues of adultery, silence, and humiliation—a complex network of deception and self-deception.)

Ruth chooses openness. In Act II, after listening to Max's recital about Jessie being "the backbone of the family" and "a slutbitch of a wife," she reaches back into her memory for an identity different from that of being Teddy's proper wife.

> *Ruth.* I was . . .
>
> *Max.* What? (Pause.) What she say? *(They all look at her.)*
>
> *Ruth.* I was . . . different . . . when I met Teddy . . . first.
>
> *Teddy.* No you weren't. You were the same.
>
> *Ruth.* I wasn't.
>
> *Max.* Who cares? Listen, live in the present, what are you worrying about? I mean, don't forget the earth's about five thousand million years old, at least. Who can afford to live in the past? (p. 50)

The past, of course, is where Max has been during much of the play, for by means of it he defines and defends himself. He also would like to escape it, to live in the present, without memories, but he cannot. So he tries to remake the past in his memories, tries to gain power over the history of desire. Ruth's presence, however, threatens him. His first response to her, in Act I, was rage as he tried to toss her out of the house, striking out verbally at her and physically at Joey (for not tossing her out). Then, after trying to deal with her in terms of the sexual category of whore, he shifted to the opposite category of mother and good wife. Having accepted her in these terms, he does not want her to slip back into the other sexual definition. But she confronts him, nevertheless, as the embodiment of youthful, feminine passion, not so unlike the way Hilde Wengel confronts Masterbuilder Solness with his own fears and failures, the memories of a life of sexual humiliation. Vengeance is veneral. Power is confounded and transformed by sexual desire. Time, the medium of self-identity, is also the power of the past over the present and the future. In Ibsen the memory of guilt, of a bad conscience, is what tends to defeat one; in Pinter the defeat comes usually when someone else's memory defines power more effectively than one's own memory (one's story) has.

This is Ruth's triumph over the men and their stories about the past. In her longest speech she begins to recall having once been "a photographic model for the body" (p. 57). In this speech she performs her turn from one sexual category to the other. This memory with its pastoral images provides a suggestion of freedom from restraints, an image of the body, possibly nude, outside in nature—sensually. At this point in the play she begins to dance with Lenny, kissing him in front of Teddy. She then rolls about the floor in an embrace with Joey— while Teddy, Lenny, and Max watch and comment. Alignments shift. Ironically, Max's suggestion to her to forget the past brings about the new power base between

Ruth and Lenny, and thus his downfall, because Ruth's immediate past that she forgets or abandons is the six years in sterile America as obedient wife and good mother. There as Teddy's helpmate, in a life as constricted as Nora's in *A Doll's House*, she was the proper mother of three children. Teddy appeals to her to return to her dutiful life there by defining her according to his needs: "You can help me with my lectures when we get back" (p. 55), but that is a role more appropriate for Mrs. Elvsted in *Hedda Gabler* than for Ruth. Having made the shift in her mind from one category of sexual identity to another, she sacrifices Teddy and the children without apparent conscience.

Teddy, in turn, is quite prepared to make his own sacrifices, including his wife to his father and brothers, in order to avoid the appearance or the acknowledgment of defeat. Once he sees that Ruth intends to stay, he quickly detaches himself from emotional involvement and moral judgment. Although she is his wife, her actions, like many aspects of philosophy, do not fall within his province. He interprets her action as a rejection of him, not so surprisingly, so he defensively cuts himself off from her. His identity is maintained by distancing himself not only from others but also from his own emotions. He has become the embodiment of his philosophical methodology: "It's a way of being able to look at the world. It's a question of how far you can operate on things and not in things" (p. 61). His cool control is a match for Ruth's, but while she uses hers offensively for commanding a situation, he uses his for removing himself from the control of others. He observes.

> Teddy. To see to be able to *see!* I'm the one who can see. That's why I can write my critical works. Might do you good . . . have a look at them . . . see how certain people can view . . . things . . . how certain people maintain . . . intellectual equilibrium. Intellectual equilibrium. You're just objects. You just . . . move about. I can observe it. I can see what you do. It's the same as I do. But you're lost in it. You won't get me being . . . I won't be lost in it (BLACKOUT.) (p. 62)

He won't be caught "being." He won't become lost in subjective feeling. Committed to the "eye" (and "I"), Teddy becomes not only an observer but an object for himself. Sight dominates, even rules out, emotion. Sight provides distances, putting "things" in a spatial rather than temporal perspective. He lives in a sanitized present, unlike the others, denying the past. He lives outside the family home, free from family history. He does not talk about Jessie, as the others do. Out of sight, out of mind—this is Teddy's philosophy. Lucidity and self-control depend upon an objective vision that denies the dark, temporal life of being. The "eye" must rule. How nicely comic, therefore, is that "BLACKOUT" that follows immediately after his long speech—another example, like Sam's fall into a heap of exhaustion after expressing his one source of power, of Pinter's use of theatrical functions for ironic meaning.

Teddy is all mask, all role. He fears humiliation, we must assume, more than he needs others. Even Lenny, who stalks, mocks, and attacks him throughout the play, can only score a few comic points against Teddy, not penetrate his guard. Nothing engages him, at least for very long. Distance triumphs, so fittingly he lives in distant America, the land of empty spaces and little history. As Ruth says: It's all rock. And sand. It stretches . . . so far . . . everywhere you look" (p. 53). As far as the eye can see. Or as Teddy puts it: "It's so clean there" (p. 54). London is dirty to Teddy, "a filthy urinal" (p. 54), which he identifies with the dirty history of his family, from which he has removed himself physically and emotionally. His one mistake was to return for a visit, to step back into the past. Unlike, however, other homecoming sons in drama (Orestes, Hamlet, Osvald), he escapes contamination and suffering by cutting himself off from family ties. He walks out the door, an island unto himself. And Ruth, no less self-contained, even though she makes a contract for her body (but not her mind), chooses to stay in the world that Teddy abandons because it offers her power over self in a family of servants.

IV

In *A Doll's House* Nora states: "I've lived by doing tricks for you, Torvald."[8] Tired of that, she walks out of his house and slams the door. Ruth walks out of one house too, but she walks into another with the decision to turn a few tricks. Almost one hundred years after *A Doll's House* started the modern revolution in drama (and the convention of characterization that gives us the frustrated housewife struggling to know herself and her condition), the dramatic action has come full circle: Ruth turns Max's home into a doll's house, but the kind of doll that Lenny knows how to manage. The bourgeois home, based upon a capitalist economy (as in *A Doll's House* with its plot depending upon social position and honor tied to financial contracts), has become in Pinter's play all contract and calculation, stripped bare of false sentiment and moralism. Everybody must pay his way (as Max warns Sam) or out the door with him. And ironically, it is not the wife but the husband, Teddy, who goes out the door—to care for his three children just as Torvald must care for his. Both of course seem emotionally incapable of their task.

Nora's skills at money management (the secret buried in the past) are now Ruth's great bargaining skills (the power openly proclaimed):

> *Ruth.* I would naturally want to draw up an inventory of everything I would need, which would require your signature in the presence of witnesses . . . All aspects of the agreement and conditions of employment would have to be clarified to our mutual satisfaction before we finalize the contract. (pp. 78-79)

In this parody of banker's and lawyer's jargon, Pinter makes the bourgeois home into the bourgeois business.

And pimp and whore are the easy symbols of such family life, symbols that were implied by Ibsen's drama. The secretive and money-based world of immoral contracts that Nora discovers embedded in her marriage contract is openly dramatized by Pinter—with a touch of cynicism and a leaven of comic irony—as essentially a sexual proposition with a desire for power at the heart of an amoral contract. The home has once again become a cottage industry.

Ruth and Lenny have replaced Jessie and Max as family rulers, *in loco parentis,* and without the worries and fears of raising three children who may in time wish to overthrow their parents. The next generation is isolated in America, so of little threat. Max and Jessie had a false marriage. Lenny and Ruth, in subversion of the secretive life of sex and power, negotiate a business deal that is a parody of marriage and sexual contracts—not only of the one that ends *The Way of the World* but also of the arrangement by which Judge Brack tries to blackmail Hedda. Now sex is a money-making proposition, free of emotions and false pieties.

Pinter thus makes explicit, with comic purpose, the themes in Ibsen's drama. The sexual politics of bourgeois family life are here with a vengeance made the sole terms for establishing power and control. Self-protection is self-profit. Pinter strips the family conflict of its traditional moral categories, making expediency rather than right and wrong the basic measure of all things. While Ibsen's drama provides a moral critique of social institutions, of the concept of respectability, of social pieties masking personal profit, Pinter's drama provides a demonstration of the expediency of ignoring such social conventions. The personal conflict in Ibsen's plays centers on guilt. In Pinter's plays this conflict has shifted to humiliation. Of course, humiliation in terms of social disgrace is a major aspect of Ibsen's drama, but there the action connects to moral issues, to repressed or suppressed acts, to bad consciences, to shameful desires. In Pinter's drama such guilt is not determining. What we discover thus at the end of *The Homecoming* is neither explicable motivations nor hidden truths as the characters struggle with social roles and personal histories, but instead simply the uses of memory in the service of power and desire.

What Pinter's play shows us, then, in terms of the Ibsenite tradition is how memory and sexual power shape the linked elements of plot, characterization, and theme. Ruth's possessive power, inspired in part by Jessie's ghostly presence in the minds of the men, represents the successful transformation of the conventions of female characterization, the turning of the male categories against the men. Fight fire with fire, control desire with desire. Ruth appropriates the way men classify women and uses these rigid codes against them. The prison keepers become the prisoners.

What is a home?—more a trollish cave apparently than a castle in the sky. The home life is not for these characters a moral theater. It is not a haven from a heartless world. Instead, the heartless world is found to exist and to thrive in the intimacy of the family. Pinter shows, as dramatists since the Greeks have also shown, that family life is not only the mirror of public and political life but also the source of much of its ways. Microcosm and macrocosm are bound together. The home is not a haven from the public world and its capitalist values because such values are in the human heart as well as in a historical culture called "bourgeois." The profit principle and the pleasure principle, Marx and Freud, are in the marriage contract and thus are in family life, not just during the last few generations but throughout history. Power and desire contend with one another in all families, and are not merely imposed from outside—by either intruders or large social and economic forces.

Danger is everywhere. Families are not havens from it, but nor are they just ogres, as Teddy's says. Of course they can be trollish. This is Ibsen's point:

> To *live* is to war with trolls
> in the vaults of the heart and the brain.
> To *write:* that is to sit
> in judgment over one's self.[8]

The battle cannot be avoided in the rooms because these rooms are the vaults of the heart and the brain. This Pinter knows too. *The Homecoming* reveals not an anomalous family of ogres, unlike "normal" families, but a family that has much in common with the families we find in Ibsen's drama. We may at first agree with Shakespeare's old Adam in *As You Like It,* when he warns Orlando against his brother:

> This is no place, this house is but a butchery;
> Abhor it, fear it, do not enter it.
>
> (II.iii.27-28)

Max is a butcher, and the family members go at one another with bloody passion, but as Ruth shows they can be controlled. Power and passion, profit and pleasure, money and sex—these are the concerns and the basis for conflict. But not just in this family. The symbolism of a whore and a pimp triumphing may seem strange to us, given the conventions of female and male behavior in family drama, but even with Pinter's seemingly amoral treatment of this family conflict we should be able to see that he is writing his own disguised version of a *Play Ibsen.* He is, in fact, making explicit a major theme and mode of characterization in Ibsen's plays: the female body as a commodity in a conflict between power and desire. What is a home? The place where this struggle must occur.

NOTES

[1] Christopher Lasch, "The Family as a Haven in a Heartless World," *Salmagundi,* 35 (Fall 1976), 44-45.

[2] Henrik Ibsen, letter to Georg Brandes, 3 June 1897, *Ibsen: Letters and Speeches,* ed. Evert Sprinchorn (New York: Hill and Wang, 1964), p. 324.

[3] Ibid.

[4] Henrik Ibsen, *A Doll's House,* in *Henrik Ibsen: The Complete Major Prose Plays,* ed. and trans. Rolf Fjelde (New York: Farrar, Straus, and Giroux, 1978), p. 125.

[5] E. M. Forster, "Ibsen the Romantic," *Abinger Harvest* (New York: Harcourt, Brace, and World, 1936); reprinted in *Ibsen: A Collection of Critical Essays,* ed. Rolf Fjelde (Englewood Cliffs, N. J.: Prentice-Hall, 1965), p. 175.

[6] Henrik Ibsen, *Hedda Gabler,* in *The Complete Major Prose Plays,* p. 726.

[7] Harold Pinter, *The Homecoming* (New York: Grove Press, 1966), p. 34. All subsequent references to this play are noted parenthetically in the text. The ellipses are Pinter's. I have found little mention of Ibsen's influence on Pinter's drama, but the following useful essays make at least some initial comparisons between the two dramatists: Rolf Fjelde, "Plotting Pinter's Progress," *A Casebook on Harold Pinter's The Homecoming,* ed. John Lahr (New York: Grove Press, 1971), pp. 87-107; Kelly Morris, "The Homecoming," *Tulane Drama Review,* 11 (1966), 186; Hugh Nelson, "*The Homecoming:* Kith and Kin," *Modern British Dramatists,* ed. John Russell Brown (Englewood Cliffs, N. J.: Prentice Hall, 1968), p. 150; Arthur Ganz, "Mixing Memory and Desire: Pinter's Vision in *Landscape, Silence,* and *Old Times,*" *Pinter: A Collection of Critical Essays,* ed. Arthur Ganz (Englewood Cliffs, N. J.: Prentice Hall, 1972), pp. 161-78.

[8] Henrik Ibsen, *A Doll's House,* in *The Complete Major Prose Plays,* p. 191.

Maurice Charney

SOURCE: "What Did the Butler See in Orton's 'What the Butler Saw?," in *Modern Drama,* Vol. XXV, No. 4, December, 1982, pp. 496-504.

[*In the following essay, Charney focuses on Joe Orton's play* What the Butler Saw *as a black-comedy farce concerned with sexual identity and lurid sexual behavior.*]

What the Butler Saw by Joe Orton (written in 1967 and produced posthumously in 1969) is, of course, a farce without a butler, which should more properly have been called *What the Butler Might Have Seen* had there been a butler and had he been privileged to oversee the strange goings-on in Dr. Prentice's private clinic. Like Stoppard in *The Real Inspector Hound,* Orton is parodying the whodunit conventions without actually writing a mystery story. We need the invisible butler in *What the Butler Saw* as a stand-in for the cozy and complacent amenities of upper-middle-class drawing-room life. Dr. Prentice's establishment is actually a private lunatic asylum, which Orton establishes in his epigraph as a

microcosm of the world: "Surely we're all mad people, and they / Whom we think are, are not" (p. 361).[1] By invoking Cyril Tourneur's Jacobean play *The Revenger's Tragedy* (from about 1607), Orton is setting up as a model one of the strangest and most extravagant of seventeenth-century black comedies, which is also a play much influenced by Shakespeare's *Hamlet.* It is a wildly, almost hysterically rhetorical play that passes for tragedy only by certain technicalities of the ending. Even better than *The Jew of Malta,* for which T. S. Eliot coined the term, it exemplifies all of the bizarre and unanticipable shifts in tone that are associated with "tragic farce."[2] *What the Butler Saw* is hardly tragic—it is, in fact, close to *The Importance of Being Earnest* both in style and plot (especially the lurid denouement)—but it plays with large concepts of identity (preferably sexual identity), incest, authority, and maintaining one's sanity in a mad world. These are all farcical themes with a certain natural relevance to tragedy.

In his recent short book on Orton in Methuen's Contemporary Writers series, C. W. E. Bigsby calls Orton "the high priest of farce in the mid-sixties"[3] and points to his development of a new kind of farce:

> But it was Orton's achievement to give farce a new meaning, to make it something more than the coy trysting with disorder it had once been. For Orton, farce became both an expression of anarchy and its only antidote. In his play, role playing is not a series of false surfaces concealing a real self; it is the total meaning or unmeaning of protagonists who survive by refusing all substance. (p. 17)

This is further defined in terms of entropy:

> The protagonists of this new farce-world are therefore themselves marginal, irrelevant to the slow unwinding of an entropic process, while the form itself is self-destructive, implying the existence of no Platonic idea in the mad logic of its own configurations. (p. 52)

This is a different kind of farce from the comfortable, domestic assumptions of Plautus's New Comedy, where all the formulas are worked out to produce the happy ending and perturbations are merely a plot device. In Aristophanes' Old Comedy, the endings generally celebrate the triumph of a splendid wish-fulfillment idea like peace, sexual bliss, and the values of Cloud Cuckooland.

Orton's endings are sardonic. In *Entertaining Mr. Sloane,* the hoodlum picaro is, through murder, tamed into a bisexual stud forced to be shared between brother and sister. *Loot* ends with the bank robbers, the homicidal nurse, and the model detective from Scotland Yard parceling out the loot among themselves, while the honest but pompous widower, Mr. McLeavy, is conveniently framed and sent to prison. *What the Butler Saw* has an extraordinarily Dionysiac—or mock Dionysiac—ending, as Sergeant Match, clad only in the leopard-spotted dress of Mrs. Prentice and the god Hercules, leads all the characters on stage to an apocalyptic exit through the skylight: *"They pick up their clothes and weary, bleeding, drugged and drunk, climb the rope ladder into the blazing light"* (p. 448). Lahr sees in the action a "wink at Euripides,"[4] whose *Bacchae* was the inspiration for Orton's bitter, adult-camp farce, *The Erpingham Camp.* Sergeant Match qualifies as spiritual guide by his remarkable discovery of the missing parts of the statue of Sir Winston Churchill. In Geraldine's cardboard box, with which she enters from the Friendly Faces Employment Bureau and which she totes about with her throughout the play, is the more than life-size penis of the great wartime leader of the valiant Britons, which was miraculously "embedded" in the remains of Geraldine's stepmother (echoing the apocalyptic ending of *Candy,* published in 1964). As the phallic Dionysus/ Hercules, Sergeant Match *"holds high the nation's heritage,"* while *"The dying sunlight from the garden and the blaze from above gild"* him with a mysterious halo (p. 448).

In literature as in life, Orton was obsessed with the idea of comic festivity and celebration. Drawing on a distinction from Nietzsche's *Birth of Tragedy,* Orton elevates the values of comedy over those of tragedy:

> I always say to myself that the theatre is the Temple of Dionysus, and not Apollo. You do the Dionysus thing on your typewriter, and then you allow a little Apollo in, just a little to shape and guide it along certain lines you may want to go along. But you can't allow Apollo in completely. (Interview with Alan Brien, BBC Radio, 14 July 1964, transmitted 28 July, Lahr, p. 15)

The Dionysiac enters *What the Butler Saw* through its enormous sexual energies. Orton recreates the raucous animal spirits of Aristophanes and Plautus rather than the refined bedroom farce of Feydeau, where an almost maddening barrage of titillation replaces any possibility of vulgar consummation. Polymorphous perversity is the guiding principle of *What the Butler Saw,* and imaginative variety defines sexual value. The question of identity that is so crucial in tragedy is now translated into its farcical equivalent: sexual identity. The characters try vainly to establish their maleness or femaleness, only to discover that it hardly matters in view of the madly incestuous climax that is being prepared.

When Dr. Prentice insists that he is a heterosexual, Dr. Rance, the inspecting government psychiatrist, objects to such an overbearing abstraction: "I wish you wouldn't use these Chaucerian words. It's most confusing" (p. 411). In the classic tradition of farce, transvestism is rampant, as if the costumes themselves were the only sure guide to the sexual identities of the characters. When Geraldine is dressed in the uniform of Nick, the bellhop of the Station Hotel, she cannot logically convince anyone that she is either a girl or a boy, and she floats frustratingly in that epicene middle state where the categories of masculine and feminine lose their clear outlines. This is definitely not bisexuality, but rather a comic release from the burdens of a narrow sexual identity. As an avowed homosexual, Orton could mercilessly twit both the gay and the straight worlds, and sexuality in his plays becomes a synonym for the imagination.

Dr. Rance is the representative of the real world—"Your immediate superiors in madness," as he puts it (p. 376)—but he is, of course, the most insane of all the characters in this private psychiatric clinic. His attempts at logic and common sense are the maddest thing about him, as he quizzes Geraldine on her sexual identity:

> RANCE . . . Do you think of yourself as a girl?
>
> GERALDINE No.
>
> RANCE Why not?
>
> GERALDINE I'm a boy.
>
> RANCE *(kindly)* Do you have the evidence about you?
>
> GERALDINE *(her eyes flashing an appeal to* DR PRENTICE*)* I must be a boy. I like girls.
>
> DR RANCE *stops and wrinkles his brow, puzzled.* (p. 413)

True to the spirit of farce, what is most obvious to the audience is most puzzling to the characters on stage, as Dr. Rance, by the conventions of the form, is forbidden to see through even the simplest of the multitudinous disguises. He cannot follow Geraldine's artlessly heterosexual reasoning, and, as a last resort, he insists on the evidence of the senses:

> RANCE . . . Take your trousers down. I'll tell you which sex you belong to.
>
> GERALDINE *(backing away)* I'd rather not know!
>
> RANCE You wish to remain in ignorance?
>
> GERALDINE Yes.
>
> RANCE I can't encourage you in such a self-indulgent attitude. You must face facts like the rest of us. (p. 413)

But when, *"Provoked beyond endurance,* GERALDINE *flings herself into* DR RANCE*'s arms and cries hysterically . . .* Undress me then, doctor! Do whatever you like only prove that I'm a girl," Dr. Rance *"pushes away and turns, frigidly to* DR PRENTICE*"* (p. 414). He recoils with horror from the real life about which he is constantly talking.

Orton goes beyond classic farce to energize his play with all possible varieties of sexual behavior: buggery, necrophilia, lesbianism, exhibitionism, hermaphroditism, rape, sadomasochism, fetishism, transvestism, nymphomania, and the very triumphant incest which crowns the mock Wildean recognition scene. Sex is entirely separated from guilt. With yeasty complications that multiply with alarming rapidity, sex symbolizes the world of impulse on which comedy is based: at its heart, it is dreamlike, self-gratifying, wish-fulfilling, and narcissistic. Thus, Mrs. Prentice's exclamation, "I want account taken of my sexual nature" (p. 423), is the real theme of the play, which seems to cure both her frigidity and her husband's impotence: the play itself acts out the sexual therapy. One of Prentice's first remarks about his wife is an appeal for sympathy from Geraldine, who is just on the point of trying out his contraceptive device: "My wife is a nymphomaniac. Consequently, like the Holy Grail, she's ardently sought after by young men" (p. 368). This is a typically Orton epigram that echoes *The Importance of Being Earnest,* a play that looms behind *What the Butler Saw* as distinctly as it does behind Stoppard's *Travesties.* Both Orton and Stoppard are invoking the archly polished wit of Restoration comedy as it is refracted through Wilde's Victorian *rifacimento* of that style.

Is Mrs. Prentice a nymphomaniac? Hardly. Although Dr. Prentice claims, "You were born with your legs apart. They'll send you to the grave in a Y-shaped coffin" (p. 371), his wife seems to be dabbling in sex to entice him back to his marital duties. When she "*advances on* DR PRENTICE" with a gun, we have a homosexual's farcical hyperbole of the phallic woman attempting by force to seduce an unwilling male:

> MRS PRENTICE *(waving the gun)* Come with me and lie down!
>
> PRENTICE The woman is insatiable.
>
> MRS PRENTICE Unless you make love to me I shall shoot you.
>
> PRENTICE No husband can be expected to give his best at gun-point. *(Backing away.)* (p. 436)

Throughout the play Mrs. Prentice keeps encountering naked men—"Doctor, doctor! The world is full of naked men running in all directions!" (p. 437)—that Dr. Rance, with professional unction, assures her are delusions. All this priapic and Dionysiac exhibitionism prepares Mrs. Prentice for a sexual reconciliation with her husband:

> DR PRENTICE *seizes her, smacks her face and tears the dress from her. She struggles.*
>
> MRS PRENTICE *(gasping as he slaps her)* Oh, my darling! This is the way to sexual adjustment in marriage. (p. 431)

This mock sadomasochistic scenario is as close to sexual fulfillment as the play ever comes.

Like Molière's Doctors (in *Le Médecin Malgré Lui, L'Amour Médecin,* and *Le Malade Imaginaire*), Orton's psychiatrists in *What the Butler Saw* also represent an arcane, technological system that has no relation to any

living reality: in other words, they are pious, jargonizing, mystifying, professional humbugs. Dr. Rance—with a pun on "rants"—is the chief spokesman for psychiatric mumbo jumbo, with Dr. Prentice functioning as his apprentice. The puns are self-consciously mischievous, and Orton is constantly doodling with wordplay, especially the clichéd double-entendres and euphemisms of British popular speech like "service" (pp. 390 and 445), "disturb" (p. 396), "interfere" (p. 408), and "misbehave" (p. 443). In the spirit of David Lodge's *The British Museum Is Falling Down* (1965), Mrs. Prentice is said to be "harder to get into than the reading room at the British Museum" (p. 396).

Like *Hamlet,* the whole plays turns on the question of the missing father, as in the very first exchange between Dr. Prentice and Geraldine: "Who was your father?" (p. 363). To spectators schooled in melodrama, this question discloses that incest will be the central theme, a point that Rance belabors with uncanny foresight. Rance is the coldly theoretical observer, the authority figure, whose speculations lie outside the ascertainable facts of the play. Almost immediately upon seeing the naked Geraldine, he certifies her as insane and prepares to admit her as a patient. There is no way of interrupting the barrage of psychoanalytic jargon by which Rance hypothesizes her case. The questions require no answers, and we are snugly ensconced in the black-comedy world of Joseph Heller's *Catch 22* (which has similar psychiatric interviews):

> RANCE . . . Who was the first man in your life?
>
> GERALDINE My father.
>
> RANCE Did he assault you?
>
> GERALDINE No!
>
> RANCE *(to* DR PRENTICE She may mean "Yes" when she says "No". It's elementary feminine psychology. *(To* GERALDINE.) Was your stepmother aware of your love for your father?
>
> GERALDINE I lived in a normal family. I had no love for my father.
>
> RANCE *(to* DR PRENTICE) I'd take a bet that she was the victim of an incestuous attack. She clearly associates violence and the sexual act. Her attempt, when naked, to provoke you to erotic response may have deeper significance. (p. 382)

Like Freud, Dr. Rance wants to displace the "erotic response" onto some "deeper significance" and not to regard it directly as a sexual expression. So we wind up with the farcial displacement of reality, by which all literal meanings and truths disappear and everything means something else.

Orton saw psychiatry as a mad system of pseudo-meanings, a way of suffocating experience in language that has no relation to any perceivable reality. On 9 June

1967, he said in an interview in the *Evening News:* "Everybody is a little like psychiatrists today. They've got this enormous wish to explain everything. Religion—especially Christianity—tries to show things following a logical progression. And for all we know the whole thing may turn out to be some vast joke" (Lahr, p. 261). In Dr. Rance's world, sexuality as primitive impulse and energy disappears to be replaced by myth-making and fictionalizing. It looks as if Dr. Rance's chief function in *What the Butler Saw* is to gather materials for a lurid best seller:

> The ugly shadow of anti-Christ stalks this house. Having discovered her Father/Lover in Dr Prentice the patient replaces him in a psychological re-shuffle by that archetypal Father-figure—the Devil himself. Everything is now clear. The final chapters of my book are knitting together: incest, buggery, outrageous women and strange love-cults catering for depraved appetites. All the fashionable bric-à-brac. A beautiful but neurotic girl has influenced the doctor to sacrifice a white virgin to propitiate the dark gods of unreason. "When they broke into the evil-smelling den they found her poor body bleeding beneath the obscene and half-erect phallus." (p. 427)

Like Stoppard, Orton delights in the merging and conversion of fiction into reality. By the logic of New Farce, the play proper has stopped and Dr. Rance is doing his turn, a little set piece exhibiting the "growing menace of pornography," on which he is determined to cash in. We are in the self-conscious, metatheatrical world of artifice and literature as Dr. Rance rises to his moral peroration: "The whole treacherous avant-garde movement will be exposed for what it is—an instrument for inciting decent citizens to commit bizarre crimes against humanity and the state!" (p. 428). This is like Orton's obscenely moralizing letters under the name of Mrs. Edna Welthorpe, including a scathing attack on Orton's own play *Entertaining Mr. Sloane* (printed in the Letters to the Editor column of the *Daily Telegraph*):

> I myself was nauseated by this endless parade of mental and physical perversion. And to be told that such a disgusting piece of filth now passes for humour.

> Today's young playwrights take it upon themselves to flaunt their contempt for ordinary decent people. I hope that the ordinary decent people will shortly strike *back!* (Lahr, pp. 166-67)

Thus Rance delights in the lurid denouement, with its split elephant brooch and sentimental memories of a rape in the linen cupboard on the second floor of the Station Hotel during a blackout: "Double incest is even more likely to produce a best-seller than murder—and this is as it should be for love *must* bring greater joy than violence" (p. 446).

Is this the final meaning of Orton's farce, that "love *must* bring greater joy than violence"? In some way the climax of *What the Butler Saw* is a structural device for converting violence into love. The play ends "*in a great blaze of glory*" (p. 446), as the characters embrace one another and prepare for their ritual ascent on the rope ladder through the skylight. Dr. Rance, the inquisitorial inspector-general of psychiatry, is revealed as the author-in-the-play, who was not only seeking out enormities, but also trying to create them for the sake of his steamy plot. He is disarmed by his own fictions. Sexual fulfillment awaits all these "*bleeding, drugged and drunk*" characters, weary and sore, as they wend their naked ways to a heaven of polymorphously perverse indulgences. The ending is wonderfully satisfying, but ironic. Can the power of Winston Churchill's phallus, waved triumphantly over the celebrants, bring eternal happiness? As Mrs. Prentice says in another connection: "the pleasures of the senses quickly pall" (p. 431); and as Geraldine exclaims very near the end: "I'm not a patient. I'm telling the truth!" We need especially to heed Dr. Rance's wise answer: "It's much too late to tell the truth" (p. 437). Orton establishes his credentials as a dramatist far beyond mere truth-telling.

In Orton's brief and meteoric career (compressed between the years 1963-1967), we see the playwright struggling with a characteristically modern problem: how to make literature out of life, but also how to disentangle literature and life so that one is not an abrasive simulacrum for the other—in other words, how to escape from the trap of autobiography. Orton's solution in his earlier plays, especially *Entertaining Mr. Sloane* and *Loot,* was to distance the events of his life by a blank, occulted, Pinteresque style. The characters are all menacing masks with an uncomfortable relation to Orton's unloving, coquettish, mother; his ineffectual, horticultural father; and the dramatist himself in his ruffian/poet guise—there is an unacknowledged debt to the personae of Tennessee Williams.

What the Butler Saw, Orton's last play, is a new departure, and it represents a way out of the problems both of autobiography and of the heavy indebtedness to Pinter. By writing a farce, Orton is able to mute the large significances of his earlier work and to distance any intrusive sense of propinquity either to his own life or to his literary sources, especially Pinter. As a genre, farce lends itself to depersonalization and to the ritual enactment of the values of comedy. Saturnalia replaces satire, and the wish fulfillment of polymorphous perversity, both in sex and in language, is vigorously celebrated. In *What the Butler Saw* Orton manages to combine, with brilliance and originality, the virtues of Old and New Farce. There is the tumultuous sexual energy of Aristophanes, the careful intrigue-plotting of Plautus, and the self-conscious, parodic, histrionic clowning of modern black comedy in the style of Beckett, Pinter, Ionesco, Stoppard, and especially Brecht.

We know from Lahr's incisive biography, *Prick Up Your Ears,* that Orton read much more widely than is generally believed, and he had a literate sense of his own place in the history of stage comedy. He was most conscious of his relation to Wilde, whom he admired for taking "great pains" with his work (Kenneth Williams, in Lahr, p. 202), but whom he faulted for being "flabby and self-indulgent" in his life (Orton in *Evening Standard,* 30 Oct. 1966, Lahr, p. 126). Ronald Bryden cleverly labeled Orton the "Oscar Wilde of Welfare State gentility" (Lahr, p. 221). Perhaps with the example of Ben Jonson, the "bricklayer of Westminster," in mind, Orton aspired to be "as tough as a bricklayer": "There is this complete myth about writers being sensitive plants. They're not. It's a silly nineteenth century idea, but I'm sure Aristophanes was not sensitive" (Orton in *Evening Standard,* 30 Oct. 1966, Lahr, p. 126). Orton the body-builder and physical culturist admired Wilde and Congreve for some very surprising qualities:

> Oscar Wilde's style is much more earthy and colloquial than most people notice. When we look at Lady Bracknell, she's the most ordinary, common, direct woman; she's not an affected woman at all. People are taken in by "the glittering style." It's not glitter. Congreve is the same. It's real—a slice of life. It's just very brilliantly written, perfectly believable. Nothing at all incredible. (Interview with Barry Hanson, Lahr, pp. 106-107)

This is exactly the criterion Orton held up for farce. In response to a wretchedly arty production of Feydeau's *A Flea in Her Ear,* Orton insisted that "in Farce everything (the externals) must be believed" (Diary, 7 June 1967, Lahr, p. 143). Without this core of credibility, the farce would degenerate into meaningless and chaotic motion without any purpose. Orton plays with a concept of reality strongly enunciated in Lewis Carroll's *Through the Looking-Glass:*

> "I *am* real!" said Alice, and began to cry. . . .

> "If I wasn't real," Alice said—half laughing through her tears, it all seemed so ridiculous—"I shouldn't be able to cry."

> "I hope you don't suppose those are *real* tears?" Tweedledum interrupted in a tone of great contempt.[5]

To Mrs. Prentice's desperate question, "Is this blood real?" (showing her hands), Tweedledum Rance of course answers, "No" (p. 439), and when Nick is shot in the shoulder, presumably by Rance, he confronts the psychiatrist's vapid fictionalizing with pain and blood:

> NICK I can't be an hallucination. (*He points to his bleeding shoulder.*) Look at this wound. That's real.

> RANCE It appears to be.

> NICK If the pain is real I must be real.

> RANCE I'd rather not get involved in metaphysical speculation. (p. 443)

The bleeding Mrs. Prentice, Nick, and Sergeant Match challenge the impunity rule of traditional farce. In the mock triumphant ending of *What the Butler Saw,* the characters are nevertheless "*weary, bleeding, drugged and drunk*" (p. 448).

In what sense can farce be "real—a slice of life," "perfectly believable"? The point of New Farce as one finds it in Ionesco and Stoppard and Orton is to uphold the old Ciceronian ideal that comedy should be an image of the world, a mirror of manners, and a model for how the rational man can conduct his life in an irrational world. Even though less overt than *Entertaining Mr. Sloane* and *Loot, What the Butler Saw* is still a bitter indictment of a world gone mad. Like Wilde, Orton did not make any tedious and artificial distinctions between earnestness and levity. Orton thought of himself as a very traditional and moral exponent of the well-made play, and it is Rance, the inspector-general who comes from afar, who speaks the final words of the play, an affirmation of the reality principle: "I'm glad you don't despise tradition. Let us put our clothes on and face the world" (p. 448).

NOTES

[1] All quotations from *What the Butler Saw* are from Joe Orton, *The Complete Plays,* introd. John Lahr (New York, 1977). Orton is quoting very freely from Tourneur's play. All subsequent references will be given in the text.

[2] T. S. Eliot, "Christopher Marlowe," in *Essays on Elizabethan Drama* (New York, 1956).

[3] C. W. E. Bigsby, *Joe Orton* (London, 1982), in Contemporary Writers series.

[4] John Lahr, *Prick Up Your Ears: The Biography of Joe Orton* (New York, 1978), p. 15. The Orton documents are quoted from Lahr with page references in the text.

[5] Lewis Carroll, *Alice Through the Looking-Glass* (New York, 1977), p. 85.

Una Chaudhuri

SOURCE: "Private Parts: Sex, Class, and Stage Space in 'Miss Julie'," in *Theatre Journal,* Vol. 45, No. 3, October, 1993, pp. 317-32.

[In the following essay, Chaudhuri explores the determinism of sexual, social, and spatial transgression in August Strindberg's naturalist drama Miss Julie.]

The plot of *Miss Julie* turns on an unusual conjunction of sexual and spatial determinism, an association which also includes the issue of class. The aristocratic Julie and her valet Jean are literally and figuratively trapped into intercourse when, to avoid being seen together alone, they are forced into hiding in Jean's room. This fateful concealment, which Strindberg is at pains to characterize also as a *fated* development, renders the disruption of class roles as *sexuality,* and sexuality (that is, transgressive, forbidden, *fatal* sexuality) as the inevitable outcome of a momentary and enforced *privacy.* In acting according to the taboos and dictates of a rigid class society, it would seem, the characters are doomed to transgress two of the orders in which that society inscribes itself, the orders of sexuality and territoriality.

The actual class situation prevailing in Sweden at the time the play was written was, of course, a good deal more complex than such generic terms as "aristocratic" and "valet" can capture. Miss Julie, for instance, belongs to the nobility and can thus claim the title "*Fröken,*" but it is clear that her family is not without its economic and social vulnerabilities and that the upper-class privilege they enjoy is in the process of unravelling. However, in developing the action that puts Julie into Jean's room, Strindberg generally erases the historical specificities which in reality would have qualified the class opposition between the protagonists. It is not only that both Julie and Jean seem to have a psychological stake in maintaining an extremist account of class difference: the play itself has a similar stake, which is however not psychological but ideological and theatrological.

Julie agrees to take refuge in Jean's room when he persuades her that the servants and farm workers who are headed into the kitchen for refreshment are mocking her in their song. Jean insists that they do not love her, as she thinks; her sentimental trust in them is misplaced, he says, made impossible by the divisive forces of class difference: "They take the food you give them, but they spit on it as soon as your back is turned."[1] Having made his point, Jean then dictates the course of action with reference to this typically extremist estimation of class relations: "That's what the mob always is—cowards! You can't fight them; you can only run away" (89). Julie's answer then enunciates the play's linking of class difference to spatial determinism: "Run away? Where? There's no way out of here" (239).

The knotting together of the separate systems of sex, class and space in a dense relation of inevitability is not only the plot of *Miss Julie;* it is also the plot—the ideological project—of naturalism. Both turn on the attempt to renegotiate *and to fix in place* the relationship between individual, private experience and its public meaning. The supposedly private parts of the house in which Miss Julie's personal destiny is played out are in fact as public, as fully determined by social definitions, as are the private "parts" or roles played by the characters of this play and the actors of naturalist theatre.

The notion of private selves, subjective identities—upon which, since Stanislavsky, the theatrology of realism rests—is as much in crisis (already) in *Miss Julie* as is the general concept of privacy, of spaces and experiences to which one has exclusive claims. Within the play (but clearly deriving from its socio-historical context) an unresolvable contradiction emerges between the idealization of the principle of privacy and its simultaneous qualification. Precisely this contradiction is also the source of a certain discordance within the theoretics of naturalism, and can be found structured into its paradigmatic stage space.

The naturalist stage adumbrates a specific relationship between the performance and the spectator, connecting them to each other with an ambitious new contract of total visibility, total knowledge. The promise of the well-stocked stage of naturalism is a promise of omniscience, indeed of a transfer of omniscience from dramatist to spectator. Having been impregnated with "reality," in the form of all those little touches of "innocent verisimilitude" which Bert States memorably describes as "the casual masquerading as the casual,"[2] the stage space of naturalism seems ready to deliver the whole truth, to dispel the enigmas of past and future from a firmly drawn present. The theatre's self-insertion into the naturalistic project sets it "marching," as Zola announced, "from the known to the unknown." The action of *Miss Julie*— the action which puts Julie in Jean's room—is arranged in such a way as to affirm this intrepid new account of theatrical signification and of spectatorship. Yet, even as it highlights and foregrounds its multi-faceted assault on the unknown, the play also demonstrates that the unknown (be it the psychological unknown of character and motivation or the socio-political unknown of class history) returns, like the repressed, in disguise. The mask it wears is hard to recognize as a mask because of its history as Truth: the mask is tragedy. However, the tragic lineaments of this play outline a pseudo-tragedy only, marking an ideological crisis that reveals itself as a profound ambivalence about, precisely, the age-old gifts of tragedy: truth, knowledge, certainty. It is this ideological crisis, inscribed in the play's unusual stage space as well as in its final moments, that makes *Miss Julie* exemplary of naturalism.

Naturalism as ideological crisis rather than as aesthetic project is enacted at every level of Strindberg's play, not least at the level of its theoretical status, which is derived from its extraordinary relationship to the monumental "Author's Preface." Strindberg's forceful theorization of his experiment[3] has produced a sort of permanent transgressive structure around the play, a confusion of outside and inside that characterizes many other features of the play as well, including its physical space and its theoretics. The preface is wrapped around and folded into the play it introduces to a degree unusual even for the heavily prefaced documents of a self-conscious dramatic modernity. It was written after the play but has accompanied the published version from the start, thus determining an interpretive future that is probably radically discontinuous with the play's compositional past.[4]

The on-going historical relationship between the play and the preface constitutes the conceptual or theoretical space of *Miss Julie,* and has, like a physical space, an inside and an outside. In this space as in the literal spaces of the play, inside and outside, as well as visible and invisible, are linked by a hidden logic, a logic of *partial*—not total—visibility. The rhetorical process of the play (and, I am arguing, of naturalism itself) is one that takes these literal spatial oppositions (along with other more figurative ones, especially private and public, known and unknown) and rewrites them so that they are not mutually exclusive opposites but rather versions of each other. In the staging and meaning of the play—just as in the logic of naturalism—"inside" is not merely contiguous and continuous with "outside" but thoroughly penetrated by it; similarly, the private is not a realm withdrawn and protected from the public but fully determined by it. In the fiction as much as in the staging of this play, what is performed is the problematic lodged in Strindberg's oxymoronic appellation, the Intimate Theatre.

The inside of the conceptual space of *Miss Julie* is occupied, of course, by the proclaimed ideals of naturalism. Naturalism is "located" in this work (that is, the preface + the play) as in few others.[5] Indeed by this time in the historiography of dramatic modernism the coincidence between this work and the program of naturalism seems so overdetermined as to be almost a relation of caricature. Certainly the heart of the preface is an encapsulated encyclopedia of the dramaturgical and theatrical devices that have come to be identified with the school of Zola: psychosocial complexity and "real doorknobs on the doors."

But Strindberg's rhetorical choices in the preface—notably his wavering between claims of radical innovation and expressions of humility, even despair—position naturalism as a paradoxical, self-contradictory and transgressive discourse. Strindberg's preface utterly disproves the assumption that a prefatory essay is inherently more univocal and less ambiguous than a literary work.[6] In this text, naturalism appears not as a closed and coherent system but precisely as an *opening,* a gap between two historical systems, one exhausted and moribund, the other still to emerge. In a quite urgent way, Strindberg's preface represents itself as the aperture from which one can begin to glimpse "the repertory that one day shall come" (217). Here and elsewhere, naturalism situates itself on the emergent horizon of theatre history, awaiting what Antoine called "the hoped-for generation of new playwrights." What distinguishes this and other manifestos of modernism is the presence here of an overriding "futurology," a movement of projection and compulsive displacement into the unknown. Strindberg's preface—but not, significantly, his play—is soaked with future reference, even down to its last lines, which read: "Here is my attempt! If I have failed, there is still time to try again" (217).

The terms I have just used to describe this futurology (projection, displacement, compulsion) indicate how easily this impulse can be and has been thematized, contributing some of modern drama's most fertile tropes: the inadequacy of home, the exhilaration of exile, the new victimage of location, the new heroism of departure. All these motifs haunt this play as well, most explicitly in Jean's lengthy fantasy, temporarily shared by Julie, of a future life as a hotelier. But the desired displacements, so crucial to writers like Ibsen and Chekhov, have an insubstantial hold on Strindberg's dramaturgy, in which a claustrophobic entrapment prevails. I would suggest that this reflects the much more complicated relationship that Strindberg had with the unknown, and his uneasiness with its new, positivist definition.

As the new frontier of scientific and secular humanism, the unknown presents a deceptively tamer aspect than it had in the past. Once contextualized outside of religious ideology, the unknown appears not as mystery but as enigma, conundrum, and puzzle, a region not merely hospitable to but positively begging for colonization by powerful explanatory systems. Such systems (in *Miss Julie* they are sex and class) are the true protagonists of the drama of naturalism, which, having set as its goal the observation, exposition and explication of life as it is, must at every moment engage and overcome the unknown. This project involves both the stage and the audience, connecting them to each other in a new and impossible contract of total visibility.

One feature of this contract is the necessary reduction of the characters to the status of signs within the plays' philosophical discourses. Unlike their classical predecessors, the inhabitants of naturalistic drama do not participate in the philosophical inquiries embodied by their fates; rather, they are merely the raw material, the data, of the audience's discoveries. The agonized question asked by Miss Julie (both the person and the play)—"Who's to blame for what has happened?" (265)—is really only asked of the spectator. Miss Julie herself quickly dismisses the question, recognizing that it is rendered irrelevant by the determinism of her position: since "I'm still the one who has to bear the guilt, suffer the consequences" (265). However, this is certainly not the attitude that is urged on the spectator or the reader, either by the play or the preface, both of which valorize and encourage a search for systematic understanding. In this way, the naturalist agenda transfers the function of recognition from the protagonists to the spectator; here discovery and revelation are of a purely hermeneutic order, within the theatre but outside the drama.

Miss Julie is clearly marked as a hermeneutic construct; its events are accompanied by a persuasive interpretive map, presented mainly in the two dreams that the protagonists recount to each other.[7] Yet these dreams do nothing to *explain* the reversal of positions between Julie and Jean; rather, they *allegorize* it, and they do so in the starkest possible way. As such, they are part of the hermeneutic determinism of the play, that structure that puts the spectator in the position once held by the tragic hero. The crude symbolism of these dreams, their imagery of high and low, up and down, climbing and falling, offers a convenient and schematic key to interpreting the plot, inviting us to read the sexual encounter as a moment of class reversal. That reading is reinforced towards the end of the play with references to a Christian schema whereby "the last shall be first" (264) and "the first shall be the last" (267). Thus the play's answer to Julie's question—'Who's to blame for what has happened?" (265)—is an abstract, structural answer, which reads change in terms of stark oppositions and which emphasizes the extreme points of these oppositions: high and low, first and last. The spaces of the play, however, diagnose the situation quite differently. They bespeak a problem not of hierarchical displacements but of *lateral* movement, a problem of the unavoidable violation of contiguous, mutually exclusive yet mutually dependent spaces.

But before one can read the stage space of *Miss Julie* it is necessary to describe what I have called its conceptual space, characterized by a similarly transgressive structure. The inside of this conceptual space is occupied, as I have said, by the emergent ideal of naturalism. The futurology that frames this ideal, keeping it hazy and indistinct while asserting its necessity, is one way in which its "outside" leaks in. The main substance of this outside, the irrationalism which is programatically excluded from the positivistic domain of naturalism, is, of course, not alien to modernism in general (and certainly not to Strindberg, who in the years to come was to plumb its depths[8]). My purpose here is to show the extent to which this irrationalism shores up the self-representation of naturalism, making *Miss Julie* a cryptic enactment of both the naturalistic theatre and its "double."[9]

This double (or, as I have called it, this "outside") is invoked in the very first lines of the preface, in terms that immediately reveal its dismal features—ignorance and religious superstition: "Like the arts in general, the theatre has for a long time seemed to me a *Biblia pauperum,* a picture Bible for those who cannot read" (204). Thus illiteracy, which openly adheres to the irrationalist outside of naturalism, is covertly linked to a central feature of the naturalistic construct, iconicity. The relation of a retrograde illiteracy to a productive, enlightening literalism is established through and across a category with which Strindberg regularly did battle, that of Woman. The link between women and illiteracy, as well as the further connection of both to an illusionistic dramaturgy is spelled out without delay: "That explains why the theatre has always been an elementary school for youngsters and the half-educated, and for women, who still retain a primitive capacity for letting themselves be deceived" (204). While appearing to herald a departure from the kind of crudely illusionistic—or "deceiving"—drama of a "primitive" past, a drama that had been geared to the "rudimentary and undeveloped mental processes" (204), the preface nevertheless projects a future whose terms remain close to certain categories that it has begun by associating with ignorance and with femaleness, especially the capacity "for succumbing to illusions" (204). For example—and it is an example that will finally bring onstage the equivocal figure whom I read as a deconstruction of naturalism— a little later in the preface, Strindberg explains his innovative abolishing of act divisions and intermissions as follows: "I was afraid that the spectator's declining susceptibility to illusion [a development he has previously characterized as an evolution "to the level of reflection, research and experimentation" (204)] might not carry him through the intermission, when he would have time to think about what he has seen and to escape the suggestive influence of the author-hypnotist" (213).

The author-hypnotist is the site of a turbulent ambivalence in Strindberg's theorizing, the point of conflict between two incommensurate views of theatre: one as an enlightening and demystifying display of meaningful causalities, and the other as a symptom of certain inexorable and mysterious historical forces that exert their influence on both the form and the content of dramatic art.[10] This vacillation disturbs the entire conceptual space of *Miss Julie,* both the play and its accompanying theoretics, in spite of Strindberg's attempt to stabilize his play by calling it "an exception . . . but an important exception of the kind which proves the rule" (206). A vivid example of this ambivalence is in the preface's much-cited passage on modernist characterology, in which the choice of imagery (and its ostentatious proliferation) suggests an overleaping of Zola's earnest positivism into something much like Brechtian irony: "I have noticed that what interests people most nowadays is the psychological action. Our inveterately curious souls are no longer content to see something happen; we want to see how it happens. We want to see the strings, look at the machinery, examine the double-bottomed drawer, put on the magic ring to find the hidden seam, look in the deck for the marked cards" (212). While claiming to further the cause of a new theatre of total visibility and total knowledge, this catalogue of stage tricks keeps dramatic representation firmly lodged in a juvenile and slightly sleazy pre-history of side-shows and mindless entertainments.

This ironic and alien presence within the conceptual space of *Miss Julie* comes unexpectedly to dominate the final moments of the play itself, which are explicitly framed in terms of a certain kind of popular performance. Just before going off to perform her own "ending" offstage, Julie asks Jean, "Have you ever been to the theater and seen a hypnotist?" (266). In fact, the preface's figure of hypnosis[11] is woven into the fabric of Strindberg's play, and, as John Greenway has shown, contemporaneous theories, debates and terms about the subject are used to structure the dialogue between Jean and Julie even prior to the explicit reference just mentioned.[12]

More importantly, hypnotism is used in *Miss Julie* to correlate the categories of class and sex in a way that is crucial to the formulation of naturalist ideology. Here sex and class are first established as powerful explanatory systems, a power that is then subtly redefined when both kinds of relations, the relations between the sexes and the relations between the classes, are represented as being in some way analogous to the enigmatic relationship between hypnotist and hypnotic subject. The analogy is not merely poetic, and Strindberg's well-known interest in what he sometimes called "the battle of the brains" is only superficially as idiosyncratic as it seems. Hypnosis is, in fact, the perfect figure with which to represent the modernist construction of power along the mutually contradictory axes of freedom and determinism. Here, by being likened to hypnosis, the power-systems of sex and class appropriate a certain uncanniness, which will later be used to spawn the play's eventual pseudotragedy. That particular generic outcome will, of course, give naturalism the stamp of aesthetic truth.

However, the protocols of hypnosis inform naturalistic stage space even before Strindberg thematizes them. The kitchen set of *Miss Julie* is, in the first instance, an example of the deterministic[13] single set of realism, whose functioning Strindberg himself characterized with the phrase "the impact of the *recurring* milieu."[14] According to Bert States, the role of the single set is "the imprisonment of the eye [such that] . . . one of the two senses through which theatre comes to us is locked into a hypnotic sameness."[15] In this play, the spell cast by the hypnotic single set is as strong as ever, but another and crucial effect is present as well, a *reflexivity* about the single set, produced by the way this particular one *stages its limits*. Invoking the impressionist painters and their "idea of asymmetrical and open composition" (214), Strindberg breaches the naturalistic contract of total visibility in its own name, substituting a partial visibility offered as an invitation to the spectator's cooperative imagination: "Because the audience cannot see the whole room and all the furniture, they will have to surmise what's missing; that is, their imagination will be stimulated to fill in the rest of the picture" (214). In a movement that is also typical at the level of the play's meaning, the spectator's attention is distracted from its hypnotic fixity, drawn towards the limits and margins of the stage. Upon these margins are inscribed the ideological limitations of naturalism.

The famous partial room of *Miss Julie* is the deliberately deficient space of several hypnotic enthrallments, which function in a way that echoes the unusual stage space: they engage a logic of *partial* visibility, of an attenuated pictorialism by which so much is exposed to view and so much occluded, so many perspectives made available and so many denied, that the persisting enigma of the play seems to record a failure.[16] This is one of the liabilities that *Miss Julie* shares with naturalism, and its traces mark the preface as much as the play. In the former, the stubborn persistence of enigma reveals itself just when Strindberg's positivism is cranked up to its highest pitch: in the famous passage on motivation and causality in naturalism. Just before introducing his own

catalogue of "circumstances" motivating "the tragic fate of Miss Julie" (206), Strindberg makes the claim—which he calls "a fairly new discovery"—that "an event in life . . . is the result of a whole series of more or less deep-rooted causes." The example that follows, however, is not one of multiple causation but rather of multiple *interpretation,* specifically of the determinism of interpretation ("Consider a case of suicide. 'Business failure,' says the merchant. 'Unhappy love,' say the women." And so on.) The conclusion that Strindberg reaches represents a significant slippage from the positivism from which he began and to which he is headed: "But it may be that the reason lay in all of these or in none of them, and that the dead man hid his real reason behind a completely different one that would reflect greater glory on his memory" (206). The sibylline dead man is, I would suggest, the exemplary figure of Strindberg's imagination, and his characteristic space is the partially visible.

Of those instances of hypnotic influence which are incorporated into the plot, the most important is obviously the mutual seduction of Julie and Jean (an influence asserted with reference to several items which were, in Strindberg's time, widely regarded as being conducive to the hypnotic state, including alcohol, somnolence,[17] ocular fixation, and menstruation.[18]) The final seduction occurs, of course, in Jean's room, offstage and invisible. However, the privacy required by and signified by this consummation does not belong inherently to that space. In fact, the sexual union of Jean and Julie is also the occasion for Jean to *assert* his rights to a private space, however contested these may be: "I'll bolt the door. If they try to break it down, I'll shoot!" (239).

Until this moment of fierce assertion, Jean has been pointedly associated not with places of his own but rather with spatial *transgression,* and with various incursions of privacy. The most scandalous of these is the story he himself tells of how, as a boy, he once sneaked into the Turkish pavilion, the "Count's private privy" (234), in the garden of the great house. The humiliating outcome of that adventure not only teaches Jean the lesson that Julie is yet to learn—that the only privacy in the play, that *all* privacy in the play belongs to the Count—it also prefigures (in significantly scatological terms) Julie's "escape" into Jean's room: "And just then I heard someone coming! There was only one way out—for the upper class people. But for me there was one more—a lower one. And I had no other choice but to take it" (234).

Certain actions explicitly called for in the text suggest that Jean's painful lack of privacy as a child ("I lived with seven brothers and sisters and a pig" [233]) has not been overcome but continues in a more subtle form. Twice the text calls for Jean to perform an action while partly visible in the wings. In the first instance, the action deals explicitly with the issue of privacy. Simultaneously, and through the same action, a muted metatheatrical point is made about visual access to stage space, with Julie standing as the fulcrum between Jean's claim to privacy and his vulnerability to (the audience's) view. It is a perfect demonstration of the problematic of total visibility:

> Miss Julie: You're not embarrassed because I'm here, are you? Just to change? Go in your room and come right back again. Or else stay here and I'll turn my back.
>
> Jean: If you'll excuse me, Miss Julie. *(He goes off to the right. His arm can be seen as he changes his jacket.)* [226]

(Although the stage directions do not specify what Julie's reaction to Jean's choice is, I would think that this would be an important moment of choice for the actress playing the role. Does she allow Jean a measure of privacy, or does she insist on sharing the audience's transgressive view? The choice is sure to have far-reaching effects on the developing relationship: the issue of a personal space is not a light subject for Jean, a man whose self-construction—or at least self-presentation, to Julie—is largely a matter of spaces that he has been denied access to or spaces that he has occupied illicitly. As for Julie, her apparent power over the space of the play turns out to be illusory when it is revealed that she owns nothing. Privacy here is a luxury contingent on *private property,* and the only owner in the play is the absent Count.)

The second instance of Jean's partial visibility occurs late in the play, when Jean, who has "slip[ped] out to the right, . . . can be seen in the wings at the right, sharpening his straight razor on a strop held between his teeth and his left hand." From this partially visible position, he "listens to [the conversation between Christine and] Miss Julie with a satisfied expression on his face, now and then nodding approvingly" (261). It is hard to overlook the contrast between this use of the same marginal space, as a site for overhearing, from the first one, as a site for hiding. The difference is also, of course, a difference in Jean, a sign that he has changed, as it were, dramatically: over the course of the play he has performed as a protagonist is supposed to, making of a series of actions, a destiny. The event that has wrought this apparent transformation is the sexual encounter, before which his status was such as to give him hardly any control even over his own tiny space. The most obvious explanation for the reversal rests on a profoundly misogynistic logic: Jean becomes Julie's superior when she "falls," through sex, to the condition of a mere woman; in identifying herself sexually, she forfeits the immunity her class had given her from the usual debasement associated with being of the wrong sex. Needless to say, this is precisely the interpretation most commonly proferred by critics; it is the one prepared and positioned by the play's "vertical" hermeneutic apparatus. It is, moreover, bluntly stated by Strindberg in the preface: "Apart from the fact that Jean is coming up in the world, he is also superior to Miss Julie in that he is a man" (211).

However, the way in which the play deploys its figure of hypnosis—and the way Jean is positioned and is behaving in this moment of power—suggests a somewhat different and less heroic plot. In a novel entitled *Short Cuts* that he wrote in 1887 (the year before *Miss Julie*), Strindberg says: "The hypnotist says sleep and the person sleeps, or at least behaves like someone asleep. The hypnotist puts a broom in his hand and the broom sways about. *But this is no more remarkable than when a recruit presents arms at a corporal's order!*"[19] If (as Strindberg seems to be implying here) the orders given to social inferiors are a form of hypnotic suggestion, then Julie has quite simply been hypnotizing Jean during the whole first half of the play. Several times during that section, the giving and obeying of orders is discussed and enacted, with Jean being, of course, on the receiving end. Thus when, after the sexual encounter, the power positions are reversed, Jean's new power is actually the result of an *exchange* of power, a transfer of control from one "hypnotist" to another. After sex with Miss Julie, Jean seems to have acquired the position of hypnotist (which, let us not forget, the preface has identified as belonging to the author). Indeed, the tale that he is overhearing from his partly visible position in the wings is a kind of post-hypnotic suggestion, for Julie is repeating to Christine what Jean had said to her moments before. The repetition signals Jean's influence and power, and, by association, the power of that partly visible, marginal space that Jean mistakenly thinks is his. To learn who really controls the logic of partial visibility, and how, one must return to the role of transgression—the confusion of inside and outside, public and private, absent and present—in the play's structure as well as (and this requires a brief detour) in its history.

Problematic spatial relations and decisions have marked *Miss Julie* from the first. As soon as it was offered for performance, the play engaged the issue of what can be presented to the public and what must remain restricted, private. Karl Otto Bonnier judged it "too risky" even to publish and ventured the opinion that "you will find difficulty in getting it produced."[20] Bonnier was right: Strindberg's play was exiled from its native Sweden for sixteen years. Its first performance occurred in Denmark, but even there it was displaced by court order from the theatre where it was scheduled, and it finally found a home, for one night only, at the Copenhagen University Students' Union. Thus *Miss Julie* was first brought to the public as a private performance.

This initial transgression was the first of many produced by *Miss Julie.* Notorious among these is the transgression of autobiography, whereby the empiricist, representative stage of naturalism is suddenly required to display the personal scandals and private demons of a man as peculiar as Strindberg. Not only is there so much biography in *Miss Julie* as to make *both* the protagonists easy to read as representatives of the author,[21] but the play itself produced further transgressive effects: Strindberg was convinced that his wife, who played Julie in the first performance, was having an affair with the man who played Jean. According to a reporter who attended both the first performance and the party following it, Strindberg "stood half-hidden behind a door, his face pale and twisted with jealousy."[22] It is hard to resist assimilating this image of the half-hidden author to the play's logic of partial visibility, especially when we further read, in the same account of the first performance, that "we search in vain for August Strindberg, though it has been announced that he is to attend the performance."[23]

In literal fact as in the discursive logic of naturalism, the author-hypnotist, who must prevent reflection and encourage projection,[24] presents himself as an absense. His power is inscribed as a series of "suggestions" that elicit the spectator's cooperation, even her intellectual assent, and that lead to an inevitable conclusion, *legitimized precisely by the author's absence*. In *Miss Julie*, the ideological meaning of this authorial absence is *staged* through the figure of the Count and his relationship to the fictional space of the play.

Among the most obvious markings of this space are class signs: the stage represents the kitchen of a Swedish manor house. It is the domain of servants, although their dominion is ironic indeed, as we see early in the play when Jean enjoys the "little bit of kidney [that Christine] cut from the veal roast," along with a stolen bottle of the Count's wine (221). While the kitchen is the space of the servants' domesticity and privacy, it is not a home to them, not a place they have chosen and arranged for themselves.[25] The privacy that it affords is seriously circumscribed, as is demonstrated so dramatically when the kitchen is invaded by a crowd of merrymaking peasants, forcing Miss Julie and Jean into their fateful hiding. It is worth noting that the kitchen does not offer itself as a refuge to Miss Julie either, although she may seem to be, like her mother, "most at home in the kitchen and the cowsheds" (78). Like its partial representation, the kitchen connotes an inviting openness; like its representation, its accessibility is limited and determined by the interests of the person in ultimate control. In terms of the stage space, that person is the "author-hypnotist;" in terms of the kitchen, it is the Count.

The most impressive and permanent signs of the actual power structure governing this space are those that evoke the absent Count: the notorious boots—placed from the start "where they are clearly visible [to the audience]" (220)—and the bell and speaking tube, both silent until the last moments of the play, then horrifyingly alive. These latter two elements of the set relate directly to the position and signification of the play's space, especially to the fact that the kitchen has very limited access to the rest of the house. It seems to be linked to the house only through the courtyard that is partly visible through the large glass door in the back wall. This door is the only way to the rest of the house.[26]

Thus the kitchen is a kind of relegated space, an architectural *cul-de-sac* held at a physical and psychological distance from the rest of the house. According to

Lawrence Stone, this kind of arrangement, made possible by technological inventions like the bell wire and the speaking tube, was part of a process of physical distancing between servants and owners that occurred in the course of the nineteenth century.[27] The owners' desire to guard their privacy against the intrusions of their servants, without at the same time sacrificing the convenience of having ready access to the servants, was reflected in this new configuration of physical distance and technological proximity.

This arrangement was in itself the reflection of a changing class relation, whereby the feudal system of generations of servants was being replaced by a more capitalistic system of servants as workers, often itinerant (like Jean) and temporary. The old kind of servant, familiar to us from Chekhov, the loyal, trustworthy and self-sacrificing family retainer, is nowhere to be found in *Miss Julie;* he has been replaced by people who feel no devotion to their masters, no sense of obligation.[28] In fact the relation between masters and servants is staged here as one fraught with suspicion, contempt, and mutual fear, an alienated relation entirely dependent on formal bonds and regulations. Jean's professions of dutiful obedience sound as phony as his pretensions to culture; in fact the latter directly contradict the former. For all his lectures to Julie about the importance of knowing her place, Jean's own identification with his place has clearly been irreversibly disrupted.[29]

As a servant, Jean is in an asymmetrical relation to his position, out of step with its traditional meaning. A great deal of the dialogue between Jean and Julie is the articulation of this asymmetry, for Julie constructs class along certain quaint and sentimental lines that Jean treats with some irony:

> Jean: And there I caught sight of a pink dress and a pair of white stockings. You! I crawled under . . . thistles that pricked me and wet dirt that stank to high heaven. And all the while I could see you walking among the roses. I said to myself, "If it's true that a thief can enter heaven and be with the angels, isn't it strange that a poor man's child here on God's green earth can't enter the count's park and play with the count's daughter."
>
> Miss Julie: *(sentimentally)* Do you think all poor children have felt that way?
>
> Jean: *(hesitatingly at first, then with mounting conviction)* If all poor ch—? Yes—yes, naturally. Of course!
>
> Miss Julie: It must be terrible to be poor.
>
> Jean: *(with exaggerated intensity)* Oh, Miss Julie! You don't know! A dog can lie on the sofa with its mistress; a horse can have its nose stroked by the hand of a countess; but a servant—! [235]

Jean is both hyperconscious of class difference (and the behavior proper to each class) and yet free of essential class identity. Strindberg's own explanation of what he calls Jean's "unformed and divided" character (210), emphasizes his class-transgressive nature: he is said to despise his peers yet fear them "because they know his secrets," and "he is familiar with the ins and outs of good society" (210). A great deal of the action of the play, especially everything that leads up to the sexual encounter, seems to be a demonstration of Jean's notion that class differences are superficial, and that "maybe at bottom there isn't such a big difference as we think, between people and people" (236).

But what, then, is the meaning of the play's conclusion, when Jean's class transgression is so decisively quelled? Significantly, this rout of Jean's (and indeed all modernity's) attempt to de-essentialize class is played out as yet another transfer of hypnotic power, this time from Jean to the now-present (but still diegetic) Count. The Count's peculiar contribution to the play's completion is unmistakably linked to the figure of hypnosis, a relation that had been explicitly anticipated earlier, in Jean's confession that "I only have to look at his boots standing there so stiff and proud and I feel my spine bending" (241). In the play's final moments, Jean has what amounts to a hypnotic epiphany, a recognition of the "truth" of the trance, (*but from within the trance,* making it more demonstration than recognition): "What?! I thought I saw the bell move . . . Afraid of a bell! but it isn't just a bell. There's somebody behind it. A hand that makes it move. And there's something that makes the hand move" (267). While the overall effect of this passage is to enact, one last time, Jean's inbred servility, its oddly theoretical content—its assertion of a signal truth—draws attention to the figure of the Count, and specifically to his functioning in a way that reminds us of the preface's "author-hypnotist."

Strindberg's partly (metonymically) visible Count controls the partly visible space of the play, exerting his influence from the wings. While the stage signs—the bell and speaking tube—link his power to sound and aurality, his silence keeps that power diffused, pervasive. The private parts of the house sought out by the protagonists in their bid for self-definition are no more secure from this power than the private parts or roles they try to script for themselves (for example, in the very obviously stereotypical fantasy of a future happy life in a hotel). It is not simply that the Count orchestrates the protagonists' failure to make connections with levels similar to one's own (although the failed alliance of Julie and Jean does mark the triumph of a hegemonic patriarchy over women and workers); what is much more devastating is the ultimate removal of responsibility from characters who have largely been formed around the question of responsibility, of personal agency ("Who's to blame for what has happened?").

The protagonists' common enemy, the Author-Hypnotist/Count, manipulates them by rendering them abstract, by returning them to the schematic, even archetypal, categories (high and low, etc.) from which a truer

class identification (a self-identification in economic terms, for example) could have rescued them. That is to say, abstraction, typicality, and representativeness, all of which are (dis)embodied in the Count himself, are gradually transferred to the two protagonists, dissolving their ostentatiously constructed social and sexual identities into a hypnotic tautology:

> Miss Julie: What would you do if you were in my place?
>
> Jean: In your place? Let me think. . . . An aristocrat, a woman, and fallen. . . . I don't know.—Or maybe I do.
>
> Miss Julie: (*picks up the razor and makes a gesture with it*) Like this?
>
> Jean: Yes. But I wouldn't do it, you understand. That's the difference between us.
>
> Miss Julie: Because you're a man and I'm a woman? What difference does that make?
>
> Jean: Just the usual difference—between a man and a woman. [265]

The "usual difference"—this one as well as the other supposedly "usual" difference, between master and servant—is reinstalled here as the closure (in both senses: the denouement and the failure) of a drama of attempted displacement. Here, as Jean formulates it and as Julie embraces it, truth is simply, even trivially, the power of *place.* Now, all that idle talk early in the play about "knowing one's place" is offered as a quasi-supernatural law. In the new tragic universe envisioned by naturalism, place, it would seem, is fate; the power of place (in both its senses, as location and as position) seems to be offering itself as the great truth spawned by the theatre of total visibility.

The flicker of revolt recorded in the brief union of Jean and Julie is quickly rewritten as tragedy. But with a qualification. Occluded authority cannot fully disguise itself as occult power. Once he has been glimpsed, the absent puppet master cannot disappear, cannot restore the illusion of total visibility which depends on his absence. Razor in hand, Miss Julie can only mimic, not emulate, the tragic heroines of antiquity, who pay with their lives for knowledge bestowed upon them from another world. The rewriting of fate as place is revealed as merely the final illusion of the author-hypnotist. His control of the play's space of partial visibility is felt one final time, not only in the sound of two sharp rings of the Count's bell—which remind us that the other world of tragedy is here only another room—but in the blatantly metatheatrical curtain line: "It's horrible, but there's no other way for it to end.—Go!" (267).

The author-hypnotist exerts his influence by making place within his representational domain for the signs of various bids for self-determination. The logic is the very same as that which (in the preface) justifies the improvised monologue, as giving "the actor a chance to work on his own for once and *for a moment* not to be obliged to follow the author's directions" (213, emphasis added). In structuring the conceptual space of *Miss Julie* around a similar logic of momentary freedom, Strindberg staged the transgressive desires—sexual, social and mimetic desires—of modernity. In this play, naturalism proposed a world of total visibility—and them performed its limits.

NOTES

[1] August Strindberg, *Miss Julie*, in *August Strindberg: Selected Plays,* ed. and trans. Evert Sprinchorn (Minneapolis: University of Minnesota Press, 1986), 237. All quotations from the play and the preface are from this edition; hereafter, page numbers will appear in parentheses after the quotations.

[2] Bert O. States, *Great Reckonings in Little Rooms* (Berkeley: University of California Press, 1985), 67.

[3] With an ambivalence that is typical of all his pronouncements on *Miss Julie,* Strindberg made contradictory claims about the play's position between the poles of tradition and innovation. In the preface to the play Strindberg insists: "In the play that follows I have not tried to accomplish anything new—that is impossible. I have only tried to modernize the form to satisfy what I believe up-to-date people expect and demand of this art" (205). On the other hand, and in keeping with modernism's privileging of originality, Strindberg was at pains to assert the novelty of his play. In a letter to the publisher K. O. Bonnier on August 10, 1888, Strindberg made the famous claim that *Miss Julie* was "the first Naturalistic Tragedy in Swedish Drama." (Quoted by Martin Lamm in *August Strindberg* (New York: Benjamin Blom, 1971), 212).

[4] According to Martin Lamm, "The preface was written after the play, and Edvard Brandes was probably correct in his suspicion that *Miss Julie* was not the result of the application of conscious theory" (*August Strindberg,* 216). In *Strindberg as Dramatist* (New Haven: Yale University Press, 1982), Evert Sprinchorn says that the "preface was written to sell the play rather than to explain it" (28). In *The Social and Religious Plays of August Strindberg* (London: Athlone Press, 1980), John Ward hypothesizes that the preface was developed as a frame for the play which would counter Zola's criticism of Strindberg's earlier attempt at naturalist drama, *The Father* (58). As is well known, Zola found the characters of *The Father* to be too abstractly drawn. (See Michael Meyer, *Strindberg: A Biography* (Oxford: Oxford University Press, 1985). A good summary of this issue is presented by Egil Tornqvist and Barry Jacobs in *Strindberg's "Miss Julie": A Play and its Transpositions* (Norwich: Norvik Press, 1988). Torqvist and Jacobs show how extremely complex the relationship between the play and the preface really is, concluding that it should "teach us that we ought to be on our guard not only against the 'intentional' fallacy but also the

'post-intentional' fallacy" (60). Finally, an important new perspective on the matter is suggested by Alice Templeton, in "*Miss Julie* as 'A Naturalistic Tragedy,'" *Theatre Journal,* 42 (1990): 469-80, who says, "In adding the preface to the play, Strindberg may have been more interested in positioning himself as an artist *and as a male* than in precisely representing the complexity of the play itself" (9; emphasis added).

[5] According to Evert Sprinchorn ("Introduction to *Miss Julie,* in *August Strindberg: Selected Plays,* 200), Strindberg's preface to *Miss Julie* "is undoubtedly the most important manifesto of naturalistic theatre." Tornqvist and Jacobs (*Strindberg's "Miss Julie,"* 39) assert that "far from being merely a commentary on the 'naturalistic tragedy,' the preface is in fact the most pregnant exposure of the ideas underlying naturalistic drama—even compared to the statements by Strindberg's precursor Zola."

[6] Torqvist and Jacobs (*Strindberg's "Miss Julie,"* 39) remark: "There is an important generic difference between the play and the preface; while the former is an 'open,' strongly connotative text, the latter is a fairly 'closed,' mainly denotative one." Their ensuing analysis of the preface, however, seems to me to contradict this idea.

[7] In Julie's dream, she is "sitting on top of a pillar. I've climbed up it somehow and I don't know how to get back down. When I look down I get dizzy. I have to get down, but I don't have the courage to jump. I can't hold on much longer and I want to fall; but I don't fall. I know I won't have any peace until I get down; no rest until I get down, down on the ground! And if I did go down on the ground, I'd want to go farther down, right down into the earth" (230-31). Jean's dream is the diametric opposite to Julie's: "I used to dream that I'm lying under a tall tree in a dark woods. I want to get up, up to the very top, to look out over the bright landscape with the sun shining on it, to rob the bird's nest up there with the golden eggs in it. And I climb and I climb, but the trunk is so thick, and so smooth, and it's such a long way to that first branch. But I know that if I could just reach that first branch, I'd go right to the top as if on a ladder. I've never reached it yet, but someday I will—even if only in my dreams" (231).

[8] That Strindberg's post-naturalistic work emerged from an extension rather than a repudiation of his naturalistic interests is persuasively argued by Evert Sprinchorn in "The Zola of the Occult," in *Strindberg and Modern Theatre* (Stockholm: Strindberg Society, 1975). In "Rereading *Fröken Julie:* Undercurrents in Strindberg's Naturalist Intent," *Scandinavian Studies* 60 (1988): 1-11, John Eric Bellquist traces Strindberg's interest in mythopoesis to his naturalistic plays, "at least a decade earlier than his celebrated Inferno crisis and his recognized turn to occultism and religious myth" (1).

[9] Alice Templeton ("*Miss Julie* as 'A Naturalistic Tragedy,'" 471) reads the play as "an indictment of the naturalistic vision the preface claims the play celebrates,"

but acknowledges that "the preface is more complicated than its overt naturalistic claims would make it appear" and that it is "possible and perhaps desirable to read the preface *against* Strindberg's naturalistic claims, just as it is possible to read the play itself against those claims" (480). I believe that it is *the naturalistic claims themselves*—both as articulated in the preface and as realized in the play—that are fraught with contradictions, and are based *upon* (not in opposition to) certain processes (including irrationalism) which are traditionally excluded from the construction of naturalism.

¹⁰ In "Fairy Tales, the Unconscious and Strindberg's *Miss Julie*," *Literature and Psychology* 28 (1978): 145-50, Philip Dodd notes the preface's "ambivalence of tone . . . towards the reasoning faculties," attributing it to Strindberg's "fear of the consequences for the theatre of the supremacy of 'judgement'" (148). Strindberg's own sense of his creative process was always diametrically opposed to Zola's ideal of the playwright as dispassionate observer of a laboratory-like empirical reality. His commitment to an essentially non-rationalist world-view predates by many years the so-called "mystical" or "expressionistic" plays with which it is usually associated. Even before *Miss Julie*, Strindberg was describing his practice in terms antithetical to the emerging dramatic ideal; in a letter to Jonas Lie on May 24, 1884, quoted by Michael Meyer in *File On Strindberg* (London: Methuen, 1986), Strindberg admits: "I have discovered that I am not a realist. I write best when I hallucinate" (51).

¹¹ Besides two references to the "author-hypnotist," the preface also contains the following extended reference to hypnosis: "I have even supplied a little source history into the bargain by letting the weaker steal and repeat words of the stronger, letting them get ideas (suggestions as they are called) from one another, from the environment (the songbird's blood), and from objects (the razor). I have also arranged for *Gedankenubertragung* [thought transference] through an inanimate medium to take place (the count's boots, the servant's bell). And I have even made use of 'waking suggestions' (a variation of hypnotic suggestion), which have by now been so popularized that they cannot arouse ridicule or skepticism as they would have done in Mesmer's time" (208).

¹² John Greenway, "Strindberg and Suggestion in *Miss Julie*," *South Atlantic Review* 51 (1986): 21-34. According to Greenway, "A physician familiar with Bernheim's radically new work [Hyppolyte Bernheim, author of *De la suggestion et de ses applications a la therapeutique* (1886), which was in Strindberg's library] . . . would understand the dialogue and stage directions almost from the beginning as a series of suggestions and responses between the two characters that subtly underscore the play's more easily recognized actions and symbols" (25). Greenway then goes on to discuss these references in detail (26-28).

¹³ As Bert O. States (*Great Reckonings,* 69) notes, "We know that human dramas do not unfold in one or two rooms. But when a play seduces us into believing that they do . . . we have the spatial counterpart of the radical improbability that Fate preforms in the temporal action. Space is destiny, the visual proof that order lurks in human affairs."

¹⁴ August Strindberg, "On Modern Drama and Modern Theatre," in *Playwrights on Playwriting: The Meaning and Making of Modern Drama from Ibsen to Ionesco,* ed. Toby Cole (New York: Hill and Wang, 1963), 16.

¹⁵ States, *Great Reckonings,* 69.

¹⁶ In *Theatrical Space in Ibsen, Chekhov and Strindberg: Public Forms of Privacy* (Ann Arbor: UMI Research Press, 1983), Freddie Rokem discusses the manipulation of point of view in Strindberg's drama, comparing his practice to cinematography, which allows for the presence of multiple and changing focal points (52-56). This is indeed what happens in the later plays (such as *A Dream Play*), but not in the naturalistic dramas (especially not in *Miss Julie*) where only one plane of the cubistic space of cinema is presented. My point is precisely that the multiple space of cinema, which is the actualization of the contract of total visibility established by naturalism, is only *evoked,* not realized, in *Miss Julie*. The space of this play is, we might say, only potentially cubistic, striving for (but necessarily missing) a representation of total visibility.

¹⁷ Greenway ("Strindberg and Suggestion," 25) notes that "while it is technically necessary for Strindberg to take the cook Kristin off-stage, he does so in a peculiar manner. Both characters notice that she stumbles off in a quasi-somnambulistic state. While Kristin has not been subject to suggestion, Bernheim would observe that both characters now have the idea in their minds." It should also be noted that Kristin is included in the general topic of hypnotism through the reference to her sleeptalking. For much of the nineteenth century, artificial somnambulism was regarded as a necessary precondition to hypnosis. It is also significant, I think, that the one example of Kristin's somnambulism takes the form of a repetition of her menial duties: "Count's boots are brushed . . . put on the coffee . . . right away, right away . . ." (229). Here as at the end of the play, hypnosis is used to rewrite class difference as fate, uncanny and absolute; in this way a tragic outcome can be managed without sacrificing the rationalistic sociological analyses of naturalism.

¹⁸ Greenway, "Strindberg and Suggestion," 31.

¹⁹ Quoted in Lamm, *August Strindberg,* 202, emphasis added.

²⁰ Quoted in Michael Meyer, "Introduction to *Miss Julie*," in *August Strindberg: Plays One* (London: Methuen, 1964), 84.

²¹ In his "Introduction" to *Strindberg: Five Plays,* trans. Harry C. Carlson (Berkeley: University of California

Press, 1983), Harry Carlson writes: "Strindberg's own divided sense of political allegiance—democratic on the one hand, elitist on the other—is present in *Miss Julie,* where his sympathies alternate between Jean, the servant, and Julie, the aristocrat" (5).

[22] Quoted in Meyer, "Introduction," 87.

[23] Quoted in Meyer, "Introduction," 86.

[24] This idea comes across more clearly in Harry Carlson's translation *(Strindberg, Five Plays):* "during [intermissions] the spectator has time to reflect and thereby escape the suggestive influence of the author-hypnotist" (57) and "when we see only part of a room . . . imagination goes to work and complements what is seen" (59).

[25] In *Strindberg's Naturalistic Theatre: Its Relation to French Naturalism* (Seattle: University of Washington Press, 1962), Borge Gedso Madsen finds it "debatable to what extent the characters are 'determined' by the milieu of the Count's kitchen" (91), and asserts further that "this location is accidental as far as Julie is concerned and has nothing to do with 'determining' her hysterical split personality" (92). My point here is that the determinism at work is more complex than the literalistic one called for by Zola: in *Miss Julie* the characters as well as the space are "determined" by the ideological program underlying naturalism, which must create an illusion of access and clarity (what I have been calling total visibility) but can only do so by actively repressing its own constitutive processes. In this play, that interplay—between a represented Truth and the truth of representation—is not only engaged (as it is in all naturalistic plays), but also *staged*—through the figure of the Count.

[26] Elizabeth Sprigge is the only translator who makes this fact explicit, adding a line of her own to the opening stage direction to the effect that the double doors leading into the courtyard represent "the only way to the rest of the house." *(Six Plays of Strindberg,* trans. Elizabeth Sprigge [Garden City: Doubleday Anchor, 1955], 75.) This inference seems to me to be correct, borne out by the dialogue which precedes Julie's going into Jean's room: Julie says explicitly that the only other exits are into the courtyard and into Christine's room.

[27] Lawrence Stone, "The English Country Home and the Concept of Privacy 1600-1990" (paper delivered at the conference "Home: A Place in the World," New School for Social Research, New York City, October 27, 1990).

[28] The need for privacy increased as the positions of domestic servants were filled not only by members of families who had worked for the house for generations but by new, unknown people. In *Miss Julie,* the dangerous proximity of servants is evoked in the following exchange: *"Jean:* . . . I've also listened to educated people talk. That way I learned the most. *Julie:* You mean to tell me you stand around listening to what we're saying! *Jean:* Certainly! And I've heard an awful lot, I can tell you" (235). Earlier in the play, Jean tells Christine about spying on Miss Julie and her fiance: *"Jean:* I saw the whole thing. Of course, I didn't let on. *Christine:* You were there? I don't believe it. *Jean:* Well I was" (220).

[29] Actually, the class identity that Strindberg has constructed for Jean is a curious combination of several historical stages: Jean is the son of an estate-worker (the *statare* were serfs who belonged to the estate on which they were born and were paid for their labor in kind). He grew up, he tells us, on this very estate; however, his relationship to this estate has been interrupted (he has travelled and worked abroad) and altered (he works as a valet, not a farm hand). We are never told why he returned to this estate, so that his relationship to this family and this place has a somewhat unclear and transgressive quality. I would suggest that the mixture of intimacy and alienation that Jean evinces towards this family reproduces the logic of partial visibility that structures the play.

David Skeele

SOURCE: "The Devil and David Mamet: 'Sexual Perversity in Chicago' as Homiletic Tragedy," in *Modern Drama,* Vol. XXXVI, No. 4, December, 1993, pp. 512-18.

[*In the following essay, Skeele describes David Mamet's drama* Sexual Perversity in Chicago *as a homiletic tragedy--a late, darker form of the medieval morality play--with the "degrading or dehumanizing use of sex" as its subject.*]

It has frequently been noted that David Mamet is a moralist, a keen social critic who uses the groping inarticulations and dizzying verbal constructions of his characters to form a chorus of complaint against the spiritual emptiness at the core of America. What has less frequently been noted is that Mamet is sometimes very nearly a *medieval* moralist, using themes, structures, and characterizations that recall actual morality plays of the fifteenth and sixteenth centuries.

The influence of medieval drama is perhaps most overt in his *Bobby Gould in Hell,* a play which features the Devil as a character and a plot lifted directly from the medieval morality formula. Some of his earlier works, however, foreshadow this appropriation of morality-play techniques, and in fact they express the debt in subtler, more interesting ways. Perhaps the most intriguing example of this medievalism in Mamet's early works exists in his *Sexual Perversity in Chicago.* Virtually every element of this play, from its title down to its structure and characters, contains clear echoes of the medieval morality play, and more specifically, of the sixteenth-century subgenre known as the "homiletic tragedy."[1]

Before proceeding to make specific comparisons between *Sexual Perversity in Chicago* and the earlier dramatic forms, it might be useful to offer a general description of the qualities that define both the morality play and the homiletic tragedy. In the well-worn words of W. Roy Mackenzie: "A Morality is a play, allegorical in structure, which has for its main object the teaching of some lesson for the guidance of life, and in which the principal characters are personified abstractions or highly universalized types."[2] Examining these elements one at a time, the moralities' "lesson for the guidance of life" tends to vary little from play to play. It usually consists of a warning about the dangerous temptations to sin which surround us, coupled with reassurances that redemption is always possible, no matter how great the fall. The "personified abstractions" and "universalized types" are similarly formularized, tending to fall into three different categories. First, there are those representing specific virtues or forces of good—allegorical beings such as God, Good Angel, Mercy, Temperance, and Pax. Second, there are those from the other side of the fence, characters representing the forces of iniquity—Bad Angel, Mischief; Worldliness, etc. The actions of these forces are usually orchestrated by a leader—either the Devil himself or a particularly potent allegorical evil who is sometimes simply referred to as Vice. The third category is of course the protagonist, the "universalized type" representing all of humanity, known variously as Man, Mankind, Everyman, and Humanum Genus. The "allegorical structure" that Mackenzie speaks of is generally Psychomachean in nature,[3] and the allegory it enacts is usually that of a "war" between vice and virtue for the soul of mankind. One might add that this structure is also essentially comic—the obstacles and complications resulting from the protagonist's sins are eventually resolved by a kind and forgiving divinity who ends the play by welcoming him into heaven (in this regard, the morality play surpasses traditional comedy, not only implying "happily ever after," but actually assuring it).

As its name suggests, the homiletic tragedy differs in structure from its comic prototype. Homiletic tragedy was a fairly late development, reflecting the sixteenth-century rise of Calvinism and its attendant emphasis on the solitude of the individual in dealing with his or her own spiritual fate. In plays of this type, far less stress is placed on redemption, far more on punishment. While these dramas still feature a protagonist who is guaranteed entry to heaven at play's end, they differ from their predecessors in that they also feature a *second* protagonist, whose fate is a tragic mirror of the first. An unrepentant sinner, he inevitably winds up being driven off, his Vice in tow, to suffer the eternal torments of hell. This dark plot twist is important, for it is in this tragic form that the morality play has the most relevance to *Sexual Perversity in Chicago.*

Obviously, the moral message in Mamet's plays is somewhat more ambiguous than the dogmatic sermons of the moralities. Though he often addresses specific sins in his plays (rampant greed is the most common), he seldom tells us directly that he is doing so, and even more rarely offers any kind of clear solution to the problems that succumbing to the sin creates. *Sexual Perversity in Chicago* is unique in this regard, however. For one thing, its overtly allegorical title precisely pinpoints the offending sin: "Sexual Perversity" is unquestionably the dominant force in the world of the play. Although this title suggests sexual pervers*ion* (the play's opening in London was attended primarily by men in raincoat),[4] Mamet clearly uses the term "sexual perversity" to refer to any degrading or dehumanizing use of sex. The perversity is that sex, which should be the ultimate act of union, often exists as an insurmountable barrier between men and women.

Yet, ironically, in this play it is sex that seems to offer the clearest road to redemption, a condition which might exist, Mamet suggests, in the genuine connection between two people. As Dennis Carroll has noted, "contact ripening into communion is the salvation that Mamet hints at."[5] Unlike a morality play, which inevitably contrasts the purity of the soul with "that stinking dunghill" of the body[6] and its animal needs, *Sexual Perversity in Chicago* offers sex as both sides of the moral equation, as both sin *and* salvation. The split is not so much between soul and flesh as it is between Healthy Sex (or sex that connects), represented in the brief flowering of human understanding that occurs between Danny and Debby in the middle of the play, and Sexual Perversity (or sex that distances), exemplified by the swaggering sexual violence of Bernie and (to a lesser extent) the prim hostility and anxiety of Joan.

The play's characters also contain echoes of the morality formula. Though each is drawn in recognizably lifelike hues, they also fulfil an important allegorical function within the moral framework of the play. For instance, as the protagonist of *Sexual Perversity,* Danny bears an uncanny resemblance to the Humanum Genus figure. Though ostensibly a realistic, individualized character, Danny too is almost a universalized type, as Mamet has endowed him with a curious facelessness. While an actor playing Danny would obviously have to supply internal motivations and specific character traits, he would be doing so with little help from the playwright. For this reason, young actors are sometimes perplexed by the role, finding Danny to be something of a cipher.[7] This is particularly true in the beginning of the play, where we see him engrossed in Bernie's fantastic sexual tale. It is immediately obvious that Danny is completely subordinate in this relationship, a wide-eyed novice in the medium of sexual exploits sitting at the feet of a master teacher. While Danny does join Bernie in the sexual talk, his comments and questions serve merely to prop up Bernie's story—he even makes suggestions to help (consciously or unconsciously) patch up the story's inconsistencies. Walter Kerr commented on this in his review of the original production, saying his responses "are the quick, liquid, uninterruptive assents of a dummy sitting on a ventriloquist's knee, and it is the story-teller who is dictating the questions he should be asked."[8] Like the innocent, newborn Humanum Genus in *The Castle of Perseverance,* Danny is introduced to the world of the play as a blank slate, ready to be filled up by the most persuasive voice. And as with his medieval counterpart, it is the Dark Angel who first captures Danny's ear.

It is the parallel between Bernie and the Vice figure, however, that gives the play its strongest ties to the medieval morality. Alan C. Dessen defines the Vice as "a character who embodies a quality, force, idea or sin pervasive in the world of the play, something to be acted out in a variety of ways, one of which may be the corruption of individual figures."[9] This definition fits Bernie *precisely,* for his main action throughout the course of the play is to corrupt Danny, tearing him away from his one chance at salvation. And as the play's main corrupter, it is almost entirely through this character that the allegorical force suggested by the title manifests itself—Bernie *is* Sexual Perversity.[10] In the first scene we see him spellbinding Danny with a sado-masochistic tale that equates sex with the violence of war. In his next scene with Danny, he continues his instruction in the ways of women, informing Danny that "The Way to Get Laid is to Treat 'Em Like Shit."[11] From there he goes on to descriptions of women having sex with dogs, equation of women with animals ("time she's twenty two-three. You don't know *where* the fuck she's been" [39]), diatribes against the Equal Rights Amendment, and so on and so forth. As Sexual Perversity, he is a being who seems to exist solely for the purpose of dehumanizing the idea of sex with a woman.

Another element Bernie shares with his medieval counterpart is what Dessen calls the "two phased"[12] relationship between the Vice figure and the audience. In the odd blend of moral instruction and popular entertainment that made up the average morality play, the Vice served a double function, existing as both the play's primary symbol of evil and as its primary entertainer. It was this latter function that made up the first phase of the Vice's relationship with the audience—it was his job to delight the audience with his pranks and his obscenity (making a refreshing contrast to the dull Virtues and the faceless Humanum Genus), in this way seducing the audience into his world of sin just as effectively as he seduced the Humanum Genus (who is in fact a symbol of the audience). At some point, however, the hilarious antics of the Vice began to lose their humour, eventually degenerating into something downright sinister. Theoretically, when this second phase was reached, the dullness of the virtuous figures suddenly appeared to be highly desirable, a haven from the chaos and wanton destruction that the Vice had come to represent.[13] Perhaps the best example of this "two-phased" relationship comes from the play *Mankind,* which begins with a tedious, latinate sermon being given to the audience by Mercy, the play's chief Virtue. This is soon interrupted by the Vice Mischief and his friends. They proceed to make fun of Mercy, hilariously mocking his speechify-

ing with a sermon of their own—one that consists of a colloquial blend of sexual and scatological humour. The protagonist, Mankind, begins the play in Mercy's corner, but Mischief and company woo him as easily as they undoubtedly did the audience, and soon he becomes a world-class libertine, drinking, whoring, and gambling. When the plans change from sex and ale to thieving and killing, however, the vices' true colours begin to show, and they actually become frightening, nearly destroying Mankind before Mercy miraculously reappears.

Bernie's relationship to the audience is two-phased in exactly the same way as Mischief's. Initially he is an immensely appealing figure. His opening story, for all its violence, is hilarious and captivating. The same is true of his vicious diatribe against Joan in the second scene—it somehow manages to be extremely funny. In fact, for the first half of the play, Bernie is the most amusing and compelling character we see, achieving this distinction in the same manner Mischief achieves it in *Mankind*—through language. Mamet's gorgeous sense of sound, dynamics, and rhythm in language has been well documented and it needs little explication here except to say that Bernie, with lines such as "A lot of these broads, you know, you just don't know. You know?"(39), is one of the prime repositories of Mamet's special brand of poetry. Just as Michief's colourful country vernacular would have been far more appealing to a rustic medieval audience than Mercy's dull didacticism, Bernie's colloquially poetic flair makes the other characters sound particularly terse and bland. Interestingly, just like his medieval counterpart Mischief, Bernie often presents his arguments in a kind of parody of religious speech. His pronouncements to Danny are sometimes printed with the first letter of every word capitalized, as if they were commandments coming down from the Mount. And in his short monologue between the scene in which Danny picks up Debby and the one in which they first make love, he lords over their union like a preacher, delivering a veritable sermon on the necessity of "[giving] thanks to a just creator" every time one is able to "moisten the old wick" (24). Again, this parodic pseudo-religious commentary is engaging and funny, and through his Vice-like antics Bernie is able to seduce both audience and protagonist, drawing us towards him just as he does Danny.

Inevitably, however, our Vice figure manifests his second phase, becoming less funny and attractive and more dangerous and destructive. This begins to happen when the focus shifts from the Danny/Bernie relationship to the Danny/Debby relationship. The budding romance appears to us as something at once highly desirable and extremely fragile. As Bernie's sabotage attempts grow less subtle, we perceive him as more and more of a threat, until at the end he clearly stands as the primary agent of Danny's fall.

Debby's place within the Psychomachean scheme of the play is somewhat more complex. If we accept Danny as the *main* protagonist (and considering the disproportionate amount of time that Mamet spends on him, this is not unreasonable), then Debby takes on some of the characteristics of a force of virtue. For she represents Danny's one true hope for a non-perverse relationship— his short-lived salvation reaches its zenith in a beautiful and playful scene in which he and Debby exchange the secrets of maleness and femaleness. Her most obvious function, however, is that of a Humanum Genus-like protagonist alongside Danny. As in a homiletic tragedy, Mamet has bifurcated his protagonist, giving us two parallel journeys to follow. Interestingly, Mamet has even followed the medieval practice of giving the dual protagonists like names, his Danny and Debby recalling similar oppositions in the earlier form such as Lust and Just, and Heavenly Man and Worldly Man. In the homiletic tragedy, the line of demarcation between the two protagonists is sharp, with one a successful resister of temptation and the other an irredeemable sinner. Yet *Sexual Perversity* is even more pessimistic than the average homiletic tragedy (which was fairly pessimistic), and in this *modern* morality play Debby hardly exists as an exemplar of virtuous living. The moral difference between Debby and Danny is a matter of slight shading rather than stark contrast, and really only manifests itself in the final two scenes of the play.

It is these scenes that most closely ally the play with homiletic tragedy, as each represents a "fall" for its respective protagonist. In Debby's final scene, we find her back in her old apartment, trying to recover from the breakup with Danny. She is sitting dismally in the company of lonely, embittered Joan, who has succeeded in wresting her friend away from Danny through her own brand of Sexual Perversity (a profound, generalized distrust of men). Joan is giving her an "I told you so" lecture when Debby suddenly bristles, forcing Joan to back off nervously. In this reaction, Debby registers some level of perception about the situation—some recognition of the Perversity that helped to destroy her relationship.

If there is a modicum of hope suggested in Debby's vague awareness, Danny's wilful obliviousness suggests a far grimmer future for him. Danny's final scene finds him and Bernie on the beach cruising chicks, united bachelors once again. This time, however, we see a change in Danny. He is no longer merely a listener, echoing Bernie and feeding him lines. He now initiates conversation as well as returns it, matching Bernie crude observation for crude observation, until in his final line he almost out-Bernies Bernie. When a passing woman ignores his greeting, he snarls out "Deaf *bitch!*" (69). Here Danny has reached the nadir of his sexual development. Where Mankind eventually signifies his salvation by taking on the ornate speaking style of Mercy, Danny signals his fall by adopting the language of Sexual Perversity. As in any homiletic tragedy, Danny and his Vice finish the play in hell, and it is a hell that is particularly appropriate for them: sitting in blazing heat, surrounded by beautiful women that they will never be able to touch. In the Psychomachean world of the play, Vice may win the battle for the protagonist's soul, but David Mamet, the medieval moralist, does not allow Sexual Perversity to go unpunished.

NOTES

[1] Coined by David Bevington, in *From Mankind to Marlowe: Growth of Structure in the Popular Drama of Tudor England* (Cambridge, Mass., 1962), 161.

[2] W. Roy Mackenzie, *The English Moralities from the Point of View of Allegory* (Boston, 1914), 9. Mackenzie's definition has been nicely deconstructed in recent years, most notably by Natalie Crohn Schmitt, in *Drama in the Middle Ages* (New York, 1982), who takes him to task point by point. For instance, she argues with the term "abstraction," arguing that moralities in fact constitute "medieval realism" of a sort, as the earthly world was held to be much less substantial than the divine (305).

[3] Robert Potter, in *The English Morality Play: Origins, History and Influence of a Dramatic Tradition* (Boston, 1975), has rightly questioned the primacy of the *Psychomachea* as an influence on the morality play, noting, for instance, that Virtues and Vices rarely confront each other directly in a morality (37-39).

[4] Related by C. W. Bigsby at American Society for Theatre Research conference, Newport, R.I., November 1992.

[5] Dennis Carroll, *David Mamet* (New York, 1985), 21.

[6] From *Mankind,* in Glynne Wickham, ed., *English Moral Interludes* (New Jersey, 1976), 12.

[7] Based on my observations as a teacher of "Introduction to Performance" at the University of Pittsburgh, 1987-91.

[8] "Easy Does It Playwriting Comes of Age," *New York Times,* 15 Aug. 1976, 14.

[9] Alan C. Dessen, *Shakespeare and the Late Moral Plays* (Nebraska, 1986), 34.

[10] Attilio Favorini, in a lecture at the University of Pittsburgh (12 Nov. 1989), added some interesting observations to the idea of Bernie as Vice. He noted the closeness of the name Bernie to the word "burn" (and Danny to the word "damned"), and pointed out Bernie's association with heat and flames in several of the scenes. His opening tale ends with the room in flames, and in another tale he has chained a woman to the radiator.

[11] *Sexual Perversity in Chicago and The Duck Variations* (New York, 1974), 22. Subsequent references will appear in the text.

[12] Dessen, 24.

[13] C. L. Barber, in *Shakespeare's Festive Comedy: A Study of Dramatic Form and Its Relation to Social Custom* (Princeton, 1959), calls this process "release to clarification" (29), meaning that the initial sense of joyous release at the overturning of societal norms is soon replaced by the realization that such a situation is inadequate as a permanent living condition, and one is then able to return to those norms with a fresh appreciation of them.

Verna Foster

SOURCE: "Sex, Power, and Pedagogy in Mamet's 'Oleanna' and Ionesco's 'The Lesson'," in *American Drama*, Vol. 5, No. 1, Fall, 1995, pp. 36-50.

[*In the following essay, Foster compares David Mamet's* Oleanna *and Eugène Ionesco's* The Lesson, *concentrating on how the former dramatizes the ambiguities of sexual politics and conflict.*]

The veneer of realism in David Mamet's plays can tempt audiences to ask questions or make assumptions about the characters' affiliations, values, and motives that the dramatist has deliberately left vague. The recent controversy over *Oleanna* is a case in point. Theatre critics and audiences, filling in the gaps in *Oleanna* with yesterday's headlines, have overdetermined motives and ideological positions that Mamet constructs as richly ambiguous. Seen only in light of the Anita Hill-Clarence Thomas hearings and their aftermath, the play becomes an ephemeral contribution to the current conversation about sexual harassment and political correctness and as such can function only as antifeminist backlash (Showalter, Burkman).[1] If, however, we examine *Oleanna* through an historical and dramaturgical—as well as a contemporary political—lens, we can reevaluate Mamet's achievement and understand his play as a more complex or indeed a different work than has thus far been placed on offer. An exploration of the relations among sex, power, and pedagogy in Eugene Ionesco's *The Lesson* and *Oleanna* suggests that Mamet's play is less an antifeminist statement than it is an indictment of an educational culture in which, in Mamet's view, power-roles and power-games played by both professors and students make teaching destructive and learning impossible.

The close similarities, which extend even to details, between *The Lesson* (1951) and *Oleanna* (1992) permit the earlier play to function as an illuminating gloss on the cultural issues explored in the later one. In both plays a stereotypical female student visits a stereotypical male professor for a tutorial. Ionesco's pupil, who is lively but not very bright, implausibly wants the professor to help her pass her "total doctorate." Mamet's student simply wants to pass the course she is currently failing. In each play one character weakens as the other saps his or her strength. In *The Lesson* the pupil's "almost aggressive" (46) vitality passes to the "timid" pro-

fessor (46). In *Oleanna* the "arrogant, pompous, self-obsessed" professor (as he was described by David Suchet, who played the part in Harold Pinter's British production of the play [*Daily Telegraph*]) loses control of the dialogue between himself and the student and grows more disheveled through the play's three scenes, while the student becomes more aggressive and dresses in a progressively more masculine way.[2]

In both plays the power inherent in the professor's role as controller and purveyor of knowledge (represented in part by his authority over the meaning of words) is ultimately expressed as sexual power over the student. This is so even in *Oleanna*, in which political control passes to the student. For both plays end with an outburst of violence in which the male attacks the female. In *The Lesson* the professor rapes and murders his pupil, who turns out to be his 40th victim. In *Oleanna* the student first accuses the professor of sexual harassment and then of attempted rape. From the professor's point of view, and probably the audience's as well, he is guilty of neither charge, though his behavior has been reprehensible in other ways. At the very end of the play, driven too far by the student's accusations, her demand that he censor his reading list, and—the final straw—her objection to his calling his wife "baby," the professor calls the student a "*cunt*" (79) and brutally strikes her, thereby exhibiting the sexual violence of which she accused him in the first place.

Where Ionesco's dramaturgy is absurdist and requires a presentational acting style, Mamet's dramaturgy comprises a kind of Pinteresque stylized realism inflected by absurdism that calls for both presentational and representational acting styles. Sometimes, however, Mamet's plays have appeared to critics to be more realistic than they actually are. This is because of the quintessentially "American" themes and lifestyles depicted in plays such as *American Buffalo* and *Glengarry Glen Ross* and especially because Mamet's fine ear for the rhythms of various class and occupational dialects is at first more obvious than his careful patterning of dramatic language (Bigsby 82, 124). The problem is exacerbated in *Oleanna* because of the contemporaneity of its engagement with issues of sexual harassment and political correctness. It becomes too easy to see John and Carol (in *The Lesson* the Professor and the Pupil are not given names) as designedly realistic portraits and to judge Mamet's characterization accordingly. (For example, some critics have commented on the plausibility of the change in Carol's attitude between acts one and two [Lahr 352; Christiansen 22].) In fact, Mamet typically presents two-dimensional, representative characters rather than psychologically detailed portraits because, like the dramatists of the absurd, he wants to get at what he sees as essential in their situation (Bigsby 65; Carroll 29-30).

The superficial realism of *Oleanna* partly obscures the play's identification of pedagogical, sexual, and political oppression that Ionesco's absurdist dramaturgy renders explicit in *The Lesson*. It is apparent early in

Ionesco's play that the Professor aims to dominate his Pupil sexually as well as intellectually: there is an intermittent lewd gleam in his eye, and he relishes the *double entendre* in the young woman's being at his "disposal" (50). At first obsequious, the Professor gradually takes advantage of the Pupil's ignorance to subdue her spirit with his superior knowledge of math and linguistics. The math is at first-grade level and the linguistics is a marvellous parody of a lecture on comparative philology, with Spanish taking the place of Indo-European. The Professor is speaking nonsense, but that makes no difference to his ability to *"enchant"* (62) and finally subject the Pupil to his (bogus) authority. The Pupil's willingness to please, to conform to the rules of the Professor's game, to accept, however imperfectly, nonsense as intellectual truth predisposes her to sexual and political oppression. Appropriately, then, the Professor's growing intellectual power over the Pupil manifests itself in her toothache and other physical pains—in other words, in her body. When at the end of the play the Professor strikes the Pupil with the phallic knife that he has ordered her to pronounce in all the neo-Spanish languages, the identification of pedagogical authority with sexual domination is complete. In its closing moments Ionesco makes *The Lesson*'s political allegory explicit as the Professor and his maid don armbands that, Ionesco suggests, can display the Nazi swastika, and the maid reassures the Professor that "people won't ask questions" about all the coffins because "they're used to it" (77).

In Donald M. Allen's translation of *The Lesson*, the Professor shouts, "That'll teach you!" (75), as he plunges the knife into the Pupil.[3] Mamet uses the same frightening pun in *American Buffalo:* "The only way to teach these people is to kill them" (11), says the character nicknamed Teach of the (female) friends who have offended him (Hubert-Leibler 80). As Pascale Hubert-Leibler has pointed out, *American Buffalo* is one of several plays written prior to *Oleanna* in which Mamet depicts some kind of quasi-teacher-student relationship that is also explicitly a power relationship and sometimes, as in *A Life in the Theatre,* involves a reversal of roles. In Mamet's earlier plays teacher and student are almost invariably an older and a younger male. While there is often an implication of homoerotic feelings in this relationship, the theme is not fully developed. The gender difference between professor and student in *Oleanna,* by contrast, foregrounds the potential for both sexual politics and, according to Mamet's views, even a violent outcome in the struggle for power between teacher and pupil. Mamet has observed that "the true nature of the world, as between men and women, is sex, and any other relationship between us is either an elaboration, or an avoidance" (*Some Freaks* 90) and that in husband-and-wife arguments "the ultimate response the man feels is, of course, physical violence" (*Writing in Restaurants* 44).

The student in *Oleanna,* Carol, from the start recognizes the sexual possibilities of her relationship with the professor, John, and is cynically willing to manipulate them, especially after meeting with her "group" between acts one and two. When John says that the only way he can explain something to her is to be "personal" (19), she responds, "Why would you want to be personal *with me?*" [my emphasis] (19), thereby adding a sexual dimension to the word *personal.* Her subsequent identification of John's words and behavior during their first meeting as sexual harassment is shocking but not surprising. John is perhaps less conscious of the sexual dynamics of their relationship than Carol, but nonetheless he implicitly puts Carol in a sexually as well as pedagogically inferior position. After first ignoring her presence while he talks to his wife on the phone, he tells her that he understands how "potentially *humiliating*" (5) her visit to his office is for her. His use of the odd word "'obeisance'" at the beginning of their interview ("You paid me the compliment, or the 'obeisance'—all right—of coming in here" [5]) similarly evokes a sexually charged relationship of lord and vassal. John's choice, too, of an illustrative, but irrelevant, anecdote about the sexual habits of the middle and lower classes ostends his own sexuality; and his offer to tutor Carol because he "like[s]" (21, 27) her (rather than out of professional commitment, say), however kindly meant, again demonstrates his arbitrary power over her.[4] In the sexually ambiguous context that Mamet has created, John's comforting arm around Carol's shoulder offers multiple interpretative possibilities. John exercises or attempts to exercise sexual power over other women, too. His attitude towards his wife is paternal and patronizing, and his anger with his female Realtor is expressed to his lawyer over the phone as *"screw* her" (39), which, while a common expletive, points to John's underlying sexual violence that erupts at the end of the play.

For both John and Carol, then, the manipulation of sexual counters is part of a broader power struggle. Despite the pronounced concern with sexual politics in *Oleanna,* the play does not in the end center on the issue of sexual harassment. The Hill-Thomas hearings, invoked by a number of critics, are a red herring in this respect because the primary issue in *Oleanna* is not evidentiary—whom to believe. In Mamet's play we know who said what, though not always with what motive. It is power, not sex, that is of the essence of the relationship between John and Carol. Carol is not, for example, sexually fascinated by John as the Pupil is by Ionesco's Professor, but she does manipulate his sexual vulnerability in order to gain control of the teacher-student relationship and ultimately for the political ends of her "group." Equally, the sexual subtext of John's dialogue serves not to get him sex, but to reinforce, somewhat sadomasochistically, his hierarchical status. Each of the roles that John tries on with Carol—firm but understanding professor, wise father, benign mentor—underscores his position of authority and bolsters his own ego. Thus far, then, the conflict between John and Carol is a power struggle similar to that between the teacher-student pairs in Mamet's earlier plays. But in this play, in which Mamet depicts his characteristic teacher-student relationship between a *literal* teacher and a *literal* student, their conflict is no longer primarily a metaphor for some other form of political power, as it is in *The Lesson* and in Mamet's earlier plays. Rather *Oleanna* is, in fact, *about* education. Sexual politics necessarily enters into the tension between male and female characters of unequal status, and if Mamet is following Ionesco's political stance, then his portrayal of American education does have chilling implications for a free society. But the core of the play is Mamet's bleak vision of contemporary academic life in America.

The epigraph from *The Way of All Flesh* that appears in the printed text of *Oleanna* ("So the absence of a congenial mental atmosphere is not commonly recognized by children who have never known it") points to the similar absence of a free exchange of thought, as Mamet sees it, in American universities and the professors' and especially students' lack of awareness of this intellectual stagnation. The ironic title, *Oleanna,* too, underscores both the allegorical quality of Mamet's play and the hopelessness of his vision. In the Norwegian folk-song, "Oleanna" refers to an American utopia, a place of freedom where one need no longer "drag the chains of slavery." In fact, John and Carol, representative professor and representative student, have put themselves into mental chains by molding themselves into their expected roles. Both are playing games. Carol wants to be told what to do and expects that if she follows the rules—"And I read your book" (14)—she will be rewarded accordingly. John *says* he wants "to take off the Artificial *Stricture,* of 'Teacher' and 'Student'" (21), but his offer to abolish the usual academic expectations of his course and give Carol an automatic 'A' and some private tutoring is possible not because he *forgoes* the role of professor but because he *is* the professor and has the power to act in an arbitrary way occasionally. This exercise throws into relief the hierarchical rules by which his status is normally maintained. Carol later tells him, not unjustly, "You love the Power. To *deviate.* To *invent,* to transgress . . . whatever norms have been established for us" (52). The play suggests that neither communication nor education is possible in a relationship in which each party attempts to use the rules for his or her own advantage, but also that there is no way in which either teacher or student can shake off their assigned roles—the "norms that have been established for us"—even if they want to and that it is dangerous to try. John's attempts to be "personal" (19) rather than professional—the story he tells about his own youthful inadequacies, the comforting arm round the young woman's shoulder—leave him open to Carol's charge of sexual harassment. John and Carol cannot communicate as human beings when John controls Carol's grade and thus has the power, as Carol puts it, to deprive her and his other students of "that same dream of security *you* pursue" (69). And when Carol reverses the power roles by making the accusation that costs John his tenure, John so hates the power that she now has over him that, as Carol again points out, "any atmosphere of free discussion is impossible" (69).

Much of the conflict between John and Carol concerns the purpose of education itself. John feels that for many American students a university education is pointless and amounts to "virtual warehousing of the young" (11), in which they are subjected to various arbitrary tests that, like the Professor's quizzing of the Pupil in *The Lesson,* are no better than "hazing" (28). It is not clear whether the audience is supposed to sympathize with John as offering a radical humanist critique of American education or condemn him as an "ambitious, talentless nonentity" *(Guardian)* who uses the system he says he despises for his own self-aggrandizement. In offering to tutor Carol and give her an automatic "A" so that she can learn something without being concerned about her grade, John is acting in accord with the principles set forth in his book; but, equally, he has also conformed to the traditional expectations of his university in order to earn tenure and buy a new house and a comfortable lifestyle. As a teacher he aims to "provoke" (32) his students into questioning the notion that "higher education is an unassailable good" (32-33), but at the same time he sends his own child to a private school. Carol, coming from a "different" (8) social and economic background, sees his "provocation" as a "*mock*[ery]" of *hardworking students* who "*slave* to come here" (52). She later tells him,

> You believe *not* in 'freedom of thought,' but in an elitist, in, in a protected hierarchy which rewards you. And for whom you are the clown. And you mock and exploit the system which pays your rent. (67-68)

John's critique of American higher education is undercut both by the contradictions inherent in his position and by the resentment and confusion he instills in Carol and his other students, who, understandably, dislike being told that the education they have worked so hard to attain may be inappropriate and useless for them. Carol's inability to understand John's lectures and his book seems to stem at least in part from her unwillingness to accept his radical questioning of why she should be in college in the first place. Her pain and her anger, then, are certainly justified. As the object and victim of John's inchoate educational philosophy, Carol is sympathetic if at times maddeningly obtuse. But when she herself takes on the role of teacher—"I came here to instruct you" (67)—at the end of the play, her abuse of her power over John makes her "teaching" just as destructive as his has been.

The site of contention between Carol and John is the medium of communication itself. At the beginning of the play, Mamet foregrounds the contingency of meaning when Carol, overhearing John's telephone conversation about his new house, asks him what a "term of art" is. John replies, in effect, that the meaning of the phrase is a matter of convention agreed upon only by the initiated: "It seems to mean a *term,* which has come, through its use, to mean something *more specific* than the words would, to someone *not acquainted* with them . . .

indicate" (3). John's control over the choice and meaning of words renders Carol inarticulate in the first scene. "What can that mean?" (8) he asks, after reading a garbled sentence from Carol's essay. Instead of explaining, Carol can only stammer, "I, the best that I . . ." (8). Deprived of her own meaning, Carol has also to ask John the meaning of his words: "index" (24) and "predilection" (31), even though she knows that the latter word means "liking." And she is apparently afraid to use her own words to paraphrase John's ideas (27), though, in retrospect, we might see her unwillingness to do so as a sign of her resistance to views that she finds wholly offensive. In the second scene, as power passes from professor to student, Carol begins to question John's choice of words:

JOHN: I'm always looking for a *paradigm* for . . .

CAROL: I don't know what a paradigm is.

JOHN: It's a model.

CAROL: Then why can't you use that word? (45)

By the play's last scene it is Carol who determines, rather carefully, the terms in which she will communicate with John. She tells him that the charges she brought against him are not "alleged" (his word), but "proved" (63). Similarly, when suggesting that her group might speak on John's behalf to the tenure committee, she rejects "'If' what?" (John's way of introducing the group's condition) and says instead, "'Given' what. Perhaps. I think that that is more friendly" (73). Not only does Carol choose the vocabulary, but she also asserts her power and right to control John's meaning as well as her own. When John tells her that putting his hand on her shoulder was "devoid of sexual content," she replies emphatically: "I say it was not. I SAY IT WAS NOT. Don't you begin to *see* . . . ? Don't you begin to understand? IT'S NOT FOR YOU TO SAY" (70). When he is not allowed to be the arbiter of his own meaning, John, like Carol in the first scene, is rendered inarticulate: "Well, I . . . I . . . I . . ." (71). First John and then Carol follow the lethal path of Ionesco's Professor: the teacher who completely dominates the discourse, effectively destroys the pupil.[5]

Carol's drive for domination leads her finally beyond the individual teacher-student power struggle. By demanding the right to censor her professor's reading list, she is attempting to take control of the whole educational process:

JOHN: You want to ban my book?

CAROL: We do not . . .

JOHN *(Off list):* It says here . . .

CAROL: . . . We want it removed from inclusion as a representative example of the university. (75)

The doublespeak is chilling. But worse is to come when Carol inserts herself even into John's relationship with his wife: "Don't call your wife baby" (79). At this point John calls Carol a "vicious little bitch" (79), beats her, and threatens her with a chair. And audiences, sometimes shocking themselves, have applauded this act of violence with which the play ends ("He Said . . . She said"; *Daily Telegraph*). If we do applaud (and it is difficult not to make some such emotional gesture), it is because Mamet in the closing moments of the play has stacked the deck in favor of John by making Carol a caricature of politically correct feminism intruding upon the sanctities of academic freedom and private life. Until the end of the play, however, sympathy or antipathy for John and Carol is more equally balanced (though any given production can be weighted to some degree). Throughout the play both are more interested in scoring points than in teaching or learning anything. And even at the end, though an audience most likely perceives that Carol has *manipulated* John into enacting the sexual violence of which she originally accused him, it is equally appropriate to say that John has *fulfilled* the potential for sexual violence that was always within him. As Carol notes: "Yes. That's right" (80).

For all the similarities between Ionesco and Mamet, there is one significant difference. In *The Lesson* it is clear who is the oppressor and who the oppressed; in Mamet's play we cannot tell which is which. The problem of sympathy in *Oleanna* arises in part from the peculiarities of Mamet's dramaturgy. The Pinteresque blend of stylized realism, absurdism, and allegory simultaneously invites and confounds any assumptions we may make about Carol's motives or John's educational philosophy. Thus what the audience brings to *Oleanna* becomes more than ordinarily crucial in determining not only how they interpret the drama but also the value they place upon it. The contemporaneity of *Oleanna*'s engagement with sexual politics and political correctness has for many critics obscured the play's central concern with what Mamet sees as the moral bankruptcy of American higher education when it is reduced to nothing more than politics. The analogy between Ionesco's more explicitly allegorical play about sex, power, and pedagogy and *Oleanna* enables us to assign Mamet's controversial drama to its appropriate place in the mainstream of Mamet's work. As an allegory of higher education, *Oleanna* forms part of Mamet's ongoing critique of contemporary America, along with his other dramas of American collective culture such as *American Buffalo, Glengarry Glen Ross,* and *Speed-the-Plow.* But in the first two of these at least, as critics have noted, there is something appealing about the vitality of Mamet's predators. There is little that is attractive about John and Carol, though there is much to be pitied and perhaps more to be feared.

NOTES

[1] Many reviews of the New York production, collected in *New York Theatre Critics' Reviews,* variously refer to contemporary concern with sexual harassment and po-

litical correctness. *Oleanna* is often seen as a gloss on the Anita Hill-Clarence Thomas hearings. See also the collection of comments in "He Said . . . She Said . . . Who Did What?"

[2] In the New York production (1992) Carol wore "a mousy ankle-length dress" in the first scene, changed into "trousers and a vest" in the second, and added a "boxy blazer" in the third (Solomon 355); by the third scene John is "dishevelled, in his shirtsleeves, and distraught," while Carol is "neatly garbed in a man's suit" (Showalter 16). I observed a similar use of the semiotics of costume in the Chicago production (1993).

[3] The French original is "tiens!" (92).

[4] A parallel situation in Mamet's film *House of Games* clarifies how John is actually asserting his arbitrary and implicitly sexual power over Carol when he tells her that he wants to help her because he likes her. In the film Mike deliberately uses the same line as part of the process by which he cons Margaret Ford out of her money: "I'm showing you this 'cos I like you. Okay? 'Cos you got blonde hair."

[5] Rosette Lamont comments that in *The Lesson* "it is clear that power will be held by the one who controls the use of language" (57). Michael Maggio, director of the Chicago production of *Oleanna,* makes a similar remark about Mamet's play: "those who control the language win" (qtd in Fishman 16).

WORKS CITED

Bigsby, C. W. E. *David Mamet.* London and New York: Methuen, 1985.

Burkman, Katherine H. "Misogyny and Misanthropy: Anita Hill and David Mamet." Paper delivered at the annual meeting of the Midwest MLA, Minneapolis, Nov. 1993.

Christiansen, Richard. "Battle of the sexes." *Chicago Tribune.* 14 Sept. 1993: 1: 22.

Carroll, Dennis. *David Mamet.* London: Macmillan, 1987.

The Daily [London] *Telegraph.* 15 Sept. 1993.

Fishman, Ted C. "Sex, Lies, No Videotape." *Stagebill.* Chicago: B&B Enterprises, Inc., October 1993: 6, 16.

The [London] *Guardian.* 16 Sept. 1993.

"He Said . . . She Said . . . Who Did What?" *New York Times.* 15 Nov. 1992, sec. 2: 6.

Hubert-Leibler, Pascale. "Dominance and Anguish: The Teacher-Student Relationship in the Plays of David Mamet." *David Mamet: A Casebook.* Ed. Leslie Kane. New York: Garland Publishing, Inc., 1992. 69-85.

Ionesco, Eugene. *Four Plays by Eugene Ionesco.* Trans. Donald M. Allen. New York: Grove P, Inc., 1958. *Theatre 1.* France: Gallimard, 1954.

Lahr, John. "Dogma Days." *The New Yorker.* 16 Nov. 1992. *New York Theatre Critics' Reviews* 53 (1992): 351-353.

Lamont, Rosette C. *Ionesco's Imperatives: The Politics of Culture.* Ann Arbor: U of Michigan P, 1993.

Mamet, David. *American Buffalo.* New York: Grove P, Inc., 1976.

————. *House of Games.* Orion Pictures Corp. 1987.

————. *Oleanna.* New York: Vintage Books, 1993.

————. *Some Freaks.* New York: Viking, 1989.

————. *Writing in Restaurants.* New York: Viking, 1986.

New York Theatre Critics' Reviews 53 (1992): 351-363.

Showalter, Elaine. "Acts of Violence." *Times Literary Supplement.* 6 Nov. 1992: 16-17.

Solomon, Alisa. "Mametic Phallacy." *Voice.* 24 Nov. 1992. *New York Theatre Critics' Reviews* 53 (1992): 355-356.

POETRY

Thaïs E. Morgan

SOURCE: "Swinburne's Dramatic Monologues: Sex and Ideology," in *Victorian Poetry,* Vol. 22, No. 2, Summer, 1984, pp. 175-95.

[*In the following essay, Morgan analyzes Algernon Charles Swinburne's critique of Victorian sexual ideology in the dramatic monologues of his* Poems and Ballads.]

In reply to Victorian critics who found *Poems and Ballads, First Series* (1866) both "indecent" and "blasphemous," Algernon Charles Swinburne stated quite firmly that his poetry is "dramatic, many-faced, multifarious" and that "no utterance of enjoyment or despair, belief or unbelief, can properly be assumed as the assertion of its author's personal feeling or faith."[1] This public defense in *Notes on Poems and Reviews* (1866) establishes Swinburne's own definition of the mask or the fictional persona and shows that he was deliberately working with the dramatic monologue as a genre in his first collection of poems. Moreover, Swinburne was sensitive to the difference between the distancing of poet from fictional persona in the Victorian dramatic monologue and the relatively direct self-expression in the Romantic lyric. "Byron and Shelley," he notes, "speaking in their own persons . . . openly and insultingly mocked and reviled what the English of their day held most sacred. I have not done this" (p. 18). Fully aware of the iconoclasm of *Poems and Ballads, First Series* (hereafter, *Poems and Ballads*), Swinburne deploys the dramatic monologue as a rhetorical strategy to deliver his own ideological message. In the poems denounced as the most "indecent" and "blasphemous"—"Anactoria," "Laus Veneris," and "Hymn to Proserpine"—the controversial opinions and acts of the imagined speakers should not and cannot be construed as simply autobiographical confessions of the poet. Like the twentieth-century roman à thèse, the nineteenth-century dramatic monologue depends on a tension between fictional representation and ideological statement.[2] Through the voices of characters reconstructed from classical and medieval literature, Swinburne exposes the deep contradictions he finds in Victorian moral and religious values. That he was so widely and vociferously condemned by contemporary readers is testimony to the very perspicacity of his critique.

Despite historical and textual evidence pointing to polemic as Swinburne's primary aim in *Poems and Ballads,* literary critics have persisted in regarding his first poems as the fictionalized autobiography of a sexually and socially maladjusted individual.[3] Consequently, Swinburne is not granted the skill of aesthetic distancing that critics readily find in the dramatic monologues of Browning and Tennyson. For example, Wendell S. Johnson refuses to accept Swinburne's defense of *Poems and Ballads* as a series of fictional "monodramas," insisting rather that "a good deal of personal belief and disbelief, or, at least, very personal emotion does shine through its dramatic masks."[4] An important exception to this approach is Jerome J. McGann who has recognized that *Poems and Ballads* follows an ironic pattern, using beautifully versified and metaphorically dazzling language to attack "all the moral confusions and hypocrisies which . . . had become settled truths" for the Victorian audience.[5] Nevertheless, it is remarkable that both Browning and Tennyson, in "Porphyria's Lover" and "Maud," for instance, draw on several of the same risqué themes as "Anactoria" and "Hymn to Proserpine"—necrophilia and the connection between sexual and socio-political repression—yet neither of these poets was censured in the way that Swinburne was. Again, one suspects that Swinburne's work hit a very tender spot in the Victorian conscience: a consciousness of the gap between sexual practice and moral discourse which still lingers in the minds of those modern critics who refuse to acknowledge the intelligence of Swinburne's sexual politics.

Even granting that *Poems and Ballads* have some basis in Swinburne's personal experience and his predilection for sado-masochism and homoeroticism, the point remains that Swinburne perceived a general crisis in sexual mores in mid-Victorian England and decided to take public action through the rhetoric of his poetry. Swinburne uses his dramatic monologues to draw attention to the disturbing correlation between Christian society's zealous repression of sexuality and its simultaneous indulgence in perversions behind closed doors. As Steven Marcus observes in his landmark study, *The Other Victorians,* the "combination of anticlericalism with pornography" in underground literature of the day manifests a series of cultural contradictions.[6] The most sanctimonious and respectable Victorian gentlemen were likely to be the most avid clientele of brothels and flagellation clubs. If we consider Swinburne as part of a rising counterculture in its critical rather than its popular aspect, we can understand the strategy of his dramatic monologues in *Poems and Ballads* as parallel to that of the famous Victorian pornographer, Pisanus Fraxi (alias Henry Spencer Ashbee), who used pseudonyms, deceptive titles, and erroneous publication dates to sell his books. The classical and medieval characters and settings in "Anactoria," "Laus Veneris," and "Hymn to Proserpine" are ironic masks, calculated to take the publicly prudent but privately prurient Victorian reader unaware, as he or she finds himself or herself silently identifying with the sexual aberrations and the religious doubtings of Sappho, Tannhäuser, and the late Roman.

Shortly after the first edition of *Poems and Ballads* appeared, an anonymous critic protested:

> Mr. Swinburne deliberately selects the most depraved stories of the ancient world . . . and dwells upon them with a passionate zest . . . which is only less shocking than the cold, sarcastic sneer with which (after the fury of sensual passion has vented itself in every form of libidinous metaphor) he assures us that these are not only the best things in the world, but better than anything we can hope for or conceive beyond the world.[7]

Ironically, the clear-sightedness of this review originates in the critic's very moral outrage. He recognizes the form and purpose of Swinburne's main rhetorical strategies: 1) the distancing of the polemic on Victorian issues by setting the fictional speaker of the dramatic monologue in a historically distant time; 2) the use of "every form of libidinous metaphor" in order to convey the extent of the perversions that result from a sexually repressed culture; and, 3) the non-resolution of the deep ideological conflicts presented in the dramatic monologue, with the specific result that the Christian consolation of salvation—"anything we can hope for or conceive beyond the world"—seems inefficacious and even false.

Of all the experiments in *Poems and Ballads,* "Anactoria" shocked the public most due to its association of "aberrant" sexual acts with "atheistic" questionings. "Anactoria" can thus be taken as a critical model of Swinburne's use of the dramatic monologue in *Poems and Ballads*: it launches a devastating attack on Victorian values through a series of interrelated metaphors that mix sexual and religious codes in ways already implicit in Christian discourse and iconography.

In "Anactoria," the classical Greek poetess, Sappho, argues for an ideological as well as a practical equivalence between love and punishment in sex and religion:

> My life is bitter with thy love; thine eyes
> Blind me, thy tresses burn me, thy sharp sighs
> Divide my flesh and spirit with soft sound.

(11. 1-3)[8]

Sappho's description of her lesbian relations with her disciple, Anactoria, is contradictory. Her "copulaic" metaphor links sensual love to pain ("bitter") and sorrow ("sighs")—a conventional moral sentiment—but Sappho's prolonged play on the paradox of "odi et amo" also suggests that she enjoys the precarious balance between pain and pleasure in the lovemaking. As a pagan thinker, Sappho does not view corporeal pain as a reminder of the transience of the flesh and the eternity of the soul, as Swinburne's Christian readers would. Rather, Sappho throughout the first section of her monologue (ll. 1-58) celebrates the division of "flesh and spirit" that occurs during sado-masochistic exchanges with Anactoria, as though sexual consummation were equal to Christian salvation in terms of self-transcendence. Indeed, as the lovers take turns at the roles of agent and object ("my pain / Pains thee, and lips bruise lips, and vein stings vein" '[ll. 11-12]), their excitement generates a "music" not unlike that of the celestial spheres when the soul of the blessed rises to heaven:

> Vex thee with amorous agonies and shake
> Life at thy lips, and leave it there to ache;
>
> . . . . .
>
> Relapse and reluctation of the breath,
> Dumb tunes and shuddering semitones of death.

(ll. 29-30, 33-34)

Sappho's portrait of her lady, Anactoria, is the first of several parodic passages in the poem. Swinburne can rely on the Victorian reader's familiarity with Christian typology in literature and painting for maximum effect as he demonstrates—always through Sappho's voice and eyes—the kinship between pornography and religious iconography.[9] Although Sappho admits herself "weary" from lovemaking, she notices with malicious glee that the younger woman, Anactoria, looks like a debauched Virgin Mary:

> eyes the bluer for all those hidden hours
> That pleasure fills with tears and feeds from flowers,
> Fierce at the heart with fire that half comes through,
> But all the flowerlike white stained round with blue.

(ll. 39-42)

Blue, red, and white are the colors traditionally assigned to the Virgin's garments and her flower, the lily, symbolizing her divinity, suffering (here ironically understood as her sensual passion), and purity. The contradictory denial/assertion of sexuality in the doctrine of the Immaculate Conception, with its implication that all women should have sex to reproduce but never for pleasure alone, is reversed in Anactoria's appearance. Indulgence in the pain and pleasure of sex with Sappho has transformed her from a "white" maiden with innocent "blue" eyes into a bruised and fallen woman (the latter a pun on "stained") with deep "blue" circles under her eyes and "ruinous lilies in thy languid hair" (l. 58).

More daring is the parody of the central Christian myth of the Passion which Sappho utters in defiance of her patron goddess, Venus, at the beginning of the second section of the poem (ll. 59-187). First, Sappho challenges Venus's exclusively heterosexual cult of love: "Are there not other gods for other loves?" (l. 101). She then secures the allegiance of her own worshipper, Anactoria, by a bit of perverse psychology: "Yea, though she scourge thee, sweetest, for my sake, / Blossom not thorns and flowers not blood should break" (ll. 103-104). In the dramatic context, Sappho is promising to give her lover more pleasure through a liberated lesbianism (the "thorns" and "blood" of sado-masochism) than Venus, representing conventional heterosexuality, ever can (the "blossom" and "flowers" of romantic love). However, during her tirade, Sappho has called Venus not only a "god" of love in the pagan sense but also a "God" in the Christian sense: "Nay, sweet, for is she God alone?" (l. 88). The typographical switch should alert the reader to the theological import of the mixed metaphors here. The series "scourge," "thorns," "blood," and "break" suggests a shocking equivalence between the role of God the Father in Christ's Passion and the role of the sadistic partner, Sappho, in Anactoria's masochistic pleasures.

When Sappho turns away from the cult of Venus to celebrate her rebellious lesbianism, she addresses Anactoria in sexually explicit terms that would, nevertheless, sound disturbingly familiar to the most proper Victorian reader:

> Ah that my mouth for Muses' milk were fed
> On the sweet blood thy sweet small wounds had bled!
> That with my tongue I felt them, and could taste
> The faint flakes from thy bosom to the waist!
> That I could drink thy veins as wine, and eat
> Thy breasts like honey! that from face to feet
> Thy body were abolished and consumed,
> And in my flesh thy very flesh entombed!

(Anactoria," 11. 107-114)

> Oh to feel the kiss of your lips,
>   For your love is better than wine!
>   Sweet to the smell are your ointments:
>   Your name is as perfume poured forth.
>
> . . . . .

Your lips drip syrup, O my bride:
Milk and honey are in your tones;

. . . . .

I am licking honey from the comb,
And quaffing my wine and my milk.

("The Song of Songs," I. 91; VII. 108, 111)[10]

In this brilliant parody of "The Song of Songs," Swinburne desacralizes the erotica of the Bible and exposes the sensualism and sadism latent in Christian discourse by shifting the vehicle of the metaphors for love. Instead of love as a divine consummation or transcendence which is allegorically depicted by the ecstasies of the flesh in eating (consumption) and lovemaking (consummation), we have metaphors for love as a purely physical consummation/consumption that skirts the edge of death in its extremities of pleasure and pain. Since "Anactoria" aroused the greatest protest from Swinburne's critics, we may conclude that Victorian readers were well aware of the inter-textual irony of such passages and, moreover, that they felt particularly vulnerable to his suggestive mingling of Christian and pornographic codes.

The repeated incursions of Christian theology into the pagan erotica of Sappho in the first part of "Anactoria" establish a metaphorical ground for the bold anti-theodicy presented in the second part of the poem. Critics have often complained about the anachronism of "Anactoria," but the fact that the classical Greek poetess discusses the Christian God's responsibility for the "mystery of the cruelty of things" (1. 154) supports the thesis that Swinburne is using Sappho as a distancing device to disarm the Victorian reader as he proposes his highly iconoclastic views. Swinburne's extended discussion of the various mis-translations of Sappho's odes to unconventional loves in *Notes on Poems and Reviews* (pp. 20-22) is a similar rhetorical subterfuge: the mask of Sappho in the poetry is redoubled by the mask of "your humble translator" in the prose. "I have striven to cast my spirit into the mould of hers, to express and represent not the poem but the poet" (p. 21). As Swinburne wryly observes, Sappho's "indecent" and "blasphemous" odes were standard fare for proper English schoolboys learning Greek. The hypocrisy of Victorian society about moral do's and don't's in this case is all too evident.

Having rejected Venus and pagan religion for their narrow, heterosexual definition of love, Sappho challenges Christian theology and its authority to condemn all modes of sexuality as innately sinful. Metaphors previously applied to the pain/pleasure paradox of lovemaking ("bitter," "break," "cruel") are now reworked in order to portray God as a sadist who takes a perverse pleasure in the pain of our mortality:

Cruel? but love makes all that love him well
As wise as heaven and crueller than hell.

Me hath love made more bitter toward thee
Than death toward man; but were I made as he
Who hath made all things to break them one by
one,

. . . . .

God knows I might be crueller than God.

(11. 145-149, 152)

Neither was the creation of the body a benevolent act, nor will the Creator offer us the final consolation of salvation for the soul. God has "made" man to "break" him: His Providential Plan is to satiate the "mute melancholy lust of heaven" (1. 170). The alternation of pain and pleasure suffered by Anactoria at the hands of Sappho parallels and parodies our vacillation between hope and terror before the Christian alternatives of "heaven" and "hell." The rites of the Church can barely conceal the connection between love of God and love of suffering and death: "Is not his incense bitterness, his meat / Murder?" (11. 171-172). The cunnilingual consummation of the love object by the sadistic lover is no more "cruel" or unusual than the consummation of the passive Christ, spreadeagled on the Cross, by the lustful God, nor more "cruel" than holy ritual of eating the body of Christ during Mass. In short, Sappho reasons, the dominant partner behaves toward the submissive partner in so-called perverse sexual acts in exactly the same manner as God treats mankind: homoeroticism and monotheism are ideologically, if not practically, equivalent. But, whereas Sappho openly admits her sado-masochistic desires through her poetry, the Christian religion on behalf of God promises "caritas" while supporting a spectacle of "cruelty."

Sappho's exposure of the inconsistencies in Christian ethics also invites reexamination of the teleology that it presupposes. The assumption that the transitory life of the body will be superseded by the immortal life of the soul through God's grace is undermined by the observation that His Love leads in the same direction as sins of sensuality—to suffering and death. In an ironic reversal of the myth of the Fall and the Redemption, God bids "sink the spirit and the flesh aspire" (1. 179), the better to grimly enjoy our devoted suffering "in imitatio Christi." In this context, the Victorian reader who clings to traditional religious beliefs is placed in the position of a masochist who, like Anactoria, willingly accepts the "thorns" along with the "blossoms." By metaphorical equivalences set up throughout the poem, the practice of mortification of the flesh is made to seem just as aberrant as its complements in Victorian flagellation literature and in Victorian social proprieties. As the anonymous reviewer quoted above indignantly remarked, "Anactoria" exemplifies Swinburne's attack on the Christian system of values from the viewpoint of a disaffected insider who flaunts "a faith that laughs at itself, that insults its own deities and defiles its own temples" (Hyder, 1970, p. 36).

Sappho's rejection of both pagan and Christian frameworks creates a metaphysical impasse that is designed to trouble the Victorian reader in a way that recalls the "void" experienced by several of Tennyson's dramatic personae during, for example, "Supposed Confessions" and "Despair." In the third and final section of "Anactoria" (11. 189-304), Sappho contrasts the Christian world and her own vision, offering the latter as a difficult but more honest alternative. Kerry McSweeney has recently argued that all of Swinburne's poetry, early and late, is organized around a "core of naturalistic beliefs (and belief in the poetic vocation)" that grows out of the Romantic tradition.[11] Reading "Anactoria" as "another dramatic monologue about an unhappy poet," McSweeney discounts the "sadistic effusion" of the speaker in the first part of the poem and relegates Sappho's lengthy discussion of God in the second part to an inartistic "intrusion" (p. 128). Despite the fact that Sappho does not present her poetics until the third part of the poem, McSweeney concludes that the main point of "Anactoria" is to show the poetess transcending her sensuality in a triumph of the spirit: "her initial, almost total submersion in her compulsive love gradually gives way before an increasingly exultant realization of her poetic powers" (p. 129). Although it is true that Sappho defines her poetics through a description of a landscape and a seascape at the end of the monologue, a critical application of the Romantic paradigm of self-transcendence through communion with Nature presupposes the very dichotomy of spirituality versus carnality which Sappho's diatribe against the hypocrisy of Christian values has sought to explode. Rather than "Romantic naturalism," then, Sappho offers the iconoclastic alternative of "sleep," a metaphor for the decision to suspend traditional dualisms in order to attain a radical freedom from Hellenic as well as Hebraic-Christian ideologies.

Sappho first defines her poetics through the body of Anactoria:

> Yea, thou shalt be forgotten like spilt wine,
> Except these kisses of my lips on thine
> Brand them with immortality.

> (11. 201-203)

Sexual experience cannot be divorced from the highest art: sexuality *is* poetry, or "music" ("thy body is the song, / Thy mouth the music" [11. 74-75]). Consequently, Anactoria's body, earlier metaphorized ironically as a bruised "lily" and a fallen "rose," now becomes a "Pierian flower," or morally neutral work of art. Sappho's poetry aims to leave behind the conflict between temporal and eternal, sinful and pure, immoral and moral, symbolized by the opposition of rose and lily in Christian iconography.

Next, Sappho defends her poetics through a contrast between the gloomy, sterile world of Christianity and her own reanimation and eroticization of the world:

> the earth,
> Filled full with deadly works of death and birth,
> Sore spent with hungry lusts of birth and death,
> Has pain like mine in her divided breath.

> (11. 233-236)

Familiar religious metaphors for the transitoriness of life in this vale of tears are recontextualized and shown to be perversely obsessed with the very sensuality of death. The earth "lusts" after the bodies of dying generations, just as God "lusts" after the "bitterness" of mankind who suffers a "violent fate." By metaphorical logic, if we condemn Sappho's "lust" for the erotic death of her lesbian lover, Anactoria ("I would earth had thy body as fruit to eat, / And no mouth but some serpent's found thee sweet" [11. 25-26]), then we must also condemn the sexual overtones of Christian discourse on the body and its mortality. Ultimately, Sappho wishes to discredit the view of the body as evil, for such ideas lead to hypocrisy and to repression of that free expression of sexuality which is the basis of her art. Thus, Sappho once and for all denies God and the authority of theology:

> —albeit I die indeed
> And hide myself and sleep and no man heed,
> Of me the high God hath not all his will.

> (11. 265-267)

Instead, Sappho proposes a fully erotic world, in which Keatsian nightingales sing "louder for love's sake" and stars "swooning with desire" respond to the "shudder of water."

In an apotheosis that owes little to Romantic-Christian modes of transcendence, Sappho wills herself into immortality, appealing not to God or to Nature, but to the poem and to the reader as her witness:

> but me—
> Men shall not see bright fire nor hear the sea,
> Nor mix their hearts with music . . .

> . . . . .

> But in the light and laughter, in the moan
> And music, and in grasp of lip and hand

> . . . . .

> Memories shall mix and metaphors of me.

> (11. 203-205, 210-211, 214)

Subtly, the audience has been implicated not only in the forbidden acts of love, but also in the overturning of cultural constraints that these acts signify throughout the monologue. "Memories" of the deep relationship or "mix" discovered between religious and sexual "metaphors," between desire for God and desire for erotic pain with pleasure, will trouble the reader until he or she is no longer sure of the demarcation between morality and immorality. Although the immortalization of the poet through art is a conventional topos, "Anactoria" gives it an ironic twist:

> my songs once heard in a strange place,
> Cleave to men's lives, and waste the days thereof
> With gladness and much sadness and long love.

(11. 278-280)

Just as Sappho relentlessly "cleaves" to the body of Anactoria in order to create the "music" of her sexually liberated poetry, so the daring message of her "song" will "cleave" the bad conscience of the Victorian—and modern—reader who professes to be shocked at such "indecency" and "blasphemy."

The conclusion to "Anactoria" remains problematic, however. While the speaker does solve the ontological threat of death through her art, the ideological contradictions raised during the monologue are left wide open:

> Alas, that neither moon nor snow nor dew
> Nor all cold things can purge me wholly through,
> Assuage me nor allay me nor appease,
> Till supreme sleep shall bring me bloodless ease;
> Till time wax faint in all his periods;
> Till fate undo the bondage of the gods,
>
> . . . . .
>
> And shed around and over and under me
> Thick darkness and the insuperable sea.

(11. 295-300, 303-304)

David A. Cook speaks for the critical consensus when he describes Sappho as a frustrated artist: "Where love and art have failed equally to satiate, the only true fullness . . . is death."[12] Yet, as Sappho's vindication of her sexual politics against a fatalistic, repressive theology has affirmed throughout the monologue, neither her love nor her art has failed. Rather, it is the false and perverting division of body and spirit in the Hellenic-Christian tradition that has failed to respect the individual's right to self-fulfillment. If read in a polemical context, then, Sappho's final vision of "sleep" in the "insuperable sea" is not decadent nihilism but dignified resignation to the "intellectual dislocation" caused by her acute recognition of the conflict between sexuality and social structures in Hellenic-Christian culture (McGann, p. 180). She rejects the standard symbolism for transcendence or purification of the flesh—"neither moon nor snow nor dew / Nor all cold things can purge me wholly through"—because it assumes that sex is innately sinful and, by implication, alien to the realm of "high" art. Adopting a stance of "insuperable" revolt, therefore, Sappho looks forward to "sleep" as a new teleology that will replace the vicious circle of man's sadomasochistic "bondage" to the gods and to God. Her espousal of the amoral condition of "sleep" and her definition of "music" or poetry as beyond morality or immorality challenges the reader to reconsider the polarities presup-

posed by Christian discourse on love and on art. In fact, Sappho's open ideological position at the end of "Anactoria" exemplifies the conclusions reached by several other fictional speakers in *Poems and Ballads,* including those in "The Triumph of Time," "Laus Veneris," and "Hymn to Proserpine."

The rhetorical strategy of "Laus Veneris" is structurally similar to that of "Anactoria." Whereas Swinburne uses the voice of the classical poetess, Sappho, to denounce God and praise eroticism from a pagan point of view, he uses the mask of the medieval knight and lover, Tannhäuser, to reveal the contradictions of Christianity from within. In each case, the polemic on contemporary Victorian issues is distanced by setting the speaker in a partly historical, partly mythical past. Secondly, "Laus Veneris" and "Anactoria" share Swinburne's characteristic deployment of mixed metaphors to collapse moral distinctions held sacred by his readers. The effect is all the more devastating when Tannhäuser discredits the authority of doctrinal language because he sincerely considers himself one of the faithful in his role as a representative of the Church Militant, or "God's knight." Likewise, Tannhäuser's calm resolution in favor of deliberate sin in the finale of "Laus Veneris" is calculated to shake the reader and cast doubt on the foundations of his or her beliefs in a way parallel to Sappho's well reasoned anti-theodicy in "Anactoria."

"Laus Veneris" is preceded by an excerpt from a bogus Old French book of romances. This elaborate parody is not aesthetic medievalizing for its own sake but rather constitutes part of the mask which Swinburne adopts in the poem.[13] Just as he claims in *Notes on Poems and Reviews* that the supposedly "unclean detail" in "Anactoria" merely reflects his faithful translation of Sappho's odes, so Swinburne steps back from the eroticism and blasphemy in "Laus Veneris" by assuring the audience that his interest in the "legend of Venus and her knight" is only to "rehandle the old story in a new fashion" (p. 26). In the latter defense, however, Swinburne's irony penetrates much further: explaining that he has picked up the story just when the "tragic" hero recognizes his plight, Swinburne maintains that "Laus Veneris" should be read as a moral parable "comparable only to that of the foolish virgins, and bearing the same burden" (p. 26). Interestingly, we see Swinburne turning Biblical typology against itself both in his poems and in his prose. The main plan of "Laus Veneris" is precisely to twist the exemplum of the Christian knight who damns his soul through lust for Venus into a counter-example of how the deeply sensual aspects of Christianity pervert its adherents. Thus, religion paradoxically ensures our eternal perdition, rendering the immortality of the soul a cruelly deceptive concept.

"'Laus Veneris' is a fine piece of macabre wit in which Swinburne dramatically accepts the Christian perspective in order that it might be self-condemned" (McGann, p. 255). Like "Anactoria" and many of Browning's dramatic monologues, "Laus Veneris" has three interlocking main sections: first, the speaker, Tannhäuser, describes the attractions of Venus and his guilty sins with her; second, he recalls the bitter revelations about the hypocrisy of knighthood and the Catholic Church that drove him from God back to Venus; and, third, he redescribes the body of Venus and takes his final iconoclastic stance. Because Tannhäuser addresses the reader directly throughout most of the poem, pausing only here and there to address Venus herself, we are placed in the position of voyeurs, looking in through the bedroom window at the two lovers. At the same time, we move with Tannhäuser through an agonizing process of religious and moral questioning that leads not to reaffirmation of faith, as it does for the speakers in several of Tennyson's dramatic monologues, but to a gradual desacralization of fundamental Christian myths and icons.

In the opening six stanzas, the sleeping Venus, "Kissed over close, wears yet a purple speck" (1.2) on her throat, reminding Tannhäuser of the ritual worship of the dead body of Christ on the Cross:

> All lips . . . now grow sad with kissing Christ,
>   Stained with blood fallen from the feet of
> God,
> The feet and hands whereat our souls were
>   priced.

> (11. 14-16)

As Robert Peters explains in his fine article on "Laus Veneris," Tannhäuser vacillates constantly between desire and guilt, between pagan and Christian evaluations of love, until their distinctions are blurred.[14] However, Peters' assessment of Tannhäuser in terms of a Romantic "antinomian artist" who speaks the language of a Pre-Raphaelite aesthete seems off the point.[15] Swinburne is using complex, mixed metaphors here to draw attention to the similarities between the sensual poses of Venus and the holy icons of Christ: "And thou didst heal us with thy piteous kiss; / But see now, Lord; her mouth is lovelier" (11. 19-20). How different is kissing the red bloody feet of Christ in agony from kissing a woman in the agony of desire until blood appears on her neck? Why must the kiss of Christ be considered pure and saving, while the kiss of Venus, "my soul's body," is branded as impure and sinful?

In the extended description of Venus's otherworldly domain, or the "Horsel," which follows (stanzas 7-52), Swinburne subverts several other major Christian symbols through mixed metaphors. Christ's Sacred Heart of divine pity and mercy becomes the lover's heart which Venus holds "in her sweet open hands / Hanging asleep" (11. 33-34), or beyond moral concerns. Presiding over this inverted ritual is the god of "Love" who takes sadistic delight in stoking the "fire" of desire in the exhausted couples who populate the Horsel, their mouths "panting" with "dry desire." In a demonic parody of Christ, "Love"—here charity transformed to lust, grace to sin—wears a crown of "gilt thorns," suggesting that Christ in his double role as Judge and Redeemer enjoys not only administering pain but suffering flagellation as a form of pleasure. Significantly, the Horsel itself is organized on the same plan as hell, with separate areas for various types of carnal activities that yield "Exceeding pleasure out of extreme pain" (1. 120). The eternal fornication among the assembly of legendary lovers offers an ironic comment on the medieval Christian topos of "ubi sunt," or the pious warning that the body is mortal and frail: in the Horsel, the soul has passed away, leaving a tortuous perpetuity of physical desire. Foreshadowing the conclusion of "Laus Veneris," Tannhäuser surveys this scene and asks: "Sin, is it sin whereby men's souls are thrust / Into the pit?" (11. 173-174). Because the Horsel shares so many features with hell, just as lovemaking does with religious worship, the speaker grows increasingly confused about the definition of evil, the nature of heaven, and even about the intentions of God:

> Day smiteth day in twain, night sundereth night,
> And on mine eyes the dark sits as the light;
>   Yea, Lord, thou knowest I know not, having
>   sinned,
> If heaven be clean or unclean in thy sight.

> (11. 157-160)

In effect, the underworld of Venus is a mythical version of the Victorian sexual underground. The very obsession with avoiding sins of the flesh has produced them a thousandfold: the rigid proprieties of the Protestant English middle class have created a clandestine subculture that stubbornly pursues its guilty pleasures in moral anxiety and pain.

It has not often been recognized that the most serious blow to Tannhäuser's faith is not delivered by his sexual involvement with Venus but by the displaced sensuality that he unwittingly uncovers in the program of the Crusades and in the doctrines of the Catholic Church. In the central section of his monologue (stanzas 53-96), Tannhäuser recalls "the clean great time of goodly fight" when he was a proud knight "of Christ's choosing." He traces his disaffection from Christianity to the moment in which his "fair pure sword" suddenly appeared not as the straight rod of God righteously raised against the infidel, but as the sinuous, phallic snake of Satan whose work is not to redeem but to destroy:

> Most like a snake that takes short breath and dips
>   Sharp from the beautifully bending head,
> With all its gracious body lithe as lips
>
> That curl in touching you.

> (11. 218-221)

The first section of "Laus Veneris" ends with a description of the most lovely courtesans in Venus' underworld: in stanzas 50-51, the queen, Semiramis, is portrayed with "large pale lips" which are "Curled like a tiger's that curl back to feed" on the bodies of her dying lovers. Since the same metaphor is applied to the shape and motion of Tannhäuser's sword in stanzas 54-56, the knight's slaughter of men for the glory of God seems just another kind of erotic sadism, thinly disguised under the "pure" veil of religious belief. The confusion of values that the speaker experiences increases when he associates the blood and "fire" of the Crusades with the blood and "fire" of the Horsel. Terrified, Tannhäuser finds himself poised over the mutilated body of a foe whose "caught-up choked dry laughters" in death sound like the sobs of sexual ecstasy as he feels his own "fighting face . . . grown a flame / For pleasure" (11. 226-227). In short, the knight realizes that his holy wars have been nothing but sado-erotic gratifications sanctioned by the ideal of Christ Militant. Christ himself, then, is exposed as a deceptively passive God who suffers Crucifixion the better to assert his cruel power as an aggressive God who, in Sappho's words, "Feeds the mute melancholy lust of heaven" (1. 170) on the death agonies of men.

Significantly, it is only after this vision of the evil in supposed good that Tannhäuser succumbs to the temptation of Venus in an allegorical garden that clearly echoes the original Fall of man through carnal knowledge. Swinburne implies, however, that the perversion of love is not anterior but posterior to the Christian value system. This iconoclastic view provides the mainspring of the irony in his defense of "Laus Veneris" in *Notes on Poems and Reviews*. Swinburne calls Tannhäuser's crisis of faith "tragic" and defines "the mediaeval Venus" as "diabolic" because the natural sexuality represented by the pagan conception of the goddess has been repressed and hence distorted by the false morality of Christianity (p. 26). Tannhäuser's encounter with the Pope at the end of the central section of the poem (stanzas 83-96) also supports this view. After fleeing the Horsel to join a pilgrimage to Rome on which he devoutly hopes to purge his soul of the sins of lust and doubt, Tannhäuser is distressed to find that the Palatine Hills look "like outer skirts of hell" (1. 342), or a sort of Golgotha of "White cursed hills" which obscenely suggest the private parts of Venus: "Like a jagged shell's lips, harsh, untunable, / Blown in between by devils' wrangling breath" (11. 344-345). Furthermore, although Tannhäuser confesses his "great sin" with Venus and begs for absolution, the Pope refuses him grace and offers him a death-in-life of penance that is an ironic inversion of the life-in-death of desire offered by Venus. His voice resounding like that of the Anti-Christ, in "a great cry out of hell" (1. 367), the Pope demands an indefinite period of self-mortification from Tannhäuser yet promises no certain salvation as its reward:

> "Until this dry shred staff, that hath no whit
> Of leaf nor bark, bear blossom and smell sweet,
>   Seek thou not any mercy in God's sight,
> For so long shalt thou be cast out from it."

(11. 369-372)

The "dry" phallic staff underscores the sterility of God in contrast to the fertility of Venus whose body is repeatedly metaphorized as a "flower." Sexual self-fulfillment now appears surer and more "sweet" than the vagaries and abstinence of religious grace. At the same time, the bondage of Tannhäuser's heart, "Hanging asleep" in Venus' hands, so closely resembles the bondage of his soul, imprisoned by the laws of the Vicar of God who "bears the keys / To bind or loose" (11. 350-351), that sensuality and religiosity become almost indistinguishable modes of masochistic suffering. It is on such metaphorical thinking about the deep relation of pornography and iconography, sin and salvation, that Tannhäuser will base his final denunciation of Christianity.

Earlier in his monologue, while contemplating the eternal cycle of pleasure and pain in the Horsel, Tannhäuser had called out to Nature, wishing for the "sleep" of death as the only state in which his moral conflicts might be suspended, just as his body would be dissolved into earth:

> Ah yet would God this flesh of mine might be
> Where air might wash and long leaves cover me,
>   Where tides of grass break into foam of
>   flowers,
> Or where the wind's feet shine along the sea.

(11. 53-56)

Unlike the pagan Sappho, who can mock outright the ritual purgation of the "fire" of sexuality by "all cold things," Tannhäuser speaks from within the Christian world view and so necessarily uses its metaphors of baptism and purification—"wash," "tides"—to express his despair, even though he no longer fully believes in the doctrines that this language presupposes. Furthermore, death in this context is itself a metaphor: "death" and "sleep" are interchangeable figurations for the speaker's ideological impasse as he realizes that the very structure of language in his culture will not permit him to think about "this flesh" in an amoral, truly natural sense, but will always force upon him the pain/pleasure complex of desire and guilt. Tannhäuser's predicament is conveyed by his unwitting insertion of erotic metaphors, previously used to describe Venus and the carnal activities in the Horsel, into his pious prayer to God for release from mortal suffering. For instance, the traditional site of death, or the hard, earthy grave, is transformed into a sensuous "foam of flowers." Notably, Tannhäuser regards the "sea" as his proper resting place, in opposition to the Christian alternatives of the heavenly air and the hell fire. This allies him with the iconoclast, Sappho, and suggests that his hope for the "seal of sleep" is a metaphor for the resolution of moral and metaphysical dualisms, to be taken in the same sense as Sappho's welcoming of "Thick darkness and the insuperable sea" at the end of "Anactoria."

Swinburne makes the metaphor of the "seal" a major pivot of Tannhäuser's argument against Christianity. In the first section of "Laus Veneris," Tannhäuser borders on blasphemy when speaking of his suicidal impulses in terms of a sensuous "seal of sleep" on the body, to be sent by God. In the second section of the poem, after he has reviewed what he has learned about the hypocrisy of virtue and faith during his exploits as knight and pilgrim, Tannhäuser turns away from God to Venus, asking her to "Seal my lips hard from speaking of my sin" (1. 323), as he tries to accept sexuality without the self-defeating contradictions of Christian values. In the final section (stanzas 97-106), Tannhäuser completes the desacralization of moral and religious ideas that he began in the opening stanzas of the poem. He converts the "seal" of apocalyptic revelation into the "seal" of absolute lust:

> I seal myself upon thee [Venus] with my might,
> Abiding alway out of all men's sight
>   Until God loosen over sea and land
> The thunder of the trumpets of the night.

(11. 421-424)

Like Sappho who is determined to defy gods and God in order to uphold her rights as a lesbian and an artist beyond morality, Tannhäuser proposes to stay with Venus and repeatedly commit his sins in defiance of a Last Judgment which he still fears may come to pass but which will be issued by a God in whom he no longer has positive faith. Ironically, then, Tannhäuser does achieve a state of revelation at the end of "Laus Veneris," but it is the revelation of the fraudulence of the entire Christian culture and his victimization by that culture.

The several structuring metaphors shared by "Anactoria" and "Laus Veneris" lead one to conclude that Swinburne wrote these poems as an ideological pair: the former as an attack on Victorian morality from the outside, the latter as an exposure of Victorian morality from the inside. A particularly striking example of the polemical connection between "Anactoria" and "Laus Veneris" is Swinburne's use of the punning metaphor, "cleave." Sappho triumphs over the conservative reader when she reminds us, in the last moments of her monologue, that we have silently been party to the aberrations of her lovemaking as well as to the revolt against cultural norms which her speech and behavior imply: "my songs once heard in a strange place [say, Victorian England], / Cleave to men's lives" (11. 278-279). The metaphor "cleave" also provides the keynote of Tannhäuser's last remarks. Abandoning "prayers and perished thanksgivings" to a discredited God, Tannhäuser fully embraces Venus:

> Feeling her face with all her eager hair
> Cleave to me, clinging as a fire that clings
>
> To the body and to the raiment, burning them;
> As after death I know that such-like flame
>   Shall cleave to me for ever; yea, what care,
> Albeit I burn then, having felt the same?

(11. 403-408)

The deeply rooted guilt that accompanies his sexual self-fulfillment makes every act of pleasure painful for Tannhäuser. Even though he bravely denies the Christian religion, he remains divided or "cloven" between his new-found skepticism and the old, culturally reinforced habit of judging everything according to the categories of purity and sin. Thus, when Venus "cleaves" or "clings" to him in "love," the "fire" of natural physical desire becomes twisted in his mind into the "flame" of hell which he has been taught will "cleave" or punish him for his "lust." In *Notes on Poems and Reviews*, Swinburne cagily interprets "Laus Veneris" as a moral exemplum, yet it is quite clear from the context and especially the play on the metaphors "cleave" and "burn" that Tannhäuser is arguing against morality. The thoroughly indoctrinated Christian conscience—whether Catholic or Protestant—can never enjoy sexuality for its own sake. Since the state of guilty passion ("fire") is identical in feeling to the state of spiritual purgation ("flame"), the distinction between moral and immoral behavior, or between the pain of abstinence and the pain of indulgence, collapses: "yea, what care, / Albeit I burn then, having felt the same?" In sum, Swinburne's medieval persona in "Laus Veneris" reaches the same open ideological position, or amorality, as his classical persona in "Anactoria." The iconoclasm of both dramatic monologues stems from the debunking of traditional values and the refusal to set up substitute dichotomies that would comfort and hence deceive the public in the same way as Christianity has.

The rhetorical strategy employed in "Hymn to Proserpine" follows much the same pattern as "Anactoria" and "Laus Veneris," with one important exception. Although adopting the mask of a late Roman thinker guarantees a certain distancing from Victorian topics of faith and doubt, morality and decadence, there is no narrative action in "Hymn to Proserpine" to match the battles and wanderings of Tannhäuser, nor even any implied action like the lovemaking between Sappho and Anactoria. This has the effect of focusing the speaker's and also the reader's attention completely on the political, moral, and theological issues raised by the advent of Christianity in late pagan culture. Consequently, "Hymn to Proserpine" is more transparently polemical than either "Anactoria" or "Laus Veneris" and typically elicited the charge of "atheism" from critics such as the anonymous reviewer mentioned earlier who strongly condemned "that hopeless mode of looking at life which Mr. Swinburne seems now to have erected into a species of faith" (Hyder, 1970, p. 37). Swinburne also uses mixed metaphors in a slightly different way in "Hymn to Proserpine": parallel pairs and triads of figurations for pagan and Christian gods and values, always angled at the expense of the latter tradition, give the poem an almost programmatic tone.

Swinburne chooses to rework the classical myth of Proserpine for roughly the same reason that he selects the medieval legend of Tannhäuser and Venus: each is based on a structure of ambiguities which he can develop to convey his own criticism of Victorian attitudes. Whereas the double function of the medieval knight-lover implies the hidden sensuality in Christian culture in "Laus Veneris," Proserpine's curiously neutral position in the classical pantheon suggests a perfect amorality, or absolute freedom, which escapes the polarity between immorality, represented by the cult of Venus, and morality, represented by the cult of the Virgin, in "Hymn to Proserpine." In the first section of the poem (ll. 1-64), the cautiously anonymous speaker invokes the goddess "Proserpina" and looks forward to an ideal state of "sleep" or "peace" in her underworld. As a stoical individualist, he has made the best of the "Gods," Venus and Apollo, who "are cruel as love or life, and lovely as death" (l. 12), but whose reign has at least permitted the Romans to enjoy and express their natural passions in public rituals: "All the feet of the hours that sound as a single lyre, / Dropped and deep in the flowers, with strings that flicker like fire" (ll. 27-28). At this early point in his monologue, the pagan speaker sounds very much like a nineteenth-century English Decadent, with his emphasis on the "grievous pain and pleasure" of love. Swinburne is setting up an ironic framework here: the pejorative use of the labels "pagan" and "decadent" by moralists will have to be revaluated in light of this exposure of the fascination in the poem with sensuality and morbidity at the very origin of Christianity.

In the second section of "Hymn to Proserpine" (ll. 65-90), the speaker criticizes the new faith in Christ for its obsession with martyrdom which he interprets as a sado-masochistic spectacle:

> O lips that the live blood faints in, the leavings
>   of racks and rods!
> O ghastly stories of saints, dead limbs of
>   gibbeted Gods!
>
>   . . . . .
>
> I kneel not neither adore you, but standing, look
>   to the end.
>
>   (ll. 43-44, 46)

To a pagan mind, unconvinced of the sinfulness of the flesh and unbelieving in the transcendence of the soul, Christ as the martyred Savior appears to be a travesty of the divine. The notion of a God who proves his immortality by dying for mankind is a logical contradiction. Christ will never truly oust Venus, for we will never prefer death over life: "Though before thee the throned Cytherean be fallen, and hidden her head, / Yet thy kingdom shall pass, Galilean, thy dead shall go down to thee dead" (ll. 73-74). Characteristically, Swinburne parodies the language of the Bible, demonstrating that the doctrine of the salvation of the soul still leaves the problem of the mortality of the body unsolved. The late Roman thinker goes even further than the skepticism of Sappho or the disillusionment of Tannhäuser, however. In an extended metaphor of "Time" as a "sea" that masters and determines all things, he argues that both

paganism and Christianity are transient historical phases that "will pass." Since all religious systems are relative, depending as they do on the evolution of time, it follows that the political authority of Christianity will "fall" some day just as the power of Venus is now waning in the Roman state: "Ye are Gods, and behold, ye shall die, and the waves be upon you at last" (l. 68).

Although the lesbianism of "Anactoria" and the blasphemy of "Laus Veneris" are daring enough, the relativity of all religious and moral values proposed in "Hymn to Proserpine" is surely the most iconoclastic position of all. The reader may object to the drift of the late Roman's argument, but we cannot deny the persuasiveness of his logic as he carefully dissects the central beliefs and icons of Christian culture and finds them either perverse or contradictory or both. In the third section of his monologue (ll. 91-110), the speaker compares the Virgin Mary and Venus by way of illustrating the morbidity and unhealthiness of the new morality. Just as Christ the "king" usurps the "throne" of Apollo, so Mary seeks to replace Venus as the "queen" of Rome. But whereas Venus represents "the world's desire" in her double role as majestic "goddess" and "mother" of eroticism, Mary remains an unfulfilled "maiden" and a common pauper, "a slave among slaves, and rejected." The contrast between the natural fertility of Venus' cult of coition and the life-threatening sterility of the Virgin's cult of continence is underscored by a series of mixed metaphors. Born from the life-giving sea, Venus bears the "white rose of the rose-white water" and brings sexual "joy" to all her followers. Associated with the "ghastly glories" of the Passion, Mary comes "pale" and "a sister to sorrow," with no "odour and colour of flowers" at all.

The oppositions established between Venus and Mary serve not only to remind the reader of the lugubriousness of the Christian religion, but ultimately to foil the more wholesome, neutral world view represented by Proserpine. "Goddess and maiden and queen," Proserpine subsumes the polar values symbolized by Venus ("goddess" and "queen") and Mary ("goddess" and "maiden"). In Proserpine's underworld, the "red rose" of eroticism becomes interchangeable with the "white rose" of transcendence. Likewise, her offer of "sleep" supersedes the pleasures of pagan sybaritism and the pains of Christian martyrdom. "Sleep" and its correlative "death" are metaphors for a freedom from both ideologies, leaving only a state of inner "peace." The "soul" that is not restricted by norms or beliefs attains the only true immortality, for all such systems must eventually "pass away," thereby proving their relative falsehood. When the late Roman thinker concludes by calling for "death," therefore, he is repeating the brave gesture of liberation made by Sappho at the end of her monologue:

> Till fate undo the bondage of the gods,
> And lay, to slake and satiate me all through,
> Lotus and Lethe on my lips like dew.
>
>   ("Anactoria," ll. 300-302)

For there is no God found stronger than death;
  and death is a sleep.

("Hymn to Proserpine," l. 110)

Both speakers reject "gods" and "God," or the very notion of theology and the perverse reactions that moral strictures foster. Both speakers also challenge Christian teleology by anticipating death as a positive or rather a neutral condition beyond the vicissitudes of moral judgments. Just as Sappho welcomes death under the "insuperable sea" after the "Lotus" of forgetfulness has "purged" her mind of its "bitter" struggle against sexual and aesthetic repression, so the late Roman awaits the cancellation of the conflict between Hellenic and Christian values once the "poppies" of Proserpine have put to "sleep" all allegiance and all doubt.

In a provocative essay entitled "Victorian Counterculture," Morse Peckham claims that the England of Swinburne's day manifested not two but three competing cultural complexes.[16] Granting that "there were two sexual cultures in nineteenth-century Europe, a *public* culture of constraint and a *private* one of license," Peckham, using Philip Rieff's terminology, calls the latter a "*remissive* culture" and distinguishes it from a third level, or the "*counterculture*" (pp. 258-259, my emphases). The true counterculture, he maintains, arises in England with the evangelical movement whose aim was widespread "sexual repression which by the end of the century was becoming dominant and beginning to be able to enforce its cultural values upon . . . public culture" (p. 259). Whether there is an essential difference between the social and psychological effects of the "constraint" on sexuality imposed by the Victorian "public culture" and the effects of the "repression" of sexuality sought by various religious groups is a moot point. However, Peckham's theory of the doubling of the "remissive" by a "counterculture" may be usefully applied to draw a distinction between the popular underground of sexual practices that Steven Marcus discusses in *The Other Victorians* and the underground of iconoclastic criticism in contemporary literature that *Poems and Ballads, First Series* exemplifies.

"Laus Veneris" and "Hymn to Proserpine" are complementary examinations of the remissive and counter cultures, respectively. As Peckham notes, the mainstream of Victorian discourse carefully separates the rhetoric of religion from the rhetoric of sexuality. Swinburne perceives the gap between public and remissive behavior and language, and in his dramatic monologues he tries to expose their dangerous contradictions. His most characteristic technique is mixing metaphors from Christian typology and doctrine with pornography, as in "Anactoria" and "Laus Veneris." In "Hymn to Proserpine," however, Swinburne supplements his critique of the two Victorian cultures with a truly countercultural proposal: an assertion of the individual's freedom from traditional ideologies, based on the premise that moral values and religious systems are historically relative, hence unreli-

able. Metaphorically, then, the underworld of Proserpine in "Hymn to Proserpine" replaces the underworld of Venus in "Laus Veneris" as, in Swinburne's estimation, critical self-determination—counterculture—should supersede the double standards—public versus remissive—of the past. The iconoclastic aim of the major dramatic monologues in *Poems and Ballads, First Series* is restated toward the end of *Notes on Poems and Reviews* when Swinburne declares: "Nothing is so favorable to the undergrowth of real indecency as this overshadowing foliage of fictions, this artificial network of proprieties" (p. 30). Recognizing that the perversities of the remissive culture—"the undergrowth of real indecency"—are a necessary reaction against the unnatural "network of proprieties" invented by the Christian Victorian mind, Swinburne challenges the reader to imagine a radical alternative: the "sleep" or suspension of morality itself.

NOTES

[1] All quotations of Algernon Charles Swinburne's *Notes on Poems and Reviews* (1866) are taken from the critical edition by Clyde K. Hyder, *Swinburne Replies* (Syracuse Univ. Press, 1966). The present quotation is found on p. 18.

[2] Susan R. Suleiman, *Authoritarian Fictions: The Ideological Novel as a Literary Genre* (Columbia Univ. Press, 1983), pp. 1-23.

[3] Morse Peckham's "Introduction" to one of the standard paperback editions of *Poems and Ballads, First Series* has been very influential (Indianapolis, 1970 [pp. xi-xxxv]). Taking a psychocritical approach, Peckham maintains that the erotic subject matter of Swinburne's poems is directly traceable to the poet's personal inclinations and practices. Peckham does pose the question "whether or not these poems are to be considered . . . as analyses not merely of masochism and other perversions but also of the relation of such non-normal behavior to the rest of human behavior" (pp. xix-xx). In another essay, entitled "Eroticism=Politics: Politics=Eroticism" (in *Victorian Revolutionaries: Speculations on Some Heroes of a Culture Crisis* [New York, 1970]), Peckham brilliantly demonstrates the connection between Swinburne's erotic writings, de Sade, and the "culture crisis" over sexuality which both authors address. Unfortunately, most critics of Swinburne before and after Peckham have preferred the psychological and autobiographical to the cultural approach. See, for example, the special issue of *Victorian Poetry* on Swinburne (*VP*, 9, Nos. 1-2 [1971]).

[4] *Sex and Marriage in Victorian Poetry* (Cornell Univ. Press, 1975), p. 102.

[5] *Swinburne: An Experiment in Criticism* (Univ. of Chicago Press, 1972), p. 203.

[6] *The Other Victorians: A Study of Sexuality and Pornography in Mid-Victorian England* (New York, 1964), p. 40.

[7] All quotations from the anonymous review (*London Review*, August 4, 1866) of Swinburne's *Poems and Ballads, First Series* are taken from Clyde K. Hyder, ed., *Swinburne: The Critical Heritage* (London, 1970). The present quotation is found on p. 36.

[8] All quotations from Swinburne's *Poems and Ballads, First Series* are taken from the Chatto and Windus edition (1904) of his *Poetical Works,* volume I. Line numbers are given in parentheses.

[9] I am indebted for several ideas on Christian typology to George P. Landow, *Victorian Types, Victorian Shadows: Biblical Typology in Victorian Literature, Art, and Thought* (Boston, 1980).

[10] Trans. Hugh J. Schonfield (New York, 1959).

[11] *Tennyson and Swinburne as Romantic Naturalists* (Univ. of Toronto Press, 1981), p. 124.

[12] "The Content and Meaning of Swinburne's 'Anactoria'," *VP,* 9, Nos. 1-2 (1971), 92.

[13] On Pre-Raphaelite medievalism, see John Dixon Hunt, *The Pre-Raphaelite Imagination, 1848-1900* (Univ. of Nebraska Press, 1968).

[14] "The Tannhäuser Theme: Swinburne's 'Laus Veneris'," *PRR,* 3, No. 1 (1979), 12-28.

[15] For Peters, Swinburne's "knight-artist" exemplifies "the creative process" in which a "sense of beautiful design and aesthetic effect is enhanced rather than diminished by personal traumas" (p. 26). The combination of simple psychologizing and stereotypes of the aesthete is another approach frequently applied, with limited success, to *Poems and Ballads, First Series.* See also Hunt.

[16] *VS,* 18 (1975), 257-276.

Lynne McMahon

SOURCE: "Female Erotics," in *American Poetry Review*, Vol. 20, No. 3, May/June, 1991, pp. 9-14.

[*In the following essay, McMahon examines two poems which offer critical views of sex and matrimony, Marianne Moore's "Marriage" and Sandra McPherson's "Streamers."*]

Marianne Moore

Elizabeth Bishop, in her essay "Efforts of Affection," gives us the most complete picture we have of Marianne Moore, and also points out the largest gaps in our understanding of Moore's difficult poetic:

> Lately I have seen several references critical of [Moore's] poetry by feminist writers, one of whom

describes her as 'a poet who controlled panic by presenting it as whimsy.' Whimsy is sometimes there, of course, and so is humor (a gift these critics sadly seem to lack). Surely there is an element of mortal panic and fear underlying all works of art? Even so, one wonders how much of Marianne's poetry the feminist critics have read. Have they really read "Marriage," a poem that says everything they are saying and everything Virginia Woolf has said? It is a poem which transforms a justified sense of injury into a work of art. . . .

"Marriage" details not so much a sense of mortal panic (the author has, after all, avoided marriage) as one of infantilizing and inescapable entrapment:

> I wonder what Adam and Eve
> think of it by this time,
> this fire-gilt steel
> alive with goldenness;
> how bright it shows—
> "of circular traditions and impostures,
> committing many spoils,"
> requiring all one's criminal ingenuity
> to avoid!

It's hard to see a wedding band ever again as anything other than "this fire-gilt steel / alive with goldenness"— not only is gold alloyed, "gilt" (and, of course, the intended homophonic pun), it is taken down one element further, revealed to be not gold at all, but steel, with the *appearance* of goldenness. Moreover this is a steel band emerging from fire, alive. It is searing and idolatrous, echoing the golden calf and the whole nature of dowry, "the spoils," which requires all one's criminal ingenuity to avoid! "Criminal" is the key adjective here, for if marriage is the honorable estate, what can spinsterhood be? "Psychology which explains everything / explains nothing, / and we are still in doubt" the poem continues, and we ask—doubt about what? Eve, the poem tells us, and why she ever consented to the proposition that marriage was desirable:

> "*I*" [i.e. Eve] should like to be alone";
> to which the visitor replies,
> "I should like to be alone;
> why not be alone together?"
> Below the incandescent stars
> below the incandescent fruit,
> the strange experience of beauty;
> its existence is too much;
> it tears one to pieces
> and each fresh wave of consciousness
> is poison.

The leap from the proposal to the incandescent, strange experience of beauty and then to poison might be the paradigm for Marriage itself. First, the promise of liberty ("alone"ness) *and* company, which is irresistible; Eve says yes. Then that wonderful Edenic moment— sexual intercourse?—taking place below the incandescent stars, below the incandescent fruit (beneath the Tree of Knowledge), that strange experience of beauty

whose existence is too much, it tears one to pieces. And
we jump to Louise Glück's "Mock Orange":

> I hate them [the orange blossoms] as I hate sex,
> the man's mouth
> sealing my mouth, the man's
> paralyzing body—
>
> and the cry that always escapes,
> the low, humiliating
> premise of union—

Coming to consciousness is poison, the low humiliating
premise of union, for the idea of union is an impossibility. For Moore's Eve, the strange beauty under the incandescent stars and fruit is now tainted, "See her, see
her in this common world, / the central flaw / in that
first crystal-fine experiment,"—for the crystal-fine Eve
is common now, divided back into her sole self, but no
longer exquisitely virgin. Moore makes another of her
wild leaps here, quoting (ironically) from Richard
Baxter's *The Saints' Everlasting Rest,* perhaps to show
us Adam's (not Eve's) postcoital peace:

> describing it
> as "that strange paradise
> unlike flesh, stones,
> gold or stately buildings,
> the choicest piece of my life:
> the heart rising
> in its estate of peace
> as a boat rises
> with the rising of the water";

"That strange paradise" is the idea of union, an "amalgamation" Moore says, "which can never be more / than
an interesting impossibility"—but one which Adam can
act upon again and again. The situation for Eve is different; she is forever implicated, tainted, in that strange
experience of beauty—she has been the more culpable in
the expulsion from the garden, an exit Moore sardonically sums up as the "shed snakeskin in the history of
politeness / not to be returned to again— / that invaluable accident / exonerating Adam." This is very witty
indeed; the relation between the sexes has now become
the received forms of politeness. Adam will gallantly not
remark upon Eve's responsibility for their exiled state,
"that invaluable accident exonerating Adam"! He is free to
be the magnanimous nobleman, dispensing largesse wherever he goes. The trouble is, Adam can't be entirely and
ironically written off, for, as the poem notes, "He has
beauty also; / it's distressing—the O thou / to whom from
whom / without whom nothing—Adam;"—he is, after all,
the measure, the Other against whom Eve judges herself;
he is the "to whom from whom without whom nothing."
He is the standard, and the namer, the wielder of language
(and so the originator of the language of patriarchy.) In
these next excerpted speeches, Moore makes of Adam an
amalgam of sources as diverse as Hazlitt on Kenneth
Burke, Richard Baxter (again quoting *The Saints' Everlasting Rest*), Anatole France, Hagop Boghossian, William
Godwin and Edward Thomas (from his essay "Feminine
Influence on the Poets"):

> he goes on speaking
> in a formal customary strain,
> of "past states, the present state,
> seals, promises,
> the evil one suffered,
> the good one enjoys,
> hell, heaven,
> everything convenient
> to promote one's joy."

One can almost see the Victorian papa puffing out his
chest here, and Moore clinches it in the next passage:
"he experiences a solemn joy / in seeing that he has
become an idol." The married life suits him very well.

But that edifice constructed on matrimony is not entirely
safe. Eve is a subversive:

> "Treading chasms
> on the uncertain footing of a spear,"
> forgetting that there is in woman
> a quality of mind
> which as an instinctive manifestation
> is unsafe

the husband unwisely goes on his proclamatory way,
until he stumbles over the image and memory of that
first sexual heat in the Garden. He becomes unnerved by
a nightingale:

> Plagued by the nightingale
> in the new leaves,
> with its silence—
> not its silence but its silences,
> he says of it:
> "It clothes me with a shirt of fire."
> "He dares not clap his hands
> to make it go on
> lest it should fly off;
> if he does nothing, it will sleep;
> if he cries out, it will not understand."
> Unnerved by the nightingale
> and dazzled by the apple,
> impelled by "the illusion of a fire
> effectual to extinguish fire,"
> compared with which
> the shining of the earth
> is but a deformity—a fire
> "as high as deep
> as bright as broad
> as long as life itself,"
> he stumbles over marriage,
> "a very trivial object indeed"

No marriage can possibly live up to the burning of
that original passion, a fire so bright the shining of
the earth is but a deformity. Against that magnificence,
marriage is a very trivial object indeed. Adam, in
memory and desire, is as "dazzled by the apple" as Eve
was; he's on fire with it. But there is no path to that
first strange experience of beauty—it has been reduced, in the real world, to insignificance "by that experiment of Adam's / with ways out but no way
in— / the ritual of marriage." There are ways out but no
way in.

This is one way of reading the phrase "dazzled by the apple"—as memory of that incandescent fruit and the strange experience of beauty—sexual love, in short. But there is another, perhaps opposite, reading that takes the apple not as temptation to bodily pleasure, but as mental intoxication. For this Adam is a philosopher, and very like Virginia Woolf's Mr. Ramsey. He is impelled by a fire "as high as deep / as bright as broad / as long as life itself," a fire of the mind. Just as Mr. Ramsey walks up and down in front of his house, trying to get past Q, trying to make his way into the brighter abstractions, too rapt by his own mental gymnastics to see his wife, so too does Moore's Adam, dazzled by the brightness of his own mind, "stumble over marriage":

> "a very trivial object indeed"
> to have destroyed the attitude
> in which he stood—
> the ease of the philosopher
> unfathered by a woman.

"The ease of the philosopher / unfathered by a woman"—doesn't that sound like Mrs. Ramsey's speculations on the masculine mind, that it appears (to itself) as springing from its own fine maleness? Both Woolf and Moore are superb ironists; these self-engendered philosophers, at rest in the bosoms of their families, "experience a solemn joy / in seeing that they have become an idol."

Whether the fire is sexual or intellectual, the exclusion of Eve from Adam's passion remains a given. And that is the segue into Moore's next examination—domestic friction. What began as the wedding's lavish display ("fiddle-head ferns / lotus flowers, opuntias, white dromedaries / its hippopatamus"-a list that gets increasingly, excessively absurd, and ends with the original twinning, "the snake and the potent apple") shifts into the friction we must not call calamity, "the fight to be affectionate":

> "no truth can be fully known
> until it has been tried
> by the tooth of disputation"

Robert of Sorbonne is quoted as saying, and Moore takes that tooth and makes it the most unnerving image in the poem:

> The blue panther with black eyes,
> the basalt panther with blue eyes,
> entirely graceful—
> one must give them the path—
> the black obsidian Diana
> who "darkeneth her countenance
> as a bear doth,"
> the spiked hand
> that has an affection for one
> and proves it to the bone. . . .

That brute tooth of disputation, the friction in marriage, is a spiked hand whose affection it proves to the bone. And yet this darkness is entirely graceful, and beautiful,

and incredibly dangerous (one must give these panthers the path). At least that is how it appears to the outsider. But the spiked hand is also "impatient to assure you," Moore says, "that impatience is the mark of independence, / not of bondage." We return to Adam's proposal—"why not be alone together?" "'Married people often look that way'" (Moore is quoting again) "seldom and cold, up and down, / mixed and malarial / with a good day and a bad." But that description, meant to be commonsensical and reassuring, surely contains more negative than positive elements? Seldom, cold, down, mixed, malarial—Moore lets it resonate there.

And follows with another kaleidoscope of quotations, from *The Expositor's Bible,* "The Tempest," a friend's parody of "Rape of the Lock" (with suggestions from Marianne Moore herself), punctuated by straight declarative sentences: "experience attests / that men have power / and sometimes one is made to feel it." One feels it indeed in the excerpt from Carey Thomas's *Founders Address* (given at Mt. Holyoke College in 1921) which Moore introduces by way of the Oriental adage that "the fact of woman / is 'not the sound of the flute / but very poison'":

> She says, "Men are monopolists
> of 'stars, garters, buttons
> and other shining baubles'—
> unfit to be the guardians
> of another person's happiness."
> He says, "These mummies
> must be handled carefully—
> 'the crumbs from a lion's meal,
> a couple of shins and the bit of an ear'";

What she says and what he says have no immediate connection; she rages against man's infantile urge to gather the baubles of power (medals, etc.), and dismisses the entire sex as "unfit to be the guardians of another person's happiness." *He* says these mummies must be handled carefully. What has archaeology to do with the war between the sexes? Maybe the remains he handles—the ravages of a lion's feast—are another kind of bauble? Perhaps, but it is more likely that we are *not* meant to see a connection, or, rather, to see that there is no possibility of connection. *She* speaks and *he* speaks. There is no common ground; marriage is impossible. "Turn to the letter M," the poem instructs us, "and you will find / that 'a wife is a coffin'" (she is quoting Ezra Pound). That boldface M turns us back to Elizabeth Bishop's essay on Moore, the last paragraph when Bishop recounts a dream she has of a kind of parchment with letters marching across it:

> I have a sort of subliminal glimpse of the
> capital letter M multiplying: Marianne's
>   monogram;
> mother, manners; morals; and I catch myself
> murmuring "Manners and morals; manners as
>   morals?
> Or is it morals as manners?"

They are so intertwined they are inextricable. Like the snake and the apple, marriage too is mired in multiplications, "mixed and malarial." But the poem's letter M is "that severe object," the coffin, "with the pleasing geometry / stipulating space not people / refusing to be buried / and uniquely disappointing." Marriage has a pleasing geometry (the symmetry of pairing) but it stipulates space, not people. The actuality of marriage refutes the concept. Man and Woman are hopelessly estranged, and each sees only self-concern in the other:

> he loves himself so much,
> he can permit himself
> no rival in that love.
> She loves herself so much,
> she cannot see herself enough—
> a statuette of ivory on ivory,
> the logical last touch
> to an expansive splendor
> earned as wages for work done:

Both are certain their condemnation of the other is justified; they are both therefore impoverished, for, as the poem tells us, "one is not rich but poor / when one can always seem so right." Scorning the other for selfishness only perpetuates selfishness. Marriage is hopeless:

> What can one do for them—
> these savages
> condemned to disaffect
> all those who are not visionaries
> alert to undertake the silly task
> of making people noble?

Surely she is talking about those who marry thinking they can change the other (all those savages taking on the silly task of making people noble)—those who are not visionaries. This is intriguing—does it mean that visionaries are the only ones who should wed? Or, and this is more likely, that everyone goes into marriage thinking he or she *is* a visionary, insofar as the idea of marriage is itself a vision, or illusion, or great duplicitous twinning of the apple and the snake. "Everything to do with love is mystery," La Fontaine says, "it is more than a day's work / to investigate this science."

"One sees that it is rare," Marianne Moore continues,

> that striking grasp of opposites
> opposed each to the other, not to unity,
> which in cycloid inclusiveness
> has dwarfed the demonstration
> of Columbus with the egg—

It is a rare visionary couple indeed who go into marriage opposed each to the other—opposed, not in the bellicose sense of the word, but the "contrapositional" one: to contrast or counterbalance by antithesis. To engage each other *as* other, and not suffer under the illusion of unity (which in its inclusive circularity has dwarfed even Columbus's discovery that the earth is round). That kind of opposition is an equality, a counterbalance, but a marriage of that sort is rare. Most often marriage is undertaken as if it were a truth and not a

posture; the "essence of the matter" remains, for Moore, in the struck pose of that smug Victorian Adam:

> 'Liberty and union
> now and forever';
>
> the Book on the writing-table;
> the hand in the breast-pocket."

STREAMERS

"Marriage" may be the best means of teaching ourselves how to read Sandra McPherson's "Streamers." We've grown accustomed now to Moore's kaleidoscope of quotations radiating out from an elusive center, her leap from image to flat declarative statement, her irony. McPherson proceeds in a similar manner. And like Moore (like Wordsworth) Sandra McPherson begins in the real descriptions of the real world; she shares with both poets an insistence on accuracy, for without an accurate apprehension of the natural world, moral vision is impossible. In "Streamers" (as in "Marriage") the moral center we confront is the failure of marriage. Moore traces that failure back to the first couple, Adam and Eve; McPherson takes as her starting point an ordinary woman (her divorced friend) and herself. Whereas Moore's poem follows bits of dialogue to emphasize the impossibility of communications between husband and wife, McPherson's poem dramatizes the sympathetic conversation between two now unmarried women. Moore's poem begins in the Garden of Eden and ends in the Victorian drawing room. McPherson's begins and ends on a seaside dock which dangles from its piling a medusa, a jellyfish "kicking / her warp of tentacles / slowly out across the current." In effect, "Streamers" begins where "Marriage" leaves off, with "ways out but no way in."

Moore's beautifully dangerous panthers, the image for domestic friction (which we must not call calamity, "the fight to be affectionate"), has become in McPherson the delicately beautiful *cyanea*, a jellyfish/medusa whose root is also the root for cyanide, whose tentacles are "as long as my friend's old bridal veil / (I wore a scarf) / perishing under woolens in a steamer trunk/on an attic voyage." The parenthetic aside is intriguing—a scarf is certainly less alarming and totemic than a bridal veil; it's humble, not expecting as much as full regalia expects. But the parenthesis insists on its importance even as it makes its disclaimer; don't we think of Marianne Moore's lavish wedding display (and those ludicrous dromedaries) and the bride's subsequent fall into disillusion? Perhaps McPherson is saying that she was less a visionary (in Moore's ironic sense of the word) than her filmily-veiled friend, but the result for both was divorce.

That "attic voyage" tersely sums up the entire marriage; landlocked, the veil packed away with its companion exotica:

> The rest of its ensemble imports
> from Spain: tiered flounces, bunched bodice,

and bolero, mostly
of a salmon-watermelon-shrimp
or peach-ginger pastel; lips
and gonads tucked into a skirt
scalloped into eight notched lappets

weighted with a crystalline rhopalium.
Such is the fashion.

This sounds a lot like Marianne Moore—the delight in the absolute right word (notched lappets and crystalline rhopalium), the heaping up of ever more precisely shaded adjectives (salmon-watermelon-shrimp or peach-ginger pastel), the abrupt halt to the waterfalling description (Such is the fashion). And like Moore, Sandra McPherson precipitates us into metaphor before we're quite aware we've left the actual. Those are real bridal flounces and bodice in the steamer trunk, but surely the lips and gonads are tucked into the cyanea's skirt, and suddenly we're in the ocean again, and the bride is a medusa.

Here we have a real departure, for in "Marriage" the man "has power / and sometimes one / is made to feel it." In "Streamers" the woman has power:

"Women have so seldom
been an attraction to me,"
said Sherlock Holmes in "Lion's Mane,"
"for my brain has always governed my heart,

[—that arch misogynist Sherlock Holmes sounds a bit like Marianne Moore's philosopher, or Virginia Woolf's Mr. Ramsey, the man who prides himself on his mental acuity (as if "unfathered by a woman"), who would be brought low by domesticity]:

"but I could not look upon
her perfect clear-cut face,
with all the soft freshness of downlands
in her delicate colouring

"without realizing
no young man would cross her path unscathed."

McPherson uses Arthur Conan Doyle in much the same way Moore uses Robert of Sorbonne or William Godwin and Ezra Pound, to portray the man's vision of the poisonous woman. Moore's Diana wears a spiked glove to prove her affection to the bone. McPherson's cyanea wears her poison in her spiked tentacles. But Moore's amalgam of Eve/Diana/Any Bride never moves beyond her capacity to harm and be harmed. McPherson's offers (albeit ironically) a kind of remedy for her sting:

Ah, friend,
not only must we scathe,
we must also know the remedies:

Ammonia, vinegar, or meat tenderizer,
papaya juice, gasoline, olive oil,
ocean water (never fresh).

Remove tentacles with a gloved hand,

apply flour, baking powder,
shaving soap.

Come to the sea with these.
Then scrape.

The spiked hand has become the gloved hand, but one administering caustics; the remedy is also an affliction. And the tone shifts from the neutral listing of a kind of Housewife's Almanac of Simples to the ominous imperative: "Come to the sea with these." (Pause.) "Then scrape." The bitterness of that action, scraping away the harm we (as wives) have inflicted in marriage, makes us inescapably culpable. Like Moore's Eve, we are responsible for the expulsion from Paradise. The cyanea poisons. "And yet her clear head / of flawless Orrefors. . . ." And we're reminded of Moore's first depiction of Eve, the beautiful woman in that "crystal-fine experiment" *before* she becomes opaque—through marriage—a "statuette of ivory on ivory." Like Orrefors crystal, clear headed, but wedded to those lethal streamers—the jellyfish is the image for marriage itself, dangerous, with a dangerous consequence: the poem plunges to this one line stanza:

Dilation, contraction.

Childbirth is certainly the most enormous result of marriage, and here for the first time "Streamers" put the pain of marriage (the man's pain, that is, the sting from the medusa's tentacles) into perspective. Nothing more is elaborated; nothing more is needed. The pain from those bridal streamers can't begin to compete with that simple two-word enormity. Dilation, contraction.

Then the triangle we expect—husband, wife, child—shifts. Suddenly the two women who begin the poem, the poet and her friend, are tied by telephone lines to the poet's husband. He is the fulcrum, an intimate of both women with the Adamic (and ironic) gift of naming:

Do you recall the day
of our equal depressions?
My husband telephoned back and forth,
listened to you then to me,
unable to synchronize our calls.

He described us to each other.

That last is a staggering presumption, and a betrayal on several levels. Like Moore's Adam, however, this husband can't be entirely written off: he remains the standard, the Other, against whom the speaker measures herself. What he says matters: "You and I [the two women] were in some depth together / miles apart, he said // and it helped." We can only speculate as to how it helped—because there was another woman at sea, in the same depth, feeling what the poet was feeling? Or the fact that the women were "miles apart"? But the poem draws the women together despite, or even because of, the now-absent husband. The poem casts him off in his manly pursuits: "he described us to each other. / Then he went fishing."

This is an exclusion as final as any we see in "Marriage," but this Adam isn't completely untouched. His fishing takes him through the Lion's Manes, another sea creature who, like the medusa, is "obnoxious, cursed— / one cannot touch them, tear them / off a line—"The connection to Sherlock Holmes's in "The Lion's Mane" is of course explicit—these beautiful creatures (women, cyanea, medusae) are dangerous. And we're also reminded of the archaeologist in "Marriage" who says "These mummies / must be handled carefully— / 'the crumbs from a lion's meal, / a couple of shins and the bit of an ear.'" The remains from a marriage are all that's left of the lion's meal. Marriage has mummified, or, in the medusa's terms, turned to stone the hapless couple, man and wife.

That's the mythology at any rate. But in "Streamers" the received wisdom is never the whole story. The bride/medusa is finally just a woman, toxic, perhaps, but also simply tired, an ordinary woman who watches over her children, who ends up, at the end of the poem, completely alone. And her ability to turn men to stone turns out to be only a male myth. Men are turned to stone by the *inaccuracy* of their own perceptions; they never really see her. They are frozen by their own lack of vision. This is a rather long quotation, but necessary, I think, to show Sandra McPherson's reversal of the myth:

> The woman in the Marine Science Center
>   welcomes
> these medusae every August warmth,
> holds out her arms to show
>
> how big she's witnessed them.
> But for now our arms and legs support
>
> not any frozenness

Lynne McMahon

SOURCE: "The Sexual Swamp: Female Erotics and the Masculine Art," in *The Southern Review,* Vol. 28, No. 2, April, 1992, pp. 333-52.

[*In the following essay, McMahon investigates the origins and implications of female sexuality and a female aesthetic in the poetry of Louise Glück, Marianne Moore, and Elizabeth Bishop.*]

For some time now feminist and Marxist and psychoanalytic critics have been exploring the language of patriarchy, trying to unearth a female aesthetic from phallogocentric digs. The lexicon is often funny ("phallocrat" is one of my favorites; another is "phallogocentric," Jacques Derrida's neologism linking phallus, logos, and center, all three of which deconstruction attempts to undo). More often the language is clunky (how many of us doze off at the first assault of Signifier and Signified, or grind our teeth at the torturous infinitive "to privilege"?), or simply and drily obscure. But whatever the failures of the language,

the idea behind it is not quite dismissible. The question is an intriguing one: *Is* there an aesthetic difference between women and men? And does that mean it is located in the sexual body? Is a marriage between the masculine art and the female body possible? Louise Glück and Marianne Moore appear to say No. Female sexuality is a paralysis, obliterating Art. Elizabeth Bishop finds something else.

Louise Glück's poems make the most explicit case for the uncrossable chasm between Eros and Art. Her landscape is the bombed-out world after sex. In *The Triumph of Achilles* passion does not unlock art; indeed, it strangles it. The dream of romance—long the province of the feminine—gives way to the "actual flesh" of love, which leads to silence and immobility: "What is a poet / without dreams? / I lie awake; I feel / actual flesh upon me, / meaning to silence me—" ("The Reproach"); "the man's mouth / sealing my mouth, the man's / paralyzing body" ("Mock Orange"); "Then I know what lies behind your silence: / scorn, hatred of me, of marriage. Still, / you want me to touch you; you cry out" ("Horse"). The body betrays the mind; the man suffocates the woman; and yet the woman in these poems falls again and again under the affliction of desire, the will paralyzed by sex.

The nine-part poem "Marathon" anatomizes desire and paralysis, not in progression—the movement from love to loss, say—but in stasis. The poem begins with "Last Letter"; abandonment and betrayal attendant from the inception:

> Without thinking, I knelt in the grass, like
>   someone meaning to pray.
> When I tried to stand again, I couldn't move,
>   my legs were utterly rigid. Does grief change you
>   like that?

The poet, betrayed and abandoned, is frozen in an effigy of prayer. Her sexual nature has led to this, a Medusa self-immobilized. Slowly she regains movement, the physical rigor released, but the psychic paralysis is complete:

> I got up finally; I walked down to the pond.
> I stood there, brushing the grass from my skirt,
>   watching myself,
> like a girl after her first lover
> turning slowly at the bathroom mirror, naked,
>   looking for a sign.
> But nakedness in women is always a pose.
> I was not transfigured. I would never be free.

The sexuality in this book loops like a Möbius strip around the twinned notions of death and freedom: the first a search for the father (the birth-right, the patronymic), the second a release from him; both of these in turn tied to the hunger for vision unobscured by physical desire. The erotic longing for the father finds its most acute expression in the sixth poem of "Marathon," titled "The Beginning." The poem presents itself as a dream addressed to the father, but the dream occurs outside time—before birth, but after sexual identity. The speaker takes on the sentient aspect of Wordsworth's infant-angels, waiting to be clothed in human flesh. But Glück's speaker knows she is female, knows she is doomed to be divided from the male. She comes, not trailing clouds of glory, but armed with pathetic knowledge:

> I had come to a strange city, without belongings:
> in the dream, it was your city, I was looking for
>   you.
> Then I was lost, on a dark street lined with fruit
>   stands.
>
> There was only one fruit: blood oranges.
> The markets made displays of them, beautiful
>   displays—
> how else could they compete? And each
>   arrangement had,
>   at its center,
> one fruit, cut open.
>
> Then I was on a boulevard, in brilliant sunlight.
> I was running; it was easy to run, since I had
>   nothing.
> In the distance, I could see your house; a woman
>   knelt
>   in the yard.
> There were roses everywhere; in waves, they
>   climbed
>   the high trellis.
>
> Then what began as love for you
> became a hunger for structure: I could hear
> the woman call to me in common kindness,
>   knowing
> I wouldn't ask for you anymore—
>
> So it was settled: I could have a childhood there.
> Which came to mean being always alone.

The poignance of women, blood oranges, lies in their defeated similarity: "the markets made displays of them, beautiful displays— / how else could they compete?" Then the terrible, and surgically revealed, heart: "And each arrangement had, at its center, / one fruit, cut open." This seems an intentional mixing of the body of the metaphor, for the heart of this fruit is genital and menstrual, centered not in the chest but in the womb.

These blood oranges carry a wealth, or burden, of Western poetic tradition as far back as Aristophanes. Anne Carson's essay in *Before Sexuality,* "Putting Her in Her Place: Woman, Dirt and Desire," traces the etymology of "ripeness" and female fruit from its Greek roots in drama and verse. In Greek society, she writes, a woman went directly from underripe (virginity) to overripe; there was no mid-point at all:

> [A] woman's first sexual experience catapults her into uncontrolled sexual activity and out of the category of desirable sex-object, for she is past her peak the moment the αvθs (flower) falls.

A comparable distortion can be seen in Greek usage of the word ὀπώρα. This word means "fruit-time," the time between the rising of Seirios and of Arktouros when the fruit ripens," and also the fruit itself. When used metaphorically of males, ὀπώρα signifies "the bloom of youth" or "ripe manhood," and does not exclude the pursuit of sexual fulfillment. But when used of females, ὀπώρα means virginity and is to be withheld from all erotic experimentation. . . . When not guarded, a woman's ὀπώρα becomes blackened (as an overripe fruit), undesirable and accursed. . . .

Within these usages is operating an identification of female sexuality with voracious promiscuity and of virginity with the best moment of female life. Implicit here is a denial that free sexual activity and "blooming" are compatible for a woman. There is no such thing as sexually vigorous ripe womanhood in the Greek view. At her peak a woman is sexually untried. . . . As soon as she lets her αvθs (flower) fall, the female is translated to the slippery slope of overripeness: "A woman's prime is an inch of time!" wails Lysistrata.

In Louise Glück's poem, there's not even an inch of time. Each display has one fruit, already cut open. In ancient Greek verse, Carson says, "a woman who is being compared to an apple on a tree or a flower in a field can be said to wither the moment she is 'plucked.' Plucking is defloration." But here we haven't even the joy or erotic drama of plucking; "cut open" insists, in fact, on the violence of sexuality. "Plucking" summons the rhyme, of course, but beyond that carries the notion of human *touch.* "One fruit, cut open" has been removed from the realm of the human altogether. Some agency has mounded the display, some agency has sliced the center fruit. This "dark street lined with fruit stands" stretches all the way back to the earliest examination of sexual difference, and then forward to the poet's own individual imagining. The "I" descends to a reality already and forever inscribed by that cut-open fruit. That's the pathos and power of these poems: that whatever psychic, societal, legal inroads feminism has made into the depiction of female sexuality, this "I" remains confined in the reality of the body. The ancient world is the future world.

And this world belongs to the father; "in the dream, it was your city, I was looking for you." But erotic longing gives way to civilized forms; the woman kneeling in the yard, gardening, will become the mother: "I could hear / the woman call to me in common kindness, knowing / I wouldn't ask for you anymore—" The mother can call in "common kindness" because she knows the child cannot seriously compete for the father's sexual attention. "So it was settled: I could have a childhood there." Those are the prescribed conditions, and the daughter accepts them, indeed, she *desires* them:

> Then what began as love for you
> became a hunger for structure:

"A hunger for structure" may be the key element in all of Louise Glück's poems, for the terror of erotic love lies in its *lack* of structure, its boundarylessness. But the safety of civilized restraints proves to be illusory. The succeeding poem, "First Goodbye" (we're to think back to the first poem in the sequence, "Last Letter") presents the display of blood oranges in a new configuration, violent in its overdetermination. The lover, appropriately, has taken the place of the father; the proscriptions are in place; the foundations of civilization are intact. But beneath the order lies self-destruction. The poem begins in betrayal:

> You can join the others now,
> body that wouldn't let my body rest,
> go back to the world, to avenues, the ordered
> depths of the parks, like great terminals
> that never darken: a stranger's waiting for you
> in a hundred rooms. Go back to them,
> to increment and limitation: near the centered
>   rose,
> you watch her peel an orange
> so the dyed rind falls in petals on her plate. This
> is mastery, whose active
> mode is dissection: the enforced light
> shines on the blade.

Go back to the world, back to the displays of oranges, back to the marketplace of women to choose a new one, a new hundred of them, what you'll find is . . . increment and limitation. Odd and unpoetic, the language of measurement, like the language of society, appears safe. But near the center of the display ("near the centered rose"—Dante's celestial flower reduced to this fruit-stand arrangement) a woman is dissecting herself. "This / is mastery, whose active / mode is dissection:" How are we to read this? As self-mutilation? As an erotic masochism specifically female? And yet "mastery" remains ironically masculine and dominant, or, in terms of the Medusa legend, Athenian. The mind's will over the body's desire. Athena, sprung from the dry head of Zeus, identifies with the will and intellect of the father; she cannot do otherwise. But Athena knows what it is to be afflicted with desire; the head of Medusa blazes from her shield, both protecting and violating her sexual integrity. She wars with her passionate double. In "First Goodbye" the Athenian side of "I" speaks, but only because her other sexual self has suffered betrayal. She has managed to climb back into her head, from which prospect (and vast remove) she can see her former lover and all his subsequent women:

> And the women lying there—who wouldn't pity
>   them,
> the way they turn to you, the way
> they struggle to be visible. They make
> a place for you in bed, a white excavation.
> Then the sacrament: your bodies pieced together,
> churning, churning, till the heat leaves them
>   entirely—

This is indeed a clinical remove, whose active mode is the dissection of analysis. And this analytical vista opens out into Athena's revenge, for she can see into the future:

> Sooner or later
> you'll begin to dream of me. I don't envy you
> those dreams. I can imagine how my face looks,
> burning like that, afflicted with desire—lowered
> face of your invention—how the mouth betrays
> the isolated greed of the lover
> as it magnifies and then destroys:
> I don't envy you that visitation.

To possess again what one has lost—that's the impossibility of Eros. And it's made doubly impossible by the realization that there never *was* that particular reality. The lover invented the beloved:

> Sooner or later you will call my name,
> cry of loss, mistaken
> cry of recognition, of arrested need
> for someone who exists in memory; no voice
> carries to that kingdom.

What a satisfying revenge: no voice carries to that kingdom. And yet the undertone is unmistakable—this is the kingdom of the dead. The speaker dissects herself even as she coldly dissects the lover's future. Everyone loses.

To dissect one's self means to control one's destiny. Some medical experts say that, like anorexia, this kind of destructive control over the body is a sexual perversion. In societal terms, this "mastery"—ironic and masculine—signals the final female subjugation. In mythic terms, it signals the shifting dominances of female erotics, the duality personified in Athena and Medusa. In Glück's poetic, the mastery of self-dissection means poetry. Only by conquering the body—the sexuality that blurs distinctions, making poetry impossible—can the mind be free. The body glories in union, in coupling; the mind requires singularity. The body does not write poetry but effaces vision, leaving nothing to describe. "Song of Invisible Boundaries," the penultimate poem in "Marathon," clarifies the derailment effected by Eros:

> Last night I dreamed we were in Venice;
> today, we are in Venice. Now, lying here,
> I think there are no boundaries to my dreams,
> nothing we won't share.
> So there is nothing to describe. We're
>   interchangeable
> with anyone, in joy
> changed to a mute couple.
>
> Then why did we worship clarity,
> to speak, in the end, only each other's names,
> to speak, as now, not even whole words,
> only vowels?

The reduction of speech to mere vowels, the O's of sexual excitement, remind us of the earlier poems of muteness and suffocation, the "man's paralyzing body," the "man's mouth sealing my mouth"; the physical power of the man "meaning to silence me." Yet here the muteness is a "joy," which is why passion is so subversive. The speaker colludes with her own undoing:

Finally, this is what we craved,
this lying in the bright light without
    distinctions—
we who would leave behind
exact records.

Exactitude, of course, is impossible without distinctions. The bright light obliterates all boundaries, shapes, contours; it obviates the need or desire to "see." It frees the speaker from the hard, divisive work of poetry. In this aesthetic, the act of poetry belongs to the distinct and bounded world of the masculine, of cerebral Athena. The eros of the female, described as wet and unbounded in some poems, as blurred and lost in others ("The bed was like a raft," the poem "Summer" concludes, "I felt us drifting / far from our natures, toward a place where we'd discover nothing"), obscures vision. Glück's "hunger for structure"—which for her makes poetry possible—inclines toward the classical view. Anne Carson summarizes the Platonic model:

[W]e see that woman is to be differentiated from man, in the ancient view, not only as wet from dry but as content from form, as the unbounded from the bounded, as polluted from pure. . . .

The image of woman as a formless content is one that is expressed explicitly in the philosophers. Plato compares the matter of creation to a mother, in his *Timaios,* for it is a "receptacle," "reservoir," "admission," which is "shapeless," "viewless," "all-receiving" and which "takes its form and activation from whatever shapes enter it." Aristotle accords to the male in the act of procreation the role of active agent, contributing "motion" and "formation" while the female provides the "raw material," as when a bed (the child) is made by a carpenter (the father) out of wood (the mother). Man determines the form, woman contributes the matter. Aristotle expresses a similar view in his *Physics,* and we might note that the Pythagorean table of oppositions sets πέρας ("boundary" or "limit") and αρρεν ("masculine") against απειρον ("the unbounded") and θῆλν ("feminine").

To be an artist, then, means to adopt the masculine imposition of boundary—how else can one survive the extinction of passion? But to take on the masculine notion of form does not mean the banishment of the female eros; nor does it mean an entirely successful self-mastery. In the dissection image of "First Goodbye" we're given the cryptic corollary: "the enforced light / shines on the blade." Again Glück points to an extra-human agency that sets the wheels of destruction circling. Who or what enforces the light? The male dominance we're born into, instituted, as the earliest records attest, from the first structures of civilization? God? Or, in the intimate terms of "The Beginning," is it simply and irrevocably the father? Whatever forces conspire to focus the light on the blade, the *use* of that blade becomes the poem.

Divided from the father, using the tools of the father, succumbing to the father (or the lover that is his proxy)—all this seems to make a case for masculine power that cannot be equaled, or even approached, by the feminine. Analysis appears to win over passion. And yet the last, and most important, poem in "Marathon" (called "Marathon") eerily sabotages what we think we have been thinking through these nine stages. Here's the entire poem:

I was not meant to hear
the two of them talking.
But I could feel the light of the torch
stop trembling, as though it had been
set on a table. I was not to hear
the one say to the other
how best to arouse me,
with what words, what gestures,
nor to hear the description of my body,
how it responded, what
it would not do. My back was turned.
I studied the voices, soon distinguishing
the first, which was deeper, closer,
from that of the replacement.
For all I know, this happens
every night: somebody waking me, then
the first teaching the second.
What happens afterward
occurs far from the world, at a depth
where only the dream matters
and the bond with any one soul
is meaningless; you throw it away.

Beyond the obvious (woman as sex-toy, plaything to be shared between men), lies the poet's astounding decision to remain still and study the voices, to analyze, in effect, her own erotic. And here the significance of the word "marathon" takes on greater dimension. In Greek Olympiads, of course, the marathon runners were men, testing their strength, endurance, prowess, all based on their own knowledge of their own bodies—how they responded, what they would and would not do. They competed against other runners, but they raced against themselves. Louise Glück shifts the grounds of the metaphor. Here the sexual engine is female; the males must run in relay, as they haven't the stamina or endurance to perform singly. The body of the woman (in her sleeping state, the normal one when she is "not supposed to hear" the men discussing her) is presented simply as object, a baton passed between teammates as they run. And therefore we expect the indictment. Socially, politically, psychically, poetically this condition of "object" is unacceptable. Acquiescence is unthinkable. And yet the speaker in the poem does not move: "For all I know, this happens / every night: somebody waking me, then / the first teaching the second." Could it be that we're misreading this phallic relay? That in fact the *men* are objects, mere erotic instruments? The poet doesn't say. "What happens afterward / occurs far from the world," far from our notions of the politically correct, far, even, from the speaker's Athenian ability to analyze and dissect her own sexuality. The world of the father, with its civilizing restraints, its *boundaries,* its specific attachments, recedes; passion takes the "I" to a depth "where only the dream matters / and the bond with any one soul / is meaningless; you throw it away." That's a terrifying conclusion. The anchor of fidelity, marriage, normal sexual response—all lost. The exactitude necessary for art—gone. "The bond with any one soul is meaningless; you throw it away." The nihilism of Eros means social abdication—the death of the Father—but it also means the dissolution of self and thus the death of art. In a way, this marathon races between the poet's two selves, where the line distinguishing male and female, will and genitals, art and passion, is crossed and recrossed, whose only finish is death. "It will run its course," Glück says in "The Encounter,"

> the course of fire,
> setting a cold coin on the forehead, between the
>   eyes.
> You lay beside me; your hand moved over my
>   face
> as though you had felt it also—
> you must have known, then, how I wanted you.
> We will always know that, you and I.
> The proof will be my body.

Although Marianne Moore's "In The Days of Prismatic Color" doesn't present itself as physical (that is, specifically sexual) or in the first person, the poem does seem to take place in the same metaphorical arena as Glück's "Marathon," exploring the blurring and falsifying effects of sex. "In The Days of Prismatic Color" begins:

> not in the days of Adam and Eve, but when Adam
>   was alone; when there was no smoke and color
>   was
> fine, not with the refinement
>   of early civilization art, but because
> of its originality; with nothing to modify it but
>   the
>
> mist that went up, obliqueness was a variation
>   of the perpendicular, plain to see and
> to account for: it is no
>   longer that; . . .

A lot happens in this opening, serious and witty at once. Immediately we're placed in the garden before Eve, "when there was no smoke." Surely we're to think of fire, of Eve, of that sexual incandescence in "Marriage" which Moore calls a fire "as high as deep / as bright as broad / as long as life itself"—passion, in short, and the subsequent expulsion from Paradise and entry into human history. Eve is the complication of smoke which obscures color. When Adam was alone, Moore says, color was fine because it was original, "with nothing to modify it but the // mist that went up." This seems to be a contradiction, for doesn't mist operate like smoke, blurring and distorting? But the poem says that the obliqueness caused by mist is "a variation / of the perpendicular, plain to see and / to account for." This puts Eve in yet another culpable light, for her smoke must not be plain to see or easy to account for; worse, it must not be merely a "variation of the perpendicular." And perhaps Moore is making a sly sexual joke here; the perpendicular must be Adam, vertical, phallic, upright;

and Eve's obliqueness now geometric, "diverging from a given straight line," Webster's has it, "devious or underhand, perverse." The world, before Eve came to distort it, was fine, but "it is no / longer that,"

> nor did the blue-red-yellow band
>   of incandescence that was color keep its stripe: it
>   also
>   is one of
>
> those things into which much that is peculiar can
>   be
>   read; complexity is not a crime, but carry
>   it to the point of murkiness
>   and nothing is plain.

Peculiar, complex, murky—those are the adjectives for reality now, though at this point in the poem Moore carefully adds that they're not necessarily criminal. Befuddling, perhaps. But the ramifications for art are enormous. What happens when the "blue-red-yellow band / of incandescence" loses its stripe? The obliteration of boundaries into the murkiness we call Eve obscures vision. This is what Louise Glück laments, the sexual "lying in the bright light without distinction" that makes "exact records" impossible. The masculine imposition of boundaries keeps the world clear. The world of Adam-without-Eve is pure. There exists only his perception, with "nothing to modify it." This, then, we might say, is Truth: Adam alone, perpendicular, stripes intact. As in Louise Glück's poem, only the mind, solitary and masculine, can achieve vision. Eve, that erotic swamp, undoes distinctions, and alloys everything.

And here the miasma of sexual murkiness deepens into something much more threatening; civilization based on a distortion of the perpendicular truth. "[C]omplexity is not a crime," the poem admits,

> but carry
> it to the point of murkiness
> and nothing is plain. Complexity,
> moreover, that has been committed to darkness,
>   instead of
> granting itself to be the pestilence that it is,
>   moves all a-
>   bout as if to bewilder us with the dismal
> fallacy that insistence
>   is the measure of achievement and that all
> truth must be dark.

Eve may have toppled Truth, but Adam is now in charge of policing the ruins. Together, Adam and Eve become civilization, the complexity committed to darkness, a pestilence bewildering us with the dismal fallacy "that insistence / is the measure of achievement and that all / truth must be dark." Insistence and achievement, force and progress, the phallic straight line has now become fallacious, no longer pure.

And this pestilence finds its most insidious shelter in Art, that sanctuary and sublime affirmation of the soul, to diminish it to mere "sophistication." Sophistication is anathema to Moore, particularly in art; that much looks clear. But Moore's use of the *body* to locate these abstractions takes the reader aback. Principally throat, sophistication is as it always has been—at the antipodes from the initial great truths. It's very tempting indeed to try a physical reading. What would be the "antipodes" of "throat"? A sexual reading would say genitals; Freud, of course, specifically links throat and genital sexual response. And in terms of the metaphor, one could make a case that the "initial great truths" point to origin, sexual origin, our ineluctable biology. And language/voice/throat, therefore, the masking or distortion of that origin. So civilization becomes that "dark pestilence," a phallocentric universe moving far from Origin, from Truth, to proclaim that "insistence / is the measure of achievement and all / truth must be dark." This Freudian reading seems underscored by Moore's next line (a quote from the Trojan War's Nestor, the annotations unhelpfully explain), "Part of it was crawling, part of it / was about to crawl, the rest / was torpid in its lair." That certainly has a Darwinian, Freudian swampiness about it, as does the next description: "In the short-legged, fit / ful advance, the gurgling and all the minutiae." We seem almost to be dragging ourselves up from the sea, evolving on the beach, sexually, culturally, poetically. These Freudian antipodes of throat and genitals look possible.

But Marianne Moore is much more interested in etymology than sexuality (which, in any case, she would find totally inappropriate in the public realm of the page. She did, after all, chastise Elizabeth Bishop for using the impolite "water closet" in a poem). And when we read "antipodes" we're meant to see the "podes" in it, and know she is referring to feet. "In the short-legged, fit / ful advance, the gurgling and all the minutiae—we have the classic / multitude of feet." We are still in the field of Darwin, but Freud has vanished altogether. The "classic multitude of feet," up the evolutionary ladder from the short-legged fitful advance, the gurgling and minutiae, is both a summary of civilization (contemporary and ancient) and a statement of poetics. "The classical multitude of feet" is the old way of measuring poetic achievement; and insofar as any poetic form is *a priori* artificial, it is useless in the journey toward Truth. The poem's vehement conclusion speaks of all form (and therefore all art):

> Truth is no Apollo
> Belvedere, no formal thing. The wave may go
>   over it if it
>   likes.
> Know that it will be there when it says,
> "I shall be there when the wave has gone by."

Truth cannot be contained in a formal thing, not a poem (with its classic multitude of feet), not even the Apollo Belvedere. Truth is no thing at all; the wave can go over it, and it will be there when the wave has gone. Our entire notion of what Art unlocks for us has been cast into doubt. Color, the essential requisite for Art, was true only when Adam was alone. The sole vision, the solitary perpendicular, the Adam before Eve, was Origin. And Origin was Truth. It exists still; it will be there when the wave has gone over it; but no poem or sculpture will yield it.

So where does that leave the artist? For Louise Glück, "exact records," the fossils of Origin, are an approachable reality, and the closest we can get to Truth; but the approach is possible only if the artist gives up the complexity of passion. Only if the body (Eve) retreats can the mind (Adam) find again the perpendicular ascent that is vision. A marriage of Eros and Art, of Sexuality and Truth, is impossible. For Marianne Moore, the recounting of the losses accruing under the combined destructiveness of Eve-with-Adam is perhaps all that poetry can accomplish. Truth may be felt (and in Moore's Christian faith that is a given) but it cannot be held. "No formal thing" translates into no thing, no form, no poem at all. For such poets as these, with their strict geometries, their angular investigations of the boundaries which allow them to work, "truth" must be terrifyingly liquid and shapeless. Like the ocean, perhaps, which for Moore is drowning. Or like female wetness, Glück's drowning. Though Moore steadfastly insists that Truth will be there when the wave has gone by, though Glück struggles up from sexual wetness into the dry region of the intellect, both are pulled again and again into the vastness. It's not the wave's receding we're left with at the end of the poem. It's anticipation of the wave's return.

Elizabeth Bishop is doing something entirely different with the sexual landscape; she seems somehow to have gone all the way back into the Terror of Origin and emerged a celebrant. Clearly the sexual surge remains, the Darwinian stew remains, but instead of paralyzing the voice, this Origin retrieves it. Far from being locked into the dichotomized patriarchal world, her poems take female sexuality out of the heterosexual notion of Adam and Eve altogether. Look, for example, at two of her tropical poems, "Little Exercise" and "Florida."

Like Marianne Moore's glacier (inching forward "with the concentric crushing rigor of the python"), this slow-moving, powerful, primitive state (a pun both on "condition" and body of government) moves down into the mangrove swamps, the wild keys, the man asleep in the boat, into the chiaroscuro of lightning-lit cypress. We move far away from innocence (though this is the state with the "prettiest" name), far from flowers (that sentimental feminine image), into the five calls of the alligator in the throat of the Indian princess. The power here is female, autoerotic (in Irigaray's sense of the word), a voluptuary creating out of the miasma of the Everglades the voice of the princess.

The conventionally pretty "feminine" gives way at once to the darker "female":

> The state with the prettiest name,

the state that floats in brackish water,
held together by mangrove roots
that bear while living oysters in clusters,
and when dead strew white swamps with
    skeletons,
dotted as if bombarded, with green hummocks
like ancient cannon-balls sprouting grass.

Bishop gives us the real account; those are actual mangrove roots in the actual swamp. But the real resonates with the old voodoo and summons that Eurasian plant, mandrake, whose branched root (thought to resemble the human body) looks remarkably like the mangrove. It's this exotic root, rising on stilts from the water, that moors the feminine state, keeps it from floating away. And it bears oysters—that ancient aphrodisiac—and skeletons (Eros in the arms of Thanatos again and again). But this is not only Halloween witchery; there's Bishop's sly humor as well, those comical "green hummocks / like ancient cannon-balls sprouting grass." Are we to think of Whitman's grass perhaps? Bishop nudging his lyrical "long hair of the dead" into cartoon, perhaps even into sexual, masculine pun? In any case, this is funny, as is the description of birds:

The state full of long S-shaped birds, blue and
    white,
hysterical birds who rush up the scale
every time in a tantrum.
Tanagers embarrassed by their flashiness,
and pelicans whose delight it is to clown; . . .

This primeval Origin is not predicated on sexual divisiveness, the donnée in Glück and Moore, but on that state *anterior* to intercourse, the fecund surge of self-generating pleasure (to use Freud's language) which isn't yet "conscious" or dependent on the physical presence of the Other. Origin may be cast in the metaphor (though, of course, always and insistently real—the actual before the figurative) of an inchoate, lightning-lit tropical storm, but the *effect* of that Origin is not terror. "Think of someone sleeping in the bottom of a row-boat," "Little Exercise" instructs us, "tied to a mangrove root or the pile of a bridge; / think of him as uninjured, barely disturbed." The psychic maelstrom takes place far below consciousness, barely disturbing the man asleep in the boat. He's as anchored to the piling or mangrove root as Florida is—safely afloat, uninjured. The "conscious" presence hardly registers at all. In "Florida" it is the indigenous, primitive, "original" life or death that gives the state its peculiar power: "Enormous turtles, helpless and mild, / die and leave their barnacled shells on the beaches, / and their large white skulls with round eye-sockets / twice the size of a man's." Man is here only to provide scale (in this case, diminishment) for the relics of a far older species.

This seems a kind of reverse psychological Darwinism—if Florida is a state of consciousness, or, rather, subconsciousness, then the enormous eye sockets of these skulls might be the vestiges of a capacity to "see." And the "barnacled shells on the beaches" recall us to

Marianne Moore's very Freudian sea in "A Grave," where "the tortoise-shell scourges about the feet of cliffs"—the motion only apparently lifelike, in that ocean "in which / dropped things are bound to sink— / in which if they turn and twist, it is neither with volition nor consciousness." In Moore's poem the sea is rapacious, encompassing ("you cannot stand in the middle of this"), frightening, death; the tortoise-shell a chilling prescience of motion without volition. The sea is at once Origin and Future, both annihilating. But Bishop's brackish, inland salt water isn't terrible at all, despite the skulls and skeletons and "thirty or more buzzards drifting down, down, down, / over something they have spotted in the swamp, / in circles like stirred-up flakes of sediment / sinking through water." In fact, Florida is rather wonderful in its awfulness ("awful but cheerful" as Bishop says in "The Bight"). This is physical Florida, political Florida, careless and corrupt, but it is also metaphorical, leading us back into the psychic terrain that ends the poem:

After dark, the pools seem to have slipped away.
The alligator, who has five distinct calls:
friendliness, love, mating, war, and a warning—
whimpers and speaks in the throat
of the Indian princess.

And here, I think, we have left both awful and cheerful behind. "After dark, the pools seem to have slipped away." Those little circles reflecting the moon, locating us, allowed us a kind of superiority (the moonlight revealed Florida to be the poorest postcard of itself; two-dimensional, harmless), but now those pools have slipped away. It's dark. And surely the alligator in the dark is fearsome.

But even more disconcerting is the list of the alligator's calls: friendliness, love, mating, war, and a warning. The first four are dramatic and straightforward enough, lethal though the last two may be; it's that "warning" that makes the skin creep. Our reptilian brain is alerted: what or who is being warned? where does the danger lie? Warning is protective, in a way, and territorial; it keeps boundaries intact. Moreover this alligator "whimpers and speaks in the throat / of the Indian princess." Suddenly the nightcreature, the swampterror, has become the voice of the female presence in this poem. Florida has been the ground for Eros and Thanatos all along, but always at a remove. The reader has been a tourist, looking at the hysterical birds, the collection of shells, the barnacled turtles and skulls dotting the ragged calico hem of the state, but detached from them; asleep, like the man in the boat, barely disturbed by the riot of the primitive. And perhaps that is where the warning lies; that the man not wake up? Not disturb the erotic swamp with its mists and deaths and mosquitoes and birds; its oysters and skeletons caught in the Vs of those stiltlike mangrove roots? Perhaps the abundant sexual life here—careless and corrupt—is possible only because it stays below the surface of the conscious. The Indian princess is the queen of this swamp—the alligator whimpers and speaks in *her* throat—and her voices,

Love and Death, drive toward the warning. This underworld is autoerotic, rich because it is self-contained—"polymorphous perverse," Freud would say—and sufficient in itself.

But the "polymorphous perverse" of our first state gives way to "normal" adult sexuality, according to Freud. And we are dependent on the Other. Luce Irigaray insists, however, that that "normalcy" is in fact a phallic paralysis, an hysteria. In her essay "Plato's *Hystera*" she traces the metaphor of the cave (the womb) and re-imagines the inhabitants:

> So men have lived in this cave since childhood. Since time began. . . . Chained by the neck and thighs, they are fixed with their heads and genitals facing *front, opposite*—which in Socrates' tale is the direction toward the back of the cave.

This is certainly a startling take—men made immobile by female sexuality *since time began*. And since they are chained facing the back of the cave, they are incapable of turning toward origin; they cannot really see:

> The only thing they can still do is to look at whatever presents itself before their eyes. Paralyzed, unable to *turn round or return* toward the origin, toward the *hystera protera* they are condemned to look ahead. . . . Heads forward, eyes front, genitals aligned, fixed in a straight direction and always straining forward, in a straight line. A phallic direction, a phallic line, a phallic time, backs turned on origin.

But, one may ask, what is wrong with straining forward in a straight line? Isn't that how we usually portray progress? Isn't the straight line (or the vertical axis, the phallic direction) the most expedient and effective means of achieving whatever it is that needs achieving? For Irigaray, that straight line is an illusion: "Chains, lines, perspectives oriented straight ahead—all maintain the illusion of constant motion in one direction. Forward. The cave cannot be explored in the round, walked around, measured in the round. Which means that the men all stay in the same spot." They are paralyzed by the phallic line; they cannot explore the cave. Progress is only a dark illusion.

But Irigaray, for all her intriguing metaphor-making, is at times as dogmatic and leaden as the prisoners she addresses. Contrast Irigaray's pages-long critique of male dominion with Marianne Moore's lines on the same theme: "the dismal / fallacy that insistence / is the measure of achievement and that all / truth must be dark." Insistence and achievement, the masculine straight line. And though Moore would never use the word "phallic," perhaps "fallacy" implies the rhyme. In any case, many of Moore's poems worry the vertical axis, the myth of progress achieved by linearity. One could make a case that the *form* of Moore's poems (rarely a straight fall) as well as her leaps of image are ways of circumventing what Irigaray calls the masculine mode, of transcending it.

The transcendental leap (for both Marianne Moore and Elizabeth Bishop) achieves finally what feminist theory cannot—a new place to live. And both "Florida" and "Little Exercise" examine our sexual/psychic/metaphoric landscape with humor, something, as Elizabeth Bishop remarks, feminist critics seem sadly to lack. "Florida" celebrates in devious and lively (and implicit) ways what Irigaray's "This Sex Which Is Not One" explicitly demands: that there be an erotic state anterior to the proscriptive, male-dominated, "normal" one. For Bishop, it is not even a question. That state is always already there; Origin afloat in brackish water, moored by mangrove roots, and presided over by the powerful Indian princess who keeps her domain inviolate.

This wet world calls us back, of course, to the oldest thinking on the differences between women and men, particularly in the area of boundaries. Bishop's Indian princess, with her alligator warning, rules an inland brackish sea, fertile with life and death. Her kingdom is mysterious and dangerous and, above all, wet. Anne Carson's studies of Homer and Aristotle trace man's fear of female wetness from the earliest documents. "The Greek poets," she writes,

> find sexuality in women a fearsome thing; it threatens the very essence of a man's manliness. The foundations of the threat appear to be two.
>
> Congenitally more susceptible to the inducements of appetite than men, women do not experience either of the constraints which check the male. Women feel no physical need to control desire, since, by virtue of innate wetness, female capacity is virtually inexhaustible. In addition, the female nature lacks the *sophrosyne* ("soundness of mind" or "sobriety and self-control") by which men subject desires to rational mastery from within. A woman cannot control herself, so her *sophrosyne* must consist in submitting herself to the control of others. . . . [As Aristotle tells us] once initiated, women revel in sex and do not wish to stop. Having no *sophrosyne* they do not *think* to stop.

Thus the institution of marriage, which provides woman the self-control and physical boundaries she can not overstep. Carson goes on to point out that even Freud leans, at least in part, to the classical view. In a letter to Eduard Silberstein, Freud writes: "A thinking man is his own legislator and confessor, and obtains his own absolution, but the woman, let alone the girl, does not have the measure of ethics in herself. She can only act if she keeps within the limits of morality, following what society has established as fitting. She is never forgiven if she has revolted against morality, possibly rightly so." Her boundaries must be imposed from the outside, as her innate wetness debars any internal form.

Bishop's Indian princess, however, confounds the imposition of boundaries. The footing in her swamp is too uncertain for any outsider to risk. And her alliance with the alligator is scary. But it is primarily her wetness that precludes a civilizing restraint. Her domain is the swamp, after all, not quite sea, not quite land, a viscous in-between suggestive of sexual wetness. Though of course there are some who would enter this preserve willingly, passionately, despite the alligator's warning, more might feel like Sartre, in his essay on stickiness, when he tells us,

> Viscosity repels in its own right, as a primary experience. . . . The viscous is a state halfway between solid and liquid. It is unstable, but it does not flow. It is soft, yielding and compressible. . . . Its stickiness is a trap, it clings like a leech; it attacks the boundary between myself and it. Long columns falling off my fingers suggest my own substance flowing into the pool of stickiness. . . . I remain a solid, but to touch stickiness is to risk diluting myself into viscosity. Stickiness is clinging, like a too-possessive dog or mistress.

To be lost in a woman's sexuality is to be truly lost. This swamp of oysters and skeletons does not invite the faint hearted. Elizabeth Bishop's Florida, the feminine state with the prettiest name, is finally not for tourists. And the poem moves far beyond the phallocratic or phallocentric, the gynocratic or gynocentric, far beyond the theories content to doze in such categories.

FICTION

Wendell V. Harris

SOURCE: "Molly's 'Yes': The Transvaluation of Sex in Modern Fiction," in *Texas Studies in Literature and Language,* Vol. X, No. 1, Spring, 1968, pp. 107-18.

[*In the following essay, Harris discusses the rising importance of sexuality in late nineteenth- and early twentieth-century fiction.*]

" . . . and first I put my arms around him yes and drew him down to me so he could feel my breasts all perfume yes and his heart was going like mad and yes I said yes I will say Yes."[1] Any devoted reader of the twentieth-century novel will immediately identify that passage as the closing words of Joyce's *Ulysses,* and any who have followed the critics' discussion of Joyce know that the passage constitutes a rather engaging crux. One position is represented by Stuart Gilbert's triumphant assertion that "it is significant for those who see in Joyce's philosophy nothing beyond a blank pessimism, an evangel of denial, that *Ulysses* ends on a triple paean of affirmation."[2] D. S. Savage, on the other hand, ridicules such an interpretation, refusing to "sentimentalize the concupiscent meanderings of the blowsy trollop of Eccles Street."[3]

The question once raised suggests a number of avenues of reflection on contemporary criticism and literature, not the least of which is the validity of judging the degree of pessimism or optimism in a novel of some seven hundred pages by the last seven words. However, the most interesting reflection is that, after all, the seemingly divergent interpretations of Gilbert and Savage not only complement each other but sum up a theme implicit or explicit in the mainstream of the twentieth-century English novel. Both views are correct; while literally saying yes simply to fornication, Molly is metaphorically saying yes to life, affirming the possibility of some sort of fulfillment by means of the one affirmation not seriously challenged in the twentieth century.

It has been one of the diversions of critics of both literature and morals to attempt to account for the emphasis on the delights of the sexual relationship in this century's literature. What has not been clearly enough noticed, especially by those who decry the importance of sex in modern literature as a sign of a reign of lubricity or who praise it as a triumph over prudery, is the degree to which the decline of almost all other values shifted greater and greater importance to the sexual experience, leaving it not one among possible values, but the only unquestioned value, the only unquestioned criterion for judging success and failure, or even happiness and unhappiness. The suspicion under which almost all of the old standards have fallen requires no documentation; the twentieth century's almost universal skepticism has been examined in learned sociological studies, made a central theme of contemporary literature, and been driven home to some of us daily by the responses of the undergradutes who appear in our classes. What this essay proposes to trace through some of the key fictional works in which the process appears in its most recognizable form is an evolution from the insistence that sexual satisfaction is important for happiness to the use of the successful sexual act as a symbol of fulfillment, and thence to the confusion of this symbolic representation with complete fulfillment of the human personality.

The symbolization of human felicity by sexual fulfillment can be found in the literature of all ages. However, at the close of the nineteenth century erotic symbolism begins to become more explicit and pervasive than it had been for at least a hundred years. A convenient starting point for tracing the process is the 1890's, by which time English writers were actively and self-consciously contending with the restrictions which had imposed themselves on the treatment of the sexual relationship in the nineteenth century. This desire to insist upon the importance of sexual satisfaction was made all the stronger, somewhat paradoxically, by the success of Victorian literature in depicting the possibility of achieving a full and satisfying life without much concerning oneself with the sexual drive. Perhaps the clearest example is Tennyson's Ulysses, who, while recalling with satisfaction that he had "drunk delight of battle with my peers, / Far on the ringing plains of windy Troy," coyly omits mention of the delights of Circe or Calypso. Obvious examples from fiction are Dickens' happy benefactors of humanity (the Cheeryble brothers, John Jarndyce,

Joe Gargery), or Trollope's men who have found success in their vocation (Archbishop Grantly, Plantaganet Palliser). Of course part of the certificate of success for the younger men and women approvingly portrayed by poets and novelists was marriage to a desirable mate (in the most unexceptionable sense of the word "desirable"), as in the cases of Esther and Woodcourt in *Bleak House* or of Arabin and Lucy Bold in *Barchester Towers,* but no one, either author or reader, ever inquired whether the young lovers would prove sexually compatible after marriage. Indeed, it would seem not only impertinent but depressing to analyze the sexual capabilities of an Esther Summerson.

That *Esther Waters* was regarded as a shocking book, that the reception of *Tess* and *Jude* was so hostile that Hardy abjured fiction henceforth, and that Grant Allen was regarded as beyond redemption after the mild propaganda of *The Woman Who Did* are well-worn bromides in English literary history. But it is with something of a shock that one finds as late as 1897 an educated man of letters, Laurence Oliphant, arguing in the preface to *Victorian Novelists* that Fielding, Smollet, and Sterne were clearly too lubricious for the fortunately more refined taste of the nineteenth century,[4] or reads James Ashcroft Noble's argument in 1895 that the sexual passion is not half of life, as Henry James had suggested, not even a tenth part of it, and is therefore properly excluded from fiction (and presumably other literature) as being of insufficient importance to occupy the writer.[5] Though many writers of the nineties asserted the importance, often indeed the predominance, of sexual satisfaction in human happiness, the attempt was premature. Wilde's conviction for homosexuality in 1896, though one would have thought it somewhat irrelevant to the indictment of those thought to be taking too great an interest in the fascinations of heterosexual love, temporarily retarded the explicit literary exploration of the phenomena of the sexual passion.

The interest was of course simply driven below the obvious surface of the ensuing fiction, and those who look for its partially concealed manifestations in the work of the Edwardians will be amply rewarded. Consider, for instance, Arnold Bennett's *Clayhanger.* Primarily a story of Edwin Clayhanger's simultaneous emergence from boyhood into manhood and from the Victorian ethos into the twentieth-century dispensation (it is remarkable how often these two developments were seen as complementary), the book treats Edwin's sexual maturation discreetly but engagingly. The day after leaving school he finds himself by chance in the Dragon tavern during a meeting of the Bursley Mutual Burial Club and witnesses an exhibition by Florence Simcox, "the champion clog-dancer of the Midlands." It is, for the respectable citizens of Bursley, rather a daring entertainment: "When Florence shone suddenly at the service-door, the shortness of her red-and-black velvet skirts, and the undeniable complete visibility of her rounded calves produced an uneasy but agreeable impression that Enoch Peake, for a chairman of the Mutual

Burial Club, had gone rather far, superbly far. . . ."[6] And thenceforth, whenever Bennett wishes to hint that certain desires have seized upon Edwin, momentarily at least suggesting that there is a good bit more to life than the printing business and the Young Man's Debating Society, the disturbing figure of Florence Simcox drifts into his thoughts.

Now this vision of Florence Simcox is not only a coy—and aesthetically happy—means of indicating the presence in Edwin's mind of those mental currents which Freud has made so banally explicit; it is a fine example of the cross-fertilization between a symbolic representation of an ideal and a concrete representation of a more venereal signification. Florence represents more than the romanticized object of Edwin's sexual desires; she also represents, in an obscure way, all the private associations and impulses toward rebellion which constitute collectively the rejection of the values of Clayhanger senior and, by extension, of the Victorian ideal, in favor of what is made to seem a wider, more vital, and ultimately more humane ideal.

A similar phenomenon occurs in Galsworthy's *Forsyte Saga,* for although the sexual relationship is barely alluded to in the trilogy, the increasing subordination of all other values to that of sexual love is clear enough. To marry romantically, to gamble "all for love," would be an offense against the strongest instincts of the older generation of Forsytes. But it is only those who are capable of so gambling whom the reader is led to admire—Bosinney, Irene, and Young Jolyon—and only by such gambling is the highest happiness won: Bosinney loses his stake, but Irene and Jolyon win over all. All three speak of course for the claims of art, beauty, and a wider humanity against those of materialism and unimaginative practicality, but, though they thus represent and fight for what is in the last analysis the freedom of the human personality, they exercise that freedom most dramatically and most completely in the choice of their mates and lovers. The figure of Soames reinforces this analysis. Soames is obviously the embodiment of the materialist's possessive personality; yet, in many ways he is an estimable human being, as Galsworthy makes us see more and more clearly in the latter volumes of the trilogy—he lacks principally only the quality of knowing how to give up all other values for love. This is his tragedy: although he finds that love for a woman is the dominating force in his life—as it was for none of the older generations of Forsytes (and for very few of the previous generations of fictional characters, if they are carefully analyzed)—he can never quite disassociate that love from the other goals of his class. Galsworthy's own position of course remains partly ambiguous. Though endorsing the choice of those who count the world well lost for love, he is never quite sure how frankly sexual to make that love, nor is he able to make love entirely its own reward: one of the primary emblems of Irene and Young Jolyon's ultimate success is their return to relative affluence and their possession of the house at Robin Hill.

In both *Clayhanger* and *The Forsyte Saga* then, sexual desire appears, though ambiguously and diffidently, as the antithesis to the accepted values of the nineteenth-century Protestant, commercial, conservative mind. The Edwardian ambiguities yet remain in the next novel to which I wish to call attention, but the ambiguities are clearly on the way to one possible solution. Like Edwin Clayhanger, Maugham's Philip Carey is engaged in freeing himself, if not from as many bonds as the title *Of Human Bondage* might seem to imply, at least from a wide range of illusions, prejudices, and conventionalities. Obviously Philip's rejection of the established values and cherished ideals of society occurs in a sequence which so nearly coincides with the historical chronology of nineteenth-and twentieth-century man's disillusionment as to be almost allegorical. First to fall are Philip's religious convictions and his anticipation of a career at Oxford—the comfortable confidence in the efficacy of the religious communion and of the value of gentlemanly scholarship which was dying so painfully through the latter half of the nineteenth century. Next falls the aesthetic stance represented by Hayward; the answer of the 1880's and 1890's will not serve. Finally both commerce and art are dismissed (it is true that Philip as an individual abandons these fields because he has insufficient aptitude, but success in neither field is seen as an intrinsically valuable goal or as a source of happiness). The rejection of commerce, perhaps the most tenacious of the nineteenth-century values, brings us well into the twentieth century, as does the denial of a transcendent value in art, a denial which in part prophesies the increasingly ironic attitude of the twentieth-century artist toward his art as his belief in himself as prophet is undermined. The affair with Mildred is both a denial of faith in man's power to exercise his will rationally (a phenomenon which happily is presented by Maugham in far more universal and lasting terms than Freud's) as well as an explicit assertion of the dominant role of sexual desire.

Having rejected the goals, ideals, and values which have been presented to him by society, Philip at last understands Cronshaw's enigmatic comparison of life to a Persian carpet, but he is redeemed from complete nihilism by Sally Athelney. Philip comes to think that "the simplest pattern, that in which a man was born, worked, married, had children, and died, was likewise the most perfect," but he sees the beauty of this pattern only after Sally has given herself to him among the hedges at the edge of the field. Philip's moments of greatest satisfaction have been in sexual relationships with Sally, Norah, and even Mildred (in fact the great drawback to June Wilkinson consisted ultimately in her undesirability as a sexual partner). And indeed, one of Sally's greatest attractions is her ability to provide physical satisfaction without raising difficulties and demanding more than honest sensuous response.

It is of some interest to measure Maugham's novel against two earlier novels which arrive at a position outwardly very much like it: Wells's *Love and Mr.*

Lewisham and Butler's *The Way of All Flesh*. At the end of Wells's novel, suddenly seeing the role of husband and father as that to which he must devote himself, forgetting his dreams of a splendid career, Lewisham thinks: "Yes. This is life. This alone is life! For this we were made and born. All these other things—all other things—they are only a sort of play . . ."[7] Despite a very obvious similarity, Wells's novel is a distinctly light and somewhat condescending treatment of the process of maturation beside Maugham's much deeper analysis. The relevant point for the purpose here, however, is that the difference between the two novels largely depends on the addition by Maugham of just the two thematic elements this essay traces: the repudiation of a large portion of the world's values and the discovery of the importance of physical love. Well's protagonist on the other hand is led only to what are essentially Victorian ideals: the recognition of flaws in himself and the acquiesence in the scheme of birth, marriage, and parenthood which steadfastly avoids too explicit recognition of the physical bases of these phenomena.

The case is similar in Butler's *The Way of All Flesh*. Ernest Pontifex has, by the close of the novel, convincingly rejected a number of values as false, but he has failed to discover any value to espouse. Thus it is that Ernest's wisdom finally comes to no more than seeing that "he is the most perfect saint who is the most perfect gentleman"[8] and Overton's wisdom itself extends only to hoping that Ernest will come to see that "common sense" is the only safe ground. After the power of the first three-quarters or so, the novel ends weakly enough with Ernest devoting himself to writing on topics specified little more exactly than as "things which not another man in England except myself will venture to say, and yet which are crying to be said."[9] Having denied throughout the novel that happiness is to be sought in love, marital or otherwise (the novel does admit frankly the power of the sexual drive but is most reticent to say anything more about it), Butler has cut himself off from what seems the central accepted value in the modern novel and finds himself with no true affirmation to make, though Ernest does weakly anticipate Joyce's dedication to art—one of the few other values resoundingly announced by the twentieth-century English novel.

The end of *Of Human Bondage* also portrays the shift of ideals which restored woman to one of her archetypal roles, that of savior to the fallen man, and which, somewhat paradoxically, ultimately reinforced the tendency to emphasize the importance of sexual love. In the figure of Sally the assertion of the supreme value of sexual pleasure is combined with the idealization of woman as the source of man's spiritual salvation. In his chaotically brilliant *Love and Death in the American Novel*, Leslie Fiedler has traced the progress of the "sentimental love religion" in which the chaste woman, through the virtue of her virginity, redeems the evil and weakness in the man she loves. Taking Clarissa as the archetype of the virtuous woman, he pursues her avatar through American fiction up through the nineteenth century, but finds that by the twentieth this sentimentalization has been rejected and such writers as West, Fitzgerald, and Faulkner have not only savagely attacked the myth but again shown woman as the tempter and destroyer of the Garden of Eden. However, though there are undoubtedly Clarissa-like figures enough in the English novel, it was not Richardson's but Fielding's treatment of women which carried the day—Sophia Western is the prize, in herself desirable, courageous, and admirable, but still the prize for, not the primary cause of, Tom's final victory over himself and his environment. And though Sophia has the courage to act, even to leave home, her descendants in the English novel tended to become less and less active. This is true of David Copperfield's Agnes, of Harry Bertram's Julia, of George Dobbin's Amelia, not to mention the women of a Jane Austen or an Anthony Trollope. The assertion of the female as either stronger than, or at least the source of strength for, a weak, confused, or despairing male returns clearly only in the beginning of the twentieth century. Thus in the same year (1915) in which *Of Human Bondage* presented Sally as the realization of Philip's search, Lena appeared as the necessary bracing force for Heyst in Conrad's *Victory.*

The tendency to endow women with a mysterious strength can be seen actually developing in the figure of Irene in *The Forsyte Saga.* Daring but essentially tragic in *The Man of Property* (1906), she emerges as a woman of considerable strength in the two later volumes (1920 and 1921). Similarly, the strongest figures in Graham Greene's *The Man Within* and *The End of the Affair* are, respectively, Elizabeth and Sarah, just as Mrs. Ramsay dominates Woolf's *To the Lighthouse.* Indeed, it would seem that not since the capable heroines of Shakespeare's comedies has the role of woman appeared to such good advantage in English literature. Sean O'Faolain has pointed to the phenomenon of the "vanishing hero" in the twentieth-century novel;[10] we must recognize also the additional phenomenon of the "emerging heroine."

However, during the same period that this idealization of woman was going forward, the naturalistic, satiric, debunking spirit was hard at work driving a wedge between the sexual desire and all its traditional romantic concomitants. Francis Chelifer, who more often than anyone else seems to speak for Huxley in *Those Barren Leaves,* sums up the reaction while musing over his affair with Barbara Waters:

> But in those days I imagined that love ought always to be mixed up with affection and admiration, with worship and an intellectual rapture, as unflag-ging as that which one experiences during the playing of a symphony. Sometimes, no doubt, love does get involved with some or all of these things; sometimes these things exist by themselves, apart from love. But one must be prepared to swallow one's love neat and unadulterated. It is a fiery, crude and somewhat poisonous draught.[11]

Strangely, this antiromanticism and the idealization of womanhood seem hardly to have conflicted at all—a compromise was affected between them in which the idealization was transferred from woman per se to the act of love itself. Further, the act of love could now become not merely the symbol for the satisfaction and fulfillment in life for which all men presumably search, but the only viable means of achieving it. No longer is the healing virtue seen to reside in woman; it is now to be found in the process of love-making, not the partner. And nowhere is this amalgamation of the ideal of the mentally, emotionally, and spiritually satisfying woman with the physically satisfying bed-partner more apparent than in D. H. Lawrence.

The hue and cry over *Lady Chatterly's Lover* has partly obscured the clear significance of that novel in the process here being traced, but what one actually finds in the novel is a demonstration of the bankruptcy, not of morals, but of belief in the efficacy of social, aesthetic, and political ideals as forces opposed to the massed ugliness of the twentieth century. From beginning to end the novel wrestles with the physical ugliness and spiritual blight imposed on both men and society by the industrialism and greed of the twentieth century. Yet, the only positive answer that the novel can suggest is the refuge of a successful sexual relation such as exists between Mellors and Constance. Thus Mellors tells Constance (in a bit of moralizing as dull as that which the most inartistic and idealistic of Victorians could have tacked to the end of a novel) that he believes in "the best bit" of himself, "the little flame between us."[12] And for the working man with whom Mellors so strongly commiserates, the most he can offer is that they "ought to learn to be naked and handsome, and to sing in a mass and dance the old group dances, and carve the stools they sit on, and embroider their own emblems. . . . They should be alive and frisky, and acknowledge the great god Pan."[13] Such a doctrine, evoking as it does a vision of a Kelmscott with adjoining pagan temple for the celebration of joyful festivals—to which each man comes bringing his hand-carved ritual wooden phallus—is clearly a repudiation of the possibility of solving the problems decried. Even the confusion of the Greek pantheon did not countenance the confounding of Hephaestus and Dionysus. Though it is true that *Lady Chatterly's Lover* presents this doctrine in an exaggerated form equalled only by that in *The Plumed Serpent,* the analyses of Morel in *Sons and Lovers* and Ursula in *The Rainbow* enunciate the same hope based precariously on the foundation of a sexual mystique.

The equally unequivocal use of sexual consummation as equivalent to a sort of spiritual consummation occurs in the short stories of Eudora Welty. Sexual frustration is a prominent dilemma and sexual satisfaction a frequent apotheosis in all four volumes of her short stories, but the clearest examples are the last two short stories of her second volume, *The Wide Net.* "Livvie" describes the emancipation of an unbelievably innocent young Negro woman from her ancient husband. Her life has been monotonous and without content for the nine years of their strange marriage, the first step in her awakening occurring the day of his death, when, through the application of lipstick, she begins to become aware of herself. Her development is rapid: a single moment after the husband's death she abandons herself to an insensitive but gorgeously caparisoned and alarmingly virile field hand, and one is sure that such experience as has been heretofore denied Livvie will be amply compensated for. To be sure the point is not missed, Miss Welty closes the story with a reminder that the scene takes place in the fecund season of spring: "Outside the redbirds were flying and criss-crossing, the sun was in all the bottles on the prisoned trees, and the young peach was shining in the middle of them with the bursting light of spring."[14]

Even more direct is "At the Landing," which is built around a very similar situation—the emancipation of a sheltered Southern girl, this time through the death of her grandfather, her last relative. Again the process consists of stages—initially the dawning of her admiration for the wastrel Billy Floyd, next his violation of her on the night of the great flood, and finally her journey to the river which flows now three miles from its old course by the increasingly moribund town (a river which a little too obviously represents the stream of life opposing the decadence of the town). There, while waiting for the return of Billy Floyd, she receives a further initiation from a group of fishermen who, though stolid and uncommunicative, capitalize on their opportunity. As in the previous story, what is obviously intended as a symbol of initiation into the meaning and mysteries of life becomes, through emphasis and iteration, an implicit assertion that sexual consummation constitutes the core of life.

Perhaps the final reduction of the meaning of life to the sexual experience occurs in Durrell's *Alexandria Quartet.* The structure of each of the novels composing the quartet is an adaptation of the favorite device of such satirists as Aldous Huxley: the gathering together of a group of minds so that they may play with interesting or picturesque ideas, and of course ultimately deliver themselves of contradictory profundities on the meaning of life. However, what is in Huxley, especially in the early novels, a less than serious analysis of human life (an analysis that is more obviously shallow and frivolous when one returns to Huxley) becomes in Durrell an apparently quite serious analysis of human love. Three things have happened. Satire, which depends for greatness upon objectivity, has been replaced by painful subjective analysis. The range of interest has been markedly narrowed from the examination of the significance of human life to an analysis of one aspect of that life, to an analysis, moreover, which excludes, by implication, all other areas of interest. (Discussion of the meaning and significance of love has historically tended to widen to somewhat broader issues, if not to the cosmic sweep of the *Symposium,* but this does not happen in the *Quartet.* And yet, one hears undergraduates talking of the philosophy of life enunciated in the *Quartet.*) And thirdly,

whereas Huxley's characters and their speculations generally have little enough effect on each other, especially in the early novels, Durrell's characters not only speculate about love but by their incessant practice of it profoundly influence one another. Obviously Durrell has chosen Alexandria for his setting partially because he is at home writing about it and partially because its picturesqueness provides an interest in itself. But it seems evident that the primary reason for the choice of setting is that it lends itself to the stripping away of all the paraphernalia of ordinary life which would clutter the scene, and thus is perfectly adapted as a background against which Durrell can portray his characters' obsessive and almost uninterrupted experimentation with and analysis of love and sex. The quartet is a framework in which to suspend aphorisms about love, such as these from *Justine:* "I realized then the truth about all love: that it is an absolute which takes all or forfeits all." "We use each other like axes to cut down the ones we really love." "Love is horribly stable, and each of us is only allotted a certain portion of it, a ration."[15]

Of course, there is in a way a hint of a larger, indeed the largest, frame of reference, for the other area which Durrell's characters attempt to explore and illuminate through their epigrammatic analysis is the nature of God. "We are all hunting for rational reasons for believing in the absurd." "One needs a tremendous ignorance to approach God. I have always known too much I suppose."[16] The enigma is approached not by way of the altar but by way of the constant analysis of one's own experience. But inasmuch as the experience Durrell's characters devote themselves to analyzing is of course love, it would seem that the answer to the riddle at which they arrive is summed up fairly clearly in the title of Pursewarden's trilogy, *God Is a Humorist.* To them, sexual love, especially its climax, is His great tragicomic jest. The narrator describes the couple he has seen in the prostitute's booth: "Their posture, so ludicrous and ill-planned, seemed the result of some early trial which might, after centuries of experiment, evolve into a disposition of bodies as breathlessly congruent as a ballet-position. But nevertheless I recognized that this had been fixed immutably, for all time—this eternally tragic and ludicrous position of engagement."[17]

Obviously, the large role that sex plays in contemporary fiction is due in great part to the desire of second-through tenth-rate writers to avail themselves of the success that commercial exploitation of lubricity continues to be able to ensure. On the other hand, so strongly has this value established its primacy in the twentieth-century English novel that it would seem that even a serious and conscientious novelist is hard put to find a viable alternative. An excellent case in point is Graham Greene, who implicitly rejects the values of physical sexuality in *The Man Within* and, while using a somewhat delicious chronicling of an adulterous affair as bait in *The End of the Affair,* explicitly denies any final value to the sexual experience. However, having refused to honor the usual twentieth-century absolute value,

Greene must affirm values completely beyond those experienced in this life to take its place. It is not simply that Greene feels that this world is well lost for the next, that all values derive ultimately from that world which we shall know only after death—all religious men of whatever persuasion presumably see the world in this way—but Greene's characters simply can find no temporal values to cling to and must hasten out of this world. Elizabeth sacrifices herself, and Andrews is brought to the point of committing suicide in *The Man Within* simply because, a reader can hardly avoid feeling, Greene finds it impossible to affirm any values in this life. In *The End of the Affair,* Sarah almost perversely chooses to die, and Bendrix, having by the close of the novel been brought to acknowledge God's existence and power, is left bereft of the possibility of finding anything of worth or joy in this world.

How long the sexual experience can maintain its preeminence unchallenged is a question for the future to answer; but one must note the curious impregnability of the position. In a world in which the religious man is dismissed as a hypocrite, the economically successful man as a sophisticated swindler, the humanitarian as a crank, the politician as a contemptible manipulator of pressure groups and lobbies, and the putatively satisfied member of the middle class as either a dolt or a seething cauldron of repressed desires, the man who boasts of personal happiness based upon the success of his sexual life has the great practical advantage of resting his claim on a foundation hardly susceptible to objective analysis. The difference between a man's professed values and goals and his actions and accomplishments is readily discoverable; it is more difficult to give the lie to the man who boasts that the great source of happiness is sexual satisfaction such as he has attained. Thus, though it seems to some of us that it is the critic's clear duty to deny the ultimate importance of so limited an attainment, the critic who does so, like the doubted who questions the mystic experience, is likely to be met only with the scornful glance reserved for the uninitiated, a glance softened perhaps by a touch of pity.

NOTES

[1] *Ulysses* ([Modern Library Edition] New York, 1946), p. 768.

[2] *James Joyce's Ulysses* (New York, 1952), pp. 388-389.

[3] *The Withered Branch* (London, 1950), pp. 194-195.

[4] (London, 1897), pp. 13-14.

[5] "The Fiction of Sexuality," *Contemporary Review,* LXVII (April, 1895), p. 497.

[6] Arnold Bennett, *Clayhanger* (New York, 1910), p. 97.

[7] H. G. Wells, *Love and Mr. Lewisham* (New York, 1924), p. 322.

[8] Samuel Butler, *The Way of All Flesh* ([Modern Library Edition], New York, 1950), p. 322.

[9] *Ibid.,* p. 531.

[10] *The Vanishing Hero* (London, 1956).

[11] Aldous Huxley, *Those Barren Leaves* (New York, n.d.), p. 146.

[12] D. H. Lawrence, *Lady Chatterly's Lover* (New York, 1959), p. 364.

[13] *Ibid.,* pp. 362-363.

[14] Eudora Welty, *The Wide Net* (New York, 1943), p. 177.

[15] (New York, 1960), pp. 105, 112, 130.

[16] *Ibid.,* pp. 92, 118.

[17] *Ibid.,* p. 187.

Arthur Boardman

SOURCE: "Howellsian Sex," in *Studies in the Novel,* Vol. 11, No. 1, Spring, 1970, pp. 52-60.

[*In the following essay, Boardman argues that, despite his well-known dedication to theoretical and artistic Realism, William Dean Howells held vastly different opinions about sexuality among the upper and lower classes, associating upper class sex with "ideal love" and lower class sex with animalism.*]

To the twentieth-century mind, for a writer to be prudish, as William Dean Howells was by most standards, makes him hardly worth thinking about. Certainly, it tends to shut off investigation of what he thinks and feels about sex, and thus there is little serious study in print of Howells's attitude toward sex.[1] Yet courtship is invariably a theme in his novels, often a central theme. Understanding what Howells thought about sex is essential to a clear apprehension and appreciation of his work.

A clue to what sex means in Howells's fiction appears in *Their Wedding Journey* (1872), his first novel, in a passage which ends with the famous question, to which I shall return, "Ah, poor Real Life, which I love, can I make others share the delight I find in thy foolish and insipid face?" The passage is set on a steamer going up the Hudson, and it begins with Basil and Isabel March, the journeying newlyweds, praising themselves for their own quiet behavior, which is especially commendable, according to Howells, in view of the behavior of "a young man of the second or third quality" and a country girl (accompanied by a younger sister) who are "carrying on a vivacious flirtation," talking "to each other and at all the company within hearing" and exchanging speeches having "for them all the sensation of repartee." At this point Howells presents some of the repartee in dramatic form, adding parenthetical remarks, like stage directions, to describe the action and to comment upon it. He closes the exchange of remarks with a quip from the young man, a specially vigorous sally from the girl, and a description of and comment upon what follows:

> *Young Man.* "Whole team and big dog under the wagon," as they say out West.
>
> *Young Woman.* Better a big dog than a puppy, *any* day.
>
> (Giggles and horror from the younger sister, sensation in the young man, and so much rapture in the young woman that she drops the key of her stateroom from her hand. They both stoop, and a jocose scuffle for it ensues, after which the talk takes an autobiographic turn on the part of the young man and drops into an unintelligible murmur. Ah, poor Real Life. . . .)[2]

No doubt there is to some eyes something pretty meaty in the dropped key, but I am going to pass all *that* business over, for the important sexual implications of the passage are not in the "symbolism" of the key: rather, they are in the fact of the "jocose scuffle," in the condescending, disapproving, and amused tone in which the incident is told, and in the low social status of the flirting couple as compared to the Marches.

The scuffle puts into physical terms the battle of wit— granted, not very witty—that has engaged the young people; and, if it does not symbolize sexual intercourse, it stresses the fundamentally sexual nature of the flirtation. Although the scuffle is playful and therefore comparatively gentle, as a scuffle it involves violence, and thus, consciously or not, Howells in the passage associates sex with violence. In doing so, he associates sex with behavior on an animal level as distinct from a civilized level. To support the inference, there is not only the contrast between the boisterousness of the young people and the decorum of the Marches, who are very civilized, but also and more specifically the dog and puppy imagery in the quips that come just before the scuffle—imagery which explicitly puts the idea of animals into the context. In short, sex as symbolized in the passage from *Their Wedding Journey* is animal.

For Howells the notion that sex links man with the animals was apparently so acutely disturbing that he referred to it covertly, and perhaps unconsciously, rather than openly. Further, he implied, again perhaps unconsciously, that the notion applies to some people only— people at the lower end of the social scale, like the flirting couple. The implication appears in the tone of the passage and in the social distance gaping between the couple and the Marches. I have quoted enough, I believe, to show Howells's condescension toward the couple and his disapproval of their behavior, a disapproval tempered by amusement. His attitude toward

them is clearly that of a superior. More important, he expects the reader to share his attitude and, in effect, to join him and the Marches in condemning and laughing at the flirting couple.[3] The tone puts them at some distance from the observers—Howells, the Marches, and the reader—and by putting them off in the distance indicates that the behavior characteristic of them is not characteristic of the observers.

The social distance between the flirting couple and the Marches, which is obviously considerable though Howells does not measure it exactly, has the same effect as the tone and has it, paradoxically, by stressing the only significant likeness between the couple and the Marches. At first glance, the contrast in behavior and the social distance might appear to suggest that the two couples have no relevance to each other, but in fact they have a great deal, for both are in some stage of courtship, the young man and the country girl having just found each other and the Marches having recently been married. In other words both couples are "in love" (how deeply is beside the point). The condition of being in love as shown in those low in the social order means sex, animal sex, whereas the same condition as shown in those considerably higher in the order, the Marches, certainly does not mean animal sex, as is plain from the contrast in behavior, and apparently does not mean or even involve sex at all—indeed means something else.

What the something else is is a card I shall hold for the moment. Meanwhile, to review briefly, it is enough to realize that in the passage from *Their Wedding Journey* sex has animal quality and that as such it is an aspect of the behavior of the lower social orders, having nothing—except by way of contrast—to do with civilized society, which disapproves of it but can be amused by it.

The question now is whether the attitudes implied in the passage from Howells's first novel are typical of his work. I believe that they are. Though the incident I have discussed is not unique—it is in fact the second and more elaborate of two having identical elements of subject, tone, and attitude in *Their Wedding Journey*[4]— neither is it one of a long series. Nevertheless, hints of the animal quality in sex occur elsewhere in Howells's novels, as in Marcia's kissing the doorknob her lover's hand has turned in *A Modern Instance* (1882) and the "feline pass" terminating the flirtation between Christine Dryfoos and Angus Beaton in *A Hazard of New Fortunes* (1890).[5] Nearest to repeating the themes apparent in the passage I have discussed are incidents in three separate works—*The Coast of Bohemia* (1893), *The Landlord at Lion's Head* (1897), and *The Kentons* (1902)—of girls being kissed against their will. The tone of amusement evident in *Their Wedding Journey* is absent,[6] but just as obviously violence of some degree is present in each instance, and so are the social implications, for invariably the man who does the kissing is of low social rank and is also of aggressive and brash personality, like the "young man of the second or third quality."

Howells develops the scene in *The Landlord at Lion's Head* more fully and at greater length than he does the other two, and he is correspondingly more explicit there about the meaning of what happens. The violence is minimal, incidentally, for the man kisses the girl against her will in the sense that he kisses her unexpectedly and with no pleasure to her. Howells reports what goes through the mind of the aristocratic though (anomalously) flirtatious Bessie Lynde after Jeff Durgin's kiss, and here is most of what he says:

> She realized . . . that she had been kissed as once she had happened to see one of the maids kissed by the grocer's boy at the basement door. In an instant this man had abolished all her defences of family, of society, of personality, and put himself on a level with her in the most sacred things of life. . . . It ought to be known, and known at once. . . . Then she reflected with a start that she could never tell any one, that in the midst of her world she was alone in relation to this; she was as helpless and friendless as the poorest and lowliest girl could be. She was more so, for if she were like the maid whom the grocer's boy kissed she would be of an order of things in which she could advise with some one else who had been kissed. . . . [7]

Howells here associates sex, as symbolized by the unwanted and sudden kiss, with the "order of things" to which a maid and a grocer's boy belong—that is, to a social level much lower than Bessie Lynde's. At that low level, Howells gives us to understand, girls are likely to be poor and helpless and friendless *and* are likely to have experience of unwanted kisses. All the qualities of life that characterize the lower level of society are in strong contrast to those that characterize the level to which Bessie belongs, and the one most in contrast is the experience of the unwanted kiss, for that one in particular now isolates Bessie, making her "alone" "in the midst of her world."

Her experience might make a reader think that only the violence accompanying the kiss is typical of a low social level and unknown at a high level. But such a view would be mistaken, as the thoughts Howells attributes to Bessie show.[8] Sex, the context of the thoughts running through her mind suggests, is one of the things which are among "the most sacred things in life." Since things are sacred because they are so considered or because they are inherently so, something—some force—makes them considered sacred or makes their sacredness perceptible. The force, given the contrast between Bessie and the "poorest and lowliest girl," consists of "family," "society," and "personality." These, it would seem, work together in some undefined way to idealize sex for Bessie and girls at her social level, for a sacred thing is holy and thus something belonging to or touched with the ideal. Sex idealized is sex without the body. And sex without the body is not sex: it is something else—ideal love.

Howells's account of Bessie Lynde's thoughts confirms the impression, given by *Their Wedding Journey,* that he associates animal sex with the lower levels of society in his fiction; it also implies strongly what is only vaguely hinted in the early novel, that he tends to think of sex in connection with the high levels of society as something else, namely ideal love. The absurdity of the tendency, for a writer who thought himself a realist, makes it probable that it was inadvertent (perhaps a kind of unconscious wishful thinking) and makes it unlikely that explicit corroboration could be found anywhere in Howells's work for the implication.

Yet corroboration exists, though it is not explicit.

It can be found, first, in a general, essentially negative tendency having to do with characters on the highest level of the society presented in Howells's fiction. Such characters appear often in his work, and it is remarkable that there is among them an almost total absence of sexual irregularity. The only certain exception is Bessie Lynde, whom Howells presents as something of a flirt—and by no means a desperate one. It is true that sexual irregularity does not abound in Howells's novels; still, there is some, and furthermore characters whom the author clearly thinks despicable tend to have in their catalog of faults that of departing from the strictest sexual conventions—Bartley Hubbard of *A Modern Instance,* for example, or Angus Beaton of *A Hazard of New Fortunes,* or Bittridge of *The Kentons.*[9]

More specific corroboration than the negative tendency can be found by examining a few love scenes. In such scenes, Howells stresses sex more when the characters are on a relatively low social level than when they are on a high one. The following scene involves Marcia Gaylord and the man she soon marries, Bartley Hubbard, of *A Modern Instance:*

> She took up the lamp to light him to the door. "I have tired you," he said, tenderly, and he passed his hand around her to sustain the elbow of the arm with which she held the lamp; she wished to resist, but she could not try.
>
> At the door he bent down his head and kissed her. "Good night, dear—friend."
>
> "Good night," she panted; and after the door had closed upon him, she stooped and kissed the knob on which his hand had rested.[10]

In this scene, Howells emphasizes physical contact which plainly has sexual connotations: the arm around Marcia's waist and the kiss, which is their first. Marcia's behavior after Hubbard leaves continues the emphasis.

Here is another first kiss, this one from *The Minister's Charge,* with like emphasis: "Statira tottered against Lemuel, with that round, soft shoulder which had touched him before. He put out his arms to save her from falling, and they seemed to close round her of themselves. She threw up her face, and in a moment he had kissed her. He released her and fell back from her aghast."[11]

The following scenes are different. In *The Rise of Silas Lapham,* when Tom Corey declares his love to Penelope Lapham, she in effect admits that she loves him, though she thinks she cannot accept him as a suitor because she and her family have believed him to be in love with her sister, who is in love with him. This is the form her admission takes: after saying goodby to him, in dismissal, "She suddenly flung her arms around his neck, and pressing her cheek tight against his, flashed out of the room. . . ."[12] Near the end of the novel Penelope accepts Tom thus:

> All at once she flung herself on his breast. "I can't even give you up! I shall never look anyone in the face again. Go, go! But take me with you! I tried to do without you! I gave it a fair trial, and it was a dead failure. O poor Irene! How could *she* give you up?"
>
> Corey went back to Boston immediately. . . .[13]

The love scenes in *The Rise of Silas Lapham* do not record a kiss. In *April Hopes,* there is a kiss, but it takes place between chapters. As the young couple walk down a dim hallway to the girl's apartment,

> "So dark here!" murmured Alice, in a low voice, somewhat tremulous. "But not too dark." [End of chapter 24.]
>
> She burst into the room where her mother sat looking over some housekeeping accounts. His kiss and his name were upon her lips; her soul was full of him.[14]

When the four novels from which I have taken the scenes are compared, the difference in the social position of the characters is as obvious as the difference in the explicitness of sexual content. Although Marcia is at the very top of the social scale of her village, in which Bartley has had a considerable social success, in Boston, where they go on being married, they are even after several months "still country people, with scarcely any knowledge of the distinctions and differences so important in the various worlds of any city."[15] In the larger world their social position remains comparatively low throughout *A Modern Instance.* Lemuel Barker of *The Minister's Charge* is a poor and ignorant country boy who comes to Boston in a desperate effort to make a living; Statira, the girl he kisses, is almost as poor and works mainly as a sales girl; both are at a very low social level.

In contrast, Tom Corey of *The Rise of Silas Lapham* is a member of a family which, especially through Bromfield Corey (Tom's father), symbolizes Bostonian aristocracy in several novels by Howells, including *The Minister's Charge.* Penelope Lapham, whom Tom marries, is not on the same social level: her father is one of the new rich, and her background is roughly like that of Marcia Hubbard of *A Modern Instance.* But when she joins Corey's family by marrying him she in effect rises to his social level, and I think it fair to say that she begins to

rise socially when they show their love for each other. The young people of *April Hopes,* Dan Mavering and Alice Pasmer, are unequivocally on the highest social level.

The pattern is clear, and it is compatible with the implications of the passages from *Their Wedding Journey* and *The Landlord at Lion's Head.* In Howells's fiction, sex is animal. Neither that notion nor his unhappiness about it is startling. What is startling is his associating sex, by implication, with only the lower levels of the society he presented in his novels. And even more startling is his implied transformation of sex into ideal love at the upper level of that society, a transformation amounting to a denial that sex exists at that level.

But what Howells does with sex in his novels has more in it than the power to astonish. His handling of sex is contrary to the main tendency of his fiction, and it contradicts his own critical theories.

As an American realist Howells was strongly influenced by the ideas of Ralph Waldo Emerson. In *Criticism and Fiction,* he quotes with approval Emerson's spirited exhortation, from "The American Scholar," to embrace and explore the familiar and the low, and, though he leaves out Emerson's statement that to know the low will be to see how "one design unites and animates the farthest pinnacle and the lowest trench,"[16] he makes clear earlier in his own words that he accepts a monistic view of the universe: the "true realist," he says, "is careful of every fact, and feels himself bound to express or to indicate its meaning at the risk of over-moralizing. In life he finds nothing insignificant; all tells for destiny and character; nothing that God has made is contemptible." The realist "feels in every nerve the equality of things and the unity of men; his soul is exalted, not by vain shows and shadows and ideals, but by realities, in which alone the truth lives."[17] "Ideals" here means something divorced from reality, something akin to "vain shows and shadows" and therefore a kind of lie, whereas the notion that truth lives only in reality implies another kind of ideal, the kind that in its absoluteness is the utter reality. Howells, then, believed—or believed that he believed—in the oneness of the ideal and the real, which is to say also the oneness of reality—and there is no need here to labor the point that he attempted in his novels to show "realities, in which alone the truth lives." As a realist he found the ideal in the real.

Clearly, however, to keep the promise I made early in this essay, the assumption that the ideal and the real are one does not underlie the question asked in Howells's first novel, *Their Wedding Journey,* "Ah, poor Real Life, which I love, can I make others share the delight I find in thy foolish and insipid face?" The question assumes, in fact, two kinds of reality: one includes the young man of the second or third quality and the girl with whom he flirts, and the other includes Howells, the Marches, and the reader. The first is "poor Real Life," personified as foolish and insipid, and kept at rather more than arm's length by and from the second. It is for "delight," in other words for amusement and humorous comment, not for real. The second reality is the basis from which judgment is made. In the second, therefore, "truth lives," and truth is characteristic of the reality which is ideal. In asking his question, Howells assumes that the real is to be found in the ideal.

I must not, of course, hold Howells to account in *Their Wedding Journey* for ideas he did not set down until fifteen to twenty years after writing that novel, but all the same I do not think it unfair to him to believe that his statement of the realist's aims, as given in *Criticism and Fiction,* describes not only what he hoped to do himself but also what he actually had been doing, in the main. What's more, the assumption underlying the question to "Real Life"—to the effect that there are two realities, one "low" and trivial, the other "high," ideal, and thus truly real—is the basis also for all the episodes I have referred to: just as the "Real Life" of the question includes the young man with the country girl and their behavior, so would it include Jeff Durgin and his kiss, Bartley Hubbard and Marcia Gaylord, Lemuel Barker and Statira; and just as the reality from the basis of which the young man and the country girl are judged includes the Marches, so would it include Bessie and her thoughts, Tom Corey with Penelope Lapham, and the young couple of *April Hopes.* The intrusion into the fiction of a tendency contrary to Howells's usual practice of realism is clear, and so is the contradiction between theory and practice.

NOTES

[1] Three important studies are the chapter in Everett Carter's *Howells and the Age of Realism* (Philadelphia, 1954), pp. 139-52, which argues that Howells was rather daring in his time and place; Kenneth E. Eble's "Howells' Kisses," *American Quarterly,* IX (Winter 1957), 441-47, which maintains that Howells's reticence about sex cannot be explained away; and Kermit Vanderbilt's "Marcia Gaylord's Electra Complex: A Footnote to Sex in Howells," *American Literature,* XXXIV (Nov. 1962), 365-74, which examines *A Modern Instance* from a Freudian point of view.

[2] Howells, *Their Wedding Journey* (Boston & New York, 1895), pp. 79-81.

[3] For an analysis of the fictional point of view in the passage, see my "Social Point of View in the Novels of William Dean Howells," *American Literature,* XXXIX (March 1967), 44.

[4] For the first incident, see p. 13.

[5] *A Modern Instance,* ed. William M. Gibson (Cambridge, Mass., 1957), p. 10; *A Hazard of New Fortunes,* II (New York, 1899), 325.

[6] Everett Carter's argument in *Howells and the Age of Realism,* pp. 148-50, that the kiss in Howells's fiction symbolizes sexual possession is surely valid; it accounts for the lack of amusement in Howells's treatment of forced kisses.

[7] *The Landlord at Lion's Head* (New York & London, 1911), pp. 300-301.

[8] Howells agrees fully with her. Here is what he says about Jeff Durgin's feeling, at the same time: "Another sort of man, no matter what he had believed of her, would have felt his act a sacrilege then and there" (p. 300).

[9] The figure in Howells's fiction most guilty of sexual irregularity, for he has kept a mistress and fathered a bastard, is a memory rather than a character and is of ambiguous social position. This is Royal Langbrith of *The Son of Royal Langbrith* (New York and London, 1904), who died long before the action of the novel opens and who founded the wealth that has made his son a kind of crown prince under the regency of his mother. Judging by the son, James, who is very consciously aristocratic, Royal Langbrith would himself be called an aristocrat; judging, however, by his history he would be called one of the new rich who, starting from obscure and humble beginnings, have rapidly amassed wealth equaling or surpassing that of the established aristocracy but who have not, understandably, acquired education, manners, and associations like those of the people of established wealth. I think it possible that Howells could not imagine a place in society for a person whom he considered guilty of a serious sexual crime. His cancelling a dinner for Maxim Gorky, in 1906, because Gorky was accompanied by the woman with whom he had lived for years but had not married, is pertinent.

[10] *A Modern Instance,* p. 10.

[11] *The Minister's Charge* (Boston, 1887), p. 165.

[12] *The Rise of Silas Lapham,* intro. by Everett Carter (New York, 1958), p. 230. I should be grateful to anyone who could explain the sexual significance of the grammatical hiatus.

[13] *Ibid.,* pp. 373-74.

[14] *April Hopes* (New York, 1888), pp. 220-21. It must be granted that *April Hopes* is a satirical novel and that in it Alice, the heroine, is treated with rough hands. At this point, however, Howells does not make fun of her love; he soon makes fun of her (pp. 222-23), and the implication is not that her way of loving is wrong but rather that she is unworthy of it because she is slight and unreasonable.

[15] *A Modern Instance,* p. 143.

[16] *Criticism and Fiction,* eds. Clara Marburg Kirk and Rudolf Kirk (New York, 1959), p. 40. For Emerson's full statement, see *Selections from Ralph Waldo Emerson,* ed. Stephen E. Whicher (Cambridge, Mass., 1960), p. 78.

[17] *Ibid.,* p. 15.

Jeffrey F. Thomas

SOURCE: "Bret Harte and the Power of Sex," in *Western American Literature,* Vol. VIII, No. 3, Fall, 1973, pp. 91-109.

[*In the following essay, Thomas focuses on the dynamic power of erotic desire in Bret Harte's short fiction.*]

Reflecting dolefully on his life and times, Henry Adams seized upon the Virgin Mary and the electric dynamo as crucial symbols of the contrast he saw between the moral unity of the Middle Ages and the soulless multiplicity of the nineteenth and twentieth centuries. In "The Dynamo and the Virgin," the twenty-fifth chapter of his autobiography, *The Education of Henry Adams,* Adams discussed the nature and meaning of these two symbolic forces: the Virgin, whose works he had studied reverentially at Chartres and the Louvre, and the Dynamo, which he had contemplated with awe and misgiving at the Chicago Exposition of 1893 and the Paris Exposition of 1900. In the course of his discussion, Adams compared the attributes of these two great sources of power; prominent among them is a quality he felt to be fundamental to the Virgin and her pagan predecessors—notably Venus—but entirely lacking in the sterile dynamo: the quality of sex.

It was through the female power of sex, Adams argued, that Venus and the Virgin had been effective moral forces over mankind. But this great female sexual energy had waned in Europe and, curiously, was quite unknown in America. Americans had never been subject to the power of Venus and the Virgin, according to Adams, because his countrymen were ashamed of sex—especially in women—and resisted its influence at all times. Adams went on to assert that recognition of the female power of sex survived in the nineteenth century only as art. But even in this area Americans rigorously kept closed their eyes and minds. Ruminating on the problem in his customary third-person posture, Adams passed a severe judgment on the honesty and courage of America's creative artists:

> Adams began to ponder, asking himself whether he knew of any American artist who had ever insisted on the power of sex, as every classic had always done; but he could think only of Walt Whitman; Bret Harte, as far as the magazines would let him venture; and one or two painters, for the flesh-tones. All the rest had used sex for sentiment, never for force; to them Eve was a tender flower, and Herodias an unfeminine horror.

American art, like the American language and American education, was as far as possible sexless.[1]

As far as I have been able to discover, Henry Adams never elaborated on these brief and blunt remarks, but the passage is certainly provocative. It might reasonably be expected that the curiosity of any alert reader would be aroused, not so much by the reference to Whitman, whose appreciation of sexual power in all its forms in his poetry is pretty well recognized, as by Adam's inclusion of Bret Harte in his exceedingly exclusive list.[2] By 1905, when Adams wrote the first draft of the *Education,* Harte had been dead for three years and, as far as almost all critics and students were concerned, his literary reputation had expired at least a quarter of a century earlier. He was—then as now—widely regarded as a pathetic example of a minor talent that burned itself out early and produced nothing but trivial hackwork thereafter. And yet Adams went out of his way not merely to cite Harte but to qualify carefully his citation. His praise of Harte's writings refers to an aspect of those works that still attracts little attention. Had Adams wished merely to pay passing tribute to Harte (as he does eleswhere in the *Education*[3]), it would have been far more convenient for him to praise some well-known attribute of Harte's stories rather than so startlingly to place him on a lonely pedestal with Walt Whitman as a daring spokesman for the power of sex.

Just what Adams conceived to be an adequate literary expression of the sexual potency he identified with Venus and the Virgin cannot be precisely defined, but we can be confident that he demanded something more substantial than innuendo or risqué titillation. It would be easy to try to explain away the allusion to Harte by suggesting that Adams was merely referring to the prostitutes, generally with hearts of gold, who appear in several of Harte's early tales.[4] But this is too trivial; surely we must seek something vastly stronger and more compelling. It is not the sex but the force of it that matters to Adams; it is the power of sex, particularly the fecund sex of woman, that drives men *and* women as the electricity from the dynamo energizes machinery. It is a force that compels individuals to think and act in certain ways that would not occur to them in the absence of that force. This power cannot be represented as sentimental or romantic but must be recognized as intense, erotic and irresistible.

II

One of the most common character types in Harte's tales is the ruthless woman who wreaks havoc through the force of her sexual desires, while the men she confronts are almost helpless to save themselves. These females often seem to be more interested in the triumphant power of their sexual allure than in mere sensual gratification. Although the wife of "Brown of Calaveras," one of Harte's lesser known *Overland Monthly* stories, bears some of their traits, the prototype of these vixens is Mrs. Skaggs, the offstage villainess of "Mrs. Skaggs's Husbands"; she never appears in that confused tale of 1871, but manages to destroy a number of men, including the ordinarily redoubtable stage-driver, Yuba Bill, in the course of her many marriages and affairs. In another story of that year, "A Passage in the Life of Mr. John Oakhurst," the gambler is attracted to a pretty invalid and arranges for her cure and convalescence. Having regained her health, the woman cuckolds her trusting husband with Oakhurst and another man, savoring her ultimate triumph when Oakhurst kills the rival lover in a duel and must flee the district.

The list of such maneaters includes Joan Blandford of "The Argonauts of North Liberty," who seduces her husband's best friend in New Jersey, emigrates with him to California—where she indulges in other affairs—and finally returns alone to North Liberty to enjoy her reputation as a paragon of feminine virtue. In "The Bell-Ringer of Angels," the restless wife of a misanthropic sharpshooter finds herself trapped in a distinctly perverse sort of triangle: her husband selects her former fiancé, now tiresomely reformed and priggish, to be her only visitor and confidant. The grotesque relationship between the two men, who incessantly profess their mutual regard and respect with a desperate fervor that clearly exposes their repressed hatred and jealousy, quite properly exasperates the confined but frisky wife, who contrives to seduce the scapegrace younger brother of her former suitor. The tale concludes with all the characters either dead or miserable, but the sexually neurotic highpoint is a scene in which, the husband being away, the older brother finds himself irresistibly drawn to the woman's cabin. As he babbles to himself that his purpose is to exhort his former sweetheart to practise modesty and fidelity, his actual lustful motivation becomes increasingly apparent. When he finally arrives at the cabin, the bell-ringer's wife is entertaining another man, who flees into the bushes. The latecomer, maddened by jealousy and rage, shoots the fugitive with the husband's rifle and only later realizes he has killed his brother.

Another coldly adulterous wife appears in "A Mercury of the Foothills." This one beguiles an admiring boy into serving as her messenger during her affair with the gambler Jack Hamlin and later tries to murder her husband with the youth's pet rattlesnake. Perhaps the most striking representation of one of these succubae is found in "A Rose of Glenbogie," one of Harte's few stories set in Scotland. Studying the hard beauty of Lady Deeside (whom he later learns to be the prowler and plotter who has been regularly disturbing his rest as she pursues her extramarital activities during a weekend holiday), an observer takes note of her cruel mouth: "Her mouth was firm, the upper lip slightly compressed in a thin red line, but the lower one, equally precise at the corners, became fuller in the centre and turned over like a scarlet leaf, or, as it struck him suddenly, like the telltale drop of blood on the mouth of a vampire."[5] This complex orifice embodies the lady's personality, which dangerously combines precision, austerity, voluptuousness, and ruthlessness.

Many of the women who embody the power of sex in Harte's writings are not conscious villainesses but are suddenly possessed by drives and appetites they cannot control. "A Drift from Red-wood Camp," which appeared in French before its publication in England or America, is a curious precursor of *Lord Jim:* a despised hanger-on in a mining camp fortuitously becomes the shaman chief of a tribe of backwoods Indians and proves to be a wise and moderate leader, until his passion for a white woman brings about tragedy and disaster. The woman, who is the wife of a government agent, does not seek to kindle the holocaust that ensues, but her satisfaction with the power she wields over the infatuated white chief makes such a climax inevitable.

The burgeoning sexual maturity of adolescent girls and its effect on weak and impressionable males are frequently portrayed in Harte's tales. The heroine of "M'liss" is only twelve years old, but the latent sexual nature of her relationship with the schoolmaster in this early story is apparent; in the first, or *Golden Era,* version a bounder even accuses the schoolmaster openly of harboring indecent intentions toward the child. Another, slightly older child-heroine in "Flip: A California Romance" expresses her sexual vigor through her tantalizing spiciness (in freckles, hair, *etc.*), a quality she shares with the woodsy bower where she and her lover, another fugitive murderer, hold their trysts. In addition to his frequent tributes to Flip Fairley's spicy beauty, Harte treats the reader to a discreet (or soft-core) exhibition of his heroine bathing in a pool within the bower, where she begins to undress:

> A slight wind followed her and seemed to whisper to the circumjacent trees. It appeared to waken her sister naiads and nymphs, who, joining their leafy fingers, softly drew around her a gently moving band of trembling lights and shadows, of flecked sprays and inextricably mingled branches, and involved her in a chaste sylvan obscurity, veiled alike from pursuing god or stumbling shepherd. Within these hallowed precincts was the musical ripple of laughter and falling water, and at times the glimpse of a lithe brier-caught limb, or a ray of sunlight trembling over bright flanks, or the white austere outline of a childish bosom (III, 321).

Thus combining spicy charm and "bright flanks," Flip is a highly desirable creature, and her lover, Lance Harriott, is rendered defenseless.

Another pubescent seductress is Cressy McKinstry in "Cressy," a long story that received oddly rapturous praise from Oscar Wilde; in a review for *Woman's World* in April, 1889, he called it "one of Harte's most brilliant and masterly productions" and hailed its heroine as "a wonderful nymph from American back-woods, who has in her something of Artemis, and not a little of

Aphrodite."[6] Not content with her conquests over her older schoolmates, this precocious temptress vamps the young school-master, who is utterly enraptured until a rendevous in a barn humiliatingly involves him in a family feud and almost brings him to his senses.

Sometimes the power of sex manifests itself to the surprise of—and, indeed, against the will of—Harte's sympathetic female characters. Jinny M'Closky, in "The Rose of Toulumne," believes herself to be in complete control of her emotions and indifferent to men, until she meets an equally self-sufficient male and walks with him in the fragrant, moonlit night.

In one of Harte's more ambitious literary efforts, the story "Maruja," the Spanish-American heroine, constrained by a family curse, limits herself to cool flirtation until she meets a mysterious and laconic stranger. Their encounters are brief, few, and sometimes wordless, but they result in an ecstatic yearning that passes beyond sentiment. Once they meet in a conservatory of jungle-like atmosphere, where the man helps Maruja unsnarl the black lace of her skirt, which has been caught in the spines of a "snaky-looking cactus" (V, 103). Later they return to pluck a blossom from the cactus—"a bright red blossom like a spot of blood drawn by one of its thorns" (V, 108-109). They exchange a few formal phrases, and then the mood of the place seems to overpower them. As usually occurs, this moment of passion leads only to a single kiss, a chaste symbol of the love-making which they clearly intend. Weeks later, during the confused flurry of melodrama that ends the long story, the two exchange another kiss and Maruja collapses into a chair, as her lover gazes at her with "dark half-savage eyes." "Well might he have gazed. It was no longer a conscious beauty, proud and regnant, seated before him; but a timid, frightened girl, struggling with her first deep passion" (V, 128).

Yet another instance of this transformation of character through the power of sex occurs in "Salomy Jane's Kiss." The titular osculation is delivered by Salomy Jane, "a tall, handsome, lazy Kentucky girl" (XV, 239), as an audacious gesture made to a friendless youth about to be hanged as a horse-thief by a California mob. The condemned man is inspired by the embrace to escape his lynchers and start a new life, and the effect on the girl is equally profound. That night, as the pines outside her father's cabin "sighed their spiced breath in the windows" (XV, 249), she and the fugitive meet again. He tells her of his reformation and begs for another encouraging kiss:

> She tried to laugh—to move away. She could do neither. Suddenly he caught her in his arms, with a long kiss, which she returned again and again. Then they stood embraced as they had embraced two days before, but no longer the same. For the cool, lazy Salomy Jane had been transformed into another woman—a passionate, clinging savage (XV, 252-253).

Soon afterwards, perilously involved in a complex feud and a mistaken-identity murder, Salomy Jane must flee with her lover, and they eventually settle down back in Kentucky.

Although the motivations presented in the situations I have been describing are almost incontrovertibly dependent on erotic drives, it might plausibly be argued that these sexual convulsions are only fleeting moments in narratives which are for the most part concerned with less explosive moods and attitudes. It may be useful, therefore, to examine in minute detail a story that seems to insist on the power of sex not in a few brief scenes but throughout the course of the narrative. Such a story is "The Mystery of the Hacienda," first published in the December, 1893, issue of the *Pall Mall Magazine*. The publication date indicates that this extraordinary narrative appeared as a Christmas treat, a light romance intended to be read to the family circle.

On the surface the plot of "The Mystery of the Hacienda" is quite simple: a young American and his nubile cousin, along with an elderly aunt, take up residence in a stately old hacienda; a beautiful Spanish girl and a handsome vaquero appear mysteriously to them, and the young Americans hold secret, separate trysts with the strangers; eventually they realize that their visitors are ghosts and decide they prefer to love one another. The psychosexual overtones even in this stark synopsis are, I think, obvious, and Harte overlooks no opportunity to exploit them.

At the core of the story is a confrontation between American sensibilities and Spanish-California customs, and the confrontation is abrupt: the hero, Dick Bracy, does not deliberately select the hacienda to be his home; it is lent to him and his family by a wealthy acquaintance who uses only the ranchland around the building. Despite some misgivings about the unfamiliar way of life he will be encountering, Dick is enthusiastic about the place; he looks forward to living here with his pretty cousin, with whom he is on the verge of love, but is concerned about his aunt, a straightlaced Yankee widow with little sympathy for alien ways. In obvious contrast to the inhibited young people, however, the aunt quickly adapts to life on the rancho. As she does so, Dick and his cousin Cecily seem to spend most of their time riding on the flat plains around the hacienda and preparing to fall chastely in love.

One afternoon during their ride, Dick finds himself becoming intensely aware of Cecily, who has bloomed in the fresh air:

> . . . mounted on her fiery little mustang, untrammeled by her short gray riding-habit, free as the wind itself that blew through the folds of her flannel blouse, with her brown hair half loosed beneath her slouched felt hat, she seemed to Dick a more beautiful and womanly figure than the stiff buckramed simulation of man's angularity and precision he had seen in the parks (X, 131).

Equally excited, Cecily "detected this consciousness too plainly in his persistent eyes," and, as though fearful Dick may attempt to emulate the freedom of the wind, she panics: " . . . it seemed to her now that an intruder had entered the field,—a stranger before whom she was impelled to suddenly fly, half laughingly, half affrontedly" (X, 132), and she gallops back to the house. Plainly she has recognized for the first time that Dick's love must include sexual desire, and she cannot cope with this discovery. (Much later, she confesses that she had been seized by an irrational, indefinable terror.)

The next day Cecily refuses to go riding with Bracy, and he goes out alone, angry and frustrated. As he sullenly rides back to the hacienda in the early evening, he sees the figure of a girl moving along the garden wall, though she vanishes around a corner before he can get close enough to speak to her. After dinner that evening Dick walks with Cecily into the rose garden, where they sit on an old stone bench. "It was still warm from the sun; the hot musk of the roses filled the air; the whole garden, shielded from the cool evening trade-winds by its high walls, still kept the glowing memory of the afternoon sunshine" (X, 133). Both Dick and his cousin are eager to make some sort of amorous avowal, but they cannot overcome their inbred inhibitions. They make inane conversation, while Dick gazes longingly at "the curves of her pretty arms and hands, clasped lightly in her lap" (X, 134), and she stares fixedly at the tip of her shoe. At last Cecily, with a blush, makes a leading remark that invites a gallant response. But Dick is paralyzed with fear:

> If he had only spoken then! The hot scent of the roses hung suspended in the air, which seemed to be hushed around them in mute expectancy; the shadows which were hiding Aunt Viney from view were also closing round the bench where they sat. He was very near her; he had only to reach out his hand to grasp hers, which lay idly in her lap. He felt himself glowing with a strange emanation; he even fancied that she was turning mechanically towards him, as a flower might turn towards the fervent sunlight. But he could not speak; he could scarcely collect his thoughts, conscious though he was of the absurdity of his silence. What was he waiting for? what did he expect? He was not usually bashful, he was no coward; there was nothing in her attitude to make him hesitate to give expression to what he believed was his first real passion. But he could do nothing. He even fancied that his face, turned towards hers, was stiffening into a vacant smile (X, 135).

Quite understandably, this insipid silence exasperates Cecily, who stalks off in disgust, while the youth half-heartedly tries to stop her. "Dick fell back dejectedly into his seat, yet conscious of a feeling of *relief* that bothered him. But only for a moment. A recollection of the chance that he had impotently and unaccountably thrown away returned to him" (X, 136). He slinks off to his bedroom, where he berates himself for lacking the courage to reveal his feelings to Cecily—"And yet—and

it disgusted him with himself still more—he was again conscious of the feeling of relief he had before experienced" (X, 136). This sensation of relief does not mean he does not really love Cecily; surely it is meant to suggest that he is so frightened of the sexual implications of love and marriage that he prefers to renounce the girl he loves rather than confess, even to himself, his physical desires.

Finally emerging from his bedroom, Dick tries to find Cecily, whom he believes to be still in the moonlit garden. Passing through a gate, he walks along an alley of rosebushes.

> Their strong perfume—confined in the high, hot walls—at first made him giddy. This was followed by an inexplicable languor; he turned instinctively toward the stone bench and sank upon it. The long rows of calla lillies against the opposite wall looked ghost-like in the darkness, and seemed to have turned their white faces towards him. Then he fancied that *one* had detached itself from the rank and was moving away. He looked again: surely there was something gliding along the wall! (X, 137).

Presuming it to be Cecily, Dick pursues the figure, which slips through an outer gate and turns to face him in the moonlight. It is a stranger, a young and beautiful girl dressed in Spanish garb. Dick is transfixed by her Latin beauty, which is described in detail. She gazes coolly at the bewildered American, who is intensely aware of her "deep, passionate eyes" (X, 137) and other physical charms. "And yet she was like a picture, a dream,—a materialization of one's most fanciful imaginings,—like anything, in fact, but the palpable flesh and blood she evidently was, standing only a few feet before him, whose hurried breath he could see even now heaving her youthful breast" (X, 138).

Dick's youthful breast also heaves as the beautiful stranger smiles at him for a few moments, provocatively draws her fan across her face, and vanishes into the darkness. When he recovers from his stupefaction, Dick persuades himself that the apparition was merely some mischievous local girl and continues to seek Cecily. Still he cannot find her, " . . . and again he experienced the old sensation of relief" (X, 139). When Cecily does turn up, she looks "pale and abstracted" (X, 139) and talks vaguely of the pleasures of her moonlit stroll on the deserted plain. Dick is too preoccupied with his own adventure to pay much attention, but the reader can hardly fail to realize that she has had some similar emotional experience.

That night Dick lies awake, thinking of the girl he has seen and indulging in amorous fantasies. "He felt himself turning hot with an indefinite uneasiness. Then he tried to compose himself. . . . Was his head turned by the witcheries of some black-eyed school-girl whom he had seen but once? Or—he felt his cheeks glowing in the darkness—was it really a case of love at first sight, and she herself had been impelled by the same yearning that now possessed him? A delicious satisfaction followed, that left a smile on his lips as if it had been a kiss" (X, 143). Having relieved his tensions with a bout of what seems to be at least emotional masturbation, Dick is able to sleep.

The next day he tries to learn the stranger's identity but finds that no girl of that description lives in the vicinity. Cecily agrees to go riding with him again, and away from the intoxicating fragrances of the garden Dick can suppress his erotic fever. "The dry, incisive breath of the plains swept away the last lingering remnants of yesterday's illusions. Under this frankly open sky, in this clear perspective of the remote Sierras, which admitted no fanciful deception of form or distance—there remained nothing but a strange incident—to be later explained or forgotten" (X, 146). Dick can even revive his affection for the "wholesome, pretty girl at his side" (X, 145), although he is a little disconcerted by her air of vague preoccupation.

After dinner that evening Dick and Cecily can hardly wait to excuse themselves and head outside. But their purpose is not to resume the aborted romantic interlude of the previous evening. Dick briefly contemplates making the avowal he could not then articulate, but he is quickly overcome by the setting:

> They had come out later than on the previous night; and the moon, already risen above the high walls of the garden, seemed a vast silver shield caught in the interlacing tops of the old pear-trees, whose branches crossed its bright field like dark bends or bars. . . . Damp currents of air, alternating with drier heats, on what appeared to be different levels, moved across the whole garden, or gave way at times to a breathless lull and hush of everything, in which the long rose alley seemed to be swooning in its own spices. . . . Cecily's voice faltered, her hand leaned more heavily on his arm, as if she were overcome by the strong perfume. His right hand began to steal toward hers. But she had stopped; she was trembling (X, 147-148).

She is, of course, excited by something other than Dick's presence, and she soon dismisses him and vanishes. He realizes that she has slipped out through the gate opening on the plain, but he doesn't much care what she does, for he suddenly beholds his mysterious beauty seated on the stone bench. As he hurries toward her, he observes the most minute details—some tiny freckles on her cheek, her moist and parted lips, her long, curving eyelashes—" . . . all this he had noted, drawing nearer and nearer, until near enough to forget it all and drown himself in the depths of her beautiful eyes. For they were no longer childlike and wondering: they were glowing with expectancy, anticipation—love!" (X, 149).

A few moments earlier Dick had made a halfhearted and unsuccessful attempt to take Cecily's hand; he has better luck now:

He threw himself passionately on the bench beside her. Yet, even if he had known her language, he could not have spoken. She leaned towards him; their eyes seemed to meet caressingly, as in an embrace. Her little hand slipped from the yellow folds of her skirt to the bench. He eagerly seized it. A subtle thrill ran through his whole frame. There was no delusion here; it was flesh and blood, warm, quivering, and even tightening around his own. He was about to carry it to his lips, when she rose and stepped backwards. He pressed eagerly forward. Another backward step brought her to the pear-tree, where she seemed to plunge into its shadow. Dick Bracy followed—and the same shadow seemed to fold them in its embrace.

. . . . .[7]

He did not return to the veranda and chocolate that evening, but sent word from his room that he had retired, not feeling well (X, 149).

Cecily, though able to cope with her chocolate, is "a little nervously exalted" (X, 149) when she returns from her stroll. She confesses that she too feels unwell; evidently, she suggests, "the close odors of the rose garden had affected them both" (X, 149). Again the reader is offered a laborious hint that Cecily has been enjoying a similar passionate experience out on the dark plain, and even the discreet aunt realizes "that Cecily was in some vague way as disturbed and preoccupied as Dick" (X, 150).

For several days this pattern persists. During the day Dick and Cecily go for long rides on the sunny, windswept plain; these spartan excursions are clearly the equivalent of cold showers for the ardent cousins. After dinner each evening they rush outside, Bracy heading for the bench and Cecily hastening to her rendezvous in the open air. One evening, however, the aunt, piqued by the young people's failure to show up for their postprandial chocolate, decides to find out what preferable diversion they have found. In the garden she hears Dick Bracy ranting amorously in the shadow of the pear-tree and realizes that he is not addressing Cecily. Later, as she is pondering this infidelity, she is further startled to see Cecily returning from her evening walk, her face flushed "and her delicate lips . . . wreathed at times in a faint retrospective smile" (X, 153).

Hoping to clear up the mystery of this odd development, the aunt invites some local Spanish-Californians to dinner. One of these, a giddy young girl, tells Dick and Cecily a ghost story about the hacienda: two thwarted lovers pined away there a century before and their spirits still haunt the property. Cecily faints in the middle of the account. Late that night she comes to Dick's bedroom. She tells him of having encountered a handsome, mute *caballero* in the garden and of meeting him nightly on the plain and letting him kiss her. She realizes now that her taciturn lover was one of the resident ghosts, and she is terrified. Dick tries to reassure her, and as they sit holding hands in the dark bedroom he gains confidence from her consternation: "Foolish she no doubt had been; pretty she certainly was, sitting there in her loosened hair, and pathetic, appealing earnestness. Surely the ghostly Rosita's glances were never so pleading as those actual honest eyes behind their curving lashes. Dick felt a strange, new-born sympathy of suffering, mingled tantalizingly with a new doubt and jealousy, that was human and stimulating" (X, 164). He is at last sufficiently stimulated to embrace and then to kiss her. This long-delayed amorous gesture exorcises the ghosts, who are seen no more. Dick and Cecily marry and settle down happily in the hacienda.

One would like to be able to ask Bret Harte if he was fully aware of the erotic and psychological undertones of "The Mystery of the Hacienda." What is extraordinary is not the nocturnal hanky-panky with the ghosts—nothing more sensational than a few kisses is specifically confessed, and the reader is permitted to believe that the trysts went no further than such chaste recreation. That is unimportant; what matters is the meticulous care Harte takes to show that the ghosts are emanations of the unsatisfied erotic desires of Dick Bracy and his cousin. They first see their respective ghosts as they return from rides, Cecily on the afternoon when she recognizes Dick's ardor and gallops home in a panic, and Dick the following day as he canters furiously around the hacienda where Cecily is hiding from him. Later Cecily meets her *caballero* out on the plain, evidently close to the spot where she had her terrifying insight. Dick meets his female spectre on the stone bench in the garden where he was unable to find the courage to voice his love for his cousin. Thus the apparitions are intimately linked to locations where one or the other frustrated lover suffered a traumatic conflict between passion and fear. And of what were they terrified? Obviously not just of love—Harte takes pains to make it clear that the young couple had been eagerly looking forward to falling in love. They can only have been in the grip of their indoctrinated fear of physical, sexual passion, and they are emotionally paralyzed by this fear. So the silent seductive ghosts give them rapturous nocturnal satisfaction of their erotic appetites and enable them to pass the daylight hours together free of shame or guilt.

Dick and Cecily's spectral liaisons could be condemned as an adolescent sublimation of their sexual longings. But adolescence is a natural step in maturation, and at the end of the story both cousins have gained the emotional maturity to abandon their fantasy outlets and accept the full significance of love between two young and corporeal individuals. One symbol of their development is that basic animal attribute, hair. Early in the story the prim and sexless Cecily realizes that Dick is staring at her and asks vexedly, "What are you looking at? Is my hair coming down?" (X, 141). In contrast to Cecily's preoccupation with harnessing and confining her hair, Rosita flamboyantly wears a bright yellow rose in her "heavy hair" (X, 137), her "lustrous black hair" (X, 138), "her lustrous hair" (X, 148). At the story's end, when Cecily comes to Dick's bedroom, he is charmed by

"her disordered chestnut hair" and finds her "very human, womanly, and attractive in her disorder" (X, 161). By this point Cecily is not ashamed to let her hair hang down; she is cured of that inhibition, among others.

If Rosita and the *caballero* can be interpreted as comforting incarnations of the sexual drives of Dick and Cecily, a similar analysis may be offered for the man-destroying beast that accompanies the pubescent Cota Ramierez in "What Happened at the Fonda," an astonishing little tale that first appeared in the *Saturday Evening Post* in the issues of August 12 and 19, 1899. Superficially the story is a feeble mystery about an unknown assailant that attacks and mangles a pair of men in an inland California community before it is identified as a vicious horse. But below the surface lurks a disquieting theme that may have eluded many readers of the *Post*.

The victims of the assaults are Colonel Culpepper Starbottle, the florid but not always foolish Kentuckian who appears in many of Harte's tales, and a naive pressman from the local newspaper. Starbottle has been courting the wife of a Mexican innkeeper; he is attacked, in fact, while riding home from a tryst on a borrowed horse belonging to this lady's daughter. The pressman is almost strangled by an unseen attacker shortly after he has been infatuated by the blossoming beauty of the fourteen-year-old girl. Curious about these violent incidents, the newspaper's editor goes to the fonda to investigate. Here the innkeeper and his wife tell him that their splendidly pubescent daughter has just returned from four years of ensconcement in a convent and that since her arrival she has been inseparable from her horse.

Soon the girl, Cota, arrives, galloping bareback astride her mustang. The editor gazes at girl and horse in perplexed admiration:

> She was indeed dangerously pretty, from her tawny little head to her small feet, and her figure, although comparatively diminutive, was perfectly proportioned. Gray eyed and blonde as she was in color, her racial peculiarities were distinct. . . . But he was the more astonished in noticing that her mustang was as distinct and peculiar as herself—a mongrel "calico" horse, mottled in lavender and pink, Arabian in proportions, and half broken! Her greenish gray eyes, in which too much of the white was visible, had, he fancied, a singular similarity of expression to Cota's own! (XVII, 62-63).

Marveling at this phenomenon, the editor stammers a few words of praise for the mare, and Cota mockingly invites him to take it for a ride. He understands the "malicious mischief" of the girl's offer but accepts it, for " . . . he was a singularly good rider of untrained stock, and rather proud of his prowess" (XVII, 63).

The implications of these passages now culminate in a startling series of energetic paragraphs. The astute editor declares that he will wear his own sharp American spurs rather than the Mexican spurs, with their large but blunt rowels, to which the horse is accustomed. This decision does not at first ruffle Cota's malicious smugness, but she quickly learns its significance, as the editor approaches the horse:

> For, without attempting to catch hold of the mustang's mane, Grey in a single leap threw himself across its back. The animal, entirely unprepared, was at first stupefied. But by this time her rider had his seat. He felt her sensitive spine arch like a cat's beneath him as she sprang rocket-wise into the air.
>
> But here she was mistaken! Instead of clinging tightly to her flanks with the inner side of his calves, after the old vaquero fashion to which she was accustomed, he dropped his spurred heels into her sides and allowed his body to rise with her spring, and the cruel spur to cut its track upward from her belly almost to her back.
>
> She dropped like a shot, he dexterously withdrawing his spurs, and regaining his seat, jarred but not discomfited. Again she essayed a leap; the spur again marked its height in a scarifying track along her smooth barrel. She tried a third leap, but this time dropped halfway as she felt the steel scraping her side, and then stood still, trembling. Gray leaped off! (XVII, 64).

(If by this point the reader does not suspect there is more going on here than meets the eye—note the female pronouns throughout—I can only apologize for having wasted his time. If the above passage is concerned only with equitation, it must follow that E. E. Cummings's well-known comic poem "she being Brand-new . . ."[8] is of interest solely to motoring enthusiasts.)

Having had his way with his mount, the editor tries to apologize to Cota. "To his surprise she glanced indifferently at the trickling sides of her favorite, and only regarded him curiously. 'Ah,' she said, drawing in her breath, 'you are strong—and you comprehend!'" (XVII, 64). The two start to walk the bleeding animal to its stall; abruptly Cota pushes the editor through a door and slams it. He hears scuffling noises outside, and soon the girl reappears and apologizes: ' "I was rude! Santa Maria! I almost threw you, too; but . . . you must not punish me as you have her!" ' (XVII, 65).

After this highly suggestive confrontation the rest of the story is anticlimactic. The pressman courts Cota, and she dares him to ride the mustang. Thrown by the intractable beast, the pressman is again attacked as he lies dazed on the ground. But he manages to draw his pistol and kill his assailant, which proves to be the horse itself. Outraged by the killing of her beloved mount, Cota spurns the wretched pressman and returns to the convent.

Now I think it can hardly be questioned that in this story the mongrel mustang mare, little-used to being ridden and dangerous to men, somehow embodies the ripening sexual power of the lovely and malicious Cota.

Only such an interpretation can explain Harte's insistence on so many details emphasizing the bizarre affinity of the adolescent girl and the half-wild mare. I can offer no allegorical explanation for every aspect of the narrative, but it seems clear that Starbottle and the pressman fall victim to the horse's onslaughts because they are rendered vulnerable by their erotic desires and preoccupation. The editor, who regards Cota as merely "a malicious flirt" (XVII, 66), is not weakened by any such passion, and, placing himself confidently "in the saddle" (a venereal term that dates back at least to 1704[9]), he overpowers his mount by exploiting her own frantic responses and achieves a symbolic defloration of the fierce adolescent virgin. Later the virtuous pressman slays the vicious animal in self-defense. Having lost her sexual dominance over man, Cota can only retreat to her convent, chastened if not chaste.

There is an obvious and tantalizing relationship between "The Mystery of the Hacienda" and "What Happened at the Fonda": the titles are virtually interchangeable. Each concerns some unspecified (because largely sexual?) quality or activity connected with a venerable Spanish California estate. (In the latter story the fonda is a rundown Mexican saloon, but it occupies the structure of the decaying hacienda of a former rancho.) The titles strongly imply that the mysterious qualities and the Hispanic settings are more than coincidentally linked. Throughout Harte's writings, Spanish California ranchos, haciendas and even missions possess the sheltering, protective qualities that Dick Bracy recognized in the *Hacienda de los Osis* in the opening of "The Mystery of the Hacienda." These thick-walled adobe mansions offer protection from the burning sun and the desiccating winds; they have the dignity of age and tradition; they are solid, secluded and silent. Behind the walls a harried man can find solace, sanctuary and repose; in the dim shadows and fragrant gardens two people can find the privacy to enjoy the ecstacies of intimacy. In such surroundings Maruja Saltonstall and her taciturn lover hold their trysts in "Maruja"; the convalescent revival preacher Stephen Masterson pursues and embraces the flirtatious Pepita Ramirez in "A Convert of the Mission"; Clarence Brant confusedly courts both Mrs. Peyton and her adopted daughter in "Susy" and "Clarence"; and a very curious relationship forms between a mission priest and his favorite acolyte in "At the Mission of San Carmel."

It is not, however, essential that the power of sex manifest itself in Spanish surroundings and characters. The primary consideration is a setting that offers seclusion and comfort to two willing partners. In "When the Waters Were Up at 'Jules'" a supercilious Eastern engineer and a hearty Western girl find themselves adrift and alone in a log-floored cabin during a flood. Their cosy isolation awakens the engineer to the girl's attractions, and she shows an equal readiness to take advantage of their situation. The Easterner dithers too long, however, and they exchange only a preliminary kiss before the girl's fiancé rows up to rescue them. A well-timed blizzard in "Snow-Bound at Eagle's," a long tale written in 1885, strands John Hale, a pompous Bostonian, for ten days in a remote cabin with a lusty Amazon named Zenobia, while his wife and sister-in-law unwittingly entertain two fugitive stage-robbers at the snowbound Hale ranch. As often occurs in Harte's fiction, the relationships here are more explicitly curative and consolatory than they are erotic, for the women are busy ministering to the men's infirmities: Hale is all but immobilized by his self-conscious stuffiness, and one of the fugitives is frantic with remorse and despair, while the other has a physical wound—he has been shot in the leg. But there are strong indications that the power of sex is inherent in these ministrations, especially during a scene in which Mrs. Hale and the incapacitated bandit exchange heavy-breathing remarks about personal freedom as she tends to his afflicted member.

III

Only once in his writings, it appears, did Bret Harte offer an explicit definition of the sexual dynamism that so often motivates his characters. This passage occurs near the end of "The Judgment of Bolinas Plain," a tale first published in the *Pall Mall Magazine* of January, 1895. "The Judgment of Bolinas Plain," which later became the source of the closest approach to a successful play Harte ever achieved, concerns Sue Beasley, a young, pretty but fading woman who lives with her extravagantly maimed and homely husband on a drab and lonely farm. The single adventure of her life begins with the arrival at the farm of a circus acrobat fleeing a murder charge. She conceals him in the barn, and the thrill of the exploit and a glimpse of his lithe, half-naked body soon arouse a new excitement in her, kindling a desire that becomes ungovernable during an interlude in the hay-loft that is interrupted by her husband's return from a search for the fugitive. When Sue returns to the barn later that night, lusting for another romp with the acrobat, she is followed by the suspicious and lecherous deputy who has been leading the posse in pursuit of the murderer. The husband, jealous and confused, kills the still-innocent deputy. Sue and the acrobat flee into the night, apparently together. (Eventually, deserted by the acrobat, a chastened Sue returns to her husband and enjoys dominance over him by letting him believe her flight was motivated by an unlikely desire to avoid having to testify against him in a murder trial.)

Harte does not adorn this sordid tale with any mitigating sentimentality. The three men involved have dull and complacent natures. The husband observes his wife's apparent infidelity with the same astonishment he would have felt if his two cows, "bought with his own money or reared by him, should suddenly have developed an inclination to give milk to a neighbor. . . ." (XV, 271). The acrobat, intent only on saving his own handsome skin, is oblivious to the erotic possibilities of the hay-loft until Sue's feverish excitement conveys itself to him; and the deputy is only a preening fool who

believes himself to be irresistible to women. Sue, on the other hand, is throughout the story motivated by a single, though complex motive: her previously unaroused sexual drive. Her desire for the acrobat does incorporate a naïve belief that he represents a world of glamorous adventure such as she has never known, but her sensual yearning is concentrated on the man himself. When he tries to justify the crime from which he is fleeing, she silences him abruptly—"She wanted no facts to stand between her and this single romance of her life" (XV, 269). When she must entertain her husband and the posse while awaiting a chance to rejoin the acrobat in the barn, her excitement is so intense that even her cloddish husband senses it: "The atmosphere of the little house seemed to him charged with some unwholesome electricity" (XV, 271). Later Sue snuggles in the hay with her sleek lover, whom she worships as a gorgeous emissary from a world of satisfied desires: "To this world belonged the beautiful limbs she gazed on,—a very different world from that which had produced the rheumatic deformities and useless mayhem of her husband, or the provincially foppish garments of the deputy" (XV, 274). During this tryst in the hay-loft that phenomenon occurs which unfailingly signals the onset of an erotic episode in Harte's fiction: the air becomes permeated with spicy and overpowering aromas.

Eventually, Sue's husband is tried by a lynch mob for the murder of the deputy. Confessing his crime, the husband explains that his motive was to punish the deputy for his supposed adulterous affair with Sue. The deputy's assistant testifies that the charge might be true, for the deputy had his appetites like other men. At this admission the mob erupts in laughter and frees the prisoner, as the author pensively remarks: "That the strongest and most magic of all human passions should always evoke levity in any public presentment of or allusion to it was one of the inconsistencies of human nature which even a lynch judge had to admit" (XV, 285). This rhetorical pomposity in the context of an intended lynching is surely supposed to be humorous, but there seems to be nothing comic about Harte's formulation of the terse definition: "the strongest and most magic of all human passions." It has the ring of deeply-pondered sincerity, and it is unquestionable that Harte is here paying sober tribute to the erotic drive, or to what Henry Adams called "the power of sex." Clearly Adams knew what he was talking about when he saluted Harte for insisting in his writings on the dynamic importance of that power.

NOTES

[1] Henry Adams, *The Education of Henry Adams,* Sentry Edition (Boston, 1961), 385.

[2] Most surprisingly, the usual response to the passage has been simply to drop Bret Harte from it. The thirteen instances of this inexplicable suppression of Harte that the writer has seen include these four: F. O. Matthiessen, *American Renaissance* (New York, 1941), 524; R.

P. Blackmur, "The Virgin and the Dynamo," *Magazine of Art,* 45 (April, 1952), 150; Gay Wilson Allen, *The Solitary Singer,* Revised Edition (New York, 1967), 226; and Alfred Kazin, "History and Henry Adams," *New York Review of Books,* October 23, 1969, 28. Several writers, notably biographers or students of Bret Harte, have called attention to the remark, but I have seen no extended inquiry into its significance or validity.

[3] *Education,* 259, 315. Similar praise of Harte's personality and writings appears in Adams's letters. See *The Letters of Henry Adams, 1892-1918,* Worthington Chauncey Ford, ed. (Boston, 1938), 293-294, 391, 619-620, 634, and *Henry Adams and His Friends,* Harold Dean Cater, ed. (Boston, 1947), 110. Also Henry Adams, "King" in *Clarence King Memoirs* (Century Club, New York, 1904), 159-60.

[4] See *The Education of Henry Adams,* Ernest Samuels, ed., Riverside Edition (Boston, 1973), 653, note 27. In this recently published annotated edition the editor suggests that Harte "portrayed sympathetically the gamblers and prostitutes of California 'Gold Rush' days."

[5] *The Writings of Bret Harte,* 20 vols. (Boston, 1896-1914), vol. XI, 311. This edition is hereafter cited in the text by volume and page number.

[6] Reprinted in *The Works of Oscar Wilde,* Sunflower Edition (New York, 1909), Vol. XII: *Essays, Criticism and Reviews,* 225.

[7] Harte's dots.

[8] E. E. Cummings, *Poems, 1923-1954* (New York, 1954), 178.

[9] See *Slang and Its Analogues Past and Present,* John S. Farmer and W. E. Henley, comps. and eds., 7 vols. (London, 1890-1904), vol. 6, 91. Similar constructions are noted from as early as 1611.

Sarah Blacher Cohen

SOURCE: "Sex: Saul Bellow's Hedonistic Joke," in *Studies in American Fiction,* Vol. 2, No. 2, Autumn, 1974, pp. 223-29.

[*In the following essay, Cohen comments on Bellow's depiction of sex as "the comic leveler" in* The Adventures of Augie March, Herzog, *and* Mr. Sammler's Planet.]

The humor in the relationship between men and women in Saul Bellow's novels rests not so much on the pandemonious clashes between male and female, but on Bellow's portrayal of the laughable nature of sex itself. The young Bellow protagonist regards copulation as a rollicking animal game in which he eagerly participates. Although he experiences some difficulty in learning the

rules and familiarizing himself with the other players' techniques, he plunges headlong into the game. He enjoys taking an amoral holiday from his quest for a distinctive fate; he welcomes the refuge it affords from those "imposers-upon, absolutists"[1] who want to conscript him to their versions of reality. He also views sex as an expression of love, a way of breaking out of his solitude and merging with another human being. But after the dissolution of one love affair after another, he realizes that he is not the selfless devotee of Eros. He only turned to love to avoid the grimness of the impersonal world. He had permitted sex to fool him into thinking that he had fused with another person and was not alone.

The middle-aged Bellow protagonist regards the human being in the act of mating as a funny creature, what with the devious stratagems and the awkward positions he must adopt to attain so ephemeral a bliss. Viewing copulation as a clumsy, undignified activity, he mocks his own and especially his female partner's tendency to invest it with romantic feelings and elevate it to the status of a universal panacea. Despite his ridicule of the sex act, after weighty internal debate and labyrinthine rationalizations, he indulges in it. It is not so much the physical pleasure that he seeks; rather he deludes himself into believing that he can escape from the anxiety and ambiguity of man's middle position between beast and god by losing himself in the animal. When his brief metamorphosis ends, he is all the more oppressed by his human state. More shame-ridden and constrained than ever, he now sees sex as a joke which his own nature and civilization, notably women, play on him. His distress is short-lived, however, for he soon allows himself to be the butt of another sexual joke. And so the delusion-disappointment pattern continues.

The older Bellow protagonist views sex not as a joke, but as the most vile plague on earth, with women and blacks as the chief contaminators. Trying desperately to dissociate himself from the debased mortal state by denouncing the bestial and choosing the divine, he is not able to quarantine himself from the noxious presence of sex. Although he is not a participant of the hedonistic revels of the time, he is still the voyeuristic spectator of them and experiences the lurid thrill of the carnal. Much as he tries to be a god, his reaction to the sexual—either his shrill condemnation of it or his furtive titillation by it—does not allow him to transcend his human nature. Against his will, he, too, is the butt of the sexual joke.

Augie March, Bellow's larky young hero, is primarily concerned with discovering a worthwhile destiny for himself. Most of his time is spent, however, not in self-scrutiny, but in fleeing from the Machiavellis in his life, those "heavy-water brains" (p. 524) who want him to play a supporting role in their fantasies. Often tiring of charting his life's voyage while having to dodge his relentless drafters, he engages in sex as a diversion. Though he is the "by-blow of a traveling man" and "well-stocked, probably by inheritance, in all the materials of love" (p. 47), he does not always have an easy time of it. His sexual initiation is obstacle-ridden and far from idyllic. Unlike a Tom Jones who chances upon ready sexual gratification, Augie must first hoist his invalid employer Einhorn on his back, walk up a tortuous flight of icy stairs in the dark, deposit Einhorn before an astonished whore, choose a nameless woman himself, and then seek his own pleasure. And this pleasure Augie claims "*didn't* have the luster it should have had, and there *wasn't* any epithalamium of gentle lovers" (p. 124). Yet this first carnal adventure does not deter Augie from getting into one erotic entanglement after another. Almost overnight he is transformed from the swain suffering from the pangs of unrequitted love for rich girl Esther Fenchel to the Don Juan whose love is very much requitted by chambermaid Sophie Geratis. Right after he is trounced by anti-union men for his association with Sophie Geratis, he is restored to his vigorous self by the higher love of the unchaste hunting goddess, Thea Fenchel. Soon after he is critically injured in Thea's iguana-hunting expedition, he recovers to become the very healthy lover of movie star Stella Chesney.

Although Augie initially considers each of these sexual relations as a pleasurable release from the more painful task of self-discovery, he soon views them more as affairs of the heart than of the groin. Believing himself to be the "sincere follower of love" (p. 401), he regards each woman with whom he is intimate as a potential life-long companion to share his lonely "pilgrimage." But after he abandons one companion after another, he realizes he is a more fickle than faithful servant of Venus. Rather than desiring any permanent unions, he sought only "temporary embraces" from any woman who would give him cover from the world's "mighty free-running terror and wild cold of chaos" (p. 403). The magic of sex had charmed him into believing he could be free of this "bondage of strangeness" (p. 523). Though he eventually marries Stella and claims to love her, at the novel's end he is still the solitary "Columbus" exploring the external and internal *"terra incognita"* (p. 536). But since he is Bellow's *"animal ridens, the laughing creature, forever rising up"* (p. 536), he has his comic sense to keep him company.

Moses Herzog is not a "young and glossy stud"[2] like Augie, but a middle-aged cuckolded intellectual who is suffering from the break-up of his marriage and the collapse of his stability. Unable to perform his scholarly duties, let alone govern himself, he heeds the promptings of his lawless id. Unable to cope with the more complicated issues of life, he copes with women. Having writhed in pain under the "sharp, elegant heel" of his former wife Madeleine, he now writhes in pleasure having sex with Ramona Donselle, "true sack artist" (p. 17). Yet Herzog is not consumed with achieving what Mailer in "The White Negro" describes as the "orgasm more apocalyptic than the one which preceded it."[3] His need for order is stronger than his need for orgy. Although he doesn't share the extreme view of Moses Maimonides, the twelfth-century Jewish philosopher who claimed that the Hebrew language was holy because it contained no words for sexual activity or the sexual organs, Herzog does agree with Maimonides that man should control his sexual desires and not be controlled by them. Herzog states that lust is the "most wretched form of human struggle, the very essence of slavery" (p. 219). Yet he cannot free himself from this slavery. It is not that he is driven only by the craving for sensual delight. As a "prisoner of perception" (p. 72) who is "sick with abstractions" (p. 123), Herzog looks to sex as a release from the cerebral. Plagued with so many human difficulties, he hopes through sex to become the insouciant animal. He therefore ingeniously convinces himself that sexual gratification is essential to his health and well-being. He further rationalizes his personal need by generalizing it to a societal need. "The erotic," he authoritatively claims, "must be admitted to its rightful place, at last in an emancipated society which understands the relation of sexual repression to sickness, war, property, money, totalitarianism" (p. 166). Bellow undoubtedly had such a remark in mind when he jocosely informed a French reviewer: "En Amérique, la sexualité est moins plaisir érotique qu'hygiène indispensable."[4]

Herzog's comic sense, however, does not allow him to remain satisfied with his impressive-sounding rationalization. He soon punctures his high-flown justification for sex by suggesting the *reductio ad absurdum* conclusion that can be drawn from it. "Why, to get laid," he states with tongue in cheek, "is actually socially constructive and useful, an act of citizenship" (p. 166). Although Herzog in his more rational moments mocks the value of sex, in his less rational moments he is persuaded otherwise by Ramona, theoretician of sex and sensibility. Trusting in the power of positive love-making, she urges Herzog to give full expression to his instincts and revel in her style of hedonism. She firmly believes that sexual release cannot only eliminate man's "constitutional tension of whatever origin" (p. 201), but it can also cure the world of most of its ills. One's failure to satisfy the needs of the body, she insists, amounts to a "surrender to malignancy . . . [and] capitulating to the death instinct" (p. 185). To lend support to her claim, Ramona quotes both "Catullus and the great love poets of all times" (p. 202), and cites the unimpeachable arguments of such neo-Freudians as Herbert Marcuse and N. O. Brown. Along with lecturing about sex, Ramona gives practical demonstrations as well. Appearing as a "tough Spanish broad," a "girlie magazine" tart, or a priestess of the "Mystical body," she presents a vast repertoire of "erotic monkeyshines" (p. 17). Herzog, in turn, is captivated by these "monkeyshines" and responds with "a lustful quacking in his depths" (p. 337). Thus, despite his mockery of the worth of sexual therapy, he is "powerless to reject the hedonistic joke of a mammoth industrial civilization" (p. 166) and eagerly puts himself in the hands of Ramona, therapist *par excellence*. But after a night-long treatment, he is still the same idiosyncratic Herzog with "his problems unsolved as ever," in addition to "a lip made sore by biting and kissing" (p. 207). He had only been a "petit-bourgeois Dionysian" (p. 17) who carried a "heavy-buttocked woman to . . . bed" (p. 154) and awkwardly experienced his spasm of rapture. Herzog therefore blames Ramona for having misrepresented sex, for convincing him that the "body is a spiritual fact, the sinstrument of the soul" (pp. 208-09). Sharing Freud's belief that woman is incapable of denying her instinctual demands for the sake of civilization, Herzog claims that Ramona's sexual theorizing and practices represent a "dangerous temptation which can only lead to more high-minded mistakes" (p. 209). Apparently Herzog will keep on making these mistakes, for after he has served his sentence of hard mental labor and returned to his Berkshire garden of Eden, he has arranged for Ramona-Eve to join him. When he sees her, he hears within himself "the deep, the cosmic, the idiotic masculine response—quack" (p. 337). The fact that he describes this *quack* as "idiotic" lets us know that as much as he would like to revert to the animal, he cannot. His comic self-awareness prevents him from possessing the spontaneous enjoyment of sex so natural to the animal and forces him to admit what a calculating, yet bungling mortal he is. His recognition of the humorous nature of sex thus transforms the sex act into something more than just the purely animal. It establishes his imperfect human state. For man, according to Bellow, affirms his middle position between beast and god by attempting through sex to deny this position.

Mr. Sammler, Bellow's seventy-plus "post-coital" man, cannot, like Herzog, look with humor upon the sex act. Suffering from a hardening of his jocular arteries, Artur Sammler has the same contemptuous regard for sex which his namesake, Artur Schopenhauer, expressed: "[Copulation] is an action of which in cold reflection one generally thinks with dislike and in a lofty mood with loathing."[5] Indeed throughout the novel Sammler is in "a lofty mood" and abhores "creatureliness." A sworn upholder of Apollonian values, he assails what to him are the Dionysian excesses of the times: "the right to be uninhibited, spontaneous, urinating, defecating, belching, coupling in all positions, tripling, quadrupling, polymorphous."[6]

The culprit whom Sammler chiefly blames for these excesses is woman. Like the fifteenth-century inquisitor, Jacob Sprenger, who claimed that all "witchcraft comes from carnal lust, which is in women insatiable,"[7] Sammler believes that women are infernal sex machines, whipping up this libidinal frenzy. The female in the novel who bears the principal brunt of Sammler's misogyny is Angela Gruner, his spoiled and dissipated grand-niece. Although she is Bellow's caricature of the emancipated woman who is more enslaved than liberated by the free expression of her sexuality, Sammler in his unvocalized monologues upbraids her for being a vile temptress of the flesh. Like the prophet Isaiah, castigating the "daughters of Zion" for their "stretched-forth necks . . . wanton eyes" and provocative adornments,[8] Sammler censures Angela for her stretched forth bust, whorish eyes, and "microskirts." Disgusted by her "experiments" in "sexology" (p. 278), he regards her lewdness as the worst form of the Roman paganism sweeping the country.

Herzog had good cause for his character assassinations of Madeleine, who for such a long time ground her heel into his groin. But Sammler has never been personally wronged by Angela and thus his criticism of her seems unduly harsh. Obviously he needs to vilify Angela to dissuade himself from being attracted to her. Whenever he meets her, he is particularly responsive to her "powerful message of gender" (p. 70). He notes the brand of tights she wears, the kind of Arabian musk she uses, and the type of swagger she employs to "enhance the natural power of the bust" (p. 31). In addition to being taken with her undisguised sensuality, he derives a vicarious thrill from listening to her disjointed tales of unbridled eroticism. If for some reason she neglects to describe all the graphic particulars of her affairs, he imagines the lurid details.

It is Angela and women like her, Sammler believes, who have elevated black men to the position of erotic leadership in the sexual revolution they have started. For Angela's notion of what constitutes the perfect man for women—"a Jew brain, a black cock and a Nordic beauty" (p. 66)—has become the sexual ideal for society at large. And the black man, once he realizes he is so prized for his virility, becomes arrogant and flaunts his sexual prowess.

Sammler does not have to rely on secondhand reports of black genital supermen. A black pickpocket, discovering that Sammler has witnessed his operations, corners him in a vacant hotel lobby, makes public his privates, and threatens him with his formidable penis. The symbolic intent of the confrontation is obvious: in this day and age reason and decency are subject to intimidation by brute, lawless forces.[9] What is not so obvious is the fascination the supposedly righteous feel for those of sexual and criminal abandon. On the one hand, Sammler, sharing Schopenhauer's view that the organs of sex are the instrument of the powerful, unprincipled will, shrinks in dread and horror before the thief exhibiting his weapon of malevolent potency. But, on the other hand, Sammler purposely takes the same bus, secretly desiring a reenactment of the thief's masterful exploitation of the "slackness, the cowardice of the world" (p. 47). Similarly, Sammler has mixed reactions about the thief's capture. When he sees him throttling Lionel Feffer, the sensation-and-money-hungry college student who tried to photograph him in action, Sammler regards the black thief as a lethal beast whose glaring sexuality makes him even more repugnant. But when Eisen, his ex-son-in-law almost destroys the thief, Sammler finds "a certain princeliness" in the black man and admires his "barbarous-majestical manner" (p. 294).

Sammler does not want to acknowledge the "ludicrous inconsistency" (p. 291) of his attitude toward the black thief or Angela. At the time it is less disturbing to dismiss them as warped entertainers "in the great fun fair" who "do this droll mortality with one another" (p. 294). When, however, his nephew Elya Gruner dies, a man whom Sammler considers a fallible, yet saintly being, he is compelled to recognize that he himself is not a flawless divine collector of deviants. By claiming to prefer "lunar chastity" (p. 67), while furtively relishing earthly prurience, he has acted less than human and certainly has not adhered to his original intention of acting more than human. Looking to Gruner as his model, he hopes now to act exactly human, which means he will not deny having "galloping impulses" and will not remove himself from "crazy streets, filthy nightmares, monstrosities come to life" (p. 74). As long as he inhabits this planet, Sammler vows he will be openly involved in its "confusion and degraded clowning" (p. 313).

In *The Adventures of Augie March, Herzog* and *Mr. Sammler's Planet,* Saul Bellow depicts sex as the comic leveler, preventing individuals from viewing themselves as brutes of the flesh or aristocrats of the spirit. Initially fooled by the alleged powers of sex, the youthful and middle-aged Bellow heroes look to it as a source of perpetual ecstasy, an end to loneliness, a reprieve from thinking and a release from all fears. The older Bellow hero recoils in disgust from it and considers himself infinitely superior for his celibacy. But when indulgence in sex or abstinence from it does not improve their lives, they chastize themselves for their gullibility. If, however, they have a sense of humor, they soon laugh at themselves for being taken in by the joke of sex. Made aware that they cannot become at one with the beasts or the angels, they struggle to come to terms with their more taxing, yet more fulfilling, mortal state.

NOTES

[1] Saul Bellow, *The Adventures of Augie March* (New York: Viking Press, 1953), p. 524. Subsequent references to this edition will be made in the text.

[2] Saul Bellow, *Herzog* (New York: Viking Press, 1964), p. 154. Subsequent references to this edition will be made in the text.

[3] Norman Mailer, "The White Negro," *Advertisements for Myself* (New York: Berkeley Publishing Corporation, 1966), p. 321.

[4] Pierre Dommergues, "Recontre avec Saul Bellow," *Preuves,* 17 (January, 1967), 41.

[5] Artur Schopenhauer, *The World as Will and Idea,* Vol. 3, "On the Assertion of the Will to Live," quoted in Eva Figes, *Patriarchal Attitudes* (New York: Stein and Day Publishers, 1970), p. 122.

[6] Saul Bellow, *Mr. Sammler's Planet* (New York: Viking Press, 1970), p. 33. Subsequent references to this edition will be made in the text.

[7] Jacob Sprenger, *Malleus Maleficarum* ("Hammer of Witches"), quoted in Eva Figes, *Patriarchal Attitudes,* p. 64.

[8] Isaiah 3:17, King James Version.

[9] For further discussion of what the black thief represents see my book, *Saul Bellow's Enigmatic Laughter* (Urbana: University of Illinois Press, 1974), pp. 181, 189-91.

Taylor Stoehr

SOURCE: "'Mentalized Sex' in D. H. Lawrence," in *Novel: A Forum on Fiction,* Vol. 8, No. 2, Winter, 1975, pp. 101-22.

[*In the following essay, Stoehr examines D. H. Lawrence's thoughts on sexuality in literature as they are expressed in his fiction as opposed to the opinions of his public statements and essays.*]

> "And I, who loathe sexuality so deeply, am considered a lurid sexuality specialist."

I

D. H. Lawrence is probably the most notoriously censored author in all of literary history. His very first novel, *The White Peacock,* had to be toned down, words like "mucked" and "passionate" changed to "dirtied" and "infatuated." From then on it was one suppression after another. When the police confiscated the first edition of *The Rainbow* in 1915, Lawrence automatically became the inspiration (though not quite the spokesman) for a new generation of writers who wished to establish sex as a legitimate subject of literature—with what effect everyone knows.

Lady Chatterley's Lover, his last novel, was Lawrence's major effort in this struggle. "I always labour at the same thing, to make the sex relation valid and precious, instead of shameful. And this novel is the furthest I've gone. To me it is beautiful and tender and frail as the naked self is, and I shrink very much even from having it typed. Probably the typist would want to interfere—."[1] In 1928 he had it printed in Florence, privately, having first explained all the dirty words to the Italian printer—who said he knew of such words himself and saw no reason to be squeamish about setting them in type. At first Lawrence had thought that he might do an expurgated edition for his British and American publishers, but it proved impossible. He said the book bled when he tried to clip it.[2] No legitimate publisher dared to bring out an uncensored edition until 1959 in the United States and 1960 in Great Britain—that is, 30 years after Lawrence's death. One wonders what he would have thought of the way publishers and readers have finally made use of his "frail" classic.

Lawrence said that he had "put forth" *Lady Chatterley* "as an honest, healthy book, necessary for us today."[3] He wanted "men and women to be able to think sex, fully, completely, honestly, and cleanly."[4] He was not so much advocating any sort of action as he was undertaking a cleansing of men's minds. "The mind has to catch up, in sex. . . . Balance up the consciousness of the act, and the act itself. Get the two in harmony. It means having a proper reverence for sex, and a proper awe of the body's strange experience. It means being able to use the so-called obscene words, because these are a natural part of the mind's consciousness of the body."[5]

Unwelcome as *Lady Chatterley* and its purpose were in polite circles of the late twenties, there was a large underground public waiting for the many pirated editions of the book with open arms. No doubt some of its readers misused the novel just as the censors said they would, but others embraced it for more respectable reasons. Edmund Wilson ended his review of the contraband Florence edition with a characteristically shrewd prediction: "All serious writers in the English-speaking countries are much in Lawrence's debt, for even the limited circulation of *Lady Chatterley's Lover* cannot fail to make it easier in future to disregard the ridiculous taboo that the nineteenth century imposed on sex."[6] Long as it took to get *Lady Chatterley* legally in print, it was widely read among young literary people during all those years, and probably did exert the influence Wilson said it would. Whether or not it had quite the effect that Lawrence himself intended is a more complicated question, for he was after more than merely opening up the genre to frank descriptions of love-making. He wanted to reform the love-making itself.

Some readers of *Lady Chatterley* have supposed that Lawrence was an advocate of sexual promiscuity, if not himself lewd. The truth is that he was a faithful and even a puritanical husband, though he had come by the role rather dishonorably, having run off with his French professor's wife. He believed in lifelong monogamy, and he never wrote approvingly about any sexual practice that went against it. "Nothing nauseates me more than promiscuous sex in and out of season."[7] Of course in *Lady Chatterley* his heroine twice commits adultery, but in the first instance she is condemned for it, and in the second she is only forgiven because her own marriage is both loveless and sexless, while she and her new lover intend to marry as soon as possible. "I realize," he said in his defense of the book, "that marriage, or something like it, is essential, and that the old Church knew best the enduring needs of man, beyond the spasmodic needs of today and yesterday. The Church established marriage for life, for the fulfilment of the soul's living life, not postponing it till the after-death."[8] So Lawrence's advocacy of more honesty and more genuine passion in sexual life should not be read as a defense of all sexual activity. Indeed, he thought that until the mind "caught up" with the body, in sexual matters, it might be reasonable for people to refrain from intercourse altogether.[9]

What then did Lawrence believe the sexual life of man ought to be, once the catching up was accomplished? What was the ultimate advice of *Lady Chatterley's Lover?*

One answer might be hinted in the famous scene in which Connie Chatterley and her lover weave forget-me-nots in one another's pubic hair. Some readers have found that idyllic interchange ridiculous, but I suppose even they recognize the accents of innocent fun-in-bed that Lawrence was attempting:

> He fastened fluffy young oak-sprays round her breasts, sticking in tufts of bluebells and campion: and in her navel he poised a pink campion flower, and in her maidenhair were forget-me-nots and woodruff.
>
> "That's you in all your glory!" he said. "Lady Jane, at her wedding with John Thomas."[10]

Successful or not as a literary effect, its charm is not lost on all readers. What complicates matters is the juxtaposition of such frolics with heavier moments. Could the following equally well-known passage in *Lady Chatterley* be an example of Lawrence's ideal sexual encounter?

> It was a night of sensual passion, in which she was a little startled and almost unwilling: yet pierced again with piercing thrills of sensuality, different, sharper, more terrible than the thrills of tenderness, but, at the moment, more desirable. Though a little frightened, she let him have his way, and the reckless, shameless sensuality shook her to her foundations, stripped her to the very last, and made a different woman of her. It was not really love. It was not voluptuousness. It was sensuality sharp and searing as fire, burning the soul to tinder.
>
> Burning out the shames, the deepest, oldest shames, in the most secret places. It cost her an effort to let him have his way and his will of her. She had to be a passive, consenting thing, like a slave, a physical slave. Yet the passion licked round her, consuming, and when the sensual flame of it pressed through her bowels and breast, she really thought she was dying: yet a poignant, marvelous death.[11]

This was one of the scenes that the prosecuting attorneys in the British trial of *Lady Chatterley* saved for trumps in their summation speech. They quoted still more of it:

> In the short summer night she learnt so much. She would have thought a woman would have died of shame. Instead of which, the shame died. Shame, which is fear: the deep organic shame, the old, old physical fear which crouches in the bodily roots of us, and can only be chased away by the sensual fire, at last it was roused up and routed by the phallic hunt of the man, and she came to the very heart of the jungle of herself.

She felt, now, she had come to the real bedrock of her nature, and was essentially shameless. She was her sensual self, naked and unashamed. She felt a triumph, almost a vainglory. So! That was how it was! That was life! That was how oneself really was! There was nothing left to disguise or be ashamed of. She shared her ultimate nakedness with a man, another being.

And what a reckless devil the man was! really like a devil! One had to be strong to bear him. But it took some getting at, the core of the physical jungle, the last and deepest recess of organic shame.[12]

"What does it mean?" the prosecutor coyly asked. "I do not know, I do not suggest. There is more than one meaning which you can put to those two pages, if you want to take offense. Who knows what is the effect on the young man or woman reading those two pages? What is he or she going to think? Is it going to be a good influence, or can it only corrupt and deprave? What is the tendency of it? Where is the justification contained? Where again is the good that a book can do, any book which contains a passage such as that?"[13]

Did the prosecution blunt this particular bullet in order to do more damage, or simply out of an unwillingness to be more precise about so unmentionable an act as Lawrence was apparently describing? However the authorities might come to terms with it, at least in part the passage must be intended symbolically, to suggest Lawrence's own activity as a writer, in searching out the secret places, "the last and deepest recess of organic shame," just as in part it is a description of Mellors buggering Connie. How could he not have known what he was saying, on both scores? But supposing Lawrence to have known what he was saying, why do we suddenly have these evasive terms to describe matters surely just as deserving of plain Anglo-Saxon as other comming-lings of these same lovers? Why mince words here if not there?

The trouble with the forget-me-not passage—if there is any trouble with it—must come down to its being too cute. And the problem with the "deepest recess" passage—if there is anything wrong with it—is that it is too suggestive, too teasing, too discreet. There is something dangerously posed and poised about both passages, something that goes against the unguarded speech and act that Lawrence was advocating.

Several years before writing *Lady Chatterley* Lawrence had stated the case for frank expression with admirable clarity, in a letter to a female friend: "The word penis or testicle or vagina doesn't shock me. Why should it? Surely I am a man enough to be able to think of my own organs with calm, even with indifference. It isn't the names of things that bother me; nor even ideas about them. I don't keep my passions, or reactions or even sensations *in my head.* They stay down where they belong."[14] The argument was carried further in another letter, to another woman, at the time of *Lady Chatterley:*

I want, with *Lady C.,* to make an adjustment in consciousness to the basic physical realities. I realise that one of the reasons why the common people often keep—or kept—the *good natural glow* of life, just warm life, longer than educated people, was because it was still possible for them to say fuck! or shit without either a shudder or a sensation. If a man had been able to say to you when you were young and in love: an' if tha shits, an' if tha pisses, I'm glad, I shouldna want a woman who couldna shit nor piss—surely it would have been a liberation to you, and it would have helped to keep your heart warm.[15]

All this seems reasonable enough until one begins to notice the repeated denial of any room "in the head" for sexuality. The notion that "uneducated" people were able to keep their lives "warm" longer than others is obviously false—worship of a primitive, unconscious, "natural" man who never really existed. The short-circuiting of the head that Lawrence advocated as an ideal of sexuality is not really bestial—despite the opinions of his enemies—so much as it is simply impossible; and impossible not merely to educated, modern men, but to all men. The mind and the body are not separable in the way Lawrence seems to imagine. "Passions," "reactions," "even sensations" do not "belong" somewhere "down" below the waist, but transpire in the entire organism.

Lawrence argued that "thought and action, word and deed, are two separate forms of consciousness, two separate lives which we lead."[16] He admits the need "to keep a connection" between these separate lives of mind and body. "But while we think, we do not act, and while we act we do not think. The great necessity is that we should act according to our thoughts, and think according to our acts. But while we are in thought we cannot really act, and while we are in action we cannot really think."[17]

Whatever common sense may seem to reside in these theories, they are at best metaphorical, simply a means of distinguishing attitudes and values. There are different kinds of mental activity, and different kinds of physical activity, but they are not necessarily opposed, only different aspects of existence—or different ways of describing what life is like. Lawrence put his objections to "mentalized sex" much more intelligibly a little further on in the same essay when he said: "When people act in sex, nowadays, they are half the time acting up. They do it because they think it is expected of them. Whereas as a matter of fact it is the mind which is interested, and the body has to be provoked."[18] It is true that sometimes people think and act according to prescriptions rather than feelings or desires; and of course prescriptions have a sort of "mental" cast to them, since they get formulated and passed around in language. "How different they are, mental feelings and real feelings. Today, many people live and die without having had any real feelings—though they have had a 'rich emotional life' apparently, having showed strong mental feeling. But it is all counterfeit. . . . Our education from the start has *taught* us a certain range of emotions, what to feel and what not to feel, and how to feel the feelings we allow ourselves to feel. . . . The higher emotions are strictly dead. They have to be faked." Lawrence's point, although obscured even here by his mental/physical dichotomy, comes across with plenty of force: sexual life has become conventionalized, trivialized, commercialized. " . . . The radio and the film are mere counterfeit emotion all the time, the current press and literature the same. People wallow in emotion; counterfeit emotion. They lap it up: they live in it and on it. They ooze with it."[19] What Lawrence wants is a new sexuality, freed from the self-indulgent pattern of popular romance. But how does he imagine his own work—also popular and romantic, though perhaps not so obviously—how does he imagine *his* novels effecting the changes he wants?

Long before *Lady Chatterley,* Lawrence wrote an elaborate satire on such faked feelings and counterfeit emotions, in the form of a burlesque novel called "Mr. Noon." The satiric manner was not really suited to his talents or message, and so Lawrence never finished this book, but the 100 pages he wrote are interesting. To get the full effect, one must take a pretty strong dose; here are several paragraphs from the chapter called "Spoon," in which the hero goes in for some heavy necking with the heroine:

> Ah, dear reader, you don't need me to tell you how to sip love with a spoon, to get the juice out of it. You know well enough. But you will be obliged to me, I am sure, if I pull down that weary old scarecrow of a dark designing seducer, and the alpaca bogey of lust. There is no harm in us any more, is there now? Our ways are so improved; so spiritualized, really. What harm is there in a bit of a spoon? And if it goes rather far; even very far; well, what by that? As we said before, it depends how you go, not where you go. . . .

> Mr. Noon was a first-rate spoon—the rhyme is unfortunate, though, in truth, to be a first-rate spoon a man must be something of a poet. With his mouth he softly moved back the hair from her brow, in slow, dreamy movements, most faintly touching her forehead with the red of his lips, hardly perceptible, and then drawing aside her hair with his firmer mouth, slowly, with a long movement. She thrilled delicately, softly tuning up, in the dim, continuous, negligent caress. Innumerable pleasant flushes passed along her arms and breasts, melting her into a sweet ripeness. . . .

> A deep pulse-beat, a pulse of expectation. She was waiting, waiting for him to kiss her ears. Ah, how she waited for it! Only that. Only let him kiss her ears, and it was a consummation.

> But no! He had left her, and wandered away to the soft little kiss-curls in the nape of her neck; the soft, warm, sweet little fibrils of her hair. She contracted with a sharp convulsion, like tickling. Delicious thrills ran down her spine, before he gave her the full assurance, and kissed her soft, deep, full among the fine curls centred in the nape of her neck. She seemed to be lifted into the air as a bit of paper lifts itself up to a piece of warm amber. Her hands fluttered, fluttered on his shoulders; she was rising up on the air like Simon Magus. Let us hope Mr. Noon will not let her down too sharp.

> No! No! Even as she rose in the air she felt his breath running warm at the gates of her ears. Her lips came apart; she panted with acute anticipation. Ah!—Ah!—and softly came his full, fathomless kiss; softly her ear was quenched in darkness. He took the small, fine contours subtly between his lips, he closed deeper, and with a second reeling swoon she reeled down again and fell, fell through a deeper, darker sea. Depth doubled on depth, darkness on darkness. She had sunk back to the root-stream, beyond sight and hearing. . . .

> His mouth was coming slowly nearer to her mouth; and yet not approaching. Approaching without disclosing its direction. Loitering, circumventing, and then suddenly taking the breath from her nostrils. For a second she died in the strange sweetness and anguish of suffocation. He had closed her nostrils for ever with a kiss and she was sleeping, dying in sweet fathomless insentience. Death, and the before-birth sleep.

> Yet, not quite. Even now, not quite. One spark persisted and waited in her. Frail little breaths came through her parted lips. It was the brink of ecstacy and extinction. She cleaved to him beyond measure, as if she would reach beyond herself. With a sudden lacerating motion she tore her face from his, aside. She held it back, her mouth unclosed. And obedient down came his mouth on her unclosed mouth, darkness closed on darkness, so she melted completely, fused, and was gone.[20]

What Lawrence hates in all this is the scripted quality of the love-making, the self-consciousness and the posturing, as if the whole thing had been written out by a playwright, cast by a director, and were now being played by rather indifferent actors: " . . . all the time, of course, each of them had a secondary mundane consciousness. Each of them was aware of the entry, the other spooners, and the passers-by outside. Each of them attended minutely when one pair of spooners crept through the gap in the big doors, to go home. They were all there, mark you. None of your bestial loss of faculties."[21] Later on, when the heroine makes plans to get married, she thinks of it this way: "She decided, if possible, to open the last long chapter of a woman's life, headed Marriage. She intended it to be a long and quite banal chapter, cauliflower and lovey-doves."[22] It is this that Lawrence calls "acting up" to sentimental myths of sexuality, love, and marriage.

Obviously, one must agree with Lawrence that such self-dramatizations are loathsome. The difficulty comes when we try to understand the difference between honest and dishonest accounts (fictional or not) of such matters. How, for example, do we distinguish the self-indulgent quality of "The Spoon" in the passages just quoted, from a description such as the following in *Lady Chatterley's Lover?*

> And it seemed she was like the sea, nothing but dark waves rising and heaving, heaving with a great swell, so that slowly her whole darkness was in motion, and she was ocean rolling its dark, dumb mass. Oh, and far down inside her the deeps parted and rolled asunder, in long, far-travelling billows, and ever, at the quick of her, the depths parted and rolled asunder, from the centre of soft plunging, as the plunger went deeper and deeper, touching lower, and she was deeper and deeper and deeper disclosed, and heavier the billows of her rolled away to some shore, uncovering her, and closer and closer plunged the palpable unknown, and further and further rolled the waves of herself away from herself, leaving her, till suddenly, in a soft, shuddering convulsion, the quick of all her plasm was touched, she knew herself touched, the consummation was upon her, and she was gone.[23]

Isn't Connie Chatterley just as self-regarding in this scene as Emmie Bostock is as she waits for her ear to be "quenched" in the Co-op entry? What precisely is the difference between "she knew herself touched, the consummation was upon her, and she was gone" and "darkness closed on darkness, so she melted completely, fused, and was gone"? As it turns out, of course, we are to understand that Connie's orgasm is genital, not to say vaginal, while Emmie's is merely literary—but anatomy aside, who can tell them apart? In "Mr. Noon" the author comes round on the reader from behind and nudges him: Aha, caught you having lascivious thoughts there, didn't I? Or, no less sneaky, Lawrence and the reader tut and gloat together over the foolish girl in the entry, whom we knew all along was just titillating herself, not really letting go. Again it is necessary to ask whether either of these passages is consistent with Lawrence's desire to open up the novel, and the minds of his readers, to frank and unself-conscious sexuality.

The problem goes deeper even than this. Were it only a matter of inconsistency—passages that seem to go against the spirit of his announced values—we could write them off as lapses or confusions that Lawrence, like any prophet, had to risk. But the difficulty really lies in the medium itself, the form that Lawrence chose to work in—the novel. Is it possible to render a scene of sexual feeling in fiction without indulging in "mentalized sex" of the kind that he despised?

II

In "Pornography and Obscenity," his chief manifesto on the subject of sex in literature, Lawrence begins with the obvious point, that pornography "is an invariable stimulant to the vice of self-abuse, onanism, masturbation," and goes on to assert that "there is an element of pornography in nearly all nineteenth-century literature," while "the mass of our popular amusements just exists to provoke masturbation." "And this," he insists, "is,

perhaps, the deepest and most dangerous cancer of our civilization."[24] The trouble with pornography and masturbation, according to Lawrence, was the "desire to spite the sexual feeling, to humiliate and degrade it." As a result, "the sex flow is dying out of the young, the real energy is dying away."[25] Masturbation was supplanting healthy sexuality, pornography was usurping the true novel.

The novel might yet reform itself, and survive. If so, that would make a difference to civilization. The idea of *Lady Chatterley's Lover* was that it would function as anti-pornography. What was needed, as Lawrence put it in the title of an essay, was "Surgery for the Novel—or a Bomb." The "serious novel" was dying. "'Did I feel a twinge in my little toe, or didn't I?' asks every character of Mr. Joyce or of Miss Richardson or M. Proust. . . . The audience round the death-bed gapes for the answer. And when, in a sepulchral tone, the answer comes at length, after hundreds of pages . . . the audience quivers all over, and murmurs: 'that's just how I feel myself.'"[26] Lawrence had good reason to include Proust in his rogues' gallery of "serious" new novelists who took more pleasure in art than life, for not only was he the worst offender in the sin of prying into his own sensations and thoughts, but he was also a self-conscious defender of fantasy, worse than any of the nineteenth-century romanticists in this regard. Lawrence justified the novel as a means to life, a sort of shock treatment to wake readers up. Proust thought of it rather as access to dreams more real than life:

> Alas, it was in vain that I implored the dungeon-keep of Roussainville, that I begged it to send out to meet me some daughter of its village, appealing to it as to the sole confidant to whom I had disclosed my earliest desires when, from the top floor of our house at Combray, from the little window that smelt of orris-root, I had peered out and seen nothing but its tower, framed in the square of the half-opened window, while, with the heroic scruples of a traveller setting forth for unknown climes, or of a desperate wretch hesitating on the verge of self-destruction, faint with emotion, I explored, across the bounds of my own experience, an untrodden path which, I believed, might lead me to my death, even—until passion spent itself and left me shuddering among the sprays of flowering currant which, creeping in through the window, tumbled all about my body. In vain I called upon it now. In vain I compressed the whole landscape into my field of vision, draining it with an exhaustive gaze which sought to extract from it a female creature. . . . And if she had appeared, would I have dared to speak to her? I felt that she would have regarded me as mad, for I no longer thought of those desires which came to me on my walks, but were never realised, as being shared by others, or as having any existence apart from myself. They seemed nothing more now than the purely subjective, impotent, illusory creatures of my temperament. They were in no way connected now with nature, with the world of real things, which from now onwards

lost all its charm and significance, and meant no more to my life than a purely conventional framework, just as the action of a novel is framed in the railway carriage.[27]

Proust describes here his first experiments with masturbation, and then his subsequent withdrawal from ordinary life and "nature," and his growing dependence upon imagination for both sexual and emotional gratification. He is clearly one of those perverts of self-analysis who according to Lawrence prefer fantasy to reality, the pleasures of imagination to health and nature:

> The only positive effect of masturbation is that it seems to release a certain mental energy, in some people. But it is mental energy which manifests itself always in the same way, in a vicious circle of analysis and impotent criticism, or else a vicious circle of false and easy sympathy, sentimentalities. The sentimentalism and the niggling analysis, often self-analysis, of most of our modern literature, is a sign of self-abuse. . . . There is hardly a writer living who gets out of the vicious circle of himself—or a painter either. Hence the lack of creation, and the stupendous amount of production. It is a masturbation result, within the vicious circle of the self. It is self-absorption made public.[28]

According to Lawrence, the secret but widespread practice of masturbation was part of a general movement away from free and natural sexuality which, so far as Englishmen were concerned, "began only in the nineteenth century."[29] There is some reason for accepting at least part of this view, for it is fairly clear that the nineteenth century was indeed the first period during which masturbation was so thoroughly feared and outlawed as to produce reactions like Lawrence's. Thus, for example, in the long history of male infibulation—the use of various artificial constrictions of the foreskin to prevent erection—apparently the first suggestion of its use to inhibit masturbation did not occur until 1786.[30] But of course this does not mean that no one masturbated before that date, only that not so many worried about it. As it happens, it was that same year that the eminent British surgeon, Dr. John Hunter, gave it as his professional opinion that masturbation "in itself does less harm to the constitution in general than the natural" act of intercourse.[31] By the time (1810) his *Treatise on the Venereal Disease* had reached a third, posthumous edition, his editor felt impelled to announce his own belief "that Onanism is more hurtful than the author imagined."[32] Later writers went so far as to allege, falsely, that Hunter had "recanted in his future editions," because he finally realized "that the solitary masturbator can repeat his crime as often as he pleases . . . [while] the compliance of a female is not always to be obtained."[33] After Hunter the Victorian medical establishment closed ranks on masturbation for a century.

Lawrence's attitude toward masturbation, although in one sense an attack on nineteenth-century practice, is also very much indebted to official Victorian opinion on the subject. It is not surprising therefore that Lawrence sometimes sounds like the generation of prigs he despised for their anti-sexuality. Here, for example, is the typical opinion of a physician in 1839: "every one will admit that, he who is addicted to the unmanly habit of masturbation or onanism, is isolated from society, concentrates all his affections on himself, exerts none of the mutual sympathies of the different members of society, which contribute most powerfully to the good of all."[34] Compare Lawrence's own theory of the bad effects of self-abuse: "The great danger of masturbation lies in its merely exhaustive nature. In sexual intercourse, there is a give and take. A new stimulus enters as the native stimulus departs. Something quite new is added as the old surcharge is removed. And this is so in all sexual intercourse where two creatures are concerned, even in the homosexual intercourse. But in masturbation there is nothing but loss. There is no reciprocity. There is merely the spending away of a certain force, and no return. . . ."[35]

As everyone knows, masturbation is frequently accompanied by sexual fantasy. Laws against pornography are typically based on formulations of a relation between imaginative experience and sexual activity—and what the mealy-mouthed legislators have in mind when they say "sexual impurity" is simply masturbation. Thus the trial judge in Roth v. the United States instructed the jury: "the words 'obscene, lewd, and lascivious' as used in the law, signify that form of immorality which has relation to sexual impurity and has a tendency to excite lustful thoughts."[36] The prosecution in Regina v. Penguin Books Limited—the trial of *Lady Chatterley* in 1960—asked the jury in its opening remarks: "Does it suggest—or, to be more accurate, has it a tendency to suggest—to the minds of the young of either sex, or even to persons of more advanced years, thoughts of a most impure and lustful character?"[37] Victorian authorities had also made these obvious connections between masturbation, pornography, and the abuse of the imagination. The manuals they put out for parents and teachers (*What a Young Man Ought to Know, Good Morals and Gentle Manners, Dr. Foote's Plain Home Talk, Home-Treatment of Sexual Abuses, Lectures on Chastity*) invariably contained similar analyses of the dangers of reading improper literature, and the results of an inflamed imagination:

> Many a young person indulges his imagination in wandering, where in person, at present he can not follow; in hearing what he dare not tell; in seeing what shame would forbid him to disclose; and in seeking what modesty would blush to reveal. These flights of unbridled fancy can not be indulged in with safety. They are the prolific source of all crime, and sin, and shame. . . .
>
> Everything that excites the imagination, inflames the passions, stimulates the curiosity, and corrupts the heart by unchaste suggestions is to be shunned. Impure thoughts, vulgar language, vicious company, obscene books, and lascivious pictures are the bane of good society. No one who is subject, in any degree, to such influences can remain pure.[38]

It should be especially noticed that the Victorian en-emies of self-abuse did not suppose the impure exercise of the imagination was limited to young readers. To blame for the pollution of others, writers in particular—as professional *fabulateurs,* like Proust—were them-selves most obviously in masturbation's hot grip. Rousseau, who in his *Confessions* had frankly discussed the origin of *Julie* as a masturbatory fantasy, was the horrifying example everyone fixed on, until his very name began to be used instead of Onan's: "Have I not often told you that I was another Rousseau?" Ruskin confessed in a letter to a friend.[39]

Partly this susceptibility was a function of the sedentary habits of writers, which made their minds and genitals irritable and inflammable (the cold water douche, fol-lowed by brisk towelling, was recommended for the body, while the mental equivalent was "getting out more" in polite society). Rousseau was noted for the "disproportionate increase of the mind to the body," resulting "from inaction and a continued sitting pos-ture"—and the psychosomatic medicine of the day pos-tulated a set of interconnections between "languid circu-lation," "obstruction in the liver," "excite[d] . . . imagi-nation," and "melancholy character."[40] One need only add the universally accepted linkage between masturba-tion and insanity to arrive at a full etiology of the Vic-torian novelist's occupational disease.

One early symptom of this sort of madness—Rousseau provided the example again—was the upsetting discov-ery that masturbation could apparently "afford . . . greater gratification than intercourse with the other sex, the idea of whom, after all, creates the excitement. . . ."[41] This anomaly was accounted for by the power of the imagination: "as the masturbator has not a material object for the beginning and end of his pleasures, his imagination must supply and invent one. . . . Prints, statues, public exhibitions, and a variety of other sub-jects, are fixed on by the imagination; and the mechani-cal force employed is more stimulating than the natu-ral."[42] Here is the Proustian thesis once again. The ques-tion was especially intriguing to a generation fascinated with the mind/body problem: How could a mere fantasy excite someone more than the living embodiment of that fantasy? It was a central concern of psychologists from Coleridge to G. H. Lewes, and gave rise to a separate genre of fiction, from *The Monk* to *The Picture of Dorian Gray.*

At this point, of course, the terms of the discussion need no longer be exclusively sexual. The issue was the issue of consciousness itself. For all his fixation on sex, Lawrence himself saw this deeper layer: "It is no good being sexual. That is only a form of the same static consciousness. Sex is not living till it is unconscious; and it never becomes unconscious by attending to sex. One has to face the whole of one's conscious self, and smash that."[43] It was not a crisis of sexuality but of consciousness, or as he sometimes formulated it, of will. The Proustian consciousness, the Noonian conscious-

ness, the Chatterley consciousness—in short, the con-sciousness of masturbation, of spooning, of impotence—all seemed to Lawrence part of the fatal self-conscious-ness of the nineteenth century. "Today practically every-body is self-conscious and imprisoned in self-conscious-ness. . . . Fight the great lie of the nineteenth century, which has soaked through our sex and our bones."[44]

On the personal level Lawrence must have felt that his marriage somehow protected him from any charge of masturbatory solipsism. But at the very least it is prob-lematic whether he did not invest so much of his emo-tional life in Frieda, as he had earlier in his mother, that she became the "world" for him—every other relation-ship in abeyance, overshadowed, or translatable into this one, leaving him with only a projection of himself (like Emmie in the entry) and not a social relationship at all. This possibility is hinted in a dialogue between his sur-rogate Somers and his wife in *Kangaroo:*

> "I intend to move with men and get men to move with me before I die," he said. Then he added hastily, "Or at any rate, I'll try a bit longer yet. When I make up my mind that it's really no good, I'll go with you and we'll live alone somewhere together, and forget the world."[45]

This was hindsight, of course, for Lawrence had already given up Australia and moved on with Frieda to New Mexico by the time he wrote this. Later in the same novel, he analyzes his hero's situation still further: "he had an ingrained instinct or habit of thought which made him feel that he could never take the move into activity unless Harriet and his dead mother believed in him."[46] This, as one might have expected, he cannot convince himself of. The female figure seems to repre-sent the world, the "all-in-all" to him, and precludes any social "activity."

Monogamy, exclusive love—the institutions Lawrence championed as bulwarks against masturbation and the isolated consciousness—may not have been quite the defenses he hoped. Although monogamy obviously does not necessarily interfere with social or communal life, it is not an infallible sign of it either. There can be too much adjustment and accommodation in romantic love, so that the partners play into one another's fantasies (if only by preserving their privacy), and the supreme sus-ceptibility for Lawrence, to be touched by the "other," may be faked in the mirror of sexual intimacy.

At some level Lawrence probably knew all this too. Both *Kangaroo* and *The Plumed Serpent* are full of reserva-tions about love as a means to mutuality: " . . . human love as an all-in-all, ah, no, the strain and the unreality of it were too great."[47] "Though a woman be dearer to a man than his own life, yet he is he and she is she, and the gulf can never close up."[48] Indeed, the collection of little newspaper essays published in 1930 as *Assorted Articles* is largely comprised of attacks on the modern conception of love, much in the old vein of "Mr. Noon."

Lawrence wrote two books—*Psychoanalysis and the Unconscious* and *Fantasia of the Unconscious*—in an attempt to rehabilitate "consciousness" by dementalizing it, discovering new "centers of consciousness" that have nothing to do with the enemies, knowledge and reason, but divide up the realm of the traditional unconscious into provinces and estates, known by mystic names like "blood consciousness." In *Fantasia* there is an especially interesting treatment of dreams—which, oddly enough for an anti-rationalist, Lawrence thought much over-emphasized in psychoanalytic theory. "Most dreams are purely insignificant, and it is the sign of a weak and paltry nature to pay any attention to them whatever."[49] He argued that dreams—even the more authentic "soul-dreams" that return over and over to "haunt the soul"—are largely mere mechanisms of the psyche, without relevance or truth to the waking life, "sheer automatic logic."[50] At first glance, Lawrence's attitude might seem inconsistent, for after all dreams are "the royal road to the unconscious," and it is the unconscious that Lawrence is always urging us to enter. But of course the "royal road" Freud had in mind was a well-lighted thoroughfare, and the point was to illuminate the irrational with theory and analysis. Lawrence wanted to plunge into the darkness.

In *Kangaroo* there is a passage of autobiography that helps explain his attitude:

> In his full consciousness, he was a great enemy of dreams. For his own private life, he found his dreams were like devils. When he was asleep and off his guard, then his own weaknesses, especially his old weaknesses that he had overcome in his full, day-waking self, rose up again maliciously to take some picturesque form and torment and overcome his sleeping self. He always considered dreams as a kind of revenge which old weaknesses took on the victorious healthy consciousness, like past diseases come back for a phantom triumph.[51]

Lawrence fears dreams, one suspects, for the same reasons that he fears masturbation, and indeed all flights of fancy, from William Blake to James Joyce. Like the rest of imaginative life, dreams were too self-indulgent, too close to one's secret sins.

The Victorians also understood these connections, for they saw the same danger of sexual arousal inherent in dreams as in waking fantasies or "imaginative" literature. Some authorities went so far as to maintain that dreams should be suppressed, just as pornography: "Patients will tell you that they *cannot* control their dreams. This is not true. Those who have studied the connection between thoughts during waking hours and dreams during sleep know that they are closely connected. The *character* is the same sleeping or waking. . . . A will which in our waking hours we have not exercised in repressing sexual desires will not, when we fall asleep, preserve us from carrying the sleeping echo of our waking thought farther than we dared to do in the daytime."[52]

Lawrence's own attitude is not far from this. "To sleep is to dream: you can't stay unconscious," he wrote in one of his essays—not quite convinced perhaps, certainly not pleased about it, but seriously.[53] Dreams then are not unconscious at all, but, as I think Lawrence saw, the purest state of consciousness; consciousness and fantasy are thus crucially linked in their deepest nature.

Consciousness is symbolically mediated awareness. When we speak, for example, of "feelings" and "emotions," using metaphors of control and isolation such as "harbor," "cherish," "nurse," or, in another direction, "stifle," "smother," "fan," "air," "erupt," we reveal our sense of being locked in our mental space, so that it seems as if we "have" the feelings, possess rather than experience them. Similarly with other mental activity, at the level of conscious awareness. Feelings are a good example because we tend to think of them as antithetical to consciousness, as in the cases of Connie Chatterley and Emmie Bostock. In fact Emmie remains conscious all along, as Lawrence complains, and this is because she focuses her awareness on the symbolic significance rather than losing herself in the simple pleasure of what she experiences. Connie, on the other hand, is supposed to "lose consciousness" through giving herself to unmediated rhythmic activity, becoming at one with her physical present. The distinction is between feelings attended to by the self-conscious "I," and passions engaged in at the surface of awareness, in the motions and chemistry of the appropriate parts of the body. This is not a mind/body distinction, though it may sound like one. The mind is engaged in the passions too, but not self-reflexively, "watching itself." Mind and consciousness are not identical—that is the key to the distinction. But in spite of *Fantasia of the Unconscious* Lawrence wanted his categories lined up in the military formation of traditional psychology, so that he could take his stand for passion over feeling, for unconscious against conscious life, for the deep rhythms of sleep instead of the rapid play of dreams on the surface of awareness. The irony was that this stand was also a stand against the novel.

III

We have already been introduced to Lawrence's opinion that "there is an element of pornography in nearly all nineteenth-century literature"—that is, in the novel as a genre—and that there is something "slightly indecent . . . in *Pamela* or *The Mill on the Floss* or *Anna Karenina*."[54] This "indecency" comes from "a desire to spite the sexual feeling, to humiliate and degrade it," and the examples chosen are obvious cases of the exploitation of sexual subject matter, whatever we might think of the various codes of sexual ethics they present. Lawrence pushes his attack on his predecessors rather unfairly, not to say recklessly, but nonetheless, from a certain point of view, *Pamela* probably is somewhat indecent—a story of a pure virgin successfully resisting seduction until finally her would-be seducer agrees to marry her—and even *Anna Karenina* is not totally free of such teasing "puritanism," nor *Jude the Obscure* nor *Middlemarch* nor many nineteenth-century novels. So there is a truth in Lawrence's judgment—one that even helps to explain why his own experiments with the "frank" description of sexual activity fail to avoid self-consciousness.

It is worth keeping in mind that *Lady Chatterley's Lover* itself was acquitted of being pornographic only a dozen years ago, and that the continued sales and the favored spot on the drug-store racks must depend on its reputation if not its actual usefulness as a dirty book. How then does it differ from novels that, by Lawrence's lights, deserve the reputation *Lady Chatterley* has unfairly acquired?

Lawrence thought the sexuality of Boccaccio and similar Renaissance storytellers might be a healthy antidote to the pornographic tendencies he saw in modern fiction. We can see from this opinion at least one side of Lawrence's intentions in *Lady Chatterley*—namely, to "talk dirty" and to describe sexual "bouts" (as they have been called) without allowing the reader to "get involved." But the vagueness of these concepts and intentions can be seen in the quotation marks blurring that last sentence. Even more or less graphic descriptions of "bouts" may be chaste so long as the aesthetic distance is preserved, and the encounter remains on the page instead of in the reader's imagination. To call a sexual encounter a "bout" is one way of distancing oneself from it; another is to treat it as a "bout," in the manner of Boccaccio. So long as "getting involved" is more a matter of amusement or enlightenment than of the willing suspension of disbelief, a reader is protected from his own viciousness. Thus Lawrence naturally prefers Fielding to Richardson, the distanced classicist to the absorbed gossip. And yet, taste aside, Lawrence is willy-nilly in the tradition initiated by Defoe and Richardson—since that is the mainstream of the novel. The genre could not take the direction that Fielding tried to lead it in, simply because the open, hearty mode of epic satire did not confront the problem of consciousness, merely laughed at it—as if you could reverse the tide of literacy and get people to stop reading and writing in their "closets" or "under the stairs." The new audience was not simply an economic phenomenon, nor was its new form of literature merely a symptom of the "privatization of experience," as social historians have sometimes supposed. These new readers were offering up their imaginations to imitations of life with peculiar zest. Fielding satirized the vulgar playgoer who takes the actors for real people, and the scenes for real events; but behind such naiveté lay a newly sophisticated literary consciousness, a new desire to enter seriously into the thoughts and feelings of characters whose lives made ordinary existence seem an adventure. Dr. Johnson, that morbid solitary, saw the matter clearly enough, though with jaundiced eyes, when he pronounced for Richardson's combination of realism and sentiment; and these virtues proved inextricable as well as indispensable in the novel.

Dr. Johnson's formulation was revealing: we do not read novels for plot but for sentiment. The implication, of course, was that nothing happens until Pamela's letters produce their remarkable effect on Mr. B. Pamela's self-analysis, her probing and recording every vibration of her consciousness as it tingles to Mr. B.'s thrusts of will—*that* was the novel, as Richardson conceived it. The hero-villain wants something to happen, but Pamela's virtue, ingenuity, and duplicity balk him at every turn, and these failures provide a series of occasions for the expression of sentiments—that is, feelings brought to consciousness, to verbalization—dealing with the actions proposed and frustrated in the plot. The epistolary novel offers a medium especially suited to such a structure, since the sentiments that are the by-product of these frustrations can have a dual existence, both as the literal novel under the reader's eyes, and also as the packet of letters that becomes a major prop in the plot as it unfolds. The connection between sexuality and self-conscious writing is perfectly defined when Pamela sews her "papers" in her petticoats. The emphasis on imaginative mediation of sexual excitement is made clear in the structure of the episodes: Pamela hastens to pen and paper after each attack by Mr. B.— so quickly indeed that verisimilitude is strained for the sake of urgent and hot response to event. Her experiences must give the sense of immediacy, but are also something to be rolled on the tongue, at leisure and in retrospect. It is the most intense case possible of dramatic irony—the reader knowing something that a character does not know—for the reader has the coveted letters in his hands throughout, and is in intimate touch with Pamela's consciousness at every moment—the ultimate end of Mr. B.'s desire. Perhaps the situation is best summed up in the fact that her adventures are recounted to her parents, who cannot do anything but look on, horrified, after the fact—the primal scene reversed.

In a novel like *Clarissa* a number of points of view are laid before the reader in this way—seducer, seduced, friends and relatives—and in later sentimental novels, for example Flaubert's *Sentimental Education,* this variety of response is again exploited, though usually with more or less focused attention to the sentiments of the hero, who is typically the frustrated sentimentalist. Marcel in *Remembrance of Things Past* is the classic case, a "giant of sentiment" as he has been called. Pamela is a more complicated instance since she is apparently not the frustrated party in the novel; there is no structural reason for her to have sentiments, which are little more than unacted desires, the whiff of language as they dissipate, or the path of thought around the impasse of will. In so far as *Pamela* ignores Mr. B.'s feelings, while exploiting Pamela's, it is the author's novel, its events being manipulated by Richardson for the sake of the thrills of sentiment he can extract from an essentially voyeuristic situation. It is from this point of view that Lawrence's accusation of pornographic intent is most justified. In the usual sentimental novel the hero's inability to act, with its consequences in verbal consciousness, is a result of ambiguity or conflict within his own character—thus the *Bildungsroman* is based on the hero's progress through a series of self-discoveries and consolidations, more or less dialectically structured as: desire: conflict or inhibition: impasse: sentimental commentary: reorganization of character: newly emergent desire: and so on. The structural necessity of allowing the reader relatively free observation of the hero's consciousness is obvious. But Pamela is less a developing sensibility than a trapped mentality, and our interest in her thoughts has, unfortunately, less to do with any growth or maturing of her character than it does with her plight—at best the reader is in the position of moral investigator, and of course there are more derogatory terms available for such roles and tastes.

Lawrence's own novels are typically sentimental in their structures, and their heroes are afforded many opportunities to vent desires that circumstances of character and plot prevent them from enjoying except in words. Plots themselves, in his novels, tend to consist of little more than the movement of the hero's disposition from relatively self-conscious aimlessness and indecision (for example, in *The Plumed Serpent*, Kate Leslie's restless tourist's attitude toward Mexico, or in *Lady Chatterley*, Connie's dissatisfaction with her life, and her experiment with a lover), through a period of elaborately contemplated and rationalized encounters with parts of the self that must be exorcised (Kate's struggle with her own feminine will, Connie's passing "beyond shame"), in order to arrive finally at a mature and undivided character, one which acts on desire directly and immediately, does not raise obstacles or consider alternatives for itself. The focus is usually on the hero as he works at disciplining his consciousness toward its silent perfection. He is never a victim, as Pamela has to be regarded.

All this is consciousness as a phenomenon of inner life, but consciousness had its social aspects as well. "A man must be self-conscious enough to know his own limits, and to be aware of that which surpasses him," Lawrence admitted in "Pornography and Obscenity." The effect of *this* awareness was to undermine the self-consciousness that gave rise to it, and to turn the soul outward, toward society. "What surpasses me is the very urge of life that is within me, and this life urges me to forget myself and to yield to the stirring half-born impulse to smash up the vast lie of the world, and make a new world. If my life is merely to go on in a vicious circle of self-enclosure, masturbating self-consciousness, it is worth nothing to me."[55] So, to combat self-consciousness, the prescription was to come to its limits, whatever that might mean. "Smash that."

Sometimes the smashing seemed to be a fairly traditional revolutionary goal, as in a letter to Bertrand Russell during the period when Lawrence thought he and Russell might join forces against the war and the establishment:

> Now either we have to break the shell, the form, the whole frame, or we have got to turn to this

inward activity of setting the house in order and drawing up a list before we die.

> But we shall smash the frame. The land, the industries, the means of communication and the public amusements shall all be nationalized. Every man shall have his wage till the day of his death, whether he work or not, so long as he works when he is fit. Every woman shall have her wage till the day of her death, whether she work or not, so long as she works when she is fit—keeps her house or rears her children.

> Then, and then only, shall we be able to *begin* living. Then we shall be able to *begin* to work. Then we can examine marriage and love and all. Till then, we are fast within the hard, unliving, impervious shell.[56]

It was during this same period that Lawrence was most serious about getting a small group of friends together in an utopian community he called Rananim, to be set up in Florida, or some other distant "island." But he was continually sorting and sifting his friends, so that the lists of potential Rananimians changed as fast as its prospective locations. Years later, whenever Lawrence felt that he could break through to a Jungian "social unconscious," he would revive this utopian fantasy. But it faded quickly: "Myself, I suffer badly from being so cut off. But what is one to do? One can't link up with the social unconscious. At times, one is *forced* to be essentially a hermit. . . . One has no real human relations—that is so devastating."[57] Or again, "What ails me is the absolute frustration of my primeval societal instinct. The hero illusion starts with the individualist illusion, and all resistances ensue. I think societal instinct much deeper than sex instinct—and social repression much more devastating. There is no repression of the sexual individual comparable to the repression of the societal man in me, by the individual ego, my own and everybody else's. I am weary even of my own individuality, and simply nauseated by other people's."[58]

These last letters, written toward the end of his life, express more of Lawrence's personal fears and loneliness than he was usually willing to reveal. Lawrence had spent his life wandering, rootless and often friendless, from cottage to cottage, country to country. He collected experiences, but never gathered friends or planted roots. He allowed no place to become his locale, but botanized everywhere. Thus his best nature poems are like "Humming-Bird," fantasies totally abstracted from the natural scene, part of a bestiary of the imagination. It was no different with people. He had followers of course, who would camp on his trail, but they could count on being turned away at some early juncture, if not by Lawrence himself, then by Frieda. To any ordinary observation, it would seem that he was searching for something, some ideal or culmination like his Rananim. But so much of his failure to find it seems willed, that some other interpretation must be necessary. The "social unconscious" that he thought might satisfy him was never achieved, even in his novels. Instead there were struggles among individual wills for mastery, in life with friends such as Russell or J. Middleton Murry and Katherine Mansfield, or in fiction between characters such as Birkin and Ursula, Gerald and Gudrun. The implication is that his real goal was to rehearse these struggles over and over, to reaffirm whatever truth it was that they held for him.

In *Kangaroo,* perhaps his most self-revealing novel, the social unconscious is explored in its traditional terms, as a movement toward a total state, an identification of every person with the group will. But the long central passage of the novel, the "Nightmare" chapter, in which Lawrence recounted all his personal difficulties with the state and the state-mentality in 1915, interrupts him from settling comfortably into a unanimous fascist movement. By the end of the novel the flirtation with totalitarianism seems to have never been more than another struggle of wills, between "Kangaroo," the leader of the fascist movement in Australia, and the hero, Somers, a recalcitrant "writer" whose longings for a religiously organized world are only less strong than his instinctive pan-individualism, his sense of the "dark gods" within himself.

> That was now all he wanted: to get clear. Not to save humanity or to help humanity or to have anything to do with humanity. No—no. Kangaroo had been his last embrace with humanity. Now, all he wanted was to cut himself clear. To be clear of humanity altogether, to be alone. To be clear of love, and pity, and hate. To be alone from it all. To cut himself finally clear from the last encircling arm of the octopus humanity. To turn to the old dark gods, who had waited so long in the outer dark.[59]

Self-consciousness of Somers' type wins out over the social unconscious of Kangaroo. There is a sort of wan and wistful sense of impossibilities, but the final choice is made clearly enough for the private, inward life. "Man's isolation was always a supreme truth and fact, not to be forsworn. And the mystery of apartness."[60]

Having brought his hero to this crisis in *Kangaroo,* Lawrence suddenly reveals a terrible impatience with the demands of denouement that must follow. "Now a novel is supposed to be a mere record of emotion-adventures, floundering in feelings," he sneers. "We insist that a novel is, or should be, also a thought-adventure, if it is to be anything at all complete."[61] But the adventure is not so engaging from this point on, and Lawrence cannot repress a growl of annoyance as he begins the next chapter: "Chapter follows chapter, and nothing doing. . . . To be brief. . . ."[62] In other words, the important part of the novel is apparently over, and the rest—a fourth of it—is merely tidying up. The texture of versimilitude is pulled back together, though never again so tightly as it was in the "Nightmare" chapter just preceding the unravelling. This impatience with "emotion-adventure" is really an impatience with "thought-adven-

ture," that is, with the need to clothe his theoretical resolution in narrative garb once he had recounted the memories of 1915 that lay behind the novel's political passion. In other novels, where the resolution is less clear by this point in the plot, Lawrence maintains his interest in his characters and their doings until the end. But here, having allowed a huge hole of flashback to gape in the center, giving a view back into his own political past, Lawrence has exhausted himself in dramatizing the remembered reality, and seems to have no energy left for fantasizing a present to conclude his story. In a way it is the opposite of the structure of *Pamela,* in which, once the long fantasy siege laid to Pamela's conscience has been raised, and the impasse removed by allowing her consciousness to come into contact with Mr. B.'s, through her letters—once these climaxes have occurred, there is suddenly an overwhelming access of dramatic energy in the novel, in the confrontation of Pamela and Mr. B.'s sister Lady Davers, and the excitement seems strangely healthy, as if we had finally gotten out in the fresh air of social life, out of the closet of Pamela's imagination. In *Kangaroo,* the denouement is stifling, a corridor whose turnings are only too well known in advance. This is interesting, because it suggests just how deeply Lawrence's hatred of the novel went: so long as he could keep his characters struggling toward each other, throwing themselves upon one another in an effort to blot out their individualities, just so long could he maintain his own excitement in the "adventure." But at some point in most of his work— and it comes quite clearly in *Kangaroo*—the failure of such efforts to permanently obliterate consciousness must be faced, and that is the moment that the heart goes out of the fiction. It is as if the goal of the typical sentimental hero—to achieve a fixed character, to fulfill his disposition to a moral nature and take his place as a mature individual in a social world—is precisely what Lawrence most desires to avoid. But he cannot avoid it, for he writes novels, novels quite as much in the mainstream of English fiction as those of Richardson. He may not have been satisfied with the genre, but he could neither change it nor abandon it.

Whatever their differences in resolution and energy, the interest of Lawrence's novels, as of *Pamela* and other examples of the genre, chiefly lies in the experience of becoming totally absorbed in the movement of another person's thoughts and emotions, those of the author or of his hero, to the exclusion of any awareness of extra-literary reality. It is in this respect that the conditions of the novel approach those of fantasy and dream: and of course the emphasis in the mainstream of the genre, on the sentimental display of the hero's consciousness, is clearly a development fostered by the peculiar combination of abstractness and closely-textured concreteness afforded by the medium. Thus it is that Lawrence's complaints about most novels, as well as all sorts of self-conscious fantasy experiences, must seem odd to us, coming as they do from a man who exploits the very modes and structures he attacks, and who heats the imagination in his fiction no less than Richardson or

Tolstoy do in theirs. Lawrence was shrewd enough to see that a heated imagination might come as easily from eavesdropping on the mental life of, say Lambert Strether, as on that of Pamela Andrews. But we must add Connie Chatterley, Kate Leslie, Rupert Birkin, and others, to the list. It is extenuating perhaps that their author's brightest hopes for them is that they may achieve wholeness, unconsciousness, and silence, but to tell the story of their successes Lawrence must use words. And a further irony is that he cannot really communicate to us any very helpful notion of the goal he has in mind, since it is itself pure experience, unmediated by language. As Kafka said, experience cannot be written, only lived.

Of course much modern fiction, including that of Lawrence and Kafka, has had as its chief aim the expression, or indication, of this inexpressible, the breaking of the bounds of the medium, in order to spill over into real life and provoke readers into some non-literary response, some incommunicable living of their own. Indeed this last is even the presumed intention of the pornographer Lawrence despised, to throw a verbal net over the reader's consciousness and to drag it into the darkness and oblivion of orgasm. Lawrence tries for a less momentary consummation, to help us back to the "dark gods" within us, but the means he takes to bring us there are necessarily part of consciousness, appealing to our reason, caressing our sympathies, provoking our feelings—whatever it takes to move a reader to give up his own verbal world and risk the ego in an unformulated terrain.

NOTES

1 *Letters,* ed. Harry T. Moore (London, 1962), p. 972. The first typist *did* interfere; Nelly Morrison refused to go on after five chapters, and Lawrence had to farm it out to his friends.

2 *Letters,* p. 1035. "A Propos of *Lady Chatterley's Lover,*" in *Sex, Literature, and Censorship,* ed. Harry T. Moore (New York, 1959), p. 84.

3 "A Propos . . . ," p. 84.

4 *Ibid.,* p. 85.

5 *Ibid.,* p. 86.

6 Edmund Wilson, "Signs of Life: *Lady Chatterley's Lover*" [1929], in *Shores of Light* (New York, 1961), p. 407.

7 *Letters,* p. 1111.

8 "A Propos . . . ," p. 99.

9 *Ibid.,* p. 85.

10 *Lady Chatterley's Lover* (New York: Grove Press, 1959), p. 290.

11 *Ibid.,* pp. 311-312.

12 *Ibid.,* pp. 312-313.

13 *The Trial of Lady Chatterley,* ed. C. H. Rolph (Baltimore, 1961), p. 224.

14 *Letters,* p. 725.

15 *Ibid.,* p. 1111.

16 "A Propos . . . ," p. 84.

17 *Ibid.,* p. 84.

18 *Ibid.,* p. 85.

19 *Ibid.,* pp. 88-89.

20 "Mr. Noon," in *Phoenix II,* ed. Warren Roberts and Harry T. Moore (New York, 1968), pp. 125-127.

21 *Ibid.,* pp. 127-128.

22 *Ibid.,* p. 169.

23 *Lady Chatterley's Lover,* p. 229.

24 "Pornography and Obscenity," in *Sex, Literature, and Censorship,* pp. 71-73.

25 *Ibid.,* pp. 71, 77.

26 "Surgery for the Novel—or a Bomb" [1923], in *Phoenix,* ed. Edward D. McDonald (London, 1936), p. 517.

27 Marcel Proust, *Swann's Way,* trans. C. K. Scott Moncrieff (New York, 1928), pp. 226-227.

28 "Pornography and Obscenity," pp. 71-74.

29 *Ibid.,* p. 74.

30 E. J. Dingwall, *Male Infibulation* (London, 1925), p. 51. The uses of infibulation, from classical times, were chiefly to prevent fornication by actors, singers, and athletes, whose continence was thought beneficial to their arts. I might point out here that various methods of discouraging masturbation by females were also entertained in the nineteenth-century—notably the excision of the clitoris—but Lawrence is not interested in that side of the story, and the terms of his discussion tend to be masculine, not to say "chauvinist."

31 John Hunter, *A Treatise on the Venereal Disease* (London, 1786), p. 200.

32 *Ibid.,* 3rd edn., ed. Everard Home (London, 1810), p. 214.

33 Michael Ryan, *Prostitution in London* (London, 1839), p. 273.

[34] *Ibid.,* p. 267.

[35] "Pornography and Obscenity," p. 73.

[36] Quoted in Alec Craig, *Suppressed Books* (Cleveland, 1963), p. 226.

[37] *Trial,* p. 13.

[38] Alexander M. Gow, *Good Morals and Gentle Manners* (New York, 1873), pp. 51-53.

[39] Quoted in Ronald Pearsall, *The Worm in the Bud* (Toronto, 1969), p. 515.

[40] Chandler Robbins, *Disorders of Literary Men* (Boston, 1825), pp. 18-19.

[41] William Acton, *The Functions and Disorders of the Reproductive Organs,* 5th edn. (London, 1871), p. 159.

[42] Ryan, p. 259.

[43] *Letters,* pp. 373-374.

[44] "Pornography and Obscenity," p. 79.

[45] *Kangaroo* (New York, 1960), p. 64.

[46] *Ibid.,* p. 95.

[47] *Ibid.,* p. 335.

[48] *The Plumed Serpent* (New York, 1951), p. 277.

[49] *Psychoanalysis and the Unconscious and Fantasia of the Unconscious* (New York, 1960), p. 194.

[50] *Ibid.,* pp. 196-197.

[51] *Kangaroo,* p. 95.

[52] Acton, p. 230.

[53] *Studies in Classic American Literature* (New York, 1961), p. 132.

[54] "Pornography and Obscenity," p. 71.

[55] *Ibid.,* p. 79.

[56] *Letters,* p. 320.

[57] *Ibid.,* p. 993.

[58] *Ibid.,* p. 989-990.

[59] *Kangaroo,* p. 271.

[60] *Ibid.,* p. 334.

[61] *Ibid.,* p. 285.

[62] *Ibid.,* p. 289.

Eugene M. Langen

SOURCE: "Dickey's 'Deliverance': Sex and the Great Outdoors," in *The Southern Literary Journal,* Vol. IX, No. 2, Spring, 1977, pp. 137-49.

[*In the following essay, Langen describes sex as a primal source of power that pervades James Dickey's novel* Deliverance.]

The homosexual rape scene in James Dickey's *Deliverance* is stunningly crude and unforgettable. It is hard not to think of this act of sex when we think of the novel in general—and this seems precisely Dickey's intent. But the sexual episode with the mountain men, with all its brutality and violence, is not simply the first in a twenty-four-hour series of nightmare adventures. It is part of the pervasive theme of sex which Dickey uses to convey an understanding of what life in the so-called great outdoors—or anywhere—is all about when the chips are down. It means that once the superstructure of courtesy, of convention, of ethics has been stripped away, what remains is life, meaningful and operative primarily in physical, sexual terms. Dickey is not suggesting that this is all that life can be; he is reminding us of what he thinks it fundamentally is. The simple fact of this sexual perspective in the novel is the first point I should like to explore.

An act of sex initiates the account of this whole weekend adventure. Ed Gentry, the narrator, and his wife Martha waken around six in the morning on the Friday when Ed is to meet three friends and head for the rugged blue mountains of north Georgia. They are sleepy but aroused. Martha "put a pillow in the middle of the bed, threw back the covers with a windy motion and turned facedown on the pillow. I knelt and entered her, and her buttocks rose and fell."[1] This act of intercourse, particularly with the rear entry position described explicitly, seems clearly intended by Dickey to contrast with the homosexual rape that occurs later.[2]

A fantasy accompanies this act in Ed's mind. The day before in his studio he had photographed a nearly nude model. She had "a peculiar spot, a kind of tan slice, in her left eye" which struck Ed with "strong powers" (p. 21). This goldflecked eye is Ed's fantasy: "It was the heat of another person [Martha] around me, the moving heat, that brought the image up. The girl from the studio threw back her hair and clasped her breast, and in the center of Martha's heaving and expertly working back, the gold eye shone, not with the practicality of sex, so necessary to its survival, but the promise of it that promised other things, another life, deliverance" (29-30). This is the only passage in the novel in which the word "deliverance" occurs. It is Ed's word. It is interrelated with his having intercourse with his wife and with his having an erotic fantasy about a girl's tan-slitted eye that promises "another life." The thought in Ed's mind seems to be that sex, in its nakedness and intimacy and physicality, is one of the few occasions left to civilized man when he can be in touch with his whole being—body and spirit—when he can shed the strait jacket of social conventions that dictate what he must do, where he must go, when, how fast, and how often, and when he can feel himself alive all the way to his fingertips. When sex does this, it is a deliverance. And it is the hope of some such deliverance that attracts Ed to the model and the model's eye. Dickey seems to be suggesting that it is this possibility of deliverance through contact with someone outside oneself that is the fundamental appeal of sex. But is it? The fact that Ed has this fantasy of the model while having intercourse with his wife would seem to belie the actuality of any real deliverance in sex. Presumably, Martha also had once appealed to Ed in such a way. If that is so, then the erotic gleam in the model's eye which so attracts Ed seems to be only an illusory device of human nature, the real purpose of which is simply to induce coupling.

Ed has intercourse with a woman (his wife Martha) and fantasizes during that act of intercourse about a woman (the model). This sexual relationship, whatever its variants, is clearly heterosexual. The matter-of-fact manner in which it is related and the fact that it occurs in Ed and Martha's bedroom, in the city, in the confines of civilized society, indicate that it represents a kind of norm of sexual behavior. Heterosexuality, we may then conclude, at least from Ed's viewpoint, represents normalcy. At the beginning of the trip down the river, while events still are occurring more or less normally, we encounter a symbolic heterosexual image which reflects that normalcy. In the morning after the first night of camping out, when the canoes are again on the Cahulawassee, we read:

> We . . . floated out into a calm broad stretch of a long turn that slid us into a dim underpass of enormous trees, conifers of some kind, spruce or fir. It was dark and heavy in there; the packed greenness seemed to suck the breath out of your lungs. . . .

> We came out among some fields grown up six or seven feet high in grass. A mottled part of the bank slipped into the water, and it took me a minute to realize it was a snake. He went across about twenty feet in front of us, swimming as if crawling, his head high, and came out on the opposite bank without changing his motion at all, a thing with a single spell, a single movement, and no barriers. (93)

The dense tunnel of firs is a vaginal image; the erect moving snake, a phallic image. This heterosexual pair of images symbolizes the still prevailing normalcy of events. However, it is a normalcy that is to be short-lived. Within two hours Ed and Bobby Trippe will be looking fearfully at the raised shotguns of the two mountain men.

Ed is terrified when he and Bobby fall into the hands of the mountain men. The tall, lean man belts Ed tightly to a tree and holds a knife to his neck. The blood trickles down from where the knife touches. Ed recalls his feelings: "I had never felt such brutality and carelessness of touch, or such disregard for another person's body. It was not the steel or the edge of the steel that was frightening; . . . the knife only magnified his unconcern" (98). It is this unconcern that establishes the horrific atmosphere of the whole episode. It is this unconcern that defines the anal intercourse between Bobby and the other mountain man as brutish and ugly. There is no respect of persons here, and the utter absence of such respect is the primary difference between this act of intercourse and the earlier act of intercourse between Ed and Martha. Even if we grant that the attraction between Ed and Martha or between Ed and the model is merely a falsely beguiling inducement to copulate, still it is clear that even the copulation has no dignity and is somehow entirely unbecoming to human beings if it does not include some minimal mutual respect between the persons involved. Between the mountain men and Ed and Bobby there simply is no such respect. But the particular importance of this unconcern in this story is that it is just such unconcern that also characterizes the forces of nature with which Ed and his companions struggle in their trip down the river. Rivers and mountains obviously have no respect for men as individuals. Though there is a figurative sense in which one may regard nature in moral terms (for example, as benign and generous), it is a plain mistake to think that nature is moral in any real sense. And this mistake can easily become fatal for anyone who must deal with the forces of nature in a life-and-death encounter.

When the guitar-strumming Drew Ballinger is shot in the head and the muscular Lewis Medlock becomes helpless with a broken leg and fat Bobby panicks, the responsibility for trying to save the three who still are alive devolves on Ed. One of the main reasons he stands half a chance of succeeding is his realization that the forces he is dealing with are unconcerned and essentially physical and that his response must also be unconcerned and essentially physical—that is, in the most crudely elemental sense of the word, sexual. An example is Ed's climb up the face of the gorge wall. We perceive it as a physical union of himself and the cliff because he describes it in sexual terms. Standing alone on the bottommost ledge, he says he was possessed of "a deep feeling of nakedness and helplessness and intimacy" (137). Then he begins to move upward. "With each shift to a newer and higher position I felt more and more tenderness toward the wall" (139). Slowly, insistently, he mounts the wall. By his own estimates he is a hundred, then a hundred and fifty feet above the river. He finds a crevice and crawls into it to rest. Then he starts climbing again: "I would begin to try to inch upward again, moving with the most intimate motions of my body, motions I had never dared use with Martha, or with any other human woman. Fear and a kind of enormous moon-blazing sexuality lifted me, millimeter by millimeter" (150-51). When, grateful and relieved, he reaches the top of the cliff and safety, he thinks to himself: "I was crawling, but it was no longer necessary to make love to the cliff, to fuck it for an extra inch or two in the moonlight. . . . I could offer it a kick or two, even, and get away with it" (151). This whole episode is sometimes referred to as "fucking the mountain." The vulgarity of the expression is apt. It emphasizes the nature of Ed's intimacy with the cliff. He uses the cliff; and when he is finished, he would be happy to kick it, even as the mountain men would probably have been content to shoot him and Bobby, once they had had their way with them. But Ed's physical fusion with the cliff is also his only means of survival. The sexual nature of his feelings as he climbs the mountain wall underscores his intensely intimate and intensely physical involvement with it, the only sort of involvement that is meaningful in his desperate situation.

When Ed succeeds in reaching the top of the cliff, he finds himself in a position that would allow him to survive without a great deal of risk. He could walk away. Survival would still entail an arduous effort, but it would no longer be a matter of life and death. Still, something in him makes him stay: "I thought about starting the trek out of the woods now, but the back of my mind told me that I had not gone through enough of the right motions yet; if Bobby and Lewis died, I wanted to be able to say to myself that I had done more than just climb up a gorge side and leave them helpless" (156). He stays to help his friends, even though he thereby leaves his own life still hanging in the balance. In the midst of a situation in which he has felt primarily an overriding need to survive at any cost, he suddenly is moral. He stays because he feels it is the right thing for him as a person to do; it is the right way for him to act towards his companions. Under the circumstances, it is a delicate choice. This certainly seems to be one point at which Dickey is concerned to tell us less how crude life elementally is and more how full and meaningful it can be.

Ed stays on the cliff above the river and eventually he kills the mountain man.[3] This event, also presented in a sexual perspective, is of critical importance. In terms of the narrative, it leaves Ed and Lewis and Bobby free to pass on down the river without further threat of being shot at, and in this sense it represents a kind of deliverance for them. It is the climax of Ed's personal experience. It explains fully the intention behind Dickey's use of sexual imagery. It explains the meaning of the title of the novel.

Preliminary to the actual killing, there occurs, so it seems to Ed, what might be termed an instinctual fusion of minds between him and the mountain man, a kind of psychological foreplay one might engage in with an intended victim: "I had thought so long and hard about him [the mountain man] that to this day I still believe I felt, in the moonlight, our minds fuse. It was not that I felt myself turning evil, but that an enormous physical indifference, as vast as the whole abyss of [moon] light at my feet, came to me: an indifference not only to the other man's body scrambling and kicking on the ground with an arrow through it, but also to mine" (154). Ed's thoughts continue with a reflection on the sort of perverse union that would have occurred between himself and this man at their first meeting, had Lewis's arrow not rescued him in time. "If Lewis had not shot his companion, he and I would have made a kind of love, painful and terrifying to me, in some dreadful way pleasurable to him, but we would have been together in the flesh, there on the floor of the woods, and it was strange to think of it" (154). Ed, imagining himself forced to perform fellatio, refers to the act with expressions like "a kind of love" and "together in the flesh." It is as though he discovers, even in an act that for him would obviously have been degrading and repugnant, an orgasmic quality.

Ed chooses a pine tree and arranges a place in it from which he guesses he will be able to kill the mountain man. He thinks to himself: "Being alive in the dark and doing what I was doing was like a powerful drunkenness, because I didn't believe it. There had never been anything in my life remotely like it" (157). Taking a position in the tree, he waits, hoping and not hoping that he has guessed correctly. As if to prove that his mind had indeed fused with that of his enemy, the man appears. Ed takes a bead on him with his bow: "We were closed together, and the feeling of a peculiar kind of intimacy increased, for he was shut within a frame within a frame, all of my making: the peep sight and the alleyway of needles, and I knew then that I had him . . ." (163). However, Ed delays long enough for the man to turn gradually in his direction and, only split-seconds after Ed releases his arrow, to fire his gun.

> What happened next I was not sure about, and still am not. The tree thrummed like an ax had struck it, and the woods, so long quiet around me, were full of unbelievable sound. The next thing I knew there was no tree with me anymore, nor any bow. A limb caught my leg and tried to tear it off me, and I was going down the trunk backwards and upside down with many things touching and hitting upward at me with live weight, like arms. . . .
>
> I tried also to turn in the air so as not to strike on the back of my head, and was beginning to turn, I think, when I hit. Something went through me from behind, and I heard a rip like tearing a bedsheet. Another thing buckled and snapped under me, and I was out of breath on the ground, hurt badly somewhere as the gun went off again, and I could not get to my feet but clawed backward, dragging something. The gun boomed again, then again and again. . . . (163-64)

Ed then sees the man staggering toward him, blood streaking down from his mouth and neck. The arrow, having passed through the front of the neck, dangles down his back.

> I put my head down, and was gone. Where? I went comfortably into the distance, and I had a dim image in my head of myself turning around, disappearing into mist, waving good-bye.
>
> Nothing.
>
> More nothing, another kind, and out of this I looked up, amazed. In front of me a man was down on his hands and knees giving up his blood like a man vomiting in the home of a friend, careful to get his head down or into the toilet bowl. I put my head back and went away again. (165)

Consider the event as Ed experiences it: his mind fuses with the mind of the mountain man; he experiences an excitement like drunkenness; he shoots his arrow at the man and simultaneously there is an explosion; he becomes confused and uncertain about what is happening; he experiences a literal sensation of falling along with breathlessness and sensations of severe pain; he hears the gun explode repeatedly; he sees the man before him, pierced by his arrow and streaming blood; he blacks out, revives, sees the man again, this time closer, bloodier, more helpless; again he blacks out. The event for Ed is orgasmic. It rocks him to the foundation of his physical being. It is a profound experience because it is a matter of survival or death. Moreover, it is a matter whose issue depends entirely on himself. It is in this moment that he proves himself to himself. This is his quintessential moment of deliverance. This event is crucial both in the story as a whole and in Ed's personal experience. The sexual perspective in which it is so emphatically presented merely caps a perspective that has persisted from the very beginning. We know, therefore, that sex is an important theme in this novel. What remains is to discover more precisely *how* sex is important.

Ed himself does not immediately realize the full significance of his experience. For one thing, his situation is too desperate. He is still involved in a struggle for survival. Ahead of him and Lewis and Bobby is one final set of vortiginous rapids, a last terrifying challenge from the river. Thereafter, he must dispose of two bodies, that of the man he killed and that of Drew Ballinger, and devise a story that will protect him and Lewis and Bobby from the hostility of local authorities. All of this is part of a continuing, exhausting effort he must make simply to survive. Reflection and understanding do not occur until after the ragged hole in his side has been cleaned and bandaged, and Lewis's leg has been treated by a doctor, and Bobby has begun to recover from fright.

"And so it ended," Ed tells us, "except in my mind, which changed the events more deeply into what they were, into what they meant to me alone" (233). Time passes. The Cahulawassee becomes smothered in the waters of the new lake that forms behind the dam. In

Ed's mind this happens: "The river and everything I remembered about it became a possession to me, a personal, private possession, as nothing else in my life ever had. Now it ran nowhere but in my head, but there it ran as though immortally. . . . In me it still is, and will be until I die, green, rocky, deep, fast, slow, and beautiful beyond reality" (233-34). On the river Ed had met a double threat of death: one, from the river itself; the other, from the man who stalked him and his companions along its banks. He engaged in a life-and-death struggle and survived. Thus he won deliverance.

The deliverance that Ed won was of a sexual nature. As he gradually realizes this, he recognizes also a mistaken assumption he had had about where he could find self-renewal. He originally regarded the canoe trip as a chance to escape from the banal quality of ordinary city life. Now he knows that life in the outdoors can be every bit as harsh, impersonal, and oppressive as life in the city. He knows that it is no mere change of place or activity that can really renew a man. He recognizes that even the deliverance promised by sexual intercourse at its best is largely illusory, to say nothing of the tame, momentary exhilarations that he and Martha know. When he had thought of the model's eye, he was attracted by the idea of sex that promised "another life," but now "her gold-halved eye had lost its fascination. Its place was in the night river. . . . That's where its magic was for me" (235). What Ed had hoped for from the golden slice in the model's eye, he had discovered in the river. The deliverance that he at one time had thought to find in sex, he did in fact find on the trip down the Cahulawassee. But what exactly did he find? In an interview Dickey has suggested an answer:

> . . . in this country a man can live his whole life without knowing whether he's a coward or not. And I think it's important to know. And what you're supposed to believe, gradually, and to see about Ed Gentry, is that he . . . is really a born killer. He figures it out exactly right as to how to kill this guy, and he does it. He carries it out, and he gets away with it. . . . That's all he needs to know, that he's capable of it. And as you see in the last few pages, it's a quietly transfiguring influence on him.[4]

Indeed Ed learns he is not a coward. He has taken the measure of himself in terms of a world that is violent and indifferent. He has tested himself, even to death's limits, and not been found wanting. He has encountered the world on its most basic terms. He knows where he stands and what he is in relation to the world. There is comfort in such knowledge. However, the meaning of his experience on the river, the nature of his deliverance, goes still deeper. Not only has Ed come to grips with the dark wild forces in the world around him, he also has come to grips with the dark wild forces in himself. Lewis's greeting to Ed the morning after their first night off the river is "Hello, killer" (212). Ed is a killer, not from force of circumstances, but by reason of his response to a powerful impulse within himself. The same situation does not make Bobby a killer. But in Ed it brings to the fore a killer-capability that has always been present. If we think back, even as Ed thinks back, on the nature of his experience, the presence of this formidable power becomes evident.

On the morning after their first night of camping on the riverbank, Ed shoots at a deer and misses. His explanation at the time is that he "psyched out. . . . Something said raise your hand, and before I could do anything about it, I did it" (87). Might not the real reason have been his fear of discovering that he could really kill and, moreover, that he could be elated by it? This is not the sort of admission that a civilized man readily makes. When Ed makes the perilous climb up the cliff, he makes love to the mountain, but when he reaches the top, he wants to kick the mountain. Why? His impulse is as inexplicable in rational terms as it is genuinely felt. When, during the night, he is on top of the cliff waiting for the mountain man, he at one point imagines "the other man's body scrambling and kicking on the ground with an arrow through it," and he feels "an enormous physical indifference." What sort of civilized response is this to such a brutal fantasy? It is no civilized response at all. In retrospect it tells Ed how strong and operative in him are certain forces that exceed the control of his consciousness and reason. When he finally kills the mountain man, it is Ed's own words as narrator that suggest the similarity between that climactic event and sexual orgasm. He recognizes that he is exhilarated by the act of killing.[5] There is a part of his being that is non-rational and prone to violence. There is a part of him that is as turbid and uncontrolled as that part of the Cahulawassee down which he and his friends have passed. There is in him something of the mountain man, too, something lurking darkly in his subconscious that could impel him to the same crude and vicious behavior that he and Bobby were subjected to.[6] And may we not here be led to a deeper understanding of what was suggested earlier as the fundamental appeal of sex, that chance for a person to feel himself alive all the way to his fingertips, to be in some full and real sense himself? In sex it is not just one's conscious rational self that one comes more fully into contact with. It is one's dark, mysterious side as well. Dickey is suggesting, I believe, that the appeal of sex is precisely the possibility, even if rarely realized, of the surrender of reason to a power and a feeling that completely overwhelm it, even if only for a moment. This, potentially, is the nature of deliverance in sex.[7] This is the sexual nature of Ed's deliverance when he kills the mountain man.[8]

When Ed later reflects on all that has happened, he recognizes that dark mysterious part of himself, like an underground river of great depth and power.[9] He realizes that the weekend trip to the rugged north Georgia woods has been a trip into a little known area of himself. Having come to grips with what is really in himself is, in the deepest sense, his deliverance. The opportunity for such deliverance may exist best in a confrontation with nature. But deliverance itself occurs only within each individual.

NOTES

[1] James Dickey, *Deliverance* (New York: Dell, 1970), p. 29. All subsequent references to the novel are to this edition.

[2] The contrast between the two acts of sex is even more sharply focused if one understands that it is anal intercourse that occurs between Ed and Martha. This understanding, however, is not strictly warranted by the text of the novel, though neither is it unwarranted. Ed's image throughout the novel is that of a man with his head on his shoulders, a sort of pole of normalcy. Anal intercourse would appear to be at odds with this general image. On the other hand, part of Dickey's concern in the novel is a fresh consideration of just what *is* normal behavior, and when, and why.

[3] It is an unresolved question whether the man Ed kills is the one he intends to kill. Under the circumstances, he has no opportunity to make preliminary inquiries. For that reason, the meaning of the killing, so far as Ed personally is concerned, is essentially unchanged. The factual doubt about the victim's identity serves only to emphasize further the chilling impersonality of the outdoors as a milieu in which to survive.

[4] William Heyen, ed., "A Conversation with James Dickey," *Southern Review,* 9 (1973), 154-55.

[5] There are other instances, following the slaying, that show this impulse asserting itself in Ed: he thinks about mutilating the corpse of the mountain man (170); he deliberately tempts himself to shoot Bobby with the mountain man's gun (171-72).

[6] It is perhaps in this perspective that the question of Ed's latent homosexuality, if indeed it is a question, should be considered. (Cf. André Bleikasten, "Anatomie d'un Bestseller: A propos de *Deliverance,*" *Recherches Anglaises et Américaines,* 4 [1971], 116-29.) In the episode with the mountain men the homosexuality simply represents the perverse and brutal behavior of which men, in certain circumstances, are capable. But Ed's recognition that he also is capable of perverse and brutal behavior *and* that he is latently homosexual (if he really is and if he recognizes the fact) are not the same thing. If we are meant to understand that Ed does not cultivate his sexual attraction to Lewis because such an attraction is by its very nature perverse and ugly, then we can only conclude that Ed's vision of himself, which in the end seems admirably unclouded and direct, is in this respect singularly myopic. However, the whole matter is insinuated so vaguely in the novel that there seems little point in raising one's hackles about it.

[7] A necessary corollary of this conclusion is that the partner in a sexual relationship functions primarily as a means for an individual to come more fully into contact with himself. In Dickey's terms, then, human sex is not *primarily* an exchange or sharing with another person. It is basically a lonely experience.

[8] Paul Italia ("Love and Lust in James Dickey's *Deliverance*," *Modern Fiction Studies,* 21, No. 2 [1975], 203-213) also stresses the sexual nature of Ed's deliverance when he kills the mountain man. He says that "Gentry's catching sight of his quarry's face turns the scene . . . from rape to love" (209). In piercing with his arrow the throat of the man who had intended to "pierce" Ed's throat with his penis, in killing the man who wanted to kill him, Ed "has shucked off that part of himself that might kill or rape anything that turns its back on him" (210). Ed, according to Italia, is humanized when he destroys another man; he learns to love when he kills. Such an experience does not seem impossible. And its paradoxes are attractive. But is it what happens in the novel? Sex abounds, to be sure, but love—well, what does Italia himself mean by love, love that is the obverse side of rape? Dickey deliberately and discreetly does not discuss the matter.

[9] This dark, powerful force in the human individual is the same force that Rollo May, in his *Love and Will* (New York: Dell, 1969), calls "the daimonic." Both Dickey and May would agree that this force is the substrate of vitality in the human being. But whereas Dickey seems to understand this force as something tending only to make a man hostile and destructive, May understands it as something that can be "either creative or destructive" (121) and which, when directed positively, can make a man constructively dynamic. I do not think Dickey's view springs from cynicism, but it is more limited. And it explains why Ed, at the novel's end, seems a person so little enriched by his new self-knowledge: what he has discovered in himself is an essentially negative force and the most he, as a decent human being, can do with it is keep it in control.

Michael Gessel

SOURCE: "Katherine Anne Porter: The Low Comedy of Sex," in *American Humor: Essays Presented to John C. Gerber,* edited by O. M. Brack, Jr., Arete Publications, 1977, pp. 139-52.

[*In the following essay, Gessel sees Katherine Anne Porter's novel* Ship of Fools *as revealing the delusions of the western world and offering "brief salvation" to its characters through unsentimentalized sex.*]

Katherine Anne Porter has the unpleasant power to involve an audience against its will, and in her writings, as in much of modern literature, it is death to the reader who identifies. For the reader is the butt of the writer, who involves him in order to shake him up. We are likely to find a character with whom we may identify at the outset of a work—perhaps this character is open and charming—but we are likely to suffer discomfort later in the work when our character hangs out his deformities and in his emotional monstrosities we recognize our own.

It is easy to be taken in, for instance, by Herr Freytag's roseate vows and views of love and his absent wife Mary Champagne in *Ship of Fools* and it is almost impossible to see the grim realities of his case emerge, and not resent Porter's having desecrated Freytag's shrine of self-delusion.

I resent Porter, not because I was worried about myself but because I couldn't put my finger on what was wrong with her. Now it's very clear to me that it was simply a case of our mutual ignorance, only the problem was complex because our ignorance is the characteristic ignorance of our modern Western world—hers is the logical low extreme of everything we have been taught. Knowledge has great strength, even when it is only partial knowledge; even when it is false.

So I was caught in a fix, and I didn't know how to cope with it; Porter's writings had truly shaken me, the reader, as the writer intended. I was caught in the same general fix the modern audience is caught in when it comes away from an experience in the modern theater of skeptical empiricism, absurdity, futility, absolute relativity, impotence and despair. We do not leave feeling purged and together, full of a sense of well-being after having relieved our emotional bladders and psychic bowels; no, we are much more likely to stagger out with our metaphorical and metaphysical bladders and bowels aching and grumbling, more full of confusion and doubt than ever.

A similar fate is in store for almost any reader who attends the theater of Porter's fiction. He is shown the Medusa in a cruel mirror, which she holds at such an angle that he may look the Medusa straight in the eye, and thereby become as stony and cool as Porter herself. In any case we are sure to hear her say, This is the truth because it is and it happens. . . . And we are fully aware that she is herself a casualty. Perhaps we come to admire her for having given up seeking the hero who can slay the monster and solve the riddle of the sphinx, for having accepted the grim facts of her condition, the fate which has hardened her heart and toughened her mind. Perhaps we admire her for having faced and accepted "the terrible failure of the life of man in the Western world,"[1] which is not just an accident but a "total consent."[2] It is neither fashionable nor sensible to deny that the world is in a mess. But few of us enjoy having it rubbed in our faces.

"If every thing that went wrong," said William Hazlitt in 1819,

> if every vanity or weakness in another gave us a sensible pang, it would be hard indeed: but as long as the disagreeableness of the consequences of a sudden disaster is kept out of sight by the immediate oddity of the circumstances, and the absurdity or unaccountableness of a foolish action is the most striking thing in it, the ludicrous prevails over the pathetic, and we receive pleasure instead of pain from the farce of life which is

played before us, and which discomposes our gravity as often as it fails to move our anger or our pity![3]

But today we are more likely to receive pain than pleasure from the farce of life which is played before us in modern literature—or if we don't we might be tempted to call it "sentimental comedy." We don't find much to laugh about, many of us, and today serious literature such as *Ship of Fools* (which perhaps could be called a depressing comedy) often works upon us in such a way that every vanity or weakness in a character tends to give us a sensible pang—and it is hard indeed. We who are aware of the oppressive atmosphere of world-wide tension and the constant threat of nuclear holocaust find little to laugh about in the absurd and unaccountable actions of a character such as Captain Thiele of Porter's novel—for though he impresses us as a ludicrous and foolish man, we are forced to see, on the one hand, the true nature of his feelings which at bottom are monstrous and terrifying, and on the other hand, the very real potential for disaster in a world piloted by such men as he.

There is no escape. Read "Magic," read "That Tree," read *Ship of Fools*—escape is an illusion: we uproot ourselves thinking we have left our monstrous past behind us when in fact we have merely displaced it into our future—we think we turn when in fact we only return. And when the grim joke has played itself out perhaps we learn that we can't escape the problems that are truly ours, and the sooner we know what they are the better; and perhaps we also learn that we are fools if we don't run like hell from the problems that are not our own. In any case, this is what Porter has learned.[4]

Absurdities and incongruities and follies, which in another time went into the making of a socially corrective laughing comedy, today serve creations which expose and represent our grim social and personal reality, our sense of futility, our laughter of despair. Humor today is not really a laughing matter so much as it is a just exposure of what is real, however ugly it may be—and in fact Porter says the humor which softens to baseness and pats it on the head is perverse, for it nourishes evil instead of giving it a swift well-placed kick. Roses are sickly sentimental obscenities of a perverted tenderness which pollutes the mind with an image of beauty which all too often causes us to take offense at the dirt and turds which nourish the false bloom; the bloom wilts and becomes a part of the offal which endures, and all perfumes are but ephemeral vapors which cover the real stench. Pure dung does not smell foul, but vigorous and healthy, while the false rose, that damn false rose, betrays the unpolluted chemistry of noses by fouling our smell with illusions. The laughter of release is a false rose which blinds us to the truth in the very act of its release. It is very pleasant to laugh, but it is ugly to cling to laughter, and it is perverse to make laughter and sweetness the object of humor and comedy, for to do so is but to avoid exposures of our grim and continuing

reality. And when it is a choice between laughing and exposing, choose to expose. Be merciless: make laughter expose itself as the hag it flees.

Porter's comments on one of Eudora Welty's short stories is revealing:

> "The Petrified Man" offers a fine clinical study of vulgarity—vulgarity absolute, chemically pure, exposed mercilessly to its final subhuman depths. Dullness, bitterness, rancor, self-pity, baseness of all kinds, can be most interesting material for a story provided these are not also the main elements in the mind of the author. There is nothing in the least vulgar or frustrated in Miss Welty's mind. She has simply an eye and an ear sharp, shrewd, and true as a tuning fork. She has given to this little story all her wit and observation, her blistering humor and her just cruelty; for she has none of that slack tolerance or sentimental tenderness toward symptomatic evils that amounts to criminal collusion between author and character. Her use of this material raises the quite awfully sordid little tale to a level above its natural habitat, and its realism seems almost to have the quality of caricature, as complete realism so often does. Yet, as painters of the grotesque make only detailed reports of actual living types observed more keenly than the average eye is capable of observing, so Miss Welty's little human monsters are not really caricatures at all, but individuals exactly and clearly presented. . . .[5]

This statement shows that the logic which underlies Porter's comic sense—in theory at least—is the logic of "complete realism."

Complete realism—if we may use the phrase before really coming to terms with what Porter means by it—proves to be the logic of her fiction taken as a whole, not merely of her comic sense. For instance: though she has indicated that the problem of the artist is to draw, by a geometry of his own, the circle around relations which really are endless and thereby to create the illusion of truth,[6] the illusion of truth she creates in her novel is an illusion of endless relations. The "Embarkation" section of her novel does not create the illusion of departure so much as it suggests the reality of continuing, with but a change in setting (a little purgatory of Veracruz is exchanged for a little purgatory of the ship); just as the "Harbors" section of her novel does not let the illusion of arriving overshadow reality continuing with its human problems still unresolved. If the reader senses he has completed a number of shorter but similar cycles, which by repetition have revealed themselves to possess a common denominator, now perhaps he sees the same essential thing beginning all over again; and if he were to read the book through again he would see the same thing in its continuous state while it is going through its phases and various changing relations. The reader may or may not be aware that his own journey through the book is a matter of undergoing various changing relations: perhaps this helps him to accept the "realism" of "endless relations" as an observation of what is rather than as merely a philosophical view. Let the "is" and the "happens" interpret themselves; this is the philosophical attitude of the book's realism.

This "realism" is punctuated by the ironical wit so sharply felt in the mottoes which head the three sections. "*Quand partons-nous vers le bonheur*" (when do we set out for happiness?) suggests the feebleness of despair, the continuing frustration of desire and hope, futility; the quotation (Baudelaire) raises all sorts of ambiguities, all of which stem from the same impulse which brings such a question into being and raises it to a position of importance: the "impulse" is confusion and the "importance" stands as an invitation to take the journey man *can* take, the one into hell, rather than living the life of frustration and inertia which is the reality of any modern quest for the Holy Grail; and this, as it is beginning to seem, is the very quest which caused the confusion which raised the question, and seen in this light the good Holy Grail is exposed realistically as the cause of a whole lot of frustration and despair since happiness is an impossible dream. All this is made particularly clear to us in the long second section, "High Seas" whose motto "*Kein Haus, Keine Heimat*" (No house, no home) suggests the unpleasant reality of the voyage, especially coming after the sickly, ennervated, clinging and self-pitying wringing tone in the French words, the Romance language; and the more so coming in a tear-choked gush of song (Brahms) sung in the thick maudlin voice of German nostalgia, which is a sentimentality and an avoiding of present reality—the awaiting of return to a homeland paradise of sweetness and tender hearth-warmth which never existed except in memory's rosy glow preciously protected and lovingly preserved in the sweet pickling-solution of a song such as *Tannenbaum*—and the last section, "The Harbors," which is given a motto which does away with the viability of salvation altogether by way of a quotation from one of salvation's most famous spokesmen, Saint Paul: "For this is no continuing city. . . ." The language, finally, is plain English. The language is flat, the statement is plain, the utterance is unremarkable, the tone is impersonal, and the sense is common realism.

It is easier to get a general impression of Porter's realism than it is to generalize what it is. It is not really pure and honest skepticism, though Porter calls herself a Questioner and pits herself against Answerers; for she answers Answerers with a flat denial of their answers wherever their answers threaten her way of unfrustrating herself. She denies heaven in order to believe absolutely in earth where she finds her only solid ground, and she is fixed in the conviction that the various sacred and hallowed beliefs men cherish have in fact done more to render them feeble and fill them with despair than to give them even much comfort, much less "salvation." Earth to her, here, means carnal and physical matter, plain facts, specific cases—everything that is and happens as perceived by our real physical senses

and experienced in our mind and imagination. Porter's complete realism denies the possibility of an Absolute Reality and thereby she frees herself to live the life of a human being—which is exactly what the life of man in the modern Western world has failed to do.

Or so Porter sees it, having found what works for her as solid ground. And firm in her viable ground, she comprehends modern man with a "complete realism" which can depict frustration and vulgarity for what it really is in living cases and which can see how imagination pollutes a person's life by shaping sacred idols for him to worship as bringers of joy, thus simultaneously robbing himself while projecting various fantasies of terror onto innocent people. In short, Porter comprehends and depicts the distortions, delusions, deceptions, perversions, and monstrosities of mind, imagination, emotion and sex as the realities they are in themselves and in their consequence of "majestic and terrible failure in the life of man" on a Western world *Ship of Fools*. And where does she place the onus of the blame? Not on the evil workings of the universe or its stars and planets, not on the inevitable evil of the world, not on the evils of nations, societies, or families—but on the individual himself, the failure of whose life she sees as unnecessary. Her ship really is populated by fools and Porter is careful to point out that she herself is a passenger on the Vera. These various sublimations, distortions and emotional ugliness and perverse obscenities (such as tenderness and sentimentality in love), must now be seen in their relation to the low comedy of sex.

The "complete realism" must be understood as an interaction and also as a process; it is an interaction between mind and experience in an attempt to explain the logic of what is and what occurs while clearing the field for living the life of a human being, and it is a process of a downward path to the working wisdom which accurately explains and prepares us for the specific cases of experience. A good many of the passengers on the Vera develop explanations—Dr. Schumann, Herr Hutton, Herr Graf, La Condesa, Arne Hansen, Frau Rittersdorf, Jenny and David and others including Porter herself, of course—and these explanations are to varying degrees successful or unsuccessful in preparing their minds to deal with the realities that are truly theirs. Some of these views are more obviously self-delusions than others, take for instance Captain Thiele's, but all of them to some extent make living life much more of a problem than it need be—for all of the views are to some extent fixed, and therefore must come into conflict with the facts of experience which threaten the viewer himself insofar as he is attached to his views and his own self-image. It could also be said that the facts of experience are not to blame; nor are the views and self-images themselves to blame, however false, but rather the individual's attachment to his image of the truth is to blame, his attachment even in the face of grim facts and contradictory cases. His attachment is to blame because it is arrogant, stubborn, vain, self-defeating, stupidly cruel, and smothering.

This is not to denounce any attachment at all, which itself would be vain since most humans cannot help themselves from forming attachments to people, things, ideas, vanities, self-images; it is natural to form attachments. No one denies this. The trouble is that we are not willing to renounce unnatural attachments or to admit that natural attachments can go bad and turn to poison; nor are we willing to view withdrawal from attachment as a natural phenomenon like that of attaching. When old views fail it is always possible to withdraw from them and form new ones which explain facts and cases more realistically. And if our phase II views are not completely realistic there will be a tendency for them to fail and be superceded by phase III views. And so on. Clearly, the process is one of evolving.

In Porter's fiction, the evolution is toward complete realism, and it takes what seems to be a downward direction because all the images of "higher" wisdom fail in her fiction; they cannot stand up to the facts of what is and what happens in specific cases. Let us take, for illustration, Dr. Schumann's wisdom, which is "high," as seen next to La Condesa's "low" views. Her views threaten him, her way of living tempts him, while neither he nor his views threaten hers or her way of living. In fact, Dr. Schumann's views are portrayed in the process of their evolution towards La Condesa's realism.

On the surface, La Condesa seems rather low, corrupt and obscene. She is fallen nobility. She is a political exile being deported from Cuba, escorted by a group of Cuban students representative of the rising bourgeoisie. Symbolically, the reformers indulge and thoroughly enjoy the very "evil" which they are deporting, escorting La Condesa into her island isolation. In fact, she is not evil, corrupt, or obscene, although she obviously enjoys sexual lust and the sensual gratification she finds in drugs. She is not evil, corrupt or obscene because her mind is free from frustration and vulgarity, which is one of the reasons she can enjoy sexual lust. Moreover, she understands Dr. Schumann much better than he understands himself, and she is as frank with him about this understanding as she is about her love of drugs and about the fact that she would enjoy indulging in sexual relations with him. She offers herself to him, but does not get pushy. She likes him and finds him charming and sweet but is not at all fooled by his sweetness and charm and high humane thoughts which she knows as the symptomatic evils which support and protect his inner frustrations and corrupted ideas of sex. He, in fact, is far more corrupt, obscene, and evil than she is, for he sees in her all the sin and temptation in himself—of which she, in fact, is free. She is pure in this regard, and her low comedy of sex is also pure; while finally, Dr. Schumann's love for her not only proves polluted with frustrations, but produces in him a false tenderness for her, false in that it is corrupt, and corrupt in that it prompts him to please her instead of trying to help her overcome her drug lust. If he had injected her with his sex instead of with his syringe she might not have needed his drugs.

La Condesa is the passenger who most closely resembles Porter herself, so far as Porter is reflected in the novel, the stories, and the critical writings. The Spanish-American blood passion and soil is native to her, more so than her homeland, or at least potentially so—one need only read "Maria Concepcion" to feel how deep the roots of this potentiality go—and why else would she have said, as she did in one of her published statements, that in Mexico there was always the possibility of salvation?[7] She saw Hitler in Mexico, and in Mexico Hitler was nothing—a clown, who fooled nobody. The possibility of salvation—not the false salvation which D. H. Lawrence represents to her and which she attacks in her critical essay on his novel of Mexican phallic salvation, attacks him for so thoroughly misunderstanding Mexico, salvation, and himself; and not any other false salvation which she exposes—but the possibility of salvation in "Maria Concepcion," a salvation which accepts the reality of cool, murdering hatred and the liberation of just revenge. It is the total picture of which a low comedy of sex is but a chemically pure part. It is a salvation which might be termed the complete realism of just primitivism.

But no one can be completely "human," as Porter means it, so La Condesa must have erred with some false hope or unrealistic generosity. Her drug habit won't really do. What we are really looking for is some perverse obscenity like her doctor's being in love or some corrupt belief such as the Cuban students' zeal for social reform or Herr Graf's religious enthusiasm. Wherein does La Condesa tolerate the symptomatic evils of others in such a way as to reveal them in herself? How about her tolerant attitude toward Ric and Rac, the incestual twins? Her protective sympathy, when they were caught in their incestual orgy, was not for them, really, but for the sex act, which in their case was a symptomatic evil and not pure frank lust—the symptomatic evil of the little human monsters they are. La Condesa errs the way an author can err, in an error of sympathy which amounts to criminal collusion with the symptomatic evils of Ric and Rac, the little human monsters who lure a cat and lull him drowsy with pleasure in order to drown him. Theirs is a case of vulgarity to expose, to be treated with just cruelty and mercilessly complete realism. La Condesa has to pay the price of her necklace of pearls in order to learn the blindness of her sympathy, her trust. The world has robbed her, stripped her of her class, made her a political exile, and now she still lets Dr. Schumann use her and abuse her by accusing her of using him as a drug source when he in fact needs to be her supplier; and now, after her protective sympathy toward Ric and Rac, they steal her pearls. Her story could well have ended with a statement like the one found at the conclusion of "Theft": "I was right not to be afraid of any thief but myself, who will end by leaving me nothing."[8]

There is a difference between the healthy, frank, pure low comedy of sex and an act of sex which in appearance is not terribly different but which in reality is not human but subhuman and monstrous. Porter views "love" as a creation of the human imagination, a sweet and illusory sublimation of the incestuous urge which she sees as the root of all love, which poisons and pollutes a human attachment with its underlying fear of sex taboo. Poor Jenny and David! And to think that all the voyage long the honeymoon beauty of the newlyweds did bloom—but we know what is in store for them after they disembark, for Herr Graf pointed his forefatherly finger at them in a blessing the bride felt as a curse. And it was.

The connection between the incest taboo and religion and religious magic is made clear by Herr Graf, who before the voyage began, bloomed in the polluted sweetness of sex-sublimation which he named God's own power calling him to heal by touch—but the incestuous pollution, the thorn of sex taboo is all that endures of his salvation, and with it he smothers and poisons his nephew Johann. Moreover Porter categorically denies any god other than the man-made ones and any love other than the illusion of transcendence which comes from sex-sublimation. She mercilessly exposes the frustration and vulgarity to its subhuman depths with all the just cruelty of a surgeon, and analyzes the symptoms of failure by tracing them back to their causes, rooted in early childhood.

There is little doubt that Porter finds sex-frustration and incest neurosis to be the roots of the world's failure (which she sees as a sum or multiplication of all individuals' failures), its feebleness and impotence to cope with fate, its despair, dullness, bitterness, rancor, all its basenesses, all its delusions, anxieties, paranoias, and delusions of grandeur, its wars and its marital strife and hatred and angry rages and oppressive tensions and hideous emotional monstrosities and stubborn blindness—in short, its majestic and terrible failure to live, in each of its men, a more really human life instead of trying to live divinely but managing to behave with monstrous vulgarity, like fools.

Porter has a version of this kind of vulgarity based on sexual frustration in "The Martyr." But her position is made even clearer by an observation on Lawrence:

> I would not object . . . to D. H. Lawrence's obscenity if it were really that. I object to his misuse and perversion of obscenity, his wrong headed denial of its true nature and meaning. Instead of writing straight, healthy obscenity, he makes it sickly sentimental, embarrassingly so, and I find that obscene sentimentality is as hard to bear as any other kind. I object to this pious attempt to purify and canonize obscenity, to castrate the Roaring Boy, to take the low comedy out of sex.[9]

I'm going to give you a bit of secret knowledge. When Porter was a little girl playing with the sand while the surf roared in, and it was twilight with the sky pale blue and only a few stars could be seen, one being Venus actually, large enough in the deepening sky that you could see it was like a tiny half moon and by the tilt of the little hemisphere of reflected sunlight, you knew just where the sun was on the other side of the earth but Callie was too little to know this or to know that the surf was caused by the pull of the moon and she was too wrapped up in making lovely sand castles to care about the surf or Venus or the sun and moon—and the bit of secret knowledge is, she made several very charming sand castles and then she knocked them down because their beauty was sickly sentimental romanticizing.

This little bit of secret knowledge is true but not real—that is, it has no foundation in biographical facts, and it is a picture which sentimentalizes the reality of Katherine Anne Porter in her fiction. The sun, moon, sky, surf, sand, and Venus are true and real—the isolated little girl kicking down sand castles is a sentimentalization of Porter as an adult. As a child named Miranda in her fiction she is very dreamy, full of romantic ideas; in love with the True but Not Real such as represented by Amy (the family myth of romantic beauty who lived in love with the True but died in the sickbed of the Real—she is Miranda's aunt, the father's sister), the attitudes of the father's side of the family (only the beautiful is true, one never admits an ugly fact, one never acknowledges that a feminine face on the father's side of the family may be ugly or her body fat), the rosy glowing past which the present can never quite equal, and a host of other True but Not Reals such as God, Love, and Immortality. The reality of Porter in her fiction is one of an exacting vengeance against family for its numerous ways of betraying and smothering the individual in love and hatred.

Everywhere you look in her fiction she is becoming the dark mirror image of the True but Not Real, the false paradise planted in the formative years, a preparation one can never really undo completely or run away from. It's futile to run: "But I've had a good run for my money—a free field in the things that matter: the will to be an artist and to live as a human being."[10] She speaks these words less than two months before her 72nd birthday, and these words bespeak the strength of her integrity. Her *Ship of Fools* has just been published, and in it she has at last created a *magnum opus*-sized dark mirror image of the True but Not Real which she finds in the "family" life of the man in the Western world. She's had a good run for her money indeed, and its ironic triumph is a perfection of opposition; it does not rise above or escape, nor does it obliterate the false truth of dawn with the complete reality of deep dusk. It denies. It denies in the following manner: Miranda was given the picture of True Love from which real sex was forbidden; Porter returns with a complete realism of sex which forbids any love at all. For love, at bottom, is frustrated sex. Therefore, to live as a human being, deny love, avoid all smothering attachments in the name of love. Don't keep repeating that old mortal family suffocation. Keep a free field for the things that matter: the will to deny family smothering by tracing its logic in art (and thereby you prove the validity of your denial), and the will to deny smothering love by living your life as if it were a low comedy of sex.

It is as if her father betrayed her, just as Miranda's father did. Betrayed Miranda's mother, too, for that matter—fell eternally in love with Amy, next to whom Miranda's mother seemed but a hardened whore, what with Amy like a Dresden-china doll come to life in a voluptuous peony bloom of sexy innocence and Miranda's mother dressed in black and wearing a red rose in her hair and a grim look on her face like the look of a Spanish prostitute, an early model of the Spanish dancers on the *Ship of Fools*. Daddy made whores of 'em all, Amy too—after all, wasn't it Miranda's father, wasn't it Harry himself who took a pot shot at Amy's hotshot lover Raymond? Wasn't it Harry drove Raymond away, made Amy marry that fat sweaty drunk friend of Harry's named Gabriel (so to speak), and in a sense caused Amy's death? Hateful father!

The whole thing happens again in "Maria Concepcion," the first story Porter published. Harry now is Juan Villegas, and he marries Miranda's mother in the form of Maria Concepcion, but runs away with Amy in the form of that hatefully blossom-blemished Maria Rosa (*Maria* is a name which means "bitter"); and Miranda's mother now is Maria Concepcion betrayed and exacting a cool, grim justice of revenge by killing her rival, taking her rival's child, squashing her husband (Miranda's father and, for the most part, all men in the sexual-marital role), and finding serene happy tranquillity in the solitude of fulfilling isolation.

Many of Porter's stories deal with the foolish involvement of a character with others' problems, and several deal with the truth that we do not run from our own. Dignity, then, which manifests itself in her "free field in the things that matter: the will to be an artist and to live as a human being," is really a product of separating herself from the problems of others, from people or noble causes, from all forms of commitment and attachment which always cause trouble and usually much more trouble than they are worth, due as much as anything else to the various individuals' self-delusions and pre-conceptions which lead one into danger—trusting others, for instance. What it really boils down to is that any emotional attachment, any attachment of the heart or of the imagination is perilous, deceitful, wearing, and withal destructive to the self, the all important terribly fragile self which values its own dignity above all else and which raises this value (or rather inflates it) to the level of a principle which might be named complete realism. Thus she has managed pretty much to harden her heart which was perhaps particularly fragile prey, to rectify her vision of reality lest she fall into a dead-end belief, and to train her emotions away from smothering ties and sentimental attachments which are incestual obscenities in disguise; physical coupling is all she wants of love as anything more might court the danger of total surrender of self and catastrophic damage to dignity.

Now, since attachments are so threatening, and belief, creed, or other creations of the human imagination support, urge and enforce an unhealthy bondage to an unhealthy connection, they ought to be attacked in the most effective way possible. Thus, emotions of defense are allowable for self-preservation on the streets of one's personal concrete jungle in life, and also allowable are the illusions of truth which justify one's flight back into the "free field in the things that matter." Satire (justly cruel), grim comedy, bristling humor, and sharply accurate (according to *her* system of illusions) vituperative bursts of a burp-gun anger of words are excellent weapons against those who pervert the low comedy of sex with obscene ideas and sentiments of love.

So it is here, as we can see, that Porter emerges most clearly as clown, as fool, as comic writer. The purest form of love is, in her comic sense, a good honest lusty fuck, whose attachment is real because it is physical, chemical, and hormonal, and honest only if it is not binding beyond the orgasm. The love attachments which the world normally considers to be on a higher plane are seen, in Porter's comic exposures, as displaying various degrees of vulgarity and varying degrees of perverted obscenity (such as tenderness and special attentions).

For this reason the sanest, realest most fulfilling moments in the *Ship of Fools* are the ones which come in a cluster of sexual encounters nearing the end of the book. The Baumgartners have good sex and their anxiety-jangled son Hans experiences a much needed release from his parents' tensions for at least one night's sleep. Or Johann, the nephew of the obscene healer Herr Graf, wakes the morning after his good sex "warm and eased all over; he stretched and yawned and rolled like a cat, making luxurious noises in his throat." The Huttons' feelings are freshened and purified by a good bout in bed. The newlyweds are the least sexually frustrated, and the most detached from entanglements in the ship's panorama of follies—but they are just in the rosy phase of the bondage which smothers. Herr Graf drowns them too, symbolically, with a touch of his father-figure finger of the power of father-figure god poisoning sex with a curse and a taboo. In the cases of the Baumgartners and the Huttons, the brief salvation through the low comedy of sex is followed by returns to the old stale incestuous smothering. And Johann allows himself to be drowned by his uncle again.

Some court jesters no doubt stood on their heads to amuse the king and court—Porter, insofar as love and sex go, is a court jester who turns the world upside down and makes it stand on its head; or rather, the world already is standing on its head, and Porter sets herself upright and walks on her feet in order to live as a human being. She finds that most of her problems come through trying to live according to the illusions, which make her stand on her head, but when she finally admits that the headstand is not a good position for intercourse or anything else but headstanding, she simply uprights herself and gets a good run for her money, however much of a whoring fool she may appear to the world in her low comedy of sex.

Herein her comedy is true comic and it is classic, for the most memorable fools are the wise, sane ones who ironically point up the folly of their insane kings and courts.

NOTES

[1] Katherine Anne Porter, *The Collected Essays and Occasional Writings* (New York: Delacorte, 1970), p. 457.

[2] James Ruoff and Del Smith, "Katherine Anne Porter on *Ship of Fools,*" *College English,* 24 (February, 1963): 397.

[3] William Hazlitt, *Lectures on the English Comic Writers,* "Introductory—On Wit and Humour," *Complete Works,* ed. P. P. Howe (London: Dent, 1931), 6:5.

[4] See the opening passage of "Holiday," Katherine Anne Porter, *The Collected Stories* (New York: Harcourt, Brace & World, 1965), p. 407.

[5] "Eudora Welty and *A Curtain of Green,*" in *Collected Essays,* p. 289.

[6] This is a passage from Henry James' Preface to *Roderick Hudson* discussed by Porter in "The Days Before"; *Collected Essays,* pp. 247-48.

[7] Ruoff and Smith, p. 397.

[8] *Collected Stories,* p. 65.

[9] "A Wreath for the Gamekeeper," in *Collected Essays,* p. 20.

[10] Maurice Dolbier, "I've Had a Good Run For My Money," *New York Herald-Tribune Books,* 1 April 1962, pp. 3, 11, quoted by George Hendrick in *Katherine Anne Porter* (New York: Twayne, 1965), p. 120.

Igor Webb

SOURCE: "Marriage and Sex in the Novels of Ford Madox Ford," in *Modern Fiction Studies,* Vol. 23, No. 4, Winter, 1977-78, pp. 586-92.

[*In the following essay, Webb observes the pessimistic attitude toward a "search for personal satisfaction through sexual relations" portrayed by Ford in his fiction.*]

"Ford's best novels," according to Kenneth Rexroth, "are concerned with the struggle to achieve, and the tragic failure of, sacramental marriage."[1] Marriage as a sacrament, as an especial sexual relation dignified by custom, law, and religion intrigues Ford; but while he is attracted by the vision of a sanctioned sexual happiness fully in harmony with social tradition, he is equally, if not more, attracted by the kinds of extravagant relationships dramatized in the troubadour lyrics he loved and in the accounts of the Courts of Love. His stories of wordly men and women contain within them the wilder passions of troubadour romance.[2] Set against Provençal sagas such as the story of Peire Vidal, the quotidian orderliness of marriage appears an unfitting accompaniment to passion; and it is, consequently, not surprising to find that in Ford's novels the love relationship occurs invariably outside marriage, while the marital relationship is experienced as destructive and deathly.

Love and hate, vitality and death—these are the antitheses of Ford's sexual dialectic. Like the troubadours, Ford holds in balance two contradictory ideas: that since love is the most ennobling moral experience, salvation, for a man, depends on his relation with "a good woman"; but, conversely, that women are vicious and that to love is to suffer. In this regard marriage assumes its central place in Ford's work—for marriage represents at once the effort to realize, one might say, to harness the possibilities of love, to make a stable social place for the greatest passions; and the debasement of love by money or "utility" or, most importantly, by what Ford sees as the inherent possessiveness and viciousness of women. Each of his major novels is concerned, then, not exactly with the struggle to achieve sacramental marriage but with the hero's search for love, a search Ford understands, very much in the terms of the troubadour heresy, as involving chiefly a choice between adultery and marriage, constructive and destructive sexuality, mistress and wife.[3]

A particularly illuminating example of such a situation of choice occurs in Ford's novel *A Call* (1910). The hero of *A Call,* Robert Grimshaw, is in love with two women: Katya Lascarides and Pauline Lucas. For him Katya represents vigor, action, companionship; Pauline "tenderness, fidelity, pretty grace, quaintness, and, above all, worship."[4] As Grimshaw tells Katya's sister Ellida, he wants them both:

> "I suppose what I really want is both Katya and Pauline. That sort of thing is probably in our blood—yours and mine [they are cousins]—and no doubt in the great days of our race I should have had them both, but I've sacrificed physical possession of one of them to the amenities of a civilization that's pleasant enough, and that's taken thousands of years to bring together." (*AC,* p. 34)

Grimshaw's weary and slightly irritated complaints about the "amenities of a civilization . . . that's taken thousands of years to bring together" imply a yearning for something grander than marriage, more akin to the (one assumes) polygamous practice of the "great days" of his race. But as the novel develops Grimshaw's talk of "physical possession," and his difficulty in choosing between two women, turns into a distaste for the whole business of sexual relations. He appears no longer to want either woman; if only God, he thinks,

> could achieve the impossible, could undo what had been done, could let him watch over Pauline, which was the extent of possession of her that he thought he desired, and wait for Katya, which was also, perhaps, all he had desired to do. (*AC*, p. 284)

What appeared initially as Grimshaw's inability to choose between two women, or his desire for both, emerges as an inability to pursue full sexual relations.[5] Grimshaw disposes of Pauline by marrying her off to his alter-ego Dudley Leicester; but Katya proves more intractable and in the end Grimshaw agrees wearily to marry her.

This is an astonishing turn of events in a Fordian novel, for Ford believes Grimshaw has fallen to the wrong woman. In an epilogue to *A Call,* addressed to "My Dear" (Violet Hunt), he writes:

> It is perfectly true as you complain of me that I have not made it plain with whom Mr. Robert Grimshaw was really in love, or that when he resigned himself to the clutches of Katya Lascarides, whom personally I extremely dislike, an amiable but inwardly conceited fool was, pathetically or even tragically, reaping the harvest of his folly. (*AC*, p. 301)

Ford here pictures Katya as destructive, a woman in whose "clutches" Grimshaw reaps the harvest of his folly. Yet Ford's characterization of Grimshaw suggests nothing short of total approbation. Certainly Ford's narrative voice nowhere slips into such an equivocal tone that we might be led to believe he views Grimshaw as a fool. Moreover Pauline, whom Ford in his epilogue asks us to value more highly than Katya, appears on the stage of the novel as a woman whose virtues—fidelity, pretty grace, and worship—command no special attention. She is portrayed as a woman lacking character and vitality, as a nurse whose banality renders her sexually "safe."[6]

Katya, in contrast, represents for Grimshaw (and for us) vigor, life, and companionship. She is sexually vital. She seems the only person in the novel capable of direct, forceful action, a woman gifted with a kind of magic potency. By profession a physical therapist, she performs in the novel two miraculous cures, one of Ellida's daughter Kitty, whose dumbness has baffled the experts, and the other of the stricken Dudley Leicester. Grimshaw's rejection of Pauline, or perhaps more accurately Katya's triumph over her, appears inevitable and completely convincing. In this respect the plot asserts the claims of action over passivity, life over death.

Ford's dislike for Katya exposes a serious ambiguity in his view of destructive and constructive sexuality. What Ford here styles constructive seems no more than a self-

effacing adoration; as Grimshaw says: "Katya would give me companionship; but wouldn't Pauline give me worship?" (*AC*, p. 15). On the other hand, what Ford believes to be destructive is vital and potent; Katya can be seen as insidious only insofar as she threatens Grimshaw's depleted manhood.

In Ford's novels after *A Call,* especially in *The Good Soldier* and *Parade's End,* sexual relations are presented no longer as meaningful in themselves but as an aspect of the broader cultural crisis of English society in the years between 1910 and 1930. Nonetheless, the themes of *A Call* continue to obsess Ford and the patterns of sexual choice of the earlier novel reappear in the later ones. In *The Good Soldier* Ashburnham must choose between his avaricious wife, Leonora, and the innocent Nancy. In *Parade's End* Christopher Tietjens must choose between his wife, Sylvia, who is characterized as La Belle Dame Sans Merci and whose love Ford labels "efficiency in killing," and his mistress, Valentine Wannop, whose love Ford calls "constructive desire."[7]

At the same time we find in these later novels a new depth of sexual observation. On the one hand, the differences between wife and mistress are detailed more sharply than before; and, indeed, Ford establishes a pattern of mythical allusion to clarify his distinction, identifying the wife with Venus and the mistress with Diana. On the other hand, these novels transcend such elusive and rigid distinctions, stressing complicating traits in Ford's feminine types, especially the "chastity" of his wives and the viciousness of his mistresses. In this way a composite of Ford's picture of Woman emerges.

In their roles as Venus, Ford's women display what John Dowell calls "the sex instinct that makes women be intolerably cruel to the beloved person."[8] They express their passion in a vindictive and violent torturing of the male. As Diana, Ford's women are, in contrast, wholesome, "clean-run," and chaste. Sylvia Tietjens is Ford's clearest example of a woman associated with the cruelty of Venus. In *Some Do Not* Father Consett specifically identifies her with Astarte; in *No More Parades* Major Perowne says to her: "There's a picture that my mother's got, by Burne-Jones . . . A cruel-looking woman with a distant smile . . . some vampire . . . La Belle Dame Sans Merci. That's what you're like'" (*PE*, p. 386, Ford's ellipses). Yet Sylvia is not wholly vampire. Indeed her son Michael says *she* is Diana, and we observe in Sylvia, as in so many of Ford's women, an almost fanatical interest in physical fitness, cleanliness, and chastity:

> Her personal chastity she now cherished much as she cherished her personal cleanliness and persevered in her Swedish exercises after her baths before an open window, her rides afterward, and her long nights of dancing. (*PE*, p. 149)

Valentine Wannop, Sylvia's opposite, epitomizes the Diana-like woman. She is an athlete by training and profession, chaste, and plain: "No one had ever tried to seduce her. That was certainly because she was so clean-run" (*PE*, p. 219). But Valentine can be identified with Venus as well. Although prior to her putative seduction she is neither cruel nor selfish, once she becomes Tietjens' mistress she begins to badger him by insisting increasingly on material pleasures. Her aversion to Tietjens' extravagant altruism surfaces early in the tetralogy: "It was demoralizing for a weak little man like Vincent [Macmaster] to have a friend with an ever-open purse beside him. Tietjens ought not to have been princely; it was a defect, a quality she did not personally admire in him" (*PE*, p. 244). When Christopher makes his one appearance in *The Last Post*, weary from travel and the mental shock of having discovered Groby Great Tree had been cut down, Valentine lashes into him for not being a responsible father:

> "You left the prints for Lady Robinson in a jar you gave the Hudnut dealer. How could you? Oh, how could you? How are we going to feed and clothe the child if you do such things?"
>
> He lifted his bicycle wearily around. You could see he was dreadfully weary, the poor devil. Mark almost said:
>
> "Let him off, the poor devil's worn out!"
>
> Heavily, like a dejected bulldog, Christopher made for the gate. As he went up the green path beyond the hedge, Valentine began to sob.
>
> "How are we to live? How are we to live?" (*PE*, p. 835)

Significantly, Sylvia calls her "a provincial miniature of herself, Sylvia Tietjens" (*PE*, p. 166).

In *The Good Soldier* Leonora is portrayed as an avaricious shrew, but at the same time as one of a family of girls who were "so clean-run that," as Dowell tells us, "in a faint sort of way, Edward seems to have regarded them rather as boys than girls" (*TGS*, p. 139)—a description that brings Diana to mind, not Venus. Leonora's opposite, Nancy, undergoes a transformation from innocence to cruelty more dramatic than Valentine's. Prior to the introduction of possible sexual relations, Nancy admires and loves Edward. She views him, grandiloquently, as a cross between Lohengrin and the Chevalier Bayard (*TGS*, p. 195). Her innocence and her adoration of Edward render her sexually safe; as Dowell says, "She didn't in the least know what it meant—to belong to a man" (*TGS*, p. 209). In many ways, Nancy seems a finer version of Pauline Lucas. Both women are boringly sweet, submissive, reticent angels. Both are pitted against more mature, more passionate women whose intelligence and resourcefulness they cannot approximate. But most significantly, both women are as "destructive" as their rivals. Consider the following description of Pauline entering Dudley Leicester's room:

> Pauline was closing the door after her silent entry.

> It was a long, dusky slice of the rear of the house, and he watched her approach, wide-eyed and panic stricken, as if she held an animal-trainer's whip. The little smile was above her lips when she stood over his huddled figure. (*AC*, p. 136)

Similarly, Nancy's pleasant triviality is sharpened by the sole active agent in her character—her viciousness. Dowell writes:

> What would Nancy have made of Edward if she had succeeded in living with him; what would Edward have made of her? For there was about Nancy a touch of cruelty—a touch of definite actual cruelty that made her desire to see people suffer. Yes, she desired to see Edward suffer. And, by God, she gave him hell. (*TGS*, pp. 205-206)

Nancy gives him hell—but not alone; Edward suffers at the hands of both Nancy *and* Leonora, the two women, joining together, as Dowell says, "to do execution, for the sake of humanity, upon the body of a man who was at their disposal" (*TGS*, p. 209).

How can we account for this apparent union of opposites? One answer lies in the remarkably similar sexual biographies that Ford outlines for most of his women, biographies whose central feature is a fear of sex. This is clear in the cases of Nancy, Leonora, Valentine, and Sylvia. All four enter the mature world totally ignorant of sex, and for all of them their first knowledge of sex is violent and brutal; it warps each of their personalities. Sylvia is raped by Drake; the innocent Nancy is raped in imagination as a result of Leonora's insistence that she sleep with Edward; Leonora is unaware of how babies are made until years after her marriage, and she seems to learn about sexual relations through Edward's affairs with other women; Valentine's full awareness of sex comes through Edith Ethel's virulent denunciations of Macmaster for making her pregnant and her demand that Valentine tell her how to abort her child. As a result of these early experiences all four recoil from sex: after her break with Tietjens, Sylvia resolves never to have a man again and becomes first a nun and then a devotee of chastity and athletics; Nancy goes mad; Leonora retreats into puritanical Catholicism and family finance; Valentine also substitutes chastity and athletics for sex. At one with their recoil from sex, however, is their natural desire for intercourse. Thus Sylvia quits her convent to pursue Tietjens at the front; Leonora hopes her financial wizardry will bring Edward back home and is, on occasion, "within a hair" of yielding to her passion for him (*TGS*, p. 157); Valentine waits hopefully for Tietjens to end the sexual innocence of their adultery.

Tietjens and Edward do not respond to Sylvia and Leonora, and out of the contraries of their coldness and their wives' persistence, Ford fashions his final statement about the possibilities of love in marriage. Sylvia's and Leonora's reaction to their husbands' neglect is complex. First, after years of abstinence, they react in a normal hunger for sexual satisfaction. In part their frustration expresses itself in an attack on their men's insistence on "keeping mum," their refusal to engage in emotional interchange. In *Some Do Not,* where Sylvia is at her most sympathetic, she denounces Tietjens for his taciturnity:

> "[If] you had once in our lives said to me: 'You whore! You bitch! You killed my mother. May you rot in hell for it . . . If you'd only said something like it . . . about the child! About Perowne! You might have done something to bring us together!" (*PE*, p. 172)

This is not only Sylvia speaking, but the whole galaxy of Ford's "destructive" women. If we look back to the first novel of Ford's maturity, *The Benefactor* (1905), we find the following attack by Mrs. Gregory Moffat against her husband:

> "No, you don't complain, of course. You never do. That's just what *I* complain of. How do I know what you're thinking of? How can I tell? It's like living with—with--" as her eyes roamed round the room her husband regarded her with amused admiration and affection--" with a blotting pad."[9]

Since "keeping mum," not complaining, is not only the central credo of what Ford calls "the tradition" but the most visible manifestation of emotional repression in Ford's books, Sylvia's and Mrs. Moffat's attacks are, in effect, incensed complaints on the part of Ford's women against his men. The women cry out for emotional contact and often go to great lengths to get it; the men, unable to confront their emotional selves, refuse to acknowledge their wives' attention-seeking extravagances and thereby stir their wives to ever more fantastic behavior. Consequently, the distance between frustration and vengeance becomes drastically foreshortened; the sex-starved wife merges imperceptibly into the Fury, La Belle Dame Sans Merci, Astarte; the women become, like Diana, hunters; the men, like the troubadour Peire Vidal, become betrayed, hunted courtly lovers.

Nancy and Valentine, initially, do not strictly correspond to this pattern. Their primary appeal for Edward and Christopher is their relative quiescence and innocence: at first glance both women, like Clara Brede of *The Benefactor* and Pauline Lucas of *A Call,* appear undemanding, comforting, perhaps even sexless. Both men gravitate towards them out of a courtly Platonic impulse. But after their relations turn sexual, both Nancy and Valentine become, like Leonora and Sylvia, cruel and vindictive, and both men relapse into their roles as hunted courtly lovers.

This stalemate announces the end of Ford's pilgrimage in the land of courtly romance. Rexroth argues that Ford was intent on a different kind of exploration, "the struggle to achieve . . . sacramental marriage." But it seems to me Ford believed from the outset that in

woman was to be found both man's salvation and his doom. His obsession with this contradictory idea sent him on his long search for an innocent, "clean-run," constructive woman, a woman with whom some one of his unengaging heroes would, at last, find true love. But in novel after novel Ford's heroes discover that even worshipful constructive heroines demand a full sexual life and a lasting personal commitment—a demand that seems in each novel to expose the inadequacy of Ford's heroes and to rouse a kind of bitter disenchantment in Ford himself.[10] Adultery remains attractive in the novels only during the period of innocent, awe-struck courtship; afterwards the distinction between marriage and adultery, wife and mistress vanishes and we discover yet again the anguished confrontation between a weak hero, unequal to the demands of the woman he loves, and a frustrated wife/mistress whose frustration brings her to act as a soul-destroying fury. The tragedy of Ford's novels thus extends beyond the failure of marriage to a more devastating failure—what Ford sees as the necessarily disastrous conclusion of any search for personal satisfaction through sexual relations.

NOTES

[1] Ford Madox Ford, *Buckshee,* with introductions by Robert Lowell and Kenneth Rexroth (Cambridge, MA: Pym-Randall Press, n.d.), pp. xix-xx.

[2] See Caroline Gordon, *A Good Soldier: A Key to the Novels of Ford Madox Ford* (Davis: University of California Library, 1963) and James Trammel Cox, "Ford's 'Passion for Provence,'" *ELH,* 28 (December, 1961), 383-398.

[3] In his *Provence* (Philadelphia, PA: J. B. Lippincott, 1935), p. 53, Ford writes of himself as a young man: "I had the conviction for all the world like that of Boccaccio or the Courts of Love—that husbands were ignoble beings when they were not villainous. Their function was, in the Mews beyond the hundred foot wall, to throw buckets of water over the cab wheels while their ladies in white satin trains handed chalices to Troubadours in black velveteen . . . And then to be condemned by the Courts of Love and for ever stink in memory." Ford's novels alter this youthful picture by telling the story from the point of view of a husband who, paradoxically, sees himself as a courtly lover.

[4] Ford Madox Ford, *A Call* (London: Chatto and Windus, 1910), p. 14. Ford published this novel under his original name, "Hueffer." Further references to it are found in the text.

[5] The sexual aspect of Ford's novels prior to *The Good Soldier* are best discussed in Thomas C. Moser, "Towards *The Good Soldier:* Discovery of a Sexual Theme," *Daedalus,* 92 (Spring, 1963), 312-325, and Carol Ohmann, *Ford Madox Ford: From Apprentice to Craftsman* (Middletown, CT: Wesleyan University Press, 1964).

[6] Ohmann, p. 59.

[7] Ford Madox Ford, *Parade's End* (New York: Knopf, 1961), p. 128. Further references are found in the text.

[8] Ford Madox Ford, *The Bodley Head Ford Madox Ford,* Vol. 1: *The Good Soldier, Selected Memories, Poems,* ed. Graham Greene (London: Bodley Head, 1962), 210. Further references are found in the text.

[9] Ford Madox Ford, *The Benefactor* (London: Brown, Langham and Co., 1905), p. 129. This novel was first published under the name "Hueffer."

[10] In *The Other Victorians* (New York: Bantam Books, 1967), p. 32, Steven Marcus quotes the following from Dr. William Acton: "As a general rule, the modest woman seldom desires any sexual gratification for herself. She submits to her husband, but only to please him; and, but for the desire of maternity, would far rather be relieved from his attentions. No nervous or feeble young man need, therefore, be deterred from marriage by any exaggerated notions of the duties required of him. The married woman has no wish to be treated on the footing of a mistress." Acton's view may no longer have prevailed in Ford's late-Victorian world; but the fear Acton expresses of the sexual demands of women is precisely the fear we find in Ford's novels. And, like Acton, Ford's heroes seem to expect that their wives will behave modestly. How much of their bitterness can we trace to the discovery that women as well as men demand sexual gratification?

C. L. Sonnichsen

SOURCE: "Sex on the Lone Prairee," in *Western American Literature,* Vol. XIII, No. 1 Spring, 1978, pp. 15-33.

[In the following essay, Sonnichsen presents an overview of sex in novels of the American West.]

Western fiction has traditionally been clean. Where the coyotes howl and the wind blows free was never a place for promiscuous sex, kinky sex, or perversion. Since the early sixties, however, all this has changed. Western novelists have not gone as far out on the pornographic limb as some of their counterparts in the East and in California, but they have done their best and are still doing it in the late seventies, although there are signs that the urge to show all and tell all is slowing down—in the Great Open Spaces as well as nationally.

Sex has always been a commodity and sometimes a literary commodity, and its appearance in works of fiction has provoked intermittent controversy for at least a century. It is only in recent times, however, that it has been put into a book like chile or oregano into a *sopa,* and with just about as much emotional involvement. This cold, commercial use of sex began even before the courts decided that *Lady Chatterley's Lover* was not obscene and might be fruitfully persued by precocious babes in arms. It achieved status with *Portnoy's Complaint,* which recognized masturbation as a normal adolescent activity, like brushing one's teeth. The result in American fiction is that adultery is what everyone is living in and rape is a spectator sport, like boxing or basketball.

We who live west of the Mississippi are not surprised that such things exist in the blasé East or among the porno sheets and underground newspapers of Los Angeles, but who would look for them in Texas or Arizona or Montana? There can be no doubt, however, that Santa Fe and San Antonio are following New York and Philadelphia in this respect, though without much hope of catching up. Larry McMurtry and a sedulous company of younger novelists have gone just about as far as they can in the pursuit of "realism," and lovely ladies from Austin, Texas, and Tucson, Arizona, are tiptoeing into what used to be forbidden territory—and are doing it for money. Westerns, gothics, murder mysteries, anti-establishment blasts, rural epics, family sagas—whatever the category, the doors are open and the obscure corners of human sexuality are on view. An ordinary unsophisticated reader (a few still exist) who picks up a modern novel about the American West feels like Kipling's color sergeant at the hanging of Danny Deever: "I'm dreadin' what I've got to watch."

As a result, people with a respect for Literature (with a capital "L")—and some of them do indeed survive—are thrown into convulsions by the books that come to hand. The editor of a book-review department in a Southwestern daily newspaper, a Southern Lady from Dallas, sent me a copy of David Helton's *King Jude* (1969) with this comment: "I don't want *any* review of this loathsome book. I give to you for your Texas collection."

Perhaps it is good for Southern Ladies to be jolted out of their complacency by Mr. Helton's portrait of a brawling singer of "down-home music" with "king-size sexual prowess." Perhaps not. Whether this opening of doors is good or bad will have to be decided by posterity. The point is that the doors are open in Western fiction, as elsewhere, and the way it has happened can be noted and described. A few preliminary points must be made, however, before the matter can be intelligently discussed.

First of all, it should be noted that the revolution of the sixties and seventies was not just the result of a number of court decisions recognizing the freedom of the press. It followed the disintegration of a once-powerful set of taboos. The whole structure of the unmentionable, the unnamable and the unthinkable has crumbled, and the sewage of centuries appears to be assaulting our ears, noses and imaginations. The sewage is of our own creation, of course. Nothing is unclean unless we agree that it is. If most of us believed that it was clean and permitted, it would be clean and permitted. Southern Ladies and their equivalents forget that it is all in our minds.

Two basic human activities cause most of the trouble—elimination and copulation. The simple, sturdy monosyllables by which our ancestors referred to them became indecent as "civilization" progressed and they were replaced in polite conversation by circumlocutions, euphemisms, Latin equivalents and the language of the nursery. These "quadriliterals," as *Time* magazine once described them, were surprisingly few in number, but their strength was as the strength of ten and they were taboo for centuries—familiar in the barnyard and the brothel but carefully avoided in other circles. "Gentlemen, there are ladies present!" and the vulgarians quieted down.

Now all is changed. Young people use the words as casually as they say "sugar" and without any feeling of barriers broken, but it took a long time for this to happen and one wonders why. One reason maybe that elimination and copulation are exceptionally personal and private matters. A man engaged in either one of them is defenseless—with his pants down—and if any publicity is attached to the interruption of either pursuit, he is at the very least ridiculous. So our ancestors agreed that under ordinary circumstances they would not talk in plain terms about these two important aspects of human experience.

The breaking of verbal taboos is part of the enlarged liberty which we now enjoy—or deplore—but even more awesome is the elimination of the visual taboo—the restriction on what can be shown or described. This is where "explicit" sex comes in. Earlier novelists took us to the bedroom door. Their successors have removed the door, and sometimes they walk right through the bedroom into the barn.

Look, for example, at Larry McMurtry's much-admired and much-imitated novel *The Last Picture Show,* published in 1966 and transformed into a popular motion picture. It is set in a small Texas town where all the inhabitants—small boys, adolescent girls, housewives, civic officials—are sex ridden and doing something about it. I grew up in a small town about the size of Thalia and went to the picture shows and the high-school entertainments. All of us were discovering sex, but we were not in the same league with McMurtry's adolescents. Take the matter of zoophily—intercourse with animals. We sometimes told stories about sexually deprived sheepherders, but we never thought of these situations as being absolutely for real. Nobody that I knew, and many of us were country boys, engaged in such practices. Yet McMurtry makes a sort of specialty of zoophily and implies that when you say "Boys will be boys," this is one of the things you mean.

The implication is always that McMurtry and his tribe are telling it truly—at last. The publishers call *The Last Picture Show* "a sensitive, poignant and powerful work of fiction" which portrays accurately "the wild, heartbreaking condition called adolescence" as experienced in Texas. I believe the publishers are wrong. I do not

agree that McMurtry's primary object is to describe Things as They Are. I wonder sometimes if he may not have been outside his peer group in high school and is out for revenge, but probably his aim is simply to shock the reader. He knows that people over fifty and some not over twenty are often scandalized by what he talks about and uncomfortable with the language he uses but keep on reading to see what he will come up with next—like a bird fascinated by a snake. It amuses him to think up a new sexual irregularity, a new obscenity, as if he were saying to himself, "This will panic them!" And of course it does. If it did not, he would lose much of his reason for writing and might even be out of business.

In their hearts his admirers know that this is true. When McMurtry won his second Carr P. Collins Award from the Texas Institute of Letters in 1968, he was introduced, with a sort of shy pride, by a Houston matron as "our *enfant terrible*"—as if to say, "our *enfant terrible* is more terrible than your *enfant terrible.*" The reviewers and the critics know it too, but they seldom say so. They ignore his seamy side and concentrate on his real gifts as a narrative artist. Thus he and his imitators are left with the conviction that the field is theirs and what they are writing is what everybody wants to read. So the public is stuck with them.

Having proclaimed these truths to be self evident, one can look with increased understanding at the sexual side of the Western novel and proceed to a few generalizations. First, it is obvious that since the early sixties "explicit" sex has been permitted and even encouraged. What the Victorians barely suggested is now described in detail. As a result we are much better informed than our forebears were, but not necessarily better served. Whether they know it or not, people like to have something left to their imaginations. Suggestion plus imagination is a better stimulant than revelation—something the inventor of the bikini failed to realize.

Western novelists, by and large, do not realize it either, and it is hard to think of a single recent writer, aside from the begetters of assembly-line westerns, who does not feel obliged to make a public display of the mating ritual somewhere in his work. And the commercial western is not as pure as it was.

There used to be stopping places. Now there are none. Seventeen-year-old Eli Russell elopes with twenty-year-old Ginny Harris in Lucas Webb's 1971 novel *Eli's Road.* They camp for the night. Ginny says, "A man has rights offen a woman who goes off with him," and she starts to "shuck." This would be a good place to leave them, but Mr. Webb moves right on. In Jack Bickham's *A Boat Named Death* (1975), Faith Socumbe offers herself to the murderer Shed if he will try to get her and her two boys out of their wilderness cabin and back to the settlements down the flooded Buttermilk River. "You can't give a man what he's already made up his mind to take," says Shed, but Faith has fully committed herself and "her fingers reached the top button of her dress." There really is no need to describe what happens next, but Mr. Bickham insists and the reader has to watch, like it or not. Gabe Wyld and Kala Fields in Jesse Bier's pleasant novel *The Year of the Cougar* (1976) are a Montana Romeo and Juliet who fall in love in spite of serious rivalry between their fathers. They have their meeting in her father's barn. "Just hold me first," she says, and Gabe does so. This would once have been the end of the chapter, but not now.

Any number of examples come to mind. Look at Edward Abbey's *The Monkey Wrench Gang* (1975), a sumptuous satire on American "civilization" with special emphasis on the havoc wrought by road-and-dam builders, where explicit sex is hardly needed to make the point. Look at William Eastlake's *Dancers in the Scalp House* (1975), aimed in the same direction; at Matt Braun's *The Kinkaids;* at Evan Hunter's *The Chisholms;* even at Colin Stuart's Indian novel *Walks Far Woman*—all published in 1976, each one intent on taking the reader to bed. The problem, obviously, is not to find a novel with explicit sex but to find one without it.

Since the fiction writer is charged with depicting life as viewed in his time, and since the country is obsessed by sex, it must be admitted that Western novelists have risen nobly to meet their great challenge. If any aspect of the subject remains unexplored, it is probably because the writers have never become aware of the resourcefulness of human beings in finding ways to improve and extend their carnal comforts. In some cases, however, Western writers with unusual endowments of instinct or experience have been able to venture out beyond the bounds of the conventional and "normal" and rival John Updike, or even Barbara Rogers or Erica Jong in putting novelty and adventure into the bedroom.

For openers, consider the matter of adolescent sex. People respond emotionally to Romeo and Juliet, to Holden Caulfield and Alex Portnoy and Lolita. Young people, beautiful and unused, are always sexually interesting. We are told that the potentates enthroned in the Alhambra during Moorish times stocked their harems with ladies no more than twelve years old, and that when these ladies reached the age of fifteen, they were considered superannuated and were retired to housekeeping duties. Men in Granada—or in Great Falls, Montana, or Guthrie, Oklahoma—would probably do as the Moors did if they could, but since they live in an age too late, they are obliged to settle for looking, dreaming and reading.

Western novelists have done their best to help them. J. P. Miller in his 1968 novel *The Race for Home* is one who gave his all for these voyeurs. Laddy, his viewpoint character, is a fifteen-year-old sexually precocious waif who comes to the Texas Gulf Coast town of Espada and becomes part of the family of well-to-do farmer Tom Calvin. Laddy has developed "an amazing monodexterity" from keeping one hand constantly in his pocket to conceal his unremitting sexual excitement. He is a

Texas Portnoy. His opposite number is Tom's adolescent daughter Polly, a bombshell primed to go off at any moment. Masturbation is a way of life with her, as it is with Laddy, but she is eager for more meaningful experience. Laddy offers a way out, but she considers him beneath her and uses him only on an experimental basis until her father dies, leaving her under the thumb of her domineering Aunt Caroline. It occurs to her then that if she can become pregnant, she can escape from her legal dependency. Taking refuge in the barn, she does her best with Laddy's assistance to avail herself of this avenue of escape. The reader has no need to take any part of her campaign on faith.

The blurb calls the book "a Rabelaisian portrait of an era"—the Depression. Rabelaisian it is, but it is more than a portrait. It is a symptom.

Western novels spotlighting the sexual experiences of the young are easy to find. They came along with some regularity in the sixties and multiplied during the seventies. One could start with Patricia Gallagher's *The Sons and the Daughters* (1961), showing what goes on in Shady Bend, Texas, or with Tom Mayer's *Bubble Gum and Kipling* (1964), a collection of short stories which does the same for Santa Fe, New Mexico. The list would include *The Last Picture Show* (1966) and *The Race for Home* (1968). In the seventies stories of adolescent love continued to be written but the best of them were not blatantly carnal. David Wagoner's amusing *The Road to Many a Wonder* (1974) is a sample. Ike Bender is a twenty-year-old innocent who starts out for the Colorado gold fields in 1859 with all his worldly possessions in a wheel-barrow. Fifteen-year-old Millie Slaughter, a determined but conventional heroine, runs him down and marries him en route.

In another 1974 novel, Barbara Moore's *Hard on the Road,* Pepper Fairchild has to leave his Louisiana home in post-Civil War days and travels through the West with his eccentric Cousin Calvin, an itinerant photographer. His temperature is raised by Emma Prosser, a redheaded crusading female journalist whom Pepper rescues from molasses-and-feathering by townspeople outraged by her efforts at reform. Emma is too old for him, however, and Mrs. Moore keeps it clean. John Reese's *Blacksnake Man* (1976) features another fifteen-year-old heroine named Wanda Archambo who falls in love with Ike Hazen, "a young Eastern dude" who joins forces with her crude and violent family of moonshiners in Western Nebraska. Ike is an expert with a blacksnake whip and uses it effectively instead of a six-shooter. Wanda is not wicked or wanton. She just knows what she wants and goes after it. In such novels as these, there is little to alarm a sensitive reader. The norm, however, seems to be the kind of brush-and-cotton-patch Lolita found in Darby Foote's *Casey Love and Baby Blue* (1975), in which the most interesting character is a young girl named Amy Sunshine. "If Amy Sunshine was a whore," says nine-year-old Leah Ann (Baby Love) Blue, the viewpoint character, "then a whore was exactly what I wanted to be when I grew up. I thought she was beautiful." C. W. Smith's *Country Music* (1975) raises the pitch considerably as he follows the fortunes of Bobby Joe Gilbert, "out of high school and hanging around," who has "a '51 Ford with full skirts and duals and a girlfriend in penny loafers who goes all the way." It hardly needs to be pointed out that Smith has learned a great deal from Larry McMurtry.

One promising aspect of juvenile sex which has been more or less neglected involves rape, including parental abuse, of little girls. It has been tried. John Irsfeld tried it in his 1975 novel *Coming Through* (also "evoking comparison with . . . Larry McMurtry," according to the dust jacket), in which LaWanda Lutts, fourteen years old, enters the story as a fugitive from molestation by her father. It turns out that Tudor Lutts, a brute in most other ways, is innocent of this particular charge. La-Wanda, however, is ready to take an advanced degree in sexology.

A bona fide victim is Jansie, the little Texas heroine of R. G. Vliet's *Rockspring* (1974). Jansie is captured in the year 1830 by three Mexican bandits when she wanders too far from home. She is forced to spend the winter with them in their hideout far back in the hills. They use her and abuse her, and she suffers all the torture they can inflict on a sensitive child. She lives and learns, however, and finally comes to love the youngest of the outlaws, who is only a boy himself. They escape and she takes him back to her home, but one of her neighbors, not understanding the situation, kills him on sight and leaves Jansie doubly desolate.

Vliet is no pornographer. Even the rape scene is transmuted into poetry, and the story is told with such simplicity, sensitivity and refinement that Malcolm Cowley calls it "a lovely novella." The field is open for less sensitive writers, however, and at least one of them has used the rape of an adolescent to rise to new heights of the unspeakable. This is Forrest Carter, the part-Indian creator of Josey Wales, the outlaw hero of *Gone to Texas* (1973) and *The Vengeance Trail of Josey Wales* (1976). Wales is a Missouri farmer who lost his wife and baby when the Kansas Redlegs burned his log house in 1858. He gets his revenge by making a career of banditry, robbing banks and dodging the Yankee cavalry during the Civil War years. At the beginning of the second novel, Josey learns that two of his friends have been done in by a renegade Mexican general named Escobedo and he invades Mexico in search of revenge.

A climactic moment comes when Escobedo rapes the captured Apache girl En-lo-e, still a child but a wise one. He lets her know that he is going to strangle her because the final convulsions of a dying woman give the rapist his supreme pleasure. She counterfeits the ultimate paroxysm just before she is about to experience the real thing, empties her bowels to show that she is dead, deceives the sadistic general and escapes to join Josey and help him attain his revenge. It would be hard to equal the sheer horror of this revolting scene, which seems to have achieved the ultimate in indecency, but Western writers are resourceful and may find ways to add new shudders to a promising subject.

Rape and attempted rape of mature women, often presented in graphic detail, are common enough. An example would be David Case's *Plumb Drillin'* (1975) about a hunt for a lost gold mine near Mexican Hat, Utah. Jane Turner has been raped by Turk Strange in the presence of her blind husband. Turk is a gunslinger and the nastiest kind of a villain but he joins the treasure hunt and Jane has to put up with him and her memories until Luke Adam DeCaire takes care of the situation. A white woman raped by Indians has been a favorite subject of Western fictioneers for years. It has remained for contemporary novelists, however, to enable the reader to watch it happen.

It may be a comfort to concerned individuals that the Western novel has not yet gone in for much really "kinky" sex. It has not even paid much attention to lesbianism and homosexuality. Leslie Fiedler in *The Return of the Vanishing American* (1968) tried to redefine the western to include a possibly homosexual relationship between a white man in search of freedom and a darker companion who humanizes him and leads him into larger life. On his list of "new westerns," along with *One Flew Over the Cuckoo's Nest,* was J. L. Herlihy's *Midnight Cowboy* (1965) in which a Houston dishwasher moves to New York, dresses up in Western garb and becomes a male prostitute—a hustler. He forms a friendship with a consumptive Black who gives him some new perspectives. The story is not a western by anybody's definition but Fiedler's but it does open a door.

It might be worth mentioning that John Rechy, the novelist laureate of the male hustler in the big city, grew up in El Paso but doesn't bring his business home to Texas. Edwin Shrake of Fort Worth, however, takes his readers on a guided tour of the gay world which will be hard to equal for savage satire and bitter laughter. The narrator of *Peter Arbiter* (1973) is a bisexual interior decorator (named with an eye cocked toward Petronius) who moves about among Texas millionaires and their ample, amorous wives. His companions are an old poet who cons his greedy friends for millions and a fifteen-year-old runaway youth who likes to live with men. Early in the story two ambidextrous lesbians tie Peter up at the point of a pistol and try to rape him. Many bizarre scenes follow but probably the most bizarre of all is set in a "clinic" where two strange women try to restore Peter's potency and enable him to resume his abnormal life. The men have names like Guy-Guy and Poo Poo Roote and Dr. Scrodmuir, and the life they lead is something no "normal" person would believe. The blurb writer for the Encino Press calls the book "a hilarious romp as power and money, in the form of some devilish caricatures of well-known Texas personalities, try to cope with the exuberance and energy of these three cavalier interlopers."

Whatever else a reader may have to say about *Peter Arbiter,* it stands pretty much alone in Western fiction—at least up to the time of its publication—in its intense concentration on peripheral or far-out sex. When these irregularities come up in most novels, they are incidental—a sort of fringe benefit. For an illustration take Richard Martin Stern's *Power* (1975), a novel about third-generation heirs of a big ranch in New Mexico. Will, the weak brother, is married to Sue, a beautiful creature who can go either way and frequently does. She has a lesbian relationship with Ethel Wilding and we catch a glimpse of them in a huge bathtub, once a fixture in a Denver bawdy house, soaping each other's bodies. A glimpse, however, is all we get.

Without getting deeply involved in the gay community, a fair proportion of recent Western novelists have experimented with what might be called unorthodox sex as public tolerance has grown and authors have probed deeper into the Formerly Forbidden. Take the matter of what has come to be termed "oral sex." A pioneer venture into this once undiscussable area is Marilyn Harris' *In the Midst of Earth* (1969). Myra Cinrus comes as a foundling to the house of "Mr. Jack" Cinrus somewhere on the parched Southwestern prairies. At first this intelligent, disillusioned, highly educated outcast ignores her—then decides to bring her up in his own image. They come to value and finally to love each other, but dark forces are at work in both of them. At night Myra is swept away in the "floodwaters of perverted sexuality," even in her girlhood. Mr. Jack is having experiences of his own in the cottage he keeps for his pleasures away from the big house. The truth comes out in their last encounter, which involves oral sex. When it is over, Mr. Jack goes back to his study and shoots himself.

Seven years later, this indulgence is no longer scandalous but is taken as a matter of course. To Shelby Hearon, wife of a lawyer in Austin, Texas, it is a natural part of human relations and a potential refreshment, like water on a thirsty land. In Mrs. Hearon's family chronicle *Now and Another Time* (1976) Louisa follows Sam Tabour to his house after a party for her father and takes part in a scene of animal passion which goes on for "hours and hours," most of the time "with her begging" before she gets what she wants. Mrs. Hearon watches it all with the detached interest of one watching a snake shed its skin or a banker foreclosing on a mortgage.

Jeanne Williams in *A Lady Bought with Rifles* (1976), a novel of the revolution in northern Mexico, brings young Miranda Greenleaf from school in England to the hacienda of Las Coronas. Before she is forced into marriage with the depraved and sadistic Court Sanders, she meets Trace Winslade, who gives her lessons in love. He leaves her a virgin but makes considerable contributions to her education and her pleasure, sending "liquid fire" through her until she bursts into "lovely, pulsating explosions." It would seem that this particular indulgence is now a creature comfort, much like a fire in the fireplace when one is cold, or a good hot bath when one is tired. Sexual eccentricities have become tolerable, almost respectable. Nobody shoots himself now.

It might even be demonstrated that a quiet competition is going on to see who can go farthest in discovering and exploiting new quirks of human sexuality. An example comes to hand in Kathryn Marshall's 1977 novel *Desert Places,* conceived in the spirit of the Larry McMurtry school of realism. Beatrice Lawrence is a rich, self-centered Texas woman whose roughneck husband Quinn chases every female in sight. She gets even by making herself available to a traveling salesman whom she despises, charges him $200, and makes sure the whole town knows about it. Her victim is partially compensated for the humiliation he endures, however, by a trick with a knotted scarf which multiplies his pleasure. The device is a plus for Marshall, who must have spent some time in the field finding out about it. It remains to be seen whether any of her fellow craftsmen do better. It is worth remarking, however, that she is a teacher of writing and some bright student may be expected to go beyond his teacher, as bright students do.

It is perhaps not fair to leave Marshall without some mention of her tragic view of life and her picture of Texas as a wasteland in which sick, sadistic, sex-driven characters pass their frustrations on to their children. In such a desert place erotic aberrations might be expected. The point here, however, is that Marshall seems to be trying to outdo her competitors.

Not many Western novelists are willing to drift even this far out, but they are willing to experiment with new sexual relationships to make sure of the reader's interest. Sex between members of different racial groups has been useful to some of them. Richard Martin Stern, who got his start writing literate and successful whodunits with Santa Fe as a locale, beginning with *Murder in the Walls* in 1971, features Johnny Ortiz of the San Cristo police department. Johnny is part Mexican and part Apache with the "gifts," as James Fenimore Cooper called them, of both racial groups. He is emotionally attached to Cassie Enright, black, beautiful and beguiling, with a Ph.D. in anthropology. Stern does not play up their sexual relations but he makes sure the reader knows they have them.

Indian men have been falling in love with white girls, and sometimes vice versa, ever since Marah Ellis Ryan's *Indian Love Letters* (1907)—or Harold Bell Wright's *The Mine with the Iron Door* (1923) or Zane Grey's *The Vanishing American* (1925) or Edgar Rice Burroughs' *The War Chief* (1927). Elliott Arnold imagined Tom Jeffords into a sexual relationship with Sonseeahray, the beautiful Apache girl, in *Blood Brother* (1947), and in 1953 Dorothy Johnson's nameless Bostonian in *A Man Called Horse* becomes the husband of Pretty Calf and functions successfully as a member of the Crow tribe. A new twist was given to an Indian-white marriage in Jane Barry's *A Time in the Sun* (1962) when Joaquin, half Apache and half Mexican, becomes the husband of

Anna Stillman, a white captive, with her full consent. The hero of *Little Big Man* (1964) is the enthusiastic spouse of a Cheyenne woman, though author Thomas Berger plays his sex life mostly for laughs. Jay Grobart in Marilyn Durham's *The Man Who Loved Cat Dancing* (1972) has two children by his Shoshone wife. Walks Far Woman in Colin Stuart's novel of that name (1976) marries a white man and lives in both worlds.

Most of these earlier authors were untroubled by demands for explicit sex, but later novelists could not escape. In Jean Rikhoff's *The Sweetwater* (1976) Benjie Klomp becomes the wife of the Sioux Bone Hand and bears him two children. We learn a good deal about how they were conceived. With William Eastlake's *Dancers in the Scalp House* (1975) there is more to see as red-headed Mary-Forge teaches Navajo children to be proud of themselves and spends her off-duty hours making love with Tom Charles at his place (which he calls The Scalp House) and dancing with him naked afterward. Tom Charlie has gone to the university and learned about science and spends *his* leisure hours making an atomic bomb with which to blow up the Atlas (read Glen Canyon) Dam. The couple's love making is subjected to close scrutiny.

Perhaps the most sensational of all these racially integrated recent novels is Paul King's *Hermana Sam* (1977) about an attractive little Irish nun from Boston who has received a medical education and comes to Santa Fe in 1847 to start a hospital. Once the reader accepts this obvious impossibility, he is called on for even greater acts of faith as Sister Samantha (Hermana Sam to her Mexicans) meets with the Apache leader Mangus out on the plains, where he has been chasing Comanches. Mangus is immobilized by a bullet lodged near his spine and Sister Samantha has to cut it out or die. She cuts it out. The result is an attachment between the Indian and the white girl which leads to their living together as man and wife when the Apaches rescue her during the Taos Rebellion of 1847. She even has a child by him and is content to be an Apache mother, but he appreciates her gift for healing, sends her back to her people and arranges for his own death because he can't go on without her. Their union strains credulity but the idea of a sexual attachment between an Apache chief and a Roman Catholic nun is bound to arouse interest and King makes sure it is interesting by giving a play-by-play account of their encounters—the first one taking place chest deep in a stream of water.

Neil Claremon in his poetic novel *Borderland* finds still another way to deal with a mixed marriage. J. P., an American hydrologist brought to northern Mexico to start an irrigation project for the benefit of a community of Opata Indians, is half of the equation. He falls in love with Tsari, a *curandera* (healer) with all sorts of other-worldly gifts and powers. Claremon not merely offers the reader a clear view of their love making—he makes J. P. violate tribal taboos and assist at the birth of their twin sons. Explicit sex is one thing. Explicit birth goes a step farther.

Nothing has been said up to this point about the traditional or "commercial" western, with a small "w." A number of examples have been cited from Doubleday's Double D list of westerns, but these are a step ahead of the multitude of soft-cover examples which carry on more or less in the tradition of the twenties and thirties. One might guess that nothing needs to be said and that the most unlikely place to look for explicit sex would be in the shoot-em-up, hayburner or oater. The printed horse opera used to be satisfied with the most modest suggestion that the cowboy wanted more than friendship from the schoolteacher, or that the teacher had more than friendship to offer. It is not satisfied with such meager fare any more.

The change came on gradually. Nelson Nye, with a hundred tales to his credit, says the first "sexy" western was Homer Croy's *West of the Water Tower* (1923), which was about a seduction. He claims credit for number two himself—*Riders by Night* (1950). The idea of "sexy," of course, has to be considered relatively. What was sexy in 1920, or even 1951, may seem timidly reserved twenty or thirty years later, and it is true that the growing tolerance—or numbness—of the reading public has spurred ambitious writers on to new levels of explicitness and specificity. In the old days when the frontiersman headed into the wilderness in search of the lost mine or the lost relative, or whatever was lost, he went by himself or with a small company of males. Now the female lead insists on coming along, unprepared as she is for what lies ahead, and the author lets her go with just one thing in mind. After a week or two on the trail, transformed and humanized by dangers and hardships, she yields to passion beside a mountain stream, sometimes with death just around the bend, and it is suggested that a good and beautiful thing has taken place.

T. V. Olsen's *Savage Sierra* (1962) used this formula. Will Angsman is the tough frontiersman. James and Judith Amberley from Boston are the tenderfeet who wish to go into dangerous Indian country to look for their brother Douglas, who disappeared a year before while searching for a lost Spanish mine. Bonito, the great Apache leader, is tired of fighting and has retired to his mountain fastness, but he has warned the white man to stay away or take the consequences. Angsman, against his better judgment, agrees to guide the Easterners. Wicked white men, as well as hostile Indians, pursue them and much blood is shed before they get out, but love does come beside the mountain stream.

John Benteen's *Apache Raiders* (1970) follows the fortunes of Neal Fargo, a super-tough frontiersman who is looking for a treasure hidden in the Big Bend of Texas. Nola Shane, a Pennsylvania school-teacher, has come to El Paso on the trail of her brother, a mining engineer held for ransom south of the border. She tags along when Fargo leaves. Nola turns out to be a seductive and voluptuous woman who can't wait to get in bed with the hero, and she gets him back in at every opportunity. He is not hers to keep, however. Mr. Benteen's motto, where Fargo is concerned, is "He who makes love and runs away. . . ."

Westerns featuring raw sex and violence keep on coming. William James is the instigator of a series called "Apache," spotlighting a mighty warrior named Cuchillo Oro from his favorite weapon, a golden Spanish knife. Number seven in the series, titled *Blood Line* (1976), begins its action in 1864 as the lone Apache watches six Indian renegades gang rape a white woman. The action, including some abnormal sex, is described in detail. After giving the reader time enough to get his money's worth, Cuchillo Oro shoots one of the gang and sends the others on their way. He is not particularly shocked by what has taken place, since he is no lover of white people himself, Captain Cyrus Pinner of the United States Cavalry having killed his wife and child. He does not war on white women, however, and he saves Linda Daughton before moving on to more bloody encounters in the town of Angus Wells.

Many more examples of this sort of sex-with-violence could be cited from the 150-plus novels which have been written about the Apache wars in the Southwest, and sexual frankness is not hard to find in other types of westerns. The majority of them, however, avoid heavy sex. Steve Overholser's Spur-Award-winning *A Hanging in Sweetwater* (1974) is about an ex-soldier and a saloon girl who preempt some rich Wyoming bottom land in 1879 in defiance of a big cattleman. They are obviously in love, but Boomer Jones, the narrator, is only fifteen years old and is not in a position to describe their intimacies in detail. Will Bryant in *Blue Russell* (1976) does not get all the mileage he can out of young Blue's first sexual experience. Jefferson Hewitt, hero of John Reese's series about the adventures of a private detective in the turn-of-the century West (*Sequoia Shootout*, 1977, for example) takes pains to keep Jeff out of the bedroom. Milton Bass brings his adolescent leading man (*Mist'r Jory,* 1976) into contact with aggressive women but keeps him from getting seriously involved. It would seem that the western preserves its heart intact though the forces of change have crumbled its outer works. What the future holds for the traditional horse opera remains unrevealed, but its readers have always been conservative and may discourage further experimentation.

There are, in truth, signs that the wave of permissiveness has begun to recede. In 1977 the verdict of guilty against Larry Flynt and his *Hustler* magazine, controversial though it was, indicated that the tide might be turning. Syndicated newspaper columnists, who represent in some degree the conscience of the country, are unhappy about the flood of smut that blankets the land. Jon-Michael Reed, for instance, is outraged because TV serial writers "get away with murder, not to mention abortion, incest, child abuse, prostitution, rape, interracial relationships, sexual promiscuity, sibling and parental rivalry, illegitimacy, insanity, as well as more mundane staples, infidelity and divorce" (*Arizona Daily Star,* February 21, 1977). Mike Royko (*Star,* July 27, 1976) regrets that "in order to preserve the right of Walter Cronkite to report the news, we must defend the right of Strange Oscar, who likes to dial the phone numbers of young ladies and pant."

The reaction may be beginning, but it has a long way to go. People will have to get fed up with pornography, or lose interest, before any significant slowdown in production may be expected. Time may be on the side of purity, however, as two forces work together for good for those who hate smut.

The first is the natural and normal tendency of any movement to go too far. The purveyors of heavy sex assume that since their books have sold, the way to sell more books is to make the sex heavier. Thus they hasten their own downfall, and the way to get rid of them entirely is to spur them on to new efforts. Apparently they do not need much urging—are, in fact, eager to get on with it. *Time* magazine in a review of Rosemary Rogers' 1976 novel *Wicked Loving Lies* (January 17, 1977) reports that the heroine is raped on page 62, on page 86, on page 192, and on page 277. She is "violated twelve times on three continents by five men." On page 654 she announces, "I am tired of being raped." This sort of thing will bring the cleanup a good deal nearer. Readers get tired of being raped too.

The second Force for Fumigation of Fiction is the fact that anything overdone becomes ridiculous, and ridicule is the best weapon against it. People kept insisting, when the Portnoy craze was at its height, that this performance was hilarious. Perhaps it was, in a sad sort of way, but in other novels, even Western novels, sex began to be played in the 1960s for heartier laughs. As early as 1965 David Markson did it in *The Ballad of Dingus Magee*. On page 66 Dingus completes a seduction which we learn about from the broken utterances of both parties as they pretend they don't know what they are doing. A passage like that is a big help in the Fumigation campaign.

Even Larry McMurtry, after sixteen years of trying to outdo himself, seems to have come to the end of the trail. His 1972 novel *All My Friends Are Going to Be Strangers* is a sort of *ne plus ultra*. In a chapter regarded by some connoisseurs as particularly funny, Danny Deck plays a visit to his uncle, who lives in a decayed Victorian mansion out in the desert fifty miles south of Van Horn, Texas. Among his uncle's retainers is a Mexican named Antonio who goes farther than any other McMurtry character in sexual eclecticism. He finds zoophily a welcome diversion, but ranges much farther afield. Anything with a visible opening is a challenge to him—he even goes for postholes and the intake to a gasoline tank. It is almost as if McMurtry has thrown up his hands and admitted that he has done all he can—there are no more sexual oddities to explore. A little of this sort of thing may go a long way toward restoring reserve to fiction.

Once the break is made, anything can happen. It has long been axiomatic among religious people that the worst sinners make the best evangelists, and it is not beyond the bounds of possibility that McMurtry and his disciples may become the spearhead of a new reform effort. The movement seems to have begun and may need only a few enthusiastic converts to become a crusade. Consider Barbara Cartland, who in 1975 wrote nineteen novels *without* explicit sex for a public demanding more. BRITISH AUTHORESS BARBARA CARTLAND FINDS PUBLIC CLAMORS FOR CHASTITY, says the headline in the *Wall Street Journal* (September 1, 1976). "My heroines are all virgins," Mrs. Cartland told the reporter. "Many publishers thought that Cartland innocence wouldn't sell. Many publishers were wrong."

If the word gets out that she is making it big with such material, and sooner or later it will, a revolution may be expected, maybe overnight. And if virginity does well at the cash register and the box office in the East, it will have its day in the West. Southern Ladies from Dallas will be happy again and purity will return to the Lone Prairee.

Gus Lenniger of the Lenniger Literary Agency in New York says it has already returned. In a letter dated March 8, 1977, he comments:

> The "sex & violence" western was really used only by the shyster paperback original publishers . . . who tried to become legitimate by introducing "category" lines like mystery and westerns when hard-core pornography killed their sales of silly bed-hopping soft-core porno! . . . All are out of business . . . only one still continuing a couple of sex-and-violence type *series* they started during the era when "spaghetti westerns" flooded the movie and TV shows and practically ruined public acceptance of westerns. . . .

> In a serious, believable western historical or family saga set in the West, sex may rear its lovely head if integral part of story line, necessary to motivation, honest realism, as it does in all types of novels today. But I fully agree with you that the *cheap* sex-and-violence western is not only on way out, but *out.* We would not attempt to market such a manuscript at present; would wish the author luck in peddling it himself.

"What in the hell does that mean?" demanded Gail Gardner, cowboy sage and singer of Prescott, Arizona, on seeing for the first time the phrase "oral sex" in a newspaper. "Does it mean they are just going to talk about it?" If Gus Lenninger is right, Gail may never have to know.

Lewis P. Simpson

SOURCE: "Sex & History: Origins of Faulkner's Apocrypha," in *The Maker and the Myth: Faulkner and Yoknapatawpha,* 1977, edited by Evans Harrington and Ann J. Abadie, University of Mississippi Press, 1978, pp. 43-70.

[*In the following essay, Simpson examines William Faulkner's works as they demonstrate the fusion and interiorization of history and sexuality in the modern consciousness.*]

As defined by the distinguished British historian R. W. Southern, the stages of the historian's experience of history are as follows: "first the individual perceptions which are the bricks out of which our historical edifices are built; then the ramifications of these perceptions to every area of social or private life to form large areas of intelligibility; and finally the arranging of this material to form works of art of a special and distinctive kind."[1] Reading Professor Southern's analysis of the historical experience at a moment when I was thinking about the great historical construct Faulkner wrought out of his literary art, the tales of Yoknapatawpha (and thinking too about how often Faulkner compared his work as a novelist to that of the carpenter), I found myself asking if the pattern of the historian's experience of history as set forth by Southern would fit Faulkner's experience of history. The question I was asking being in totality far too large to be taken up in the project immediately before me—that of exploring further the subject of sex and history in relation to the origins of Yoknapatawpha[2]— I turned to Professor Southern's prescription for his own lecture: "But here I shall examine only the first and most primitive stage of all—the sources and characteristics of the initial perceptions." I impose this prescription as my own here, and ask only this: if one tries to adapt Southern's formula of the historical experience to Faulkner, what does one set down as the record of the initial, or primitive, stage?

Professor Southern characterizes this initial stage as that in which the historian confronting a chaos of information glimpses a "small area of intelligibility."[3] Of course a novelist—although all novelists are historians—does not work by accumulating information, hoping to put it together in such a manner as to deduce significant meaning from it. The early task of the novelist is more awesome. Unless he is a truncated novelist who limits himself to writing colorful fictions about certain historical periods and so is hardly a novelist at all, the novelist seeks to perceive areas of intelligibility in the raw history of the streets and rooms he lives in or enters—of the areas of human activity he knows, being born into them or coming into them in the course of living. The novelist from the beginning of his career has an impulse to a greater intimacy with history than the historian proper. This may be more true if, like Faulkner, the novelist in his early stage of development goes through a period when he tries to be a poet. In this effort he intensifies his concern with language—with individual words—for poems live almost solely in the preciseness of their cultural evocation. While Faulkner was not a markedly successful poet, and recognized this before he had written very many poems, he did publish two volumes of poetry and always attached considerable significance to his having tried his hand at making poems. He did so with justification, for it is in the poems that the initial stage of his perception, or experience of history, is defined. More than foreshadowed in them, it is in effect formulated in their attempt to express with poetic precision the fundamental connection of sex and history. To see how this is so illuminates the essential inception (before any one of them was written) of the emotional—let me say, spiritual—character of the series of fictions set in Yoknapatawpha, which Faulkner came to call, in more than a nominal sense, "my apocryphal county."[4]

Perhaps I can get most directly into the early perception of the nexus of sex and history in Faulkner by referring to one of his irregular Italian sonnets. Written before 1925, possibly in 1924, this poem is numbered XLII in *A Green Bough*. (Although not published until 1933, this volume collects poems written during Faulkner's poetic period several years earlier.) The octave of the sonnet (rhymed in the Shakespearean rather than the Italian style) interprets the symbolism of the story of the Hebraic Garden of Eden in a literal way.

> Beneath the apple tree Eve's tortured shape
> Glittered in the Snake's, her riven breast
> Sloped his coils and took the sun's escape
> To augur black her sin from east to west.
> In winter's night man may keep him warm
> Regretting olden sins he did omit;
> With fetiches the whip of blood to charm,
> Forgetting that with breath he's heir to it.

The sestet expands and comments on the theme of the octave—the seduction of Eve by Satan and the consequent repression of the instinctive desires of the blood—as follows:

> But old gods fall away, the ancient Snake
> Is throned and crowned instead, and has for
>   minion
> That golden apple which will never slake
> But ever feed man's crumb of fire, when plover
> And swallow and shrill northing birds whip over
> Nazarene and Roman and Virginian.[5]

The defeat of the old gods of the Greco-Roman mythology and the enthronement of the power of the Hebraic snake, the power of the knowledge of good and evil, paradoxically does not suppress man's cosmic "crumb of fire" but, opposing it, feeds it. Flaring up when the birds go north in the spring to nest and to renew life, it whips "over Nazarene and Roman and Virginian." That is, it wields the "whip of blood" over the dominion of Christian history. Faulkner's imagery is clumsy and its implication obvious: under the dominion of the Hebraic snake, man becomes a self-conscious sexual creature and a self-conscious historical being. A less obvious implication is that in the seduction of Eve every sexual act, like every act of man, becomes a historical act. At the time he had his vision of Eve's tortured shape beneath the apple tree, I doubt that Faulkner quite under-

stood its more subtle implication. Probably he never did in a sharp, rational way—not, I should say, because he was incapable of such perception but because he was never entirely reconciled to Eve's seduction. His irreconciliation created in his vision of Yoknapatawpha a myriad tension between the cosmological and historical modes of existence.

Yet I do not intend to say that Faulkner opposed the cosmological to the historical. I mean that his perception of history found a focus in the tension generated in the literary imagination by the conquest of the cosmic sexuality of the Greco-Roman garden by the historicism of the Hebraic-Christian interpretation of sexuality. In his response to this tension is to be discovered Faulkner's shaping experience of history.

But I am getting ahead of the story. The earliest stage of Faulkner's historical perception is a vision simpler than that of the historicism of Hebraic-Christian sexuality. It is simply a vision of the world grown old, a world which has lost the vitality of cosmic unity. The theme of the aging world is graphically present in a nine-line poem in *The Green Bough* (number XXVI), in which the withdrawal of the moon goddess is the subject.

> Still, and look down, look down:
> Thy curious withdrawn hand
> Unprobes, now spirit and sense unblend,
>   undrown,
> Knit by a word and sundered by a tense
> Like this: Is: Was: and Not. Nor caught between
> Spent beaches and the annealed insatiate sea
> Dost myriad lie, cold and intact Selene,
> On secret strange or old disastrous lee
> Behind the fading mistral of the sense.[6]

In this short poem, possibly the best poem Faulkner ever wrote, the austere behavior of Selene, the moon goddess, is associated with the modern rupture of sense and spirit. It is an effective symbol of the estrangement from the world which occurs as, becoming a part of the historical consciousness, the world ceases to be a cosmos.

In Faulkner's first book of poems (and in his first published book, The *Marble Faun,* 1924), the aging of the world is the predominant theme. In fact the world has grown so old there is virtually no sexual activity. Both the Faun imprisoned in his "marble bonds" and dreaming of pastoral freedom and the Pan who appears in his dreaming are chaste creatures. The Faun sees but does not pursue the golden nymphs. Pan, far from being the "goat god," is present in the voice of his pipe, invoking a beautiful but strangely empty Arcadia. Yet in spite of its sexual passivity, *The Marble Faun* displays a certain tension between the Faun's recollection of the cosmic garden and a sense of the Edenic garden. In the Prologue, the Faun complains that he cannot break his "marble bonds" yet "That quick keen snake / Is free to come and go." In a later passage the Faun, hearing the pipes of Pan, glides "like a snake" to "peer" into the "leafy depths" where Pan sits on "a chill rock gray and old" as he had "since the world began."[7] The triumphant snake is present, it would seem, in the gray garden of the Faun's imprisonment. Locked in the statue in the garden, the Faun is a creature of his consciousness of art and history. He imagines his situation, so to speak, as an experience of history.

In general, Faulkner's poems—and for that matter several of the prose sketches he wrote in his youth—indicate clearly that the earliest stage of his perception of history occurs in his experience of the world alienation, which (under the rubrics of romanticism, impressionism, surrealism, etc.) dominates the mood and subject matter of modern literature and art. In spite of the fact that in his youth Faulkner's literary attitudes reek of Edwardian decadence, his early sensibility cannot be dismissed as merely imitative. Seeking the displaced connection between sense and spirit, the young Faulkner was fascinated by the drama of "Is, Was, and Not." Whether or not Selene might return her hand to the world was no mere idle dream of an imagination stuffed with the poems of Swinburne and old numbers of the *Yellow Book*. Faulkner early made a heavy emotional investment in Arcadia and in all the beings who populated the Greco-Roman imagination of the cosmos. From first to last these mythical beings are present in his writings. At times visible, at times invisible, they are always there. But they are never invoked by Faulkner's imagination as pure cosmic presences. Not even in the earliest writings does Faulkner have the illusion that Arcadia still exists in the human consciousness; save, that is, as illusion.

In the poetic schema suggested in Faulkner's poems, Arcadia became a part of the historical consciousness when the Western imagination transformed the cosmological garden into the Garden of Eden; when Satan entered the garden, seduced Eve, and forever sundered sense and spirit in the self-conscious act of sexuality. As the first poem I have referred to says, the old gods fell away. Pan was transformed into Satan, and the rest is history. Faulkner, in other words—in what may be termed the second stage of his historical experience—perceived the historicizing of sexuality as the key element in the differentiation of the human consciousness of existence in a historical society from existence in the organic, or compact—the undifferentiated—society. Equating the differentiation of self-conscious sexuality and the differentiation of history (although surely with no deliberate knowledge that he was doing this), Faulkner in his initial writings entered into the literary and artistic experience of world historical alienation. And like all the great modern writers, including Joyce, Eliot, and Mann, he took this as his subject. The development of Faulkner's own version of the modern estrangement and the making of this into his novelistic substance is the third stage of his primary historical experience.

In this stage Faulkner discovered a symbol of alienation in the difficulty the modern historical consciousness has in responding to sexuality and began with increasing complexity to employ specific sexual situations as emblems of the estrangement of modern consciousness from a unified or harmonious order of sense and spirit. I will pass over the interesting foreshadowing of this kind of symbolization in Faulkner's little poetic drama, *Marionettes* (1920),[8] and remark on it in his first two novels, *Soldiers' Pay* and *Mosquitoes*, and in the inaugural works of the Yoknapatawpha series: the fragment called *Father Abraham*, *Flags in the Dust* (published as *Sartoris*), and *The Sound and the Fury*.

A story set in a small town in Georgia right after the First World War, *Soldiers' Pay* has varied facets, but it is not misleading to emphasize the theme of sexual frustration. The novel is fundamentally about the defeat of the spirit of wonder and of desire, of the poetry of living, by modern history. Donald Mahon, an American aviator shot down over Flanders and lying in a comatose state in the home of his father, an Episcopal priest and rector, is not only a type of the poet but a faun returned into history. Swimming naked in the creek with the pretty servant girl Emmy, running with her in the night, and making love to her, he has converted her into a nymph. Januarius Jones, a fat and repulsive satyr returned into history, corrupts Emmy. A ridiculous figure yet a sinister force of lust, Januarius is the most strongly conceived character in the novel. The element of fantasy in his makeup is more successfully assimilated to his reality as a creature of history than it is in the cases of Donald and Emmy. All three characters are aspects of the great god Pan, who returns, or tries to return, into a world in which he is as dead as Christ is.[9] The reiteration of the motif of "sex and death and damnation" in *Soldiers' Pay* provides for the feeling of a dead-end historical situation. Falling within the ambiance of the waste land as projected by Eliot, *Soldiers' Pay* proclaims the damnation attendant upon the triumph of a pervasive "ennui" in the aftermath of the First World War and the general victory of an industrialized and spiritually trivialized society.[10] There is a suggestion, however—and I think this may be the most significant part of *Soldiers' Pay*—of an association between the generalized historical situation and its relation to the historical situation in the American South. This occurs in a description of the courthouse square of Charlestown, Georgia. The depiction of the somnolent scene of southern apathy is climaxed by an effusive image: "And above all brooded early April sweetly pregnant with noon."[11]Ridiculous as it is, the image declares an increasing boldness in Faulkner's imagination. By the time he wrote *Soldiers' Pay* he was trying for an ironic juxtaposition of historical actuality and pastoral sexuality that he had not before attempted. He not only brings the pastoral deities back to the rose garden of the Reverend Mr. Mahon but into a courthouse square in Georgia. Soon this would be the square in Jefferson, Yoknapatawpha County, Mississippi. Across the Jefferson square would walk avatars of the gods, goddesses, and minor deities of the lost Arcadia who are among the most memorable characters in American novelistic literature.

But Faulkner's perception of the complex fate of creatures from the pastoral cosmos who return into modern history had yet to be refined or even substantially developed. In his second novel, *Mosquitoes,* he is no longer interested in the more or less literal return of fleet fauns, virginal nymphs, and wanton satyrs consumed with nympholepsy. He creates more subtle avatars of the pastoral figures, especially in the nymphlike Pat Robyn, and, more especially, in the sculptor Gordon. Gordon is a tall, angular man with a hawk face (in the moonlight a "silver faun's face") and a dark-bearded head (something like a Laurence Housman version of Pan in the *Yellow Book*). He is a full-fledged yet elusive suggestion of the modern artist as avatar of Pan. But Faulkner also identifies Gordon with the Christian myth of history, precisely with Christ and the Passion Week. In so doing, Faulkner rather forcibly but with some success unites concepts of the sexuality of art and the sexuality of history. He accomplishes this primarily by means of two symbols. One is a representation of a female figure in marble which Gordon has done and which he greatly prizes.

> As you entered the room the thing drew your eyes: you turned sharply as to a sound, expecting movement. But it was marble, it could not move. And when you tore your eyes away and turned your back on it at last, you got again untarnished and high and clean that sense of swiftness, of space encompassed; but on looking again it was as before: motionless and passionately eternal—the virginal breastless torso of a girl, headless, armless, legless, in marble temporarily caught and hushed yet passionate still for escape, passionate and simple and eternal in the equivocal derisive darkness of the world. Nothing to trouble your youth or lack of it: rather something to trouble the very fibrous integrity of your being.[12]

The other symbol is a clay mask of Mrs. Maurier, the patron of New Orleans writers, artists, and intellectuals. Her invitation to a mixed bag of them to spend a week aboard her yacht, the *Nausikka,* provides what little plot *Mosquitoes* has, the record of an aborted odyssey on Lake Pontchartrain.

> It was clay, yet damp, and from out its dull, dead grayness Mrs. Maurier looked at them. Her chins, harshly, and her flaccid jaw muscles with savage versimilitude. Her eyes were caverns thumbed with two motions into the dead familiar astonishment of her face; and yet, behind them, somewhere within those empty sockets, behind all her familiar surprise, there was something else—something that exposed her face for the mask it was, and still more, a mask unaware.[13]

The marble abstraction of the female body represents a passionate erotic grief in Gordon's life that is never revealed beyond hints given in the rhetoric of a second-rate Cyrano de Bergerac. Nonetheless the highly wrought and perfected virginal torso is the source of the perception of the mask, and still more, the mask unaware which is Mrs. Maurier's face. Gordon's explora-tion of the depths of the personal consciousness has given him the power (suggested to Faulkner by Bergson)[14] to intuit human experience in its historical fullness and actuality.

Faulkner reinforces the point by having the Semitic man, a figure of the literary intellectual in *Mosquitoes,* tell the story of Mrs. Maurier. It is a story involving the unwilling marriage of a New England girl to a much older man, who during the Civil War had disappeared from the plantation where he was an overseer. After the end of hostilities he turned up astride a Union cavalry saddle and with a hundred thousand dollars in uncut federal notes in his possession. Forced by her parents to desert her true love for a marriage of convenience to this nouveau addition to the southern gentry, Mrs. Maurier has long outlived her husband. Yet as the Semitic man sees and Gordon has discerned, this aging childless widow is yet alive to life. What Gordon has caught in her mask is fundamentally the thing he has caught in the marble abstraction of the young girl, the mystique of virginity and desire and the grief of unfulfillment. At first, the Semitic man says, you may think that Mrs. Maurier's penchant for collecting writers and artists is "just silliness, lack of occupation—a tub of washing, to be exact." But he says he has come to "see something thwarted back of it all, something stifled, yet which won't quite die." Dawson Fairchild, a novelist who is listening intently to the Semitic man's divination, exclaims, "A virgin. . . . That's what it is, exactly. Fooling with sex, kind of dabbling at it, like a kitten at a ball of string. She missed something: her body told her so, insisted, forced her to try to remedy it and fill the vacuum. But now her body is old; it no longer remembers that it missed anything, and all she has left is a habit, the ghost of a need to rectify something the lack of which her body has long since forgotten about." Fairchild remonstrates with himself for having failed to understand his hostess's motive. "Missed it clean," he thinks. But a few minutes later, standing before Gordon's statue of the naked torso, Fairchild misses it again. He sees in the abstraction a nymph "on a May morning, bathing in a pool where there were a lot of poplar trees." And he exclaims, comparing the statue with the mask of Mrs. Maurier he has just been looking at, "Now, this is the way to forget your grief." Gordon, who has remained silent, cries out a sentiment that Faulkner was to repeat several times: "Forget grief. . . . Only an idiot has no grief; only a fool would forget it. What else is there in this world sharp enough to stick to your guts?"[15]

The movement in *Mosquitoes* out of Gordon's sublimation in art of his personal erotic suffering toward a more comprehensive grasp of the suffering of the human heart is consummated in the nighttown scene which follows the conversation in Gordon's studio. Taken out of context the scene in which the Semitic man, Fairchild, and Gordon, all drunk, wander about the French Quarter represents probably the silliest writing Faulkner ever allowed to get into print; but in the framework of the novel, which however flawed is deliberate, it serves its purpose: to provide an ironic contrast between a redemptive vision of art, history, and sexuality fused in the image of a "Passion Week of the heart"—a transcendent "instant of timeless beatitude"—and the modern sexual incapacity.[16] The nighttown scene is immediately preceded by the account of the visit the dilettantish poet Mark Frost makes to the quarters of Miss Jameson, whose efforts to seduce Mark are singularly nonproductive. The nighttown scene is immediately followed by a further episode (and this episode concludes the novel) in the blundering sexual career of Mr. Talliaferro. Tricked into Mrs. Maurier's cabin during the journey aboard the *Nausikka,* he is to marry her. But he is still trying to make a conquest of Jenny, one of the desirable young creatures on the voyage. In the total context of *Mosquitoes* you might say that a kind of world historical failure of sexuality emerges as its dominant theme.

It is important to note that the setting of *Mosquitoes* is not simply that of an exotic but anonymous city. It is no doubt far more appropriate for Pan to return to the Vieux Carré than to the courthouse square in a Georgia village; and Faulkner makes the most of the exoticism of a place which broods "in a faintly tarnished languour like an aging yet still beautiful courtesan in a smoke-filled room, avid yet weary too of ardent ways."[17] But for all that he makes of its exotic qualities, New Orleans is a historical actuality in *Mosquitoes.* Faulkner knew it as the great port city of the Mississippi valley culture, integral in the history of Mississippi—even though to a north Mississippian like himself, Memphis was the basic metropolitan reference. Faulkner, moreover, knew the French Quarter in the 1920s as the historical setting of a literary and artistic life of some consequence. His involvement in this life was brief, but it was enough for one who assimilated experiences as rapidly and fully as the precocious young writer did. While *Mosquitoes* can be dismissed as an inconsequential, talky novel about arty people (Faulkner himself once referred to it as "transhily smart"),[18] I feel it represents the most substantial experience of modern cultural history Faulkner had had up to the point when he wrote the book. In it the young literary artist not only confirmed his initial perception of sexuality as a fundamental motive in the continuum of the historical consciousness but reinforced his feeling that this continuum cannot be transcended. The tensional relation between Gordon's marble statue of the young girl and the clay mask of Mrs. Maurier symbolizes the way in which even the perfected work of art is in and of history. However awkwardly, *Mosquitoes* presents a myth of the artist as creature of history. Writing this novel, after first living it as a resident of the French Quarter, Faulkner became a self-conscious participant in what many years later he would refer to as the "literary history of man's spirit."[19]

At about the time he completed *Mosquitoes,* Faulkner conceived a more subtle and intricate return of the classical deities into history: this time into northern Mississippi, the country of his nativity, and as it proved to be

(after his sojourn in New Orleans and a tour of Europe), the site of his permanent residence. He began work on two stories, one set in Jefferson, the seat of Yoknapatawpha County, the other in Frenchman's Bend, a settlement about ten miles away. The latter story, called *Father Abraham,* introduced a character named Flem Snopes, president of the bank in Jefferson. Several years earlier this son of the tenant farming class had "appeared unheralded" in Jefferson "behind the counter of a small restaurant on a side street, patronized by country people. With this foothold and like Abraham of old, he led his family piece by piece into town."[20] In the course of his rise the impotent Flem marries Eula Varner, pregnant daughter of Will Varner, owner of the general store in Frenchman's Bend and lord of the region. Supplying Eula's need for a husband, Flem gains a hold on Varner. A "softly ample girl with eyes like cloudy hothouse grapes and a mouth always slightly open,"[21] Eula is more than a nymph; she is potentially an earth goddess. And so she becomes fifteen years later in *The Hamlet,* the first volume in the Snopes trilogy.

In the resumption of the Snopes story (which Faulkner soon suspended in the 1920s in favor of *Flags in the Dust*), Flem also assumes something of a supratemporal aspect. This is obliquely suggested in the tall tale Ratliff imagines or dreams about the money-obsessed Flem usurping the throne of the Prince of Darkness. In *The Hamlet* Flem is not only a kind of demonic presence but, in the context of Faulkner's subtle parody of pastoral, he may be an instance of Pan transformed into the devil. The possibility of such a transformation is to be found in the Gothic lore and legend of Pan. At about the time Faulkner was writing the *Father Abraham* fragment, the Gothic Pan was being employed directly by Eugene O'Neill in one of his major dramas, *The Great God Brown* (first produced in 1925). In this play, one surely familiar to Faulkner (who admired O'Neill and was, as Blotner shows, influenced by him earlier), the elaborate employment of Greek dramatic masks includes Dion Anthony's exchange of the mask of Pan for that of Mephistopheles. As it is put in the play, "When Pan was forbidden the light and warmth of the sun he grew sensitive and self-conscious and proud and revengeful—and became Prince of Darkness."[22] Further evidence that Faulkner had Flem and Eula in mind as avatars of pastoral deities when he began *Father Abraham* appears in a "highly emblematic" sketch on the back of one page of the manuscript. This depicts Faulkner himself as a faun, or it may be as Pan, piping music to dancing lambs.[23]

By the time he wrote *The Hamlet,* Faulkner knew how the intracosmic beings become creatures of the historical consciousness, and he understood their continuity in the human consciousness of sexuality. He knew that in their return they represent an ironic nexus of the cosmological and historical modes of consciousness. But such comprehension came after Faulkner had explored the representation of the nexus through characters more intimately accessible to his imagination than the "peasants" of Frenchman's Bend, namely the Sartorises and the Compsons. Upon discovering the greater accessibility of characters closer to his own class and education, it can be plausibly conjectured, Faulkner temporarily abandoned the "peasants" for the "aristocrats." Thus he found his way directly into the drama of the modern juncture of cosmic and historical. An excited letter he wrote to his publisher Horace Liveright as he finished *Flags in the Dust* seems to confirm this observation: "I have written THE book, of which those other things [*Soldiers' Pay* and *Mosquitoes*] were but foals. I believe it is the damdest best book you'll look at this year, and any other publisher."[24] Having created the foals, Faulkner had now created the mare. Growing in his perception of the ironic complexities involved in the novelist's experience of modern history, he had for the first time in the story of the Sartorises and the Jefferson community fully perceived at its center a crisis in sexuality; and not only this but had found in the history of the South a singular yet compelling representative exemplification of this crisis. He had discovered in the post-Civil War southern consciousness, as embodied in Yoknapatawpha County, an emblem of the modern experience of psychic—of spiritual—estrangement from a unified human existence.

In *Flags in the Dust* the crisis in the historical consciousness of sexuality is located in the character of the matriarchal society that arose in the South after the defeat of the southern men. It was the men, Faulkner once explained, "that couldn't bear being—having lost the war. The women were the ones that could bear it because they never had surrendered. The men had given up and in a sense were dead and even generations later were seeking death."[25] (Of course the time scheme here is exaggerated; the post-Civil War generations may be reckoned realistically as confined to two, or no more than three. Yet those who know the South may well feel that the search for death is not an extinct motive in white southern males, even in the fourth and fifth generations.)

The most interesting character in *Flags in the Dust,* surely the chief character, is Narcissa. A feminine avatar of the mythological youth Narcissus, while her brother Horace is the male avatar, Narcissa falls prey by her own volition to an avatar of the satanic Pan, the obscene letter writer, Byron Snopes. She is a corruption of the matriarchal order (represented in its purity by Aunt Jenny Dupre, Colonel Sartoris's widowed sister) and its struggle to preserve the sacramental family in the face of an abdicated masculinity. She may be a greater corrupter of the family order than the scheming Belle Mitchell, who lures the idealistic Horace from his submissive and basically incestuous relation with his sister into the trap of a long and unhappy marriage. Narcissa is enigmatic in her ways. Having married the death-seeking Bayard Sartoris, borne Bayard's son and on the same day learned of her husband's death in an air crash, she names the son Benbow, instead of giving him his grandfather's name, John, as was expected. Her motive would seem to lie in the hope of removing her

son from the Sartoris destiny, but the act may be prompted by a motive that will damn the son more than the Sartoris blood: her desire to enclose him in her own incestuous nature.

> All of Narcissa's instincts had been antipathetic to him [Bayard]; his idea was a threat and his presence a violation of the very depths of her nature: in the headlong violence of him she had been like a lily in a gale which rocked to its roots in a sort of vacuum, without any actual laying-on of hands. And now the gale had gone on; the lily had forgotten it as its fury died away into fading vibrations of old terrors and dreads, and the stalk recovered and the bell itself was untarnished save by the friction of its own petals. The gale is gone, and though the lily is sad a little with vibrations of ancient fears, it is not sorry.[26]

Narcissa's inviolable narcissism may be taken as a singular phenomenon, but in its context in *Flags in the Dust* it suggests the final stage of a South living its death in history, a closure of the southern matriarchy in itself. In this suggestion Faulkner at last clearly sounds a theme he had been seeking to articulate: the internalization of sexuality in the individual of the modern historical society. Faulkner was on the verge of perceiving that the modern sexual situation—as exemplified in the fragmentation of the sacramental family in the twentieth-century South—not only signifies an isolation of the individual in history but an isolation of history in the individual, a closure of history in the self. When at the end of *Flags in the Dust* Faulkner envisioned Narcissa—her child asleep in its crib upstairs in Narcissa's room—quietly playing the piano in the Mississippi twilight, "her white dress with its black ribbon at the waist vaguely luminous in the gloom," and the smell of jasmine drifting in through the window and Miss Jenny listening,[27] he made his final preparation for a very different, far more complex, but congruent vision: that of a fourteen-year-old girl in a flowering pear tree. She has on a "prissy dress" and wears a hat with flowers on it, but her most obvious article of apparel to the children, white and black, who watch from below as she stands precariously in the tree outside a room in the Compson house in Jefferson, is her muddy white drawers.

> A snake crawled out from under the house, Jason said he wasn't afraid of snakes and Caddy said he was but she wasn't and Versh said they both were and Caddy said to be quiet, like father said. . . .
>
> We stopped under the wet tree by the parlor window. Versh set me down in the wet grass. It was cold. There were lights in all the windows.
>
> "That's where Damuddy is." Caddy said. "She's sick every day now. When she gets well we're going to have a picnic."
>
> "I knows what I knows." Frony said.
>
> The trees were buzzing, and the grass.

"The one next to it is where we have the measles." Caddy said. "Where do you and T. P. have the measles, Frony."

"Has them just wherever we is, I reckon." Frony said.

"They haven't started yet." Caddy said.

They are getting ready to start, T.P. said. You stand right here now while I get that box so we can see in the window. Here, les finish drinking this here sassprilluh. It make me feel just like a squinch owl inside.

We drank the sassprilluh and T.P. pushed the bottle through the lattice, under the house, and went away. I could hear them in the parlor and I clawed my hands against the wall. T.P. dragged the box. He fell down, and he began to laugh. He lay there, laughing into the grass. He got up and dragged the box under the window, trying not to laugh.

"I skeered I going to holler." T.P. said. "Git on the box and see is they started."

"They haven't started because the band hasn't come yet." Caddy said.

"I knows what I knows." Frony said.

"You dont know anything." Caddy said. She went to the tree. "Push me up, Versh."

"Your paw told you to stay out that tree." Versh said.

"That was a long time ago." Caddy said. "I expect he's forgotten about it. Besides, he said to mind me tonight. Didn't he say to mind me tonight."

"I'm not going to mind you." Jason said. "Frony and T.P. are not going to either."

"Push me up, Versh." Caddy said.

"All right." Versh said. "You the one going to get whipped. I aint." He went and pushed Caddy up into the tree to the first limb. We watched the muddy bottom of her drawers. Then we couldn't see her. We could see the tree thrashing.

"Mr. Jason said if you break that tree he whip you." Versh said.

"I'm going to tell on her too." Jason said.

The tree quit thrashing. We looked into the still branches.

"What you seeing." Frony whispered.

I saw them. Then I saw Caddy, with flowers in her hair, and a long veil like shining wind. Caddy. Caddy. . . .

"Who in that tree." Dilsey said. She came and looked up into the tree. "Caddy." Dilsey said. The branches began to shake again.

"You, Satan." Dilsey said. "Come down from there."

"Hush." Caddy said, "Dont you know Father said to be quiet." Her legs came in sight and Dilsey reached up and lifted her out of the tree.[28]

This sequence comes, as you know, from the pear tree episode in the Benjy section of *The Sound and the Fury*. Transpiring in the decayed garden of the Compson place with its "weedchoked traces of the old ruined lawns and promenades,"[29] this episode is a memory of the story of the Edenic fall. This was a fall not into simple human mortality but into the linear sexuality of familial generations. It marks the beginning of history in the "generations of Adam." Following the emphasis in Faulkner's poem "Beneath the apple tree Eve's tortured shape," the story of Caddy in the pear tree envisions the subjection both of man and the old non-Edenic gods to the god of human history, the Hebraic Satan. As she comes to us in Benjy's re-creation, Caddy is an avatar of all the women who have borne heirs to the Compson lineage, a Compson princess, a sacred vessel of the family's perpetuation and a symbol of living motherhood. She is also an avatar of Persephone, the goddess of fertility and queen of Hades.[30] She is also an avatar of the Grecian nymphs of the woods and waters. She is also herself, a daring little girl, who is braver than her brothers and who is almost a woman.

At this point in *The Sound and the Fury* she is none of these things save in a consciousness in which time does not exist; yet which, although responsive to pasture and firelight, is locked in the reverberations of a bodiless name, "Caddy. Caddy" (bodiless because Benjy remembers only the loss not the person) that echoes the historical doom of the Compsons. Like Herman Melville, Thomas Mann, Robinson Jeffers, and Eugene O'Neill, Faulkner was attracted to the relationship between brother and sister as a profound symbol of the modern internalization of history. In the Compson family the symbol is connected with the lapse of the southern matriarchal order as signified by the death of Damuddy, the neurosis of Mrs. Compson, and, most of all, by the fate of Caddy and her daughter, the last Quentin. Faulkner forcefully pursues the symbol of the brother-sister relation into the consciousness of Quentin in the second section of *The Sound and the Fury*, achieving what may well be an unmatched realization of his novelistic powers. In Quentin's story the self (in old-fashioned terminology the "soul") is closed not in the obsessive memorialization of loss, a characteristic of the modern society of science and history, but in a more central, perhaps *the* central imperative of this society: the compulsion, common alike to Francis Bacon and Cotton Mather, to destroy myth and tradition, ritual and liturgy, the wholeness of the sacramental world, in the interest of purifying the consciousness of everything that is not historical. Or, put another way, in the interest of making the individual consciousness absolutely historical.

The compulsive fusion of historical consciousness and self-consciousness, or history and self—this is the meaning of the matchless beginning of the Quentin section: "When the shadow of the sash appeared on the curtains it was between seven and eight o'clock and then I was in time again, hearing the watch. It was Grandfather's and when Father gave it to me he said, Quentin, I give you the mausoleum of all hope and desire."[31] Identifying death, the Crucifixion, and incest with watch and clock, twisting the hands off his watch, recollecting the watch charm from the great world's fair (symbol of the society of science and history), breaking the crystal of his watch and leaving the mark of his blood on the dial—in doing these things Quentin prepares for the consummation of his unwilling, agonizing, but fierce and dedicated compulsion to purify history by drowning himself. Thereby he fulfills what his psychic incest with his sister had signified: the ultimate historical act, a pure identification of his consciousness with the historical death of the Compson family and the South.

In the Jason section of *The Sound and the Fury*, Jason's relation with Caddy becomes a symbol of the closure of history in the self through the purity of Jason's absorption in the money ethic of modern rationalistic society, which, cleansed of myth and tradition and the sacramental connection of life to its sources in nature, makes money the nexus between human beings, even between brother and sister. Told from the authorial point of view, the last section of *The Sound and the Fury* develops the climactic moment in the novel when, in the Easter service in Dilsey's church, the story of Caddy and her brothers is brought into conjunction with the celebration, not of the sacrament of the mass and the transubstantial reality of Christ's presence, but with the historical reality of the events of the Crucifixion and the Resurrection—with Dilsey's endurance of history, its beginning and ending, as sustained by "the annealment and the blood of the remembered Lamb."[32] In his Easter sermon, abandoning his educated manner and becoming the vernacular black preacher, the Reverend Shegog (of Chicago) tells the story of Jesus and the Roman Empire, offering a pure—a puritan, a Pauline—version of the apocalyptic closure of history in the Christ.

In the final moment of the fourth section of *The Sound and the Fury* the order of Benjy's world is associated with the South's attempt to close history in its dream of a modern, world beneficent slave society, and with the defeat of this dream. Luster drives Benjy—gelded, completely innocent of history, yet the complete historian—around the Confederate monument in the courthouse square of Jefferson. The soldier gazes with empty eyes beneath his marble hand, and Benjy, his eyes empty and serene, sees everything in its ordered place. History is closed in the consciousness of a world-historical idiot.

In a remarkable comment on his writing of *The Sound and the Fury*, composed in 1933 but not published until recently, Faulkner says: "The story is all there, in the first section as Benjy told it. I did not try deliberately to make it obscure; when I realised that the story might be printed, I took three more sections, all longer than Benjy's, to try to clarify it." The last section, he says, is an effort "to get completely out of the book." In making this endeavor, Faulkner realized "that there would be compensations, that in a sense I could then give a final turn to the screw and extract some ultimate distillation."[33]

If there is an ultimate distillation of the meaning of *The Sound and the Fury*, it comes in the coda to the novel Faulkner wrote some fifteen years after its completion, the Compson genealogy, notably in the entry on Candace Compson. In reporting on Caddy's life after she has left Jefferson, Faulkner presumably moves as far outside his novel as he could ever have gotten without starting over and rewriting it. His movement outward comprehends a further attempt to clarify the Benjy section. After recording Caddy's marital career up to the time of the Nazi invasion of France, where she is living at the time, Faulkner reports that she has vanished in the occupation. But there is a definite clue as to her whereabouts as late as 1943, when Melissa Meek, the town librarian of Jefferson, finds a picture in a slick magazine. It is "a picture filled with luxury and money and sunlight—a Cannebière backdrop of mountains and palms and cypresses and the sea, an open powerful expensive chromium-trimmed sports car, the woman's face hatless between a rich scarf and a seal coat, ageless and beautiful, cold serene and damned; beside her a handsome lean man of middle-age in the ribbons and tabs of a German staff-general." Melissa clips the picture, puts it in her purse, and goes to Jason. Unfolding it before him she whispers, "It's Caddy. . . . We must save her!" Jason says, "It's Cad, all right"; but then he denies his sister, "That Candace? . . . That bitch aint thirty yet. The other one's fifty now." Desperate, Melissa gets on a train and goes up to Memphis, where Dilsey now lives in the care of Frony. But Dilsey says she is too blind to look at the picture. Melissa comes back to Jefferson, "crying quietly *that was it she didn't want to see it know whether it was Caddy or not because she knows Caddy doesn't want to be saved hasn't anything anymore worth being saved for nothing worth being lost that she can lose.*"[34]

The story of the Compson family ends in Caddy's identification with the unspeakable Nazi endeavor to effect a final purification of history. Serene in her prolonged beauty, Caddy knows her damnation. One more turn of the screw. Dilsey not only knows that Caddy has nothing to be saved for, she knows that Caddy could never have been saved. She recognized this long ago when she said to the little girl in the blooming pear tree. "You, Satan . . . Come down from there." And Caddy said, "Hush. . . . Don't you know Father said to be quiet." Finally recognizing what Dilsey had said, Faulkner got out of *The Sound and the Fury* by turning the story over to the snake in the Compson garden. The only one of the Compsons capable of loving another person (save the servant Dilsey), Caddy emerges in her last appearance in the Compson record as an avatar of Satan. Far from being an Arcadian nymph, far even from being Per-sephone, goddess of the classical underworld, she is an empress of the dark dominion of modern history—the queen of the twentieth-century version of the Hebraic-Christian hell.

In all this oblique emblematizing there is a bizarre but logical extension of what Faulkner refers to in the 1933 introduction to *The Sound and the Fury* as the "symbology of the soiled drawers"—of the "muddy bottom of a little doomed girl climbing a blooming pear tree in April to look in the window at the funeral."[35] The sexuality of the Compsons has become symbolic not simply of the history of the South but, identified with the Nazi imperatives, of the modern drive to control history through the power of the human will. Closed in Caddy, the tale of the Compsons becomes a pure distillation of the terrible intimacy between the individual and modern history. As in her brother Quentin's case, Caddy is not only isolated in history but history is isolated in her.

His perception of the situation of Quentin and Caddy dramatizes the fundamental insight Faulkner attained in writing *The Sound and the Fury*: the knowledge of his own internalization of history, of the closure of history in himself. Exploring the sexuality of southern history, Faulkner underwent a deep experience of the historicism of his own consciousness. This experience is more or less overtly recorded in the 1933 commentary on the composition of *The Sound and the Fury*. (By the time this commentary was written, the experience of history it sets forth had been confirmed in the writing of *As I Lay Dying, Light in August,* and *Sanctuary,* and it was going to be still more deeply confirmed in the writing of *Absalom, Absalom!*) "Because it is himself that he is writing about, not about his environment," the author says in the 1933 document, "he has, figuratively speaking, taken the artist in him in one hand and his milieu in the other and thrust the one into the other like a clawing and spitting cat into a croker sack."[36]

Like Joyce, Faulkner responded directly to the interiority of history first detected by Shakespeare and Cervantes. This followed upon the loss of the cosmic sacramentalism which the medieval society of myth and tradition had perpetuated, but which could not survive the attack on it by the sixteenth- and seventeenth-century reformers bent on redeeming Christianity by reclaiming the apocalyptic historicism of St. Paul. Like Joyce, Faulkner was attracted to the notion that the apocalypse of history in the self of the artist dispenses with God and elevates the artist to the throne. Indeed, Faulkner in one well-known statement (1959) ironically assumes the whole foundation of Yoknapatawpha to rest on his godlike power paradoxically to create a sacramental cosmos out of his particular experience of the historicism of consciousness:

With *Soldiers' Pay* I found out writing was fun. But I found out afterward that not only each book had to have a design but the whole output or sum of an artist's work had to have a design. With *Soldiers' Pay* and *Mosquitoes* I wrote for the sake of writing because it was fun. Beginning with *Sartoris* I discovered that my own little postage stamp of native soil was worth writing about and I would never live long enough to exhaust it, and that by sublimating the actual into the apocryphal I would have complete liberty to use whatever talent I might have to its absolute top. It opened up a gold mine of other people, so I created a cosmos of my own. I can move these people around like God, not only in space but in time too. The fact that I have moved my characters around in time successfully, at least in my estimation, proves to me my own theory that time is a fluid condition which has no existence except in the momentary avatars of individual people. There is no such thing as *was*—only *is*. If *was* existed, there would be no grief or sorrow. I like to think of the world I created as being a kind of keystone in the universe; that, small as that keystone is, if it were ever taken away the universe itself would collapse. My last book will be the Doomsday Book, the Golden Book, of Yoknapatawpha County. Then I shall break the pencil and I'll have to stop.[37]

Saying that beginning with *Sartoris* ("the germ of my apocrypha")[38] he sublimated the actual—that is to say the basic sexuality of southern history he discovered in the initial Yoknapatawpha novel, or more precisely, the matriarchal culture of Mississippi—into the apocryphal, is not Faulkner wryly saying more than that he translated social reality into fiction or, for that matter, that he elevated it into myth? Does he not imply something like the transformation of the actual into a secular testament—into pseudo, or, it may be, uncanonized scripture? In the sense either of that which is testamentary or of that which has "hidden meanings" (the more literal sense of the term), "apocryphal" may appropriately characterize stories which in total design constitute a massive replication of the conjunction of the cosmic and historical modes of existence—and not less the result of this conjunction in the literary imagination, the recognition of the absorption of the cosmic in the historical. Yoknapatawpha, Faulkner's apocryphal world, is a great, ironic, often enigmatic testament to the capacity of the literary imagination to conceive the drama of the historical consciousness in its formation and in its completion and to conceive this as a tale told by the modern literary artist. To return to the metaphor with which I began, Yoknapatawpha is a part of the large edifice of Western secular literature. Since the age of Marlowe and Shakespeare and Cervantes and before, since the time when Christendom began to purify itself of the medieval cosmic sacramentalism (and since the time when the purifiers came to America to establish New England and eventually the South, which today is the American homeland of the "born again") this construct has always been enlarging and more and more assuming the status of secular scripture. Not opposite to but apposite to the religious structure erected on the Protestant vision of the Bible, it is itself, like this vision, a source and integral part of the Western imagination of history.

NOTES

[1] R. W. Southern, "The Historical Experience," *Times Literary Supplement,* June 24, 1977, p. 771.

[2] See Lewis P. Simpson, "Faulkner and the Legend of the Artist," in *Faulkner: Fifty Years After The Marble Faun,* ed. George H. Wolfe (Tuscaloosa: University of Alabama Press, 1976).

[3] Southern, "The Historical Experience," 771.

[4] For instances of the use of the term see Faulkner to Harold Ober, January 5, 1946, February 1, 1948, in Joseph Blotner (ed.), *Selected Letters of William Faulkner* (New York: Random House, 1977), 218, 262.

[5] *A Green Bough* (New York: Harrison Smith and Robert Haas, 1933). 65.

[6] *Ibid.,* 48.

[7] *The Marble Faun* (Boston: The Four Seas Company, 1924), 12, 16.

[8] See Noel Polk, "William Faulkner's *Marionettes,*" in *A Faulkner Miscellany,* ed. James B. Meriwether (Jackson: University Press of Mississippi, 1974), 3-36.

[9] Many aspects of the Pan-Christ identification are discussed in Patricia Merivale, *Pan the Goat-God: His Myth in Modern Times* (Cambridge: Harvard University Press, 1969), 14-16 *passim.*

[10] The sense of "ennui" is an implied motif in both *Soldiers' Pay* and *Mosquitoes.* A major study of the motif in Western culture is provided in Reinhard Kuhn, *The Demon of Noontide: Ennui in Western Literature* (Princeton: Princeton University Press, 1976).

[11] *Soldiers' Pay* (New York: Liveright Publishing Company, 1954), 112.

[12] *Mosquitoes* (New York: Liveright Publishing Company, 1955), 152, 11.

[13] *Ibid.,* 322.

[14] See Joseph Blotner, *Faulkner: A Biography* (New York: Random House, 1974), 11, 1440-41.

[15] *Mosquitoes,* 326-29.

[16] *Ibid.,* 339. See pp. 335-40 for the nighttown scene.

[17] *Ibid.,* 10.

[18] Faulkner to Horace Liveright, February, 1928, in Blotner (ed.), *Selected Letters of Faulkner,* 40.

[19] Frederick L. Gwynn and Joseph Blotner (eds.), *Faulkner in the University* (New York: Vintage Books, 1965), 130.

[20] *Flags in the Dust,* ed. Douglas Day (New York: Random House, 1973), 154.

[21] Blotner, *Faulkner,* I, 528.

[22] *Ibid.,* 331-32; Merivale, *Pan the Goat-God,* 220.

[23] Blotner, *Faulkner,* I, 529-31.

[24] *Ibid.,* 557.

[25] Gwynn and Blotner (eds.), *Faulkner in the University,* 254.

[26] *Flags in the Dust,* 368.

[27] *Ibid.,* 369.

[28] *The Sound and the Fury* (New York: Vintage Books, 1946), 45-54.

[29] *Ibid.* (Appendix), 409.

[30] Cf. André Bleikasten, *The Most Splendid Failure: Faulkner's The Sound and the Fury* (Bloomington: Indiana University Press, 1976), 43-66. Bleikasten sees the treatment of Caddy as "the quest for Eurydice." The association is possible, but it seems unlikely that it was in Faulkner's mind.

[31] *The Sound and the Fury,* 93.

[32] *Ibid.,* 371.

[33] "An Introduction to *The Sound and the Fury,*" in Meriwether (ed.), *A Faulkner Miscellany,* 160-61.

[34] *The Sound and the Fury* (Appendix), 415-20.

[35] "Introduction to *The Sound and the Fury,*" 159, 161.

[36] *Ibid.,* 158.

[37] Jean Stein Vanden Heuvel, "William Faulkner" [interview], in *Writers at Work: The Paris Review Interviews,* ed. Malcolm Cowley (New York: Viking Press, 1959), 141.

[38] Gwynn and Blotner (eds.), *Faulkner in the University,* 285.

Harold Fromm

SOURCE: "Virginia Woolf: Art and Sexuality," in *The Virginia Quarterly Review,* Vol. 55, No. 3, Summer, 1979, pp. 441-59.

[*In the following essay, Fromm responds to critics who see Virginia Woolf's writing as characteristically "sexless."*]

Since the publication in 1941 of her last novel, *Between the Acts,* Virginia Woolf's reputation has undergone radical transformation. At first characterized as "experimental" and treated from an esthetic vantage point, her novels received serious, if somewhat limited, examinations as literary productions, while a view prevailed of her as a rather precious Bohemian associated with slightly disreputable characters from Bloomsbury. But even as late as the sixties, when *Mrs. Dalloway* and *To the Lighthouse*—and by some, *The Waves*—were considered major works, she herself was not regarded as one of the major figures of 20th-century literature, and as recently as 1975 the *Norton Anthology* did not consider her a "major author." Still, with the gradual appearance in the sixties of Leonard Woolf's five-volume autobiography and the emergence of women's and gay liberation movements, Woolf's reputation began to grow, rapidly accelerating after the publication in 1972 of Quentin Bell's biography and the many reminiscences and biographical essays which began to flood the market shortly thereafter.

As an intrinsically interesting personality, as a figure of sociological interest, as a writer who seemed to have some measure of importance in literary history, and as an embodiment of a number of unconventionalities currently becoming conventionalized, Woolf has become virtually a cult celebrity. But if she is now regarded as a Major Literary Figure, it is more the case of a Major Figure who also happens to be Literary than a Literary Figure who happens to be Major. Indeed, her current status may turn out to have been achieved at a high price once her fortuitous enmeshment with present obsessions has had its day. For she now occupies the position with the ruling intelligentsia that Herman Hesse occupied during the late sixties with the student revolution. And so we see again a principally polemical use being made of a literary figure, this time with grossly disproportionate emphasis being placed on her life and its adaptability to current political-psychological programs. Nor is close scrutiny required to realize that most of the attention these days falls upon peripheral works by and about her: *A Room of One's Own, Three Guineas, The Years, A Writer's Diary,* Bell's biography, Nicolson's *Portrait of a Marriage,* Woolf's letters and now her journals, as well as *Moments of Being,* an admittedly striking collection of previously unpublished autobiographical essays by Woolf herself. Far from being seen these days as an eccentric from Bloomsbury, a highbrow grafted away from her ancestral upper-middle-class roots, she is widely regarded as a patrician intellectual, a strong-minded and determined profes-

sional, and a somewhat sexually ambiguous feminist. Even her bouts with madness have served as a wound that can be shared with today's educated and psychologically sensitized middle class.

Among the extraordinary quantity of writings about Bloomsbury that have recently pressed her into eminence can be found a number of journals and newsletters devoted exclusively to Woolf and her circle, founded in the main by women who are apt to be feminists and who frequently (though by no means always) indulge themselves in minute worryings of the details of Woolf's life, visiting Monks House, rifling through her papers, rubbing elbows with Quentin Bell, and then descending from this Parnassus to write reminiscences of tiresome inconsequence. With the widespread changes in social roles now being undergone by educated and academic women, their experiences in or with psychoanalysis, the availability of alternate sexual lifestyles, the possibility of escape from domesticity, the commonplaceness of divorce, and the earning of their own living, there is very strong identification with and admiration for Woolf in much of current female writing about her, an identification intensified by Woolf's own psychological and sexual problems. This phenomenon can be seen in such books as Nancy Bazin's *Virginia Woolf and the Androgynous Mind,* Jane Novak's *The Razor Edge of Balance,* and Joanne Trautmann's *Jessamy Brides,* to mention a few. One of the most startling of essays, "Mrs. Virginia Woolf," by Cynthia Ozick, appeared several years ago in *Commentary* and castigated Leonard Woolf as a tyrannical and repressive husband who was virtually an anti-Semite. For now, at any rate, this essay would seem to represent the limits of appropriation.

With so much of Woolf's current status derived from extraliterary valuations, one finds that despite some recent signs of shifting here and there the novels still tend to be seen as they have been for a long time. In other words, the *literary* identity of the novels has not changed a great deal, but a reshuffling of their importance has resulted from those examinations which appropriate them as feminism, mythopoetic thought, polemics for androgyny, attacks on the social system, etc.

One of the greatest impediments to a just literary revaluation of Woolf's novels has been, even from the earliest years, the objection that they are lacking in sexuality, deficient in earthy vitality, that they are precious and rather weak in the kind of human interest that *is* present in her contemporaries, Joyce and Proust. There is nothing in Woolf's novels, her denigrators might remark, that quite corresponds in its impact to Stephen Dedalus picking his nose or Leopold Bloom masturbating. Despite the contemporary agreement, at least in theory, that literary "realism" is a convention as "artificial" as any other, the imputed absence of such an impact has cost Woolf a lot. If you scratch even a sophisticated contemporary reader, it would seem, you are bound to find a die-hard representationalist under the skin. Mimeticism still reigns supreme. For all of the involutedness and stylization of Joyce, he is felt to be a "realist" after all.

This representational bias against Woolf's supposed sexlessness has actually increased and been afforded greater currency as a result of Bell's biography, with its insistent emphasis on Woolf's "aetherial" character and her low sexual energies as a person. Instead of subjecting to investigation what can be meant by the term "sexuality" when it is used in connection with fiction, the reviewers of Bell's biography fixed upon Woolf's sex life, particularly the harm that supposedly was wrought by George Duckworth's erotic displays towards his half-sisters Virginia and Vanessa. Virginia Woolf alludes very unfavorably in later life to George's behavior and, in *Moments of Being,* to Gerald Duckworth's pettings as well, but the assumption that her coldness as a person and the "sexlessness" of her novels can be traced to all of this is both rash and absurd, especially since Vanessa received similar treatment and developed very differently. Surely the seeds of their sexuality were sown long before their experiences with the Duckworths. As it turns out, there is nothing Bell tells us that can account for the causes of Woolf's sexual "coolness." But once given the rash and dramatic conclusions of the reviewers of his book, it was not very difficult to move along to the conclusion that Virginia Woolf was basically a sexless person and (as if more were needed) that *that* is why her fiction itself is so sexless. Bell wrote: "Vanessa, Leonard and, I think, Virginia herself were inclined to blame George Duckworth. George certainly had left Virginia with a deep aversion to lust; but perhaps he did no more than inflame a deeper wound and confirm Virginia in her disposition to shrink from the crudities of sex, a disposition which resulted from some profound and perhaps congenital inhibition [*i.e.,* Bell knows nothing about the whole matter.]. I think that the erotic element in her personality was faint and tenuous." As for Virginia's relationship with her husband, Bell admits that beyond her coolness, he does not know the extent of their sexual activities. In a letter, shortly after their marriage, Virginia writes, "but certainly I find the climax immensely exaggerated," and Bell alludes to her subsequently as "frigid."

II

If one were to try to be as accurate as possible, there would not be a great deal that one could say with any degree of certainty about Virginia Woolf's sexuality as a flesh and blood person. To derive support from Bell's limited and sometimes self-contradictory and flimsy generalizations for the view that Woolf's novels lack sexuality is to go rather far. Indeed, a large-scaled attack is mounted against Bell's weakness in this area by Ellen Hawkes Rogat ["The Virgin in the Bell Biography," *Twentieth Century Literature,* XX, 2, April 1974], who concludes:

> When Bell and others insist on the insubstantial quality of Woolf's novels, they are stubbornly

demanding a wider domain of reference. They still insist on conventional definitions of what constitutes "reality" in fiction, even when Woolf rejected "the plausible and preposterous formulas which are supposed to represent the whole of our human adventure." Bell has sanctioned this attitude by equating the supposedly narrow sphere of her novels with her sexuality. Preoccupied with her virginity and frigidity, careless about his language, and willing to believe that her writing reflects sexual neurosis, Bell fails to understand that she "wrote as a woman, but as a woman who has forgotten that she is a woman, so that her pages were full of that curious sexual quality which comes only when sex is unconscious of itself" [quotations are from Woolf's essays]. She called this "the first great lesson" for a woman writer. Bell should have been similarly instructed; instead, his biography suffers from that tiresome sexual quality which comes from unconscious, but nevertheless predominant, stereotypes of femininity.

Before legitimate use can be made of biography to bolster literary criticism, one needs to ask what is the relationship between an artist's life and an artist's work. And immediately that such a question is raised, we are faced with the dilemma that there is no consistently observable and reliable equation between life and art. For every artist whose work bears a close and obvious relationship to his life we can find another whose work does not. For every Emily Dickinson, who wrote shocking little poems for a spinsterly recluse, we can discover a Norman Mailer, who writes just the kind of novels one would expect him to write. For every artist who reviews his life in art, there is another who lives it in art. Because an artist need not deal at all with his own visible experiences in the world, the data recordable in a biography may have little in common with the data expressed in art. And if art, like dreams, uses a language of image and metaphor in which anything can be made to stand for anything, no reliable mediation may ever be achieved between life and art. There are indeed cases—perhaps George Eliot's is one—in which the germinal experiences of the artist's life are clearly visible and lived through once again in the works. But there are other artists, and I think Virginia Woolf is one of them, who do not in any substantial way write about their visible lives, even if the data they employ can be shown to derive from their apparent milieu.

Thus it is far from clear after reading about Woolf's "sexless" life what we are to make of "sexless" as an adjective used to describe the novels. If what is meant by the charge were nothing more than the absence of overt lovemaking, then perhaps one could agree that the novels are "sexless." But more than this is usually intended: the complaint is that these works lack certain vital juices and are the productions of a virtually disembodied spirit. And it is this complaint that one cannot take seriously. For it is only from the point of view of the traditional "realistic" novel that Woolf's novels are seen as wanting in sexuality. In the language of the "realistic" novel, "sexual" means that basic sexual acts, like kissing, take place. But Woolf, in rejecting the language of the traditional novel, was concerned with forging a new set of signs and symbols. As Lily, the painter, observes in *To the Lighthouse*, "A mother and child might be reduced to a shadow without irreverence." In other words, art requires the establishment of equivalences, and new schools of art must establish new equivalents. Whereas in an earlier work of fiction a kiss might stand for relations between sexes, in a new fiction as in a new psychology, another image might serve the same function. Thus, a boat sailing down a stream, once it is taken as an image of sexual intercourse, could take the place of a kiss as a representation of human sexual relations, serving as a more appropriate image for a more lyrical and non-representational mode of art. Why not, for instance, "Look how the willow shoots its fine sprays into the air! Look how through them a boat passes, filled with indolent, with unconscious, with powerful young men"? This is the usual method of poetry—and more and more it has come to be employed in fiction. (The passage, as a matter of fact, from *The Waves,* is an instance of Neville's sexual fantasies.) Once such an allowance has been made—that fiction is free to establish new languages of equivalence—the charge of Virginia Woolf's sexlessness as a writer begins to crumble.

To settle once and for all this ubiquitous issue is a fairly straightforward matter, and it can be settled by clearing up what one means by "sexual" and then by examining the fiction itself. I have already dismissed as too narrow the equation of sexual with conventional erotic phenomena and, indeed, the general usage of the word in the present century is not customarily confined to so narrow a sense. "Sexual" is generally used to refer to the entire affective life in all its variations and permutations. We say, for example, that the nature of the lesson in Ionesco's play *The Lesson* is sexual, and we mean that the conversation between the professor and his student conveys, by its form but not by its literal meanings, the progress of a sexual violation, and in the same dramatist's play *Jack, or the Submission* we describe the conversation between Jack and Roberta as sexual because its rhythms suggest those of an orgasm, with the effect reinforced by imagery that is erotically evocative.

Here, then, I am prepared to demonstrate that far from having a "deep aversion to lust" and a "disposition to shrink from the crudities of sex" (by which Bell means sex itself), Virginia Woolf produced fiction that is among the most effectively sexual that we have. And by examining so early a work as *Jacob's Room* we can see that this erotic timbre is present in what were to become the most characteristic elements of Woolf's later art.

III

Although *Jacob's Room* deals directly with Jacob's affairs with various girls (thus satisfying even the most simpleminded sense of "sexual"), the novel's strong sexual ambiance comes not from an explicit handling of sexual relationships but from the quality of the imagery:

> After six days of salt, wind, rain, and sun, Jacob Flanders had put on a dinner jacket. . . . Even so his neck, wrists, and face were exposed without cover, and his whole person, whether exposed or not, tingled and glowed so as to make even black cloth an imperfect screen. He drew back the great red hand that lay on the table-cloth. Surreptitiously it closed upon slim glasses and curved silver forks. The bones of the cutlets were decorated with pink frills—and yesterday he had gnawn ham from the bone!

This is the characteristic imagery of the novel and if it is not redolent of sexuality, if it is not an attempt to distill, in this case, masculinity and its mysteries, then it is hard to say what its function is intended to be. Or, to use a longer but similar passage:

> Very awkward he was. And when they sat upon a plush sofa and let the smoke go up between them and the stage, and heard far off the high-pitched voices and the jolly orchestra breaking in opportunely he was still awkward, only Fanny thought: "What a beautiful voice!" She thought how little he said yet how firm it was. She thought how young men are dignified and aloof, and how unconscious they are, and how quietly one might sit beside Jacob and look at him. And how childlike he would be, come in tired of an evening, she thought, and how majestic; a little overbearing perhaps; "But I wouldn't give way," she thought. He got up and leant over the barrier. The smoke hung about him.
>
> And for ever the beauty of young men seems to be set in smoke, however lustily they chase footballs, or drive cricket balls, dance, run, or stride along roads. Possibly they are soon to lose it. . . . Anyhow, they love silence, and speak beauti-fully, each word falling like a disc new cut, not a hubblebubble of small smooth coins such as girls use; and they move decidedly, as if they knew how long to stay and when to go. . . .
>
> And isn't it pleasant, Fanny went on thinking, how young men bring out lots of silver coins from their trouser pockets, and look at them, instead of having just so many in a purse?

If one had nothing better to say, one could observe that these are the musings of an Edwardian feminist idealizing her dead brother Thoby, and just this sort of thing is remarked by Herbert Marder in his disappointing book on Virginia Woolf's feminism. But what really seems to need pointing out is that this is writing suffused with sexuality, a product of an ultraresponsive sensibility noting every curve's, every odor's, every sound's visceral impact. It is an attempt to convey the feeling of maleness and femaleness (one of Woolf's obsessions), and it comes closer to recreating that twitch in our psyches that reveals such intuitions to us than the phallic ragings of even some of the best passages in

Lady Chatterley's Lover. It is, in any event, no less sexual than they.

In the long passage quoted above, the reader should observe such words as "awkward," "firm," "unconscious," which are recurrent adjectives connected with the quality of "maleness." In the wonderful scene in which Jacob is seated in the railway carriage with an old woman who fears he will attack her (an erotic episode reflecting the mysteries of the sexes), we read: "She dwelt upon his mouth. The lips were shut. The eyes bent down, since he was reading. All was firm, yet youthful, indifferent, unconscious—as for knocking one down! No, no, no!" At first the woman is disturbed because Jacob is smoking (already established as an erotic act). But after she is drawn to his appearance—she seems a bit inflamed, in fact—he helps her out of the compartment: ". . . when the train drew into the station, Mr. Flanders burst open the door, and put the lady's dressing-case out for her, saying, or rather mumbling, 'Let me' very shyly: indeed he was rather clumsy about it." Once again, awkwardness mixed with strength, clumsiness mixed with shyness, indifference and unconsciousness and eyes bent down in reading. It is this mixture of ruthlessness and unconsciousness with intelligence, of slovenliness combined with dignity, which appears in most of the "maleness" passages of the novel. Jacob's rough hand holding the delicate dinnerware, to recall the passage quoted earlier, exemplifies a method both consistent and effective of conveying male sexuality. We see it again in the passage describing Cambridge undergraduates entering the chapel:

> Look, as they pass into service, how airily the gowns blow out, as though nothing dense and corporeal were within. [This is the spirituality and delicacy, the intelligence of maleness.] What sculptured faces, what certainty, authority controlled by piety [a bit mocking], although great boots march under the gowns. [This is male roughness, indifference, unconsciousness.]

At a dinner party where Jacob's rough hand holds the wineglass, one of the guests observes: "'He is extraordinarily awkward,' she thought, noticing how he fingered his socks. 'Yet so distinguished looking.'"

Because a large portion of *Jacob's Room* deals with the life of Cambridge undergraduates, critics have been ready to observe that the scenes at Cambridge, the kind of young men described, their intellectuality, and their mannerisms—all were familiar to a young woman like Virginia Stephen, who was introduced to the Cambridge world by her brother Thoby. Interesting as it is to know this, the novel is not "realistic" and does not attempt to give us a verisimilitudinous representation of Cambridge life. What is vital here is the author's attempt to recreate the emotional crux, the intuitive center of a particular world of experience. This vital center is conveyed not through an accurate description of Cambridge topography and customs so much as through images akin to those I have just reviewed. In a scene picturing

several undergraduates involved in an intellectual discussion, Jacob is described as sitting "astride a chair [while he] ate dates from a long box." And after another fellow makes an observation, we learn of Jacob that "taking out his penknife, he dug the point of it again and again into a knot in the table, as if affirming that the voice from the fender spoke the truth." The mode of seating and of eating are presented as distinctively male and the repeated stabbings of the knife recall both Peter Walsh and his penknife, from *Mrs. Dalloway,* and Giles Oliver's stomping of the snake in *Between the Acts.* These descriptions came close to musical phrases, making explanations on the part of the author superfluous as far as intuiting the novel is concerned—the reader gets them on the level at which they count. It is because I am making claims for Virginia Woolf that I find it needful to raise to consciousness what is properly appreciated unconsciously.

If the sexual imagery which I have been discussing were to be removed from *Jacob's Room,* the novel would fall apart, not simply because the removal of any materials from a well-wrought artifact would cause it to collapse but because these sexual images are the heart of the book, giving it its distinctive erotic flavor. And I have not bothered to deal at any length with such major elements as the episodes with Florinda, Fanny, and Sandra, nor for that matter the little clever sketches of the Cambridge professors Sopwith and Cowan—or Jacob's friend Bonamy. All pretty sappy. Besides, how shall one understand all of the *talking* that goes on at Cambridge? "Talking, talking, talking—as if everything could be talked—the soul itself slipped through the lips in thin silver discs which dissolve in young men's minds like silver, like moonlight." A passage like this brings to mind Norman Brown's treatment of language as eros in *Life Against Death.* In the context of Cassirer and Wittgenstein's views of language as play, as games, Brown writes: "The element of play in language is the erotic element; and this erotic element is in essence not genital, but polymorphously perverse." "If, in the history of every child, language is first of all a mode of erotic expression and then later succumbs to the domination of the reality-principle, it follows, or perhaps we should say mirrors, the path taken by the human psyche, namely neurosis. Language will then have to be analyzed as compromise-formation, produced by the conflict of the pleasure-principle and the reality-principle, like any neurotic symptom." And this becomes apparent in Woolf's use of talking at Cambridge as erotic by-play: "Sopwith went on talking; twining stiff fibers of awkward speech—things young men blurted out—plaiting them round his own smooth garland, making the bright side show, the vivid greens, the sharp thorns, manliness." Admittedly, the passage (like many in the novel) is a bit obscure, but one intuits its general sense well enough. The "awkward" speech of the vital and enthusiastic young Cambridge men appeals to the polished and scholarly professor, who weaves their rough fibers around his own "smooth garland" of cultivated articulateness. And what emerges for him is an eroticized experience of "manliness." The whole passage is a sexual one, erotic in the fullest sense, not the expression of a sensibility with an "aversion to lust," but of a sensibility that feels life in erotic terms.

Conceivably one might agree with Quentin Bell's remark, "I think that the erotic element in her personality was faint and tenuous," if one were considering Virginia Woolf's personality. But *Jacob's Room* is not her "personality,"—it is her creative work, a novel that does not have to be squeezed very hard to release its erotic juices. Nor is it an exception to the general tenor of the Woolf *opera,* nor characteristic of merely minor passages. Consider the well-known passage describing Clarissa Dalloway's feelings for Sally Seton: " . . . she did undoubtedly then feel what men felt."

> Only for a moment; but it was enough. It was a sudden revelation, a tinge like a blush which one tried to check and then, as it spread, one yielded to its expansion, and rushed to the farthest verge and there quivered and felt the world come closer, swollen with some astonishing significance, some pressure of rapture, which split its thin skin and gushed and poured with an extraordinary alleviation over the cracks and sores! Then, for that moment, she had seen an illumination; a match burning in a crocus; an inner meaning almost expressed. But the close withdrew; the hard softened. It was over—the moment.

This is a surprising passage from an "aetherial," a "sexless," a "frigid" writer, who may have found "the climax immensely exaggerated," but who seems to know quite well the sensibility of orgasms and who evokes one to describe Clarissa's feeling. It is not simply that she has learned from a sex manual about "swollen" and "gushed" and the "hard softened" but she has conveyed the very quality of sexual experience through lyrical language. A reader for whom this is not a sexual voice requires photographs of barnyard copulations, not literature.

IV

I have tried to suggest that in describing Woolf's fiction as deficient in eroticism one is using that concept in a sense much narrower than the one in customary use. When Bell writes,

> I would go further and suggest that she regarded sex, not so much with horror, as with incomprehension; there was, both in her personality and in her art, a disconcertingly aetherial quality and, when the necessities of literature compel her to consider lust, she either turns away or presents us with something as remote from the gropings and grapplings of the bed as is the flame of a candle from its tallow,

he is thinking of sex in the narrowest of senses, according to which only writers like Lawrence and Miller can be considered as dealing with sexual matters. And his reduction of sex to "lust," with little or nothing forming

a spectrum between "grapplings" and sexlessness is simply preposterous. His "both in her personality and in her art" is too facile, too easily spoken. There is not so generally such an easy transition from one's life to one's art that the two realms can be so unhesitatingly encompassed as Bell has done. Art is not based on the archetypes of daily action. Virginia Woolf's "aetherial quality" may very well have been present and even striking in her day-to-day life (though one also reads about day-to-day malice and bitchiness in a number of recollections), but it is a large jump to conclude that her books are equally "aetherial." The locus of her fiction is not to be found in *representations* of daily life but in the *presentation* of life's energies by means of a lyrical use of language. What various critics have regarded as sexlessness, then, is the relative absence of familiar sexual *events;* but events in general are infrequent in Virginia Woolf's fiction, and when they do appear they are usually complex metaphors for psychological states. Thus it is not so much sexlessness as eventlessness that characterizes Woolf's novels, while the *energies* of sex abound.

Although it would distend this discussion too much to explore the sexual qualities of all of Woolf's novels, it might be well to remind the reader of the extent to which sex figures as a major or a subsidiary force in *Mrs. Dalloway,* where it is pervasive (as "masculine" and "feminine"); in *To the Lighthouse,* where the natures and relationships of the sexes are central; in *The Waves,* where sex is the focus of life for at least three of the characters; in *Orlando,* where it is virtually the subject of the whole work; in *The Years,* where it is pervasive enough to be taken up by current feminists; and in *Between the Acts,* where it is a bright thread in the multithreaded tapestry of that complex work.

With regard to the homosexuality that is found in most of Woolf's fiction, it is beyond dispute that a knowledge of the milieu and character of the Bloomsbury Group explains a good deal of the *genesis* of characters and tensions in her works. It is likely that much of the particular sexual stresses in her fiction might not have been there if she had moved among a different set of men and women, for their presences and lives seem to have provided materials for insight that are not available in everyone's environment. On the other hand, information about genesis sheds little, if any, light on the meaning, the significance, of homosexuality in her novels. Quentin Bell gives us a wealth of information on the environment but none at all on the meaning. The homosexuality that thrived at Cambridge at the beginning of the century was reflected in the creative men and women associated with Bloomsbury. One is impressed (in Bell's account) that the lives of so many of these intellectuals and artists turned out as well as they did and that the suppression forced upon them by society did not destroy their art. Art may be a form of sublimation, but if the emotional life is restricted too much, there may be little left to sublimate. In an age when minority and countercultural points of view were not generally acceptable, the people connected with Bloomsbury did very well indeed, engaging in a much more open and less sinister life style than previous centuries would have exacted. Still, in their art, if we consider Forster and Strachey as representative, less openness was possible, at least if the artist intended to appeal to a general audience of the educated. And so the sublimations and transformations that we associate with artists like Michelangelo and Pater had not yet been rendered obsolete (nor had they yet been made supererogatory in Albee or Auden). Still, under the circumstances, Bloomsbury did rather well.

Virginia Woolf, however, was not among those creative people who have had to disguise their real sensibilities. Despite her living among such a polymorphous group, despite her intimacy with such an extraordinary trio as the Strachey-Carrington-Partridge ménage, she was not really one of them. As Quentin Bell suggests, her daily life might well have been relatively "aetherial," and even the much whispered-about infatuations that she had with a number of women (the most celebrated of which involved Vita Sackville-West, transfigured in *Orlando*) seem to have been fairly tame. But although her sexuality may not have exhibited itself vigorously in her personal relationships, her erotic sensibility took in everything going on around her—in Bloomsbury and elsewhere—and found a mirror for it all in her own psyche. The results of such a life are remarkable, even though they have scarcely hitherto been observed: she was able to embody a wide range of sexual feeling and behavior in her novels, ranging from the conventional to the homosexual, and she was bold enough to do this decades before a radical shift in society had made it not merely possible but fashionable to do so. While Forster and Strachey concealed what society might have regarded as perversion, and the supposedly bold Lawrence pretended (to himself above all) to disapprove of such stuff, Virginia Woolf was expressing her sensibility quite freely. While the homosexuality that appears in literature in the early part of the century was usually disguised or disapproved of by the author, Virginia Woolf dealt with it as matter-of-factly as the more approved forms of sexuality. Thus, the "gropings and grapplings of the bed" as handled by the noisier and more sexually celebrated writers now seem not quite so impressive as they once did. In the light of later knowledge, such writers as Lawrence, Hemingway, and Mailer (to cite a few) seem sullied by dishonest pretensions (if lack of self-knowledge can be regarded as a form of dishonesty), while Woolf, as a voice for sexuality, seems completely authentic. She was not subject to either a compulsive treatment *(e.g., Maurice)* or a disguised treatment *(e.g.,* Wilde's *Salome,* especially in Kate Millett's brilliant discussion of this play in *Sexual Politics)* of homosexuality in her fiction because she was not herself, in any meaningful sense, homosexual. On the other hand, that she had a polymorphous sensibility can be seen not only from her open and authentic-sounding accounts of homosexuality but from her equally authentic accounts of male and female feeling. She herself had that an-

drogynous mind which she talks about so eloquently in *A Room of One's Own,* and it enabled her to produce a body of creative work whose sympathies are extremely broad, however narrow the range of her fiction may be. Her literary tonality and timbre are the counterpart in prose of the musical sensibility of Gabriel Fauré, refined, elegant, muted, interior, while also passionate, quivering. Elegance and sensuousness, impressionism and sexuality, are not mutually exclusive. The interior life has its own range of excitements, whose colorations differ from those found in the art of a Wagner or a Lawrence. Thus, in place of the gropings and grapplings of the bed, Woolf has given us, in her explorations of the nervous qualities of the psyche, a picture of sexuality before it becomes phenomena! She has given us sexuality as that "jar on the nerves" that lies behind phenomena.

In this matter of polymorphousness, Virginia Woolf's life does not provide a key to her fiction (just as her "aetherial" daily character does not lead us to a view of her fiction as "sexless"). Rather, the contrary: a knowledge of her creative work makes it possible for us to understand what her mundane experience ultimately meant to her, an understanding which, nevertheless, remains of only secondary importance. Her esteem for the sexual variety in the Bloomsbury circle is reborn in her novels and made more general and abstract in *A Room of One's Own.* The androgyny that she so admired was a quality of mind that she took for granted as desirable, one of which she had seen admirable embodiments and one that she wished more generally to prevail among humanity at large. But Virginia Woolf did not lead a particularly repressed life as the result of being a woman, so it cannot therefore be inferred that her hopes for the androgynous mind sprang from personal grief. It is not a case of personal pleading and, indeed, there is very little in her works that can be thought of as pleading at all. She is not in the main concerned with the political range of action available to women in the mundane world so much as she is concerned with the general enlargement of consciousness. This interest in consciousness rather than action is what she is about when she writes of the response of women to contemporary male novelists (in *A Room of One's Own*): "Do what she will a woman cannot find in them that fountain of perpetual life which the critics assure her is there. It is not only that they celebrate male virtues, enforce male values and describe the world of men; it is that the emotion with which these books are permeated is to a woman incomprehensible."

While scattered insights about Virginia Woolf's representations of sexuality in her fiction have appeared over the years in critical writings about her, the prevailing attitude had been the one we have seen in Quentin Bell. Although we can no longer accept this point of view, we can, with the materials obtained from Bell's book and, even more importantly, those we obtain from Woolf's writings themselves, be in a position to understand things reasonably well; and such an understanding must conclude that however "aetherial" her daily life and however restrained her sexual activities, Virginia Woolf was an extraordinarily sentient person who was fully aware through firsthand feelings of her own of the nature and complexity of the sensual life. She may have had an innocence of the world (though I myself don't believe it), but she by no means had an innocence of the intuitive life. Without direct and fully enacted experiences of her own in the day-to-day world, her extra-sensitive artist's faculties enabled her nevertheless to present in her art a deep and broad spectrum of human sensuality, extrapolated from her own observations and nourished by her humanness. That it is presented in an "impressionistic" rather than a "realistic" manner does not make it any the less deep an exploration. With a wide and complicated scene of life taking place around her, however narrow the social circle in which she lived, she was fully apprised of as much of reality as most artists are vouchsafed.

Like Emily Dickinson, whose life was ten times more narrow, Virginia Woolf reveals in her art a sophisticated and worldly psyche, whatever the limitations of the experience of the body which maintained that psyche. And in her presentations of sexuality, she has gone far beyond the conventional conceptions of both the sexual and the emotional life. Lawrence's famous remark in *Lady Chatterley,* "The root of sanity is in the balls," once regarded as so outré, seems now somewhat narrowly Kiplingesque, with Mellors' therapeutic screwing of Connie little more than a sexualized version of "The White Man's Burden." And the rich, broad palette of the emotions experienced in Mailer is rendered curiously ineffective by the author's own inability to come to terms with it. In Virginia Woolf's fiction there is presentation rather than struggle. The author is not trying to persuade either her audience or herself of the validity of a program that she herself does not quite believe. The struggle and aggression in the work of writers like Lawrence and Mailer are aspects of an attempt to establish an identity by forcing and wresting the raw materials of reality into a shape that is pleasing to their inchoate selves. The very violence of the struggle betrays the desperateness of their personal need, and their incessant preaching conceals imperfectly a hope that, like Amphion, they will succeed in moving stones to assume a shape that serves their turn. In Virginia Woolf this absence of visible struggle, this paucity of action and wrenching events, may lead inattentive or presuppositious readers to experience her art as "sexless." But the presentation of sex by Virginia Woolf is closer to noumenal than phenomenal. It is a presentation that reveals through lyric imagery that "jar on the nerves" before it becomes phenomenal, before it is seen as "masculine" or "feminine." As a writer she deals with nerves rather than organs. Clearly, our previous assessments of the sexuality of Virginia Woolf's novels have employed too coarse a sieve.

David J. Gordon

SOURCE: "Sex and Language in D. H. Lawrence," in *Twentieth Century Literature,* Vol. 27, No. 4, Winter, 1981, pp. 362-75.

[*In the following essay, Gordon comments on the tension between sexuality and language in D. H. Lawrence's* Women in Love *and* Lady Chatterley's Lover.]

It is a mark of sophistication among literary interpreters to recognize that the verbal medium they are governed by is a means as well as an end, that language is inherently so figurative that the meaning of a text is always a matter of self-conscious rhetoric as well as direct reference. Influenced by the current authority of linguistics, some critical theorists in recent years have even attempted to discard as naïve the mimetic and referential functions of language. They would enclose us in a verbal world by declaring an impassable gulf between it and a world outside of words.

This new skepticism or linguistic autonomy can be dramatized by the following two contrasts, one literary, one psychoanalytic. First, D. H. Lawrence in 1929—"Poetry, they say, is a matter of words. . . . It is such a long way from being the whole truth that it is slightly silly if uttered sententiously"[1]—versus William Gass in 1972—"That novels should be made of words, and merely words, is shocking, really."[2] Lawrence implies that the poet expresses and evokes a subsistent physical life through language whereas Gass calls our attention to the illusory nature of any such attempt. A second contrast, Freud versus Lacan. In *An Outline of Psychoanalysis,* Freud acknowledged the challenge of epistemologists by writing: "We have no hope of being able to reach [reality itself], since it is evident that everything new that we have inferred must nevertheless be translated back into the language of our perceptions, from which it is simply impossible to free ourselves."[3] That is, he accepted a dependence on language as the condition of our knowing anything yet believed that valid inferences about a presumable reality could nevertheless be made. Lacan influentially proposed a different doctrine when he asserted that the unconscious is not something other than a language: hence psychoanalytic terms like condensation and displacement can be translated into rhetorical ones like metaphor and metonymy and hence a term like phallus, though far from abandoned, can be understood entirely without reference to a physical reality.[4]

In view of the currency of this hyper-sophisticated point of view, it seems to me important to say that the apparently naïve functions of language—imitating, referring—play an indispensable part in the appreciation of literature. For without direct, empathetic responses to the action of a novel, play, or poem, there is no aesthetic experience or value. It is true that literary art is distinguished from subliterary text by its linguistic self-consciousness. The language of art functions not merely as a window through which we perceive a palpitating reality: it calls attention to itself. But it is precisely our perception of the interplay between these two aspects of our response—the naïve and the self-conscious—that enables us to identify an aesthetic structure. In reading literature, we allow ourselves to believe that an imaginary enactment is real while knowing—and knowing its author knows—that its only reality is verbal or symbolic. The fascination of literature is that an avowed symbolization of the psychic life is temporarily made to seem real, as real somehow as the physical world.

We know of course that this experience is an illusion, that we are still enclosed in a world of words. And so the modern critic often looks with special interest at the psychoanalyst, who is faced by real persons, not merely books. True, the French Freudians tell us the psyche is a text. But unlike a text, which exists materially in separation from writer and reader, it is part of a physical body. Psychoanalysis is an interpretive art allied to criticism that seems to have kept open an avenue to a real, physical world beyond a self-enclosed world of words. It enables us to talk about a phenomenon like sexuality—which is important psychologically and yet a real physical function—with some hope of escaping the sensation of being trapped in a hall of mirrors, of being shut into what has been called the prison-house of language. The assertion that creativity is a supreme mark of our human freedom will seem like mockery unless we can believe that the created text bears a significant relation to—in effect validates—something outside of it and the reader's consciousness.

D. H. Lawrence is a novelist of exemplary interest in this connection because his obsession with sex manifests itself as a quest to discover through sex a world beyond or below words, a naïve consciousness that civilized man has crusted over with self-consciousness and the accompanying experience of separation and aloneness. At the same time, Lawrence understood very well that he was bound to language and could only pursue this quest through the sophisticated resources of civilization. Thus we reach the central paradox of his work: we must go forward through conscious, articulate realization in order to go backward to psychic fulfillment and peace. His consequent ambivalence toward language and consciousness creates the tensions that are at the heart of the aesthetic experience he affords, and I propose to examine here the working out of these tensions in two of his principal novels, *Women in Love* and *Lady Chatterley's Lover,* hoping to demonstrate the fruitful interaction between thematic stress and self-conscious rhetoricity.

Women in Love was mostly written during the Great War, which looms unmentioned in the background but lends a life-and-death urgency to the sexual battles in the dramatized foreground. The novel begins with a piquant scene of two sisters (its original title was *The Sisters*) who are discussing the question of marrying—should they or shouldn't they? According to the conventions of the Victorian novel, in view of which the scene is written, marriage is a woman's promised end or, in the most searching cases (Eliot's *Middlemarch,* Hardy's *Jude*), her anguished but still inescapable destiny. Lawrence's independent sisters mock the institution as the end rather than the beginning of experience but with a bravado that betrays their uneasiness. Marriage and love have become problematic in *Women in Love* and not just as an institution and a feeling: the meaning of those *words* is now in doubt.

The successful lovers, Birkin and Ursula, spend much of their novelistic time haggling over definition. Some readers impatiently ask, what exactly does Birkin want? On the one hand, he doesn't want too much closeness, merging, steamy domesticity, as if he fears the power of a woman. (We remember the scene in which he stones the moon's reflection, symbol of the Magna Mater.) On the other hand, he wants something as indissoluble as Victorian marriage, something you can't go back on, something that promises to cure his acute sense of separateness. What he is searching for is not exactly a way of living because like Lawrence he is scarcely interested in the social aspect of marriage. He is searching for a way of speaking, a phrase that will epitomize his combined attraction and repulsion. The phrase he invents is "star-polarity"; the gravitational action of material bodies, centripetal and centrifugal at once, expresses for him the tension of contrary psychological forces.

Almost every scene of the novel shuttles between a concern for getting at the truth and for the linguistic means of doing so, between reference and rhetoric, sex and language. Lawrence was too earnest to make writing into a language game primarily. Yet he was too sophisticated not to know that, as a writer seeking to dramatize preconscious thought and feeling, he would have to wrestle with a resistant medium unaccustomed to such use, or would have to let his characters do so. In the Foreword to the American edition, he aggressively defends this intention: "Any man of real individuality tries to know and to understand what is happening, even in himself, as he goes along. This struggle for verbal consciousness should not be left out in art. It is a very great part of life."[5] But the strain of trying to literalize what were after all metaphors is often evident, and is occasionally acknowledged during the novel: "There is always confusion in speech. Yet it must be spoken" (*WL*, p. 178).

Women in Love, broadly speaking, falls within the realistic tradition of narrative fiction. But we soon notice how urgently Lawrence's language pulls us away from narrative interest as such. In the second scene of the novel, for example, the sisters are abruptly confronted by potential lovers in whom they are interested, but Lawrence is trying for something more strenuous than what could be called an account of a budding intimacy. Here is Gudrun's first reaction to Gerald Crich, before a word has been spoken between them:

There was something northern about him that magnetised her. In his clear northern flesh and his fair hair was a glisten like sunshine refracted through crystals of ice. And he looked so new, unbroached, pure as an arctic thing. Perhaps he was thirty years old, perhaps more. His gleaming beauty, maleness, like a young, good-humoured smiling wolf, did not blind her to the significant, sinister stillness in his bearing, the lurking danger of his unsubdued temper. "'His totem is the wolf,'" she repeated to herself. "His mother is an old unbroken wolf." And then she experienced a keen paroxysm, a transport, as if she had made some incredible discovery, known to nobody else on earth. A strange transport took possession of her, all her veins were in a paroxysm of violent sensation. . . . Am I *really* singled out for him in some way, is there really some pale gold, arctic light that envelopes only us two? (*WL*, p. 9)

This style of conveying psychological reactions as if they were violent physical actions and of using incremental, almost hypnotic repetition, as if the prose were performing rather than describing—such a style is a deliberate gamble with the limits of language. Lawrence acknowledged as much in his Foreword, where he defended this style not only as natural to the author but also appropriate to his purpose: "every natural crisis in emotion or passion or understanding comes from this pulsing, frictional to-and-fro which works up to culmination" (*WL*, p. viii). By this sexualization of style, Lawrence suggests that distinctions of personality in fiction are relatively superficial and conventional, that our lives are truly characterized by a more intense but less personal flux of sensation. To be sure, in trying to register this flux with little recourse to the stigmata that readers are accustomed to rely on in distinguishing fictional persons, he runs a risk, as has often been noted, of making his persons hard to tell apart. But the point is that he understood the difficulty, and devised alternative distinctions of a more abstract, allegorical kind.

In the passage quoted, for example, we get our bearings by discerning the potential sado-masochism in the relationship between Gudrun and Gerald and by clustering the images of fair hair and arctic light into a potential symbolic meaning that will function like a concept. Ursula's reaction to Birkin, by contrast, is less certain, and is established in part by her awareness of his unwholesome dependence on Hermione, who responds to his seeming absence at a wedding party with an inner violence not unlike Gudrun's. The Ursula-Birkin relationship will also be marked by more acceptance of the sensual wisdom associated with darkness. Thus Lawrence is preparing us to understand the movement of his story—the failure of one couple and the (qualified) success of another—as a progress of states of being more than of personalities. One could fairly allegorize the central contrast of the novel as one between a narcissistic dissolution *within* an egotistic shell and a creatively destructive dissolution *of* an egotistic shell.

A brilliant device used by Lawrence to objectify states of being has been called the constitutive symbol,[6] a term referring to the central image in certain scenes that enables him to dramatize a relational tension: Gerald reining in the mare before the oncoming train and perceived differently by Gudrun and Ursula; Birkin stoning the lunar reflection and watched skeptically by Ursula; Gudrun and Gerald watching the arrogant movements of the tomcat Mino; Gerald and Birkin wrestling ritually though not quite with the same understanding. These semi-allegorical actions do not advance the plot as such but they clarify a pattern of meaning, and help set up later climactic events—notably, Gerald's death in the snow and Birkin and Ursula's purgative night in Sherwood Forest in which all sexual shame is burned away.

Although the effect of the purgative night does seem to attenuate at the end, as Birkin still hankers for male friendship to complement marriage, this finale can be interpreted instead as a characteristic Lawrentian compromise between hope and despair, a falling back to the Romantic faith in potentiality, in what Wordsworth called "something ever more about to be." Lawrence in fact had to struggle artistically with the theme of homosexual love so as to keep the finale sufficiently open. In an earlier, rejected draft of the novel, Birkin's homosexual inclinations are directly expressed, and in that light one could interpret the wrestling, which works toward a compact of blood-brotherhood rather than sexual intimacy, as an evasion on Lawrence's part, a shying away from the truth of his own temperament for lack of moral courage. But such an inference is not consistent with his characteristic audacity, and it is not necessary to make it. It is more likely, as one critic pointed out,[7] that Lawrence's refinement here was essentially artistic: the homosexual theme worked better *in*directly. So, for the most part, sexual attractiveness in the novel is viewed from the woman's point of view, and the wrestling is presented as a sublimated eroticism.

The gladiatorial scene makes the further point that Gerald, who wants to keep the social forms intact, though at bottom he feels hopeless, cannot admit to himself the value of such intimacy. This is brought, out nicely in the earlier scene ("Totem") at Halliday's flat, where again a central image, the primitive carving of the naked woman in labor, serves to dramatize differences in perspective. The interest of Halliday's friends is merely a kind of radical chic, and their homosexual manners are accordingly satirized. Birkin perceives in the statue a profoundly archaic art-speech that the white race at its peril is losing the ability to respond to imaginatively. And Gerald, though disturbed by it and surreptitiously attracted to it as to Minette, turns in hatred against "the sheer barbaric thing": "He wanted to keep certain illusions, certain ideas like clothing." To Birkin he says, "You like the wrong things, Rupert . . . things against yourself" (*WL*, p. 72).

Lawrence the artist, in other words, uses crucial images and symbolic actions as organizing principles to offset the inherent ineffability of a style that attempts to register the to-and-fro of sensation. Sex as theme and idea, one might say, balances sex as style and mode of expression.

Another organizing device, clarifying the major contrast between the two principal couples, is the perspectival use of Hermione in the first half of the novel and of Loerke in the second half. It is important to understand that these two figures, like the four principals, are Lawrentian aristocrats in that they are above the sordid business of getting and spending and are concerned primarily with the adventure of the spirit. But Hermione is incapable of real belief. She fakes commitment by mouthing the form of Birkin's words as if they expressed her own beliefs. And since she does not even know her "lie," her consciousness is hopelessly split, and she is, in Lawrentian terms, insane. Birkin for his part shows by his residual attachment to her that he is still intellectualizing his instinctual life, but he knows this and struggles against it. The incident of her bashing his head symbolically cleanses him of any further responsibility toward that source of unwholesome influence.

As for Loerke, he is a more conscious cynic. The narrator expresses a grudging admiration for him because he has accepted disillusionment and self-division so finally; he is called "the wizard rat that swims ahead" (*WL*, p. 419), which resembles a phrase later used about Michaelis in *Lady Chatterley's Lover*, "an extreme of impurity that is pure." Evidence of this easy self-division in the artist Loerke is that he can, on the one hand, deliberately create an ugly art to reflect the ugliness of a modern industrial civilization and, on the other, thrill to the elegant artistic perfections of a bygone Romantic era. The cynic and the idealist are two sides of a coin. In his idealization of the past, he strongly attracts the sympathy of Gudrun, but Ursula, speaking for Lawrence, tells him that he is too far gone to see that art is always an attempt to achieve wholeness.

The destinies of the sisters and their lovers are thus diametrically different even though Lawrence has to push and pull a little in the process of making them so. He is not altogether convincing in his effort to prevent Birkin (or sometimes Ursula) from being his own mouthpiece. And perhaps he is not quite fair in turning Gudrun at last into a demonic destroyer, as if Gerald is being punished by *her* for not accepting *Birkin's* friendship. But Gerald's death is finely done, at least on the symbolic level. If on the literal level it seems unfair to emphasize how fated he is from early childhood while burdening him most of all with the responsibility of choice, on the symbolic level he attains a certain grandeur as the vehicle of white civilized consciousness crucified by its failure to integrate the dark life of the body.

What I want to stress here regarding the resolution of Lawrence's novel is that it makes success and failure a matter both of sexuality and of speech. Gerald fails to come into new being through sexual relationship and correspondingly he falls into speechlessness. Gudrun

sidetracks a sensual rebirth and regresses appropriately to a pseudosophisticated playing with words and sentiments. Birkin and Ursula are shown on the last page of the novel still wrestling not only with love but with the meaning of love:

> "You can't have two kinds of love. Why should you!"
>
> "It seems as if I can't," he said. "Yet I wanted it."
>
> "You can't have it, because it's false, impossible," she said.
>
> "I don't believe that," he answered. (*WL*, p. 473)

It is a rather grim kind of bickering, but the point is that it's open, unresolved. These lovers may have a future.

There is a profounder parallel between sex and language intimated in the novel, for both are shown to be an incomplete but supreme means of contact between persons. After the sexual embrace we are thrown back painfully on our own separateness, but for Lawrence it is the closest we come—religion having passed—to spiritual peace. It is both a crucifixion ("Why were we crucified into sex?" he asks in "Tortoise Shout," one of his best poems) and a communion. Similarly, speech and, still more, writing imply a permanent gulf between persons, yet they are an inescapable and powerful means of attaining such a communion. "Books are not life," he asserts despairingly in "Why the Novel Matters," but adds, they are "tremulations upon the ether . . . which can make the whole man alive tremble."[8] In his recent book, *The Realistic Imagination*, George Levine rightly credits Lawrence with the dark knowledge of "the dissociation of language from being" but says "he never gave up the hope in his fiction and out of it of rebuilding a knowable community."[9]

Freud in his 1914 essay on narcissism wrote that "in the last resort we must begin to love in order that we may not fall ill."[10] Like many other literary artists of the modern period, Lawrence seems to have written so that he would not fall ill: "Art for my sake," he declared in an early letter.[11] Writing may be to some extent a substitute for loving, but it is also, as Freud and others have observed, a transfer of a primary narcissism onto an object that can be enjoyed by others and thus provide an escape from utter self-enclosure. But it is of course an indirect escape, and it is no wonder that the words language and consciousness (and synonyms for these words) are used throughout Lawrence's work in *both* a negative and a positive sense.

Lady Chatterley's Lover is a less strenuous though by no means unambitious novel. It was written three times over in the late twenties when Lawrence knew he was dying.

Its essential structure is a common fantasy—in fact a typical daydream—though one with traceable roots in the childhood situation of a man who was the son of a coal miner and of a mother with pretensions to gentility. A superior, desirable woman, wasting in a marriage to an impotent, insensitive aristocrat, meets an outsider, a natural man, with whom she enjoys an idyllic interlude culminating in her pregnancy. The daydream aspect of the book—the obviousness of the direction in which the story is going—makes it resemble popular fiction superficially, but its complications testify not only to Lawrence's awareness of the pressures of social reality but also to his sophisticated self-consciousness as an artist.

Indeed, George Levine claims that the novel is to a significant degree about the writing of a novel. He points to the parodic value of the narrator's cliché-ridden style in the first half, which reflects the artificial drawing-room talk and Clifford Chatterley's shallowly clever writing at the same time that the narrator is exposing and repudiating it.[12] One might add that, although Clifford is presented with scant sympathy, Lawrence was probably aware of putting something of himself into him, as he too was impotent at this period of his life. A similar process seems to be involved in the imagining of Connie's unsatisfactory lover, Michaelis. Although his attack on Connie for withholding her orgasm is presented as meanspirited, we recall that the narrator tartly reported her doing this with a youthful lover; and if the narrator seems to attack Michaelis for finishing too quickly, we can't help remembering that Middleton Murry hinted broadly this inadequacy was Lawrence's own.[13]

The idyllic interlude, like the idyllic moment almost always in Lawrence, is a rebirth following a painful spiritual death—rather different from the daydreams of popular fiction. And here, as in *Women in Love,* the cleansing of the unwholesome civilized consciousness is understood as both a sexual and a linguistic process. It is a matter of breaking down inhibitions of feeling and restraints of convention that have caused (as Connie realized in Wragby Hall) the great dynamic words to go dead. She and her gamekeeper must, so to speak, learn not only to fuck but also to say the word so as to recover a speech that is, in Yeats's fine phrase, "ancient, humble, and terrible."

A simple defiance of social and linguistic convention is hardly what the novel is seeking to achieve. Our lovers in the woods or in the hut are not out of *Paul et Virginie* or *The Blue Lagoon,* but are "battered warriors" in the grim game of love, particularly the older Mellors, who suffers from "a bellyful of remembering," mainly of the bullying will of his estranged wife who creates an oppressive scandal for them both that is not resolved by the end of the book. Their lovemaking is not even very successful at first. It takes time for them to weaken the inhibitions fortified by their awareness of the power of iron and coal, and to begin to recover natural beauty and "the riches of desire." In fact, of course, they never completely do so. The "pure peace" that Mellors experiences on entering the woman is soon followed by a lament that love means being broken open and exposed to a world in which there are too many people. They do

achieve a measure of tenderness ("Tenderness" was a projected title for the novel), like Birkin and Ursula, after a strenuous night of burning out the sources of shame. Whether or not the suggestion in both novels of anal intercourse as a means of rebirth is symbolically adequate, it is clear enough that, in Lawrentian, unlike popular, romance, natural love is not something merely apart from civilization but is profoundly corrupted by it. At the end of *Lady Chatterley,* we are left quite uncertain as to what kind of future is possible for Connie and Mellors. In the third, familiar version of the novel, Lawrence changed his gamekeeper, earlier called Parkin, from a mere man of the people to what Connie's snobbish sister calls "almost a gentleman," giving the relationship a chance to survive in society. But the chance is not very promising. One feels that their romance has peaked in the novel's pastoral centerpiece: a ritual of rebirth symbolized by new-hatched chicks, rain-soaked coupling, and genital flower-twining.

In its culminating moments, the lovemaking of Connie and Mellors is said to have achieved an "unfathomable silence," a "ponderous, primordial tenderness." Such phrases help to make the four-letter words ancient, humble, and terrible rather than the language of school-boy defiance. They are good examples of Lawrence's effort to use language in an effort to suggest a world beyond or below language. Connie at Wragby "hated words, always coming between her and life"—life being some sort of subsistent actuality that words at best can only evoke. Nevertheless it is clear that everywhere in the novel—in the hut as well as in the drawing room—there is talk, talk, talk. *Lady Chatterley's Lover* is a preachy novel, so much so that James Joyce sarcastically dubbed it Lady Chatterbox's Lover.[14] Lawrence knew it was preachy, and in his forthright, not to say brazen, way tried to make a virtue of the fact: "This is the real point of this book" [he wrote in "Apropos of Lady Chatterley's Lover"]. "I want men and women to be able to think sex fully, completely, honestly and cleanly."[15] No doubt this is sincere, but at the same time he was writing sarcastically of "sex in the head." And the novel itself is full of the same conflicting evidence, testifying to Lawrence's profound ambivalence toward verbal consciousness. The narrator endorses Connie's view of the mental life as a "swindle," yet in Chapter IX speaks of the power of "the novel properly handled" to "reveal the most secret places of life." And it is clear from that chapter that the properly handled novel must in our time attempt not only to evoke a pristine consciousness but to repudiate an old one through satirical particularity. In short both kinds of intercourse are required.

The novel ends significantly with a figure of speech that epitomizes the problematic relation between sex and language. Closing his letter to Connie with a playful use of colloquial names for the genitals, Mellors writes: "John Thomas says goodnight to Lady Jane, a little droopingly, but with a hopeful heart." (*John Thomas and Lady Jane* is the title of the now published second version of *Lady Chatterley's Lover.*) This pleasantry is both personification and synechdoche: the genitals are given the names of persons, and parts of the body substitute for the whole body. It thus asserts imaginatively an identity between nominal and actual physical presence, but implies at the same time, as a self-conscious figure of speech, separation and incompleteness. Language enables yet frustrates. Lawrence the vivacious rhetorician evidently finds a specific satisfaction through writing, though he is compelled to seek in thought a reality beyond words.

This dual awareness is much closer in spirit to Freud than to Lacan, though Lawrence objected vigorously to Freud's view of repression because it accepted as forever impossible a return to the Eden of wordless unity. What is important is that it does not dichotomize language and sexuality, mind and body. Lawrence was pained by the realization that writing was indirect, symbolic expression yet it was *expression:* it was of the body and arose mysteriously from the pre-verbal life of the body. Freud too did not dichotomize mind and body even after he abandoned the *Project;* he retained the conviction that "our provisional ideas in psychology will someday be based on an organic substructure."[16] There is a difference, in other words, between these recognitions of the symbolic or provisional nature of reference and a categorical Cartesian distinction between *res cogitans* and *res extensae.*

It is remarkable that the insistence on the "floating signifier" in the work of Jacques Lacan and his followers, while used to attack the Cartesian *cogito,* results in the absolute separation of mind from matter for which Descartes himself is often blamed. Lacan's argument is abstract to say the least; but the gist seems to be that the human infant first discovers selfhood as an image, in the so-called mirror-stage *(stade du miroir)* between six and eighteen months; thus, whereas the Freudian ego is an agent of synthesis, mastery, integration, and adaptation, the Lacanian ego is "*constituted* by an identification with another . . . perpetually threatened by its own otherness to itself."[17] Lacan finds this idea supposedly in Freud himself, particularly in the 1914 essay on Narcissism, but it is different in conception. It arises from a philosophical tradition of dialectic rather than from psychological observation of infantile conflict and development. For Lacan, the concepts "ego" and "unconscious" have the same status as "phallus." They are all names. None has any reference; they are all floating signifiers. Phallus Is Desire Perpetually In Search (which is true enough, from a comic point of view). The Ego is an Illusory Presence or The Absence of A Presence (a phrase which again has comic possibilities). And "the unconscious is structured like a language. . . . It is neither primordial nor instinctual; what it knows about the elementary is no more than the elements of the signifier."[18]

Lacan liked to charge the Freudians, especially the ego psychologists, with repressing repression because they tried to smooth out the contradictions in Freudian theory. He himself might be charged with repressing

repression by making it a matter of logic and discursive inconsistency rather than of dynamic, affective psychology. If Kenneth Burke was right in saying that Freud's was an essentializing rather than proportionalizing strategy, with *wish* as the key term,[19] then it might be said that Lacan adopted a parallel strategy with *word* as the key term. But one must concede that his transposition of Freud into another key—fusing conflict with dialectic, psychology with metaphysics—has transformed the French intellectual scene. Before 1950, Freud was scarcely read in France, badly translated, little commented on; since then, and due to Lacan, his work has generated a spate of amazingly resourceful and influential revisionist criticism. And the effort to absorb this into American criticism has led to many thoughtful mediations of the two contrary strategies, one little instance of which is, I hope, the present paper.

What I miss above all in literary criticism inspired by Lacan, although Jonathan Culler in his recent *Pursuit of Signs* seems to say I shouldn't even be looking for it, is some attempt to explain the *experience* of literature—to deal with self-alienation, if that is in question, as an imaginative act. I would like, for example, to think of Rimbaud's famous solecism—Je est un autre—as such an act rather than as a principle of metaphysics. And I doubt that Lacanian criticism could give me any sense of the strange beauty of the delusional system of Freud's patient, Dr. Schreber; or of Kafka's gloss on Genesis as a story of "God's rage against humanity"; or of Beckett's brilliant playlet "Not I."[20]

To return to Lawrence. He is far from the most self-conscious rhetorician among sophisticated modernist writers, but I think that *all* genuine literary artists, since Homer, have used what's now called rhetoricity to establish a framework of play and game, thus permitting us to regress temporarily to a naïve acceptance of the mimetic and referential functions of words. For without such an acceptance, the substantiation of the world (or of the word) cannot take place, and literature is not alive.

Lawrence believed with Freud, despite some resistance, that the human heart must remain in conflict, a conflict between nature and culture or between competing instincts. There is no return to a wordless, undifferentiated state in the Edenic womb. And the stoical Freud believed with the romantic Lawrence, despite some resistance, in the ongoing joy of expression, at once physical and verbal. The marvelous plasticity of Lawrence's language and the brilliant treatises on dreams, jokes, and mistakes (the very stuff of comedy) take us beyond a tragic vision. They show us that, in the endless play of the mind, the physical and verbal aspects of consciousness, though never identical, cannot be separated.

NOTES

[1] *Phoenix: The Posthumous Papers of D. H. Lawrence,* edited with an introd. by Edward D. McDonald (London: Heinemann, 1936), p. 255.

[2] William H. Gass, *Fiction and the Figures of Life* (New York: Vintage Books, 1972), p. 27.

[3] Sigmund Freud, *An Outline of Psychoanalysis,* The James Strachey translation, rev. ed. (New York: Norton, 1949), p. 53.

[4] See particularly chaps. 5 and 8 of Jacques Lacan, *Écrits: A Selection,* trans. Alan Sheridan (New York: Norton, 1977).

[5] D. H. Lawrence, *Women in Love* (New York: Viking, 1961), p. viii. Subsequent references will be cited parenthetically in the text as *WL.*

[6] By Eliseo Vivas, in *The Failure and the Triumph of Art* (Evanston: Northwestern Univ. Press, 1960).

[7] Charles L. Ross, "Homoerotic Feeling in *Women in Love:* Lawrence's "struggle for verbal consciousness" in the Manuscripts, in *D. H. Lawrence: The Man Who Lived,* Papers Delivered at the D. H. Lawrence Conference at Southern Illinois University, Carbondale, 2-5 April 1979, ed. Robert B. Partlaw, Jr. and Harry T. Moore.

[8] *Phoenix,* p. 535.

[9] George Levine, *The Realistic Imagination: English Fiction from Frankenstein to Lady Chatterley* (Chicago: Univ. of Chicago Press, 1981), p. 320.

[10] Sigmund Freud, *Collected Papers,* vol. 4 (New York: Basic Books, 1959), p. 42.

[11] *The Letters of D. H. Lawrence,* ed. with an introd. by Aldous Huxley (London: Heinemann, 1932), p. 86.

[12] Levine, *The Realistic Imagination,* pp. 324-28. Levine, of course, cites chap. IX in which Lawrence defends "even satire as a form of sympathy."

[13] See, for example, his letters to Frieda in Frieda Lawrence, *The Memoirs and Correspondence,* ed. E. W. Tedlock (London: Heinemann, 1961), pp. 321, 329 ff.

[14] James Joyce, *Letters,* ed. Stuart Gilbert (New York: Viking, 1957), p. 294.

[15] In *Sex, Literature and Censorship,* ed. Harry T. Moore (New York: Twayne, 1953), p. 92.

[16] From the essay "On Narcissism: An Introduction" (1914), rpt. in *Collected Papers,* v. 4 (New York: Basic Books, 1959), p. 36.

[17] Jeffrey Mehlman, "The 'floating signifier': from Lévi-Strauss to Lacan," in *Yale French Studies,* vol. 48 (*French Freud: Structural Studies in Psychoanalysis,* 1972), p. 19.

[18] Jacques Lacan, "The Insistence of the Letter in the Unconscious," in Jacques Ehrmann, ed., *Structuralism* (Garden City: Doubleday, 1970), p. 130.

[19] Kenneth Burke, "Freud—and the Analysis of Poetry," rpt. in *Art and Psychoanalysis,* ed. William Phillips (Cleveland: World Pub. Co., 1963), pp. 412-39.

[20] The Schreber case is found in vol. XII of the *Standard Edition;* the delusion entails an alliance with God, who murdered Schreber's soul and used his body like a strumpet (see esp. p. 19). Kafka's gloss is quoted in Ronald Hayman's recent biography (New York: Oxford Univ. Press, 1982), p. 207; it goes like this:

> God's rage against humanity. The two trees, the unexplained veto, the punishment of all (serpent, Woman and Man), the priority given to Cain, whom He provokes by addressing him.

Beckett's play, easily available, dramatizes the effort of the subject ("Mouth") to present herself authentically in the third person.

Judith Rinde Sheridan

SOURCE: "Isaac Bashevis Singer: Sex as Cosmic Metaphor," in *The Midwest Quarterly,* Vol. XXIII, No. 4, Summer, 1982, pp. 365-79.

[*In the following essay, Sheridan studies Singer's association of sex in marriage with redemption and his critical views of unrestrained sexuality and perversion.*]

The 1978 Nobel Prize in Literature granted to Isaac Bashevis Singer may be looked upon as not only deserved international recognition given to this great Yiddish author, a unique and powerful literary voice, but as a tribute to Yiddish literature as well. It is nothing new to point out that Yiddish is a language whose extinction is imminent. Singer has long parried with questions concerning his commitment to writing in Yiddish. He has said, "It's like the Jews generally. They die all the time and they keep living all the time," and "I like to write ghost stories. . . . Ghosts love Yiddish, and as far as I know, they all speak it." Nevertheless, the bravado of these remarks fails to alter the fact that inevitably and rightfully Singer will be thought of as the last in the line of such notable Yiddish writers as Mendele, Sholom Aleichem, Peretz, Asch, and I. J. Singer.

Although Isaac Bashevis Singer's position among Yiddish authors is secure, many commentators on Yiddish writing have observed that the Yiddish literary public often regards its most acclaimed writer with marked discomfort. Mostly their chagrin is rooted in Singer's seemingly obsessive interest in sexual matters as a subject for his fiction. Irving Howe has summarized this attitude:

Many Yiddish literary people have been troubled

by what they see as his exploitation of sexuality, his surrender to the irrational, his indifference to the humane ethic of Yiddishkeit, his seeming readiness to move with equal ease to the sensational or the ascetic.

In Cynthia Ozick's brilliant novella, "Envy: or Yiddish in America," two fictional representatives of the dying world of Yiddish poets and writers echo the above sentiment. Edelschtein, an untranslated and failed poet, and Baumzweig, an editor of a biannual Yiddish periodical whose survival depends on the generosity of an Episcopal philanthropist, fume at Yankel Ostrover, a successful Yiddish writer overtly modeled after I. B. Singer:

> They raged against his subject matter, which was insanely sexual, pornographic, paranoid, freakish men who embraced men, women who caressed women, sodomists of every variety, boys copulating with hens, butchers who drank blood for strength behind the knife.

This description of Ostrover's work (meant to characterize Singer's fiction) is only slightly overstated. For without question Singer's concern with sexuality and perversion is prominent. Yet the basis of his interest must be understood in terms of the ancient Jewish traditions and attitudes found in the Kabbalah. For Singer, as well as for Kabbalistic sages, sexuality provides the consummate metaphor for man's proximity to salvation or damnation. Although Kabbalistic study has been subject to an uneasiness among Jewish intellectuals similar to that felt by Singer's Yiddish readers, Singer's use of sexuality influenced by the Kabbalah is central to Jewish theological and ethical matters.

A son of a Hasidic rabbi, Singer's early education was steeped in the arcane mystical teachings of Judaism. Unlike other forms of non-Jewish mysticism, Kabbalism rejected asceticism and sought to discover sacred mysteries in lawful sexuality, sex within the constraints of marriage and Talmudic dictates. In the *Zohar,* a central text of Kabbalism, sexual union within marriage became a symbol of redemption, the reunification of the "Shekinah," a divine feminine presence who embodies the exile of Israel, and the Almighty, himself. Passionate physical love also was viewed as the means by which man could comprehend "devekuth," mystical adhesion to God. In his discussion of the relationship of sexuality to devotion in the evolution of Hasidic thought, Gershom Scholem, the famed historian of Jewish mysticism, notes the contribution of Saadia, a tenth century scholar:

> The earthly love which [Saadia] describes in considerable detail, was for the early German Hasidim a complete allegory for the heavenly passion, just as it was in a later age for Israel Baal Shem, the founder of Polish Hasidism, who is quoted as saying, "What Saadia says of love makes it possible to draw an inference from the nature of the sensual to that of the spiritual passion; if the force of sensual love is so great, how great must be the passion with which man loves God."

For Scholem this positive stance toward sexual life "represents a genuinely Jewish attitude," one that is also found in Rabbinical Judaism, where sex within the boundaries of the law was seldom considered suspicious or impure.

The Kabbalah's approach to sexuality also provides an antithetical corollary to the belief that sexual love symbolizes both worldly redemption and mystical adhesion between the individual and God. Perverted love comes to represent the broken state of the world or the fallen condition of the universe, and also occasions the generation of evil progeny. According to the *Zohar,* sin always destroys union and contributes to existing chaos. The violation of marriage, the inability of husband and wife to join spiritually and physically, can be seen as a manifestation of an unredeemed world. Moreover, abuse of the generative powers of man, especially the wasteful spilling of seed, was believed by Kabbalists to result in the population of "the other side," in evil embodied. Both these notions inform Singer's attitude toward evil, and reflect in what for some seems his obsessive concern with profanity and sexual aberration. Yet Singer's recreation of disturbed human activity is far from a glorification; rather he finds that perversion and sexual abomination provide him with powerful metaphors with which to capture what he perceives to be the prevailing evil in the world.

The positive attitude toward sexuality within marriage evident in Kabbalistic thought, and in Judaism generally, influences Singer's depiction of saintly men. While his fiction is mostly associated with the demonic, the adulterous, and the lascivious, there are significant portraits of pious rabbis and virtuous townsmen whose lives are highlighted by loving marriages. In *The Family Moskat,* Singer's first chronicle, Reb Dan, the maternal grandfather of the spiritually spent protagonist, Asa Bannet, stands as the embodiment of the old world. Despite oppression and forced dislocation, Reb Dan experiences joy and comfort through faith. Unlike the misery which marks the lives of the secular Jews, the rabbi is happy, respected by his family, revered by the community, and loved by a wife who thinks of him as a "venerable ancient, a 'tanna.'" In Singer's later two-part chronicle, *The Manor* and *The Estate,* of Calman Jacoby's four daughters, only one is happily married, Tsipele, the youngest, to the Hasidic Rabbi, Jochanon. Although filled with doubts concerning his worthiness, Jochanon is the only husband joyfully and at times ecstatically renewed through an intimacy with God. Yet another rabbi, central to the short story, "The Shadow of a Crib" *(Spinoza),* serves as an example of fulfilled religious life characterized by marital love. During a sleepless night Dr. Yaretzky, the protagonist, a Christian apostate and follower of Schopenhauer, gazes through the unnamed old rabbi's study window and witnesses a scene of love as the rabbi's wife enters the room:

> Strange, that the rabbi did not address her and kept his eyes on the book. But his face grew

gentler as he half-concentrated on his reading, half listened to his wife's movements. He raised his eyebrows and on the ceiling the shadow trembled. Dr. Yaretzky stood there, unable to move. . . . She'd roused herself in the middle of the night to tend to the coals of the rabbi's samovar. He, the rabbi, did not dare interrupt his holy studies but aware of her nearness, he offered silent gratitude.

While looking in from behind the barrier of the window, Yaretzky senses that the drama he has observed contains the answer to the restless search of his life. He, however, will choose to reject what he has seen and always remain an outsider. In anger against his inner turmoil, he spits at the sky, but significantly the spittle lands on his own body.

Of Singer's works of fiction none is as devoted to the celebration of marital bliss and spiritual sexuality as *The Slave*. This novel, a moving account of the love between Jacob, a Jew exiled during the Chmelnicki massacre, and Wanda, his pagan master's daughter, clearly expresses the connection between sexuality and the vital, divine essence Kabbalists believe exists in all within creation. By describing Wanda in natural terms, Singer suggests that Jacob's passion for her is linked to his love of nature. "Her body exuded the warmth of the sun, the breeze of summer, the fragrance of wood, field, flower, leaf, first as milk gave off the odor of grass the cattle fed on." Noting this, Jacob's lovemaking may be understood as both the consummation of his feeling for Wanda and the achievement of a mystical merging with divinity located in nature. Although at the point of consummation Jacob is outside Talmudic law, his love possesses a religious fervor. When he submits to his passion, in an awkward effort to maintain Jewish edict, he asks Wanda to cleanse herself by submersion in a clean, cold stream. The absence of understanding on her part dooms his effort. Yet as he makes love the "Song of Songs" echoes through his mind and the sacred mysteries of the body unfold. True to a mystical concept of religion, Singer implies that a commitment to God may transcend the boundaries imposed by legalities. Much to the point, later in the novel, after Jacob has been ransomed and he decides to marry Wanda, he justifies his physical desires by recalling teachings from the Kabbalah: "Coupling was the universal act underlying everything; Torah, prayer, the Commandments, God's holy names themselves were mysterious unions of the male and female principle."

In the course of *The Slave*, Jacob and Wanda, who takes the name Sarah after her marriage, confront cruelty and brutality within and without the Jewish community where they reside, yet never is their saintliness doubted. During their lives Jacob and Wanda/Sarah are unable to overcome the unfeeling character of society and the naturalistic forces of life. Nevertheless, the conclusion documents a miracle which transforms this fiction into legend and establishes the central figures as timeless models.

"Short Friday" provides another occasion in which Singer affirms the saintly potential within man as manifested by marital joy. The tale records the events of a day in the life of a couple busily preparing for the Sabbath meal on the shortest Friday in the winter of an undefined year. Smul-Leibele, an inept tailor-furrier in the "shtetl" Lapschitz, conforms to the "dos kleine menchele" figures found in Yiddish folklore; he is incompetent, unscholarly, yet unquestionably of good heart. Life for Smul consists of worship and gratitude toward God. Although impoverished, Smul's goodness is rewarded with a competent and beautiful wife, Shoshe, whose ability allows them to live comfortably. The night before the Sabbath evening is busy. Each segment of the meal is joyfully prepared. The process which occupies Smul and his wife every week becomes a celebration of their marriage. Singer conveys a spirit of the divine during the Sabbath ritual whose highest expression becomes the blessings of this marriage:

> She had already performed the benediction over the candles, and the spirit of the Sabbath emanated from every corner of the room. She was wearing her silk handkerchief with the silver spangles, a yellow and gray dress, and shoes with gleaming pointed tips. On her throat hung the charm that Smul-Leibele's mother, peace be with her, had given her to celebrate the signing of the wedding contract. The marriage band sparkled on her index finger. . . . He yearned to tell his wife how full of grace she was.

The story culminates in the physical consummation of their love, sexuality which truly reflects their spiritual oneness. Yet this story which might easily be dismissed by modern critics as sentimental, ends with their death, a death caused by fumes from the oven. Although the narrator gives assurances that they gain a heavenly reward in their after life, the fumes and their association with the Holocaust have a chilling effect on the reader. The story becomes an allegory of the Jew and his destiny in the twentieth century. Singer is unsentimentally aware of the powerlessness of belief and faith to alter the inevitability of history, but he seems to believe that the personal rewards of religious commitment provide man with his best chance at happiness.

Although Singer portrays with special warmth the simple Jew whose belief in the divinely inspired extends to the ordinary events of a day, the reader experiences a sense of a modern writer who possesses the knowledge of the Holocaust, looking backward to an imperiled simplicity. Perhaps it is significant that while *The Slave* allows a son to be born to Jacob and Sarah and to survive eventually to build a new life in Israel, in the later fiction, "Short Friday," Smul and Shoshe are childless.

An example of the redemptive power of sexuality within marriage emerges in a brilliantly realized short story, "The Spinoza of Market Street." Dr. Nahum Fischelson, the story's protagonist, a Spinozan scholar, suffers from physical and psychological decay. A prototype of scholars found throughout Singer's work, he is clothed in black; his room is littered with scholarly papers and books; insects scurry about; he is hunchbacked and suffers from heartburn, cramps and nausea. Fischelson's life has been devoted to the pursuit of the Spinozan edict that "the most moral deed a man could perform was to indulge in some pleasure which was not contrary to reason." He watches the world through a window, much as did Yaretzky. While viewing Hasidic Jews from his room, he voices contempt for these people "drunk with emotion." Yet mostly he lives entombed in his room, his life absurdly spent and wasted in pursuit of reason.

During the story Fischelson becomes acutely ill and is aided by an ugly yet kindhearted spinster called Black Dobbe. Surprisingly, they become close and decide to marry. In a skillfully wrought comic scene, Fischelson, weak with his recent illness, has difficulty performing such marriage rituals as the breaking of the goblet. But their wedding renews in Fischelson strength he no longer believed he possessed:

> What happened that night could be called a miracle. . . . Powers long dormant awakened in him. Although he had only a sip of benediction wine, he was as if intoxicated. He kissed Dobbe and spoke to her of love. Long forgotten quotations from Klopstock, Lessing, Goethe rose to his lips. The pressure and aches stopped. He embraced Dobbe, pressed her to himself, was again a man as in his youth. Dobbe was faint with delight. . . .

Fischelson experiences miraculous passion; his thoughts are filled with romantic poetry long repressed; and he transcends the boundaries of reason. The final line of the story attests to the wrongheadedness of his life before Dobbe, and affirms the irrational revealed through the sacred glories of the flesh: "Divine Spinoza, forgive me. I have become a fool." Although the degree of Fischelson's awareness is ambiguous, the reader knows that by becoming a fool Fischelson has known the mysteries of love. Hopefully, it is not an exaggeration to point out that like the Hasids he earlier derided, Fischelson celebrates the spirit through physical ecstasy.

For Isaac Bashevis Singer sexuality in marriage not only provides a metaphor for the proximity of the cosmos to redemption, but also serves as a barometer for the spiritual condition of the individual and his society. So it is not surprising that given the continuing brutality of the post-Holocaust world, Singer's landscape seems overwhelmingly populated with failed marriages and perverted love. The instances of unity in marriage are significant for they establish a strong, traditional moral center in Singer's work which shapes the reader's response to the domination of marital disharmony and disturbed sexuality. Singer's approach to evil and its manifestation in sexual behavior is rooted in Kabbalistic thought. In response to a question about the moral nature of his tales, Singer characterized the absence of morality in the world by invoking the Kabbalah:

> The Cabbalists [sic] say this world is the worst of all possible worlds. They believe there are millions of worlds, but the worst one is this one. Here is the very darkness itself. How can you expect that in the blackest darkness, in the deepest abyss of all, everything should turn out nice and proper?

As discussed earlier, the *Zohar* defines sin as that which destroyed primordial harmony and contributes to existing chaos: creation metaphorically shattered. Sin prohibits unity and redemption. Hence in Singer's work, evil is often portrayed as the force responsible for the severing of matrimonial and communal bonds. A favorite device of Singer is to depict the result of evil as the unhappy marriage of incompatible beings. Demons, like the primeval snake in "The Destruction of Kreshev" (*Spinoza*), take special delight in arranging such marriages. In "The Gentleman from Cracow" (*Gimpel*), the greed of the townsmen culminates in a mass marriage of this kind:

> twelve year old boys were mated with 'spinsters' of nineteen. The sons of substantial citizens took daughters of paupers as brides; midgets were coupled with giants, beauties with cripples.

Such obviously doomed alliances manifest a world gone amuck, a hell on earth.

Since the Kabbalah views marriage as a metaphor for the union between God and the Shekinah, a representation of redemption, the inability of husband and wife to achieve spiritual and physical oneness becomes symbolic of the fallen state of the universe. The isolation of the individual in marriage increases his spiritual alienation and removes him further from adhesion with the Almighty. Moreover, failed marriages often prohibit the fulfillment of the Biblical commandment to be fruitful and multiply. Singer's rejection of asceticism, and its implied dichotomy between body and spirit, manifests itself in his portraits of ascetics whose fears of sexuality prevent successful marriage. The absence of sympathy for Itche Nokhum in "The Fast" (*Short Friday*), and Itche Mates in *Satan in Goray*, clearly suggests he believes those who reject the flesh commit heresy. In *Satan in Goray*, the unconsummated marriage which is later severed seems to unleash an evil which taints every phase of experience: Rabbi Benish, the voice of reason and the pillar of the community, is forced into exile; townsmen cease to worship or trade; the heavens withhold rain and the earth lacks fertility. All productivity is constricted.

The presence of imps, devils and serpents in Singer's work may well be puzzling to the contemporary reader, more comfortable with the empirical demands of naturalism. Singer has characterized his use of the demonic and the supernatural as a "spiritual stenography," a short hand method of representing the evil which exists in the world and in man. But the literary reason for Singer's use of the demonic must be considered in light of his avowed belief in their actual existence; "Demons symbolize the world for me, and by that I mean human beings and human behavior, and since I really believe in their existence—that is not only symbolically but substantially—it is easy to see how this kind of literary style was born." Singer's perception of the pervasive influence and power of evil is such that for him evil must be manifested as an inversion of the divine or as a part of the Almighty and His design for the universe, another idea posited by the Kabbalah.

As alluded to earlier, Kabbalists believed that evil obtains progeny through the abuse of man's generative powers. "Blood" (*Short Friday*) serves as a prototypical Singer tale of the temptations of the flesh and the consequence of surrender. Significantly, the story begins with a direct allusion to the Kabbalah:

> The cabalists [sic] knew that the passion for blood and the passion for flesh have the same origin, and that this is the reason 'Thou shalt not kill' is followed by 'Thou shalt not commit adultery.'

Evil of one kind promulgates evil of all kinds; all abuses of the flesh are intertwined.

The tale documents the adulterous relationship between Risha, thrice married and presently wife to a pious owner of a large estate, and Reuben, the lascivious town slaughterer of animals. The lust Risha and Reuben feel is heightened by the act of slaughtering, and in the course of the story they abandon both sexual restraints and the laws governing "Kashrut," the proper slaughter of animals. Their unholy alliance not only leads to their physical deterioration, but, by the sale of unkosher meat, taints the entire community. Eventually, their sins revealed, Reuben flees and Risha commits the ultimate defiance: she converts. Years later the town kills a werewolf and discovers the beast is Risha. As the Kabbalah warns, the sins of the flesh, abuse of the generative powers of man, culminate in evil embodied. In "Blood," Singer unsympathetically portrays man's surrender to lust. Human passion emanates from a craving for blood, which allows Risha and Reuben to delight in animal slaughter (an act which always revolts the vegetarian Singer) and in the perversion of sexuality.

Singer's tales, however, often reflect his comprehension of the unbearable tension between man's will to live life fully and the restraints of Jewish Law. In his fine essay, "Sabbatai Zevi and the Jewish Imagination," Robert Alter concisely summarizes this tension as it emerges in Kabbalistic doctrine and influenced the rise of Sabbatai Zevi, the nineteenth century false messiah:

> According to a Kabbalistic tradition adopted by the followers of Sabbatai Zevi, there are two Torahs: the Torah of the Tree of Knowledge, Good and Evil, which has been revealed to us and the Torah of the Tree of Life--manifestly, beyond good and evil—which the redeemer is to reveal. Because the common image of the Jew has been a figure clinging to the first Torah, the man bound by Law,

there is a special piquancy in Sabbatianism's antithetical image of the Jew committed to a Torah which is all life, unfettered by any law. The serious danger, however, in such alluring antithesis is that life becomes arbitrarily associated with the abandonment of restraints and hence death with the general notion of imposing limits.

Throughout Singer's work, characters yield to the temptations of the flesh precisely because the passions within, which they associate with the life force, can no longer be tempered by knowledge of the law. Often the Kabbalah is invoked as a justification for sinful acts. In *Satan in Goray*, Reb Gedaliya becomes an effective spokesman for Sabbatianism because his appeals are directed to the profound desires within even the most pious Jews:

> He scolded them that so many young men and girls were still unmarried. Such neglect of the principle of fruitfulness would delay redemption. He demonstrated by means of the Cabala [sic] that all the laws in the Torah and the Schulchan Aruch referred to the commandment to be fruitful and multiply; and that, when the end of the days was come, not only would Rabbi Gershom's ban on polygamy become null and void, but all the strict "Thou Shalt nots," as well. Every pious woman would then be as fair as Abigail, and there would be no monthly flow of blood at all. . . . Men would be permitted to know strange women. Such encounters might even be considered a religious duty. . . .

In "The Destruction of Kreshev" (*Spinoza*), Shloime, a secret disciple of Sabbatai Zevi, uses similar methods to sway his wife to participate in unholy sexual acts as to appease Shloime's perverse needs:

> He assured her that it is preferable for a man to commit a sin with fervor, than a good deed without enthusiasm, and that yea and nay, darkness and light, right and left, heaven and hell, sanctity and degradation were all images of the divinity and no matter where one sunk one remained in the shadow of the Almighty, for beside His light nothing else exists.

Given the social climate of continuous oppression and poverty, the pious Jew could often be influenced by such arguments. Adherence to the law and its many taboos had not resulted in the alleviation of poverty and pain, and certainly not in a messianic age.

For Singer the passions of man and mystical belief can bring man closer to a knowledge of the Almighty, but there are dangers. These same passions when relieved of all restraints can lead to apostasy and sin justified in the name of the God who remains mysterious in the written Torah. Clearly in *The Magician of Lublin*, Singer exhibits sympathy for Yasha Mazur, an artistic magician who cannot resist the appetites of life. But even in this work, the eventual outcome of such indulgence is disaster. In the conclusion of the novel, Yasha serves a long penance, a self-imposed entombment. Through the method of Yasha's atonement Singer implies that only in complete isolation can man successfully resist the temptations of the flesh.

Singer's strong attraction to sexuality and perversion as fictional subjects is misunderstood by a discomforted Yiddish reading public. Singer has little in common with such contemporary Jewish-American writers as Philip Roth or Erica Jong, whose embattled psyches plea for a release of the "Id in Yid." Nor is he a Lawrentian who views the inhibition of primal instincts as a symptom of the failings of an industrialized world. Rather he associates unrestrained sexuality with demonic seduction or with Satanic triumph. He is a moral conservative, concerned, in an old-fashioned way, with good and evil. Yet, while Singer honors the rare individuals who lovingly respect and maintain their marital vows, often he exhibits compassion for the adulterous and the fallen. Finally, however, the world of sexual aberration which he most vividly renders, reflects Singer's vision of "gehenna," or hell, the abyss out of which mankind seems never quite to ascend.

BIBLIOGRAPHY

Alter, Robert. *After the Tradition.* New York, 1971.

Blocker, Joel, and Richard Elman. "An Interview with Isaac Bashevis Singer." In *Critical Views of Isaac Bashevis Singer.* Ed. Irving Malin. New York, 1969.

Buchen, Irving. *Isaac Bashevis Singer and the Eternal Past.* New York, 1968.

Howe, Irving. *World of our Fathers.* New York, 1976.

Howe, Irving, and Eliezar Greenberg. "Introduction." In *A Treasury of Yiddish Stories.* New York, 1953.

Ozick, Cynthia. *The Pagan Rabbi and Other Stories.* London, 1972.

Scholem, Gershom. *Major Trends in Jewish Mysticism.* New York, 1941.

———. *On the Kabbalah and Its Symbolism.* New York, 1969.

Singer, Isaac Bashevis. *Gimpel the Fool and Other Stories.* New York, 1955.

———. *Satan in Goray.* New York, 1963.

———. *Short Friday and Other Stories.* New York, 1964.

———. *The Slave.* New York, 1964.

———. *The Spinoza of Market Street and Other Stories.* New York, 1963.

Evelyn Torton Beck

SOURCE: "Kafka's Traffic in Women: Gender, Power, and Sexuality," in *The Literary Review,* Vol. 26, No. 4, Summer, 1983, pp. 565-76.

[*In the following essay, Beck explores debased female sexuality and the "androcentric" point of view in Franz Kafka's fiction.*]

When, in 1952, the Austrian writer Ilse Aichinger received the prestigious Group 47 prize, her work was so often compared to Franz Kafka's that one of the group members allowed himself a little joke and referred to her as "Fräulein Kafka," only to correct himself at once, "That isn't really the lady's name; she only writes as if it were."[1]

In spite of the high praise intended by this somewhat backhanded compliment, Aichinger was not pleased. She did not wish to be viewed as an epigone, not even a Kafka epigone. She may also have understood that what these critics thought was so good about her work was that she was able to write *like a man.* Moreover, she may have recognized that something in this renaming process was off balance, that the very process by which she had been elevated to a "Fräulein Kafka" could only work in one direction, since, as every schoolchild learns quite early, in Western culture it is *never* a compliment for a man to be dubbed a female *anything.* Such a reversal is so far from our imagination, that a witty reference to a Herr Lasker-Schüler in Germany or a Mr. Stein, or Mr. O'Keefe or Mr. Dickinson in the United States would probably be mistaken as a reference to these artists' *fathers.* Moreover, no woman's writing has, like Kafka's and the work of other male writers, ever been viewed as representative of that supposedly unmarked category, "the universal."

It is by questioning the conception of Kafka's universality that a feminist reading of Kafka must begin. We might start by asking, "What does it mean when critics, one after the other, using different formulations, all come to the same conclusion—that Kafka is the spokes*man* for modern *man?*" I have no intention of challenging the sexist language of this assertion; it is, in fact, quite correct—so long as we can agree that when Kafka and Kafka critics claim to be speaking for *man,* they do not at the same time claim to be speaking for *woman.* A poem by the late Muriel Rukeyser on this theme might prove to be instructive:

Myth

Long afterwards, Oedipus, old and blinded,
　　walked the roads.
He smelled a familiar smell.
It was the Sphinx.
Oedipus said, "I want to ask one question.
Why didn't I recognize my mother?"
"You gave the wrong answer," said the Sphinx.
"But that was what made everything possible,"
　　said Oedipus.
"No," she said.

"When I asked, what walks on four legs in the
    morning, two at noon, and three in the
    evening, you answered, Man.
You didn't say anything about woman."

"When you say Man," said Oedipus, "you include
    women too. Everyone knows that."
    She said, "That's what you think."[2]

Sobered perhaps by this feminist retelling of one of our
most revered myths, let us stand back for a moment
from our received truths about Kafka and look again
"with fresh eyes" (to quote both Bertold Brecht and
Adrienne Rich) and approach his texts from a new critical direction.

It is not difficult to show that the question of gender is
the single most ignored aspect of Kafka's work, while at
the same time it is one of his most outstanding characteristics. Let us begin with a few simple observations on
which I think we can all agree:

1. *Kafka's fictional world is male—homosocial and at
moments subtly and not so subtly homoerotic.* Think,
for example, of the Stoker chapter in *Amerika,* the
Titorelli chapter in *The Trial,* the Bürgel episode in *The
Castle.* In at least a dozen short pieces *woman is literally absent* from the text (for example, "An Old Manuscript," "Jackals and Arabs," "A Visit to a Mine,"
"Eleven Sons"). There is not even an Eve in Kafka's
Paradise parables; in Kafka's world there is only Adam
and God. When woman is not absent, *her presence is
obliterated, obscured or trivialized;* for example, in
"The Penal Colony," "A Hunger Artist," "A Fratricide."
Where she is not obscured, *she is seen as purely instrumental;* she becomes the vehicle or conduit for male
activity, specifically for the male quest which is at the
center of Kafka's works.

2. *The essential power struggles in Kafka's texts are
between the males:* Joseph K. and the representatives of
the Law in *The Trial;* K., Klamm, and the castle officials (and messengers) in *The Castle,* Georg Bendemann
and his father in "The Judgment," Gregor and his father
in "The Metamorphosis," the Officer and the Explorer
in "The Penal Colony." In the monologue pieces *a male
voice always speaks into a male ear*—"The Investigations of a Dog," or the Ape speaking to the "Honored
Gentlemen of the Academy." In the one or two instances
where a female figure seems to be the center, as in
"Josephine the Mouse" or "A Little Woman," the male
narrator speaks for her. *Nowhere in Kafka does woman
speak for herself.*

3. Because it is his male heroes who organize the text's
way of seeing, *the angle of vision in Kafka's texts is
necessarily androcentric*—i.e., male-centered. The full
import of this becomes particularly clear when that male
eye looks out at woman. What it never sees is the "person" of a woman, but always the body or part of a body.
In *The Trial,* Fräulein Bürstner, exhausted though she is
at the end of the day, having been surprised by K. in her

room, and obviously uneager to speak to him, is nonetheless seen by K. as "slowly caressing her hip," as if to
attract his sexual attentions (which he eventually forces
on her). Another example is provided by the washerwoman's "warm voluptuous body under the coarse
dress," as if it existed simply in order to invite/incite the
male eye. Woman is seen as an intrusion to the male
equilibrium; she disrupts by her very presence.

It is therefore no accident that Kafka's heroes have been
spoken of in strictly male terms, as modern day Fausts,
or *shlemiels,* or even as little boys. Woman in Kafka's
world can help or hinder the hero, but never can she
herself be an active participant in the quest. Moreover,
as Kafka represents her, she is quite incapable of understanding the impulse to act or of comprehending its
spiritual dimension. *Woman does not struggle toward
writing; she is what is written.*

If this were a longer study it would be useful to provide
a contextual history of Kafka's highly problematic relationship to women in his life—beginning with his 1913
question in a letter to Max Brod: "Could it be that one
can bind a girl by writing?" We would continue with the
recognition that Kafka used the hundreds of letters he
elicited (indeed coerced) from Felice (to whom he was
twice engaged) *as a nourishment for his own writing.*
Kafka was well aware of the fact that she, in turn, had
no idea of whom she was thus nourishing. I would also
explore more fully his desire to keep "nocturnal writing" to himself, specifically asking Felice *not* to write to
him at night because "nocturnal writing belongs to men
everywhere, even in China." We would thus see more
clearly the degree to which his understanding and representation of the world were androcentric. I would also
explore the impact of Jewish family life on his imagination, the fact that his own Jewish father was an arch-
patriarch of whom he was afraid, and that women are
structured into Orthodox Judaism in ways that place
them at the center of the culture, but outside some religious obligations and ritual participation. (For example,
women do not count as part of the ten men needed for
a *minyan,* the minimum number to start a prayer service. Women are considered "unclean" during menstruation and in the synagogue, they sit either upstairs
or at the back behind a curtain, so they do not distract
the praying men. While Kafka's family was reformed,
Kafka was fascinated with the Orthodox Law and these
attitudes, in any case, permeate the Orthodox Jewish
view of women.)

The most serious implications of the texts' male-centered angle of vision is that it makes impossible the
existence of real women, and substitutes in their place
false constructs, projections of male fears and fantasies,
idealizations and demonizations of woman, and asks us
to accept these as real representations of ourselves. Virginia Woolf, who understood much about gender/power
relationships, was distressed by the sharp discrepancy
she noted between the actual lives of historical women
and the representations of woman in male writings. In

A Room of One's Own she writes: "[Woman] pervades poetry from cover to cover; she is all but absent from history."[3] As astute as Woolf was, she was only half-right. Women are indeed absent from recorded history, but in spite of the variety of female creations, she is also absent from literature. Feminist film criticism has developed this analysis: "Man imposes meaning on the silent image of woman who is tied to her place as the bearer of meaning, not a maker of meaning."[4]

The German theorist Sylvie Bovenschen articulates the analysis in these words:

> The wealth of representations of woman is supposed to compensate for the silence of women. But even this silence has been mythologized. . . . Mostly, however, the silence of women remains unnoticed. It has been drowned out by the substitutionary dialogue about the feminine.[5]

However subversive some aspects of Kafka's vision may be, his work carries the dominant ideology about woman. By creating figures like those of Fräulein Bürstner and Leni in *The Trial,* Frieda and Olga in *The Castle,* Clara and Brunelda in *Amerika,* Frieda Brandenfeld in "The Judgment," he participates in the mythologizing process and also contributes to the substitutionary dialogue. Most fascinating in a feminist reading of Kafka is the recognition that even as he perpetuates the mythology about woman, he also unmasks it, and in so doing, lays bare the structures that bind woman. We need to be "resisting readers" of Kafka only to the extent that we continue to believe in the universality of his vision. Once we accept its partiality, we are freer to understand in what ways woman is structured into his texts, what functions she serves, and in what ways she is necessary to his discourse.

Kafka's works demonstrate the ways in which women's services are essential for male survival. It is not necessary to document elaborately that throughout Kafka's texts women are expected to, and do perform domestic and sexual services for men. In *The Trial* Leni is cook, nurse, maid, and mistress to the Lawyer, much as Frieda ministers to K.'s needs in *The Castle* (and to Jeremiah after she abandons K.). Virginia Woolf calls this woman's "civilizing" function for men. In *The Trial* Josef K. articulates it well:"'Women's hands are quietly effective,' . . . He himself might have smashed the dishes on the spot, but he certainly could never have quietly carried them away."[6] Woman provides the nurturance that keeps men going.

Kafka also understands that access to women is essential to the maintenance of male power. In a patriarchal world, men develop a sense of entitlement to women; they have rights to women that women do not have to themselves. With the exception of Amalia in *The Castle,* Kafka's women are domesticated and seen as objects of exchange between male partners. Where the phallus carries power and the meaning of difference, the phallus passes from one male to another through the medium of woman. Thus men are linked to one another through woman. She is both central and utterly peripheral. Woman, on the other hand, is not ever in a position to realize the benefits of her own circulation.[7]

Virginia Woolf also understood this pattern: What these illustrious men got from their alliance with women, aside from "comfort, flattery and the pleasures of the body" was "something that their own sex was unable to supply."[8] In Kafka's works men are the rightful owners of women's nurturing. This becomes clear when, for example, Gregor's wound (in "The Metamorphosis") begins *to throb* as he sees that his mother and sister, having left their work lying, "drew close to each other and sat cheek to cheek."[9] Similarly, after Gregor's death, Mr. Samsa is upset when he sees the mother and daughter clasping each other tightly. He interrupts their embrace, "And you might have some consideration for me!"[10] thus refocusing attention onto himself. At the end, he places himself between the two women, having successfully disrupted their alliance.

Throughout, Kafka's male characters think of women in the language of ownership. "I'm not thinking of handing the girl over to you," says the country doctor to his groom. "The body belonged to Wese . . ." in "A Fratricide." Even the weakest, most powerless male feels entitled to exercise some power over women. When Josef K. loses access to the washerwoman because the student carries her off to the Examining Magistrate, K. sees this loss of the woman as his "first unequivocal defeat." To have won the woman would have been to win power over the other men. Woman has no place in this struggle; she is the booty to be won. She does not exist for herself and she cannot speak in her own name. "There could be no more fitting revenge on the Examining Magistrate and his henchmen than to wrest this woman from her and take her himself."[11] Clearly if Josef K. had won her, he would have won power over his opponent. The woman becomes the means of his revenge. Josef K. even fantasizes that someday the woman might "belong to K. and K. alone." He also pictures using his prostitute whom he visits weekly, as a means of putting down the student. She would refuse the student her favors, the student would beg for them on his knees, and K. would then be the victor. That the body of the woman becomes the battleground for the male partners should be self-evident.

But Kafka goes one step further in annihilating woman: he allows Josef K. to speak for her, to name her experience. Angry at losing the washerwoman, and angry at what he perceives as her lack of resistance (against obviously heavy odds), K. shouts at her, "And you don't want to be set free."[12] One might well ask, what would "freedom" for her mean here? Whether she is carried off by the student or by Josef K., her position of powerlessness remains the same. Feminist theorist Andrea Dworkin suggests that in a patriarchy, woman is at the mercy of male power even if that power seems to be in warring male factions—men rape; men protect women from rape. The system operates to make women dependent on male power.[13] But the crowning blow in the washerwoman episode is K.'s reinterpretation of her behaviour: he insists that her abduction (read rape, coercion, seduction) is "her own fault" a judgment in which her husband all too readily concurs: "She's actually the most to blame of all."[14] Could there be a clearer statement of the patriarchal myth that women not only enjoy rape, but that they ask for it?

Woman is also powerless to express her own sexuality. She is called a whore if she initiates or appears to initiate sexual activity (Josef K.—"So this is all that it amounts to, she's offering herself to me. She's corrupt."[15]), but it is her refusal of the male that brings down the full force of patriarchal wrath. The Amalia episode in *The Castle,* whatever its spiritual or symbolic meanings, must also (perhaps first) be read on the literal level. "Access is one of the faces of Power. . . . Total power is unconditional access, total powerlessness is being unconditionally accessible."[16] The slave who denies access thereby declares herself not a slave. Amalia's is the story of the slave who said no.

Amalia's story is at once very simple and extremely complex. It both supports and exposes the patriarchal power system that enslaves woman. Part of its complexity arises from the narrative perspective: It is not as simple as one woman (Olga) telling another woman's story (Amalia's) to a man (K.). Kafka creates two very different female figures whom he sets off one against the other. Amalia, the pariah, whose act of refusal sets her outside the community, remains virtually silent; it is Olga, the "gentler of the sisters," the adapter, the woman who identifies with and accepts male power, who sees herself and other women through male eyes, who speaks for the rebel Amalia. Thus, though the voice that speaks is a woman's, the male value system permeates her story. It is no accident that it is Olga who introduces K. to the Herrenhof, an inn whose very name establishes it as a precinct of patriarchal power, and it is in the Herrenhof that Olga reveals her relationship to that power system. For this reason, the scene is worth quoting in some detail. K. is feeling powerful, so he orders Olga to take him home. But Olga gets caught up in her circle of friends.

> The peasants would not let her go; they had made up a dance in which she was the central figure, they circled round her yelling all together and every now and then one of them left the ring, seized Olga firmly round the waist and whirled her round and round; the pace grew faster and faster, their yells more hungry, more raucous, until they were insensibly blended into one continuous howl. Olga, who had begun laughingly by trying to break out of the ring, was now merely reeling with flying hair from one man to another.[17]

The contradictions in this picture are as glaring as they are revealing. The peasants (the men) have created a dance (a set of conventions, a pattern, a structure) in

which Olga (woman) is trapped. Though she is the central figure and is absolutely necessary to the structure, she is clearly out of her own control and at the mercy of the shouting, leering men. This image not only represents the position of woman in patriarchy, but also follows closely the dialogue in which K. admits his urge to take Frieda from Klamm. It may well provide a correlative for Frieda's passage from Klamm, to K. to Jeremiah, to who knows what man next?

It is this whirling female figure that we need to juxtapose to Amalia, the woman who stands alone, who, we are told, has a "direct and serious gaze, which is unflinching." Amalia's unabashed open gaze should warn us. If man is the owner of the gaze and woman its object, who should appropriately look down in modesty, then any woman who herself gazes, will be considered insurrectionary. Like the Medusa's, her eye will be seen as cold and hard, and monstrous. Amalia's fortune (or misfortune) is that she becomes the object of a castle official's gaze. On that day, Amalia is the only one who does not participate in the celebration of the new fire-engine (a symbol of male power?); she stands apart from the others and is thus noticed by the official who, having seen her, desired her; desiring her, he demands access to her and expects to be obeyed. (Olga tells K. "There is no such thing as an official's unhappy love affair."[18] He always gets the girl if he wants her.) If the woman in question "knows her place," she complies, as Frieda did when she herself had been called by Klamm. Sortini's request in the form of a vulgar letter which Amalia tears up and throws out the window, reveals the degree to which the official felt disrupted by his attraction to Amalia.

Olga believes that Amalia, by being chosen, is somewhat at fault. She explains to K., "Sortini was obviously enraged because the sight of Amalia had disturbed and distracted him in his work . . . even overnight he had not succeeded in forgetting her."[19] Sortini's letter has the force of rape: it commands, threatens, and brings shame on its victim, not on the perpetrator, in spite of the fact that it is widely acknowledged in the community that it represents "an abuse of power." Olga also explains that it is not simply refusing that was Amalia's crime. A woman can refuse, so long as she pretends to comply. "It wasn't that she didn't go that the curse was laid upon our family. . . . for there are many ways of getting around it, another girl might have decked herself up and wasted some time in doing it and then gone to the Herrenhof only to find that Sortini had left . . . but Amalia neither did that nor anything else. If only she had made some pretense of complying."[20] The family too could have re-established itself in the community if it had avoided ever mentioning the matter.

In order for the patriarchal power system to continue to operate, women must comply in keeping silent the violations of power. Amalia's "shamelessness," as Olga puts it, is that she refused to pretend that nothing had happened. By tearing up the letter, she fought back.

"She stood face to face with the truth and went on living."[21] The woman who speaks the truth, the woman who tries to control her own destiny, if only by refusing, becomes a pariah and calls down the wrath of the power structure. "What would happen if one woman told the truth about her life? The world would split open,"[22] is Muriel Rukeyser's articulation of this understanding. K. has a hard time accepting or understanding this truth. His own understanding is limited by his desire to find a place in the power structure. If he had to choose between Amalia and Olga, he wouldn't give it much reflection (and would choose Olga).[23] K. also refuses to see that his liaison with Frieda is no different from Frieda's with Klamm, or from what Amalia's would have been. K. wants to idealize male-female transactions. Here Kafka's analytic vision comes surprisingly close to that of Emma Goldman who first recognized that the traffic in women was a result of women being treated as a sex commodity.

> Nowhere is woman treated according to the merit of her work, but rather as a sex. It is therefore almost inevitable that she should pay for her right to exist, to keep a position in whatever line, with sex favors. Thus it is merely a question of degree whether she sells herself to one man, in or out of marriage, or to many men.[24]

There is considerable irony in Kafka's sharing such a radical critique of the uses of women's sexuality in a patriarchy, and I am not certain how much of what he represents he himself takes in as critique.

What is even more ironic, is that despite Kafka's personal sense of alienation from the sources of patriarchal power, he nonetheless embeds masculist values in his world, a world, to quote Virginia Woolf, in which "men harbor in their breasts an eagle, a vulture, forever tearing the liver out and plucking at the lungs—the instinct for possession, the rage for acquisition which drives them to desire other people's fields and goods perpetually [and, one might add, other men's women], to make frontiers and flags, battleships and poison gas."[25] Kafka may not approve of such a world, but he is undoubtedly of it: he supports and perpetuates as he unmasks. Looking at Kafka's *oeuvre* with even only slightly more open vision, we cannot fail to see that his fiction (and letters, diaries, and fragments) are filled with images and acts of mutilation, gratuitous violence, murder, rape, death, abduction, wounds, carrion, blood.

Setting aside *The Penal Colony* since that can too easily be seen as an exception, let us look at a few less well known pieces that illustrate the point amply. Consider "A Fratricide" in which one man, without any apparent motivation, murders another while the narrator watches: "Right into the throat and left into the throat and a third time deep into the belly stabbed Schmar's knife. . . . 'Done' said Schmar, and pitched the knife, now superfluous blood-stained ballast, against the nearest house front. 'The bliss of murder! The relief, the soaring ecstasy from the shedding of another's blood.' . . . Wese,

old nightbird, friend, alehouse crony, you are oozing away into the dark earth below the street. Why aren't you simply a bladder of blood so I could stamp on you and make you vanish into nothingness? Not all we want comes true, not all the dreams that blossomed have borne fruit. . . ."[26] Another example is "The Vulture" which is hacking at the narrator's feet, who overhears the narrator ask a gentleman for help, and "It took wing, leaned far back to gain impetus, and then like a javelin thrower thrust its beak through my mouth, deep into me. Falling back, I was relieved to feel him drowning irretrievably in my blood, which was filling every depth, flooding every shore."[27] A celebratory blending of violence, sexuality and death is fairly obvious here.

The same perspective holds in "The Bridge," in which the narrator is stiff and cold, stretched over a ravine. The human step he hears tells him to prepare. But when the man was on the bridge, he "jumped with both feet on the middle of my body. I shuddered with wild pain . . ." and finally, turning around to see him, "I . . . . began to fall, I fell and in a moment I was torn and transpierced by the sharp rocks."[28] A somewhat different version occurs in "An Old Manuscript" in which the butcher throws a live ox to the nomads while the narrator covers his ears with his bed clothes "to keep from hearing the bellowing of that ox, which the nomads were leaping on from all sides, tearing morsels out of its living flesh with their teeth."[29] The self-hating quality of these passages will not surprise us, especially when we also recognize their strong homoerotic component, an aspect of his sexuality which Kafka had great difficulty accepting. (We might add that he also had difficulty with heterosexuality, but he did not create such violent images in his descriptions of male-female sexuality, though Frieda and K. do "claw at each" other in a desperate attempt to find fulfillment. In these all-male pieces, the violence is always tinged with pleasure-pain. Kafka bears out the observation that the legend of male violence is the most celebrated legend of *man*kind.[30]

Most Kafka critics (except psychoanalytically oriented ones) look past the surface of these violent images to consider their "deeper meanings." My question: what could lead us to want to look past the surface, to not see what is so clearly there? Only some degree of participation in a system that naturalizes and celebrates violence, that accepts a brutalized version of sexuality. In this sense, Kafka's world is not exceptional, it is the rule.

In the heterosexual realm, there is a degree of cannibalism in Kafka's descriptions. One critic refers to "pornological" elements in Kafka which relate to male pornography. Robinson's description of Brunelda in *Amerika* is a good example: "How lovely she looked. . . . You felt you could eat her. [The German is *ablecken*—"lick her"] You felt you could drink her up."[31] In similarly imbibing and objectifying terms, Kafka describes Josef K.'s advances to Fräulein Bürstner, "He rushed out, seized her, and kissed her first on the lips, then all over the face, like some thirsty animal lapping greedily at a spring of long-sought-for fresh water."[32] If woman is the water to be imbibed, the food to be eaten, how is she to nourish herself?

This is not a question that the androcentric writer poses (nor the androcentric critic either), since his focus is on the well-being of the male psyche. For this reason, the feminist critic must focus on the small ruptures in the text that come more clearly into our vision once the male ceases to be the central and only reference point in our readings. For instance, in "A Report to an Academy," we may wish to account for the ape's wife, who turns up only at the very end of the ape's report. She is a "half-trained little chimpanzee" who waits every evening for her performing husband to return home late at night, "and I take comfort from her, as apes do. By day I cannot bear to see her, for she has the insane look of the bewildered, half-broken animal in her eye."[33]

What are we to make of this insertion? Why does Kafka bother to give his ape a wife at all? Why a half-crazed one, only half-domesticated at that? Or are all women, like Leni, "freaks of nature"? Is Kafka trying to tell us something about the situation of woman, particularly academic wives with performing husbands? Are we to take this representation as a critique—or is he simply making a report? When are the two the same? When and how do they differ?

Kafka's manipulation of the narrative perspective makes it difficult to answer these questions definitely. They are in fact, the central questions asked by feminist critics. What is the relationship between fictional representation and a writer's world view? What responsibility does the writer have? If the writer merely *represents,* is he or she responsible for perpetuating a power structure and a way of thinking that needs to be changed? Kafka's extraordinary skill as a writer whose words have the power to seduce, to make us see with him, to accept his vision, makes him a dangerous writer. The central male figures in Kafka's texts seek and struggle, but never find. For him, there is no way out *but* the struggle itself. The female is placed in a far more powerless position, for she is at the mercy of even the smallest, most inconsequential male. For her, there can be no quest; at best, she can be a conduit; her power is temporary and derivative, bestowed upon her by the male. She is never in a position to learn anything, since she herself cannot act. A male can read Kafka against the grain. He can refuse to answer the Law when it beckons, he can refuse a false trail or trial. Woman exists only on the margins, entrapped in a power system in which she is never an actor, only acted upon.

For this reason, as Rich suggests, "a radical critique of literature, feminist in its impulse, would take the work first of all as a clue to how we live, how we have been living, how we have been led to imagine ourselves. . . . how we can begin to see—and therefore live—afresh."[34]

A first step in seeing anew is our willingness to recognize that even our most canonized texts, those we have imagined to be most universal, are in fact, not gender neutral. Faust after all, is and can only be male; Gretchen "the eternal feminine that leads 'us' on high" is irrevocably female. We must be willing to recognize that gender has been a determining factor in our myth-making, in the way power and sexuality are structured into literary texts. If we recognize this, then what follows is the awareness that even our most "objective" readings of these texts are also not gender neutral. In this arena we could speak of Fräulein Hartmanns or Fräulein deMans or Fräulein Derridas and Lacans.

For women have been taught to see through an androcentric lens; it is a way of seeing we all have to unlearn. Such a paradigm shift is both exhilarating and disorienting, since it forces us to rethink our received truths about literary study and about the world. It challenges our codified values, especially about "old masters" and "eternal truths." It forces us to rethink and reconceptualize the value systems by which we live. Such disruptions are never comfortable, but to paraphrase a Kafka aphorism, a book should act on us like a sharp blow—it should serve as an ax for "the frozen sea within us." Though I would prefer less violent language, this perception well describes the kind of awakening a feminist analysis of literature can catalyze. We ought to welcome it.

NOTES

[1] See Elisabeth Endres, "Ilse Aichinger," *Neue Literatur der Frauen,* ed. Heinz Fuknus (Munich: Verlag C. H. Beck, 1980), p. 44.

[2] Muriel Rukeyser, "Myth," in *I Hear My Sisters Saying: Poems by Twentieth Century Women,* ed. Carol Konek and Dorothy Walters (New York: Thomas Y. Crowell, 1976), p. 243.

[3] Virginia Woolf, *A Room Of One's Own* (New York: Harcourt, Brace and World, 1957), p. 45.

[4] This concept is analyzed in some detail in an unpublished dissertation-in-process, on feminist criticism by Lucie Arbuthnot; probable date of completion, May 1982, New York University.

[5] Silvia Bovenschen, *Die imaginierte Weiblichkeit: Exemplarische Untersuchungen zu kulturgeschichtlichen und literarischen Präsentationsformen des Weiblichen* (Frankfurt am Main: Suhrkamp Verlag, 1979), p. 41. Translation mine.

[6] Franz Kafka, *The Trial,* definitive edition (New York: Schocken Books, 1968), p. 18.

[7] This analysis is based in part on the excellent theoretical work of Gayle Rubin, "The Traffic in Women," in *Toward an Anthropology of Women,* ed. Rayna R. Reiter (New York and London: Monthly Review Press, 1975), pp. 157-210. Rubin's work is based on a femi-

nist reinterpretation of the works of Levi-Strauss, Freud, and Lacan.

[8] Woolf, *Room,* p. 90.

[9] Franz Kafka, "The Metamorphosis," in *The Complete Stories,* ed. Nahum N. Glatzer (New York: Schocken Books, 1976), p. 125.

[10] Kafka, *Stories,* p. 139.

[11] Kafka, *Trial,* p. 56.

[12] Kafka, *Trial,* p. 58.

[13] Andrea Dworkin, *On Pornography: Men Possessing Women* (New York, 1981). Dworkin's analysis comes close to Josef K.'s recognition that the apparent parties of the Right and the Left were all colleagues, all wearing the same badge as even the Examining Magistrate (*Trial,* p. 47). What Josef K. does not comprehend is that no matter how outside the system he may perceive himself to be, as a male, he too is a colleague, wearing a male badge of power, power which he believes he ought to be able to exert on women.

[14] Kafka, *Trial,* p. 61.

[15] Kafka, *Trial,* p. 52.

[16] Marilyn Frye, "Some Reflections on Separatism and Power," *Sinister Wisdom* 6 (Summer 1978), pp. 35-36.

[17] Franz Kafka, *The Castle* (New York: Alfred A. Knopf, 1947), p. 52.

[18] Kafka, *Castle,* p. 254.

[19] Kafka, *Castle,* p. 248.

[20] Kafka, *Castle,* p. 250.

[21] Kafka, *Castle,* p. 270.

[22] Muriel Rukeyser, "Käthe Kollwitz," in *No More Masks,* ed. Florence Howe and Ellen Bass (Garden City, New York: Anchor Press, 1973), p. 103.

[23] Kafka, *Castle,* p. 298.

[24] Emma Goldman, *"The Traffic in Women" and Other Essays in Feminism* (Washington, N.J.: Times Change Press, 1970 reprinting of 1917 edition), p. 20.

[25] Woolf, *Room,* pp. 38-39.

[26] Kafka, *Stories,* p. 403. Earlier in the piece the narrator had commented, "Unriddle the mysteries of human nature" (p. 402). This seems an excellent example of a generalization about the *human* condition which is, in fact, accurate only in a description of *male* behavior in

western culture. This kind of violence is simply not condoned or encouraged in women as it is in men. It is men who have been the perpetrators of gratuitous violence; most often, women are its victims.

[27] Kafka, *Stories,* p. 443.

[28] Kafka, *Stories,* p. 412.

[29] Kafka, *Stories,* p. 417.

[30] See Dworkin, *On Pornography,* which develops this idea in some detail.

[31] Franz Kafka, *Amerika* (New York: Schocken Books, 1962), p. 234.

[32] Kafka, *Trial,* p. 29.

[33] Kafka, *Stories,* p. 259.

[34] Adrienne Rich, "When We Dead Awaken: Writing as Re-Vision," in *On Lies, Secrets, and Silence* (New York: Norton, 1971) p. 35.

Mark Sturdivant

SOURCE: "Milan Kundera's Use of Sexuality," in *Critique: Studies in Modern Fiction,* Vol. XXVI, No. 3, Spring, 1985, pp. 131-40.

[*In the following essay, Sturdivant assesses Kundera's use of sexual intercourse in his fiction to portray "the utter meaninglessness of the human condition."*]

In examining the work of Czechoslavakian author Milan Kundera, critic Philip Roth observes that "almost all [Kundera's] novels, in fact all the individual parts of his latest book, find their dénouement in great scenes of coitus" (afterword, *The Book of Laughter and Forgetting,* 236). Indeed, in Kundera's most recent effort, *The Book of Laughter and Forgetting,* the novelist follows a pattern earlier established in his highly acclaimed novel *The Joke* and his collection of short stories *Laughable Loves* by depicting sexuality as "the focus where all the themes of the story converge and where its deepest secrets are located" (afterword, 236). Kundera views sexuality and eroticism as "the deepest region of life" and therefore feels that the question of mankind's *raison d'être,* when "posed to sexuality, is the deepest question" (afterword, 237). In the expression of this belief in his three aforementioned novels, sexuality becomes a vehicle for expressing a variety of interwoven threads of commentary upon human characteristics, and for ultimately casting a pall of hopelessness and meaninglessness over mankind's fundamental existence.

Perhaps the most obvious role of sexuality in the portrayal of man involves the presentation of the characters' innermost concerns and desires, as sensed by the omniscient narrator, in scenes either during or intimately related to the sexual act. A clear example of this device, one which explores what might be termed "the sexual mentality" rather than the act of intercourse itself, arises in the story "Symposium" in *Laughable Loves.* In accordance with the chief physician's statement that "in eroticism we seek the image of our own significance and importance" (124), Nurse Alzhbeta, a woman with "a hideous face but a beautiful body" (124), protests against what she considers the "sheer absurdity and injustice" (179) of her physical fate by performing a mock striptease. Her frustration and agony increase as a doctor to whom she "brazenly [makes] advances" harshly rejects her, causing her striptease to become increasingly blatant; this progression expresses the character's emotions via a sexually related action. Another such example emerges in Part Four of *The Book of Laughter and Forgetting* as Tamina, identified by Kundera as the book's "main character and main audience" (165), vividly "displays" her concern over losing the memory of her former husband while involved in a spiritless act of sex. The narrator explains that "lately she has begun noticing with desperation that the past is growing paler and paler. All she has left of her husband is his passport picture" (83-84), which she uses, "in a sort of spiritual exercise" (84), to evoke "his skin, its color, and all its minor blemishes" (84). This habit of Tamina's is forcefully demonstrated by its domination of her sexual affair with Hugo; her suspicion that "she would see [her husband] when she made love" (88) materializes as "her husband's image [follows] her around the room as she [turns] her face. It [is] a giant image of a grotesquely giant husband, a husband much larger than life, yet just what she [has] imagined for three years" (109).

This lack of intimacy in the second example links Kundera's self-described use of sexuality to "[generate] an extremely sharp light which suddenly reveals the essence of characters" (afterword, *The Book of Laughter and Forgetting,* 236) to another prevalent theme in his work, that of an inevitable mind/body duality. Though these two points of focus may first appear contradictory, the author clearly demonstrates that although the body may serve as the ultimate spokesman for the mind, the two are by nature irreconcilable, thereby catalyzing the sense of alienation which haunts Kundera protagonists, including Tamina. Perhaps Kundera's most straightforward presentation of this inability to establish psychological and physical unity occurs in the opening short story of *Laughable Loves,* "The Hitchhiking Game." In this story, the young, unnamed female initially believes that her boyfriend "never [separates] her body from her soul" and that "she [can] live with him wholly" (5). However, Kundera suggests the implausibility of such an attitude in a game which the couple choose to play: through changing identities, and fueled by mutual possessive jealousy and relentlessly heightening eroticism, the two characters' thoughts and actions offer another example of the author's viewpoint expressed via sex-dominated circumstances. To her boyfriend, the girl

grows more attractive physically as she "[withdraws] from him psychically" (16); for as he muses that the illusion of her co-existing goodness and beauty which "he worshipped" (19) is "real only within the bounds of fidelity and purity" and that "beyond these bounds she [ceases] to be herself" (19), the young man realizes that "the girl he loved was a creation of his desire, his thoughts, and his faith and that the real girl now standing in front of him [is] hopelessly alien, hopelessly ambiguous" (21). As "the game [merges] with life" (22), the two characters—the girl a prostitute, the boy her client—plunge into frenzied intercourse in which "there [are] soon two bodies in perfect harmony, two sensual bodies, alien to each other" (25). This sexual act causes the girl to acknowledge her irreversible mind/body duality as she, feeling "horror at the thought" (25), realizes that "she [has] never known such pleasure" as that which she experiences beyond the "forbidden boundary" of "love-making without emotion or love" (25). An additional vivid example of Kundera's refuting mental and physical unity emerges in the second part of *The Book of Laughter and Forgetting,* a section described by Roth as "one long scene of three-way sex, with a prologue and epilogue" (afterword, 236). In this instance Karel and Marketa, a couple having marriage difficulties, participate in a session of *ménage a trois* with a mutual friend named Eva hoping to "[lift] the burden they [are] both struggling under" (38). However, Eva's interpretation of sexuality—a belief not in love but "only in friendship and sensuality" (33)—dominates the couple's ill-fated plans for reconciliation via sex as Marketa feels "the new and intoxicating touch of freedom" only after mentally severing Karel's "head from his body" thus escaping "the presence of the man she [loves] too much" which weighs "heavy on her and [dampens] the pleasures of the senses" (49). Thus, once again the irreconcilable nature of the mind and body causes a functioning duality as "the anonymity of their bodies [is] sudden paradise, paradise regained" (49).

At this point however, lest the reader think Kundera is promoting raw, unbridled sensuality as mankind's hope for a meaningful or at best tolerable existence, Marketa's temporary alienated yet satisfied state abruptly ceases as Karel's "headless body [stops] short" in its "vigorous motions on top of her" and loudly speaks; the sound of her husband's voice "[is] like being waked out of a dream" to Marketa, interrupting the pleasure she experienced only while "a body without past or memory" (49). Indeed, Kundera ultimately presents eroticism as but a short-lived respite from the reality of human frailty in the face of earthly existence; a fine example of the author's intentions can be found in Part Six of *The Book of Laughter and Forgetting.* In this portrayal through "magical realism" of Tamina upon an island otherwise inhabited solely by children, she closes "her eyes again and [rejoices] in her body" as it takes "pleasure in the absence of the soul" (177) while the children curiously explore the most intimate regions of Tamina's physique. She thus enjoys her sexuality as "a toy for the production of sensual pleasure" (182), for, as the omni-

scient narrator points out, "sexuality freed from its diabolical ties with love [has] become a joy of angelic simplicity" (182). However, "all at once the realm where
things are light as a breeze knows no peace" (183);
Kundera harshly depicts the hopelessness of man's destiny as Tamina's sensual haven becomes a nightmare.
The children relentlessly taunt "what not so long ago
had been her pride and weapon—her black pubic hair,
her beautiful breasts" (184), and in a scene reminiscent
of Golding's *Lord of the Flies* trap her in nets and eventually cause her to attempt escape from both her inner
torment and her oppression on the island by swimming
away. As the children watch, "wide-eyed and eager"
(191), the woman who had so recently experienced a
"quiet, cradlelike pleasure" (177) through eroticism now
disappears "beneath the surface" (191).

Rather than limit his presentation to depicting man's
hopeless existence through an inherent mind/body duality which leads to an unavoidable alienation, Kundera
broadens his philosophical approach in *The Book of
Laughter and Forgetting* by adding Part Seven. In doing
so, Kundera seems dissatisfied with the depth of his
anti-humanism stance and thus indicates human frailty
by stressing, via examples involving sexuality, that
"man passes through the present with his eyes blind-
folded. He is permitted merely to sense and guess at
what he is actually experiencing" (*Laughable Loves,*
57). However, this varied approach to proving his thesis—the utter meaninglessness of the human condition—is by no means distinctly separated from
Kundera's other thrusts; instead, a careful blending of
his major depictions of sexuality marks this intended
interrelationship. For instance, Kundera's mind/body
duality then is closely linked to his description of faces
as "blank screens," an analytical launching point for a
series of related adventures displaying human relegation
to ignorance and/or misinterpretation. An example occurs in Part Seven of *The Book of Laughter and Forgetting* as Jan depicts his wife Edwige's face as "a blank
screen" in which he can "find no answers" (195). "Of
course he might [ask] her," the narrator explains, "but
they [have] fallen into a strange pattern" of losing "the
power of speech once their bodies [intertwine]" (195).
In a strong passage, Kundera points to the abyss between Jan and his wife and the frightening contentment
with which they both approach this lack of understanding—Jan with acceptance, Edwige with ignorance: "Jan
and Edwige never understand each other, yet they always [agree]. Each [interprets] the other's words in his
own way, and they [live] in perfect harmony, the perfect
solidarity of perfect mutual misunderstanding" (227).
The author, in addition, presents his doctrine of "perfect
misunderstanding" in earlier incidents, which also demonstrate the unity and interdependence of Kundera's
approaches toward his thesis. Such an instance arises in
the affair between the student and Kristyna; the older
woman falls "in love with his (the student's) gentle
shyness and [wants] to preserve it for herself" (119)
without dragging "their relationship down to the level
(purely erotic) of her relationship with the butcher (her

husband) or the mechanic" by "surrendering her body to
the student" (120). Meanwhile, the student, while appreciating what he views as the wholeness of their relationship yet continually attempting (unsuccessfully) to
initiate sexual intercourse with Kristyna, fails to realize
that while his penchant for quoting Schopenhauer
"might charm her soul, it also [places] a barrier between
him and her body" (121). Therefore, this situation, with
its implied link to mind/body duality, portrays Kundera's
belief that "this is the way life goes: a man imagines
that he is playing his role in a particular play, and does
not suspect that in the meantime they have changed the
scenery without his noticing" (*Laughable Loves,* 229).

Instead of merely presenting man's relegation to ignorance and misinterpretation as a human shortcoming in
and of itself, Kundera further develops his thesis by
bridging this facet of his argument to the vitally important concept of "The Border," which he describes as "a
certain imaginary dividing line beyond which things
appear senseless and ridiculous" (afterword, *The Book
of Laughter and Forgetting,* 236) and which the omniscient narrator describes as a condition "constantly with
us, irrespective of time or our age" (217). The conflict
between Kristyna and the student provides an example:
after inviting Kristyna to his apartment in Prague, he
attends a gathering of famous poets in which Goethe's
opinion that "(the student's) small-town butcher's wife
is the perfect woman for a poet" (139) so fills the student with pride that "he [aches] at the very thought of
her" (140). The student then returns to his apartment
certain of establishing a satisfactory equilibrium between his tender emotions of love and his burning desire
for long-sought physical gratification. However, Kristyna
again rejects his sexual advances, and upon discovering
the cause of this sexual abstinence—her fear of getting
pregnant—the student suddenly realizes that "if only he
had said one sensible sentence, if only he had called a
spade a spade, he could have had her." He now sees that
her fear of pregnancy, rather than "the boundless horizons of their love," which the student had so romantically analyzed, is the cause of her attitude; and he, upon
"peering deep into the abyss of his stupidity," feels "like
screaming with laughter—tearful, hysterical laughter"
as he leaves with "litost, frustration, at his side" (149).
Furthermore, Kundera saves his most explicit example
of passing from ignorance to *litost* via realization for
the last part of *The Book of Laughter and Forgetting,*
aptly entitled "The Border." In portraying his belief that
"the boundary exists everywhere, in all areas of human
life and even in the deepest, most biological of all: sexuality" (afterword, 236), Kundera constructs a scenario
which vividly and forcefully attempts to answer "the
question posed by sexuality" (237). Again, in describing
the gulf between Jan and Edwige, the author relays
Jan's dance along the "fraction of an inch separating
intercourse from laughter, . . . from the border" (214).
Although ten years earlier Jan had been able to hold
"back the smile" (213), which his affair with a married
woman had nearly provoked, he now finds that "every
time something is repeated, it loses part of its meaning"

(216), thus drawing closer to "the border beyond which everything loses meaning: love, convictions, faith, history" (206). In the closing scene of *The Book of Laughter and Forgetting,* Jan strolls along a nude beach and feels that "he [is] at the line, crossing it" (226) as he is "overwhelmed by a strange feeling of affliction" caused by "the vague and mysterious idea of the border" (226). Indeed, Kundera blatantly demonstrates his intentions of displaying the meaninglessness of human existence through sexually related incidents; as "the feeling of affliction Jan [feels] at the sight of all those naked bodies on the beach [becomes] more and more unbearable" (226), his wife continually misinterprets his statements and fails to sense his turmoil as she endlessly prattles. The couple is soon joined by other beach walkers who enter into the shallow, dull routine of repeating "statements which Jan [has] heard ten, twenty, thirty . . . a thousand times before" (225). However, the significance of this meaninglessness gains greater breadth and impact as the narrator depicts the scene in stark sexual terms which lend intensity and universality to the situation: "On and on the man [talks]. The others [listen] with interest, their naked genitals staring dully, sadly, listlessly at the yellow sand" (228).

At this point in the analysis of Kundera's use of sexuality, a brief organizational review of previous arguments should aid in effectively viewing the author's multi-faceted yet interdependent approach, perhaps best described as a "tri-pronged attack." The first prong consists of Kundera presenting the general statement that human existence lacks opportunity for lasting contentment (as he portrays his characters as victims of mind/body duality, alienated and unsatisfied by either mental or physical pleasures). The second prong further develops the first prong while simultaneously, by depicting man's inherent tendency towards misinterpretation as indicative of his haphazard and ill-fated attempts to avoid crossing over the border towards meaninglessness, approaching the thesis of "mankind's hopelessness" from a related yet varied angle. Given the first two stages of Kundera's assault, the final prong involves direct approach to Kundera's thesis: by entangling his characters in situational labyrinths from which they are powerless to escape, and by displaying the transition in these instances from jokes *of* the characters to jokes *on* the characters (amid a backdrop of meaninglessness "on the other side of the border" [209]), Kundera offers his final, most pessimistic evaluation of the human existence.

A prime example of the farcical nature of human existence, in the world according to Kundera, predictably occurs in his first novel, *The Joke.* The basis for the novel's title develops as the protagonist, Ludvik Jahn, writes his girlfriend (a devout Communist) a playful note: "Optimism is the opium of the people! The healthy atmosphere stinks! Long live Trotsky!" (132). Although the postcard is sent purely in jest, the party banishes Ludvik and sentences him to forced labor in the coal mines after an impassioned prosecution by Pavel Zemanek. Ludvik, inspired by "the force of fifteen years of hatred"

(171) towards Zemanek, plots revenge in the form of a "cool and deliberate plan" (167) for seducing Zemanek's wife; in the successful climax of his plan, Ludvik feels that he has "Zemanek's very life in [his] grasp" (187) as he relentlessly drives Helena from orgasm to orgasm, ransacking "Pavel Zemanek's marriage bed! [Rummaging] through everything! [Leaving] everything in a shambles!" (190). However, Ludvik's total confidence in the "success of [his] project" (193) proves short lived and tragically inaccurate as Kundera's commentary, through sexuality, on the farcical nature of human existence unfolds. First, Zemanek is planning to divorce his wife and meets his former legal opponent accompanied by a beautiful young woman, causing Ludvik to ruminate that "life [has] mocked me by sending me, in the form of this man's lover, a reminder of the grotesque sexual contest in which only the day before I'd mistakenly thought I'd defeated him" (255). The tragic reversal of Ludvik's joke continues as he realizes that the object of his intensely maintained hatred has changed, that now Zemanek has "abandoned his former views" to the extent that Ludvik "would in any conflict, like it or not, find [himself] on his side" (251). Thus, "that bad joke—which, not content with itself, [goes] on monstrously multiplying into greater and greater grotesquery" (263) becomes painfully clear to Ludvik as he acknowledges the need "to hate him (Zemanek)" since "by hating him Ludvik [is] balancing the weight of evil that smothered [Ludvik's] youth, [Ludvik's] life" (252). Thus, Ludvik's earlier description of Helena as representative of "the endless human capacity for self-delusion" (175) ironically characterizes his own unfocused view prior to the final, devastating realization that "the entire course of [his] life was conceived in error, through the bad joke of the postcard—that accident, that absurdity" (264). Ludvik therefore expresses Kundera's evaluation, presented through circumstances linked to sexuality, of the essence of human existence as he muses: "Who then was at fault? History? Divinely rational history? Why should it have been a mistake on her part? Then I realized how feeble it was to want to annul my own joke when throughout my life I'd been involved in a monumental joke—all-embracing, unfathomable, and utterly irrevocable" (264).

Although *The Joke* may carry a more fervent political statement than *Laughable Loves,* the final story of the latter book—"Edward and God"—seems to present the author's thesis on human existence in its most forcefully despairing form. Thus, this second example of the third prong of the author's approach serves as both an ultimate declaration and as an exemplary fusion of the earlier two prongs toward the final destination of Kundera's thesis. In this tale, a lighthearted outlook on sexuality—an approach which might be expected from a book entitled *Laughable Loves*—dominates the beginning of the story as Edward, the protagonist, feigns piety and religious conviction in hopes of establishing sexual relations with the beautiful yet "very reserved and virtuous" Alice (207). Circumstances favor Edward as party members persecute him for his "religious beliefs," causing

Alice in admiration to become "warm, and passionate" (226) and agreeing to prove her affection for Edward by visiting his brother's cottage, "where they could be alone" (229). At this point, the reader, probably awaiting the "Fall of Edward," is not disappointed; however, the use of Edward's long-sought sexual encounter with Alice as the actual catalyst for this decline serves to magnify the extent of his misery and to accurately demonstrate the true magnitude of meaninglessness with which Kundera associates the human condition. Edward indeed meets success in his sexual endeavors, yet, as he realizes, "Alice's unexpected turnabout had occurred independently . . . of his argumentation . . . of any logical consideration whatsoever" (235). Representative of Kundera's belief in the farcical nature of human events, the fulfillment of Edward's consummate desire rests "upon a mistake," and Alice's change of heart had "been deduced quite illogically even from this mistake" (235). Furthermore, representative of Kundera's practice of revealing his characters' most fundamental beliefs in scenes of coitus or some other sexually related situation, Edward is haunted by thoughts of "those long, futile weeks when Alice had tormented him with her coldness" (236) in that Edward now is irritated by "how easily and remorselessly she [is] now betraying her God of No Fornication" (236). Kundera's emphasis on an inescapable mind/body duality, accompanied by an inability to achieve satisfaction in either state, again emerges as Edward realizes that he much favors the "old" Alice, whose "beautiful simplicity of her looks seemed to accord with the unaffected simplicity of her faith, and [whose] simple faith seemed to be a substantiation of her attitude" (237); however, he now "[feels] no joy at all" upon viewing her as "an accidental conjunction of a body, thoughts, and a life's course" (237). Therefore, in an episode marked by demonstration of the fluid and cyclic characteristics of Kundera's overall analysis through sexuality, Edward masters his newly-acquired outlook—using "the words 'disgust' and 'physical aversion'" (241) to attack his lover—by sending Alice home on the train.

The thoughtful reader now may recognize the abnormal (for a Kundera character) degree of control which Edward yields, a characteristic seemingly in direct opposition to the author's attempt to present human existence as farcical, meaningless, and hopelessly uncontrollable. However, Edward's dominance over the course of Alice's departure proves quite misleading: earlier in the story, Edward receives harsh admonitions from the Communist Party Organization in his town but manages to avoid serious disciplinary action through clever lies, which indicate his self-declared failure to "take them seriously" (239). However, the very depth of knowledge which distinguishes Edward from most Kundera characters creates a new degree of meaninglessness and hopeless relegation to life without control, for not only is his existence plagued by these factors, he realizes and understands that "the shadow that mocks remains a shadow, subordinate, derivative, and wretched, and nothing more" (240). Kundera seems to demand "What else can

knowledge accomplish?" as Edward realizes that "what [has] happened, [has] happened, and it [is] no longer possible to right anything" (241).

An ideal conclusion—yet Kundera apparently feels that additional "circumstantial evidence" will better hammer home his thesis. Therefore, after depicting Edward as reasonably content with his routine of sex with the directress of the Communist Party Organization (yes, yet another twist in plot) and of solitary walks, Kundera uses parenthesis to imply direct author-reader contact as he invites the reader to join him in viewing Edward visiting the local church. This final scene in *Laughable Loves,* involving Edward while sitting in the quiet sanctuary suddenly smiling a broad smile in the midst of his sorrow, might be interpreted three ways. However, two of the possible interpretations are apparently refuted by evidence given in context, leaving the third as the plausible, forceful, and rightful conclusive analysis of Kundera's evaluation of human existence. And as in his other works, the author's conclusive statement evolves from thoughts and actions based on sex-related relationships.

The first of the possible renditions holds that Edward indeed sees "the genuine living face of God" (242) and thus smiles in rapture. However, Kundera earlier insists that "Edward did not believe in God" (242) and assures the reader that "our story does not intend to be crowned with the effect of so ostentatious a paradox" (242); these inserts, coupled with another author-to-reader statement in parenthesis describing God as "alone and nonexistent" (242), severely damage the credibility of this first interpretation.

Secondly, upon recalling Kundera's penchant for surprise and his belief in man's inability to clearly judge events affecting his life, the reader might interpret the author's purpose for the final scene as "the last word" concerning Edward's lack of true judgment as he is ultimately deceived into a belief in God. Once again, however, the arguments refuting the first explanation are applicable in this case, and seem to overpower additional opposing suggestions such as the possibility of Kundera's description of God as "nonexistent" being more accurately analyzed as the author's depiction of God as a spirit rather than a member of "this unessential (but so much more existent) world" (242).

This leaves only a third evaluation, a stance supported both by the intricacies of the final scene as well as by the story, and its foundation of use of sexuality, as a whole. This final interpretation holds that Edward, in his tragic awareness, realizes the full magnitude of the hopelessly farcical and meaningless connotations of human existence and crosses The Border as he smiles a smile not of "imitation laughter" but of "original (the Devil's)" laughter (*The Book of Laughter and Forgetting,* 62), the laughter of hopeless despair. Supporting this explication of the last page of "Edward and God" and of *Laughable Loves,* the portrayal of Edward as cognizant of man's position continues as he is "too bright to concede that he [sees] the essential in the unessential" (242). But he nonetheless longs "for God . . . the essential opposite of this unessential . . . world" (242), for he is "too weak not to long secretly" (242) for a means of removing his burden of knowledge and subsequent sorrow, which has developed via his various sexual encounters. Despite this hope, he soon recognizes that which Kundera has earlier told the reader—that God is nonexistent—and the depth of his and mankind's ignominious fate is mirrored in the terrible irony of the narrator describing this revelation as the emergence of "the genuine living face of God" (242). The narrator, whose view now lacks the tone of intimacy earlier described in Kundera's comments in parenthesis, sadly misinterprets Edward's smile as "happy" (242); a more accurate approach, signified by a sense that Kundera inserts his comments since it does not smoothly follow from the previous statement (Edward as "too weak not to long secretly for the essential"), emerges in the thought that "a man lives a sad life when he cannot take anything or anyone seriously" (242).

Kundera needlessly urges the reader to "keep him (Edward) in your memory with this smile" (242).

William K. Buckley

SOURCE: "Louis-Ferdinand Céline's Novels: From Narcissism to Sexual Connection," in *Studies in the Novel,* Vol. XVIII, No. 1, Spring, 1986, pp. 51-65.

[*In the following essay, Buckley examines the failure of narcissistic love and the positive aspects of sexuality in the novels of Louis-Ferdinand Céline.*]

> "Ah, Ferdinand . . . as long as you live you will always search for the secret of the universe in the loins of women!"
>
> --*L'Eglise*

> . . . the female mystery doesn't reside between the thighs, it's on another wave-length, a much more subtle one
>
> --*Castle to Castle*

After Freud, modern novelists grew more conscious of not only their own literary expression as a kind of narcissism, but also of the narcissism in the characters they created. Distress about narcissism, therefore, can be easily detected in modern novels. "The psychoanalytic concept of narcissism," says Russell Jacoby in his study *Social Amnesia* (1975), "captures the reality of the bourgeois individual; it expresses the private regression of the ego into the id under the sway of public domination. . . . it comprehends the dialectical isolation of the bourgeois individual—dialectical in that the isolation that damns the individual to scrape along in a private world derives

from a public and social one. The energy that is directed toward oneself, rather than toward others, is rooted in society, not organically in the individual. . . . The mechanism of this shift is not the least the society that puts a premium on the hardening of each individual— the naked will to self-preservation."[1] This *naked will* to self-preservation, this *hardening* of oneself is an apt description of most protagonists in our modern novels.[2] These terms are an especially good description of Céline's main character in his first two novels: the young Ferdinand.

Still creating their storm of interest and influence after fifty years, Céline's *Journey to the End of the Night* (1932) and *Death on the Installment Plan* (1936) are good examples of modern novels which use a narrator who expresses his hardened feelings over both his narcissistic and crushed ego-ideals, and over his careful love choices. Ferdinand, like so many in modern fiction, is a character who has withdrawn his libido from the outer world because his contact with that world has brought mostly economic and emotional disaster; and, in defense, he has directed his libido to his ego. Major American scholarship on Céline has not explored the sexual behavior of Céline's characters as closely as it needs to do. Of course there have been important discussions of Céline's views on sex by many. McCarthy gives us a rather negative assessment of the author's views in his biography *Céline* (1975),[3] as does J. H. Matthews in his book, *The Inner Dream: Céline as Novelist* (1978).[4] In comparing Céline's views on sex to Baudelaire's views in *Journaux intimes,* McCarthy claims that *Journey* shows women as "predatory" (p. 69), that Céline suggests "women need to destroy men because there is a link between female sexuality and cruelty" (p. 69), and that, in the final analysis—because of the behavior of Musyne and Lola—"sex turns out to be disgusting" (p. 71) for Ferdinand, reflecting Céline's personal view that the male loses himself in orgasm with a woman because he is "weary" to have done "with himself" (p. 70). J. H. Matthews offers an equally negative view of sex in *Death on the Installment Plan.* He points to several episodes in the novel which support his point that sex "brings no consolation of any kind, no sense of release. It is a heightened form of terror. . . . Ferdinand's sexual contacts revitalize the cliche that represents sex as a form of death and likens the ecstasy of orgasm to dying" (p. 77). The client who early in the novel invites the young Ferdinand to engage her in oral sex; the sexual demands made upon Ferdinand by Madame Gorloge, and her theft of a jewel from the young boy's pocket; Gwendoline, the sex partner Ferdinand meets after crossing the Channel, and whom Matthews calls the *vagina dentata;* Nora's desperate actions with Ferdinand at Meanwell College; the astonishing scene between Antoine and his wife, to which Ferdinand and his friend Robert are voyeurs: all these scenes are examples of what Matthews calls Céline's linking of violence and eroticism. Matthews further maintains that even masturbation is "marked by terrorism" in this novel (p. 79), especially when the boys at the English boarding school cruelly beat and masturbate the retarded Jongkind for getting penalties during a soccer match. Therefore since at "no time in his life has Ferdinand felt capable of trusting women enough to love any of them," masturbation becomes the "significant feature" of his early life (pp. 79-80). "It is a direct expression of his profound need to change his destiny in a world ruled by violence and predatory sexuality, where [Ferdinand] is alternately victim and pariah" (p. 80). I agree with Matthews that in most of these scenes "tenderness has no place" (p. 77), and that masturbation, sodomy, and rape become the clear but worst examples of narcissism in this novel. One could argue, for example, that Gorloge's seduction of the little Ferdinand is an example of emotional exploitation born out of the economic brutalities which exist between the classes in Paris, or that Antoine's attempt to copulate with his wife using butter, while Ferdinand and Robert look on and laugh, is an illustration of common but secret sexual hilarities. Ferdinand's laughter in this scene, and our mix of laughter and uncomfortable surprise, is to free us from pompous judgment, to suspend our surprise in humor—much as Chaucer does in his tales on sex. And yet I believe that Ferdinand's experience with Nora, as I will show, is the exception to what Matthews and McCarthy call the predatory nature of sex in Céline's novels. In fact, his feelings over Nora are very exceptional indeed, for they begin Ferdinand's emotional education, his learning to see women as affirmations of beauty and life.

In her *Céline and His Vision* (1967), Erika Ostrovsky sees Céline as debunking sex, but for a very special reason: "Céline tends to blacken most descriptions" of sexual gratification, but in a "spirit of mockery," because the author "finds this business of 'I lo-o-ve you' vulgar, heavy-handed, and cheaply sentimental."[5] As a result, she says, Céline intends to show us that eroticism is also "quite frequently linked to violence" (p. 53): witness Hilda, the sixteen-year-old, who waits for troop trains in *Castle to Castle,* Frau Frucht, addicted to sexual perversion, in *Castle to Castle,* Ferdinand's escape from a brawl with women on board the *Bragueton* in *Journey,* or Céline's comment in *North* that the more cities burn the more crazy for sex women become.[6] Ostrovsky is quick to point out, however, that Céline can also be quite positive about sex, can even see sex as regenerative. She points to the author's descriptions of Lola, Molly, Madelon, and Sophie in *Journey,* Nora in *Death on the Installment Plan,* and Virginia in *Pont de Londres*—all characters reflecting, perhaps, Céline's comment in a letter to Eveline Pollet: "I love the physical perfections of women almost to the point of madness. It's a truth I reveal to you. It governs all the others."[7] Moreover, Ostrovsky comments on Céline's astonishingly positive description of Sophie in *Journey,* that "if anywhere in Céline's work there is a glimpse of hope and beauty, of sun and joy, it is in the sight of such women . . . only the physical perfection of a woman, an animal, a gesture, can offer affirmation or a momentary respite from horror" (p. 125).

Wayne Burns and Gerald Butler go even further in their positive estimations of Céline's treatment of sex. In his essay *"Journey to the End of the Night:* A Primer to the Novel,"* (from the recently published anthology of essays edited by James Flynn entitled *Understanding Céline* [Seattle, Washington: Genitron Press, 1984]), Burns says that "Through loving the woman's body—Sophie's, Tania's, Molly's, even Madelon's—[Ferdinand] comes to love the woman herself. Much as Céline would have disliked having Ferdinand compared with Mellors (Céline once described *Lady Chatterley's Lover* as 'a gamekeeper's miserable prick for six hundred and fifty pages') Ferdinand's attitude towards women is essentially Lawrentian in that he comes to the woman herself through her body" (p. 86). Burns also reminds us of Céline's long "lyrical description" of Sophie in *Journey.*[8] In his essay "The Feeling for Women in Céline and His American Counterparts," (also from *Understanding Céline*), Gerald Butler not only maintains that Céline's view of women is one of adoration when compared to the way women are seen in Miller and Kerouac, but also "that it is *not* true," as Julia Kristeva claims (in her chapter on Céline entitled "Females Who Can Wreck the Infinite," from her book *Powers of Horror: An Essay on Abjection*)[9] that Céline's fiction "shows all women as of only two kinds: desexualized and delightful on the one hand and sexual and terrifying on the other, so that beauty is what wards off the sexual" (p. 142). "Sophie," Butler says, "is both sexual and, in her sexuality, a miracle of delight for Ferdinand" (p. 142). Her "presence and Ferdinand's reaction to it is enough to give the lie to the 'heroism' of Robinson that is the epitome of that bitterness and 'sense of superiority' and 'heaviness' that the world. . . . teaches" (p. 156). And in his essay "The Meaning of the Presence of Lili in Céline's Final Trilogy,"[10] he says that Lili is "put forth in the novels as a guiding light for humanity," that even "her animal qualities, in the positive sense that Céline gives to 'animal'" (and here Butler means Lili is on the same "wave-length" as animals—she tunes in only those who are helpless) "do not detract from her comparison to a heroine from Dickens, for Lili's 'heart' does not exclude the 'animal' but seems to be profoundly connected with it. If that is so, then all the sexuality of human beings that Céline does not at all present in these novels in a favorable light is not an expression of animality in the sense that Lili is like an animal. Rather, the implication, the message for human beings is that they should have real animality above all by having hearts, as Lili does" (p. 184).

These are the important discussions of Céline's view of sexual feeling. My intention here is not to further discuss Dr. Destouches' views on sex and love, interesting and shadowy as this topic is turning out to be. (See, for example, Céline's own definition of love and sex in Marc Hanrez's *Céline* [Paris: Gallimard, 1961].)[11] Rather, my intention is two-fold: first, to describe how the young Ferdinand came to feel that women are regenerative, worthy of trust, and beautiful (how he learned about what Ostrovsky, Burns, and Butler are calling the *posi-*

tive aspects of sexual experience); and second, how the older Ferdinand came to realize that the sheer naked force of his will and the hardening of his heart would not help him be less narcissistic, would not help him gain sexual satisfaction. My goal is to open a more detailed investigation into those scenes of Céline's novels which describe modern sexual behavior, to look more closely at the sexual needs, desires, and secrets of Céline's characters.

In *Death on the Installment Plan,* young Ferdinand, already hardened to real connection from his brutal experiences in Paris as the son of a mother and father who want him to be a success, retains an erotic fantasy for Nora, the wife of an English school master. He has been sent by his parents to Meanwell College, in England, in order to learn English for business purposes so that when he returns to Paris he will start his business career off on the right foot. Badgered by an embittered and humiliated father, watching his mother work herself to death in their lace and furniture shop, and seduced by their female customers, Ferdinand is a tight-lipped adolescent, unable to connect with anyone, and full of childhood memories that are violent and sad. He is a classic self-preservative personality. And in this novel his masturbation preserves gratification in fantasy. He compliments his fantasies for Nora this way: "I can still see her. . . . I can bring back her image whenever I please. At the shoulders her silk blouse forms lines, curves, miracles of flesh, agonizing visions, soft and sweet and crushing. . . . The kid that came around to lap me up had his money's worth on Sunday night . . . But I wasn't satisfied, it was her I wanted. . . . Beauty comes back at you in the night . . . it attacks you, it carries you away . . . it's unbearable . . . I was soft in the head, from jerking off on visions . . . The less we had for meals, the more I masturbated. . . ."[12] Ego regresses into id under the power of parental domination, fantasy masturbation, and the sheer weight of poverty at the bankrupt English boarding school. Ferdinand's egolibido creates Nora as his "object-choice." In one scene he masturbates with a school friend, while thinking of Nora, and, as the angry narcissist, fuels his mild sadism with attacks on sentimentality in love. *At the same time,* however, his attack on sentiment exhibits a deep desire for real connection, and this is what gives this novel a complexity rarely found even in our best modern British and American fiction.

> "We did each other up brown . . . I was ruthless, I couldn't stop, my imagination kept winding me up . . . I devoured Nora in all her beauty. . . . I'd have taken all her blood, every drop . . . Still it suited me better to ravage the bed, to chew up the sheets . . . than to let Nora or any other skirt take me for a ride. . . . To hell with all that stinking mush! . . . Yak! yak! I love you. I adore you! Sure, sure! . . . Why worry, it's a party. Bottoms up! It's so lovely! It's so innocent! . . . I'd wised up when I was a kid! Sentiment, hell! Balls! . . . I clutched my oil can. . . . You won't catch me dying like a sucker . . . with a poem on my lips." (pp. 239-40)

When Nora does, at last, come to Ferdinand's room, out of her own mad loneliness and lack of connection to her husband, and abruptly flattens him out with her caresses, giving him, as Céline says, "an avalanche of tenderness," young Ferdinand does surprisingly well in responding. In bed with her he is beginning to reject, I believe, his narcissism—if only for a moment:

> I try to soothe her pain, to make her control herself . . . I caulk wherever I can . . . I knock myself out . . . I try my best . . . I try the subtlest tricks . . . But she's too much for me . . . She gives me some wicked holds . . . The whole bed is shaking . . . She flails around like crazy . . . I fight like a lion . . . My hands are swollen from clutching her ass! I want to anchor her, to make her stop moving. There. That's it. She's stopped talking. Christ almighty! I plunge, I slip in like a breeze! I'm petrified with love . . . I'm one with her beauty . . . I'm in ecstacy . . . I wriggle. . . . On her face I go looking for the exact spot next to her nose . . . the one that tortures me, the magic of her smile" (p. 266)

In feeling "love," and in "looking for the exact spot" which tortures him, Ferdinand replaces his fantasy of Nora with her reality. Unfortunately Nora "breaks loose" from Ferdinand, and runs from the school to make her way to a bridge, where she will jump into a river to her death, a "nightgown fluttering in the wind" (p. 267). This whole scene is charged with the helpless desperation of human behavior. "I knew it," says Ferdinand, "she's off her rocker! . . . Dammit to hell . . . Could I catch her? . . . But it's none of my business . . . There's nothing I can do . . . The whole thing is beyond me . . . I listen . . . I look out through the hall door . . . to see if I can see her on the waterfront . . . She must be down by now . . . There she is again . . . still screaming . . . 'Ferdinand! Ferdinand!' . . . her screams cut through the sky . . ." (p. 267). It is Céline's intention, as Wayne Burns has pointed out in *Understanding Céline,* "to make the reader hear cries he has never heard before; to make him realize that there is no end to these cries (in either time or circumstance), for they are cries which cannot be remedied by religion or philosophy or morality—much less by the paltry palliatives of social reform or even social revolution."[13]

Ferdinand does go after her, but feels helpless and endangered as he stands on the bridge with the retarded boy both he and Nora had been taking care of at the school. We hear more of her pleas as she "flits" like a "butterfly" from one street lamp to the next. Sirens and whistles blow, rescue squads arrive, but nothing has helped. She is a "little white square in the waves. . . . caught in the eddies. . . . passing the breakwater!" (p. 268). It is Céline's intention, as he later has Ferdinand say in *Journey to the End of the Night,* "to go deeper and hear other cries that I had not heard yet or which I had not been able to understand before, because there seems always to be some cries beyond those which one has heard."[14] This need to hear the "cries" of humanity is not the impulse of a narcissist, for he is not, as Freud says in "On Narcissism: An Introduction" (1914), "plainly seeking" himself "as a love-object."[15] Nor is Ferdinand seeking a Nora as males would seek women to "save," those who would fulfill the male's desire to believe that "without him she would lose all hold on respectability."[16] Even though Nora's behavior could trigger the *narcissistic* impulse in Ferdinand to rescue her, "justified by her untrustworthy temperament sexually and by the danger to her social position" (as Ferdinand might say it), it does not do so, neither in fantasy nor in reality.[17] For there has been no "skill in argument" to win Nora, to save her from Meanwell College, no real seduction on Ferdinand's part. In fact, his *self-preservative* impulse remains defiant and hostile after her death, for he fears he will take the rap for it. Freud has it that "the attitude of defiance in the 'saving' phantasy far outweighs the tender feeling in it, the latter being usually directed towards the mother. . . . in the rescue phantasy, that is, he identifies himself completely with the father. All the instincts, the loving, the grateful, the sensual, the defiant, the self-assertive and independent—all are gratified in the wish to be *the father of himself.* . . . When in a dream a man rescues a woman from the water, it means that he makes her a mother . . . his own mother."[18] Yet Nora is not rescued. The drowning is no *phantasy*. And Ferdinand, after hearing Nora's cries and feeling he was sure to get caught and blamed, runs back to the school to wake Nora's old husband out of his own torpor. The scene we see then is painful: the old man, drunk on the floor, making masturbatory gestures with the flesh on his stomach; and Ferdinand, observing, and finally giving up, leaving to pack his bags for Paris "at the crack of dawn" (p. 269).

Despite the suicide, both Nora and Ferdinand had freed themselves, momentarily, from their environments, fixed as they were to their economic realities: Ferdinand to his petit-bourgeois Paris background and Nora to her bankrupt English middle-class. Without moralizing or sentimentalizing their encounter, Céline shows us Nora and Ferdinand achieving a moment of difficult tenderness. "It seems very evident," Freud says in "On Narcissism," that "one person's narcissism has a great attraction for those others who have renounced part of their own narcissism and are seeking after object-love."[19] As an adult, Nora has rejected part of her narcissism, and a kind of vulnerable, nervous, but tender compassion remains. She is no Madame Gorloge, who, as the wife of Ferdinand's boss, *orders* Ferdinand to take his clothes off and make love to her. "She grabs me by the ears . . . She pulls me down to mother nature . . . She bends me with all her might. . . . 'Bite me, sweet little puppy . . . Bite into it!'" (p. 180).

Ferdinand *plays* "the ardent lover," and charges into her, as he had seen her husband Antoine do when he and Robert were spying on them, "but much more gently" (p. 181). "She squashed me against her tits! She was having a hell of a good time . . . It was stifling. . . . She wanted me to work harder. . . . to be more

brutal. . . . 'you're ripping me apart, you big thug! Oh rip me' . . ." (p. 181). Ferdinand did not have to play the "ardent lover" with Nora; nor could their lovemaking be called "ripping." She was not, as he characterized Gorloge, a "vampire" (p. 181). She was a "mirage of charm" (p. 241). Neither was Nora a Gwendoline, Ferdinand's "Greasy Jone" (p. 212), the English fish and chips girl he meets on the docks before finding Meanwell College. "She kept repeating her name. She tapped on her chest . . . Gwendoline! Gwendoline! . . . I heard her all right, I massaged her tits, but I didn't get the words . . . To hell with tenderness . . . sentiment! That stuff is like a family. . . . She took advantage of the dark corners to smother me with caresses. . . . We could have done our business, we'd certainly have had a good time . . . But once we'd had our sleep out, then what?" (pp. 212, 214). "Anyway I was too tired . . . And besides, it was impossible . . . It stirred up my gall . . . it cramped my cock to think of it . . . of all the treachery of things . . . as soon as you let anybody wrap you up. . . . That's all I had on my mind in the little side streets while my cutie was unbuttoning me . . . She had the grip of a working girl, rough as a grater, and not at all bashful. Everybody was screwing me. O well . . ." (p. 215).

Rather, when Ferdinand sees Nora for the first time, he is astonished at his reaction to the *gentleness* in her face: "the special charm she had, that lit up on her face when she was speaking. . . . It intimidated me . . . I saw stars, I couldn't move" (p. 224). Ferdinand's narcissism is under attack by such powerful gentleness, tenderness, and charm because it is responding to it, needing it, and weakened by it in its self-preservative inner life. For all through the Meanwell College scene, Nora will be tending to the needs of a helpless retarded boy. And even though Ferdinand's young narcissism is interested in the idealized Nora—the Nora of his dreams, the picture of her which helps him adjust to his bitterness—he still responds, physically to *her,* and not to her manipulations, as he did with Gorloge and Greasy Jone. This is especially remarkable when you consider Ferdinand's characterization of himself earlier in the novel: "you'll never know what obsessive hatred really smells like . . . the hatred that goes through your guts, all the way to your heart . . . Real hatred comes from deep down, from a defenseless childhood crushed with work. That's the hatred that kills you" (p. 144). Even more remarkably, it may be said that Ferdinand gets a bit of compassion from Nora, learns from her, as he too walks with the retarded boy Jongkind, who "whines like a dog" after Nora's death.

> I got to get the brat home . . . I give him a poke in the ass. . . . He's worn out from running . . . I push him . . . I throw him . . . He can't see a thing without his glasses . . . He can't even see the lamp posts. He starts bumping into everything . . . He whines like a dog . . . I grab him and pick him up, I carry him up the hill . . . I toss him into his bed . . . I run to the old man's door. . . . He blinks a little, his eyelids flutter . . . He don't know from nothing . . . 'She's drowning! She's

drowning!' I yell at him. I repeat it even louder
. . . I shout my lungs out . . . I make motions . . .
I imitate the glug-glug . . . I point down . . . into the
valley . . . out the window! (pp. 268-69)

Ferdinand's heart and naked self-will are now less hardened to women, and to those who are victims of biology.

In *Journey to the End of the Night*, Ferdinand, as an
adult, is the eloquent spokesman of revulsion from European colonialism and modern warfare, the voice of
revulsion from our traditional beliefs in brotherhood,
marriage, and love. He does not believe in our modern
love, which is, for him, a "poodle's chance of attaining
the infinite" (p. 4). His travels in the novel from the
front lines of World War I, to Paris, to New York City
and Detroit, to Africa, and back to Paris, have given
him an anti-idealistic view of human behavior. "The
great weariness of life," he says near the end of the
novel, "is maybe nothing but the vast trouble we take to
remain always for twenty or forty or more years at a
time reasonable beings—so as not to be merely and
profoundly oneself, that is to say, obscene, ghastly, and
absurd" (p. 416). His first relationship with a woman in
this novel is with Lola, an American nurse who believes
in the existence of the soul and in patriotism, and it is
a relationship characterized by a weariness because
Ferdinand believes only in survival after coming home
from the war. The understanding between them is of the
body not the heart because the hardened heart cannot be
trusted during war time. At first he accepts Lola for
what she is, and this is even more of a step forward for
his self-preservative personality, even less narcissistic
than his relationship with Nora, for he no longer needs
to see the female body in idealized images: "If I had told
Lola what I thought of the war, she would only have
taken me for a depraved freak and she'd deny me all
intimate pleasures. So I took good care not to confess
these things to her. . . . she hadn't only a fine body, my
Lola,—let us get that quite clear at once; she was graced
also with a piquant little face and grey-blue eyes, which
gave her a slightly cruel look, because they were set a
wee bit on the upward slant, like those of a wildcat" (pp.
49-50). When Ferdinand does admit that he is not going
back to the front, Lola leaves him, furious at his lack of
ideals, and returns to New York. But when Ferdinand
arrives in New York, he meets Lola again.

> She inquired after my genital lapses and wanted
> to know if I hadn't somewhere on my wanderings
> produced some little child she could adopt. It was
> a curious notion of hers. The idea of adopting a
> child was an obsession with her. . . . what she
> wanted was to sacrifice herself entirely to some
> "little thing." I myself was out of luck. I had
> nothing to offer her but my own large person,
> which she found utterly repulsive. (pp. 216-17)

"Really, it's a pity, Ferdinand," Lola says, "that you
haven't a little girl somewhere. . . . Your dreamy temperament would go very well in a woman, whereas it
doesn't seem at all fitting in a man . . ." (p. 217). This

is an interesting description of female narcissism, to
which Ferdinand responds with some of his own. Lola's
attitude toward Ferdinand is cool, but now she has
found a way to object-love: through a child she could
possess the ideal of what she thinks Ferdinand should
be. The desire Lola has for Ferdinand is not based on a
need to tend him, nor is the desire Ferdinand has for
Lola based on a need to protect her. There is, therefore,
no *anaclitic* object-choice here. Rather, Lola looks at
Ferdinand as a lover who should be what she wants him
to be. And Ferdinand looks at Lola as a source for adventure in America. Her body to him was an endless
source of joy because of its "American contours" (p. 49);
she is "a type" that appeals to him (p. 193). Only when
Lola gives him money and he takes off for Detroit to
work in the Ford plant, do we see a strong and more
radical change in Ferdinand's desires for women. The
mechanisms involved in his new object-choice—Molly,
the Detroit prostitute—are now *more* anaclitic than narcissistic, more dependent than independent, and not so
much concerned about being with an "American type."
And although Ferdinand's relationship with Molly
shows remarkable similarities with Freud's description
of male love for the *grande amoureuse* (especially when
Freud describes the childhood experiences, the mother-
complex, and youthful masturbatory practices of those
who have "love for a harlot"),[20] I believe that the following remarks show Ferdinand freeing himself of narcissistic self-absorption, and combining, if only for a time,
his feelings of sex *and* tenderness, despite the fact that
he is eventually fonder of his longing to "run away from
everywhere in search of something" (p. 228).

> I soon felt for Molly, one of the young women in
> this place, an emotion of exceptional trust, which
> in timid people takes the place of love. I can
> remember, as if I'd seen her yesterday, her *gentle-
> ness and her long white legs,* marvellously lithe
> and muscular and noble. . . . (p. 227, emphasis
> added)

> "Don't go back to the works!" Molly urged me,
> making it worse. "Find some small job in an office
> instead. . . . Translating, for example; that's really
> your line . . . you like books. . . ." She was very
> sweet giving me this advice; she wanted me to be
> happy. . . . if only I'd met Molly. . . . Before
> I lost my enthusiasm over that slut of a Musyne
> and that horrid little bitch Lola!" (p. 228)

At the end of the Detroit chapter, we begin to understand the causes of Ferdinand's narcissism, and his
possible solutions for his troubles:

> Molly had been right. I was beginning to under-
> stand what she meant. Studies change you, they
> make a man proud. Before, one was only hovering
> around life. You think you are a free man, but
> you get nowhere. Too much of your time's spent
> dreaming. You slither along on words. That's not
> the real thing at all. Only intentions and ap-
> pearances. You need something else. With my
> medicine, though I wasn't very good at it, I had

come into closer contact with men, beasts, and creation. Now it was a question of pushing right ahead, foursquare, into the heart of things. (p. 239)

No longer do we have a character at the mercy of narcissism—like the young Ferdinand—because the narcissist would never want to plunge "into the heart of things." Rather, the adult Ferdinand sees conventional love (i.e. ego-centric romantic love) as doomed to fail in a world where so many people have to scrape and crawl just to get by, in a world where Nature's lessons are hard to swallow, where "sex is the poor man's pocket gold mine" (p. 219).

> To love is nothing, it's hanging together that's so hard. . . . All our unhappiness is due to having to remain Tom, Dick, and Harry, cost what it may, throughout a whole series of years. (p. 335)

And near the end of *Journey,* when Ferdinand visits a bistro for some cheap fun, living, as he says, a "capitalist's existence without capital" (p. 361), we hear him comment with irony and compassion on a female singing group from England, who are bawling out their little songs of love: "They were singing the defeat of life and they didn't see it. They thought it was only love, nothing but love; they hadn't been taught the rest of it, little dears. . . ." (p. 361). Ferdinand finally realizes that conventional love, the kind we see today everywhere in American culture, richly narcissistic as it is, fails to help anyone—especially him.

What *would* help he tries to describe for us at the end of the novel, after seeing the death of his friend Robinson at the hands of a romantic lover. Ferdinand says about himself that he is just "a quite real Ferdinand who lacked what might make a man greater than his own trivial life, a love for the life of others" (p. 501). This "love for the life of others" is not at all narcissistic, and it is the kind of love which the young Ferdinand began to achieve when he took Jongkind back to the school the night Nora died, and when he banged on the door to tell Nora's old, drunken husband that she was dying. It is the kind of love which would allow death to be

> imprisoned in love along with joy, and so comfortable would it be inside there, so warm, that Death, the bitch, would be given some sensation at last and would end up by having as much fun with love as every one else. Wouldn't that be pretty? Ah, wouldn't that be fine? I laughed about it, standing there alone on the river bank, as I thought of all the dodges and all the tricks I'd have to pull off to stuff myself like that full of all-powerful resolves. . . . A toad swollen out with ideals! (p. 505)

But Ferdinand dismisses even these ideas as hopelessly idealistic for a man like him.

What *does* help him are not resolves, but what he finds in Sophie, the Slovak nurse who works at the lunatic

asylum with him. In his relationship with Sophie, I believe, we see a man nearly free of narcissism. For Sophie is a woman

> who still from time to time caught me to her, her whole body strong with the strength of her concern for me and tenderness and a heart full also and overflowing and lovely. I felt the directness of it myself, the *directness of her tender strength.* (p. 507, emphasis added)

Male narcissism could never feel the directness of *tender strength* in a woman's body, the kind of strength Ferdinand now finds that he desires to have not only for himself, but also for women. It is this tender strength in a woman's body, this sex-tenderness and a full heart, which can ease the hardened heart and cruel naked self-will of a man.

I have been looking at scenes which show Ferdinand as an individual seeking meaning and sexual fulfillment. Yet there are other kinds of scenes in Céline's novels which do not emphasize individual sexual action, but rather mass sexual action. These scenes are astonishing in their impact, and they need further study—for they show Céline as a keen observer of herd psychology. Questions, therefore, remain to be answered.

For example, what is the function of Céline's *délire*[21] and exaggeration in the episode from *Death on the Installment Plan,* where, in the Bois de Boulogne, Ferdinand and Mireille make love in public, and an orgy of sexual chaos moves and surges a crowd up to the Arc de Triomphe, where they are routed by "twenty-five thousand" policemen (pp. 35-39)? Or what is the meaning of that scene in *Guignol's Band,* where Virginia and Ferdinand are swept up in a chaos of orgy, violence, and delight in the night club, where people are copulating in a jumble of arms and legs? There are similar scenes of mass, violent delight in *North* and *Castle to Castle.* Are these "little narcissistic eccentricities," as Céline labels his writing in *Guignol's Band*? Or are they scenes which tell us to: "Palpitate, damn it! That's where the fun is! . . . Wake up! Come on, hello! You robot crap! . . . Shit! . . . Transpose or it's death! I can't do any more for you. Kiss any girl you please! If there's still time!"[22] Perhaps these mass scenes expose the flimsiness of even our most sophisticated ideas about love, or perhaps they speak of what Céline thought to be some ancient longing in sex, the "quite bestial act" of it, as he said.[23] Ferdinand (and later Céline himself in his World War II trilogy) are both swept up by such sights and crowds in every one of the novels—as if this author, as a physician, wants us to understand that he sees impulses which repeat themselves on a huge scale, as if all of human life is joyously trapped into having such feelings out of the sheer biological surgings of the species, as well as out of our small motivations, brutalized as they are by war and stupid economies. Witness this description from *Castle to Castle,* where in a railway station, Céline's favorite locale for the mob's sexual *délire,* we see that:

sadness, idleness, and female heat go together . . . and not just kids! . . . grown women and grand-mothers! obviously the hottest ones, with fire in their twats, in those moments when the page turns, when History brings all the nuts together and opens its Epic Dance Halls! . . . you've got to have phosphorus and hunger so they'll rut and sperm and get with it without paying attention! pure happiness! no more hunger, cancer, or clap! . . . the station packed with eternity![24]

Are these scenes of mass erotic action in direct conflict with Ferdinand's lessons about tenderness? Or do they, then, in their juxtaposition with Ferdinand's raptures, for example, over Sophie, show us the value of individual, sexual tenderness in the face of "History"?

More comment is also needed on the intriguing relationship between what Ferdinand enjoys about women (their astonishing bodies, their compassion and intelligence, their ability to have orgasms, and their "wave-lengths"), and what Céline says about sex for men ("it allows a guy a few seconds delirium which permits him to communicate with her").[25] How do we square Céline's striking portraits of what women have to offer men with this statement from *Rigadoon* (1961):

> all our theater and literature revolve around coitus, deadly repetition! . . . the orgasm is boring, the giants of the pen and silver screen with all the ballyhoo and the millions spent on advertising . . . have never succeeded in putting it across . . . two three shakes of the ass, and there it is . . . the sperm does its work much too quietly, too intimately, the whole thing escapes us . . . but childbirth, that's worth looking at! . . . examining! . . . to the millimeter! fucking . . . God knows I've wasted hours! . . . for two three wiggles of the ass![26]

And lastly, careful analysis is needed on the relationship between what we see as the positive aspects of sexuality in Céline, what Burns calls "the essentially Lawrentian attitude" Ferdinand gains in coming to the woman, and Céline's personal comment that "(coitus is delirium): to rationalize that delirium with precise verbal maneouvers seems to me silly."[27] Perhaps Céline sees deeper than my critical phrase "positive aspects of sexuality"—a "precise verbal maneuver" if ever I could invent one. Just how deeply and broadly Céline sees can be detected as early as 1916, the date he wrote a poem for his parents in his early twenties, while traveling to Africa. Even at this early date we see that Céline's vision of sexuality is much like the "town crier's," who remains perched in a minaret:

> Stamboul est endormi sous la lune blafarde Le Bosphore miroite de mille feux argentés Seul dans la grande ville mahométane Le vieux crieur des heures n'est pas encore couché—Sa voix que l'écho répète avec ampleur Announce à la ville qu'il est déjà dix heures Mais par une fenêtre, de son haut minaret Il plonge dans une chambre, son regard indiscret Il reste un moment, muet, cloué

> par la surprise Et caresse nerveux, sa grande barbe grise Mais fidèle au devoir, il assure sa voix[28]

This indiscreet glance, which plunges into a bedroom, and yet remains mute, frozen with surprise, is a remarkable description of not only our reaction to the sexual scenes we see in Céline's works, but it also characterizes the young Ferdinand's sights of sex behavior in *Death on the Installment Plan*, as well as the eventual mature view of sexual behavior in the later novels. For as an author, Céline continues to sing that our odd sun rises, despite what he has seen either in or out of his *délire*, and no matter how many times "History brings all the nuts together and opens its Epic Dance Halls." At every reading of his novels, Céline continues to plunge us "into the heart of things."

NOTES

[1] Russell Jacoby, *Social Amnesia* (Boston: Beacon Press, 1975), p. 44.

[2] Works by Dickens, Hardy, Lawrence, Joyce, Woolf, Forster, Sartre, Döblin, Musil, Faulkner, Hemingway, Fitzgerald, Miller, Kerouac, Roth, Mailer, Kerouac, Roth, Mailer, Kesey, Pynchon, and E. M. White all contain protagonists who are particularly narcissistic.

[3] Patrick McCarthy, *Céline* (New York: Penguin Books, 1975).

[4] J. H. Matthews, *The Inner Dream: Céline as Novelist* (New York: Syracuse Univ. Press, 1978).

[5] Erika Ostrovsky, *Céline and His Vision* (New York: New York Univ. Press, 1967), p. 53.

[6] Ostrovsky, p. 54; Matthews, p. 136.

[7] Letter to Eveline Pollet, February 1933, *L'Herne,* No. 3, p. 96.

[8] *Journey to the End of the Night* (New York: New Directions. 1934), pp. 475-76.

[9] Trans., Leon S. Roudiez (New York: Columbia Univ. Press, 1982).

[10] James Flynn, ed., *Understanding Céline* (Seattle, WA: Genitron Press, 1984).

[11] Sexual gratification is "a bonus which nature gives to coitus and reproduction: it allows a guy a few seconds' delirium which permits him to communicate with her" (Marc Hanrez, "Céline au magnétophone," *Le Nouveau Candide* [November 23, 1961]), p. 14. Quoted from Ostrovsky, p. 198. Lové is "feeling, it's an act, my God! quite bestial—and, naturally, bestial it has to be! Warding it off with little flowers seems to me crass. Bad taste, precisely, is putting flowers where none are really needed. . . . You go into a

delirium (coitus is a delirium): to rationalize that delirium with precise verbal maneouvers seems to me very silly" (Hanrez, *Céline,* p. 275). Quoted in Matthews, p. 75.

[12] Translated by Ralph Manheim (New York: New Directions, 1966), p. 239. It should be noted here that Céline's *points de suspension* are retained in these quotes. I have used four periods when omitting one or more sentences.

[13] Flynn, ed., *Understanding Céline,* p. 41.

[14] Translated by John H. P. Marks (New York: New Directions, 1934), p. 265.

[15] Sigmund Freud, "On Narcissism: An Introduction (1914)," J. Richman, ed., *A General Selection from the Works of Sigmund Freud* (New York: Liveright Publishing Corp., 1957), p. 112.

[16] Freud, "A Special Type of Object Choice Made by Men (1910)," P. Rieff, ed., *Sexuality and the Psychology of Love* (New York: Collier Books, 1963), p. 52.

[17] Freud, p. 52.

[18] Freud, p. 57.

[19] Freud, "On Narcissism," p. 113.

[20] Freud, "A Special Type of Object Choice Made by Men (1910)," pp. 51 and 54-56.

[21] See Allen Thiher's *Céline: The Novel as Delirium* (New Brunswick, NJ: Rutgers Univ, Press, 1972).

[22] Céline, *Guignol's Band* (New York: New Directions, 1954), pp. 4-5.

[23] See footnote eleven.

[24] Translated by Allen Thiher, footnote 21, p. 186.

[25] See footnote eleven.

[26] Céline, *Rigadoon* (New York: Delacorte Press, 1969), pp. 195-96.

[27] See footnote eleven.

[28] L. des Touches, "Gnomography," *Cahiers Céline 4. Letters et premiers écrits d'Afrique, 1916-17.* Ed., Jean-Pierre Dauphin (Paris: Gallimard, 1978), p. 79.

Laura Claridge

SOURCE: "Tess: A Less than Pure Woman Ambivalently Presented," in *Texas Studies in Literature and Language,* Vol. 28, No. 3, Fall, 1986, pp. 324-38.

[*In the following essay, Claridge argues that Thomas Hardy's subversion of Tess's sexual and psychological purity in* Tess of the d'Urbervilles *leads to that text's aesthetic incoherence.*]

> How strange that one may write a book without knowing what one puts into it—or rather, the reader reads into it.
>
> —Thomas Hardy

Over the years many readers have tried to solve the problem of just what, finally, is wrong with Hardy's *Tess of the d'Urbervilles.* These same critics have commonly admitted the novel to the first ranks of our literary canon, but they nonetheless feel compelled to address the niggling question of "the flaw." Weaknesses singled out with some regularity include the heavy dependence upon coincidence, the "absurdity of Alec's conversion and deconversion," and the indubitable hypocrisy of Angel Clare.[1] But with rare exceptions, criticism has failed to glean the higher fault: the novel's fundamental conflict of purposes. Indeed, Hardy's philosophy of life has been heavily indicted for its inconsistency or implausibility, but the deeper problem of textual incoherence generally has been ignored. In what is perhaps the most notable exception, Bernard Paris has offered an incisive analysis of the thematic confusion arising from Hardy's treatment of nature versus convention.[2] My thesis, however, deviates from Paris's account of the closeness of author to his protagonist by my use of this relationship to explore a complete undermining of formal coherence. Hardy's intense identification with his heroine creates an almost compulsive authorial exoneration of Tess's mistakes, mistakes that instead must function as signs of the heroine's moral culpability if the novel's unity is maintained. In spite of Hardy's efforts to present Tess as a modern-day tragic hero with whom we are meant to sympathize deeply, a subtle reading suggests too many cross currents that undermine his intention.

Such a subtle reading, however, is not (perhaps happily) always the novelist's fate. Because of the novel's undeniable poetic grandeur, it is easy for the first-time reader of *Tess* to be blinded to its textual incoherence. It is, as one early reviewer recognized, the second reading that "leaves a lower estimate than the first."[3] Lionel Johnson, one of Hardy's first serious critics, devoted himself to the novel: "I read *Tess* eight or ten times with perfect enthusiasm—it is great literature—but finally, difficulties at first unfelt began to appear."[4] Johnson's analysis is credible in part because he does acknowledge the book's beauty; he recognizes that the novel yields pleasure, *but on a different plane than that of textual consistency.* He locates as a requisite for a novel informed by didactic purpose (a purpose which Hardy denied) a particular coherence: "Either the story should bear its own burden of spiritual sorrow, each calamity and woe crushing out of us all hope, by its own resistless weight: or the bitter sentences of comment should be lucid and cogent" (389). In Hardy's indictment of society, Johnson "can see . . . but a tangle of inconsistencies" (391); Hardy's narration creates in Johnson a yearning for "definitions of *nature, law, society,* and *justice,*" for the story grants these words first one premise than another (390-91). If it is largely Hardy's philosophical inconsistencies and his reliance upon determinism that worry Johnson, it is also his "apparent denial of anything like conscience in men, that makes his impressive argument so sterile" (394), conscience in Tess as well as the other characters. Finally, Johnson alludes to Thomas à Kempis to suggest that, like Maggie Tulliver, Tess could make "true use" of her passage through "fire and water," but she never does (397).

It is because we are more attuned to the subtext upon subsequent readings, after the novel's obvious splendors dazzle us less, that we begin to sense the inconsistencies which weaken our "appropriate" author-guided identification with Tess. Bernard Paris borrows from John Stuart Mill the phrase "a confusion of many standards" to explain the undermining of the text.[5] Virginia Woolf went a step further: "It is as if Hardy himself were not quite aware of what he did, as if his consciousness held more than he could produce."[6] These critical insights direct us to the heart of the problem: the ambivalence that readers have too easily justified as a deliberate part of the novelist's art is in fact a serious weakness of authorial control. Hardy creates a heroine who does not, in the end, deserve the full sympathy that the thrust of the dominant narrative demands.

Certainly the surface movement of the plot directs us to understand Tess herself as a passive heroine, acting most often out of a last resort in order to survive. In fact, it is necessary that she function as a tractable, victimized girl in order for the characterization of Alec as stock villain to cohere. Thus we tend to downplay at best or, in some cases, suppress the startling portrait of Tess as assertive, shrewd young woman that surfaces throughout at the expense of the novel's unity.

From the beginning of what D. H. Lawrence called the most important relationship in the book, Tess is sharp-tongued and sure. As she rides to Trantridge with Alec, she exclaims angrily in response to his race downhill, "Thank God we're safe in spite of your fooling."[7] She is too quick to be taken in by Alec's teasing; her cleverness in fact suggests her way out of the dogcart: she allows her hat to blow off in order to force Alec to stop. It is Tess's strong will that must help guide our apportioning of responsibility to both Alec and Tess in the course of their relationship. It becomes somewhat difficult, for instance, to marry the headstrong Tess who, riding off with Alec, "pants in her triumph" (58) to the Tess who is so tractable that any villain can have his way with her. But Tess's malleability, singled out frequently by critics as her dominant trait, functions to sustain her necessary innocence throughout the story. Her submissiveness allows Hardy to explain—and to come close to exonerating—Tess's two accommodations

to Alec. Where the subtext insists upon a great deal of at least subtle complicity on Tess's part, the surface narrative denies it in light of her carefully established tractable nature as her only "real flaw."

As Elizabeth Langland remarks in her essay on another problematic heroine, Sue Bridehead, inconsistency within a character becomes a textual problem only if the inconsistency marks a novelist's confusion of parts rather than the identifying mark of the character's psychology.[8] That is, there are people whose identity theme might be said to consist of inconsistency. Hardy, however, errs by shifting authorial perspective on a character whose textual integrity is essential to a furthering of his plot. He creates a heroine whose "tractability" is so marked that it represents her defining characteristic, and yet at the same time he presents her as shrewd, sure, strong enough eventually to assert herself against any fate. We confront not the tragic flaw in an otherwise noble character, but a characterization formed by competing major instincts that never coalesce into an ordered, coherent personality. In 1892 *The Spectator* expressed reader displeasure in this way: "If she be 'faithfully presented,' she was not at all faithful to her own sense of duty in the course of the story. Again and again Hardy shows her shrinking from the obvious and imperative duty of the moment when she must have felt that the whole sincerity of her life was at stake."[9] This condemnation no doubt implies as much moral indignation as disinterested criticism, yet it neatly suggests the formal difficulties with the novel as well.

I

Hardy's disclaimer aside, *Tess* is a didactic novel.[10] As *Longman's* insisted from the start, it is "a story with a moral,"[11] or, as *The Speaker* more longwindedly proposed, Hardy has given us a tale that is "powerful and valuable as a contribution to the ethical education of the world."[12] What is exasperating, however, is our confusion as to the exact lesson we are meant to learn.

Certainly the author's most obvious intent was to admonish a society that lived according to restrictive rules rather than by feelings of the heart. When Hardy published the chapter on Sorrow's baptism separately and entitled it "The Midnight Baptism, a Study in Christianity," we can be sure that no one missed his indictment of hypocritical values. But what remains confused throughout his novel is his definition of sexual hypocrisy. What constitutes licit versus illicit sexuality? This question assumes great significance as Tess's erotic entanglements with both Alec and Angel increasingly come to define her fate. That her innocence is important to Hardy is clear in the novel's subtitle: *A Pure Woman Faithfully Presented.* Yet the author compromises the unity of his text through his implicit emphasis on appropriate sexual conduct as a measure of morality. He strongly indicts Alec as the treacherous thief of Tess's virginity, and he condemns Angel as a hypocrite who dares to care about that theft. But at the same time, by allowing a sense of confusion to pervade the text over the right circumstances in which a sexual encounter may occur, Hardy inevitably, if accidentally, suggests the very convention he would deny: that an unmarried woman be sexually inexperienced remains of utmost importance in judging her value.

There can be little doubt that Hardy wanted to liberate sex as a forbidden type of knowledge. Certainly the respect Hardy and Havelock Ellis entertained for each other is consonant with the novelist's real life concerns. It is in his fictional creation that the author seemed unable to decide what should constitute the norms for ethical sexual conduct. The controversy over the famous seduction scene points to his ambivalence: in spite of the heavy evidence that finally demands that the scene be read as sex by (reluctant) consent, several textual passages support critics such as F. R. Pinion in their insistence upon rape as the crime:[13] "A little more than persuading had to do wi' the coming o' t [the baby] I reckon. There were they that heard a sobbing one night last year in The Chase; and it mid ha' gone hard wi' a certain party if folks had come along" (76). What complicates our judgment is the narrator's suggestion that there is no distinction between the sexual acts of seduction and rape: "a little more, or a little less, 'twas a thousand pities that it should have happened to she."

It is as if the possibility that Tess is raped protects her from the position of having engaged in "liberated" sex, as if the idea of free choice might sully her important purity. Yet such freedom is, in a sense, precisely the concern of this novel. We are to censure Angel for his prudishness and society at large for its callous sensibilities. At the same time, however, if we are to take a more expansive attitude toward sex, then the typical reader's severe condemnation of the licentious Alec is exaggerated.

The point is that it does matter, within the textual constraints Hardy sets for himself, whether or not Tess "accepted" Alec. If Tess is seduced, if she gives in to Alec's flattering, unremitting advances that allow her the chance to flout the gypsy women upon her escape with Car's former lover, her motivation for even their short-lived initial relationship remains unclear. Perhaps Alec's local power lures her, as she insists "my eyes were dazed by you for a little and that is all" (65). Indeed, Tess justifies her escape with Alec because with "a spring of the foot" she can transform her "fear and indignation" at the gypsies into a "triumph over them" (58). If we are to read here a case of a particularly modern (sexually liberated) attitude wherein "pure" physical attraction alone warrants sexual consummation, Tess herself appears to disavow such motivation. But the conventional justification of affection does not suffice either; Tess despises herself precisely because she has *not* loved Alec. If she had, she "should not . . . hate myself for my weakness as I do now" (65). If neither love nor physical attraction, what moral code informs Tess's actions? The narrator, who never hesitates to jump to Tess's defense, especially if he considers her

blind to her own virtue, allows her perspective here to stand; for once he fails to contradict her sense of guilt over her encounter with Alec.

What does this failure of narrative control do to Tess's essential formal function as victim? She stays for two weeks after her "weakness" with Alec. Of course, there is gross inequality in the relationship: Alec's financial control over her family immediately implicates him in a coercive role. But at the same time, and at the expense of defining Tess as an innocent, the narrative implicates Tess too as bearing some kind of responsibility for a "wrong" relationship. This confusion over Tess's role surfaces as early as the garden scene in which Alec and Tess become acquainted. Here the context of an Edenic bower—a profusion of fruits and flowers—creates a frame for the story that at times will work against the dominant and necessary motif of Tess's innocence. At first glance, the garden sequence appears orchestrated solely by Alec, but upon scrutiny, it bears much in common with the later seduction/rape scene. Inevitably an "ideal" reader brings to the garden setting an awareness of the sexual complicity implicated in bowers, with the Ur-text, of course, the Edenic garden of Adam and Eve.

Victorian literature often appropriated the lushness of nature to foreground sexual initiation. In Tennyson's *Maud,* for example, the narrator and his lover meet in a garden of innocence which their liaison transforms into a lair of knowledge, passion, and death: "the honey of poison-flowers and all the measureless ill" [where Maud has] "but fed on the roses and lain in the lilies of life."[14] Nature's ripeness functions even more strongly as a prolepsis of the fallen sexual state in Christina Rossetti's fantastic *Goblin Market,* with its alignment of willful sexual initiation and the bounty of the countryside. The brilliant fruits and flowers that the goblins use to tempt innocent maids into their snare create the taste for "more" of the same, similar to Tess's quick acquiescence to the pleasure of eating strawberries. In Rossetti's tale, as in *Tess,* the maiden *chooses* whether to become an initiate or not: Laura's sister, Lizzie, remonstrates that the girls "should not peep at goblin men" but "Curious Laura chose to linger" until finally she "sucked and sucked and sucked the more / Fruits which that unknown orchard bore," becoming addicted so that the fruits are necessary food to sustain her life.[15] Similarly, Alec will become the "poisoned fruit" that sustains Tess as well.

Striking in Rossetti's narrative is the insistence that sexual initiation is always choice: even when Lizzie, the innocent sister, confronts the goblins for Laura's sake, the narrator is at pains (though she never directly indicts Laura) to emphasize the potential for resistance:

> One may lead a horse to water;
> Twenty cannot make him drink.
> Though the goblins cuffed and caught her,
> Coaxed and fought her. . . .
> Lizzie uttered not a word;

Would not open lip from lip
Lest they should cram a mouthful in.

                              (ll. 422-32)

In contrast to Rossetti's Lizzie, Tess accedes to Alec's demand that he feed her the strawberry himself: "in a slight distress she parted her lips and took it in" (34). It is precisely our sense that Tess chooses her sexual initiation—that she knows what she is about—that makes this scene highly erotic (we are not worried about the heroine, but engaged instead in her own deliberate rite of passage into womanhood) *and* that vitiates our sympathy in her later encounters with Alec. After Tess "takes in" Alec's offering, she wanders "desultorily . . . eating in a half-pleased, half-reluctant state whatever d'Urberville offered her" (34). Her willingness to sate her appetite before leaving anticipates her reaction to her "seduction" later on: thus she will stay with d'Urberville two weeks beyond the initial liaison, her eyes "dazed" a little, until she feels compelled to address other responsibilities.

When we read the subtexts of both the strawberry scene and the seduction scene, then we understand Tess as the Eve who rather too quickly yields to the temptation of the snake in the grass—or brambles—the villainous Alec. Equally interesting is the subsequent conflation of identity, wherein Tess takes on snake-like characteristics herself, a double identity that serves both to underscore the historically negative implications of "being Eve" and to emphasize her kinship with Alec at a deeper, more essential level than the mere literal relationship that she originally claims, a confused characterization that again subverts textual unity. In joltingly ugly imagery that parodies the richly sensual strawberry scene at Trantridge, Angel approaches Tess as she is yawning, at which point he sees "the red interior of her mouth as if it had been a snake's." She next stretches her arm above her *coiled-up cable* of hair (143; emphasis mine). When Alec later calls her "you temptress" and she "recoils" from him as she falsely exclaims that she could not prevent his seeing her again, we wonder how Hardy means for us to understand his heroine now (265). If Tess acts out her Edenic part as snake as well as that of Eve, it is to both Alec's and Angel's discomfort: as d'Urberville notes, it is Tess's skepticism that drives him back to his old ways, so that "your husband's teaching has *recoiled* upon him" (274).

As Hardy couches his description of Tess in serpent images, we are again forced to read Alec and Tess's earliest meeting retrospectively in light of Tess's complicity in her fate *even then,* a complicity that points more toward Hardy's own confusion over sexuality than to a formal position Tess is meant to embody. Man falls, but woman seduces, perhaps against her will, compelled by an inner sexuality that in fact defines her as female. Woman becomes, in some sense, the first term of the argument, as even the original tempter is ensnared by her beauty. Particularly since Hardy draws upon Milton,

we might recall the treatment of this same problem in *Paradise Lost,* for as Satan approaches Eve, who, like Tess in the Garden, is almost hidden by the beautiful rose thickets, he is momentarily stymied by her brilliant innocence and goodness. For a moment, Satan

                    abstracted stood
            From his own evil,
        and for the time remained
    Stupidly good, of enmity disarm'd,
Of guile, of hate, of envy, of revenge.[16]

As Tess and Alec till a humble village plot—yet another "fallen" garden—Alec quotes lines subsequent to Satan's mesmerization:

A jester might say this is just like Paradise. You are Eve, and I am the old Other One come to tempt you in the disguise of an inferior animal. I used to be quite up in that scene of Milton's when I was theological. Some of it goes—

"Empress, the way is ready, and not long,
Beyond a row of myrtles. . . .
    . . . If thou accept
My conduct, I can bring thee thither soon."
"Lead then," said Eve.

                    (p. 289 [*PL*, bk. 9, ll. 626-31])

If we read this Miltonic allusion alongside the serpent images of Tess, Hardy's concern reveals itself: in tandem with the lush sexuality at the woman's disposal, does she possess an innate "goodness" that protects her, *if she so chooses,* against the "fallenness" of sexual knowledge? Tess's purity is maintained throughout the dominant narrative line precisely on these terms: in spite of men's abuse, she is pure. Yet again, this position causes formal discontinuities: if this purity is so potent an ingredient in her makeup, why did she open up her lips and take in the strawberry—and then continue to eat? Why, finally, does Eve not refuse Satan? Hardy shifts perspectives on Tess's real responsibility for her eventual fate as he alternately defines her as an unfallen Eve or an Eve who willingly accepts the serpent. Finally, in the parodic Edenic scene, wherein Tess approaches Angel through a fallen garden, "damp and rank with juicy grass which sent up mists of pollen at a touch" (104), she becomes a conflation of Eve and the dangerous other of the snake-tempter, a function formally assigned to Alec.

What at first puzzles us in seeing Tess switch roles becomes clearer when we recognize Hardy's own uncertainty about how erotic a woman is his Tess. She is surely in part a fantasy to the author as well as to Clare, who sees her as "a fresh and virginal daughter of Nature" (102). Hardy himself admits that "I have not been able to put on paper all she was or is to me."[17] It is even possible for two sensitive and sophisticated readers to draw opposite conclusions: Geoffrey Thurley, in *The Psychology of Hardy's Novels,* claims that Tess's weakness is in fact her overwhelming sensuality, whereas

Henry James, in a letter to Robert Louis Stevenson, writes that her "pretense of 'sexuality' is only equalled by the absence of it."[18]

It is precisely the problem in *Tess* that the heroine is too often caught in the middle of Hardy's own evolving ideas, so that no one, least of all Tess herself, is quite sure how sexual a creature she is allowed to be.

II

In order to maintain Tess's sexual and psychological purity, a purity necessary (indicated even in the subtitle) for the novel to cohere, readers must condemn Alec as the worst sort of villain and allow Tess her occasional weakness at most. Alec, in fact, becomes for most readers the stock villain of melodrama. But in our condemnation of Alec that the narrative demands, we can easily fail to see Hardy's implicit, even unintentional acknowledgment of Tess's own moral failure. Hardy means to show Tess's strength through her later relationship with Alec, to dramatize her heroic attempt to "get back her own." But in so doing, he reveals her understanding to be as limited in its way as is Angel's. Tess is not the victim here, as the narrative line suggests, but the victimizer. She dangerously fails Alec in charity—charity that would in fact have saved her as well as him from destruction. Such a failure works against the ordering of the text that requires Alec and Angel alone to function as active, deliberate agents of pain to others.

It is through biblical allusions to charity that Hardy subverts the very characterizations he means to support, especially his portrait of Tess. That the novelist comments frequently on his story with quotations from the Bible is, of course, a commonplace of criticism. Yet the extent to which these quotations *undermine* his text in *Tess* has gone unexplored. Hardy describes Tess's devotion to Angel in the terms of Paul's letter to the Corinthians on charity (1 Cor. 13): she was not "unseemly; she sought not her own; was not provoked; thought no evil of his treatment of her." At this point, the narrator allows, she might well seem "Apostolic Charity" itself (202). The narrator further explains Tess's vulnerability to Angel's arguments by asserting that "[her] heart was humanitarian to its centre." This forefronting of charity serves to define this Pauline virtue as central to a moral life, as we see even upon the eve of the lovers' joint confessions, when Angel recites Paul's credo for the righteous man: "Be thou an example—in word, in conversation, in charity, in spirit, in faith, in purity" (1 Tim. 4:12). Angel's reflections, of course, overtly (and consistently) serve the narrative in defining his later hypocrisy and need for a rebirth. But it is not only Angel who fails dramatically in the Pauline charity so important a part of this novel. Earlier Angel's father has reminded him that a wife's knowledge of farm duties comes "second to a Pauline view of humanity." When we juxtapose this paternal statement with the narrator's insistence on Tess's "pure humanitarian" heart, we are clearly meant to read the father's

opinion as an unaware elevation of his son's fiancée, as well as a foreshadowing of Angel's own lack of vision. Yet events occur which suggest the Reverend Mr. Clare's inadvertent but correct indictment of Tess for a moral failure equal to her husband's: she knows her farm duties but does not know a "Pauline view of humanity" at all. With the portrait that unfolds in direct opposition to Tess's designation as "Apostolic Charity," the narrative is subverted once again—this time most seriously yet.

In her first exchange with the "converted" Alec, in which he embarrassedly tries to justify his new role, Tess reacts by scorning his suggestion of a godly mission: "Have you saved yourself? Charity begins at home, they say" (255). Alec begs her to pray for him, so that even Tess's omnipresent spokesperson, the narrator, admits that "the suppressed discontent of his manner was almost pitiable"; but Tess does not pity him (265). She withholds her charity from an Alec too grotesque for her to pity, though she had recently been on the receiving end of just such a harsh judgment:

> "Forgive me as you are forgiven! I forgive *you*, Angel."
>
> "You—yes, you do."
>
> "But you do not forgive me?"
>
> "O Tess, forgiveness does not apply to the case! You were one person; now you are another. My God—how can forgiveness meet such a grotesque—prestidigitation as that." (191)

Even earlier in the story Tess has asked that letter of the law morality be overturned by a spiritually expansive charity in order to comfort her. She desperately pleads with her pious minister to agree that Baby Sorrow has been legitimately baptized, and he subsequently yields to her need for pity. Not satisfied with only partial charity, however, Tess condemns him for not allowing her baby to be "properly buried" (82). Charity, it appears, is a demand Tess makes of others, not of herself, except where she judges it earned, quite in contrast with the Pauline injunction. Yet it is precisely their lack of charity that has informed our reactions to, even definitions of, Angel and Alec: Angel as he fails Tess upon her confession; Alec in his initial focus on his physical pleasures alone. If we attune ourselves to the underlying subversive impulses of the text, we must reevaluate "Tess as pure woman" in her lack of the same virtue whose absence condemns her two lovers.

It becomes easier to appreciate the importance that Tess's charity would hold for Alec when we unearth the surprising evidence that he has, in whatever grossly inadequate fashion, loved Tess. Such evidence works against our dominant impression of Alec as a caricatured, melodramatic villain. Yet there are incipient signs of his real affection as early as the seduction scene, where he removes the overcoat protecting him from the September chill and "tenderly" places it around Tess so that she will feel warmer (61). He wildly chases after her when she returns to Marlott—though, significantly, he fears that she will not go back with him—in order to ease her journey home and to assure her of any support she might need for the future. Her total lack of affection for him bothers Alec; he says, within the space of only a few minutes, "You didn't come for love of me [to Trantridge]" (65) and "You'll never love me, I fear" (66). The evidence of Alec's desire to make human connections—to make contact emotionally as well as sexually—helps pave the way for his desperate conversion attempt as well as for the equally fierce revival of feelings that Tess's reappearance in his life provokes.

When Alec and Tess do meet again, Alec's lips start to tremble and his eyes hang "confusedly in every direction but hers" (254). He later apologizes for his disorientation by explaining that "considering what you had been to me, it was natural enough" (255). He risks humiliation by asking Tess to marry him, and when he draws the marriage license out of his pocket, it is with "a slight fumbling of embarrassment" (261). After Alec finds out that Tess is already married, he offers to help both Tess and her husband financially even before he knows that they are separated (263). Alec chafes at his impotence in removing Tess from Groby's abuse and exclaims that he feels mad to think he has no legal right to protect her from the malevolent farmer (268). In her former lover's reflective state of redressing past iniquities lies Tess's chance for safety, but rather than seek refuge there, she (and the demands of the text) insists that he remain a villain. Tess continues to define Alec only as a sexual threat until he resumes, almost in response to her expectations, his role as predator. The sharp words that issue forth from his bedside when Tess confronts him with Angel's return are different from the sardonic laughter we might have expected earlier: he loves her, and he will finally pay "to the utmost farthing" for his surprising and textually disruptive fantasy that one day the affection might be mutual.

It is in light of such complex undercurrents that the necessary sympathy for Tess and hostility toward Alec become complicated. Indeed, it is even possible to laud Alec's fidelity of sexual desire versus Tess's "use" of Alec, a real twist to the obvious dominant demands of the narrative. Most damagingly, such confusion of character subverts the novel's climax—Tess's killing of Alec—into a dishonest narrative move: rather than the inevitable act of a manipulated, maltreated hero, instead it appears, while certainly not unmotivated, as *unnecessary* by now. Tess could run away with Angel without killing Alec. Angel's catharsis in the desert has clearly left him a changed man; even as she talks from the staircase, Tess is the one in command, both in station and in physical power, while Angel, beneath her, looks so weak that Tess infers that he is dying (315). Tess's apparent supposition that even this new Angel will not accept her in adultery is hard to credit, since she believes he will accept her in the role of murderer.

Thus what vitiates the strength of the murder scene is our uneasy intuition that *Alec does not deserve to be killed:* deserted, yes, though by now we might still flinch at what could be interpreted as injustice. After all, Angel accepts the d'Urbervilles' putative rebuke of him because "his had been a love 'which alters when it alteration finds'" (305), unlike Alec's affection which, despite its possessor's inadequacies, had been unwavering. Even the narrative description of Alec's murder creates a subtext of confusion over lover versus predator, over what roles Alec and Tess are meant to fulfill. "The wound was small, but the point of the blade had touched the heart of the victim, who lay on his back, pale, fixed, dead, as if he had scarcely moved after the inflection of the blow" (317). Yet Tess justifies her killing of Alec in her old justificatory terms of *his* power over her: " . . . you had used your cruel persuasion upon me. . . . you moved me. . . . you taunted me. . . . you have torn my life all to pieces . . . made me be what I prayed you in pity not to make me be again!" (315).

But even earlier, Tess's refusal to act upon her admitted knowledge of the Sermon on the Mount already had revealed an inner spiritual poverty rather than the moral richness a superficial reading suggests. "I believe in the *Spirit* of the Sermon on the Mount, and so did my dear husband," she tells Alec, but we know what that sermon says and that Tess acts no more in accordance with it now than Angel did upon his wife's confession:

> Ye have heard that it hath been said, An eye for an eye, and a tooth for a tooth: But I say unto you, That you resist not evil: but whosoever shall smite thee on the right cheek, turn to him the other also. (Matt. 5:38-39)

Tess's earlier reference to the following passage suggests her familiarity with the Sermon's radical message of charity and thus further indicts her selective application of its message:

> Ye have heard that it hath been said, Thou shalt love thy neighbour and hate thine enemy. But I say unto you, Love your enemies, bless them that curse you, . . . for he maketh his sun to rise on the evil and on the good, and sendeth rain on the just and on the unjust.[19] (Matt. 5:43-45)

Tess betrays fully the spirit of this passage; she scorns Alec's pitiable, even absurd attempts to give a moral direction to his life and refuses to forgive him. Certainly she had not hesitated to ask Angel to "forgive me as you are forgiven" (191) in tones resonant of the Lord's Prayer, an evocation that the narrative emphasizes, since that prayer is contained in—and central to—the Sermon on the Mount. By invoking the biblical words of Paul and Matthew, Hardy reminds us that without charity we are as nothing, and, as illustration, Angel, in fact, becomes depleted, a mere skeleton on his South American journey into the self. It is only through a painfully won vision of charity that he can come to life again. But if Hardy completes Angel Clare, he leaves us wondering what constitutes the center of Tess herself.

III

Thomas Hardy is on record as wishing his audience to read *Tess of the d'Urbervilles* for its "inner Necessity and Truth" alone. Thus he justifies our sense that he meant something, that he pointed to "a truth." Precisely such a compelling "inner Necessity" is lacking, however, and fails to control a close reading of *Tess*. And it is for this reason that the dissatisfaction with the novel exists for some readers; this is the reason some of us feel uncomfortable when its devotees explain away its weakness by the illumination of some specific, basically minor, flaw. I suggest instead that it is the whole, not the parts, that ails.

But what do we as readers have the right to expect from the text? We assume that within the context which the author creates she or he will fulfill the expectations aroused. We expect a realistic novel to function according to a particular logic that Franz Kafka, for instance, will necessarily subvert in his fiction. As Dorothy Van Ghent has pointed out, we desire an ordering of life within the realistic novel that cannot exist in the chaos of the real world. Thus we encounter the paradox of reality in the text: to make fiction real, we make artificial good sense of the environment it inhabits. It is, of course, true that readers impose coherent shape by reading backward, so that we create a unified whole a posteriori from the teleology that the closure suggests.[20] Yet in spite of current theoretical tendencies to escape the notion of determinate meaning, we must confess to making literary sense most often through a norm of ordering, even as we share Michel Foucault's dismay at the political manipulation such a system encourages.

Thomas Hardy structured *Tess of the d'Urbervilles* so that it demands to be read in a way that a careful scrutiny of its form disallows. It is true that the novel succeeds on some terms nonetheless; too many generations of "ideal readers" have indeed been enamored of the text to suggest that it does not deserve its place in the canon. But the particular pleasure of *Tess* comes from the genre it constantly evokes: the realm of poetry, not prose. It is Hardy the master of dark poetic truths who speaks so persuasively throughout this novel, and it is Hardy the novelist who works *against* his own text. Thus it is that there exists some recalcitrant coterie of critics, among whom I sit, who see the novel as giving pleasure only in spite of itself. And that pleasure, I suggest, is severely limited for part of its audience precisely to the degree in which the novel deviates from textual coherence.

NOTES

1. For these respective criticisms, see Rosemary Benzing, "In Defense of Tess," *Contemporary Review* 218, no. 1263 (1971): 202; Geoffrey Thurley, *The Psychology of Hardy's Novels* (St. Lucia, Queensland, 1975), 179; and Mary Jacobus, "Tess's Purity," *Essays in Criticism* 26 (1976): 332.

2. Bernard Paris, "'A Confusion of Many Standards': Conflicting Value Systems in *Tess of the d'Urbervilles*," *Nineteenth-Century Fiction* 24 (1969): 57-92.

3. Francis Adams, *The Fortnightly Review,* July 1892, quoted in *Thomas Hardy and His Readers,* ed. Laurence Lerner and John Holmstrom (New York: Barnes & Noble, 1968), 89.

4. Lionel Johnson, *The Art of Thomas Hardy* (London, 1895), 245-56, 262-64, 267, 269, 274-76; rpt. "The Argument," in Thomas Hardy, *Tess of the d'Urbervilles,* ed. Scott Elledge (New York: Norton, 1965), 389. All further references to this work will be included parenthetically in the text.

5. Paris, 59.

6. Virginia Woolf, "The Novels of Thomas Hardy," in *The Second Common Reader* (New York: Norton, 1932), 266-80; rpt. "Hardy's Moments of Vision," in Elledge, ed., *Tess of the d'Urbervilles,* 401.

7. Scott Elledge, ed., *Tess of the d'Urbervilles,* by Thomas Hardy (New York: Norton, 1965), 44. All further page references will be cited in the text.

8. Elizabeth Langland, "A Perspective of One's Own: Thomas Hardy and the Elusive Sue Bridehead," *Studies in the Novel* 12 (Spring 1980): 17-18. Perhaps there actually is a kinship of sorts between Sue Bridehead and Tess Durbeyfield; Michael Millgate (*Thomas Hardy: A Biography* [New York: Random House, 1982], 295) reminds us that "Tess herself was for a long time called Sue in Hardy's manuscript, and in July 1889 he was suggesting that the novel *[Tess of the d'Urbervilles]* be called 'The Body and Soul of Sue.'"

9. R. H. Hutton, *The Spectator,* Jan. 1892, quoted in Lerner and Holmstrom, 69.

10. In the preface to the fifth edition of *Tess,* Hardy claimed that "the novel was intended to be neither didactic nor aggressive" (see Elledge, 2).

11. Andrew Lang, *Longman's Magazine,* Nov. 1892, quoted in Elledge, 384.

12. *The Speaker,* Dec. 1891, quoted in Lerner and Holmstrom, 61.

13. F. B. Pinion, *Thomas Hardy: Art and Thought* (London, 1977), 122, 134.

14. Alfred Tennyson, *Maud, Selected Poems,* ed. Michael Millgate (Oxford, 1973), 11. 157, 161.

[15] Christina Rossetti, *Goblin Market* (Boston: D. R. Godine, 1981), 11. 49, 69, 134-35; all subsequent references will be cited by line from this edition and will be included in the text.

[16] John Milton, *Paradise Lost, Complete Poems and Major Prose*, ed. Merrit Y. Hughes (Indianapolis and New York: Odyssey Press, 1957), bk. 9, 11. 463-66.

[17] Gittings, 68.

[18] Thurley, 152, and Henry James quoted in Lerner and Holmstrom, 85.

[19] Tess laments to Angel that "I shouldn't mind learning why—why the sun do shine on the just and the unjust alike" (107).

[20] For an illuminating discussion of the artificial nature of formal coherence, see D. A. Miller, *Narrative and Its Discontents: Problems of Closure in the Traditional Novel* (Princeton: Princeton University Press, 1981), xiii.

Kurt Hochenauer

SOURCE: "Sexual Realism in 'The Portrait of a Lady': The Divided Sexuality of Isabel Archer," in *Studies in the Novel*, Vol. XXII, No. 1, Spring, 1990, pp. 19-25.

[*In the following essay, Hochenauer emphasizes Isabel Archer's sexually passionate and emotionally inhibited sides and the implications of this dual nature in Henry James's novel* The Portrait of a Lady.]

Isabel Archer's divided sexuality represents a literary paradigm of the struggle for sexual independence among late nineteenth-century women. Throughout *The Portrait of a Lady,* she remains caught between a stale ideology insisting women de-emphasize their sexuality to gain equal footing with men and a growing, nineteenth-century movement among feminists working to legitimize a woman's sex drive.[1] Eventually isolated between what Nancy F. Cott calls "passionlessness ideology" and her own deeply felt sexuality, Isabel cannot be interpreted as the fictional mother of morality or the femme fatale of romantic literature.[2] As an ambiguous, subtle character with an apparent but unresolved sexuality, Isabel remains a vanguard of the new realism Henry James sought in his fiction.

With her deeply split personality, however, Isabel Archer continues to represent a foil to critics who adopt a single interpretation about her sexuality. Obstinate, one-sided views have persisted since William Bysshe Stein's 1959 controversial assessment of Isabel as a "case history" of a frigid American woman.[3] By treating only one aspect of her sexuality, Stein commits the critical error repeated sixteen years later by Annette Niemtzow who argues Isabel has "an almost obscene—certainly not frigid—imagination."[4] Falling into this critical quagmire, Courtney Johnson sees her as Eve,[5] Marjorie Perloff sees her as a wicked stepmother,[6] and Daniel J. Schneider sees her as neurotic.[7] As critics argue one side or the other, Isabel Archer becomes stretched between the sexual and asexual. These interpretations about Henry James's great heroine in *The Portrait of a Lady* have in common only a desire to reconcile Isabel's sexual ambiguity to fit the narrow constraints posed by their arguments. This reconciliation is not only impossible but begs the questions raised by Isabel's two sides. In my view, when critics fail to recognize the tension between the passionate Isabel and the inhibited Isabel, James's portrait runs the risk of becoming a cheap, contrived painting rather than the epitome of the new literary realism.

If, as some Freudian critics argue, she reflects an exhibition of James's repressed sexuality, Isabel's ambiguity becomes unconscious and her realism becomes a fluke of her creator's subconscious. If, as others such as Niemtzow argue, her sexual imagination is as intrusive as neon lighting, Isabel's sexuality becomes heavy-handed and her realism is marred by James's preoccupation with her passionate side. Both interpretations, intentionally or not, diffuse the prevailing consensus that Henry James is a founding father of realism in modern American literature. If held hostage in either camp, Isabel reflects an author not conscious of his role in shaping a transition between romanticism and realism. And even those critics who view James as an anglicized elitist content to wallow the inner-consciousness of his characters into obscurity cannot doubt his self-imposed—if not sometimes self-serving—mission as a new realist in his era.

After accepting Isabel's two sides, however, there remains a lingering question about her realism. But in the debate over Isabel's sexuality, readers and critics often fall short in juxtaposing it against the prevailing sexual ideology of the late nineteenth-century. This is unfortunate. To gauge the success of James's realism through Isabel's sexuality, our own sexual views and sexual prejudices should be temporarily suspended when considering James's heroine. Further, there exists a need to go beyond the obviousness of critics, such as Edward Wagenknecht, who call on readers to simply see Isabel as "limited by the mores and standards of her time."[8] A close, historical scrutiny becomes necessary because Isabel's two sides, the passionate and the inhibited, reflect the changing sexual ideology among women in the late nineteenth century. James's portrait, under this interpretation, is the epitome of the emerging literary realism in the late nineteenth century. Isabel's divided sexuality, then, becomes the *point* not the *problem*.

The tenor of Isabel's dual sexuality can best be seen through her relationship with Caspar Goodwood. A typical Freudian interpretation holds that Isabel sees Goodwood as a "walking erection."[9] In the beginning of the novel, we are told Isabel "wished [Goodwood] no ounce less of his manhood," but a few sentences later

Isabel considers his "figure" as "too straight and stiff" (vol. 3, p. 165). While his straight and stiff figure can obviously justify a phallic-symbol interpretation, Goodwood's sexuality is not, as some would have it, merely a hallucination of Isabel's repression. From Isabel's consciousness, we have already learned that she does not deny Goodwood his "manhood." At the same time, however, she sees his masculinity as a threat. Obviously, James presents the two sexual sides of his heroine through this paradox. Isabel's initial, ambiguous response to Goodwood's physical appearance becomes a coda for her divided sexuality throughout the novel.

This becomes even more apparent when Isabel refuses Goodwood's marriage proposal. After turning him down, Isabel takes his hand and "felt a great respect for him; she knew how much he cared for her and she thought him magnanimous" (vol. 3, p. 230). A few moments later, she "intensely rejoiced that Caspar Goodwood was gone" (vol. 3, p. 232). When her divided sexuality surfaces like this, the result is powerful:

> She was not praying; she was trembling—trembling all over. Vibration was easy to her, was in fact too constant with her, and she found herself now humming like a smitten harp. She only asked, however, to put on the cover, to case herself again in brown holland, but she wished to resist her excitement, and the attitude of devotion, which she kept for some time, seemed to help her to be still. (vol. 3, p. 232)

The passionate Isabel trembles, vibrates like a smitten harp as the inhibited Isabel wraps herself with covers to enclose, smother, this intrusive sexuality. But, it is here, with this vivid passage filled with sexual symbols, where readers and critics first get tempted to delineate her sexuality into separate and extreme positions. The asexual and sexual camps can and do use the passage's ambiguity to fit their opposite theories. Trembling and vibrating, Isabel is having a sexual experience. Encased in brown holland, she is a prude if not frigid. The problem is that this temptation to reconcile Isabel's ambiguity ignores James's deliberate attempt to create a realistic character struggling with the question of sexual independence. If she gives in to her sexual passion, she becomes a femme fatale risking her reputation. If she ignores it completely, she becomes an idealized guardian or mother of morality. In either case, she becomes an overdrawn, romantic character rather than a subtle, realistic character. James's ideas of literary realism demand that we leave Isabel's sexual independence unresolved.

But the temptation is apparently too great. Schneider, for example, recognizes Isabel's divided self, but he attributes it to a schizoid personality.[10] If she suffers from a mental disorder, as Schneider argues, Isabel's sexuality becomes a sickness that can be reconciled by a Freudian interpretation. Juliet McMaster sees two Isabels as well, but again the focus is on the "morbid-desire" side, on Isabel's "perverse morality," on a sickness that can be attributed ultimately to James's uncon-

scious repressions.[11] More common, however, are interpretations ignoring altogether her two sides. To Perloff, Isabel is selfish and conceited, and she subjugates her stepdaughter.[12] To Johnson, Isabel is an Eve who never falls to the serpent-like sexuality of Goodwood, and her personal morality redeems her at the novel's conclusion.[13] All these arguments create issues that cannot be supported adequately by the text or the prevailing sexual ideology in James's day. Critics consistently interpret Isabel by twentieth-century standards without recognizing she is a character created in an era much different than our own. By dismissing historical approaches in favor of the never-ending ambiguity offered by psychological or spiritual interpretations, Isabel's detractors and worshippers give us half-empty insights.

In her important study about Victorian women, Cott argues that most American and British feminists by the mid-nineteenth century had de-emphasized the sexuality they felt could ruin their opportunities for equality.[14] By doing so, "the middle-class moralists made female chastity the archetype for human morality."[15] The passionlessness ideology held out certain advantages for women. By de-emphasizing their sexual characteristics, women focused attention on their intellectual and spiritual capabilities. Perhaps more importantly, passionlessness ideology enabled women to gain control of what Cott calls the "sexual arena" because:

> In sexual encounters women had more than an even chance to lose, whether by censure under the double standard, unwanted pregnancies and health problems, or ill-fated marriage.[16]

After 1860, however, leading feminists tried to legitimize a woman's sex drive. Still holding to the ideology, feminists rejected the idea of prudery that became associated with passionlessness. In the late nineteenth century, then, women were torn between the older sexual ideology and a progressive call for accepting the female sexual drive as normal and legitimate. In short, it would be correct to assume that many women were held hostage to this paradox. Isabel Archer's sexuality represents not only the two extremes but the confusion obviously generated by them as well.

As a proponent of the prevailing passionlessness theory, Isabel wrests control of the sexual arena by refusing Warburton and Goodwood. Her marriage to Osmond is essentially asexual. In her quest for personal independence, Isabel must check her sexuality. If she must define herself by marriage it will be her decision, a decision unclouded by sexual impulse. The man *she* will choose must recognize her intellectual capabilities, her ideas. For her potential suitors, Isabel flaunts her brain not her body. Isabel chooses Osmond because he thinks "she was the most imaginative woman he had known" not because he makes her tremble like Goodwood (vol. 4, 192). Isabel, as she makes the decision to marry Osmond, thinks herself in control of her destiny, her sexual independence. Osmond, however, tricks her. He disdains her ideas. Yet, his deception is asexual as well; he only wants her money.

Throughout the novel, however, Isabel must deal with the persistent Goodwood. He arouses the sexuality Isabel thinks she has forfeited in her search for independence. After she makes her decision to marry Osmond, for example, Goodwood makes a suitor's last-ditch effort to persuade her differently. In this episode, Isabel sees him as "straight, strong and hard" (vol. 4, p. 43), and he has a "stiff insistence" (vol. 4, p. 44). He has a "stiff help-lessness" (vol. 4, p. 48). There "was the manly staying of his hand that made her heart beat faster" (vol. 4, p. 49). He "held himself hard" (vol. 4, p. 50). After he leaves, rejected again, Isabel bursts into tears. Her sexual passion is at odds with her desire for independence.

With Osmond, Isabel adopts the prevailing sexual codes, but their marriage is, of course, a failure. With Goodwood, she fights back the overwhelming sexual impulse she never fully understands. Her sexual relationship with Osmond produces only the death of a child and the spiritual death of Isabel herself. But her sexual response to Goodwood is no better; it repeatedly drives her to tears. Caught in this miserable conundrum, Isabel has no choices. As a woman trapped in an era of changing sexual ideology, she is struggling for a freedom blurred by the tension created between the asexual and the sexual. Isabel cannot achieve her sexual independence because she is not quite sure what that independence means. Is it an imposed celibacy with a wretched husband? Is it immediate sexual gratification with Goodwood? Isabel's tragedy, so vividly delineated in the final chapter, indicates James's sympathies rested with some type of compromise between the two, a compromise between passionlessness ideology and a woman's sexuality. But the compromise remains unstated. The novel is, as James titled it, merely a realistic portrait, not an idealized, romantic account of how things should be.

But this raises the questions of how conscious James was of his character's sexuality and how aware he was of the emerging women's rights movement in his day. In an 1883 letter, Henry Adams writes of his friend that "James knows nothing of women but the mere outside; he never had a wife."[17] Nearly a hundred years later, Mary S. Schriber writes: "No American novelist of the nineteenth century better understood the complexities of a woman's place in society than Henry James."[18] Obviously, the answers to the questions I pose rest some-where between Adams's diatribe and Schriber's adulation. With his great intellectual faculties and sophistication, it would be absurd to assume, as Adams contends, that James remained ignorant of the issues facing women in his day. On the other hand, Schriber's assessment reeks of overstatement. Moreover, Leon Edel's generally accepted view that James remained celibate during his life complicates matters further. How are we to ever understand fully the sexuality of a female character created by a man who, in Edel's assessment, suffered from "latent prudery" and had "transmuted pas-

sions"?[19] One answer rests perhaps with James's own divided self. He both idealized and feared women, according to Edel, and nothing reflects better the two sides of Henry James than his personal struggle with the Europe versus America question. His celibacy, it might be assumed, posed a similar struggle. If James tried to desexualize himself, he must have known the ultimate futility of such an action. Like his heroine, then, James must have been torn between the sexual and the asexual. But this biographical interpretation remains overshad-owed by the ending of *The Portrait of a Lady,* which provides even stronger clues to James's intent.

When the novel was first published in 1881, the kiss between Goodwood and Isabel at the novel's conclusion was limited to this terse, one sentence: "His kiss was like a flash of lightning; when it was dark again she was free."[20] For the 1908 New York Edition of the novel, this became:

> His kiss was like white lightning, a flash that spread, and spread again, and stayed; and it was extraordinarily as if, while she took it, she felt each thing in his hard manhood that had least pleased her, each aggressive fact of his face, his figure, his presence, justified of its intense identity and made one with this act of possession. (vol. 4, p. 436)

The revision dispels any doubt that James remained unaware of the sexuality of his character. As Edel de-scribes it: "If erotic feeling was absent in the earlier work, the Master now made amends."[21] But the new passage also reinforces Isabel's divided sexuality. She is aroused but threatened. If she gives in to her sexual feelings, Goodwood will possess her. The inhibited and passionate Isabels merge in this kiss described bluntly by Seymour Kleinberg as the "equivalent impact of orgasm."[22] As explicit as one will ever find James, the revision also suggests he had more than just a casual interest in Isabel's sexuality. Judged against the standards and conventions of James's era, the sexu-ality here is graphic not limited, realistic not romantic. James went as far as his reading public would allow him to go.

If we are to accept Isabel's sexuality as intrinsic to a proper reading of *The Portrait of a Lady,* as I think we must, then we can assume James had more in mind than one young woman's response to her aroused passion. If the emerging realism in literature often demanded a narrow focus on individual characters, it sought also to provide greater truths on a smaller stage. As Nina Baym points out, the novel was one in a series of works deal-ing with the "woman question." Unlike other authors, James did not "employ the standard formula of saving [Isabel] from [her] delusion" by giving her a happy marriage.[23] He could not have done so and retained Isabel's realism. Isabel's sexual realism reflects what James felt to be the prevailing ideology among women in his day. If it reflected anything less, the portrait would be marred.

Passionlessness ideology required women to desexualize themselves to achieve some equality with men. But, along with some feminists of his day, James saw the futility and frustration of sexual abnegation. Isabel Archer's divided sexuality cannot be reconciled among critics because James refused to accept sexlessness as the only road to women's independence. In the end, his character is in a sexual limbo. She feels but she cannot act. Her lightning kiss repudiates the foundation of her quest for independence. But the kiss in itself is not enough. We are left with a broken woman still in search of the sexual independence denied her, and most women, in the nineteenth century.

NOTES

[1] Henry James, *The Portrait of a Lady,* vols. 3-4 of *The Novels and Tales of Henry James,* New York Edition (New York: Scribner's, 1908). Page references to this work appear in the text.

[2] Nancy F. Cott, "Passionlessness: An Interpretation of Victorian Sexual Ideology, 1790-1850," *Signs* 4 (1978): 219.

[3] William Bysshe Stein, "*The Portrait of a Lady:* Vis Inertiae," *Western Humanities Review* 13 (1959): 180.

[4] Annette Niemtzow, "Marriage and the New Woman in *The Portrait of a Lady,*" *American Literature* 47 (1975): 386.

[5] Courtney Johnson, "Adam and Eve and Isabel Archer," *Renascence* 21 (1969): 139.

[6] Marjorie Perloff, "Cinderella Becomes the Wicked Stepmother: *The Portrait of a Lady* as Ironic Fairy Tale," *Nineteenth-Century Fiction* 23 (1969): 416.

[7] Daniel J. Schneider, "The Divided Self in the Fiction of Henry James," *PMLA* 90 (1975): 447.

[8] Edward Wagenknecht, *Eve and Henry James* (Norman: Univ. of Oklahoma, 1978): p. 93.

[9] Seymour Kleinberg, "Ambiguity and Ambivalence: the Psychology of Sexuality in Henry James's *The Portrait of a Lady,*" *Markham Review* 5 (1969): 3.

[10] Schneider, p. 447.

[11] Juliet McMaster, "The Portrait of Isabel Archer," *American Literature* 45 (1973): 66.

[12] Perloff, p. 416.

[13] Johnson, pp. 134-44.

[14] Cott, p. 219.

[15] Cott, p. 223.

[16] Cott, p. 233.

[17] Henry Adams, "To John Hay, 24 Sept, 1883," *The Selected Letters of Henry Adams,* ed. Newton Arvin (New York: Farrar, 1951), pp. 84-85.

[18] Mary S. Schriber, "Isabel Archer and Victorian Manners," *Studies in the Novel* 8 (1976): 441.

[19] Leon Edel, *Henry James: A Life,* Vols. 1-5, 1950-71, revised (New York: Harper, 1985), p. xii. In this revised and condensed biography, Edel devotes much of his introduction to James's sexuality.

[20] Edel, p. 626.

[21] Ibid.

[22] Kleinberg, p. 6.

[23] Nina Baym, "Revision and Thematic Change in *The Portrait of a Lady,*" *Modern Fiction Studies* 22 (1976): 184.

Peter F. Murphy

SOURCE: "Male Heterosexuality in Hawkes's 'The Passion Artist," in *Twentieth Century Literature,* Vol. 36, No. 4, Winter, 1990, pp. 403-18.

[*In the following essay, Murphy evaluates John Hawkes's* The Passion Artist *as a work that "explores the fantasies, manifestations, doubts, and transformations of male heterosexuality in the context of a world besieged by hatred, fear, and shame."*]

A critical sequence in John Hawkes's fiction: *The Blood Oranges* (1970) to *Virginie: Her Two Lives* (1981), presents a radical theory of male heterosexuality. During this ten-year span Hawkes also published *Death, Sleep and the Traveler* (1973), *Travesty* (1976), and *The Passion Artist* (1978).[1] The first three of these novels make up what Hawkes came to call "the sex triad."

As one of the few contemporary male authors affected directly by the feminist movement, Hawkes is at the forefront of the male response. His fiction examines such issues as: domination/submission, father-daughter incest, pornography, the Lolita complex, men's relationship with their mothers, jealousy, and power. With the recent conflict within feminism over erotica vs. pornography, Hawkes gives an honest and vivid portrayal of one man's involvement; often his vision resembles that of many men.

The Blood Oranges introduces an important theme for a critical engagement with male heterosexuality. Cyril, the male antagonist, articulates an explicit theory of non-monogamous marriage. His theory diverges quite dramatically, though, from the typical double standard of most male writers. In *Death, Sleep and the Traveler* and *Travesty* Cyril's theory unravels in the specific behavior of the male characters. Cyril's suggestion that husbands and wives should make love with whom they please and that each should help the other in accomplishing their seductions becomes problematic in *Death, Sleep and the Traveler*. Allert, the husband, is quite unhappy with the knowledge that his wife has a boyfriend. As if to retaliate, Allert falls in love with Ariane who, it seems, he murders. A lovely young woman who believes in free love, Ariane seduces Allert by playing her flute in the nude. She represents another recurrent male fantasy in Hawke's novels: small, diminutive women. The Lolita complex informs this novel as it does many of his other works of fiction.

In *Travesty*, the theory of non-monogamous marriage explodes and claims for its victims not only Papa, the male protagonist, but his daughter, Chantel, and his wife's lover, Henri. Both *Death, Sleep and the Traveler* and *Travesty* demonstrate the difficulty men, not women, have with open relationships. They provide the basis to begin rethinking the recurrent male obsession with non-monogamy and free love. It is, after all, Papa who kills himself and two others, not his wife, who sleeps comfortably at home.

In *Virginie: Her Two Lives*, Hawkes relies on a female narrator for the first time in his fiction. Formalistically similar to Virginia Woolf's *Orlando*, the story describes a young girl's life during two different historical periods: 1740 aristocratic France and 1945 post-World War II Paris. In 1740, Virginie helps Seigneur operate a school for women and in 1945 she and Bocage run a surrealist bordello. As a parody of de Sade, Seigneur represents the full spectrum of male heterosexuality. An ironic perversion of a Sadeian discourse, *Virginie* can be read as a feminist text.

The Passion Artist commands a central position for a critical appreciation of Hawkes's ideas about male heterosexuality. Exploring the sexual awakening of one man, Konrad Vost, the novel focuses on the relationship between masculinity and femininity. More than any other of Hawkes's novels, *The Passion Artist* "lays bare the horrors of the masculine mind" (O'Donnell 116).

Vost's sexual development occurs in the surrealist context of a riot-torn women's prison and a stark and desolate marshland. His own life is desolate, as well. Claire, his wife, died several years earlier but he cannot accept her death. His young daughter has become a prostitute. His mother, Eva, has been imprisoned for the murder of his father. In this novel, as in much of his fiction, Hawkes combines "dislocation of cause and effect, distortion of rational processes, insistence on the psychic truth beneath the recognized surfaces" (Griener 12). In an anti-real, Kafkaesque setting, Hawkes explores relentlessly the contradictions as well as the possibilities of male heterosexuality.

Vost's transformation begins when he volunteers to help put down a riot in La Violaine, the local women's prison in which his mother is incarcerated. His experience inside the prison battering the prisoners and eventually as the captive of his mother and her best friend, Hania, provides valuable insights into Vost's sexuality in particular and male heterosexuality in general. While hunting escaped prisoners Vost fantasizes about some of the women escapees and learns firsthand the intimidating power of masculinity. These encounters force Vost to confront the ordeal of women's lives and become a better man. In this context, innocence and purity are illuminated against the setting of male violence against women, submission and domination, marriage, bestiality, and pornography.

The Passion Artist explores the fantasies, manifestations, doubts, and transformations of male heterosexuality in the context of a world besieged by hatred, fear, and shame. The novel conveys Vost's sexual awakening from the artist of dead passion (as was Papa in *Travesty*) to "an artist . . . of the willed erotic union" (*TPA* 181). Vost evolves from being a man who hates his body and denies his sexual longings to one who finally feels comfortable with his sexuality. This long and brutal voyage culminates in Vost's acceptance of his role as a man, due in no small part to his experience of what it is like to be a woman. As he endures the life of a woman, Vost learns about the potential for men's liberation.

His participation (along with many other men) in squelching a violent rebellion by the women inmates focuses many of the issues raised in this novel. What transpires between the men and the women, as well as among the men, explains much of what it means to be a man in contemporary society. Through the image of the riot, Hawkes examines male fantasies about and male bonding around violation in its various manifestations and the relationship between power and sexuality.

The volunteers represent the complete gamut of males in our society. They are "husbands, fathers, bachelors" (*TPA* 46), "workers, shop owners, professional men" (*TPA* 53). They come from all classes of society and represent every relationship men have with women, except friendship. If they were friends they would not be in the prison trying to squelch the riot; they would empathize with the women and defend their right to rebel. The possibility that such men exist is given explicit consideration.

Initially, the men seem to feel ashamed about their participation in putting down the women's rebellion; even though Vost knows two of the men they do not speak or even acknowledge each other's presence. Most of the men are relatively innocent of inflicting pain on anyone and prefer to stand far apart from each other. At the same time, however, they are "fully or partially aware of the fact that the blows [they were] about to strike would fall on the flesh and bones of a woman" (*TPA* 47). They felt either guilty about their actions or eager to begin.

These husbands, fathers, bachelors (brothers) want to beat their wives, daughters, mothers, sisters.

The extent to which Vost becomes involved with the suppression of the women and the extent to which he enjoys his brutality against them emerge as crucial points in the novel. He

> prepared to drive the stick into the face of the disbelieving woman. . . . He swung his arm with all the strength he could manage and brought the stick crashing against the side of the woman's head . . . and for a moment he wished that the rioting all around him would never cease. (*TPA* 54-55)

Vost's obsession provides a perceptive portrayal of a male fantasy and in this way enlists the reader directly into the novel's prose. The issues of power, sadomasochism, bondage, and pornography are engaged powerfully, allowing readers to confront their own complicity in such violence. At first, the reader might feel horrified. Almost immediately, though, he feels compelled to consider the accuracy of the fictional portrayal. If violation were sanctioned, especially against women, many men would find it difficult to control themselves. More than half of the men surveyed in a recent poll said that they would rape a woman if they were absolutely sure they would get away with it (Sidran 30). In light of this, Vost's behavior in the women's prison is not incredible at all. In a society in which such violation is an everyday occurrence, Vost represents Everyman.

In the context of this "sanctioned violation" (*TPA* 53) Vost "found himself wanting nothing more than to beat the woman first to surrender and then to unconsciousness. He was not given to physical exertion. . . . Yet he was determined that he himself would administer the blows that would fell this woman who had become victorious in a man's clothing" (*TPA* 51). Vost's outrage is exacerbated by the women's attire; they transgress gender boundaries when they put on men's clothes. Vost's trial, later in the novel, reveals the possibility that women have a similar confused and antagonistic response to men attired in women's clothing. Here, as elsewhere in the novel, Hawkes seems to be suggesting a similarity between the sexes. Opposition to rebellion against gender boundaries may not be innate to the male condition but rather a socially learned, culturally reinforced stereotype that neither men nor women can transcend easily.

While the riot continues, the voice of a young woman, a "young invisible victim" (*TPA* 55), can be heard in the background. The vividness with which Hawkes describes Vost's attack on his victim, combined with the description of the young woman sighing in the background, accentuates the issue of violence against women. Invisible victims remain a major problem in contemporary society: as long as they remain invisible no one has to act. If we are neither victims nor perpetrators we are innocent. But, as Hawkes makes clear throughout this novel, no one is innocent; we are all culpable and share similar fantasies of domination and submission. For Hawkes, "if we don't know our destructive potential we can't very well assume genuine responsibility for the world around us. . . . I'm just writing about the things that are most deeply embedded in the human psyche" (Fielding 45). Expanding on these ideas, Hawkes explains that his "work is an effort to expose the worst in us all, to cause us to face up to the enormities of our terrible potential for betrayal, disgrace and criminal behavior" (LeClair 27).

Vost is stimulated erotically by the stark and unbridled violence against women. Later, he changes and evolves. For now though,

> through the medium of the unbreakable length of wood the young woman's pain leapt to his clenched hands; in his hands and arms he could feel the small perfect body losing its form . . . and, as the childlike woman took random useless steps, cowering and dangling her arms, the dress fell and exposed one shoulder while on the oval face the lips began to glisten with a wetness rising from deep within that miniature anatomy. (*TPA* 56)

Even while he is battering this woman to death, her exposed shoulder remains a point of interest, of sexual excitation. As her lips begin to glisten Vost becomes even more titillated. The small, childlike woman resounds throughout Hawkes's fiction and in *The Passion Artist* it reaches new significance. Eventually, and despite her large size, Vost learns to love Hania.

One scene in particular explores the issue of submission/domination and the relationship between power and the erotic. Following the riot, Vost dreams he has been taken captive by the women in the prison. He stands trial for the crimes he has committed against these women and against one woman in particular. His accuser, a young woman, is "as small as a child yet clothed in a tight gown of a sparkling mauve colored material which exposed the diminutive anatomy that could belong only to an adult woman" (*TPA* 63). This small and childlike woman, attired in a sensually colored gown, has complete power over Vost. She charges him with not knowing anything about women, explaining that all he ever did was comment on her size but never touched her. Despite the fact that he is condemned and powerless, a victim of her every whim, Vost finds his accuser sexually arousing. Even in his discomfort and humiliation he feels a growing rapture. Though accused of sexual impotence and complete ignorance of women he realizes

> that all the agreeableness of her mannerisms concealed a petulance even more desirable than the legs, the hips, the musical voice . . . [and that] now, against his will, in the darkness of a condition that could not have been more contrary to that of erotic excitation, now he was overcome with the knowledge that in his locked and inaccessible loins the army of mice was beginning to

run through the forest that was filled with snow. (*TPA* 65-66)

In contrast to the assumption that men must dominate to obtain sexual pleasure, Vost finds himself sexually aroused to the point of orgasm, an orgasm he prefers not to have. The suggestion that men may also obtain pleasure from being submissive counters the assertion that pornography manifests an inherently male need to be the dominator. Current feminist arguments against pornography (for example, Brownmiller, Dworkin, and Griffin)[2] are confronted throughout the novel; Vost's journey examines the question of sexual difference.

Vost awakens from his dream to find himself in the hospital. He arrived there after having fallen in the ranks of the victims of La Violaine. The women had managed to rout the voluntary male militia and now control the prison. Vost leaves the hospital, decides to join the hunt for the women prisoners, and goes into the marsh after them. Here, Vost encounters the young woman in his dream. The bruises he had inflicted upon her body during the riot contribute to Vost's erotic sensations and enhance his vision of her beauty. Vost begins to fall in love with this young woman whom he had beaten unconscious and now spies upon. She brings out feelings in Konrad Vost that had always been fleeting and uncomfortable.

Vost's ambivalence about his sexual passion compels him to leave the scene immediately. As he leaves, he is threatened by one of the armed guards hunting for the escaped women. Vost betrays the young woman in an effort to save his own life: "The brute maleness of the man and dog [and] the stench of their intimidation" (*TPA* 97), remind Vost that confronted by the savage power of masculinity, one cowers. This firsthand experience of the fear and intimidation that male sexuality presents to women every day of their lives furthers Vost's sexual awareness.

From this immediate encounter with the malignant potential of masculinity, Vost confronts yet one more component of the female sexual experience: their assumed role as the means to men's sexual satisfaction. Lost in the fog that has covered the marsh, Vost stumbles upon an old abandoned barn in which he decides to spend the night. Unknown to him, he shares it with two women who have escaped from the prison. When these women giggle, Vost assumes, as would many men, that their giggling was intended for him. He believes they are flirting with him. He could not be more wrong, for these escaped women convicts proceed to "rape" Vost. They force him to fondle their breasts and vaginas so that they can have an orgasm but every time he tries to get them to reciprocate they abuse him. They maintain complete control of this sexual encounter and force Vost to satisfy them without any concern at all for his pleasure. One of the women "began squeezing rapidly the front of his trousers as if to arouse and crush desire in a single gesture" (*TPA* 106-07).

Vost's "rape" parodies the sexual experience many women have at the hands of impatient, selfish men socialized to believe that women were created to satisfy their sexual needs. At the same time, however, it explicates, vividly, the experience of rape. "Submission, revolt, attack, submission; so the darkness was consumed in revolt, attack, submission" (*TPA* 109-10), describes much female experience of sex at the hands of husbands, lovers, rapists.

Later, Vost is relieved upon awakening to discover himself a captive in La Violaine. He

> found himself exactly where he had always wanted to be without knowing it: in the world of women and in the world of the prison . . . where he would receive the punishment he deserved and desired. [Here he would] suffer at will the presence of the women he had spent his life avoiding. (*TPA* 120-21)

This direct confrontation with women, and in particular the environment of the prison within which it will occur, contributes much to Vost's awakening. Here he will "be brought to [a] rudimentary knowledge of submission, domination, the question of woman" (*TPA* 121). Within the walls of this women's prison and at the hands of Hania, his mother's best friend, Vost will learn the experience of women and will become a more sexually liberated male.

One of the first and certainly most important lessons he learns derives from his original characterizations of these two women who play such a significant role in his liberation: his mother and Hania. These women, who replace his wife, Claire, "promised him not sentimentality but flesh and light" (*TPA* 122). They will give him not tender feelings of loss or regret but sexuality and the knowledge that accompanies it. Vost becomes aware that the stereotypical view of women as virgin/whore does not work. As Eva becomes the "notorious woman revealed," she can no longer be characterized as a whore. And Hania is "identified . . . no longer as the nun [virgin] she had once been" (*TPA* 121). Vost begins to see beyond the socially accepted characterization of women as either evil and dangerous or pure and sensitive.

In his prison cell strewn with articles of women's clothing, in this "splendor of depravation," Vost recognizes for the first time "the trespasser inside himself" (*TPA* 125). Here, in confinement and at the hands of his female captors, Vost begins to comprehend his identity as a man. In La Violaine, which derives from the French *viol, violateur, violenter,* or *violer,* meaning to rape, to violate, to transgress, Vost becomes aware of his sexually prescribed role as a man—a violator and a rapist. At the same time, though, he realizes his own vulnerability. When Eva and Hania enter his cell, Vost struggles to "retain some semblance of pride in the midst of submission" (*TPA* 128). Simultaneously, he realizes that for Hania indignity does not exist. Through years of submission and brutality at the hands of the prison guards and men in general, "there could be no indignity, nothing repugnant" for Hania (*TPA* 130).

At this point, Eva shares her ideas about marriage with Vost. She explains the difficulty a woman has being a wife because most women find themselves not only married to a child but bearing children. She concludes with some radical insights into motherhood and female identity, insights echoing Simone de Beauvoir and Shulamith Firestone: "We who spend our lives in prison know three things: that the family is the first prison; that among prisons the actual is preferable to the metaphorical; and that the woman is not a mother until she leaves her child" (*TPA* 129). With this knowledge Vost becomes educated, even politicized. He realizes that he no longer grieves for Claire and that his marriage is over. Finally, he severs his ties with his dead wife, Claire. This contributes significantly to Vost's awareness. The more exposure to the female social experience Vost encounters, the more he appreciates their plight at the hands of men and patriarchy.

Eva amplifies her ideas of motherhood and of being a good wife when she relates her own experience giving birth to Vost. The ultimate moment of his recognition provides insights about himself that he needed to know, but of which he believed he would never be made aware. Eva was informed by a village doctor, who resented her small size and beauty, that her baby was dead inside her. The doctor prescribed abhorrent things for her to do to expel the fetus.[3] After much excruciating pain and violence to herself, she almost succeeds in aborting the baby. It lives, however, albeit extremely premature. Eva maintains that her son, Konrad Vost, holds the responsibility for the destruction of an otherwise beautiful experience by making it into something extremely painful and grotesque. Stressing that she had been married for a while before becoming pregnant, Eva seems to suggest that childbirth destroys innocence; not sex, but motherhood, makes a woman into a victim.

Vost is astonished by the graffiti on the walls when he awakens at dawn of his first full day at La Violaine. He reads the slogans and aphorisms written by the women inmates and is surprised by "the humorous or violent jottings of women whose vulgar cravings were the equal of the vulgar cravings of any man" (*TPA* 155). Two inscriptions in particular impress him more than the others:

> "In memory of a Sunday in summer" [made him wonder whether it was possible] that a woman, especially in this place, had been capable of such generosity. After all, the nostalgia and resignation captured in the expression were as shockingly appropriate to the mind of a man as were the obscenities that made him flush with embarrassment. (*TPA* 155)

The second inscription, "'Love is not an honest feeling,' [made him ponder] who but a man could have written these words? . . . Yet the authors of these sayings had in fact been women" (*TPA* 155). The novel reiterates the point that women have sexual fantasies and sexual cravings similar to those of men. Hawkes seems well aware that one man can be embarrassed by the sexual longings of a woman just as a woman can be disconcerted by the sexual cravings of a man. This revelation resists the radical feminist position which maintains that pornography describes only male fantasies. According to one feminist perspective, pornography, written by men and for men, is evil and oppressive. This notion oversimplifies sexuality in general and distorts male sexuality in particular. As Ellen Willis points out in her response to the feminist opposition to pornography:

> the view of sex that most often emerges from talk about "erotica" is as sentimental and euphemistic as the word itself; lovemaking should be beautiful, romantic, soft, nice and devoid of messiness, vulgarity, impulses to power, or indeed aggression of any sort. Above all the emphasis should be on relationship not (yuck) organs. This goody-goody concept of eroticism is not feminist, it is feminine. (Willis 224)

One aphorism in particular stands out for Vost: "'Between my legs I do not have a bunch of violets.'" This statement "excluded him forever; it was the clue to the object of his desperate quest; it could not have been written by a man" (*TPA* 156). Here, as elsewhere in the novel, Vost searches for the difference between men and women. For Vost, learning that the vagina is not a bunch of violets helps move him beyond his previous characterization of a vagina as "the nostril of a dead bird" (*TPA* 67) or as "a small face beaten unrecognizable by the blows of a cruel fist" (*TPA* 151). Soon, with Hania, Vost will come to realize the beauty and desirability of women's sexual anatomy.

First, however, Eva Laubenstein introduces the theories of Dr. Slovotkin, the prison doctor. Slovotkin's obsession with the difference, if any, between the man and the woman seems to echo the object of Vost's own desperate quest. Unlike Slovotkin, though, Vost is less a theorist than a simple man confused about his own sexuality as much as he is by women's. Slovotkin, on the other hand, parodies the contemporary "feminist" man. Obsessed with his theory of androgyny, Slovotkin tries to have sex with every woman in La Violaine. That "he never tired of taking his victims or stating his theories" (*TPA* 157), sounds a little like the radical man at the cocktail party who mouths feminist theories for the sake of getting laid.

Slovotkin has a theory though, and an important one for the overall meaning of this novel. Eva explains it at length:

> Slovotkin proposed, first, that the person is essentially a barren island and that for each of us life's only pleasure is the exploration of other barren islands: in this way being a man or woman

merely enhances the interesting differences of people who are in fact the same. He proposed, secondly, that in the souls of their bones the man and woman are opposites: as extreme as that. Finally he proposed that the man and woman are both the same and opposite. (*TPA* 157)

Slovotkin's opportunistic use of feminism confirms Eva's point that his "dedication to his single question was no more than a ruse to feed his insatiable craving for the bodies of women" (*TPA* 159). Slovotkin insisted, even in the face of death, that his first and third theories were correct. He asserted that, setting aside reproduction, men and women have the same capabilities. Simultaneously, he claimed that men and women are both the same and opposite. He concluded by explaining the impossibility of being the one without knowing the experience of the other.

This substantiates Eva's assertion of the similarity between Slovotkin and Vost. Vost seems to have known Slovotkin's theory, though without the premeditated opportunism of Slovotkin's work. In the women's prison, which is a metaphor for women's experience in contemporary society, Vost has encountered a woman's life: the fear of male sexuality and the tendency to cringe before it. Like many women today, he has been used as a vehicle for sexual satisfaction without having the partner concerned with his satisfaction. He has experienced the submissive role of the woman and has been dominated in the sexual encounters he has had since joining the men in their efforts to squelch the women's riot.

Slovotkin's theory remains only superficial, however, as it becomes obvious that only women are qualified to speak about androgyny or the relative equality of the sexes: they have experienced the servitude of the female at the hands of the male. In taking Slovotkin's theory one step further, Eva points to a crucial truth: "The woman is not naturally a martyr; the man is not naturally a beast" (*TPA* 160). This important addition to Slovotkin's theory highlights Eva's disagreement with the radical feminists' belief that men represent the enemy: naturally evil, inherently aggressive, and prone to violence against women. Eva maintains that women are no more naturally passive and gentle than men are naturally brutal; Vost demonstrates this insight throughout his entire experience at the women's prison.

As if remembering an important addition to any theory of sexual politics, Eva reminds Hania that only the childless woman retains her youth. Echoing her previous assertion that for women "the family is the first prison . . . [and] that the woman is not a mother until she leaves her child" (*TPA* 129), Eva stresses the importance for women not to become mothers, or at least not to remain mothers. Motherhood as a woman's sole occupation destroys women's individuality and self-worth.

The culmination of Vost's sexual awakening occurs with Hania while he is a prisoner at La Violaine. As Hania undresses, Vost finds himself confronted once again with the issue of the difference or similarity between men and women. He sees in Hania "the presence of the hidden thighs that were as large as a man's and yet of the soft line belonging only to a woman" (*TPA* 178). Parts of Hania's body, like many women's, resemble a man's just as many men resemble women. Here, as elsewhere in the novel, Hawkes seems to be pointing out the problematics of biology as destiny especially when that argument suggests that women are not physically capable of doing the same things men do.

Vost continues en route to his liberation. He has not arrived there yet. Upon seeing Hania naked he ponders:

> why was it that when a man of his age saw for the first time hair and light glistening between a woman's legs he felt both agitation and absurdity? And yet was he even now beginning to learn that what he had thought of as the lust of his middle age was in fact the clearest reflection of the generosity implicit in the nudity of the tall woman? (*TPA* 178)

Vost's middle-age crisis, or his insecurity as a man, is eclipsed by Hania's appeal as a caring, giving woman; these qualities make her attractive to him. He falls in love with Hania and, though this love has very little hope for the future, he begins to feel comfortable with his feelings. A significant moment in Vost's awakening emerges when he realizes his ability to feel comfortable with himself, to trust his emotions, and to be able to love someone.

Vost is a man in the social, cultural, and political sense of that identity. Unlike the women surrounding him in the prison, he has never learned certain things about himself as a sexual being nor, like so many men, has he learned how to express his emotions. He does not know how to sing and in particular he does not know the language of song, the discourse of celebration. And, Vost does not know how to dance. He is appalled to realize that even though he had been both a husband and a father he had never learned to dance. His male armor has not allowed him to relax and feel comfortable with himself. Like many men, Vost's sexual repression makes him afraid of his body, of his emotions, and of his feelings. Hawkes seems to suggest that while society may very well be patriarchal, men, too, are excluded from the discourse that supposedly belongs to them alone. They have to struggle against all the armor society has foisted upon them in the process of making them men. In order to do that men need to scrutinize male discourse in the same way feminists today seek a new language.

Vost's experience with Hania moves him closer to his liberation. While making love to him, Hania tells Vost to watch her as she performs fellatio on him. She points out that "passionate sensation depends on sight" (*TPA* 179). Hania confronts another stereotypical distinction between men and women: for men sexual experience is thought to be a more visible encounter than it is for women. Hania maintains, however, that the visual experience enhances sexual pleasure for both men and women.

Vost is amazed that even while continuing to take his penis in her mouth, Hania does not change her facial expression in the slightest. His confusion is exacerbated by his feelings of arousal. Vost has not recovered completely from his distress over his body and his fear of being repulsive to a woman. He still harbors feelings of doubt and apprehension about his sexuality and his attractiveness. Though on his way to a quasi-liberation he still has not arrived. Overcoming the socialization of manhood in this society necessitates a long, difficult struggle. Hawkes does not pretend that it is easy. Eventually, though, Vost becomes more comfortable with himself and his passions. As Hania takes his penis in her mouth his penis has become "that part of his anatomy that he could no longer deny" (*TPA* 180). Finally, Vost accepts his sexuality. An important moment for his awakening, this newly found ability to acknowledge his passion moves Vost much closer to at least a semblance of sexual liberation.

Hania provides Vost with additional knowledge about the difference between men and women as sexual beings. She tells him that "'In no other way . . . can a woman so reveal her eroticism as by an act of the will. . . . As for you,' she said, 'the force of amorous passion is respect. You are now aware of your own respect and mine'" (*TPA* 180). This respect is crucial for Vost, for throughout his life self-respect has been something he lacked. His love for Hania and his appreciation of himself and his body have allowed him to respect someone else as well as himself. When Hania asks Vost to perform cunnilingus on her, he discovered that her dilation was such that

> the exterior of her body could no longer be distinguished from its interior; when she encouraged him to discover that the discolorations of the blown rose are not confined to the hidden flesh of youth, it was then that in the midst of his gasping he realized that the distinction between the girl who is still a child and the woman who is more than mature lies only in the instinct of the one and the depth of consciousness of the other. (*TPA* 180-81)

These important insights help him discover not the "small face beaten unrecognizable" nor the "nostril of a dead bird" but a woman's sexuality: not just one isolated part, one organ, but rather a component of a much larger form, a part of a whole all intricately and intimately connected. Vost realizes that the difference between the young schoolgirl he was seduced by earlier in his life and the woman he has in front of him has nothing to do with physiology or age, but rather with experience. Hania's "depth of consciousness" makes her a desirable and satisfying woman.

As the night draws to a close, Vost finds himself "in the arms of the tall handsome woman who had loved him

and seduced him as well" (*TPA* 184-85). The possibility that a woman, and in this case maybe a wife, would be able to love and seduce someone at the same time provides a telling conclusion to the relationship between Vost and Hania. None of Vost's previous experiences with women had demonstrated both of these possibilities simultaneously. Most of the women he had encountered were interested primarily in seducing him. There was certainly not much love exchanged. Claire, Vost's wife, seemed capable of love toward Vost but not seduction. Hania emerges as all these women and more as she becomes the woman capable of both seduction and love. For Hania, women have vital, aggressive sexual needs upon which they are quite capable of acting.

Male sexuality, on the other hand, remains confused and uncertain. Though Vost has made progress toward sexual liberation he can share this accomplishment with very few men. His continued existence is problematic in a sexually oppressive society. As he leaves the prison early the next morning his old friend, Gagnon, shoots him down. As he dies, Vost knows "that the hole torn in his abdomen by Gagnon's shot was precisely the same as would have been opened in his flesh by the dog in the marsh" (*TPA* 184). Men's omnipotence, coupled with a fear of their sexuality and a hatred of "the woman within" (Hoch 68)[4] manifests itself in domination and control. Gagnon's response represents the pathetic desperation of threatened male power.

Vost dies because the liberated man in contemporary society is a contradiction in terms. In the first place, there cannot be a fully, completely liberated man (or woman, for that matter). In the second place, as one moves closer to becoming a liberated man, he moves further away from being socially acceptable as a man. The liberated man, like the gay man, both of whom have had the female experience of male power, cannot be countenanced in a homophobic and sexist society that fears and hates female sexuality, especially when embodied in a man.

NOTES

[1] All quotations from the novel in the text of the paper are cited parenthetically in the text as *TPA*.

[2] Andrea Dworkin highlights this position when she maintains, for example, that "the major theme of pornography as a genre is male power, its nature, its magnitude, its use, its meaning" (24). Later in this same book, Dworkin states that "male sexual aggression is the unifying thematic and behavioral reality of male sexuality" (57). Susan Griffin points out that "the world of pornography is a world of male gesture and male language and a male ethos" (52). This kind of reductionism posits a male essence and a male nature which are as damaging and reductionist as many reactionary ideas about women; for example, that biology is destiny.

3 Contemporary American feminism has spent much time examining the history of women as victims of the medical profession. For example, see Ehrenreich and English, and Drefus.

4 For a more extensive examination of "the feminine other within the male unconscious" and how it informs current literature on men and masculinity, see Murphy.

The author wishes to thank Anne Bertholf, Michael Boughn, Diane Christian, Paul Hogan, Bruce Jackson, Neil Schmitz, and Carole Southwood for their critical contributions to this essay.

WORKS CITED

Brownmiller, Susan. *Against Our Will: Men, Women and Rape.* New York: Bantam, 1975.

de Beauvoir, Simone. *The Second Sex.* New York: Vintage, 1974.

Drefus, Claudia. *Seizing Our Bodies: The Politics of Women's Health.* New York: Vintage, 1977.

Dworkin, Andrea. *Pornography: Men Possessing Women.* New York: Putnam's, 1979.

Ehrenreich, Barbara, and Deirdre English. *For Her Own Good: 150 Years of the Experts' Advice to Women.* New York: Doubleday, 1979.

Fielding, Andrew. "John Hawkes Is a Very Nice Guy and a Novelist of Sex and Death." *Village Voice* 24 May 1976: 45-47.

Firestone, Shulamith. *The Dialectic of Sex: The Case for Feminist Revolution.* New York: Bantam, 1970.

Greiner, Donald. *Understanding John Hawkes.* Columbia, SC: U of South Carolina Press, 1985.

Griffin, Susan. *Pornography and Silence: Culture's Revenge against Nature.* New York: Harper, 1981.

Hawkes, John. *The Blood Oranges.* New York: New Directions, 1970.

———. *Death, Sleep and the Traveler.* New York: New Directions, 1974.

———. *The Passion Artist.* New York: Harper, 1978.

———. *Travesty.* New York: New Directions, 1976.

———. *Virginie: Her Two Lives.* New York: Harper, 1981.

Hoch, Paul. *White Hero, Black Beast: Racism, Sexism and the Mask of Masculinity.* London: Pluto, 1979.

LeClair, Thomas. "The Novelists: John Hawkes." *New Republic* 10 Nov. 1979: 26-29.

Murphy, Peter F. "Toward a Feminist Masculinity: A Review Essay." *Feminist Studies* 15.2 (1989): 351-61.

O'Donnell, Patrick. "Life and Art: An Interview with John Hawkes." *Review of Contemporary Fiction* 3.3 (1983): 107-26.

Sidran, Maxine. "The Hating Game: Men's Response to Women's Independence: Don't Get Even, Get Mad." *Quest* Oct. 1981: 16-23.

Willis, Ellen. "Feminism, Moralism, and Pornography." *Beginning to See the Light: Pieces of a Decade.* New York: Knopf, 1981. 219-27.

Woolf, Virginia. *Orlando.* New York: Harcourt, 1928.

James Ellis

SOURCE: "Sherwood Anderson's Fear of Sexuality: Horses, Men, and Homosexuality," in *Studies in Short Fiction*, Vol. 30, No. 4, Fall, 1993, pp. 595-601.

[*In the following essay, Ellis discusses the theme of spiritualized relationships debased by "the intrusions of the brutishly sexual" in Sherwood Anderson's stories "The Man Who Became a Woman" and "I Want to Know Why."*]

In discussing Sherwood Anderson's treatment of sexuality, Ray White argues that it is Anderson's short stories, not his novels, that deserve high praise for helping to bring the "honest use of sex into American literature" (40). But to say "honest" is not necessarily to say "forthright," for Anderson sensed a mystery in human sexuality that defies an easy reduction.

Two of Anderson's most complex stories—"The Man Who Became a Woman" and "I Want to Know Why"—treat this mystery with great subtlety. Of the two, "The Man Who Became a Woman" is usually considered the superior and more challenging story, but it seems to me that, properly understood, "I Want to Know Why" is an equally challenging and complex presentation of human sexuality.

Kim Townsend's recent biography of Anderson illuminates Anderson's own confusions regarding this matter. Townsend notes the influence of Emma Anderson, Sherwood's mother, on the development of Anderson's sexuality. Anderson "would always think of her as Woman, a figure who inspired him to do good, to write. If he could not approach her when she was alive, he would approach her through his works" (Townsend 13). Anderson said of his mother, "[I] was in love with her all [my] life" (13). Yet while Anderson felt this feminine, softer, asexual impulse toward his mother as

Woman, he also felt what for him was masculine and brutish desire to exploit women sexually.

Townsend cites two occasions, one when Anderson was brought by a more experienced boy to watch through a window a girl "undress and warm herself in front of the stove before going to bed" (21). Anderson watched, and then, confused by the conflict between the beauty of the girl's body and his own sexual desires, he struck the boy and knocked him to the ground. The second occasion occurred years later when Anderson was visiting an operating room to observe an appendectomy on a young girl. Confronted with her nude body lying before him, he said he "wanted to grab the surgeon's arm . . . [and tell him], 'Don't. It's too beautiful. Don't cut it.' But he fled from the room instead" (Townsend 22). He later said that it seemed as if a voice, much like his mother's, said to him in regard to women, "Men are such brutish beings. Don't you be one of them" (23).

This conflict—the feeling that to admire a woman as beautiful seemed inevitably to invite the debasement of that beauty by man's sexual desires—turned Anderson to male friendships as an outlet for his need for spiritual communication. Anderson would have liked to think that this outlet precluded the possibility of sexuality. He tells the story of his first boyhood friend, Jim Moore, with whom he would go into the woods, "undress, play in the creek, and run naked among the trees" (19). On one occasion, however, when they were discovered by a man, they hid in the bushes, forced to lie with their bodies close together to avoid detection. Anderson said later that after the man passed they felt strange and put their clothes on and immediately turned their conversation to a boy they knew who had taken a girl into a barn and had sex with her. Both Anderson and Jim Moore instinctively felt that their awakened physical sensations had to be shifted from themselves—where it was unthinkable—to the "more natural" outlet of a boy with a girl, a man with a woman. They continued to discuss heterosexual love—more, Anderson said, than they really wanted to—all the time feeling increasingly uncomfortable in doing so, but both driven to do so because of the feeling that they must deny any possibility of homosexual attraction. They thus had to make women bear the burden of physical sexuality and thereby maintain in the purely masculine relationship a communication that would not be sullied by sexuality. It was as though with men, Anderson hoped, man could maintain a spiritual relationship that he desired with his mother and with Woman in the abstract.

Years later, when Anderson was almost 60, he returned to this need for male friendship, writing Theodore Dreiser that American artists and writers need to build up "a relationship between man and man" (Townsend 304). Writing later in that year to his friend Roger Sergel, Anderson said what he "'really wanted . . . [was] something like [a] tenderness that dares to go on and on.' What he did not mean, 'as is the case of man with woman,' was 'the going to the flesh.' . . . What he

wanted to do was block men's retreat to women and to sex" (306).

For Anderson this "male comradeship would prevent a man from using women [sexually]" and would therefore preserve a purity of human relationships that seemed impossible between man and woman. Male friendship, then, in Anderson's words, would "stand like a wall between man and a tendency to sell himself out and in doing so to sell out others" (Townsend 307).

Kim Townsend argues persuasively that what Anderson was asking for was a true "men's friendship—not male bonding, nor homosexual relations, . . . but friendship . . ." (306). But I would argue that while Anderson did indeed hope to find in male friendship an asexual communication of spirit, some of his best fiction dramatizes his own understanding that sexuality pervades not only the "natural" world of heterosexuality but also stands mysteriously implicit as a threat to the human spirit in male relationships. Anderson successfully portrayed this conflict in two of his most powerful and artistically satisfying stories—"I Want to Know Why" and "The Man Who Became a Woman."

In "The Man Who Became a Woman" Herman Dudley is a young, unmarried man of 19 working as a groom in Pennsylvania. He is befriended by a young man, also a groom and unmarried, named Tom Means whose ambition it is "to write the way a well-bred horse runs or trots or paces" (60)—in other words, to achieve the utmost purity of art in his writing. Tom becomes Herman's mentor in regard to both horses and spiritual aspiration, telling him that "[t]here isn't any man or woman, not even a fellow's mother, as fine as a horse, that is to say a thoroughbred horse" (60).

Tom Means and Herman Dudley, appropriately, are grooms not for stallions—symbols of the sexual triumph of the masculine flesh—but for geldings, like themselves, innocents before the world of male sexuality. Herman says that Tom's talks "started something inside you that went on and on, and your mind played with it like walking about in a strange town and seeing the sights, and you slipped off to sleep and had splendid dreams and woke up in the morning feeling fine" (66). For some time Tom's talks satisfy Herman's desire for spiritual fulfillment. But when Tom Means leaves for another track, Herman is left adrift.

For a while Herman Dudley clings to his remembrance of Tom Means, sublimating his relationship with him through his gelding Pick-it-boy as he walks him after a race. As he walks Pick-it-boy, Herman realizes that his relationship with the gelding brings out his own desire "to be big and grand and important maybe and won't let us just be" (67-68). The difference between the man and the horse, he understands, is that the horse will be just himself, whereas man if he triumphs as does the horse will inevitably become "proud" or "mean." For this reason the boy respects the horse and his natural purity, saying, again in sexually charged language,

> I got inside him in some way I can't explain and he got inside me. Often we would stop walking for no cause and he would put his nose up against my face.

> I wished he was a girl sometimes or that I was a girl and he was a man. It's an odd thing to say but it's a fact. Being with him that way, so long, and in such a quiet way, cured something in me a little. Often after an evening like that I slept all night and did not have the kind of dreams I've spoken about. (68)

But Herman's relation with Pick-it-boy cannot finally assuage an onslaught of sexual dreams that threaten his innocence. "[A]t night [he] kept seeing women's bodies and women's lips and things in [his] dreams and woke up in the morning feeling like the old Harry" (66).

Determined to lose his virginity and satisfy these sexual desires, Herman decides to go into town and to find himself a woman. The dream that propels him toward this satisfaction of the physical is not of the reality he knows he will find—"some cheap woman" (69)—but "a woman as [he] thought then [he] should never find in the world. She was slender and like a flower and with something in her like a race horse too, something in her like Pick-it-boy in the stretch . . ." (69).

Walking into town he finds a saloon, marked (unlike the cleanliness of the race horse and the bachelor) by the rotten stench of men who never bathe or wash their clothes. Standing at the bar he is suddenly surprised to find that his face reflected in the mirror is now the face of a woman, a girl's face, young and scared. His initial fear is that the miners in the saloon will "get on to [him]" (72) and that there will be trouble. Later after the strong red-haired man has beaten a miner for laughing at him, Herman returns to his bed in the loft above the stables and falls asleep naked. He is discovered by two black men who, "half liquored up" (80), mistake his white and slender body for a young girl's and prepare to sexually assault him. At this point Herman realizes that

> all [his] life, . . . never having had any sisters . . . [or] a sweetheart . . . [he] had been dreaming and thinking about women . . . and [that he had] always been dreaming about a pure innocent one, for [him]self, made for [him] by God. . . .

> So [he] had invented a kind of princess, with black hair and a slender willowy body to dream about. . . .

> [And now with the two black men preparing to attack him, he realizes that he has become] that woman, or something like her, [him]self. (81)

Fleeing in terror, Herman escapes and runs along the race track and across a field to the old slaughterhouse, which he identifies in the dark by its terrible lingering smell, and there he trips and falls into the skeleton of a horse. The slaughterhouse is the end of all dreams of the purity of the flesh, for as Herman tells us, even horses like Pick-it-boy and the stallion O My Man, alive so beautiful and spiritual in their flesh, are in death sold for a dollar or two and skinned for their hides, leaving their skeletons to bleach upon the field.

The result of his fall into death is that Herman experiences a sensation "like the finger of God running down [his] back and burning [him] clean . . ." (84). And, he adds, "It burned all that silly nonsense about being a girl right out of me" (84). He returns to the stable, retrieves his clothes, gives Pick-it-boy "a good-bye kiss on the cheek" (85) and lights out, leaving forever behind him the world of "the race-horse and the tramp life . . ." (85). Subsequently Herman will marry—as will Tom Means—and settle, it would seem, for a joy perhaps not so spiritually satisfying as the world of males and race horses but for a happiness more secure and realizable.

The meaning of the story, however, is not so much the happy conclusion that Anderson draws—sending Herman Dudley to a wife with all his "silly nonsense about being a girl" burned right out of him—but rather his complex rendering of the boy's desire for that spiritual fulfillment that at one time he had glimpsed in the world of horses and men but that he had also come to realize was to be intruded upon by a violent, physical sexuality.

Early in the story Herman had spoken to this spiritual quest that he had sought in Tom Means and Pick-it-boy and his love of himself in the form of a slender willowy princess, and he had defended the purity of the quest and the possibility of its attainment. He had said:

> To tell the truth, I suppose I got to love Tom Means who was five years older than me, although I wouldn't have dared say so then. Americans are shy and timid about saying things like that and a man here don't dare own up he loves another man, I've found out, and they are afraid to admit such feelings to themselves even. I guess they're afraid it may be taken to mean something it don't need to at all. (60)

Yet, as Herman later discovers, when he becomes physically the girl of his dreams, the result is not spiritual communication but rather an invitation to sexual assault. So it would seem that as much as Anderson sought in man an outlet for love without the sexual, he was aware that the sexual could and would erupt in relationships, whether it be in male-female or male-male relationships.

Anderson's earlier "I Want to Know Why" is a further and in some ways more subtle treatment of the same problem. The story turns on the experience of a young Kentucky boy who has run away from home to follow the races at Saratoga. There he meets a trainer from his home named Jerry Tillford, who has prepared the stallion Sunstreak for the big race, the Mullford Handicap. Sunstreak's only possible competition in the race is the gelding Middlestride. But on the day of the race, when the horses are being saddled, the boy and Jerry Tillford look into each other's eyes and they both know that Sunstreak will win the race.

The boy, however, has great respect for both horses. As an innocent and an adolescent just turned 15, he himself is to be identified with the gelding Middlestride, but also at his age he is on the verge of manhood and therefore ready for sexual initiation and identification with the stallion Sunstreak. The race is run and Sunstreak wins as the boy and Jerry Tillford had foreseen. That night the boy walks outside of town and finds himself at "a little rummy-looking farmhouse set in a yard" (11). Suddenly Jerry Tillford and other men associated with horse racing drive up. All are drunk and all go into the farmhouse brothel with the exception of Henry Rieback's father, the gambler, whose form of corruption is money rather than the flesh.

It is this brothel scene that gives rise to the title of the story, for the boy will discover here the dual nature of the adult: his ability to serve the spiritual by training the thoroughbred and thereby raising the horse's flesh to its animal perfection, but also his seemingly concomitant desire, not just for physical, reproductive sex, but for the sexual as either the erotic or the lubricious.

This brothel scene deserves close examination, but it must be examined in light of the earlier paddocks scene in which the boy and Jerry Tillford had looked at each other and had known Sunstreak would win. In this scene the boy describes the stallion in both spiritual and physical terms. First he describes the horse as "like a girl you think about sometimes but never see" (10). In this context Sunstreak represents the embodiment of the perfection of the flesh, which can be arrived at in the animal world of the horse because the powerful sexuality of the horse is natural and therefore does not detract from its amoral being. The idealized girl, if she were to be realized in the flesh, would evoke a sexuality in man that would debase and destroy the beauty she achieves in his ideal world of thought.

But the boy goes beyond describing Sunstreak in terms of the feminine ideal. He also describes the horse in terms of its masculine power and in terms that are to be taken literally but that surely also are very suggestive of physical, homosexual attraction and lovemaking. The boy says of Sunstreak, "He is hard all over and lovely too. When you look at his head you want to kiss him" (10). Here it is very difficult, I think, not to see the boy's description of the horse as suggestive of fellatio. At the moment that the boy and Jerry Tillford look into each other's eyes, the boy says, "Something happened to me. I guess I loved the man as much as I did the horse . . ." (10-11). He then adds of his feelings for Jerry, "It was the first time I ever felt for a man like that" (11).

In the brothel scene previously mentioned, the boy stands outside the farmhouse and looks through a window. There he sees Jerry Tillford talking to a red-haired, tall prostitute who "looked a little like the gelding Middlestride, but not clean like him" (12). Then two things happen that upset the boy very much: Jerry brags that he "made [Sunstreak], that it was him that won the race and made the record"; then Jerry's eyes "began to shine just as they did when he looked at [the boy] and at Sunstreak in the paddocks," and he kisses the prostitute (12). The boy feels so much anger with Jerry that he says, "I began to hate that man. I wanted to . . . kill him. I never had such a feeling before" (12-13).

The boy's anger is intense, of course, because he sees Jerry as having betrayed the spiritual love that had brought them together in their appreciation of Sunstreak. But I would suggest that there are two further reasons for his great anger and that they speak to Anderson's understanding of the limits of platonic love and the force of sexual and physical love. First, if the boy is still to be identified as an innocent with the male gelding Middlestride, we are justified, I think, in recognizing that on the psychological level he is jealous of his female counterpart, the prostitute who "looked a little like the gelding Middlestride, but not clean like him" (12) and that he feels dispossessed in the affections of Jerry Tillford.

Second, while he feels this jealousy, he is further angered to the point that he could kill Jerry Tillford, because in Jerry's physical and sexual advances upon the prostitute, he is also—in the sense that the boy is also to be identified with Middlestride, a clean Middlestride—forcing the repugnant demands of physical sexuality upon the boy and his desire for a spiritual relationship. Jerry Tillford's actions, therefore, signal to the boy that gelding (innocent) though the boy may be, and spiritual as his and Jerry's relationship may have been (as represented in their shared appreciation of Sunstreak), the nature of the adult male is always to debase that spiritual relationship by the intrusion of the brutishly sexual. For this reason the boy is outraged and demands to know why such a thing can be.

WORKS CITED

Anderson, Sherwood. "I Want to Know Why." Geismer 5-13.

————. "The Man Who Became a Woman." Geismer 58-85.

Geismer, Maxwell, ed. *Sherwood Anderson: Short Stories.* Clinton, MA: Hill and Wang, 1962.

Townsend, Kim. *Sherwood Anderson.* Boston: Houghton, 1987.

White, Ray Lewis. "The Warmth of Desire: Sex in Anderson's Novels." *Sherwood Anderson: Dimensions of His Literary Art.* Ed. David D. Anderson. Lansing: Michigan State UP, 1976. 24-40.

Patricia Juliana Smith

SOURCE: "All You Need is Love: Angela Carter's Novel of Sixties Sex and Sensibility," in *The Review of Contemporary Fiction,* Vol. 14, No. 3, Fall, 1994, pp. 24-29.

[*In the following essay, Smith describes Angela Carter's novel* Love *as a "postmodern pastiche" of the eighteenth-century novel of sensibility.*]

In her afterword to the revised 1987 edition of *Love,* Angela Carter reveals the obscure source of inspiration for her narrative of sixties sexual misadventure: "I first got the idea for *Love,* from Benjamin Constant's . . . novel of sensibility, *Adolphe;* I was seized with the desire to write a kind of modern-day, demotic version . . . although I doubt anybody could spot the resemblance."[1] If this connection had eluded Carter's audience, surely it is understandable. A phenomenon of the late eighteenth and early nineteenth centuries, the novel of sensibility had long fallen from vogue and reappeared, revenant-like, only in its latter-day guise of popular romance. Yet, as Lorna Sage has so adroitly observed, one of the hallmarks of Angela Carter's craft is the "grotesque, and yet . . . recognisable (borrowed, parodied) range of her symbolism [with which] she seems bent on a general stocktaking, from the earliest innocent cons to their latest camp revivals."[2] In this particular borrowing Carter effectively scrutinizes the moral ambivalences of sensibility, particularly the sinister motivations lurking behind the external display of emotionality constructed as a sign of heightened sensitivity and refined benevolence. Simultaneously, she mercilessly illustrates the similarities between the excesses of the period that gave rise to Romanticism and those of the period that gave us the sexual revolution. Through the medium of the ménage à trois comprised of Lee, Annabel, and Buzz, she takes stock of our cherished and reviled conventional gender roles and to what extent they have, while changing drastically, nonetheless stubbornly remained the same.

In a retrospective assessment of the cultural and social significance of the sixties, Carter speculated that "manners had not been so liberal and expressive since the Regency—or maybe even since the Restoration, with the absence of syphilis compensated for in the mortality stakes by the arrival of hard drugs."[3] Indeed, the sex and drugs that seem synonymous with sixties culture were simply elements of a greater phenomenon, the youth culture's valorization of total freedom (or, more precisely, license), of boundless physical and mental sensation, and of a Rousseauistic "natural" goodness unrelated to traditional social mores (or, as a number of popular songs of the era put it, being "really real"). Likewise, if less demotically, the eighteenth-century cult

of sensibility prized emotional susceptibility, heightened sensitivity, and a tremendous capacity for suffering, all regarded as the outward signs of a highly refined moral character. The novel of sensibility, as Janet Todd explains, was originally a didactic mode that "showed people how to behave, how to express themselves in friendship and how to respond decently to life's experiences," but it soon devolved into a popular form that "prided itself more on making its readers weep and in teaching them when and how much to weep."[4] Yet Carter, incorporating this mode into a postmodern pastiche, inverts this paradigm. *Love* is more likely to invoke fear and revulsion than tears and sympathy—and is, in its fatal consequences, a study in how *not* to deport oneself.

In the traditional novel of sensibility the characteristic signs of the privileged trait were most often embodied in female protagonists who were prone to weeping, fainting, and madness while being perpetually subject to threats of seduction and bodily harm. This historical model finds its postmodern reincarnation in the "mad girl" Annabel, a young woman so lost in a dream world that "even the women's movement would have been no help to her and alternative psychiatry would have only made things, if possible, worse" (113). The setting in which Annabel, in the throes of hysteria, first appears is directly analogous to the origins of the novel of sensibility and its literary first cousin, the Gothic novel: the collision between the orderly, cool rationality of Augustan neoclassicism and the pleasurable terrors of the imagination lurking at the heart of Romanticism. The park, which, "In the system of correspondences by which she interpreted the world around her . . . had a special significance" (1), constitutes the remains of a ruined eighteenth-century manor. All that remains of the once stately home is, on the south side, "a stable built on the lines of a miniature Parthenon, housing for Houyhnhnms rather than natural horses" replete with "pillared portico," and, on the north, "an ivy-covered tower with leaded ogive windows skulk[ing] among the trees," fronted by "a massive pair of wrought-iron gates decorated with cherubs, masks of beasts, stylized reptiles and spearheads" (1,2). Annabel, a creature of sensibility "suffer[ing] from nightmares too terrible to reveal," quite naturally prefers the latter Gothic setting, "for serenity bored her" (3,2).

The opening sentences of the novel reveal the depth of Annabel's sensibility, one apparently so refined that the sources of her torments would seem to be far from mundane ones: "One day, Annabel saw the sun and moon in the sky at the same time. The sight filled her with a terror which entirely consumed her and did not leave her until the night closed in catastrophe for she had no instinct for self-preservation if she was confronted by ambiguities" (1). Ambiguities, however, inform the very essence of Carter's fictions. While Annabel externally exemplifies the "feminine" traits of physical and mental frailty and passive victimage peculiar to the Gothic heroine, her interactions with her husband and brother-in-law betray her passive-aggressive sadism. The most extreme manifestation of her assumption of a quasi-masculine role is her "branding" of Lee, her wayward husband. To punish him, she forces him to submit to a tattoo of her own design, "her name indelibly in Gothic script . . . circle[d] . . . with a heart" (69) that becomes a living emblem of his subjugation. Moreover, in attempting to reduce both Lee and his brother Buzz to denizens of a realm that exists in her own fevered imagination, a realm that would exceed the combined nightmares of Emily Brontë and Edgar Allan Poe, Annabel indulges in a virtuoso display of will to power and engages the two men in a duel to the death—ironically, her own. Before reaching this end, however, she enjoys a brief tenure as the phallic mother to this sibling pair, who have been, all along, her rivals for the distinction of having the acutely tortured sensibility.[5]

After all, sensibility has never been the exclusive property of imperiled heroines. This trait has also manifested itself in certain "problematic" male characters whose feelings, Todd informs us, "are too exquisite for the acquisitiveness, vulgarity and selfishness of the world," and who "avoided manly power and assumed the womanly qualities of tenderness and susceptibility but . . . [could not] be raped and abandoned."[6] These descriptions would seem to apply to Lee Collins, the blond, blue-eyed, university-educated, correctly leftist, and sadomasochistic "very nice young working-class boy" around whom *Love* revolves.[7] His dazzling smile and frequent tears, disarming outward signs of a "feminine side," are perceived by women as evidence of his sensitivity, compassion, and travail. Like his literary antecedents, this man of feeling presents himself as an exemplar of benevolence, a rescuer of the wretched of the earth, roles no doubt the legacy of his two most significant female influences: the socialist aunt who raised him and the mother who, "in his sixth year, . . . naked and painted all over with cabbalistic signs, burst into the crowded play-ground and fell writhing and weeping on the asphalt before him" (10). Indeed, the death of his aunt and the memory of his mother predicate, both textually and psychologically, his "rescue" of Annabel, whom he discovers in a state of profound and nearly aphasic abjection at the typical sixties party scene of sex, drugs, and rock and roll.

If Lee were seeking, unconsciously or otherwise, a surrogate for his absent mother, he could not have chosen a better replacement than Annabel. What Annabel expected in a husband, however, is as unclear as her chronic mental state. From her drawings of Lee as a lion or a unicorn, we can infer a desire for a fairy-tale figure—which the man of feeling, featured as he is in popular romance, may well be. Yet if her expectation is that he simultaneously be the protector who defends her from the world outside her fantasies and a subject forever in her thrall, she must inevitably be disappointed, for the benevolent hero of sensibility is ultimately as narcissistic and hysterical as his female counterpart. That this should be the case, Carter suggests, is hardly surprising; it is the product of our social conditioning:

Women tend to be raised with a monolithic notion of "maleness," just as men are raised with the idea of a single and undifferentiated femininity. Stereotyping. *Real* men, especially when approached by women acting in ways they're not supposed to act, can behave like fifteen-year-old girls in the photostory magazines. This can come as a shock. ("Truly" 214)

As the novelty of Annabel's "strangeness" wears thin, Lee, weary of her sexual unresponsiveness and manifold needs, seeks affirmation of his beauty and benevolence from other female sources. Not surprisingly, more than a few succumb to his smile and his tears, ready to assuage his wounded, exquisite feelings. When they discover they have merely provided sexual diversion, they too are disappointed and shocked.

To punish Lee's crass and public display of infidelity, Annabel slashes her wrists and, as a result, enjoys an extended stay in the National Health Service psychiatric hospital. Lee, in order to expiate, offers himself as her sacrificial victim, abjectly submitting to her whims, particularly the pernicious tattoo, upon her release. Thus the two paragons of emotionality, now both physically as well as mentally scarred by their travails, embark upon a domestic war of abasement and self-abasement climaxing in the ritualistic enactment of "a mutual rape" (97). Although, as Todd suggests, the eighteenth-century man of sensibility was immune from the threat of rape or abandonment, it would appear that this exception no longer applies to his postmodern descendent. Women can also act in a manner inconsistent with societal gender expectations. This too "can come as a shock."

But *Love* is not merely an allegorical narrative of the traditional battle of the sexes along male-female lines. Lest anyone attempt to imagine otherwise, Carter reminds us that the sexual explosion of the sixties "wasn't just heterosex, either; o, dear, no" ("Truly" 215). In the event that, like Annabel, readers missed the clues to Buzz's homosexuality in the first edition—including his gonorrhea acquired in North Africa (where male prostitution flourished in the days before AIDS and Islamic fundamentalism) and Lee's explanation that "He's always been funny with girls" (98)—Carter makes the matter perfectly clear in the afterword. In the context of the sixties, however, Buzz's exaggeratedly ferocious demeanor, his lack of verbal facility, and his complete lack of Lee's semblance of gentility or civility give him the outward appearance of the hypermasculine sexuality attributed to the Gothic villain. While this simulacrum convinces Annabel that she can coerce Buzz into playing Heathcliff to her Cathy, it is merely the inarticulate repression of a love that dare not speak its name—one that is not only homosexual but incestuous as well. Nevertheless, as a member of what was then deemed "the middle sex," Buzz becomes the sexual third term of mediation between Annabel and Lee. It is hardly an accident that their delayed consummation finally occurs when Lee returns home to find Annabel dressed in the absent Buzz's clothes: "and for a moment he thought his brother was back unexpectedly" (32). That Buzz (or Buzz, as he has become) can announce some twenty years on, "if there is one thing he would like to do before he dies, it is to fuck [Lee]" (117), forces us to reassess the object of his jealous agony, night after night, listening to Lee and Annabel make love, and his obsessive photography of the naked couple in bed. In her solipsism Annabel infers that the sexual tension pervading the household is purely heterosexual—indeed she seems ignorant of any alternative. This blunder proves her undoing, for "It is always a dangerous experiment to act out a fantasy" (95).

Annabel plots a physical union with Buzz, as yet another exquisite torture of Lee, to complete the seeming "psychic" connection she shares with her brother-in-law. "[H]andled as unceremoniously as a fish on a slab, reduced only to anonymous flesh" (94) and sodomized, Annabel finds her power exposed and fraudulent. The phallic mother has no phallus, and, lacking any tangible, physical masculinity, she is found wanting as an object of desire. "They had imagined too often and too much and so they had exhausted all their possibilities" (94), so much so that Annabel, failing in her subsequent attempt at "real" (that is, violently passionate) heterosexuality with Lee, has no remaining possibility, save an elaborate artifice culminating in a very early death.

In the original edition of *Love* Carter left us at this point, with the brothers arguing over blame for Annabel's demise. That Carter chose two decades later to update and revise this particular text surely indicates that the novel of sensibility still retains, in defiance of the logic of its own terms, a didactic function.[8] As the adolescent Jane Austen demonstrated in her parodic "Love and Freindship" (*sic*) two centuries before, sensibility is often nothing more than a facade to disguise a refusal to accept responsibility, a means by which to "check out" and feign ignorance of the cause-and-effect relationships that govern one's environment. Through the "almost sinister feat of male impersonation" (113) from which she demurs in retrospect, Carter creates a telling and painful parody of the mores of her own generation. Lee's easy tears are, in fact, the product of nothing more profound than a chronic eye inflammation exacerbated by the smoke-filled venues he habituates, and his smile, as Annabel discovers, is merely a pose that he (or she) can put on or take off at will. Likewise, Annabel's fit is brought on not so much by the ambiguity of the sun and moon together in the sky but rather by her evasion of the ambiguities of her own problematic relationships with her cheating husband and her inscrutable brother-in-law. In all, Carter's characters approximate, in their self-created emotional fragility, the condition of moral dubiousness characteristic of Austen's self-styled heroines who, "mutually deprived of [their] Senses some minutes" by the "horrid Spectacle" of a coach accident, fail to bring about the rescue of its victims, their husbands.[9]

Lest the Carter-Austen analogy seem too much a stretch, it is simply an indication of the extent to which many of us who came of age during the sixties have become what we swore we would never be. Products of an era of young men and women who thought their own actions and feelings unprecedented, Lee and Annabel are in many ways simply self-deluded relics of a bygone age dressed in a newer fashion. Carter does not deny this: if anything, her update on her characters' fates confirms their conventionality. Lee, the erstwhile sensualist and class-conscious revolutionary, becomes the faithful, home-owning family man who "can hardly bear to think his daughters might meet young men like him" (119). Pete Townsend's motto for the youth culture, "I hope I die before I get old," is illustrated too well in Annabel to retain any of its old appeal. Given this choice, most of the generation of the sixties, who trusted no one over thirty, have themselves edged "nervously up to the middle age they thought could never happen" (113). They have become their parents; they have become the dreaded Establishment to the Generation X, which has become who they used to be. Lee's daughters "discuss in muted whispers their parents' deficiencies as human beings" (120). In this there is a lesson, however unpleasant, for all of us.

This is not to say that everything remains the same. If so, there would be no need to revise the original text. What has changed is women's sense of and access to self-determination, evinced not only by the fates of all the other female characters but also by their creator's determination to reassess the blame. Indeed, the feminist Rosie Collins, Lee's second wife, who makes her first appearance in the epilogue, requires Lee's acknowledgment of his blame in Annabel's death as a condition necessary to the continuation of their marriage. Carter observes that "it takes a lot to make a man admit he has been a bastard, even a man so prone to masochistic self-abnegation as Lee" (119), yet it is apparent that the pragmatic Rosie evokes considerable respect, cooperation, and responsibility from her husband that Annabel never did or could. In Rosie's estimate, "Lee drove his first wife mad and then killed her" (120). While this revisionist view is not altogether accurate, the social and textual changes wrought by two decades make it unavoidably clear that he is far from an innocent victim. Indeed, Carter asks us to consider whether Lee's fate, "the revenge of heterosexuality" (120), is not "almost as much a punishment as a reward" (119). The author has thus required her character to take responsibility for his actions in her earlier creation. In that, too, is a lesson for us all.

NOTES

[1] Angela Carter, *Love,* revised edition (New York: Penguin, 1988), 113; hereafter cited parenthetically.

[2] Lorna Sage, "The Savage Sideshow: A Profile of Angela Carter," *New Review,* June-July 1977, 53.

[3] Carter, "Truly It Felt Like Year One," in *Very Heaven: Looking Back at the 1960s,* ed. Sara Maitland (London: Virago, 1988), 213; hereafter cited parenthetically.

[4] Janet Todd, *Sensibility: An Introduction* (London: Methuen, 1986), 4.

[5] For an exhaustive discussion of the highly problematic Freudian figure of the phallic mother and applications of this concept to twentieth-century cultural modes, see Marcia Ian, *Remembering the Phallic Mother: Psychoanalysis, Modernism, and the Fetish* (Ithaca: Cornell University Press, 1993).

[6] Todd 4, 89.

[7] Carter, quoted in Sage 55.

[8] Lorna Sage discusses Carter's revisions and the deletion of passages "which in the original make Lee Annabel's victim" in *Women in the House of Fiction* (New York: Routledge, 1992), 172-73. Overall, Sage's analysis of *Love,* a novel ignored in much critical discussion of Carter's works, is one of the best to date.

[9] Jane Austen, "Love and Freindship," in *Minor Works,* ed. R. W. Chapman (Oxford: Oxford University Press, 1967), 99.

Elizabeth Patnoe

SOURCE: "Lolita Misrepresented, Lolita Reclaimed: Disclosing the Doubles," in *College Literature,* Vol. 22, No. 2, June, 1995, pp. 81-104.

[In the following essay, Patnoe offers a close reading of Vladimir Nabokov's Lolita *that endeavors to demonstrated how its title character is an adolescent victim of molestation rather than a young seductress.]*

> There is general agreement, among those professionals who work with adult survivors, that the effects of abuse might show themselves in the form of low self-esteem, lack of assertiveness, depression, and problems in sexual and maternal relationships. However, when we look at the research done on the socialization of women, and the norms set for female behavior (in Western culture) we find that many of the behaviors and "traits" that would be seen to characterize "neurotic" women, such as those listed above, would also be used to prescribe sex-role-appropriate behavior in women. (Jones 76)

> Where [the women's movement] is strong, incidence figures rival the shocking U. S. statistic that one in three women before the age of eighteen has been sexually abused; where the women's movement is weak, incidence figures drop, and social concern about it is minimal. (Goldner viii)

CULTURE

"She walked up to me, and she asked me to dance. I ask her her name. In a background voice she said Lola, L-O-L-A, Lola, Lo, Lo, Lo, Lo, Lo—la."

As a ten-year-old, I was intrigued by the Kinks' song about a boy liking a girl and then finding out something. What exactly was it? I didn't know for sure, but I liked its sound, its ability to urge movement at the slightest memory of its lyrics. I continued to love the name "Lola," a word that evoked memories of carefree childhood days—of sneaking squirt bottles on the school bus and dancing in the backyard. But during my first reading of *Lolita,* the name lost its playful allure, stopped making me want to sing along. Now it urges pause as I try to understand the speaker's use of "Lola" or "Lolita." The Kinks' "Lola," while about the doubling of cross-dressing, broaches issues of gender, sexuality, and interpretation, issues that also inform any discussion of *Lolita,* but I am interested in it for its exemplification of the power of intertextuality, of how one text—*Lolita*—can be even retroactively intertextualized with another—"Lola"—such that my pleasure in "Lola" is diminished, my vision of childhood changed, and my understanding of the diffuse doublings fueled by Vladimir Nabokov's *Lolita* clarified.

. . . . .

Nabokov's Lola experiences great pain because of Humbert's treatment of her, which we see in her crying every night after she thinks Humbert is asleep, in the scratches she leaves on Humbert's neck while resisting sex with him, and in her escape from him and the territory of his treatment—much of the United States. It is fitting that Lolita retreats to one of the country's borders, to a remote place where, presumably in part because its isolation precludes sophisticated medical support, she dies in childbirth. But, as if it is not enough that Humbert repeatedly violates Lolita and that she dies in the novel, the world repeatedly reincarnates her—and, in the process, it doubles her by co-opting, fragmenting, and violating her: it kills her again and again.

In 1966, *The Random House Unabridged Dictionary of the English Language* defined "Lolita" as "a girl's given name, form of Charlotte or Delores. Also Loleta." By 1992, *The American Heritage Dictionary of the English Language* offers a very different definition for "Lolita": "A seductive adolescent girl. [After Lolita, the heroine of *Lolita,* a novel by Vladimir Nabokov]." In a recent and exceptionally distorted representation of Lolita, the mythicized Lolita is not based on the novel's character who is abducted and abused, who dies at the end of the book, but a "Lethal Lolita" who attempts to murder her lover's wife. Amy Fisher has been repeatedly referred to as "Lolita"—in commercials for the three television movies about the shooting,[1] in newspapers, in *People*'s cover story, "Lethal Lolita," and even on the national evening news (CBS 12-1-92). In Japan, the term "Lolita complex" is widely used to refer to men's fascination with the sexuality of female youth—and to perpetuate the portrayal of women as ridiculously childlike. Maureen Corrigan of Georgetown University also distorted the Lolita character when, in a National Public Radio editorial, she equated one of Madonna's characters in the book *Sex* with Lolita. There, in another kind of doubling, Madonna poses as a full-breasted little girl in drop-bottom pink baby pajamas, who supposedly wants sex. What Corrigan describes as a Lolita is not the novel's Lolita, the Lolita who tries to call her mother from the inn, who scratches Humbert, who cries every night, and who finally escapes—just as my *Lolita* is not the same *Lolita* that *Vanity Fair* calls "the only convincing love story of our century" (Vintage 1989 cover). In "Time Has Been Kind to the Nymphet: *Lolita* 30 Years Later," Erica Jong says, "She has, in fact, defeated time—her enemy" (47), but time was never Lolita's enemy; it was Humbert's, one he imposed on her. And time's occupants—not time—continue to reincarnate Lolita only to batter her into their own self-validating construction, to be anything but kind to her.

Why didn't the Lolita myth evolve in a way that more accurately reflects Nabokov's Lolita? Why isn't the definition of "Lolita" "a molested adolescent girl" instead of a "seductive" one? The answer seems relatively clear, but its consequences are complex. This misreading is so persistent and pervasive because it is enabled and perpetuated intertextually, extratextually, and intratextually. The text itself promotes misreadings of Lolita because, as Wayne Booth is one of the first to note, Humbert's skillful rhetoric and Nabokov's narrative technique make it difficult to locate both Humbert's unreliability and Nabokov's moral position (389-91). While the text offers evidence to indict Humbert, it is so subtle that many readers overlook its critique of the misogyny illustrated in and purveyed by the rest of the text. Perhaps Nabokov minimized such signals in order to merge the novel's form and characterization with his attempt to illustrate and thematize what happens when an allegedly charming, clearly powerful character wreaks his egocentricity on a weaker one. Whatever Nabokov's rationale for providing such subdued messages in support of Lolita, they are often lost in an atmosphere that interprets and presents her oppositionally, and these antagonistic messages are compounded by a host of cross-cultural, diachronic narratives that precede and succeed *Lolita*, texts that purvey the notion that femaleness, femininity, and female sexuality are desirable, but dangerous—even deadly.[2]

Thus, instead of embracing the muted, violated Lolita, our misogynistic culture created and reified a violating Lolita. It made her as contrary to birthgiving and nurturing as possible: it made her lethal. Linda Kauffman says, "Lolita is as much the object consumed by Humbert as she is the product of her culture. And if she is 'hooked,' he is the one who turns her into a hooker" (160). Similarly, throughout the years Lolita has become the product of our culture beyond the book's pages,

where she has been made a murderess by characters far more powerful than Humbert. And these mythical machineries of evil Lolita narratives perpetuate a misogyny that imposes developmentally abnormal sexuality on some females and simultaneously punishes all females for any sexuality. By imposing this sexual responsibility and fault on females, they deem us unnatural, evil for having any sexuality, and, if we are young, doubly deviant, however developmentally appropriate our sexuality is.[3] Ultimately, all females are caught in a culture that bifurcates them into characters who are or are supposed to be both compassionate and lethal, asexual and hypersexual.

With so many co-opted Lolita myths circulating in our culture, readers come to *Lolita* inundated with a hegemonic reading of evil Lolita and bad female sexuality, an overdetermined reading that then imposes itself upon its own text. The Lolita Story and its discourse have become an ongoing and revealing cultural narrative, a myth appropriated in ways that validate male sexuality and punish female sexuality, letting some people avoid the consequences of their desires as they impose those desires on others. Thus, another source of the misreadings of Lolita is the reader, who is extratextual because he or she is outside the text of *Lolita*, intertextual because he or she lives between the narratives and images that bolster the misreadings of Lolita, and intertextual as he or she, submerged in these larger influences of cultures and intertextuality, brings them to *Lolita* so thoroughly that they become, for that reader, a real part of the *Lolita* text.

This dual existence of one textual Lolita and another, very different, co-opted, mythical Lolita is just one example of the doubling in and around *Lolita*, which results in fragmentations, splits, and violations of what many people experience personally or vicariously, of what many people witness, believe, and know. The cultural systems complicit in the cleaving and appropriation of Lolita also fuel a machinery of doubling that promotes the doubling of readers, students, molestation survivors, female sexuality, and the roles and perception of women in general. While critics have addressed the character doubling of Humbert and Quilty, and while some of their notions are related to the doublings that I explore, my concern is with a whole system of doubling and with the various pegs within it, an expansive doubling associated with both the mythic and the textual Lolitas, with the division and doubling of the public and private selves, the spoken and the silenced, the imagined or perceived or represented and the real—with what is often a destructive, oppressive, institutionally-condoned system of doubling that occurs in *Lolita* and that informs and is informed by it.[4]

Given a cultural context that both distorts and feeds upon Lolita, teachers must contend with the neglected doubling that occurs in these other realms and with how the book reflects on larger cultural pressures and processes. The entrenched misreadings of Lolita, women, and sexual molestation are marked by inter- and extratextual sources that become intratextual. Very personal readings are influenced by sweeping, insidious ideologies. Booth says *Lolita* misreadings "do not come from any inherent condition of the novel or from any natural incompatibility between author and reader. They come from the reader's inability to dissociate himself from a vicious center of consciousness presented to him with all of the seductive self-justification of skilful rhetoric" (390). But *Lolita* readers must also understand what is at the center of a cultural consciousness that encourages misreadings of *Lolita*. Once readers have some sense about how their readings are, at least in part, predetermined, they can confront more intimate sources of misreadings, their own interpretive systems and assumptions. And then, perhaps readers will be more receptive to *Lolita*'s covert, intratextual messages that are frequently overlooked but that are essential to our understanding of the way it functions in our culture. It would seem that the most effective resistance—whether to hegemonic readings or to challenging them—would be met and take place in the "self" realm of the extratextual, in the most personal, private, and sometimes painful realms of readings and of texts. But if we can understand the part of the extratextual realm that influences the personal part of the extratextual, then perhaps we will better access and understand the interplay of our culture, ourselves, and the texts that become our texts.

To this end, I would like to see those of us who have been excluded from the hegemonic readings of *Lolita* resuscitate the character, reclaim the book, and insist upon our experiences with and around it so we can at least begin to counter the Lolita myth distortions, to resist some of the cultural appropriations of female sexuality. For me, this means processing several of my experiences with *Lolita*: as a young listener of "Lola," a nurse for children and teenagers, a student reader of *Lolita*, and with the text itself—particularly, here, with an excerpt from The Enchanted Hunters chapter in which the double-voicing is so complete and so manipulative that it results in a double-drama rarely seen in literature but very much like the double-dramas too often played out in girls' and women's lives: the narration of an event that is countlessly described as "lovemaking" and seduction, but that can only be interpreted as rape.[5]

PEOPLE

The resounding Lolita myths have influenced many responses to *Lolita*. Critics focus on the book's aesthetics and artistry, discuss it as an American travelogue, view Humbert with compassion, as truly contrite, a tragic hero. Though diverse, these readings remain hegemonic, and they do not contend with gender issues, do not attempt to understand why and how the same text can be so pleasurable for some and so traumatic for others. While many of us celebrate the personal nature of literature, criticism has historically denied the subjective. For a long time women's voices in general, but especially women's voices of anger and pain, have not been

sounded or heard. Despite the critical history of reader response and personal criticism, for the most part our discipline still disallows even the slightest hints of personal perceptions and reactions in scholarly work: we are expected to engage intimately with some of the most emotive stories ever told, but we are also expected to squelch certain results of that engagement even as we try to articulate some of the implications of that very same engagement. We have been limited to those discussions and reactions deemed appropriate by the reigning cultural powers. Particularly noticeable in this movement is the critical history of *Lolita*, in which readers and critics almost always embrace what they consider the book's pleasures, almost always skirt its pains—Lolita's pains, as well as the readerly traumas associated with this novel.

Perhaps these issues have not been adequately addressed because readers who do not have such disturbing desires cannot imagine, cannot bear or bare the thought of them in themselves or others, and so deny or minimize such imaginings. One man I know seemed staunchly located in Humbert's narrative audience, defending him, insisting he does not rape Lolita, and calling her an "experienced seductress." I said that, while she had had sex, it was with her peer, which suggests at least the chance for a more developmentally normal, mutually-empowered experience. He said, "If my daughter ever fooled around at that age," and stopped short. I replied, "If your daughter were Lolita, you'd call it rape." He shook his head, exhaled audibly through his nose, and said, "Touché. Now I see what you mean."

Many other men praise the book's artistry, Nabokov's brilliant language. One associate said he loved the book—his favorite—for its artistry.[6] I asked him how he could feel so much pleasure from a book with this content. He said, "It's just a book." But this book is not "just a book" for everyone. For many people it represents some aspect of their reality, what has happened to them or their loved ones—or what they fear might happen. But this man seemed so seduced by the book's form that in every visible way he trivialized Lolita's experience and dismissed the trauma many readers experience with this text.

I witnessed how this book is not "just a book" for some people when, nestled in a booth one afternoon, some women and I began discussing the implications of *Lolita*. Three of us were especially passionate as we discussed its narrative strategy, its characterization, our responses. Our fourth colleague occasionally nodded her head, but remained quiet. About fifteen minutes into our talk, she abruptly rose to go home. The closest of her friends among us walked her to her car and upon her return told us why our colleague had gone: when she was a child, her father woke her, carried her from her bed to the bathroom, made her bend forward over the tub, and raped her. When she cried out, her father stuffed a washcloth in her mouth. With blood dripping down her legs, he forced her to perform fellatio on him.

When she refused to swallow his semen, he squeezed her nostrils shut until she did. When he was finished, he picked her up by the elbows, held her face to the mirror, and said, "Do you know why Daddy did this to you? Because you are such a pretty pussy."

Is this shocking to you? Do you feel that in my writing it and your reading it, this person's trauma has been re-enacted? It has—through her, through and for me, and for you. And I imposed this trauma on you, thrust it into your eyes without your consent. If you feel upset, then perhaps you can imagine how our fourth colleague felt and how others might respond to texts and discussions that catapult them into chasms of deep, secret pains—including discussions less vivid and texts far less shocking than this one.[7]

While a few critics have expressed charged sympathy for Lolita's trauma,[8] most neglect to confront the trauma Humbert inflicts on Lolita, and none contend with the trauma the book inflicts on readers. Indeed, if critics discuss trauma at all (excepting those noted in notes 13, 16, and 17), they focus on Humbert's trauma. Critics range from judging him harshly yet with much compassion,[9] to strongly sympathizing with and even identifying with him,[10] to "rooting" him on, sympathizing and identifying with him to the point of sharing his pleasures—artistic and sexual.[11] Concurrent with this is the critical move that seems to offer frightening pleasure to those who view Lolita with derision.[12] While examinations of the book that focus on more typical questions of theme and structure can enhance our understanding about some parts of this complicated text, as countless critics focus on the book's pleasure and neglect its trauma, they also neglect many of its readers and enable the violator's pleasure, reinforce it, invite it to continue without confrontation. Thus, in addition to particular critical comments that purvey the Lolita myth, the collectivity of *Lolita* criticism in some way becomes complicit in the aesthetization of child molestation perpetrated by individual people and by the culture at large.[13]

And by not contending with readers' or with Lolita's trauma in the classroom, the criticism, or the culture, the trauma is at once both trivialized and intensified for individual readers because they suffer it alone, without forum. People who have been molested have lived what Elsa Jones calls a "double reality": "In my view one of the major negative consequences of being abused as a child lies in the confusion generated for the child between what she knows to be true and what her world acknowledges to be true" (37). Similarly, some readers of this text also live a double reality in the classroom, a place where personal, often disturbing texts are routinely, matter-of-factly, and authoritatively explored, even enforced.

PEDAGOGY

On the way to class, one of my peers told me that as he read he kept saying to himself, "Yes, yes. . . . But, then

I'm a male, so I understand Humbert."[14] The first hour or more of class consisted of discussions much like published ones, about the puns, the time of narration, the time of action, the narrative audience—about everything except what Humbert really does to Lolita. One man read the frotteurism couch scene aloud, without any apparent sense of how the reading may have affected the discussion dynamics. In the second hour, the discussion, quiet and controlled, moved to whether, in the course of his narration, Humbert had come to a true understanding of and repentance for what he had done. Some men said they did not condone Humbert—and then talked at length about how we should have compassion for him, how he really comes to love Lolita, how he rehabilitates and wishes he had left her alone early on. Eventually I asked—with some measure of incredulousness—whether anyone else had had an unmitigated reaction against Humbert.

I appeared to be in the minority. Many of the women in the class remained quiet, including a usually expressive one who later told me she had been molested by her father. One woman had a strong reaction against Humbert, voiced it once, then told me later that she felt silenced by the men—and so silenced herself. Another woman, a writer, focused on Nabokov's use of language. Another argued that understanding Humbert would help us understand and deal with our own desires.[15] After class, some of us talked about feeling judged because others implied that we had insufficient compassion for Humbert, suggested that we violated the text when we could not subjugate our real reader experiences to the "desired" authorial or narrative reader experiences.[16]

Discussing this text seemed to exacerbate the typical classroom dynamic in which the teacher—however much he or she may try to share authority—remains the authority, such that almost independently of what this teacher did or did not do, in this class, what is often assumed to be or represented as the "male" perspective became the dominant perspective. As a result, those students with painful experiences—students who, in vital ways, might have been most able to understand the implications of this book—felt and were disempowered. Sitting there, in humane academia, reading this prolonged account of how a young girl is sexually enslaved for two years, there seemed no room for these responses, these lives. After class, when one of my male associates told me that I cheated the text, that my reaction was "too moral," that it silenced him, then I really wanted to yell.[17] But I stayed implosively silent, feeling embarrassed for saying anything against Humbert, even as I felt angry—with Humbert and with some of the men in class for being unable to permit, accept, even tolerate our responses, responses that I considered rational and reasonable in content and articulation. And yet, if, as Goldner reports, "one in three women before the age of eighteen has been sexually abused" (viii), can texts like *Lolita* be taught without exacerbating the trauma of relatively large numbers of mostly female students? Without dealing with what often becomes another silencing, disempowering presence in a host of discourses?

This class resounded with student splitting, as students responded to the text one way outside the room and another way within it, one way within ourselves and another way without. I am certain that some students split as they felt and denied or hid their trauma. Other discussants might have doubled as they felt and denied their pleasure, as they made public declarations against Humbert's behavior while growing privately pleased by it. And, while I am working from a generally female perspective in my attempt to contend with larger issues of pedagogically- and textually-induced trauma, I want to know more about how *Lolita* and other texts produce and exacerbate male trauma. Might some male readers of *Lolita* feel bullied? Misrepresented? Wronged? Might some be distressed by other men's arousal? By their own arousal? Might some fear that all women will think that all men want to violate girls? Might they fear for the women and girls about whom they care? Fear that their reactions might betray their peers who argue relentlessly on Humbert's behalf? And how might men who have been sexually abused feel, men who often have no forum in which to process their experiences, whose trauma is silenced perhaps more than any other? Think of how they must have doubled.[18]

The classroom is perhaps one of the most public arenas for traumatic readings. Yet, amidst a flurry of attention to various sorts of harassment and violence, pedagogical theory and methods have not yet sufficiently addressed personal trauma transmitted through and perpetuated by perfectly academic discussions and canonized texts. It is not difficult to see why some might want to overlook or repress traumatic reactions. Perhaps silence is a site, source, and sign of strength for some people. And there is the risk of classroom chaos, of cascades of shocking personal revelations, of dangerous pseudo-therapy sessions. But if teachers assign traumatic texts, it seems they are obligated to acknowledge and at least reasonably try to accommodate students' responses to them— if not entirely, then in part; if not on an individual basis, then within a general and perhaps less threatening discussion of what responses such texts "might" evoke. In the process of trying to contend with trauma, there is always the possibility of exacerbating it, but the risk of exacerbation must be greater if teachers impose and then ignore the trauma, if they banish it to some secret solitude or silence. Silence should be an option in, not a function of, such discussions.

We may not love *Lolita*. Many of the women I have talked with about it have very negative feelings about it, and many cannot re-read, write about, or teach it. But the book remains required reading in some classrooms, and were it never again assigned, we would still have to contend with its resonances and the culture that supports them. I understand why some people prefer to maintain their externally silent reactions to these issues, but I also hope that others see that voicing our responses is essential, that it is time to confront those who cannot see that, beneath Humbert's dominant sexist imaginings of Lolita, there is a kid molded to fulfill a role in a destructive fantasy, a fantasy that every day becomes, in one way or another, a very real nightmare for countless children. It is time for us to grapple with the couch scenes, to redress ourselves. While contending with *Lolita* and other Lolita texts, we can advance our understanding of broader issues of classroom and readerly trauma—and of pedagogically-imposed trauma in general—and we can contend with the whole set of Lolita myths and discourses. We can discuss the politics of representation, ingestion, response, and influence, and we can expose the complex relations of power, sex, and gender that are represented in and sometimes perpetuated by these texts. While the general and critical communities have repressed the ideological contestation imbued in this book, have turned it into a site of gross cultural appropriation—and in ways that may neither have surprised nor been condoned by Nabokov—we need to renew the contestation. As we do this, we will take an important step in refusing a cultural milieu that violates and punishes women, that denies, trivializes, and fragments the female personal—especially trauma— while hegemonically advancing the male personal—especially pleasure.

TEXTS

One of the primary debates about *Lolita* is whether we can believe Humbert's claims about Lolita. Humbert acknowledges and reveals his unreliability throughout the book, and, having been frank and honest, he expects us to believe him when he claims reliability. But I cannot believe two important claims of which he tries to convince us: that Lolita seduces him the first time they have intercourse and that he truly comes to love Lolita as a person.[19]

When Humbert recounts his first non-frotteuristic sex act with Lolita, he insists that Lolita seduces him, but a variety of textual signals suggest that Lolita and Humbert are not seeing eye-to-eye throughout the event. Because I will explicate this passage in detail, let me reproduce it for you here:

> Frigid gentlewomen of the jury! I had thought that months, perhaps years, would elapse before I dared to reveal myself to Dolores Haze; but by six she was wide awake, and by six fifteen we were technically lovers. I am going to tell you something very strange: it was she who seduced me.
>
> Upon hearing her first morning yawn, I feigned handsome profiled sleep. I just did not know what to do. Would she be shocked at finding me by her side, and not in some spare bed? Would she collect her clothes and lock herself up in the bathroom? Would she demand to be taken at once to Ramsdale—to her mother's bedside—back to camp? But my Lo was a sportive lassie. I felt her eyes on me, and when she uttered at last that beloved chortling note of hers, I knew her eyes had been laughing. She rolled over to my side, and her warm brown hair came against my collarbone. I gave a mediocre imitation of waking up. We lay

quietly. I gently caressed her hair, and we gently kissed. Her kiss, to my delirious embarrassment, had some rather comical refinements of flutter and probe which made me conclude that she had been coached at an early age by a little Lesbian. No Charlie boy could have taught her *that*. As if to see whether I had my fill and learned the lesson, she drew away and surveyed me. Her cheekbones were flushed, her full underlip glistened, my dissolution was near. All at once, with a burst of rough glee (the sign of the nymphet!), she put her mouth to my ear—but for quite a while my mind could not separate into words the hot thunder of her whisper, and she laughed, and brushed the hair off her face, and tried again, and gradually the odd sense of living in a brand new, mad new dream world, where everything was permissible, came over me as I realized what she was suggesting. I answered I did not know what game she and Charlie had played. "You mean you have never—?"—her features twisted into a stare of disgusted incredulity. "You have never--" she started again. I took time out by nuzzling her a little. "Lay off, will you," she said with a twangy whine, hastily removing her brown shoulder from my lips. (It was very curious the way she considered—and kept doing so for a long time—all caresses except kisses on the mouth or the stark act of love either "romantic slosh" or "abnormal.")

"You mean," she persisted, now kneeling above me, "you never did it when you were a kid?"

"Never," I answered quite truthfully. "Okay," said Lolita, "here is where we start."

However, I shall not bore my learned readers with a detailed account of Lolita's presumption. Suffice it to say that not a trace of modesty did I perceive in this beautiful hardly formed young girl whom modern co-education, juvenile mores, the campfire racket and so forth had utterly and hopelessly depraved. She saw the stark act merely as part of a youngster's furtive world, unknown to adults. What adults did for purposes of procreation was no business of hers. My life was handled by little Lo in an energetic, matter-of-fact manner as if it were an insensate gadget unconnected with me. While eager to impress me with the world of tough kids, she was not quite prepared for certain discrepancies between a kid's life and mine. Pride alone prevented her from giving up; for, in my strange predicament, I feigned supreme stupidity and had her have her way—at least while I could still bear it. But really these are irrelevant matters; I am not concerned with so-called "sex" at all. Anybody can imagine those elements of animality. A greater endeavor lures me on: to fix once for all the perilous magic of nymphets. (part I, end of chapter 29)

We can read this passage in at least two very different ways, believing Humbert's claim that Lolita seduces him and directs him to the act of intercourse, or challenging him by imagining Lolita's perspective, and especially by considering that Lolita does not direct him to penetrate her. Throughout *his* report, Humbert wants us to believe

that Lolita knows exactly what she does, that she directs him to intercourse, that Lolita is in control: he tells us that he acts stupid; that she is a knowledgeable and experienced teacher who has participated in a furtive world, a perilous and depraved nymphet; that she is the one who makes presumptions with him. But Humbert also participates in the doubling of this text and of child molestation by doubling himself, by being one thing and pretending to be another. From the onset, with his address, "Frigid gentlewomen of the jury!" he implies that he will employ evidentiary rhetoric directed at women, but, throughout this passage, his language is riddled with indirection and ambiguity, and he never absolutely defines the "stark act" so central to the scene.[20] Throughout the narration as well as the time of action, Humbert doubles: he "feigns" sleep and "imitates" waking; he pretends to be a powerless student while he is the powerful teacher; he says that his "dissolution" was near, that "for a while [his] mind could not separate into words the hot thunder of her whisper"; he has the sense that he is in a "mad new dream world, where everything was permissible"; he tells *us* that he "realized what she was suggesting," but he tells *Lolita* that he "did not know what game she and Charlie had played"; he feigns "supreme stupidity" and ignores Lolita's difficulties during the act; he says he is not concerned with "sex" at all, but we know that compels him. Clearly, Humbert, while wanting us to believe he is disempowered, is empowered, and he manipulates the voice and the dialogue of this passage in his effort to convince us that he is seduced, while there is covert evidence that this is not the case, that Lolita does not have intercourse in mind, but an adolescent petting game.

First, Humbert says Lolita seduces him, but he begins the caressing, and he does not indicate who initiates the first kiss. Shortly thereafter he says, "As if to see whether I had my fill and learned the lesson, she drew away and surveyed me." If we can rely on Humbert's interpretation of Lolita's look, and if she is indeed drawing away to see if he has learned his lesson, then it seems logical to infer that Lolita thinks she *has* finished giving the lesson, that she has given Humbert what she thinks *should* be his fill after the first kiss. Furthermore, if Lolita intends to teach Humbert a lesson about kissing, then presumably she would initiate the lesson. If she does initiate it—and if Humbert wants us to believe she seduces him—then why doesn't Humbert tell us she initiates it? By not identifying who kisses whom first, Humbert enables the possibility that he kisses her. We also cannot be sure of Humbert's interpretation of Lolita's look and of why she moves away from him. Could she draw—or pull—away from Humbert in surprise? Could her flush be of fear?

Throughout this passage, Humbert says he realizes what Lolita suggests when she "put her mouth to" his ear, saying that she seduces him and implying that she initiates foreplay that she wants to culminate in intercourse. Again, if Humbert's goal is to convince the jury that Lolita seduces him to intercourse and if her whisper resounds like thunder, why doesn't he conclusively tell the jury what Lolita *says* instead of what she *suggests?* When Humbert says he realizes what Lolita's *suggesting,* his sly wording whispers two possible interpretations. First, Humbert could mean that Lolita directly invites him to participate in something—that she says, for instance, "Let's make out" or "Should we make out?" But Humbert's wording could also indicate that he—and not Lolita—makes the presumptions, that he infers what Lolita might be implying, not what she is actually stating.

Even though it would be easier for Humbert if we believed his claim that Lolita initiates and orchestrates the activities that lead to intercourse, the collective effect of Lolita's perspective and Humbert's commentary suggests that her lesson, her goal, her game, her "stark act" is not to have intercourse, but only to kiss and perhaps fondle. Humbert, of course, admits to feigning ignorance throughout this scene, and even how he speaks this to her suggests kissing and petting games, not intercourse: "I answered I did not know what game she and Charlie had played." For me, *game* evokes various pre-teen kissing games—or, at the very most, some kind of fondling activity. Again, Humbert strategically does not specify what Lolita says. Instead, he reports her as saying "you never did *it* when you were a kid?" (emphasis added), which reinforces the implication that Lolita is referring to a common kids' game. Perhaps Humbert really never played the game as a kid, but surely Lolita does not think that sexual intercourse is common among youngsters—while it would be quite likely that she would believe kissing or petting games are.

One key to identifying the indeterminacy in this passage is the phrase "stark act," which Humbert uses twice. First, he says that Lolita thinks that "all caresses except kisses on the mouth or the stark act of love [are] either 'romantic slosh' or 'abnormal.'" Later he says, "she saw the stark act merely as part of a youngster's furtive world, unknown to adults. What adults did for purposes of procreation was no business of hers." While, after the first reference, *stark* act may possibly—though not necessarily—mean intercourse, the second reference undermines this possibility by suggesting even further that Lolita plans to participate in kids' petting games. This would further explain why, after suggesting them, she is surprised to learn that he had not participated in them when he was young. Humbert facilitates this alternative reading by emphasizing the kids' context of the game when he lists the influences upon this "young girl" of "modern co-education, juvenile mores, [and] the campfire racket." While Humbert wants us to believe the "depraved" Lolita wants to have intercourse with him, he also exaggerates typical "juvenile mores" and campfire experiences.

Finally, whether Lolita has had intercourse with Charlie or not, Lolita gives Humbert no clear indication that she wants to have it with him. Somewhere even Humbert recognizes this: once again, he says, "She saw the stark

act merely as part of a youngster's furtive world, unknown to adults. What adults did for purposes of procreation was no business of hers."[21] One of my associates interprets these lines to mean that Lolita believes intercourse is something about which youngsters know and adults do not care. If so, then why would Lolita want to seduce Humbert, an adult, to intercourse? My colleague claims it is to impress Humbert with her knowledge and experience. But, if she believes "it" is a common children's experience, then why would she think her experience would impress someone who also had been a kid and who, she presumes, had had similar childhood experiences? Finally, the double-voicing of the line "What adults did for purposes of procreation was no business of hers" is remarkably telling of Humbert's manipulative voice. Whether or not one accepts my associate's reading that Lolita believes intercourse is common in childhood and that she does not care about how adults procreate, Humbert's own words subvert his primary interpretation, and their double-voicing resonates loudly: *this is what adults say about kids, not what kids say about adults.*

For me, these lines and the following ones strongly suggest that Humbert knows Lolita cannot yet conceive, cannot comfortably accommodate a man—and that she is not interested in intercourse with him. The following passage is charged with possibilities:

> My life was handled by little Lo in an energetic, matter-of-fact manner as if it were an insensate gadget unconnected with me. While eager to impress me with the world of tough kids, she was not quite prepared for certain discrepancies between a kid's life and mine. Pride alone prevented her from giving up; for, in my strange predicament, I feigned supreme stupidity and had her have her way—at least while I could still bear it.

These lines describe Humbert's ultimate power twist—the twist of what he actually does and of how he narrates his actions in his attempt to convince himself and us that Lolita is in control, that he succumbs to her, and that what he does here is on some level acceptable. When Humbert says he feigns "supreme stupidity" and has "her have her way" while he can "still bear it," he might mean that he lets her fondle him until he ejaculates (and they never have intercourse) or, what I think he *wants* us to believe, that she wants to have intercourse, and that, even though Lolita is not prepared for intercourse with an adult, though this causes her pain, her pride compels her to continue having intercourse until Humbert ejaculates. I propose, however, that Lolita's "stark act" could well be the more sophisticated component of her two approved activities—a petting game that she thinks adults do not play. If we read these same lines within another possible context of Lolita as a preteen—one covertly corroborated by the text—it is quite possible that they indicate that Lolita wants to impress him with this unnamed activity from "the world of tough kids"—note that "kids" is used thrice—and that she is absolutely not prepared for a different kind of discrepancy between children and adults: Lolita's perspective of the "stark act" versus Humbert's, petting games versus child-adult intercourse.

These same lines also allow for another very different but related reading of Lolita's perspective and experience, and, considered together, the alternative readings enhance each other. Humbert uses *life* twice in the end of the excerpt. Within the dominant, more figurative reading, *life* is a metaphor for *penis*. As such, the line "My life was handled by little Lo in an energetic, matter-of-fact manner as if it were an insensate gadget unconnected with me" suggests a description of Lolita's genital fondling of Humbert, and "she was not quite prepared for certain discrepancies between a kid's life and mine" may refer to size differences in children and adults. However, what if, in a kind of reversal of Humbert's narrative trend to be strategically symbolic and indirect, we pull back his covers and consider *life* more literally. Within this reading, these lines suggest that, when they pet, Lolita obliviously alters the direction of Humbert's future life, that she makes out with him as if their behavior is in no way going to affect Humbert's future. Of course, while Humbert's syntax places the blame for these changes on Lolita, it is his molestation of her that changes both of their futures. Furthermore, the second use of *life*, considering its literal definition based in length of time (not anatomy), reiterates that a youngster may be satisfied with petting games while an adult may not be. Merging both meanings of *life* and both meanings of *stark act*, and considering that *harsh, blunt,* and *grim* are synonyms for *stark* (*Webster* and *American Heritage*), this passage underscores that Lolita is at once not prepared for Humbert's size or his ejaculatory stamina during fondling, that her pride compels her to continue petting, that Humbert goes along with her game, feigning stupidity about her limitations and her intentions, and, when *her* way—the way of a kid's life, either the kissing or the fondling—is no longer enough for him, in an abuse of both her body and her "pride," he, without her consent, directs the stark activity *his* way: he penetrates her, and, as he rapes her, feigns ignorance about her pain while he thrusts to ejaculation.

This novel, this experience, this social issue, is fraught with doubling, and this passage, with its internal doublings that are both contradictory and mutually enhancing, doubles into itself in a way that enables two different readings: the critically dominant, unchallenged one that assumes Lolita seduces Humbert to intercourse, and an overlooked reading that Lolita proposes kissing and petting games with Humbert—but not intercourse. This relative indeterminacy frustrates some readers of the novel (though most seem to unproblematically accept the hegemonic reading), and certainly my attempt to account for the latter reading will frustrate some of my readers. Of course, Humbert's passage is inherently and intentionally indeterminate. It is conveniently doubled. He claims to leave out the details because they are "irrelevant matters," but he erases them because they

are, indeed, quite relevant. Since he wants to acquit himself of the accusation of rape, wants to convince us that in this scene Lolita seduces him to intercourse, he must narrate in gaps, must not tell us who initiates certain acts, must use elusive language, must be self-protectively discreet.

While in some ways this formalist reading may seem to redeem the text and Nabokov because it identifies textual challenges to the violent seduction fantasy, I am not ready to entirely exculpate Nabokov, the text, or readers like Lionel Trilling. Perhaps Nabokov wanted me to see the "real" kid in this excerpt—or perhaps not. Certainly, where I see the raped child, others imagine a seductive little girl. While I cannot know for certain how Nabokov intended this passage to be read, in it, and perhaps with more force than anywhere else in the novel, he narratively plies two perspectives. This interweaving, this doubling, problematizes Humbert's claims and Lolita's liability—and Nabokov does this by testing the limits of what we now familiarly know as Mikhail Bakhtin's notion of heteroglossia:

> *another's speech in another's language,* serving to express authorial intentions but in a refracted way. Such speech constitutes a special type of *double-voiced discourse.* It serves two speakers at the same time and expresses simultaneously two different intentions: the direct intention of the character who is speaking, and the refracted intentions of the author. In such discourse there are two voices, two meanings and two expressions. And all the while these two voices are dialogically interrelated, they—as it were—know about each other. (324)

This passage, with Humbert so insistent upon his own view while revealing such contrary yet valid, viable variations of Lolita's perspective, exemplifies an extreme kind of personal double voicing. In the course of this narration, the doubled form both produces and enacts a doubled content—a doubled action—and the narrative consequences are that this interconnected yet gaping double-voicing reflects and produces a colliding *double drama:* two people, with two related yet relatively oppositional intentions, interact—and for the empowered one the outcome is seduction, while for Lolita, the very same interaction, the very same words, result in rape.

Some readers insist that, from the onset of this scene, Lolita wants to teach Humbert how to have intercourse, that she initiates and maneuvers penetration. While I disagree with this interpretation, even it describes an essential double drama: if Lolita consents to or even appears to direct her painful penetration by Humbert, she does so with Humbert's powerful director's hand. As he leads her to believe she is in control, he controls her—he gets power by appearing to give up power, exerts his will by appearing to relinquish his will. Finally, even within this reading of Lolita as pseudo-director, he directs her to consent to activities that he maneuvers and for which he knows she is not prepared. And this "consent" is problematic, first, because it is not clear that Lolita does consent to intercourse, and because, within the power-differential of this situation, it becomes impossible for Lolita—or for any twelve-year-old—truly to consent to what is about to happen, to consent as an informed, independent, empowered person who has a variety of implementable options from which to choose. We know the implications of Humbert's gaming with Lolita, of the power-differential that is doubly dramatized, and we know that Humbert's manipulations result in an extended bondage and violation of Lolita during which his will—his *life*—continues to penetrate and prevail.

Regardless of the indeterminacies of this passage, all readings describe Humbert's coercion of Lolita, the exertion of an adult's sexual desires upon a child—rape. This ambiguity of perception and interpretation—this double drama that concurrently reveals and conceals various truths—is both continued and undermined when Humbert reports that Lolita says *with a smile,* "You revolting creature. I was a daisy-fresh girl, and look what you've done to me. I ought to call the police and tell them you raped me. Oh you, dirty, dirty old man." Are we to entirely believe the man who believes that Lolita's second expression of pain is "reproduced" for his benefit? Does she really smile when she calls Humbert a brute? Humbert's manipulation of rape into consensual sex involves an honest portrayal of some of his liabilities, which makes it easier for him to misrepresent other liabilities, easier for him to double. Yet Nabokov reveals Humbert's role as screenwriter, director, and interpreter—as perverter—of the drama when Humbert says a few chapters after narrating the rape scene, "*The rapist* was Charlie Holmes; I am the *therapist*—a matter of nice spacing in the way of distinction" (137, emphasis added).

Nabokov continues to reveal Humbert's doubling—and unreliability—through language that exposes his ongoing pedophilia and debunks his insistence that he comes to love Lolita for her own sake.22 He says of his meeting the pregnant, married Dolly:

> I had no intention of torturing *my* darling. . . . there she was with her ruined looks and her adult . . . hands . . . *(my Lolita!)*, hopelessly worn. . . . and . . . I knew . . . that I loved her more than anything I had ever seen or imagined on earth. . . . She was only the . . . dead leaf echo of the *nymphet* I had rolled myself upon with such cries in the past . . . but thank God it was not that echo alone that I worshipped. . . . I will shout my poor truth. I insist the world know how much I loved *my* Lolita, this Lolita, pale and polluted. . . . *still mine*. . . . No matter, even if . . . her lovely *young velvety delicate* delta be tainted and torn—even then I would go mad with tenderness at the mere sight of your dear wan face, at the mere sound of your raucous *young* voice, *my* Lolita. (253, emphasis added)

Even as Humbert proclaims his love for this Lolita, as he describes a young woman ravished by the experiences he has imposed on her, key words throughout his narrative reveal his continued obsession with *possessing* a *young* Lolita, with possessing her for the sexual attraction he found in her youth—and that he still finds in other youth. He continues to think about other girls sexually both in the time of narration and the time of action at the end of the novel: in the time of action, he looks lewdly at young girls playing near Lolita's house. At the beginning of the time of narration, he thinks about the girls in the catalogue in prison. And at the end of his narration, he writes this passage, saturated with quiet clues about what still obsesses him, with clues that make clear that he does not love Lolita spiritually, nor as an individual, that his feelings for her are pathological and self-serving, and that he remains fixated on what he cannot have—a fantasy world and object that he unsuccessfully tries to disguise beneath the discourse of age and wear.

Humbert's objectification of and disregard for Lolita is reflected even in how he addresses and refers to her: throughout most of the time of action and the time of narration, Humbert calls her *Lolita,* while everyone else calls her by the name she prefers, *Dolly.* When he sees the pregnant Dolly, he calls her by her preferred name until he recognizes in her the "echo of the nymphet" and envisions the young, "velvety delta" of *his Lolita.* Finally, just before the book ends, he refers to Dolly as "*my little one. Lolita girl*" (259, emphasis added), and his last words are "my Lolita" (281). And yet, even with these clues, in the same way that Dolly's will, character, and voice are supplanted by Humbert's throughout the novel, her life, fate, and image continue to be supplanted, distorted, and used by a world that embraces and punishes its own version of Humbert's imaginary Lolita.

. . . . .

"Well, you drink champagne and it tastes just like cherry cola, *C-O-L-A,* cola."

Suddenly, this "Lola" line intertextually and ironically reflects the duality of *Lolita*—the doubled discrepancies between and the manipulated mergings of an adult's world with a child's. It reflects how, for some readers, *Lolita* is traumatic and depressing—like the alcohol in champagne—yet, for many others, it is pleasurable and stimulating—like the caffeine in cola.

Whether this book remains part of the canon or not, its repercussions will reverberate for a long time. While it might be simpler to slap the book shut, this will not silence its echoes. Instead of retreating from its trauma, I believe we—students and teachers, women and men—should confront its messages and challenges, should address its personal and cultural implications. While recognizing that there may be gender-specific reactions to the Lolita myths and the book, we must not assume them. We need to consider whether these passages and others in *Lolita* are heteroglossia at its best or its worst, to bring our own backgrounded voices to the fore, to reclaim ourselves—our voices, our interpretations, our stories. As we do this, we can confront the myths that aestheticize and romanticize molestation, that pre-sexualize kids, that make pedophilia pretty. And we can explore why, with the devastations of forced and coerced sexual behavior so evident, any person succumbs to or perpetrates it. Virginia Goldner says adequate treatment of sexual abuse "must do justice to the *double injury:* the injury of a particular person by a particular person or people, and the social injustice of the victim's exploitation because of the impersonal fact of her age or sex" (ix; emphasis added). As we understand the double injuries, and disclose and undo the doublings in and around this book—the doubling of the Lolita myth, of female sexuality, of responses to the text, of students, of survivors, and of the text itself—and as we share our differences with this text and others, perhaps we will better understand the nature of reading, of sharing readings, of textual traumas, of others and of ourselves.[23]

NOTES

[1] One, *Casualties of Love: The "Long Island Lolita" Story,* "earned a 22 percent audience share and $3.64 million in revenues" (*People* 8 Aug. 1994).

[2] Alfred Appel (*Annotated* 332) reports that Nabokov was unfamiliar with the movie *The Blue Angel* (directed by Josef von Sternberg, 1930), in which Lola-Lola, a cabaret dancer, ruins the life of a professor who falls in love with her, but it is easy to speculate about the possibility of intertextuality between this film, its 1959 remake, and the 1955 publication of *Lolita. Lolita* readers and the Lolita myth also may have been influenced by the movie version of *Lolita,* which impacted notions of what is phenotypically beautiful in North American women and models. However, while Nabokov wrote the screenplay for the movie, it is significantly different from the novel.

[3] This punishment of female sexuality is all the more ironic since the alleged sexuality of "nymphets" is what makes them, by patriarchy's own definition, desirable. And the doubling continues because Lolita's alleged nymphet quality is supposed to be essential—thus, natural (and so why not common?); but it is also supposed to be abnormal and rare—thus, unnatural.

[4] For a discussion of the Humbert/Quilty and the good/evil double, see Appel ("Lolita" 114, 131, 134) and Frosch (135-36). Also see Maddox (80), Alexandrov (161), and Tamir-Ghez (80). Critics who discuss the doubling of readers' desire or perspective with Quilty include Appel ("Lolita" 123), Packman (47), and Rampton (107). Haegert notes critics who claim that Nabokov was in part attempting to exorcise an unwanted "double" (779), among them Fowler and Pifer. They are joined by Centerwall, who argues that Nabokov was a "closet pedophile" (468).

[5] Kauffman states "it is doubtful" that Lolita seduces Humbert, and Robert Levine rejects the "misguided" arguments which "confuse virginity with innocence" (475), but critics usually claim that Lolita is a seductress, and often, in the process, confound the issue of virginity with the question of rape. Some explicitly but cursorily defend her and then sympathetically incorporate Humbert's language into their own. See: Lionel Trilling, who says, "Perhaps [Humbert's] depravity is the easier to accept when we learn that he deals with a Lolita who is not innocent, and who seems to have very few emotions to be violated" (14); Andrew Field, who says, "Humbert is himself 'seduced' by the unvirginal little nymphet" (330); Frosch, who says, "Then, too, Lolita is not 'the fragile child of a feminine novel' but a child vamp, who . . . is not a virgin" (132); Rubin-stein, who says, "Lolita's behavior supports Humbert's assertion to the effect that nymphets are depraved sorceresses" (364); Appel, who refers to the sex acts between Lolita and Humbert as "conjugal visits" and "seduction" ("Lolita" 121); and Packman, who says that by the end of part one "the initial striptease of the nymphet has been completed" (59). Others believe Lolita seduces Humbert but emphasize Humbert's responsibility, including Phelan (*Worlds* 164).

Typically, those who claim that Humbert rapes Lolita go on to subvert the claim by confounding love and rape. Gullette says that "each act" of Humbert's intercourse with Lolita is "a form of rape" (223), but describes Humbert as "loving children" (221). Maddox confounds love with hate and moral perfection with imperfection when she says, "*Lolita* is a novel about love and death in two of their most pathological forms: child rape and murder," which, when we "encounter them in a text," "can be disturbing but convincing metaphors for a desire for moral and aesthetic perfection" (67). Tamir-Ghez refers to Humbert's "design to rape" Lolita, but says he does not rape her because "she complies," and then refers to "the first time he makes love to Lolita" (72 n. 7, 80).

[6] Of course, Nabokov wants this admiration, and he uses his artistic skill to enact another kind of doubling: to represent a playful tragedy, to construct carefully and then deny the same mimetic reality, to make the story artificial and real, to foreground the synthetic aspects of the work so much that, even as he asks us to participate mimetically, he undermines our mimetic engagement—such that those who largely engage mimetically with *Lolita* are criticized for not appreciating its art. See Phelan's *Reading People, Reading Plots* for definitions and applications of the synthetic, mimetic, and thematic components of narrative.

[7] While Nabokov avoids sustained, graphic descriptions of Lolita's violations, his words throw some readers into ripping, detailed memories of their own molestations.

[8] Most notably, see Linda Kauffman. Also see Trevor McNeely, Robert Levine, and Rodney Giblett. See notes 5, 13, 16, and 17.

[9] Some of the critics who discuss readers' sympathy for Humbert include Dana Brand (19), Rampton (110), Tamir-Ghez (70), and Phelan (*Worlds* 162).

[10] See Appel, who emphasizes Humbert's victimization, entrapment, pain, despair, and horror; Bullock, who says Lolita "abandons . . . Hum for other men"; Gullette, who says Humbert's crime is aging "and wanting nevertheless to have a sexual life" (221); Jong, who says the villain in *Lolita* is time and that "Humbert is . . . every man who is driven by desire" (46-47); Tamir-Ghez, who calls Humbert a "man with whom the average reader can easily identify" who "wins us over" (71, 82); and Green, who claims that "The sexually perverse enterprises . . . are made funny, beautiful, pathetic, romantic, tragic; in five or six different ways we are made to sympathize with [Humbert] in them. Above all, they are made impressive" (365).

[11] Most notorious is Trilling's comment that "we have come virtually to condone the violation it presents. . . . We have been seduced into conniving in the violation, because we have permitted our fantasies to accept what we know to be rather revolting" (14). Others include Appel, who says, "we almost find ourselves wishing Humbert well during his agonizing first night with Lolita at The Enchanted Hunters" ("Lolita" 126); Bader, who says Humbert's "agonizing love for a slangy twelve-year-old is a delectable taboo" (63); Butler, who claims that during the couch scene "we may even fear for him the possibility of detection. Then, at the moment of orgasm, we experience a corresponding relief that the scene has passed without incident. And, finally, we may even let ourselves be swayed by Humbert's retrospective view of the scene as an artistic triumph" (433); Tamir-Ghez, who notes that "What enraged or at least disquieted most readers and critics was the fact that they found themselves unwittingly accepting, even sharing, the feelings of Humbert Humbert. . . . [T]hey caught themselves identifying with him" (65); and Toker, who says we identify and sympathize with Humbert, who pursues "a pleasure that few readers wish to give up, despite all the scornful treatment that such a pleasure may receive in various aesthetic theories" (202-03).

[12] See Trilling, who "was plainly not able to muster up the note of moral outrage" and says "it is likely that any reader of *Lolita* will discover that he comes to see the situation as less and less abstract and . . . horrible, and more and more as human and 'understandable'" (14); Parker: "She is a dreadful little creature, selfish, hard, vulgar, and foul-tempered. . . . Lolita leaves him . . . for a creature even worse than she is" (9-10); Appel: Lolita "affords Nabokov an ideal opportunity to comment on the Teen and Sub-Teen Tyranny. It is poetic justice that Lolita should seduce Humbert. . . . Lolita is a Baby Snooks who looms threateningly high above us all" ("Lolita" 121); Bader, who says Lolita "responds shrilly to Humbert's love-making" and faults her for being conventional (69); Brand: Lolita is a "little girl as vulgar, energetic, flirtatious, seemingly innocent and yet manipulative as the American commercial environment itself" (19); Jong: Lolita is "an impossible object: a banal little girl" (46); Fowler: Lolita is "quite at home as a semiliterate Mrs. Richard Schiller living in a shack and the love of her life was the disgusting Quilty, not Humbert" (174); and Gullette: "Both the cult of childhood and the discourse that has been labelled 'Freudianism' have exacerbated, if they have not created, the guilt an adult feels in longing sexually for a child. . . . And feminism has heightened the sense of potential exploitation in this longing. . . . The outcome, at any rate, is that in the Western world sex is patently another game one cannot play with children" (218).

[13] Kauffman is one of the only critics I have found truly to contest what I am calling this aestheticizing of molestation: "Aesthetic bliss is not a criterion that compensates for those crimes; instead it is a dead end, meager consolation for the murder of Lolita's childhood" (163).

[14] While there seem to be some gender-specific reactions to *Lolita,* both in students and in published critics, there are also clear and important exceptions to them, as evidenced in my notes.

[15] This response seems a dramatic manifestation of what Fetterley calls "immasculation," when "the female reader is co-opted into participation in an experience from which she is explicitly excluded; she is asked to identify with a selfhood that defines itself in opposition to her; she is required to identify against herself" (xii). This reader's response surpasses immasculation because it not only requires the reader to identify against herself as she accepts a male position, but she, in taking this stance, also positions herself in stark contrast and *opposition to* another, particularly vulnerable, female. Kauffman, citing Fetterley, notes that *Lolita* gives "feminist" (though, it seems "female" is more appropriate here) readers "the choice of either participating in their own 'immasculation' by endorsing aesthetic bliss, or of demonstrating their humorlessness and frigidity" and that "physical as well as aesthetic *jouissance* for Humbert requires anaesthesia or annihilation for Lolita" (155). While immasculation has been the norm in *Lolita* criticism, Kauffman, McNeely, and Giblett have begun to challenge it.

[16] For an articulation of these terms, see Rabinowitz. One would think that, since Lolita's pain is so acutely, though rarely, clarified, that critics would have better attended to that very large group of readers who identify with the experience of pain and trauma, not of pleasure. Most critics—male and female—focus on the pleasurable experience of reading, especially (both overtly and covertly) from a male perspective, including: Packman, Toker, Field, Appel ("Lolita"), Butler, Jong, O'Connor, and Fowler. For those who problematize the reading experience, see Rampton and Tamir-Ghez. And, for those who directly confront the "male" reading experience, see Kauffman, McNeely, Levine, and Giblett.

[17] See Booth's *Rhetoric of Fiction* for one of the earliest and most notable discussions about the book's morality. For discussions focussed on Lolita's perspective, see McNeely, Levine, and Kauffman, who says, "*Lolita* is not about love but about incest, which is a betrayal of trust, a violation of love. How have critics managed so consistently to confuse love with incest in the novel? My aim here is to show how . . . the inscription of the father's body in the text obliterates the daughter's" (152). And one of my aims is to show how the "father's" text obliterates the "daughter's" in several contexts: in the larger culture, the classroom, the actual *Lolita* text, and in its criticism.

[18] While Fetterley discusses the ways in which women identify against themselves as "immasculation" (see note 15), a related but very different move occurs when men are expected and assumed to identify with the male "standard" when that standard violates who they are as individuals. Individual men may be "immasculated," not in that they are co-opted into participating in experiences from which they are explicitly excluded, but by being co-opted into participating in experiences in which they are assumed to be included but, given their individual reactions, are not. Are some male readers of *Lolita* asked to identify with a perspective that is in opposition to themselves as individuals even though it is often assumed to represent their gender?

[19] See note 5 on Lolita as seductress and note 22 on whether Humbert abandons his pedophilia and truly comes to love Lolita.

[20] This passage is a pivotal factor in most critics' assumptions that Lolita is the unvirginal seductress, but few have noted—let alone explored and complicated—its specifics. Among those few are Levine, who says Lolita's pain after the "honeymoon night" is probably due to her menarche, not because Humbert "had torn something inside her" (472). Levine and Toker, and Tamir-Ghez comment, respectively, on "the stark act" and the "certain discrepancies" without clarifying what they think these actually are. Phelan, who indicates that he believes "life" refers to sex organ, refers to the "certain discrepancies" and the "stark act" without problematizing their meaning, although his interpretation of "life" enables us to infer that he defines them as organ size and intercourse (*Worlds* 164).

[21] There is, of course, an important distinction between intercourse and procreation (as we see in Lolita's fate), and perhaps Humbert is referring to Lolita's lack of interest in or preparedness for producing children. However, we would be remiss to discount the association of intercourse with procreation, whether conception occurs during intercourse or not. For my purposes, I will emphasize the first step in procreation, intercourse.

[22] Critics offer a range of opinions on whether Humbert experiences true "moral apotheosis" and love or whether his confession is "a virtuoso performance: an artfully contrived *apologia*" (Haegert 778), although most critics argue that Humbert's claims are genuine. Among those who believe Humbert experiences a true "moral apotheosis" or is no longer a pedophile or both are Alexandrov, Appel ("Lolita"), Bader, Bullock, Field, Fowler, Gullette, Levine, Maddox, Morton, Pifer, Tamir-Ghez, Toker, and O'Connor. Butler challenges this view, arguing that "Humbert's expression of love still functions as one of the novel's modulation" (436 n. 22, 434), and Kauffman argues that Humbert is "far from being in love with Lolita," that he is "completely obsessed with the mental image he incessantly projects with random girls and women" (159), and that what critics usually cite as signs of Humbert's love are "signs not of overpowering love but of domination" typical of father-daughter incest (161).

[23] For our fourth colleague. And with gratitude to James Phelan, Nils Samuels, and Marlene Longenecker for our provocative discussions about *Lolita* and for their keen responses to this paper.

WORKS CITED

Alexandrov, Vladimir E. *Nabokov's Otherworld.* Princeton: Princeton UP, 1991.

Appel, Alfred, Jr. *The Annotated Lolita.* By Vladimir Nabokov. Rev. ed. New York: Vintage, 1991. xi-xvii.

———. "Lolita: The Springboard of Parody." *Nabokov: The Man and His Work.* Ed. L. S. Dembo. Madison: U of Wisconsin P, 1967. 106-43.

Bader, Julia. *Crystal Land: Artifice in Nabokov's English Novels.* Berkeley: U of California P, 1972. 57-81.

Bakhtin, M. M. "Discourse in the Novel." *The Dialogic Imagination: Four Essays by M. M. Bakhtin.* Trans. Carl Emerson and Michael Holquist. Ed. Michael Holquist. Austin: U. of Austin P, 1981. 259-422.

Booth, Wayne C. *The Rhetoric of Fiction.* 2nd ed. Chicago: U of Chicago P, 1983.

Brand, Dana. "The Interaction of Aestheticism and American Consumer Culture in Nabokov's *Lolita.*" *Modern Language Studies* 17.2 (1987):14-21.

Bullock, Richard H. "Humbert the Character, Humbert the Writer: Artifice, Reality, and Art in *Lolita.*" *Philological Quarterly* 63.2 (1984): 187-204.

Butler, Steven H. "*Lolita* and the Modern Experience of Beauty." *Studies in the Novel* 18.4 (1986): 427-40.

Centerwall, Brandon S. "Hiding in Plain Sight: Nabokov and Pedophilia." *Texas Studies in Literature and Language* 32.3 (1990): 468-84.

Corrigan, Maureen. *All Things Considered.* National Public Radio. WCBE, Columbus, Ohio. 21 Sept. 1992.

Fetterley, Judith. *The Resisting Reader: A Feminist Approach to American Fiction.* Bloomington: Indiana UP, 1978.

Field, Andrew. *Nabokov: His Life in Art.* Boston: Little, Brown, 1967.

Fowler, Douglas. *Reading Nabokov.* Ithaca: Cornell UP, 1974.

Frosch, Thomas R. "Parody and Authenticity in *Lolita.*" *Nabokov's Fifth Arc.* Ed. J. E. Rivers and Charles Nicol. Austin: U of Texas P, 1982. 127-43.

Giblett, Rodney. "Writing Sexuality, Reading Pleasure." *Paragraph* 12.3 (1989): 229-38.

Goldner, Virginia. Introduction. Jones vii-x.

Green, Martin. "Tolstoy and Nabokov: The Morality of *Lolita.*" *The Kenyon Review* 28.3 (1982).

Gullette, Margaret Morganroth. "The Exile of Adulthood: Pedophilia in the Midlife Novel." *Novel* 17.3 (1984): 215-32.

Haegert, John. "Artist in Exile: The Americanization of Humbert Humbert." *ELH* 52.3 (1985): 777-94.

Jones, Elsa. *Working with Adult Survivors of Child Sexual Abuse.* London: Karnack Books, 1991.

Jong, Erica. "Time Has Been Kind to the Nymphet: *Lolita* 30 Years Later." Rev. of *Lolita* by Vladimir Nabokov. *New York Times Book Review* 5 June 1988: 3, 46-47.

Kauffman, Linda. "Framing Lolita: Is There a Woman in the Text?" *Refiguring the Father: New Feminist Readings of Patriarchy.* Ed. Patricia Yaeger and Beth Kowaleski-Wallace. Carbondale: Southern Illinois UP, 1989. 131-52.

The Kinks. "Lola." *Lola versus Powerman and the Money-Go-Round.* Reprise Records, 1970.

Kubrick, Stanley. *Lolita.* With James Mason, Shelley Winters, Peter Sellers, and Sue Lyon. MGM, 1962.

"Lethal Lolita." *People* 12 Oct. 1992.

Levine, Robert T. "My Ultraviolet Darling': The Loss of Lolita's Childhood." *Modern Fiction Studies* 25.3 (1979): 471-79.

Maddox, Lucy B. *Nabokov's Novels in English.* Athens: U of Georgia P, 1983.

McNeely, Trevor. "'Lo' and Behold: Solving the *Lolita* Riddle." *Studies in the Novel* 21.8 (1989): 182-99.

Nabokov, Vladimir. *Lolita* (1955). New York: Berkeley, 1977.

O'Connor, Katherine Tiernan. "Rereading *Lolita,* Reconsidering Nabokov's Relationship with Dostoevskij." *Slavic and Eastern European Journal* 33.1 (1989): 64-77.

Packman, David. *Vladimir Nabokov: The Structure of Literary Desire.* Columbia: U of Missouri P, 1982.

Parker, Dorothy. "Sex—Without the Asterisks." *Major Literary Characters: Lolita.* Ed. Harold Bloom. Chelsea House: New York, 1993. 9-10.

Phelan, James. *Reading People, Reading Plots: Character, Progression, and the Interpretation of Narrative.* Chicago: U of Chicago P, 1989.

———. *Worlds from Words: A Theory of Language in Fiction.* Chicago: U of Chicago P, 1981.

Pifer, Ellen. "Shades of Love: Nabokov's Intimations of Immortality." *Kenyon Review* ns 11.1 (1989): 75-86.

Rabinowitz, Peter J. *Before Reading: Narrative Conventions and the Politics of Interpretation.* Ithaca: Cornell UP, 1987.

Rampton, David. "Lolita." *Vladimir Nabokov: A Critical Study of the Novels.* Cambridge: Cambridge UP, 1984. 101-21.

Tamir-Ghez, Nomi. "The Art of Persuasion in Nabokov's *Lolita.*" *Poetics Today* 1.1/2 (1979): 65-83.

Toker, Leona. *Nabokov: The Mystery of Literary Structures.* Ithaca: Cornell UP, 1989.

Trilling, Lionel. "The Last Lover: Vladimir Nabokov's *Lolita.*" *Encounter* 11.4 (1958): 9-19.

Meryl Altman

SOURCE: "Before We Said 'We' (and after): Bad Sex and Personal Politics in Doris Lessing and Simone de Beauvoir," in *Critical Quarterly,* Vol. 38, No. 3, Autumn, 1996, pp. 14-29.

[*In the following essay, Altman assesses the unresolved sexual conflicts portrayed in Doris Lessing's* The Golden Notebook *and Simone de Beauvoir's* Les Mandarins.]

> Dans un espace courbe, on ne peut pas tirer de ligne droite, dit Dubreuilh. On ne peut pas mener une vie correcte dans une société qui ne l'est pas.
>
> —*Les Mandarins*[1]

Free! What's the use of us being free if they aren't?

—*The Golden Notebook*[2]

A taste for what has not yet been thought is not the same thing as an impasse.

—Michèle Le Doeuff[3]

In 1993, Sally Munt succinctly called the personal 'the discourse we now love to hate'.[4] Feminist theory for the last ten years (at least) has been embroiled with epistemological and ethical issues around the relation of 'I' to 'we'. For sound and healthy reasons, both pronouns often feel uncomfortable in our mouths, often sound poisoned in our ears. Yet for sound and healthy reasons, I/we still use and need them. Nor are these issues purely academic, since whenever I hear or say sentences like 'am I a feminist', 'am I still a feminist', 'is feminism still about me', 'is feminism about me yet', 'is there a group I can join', even, 'isn't there anything we can do about' (whatever awful thing has happened that day), those same problems are being posed. Because I am still hoping the answer to all these questions is 'yes', I want to bracket the forms this issue is taking now and go back behind and before 'we' (and I) got into this mess.

Different as they are, Doris Lessing's *The Golden Notebook* (1962) and Simone de Beauvoir's *Les Mandarins* (1954) occupy a similarly ambiguous place in the feminist canon (a similarly odd moment in feminist history). Many women were brought to feminism by one or another of these novels, or by novels much like them. And yet it's not quite possible, not quite historical, to call either a 'feminist novel'. (As Lessing's Anna Wulf would say, I wouldn't write that now.)

Each is: a condition of England/condition of France novel. A long novel including history, so long, and so densely cross-referenced to things students don't remember or know, that one has to think long and hard before teaching either. A long novel including politics, including women's experience, but not *quite* including the politics of women's experience.

And each is also a love story, a story in which women, through sexuality, lose control: a story that embarrasses us, that we can't seem to put down. We can always claim to be reading it for the politics, the history, the literary experimentalism (like the man who buys *Playboy* 'for the articles'?) but it is the love story, the sex story, the identification (some of it illicit) that keeps us interested for all those hundreds of pages.

Of course, I could say all those things about *Middlemarch,* too.

When I say neither novel is 'feminist', what do I mean by that word? The ability to name women as a political collectivity, as a prerequisite for calling for change. The willingness to move 'women's problems' from the pri-

vate sphere into the public sphere, to claim a space for them among the public discourses of resistance. In *The Second Sex,* Beauvoir said, 'Women do not say "we".' Soon she, and other women, *would* say 'we', on the basis of the insight into women's subordination provided by that book and others like it. But not yet.

Instead, these two books pose side by side, and in a concretely historicised way, (a) the problematic of what Nancy Miller calls the female erotic destiny (conceived of as private and literary, drawing on a tradition constitutive of the 'novel' as we know it) and (b) the problematic of political activism (conceived of as public, mainly Marxist, potentially violent, and male), in a world which seems to be going to pieces both materially and linguistically. They also both explicitly pose epistemological/ethical questions about what is now called 'subjectivity': who may write, how may one write, how can one write the truth and whose truth will it be once it is written, why write and should one write (or speak) at all. In many ways, these too are still 'questions for feminism'.

And yet the novels date themselves; our response dates, places us. Many of the essays in Jenny Taylor's anthology on rereading Lessing record a double movement of indebtedness and disappointment.[5] As Elizabeth Wilson asks in her contribution, 'Yesterday's heroines: on rereading Lessing and de Beauvoir',

> Who are these women we admired so much? In the strange cultural landscape of 1960 they loomed up, Cassandras of women's experience, an experience that was everywhere silenced, concealed and denied . . . Then, I was lost in admiration, so that I noticed neither their political isolation (as women), nor their contempt for lesbianism, nor their romanticism when it came to sexuality. . . . Now, in *The Golden Notebook* (which I first read as a manual of womanly experience), I discern attitudes towards both men and women whose ambivalence repels me.[6]

Adrienne Rich's comments about Lessing in an interview with Elly Bulkin could stand in for a whole gathering of this response.

> AR: I remember reading *The Golden Notebook,* Doris Lessing, in 1962 when it first came out. . . . *The Golden Notebook* at that time seemed like a very radical book. It doesn't anymore, but it was a radical book . . . it talked about things that had not been talked about in literature before . . . Lessing has been enormously important as a quasi-feminist writer, a writer centering on women's lives, and the failure of her novels . . . is a real failure to envisage any kind of political bonding of women and any kind of really powerful central bonding . . . [7]

Rich linked this point to Lessing's homophobia, and returned to it in her crucial essay, 'Compulsory Heterosexuality and Lesbian Existence' (1980), which starts exactly here: boldly naming the failures of venerated and canonised feminist writers to acknowledge and respect lesbianism, and clearly showing the resulting rot at the core of much of 1970s feminist theory and practice. Where the choice, the possibility, of lesbianism, is silenced, nothing true about women (any women) can be said.[8]

Feminist disappointment with *The Mandarins* is more complicated. Here the heroine's disastrous preoccupation with 'love, our subject' has been contrasted with a more heroic, more overtly feminist Beauvoir abstracted from her other writing. Carolyn Heilbrun used this contrast in one of her own early books to make an important point about the nature of literary convention, more binding and more conservative sometimes than the social conventions it might seem to mirror.

> The failure of women writers to imagine female selves as characters is . . . profound . . . Thus Simone de Beauvoir explains that her novel *The Mandarins* was to contain 'all of myself'. Yet even in this novel she cannot, she knows, herself create a positive heroine. 'Anna [sic]', she writes, 'hasn't the autonomy that has been bestowed upon me by a profession that means so much to me'. Anna 'lives the relative life of a secondary being; Henri resembles me more than Anna does'.

Heilbrun generalises from this case and others that

> women writers (and women politicians, academics, psychoanalysts) have been unable to imagine for other women, fictional or real, the self they have in fact achieved. Jane Austen cannot allow her heroines her own unmarried, highly accomplished destiny. Women writers, in short, have articulated their pain. But they cannot, or for the most part have not, imagined characters moving, as the authors themselves have moved, beyond that pain . . . Her creative imagination will fail her even when life, in her own case, does not. She therefore projects upon a male character the identity and experience for which she searches, leaving to male authors the creation of female characters who might well be called 'heroes'.[9]

Time may have modified this judgment: for one thing, biographical material since made available, and theoretical sophistication, make it less simple to assert that we know who 'Beauvoir' really was. My point here is simply that for all these commentators—and also for many of the women I have buttonholed about this question over the last two years—both the emotional importance, and the disappointment, of Lessing's work (and Beauvoir's) can be located on the same terrain: sexuality and its discontents. It complicates the matter to realise that women, feminists, women about to become feminists were so captivated by both these books precisely because of these elements that disappoint Heilbrun—because they explore the love problems of women who really know better but can't help themselves; the pain, the shame, the victimisation, the anger were recognisable.

. . . . .

It is on only one subject that she leaves me flat and that is politics. She doesn't give a damn about it. It's not that she actually doesn't give a damn about it, but she doesn't want to get involved in the political rat race.

—Sartre, interviewed by Madeleine
Gobeil in 1965

My idea of hell is a committee meeting.

—Doris Lessing to Susan Brownmiller

The relation of the individual to the collectivity; the possibility (or impossibility) of bringing about political change; the role of the intellectual (the academic); the interplay of ideological and material forces in social life, in history; the changing nature of power in the twentieth century, and of our understanding of it; the search for a discourse *about* power that will not become a discourse *of* power, a catspaw or a tool to oppress others in turn; the relative 'truth' claims of various doctrines and disciplines and how to choose among them. Surely these are (some of) our questions. And, turning to *The Mandarins* and *The Golden Notebook*, one finds ink, emotion, angst, and intelligence, massively and intensely applied to just these questions. But, never in terms of feminism, never in terms of women. *The Mandarins* particularly is a very 'talky' book: located precisely at the close of the Second World War and as inheritors of the French Resistance, Robert Dubreuilh and Henri Perron, writers and public figures, set out, argue, inhabit, reject, and retake various positions, positions we associate with Jean-Paul Sartre and his circle, particularly with their attempt at that juncture to rework his existentialist philosophy to make it compatible with political 'engagement'.

But women in *The Mandarins* never talk this talk. Paule, the classic figure of the 'femme amoureuse' whose dependence on her lover is total and nearly suicidal, refuses to hear any news, even war news, except from the lips of Henri, insists to him that in writing politically he is betraying his vocation (and thus the reason for *her* self-abnegating existence). In her autobiography, Beauvoir notes that

> Françoise d'Eaubonne, in her review of *The Mandarins,* observed that every writer has his death's head, and that mine—as exemplified by Elisabeth, Denise, and above all by Paula—is the woman who sacrifices her independence for love. Today I ask myself how much, in fact, such a risk ever existed . . . [10]

Each of her novels, most of her autobiographical books, and perhaps most crucially *The Second Sex* itself, is haunted by this figure of the dependent woman who, in basing her whole identity on love and dependency, becomes complicit with her own oppression, colludes in turning herself into the Other. As critics have noted, however, the 'femme amoureuse' is always doubled by a more lucid, self-sufficient woman character (in *The Sec-*

ond Sex this role is taken by the governing voice of the rationalist philosopher, Simone de Beauvoir). Dubreuilh's wife Anne is more sympathetic, more intelligent, and more independent—her professional identity as a psychoanalyst is important to her—and she is aware that she has been *marked* by the war, the Occupation, her personal losses and the international loss of innocence represented in the book by the dropping of the atom bomb and the beginnings of the cold war. Still, she declines to take part in the political movement the men are founding, except as a spectator. She does not speak or act; she witnesses, she suffers, she binds the wounds of others while wondering if it is right to cure patients of their bad dreams by helping them 'bear' an unbearable reality. Someone asks Anne Dubreuilh if she is a writer. And she replies, 'Thank god, no!' This in spite of two passing references to 'mon livre'—she actually does write, but isn't a Writer. In fact she says to herself with great satisfaction 'I am no-one' (Beauvoir notes that her earlier heroine, Françoise, spoke the same words in anguish[11]). Most problematically of all, she comes into her own and becomes 'someone' in the second volume when, leaving France and politics behind, she discovers sexual satisfaction in the arms of the younger American writer, Lewis Brogan. And the end of this relationship leaves her despairing, ready to commit suicide by swallowing the very poison she took away from Paule, deterred only by a reminder that it would hurt her family. Is this lucid heroine really any better off than Paule for her lucidity?

. . . . .

> 'It's shameful!' I said to myself that evening. They were having a discussion in Robert's study; they were talking about the Marshall Plan, the future of Europe, the future of the whole world; they were saying that the chances of war were increasing . . . War concerns all of us, and I didn't take those troubled voices lightly. And yet, I was thinking only of that letter, of a single line in that letter: 'Across an ocean, the tenderest arms are cold indeed.' Why, in confessing to me a few unimportant affairs, had Lewis written those hostile words? (*The Mandarins*, p. 648)

> Then I thought: the truth is I don't care a damn about politics or philosophy or anything else; all I care about is that Michael should turn in the dark and put his face against my breasts. And then I drifted off to sleep. (*The Golden Notebook*, p. 299)

Politics and philosophy are within the grasp and competence of the heroine—but she does not reach out her hand to them. Something splits, divides each book into two separate channels, erotic (feminine?) and political (masculine?). Something structural, in both cases.

In *The Golden Notebook,* especially, the somewhat experimental structure of the fiction makes this point. Parallel discourses never meet. Lessing's main character, Anna Wulf, is a committed leftist, but she keeps her communism in one notebook, her personal life and her psychoanalysis in another; in still a third notebook, she is writing a novel whose third-person heroine, Ella, resembles her in many respects, but 'has no politics' of any sort. In *The Mandarins,* half the chapters, told in the first person by Anne Dubreuilh, recount a love story, the subjective experience of having survived the Occupation, the difficulties of female friendship and of mothering an adult daughter; the political history and the debates are confined to third-person chapters, seen through the consciousness of Henri (who also has love problems, it must be said). In both books, the great events of post-war history and politics rush by, runaway trains uncomfortably close: Hiroshima, the death of Stalin, the disclosures of the Soviet labour camps, the Prague trials, the death of the Rosenbergs. Each heroine knows people, is close to people—men, mostly—for whom this history imposes a sense of responsibility, a terrifying and yet sometimes exhilarating sense of being part of their age. And each heroine refuses this sense, this role.

Lessing's Anna Wulf refuses it by refusing histrionics, heroism, by refusing and criticising what she calls 'the myth of the group'—by her irony (a quality she dislikes in herself) she refuses it. Sometimes she sees herself as a 'boulder-pusher', a kind of antitheoretical social worker within a vague progressive movement, but even this may be too noble; in Africa she plays the 'age-old role of the leader's girlfriend', who argues in literary and personal terms when she knows it is more 'correct' to take a collective, abstract, 'political' approach. She sleeps with history: first with Willi, the apparatchik in training (and the sex is bad); then with Michael, who has left the Party, betrayed and (in their eyes) betrayer, yet who calls himself 'the history of Europe in his century'. The sex is good, but he leaves her. The position she defines for herself, in this way, is often self-deprecating; never more so than when her subjectivity is sexual subjectivity, as in the quotation above. Lessing deliberately invites us, in certain places, to play the role of the communist grand inquisitor, to be shocked, to take on the voice of the party (this is the voice people hear even now in their paranoid fantasies about 'PC') and say: irresponsible, middle-class, masochistic Anna, no fit role model for us and for the new society. This is one of the voices in which Anna speaks to herself, of course. One of her many valedictions forbidding writing is her condemnation of her earlier book as 'nostalgic', as 'a little novel about the emotions'.

But this is very clever of Lessing, is in fact a key part of the amazing ideological balancing act that is *The Golden Notebook.* For the personal, the ironic, the sexual, the naïve, is part of what undermines the grand political myths; and the grand political myths are destroying Europe and the world. Even as Anna surrounds herself with newspaper clippings, forces herself not to write (and this blocked writer is dying to write—all sorts of stories pour out—because she is trying to censor the individual, to become useful, to merge with a collectivity) there is the sense that those who believe themselves to be in touch with, in control of these events, are dangerous madmen or the dupes of dangerous madmen. It is not just that what seems to be the only effective political force, the communist party, seems to require so much lying, so much lying to oneself. It is also true that when the clippings come out of the notebook and start to take over the apartment Anna is on the verge of going mad. Anna and her best friend Molly joke bitterly that in a truly revolutionary situation one of them would probably have ordered the other shot by now. Similarly, all the brave self-sacrificing politicking of the men in *The Mandarins* comes to precisely nothing, comes to the realisation that France is a third-rate power within which the intellectual has no public role to play and may not even be able to save his own freedom of conscience.

Yes, there is a weakness in refusing the leadership role, there is a feminine masochism in insisting that it is 'more my husband's game than mine' (as a prominent feminist scholar of our own day said about epistemology).[*] Still, in the post-war world, to refuse that role is also to refuse the 'necessity' of doing something awful. The personal becomes the affirmation of a genuine ethical space, involved with history but not at its mercy.

Certainly the feminist romance with the male left is over. Which might be one way of smugly rescuing these texts for feminism: see, we were right all along, the politics of orgasm is more important than how feminist concerns can harmonise with efforts to change the whole political and economic structure. Yet that would be a retreat from the darkness of the books themselves, from their assertion of the connection. Because while neither book can 'bring off' a connection between personal and political, neither is willing to cheat by pretending to resolve the tension it sets up, and each has a famously unsatisfying inconclusive ending. Denied a comfortable identification anywhere, serious readers located themselves in the space in between, with the governing consciousness who wants to be engaged but not to become a monster.

Still, these refusals on the basis of the sexual are what have made feminist readers most uneasy later. *The Mandarins,* and Beauvoir's fiction generally, has been dogged by the assertion that it is writing for shopgirls, '*midinettes*'.[12] Clearly this view trivialises all women, and our concerns. But I find a trace of the same unease in the view (beginning with Heilbrun) that Beauvoir's fiction has failed to give us strong, non-masochistic role models, that it is a retreat from, in some ways the evil twin of, *The Second Sex.* And there are sections of *The Golden Notebook* that are hard to teach to a feminist classroom for precisely the same reason, especially the section where Anna, speaking through Ella, affirms that there is such a thing as a vaginal orgasm—'It is the orgasm that is created by the man's need for a woman, and his confidence in that need' (p. 215)—and that it is vastly superior to the 'clitoral' orgasms Paul is pleased to 'give' Ella when he is backing away from emotional

commitment to her. She even says, 'for a woman, integrity is the orgasm', as if orgasm were itself utopic, and capable of breaking down barriers, the opposite of escapism. (This 'utopia' can only be articulated in the context of its failure, however.)

The two textual moments I cited above—moments where the heroine unhooks herself from politics and especially from political responsibility—are guilty moments for the heroine and for the reader. They express a 'split' in the heroine between thinking and feeling, between reason and emotion. But they are also moments of tremendous authenticity and radical truth. Female subjectivity through sexuality seems profoundly masochistic, dependent, scandalous; but it is also affirming its autonomy from male systems, breaking free. And since the ethical centre of both novels is a search for a language in which the truth could finally be told . . .

. . . . .

Both *The Mandarins* and *The Golden Notebook* contain memorable descriptions of monumentally bad heterosexual sex, depicted from a woman's point of view, in fact from the point of view of a woman's natural and healthy interest in, and right to, less-than-monumentally-bad heterosexual sex. Both discuss the female and male anatomy in a detailed and unsentimentalised way, and again from the point of view of women's subjective experience of it. In both traditions, this is pathbreaking. (It is easy to forget the shock and impact, in 1962, of what Rachel Blau DuPlessis called 'the first Tampax in world literature'.[13]) Beauvoir implies, and Lessing says straight out, that female sexual subjectivity is different from male sexual subjectivity. We need not accept this point, which has been highly contested since; or, we can accept its descriptive accuracy without seeing it as inevitable and rooted in the 'natural' (Lessing wouldn't accept that modification; Beauvoir, according to some readings of *The Second Sex,* might have). But it seems almost more important to me that each asserted that female sexual subjectivity even EXISTED, deserved to be named, talked about by women themselves (not shrinks or Sartre). I would argue there is in each text a serious point of resistance that keeps the book from turning into either Mills and Boon goop *or* a socialist-realist diatribe against the personal, and that the point of resistance, in both texts, is women's negative experiences of heterosexual sex.(Sex, not 'relationships' or 'love'.)

The Golden Notebook is almost a Sears Roebuck-sized catalogue of what we have since learned to politely call 'sexual miscommunication'. Willi and Anna in Africa are incompatible 'as if the very chemical structures of [their] bodies were hostile' (p. 70); 'the only time I could remember him making love to me with any conviction was when he knew I had just made love to somebody else' (p. 151). Molly's repellent ex-husband Richard, a bourgeois businessman whose constant cheating on his wife Marion turns her into an alcoholic basketcase and all other women into 'popsies', stands throughout the book for a certain kind of sexual (and moral) stupidity:

> 'I know there's one problem you haven't got—it's a purely physical one. How to get an erection with a woman you've been married to fifteen years?' He said this with an air of camaraderie, as if offering his last card . . .

And it is clear that he misses the point, over and over again:

> 'You should have loved her', said Anna simply. . . . 'Good lord,' said Richard at a loss. 'After all I've said—and it hasn't been easy mind you . . . ' he said this almost threatening, and went red as both women rocked off into fresh peals of laughter. 'No it's not easy to talk about sex frankly to women'. (p. 31)

American men are caricatured, first in the minor figure of Cy Maitland, with his 'oh boy, oh boy!' wham-bam-thank-you-ma'am, almost innocent in his lack of awareness that anything else is possible, puzzled why his beautiful wife wants nothing to do with him in bed. Ella 'gives pleasure' and feels like a prostitute. And the last sections of the book turn into almost a laundry list of sadisms: the man who calls Julia a castrating woman after she has taken pity on his impotence; Da Silva, who turns women into players in his own sick sexual scripts; Milt, who can't make love to a woman he likes; Nelson, who is using Anna as a pawn in his neurotic battles with his wife; most of all Saul in the last sections. Saul may be clinically 'mad' and may be infecting Anna with his madness; he has lost his sense of time, seems to be a number of different people, often seems unsure just who he is making love to when he is in bed with Anna . . . Yet part of what Anna is fighting is her own masochism and the tendency to turn all this experience into self-pity. She fights not to be a victim. And her weapons are partly formal: she turns some of her experience over to Ella, the fictional Anna character in the novel she is sort of writing, and arranges some of the rest of it in lists of possible 'stories' or scripts, as if to distance it and analyse it. Although the Anna who analyses is a stranger to the Anna who is capable of falling in love, who can 'create through naïveté'.

> Sex is essentially emotional for women. How many times has that been written? And yet there's always a point even with the most perceptive and intelligent man, when a woman looks at him across a gulf: he hasn't understood; she suddenly feels alone; hastens to forget the moment, because if she doesn't she would have to think. Julia, myself and Bob sitting in her kitchen gossiping. Bob telling a story about the breakup of a marriage. He says: 'The trouble was sex. Poor bastard, he's got a prick the size of a needle.' Julia: 'I always thought she didn't love him.' Bob, thinking she hadn't heard: 'No, it's always worried him stiff, he's just got a small one.' Julia: 'But she never did love him, anyone could see that just by looking at them together.' (p. 215)

Yet for all this focus on the 'emotional' side, and for all Ella's irritation with Paul's 'mechanical' ways of bringing her to orgasm, the worst sexual moments in this novel (and in *The Mandarins*) occur when the heroine realises that a man with whom she has felt deep sexual satisfaction shows that he actually can't tell (and doesn't care) when she doesn't. And, as depressing and frustrating as the status of 'free woman' under patriarchy is for Anna and Molly (and Ella and Julia), the book never retreats from its early assertion of the good reason to be one.

> Challenged now, I would say that every woman believes in her heart that if her man does not satisfy her she has a right to go to another. (p. 143)

None of the currently available narratives of female eroticism is acceptable to Anna; any way of talking about it turns out to be a trap; the points of resistance are that Anna names this; and that she does not give up.

. . . . .

The Mandarins makes a similar point about female sexuality by a different sort of splitting. The first sex scene in the book takes place between Henri and Paule, and is told from the point of view of Henri, who would like their affair to be over.

> He heard a rustle of silk, then the sound of running water and the clinking of glass, those sounds which once used to make his heart pound. 'No, not tonight, not tonight,' he said to himself uneasily . . . She slipped in between the sheets and without uttering a word, pressed her body to his; he could find no pretext to repulse her.[14]

Her hand on his erect penis, Paule insists that Henri tell her that he loves her, that he repeat the ritual endearments of their courtship, and he does.

> She uttered a long moan of satisfaction. He embraced her violently, smothered her mouth with his lips, and to get it over with as quickly as possible immediately penetrated her . . . He was horrified by her and by himself. Her head bent back, her eyes half closed, her teeth bared, she had given herself so totally to love, was so frightfully lost, that he felt like slapping her to bring her back to earth, felt like saying, 'It's just you and I and we're making love, that's all.' It seemed to him as if he were raping a dead woman, or a lunatic, and it took him forever to come. When finally he fell limp on Paula, he heard a triumphant moan.
>
> 'Are you happy?' she murmured.
>
> 'Of course.'[15]

This is almost a textbook example of what the existentialists call 'bad faith'. Paule lies to herself and to Henri (because she must know that he no longer loves her; she plays a role of the 'most beautiful woman in the world' loved by the 'most glorious of men' to the point where she no longer knows who she is or what she feels). It is strikingly similar to the examples (anecdotes, really) about women's frigidity which Sartre used to define the whole concept of 'bad faith' in *Being and Nothingness*. It's also very similar to Beauvoir's discussion of the bad faith and self-deception of the 'femme amoureuse' in *The Second Sex;* for Beauvoir, this is one of the very worst ways that a woman can 'assume her situation' as an oppressed person, one of the ways that implies being deeply complicit in her own oppression.

But Sartre could not have written this scene—which you can see if you compare it with the novelistic depictions of sexual disgust he did write, in *Nausea* and in the first volume of *The Roads to Freedom*. Because *Henri's* bad faith is also in evidence here: however sympathetic he is to us, he is clearly a coward, unable to acknowledge his own freedom or his own responsibility. What can be said about someone who feels as if he is raping a dead woman—but still does it?

This incident is balanced by one where Anne goes out for the evening with a minor character named Scriassine, a Russian refugee associated with their political group. It is significant that he has already made Anne uneasy, at the party which opens the book, by predicting that French intellectuals are about to find themselves at an impasse, forced to choose between the imperialisms of the Soviet Union and the US or be crushed between them; and that in the course of the book he will move further and further to the right, as the degeneration of their movement leaves Robert and Henri more and more isolated. For Anne at this moment, however, he represents more of a risk that she makes herself take because she is afraid to do so. She has been considering that her life as a woman is over; her daughter Nadine has accused her of going through life with kid gloves on; his desire reminds her that she still has a body. But:

> He took me in his arms and I felt a hard yet gentle mouth pressing against my lips. Yes, it was possible, it was even easy . . . I closed my eyes and stepped into a dream as lifelike as reality itself, a dream from which I felt I would awaken at dawn, carefree and lighthearted. And then I heard his voice: 'The little girl seems frightened. But we won't hurt the little girl; we'll deflower her, but painlessly.' These words which were not addressed to me, awakened me rudely. I hadn't come here to play at being the ravished maiden, nor at any other game. I pushed myself free.
>
> 'Wait.'[16]

Scriassine's first mistake is to insist on reading Anne as a player in his own sexual drama. But this does not destroy her sexual feelings all at once:

> His hands ripped off my slip, caressed my belly, and I abandoned myself to the black swell of desire. Carried away, tossed about, submerged, aroused, dashed headlong; there were moments when I felt as if I were plummeting through empty space, were about to be stranded in oblivion, in the blackness of night. What a voyage!
>
> His voice threw me back abruptly on the bed. 'Do I have to be careful?'
>
> 'If you can.'
>
> 'You mean you're not wearing anything?'
>
> The question was so brutal it made me start.
>
> 'No,' I replied.
>
> 'Why not? why aren't you?' he asked angrily.
>
> It was difficult to begin again. Once more I gathered myself together under his hands, welcomed the silence, clung to his body and absorbed his warmth through my every pore. My bones, my flesh were melting and peace was wrapping itself about me in silky spirals, and then he said commandingly,
>
> 'Open your eyes.'[17]

What Henri wanted to say to Paule—'open your eyes, it's only you and me making love'—Scriassine actually says to Anne; she, unlike Paule, can see his point, but it destroys her pleasure—and he holds that against her, too.

> 'You have no real love for the penis.'
>
> This time he scored a point against me.[18]

In one way, this scene is the first scene inside out, one more sympathetic to the point of view, also expressed in *The Second Sex*, that women's desire is deeply different from men's—quieter, slower, more 'situational', more emotional, less concentrated on the one organ, more diffuse. In this way Anne becomes allied with Paule and we may see that 'ouvre les yeux' is not in fact the right thing to say. In another way, and especially as things progress from bad to worse, Anne becomes allied with Henri, in that both experience themselves as subjects but are treated as objects by the other, who needs to appropriate their pleasure.

Like Henri, Anne ends up simulating a pleasure she does not feel, to get it over with; like Henri and unlike Paule, she takes a certain amount of lucid responsibility. Later, with a man she loves, she will be able to feel and express genuine sexual pleasure—including 'un vrai amour pour le sexe de l'homme'. But then, like Paule, like Anna, she will discover that she does not really know what he is feeling, that he does not really know what she is feeling, and that he is able to get sexual pleasure even without knowing and without caring. And this will be the worst betrayal.

Many possible conclusions could be drawn from this analysis. It can help us see, for example, that while there is a tragedy implied in the differences between women's sexuality and men's, as Beauvoir says in *The Second Sex,* there is also a human tragedy in the separation of consciousness each from the other—a truth the temporary reciprocity of sexual meeting can only temporarily block. And it is important, as part of a larger argument about the usefulness of *The Second Sex* and Beauvoir generally, to see how complicated her vision of this was and finally how un-Sartrean. There's a baseline authenticity to this language, simply an explicitness, that is its own point: when we read a description like, 'Inside me, I sensed a presence without really feeling it, as you sense a dentist's tool against a swollen gum', we may feel that the experience of being a sexual woman is being named with incredible specificity, and that this in itself asserts the right of women to be sexual subjects, to feel what they feel and name it.[19] It is finally this authenticity that shows resistance to conventional sexual scripts, including Sartre's, and incidentally shows that she takes refuge neither in a cosy essentialism nor in a self-denying male-identification. Like Anna Wulf, like Doris Lessing, Anne and Simone cannot solve the problems they raise. The point is that they raise them, and they don't cheat and say they have the answer. And in an era where every book about women, every book about sex, *did* claim to have the answer, and the answer for every woman, about what women wanted, what would make women sexually happy, this was (and still seems to me) breathtaking.

. . . . .

These two texts have not lost their power to disturb us, because the problems they have not solved, we have not solved (though we may have set them aside). Part of the unfulfilled promise of feminism was that sex would get better, that the sexual contract would be revised. That somehow through collective activity 'we' would bring about change so that 'I' would have better choices than Anne and Anna had in this most intimate, least obviously 'collective' area. (Though each 'I' would still have to make them.)

Looking at the young women in my class who are about to graduate, and comparing them to the young women of 1970, I see enormous economic strides. On the terrain of sexuality, I see enormous discursive change, but not much *progress.* The issue of so-called 'date rape' is rightly prominent: it signals that heterosexual activity still occurs on men's turf and on their terms, and that women are not positioned to negotiate successfully for their own pleasure.

I must admit, finally, that there has been something fishy, all along, in my account of feminist history. I've been discussing *The Golden Notebook* and *The Mandarins* as somehow pre-feminist or proto-feminist texts; this both does and doesn't make historical sense. Both Lessing, in her 1972 introduction to *The*

Golden Notebook, and Beauvoir, in the introduction of *The Second Sex* itself (1949, please note), explicitly distance themselves from 'feminism', not because it hasn't happened yet, but because it is *over,* obsolescent, boring, beside the point. (Both would express some initial unease with the feminism about to be reborn and reclaim them as its heroines; Beauvoir quickly got over hers, but Lessing continues to express her view that the 'sex war' is irrelevant to political realities, to the distress of many fans.) Can a text be both pre-feminist and post-feminist at the same time?

Certainly they're in good company: Virginia Woolf declared herself ready to scatter the ashes of a successful, obsolete, and slightly embarrassing 'feminist' movement as early as 1928, in *A Room of One's Own.* Readers will recall that this book, probably more important to feminist intellectuals in the twentieth century than any other unless that other is *The Second Sex* itself, also calls on us to stop using the word 'feminist' and to put aside our anger at women's oppression as we set aside all other obstacles to 'the white light of truth'.

When teaching, it is tempting to brush this off as a regrettable but unimportant concession to male readers (Forster, Strachey and company; Sartre and company). But there may be more to it than that. Michèle Le Doeuff, who has also noticed that 'the woman question' always 'presents itself to the conscious mind as the question-which-has-already-obviously-been-settled', links this recurring gesture to 'the point that every woman's life is lived in contradiction': one is oppressed, and one is at the same time sufficiently free of oppression to name and denounce it.[20] There may also be something about the position of the woman writer *as writer* that intensifies this contradiction, in the same way that, while it is odd to hear a woman stand up and *say,* 'I have been silenced', one hears it all the time—and rightly so, since the alternative is for women to actually remain silent. In any case, my point is that the linear progress narrative of feminism both does and doesn't ring true. Feminist history both evolves in real time and unfolds within mythic time. But this hardly makes it less powerful.

NOTES

[1] Simone de Beauvoir, *Les Mandarins* (Paris: Editions Gallimard, 1954), vol. 2, 343. 'You can't draw a straight line in a curved space,' Dubreuilh said. 'You can't lead a proper life in a society which isn't proper' (*The Mandarins,* translated by Leonard Friedman, Flamingo, London, 1993, 625). Unless noted, all further references will be to these editions.

[2] Doris Lessing, *The Golden Notebook* (New York: Bantam, 1962), 458. All further references will be to this edition.

[3] Michèle Le Doeuff, *Hipparchia's Choice: An Essay Concerning Women, Philosophy, etc.* (Oxford: Basil Blackwell, 1991).

[4] Sally Munt, Introduction, *New Lesbian Criticism* (New York: Columbia University Press 1992), p. xv.

[5] Jenny Taylor (ed.), *Notebooks/memoirs/archives: reading and rereading Doris Lessing* (Routledge, 1982).

[6] In Taylor, 57, 71.

[7] *Conditions,* April 1977, part 1, p. 60. Reprinted in Claire Sprague and Virginia Tiger (eds), *Critical Essays on Doris Lessing* (Boston: G. K. Hall, 1986), 181-2.

[8] Adrienne Rich, 'Compulsory Heterosexuality and Lesbian Existence', *Signs* (Summer 1980), 631-57.

[9] Carolyn Heilbrun, *Reinventing Womanhood* (New York: W. W. Norton, 1979), 72-3. Heilbrun says 'Anna' instead of 'Anne' throughout—coincidence?

[10] *The Prime of Life,* translated by Peter Green (Cleveland: World Publishing Company, 1962), 69.

[11] *The Prime of Life,* 269.

[12] See Toril Moi's excellent discussion of this topic in *Simone de Beauvoir: The Making of an Intellectual Woman* (Oxford: Blackwell, 1994).

[13] Rachel Blau DuPlessis, *The Pink Guitar: Writing as Feminist Practice* (London: Routledge, 1990), 10.

[14] *The Mandarins,* 33. Having worked from the original French, I was rather surprised to discover quite late in the game that many of the passages most central to my argument were silently omitted from the recent and rather classy-looking British Flamingo edition. I have supplied them from an American edition with a rather lurid cover, which is otherwise the same Leonard Friedman translation. So, beginning with 'He could find no pretext', the above comes from *The Mandarins* (New York: Popular Library Eagle Books, 1956), 22. I'll leave it to my British readers to explain this anomaly.

[15] American edition, 23. Translation further altered by me.

[16] American edition, 71, slightly altered.

[17] American edition, 72, slightly altered.

[18] My translation.

[19] American edition, 73.

[20] Le Doeuff, 3, 128.

FURTHER READING

Secondary Sources

Allen, Dennis W. *Sexuality in Victorian Fiction.* Norman: University of Oklahoma Press, 1993, 160 p.
> Studies Victorian literary representations of sexuality using the following texts: *Pride and Prejudice, Cranford, Bleak House,* and *The Picture of Dorian Gray.*

Atkins, John. *Sex in Literature: The Erotic Impulse in Literature.* London: Calder and Boyars, 1970, 411 p.
> Survey of various sexual subjects in literature, including lust, the female body, and masturbation.

Berlant, Lauren. "Re-Writing the Medusa: Welty's 'Petrified Man.'" *Studies in Short Fiction* 26, No. 1 (Winter 1989): 59-70.
> Analyzes the violence of heterosexual difference dramatized in Eudora Welty's "Petrified Man."

Brians, Paul. "Sexuality and the Opposite Sex: Variations on a Theme by Theophile Gautier and Anaïs Nin." *Essays in Literature* IV, No. 1 (Spring 1977): 122-37.
> Explores the theme of changing women's sexual roles in Gautier's *Mademoiselle de Maupin* and Nin's *A Spy in the House of Love.*

Buchen, Irving, ed. *The Perverse Imagination: Sexuality and Literary Culture.* New York: New York University Press, 1970, 296 p.
> Collection of essays on such subjects as sadism, pornography, incest, and erotica in literature.

Charney, Maurice. *Sexual Fiction.* London: Methuen, 1981, 180 p.
> In-depth study of the "fantasizing impulse of sexual writing and its stylistic and thematic assumptions."

Duffy, Maureen. *The Erotic World of Faery.* London: Hodder and Stoughton, 1972, 352 p.
> Examines the sexual component of traditional fantasy literature from the writings of St. Augustine and Edmund Spencer to those of the Brothers Grimm and Christina Rossetti.

Faris, Wendy B. "'Without Sin, and with Pleasure': The Erotic Dimensions of Fuentes' Fiction." *Novel* 20, No. 1 (Fall 1986): 62-77.
> Investigates the visionary and utopian dimension of erotic couplings in the writings of Carlos Fuentes.

Helford, Elyce Rae. "'We Are Only Seeking Man': Gender, Psychoanalysis, and Stanislaw Lem's *Solaris.*" *Science Fiction Studies* 19, No. 2 (July 1992): 167-77.
> Offers a psychoanalysis of sexuality and gender relations (informed by Lacanian and feminist theory) in Stanislaw Lem's science fiction novel *Solaris.*

Kiell, Norman. *Varieties of Sexual Experience: Psychosexuality in Literature.* New York: International Universities Press, Inc., 1976, 753 p.
Observes various aspects of sex as they are represented in literature, grouped by subject and including "olfactory eroticism, anal eroticism, phallic women, the primal scene, drugs and sex, transsexualism and transvestitism" as well as homosexuality, autoeroticism, and other forms of sexual experience.

Kopelson, Kevin. *Love's Litany: The Writing of Modern Homoerotics.* Stanford, Calif.: Stanford University Press, 1994, 194 p.
Discusses homoeroticism in the works of such writers as Oscar Wilde, André Gide, Virginia Woolf, Gertrude Stein, Mary Renault, Roland Barthes, and others.

Leach, Donald. "Sexual Conflict and Self Disintegration in the Work of J. K. Huysmans." *Literature and Psychology* XXXXI, Nos. 1 & 2 (1995): 37-51.
Presents a critique of classical, Freudian psychoanalytic theory using the works of J. K. Huysmans.

O'Connor, Eugene Michael. *Symbolum Salacitatis: A Study of the God Priapus as a Literary Character.* Frankfurt am Main: Verlag Peter Lang, 1989, 214 p.
Historical and literary analysis of Greek and Roman Priapic poetry.

Palumbo, Donald, ed. *Erotic Universe: Sexuality and Fantastic Literature.* New York: Greenwood Press, 1986, 305 p.
Contains fifteen essays on "the most salient concerns, themes, viewpoints, and motifs" related to sexuality and eroticism in science fiction and fantasy literature.

Reisner, Robert George. *Show Me the Good Parts: The Reader's Guide to Sex in Literature.* New York: The Citadel Press, 1964, 340 p.
Alphabetical approach to sexual subjects in literature from adultery to voyeurism.

Rubenstein, Roberta. "Sexuality and Intertextuality: Margaret Drabble's *The Radiant Way.*" *Contemporary Literature* 30, No. 1 (Spring 1989): 95-112.
Examines the psychological, sexual, and textual implications of Margaret Drabble's use of the Labyrinth and Medusa myths in her novel *The Radiant Way.*

Siegel, Carol. *Male Masochism: Modern Revisions of the Story of Love.* Bloomington: Indiana University Press, 1995, 211 p.
Focuses on the representation of male masochism in literature and film from the European colonial period to the postmodern era.

Stratton, Jon. *The Virgin Text: Fiction, Sexuality & Ideology.* Brighton, Sussex: The Harvester Press, 1987, 237 p.
Uses "the theoretical assumptions of psychoanalysis and of Marxism" to construct a sexualized "rewriting of the history of the novel."

Van Meter, Jan R. "Sex and War in *The Red Badge of Courage*: Cultural Themes and Literary Criticism." *Genre* VII, No. 1 (March 1974): 71-90.
Explores the relationship between sexuality and warfare in the language and imagery of Stephen Crane's novel *The Red Badge of Courage.*

Twentieth-Century
Literary Criticism

Cumulative Indexes
Volumes 1-82

How to Use This Index

The main references

Calvino, Italo
1923–1985 .... CLC 5, 8, 11, 22, 33, 39,
73; SSC 3

list all author entries in the following Gale Literary Criticism series:

BLC = *Black Literature Criticism*
CLC = *Contemporary Literary Criticism*
CLR = *Children's Literature Review*
CMLC = *Classical and Medieval Literature Criticism*
DA = *DISCovering Authors*
DAB = *DISCovering Authors: British*
DAC = *DISCovering Authors: Canadian*
DAM = *DISCovering Authors: Modules*
       DRAM: *Dramatists Module;* *MST*: *Most-Studied Authors Module;*
       MULT: *Multicultural Authors Module;* *NOV*: *Novelists Module;*
       POET: *Poets Module;* *POP*: *Popular Fiction and Genre Authors Module*
DC = *Drama Criticism*
HLC = *Hispanic Literature Criticism*
LC = *Literature Criticism from 1400 to 1800*
NCLC = *Nineteenth-Century Literature Criticism*
PC = *Poetry Criticism*
SSC = *Short Story Criticism*
TCLC = *Twentieth-Century Literary Criticism*
WLC = *World Literature Criticism, 1500 to the Present*

The cross-references

See also CANR 23; CA 85-88;
   obituary CA116

list all author entries in the following Gale biographical and literary sources:

AAYA = *Authors & Artists for Young Adults*
AITN = *Authors in the News*
BEST = *Bestsellers*
BW = *Black Writers*
CA = *Contemporary Authors*
CAAS = *Contemporary Authors Autobiography Series*
CABS = *Contemporary Authors Bibliographical Series*
CANR = *Contemporary Authors New Revision Series*
CAP = *Contemporary Authors Permanent Series*
CDALB = *Concise Dictionary of American Literary Biography*
CDBLB = *Concise Dictionary of British Literary Biography*
DLB = *Dictionary of Literary Biography*
DLBD = *Dictionary of Literary Biography Documentary Series*
DLBY = *Dictionary of Literary Biography Yearbook*
HW = *Hispanic Writers*
JRDA = *Junior DISCovering Authors*
MAICYA = *Major Authors and Illustrators for Children and Young Adults*
MTCW = *Major 20th-Century Writers*
NNAL = *Native North American Literature*
SAAS = *Something about the Author Autobiography Series*
SATA = *Something about the Author*
YABC = *Yesterday's Authors of Books for Children*

Literary Criticism Series
Cumulative Author Index

Aldanov, M. A.
See Aldanov, Mark (Alexandrovich)
Aldanov, Mark (Alexandrovich) [1886(?)-1957]
TCLC 23
See also CA 118
Aldington, Richard [1892-1962] .... **CLC 49**
See also CA 85-88; CANR 45; DLB 20, 36, 100, 149
Aldiss, Brian W(ilson) [1925-]**CLC 5, 14, 40;**
DAM NOV
See also CA 5-8R; CAAS 2; CANR 5, 28, 64;
DLB 14; MTCW; SATA 34
Alegria, Claribel [1924-]........**CLC 75; DAM**
MULT
See also CA 131; CAAS 15; CANR 66; DLB 145; HW
Alegria, Fernando [1918-] .... **CLC 57**
See also CA 9-12R; CANR 5, 32; HW
Aleichem, Sholom .... **TCLC 1, 35**
See also Rabinovitch, Sholem
Aleixandre, Vicente [1898-1984] **CLC 9, 36;**
DAM POET; PC 15
See also CA 85-88; 114; CANR 26; DLB 108;
HW; MTCW
Alepoudelis, Odysseus
See Elytis, Odysseus
Aleshkovsky, Joseph [1929-]
See Aleshkovsky, Yuz
See also CA 121; 128
Aleshkovsky, Yuz .... **CLC 44**
See also Aleshkovsky, Joseph
Alexander, Lloyd (Chudley) [1924-] **CLC 35**
See also AAYA 1; CA 1-4R; CANR 1, 24, 38, 55; CLR 1, 5, 48; DLB 52; JRDA; MAICYA;
MTCW; SAAS 19; SATA 3, 49, 81
Alexander, Samuel [1859-1938] ..... **TCLC 77**
Alexie, Sherman (Joseph, Jr.) [1966-]**CLC 96;**
DAM MULT
See also CA 138; CANR 65; DLB 175; NNAL
Alfau, Felipe [1902-] .... **CLC 66**
See also CA 137
Alger, Horatio, Jr. [1832-1899] .... **NCLC 8**
See also DLB 42; SATA 16
Algren, Nelson [1909-1981] .... **CLC 4, 10, 33**
See also CA 13-16R; 103; CANR 20, 61;
CDALB 1941-1968; DLB 9; DLBY 81, 82;
MTCW
Ali, Ahmed [1910-] .... **CLC 69**
See also CA 25-28R; CANR 15, 34
Alighieri, Dante
See Dante
Allan, John B.
See Westlake, Donald E(dwin)
Allan, Sidney
See Hartmann, Sadakichi
Allan, Sydney
See Hartmann, Sadakichi
Allen, Edward [1948-] .... **CLC 59**
Allen, Paula Gunn [1939-] ..... **CLC 84; DAM**
MULT
See also CA 112; 143; CANR 63; DLB 175;
NNAL
Allen, Roland
See Ayckbourn, Alan
Allen, Sarah A.
See Hopkins, Pauline Elizabeth
Allen, Sidney H.
See Hartmann, Sadakichi
Allen, Woody [1935-]**CLC 16, 52; DAM POP**
See also AAYA 10; CA 33-36R; CANR 27, 38, 63; DLB 44; MTCW
Allende, Isabel [1942-]**CLC 39, 57, 97; DAM**
MULT, NOV; HLC; WLCS
See also AAYA 18; CA 125; 130; CANR 51;
DLB 145; HW; INT 130; MTCW
Alleyn, Ellen

See Rossetti, Christina (Georgina)
Allingham, Margery (Louise) [1904-1966]
CLC 19
See also CA 5-8R; 25-28R; CANR 4, 58; DLB 77; MTCW
Allingham, William [1824-1889] ... **NCLC 25**
See also DLB 35
Allison, Dorothy E. [1949-] .... **CLC 78**
See also CA 140; CANR 66
Allston, Washington [1779-1843] .... **NCLC 2**
See also DLB 1
Almedingen, E. M. .... **CLC 12**
See also Almedingen, Martha Edith von
See also SATA 3
Almedingen, Martha Edith von [1898-1971]
See Almedingen, E. M.
See also CA 1-4R; CANR 1
Almqvist, Carl Jonas Love [1793-1866]**NCLC 42**
Alonso, Damaso [1898-1990] .... **CLC 14**
See also CA 110; 131; 130; DLB 108; HW
Alov
See Gogol, Nikolai (Vasilyevich)
Alta [1942-] .... **CLC 19**
See also CA 57-60
Alter, Robert B(ernard) [1935-] .... **CLC 34**
See also CA 49-52; CANR 1, 47
Alther, Lisa [1944-] .... **CLC 7, 41**
See also CA 65-68; CANR 12, 30, 51; MTCW
Althusser, L.
See Althusser, Louis
Althusser, Louis [1918-1990] .... **CLC 106**
See also CA 131; 132
Altman, Robert [1925-] .... **CLC 16**
See also CA 73-76; CANR 43
Alvarez, A(lfred) [1929-] .... **CLC 5, 13**
See also CA 1-4R; CANR 3, 33, 63; DLB 14, 40
Alvarez, Alejandro Rodriguez [1903-1965]
See Casona, Alejandro
See also CA 131; 93-96; HW
Alvarez, Julia [1950-] .... **CLC 93**
See also AAYA 25; CA 147; CANR 69
Alvaro, Corrado [1896-1956] .... **TCLC 60**
See also CA 163
Amado, Jorge [1912-]**CLC 13, 40, 106; DAM**
MULT, NOV; HLC
See also CA 77-80; CANR 35; DLB 113;
MTCW
Ambler, Eric [1909-] .... **CLC 4, 6, 9**
See also CA 9-12R; CANR 7, 38; DLB 77;
MTCW
Amichai, Yehuda [1924-] .... **CLC 9, 22, 57**
See also CA 85-88; CANR 46, 60; MTCW
Amichai, Yehudah
See Amichai, Yehuda
Amiel, Henri Frederic [1821-1881] . **NCLC 4**
Amis, Kingsley (William) [1922-1995]**CLC 1,**
2, 3, 5, 8, 13, 40, 44; DA; DAB; DAC; DAM
MST, NOV
See also AITN 2; CA 9-12R; 150; CANR 8, 28, 54; CDBLB 1945-1960; DLB 15, 27, 100, 139; DLBY 96; INT CANR-8; MTCW
Amis, Martin (Louis) [1949-]**CLC 4, 9, 38, 62, 101**
See also BEST 90:3; CA 65-68; CANR 8, 27, 54; DLB 14, 194; INT CANR-27
Ammons, A(rchie) R(andolph) [1926-]**CLC 2, 3, 5, 8, 9, 25, 57, 108; DAM POET; PC 16**
See also AITN 1; CA 9-12R; CANR 6, 36, 51;
DLB 5, 165; MTCW
Amo, Tauraatua i
See Adams, Henry (Brooks)
Anand, Mulk Raj [1905-] **CLC 23, 93; DAM**
NOV
See also CA 65-68; CANR 32, 64; MTCW
Anatol

See Schnitzler, Arthur
Anaximander [c. 610B.C.-c. 546B.C.] **CMLC 22**
Anaya, Rudolfo A(lfonso) [1937-] .. **CLC 23;**
DAM MULT, NOV; HLC
See also AAYA 20; CA 45-48; CAAS 4; CANR 1, 32, 51; DLB 82; HW 1; MTCW
Andersen, Hans Christian [1805-1875]**NCLC 7; DA; DAB; DAC; DAM MST, POP; SSC 6; WLC**
See also CLR 6; MAICYA; YABC 1
Anderson, C. Farley
See Mencken, H(enry) L(ouis); Nathan, George Jean
Anderson, Jessica (Margaret) Queale [1916-]
CLC 37
See also CA 9-12R; CANR 4, 62
Anderson, Jon (Victor) [1940-]**CLC 9; DAM POET**
See also CA 25-28R; CANR 20
Anderson, Lindsay (Gordon) [1923-1994]
CLC 20
See also CA 125; 128; 146
Anderson, Maxwell [1888-1959].....**TCLC 2;**
DAM DRAM
See also CA 105; 152; DLB 7
Anderson, Poul (William) [1926-] .... **CLC 15**
See also AAYA 5; CA 1-4R; CAAS 2; CANR 2, 15, 34, 64; DLB 8; INT CANR-15;
MTCW; SATA 90; SATA-Brief 39
Anderson, Robert (Woodruff) [1917-] .. **C L C 23; DAM DRAM**
See also AITN 1; CA 21-24R; CANR 32; DLB 7
Anderson, Sherwood [1876-1941]**TCLC 1, 10, 24; DA; DAB; DAC; DAM MST, NOV; SSC 1; WLC**
See also CA 104; 121; CANR 61; CDALB 1917-1929; DLB 4, 9, 86; DLBD 1; MTCW
Andier, Pierre
See Desnos, Robert
Andouard
See Giraudoux, (Hippolyte) Jean
Andrade, Carlos Drummond de .... **CLC 18**
See also Drummond de Andrade, Carlos
Andrade, Mario de [1893-1945] .... **TCLC 43**
Andreae, Johann V(alentin) [1586-1654] **L C 32**
See also DLB 164
Andreas-Salome, Lou [1861-1937] **TCLC 56**
See also DLB 66
Andress, Lesley
See Sanders, Lawrence
Andrewes, Lancelot [1555-1626] .... **LC 5**
See also DLB 151, 172
Andrews, Cicily Fairfield
See West, Rebecca
Andrews, Elton V.
See Pohl, Frederik
Andreyev, Leonid (Nikolaevich) [1871-1919]
TCLC 3
See also CA 104
Andric, Ivo [1892-1975] .... **CLC 8**
See also CA 81-84; 57-60; CANR 43, 60; DLB 147; MTCW
Androvar
See Prado (Calvo), Pedro
Angelique, Pierre
See Bataille, Georges
Angell, Roger [1920-] .... **CLC 26**
See also CA 57-60; CANR 13, 44; DLB 171, 185
Angelou, Maya [1928-] . **CLC 12, 35, 64, 77;**
BLC 1; DA; DAB; DAC; DAM MST,
MULT, POET, POP; WLCS
See also AAYA 7, 20; BW 2; CA 65-68; CANR 19, 42, 65; DLB 38; MTCW; SATA 49

Anna Comnena [1083-1153] .... **CMLC 25**

Annensky, Innokenty (Fyodorovich) [1856-1909] .... **TCLC 14**
See also CA 110; 155

Annunzio, Gabriele d'
See D'Annunzio, Gabriele

Anodos
See Coleridge, Mary E(lizabeth)

Anon, Charles Robert
See Pessoa, Fernando (Antonio Nogueira)

Anouilh, Jean (Marie Lucien Pierre) [1910-1987] ....
CLC 1, 3, 8, 13, 40, 50; DAM DRAM; DC 8
See also CA 17-20R; 123; CANR 32; MTCW

Anthony, Florence
See Ai

Anthony, John
See Ciardi, John (Anthony)

Anthony, Peter
See Shaffer, Anthony (Joshua); Shaffer, Peter (Levin)

Anthony, Piers [1934-] . **CLC 35; DAM POP**
See also AAYA 11; CA 21-24R; CANR 28, 56; DLB 8; MTCW; SAAS 22; SATA 84

Antoine, Marc
See Proust, (Valentin-Louis-George-Eugene-) Marcel

Antoninus, Brother
See Everson, William (Oliver)

Antonioni, Michelangelo [1912-] ...... **CLC 20**
See also CA 73-76; CANR 45

Antschel, Paul [1920-1970]
See Celan, Paul
See also CA 85-88; CANR 33, 61; MTCW

Anwar, Chairil [1922-1949] .... **TCLC 22**
See also CA 121

Apollinaire, Guillaume [1880-1918]**TCLC 3, 8, 51; DAM POET; PC 7**
See also Kostrowitzki, Wilhelm Apollinaris de
See also CA 152

Appelfeld, Aharon [1932-].......... **CLC 23, 47**
See also CA 112; 133

Apple, Max (Isaac) [1941-] .... **CLC 9, 33**
See also CA 81-84; CANR 19, 54; DLB 130

Appleman, Philip (Dean) [1926-]...... **CLC 51**
See also CA 13-16R; CAAS 18; CANR 6, 29, 56

Appleton, Lawrence
See Lovecraft, H(oward) P(hillips)

Apteryx
See Eliot, T(homas) S(tearns)

Apuleius, (Lucius Madaurensis) [125(?)-175(?)] **CMLC 1**

Aquin, Hubert [1929-1977] .... **CLC 15**
See also CA 105; DLB 53

Aragon, Louis [1897-1982] **CLC 3, 22; DAM NOV, POET**
See also CA 69-72; 108; CANR 28; DLB 72; MTCW

Arany, Janos [1817-1882] .... **NCLC 34**

Arbuthnot, John [1667-1735] .... **LC 1**
See also DLB 101

Archer, Herbert Winslow
See Mencken, H(enry) L(ouis)

Archer, Jeffrey (Howard) [1940-] .. **CLC 28; DAM POP**
See also AAYA 16; BEST 89:3; CA 77-80; CANR 22, 52; INT CANR-22

Archer, Jules [1915-] .... **CLC 12**
See also CA 9-12R; CANR 6, 69; SAAS 5; SATA 4, 85

Archer, Lee
See Ellison, Harlan (Jay)

Arden, John [1930-] .... **CLC 6, 13, 15; DAM DRAM**
See also CA 13-16R; CAAS 4; CANR 31, 65, 67; DLB 13; MTCW

Arenas, Reinaldo [1943-1990]**CLC 41; DAM MULT; HLC**
See also CA 124; 128; 133; DLB 145; HW

Arendt, Hannah [1906-1975] ..... **CLC 66, 98**
See also CA 17-20R; 61-64; CANR 26, 60; MTCW

Aretino, Pietro [1492-1556] .... **LC 12**

Arghezi, Tudor .... **CLC 80**
See also Theodorescu, Ion N.

Arguedas, Jose Maria [1911-1969]**CLC 10, 18**
See also CA 89-92; DLB 113; HW

Argueta, Manlio [1936-] .... **CLC 31**
See also CA 131; DLB 145; HW

Ariosto, Ludovico [1474-1533] .... **LC 6**

Aristides
See Epstein, Joseph

Aristophanes [450B.C.-385B.C.]**CMLC 4; DA; DAB; DAC; DAM DRAM, MST; DC 2; WLCS**
See also DLB 176

Arlt, Roberto (Godofredo Christophersen) [1900-1942]**TCLC 29; DAM MULT; HLC**
See also CA 123; 131; CANR 67; HW

Armah, Ayi Kwei [1939-] **CLC 5, 33; BLC 1; DAM MULT, POET**
See also BW 1; CA 61-64; CANR 21, 64; DLB 117; MTCW

Armatrading, Joan [1950-] .... **CLC 17**
See also CA 114

Arnette, Robert
See Silverberg, Robert

Arnim, Achim von (Ludwig Joachim von Arnim) [1781-1831] ... **NCLC 5; SSC 29**
See also DLB 90

Arnim, Bettina von [1785-1859] .... **NCLC 38**
See also DLB 90

Arnold, Matthew [1822-1888] .. **NCLC 6, 29; DA; DAB; DAC; DAM MST, POET; PC 5; WLC**
See also CDBLB 1832-1890; DLB 32, 57

Arnold, Thomas [1795-1842] .... **NCLC 18**
See also DLB 55

Arnow, Harriette (Louisa) Simpson [1908-1986] .... **CLC 2, 7, 18**
See also CA 9-12R; 118; CANR 14; DLB 6; MTCW; SATA 42; SATA-Obit 47

Arp, Hans
See Arp, Jean

Arp, Jean [1887-1966].......................... **CLC 5**
See also CA 81-84; 25-28R; CANR 42

Arrabal
See Arrabal, Fernando

Arrabal, Fernando [1932-] . **CLC 2, 9, 18, 58**
See also CA 9-12R; CANR 15

Arrick, Fran .... **CLC 30**
See also Gaberman, Judie Angell

Artaud, Antonin (Marie Joseph) [1896-1948] **TCLC 3, 36; DAM DRAM**
See also CA 104; 149

Arthur, Ruth M(abel) [1905-1979] ... **CLC 12**
See also CA 9-12R; 85-88; CANR 4; SATA 7, 26

Artsybashev, Mikhail (Petrovich) [1878-1927] **TCLC 31**

Arundel, Honor (Morfydd) [1919-1973]**C L C 17**
See also CA 21-22; 41-44R; CAP 2; CLR 35; SATA 4; SATA-Obit 24

Arzner, Dorothy [1897-1979] .... **CLC 98**

Asch, Sholem [1880-1957] .... **TCLC 3**
See also CA 105

Ash, Shalom
See Asch, Sholem

Ashbery, John (Lawrence) [1927-]**CLC 2, 3, 4, 6, 9, 13, 15, 25, 41, 77; DAM POET**
See also CA 5-8R; CANR 9, 37, 66; DLB 5, 165; DLBY 81; INT CANR-9; MTCW

Ashdown, Clifford
See Freeman, R(ichard) Austin

Ashe, Gordon
See Creasey, John

Ashton-Warner, Sylvia (Constance) [1908-1984] .... **CLC 19**
See also CA 69-72; 112; CANR 29; MTCW

Asimov, Isaac [1920-1992]**CLC 1, 3, 9, 19, 26, 76, 92; DAM POP**
See also AAYA 13; BEST 90:2; CA 1-4R; 137; CANR 2, 19, 36, 60; CLR 12; DLB 8; DLBY 92; INT CANR-19; JRDA; MAICYA; MTCW; SATA 1, 26, 74

Assis, Joaquim Maria Machado de
See Machado de Assis, Joaquim Maria

Astley, Thea (Beatrice May) [1925-] **CLC 41**
See also CA 65-68; CANR 11, 43

Aston, James
See White, T(erence) H(anbury)

Asturias, Miguel Angel [1899-1974]**CLC 3, 8, 13; DAM MULT, NOV; HLC**
See also CA 25-28; 49-52; CANR 32; CAP 2; DLB 113; HW; MTCW

Atares, Carlos Saura
See Saura (Atares), Carlos

Atheling, William
See Pound, Ezra (Weston Loomis)

Atheling, William, Jr.
See Blish, James (Benjamin)

Atherton, Gertrude (Franklin Horn) [1857-1948] .... **TCLC 2**
See also CA 104; 155; DLB 9, 78, 186

Atherton, Lucius
See Masters, Edgar Lee

Atkins, Jack
See Harris, Mark

Atkinson, Kate .... **CLC 99**
See also CA 166

Attaway, William (Alexander) [1911-1986] **CLC 92; BLC 1; DAM MULT**
See also BW 2; CA 143; DLB 76

Atticus
See Fleming, Ian (Lancaster); Wilson, (Thomas) Woodrow

Atwood, Margaret (Eleanor) [1939-]**CLC 2, 3, 4, 8, 13, 15, 25, 44, 84; DA; DAB; DAC; DAM MST, NOV, POET; PC 8; SSC 2; WLC**
See also AAYA 12; BEST 89:2; CA 49-52; CANR 3, 24, 33, 59; DLB 53; INT CANR-24; MTCW; SATA 50

Aubigny, Pierre d'
See Mencken, H(enry) L(ouis)

Aubin, Penelope [1685-1731(?)] .... **LC 9**
See also DLB 39

Auchincloss, Louis (Stanton) [1917-]**CLC 4, 6, 9, 18, 45; DAM NOV; SSC 22**
See also CA 1-4R; CANR 6, 29, 55; DLB 2; DLBY 80; INT CANR-29; MTCW

Auden, W(ystan) H(ugh) [1907-1973]**CLC 1, 2, 3, 4, 6, 9, 11, 14, 43; DA; DAB; DAC; DAM DRAM, MST, POET; PC 1; WLC**
See also AAYA 18; CA 9-12R; 45-48; CANR 5, 61; CDBLB 1914-1945; DLB 10, 20; MTCW

Audiberti, Jacques [1900-1965]**CLC 38; DAM DRAM**
See also CA 25-28R

Audubon, John James [1785-1851]**NCLC 47**

Auel, Jean M(arie) [1936-]**CLC 31, 107; DAM POP**
See also AAYA 7; BEST 90:4; CA 103; CANR 21, 64; INT CANR-21; SATA 91

Auerbach, Erich [1892-1957] .... **TCLC 43**
See also CA 118; 155

Augier, Emile [1820-1889] .... **NCLC 31**
See also DLB 192

Baron, David
　See Pinter, Harold
Baron Corvo
　See Rolfe, Frederick (William Serafino Austin
　　Lewis Mary)
Barondess, Sue K(aufman) [1926-1977]**CLC 8**
　See also Kaufman, Sue
　See also CA 1-4R; 69-72; CANR 1
Baron de Teive
　See Pessoa, Fernando (Antonio Nogueira)
Barres, (Auguste-) Maurice [1862-1923]
　TCLC 47
　See also CA 164; DLB 123
Barreto, Afonso Henrique de Lima
　See Lima Barreto, Afonso Henrique de
Barrett, (Roger) Syd [1946-] .... **CLC 35**
Barrett, William (Christopher) [1913-1992]
　CLC 27
　See also CA 13-16R; 139; CANR 11, 67; INT
　　CANR-11
Barrie, J(ames) M(atthew) [1860-1937]**TCLC
　2; DAB; DAM DRAM**
　See also CA 104; 136; CDBLB 1890-1914;
　　CLR 16; DLB 10, 141, 156; MAICYA;
　　YABC 1
Barrington, Michael
　See Moorcock, Michael (John)
Barrol, Grady
　See Bograd, Larry
Barry, Mike
　See Malzberg, Barry N(athaniel)
Barry, Philip [1896-1949] .... **TCLC 11**
　See also CA 109; DLB 7
Bart, Andre Schwarz
　See Schwarz-Bart, Andre
Barth, John (Simmons) [1930-]**CLC 1, 2, 3, 5,
　7, 9, 10, 14, 27, 51, 89; DAM NOV; SSC 10**
　See also AITN 1, 2; CA 1-4R; CABS 1; CANR
　　5, 23, 49, 64; DLB 2; MTCW
Barthelme, Donald [1931-1989]**CLC 1, 2, 3, 5,
　6, 8, 13, 23, 46, 59; DAM NOV; SSC 2**
　See also CA 21-24R; 129; CANR 20, 58; DLB
　　2; DLBY 80, 89; MTCW; SATA 7; SATA-
　　Obit 62
Barthelme, Frederick [1943-] .... **CLC 36**
　See also CA 114; 122; DLBY 85; INT 122
Barthes, Roland (Gerard) [1915-1980]. **C L C
　24, 83**
　See also CA 130; 97-100; CANR 66; MTCW
Barzun, Jacques (Martin) [1907-] .... **CLC 51**
　See also CA 61-64; CANR 22
Bashevis, Isaac
　See Singer, Isaac Bashevis
Bashkirtseff, Marie [1859-1884] .... **NCLC 27**
Basho
　See Matsuo Basho
Bass, Kingsley B., Jr.
　See Bullins, Ed
Bass, Rick [1958-] .... **CLC 79**
　See also CA 126; CANR 53
Bassani, Giorgio [1916-] .... **CLC 9**
　See also CA 65-68; CANR 33; DLB 128, 177;
　　MTCW
Bastos, Augusto (Antonio) Roa
　See Roa Bastos, Augusto (Antonio)
Bataille, Georges [1897-1962] .... **CLC 29**
　See also CA 101; 89-92
Bates, H(erbert) E(rnest) [1905-1974] .. **C L C
　46; DAB; DAM POP; SSC 10**
　See also CA 93-96; 45-48; CANR 34; DLB 162,
　　191; MTCW
Bauchart
　See Camus, Albert
Baudelaire, Charles [1821-1867]**NCLC 6, 29,
　55; DA; DAB; DAC; DAM MST, POET;
　PC 1; SSC 18; WLC**
Baudrillard, Jean [1929-] .... **CLC 60**

Baum, L(yman) Frank [1856-1919] **TCLC 7**
　See also CA 108; 133; CLR 15; DLB 22; JRDA;
　　MAICYA; MTCW; SATA 18
Baum, Louis F.
　See Baum, L(yman) Frank
Baumbach, Jonathan [1933-] .... **CLC 6, 23**
　See also CA 13-16R; CAAS 5; CANR 12, 66;
　　DLBY 80; INT CANR-12; MTCW
Bausch, Richard (Carl) [1945-] .... **CLC 51**
　See also CA 101; CAAS 14; CANR 43, 61; DLB
　　130
Baxter, Charles (Morley) [1947-]**CLC 45, 78;
　DAM POP**
　See also CA 57-60; CANR 40, 64; DLB 130
Baxter, George Owen
　See Faust, Frederick (Schiller)
Baxter, James K(eir) [1926-1972] ..... **CLC 14**
　See also CA 77-80
Baxter, John
　See Hunt, E(verette) Howard, (Jr.)
Bayer, Sylvia
　See Glassco, John
Baynton, Barbara [1857-1929] ...... **TCLC 57**
Beagle, Peter S(oyer) [1939-] ..... **CLC 7, 104**
　See also CA 9-12R; CANR 4, 51; DLBY 80;
　　INT CANR-4; SATA 60
Bean, Normal
　See Burroughs, Edgar Rice
Beard, Charles A(ustin) [1874-1948]**TCLC 15**
　See also CA 115; DLB 17; SATA 18
Beardsley, Aubrey [1872-1898] .... **NCLC 6**
Beattie, Ann [1947-] .. **CLC 8, 13, 18, 40, 63;
　DAM NOV, POP; SSC 11**
　See also BEST 90:2; CA 81-84; CANR 53;
　　DLBY 82; MTCW
Beattie, James [1735-1803] .... **NCLC 25**
　See also DLB 109
Beauchamp, Kathleen Mansfield [1888-1923]
　See Mansfield, Katherine
　See also CA 104; 134; DA; DAC; DAM MST
Beaumarchais, Pierre-Augustin Caron de
　[1732-1799] .... **DC 4**
　See also DAM DRAM
Beaumont, Francis [1584(?)-1616]**LC 33; DC
　6**
　See also CDBLB Before 1660; DLB 58, 121
**Beauvoir, Simone (Lucie Ernestine Marie
　Bertrand) de** [1908-1986]**CLC 1, 2, 4, 8,
　14, 31, 44, 50, 71; DA; DAB; DAC; DAM
　MST, NOV; WLC**
　See also CA 9-12R; 118; CANR 28, 61; DLB
　　72; DLBY 86; MTCW
Becker, Carl (Lotus) [1873-1945] .. **TCLC 63**
　See also CA 157; DLB 17
Becker, Jurek [1937-1997] .... **CLC 7, 19**
　See also CA 85-88; 157; CANR 60; DLB 75
Becker, Walter [1950-] .... **CLC 26**
Beckett, Samuel (Barclay) [1906-1989]**CLC 1,
　2, 3, 4, 6, 9, 10, 11, 14, 18, 29, 57, 59, 83;
　DA; DAB; DAC; DAM DRAM, MST,
　NOV; SSC 16; WLC**
　See also CA 5-8R; 130; CANR 33, 61; CDBLB
　　1945-1960; DLB 13, 15; DLBY 90; MTCW
Beckford, William [1760-1844] ...... **NCLC 16**
　See also DLB 39
Beckman, Gunnel [1910-] .... **CLC 26**
　See also CA 33-36R; CANR 15; CLR 25;
　　MAICYA; SAAS 9; SATA 6
Becque, Henri [1837-1899] .... **NCLC 3**
　See also DLB 192
Beddoes, Thomas Lovell [1803-1849]**NCLC 3**
　See also DLB 96
Bede [c. 673-735] .... **CMLC 20**
　See also DLB 146
Bedford, Donald F.
　See Fearing, Kenneth (Flexner)
Beecher, Catharine Esther [1800-1878]**NCLC**

30
　See also DLB 1
Beecher, John [1904-1980] .... **CLC 6**
　See also AITN 1; CA 5-8R; 105; CANR 8
Beer, Johann [1655-1700] .... **LC 5**
　See also DLB 168
Beer, Patricia [1924-] .... **CLC 58**
　See also CA 61-64; CANR 13, 46; DLB 40
Beerbohm, Max
　See Beerbohm, (Henry) Max(imilian)
Beerbohm, (Henry) Max(imilian) [1872-1956]
　TCLC 1, 24
　See also CA 104; 154; DLB 34, 100
Beer-Hofmann, Richard [1866-1945] **T C L C
　60**
　See also CA 160; DLB 81
Begiebing, Robert J(ohn) [1946-] ..... **CLC 70**
　See also CA 122; CANR 40
Behan, Brendan [1923-1964]**CLC 1, 8, 11, 15,
　79; DAM DRAM**
　See also CA 73-76; CANR 33; CDBLB 1945-
　　1960; DLB 13; MTCW
Behn, Aphra [1640(?)-1689] ... **LC 1, 30; DA;
　DAB; DAC; DAM DRAM, MST, NOV,
　POET; DC 4; PC 13; WLC**
　See also DLB 39, 80, 131
Behrman, S(amuel) N(athaniel) [1893-1973]
　CLC 40
　See also CA 13-16; 45-48; CAP 1; DLB 7, 44
Belasco, David [1853-1931] .... **TCLC 3**
　See also CA 104; DLB 7
Belcheva, Elisaveta [1893-] .... **CLC 10**
　See also Bagryana, Elisaveta
Beldone, Phil "Cheech"
　See Ellison, Harlan (Jay)
Beleno
　See Azuela, Mariano
Belinski, Vissarion Grigoryevich [1811-1848]
　NCLC 5
　See also DLB 198
Belitt, Ben [1911-] .... **CLC 22**
　See also CA 13-16R; CAAS 4; CANR 7; DLB
　　5
Bell, Gertrude (Margaret Lowthian) [1868-
　1926] .... **TCLC 67**
　See also DLB 174
Bell, James Madison [1826-1902] . **TCLC 43;
　BLC 1; DAM MULT**
　See also BW 1; CA 122; 124; DLB 50
Bell, Madison Smartt [1957-] ... **CLC 41, 102**
　See also CA 111; CANR 28, 54
Bell, Marvin (Hartley) [1937-] .... **CLC 8, 31;
　DAM POET**
　See also CA 21-24R; CAAS 14; CANR 59; DLB
　　5; MTCW
Bell, W. L. D.
　See Mencken, H(enry) L(ouis)
Bellamy, Atwood C.
　See Mencken, H(enry) L(ouis)
Bellamy, Edward [1850-1898] .... **NCLC 4**
　See also DLB 12
Bellin, Edward J.
　See Kuttner, Henry
**Belloc, (Joseph) Hilaire (Pierre Sebastien Rene
　Swanton)** [1870-1953]**TCLC 7, 18; DAM
　POET**
　See also CA 106; 152; DLB 19, 100, 141, 174;
　　YABC 1
Belloc, Joseph Peter Rene Hilaire
　See Belloc, (Joseph) Hilaire (Pierre Sebastien
　　Rene Swanton)
Belloc, Joseph Pierre Hilaire
　See Belloc, (Joseph) Hilaire (Pierre Sebastien
　　Rene Swanton)
Belloc, M. A.
　See Lowndes, Marie Adelaide (Belloc)
Bellow, Saul [1915-] **CLC 1, 2, 3, 6, 8, 10, 13,**

Author Index

See also Wilson, John (Anthony) Burgess
See also AAYA 25; AITN 1; CDBLB 1960 to Present; DLB 14, 194

Burke, Edmund [1729(?)-1797]LC 7, 36; DA; DAB; DAC; DAM MST; WLC
See also DLB 104

Burke, Kenneth (Duva) [1897-1993]CLC 2, 24
See also CA 5-8R; 143; CANR 39; DLB 45, 63; MTCW

Burke, Leda
See Garnett, David

Burke, Ralph
See Silverberg, Robert

Burke, Thomas [1886-1945] .... TCLC 63
See also CA 113; 155; DLB 197

Burney, Fanny [1752-1840] ......NCLC 12, 54
See also DLB 39

Burns, Robert [1759-1796] .... PC 6
See also CDBLB 1789-1832; DA; DAB; DAC; DAM MST, POET; DLB 109; WLC

Burns, Tex
See L'Amour, Louis (Dearborn)

Burnshaw, Stanley [1906-] ..... CLC 3, 13, 44
See also CA 9-12R; DLB 48; DLBY 97

Burr, Anne [1937-]................................ CLC 6
See also CA 25-28R

Burroughs, Edgar Rice [1875-1950]TCLC 2, 32; DAM NOV
See also AAYA 11; CA 104; 132; DLB 8; MTCW; SATA 41

Burroughs, William S(eward) [1914-1997] CLC 1, 2, 5, 15, 22, 42, 75, 109; DA; DAB; DAC; DAM MST, NOV, POP; WLC
See also AITN 2; CA 9-12R; 160; CANR 20, 52; DLB 2, 8, 16, 152; DLBY 81, 97; MTCW

Burton, Richard F. [1821-1890] ..... NCLC 42
See also DLB 55, 184

Busch, Frederick [1941-] .. CLC 7, 10, 18, 47
See also CA 33-36R; CAAS 1; CANR 45; DLB 6

Bush, Ronald [1946-] .... CLC 34
See also CA 136

Bustos, F(rancisco)
See Borges, Jorge Luis

Bustos Domecq, H(onorio)
See Bioy Casares, Adolfo; Borges, Jorge Luis

Butler, Octavia E(stelle) [1947-] ..... CLC 38; BLCS; DAM MULT, POP
See also AAYA 18; BW 2; CA 73-76; CANR 12, 24, 38; DLB 33; MTCW; SATA 84

Butler, Robert Olen (Jr.) [1945-] .... CLC 81; DAM POP
See also CA 112; CANR 66; DLB 173; INT 112

Butler, Samuel [1612-1680] .... LC 16, 43
See also DLB 101, 126

Butler, Samuel [1835-1902]TCLC 1, 33; DA; DAB; DAC; DAM MST, NOV; WLC
See also CA 143; CDBLB 1890-1914; DLB 18, 57, 174

Butler, Walter C.
See Faust, Frederick (Schiller)

Butor, Michel (Marie Francois) [1926-] C L C 1, 3, 8, 11, 15
See also CA 9-12R; CANR 33, 66; DLB 83; MTCW

Butts, Mary [1892(?)-1937] .... TCLC 77
See also CA 148

Buzo, Alexander (John) [1944-] .... CLC 61
See also CA 97-100; CANR 17, 39, 69

Buzzati, Dino [1906-1972] .... CLC 36
See also CA 160; 33-36R; DLB 177

Byars, Betsy (Cromer) [1928-] .... CLC 35
See also AAYA 19; CA 33-36R; CANR 18, 36, 57; CLR 1, 16; DLB 52; INT CANR-18; JRDA; MAICYA; MTCW; SAAS 1; SATA 4, 46, 80

Byatt, A(ntonia) S(usan Drabble) [1936-]

CLC 19, 65; DAM NOV, POP
See also CA 13-16R; CANR 13, 33, 50; DLB 14, 194; MTCW

Byrne, David [1952-] .... CLC 26
See also CA 127

Byrne, John Keyes [1926-]
See Leonard, Hugh
See also CA 102; INT 102

Byron, George Gordon (Noel) [1788-1824] NCLC 2, 12; DA; DAB; DAC; DAM MST, POET; PC 16; WLC
See also CDBLB 1789-1832; DLB 96, 110

Byron, Robert [1905-1941] .... TCLC 67
See also CA 160; DLB 195

C. 3. 3.
See Wilde, Oscar (Fingal O'Flahertie Wills)

Caballero, Fernan [1796-1877] ...... NCLC 10

Cabell, Branch
See Cabell, James Branch

Cabell, James Branch [1879-1958] . TCLC 6
See also CA 105; 152; DLB 9, 78

Cable, George Washington [1844-1925] TCLC 4; SSC 4
See also CA 104; 155; DLB 12, 74; DLBD 13

Cabral de Melo Neto, Joao [1920-] CLC 76; DAM MULT
See also CA 151

Cabrera Infante, G(uillermo) [1929-]CLC 5, 25, 45; DAM MULT; HLC
See also CA 85-88; CANR 29, 65; DLB 113; HW; MTCW

Cade, Toni
See Bambara, Toni Cade

Cadmus and Harmonia
See Buchan, John

Caedmon [fl. 658-680] .... CMLC 7
See also DLB 146

Caeiro, Alberto
See Pessoa, Fernando (Antonio Nogueira)

Cage, John (Milton, Jr.) [1912-] .... CLC 41
See also CA 13-16R; CANR 9; DLB 193; INT CANR-9

Cahan, Abraham [1860-1951]........ TCLC 71
See also CA 108; 154; DLB 9, 25, 28

Cain, G.
See Cabrera Infante, G(uillermo)

Cain, Guillermo
See Cabrera Infante, G(uillermo)

Cain, James M(allahan) [1892-1977] CLC 3, 11, 28
See also AITN 1; CA 17-20R; 73-76; CANR 8, 34, 61; MTCW

Caine, Mark
See Raphael, Frederic (Michael)

Calasso, Roberto [1941-] .... CLC 81
See also CA 143

Calderon de la Barca, Pedro [1600-1681]L C 23; DC 3

Caldwell, Erskine (Preston) [1903-1987]C L C 1, 8, 14, 50, 60; DAM NOV; SSC 19
See also AITN 1; CA 1-4R; 121; CAAS 1; CANR 2, 33; DLB 9, 86; MTCW

Caldwell, (Janet Miriam) Taylor (Holland) [1900-1985] .CLC 2, 28, 39; DAM NOV, POP
See also CA 5-8R; 116; CANR 5

Calhoun, John Caldwell [1782-1850] N C L C 15
See also DLB 3

Calisher, Hortense [1911-] ...CLC 2, 4, 8, 38; DAM NOV; SSC 15
See also CA 1-4R; CANR 1, 22, 67; DLB 2; INT CANR-22; MTCW

Callaghan, Morley Edward [1903-1990]C L C 3, 14, 41, 65; DAC; DAM MST
See also CA 9-12R; 132; CANR 33; DLB 68; MTCW

Callimachus [c. 305B.C.-c. 240B.C.]CMLC 18
See also DLB 176

Calvin, John [1509-1564] .... LC 37

Calvino, Italo [1923-1985]CLC 5, 8, 11, 22, 33, 39, 73; DAM NOV; SSC 3
See also CA 85-88; 116; CANR 23, 61; DLB 196; MTCW

Cameron, Carey [1952-] .... CLC 59
See also CA 135

Cameron, Peter [1959-] .... CLC 44
See also CA 125; CANR 50

Campana, Dino [1885-1932] .... TCLC 20
See also CA 117; DLB 114

Campanella, Tommaso [1568-1639] .... LC 32

Campbell, John W(ood, Jr.) [1910-1971]C L C 32
See also CA 21-22; 29-32R; CANR 34; CAP 2; DLB 8; MTCW

Campbell, Joseph [1904-1987] .... CLC 69
See also AAYA 3; BEST 89:2; CA 1-4R; 124; CANR 3, 28, 61; MTCW

Campbell, Maria [1940-] ....CLC 85; DAC
See also CA 102; CANR 54; NNAL

Campbell, (John) Ramsey [1946-] .. CLC 42; SSC 19
See also CA 57-60; CANR 7; INT CANR-7

Campbell, (Ignatius) Roy (Dunnachie) [1901-1957] ....
TCLC 5
See also CA 104; 155; DLB 20

Campbell, Thomas [1777-1844] ..... NCLC 19
See also DLB 93; 144

Campbell, Wilfred .... TCLC 9
See also Campbell, William

Campbell, William [1858(?)-1918]
See Campbell, Wilfred
See also CA 106; DLB 92

Campion, Jane................................... CLC 95
See also CA 138

Campos, Alvaro de
See Pessoa, Fernando (Antonio Nogueira)

Camus, Albert [1913-1960]CLC 1, 2, 4, 9, 11, 14, 32, 63, 69; DA; DAB; DAC; DAM DRAM, MST, NOV; DC 2; SSC 9; WLC
See also CA 89-92; DLB 72; MTCW

Canby, Vincent [1924-] .... CLC 13
See also CA 81-84

Cancale
See Desnos, Robert

Canetti, Elias [1905-1994] CLC 3, 14, 25, 75, 86
See also CA 21-24R; 146; CANR 23, 61; DLB 85, 124; MTCW

Canin, Ethan [1960-] .... CLC 55
See also CA 131; 135

Cannon, Curt
See Hunter, Evan

Cao, Lan [1961-] .... CLC 109
See also CA 165

Cape, Judith
See Page, P(atricia) K(athleen)

Capek, Karel [1890-1938] . TCLC 6, 37; DA; DAB; DAC; DAM DRAM, MST, NOV; DC 1; WLC
See also CA 104; 140

Capote, Truman [1924-1984]CLC 1, 3, 8, 13, 19, 34, 38, 58; DA; DAB; DAC; DAM MST, NOV, POP; SSC 2; WLC
See also CA 5-8R; 113; CANR 18, 62; CDALB 1941-1968; DLB 2, 185; DLBY 80, 84; MTCW; SATA 91

Capra, Frank [1897-1991] .... CLC 16
See also CA 61-64; 135

Caputo, Philip [1941-] .... CLC 32
See also CA 73-76; CANR 40

Caragiale, Ion Luca [1852-1912] ... TCLC 76
See also CA 157

Card, Orson Scott [1951-] ... **CLC 44, 47, 50; DAM POP**
See also AAYA 11; CA 102; CANR 27, 47; INT CANR-27; MTCW; SATA 83

Cardenal, Ernesto [1925-] ..... **CLC 31; DAM MULT, POET; HLC; PC 22**
See also CA 49-52; CANR 2, 32, 66; HW; MTCW

Cardozo, Benjamin N(athan) [1870-1938] **TCLC 65**
See also CA 117; 164

Carducci, Giosue (Alessandro Giuseppe) [1835-1907] .... **TCLC 32**
See also CA 163

Carew, Thomas [1595(?)-1640] .... **LC 13**
See also DLB 126

Carey, Ernestine Gilbreth [1908-] .... **CLC 17**
See also CA 5-8R; SATA 2

Carey, Peter [1943-] .... **CLC 40, 55, 96**
See also CA 123; 127; CANR 53; INT 127; MTCW; SATA 94

Carleton, William [1794-1869] .... **NCLC 3**
See also DLB 159

Carlisle, Henry (Coffin) [1926-] .... **CLC 33**
See also CA 13-16R; CANR 15

Carlsen, Chris
See Holdstock, Robert P.

Carlson, Ron(ald F.) [1947-] .... **CLC 54**
See also CA 105; CANR 27

Carlyle, Thomas [1795-1881] **NCLC 70; DA; DAB; DAC; DAM MST**
See also CDBLB 1789-1832; DLB 55; 144

Carman, (William) Bliss [1861-1929] **TCLC 7; DAC**
See also CA 104; 152; DLB 92

Carnegie, Dale [1888-1955] .... **TCLC 53**

Carossa, Hans [1878-1956] .... **TCLC 48**
See also DLB 66

Carpenter, Don(ald Richard) [1931-1995] **CLC 41**
See also CA 45-48; 149; CANR 1

Carpentier (y Valmont), Alejo [1904-1980] **CLC 8, 11, 38, 110; DAM MULT; HLC**
See also CA 65-68; 97-100; CANR 11; DLB 113; HW

Carr, Caleb [1955(?)-] .... **CLC 86**
See also CA 147

Carr, Emily [1871-1945] .... **TCLC 32**
See also CA 159; DLB 68

Carr, John Dickson [1906-1977] .... **CLC 3**
See also Fairbairn, Roger
See also CA 49-52; 69-72; CANR 3, 33, 60; MTCW

Carr, Philippa
See Hibbert, Eleanor Alice Burford

Carr, Virginia Spencer [1929-] .... **CLC 34**
See also CA 61-64; DLB 111

Carrere, Emmanuel [1957-] .... **CLC 89**

Carrier, Roch [1937-] **CLC 13, 78; DAC; DAM MST**
See also CA 130; CANR 61; DLB 53

Carroll, James P. [1943(?)-] .... **CLC 38**
See also CA 81-84

Carroll, Jim [1951-] .... **CLC 35**
See also AAYA 17; CA 45-48; CANR 42

Carroll, Lewis ..... **NCLC 2, 53; PC 18; WLC**
See also Dodgson, Charles Lutwidge
See also CDBLB 1832-1890; CLR 2, 18; DLB 18, 163, 178; JRDA

Carroll, Paul Vincent [1900-1968] ... **CLC 10**
See also CA 9-12R; 25-28R; DLB 10

Carruth, Hayden [1921-] **CLC 4, 7, 10, 18, 84; PC 10**
See also CA 9-12R; CANR 4, 38, 59; DLB 5, 165; INT CANR-4; MTCW; SATA 47

Carson, Rachel Louise [1907-1964] **CLC 71;**

DAM POP
See also CA 77-80; CANR 35; MTCW; SATA 23

Carter, Angela (Olive) [1940-1992] **CLC 5, 41, 76; SSC 13**
See also CA 53-56; 136; CANR 12, 36, 61; DLB 14; MTCW; SATA 66; SATA-Obit 70

Carter, Nick
See Smith, Martin Cruz

Carver, Raymond [1938-1988] **CLC 22, 36, 53, 55; DAM NOV; SSC 8**
See also CA 33-36R; 126; CANR 17, 34, 61; DLB 130; DLBY 84, 88; MTCW

Cary, Elizabeth, Lady Falkland [1585-1639] **LC 30**

Cary, (Arthur) Joyce (Lunel) [1888-1957] **TCLC 1, 29**
See also CA 104; 164; CDBLB 1914-1945; DLB 15, 100

Casanova de Seingalt, Giovanni Jacopo [1725-1798] .... **LC 13**

Casares, Adolfo Bioy
See Bioy Casares, Adolfo

Casely-Hayford, J(oseph) E(phraim) [1866-1930] ... **TCLC 24; BLC 1; DAM MULT**
See also BW 2; CA 123; 152

Casey, John (Dudley) [1939-] .... **CLC 59**
See also BEST 90:2; CA 69-72; CANR 23

Casey, Michael [1947-] .... **CLC 2**
See also CA 65-68; DLB 5

Casey, Patrick
See Thurman, Wallace (Henry)

Casey, Warren (Peter) [1935-1988] .. **CLC 12**
See also CA 101; 127; INT 101

Casona, Alejandro .... **CLC 49**
See also Alvarez, Alejandro Rodriguez

Cassavetes, John [1929-1989] .... **CLC 20**
See also CA 85-88; 127

Cassian, Nina [1924-] .... **PC 17**

Cassill, R(onald) V(erlin) [1919-] . **CLC 4, 23**
See also CA 9-12R; CAAS 1; CANR 7, 45; DLB 6

Cassirer, Ernst [1874-1945] .... **TCLC 61**
See also CA 157

Cassity, (Allen) Turner [1929-] ..... **CLC 6, 42**
See also CA 17-20R; CAAS 8; CANR 11; DLB 105

Castaneda, Carlos [1931(?)-] .... **CLC 12**
See also CA 25-28R; CANR 32, 66; HW; MTCW

Castedo, Elena [1937-] .... **CLC 65**
See also CA 132

Castedo-Ellerman, Elena
See Castedo, Elena

Castellanos, Rosario [1925-1974] ... **CLC 66; DAM MULT; HLC**
See also CA 131; 53-56; CANR 58; DLB 113; HW

Castelvetro, Lodovico [1505-1571] ..... **LC 12**

Castiglione, Baldassare [1478-1529] ... **LC 12**

Castle, Robert
See Hamilton, Edmond

Castro, Guillen de [1569-1631] .... **LC 19**

Castro, Rosalia de [1837-1885] **NCLC 3; DAM MULT**

Cather, Willa
See Cather, Willa Sibert

Cather, Willa Sibert [1873-1947] **TCLC 1, 11, 31; DA; DAB; DAC; DAM MST, NOV; SSC 2; WLC**
See also AAYA 24; CA 104; 128; CDALB 1865-1917; DLB 9, 54, 78; DLBD 1; MTCW; SATA 30

Catherine, Saint [1347-1380] .... **CMLC 27**

Cato, Marcus Porcius [234B.C.-149B.C.] **CMLC 21**

Catton, (Charles) Bruce [1899-1978] **CLC 35**

See also AITN 1; CA 5-8R; 81-84; CANR 7; DLB 17; SATA 2; SATA-Obit 24

Catullus [c. 84B.C.-c. 54B.C.] .... **CMLC 18**

Cauldwell, Frank
See King, Francis (Henry)

Caunitz, William J. [1933-1996] .... **CLC 34**
See also BEST 89:3; CA 125; 130; 152; INT 130

Causley, Charles (Stanley) [1917-] ..... **CLC 7**
See also CA 9-12R; CANR 5, 35; CLR 30; DLB 27; MTCW; SATA 3, 66

Caute, (John) David [1936-] .. **CLC 29; DAM NOV**
See also CA 1-4R; CAAS 4; CANR 1, 33, 64; DLB 14

Cavafy, C(onstantine) P(eter) [1863-1933] **TCLC 2, 7; DAM POET**
See also Kavafis, Konstantinos Petrou
See also CA 148

Cavallo, Evelyn
See Spark, Muriel (Sarah)

Cavanna, Betty .... **CLC 12**
See also Harrison, Elizabeth Cavanna
See also JRDA; MAICYA; SAAS 4; SATA 1, 30

Cavendish, Margaret Lucas [1623-1673] **L C 30**
See also DLB 131

Caxton, William [1421(?)-1491(?)] ...... **LC 17**
See also DLB 170

Cayer, D. M.
See Duffy, Maureen

Cayrol, Jean [1911-] .... **CLC 11**
See also CA 89-92; DLB 83

Cela, Camilo Jose [1916-] **CLC 4, 13, 59; DAM MULT; HLC**
See also BEST 90:2; CA 21-24R; CAAS 10; CANR 21, 32; DLBY 89; HW; MTCW

Celan, Paul ... **CLC 10, 19, 53, 82; PC 10**
See also Antschel, Paul
See also DLB 69

Celine, Louis-Ferdinand **CLC 1, 3, 4, 7, 9, 15, 47**
See also Destouches, Louis-Ferdinand
See also DLB 72

Cellini, Benvenuto [1500-1571] .... **LC 7**

Cendrars, Blaise [1887-1961] ... **CLC 18, 106**
See also Sauser-Hall, Frederic

Cernuda (y Bidon), Luis [1902-1963] **CLC 54; DAM POET**
See also CA 131; 89-92; DLB 134; HW

Cervantes (Saavedra), Miguel de [1547-1616] **LC 6, 23; DA; DAB; DAC; DAM MST, NOV; SSC 12; WLC**

Cesaire, Aime (Fernand) [1913-] **CLC 19, 32, 112; BLC 1; DAM MULT, POET**
See also BW 2; CA 65-68; CANR 24, 43; MTCW

Chabon, Michael [1963-] .... **CLC 55**
See also CA 139; CANR 57

Chabrol, Claude [1930-] .... **CLC 16**
See also CA 110

Challans, Mary [1905-1983]
See Renault, Mary
See also CA 81-84; 111; SATA 23; SATA-Obit 36

Challis, George
See Faust, Frederick (Schiller)

Chambers, Aidan [1934-] .... **CLC 35**
See also CA 25-28R; CANR 12, 31, 58; JRDA; MAICYA; SAAS 12; SATA 1, 69

Chambers, James [1948-]
See Cliff, Jimmy
See also CA 124

Chambers, Jessie
See Lawrence, D(avid) H(erbert Richards)

Chambers, Robert W(illiam) [1865-1933]

Crichton, (John) Michael [1942-]**CLC 2, 6, 54, 90; DAM NOV, POP**
    See also AAYA 10; AITN 2; CA 25-28R; CANR 13, 40, 54; DLBY 81; INT CANR-13; JRDA; MTCW; SATA 9, 88
Crispin, Edmund .... **CLC 22**
    See also Montgomery, (Robert) Bruce
    See also DLB 87
Cristofer, Michael [1945(?)-] . **CLC 28; DAM DRAM**
    See also CA 110; 152; DLB 7
Croce, Benedetto [1866-1952] .... **TCLC 37**
    See also CA 120; 155
Crockett, David [1786-1836] .... **NCLC 8**
    See also DLB 3, 11
Crockett, Davy
    See Crockett, David
Crofts, Freeman Wills [1879-1957] **TCLC 55**
    See also CA 115; DLB 77
Croker, John Wilson [1780-1857] .. **NCLC 10**
    See also DLB 110
Crommelynck, Fernand [1885-1970] **CLC 75**
    See also CA 89-92
Cromwell, Oliver [1599-1658] .... **LC 43**
Cronin, A(rchibald) J(oseph) [1896-1981] **CLC 32**
    See also CA 1-4R; 102; CANR 5; DLB 191; SATA 47; SATA-Obit 25
Cross, Amanda
    See Heilbrun, Carolyn G(old)
Crothers, Rachel [1878(?)-1958] .... **TCLC 19**
    See also CA 113; DLB 7
Croves, Hal
    See Traven, B.
Crow Dog, Mary (Ellen) [(?)-] .... **CLC 93**
    See also Brave Bird, Mary
    See also CA 154
Crowfield, Christopher
    See Stowe, Harriet (Elizabeth) Beecher
Crowley, Aleister .... **TCLC 7**
    See also Crowley, Edward Alexander
Crowley, Edward Alexander [1875-1947]
    See Crowley, Aleister
    See also CA 104
Crowley, John [1942-] .... **CLC 57**
    See also CA 61-64; CANR 43; DLBY 82; SATA 65
Crud
    See Crumb, R(obert)
Crumarums
    See Crumb, R(obert)
Crumb, R(obert) [1943-] .... **CLC 17**
    See also CA 106
Crumbum
    See Crumb, R(obert)
Crumski
    See Crumb, R(obert)
Crum the Bum
    See Crumb, R(obert)
Crunk
    See Crumb, R(obert)
Crustt
    See Crumb, R(obert)
Cryer, Gretchen (Kiger) [1935-] .... **CLC 21**
    See also CA 114; 123
Csath, Geza [1887-1919] .... **TCLC 13**
    See also CA 111
Cudlip, David [1933-] .... **CLC 34**
Cullen, Countee [1903-1946]**TCLC 4, 37; BLC 1; DA; DAC; DAM MST, MULT, POET; PC 20; WLCS**
    See also BW 1; CA 108; 124; CDALB 1917-1929; DLB 4, 48, 51; MTCW; SATA 18
Cum, R.
    See Crumb, R(obert)
Cummings, Bruce F(rederick) [1889-1919]
    See Barbellion, W. N. P.

See also CA 123
Cummings, E(dward) E(stlin) [1894-1962] **CLC 1, 3, 8, 12, 15, 68; DA; DAB; DAC; DAM MST, POET; PC 5; WLC 2**
    See also CA 73-76; CANR 31; CDALB 1929-1941; DLB 4, 48; MTCW
Cunha, Euclides (Rodrigues Pimenta) da [1866-1909] ....
TCLC 24
    See also CA 123
Cunningham, E. V.
    See Fast, Howard (Melvin)
Cunningham, J(ames) V(incent) [1911-1985] **CLC 3, 31**
    See also CA 1-4R; 115; CANR 1; DLB 5
Cunningham, Julia (Woolfolk) [1916-]. **C L C 12**
    See also CA 9-12R; CANR 4, 19, 36; JRDA; MAICYA; SAAS 2; SATA 1, 26
Cunningham, Michael [1952-] .... **CLC 34**
    See also CA 136
Cunninghame Graham, R(obert) B(ontine) [1852-1936] ....
TCLC 19
    See also Graham, R(obert) B(ontine) Cunninghame
    See also CA 119; DLB 98
Currie, Ellen [19(?)-] .... **CLC 44**
Curtin, Philip
    See Lowndes, Marie Adelaide (Belloc)
Curtis, Price
    See Ellison, Harlan (Jay)
Cutrate, Joe
    See Spiegelman, Art
Cynewulf [c. 770-c. 840] .... **CMLC 23**
Czaczkes, Shmuel Yosef
    See Agnon, S(hmuel) Y(osef Halevi)
Dabrowska, Maria (Szumska) [1889-1965] **CLC 15**
    See also CA 106
Dabydeen, David [1955-] .... **CLC 34**
    See also BW 1; CA 125; CANR 56
Dacey, Philip [1939-] .... **CLC 51**
    See also CA 37-40R; CAAS 17; CANR 14, 32, 64; DLB 105
Dagerman, Stig (Halvard) [1923-1954]**TCLC 17**
    See also CA 117; 155
Dahl, Roald [1916-1990] .... **CLC 1, 6, 18, 79; DAB; DAC; DAM MST, NOV, POP**
    See also AAYA 15; CA 1-4R; 133; CANR 6, 32, 37, 62; CLR 1, 7, 41; DLB 139; JRDA; MAICYA; MTCW; SATA 1, 26, 73; SATA-Obit 65
Dahlberg, Edward [1900-1977] **CLC 1, 7, 14**
    See also CA 9-12R; 69-72; CANR 31, 62; DLB 48; MTCW
Daitch, Susan [1954-] .... **CLC 103**
    See also CA 161
Dale, Colin .... **TCLC 18**
    See also Lawrence, T(homas) E(dward)
Dale, George E.
    See Asimov, Isaac
Daly, Elizabeth [1878-1967] .... **CLC 52**
    See also CA 23-24; 25-28R; CANR 60; CAP 2
Daly, Maureen [1921-] .... **CLC 17**
    See also AAYA 5; CANR 37; JRDA; MAICYA; SAAS 1; SATA 2
Damas, Leon-Gontran [1912-1978] .. **CLC 84**
    See also BW 1; CA 125; 73-76
Dana, Richard Henry Sr. [1787-1879] **N C L C 53**
Daniel, Samuel [1562(?)-1619] .... **LC 24**
    See also DLB 62
Daniels, Brett
    See Adler, Renata
Dannay, Frederic [1905-1982]**CLC 11; DAM

POP**
    See also Queen, Ellery
    See also CA 1-4R; 107; CANR 1, 39; DLB 137; MTCW
D'Annunzio, Gabriele [1863-1938] **TCLC 6, 40**
    See also CA 104; 155
Danois, N. le
    See Gourmont, Remy (-Marie-Charles) de
Dante [1265-1321].. **CMLC 3, 18; DA; DAB; DAC; DAM MST, POET; PC 21; WLCS**
d'Antibes, Germain
    See Simenon, Georges (Jacques Christian)
Danticat, Edwidge [1969-] .... **CLC 94**
    See also CA 152
Danvers, Dennis [1947-] .... **CLC 70**
Danziger, Paula [1944-] .... **CLC 21**
    See also AAYA 4; CA 112; 115; CANR 37; CLR 20; JRDA; MAICYA; SATA 36, 63; SATA-Brief 30
Dario, Ruben [1867-1916] .... **TCLC 4; DAM MULT; HLC; PC 15**
    See also CA 131; HW; MTCW
Darley, George [1795-1846] .... **NCLC 2**
    See also DLB 96
Darrow, Clarence (Seward) [1857-1938] **TCLC 81**
    See also CA 164
Darwin, Charles [1809-1882] .... **NCLC 57**
    See also DLB 57, 166
Daryush, Elizabeth [1887-1977] ...**CLC 6, 19**
    See also CA 49-52; CANR 3; DLB 20
Dasgupta, Surendranath [1887-1952] **T C L C 81**
    See also CA 157
Dashwood, Edmee Elizabeth Monica de la Pasture [1890-1943]
    See Delafield, E. M.
    See also CA 119; 154
Daudet, (Louis Marie) Alphonse [1840-1897] **NCLC 1**
    See also DLB 123
Daumal, Rene [1908-1944] .... **TCLC 14**
    See also CA 114
Davenport, Guy (Mattison, Jr.) [1927-] **C L C 6, 14, 38; SSC 16**
    See also CA 33-36R; CANR 23; DLB 130
Davidson, Avram [1923-]
    See Queen, Ellery
    See also CA 101; CANR 26; DLB 8
Davidson, Donald (Grady) [1893-1968] **C L C 2, 13, 19**
    See also CA 5-8R; 25-28R; CANR 4; DLB 45
Davidson, Hugh
    See Hamilton, Edmond
Davidson, John [1857-1909] .... **TCLC 24**
    See also CA 118; DLB 19
Davidson, Sara [1943-] .... **CLC 9**
    See also CA 81-84; CANR 44, 68; DLB 185
Davie, Donald (Alfred) [1922-1995]**CLC 5, 8, 10, 31**
    See also CA 1-4R; 149; CAAS 3; CANR 1, 44; DLB 27; MTCW
Davies, Ray(mond Douglas) [1944-]. **CLC 21**
    See also CA 116; 146
Davies, Rhys [1901-1978] .... **CLC 23**
    See also CA 9-12R; 81-84; CANR 4; DLB 139, 191
Davies, (William) Robertson [1913-1995]**CLC 2, 7, 13, 25, 42, 75, 91; DA; DAB; DAC; DAM MST, NOV, POP; WLC**
    See also BEST 89:2; CA 33-36R; 150; CANR 17, 42; DLB 68; INT CANR-17; MTCW
Davies, W(illiam) H(enry) [1871-1940]**T C L C 5**
    See also CA 104; DLB 19, 174
Davies, Walter C.

See Bradley, Marion Zimmer
Dexter, Martin
  See Faust, Frederick (Schiller)
Dexter, Pete [1943-] **CLC 34, 55; DAM POP**
  See also BEST 89:2; CA 127; 131; INT 131; MTCW
Diamano, Silmang
  See Senghor, Leopold Sedar
Diamond, Neil [1941-] .... **CLC 30**
  See also CA 108
Diaz del Castillo, Bernal [1496-1584] . **LC 31**
di Bassetto, Corno
  See Shaw, George Bernard
Dick, Philip K(indred) [1928-1982]. **CLC 10, 30, 72; DAM NOV, POP**
  See also AAYA 24; CA 49-52; 106; CANR 2, 16; DLB 8; MTCW
Dickens, Charles (John Huffam) [1812-1870] **NCLC 3, 8, 18, 26, 37, 50; DA; DAB; DAC; DAM MST, NOV; SSC 17; WLC**
  See also AAYA 23; CDBLB 1832-1890; DLB 21, 55, 70, 159, 166; JRDA; MAICYA; SATA 15
Dickey, James (Lafayette) [1923-1997]**CLC 1, 2, 4, 7, 10, 15, 47, 109; DAM NOV, POET, POP**
  See also AITN 1, 2; CA 9-12R; 156; CABS 2; CANR 10, 48, 61; CDALB 1968-1988; DLB 5, 193; DLBD 7; DLBY 82, 93, 96, 97; INT CANR-10; MTCW
Dickey, William [1928-1994] .... **CLC 3, 28**
  See also CA 9-12R; 145; CANR 24; DLB 5
Dickinson, Charles [1951-] .... **CLC 49**
  See also CA 128
Dickinson, Emily (Elizabeth) [1830-1886] **NCLC 21; DA; DAB; DAC; DAM MST, POET; PC 1; WLC**
  See also AAYA 22; CDALB 1865-1917; DLB 1; SATA 29
Dickinson, Peter (Malcolm) [1927-] **CLC 12, 35**
  See also AAYA 9; CA 41-44R; CANR 31, 58; CLR 29; DLB 87, 161; JRDA; MAICYA; SATA 5, 62, 95
Dickson, Carr
  See Carr, John Dickson
Dickson, Carter
  See Carr, John Dickson
Diderot, Denis [1713-1784] .... **LC 26**
Didion, Joan [1934-]**CLC 1, 3, 8, 14, 32; DAM NOV**
  See also AITN 1; CA 5-8R; CANR 14, 52; CDALB 1968-1988; DLB 2, 173, 185; DLBY 81, 86; MTCW
Dietrich, Robert
  See Hunt, E(verette) Howard, (Jr.)
Dillard, Annie [1945-]**CLC 9, 60; DAM NOV**
  See also AAYA 6; CA 49-52; CANR 3, 43, 62; DLBY 80; MTCW; SATA 10
Dillard, R(ichard) H(enry) W(ilde) [1937-] **CLC 5**
  See also CA 21-24R; CAAS 7; CANR 10; DLB 5
Dillon, Eilis [1920-1994] .... **CLC 17**
  See also CA 9-12R; 147; CAAS 3; CANR 4, 38; CLR 26; MAICYA; SATA 2, 74; SATA-Obit 83
Dimont, Penelope
  See Mortimer, Penelope (Ruth)
Dinesen, Isak .... **CLC 10, 29, 95; SSC 7**
  See also Blixen, Karen (Christentze Dinesen)
Ding Ling .... **CLC 68**
  See also Chiang, Pin-chin
Disch, Thomas M(ichael) [1940-] . **CLC 7, 36**
  See also AAYA 17; CA 21-24R; CAAS 4; CANR 17, 36, 54; CLR 18; DLB 8; MAICYA; MTCW; SAAS 15; SATA 92

Disch, Tom
  See Disch, Thomas M(ichael)
d'Isly, Georges
  See Simenon, Georges (Jacques Christian)
Disraeli, Benjamin [1804-1881] . **NCLC 2, 39**
  See also DLB 21, 55
Ditcum, Steve
  See Crumb, R(obert)
Dixon, Paige
  See Corcoran, Barbara
Dixon, Stephen [1936-] .... **CLC 52; SSC 16**
  See also CA 89-92; CANR 17, 40, 54; DLB 130
Doak, Annie
  See Dillard, Annie
Dobell, Sydney Thompson [1824-1874]**NCLC 43**
  See also DLB 32
Doblin, Alfred .... **TCLC 13**
  See also Doeblin, Alfred
Dobrolyubov, Nikolai Alexandrovich [1836-1861] .... **NCLC 5**
Dobson, Austin [1840-1921] .... **TCLC 79**
  See also DLB 35; 144
Dobyns, Stephen [1941-] .... **CLC 37**
  See also CA 45-48; CANR 2, 18
Doctorow, E(dgar) L(aurence) [1931-]**CLC 6, 11, 15, 18, 37, 44, 65, 113; DAM NOV, POP**
  See also AAYA 22; AITN 2; BEST 89:3; CA 45-48; CANR 2, 33, 51; CDALB 1968-1988; DLB 2, 28, 173; DLBY 80; MTCW
Dodgson, Charles Lutwidge [1832-1898]
  See Carroll, Lewis
  See also CLR 2; DA; DAB; DAC; DAM MST, NOV, POET; MAICYA; YABC 2
Dodson, Owen (Vincent) [1914-1983]**CLC 79; BLC 1; DAM MULT**
  See also BW 1; CA 65-68; 110; CANR 24; DLB 76
Doeblin, Alfred [1878-1957] .... **TCLC 13**
  See also Doblin, Alfred
  See also CA 110; 141; DLB 66
Doerr, Harriet [1910-] .... **CLC 34**
  See also CA 117; 122; CANR 47; INT 122
Domecq, H(onorio) Bustos
  See Bioy Casares, Adolfo; Borges, Jorge Luis
Domini, Rey
  See Lorde, Audre (Geraldine)
Dominique
  See Proust, (Valentin-Louis-George-Eugene-) Marcel
Don, A
  See Stephen, SirLeslie
Donaldson, Stephen R. [1947-]**CLC 46; DAM POP**
  See also CA 89-92; CANR 13, 55; INT CANR-13
Donleavy, J(ames) P(atrick) [1926-]**CLC 1, 4, 6, 10, 45**
  See also AITN 2; CA 9-12R; CANR 24, 49, 62; DLB 6, 173; INT CANR-24; MTCW
Donne, John [1572-1631]**LC 10, 24; DA; DAB; DAC; DAM MST, POET; PC 1**
  See also CDBLB Before 1660; DLB 121, 151
Donnell, David [1939(?)-] .... **CLC 34**
Donoghue, P. S.
  See Hunt, E(verette) Howard, (Jr.)
Donoso (Yanez), Jose [1924-1996] . **CLC 4, 8, 11, 32, 99; DAM MULT; HLC**
  See also CA 81-84; 155; CANR 32; DLB 113; HW; MTCW
Donovan, John [1928-1992] .... **CLC 35**
  See also AAYA 20; CA 97-100; 137; CLR 3; MAICYA; SATA 72; SATA-Brief 29
Don Roberto
  See Cunninghame Graham, R(obert) B(ontine)
Doolittle, Hilda [1886-1961]**CLC 3, 8, 14, 31, 34, 73; DA; DAC; DAM MST, POET; PC**

5; **WLC**
  See also H. D.
  See also CA 97-100; CANR 35; DLB 4, 45; MTCW
Dorfman, Ariel [1942-] ... **CLC 48, 77; DAM MULT; HLC**
  See also CA 124; 130; CANR 67; HW; INT 130
Dorn, Edward (Merton) [1929-] **CLC 10, 18**
  See also CA 93-96; CANR 42; DLB 5; INT 93-96
Dorris, Michael (Anthony) [1945-1997] **C L C 109; DAM MULT, NOV**
  See also AAYA 20; BEST 90:1; CA 102; 157; CANR 19, 46; DLB 175; NNAL; SATA 75; SATA-Obit 94
Dorris, Michael A.
  See Dorris, Michael (Anthony)
Dorsan, Luc
  See Simenon, Georges (Jacques Christian)
Dorsange, Jean
  See Simenon, Georges (Jacques Christian)
Dos Passos, John (Roderigo) [1896-1970] **CLC 1, 4, 8, 11, 15, 25, 34, 82; DA; DAB; DAC; DAM MST, NOV; WLC**
  See also CA 1-4R; 29-32R; CANR 3; CDALB 1929-1941; DLB 4, 9; DLBD 1, 15; DLBY 96; MTCW
Dossage, Jean
  See Simenon, Georges (Jacques Christian)
Dostoevsky, Fedor Mikhailovich [1821-1881] **NCLC 2, 7, 21, 33, 43; DA; DAB; DAC; DAM MST, NOV; SSC 2; WLC**
Doughty, Charles M(ontagu) [1843-1926] **TCLC 27**
  See also CA 115; DLB 19, 57, 174
Douglas, Ellen .... **CLC 73**
  See also Haxton, Josephine Ayres; Williamson, Ellen Douglas
Douglas, Gavin [1475(?)-1522] .... **LC 20**
  See also DLB 132
Douglas, George
  See Brown, George Douglas
Douglas, Keith (Castellain) [1920-1944] **TCLC 40**
  See also CA 160; DLB 27
Douglas, Leonard
  See Bradbury, Ray (Douglas)
Douglas, Michael
  See Crichton, (John) Michael
Douglas, (George) Norman [1868-1952] **TCLC 68**
  See also CA 119; 157; DLB 34, 195
Douglas, William
  See Brown, George Douglas
Douglass, Frederick [1817(?)-1895] **NCLC 7, 55; BLC 1; DA; DAC; DAM MST, MULT; WLC**
  See also CDALB 1640-1865; DLB 1, 43, 50, 79; SATA 29
Dourado, (Waldomiro Freitas) Autran [1926-] **CLC 23, 60**
  See also CA 25-28R; CANR 34
Dourado, Waldomiro Autran
  See Dourado, (Waldomiro Freitas) Autran
Dove, Rita (Frances) [1952-] ..... **CLC 50, 81; BLCS; DAM MULT, POET; PC 6**
  See also BW 2; CA 109; CAAS 19; CANR 27, 42, 68; DLB 120
Doveglion
  See Villa, Jose Garcia
Dowell, Coleman [1925-1985] .... **CLC 60**
  See also CA 25-28R; 117; CANR 10; DLB 130
Dowson, Ernest (Christopher) [1867-1900] **TCLC 4**
  See also CA 105; 150; DLB 19, 135
Doyle, A. Conan
  See Doyle, Arthur Conan

Echo
    See Proust, (Valentin-Louis-George-Eugene-) Marcel
Eckert, Allan W. [1931-] .... CLC 17
    See also AAYA 18; CA 13-16R; CANR 14, 45; INT CANR-14; SAAS 21; SATA 29, 91; SATA-Brief 27
Eckhart, Meister [1260(?)-1328(?)] CMLC 9
    See also DLB 115
Eckmar, F. R.
    See de Hartog, Jan
Eco, Umberto [1932-]CLC 28, 60; DAM NOV, POP
    See also BEST 90:1; CA 77-80; CANR 12, 33, 55; DLB 196; MTCW
Eddison, E(ric) R(ucker) [1882-1945] T C L C 15
    See also CA 109; 156
Eddy, Mary (Morse) Baker [1821-1910] TCLC 71
    See also CA 113
Edel, (Joseph) Leon [1907-1997] CLC 29, 34
    See also CA 1-4R; 161; CANR 1, 22; DLB 103; INT CANR-22
Eden, Emily [1797-1869] .... NCLC 10
Edgar, David [1948-] CLC 42; DAM DRAM
    See also CA 57-60; CANR 12, 61; DLB 13; MTCW
Edgerton, Clyde (Carlyle) [1944-] ... CLC 39
    See also AAYA 17; CA 118; 134; CANR 64; INT 134
Edgeworth, Maria [1768-1849] .NCLC 1, 51
    See also DLB 116, 159, 163; SATA 21
Edmonds, Paul
    See Kuttner, Henry
Edmonds, Walter D(umaux) [1903-] CLC 35
    See also CA 5-8R; CANR 2; DLB 9; MAICYA; SAAS 4; SATA 1, 27
Edmondson, Wallace
    See Ellison, Harlan (Jay)
Edson, Russell .... CLC 13
    See also CA 33-36R
Edwards, Bronwen Elizabeth
    See Rose, Wendy
Edwards, G(erald) B(asil) [1899-1976] C L C 25
    See also CA 110
Edwards, Gus [1939-] .... CLC 43
    See also CA 108; INT 108
Edwards, Jonathan [1703-1758] .. LC 7; DA; DAC; DAM MST
    See also DLB 24
Efron, Marina Ivanovna Tsvetaeva
    See Tsvetaeva (Efron), Marina (Ivanovna)
Ehle, John (Marsden, Jr.) [1925-] .... CLC 27
    See also CA 9-12R
Ehrenbourg, Ilya (Grigoryevich)
    See Ehrenburg, Ilya (Grigoryevich)
Ehrenburg, Ilya (Grigoryevich) [1891-1967] CLC 18, 34, 62
    See also CA 102; 25-28R
Ehrenburg, Ilyo (Grigoryevich)
    See Ehrenburg, Ilya (Grigoryevich)
Ehrenreich, Barbara [1941-].......... CLC 110
    See also BEST 90:4; CA 73-76; CANR 16, 37, 62; MTCW
Eich, Guenter [1907-1972] .... CLC 15
    See also CA 111; 93-96; DLB 69, 124
Eichendorff, Joseph Freiherr von [1788-1857] NCLC 8
    See also DLB 90
Eigner, Larry .... CLC 9
    See also Eigner, Laurence (Joel)
    See also CAAS 23; DLB 5
Eigner, Laurence (Joel) [1927-1996]
    See Eigner, Larry
    See also CA 9-12R; 151; CANR 6; DLB 193

Einstein, Albert [1879-1955] .... TCLC 65
    See also CA 121; 133; MTCW
Eiseley, Loren Corey [1907-1977] ...... CLC 7
    See also AAYA 5; CA 1-4R; 73-76; CANR 6
Eisenstadt, Jill [1963-] .... CLC 50
    See also CA 140
Eisenstein, Sergei (Mikhailovich) [1898-1948] TCLC 57
    See also CA 114; 149
Eisner, Simon
    See Kornbluth, C(yril) M.
Ekeloef, (Bengt) Gunnar [1907-1968]CLC 27; DAM POET; PC 23
    See also CA 123; 25-28R
Ekelof, (Bengt) Gunnar
    See Ekeloef, (Bengt) Gunnar
Ekelund, Vilhelm [1880-1949] .... TCLC 75
Ekwensi, C. O. D.
    See Ekwensi, Cyprian (Odiatu Duaka)
Ekwensi, Cyprian (Odiatu Duaka) [1921-] CLC 4; BLC 1; DAM MULT
    See also BW 2; CA 29-32R; CANR 18, 42; DLB 117; MTCW; SATA 66
Elaine .... TCLC 18
    See also Leverson, Ada
El Crummo
    See Crumb, R(obert)
Elder, Lonne III [1931-1996] .... DC 8
    See also BLC 1; BW 1; CA 81-84; 152; CANR 25; DAM MULT; DLB 7, 38, 44
Elia
    See Lamb, Charles
Eliade, Mircea [1907-1986] .... CLC 19
    See also CA 65-68; 119; CANR 30, 62; MTCW
Eliot, A. D.
    See Jewett, (Theodora) Sarah Orne
Eliot, Alice
    See Jewett, (Theodora) Sarah Orne
Eliot, Dan
    See Silverberg, Robert
Eliot, George [1819-1880]NCLC 4, 13, 23, 41, 49; DA; DAB; DAC; DAM MST, NOV; PC 20; WLC
    See also CDBLB 1832-1890; DLB 21, 35, 55
Eliot, John [1604-1690] .... LC 5
    See also DLB 24
Eliot, T(homas) S(tearns) [1888-1965]CLC 1, 2, 3, 6, 9, 10, 13, 15, 24, 34, 41, 55, 57, 113; DA; DAB; DAC; DAM DRAM, MST, POET; PC 5; WLC
    See also CA 5-8R; 25-28R; CANR 41; CDALB 1929-1941; DLB 7, 10, 45, 63; DLBY 88; MTCW
Elizabeth [1866-1941] .... TCLC 41
Elkin, Stanley L(awrence) [1930-1995]CLC 4, 6, 9, 14, 27, 51, 91; DAM NOV, POP; SSC 12
    See also CA 9-12R; 148; CANR 8, 46; DLB 2, 28; DLBY 80; INT CANR-8; MTCW
Elledge, Scott .... CLC 34
Elliot, Don
    See Silverberg, Robert
Elliott, Don
    See Silverberg, Robert
Elliott, George P(aul) [1918-1980] ..... CLC 2
    See also CA 1-4R; 97-100; CANR 2
Elliott, Janice [1931-] .... CLC 47
    See also CA 13-16R; CANR 8, 29; DLB 14
Elliott, Sumner Locke [1917-1991] .. CLC 38
    See also CA 5-8R; 134; CANR 2, 21
Elliott, William
    See Bradbury, Ray (Douglas)
Ellis, A. E. .... CLC 7
Ellis, Alice Thomas .... CLC 40
    See also Haycraft, Anna
    See also DLB 194
Ellis, Bret Easton [1964-] CLC 39, 71; DAM

POP
    See also AAYA 2; CA 118; 123; CANR 51; INT 123
Ellis, (Henry) Havelock [1859-1939]TCLC 14
    See also CA 109; DLB 190
Ellis, Landon
    See Ellison, Harlan (Jay)
Ellis, Trey [1962-] .... CLC 55
    See also CA 146
Ellison, Harlan (Jay) [1934-] CLC 1, 13, 42; DAM POP; SSC 14
    See also CA 5-8R; CANR 5, 46; DLB 8; INT CANR-5; MTCW
Ellison, Ralph (Waldo) [1914-1994]CLC 1, 3, 11, 54, 86; BLC 1; DA; DAB; DAC; DAM MST, MULT, NOV; SSC 26; WLC
    See also AAYA 19; BW 1; CA 9-12R; 145; CANR 24, 53; CDALB 1941-1968; DLB 2, 76; DLBY 94; MTCW
Ellmann, Lucy (Elizabeth) [1956-] ... CLC 61
    See also CA 128
Ellmann, Richard (David) [1918-1987] C L C 50
    See also BEST 89:2; CA 1-4R; 122; CANR 2, 28, 61; DLB 103; DLBY 87; MTCW
Elman, Richard (Martin) [1934-1997]CLC 19
    See also CA 17-20R; 163; CAAS 3; CANR 47
Elron
    See Hubbard, L(afayette) Ron(ald)
Eluard, Paul .... TCLC 7, 41
    See also Grindel, Eugene
Elyot, Sir Thomas [1490(?)-1546] .... LC 11
Elytis, Odysseus [1911-1996]CLC 15, 49, 100; DAM POET; PC 21
    See also CA 102; 151; MTCW
Emecheta, (Florence Onye) Buchi [1944-] CLC 14, 48; BLC 2; DAM MULT
    See also BW 2; CA 81-84; CANR 27; DLB 117; MTCW; SATA 66
Emerson, Mary Moody [1774-1863]NCLC 66
Emerson, Ralph Waldo [1803-1882]NCLC 1, 38; DA; DAB; DAC; DAM MST, POET; PC 18; WLC
    See also CDALB 1640-1865; DLB 1, 59, 73
Eminescu, Mihail [1850-1889] .... NCLC 33
Empson, William [1906-1984]CLC 3, 8, 19, 33, 34
    See also CA 17-20R; 112; CANR 31, 61; DLB 20; MTCW
Enchi, Fumiko (Ueda) [1905-1986] .. CLC 31
    See also CA 129; 121
Ende, Michael (Andreas Helmuth) [1929-1995] CLC 31
    See also CA 118; 124; 149; CANR 36; CLR 14; DLB 75; MAICYA; SATA 61; SATA-Brief 42; SATA-Obit 86
Endo, Shusaku [1923-1996]CLC 7, 14, 19, 54, 99; DAM NOV
    See also CA 29-32R; 153; CANR 21, 54; DLB 182; MTCW
Engel, Marian [1933-1985] .... CLC 36
    See also CA 25-28R; CANR 12; DLB 53; INT CANR-12
Engelhardt, Frederick
    See Hubbard, L(afayette) Ron(ald)
Enright, D(ennis) J(oseph) [1920-] CLC 4, 8, 31
    See also CA 1-4R; CANR 1, 42; DLB 27; SATA 25
Enzensberger, Hans Magnus [1929-] CLC 43
    See also CA 116; 119
Ephron, Nora [1941-] .... CLC 17, 31
    See also AITN 2; CA 65-68; CANR 12, 39
Epicurus [341B.C.-270B.C.] .... CMLC 21
    See also DLB 176
Epsilon
    See Betjeman, John

Ferguson, Samuel [1810-1886] ...... **NCLC 33**
See also DLB 32
Fergusson, Robert [1750-1774] .... **LC 29**
See also DLB 109
Ferling, Lawrence
See Ferlinghetti, Lawrence (Monsanto)
Ferlinghetti, Lawrence (Monsanto) [1919(?)-]
CLC 2, 6, 10, 27, 111; DAM POET; PC 1
See also CA 5-8R; CANR 3, 41; CDALB 1941-1968; DLB 5, 16; MTCW
Fernandez, Vicente Garcia Huidobro
See Huidobro Fernandez, Vicente Garcia
Ferrer, Gabriel (Francisco Victor) Miro
See Miro (Ferrer), Gabriel (Francisco Victor)
Ferrier, Susan (Edmonstone) [1782-1854]
NCLC 8
See also DLB 116
Ferrigno, Robert [1948(?)-] .... **CLC 65**
See also CA 140
Ferron, Jacques [1921-1985] .. **CLC 94; DAC**
See also CA 117; 129; DLB 60
Feuchtwanger, Lion [1884-1958] ..... **TCLC 3**
See also CA 104; DLB 66
Feuillet, Octave [1821-1890] .... **NCLC 45**
See also DLB 192
Feydeau, Georges (Leon Jules Marie) [1862-1921] ....
TCLC 22; DAM DRAM
See also CA 113; 152; DLB 192
Fichte, Johann Gottlieb [1762-1814]**NCLC 62**
See also DLB 90
Ficino, Marsilio [1433-1499] .... **LC 12**
Fiedeler, Hans
See Doeblin, Alfred
Fiedler, Leslie A(aron) [1917-] **CLC 4, 13, 24**
See also CA 9-12R; CANR 7, 63; DLB 28, 67; MTCW
Field, Andrew [1938-] .... **CLC 44**
See also CA 97-100; CANR 25
Field, Eugene [1850-1895] .... **NCLC 3**
See also DLB 23, 42, 140; DLBD 13; MAICYA; SATA 16
Field, Gans T.
See Wellman, Manly Wade
Field, Michael [1915-1971] .... **TCLC 43**
See also CA 29-32R
Field, Peter
See Hobson, Laura Z(ametkin)
Fielding, Henry [1707-1754]**LC 1; DA; DAB; DAC; DAM DRAM, MST, NOV; WLC**
See also CDBLB 1660-1789; DLB 39, 84, 101
Fielding, Sarah [1710-1768] .... **LC 1, 44**
See also DLB 39
Fields, W. C. [1880-1946] .... **TCLC 80**
See also DLB 44
Fierstein, Harvey (Forbes) [1954-]. **CLC 33; DAM DRAM, POP**
See also CA 123; 129
Figes, Eva [1932-] .... **CLC 31**
See also CA 53-56; CANR 4, 44; DLB 14
Finch, Anne [1661-1720] .... **LC 3; PC 21**
See also DLB 95
Finch, Robert (Duer Claydon) [1900-]**CLC 18**
See also CA 57-60; CANR 9, 24, 49; DLB 88
Findley, Timothy [1930-]**CLC 27, 102; DAC; DAM MST**
See also CA 25-28R; CANR 12, 42, 69; DLB 53
Fink, William
See Mencken, H(enry) L(ouis)
Firbank, Louis [1942-]
See Reed, Lou
See also CA 117
Firbank, (Arthur Annesley) Ronald [1886-1926] .... **TCLC 1**
See also CA 104; DLB 36
Fisher, M(ary) F(rances) K(ennedy) [1908-

1992] .... **CLC 76, 87**
See also CA 77-80; 138; CANR 44
Fisher, Roy [1930-] .... **CLC 25**
See also CA 81-84; CAAS 10; CANR 16; DLB 40
Fisher, Rudolph [1897-1934]**TCLC 11; BLC 2; DAM MULT; SSC 25**
See also BW 1; CA 107; 124; DLB 51, 102
Fisher, Vardis (Alvero) [1895-1968] ... **CLC 7**
See also CA 5-8R; 25-28R; CANR 68; DLB 9
Fiske, Tarleton
See Bloch, Robert (Albert)
Fitch, Clarke
See Sinclair, Upton (Beall)
Fitch, John IV
See Cormier, Robert (Edmund)
Fitzgerald, Captain Hugh
See Baum, L(yman) Frank
FitzGerald, Edward [1809-1883] .... **NCLC 9**
See also DLB 32
Fitzgerald, F(rancis) Scott (Key) [1896-1940]
TCLC 1, 6, 14, 28, 55; DA; DAB; DAC; DAM MST, NOV; SSC 6, 31; WLC
See also AAYA 24; AITN 1; CA 110; 123; CDALB 1917-1929; DLB 4, 9, 86; DLBD 1, 15, 16; DLBY 81, 96; MTCW
Fitzgerald, Penelope [1916-] **CLC 19, 51, 61**
See also CA 85-88; CAAS 10; CANR 56; DLB 14, 194
Fitzgerald, Robert (Stuart) [1910-1985]**C L C 39**
See also CA 1-4R; 114; CANR 1; DLBY 80
FitzGerald, Robert D(avid) [1902-1987]**C L C 19**
See also CA 17-20R
Fitzgerald, Zelda (Sayre) [1900-1948] **T C L C 52**
See also CA 117; 126; DLBY 84
Flanagan, Thomas (James Bonner) [1923-]
CLC 25, 52
See also CA 108; CANR 55; DLBY 80; INT 108; MTCW
Flaubert, Gustave [1821-1880] .**NCLC 2, 10, 19, 62, 66; DA; DAB; DAC; DAM MST, NOV; SSC 11; WLC**
See also DLB 119
Flecker, Herman Elroy
See Flecker, (Herman) James Elroy
Flecker, (Herman) James Elroy [1884-1915]
TCLC 43
See also CA 109; 150; DLB 10, 19
Fleming, Ian (Lancaster) [1908-1964]**CLC 3, 30; DAM POP**
See also CA 5-8R; CANR 59; CDBLB 1945-1960; DLB 87; MTCW; SATA 9
Fleming, Thomas (James) [1927-] .... **CLC 37**
See also CA 5-8R; CANR 10; INT CANR-10; SATA 8
Fletcher, John [1579-1625] .... **LC 33; DC 6**
See also CDBLB Before 1660; DLB 58
Fletcher, John Gould [1886-1950] . **TCLC 35**
See also CA 107; DLB 4, 45
Fleur, Paul
See Pohl, Frederik
Flooglebuckle, Al
See Spiegelman, Art
Flying Officer X
See Bates, H(erbert) E(rnest)
Fo, Dario [1926-]**CLC 32, 109; DAM DRAM**
See also CA 116; 128; CANR 68; DLBY 97; MTCW
Fogarty, Jonathan Titulescu Esq.
See Farrell, James T(homas)
Folke, Will
See Bloch, Robert (Albert)
Follett, Ken(neth Martin) [1949-] .. **CLC 18; DAM NOV, POP**

See also AAYA 6; BEST 89:4; CA 81-84; CANR 13, 33, 54; DLB 87; DLBY 81; INT CANR-33; MTCW
Fontane, Theodor [1819-1898] ...... **NCLC 26**
See also DLB 129
Foote, Horton [1916-]...... **CLC 51, 91; DAM DRAM**
See also CA 73-76; CANR 34, 51; DLB 26; INT CANR-34
Foote, Shelby [1916-] .. **CLC 75; DAM NOV, POP**
See also CA 5-8R; CANR 3, 45; DLB 2, 17
Forbes, Esther [1891-1967] .... **CLC 12**
See also AAYA 17; CA 13-14; 25-28R; CAP 1; CLR 27; DLB 22; JRDA; MAICYA; SATA 2
Forche, Carolyn (Louise) [1950-]**CLC 25, 83, 86; DAM POET; PC 10**
See also CA 109; 117; CANR 50; DLB 5, 193; INT 117
Ford, Elbur
See Hibbert, Eleanor Alice Burford
Ford, Ford Madox [1873-1939] **TCLC 1, 15, 39, 57; DAM NOV**
See also CA 104; 132; CDBLB 1914-1945; DLB 162; MTCW
Ford, Henry [1863-1947] .... **TCLC 73**
See also CA 115; 148
Ford, John [1586-(?)] ....**DC 8**
See also CDBLB Before 1660; DAM DRAM; DLB 58
Ford, John [1895-1973] .... **CLC 16**
See also CA 45-48
Ford, Richard [1944-] .... **CLC 46, 99**
See also CA 69-72; CANR 11, 47
Ford, Webster
See Masters, Edgar Lee
Foreman, Richard [1937-] .... **CLC 50**
See also CA 65-68; CANR 32, 63
Forester, C(ecil) S(cott) [1899-1966] **CLC 35**
See also CA 73-76; 25-28R; DLB 191; SATA 13
Forez
See Mauriac, Francois (Charles)
Forman, James Douglas [1932-] .... **CLC 21**
See also AAYA 17; CA 9-12R; CANR 4, 19, 42; JRDA; MAICYA; SATA 8, 70
Fornes, Maria Irene [1930-] .... **CLC 39, 61**
See also CA 25-28R; CANR 28; DLB 7; HW; INT CANR-28; MTCW
Forrest, Leon (Richard) [1937-1997] **CLC 4; BLCS**
See also BW 2; CA 89-92; 162; CAAS 7; CANR 25, 52; DLB 33
Forster, E(dward) M(organ) [1879-1970]**CLC 1, 2, 3, 4, 9, 10, 13, 15, 22, 45, 77; DA; DAB; DAC; DAM MST, NOV; SSC 27; WLC**
See also AAYA 2; CA 13-14; 25-28R; CANR 45; CAP 1; CDBLB 1914-1945; DLB 34, 98, 162, 178, 195; DLBD 10; MTCW; SATA 57
Forster, John [1812-1876] .... **NCLC 11**
See also DLB 144, 184
Forsyth, Frederick [1938-]**CLC 2, 5, 36; DAM NOV, POP**
See also BEST 89:4; CA 85-88; CANR 38, 62; DLB 87; MTCW
Forten, Charlotte L. .... **TCLC 16; BLC 2**
See Grimke, Charlotte L(ottie) Forten
See also DLB 50
Foscolo, Ugo [1778-1827] .... **NCLC 8**
Fosse, Bob .... **CLC 20**
See also Fosse, Robert Louis
Fosse, Robert Louis [1927-1987]
See Fosse, Bob
See also CA 110; 123
Foster, Stephen Collins [1826-1864]**NCLC 26**
Foucault, Michel [1926-1984]**CLC 31, 34, 69**
See also CA 105; 113; CANR 34; MTCW

Author Index

Gilliam, Terry (Vance) [1940-] .... **CLC 21**
  See also Monty Python
  See also AAYA 19; CA 108; 113; CANR 35;
  INT 113
Gillian, Jerry
  See Gilliam, Terry (Vance)
Gilliatt, Penelope (Ann Douglass) [1932-1993]
  CLC 2, 10, 13, 53
  See also AITN 2; CA 13-16R; 141; CANR 49;
  DLB 14
Gilman, Charlotte (Anna) Perkins (Stetson)
  [1860-1935] .... **TCLC 9, 37; SSC 13**
  See also CA 106; 150
Gilmour, David [1949-] .... **CLC 35**
  See also CA 138, 147
Gilpin, William [1724-1804] .... **NCLC 30**
Gilray, J. D.
  See Mencken, H(enry) L(ouis)
Gilroy, Frank D(aniel) [1925-] .... **CLC 2**
  See also CA 81-84; CANR 32, 64; DLB 7
Gilstrap, John [1957(?)-] .... **CLC 99**
  See also CA 160
Ginsberg, Allen [1926-1997]**CLC 1, 2, 3, 4, 6,**
  13, 36, 69, 109; DA; DAB; DAC; DAM
  MST, POET; PC 4; WLC 3
  See also AITN 1; CA 1-4R; 157; CANR 2, 41,
  63; CDALB 1941-1968; DLB 5, 16, 169;
  MTCW
Ginzburg, Natalia [1916-1991]**CLC 5, 11, 54,**
  70
  See also CA 85-88; 135; CANR 33; DLB 177;
  MTCW
Giono, Jean [1895-1970] .... **CLC 4, 11**
  See also CA 45-48; 29-32R; CANR 2, 35; DLB
  72; MTCW
Giovanni, Nikki [1943-]**CLC 2, 4, 19, 64; BLC**
  2; DA; DAB; DAC; DAM MST, MULT,
  POET; PC 19; WLCS
  See also AAYA 22; AITN 1; BW 2; CA 29-32R;
  CAAS 6; CANR 18, 41, 60; CLR 6; DLB 5,
  41; INT CANR-18; MAICYA; MTCW; SATA
  24
Giovene, Andrea [1904-] .... **CLC 7**
  See also CA 85-88
Gippius, Zinaida (Nikolayevna) [1869-1945]
  See Hippius, Zinaida
  See also CA 106
Giraudoux, (Hippolyte) Jean [1882-1944]
  TCLC 2, 7; DAM DRAM
  See also CA 104; DLB 65
Gironella, Jose Maria [1917-] .... **CLC 11**
  See also CA 101
Gissing, George (Robert) [1857-1903] **T C L C**
  3, 24, 47
  See also CA 105; DLB 18, 135, 184
Giurlani, Aldo
  See Palazzeschi, Aldo
Gladkov, Fyodor (Vasilyevich) [1883-1958]
  TCLC 27
Glanville, Brian (Lester) [1931-] .... **CLC 6**
  See also CA 5-8R; CAAS 9; CANR 3; DLB 15,
  139; SATA 42
Glasgow, Ellen (Anderson Gholson) [1873-
  1945] .... **TCLC 2, 7**
  See also CA 104; 164; DLB 9, 12
Glaspell, Susan [1882(?)-1948] ...... **TCLC 55**
  See also CA 110; 154; DLB 7, 9, 78; YABC 2
Glassco, John [1909-1981] .... **CLC 9**
  See also CA 13-16R; 102; CANR 15; DLB 68
Glasscock, Amnesia
  See Steinbeck, John (Ernst)
Glasser, Ronald J. [1940(?)-] .... **CLC 37**
Glassman, Joyce
  See Johnson, Joyce
Glendinning, Victoria [1937-] .... **CLC 50**
  See also CA 120; 127; CANR 59; DLB 155
Glissant, Edouard [1928-]**CLC 10, 68; DAM**

MULT
  See also CA 153
Gloag, Julian [1930-] .... **CLC 40**
  See also AITN 1; CA 65-68; CANR 10
Glowacki, Aleksander
  See Prus, Boleslaw
Gluck, Louise (Elisabeth) [1943-]**CLC 7, 22,**
  44, 81; DAM POET; PC 16
  See also CA 33-36R; CANR 40, 69; DLB 5
Glyn, Elinor [1864-1943] .... **TCLC 72**
  See also DLB 153
Gobineau, Joseph Arthur (Comte) de [1816-
  1882] .... **NCLC 17**
  See also DLB 123
Godard, Jean-Luc [1930-] .... **CLC 20**
  See also CA 93-96
Godden, (Margaret) Rumer [1907-] . **CLC 53**
  See also AAYA 6; CA 5-8R; CANR 4, 27, 36,
  55; CLR 20; DLB 161; MAICYA; SAAS 12;
  SATA 3, 36
Godoy Alcayaga, Lucila [1889-1957]
  See Mistral, Gabriela
  See also BW 2; CA 104; 131; DAM MULT;
  HW; MTCW
Godwin, Gail (Kathleen) [1937-]**CLC 5, 8, 22,**
  31, 69; DAM POP
  See also CA 29-32R; CANR 15, 43, 69; DLB
  6; INT CANR-15; MTCW
Godwin, William [1756-1836] .... **NCLC 14**
  See also CDBLB 1789-1832; DLB 39, 104, 142,
  158, 163
Goebbels, Josef
  See Goebbels, (Paul) Joseph
Goebbels, (Paul) Joseph [1897-1945]**TCLC 68**
  See also CA 115; 148
Goebbels, Joseph Paul
  See Goebbels, (Paul) Joseph
Goethe, Johann Wolfgang von [1749-1832]
  NCLC 4, 22, 34; DA; DAB; DAC; DAM
  DRAM, MST, POET; PC 5; WLC 3
  See also DLB 94
Gogarty, Oliver St. John [1878-1957] **T C L C**
  15
  See also CA 109; 150; DLB 15, 19
Gogol, Nikolai (Vasilyevich) [1809-1852]
  NCLC 5, 15, 31; DA; DAB; DAC; DAM
  DRAM, MST; DC 1; SSC 4, 29; WLC
  See also DLB 198
Goines, Donald [1937(?)-1974]**CLC 80; BLC**
  2; DAM MULT, POP
  See also AITN 1; BW 1; CA 124; 114; DLB 33
Gold, Herbert [1924-] .... **CLC 4, 7, 14, 42**
  See also CA 9-12R; CANR 17, 45; DLB 2;
  DLBY 81
Goldbarth, Albert [1948-] .... **CLC 5, 38**
  See also CA 53-56; CANR 6, 40; DLB 120
Goldberg, Anatol [1910-1982] .... **CLC 34**
  See also CA 131; 117
Goldemberg, Isaac [1945-] .... **CLC 52**
  See also CA 69-72; CAAS 12; CANR 11, 32;
  HW
Golding, William (Gerald) [1911-1993] **C L C**
  1, 2, 3, 8, 10, 17, 27, 58, 81; DA; DAB;
  DAC; DAM MST, NOV; WLC
  See also AAYA 5; CA 5-8R; 141; CANR 13,
  33, 54; CDBLB 1945-1960; DLB 15, 100;
  MTCW
Goldman, Emma [1869-1940] .... **TCLC 13**
  See also CA 110; 150
Goldman, Francisco [1954-] .... **CLC 76**
  See also CA 162
Goldman, William (W.) [1931-] .... **CLC 1, 48**
  See also CA 9-12R; CANR 29, 69; DLB 44
Goldmann, Lucien [1913-1970] .... **CLC 24**
  See also CA 25-28; CAP 2
Goldoni, Carlo [1707-1793] .... **LC 4; DAM**
  DRAM

Goldsberry, Steven [1949-] .... **CLC 34**
  See also CA 131
Goldsmith, Oliver [1728-1774] .... **LC 2; DA;**
  DAB; DAC; DAM DRAM, MST, NOV,
  POET; DC 8; WLC
  See also CDBLB 1660-1789; DLB 39, 89, 104,
  109, 142; SATA 26
Goldsmith, Peter
  See Priestley, J(ohn) B(oynton)
Gombrowicz, Witold [1904-1969]**CLC 4, 7, 11,**
  49; DAM DRAM
  See also CA 19-20; 25-28R; CAP 2
Gomez de la Serna, Ramon [1888-1963]**C L C**
  9
  See also CA 153; 116; HW
Goncharov, Ivan Alexandrovich [1812-1891]
  NCLC 1, 63
Goncourt, Edmond (Louis Antoine Huot) de
  [1822-1896] .... **NCLC 7**
  See also DLB 123
Goncourt, Jules (Alfred Huot) de [1830-1870]
  NCLC 7
  See also DLB 123
Gontier, Fernande [19(?)-] .... **CLC 50**
Gonzalez Martinez, Enrique [1871-1952]
  TCLC 72
  See also CA 166; HW
Goodman, Paul [1911-1972] ... **CLC 1, 2, 4, 7**
  See also CA 19-20; 37-40R; CANR 34; CAP 2;
  DLB 130; MTCW
Gordimer, Nadine [1923-]**CLC 3, 5, 7, 10, 18,**
  33, 51, 70; DA; DAB; DAC; DAM MST,
  NOV; SSC 17; WLCS
  See also CA 5-8R; CANR 3, 28, 56; INT CANR-
  28; MTCW
Gordon, Adam Lindsay [1833-1870]**NCLC 21**
Gordon, Caroline [1895-1981]**CLC 6, 13, 29,**
  83; SSC 15
  See also CA 11-12; 103; CANR 36; CAP 1;
  DLB 4, 9, 102; DLBY 81; MTCW
Gordon, Charles William [1860-1937]
  See Connor, Ralph
  See also CA 109
Gordon, Mary (Catherine) [1949-]**CLC 13, 22**
  See also CA 102; CANR 44; DLB 6; DLBY
  81; INT 102; MTCW
Gordon, N. J.
  See Bosman, Herman Charles
Gordon, Sol [1923-] .... **CLC 26**
  See also CA 53-56; CANR 4; SATA 11
Gordone, Charles [1925-1995]**CLC 1, 4; DAM**
  DRAM; DC 8
  See also BW 1; CA 93-96; 150; CANR 55; DLB
  7; INT 93-96; MTCW
Gore, Catherine [1800-1861] .... **NCLC 65**
  See also DLB 116
Gorenko, Anna Andreevna
  See Akhmatova, Anna
Gorky, Maxim [1868-1936] .. **TCLC 8; DAB;**
  SSC 28; WLC
  See also Peshkov, Alexei Maximovich
Goryan, Sirak
  See Saroyan, William
Gosse, Edmund (William) [1849-1928]**T C L C**
  28
  See also CA 117; DLB 57, 144, 184
Gotlieb, Phyllis Fay (Bloom) [1926-] **CLC 18**
  See also CA 13-16R; CANR 7; DLB 88
Gottesman, S. D.
  See Kornbluth, C(yril) M.; Pohl, Frederik
Gottfried von Strassburg [fl. c. 1210-]**C M L C**
  10
  See also DLB 138
Gould, Lois .... **CLC 4, 10**
  See also CA 77-80; CANR 29; MTCW
Gourmont, Remy (-Marie-Charles) de [1858-
  1915] .... **TCLC 17**

Hearne, Vicki [1946-] .... **CLC 56**
See also CA 139
Hearon, Shelby [1931-] .... **CLC 63**
See also AITN 2; CA 25-28R; CANR 18, 48
Heat-Moon, William Least .... **CLC 29**
See Trogdon, William (Lewis)
See also AAYA 9
Hebbel, Friedrich [1813-1863] ..... **NCLC 43;**
DAM DRAM
See also DLB 129
Hebert, Anne [1916-] ... **CLC 4, 13, 29; DAC;**
DAM MST, POET
See also CA 85-88; CANR 69; DLB 68; MTCW
Hecht, Anthony (Evan) [1923-]**CLC 8, 13, 19;**
DAM POET
See also CA 9-12R; CANR 6; DLB 5, 169
Hecht, Ben [1894-1964] .... **CLC 8**
See also CA 85-88; DLB 7, 9, 25, 26, 28, 86
Hedayat, Sadeq [1903-1951] .... **TCLC 21**
See also CA 120
Hegel, Georg Wilhelm Friedrich [1770-1831]
NCLC 46
See also DLB 90
Heidegger, Martin [1889-1976] .... **CLC 24**
See also CA 81-84; 65-68; CANR 34; MTCW
Heidenstam, (Carl Gustaf) Verner von [1859-
1940] ....
TCLC 5
See also CA 104
Heifner, Jack [1946-] .... **CLC 11**
See also CA 105; CANR 47
Heijermans, Herman [1864-1924] . **TCLC 24**
See also CA 123
Heilbrun, Carolyn G(old) [1926-] .... **CLC 25**
See also CA 45-48; CANR 1, 28, 58
Heine, Heinrich [1797-1856] ...... **NCLC 4, 54**
See also DLB 90
Heinemann, Larry (Curtiss) [1944-] **CLC 50**
See also CA 110; CAAS 21; CANR 31; DLBD
9; INT CANR-31
Heiney, Donald (William) [1921-1993]
See Harris, MacDonald
See also CA 1-4R; 142; CANR 3, 58
Heinlein, Robert A(nson) [1907-1988]**CLC 1,**
3, 8, 14, 26, 55; DAM POP
See also AAYA 17; CA 1-4R; 125; CANR 1,
20, 53; DLB 8; JRDA; MAICYA; MTCW;
SATA 9, 69; SATA-Obit 56
Helforth, John
See Doolittle, Hilda
Hellenhofferu, Vojtech Kapristian z
See Hasek, Jaroslav (Matej Frantisek)
Heller, Joseph [1923-]**CLC 1, 3, 5, 8, 11, 36, 63;**
DA; DAB; DAC; DAM MST, NOV, POP;
WLC
See also AAYA 24; AITN 1; CA 5-8R; CABS
1; CANR 8, 42, 66; DLB 2, 28; DLBY 80;
INT CANR-8; MTCW
Hellman, Lillian (Florence) [1906-1984]**C L C**
2, 4, 8, 14, 18, 34, 44, 52; DAM DRAM;
DC 1
See also AITN 1, 2; CA 13-16R; 112; CANR
33; DLB 7; DLBY 84; MTCW
Helprin, Mark [1947-]**CLC 7, 10, 22, 32; DAM**
NOV, POP
See also CA 81-84; CANR 47, 64; DLBY 85;
MTCW
Helvetius, Claude-Adrien [1715-1771] **LC 26**
Helyar, Jane Penelope Josephine [1933-]
See Poole, Josephine
See also CA 21-24R; CANR 10, 26; SATA 82
Hemans, Felicia [1793-1835] .... **NCLC 71**
See also DLB 96
Hemingway, Ernest (Miller) [1899-1961]**CLC**
1, 3, 6, 8, 10, 13, 19, 30, 34, 39, 41, 44, 50,
61, 80; DA; DAB; DAC; DAM MST, NOV;
SSC 25; WLC

See also AAYA 19; CA 77-80; CANR 34;
CDALB 1917-1929; DLB 4, 9, 102; DLBD
1, 15, 16; DLBY 81, 87, 96; MTCW
Hempel, Amy [1951-] .... **CLC 39**
See also CA 118; 137
Henderson, F. C.
See Mencken, H(enry) L(ouis)
Henderson, Sylvia
See Ashton-Warner, Sylvia (Constance)
Henderson, Zenna (Chlarson) [1917-1983]
SSC 29
See also CA 1-4R; 133; CANR 1; DLB 8; SATA
5
Henley, Beth .... **CLC 23; DC 6**
See also Henley, Elizabeth Becker
See also CABS 3; DLBY 86
Henley, Elizabeth Becker [1952-]
See Henley, Beth
See also CA 107; CANR 32; DAM DRAM,
MST; MTCW
Henley, William Ernest [1849-1903] **TCLC 8**
See also CA 105; DLB 19
Hennissart, Martha
See Lathen, Emma
See also CA 85-88; CANR 64
Henry, O. .... **TCLC 1, 19; SSC 5; WLC**
See also Porter, William Sydney
Henry, Patrick [1736-1799] .... **LC 25**
Henryson, Robert [1430(?)-1506(?)] ... **LC 20**
See also DLB 146
Henry VIII [1491-1547] .... **LC 10**
Henschke, Alfred
See Klabund
Hentoff, Nat(han Irving) [1925-] ...... **CLC 26**
See also AAYA 4; CA 1-4R; CAAS 6; CANR
5, 25; CLR 1, 52; INT CANR-25; JRDA;
MAICYA; SATA 42, 69; SATA-Brief 27
Heppenstall, (John) Rayner [1911-1981]**C L C**
10
See also CA 1-4R; 103; CANR 29
Heraclitus [c. 540B.C.-c. 450B.C.] **CMLC 22**
See also DLB 176
Herbert, Frank (Patrick) [1920-1986]**CLC 12,**
23, 35, 44, 85; DAM POP
See also AAYA 21; CA 53-56; 118; CANR 5,
43; DLB 8; INT CANR-5; MTCW; SATA 9,
37; SATA-Obit 47
Herbert, George [1593-1633] .. **LC 24; DAB;**
DAM POET; PC 4
See also CDBLB Before 1660; DLB 126
Herbert, Zbigniew [1924-] **CLC 9, 43; DAM**
POET
See also CA 89-92; CANR 36; MTCW
Herbst, Josephine (Frey) [1897-1969]**CLC 34**
See also CA 5-8R; 25-28R; DLB 9
Hergesheimer, Joseph [1880-1954] **TCLC 11**
See also CA 109; DLB 102, 9
Herlihy, James Leo [1927-1993] .... **CLC 6**
See also CA 1-4R; 143; CANR 2
Hermogenes [fl. c. 175-] .... **CMLC 6**
Hernandez, Jose [1834-1886] .... **NCLC 17**
Herodotus [c. 484B.C.-429B.C.] .... **CMLC 17**
See also DLB 176
Herrick, Robert [1591-1674]**LC 13; DA; DAB;**
DAC; DAM MST, POP; PC 9
See also DLB 126
Herring, Guilles
See Somerville, Edith
Herriot, James [1916-1995] ... **CLC 12; DAM**
POP
See also Wight, James Alfred
See also AAYA 1; CA 148; CANR 40; SATA
86
Herrmann, Dorothy [1941-] .... **CLC 44**
See also CA 107
Herrmann, Taffy
See Herrmann, Dorothy

Hersey, John (Richard) [1914-1993]**CLC 1, 2,**
7, 9, 40, 81, 97; DAM POP
See also CA 17-20R; 140; CANR 33; DLB 6,
185; MTCW; SATA 25; SATA-Obit 76
Herzen, Aleksandr Ivanovich [1812-1870]
NCLC 10, 61
Herzl, Theodor [1860-1904] .... **TCLC 36**
Herzog, Werner [1942-] .... **CLC 16**
See also CA 89-92
Hesiod [c. 8th cent. B.C.-] .... **CMLC 5**
See also DLB 176
Hesse, Hermann [1877-1962]**CLC 1, 2, 3, 6, 11,**
17, 25, 69; DA; DAB; DAC; DAM MST,
NOV; SSC 9; WLC
See also CA 17-18; CAP 2; DLB 66; MTCW;
SATA 50
Hewes, Cady
See De Voto, Bernard (Augustine)
Heyen, William [1940-] .... **CLC 13, 18**
See also CA 33-36R; CAAS 9; DLB 5
Heyerdahl, Thor [1914-] .... **CLC 26**
See also CA 5-8R; CANR 5, 22, 66; MTCW;
SATA 2, 52
Heym, Georg (Theodor Franz Arthur) [1887-
1912] .... **TCLC 9**
See also CA 106
Heym, Stefan [1913-] .... **CLC 41**
See also CA 9-12R; CANR 4; DLB 69
Heyse, Paul (Johann Ludwig von) [1830-1914]
TCLC 8
See also CA 104; DLB 129
Heyward, (Edwin) DuBose [1885-1940]**TCLC**
59
See also CA 108; 157; DLB 7, 9, 45; SATA 21
Hibbert, Eleanor Alice Burford [1906-1993]
CLC 7; DAM POP
See also BEST 90:4; CA 17-20R; 140; CANR
9, 28, 59; SATA 2; SATA-Obit 74
Hichens, Robert (Smythe) [1864-1950]**T CLC**
64
See also CA 162; DLB 153
Higgins, George V(incent) [1939-] **CLC 4, 7,**
10, 18
See also CA 77-80; CAAS 5; CANR 17, 51;
DLB 2; DLBY 81; INT CANR-17; MTCW
Higginson, Thomas Wentworth [1823-1911]
TCLC 36
See also CA 162; DLB 1, 64
Highet, Helen
See MacInnes, Helen (Clark)
Highsmith, (Mary) Patricia [1921-1995]**C L C**
2, 4, 14, 42, 102; DAM NOV, POP
See also CA 1-4R; 147; CANR 1, 20, 48, 62;
MTCW
Highwater, Jamake (Mamake) [1942(?)-]**CLC**
12
See also AAYA 7; CA 65-68; CAAS 7; CANR
10, 34; CLR 17; DLB 52; DLBY 85; JRDA;
MAICYA; SATA 32, 69; SATA-Brief 30
Highway, Tomson [1951-] ..... **CLC 92; DAC;**
DAM MULT
See also CA 151; NNAL
Higuchi, Ichiyo [1872-1896] .... **NCLC 49**
Hijuelos, Oscar [1951-]**CLC 65; DAM MULT,**
POP; HLC
See also AAYA 25; BEST 90:1; CA 123; CANR
50; DLB 145; HW
Hikmet, Nazim [1902(?)-1963] .... **CLC 40**
See also CA 141; 93-96
Hildegard von Bingen [1098-1179]**CMLC 20**
See also DLB 148
Hildesheimer, Wolfgang [1916-1991]**CLC 49**
See also CA 101; 135; DLB 69, 124
Hill, Geoffrey (William) [1932-]**CLC 5, 8, 18,**
45; DAM POET
See also CA 81-84; CANR 21; CDBLB 1960
to Present; DLB 40; MTCW

Hill, George Roy [1921-] .... **CLC 26**
  See also CA 110; 122
Hill, John
  See Koontz, Dean R(ay)
Hill, Susan (Elizabeth) [1942-] . **CLC 4, 113;**
  DAB; DAM MST, NOV
  See also CA 33-36R; CANR 29, 69; DLB 14,
  139; MTCW
Hillerman, Tony [1925-] **CLC 62; DAM POP**
  See also AAYA 6; BEST 89:1; CA 29-32R;
  CANR 21, 42, 65; SATA 6
Hillesum, Etty [1914-1943] .... **TCLC 49**
  See also CA 137
Hilliard, Noel (Harvey) [1929-] .... **CLC 15**
  See also CA 9-12R; CANR 7, 69
Hillis, Rick [1956-] .... **CLC 66**
  See also CA 134
Hilton, James [1900-1954] .... **TCLC 21**
  See also CA 108; DLB 34, 77; SATA 34
Himes, Chester (Bomar) [1909-1984] **CLC 2,**
  4, 7, 18, 58, 108; BLC 2; DAM MULT
  See also BW 2; CA 25-28R; 114; CANR 22;
  DLB 2, 76, 143; MTCW
Hinde, Thomas .... **CLC 6, 11**
  See also Chitty, Thomas Willes
Hindin, Nathan
  See Bloch, Robert (Albert)
Hine, (William) Daryl [1936-] .... **CLC 15**
  See also CA 1-4R; CAAS 15; CANR 1, 20; DLB
  60
Hinkson, Katharine Tynan
  See Tynan, Katharine
Hinton, S(usan) E(loise) [1950-]**CLC 30, 111;**
  DA; DAB; DAC; DAM MST, NOV
  See also AAYA 2; CA 81-84; CANR 32, 62;
  CLR 3, 23; JRDA; MAICYA; MTCW; SATA
  19, 58
Hippius, Zinaida .... **TCLC 9**
  See also Gippius, Zinaida (Nikolayevna)
Hiraoka, Kimitake [1925-1970]
  See Mishima, Yukio
  See also CA 97-100; 29-32R; DAM DRAM;
  MTCW
Hirsch, E(ric) D(onald), Jr. [1928-] .. **CLC 79**
  See also CA 25-28R; CANR 27, 51; DLB 67;
  INT CANR-27; MTCW
Hirsch, Edward [1950-] .... **CLC 31, 50**
  See also CA 104; CANR 20, 42; DLB 120
Hitchcock, Alfred (Joseph) [1899-1980] **C L C**
  16
  See also AAYA 22; CA 159; 97-100; SATA 27;
  SATA-Obit 24
Hitler, Adolf [1889-1945] .... **TCLC 53**
  See also CA 117; 147
Hoagland, Edward [1932-] .... **CLC 28**
  See also CA 1-4R; CANR 2, 31, 57; DLB 6;
  SATA 51
Hoban, Russell (Conwell) [1925-]**CLC 7, 25;**
  DAM NOV
  See also CA 5-8R; CANR 23, 37, 66; CLR 3;
  DLB 52; MAICYA; MTCW; SATA 1, 40, 78
Hobbes, Thomas [1588-1679] .... **LC 36**
  See also DLB 151
Hobbs, Perry
  See Blackmur, R(ichard) P(almer)
Hobson, Laura Z(ametkin) [1900-1986] **C L C**
  7, 25
  See also CA 17-20R; 118; CANR 55; DLB 28;
  SATA 52
Hochhuth, Rolf [1931-] **CLC 4, 11, 18; DAM**
  DRAM
  See also CA 5-8R; CANR 33; DLB 124; MTCW
Hochman, Sandra [1936-] .... **CLC 3, 8**
  See also CA 5-8R; DLB 5
Hochwaelder, Fritz [1911-1986] ..... **CLC 36;**
  DAM DRAM
  See also CA 29-32R; 120; CANR 42; MTCW

Hochwalder, Fritz
  See Hochwaelder, Fritz
Hocking, Mary (Eunice) [1921-] .... **CLC 13**
  See also CA 101; CANR 18, 40
Hodgins, Jack [1938-] .... **CLC 23**
  See also CA 93-96; DLB 60
Hodgson, William Hope [1877(?)-1918]**TCLC**
  13
  See also CA 111; 164; DLB 70, 153, 156, 178
Hoeg, Peter [1957-] .... **CLC 95**
  See also CA 151
Hoffman, Alice [1952-].**CLC 51; DAM NOV**
  See also CA 77-80; CANR 34, 66; MTCW
Hoffman, Daniel (Gerard) [1923-]**CLC 6, 13,**
  23
  See also CA 1-4R; CANR 4; DLB 5
Hoffman, Stanley [1944-] .... **CLC 5**
  See also CA 77-80
Hoffman, William M(oses) [1939-] ... **CLC 40**
  See also CA 57-60; CANR 11
Hoffmann, E(rnst) T(heodor) A(madeus) [1776-
  1822] ....
  NCLC 2; SSC 13
  See also DLB 90; SATA 27
Hofmann, Gert [1931-] .... **CLC 54**
  See also CA 128
Hofmannsthal, Hugo von [1874-1929] **T C L C**
  11; DAM DRAM; DC 4
  See also CA 106; 153; DLB 81, 118
Hogan, Linda [1947-] **CLC 73; DAM MULT**
  See also CA 120; CANR 45, 69; DLB 175;
  NNAL
Hogarth, Charles
  See Creasey, John
Hogarth, Emmett
  See Polonsky, Abraham (Lincoln)
Hogg, James [1770-1835] .... **NCLC 4**
  See also DLB 93, 116, 159
Holbach, Paul Henri Thiry Baron [1723-1789]
  LC 14
Holberg, Ludvig [1684-1754] .... **LC 6**
Holden, Ursula [1921-] .... **CLC 18**
  See also CA 101; CAAS 8; CANR 22
Holderlin, (Johann Christian) Friedrich [1770-
  1843] ....
  NCLC 16; PC 4
Holdstock, Robert
  See Holdstock, Robert P.
Holdstock, Robert P. [1948-] .... **CLC 39**
  See also CA 131
Holland, Isabelle [1920-] .... **CLC 21**
  See also AAYA 11; CA 21-24R; CANR 10, 25,
  47; JRDA; MAICYA; SATA 8, 70
Holland, Marcus
  See Caldwell, (Janet Miriam) Taylor (Holland)
Hollander, John [1929-] .... **CLC 2, 5, 8, 14**
  See also CA 1-4R; CANR 1, 52; DLB 5; SATA
  13
Hollander, Paul
  See Silverberg, Robert
Holleran, Andrew [1943(?)-] .... **CLC 38**
  See also CA 144
Hollinghurst, Alan [1954-] .... **CLC 55, 91**
  See also CA 114
Hollis, Jim
  See Summers, Hollis (Spurgeon, Jr.)
Holly, Buddy [1936-1959] .... **TCLC 65**
Holmes, Gordon
  See Shiel, M(atthew) P(hipps)
Holmes, John
  See Souster, (Holmes) Raymond
Holmes, John Clellon [1926-1988] ... **CLC 56**
  See also CA 9-12R; 125; CANR 4; DLB 16
Holmes, Oliver Wendell, Jr. [1841-1935]
  TCLC 77
  See also CA 114
Holmes, Oliver Wendell [1809-1894]**NCLC 14**

  See also CDALB 1640-1865; DLB 1, 189;
  SATA 34
Holmes, Raymond
  See Souster, (Holmes) Raymond
Holt, Victoria
  See Hibbert, Eleanor Alice Burford
Holub, Miroslav [1923-] .... **CLC 4**
  See also CA 21-24R; CANR 10
Homer [c. 8th cent. B.C.-] **CMLC 1, 16; DA;**
  DAB; DAC; DAM MST, POET; PC 23;
  WLCS
  See also DLB 176
Hongo, Garrett Kaoru [1951-] .... **PC 23**
  See also CA 133; CAAS 22; DLB 120
Honig, Edwin [1919-] .... **CLC 33**
  See also CA 5-8R; CAAS 8; CANR 4, 45; DLB
  5
Hood, Hugh (John Blagdon) [1928-]**CLC 15,**
  28
  See also CA 49-52; CAAS 17; CANR 1, 33;
  DLB 53
Hood, Thomas [1799-1845] .... **NCLC 16**
  See also DLB 96
Hooker, (Peter) Jeremy [1941-] .... **CLC 43**
  See also CA 77-80; CANR 22; DLB 40
hooks, bell .... **CLC 94; BLCS**
  See also Watkins, Gloria
Hope, A(lec) D(erwent) [1907-] ..... **CLC 3, 51**
  See also CA 21-24R; CANR 33; MTCW
Hope, Anthony [1863-1933] .... **TCLC 83**
  See also CA 157; DLB 153, 156
Hope, Brian
  See Creasey, John
Hope, Christopher (David Tully) [1944-]**CLC**
  52
  See also CA 106; CANR 47; SATA 62
Hopkins, Gerard Manley [1844-1889]**N C L C**
  17; DA; DAB; DAC; DAM MST, POET;
  PC 15; WLC
  See also CDBLB 1890-1914; DLB 35, 57
Hopkins, John (Richard) [1931-]........ **CLC 4**
  See also CA 85-88
Hopkins, Pauline Elizabeth [1859-1930]
  TCLC 28; BLC 2; DAM MULT
  See also BW 2; CA 141; DLB 50
Hopkinson, Francis [1737-1791].......... **LC 25**
  See also DLB 31
Hopley-Woolrich, Cornell George [1903-1968]
  See Woolrich, Cornell
  See also CA 13-14; CANR 58; CAP 1
Horatio
  See Proust, (Valentin-Louis-George-Eugene-)
  Marcel
Horgan, Paul (George Vincent O'Shaughnessy)
  [1903-1995] .... **CLC 9, 53; DAM NOV**
  See also CA 13-16R; 147; CANR 9, 35; DLB
  102; DLBY 85; INT CANR-9; MTCW;
  SATA 13; SATA-Obit 84
Horn, Peter
  See Kuttner, Henry
Hornem, Horace Esq.
  See Byron, George Gordon (Noel)
Horney, Karen (Clementine Theodore
  Danielsen) [1885-1952] .... **TCLC 71**
  See also CA 114; 165
Hornung, E(rnest) W(illiam) [1866-1921]
  TCLC 59
  See also CA 108; 160; DLB 70
Horovitz, Israel (Arthur) [1939-] ... **CLC 56;**
  DAM DRAM
  See also CA 33-36R; CANR 46, 59; DLB 7
Horvath, Odon von
  See Horvath, Oedoen von
  See also DLB 85, 124
Horvath, Oedoen von [1901-1938] **TCLC 45**
  See also Horvath, Odon von
  See also CA 118

See also DLB 133

Inchbald, Elizabeth [1753-1821] ... **NCLC 62**
See also DLB 39, 89

Inclan, Ramon (Maria) del Valle
See Valle-Inclan, Ramon (Maria) del

Infante, G(uillermo) Cabrera
See Cabrera Infante, G(uillermo)

Ingalls, Rachel (Holmes) [1940-] ...... **CLC 42**
See also CA 123; 127

Ingamells, Rex [1913-1955] .... **TCLC 35**

Inge, William (Motter) [1913-1973]**CLC 1, 8, 19; DAM DRAM**
See also CA 9-12R; CDALB 1941-1968; DLB 7; MTCW

Ingelow, Jean [1820-1897] .... **NCLC 39**
See also DLB 35, 163; SATA 33

Ingram, Willis J.
See Harris, Mark

Innaurato, Albert (F.) [1948(?)-] **CLC 21, 60**
See also CA 115; 122; INT 122

Innes, Michael
See Stewart, J(ohn) I(nnes) M(ackintosh)

Innis, Harold Adams [1894-1952] . **TCLC 77**
See also DLB 88

Ionesco, Eugene [1909-1994]**CLC 1, 4, 6, 9, 11, 15, 41, 86; DA; DAB; DAC; DAM DRAM, MST; WLC**
See also CA 9-12R; 144; CANR 55; MTCW; SATA 7; SATA-Obit 79

Iqbal, Muhammad [1873-1938] ..... **TCLC 28**

Ireland, Patrick
See O'Doherty, Brian

Iron, Ralph
See Schreiner, Olive (Emilie Albertina)

Irving, John (Winslow) [1942-]**CLC 13, 23, 38, 112; DAM NOV, POP**
See also AAYA 8; BEST 89:3; CA 25-28R; CANR 28; DLB 6; DLBY 82; MTCW

Irving, Washington [1783-1859]**NCLC 2, 19; DA; DAB; DAM MST; SSC 2; WLC**
See also CDALB 1640-1865; DLB 3, 11, 30, 59, 73, 74, 186; YABC 2

Irwin, P. K.
See Page, P(atricia) K(athleen)

Isaacs, Jorge Ricardo [1837-1895] **NCLC 70**

Isaacs, Susan [1943-] .... **CLC 32; DAM POP**
See also BEST 89:1; CA 89-92; CANR 20, 41, 65; INT CANR-20; MTCW

Isherwood, Christopher (William Bradshaw) [1904-1986] . **CLC 1, 9, 11, 14, 44; DAM DRAM, NOV**
See also CA 13-16R; 117; CANR 35; DLB 15, 195; DLBY 86; MTCW

Ishiguro, Kazuo [1954-]**CLC 27, 56, 59, 110; DAM NOV**
See also BEST 90:2; CA 120; CANR 49; DLB 194; MTCW

Ishikawa, Hakuhin
See Ishikawa, Takuboku

Ishikawa, Takuboku [1886(?)-1912]**TCLC 15; DAM POET; PC 10**
See also CA 113; 153

Iskander, Fazil [1929-] .... **CLC 47**
See also CA 102

Isler, Alan (David) [1934-] .... **CLC 91**
See also CA 156

Ivan IV [1530-1584] .... **LC 17**

Ivanov, Vyacheslav Ivanovich [1866-1949] **TCLC 33**
See also CA 122

Ivask, Ivar Vidrik [1927-1992] .... **CLC 14**
See also CA 37-40R; 139; CANR 24

Ives, Morgan
See Bradley, Marion Zimmer

J. R. S.
See Gogarty, Oliver St. John

Jabran, Kahlil

See Gibran, Kahlil

Jabran, Khalil
See Gibran, Kahlil

Jackson, Daniel
See Wingrove, David (John)

Jackson, Jesse [1908-1983] .... **CLC 12**
See also BW 1; CA 25-28R; 109; CANR 27; CLR 28; MAICYA; SATA 2, 29; SATA-Obit 48

Jackson, Laura (Riding) [1901-1991]
See Riding, Laura
See also CA 65-68; 135; CANR 28; DLB 48

Jackson, Sam
See Trumbo, Dalton

Jackson, Sara
See Wingrove, David (John)

Jackson, Shirley [1919-1965]**CLC 11, 60, 87; DA; DAC; DAM MST; SSC 9; WLC**
See also AAYA 9; CA 1-4R; 25-28R; CANR 4, 52; CDALB 1941-1968; DLB 6; SATA 2

Jacob, (Cyprien-)Max [1876-1944] . **TCLC 6**
See also CA 104

Jacobs, Harriet A(nn) [1813(?)-1897] **NCLC 67**

Jacobs, Jim [1942-] .... **CLC 12**
See also CA 97-100; INT 97-100

Jacobs, W(illiam) W(ymark) [1863-1943] **TCLC 22**
See also CA 121; DLB 135

Jacobsen, Jens Peter [1847-1885] .. **NCLC 34**

Jacobsen, Josephine [1908-] ..... **CLC 48, 102**
See also CA 33-36R; CAAS 18; CANR 23, 48

Jacobson, Dan [1929-] .... **CLC 4, 14**
See also CA 1-4R; CANR 2, 25, 66; DLB 14; MTCW

Jacqueline
See Carpentier (y Valmont), Alejo

Jagger, Mick [1944-] .... **CLC 17**

Jahiz, Al- [c. 776-869] .... **CMLC 25**

Jahiz, al- [c. 780-c. 869] .... **CMLC 25**

Jakes, John (William) [1932-]**CLC 29; DAM NOV, POP**
See also BEST 89:4; CA 57-60; CANR 10, 43, 66; DLBY 83; INT CANR-10; MTCW; SATA 62

James, Andrew
See Kirkup, James

James, C(yril) L(ionel) R(obert) [1901-1989] **CLC 33; BLCS**
See also BW 2; CA 117; 125; 128; CANR 62; DLB 125; MTCW

James, Daniel (Lewis) [1911-1988]
See Santiago, Danny
See also CA 125

James, Dynely
See Mayne, William (James Carter)

James, Henry Sr. [1811-1882] .... **NCLC 53**

James, Henry [1843-1916]**TCLC 2, 11, 24, 40, 47, 64; DA; DAB; DAC; DAM MST, NOV; SSC 8; WLC**
See also CA 104; 132; CDALB 1865-1917; DLB 12, 71, 74, 189; DLBD 13; MTCW

James, M. R.
See James, Montague (Rhodes)
See also DLB 156

James, Montague (Rhodes) [1862-1936] **TCLC 6; SSC 16**
See also CA 104

James, P. D. .... **CLC 18, 46**
See also White, Phyllis Dorothy James
See also BEST 90:2; CDBLB 1960 to Present; DLB 87

James, Philip
See Moorcock, Michael (John)

James, William [1842-1910] ..... **TCLC 15, 32**
See also CA 109

James I [1394-1437] .... **LC 20**

Jameson, Anna [1794-1860] .... **NCLC 43**
See also DLB 99, 166

Jami, Nur al-Din 'Abd al-Rahman [1414-1492] **LC 9**

Jammes, Francis [1868-1938] .... **TCLC 75**

Jandl, Ernst [1925-] .... **CLC 34**

Janowitz, Tama [1957-] **CLC 43; DAM POP**
See also CA 106; CANR 52

Japrisot, Sebastien [1931-] .... **CLC 90**

Jarrell, Randall [1914-1965]**CLC 1, 2, 6, 9, 13, 49; DAM POET**
See also CA 5-8R; 25-28R; CABS 2; CANR 6, 34; CDALB 1941-1968; CLR 6; DLB 48, 52; MAICYA; MTCW; SATA 7

Jarry, Alfred [1873-1907]**TCLC 2, 14; DAM DRAM; SSC 20**
See also CA 104; 153; DLB 192

Jarvis, E. K.
See Bloch, Robert (Albert); Ellison, Harlan (Jay); Silverberg, Robert

Jeake, Samuel, Jr.
See Aiken, Conrad (Potter)

Jean Paul [1763-1825] .... **NCLC 7**

Jefferies, (John) Richard [1848-1887] **NCLC 47**
See also DLB 98, 141; SATA 16

Jeffers, (John) Robinson [1887-1962]**CLC 2, 3, 11, 15, 54; DA; DAC; DAM MST, POET; PC 17; WLC**
See also CA 85-88; CANR 35; CDALB 1917-1929; DLB 45; MTCW

Jefferson, Janet
See Mencken, H(enry) L(ouis)

Jefferson, Thomas [1743-1826] ..... **NCLC 11**
See also CDALB 1640-1865; DLB 31

Jeffrey, Francis [1773-1850] .... **NCLC 33**
See also DLB 107

Jelakowitch, Ivan
See Heijermans, Herman

Jellicoe, (Patricia) Ann [1927-] .... **CLC 27**
See also CA 85-88; DLB 13

Jen, Gish .... **CLC 70**
See also Jen, Lillian

Jen, Lillian [1956(?)-]
See Jen, Gish
See also CA 135

Jenkins, (John) Robin [1912-] .... **CLC 52**
See also CA 1-4R; CANR 1; DLB 14

Jennings, Elizabeth (Joan) [1926-]**CLC 5, 14**
See also CA 61-64; CAAS 5; CANR 8, 39, 66; DLB 27; MTCW; SATA 66

Jennings, Waylon [1937-] .... **CLC 21**

Jensen, Johannes V. [1873-1950] ... **TCLC 41**

Jensen, Laura (Linnea) [1948-] .... **CLC 37**
See also CA 103

Jerome, Jerome K(lapka) [1859-1927]**TCLC 23**
See also CA 119; DLB 10, 34, 135

Jerrold, Douglas William [1803-1857]**NCLC 2**
See also DLB 158, 159

Jewett, (Theodora) Sarah Orne [1849-1909] **TCLC 1, 22; SSC 6**
See also CA 108; 127; DLB 12, 74; SATA 15

Jewsbury, Geraldine (Endsor) [1812-1880] **NCLC 22**
See also DLB 21

Jhabvala, Ruth Prawer [1927-]**CLC 4, 8, 29, 94; DAB; DAM NOV**
See also CA 1-4R; CANR 2, 29, 51; DLB 139, 194; INT CANR-29; MTCW

Jibran, Kahlil
See Gibran, Kahlil

Jibran, Khalil
See Gibran, Kahlil

Jiles, Paulette [1943-] .... **CLC 13, 58**
See also CA 101

Jimenez (Mantecon), Juan Ramon [1881-1958]
TCLC 4; DAM MULT, POET; HLC; PC
7
See also CA 104; 131; DLB 134; HW; MTCW
Jimenez, Ramon
See Jimenez (Mantecon), Juan Ramon
Jimenez Mantecon, Juan
See Jimenez (Mantecon), Juan Ramon
Jin, Ha [1956-] .... CLC 109
See also CA 152
Joel, Billy .... CLC 26
See also Joel, William Martin
Joel, William Martin [1949-]
See Joel, Billy
See also CA 108
John, Saint [7th cent. -] .... CMLC 27
John of the Cross, St. [1542-1591] ...... LC 18
Johnson, B(ryan) S(tanley William) [1933-
1973] .... CLC 6, 9
See also CA 9-12R; 53-56; CANR 9; DLB 14,
40
Johnson, Benj. F. of Boo
See Riley, James Whitcomb
Johnson, Benjamin F. of Boo
See Riley, James Whitcomb
Johnson, Charles (Richard) [1948-]CLC 7, 51,
65; BLC 2; DAM MULT
See also BW 2; CA 116; CAAS 18; CANR 42,
66; DLB 33
Johnson, Denis [1949-] .... CLC 52
See also CA 117; 121; DLB 120
Johnson, Diane [1934-] .... CLC 5, 13, 48
See also CA 41-44R; CANR 17, 40, 62; DLBY
80; INT CANR-17; MTCW
Johnson, Eyvind (Olof Verner) [1900-1976]
CLC 14
See also CA 73-76; 69-72; CANR 34
Johnson, J. R.
See James, C(yril) L(ionel) R(obert)
Johnson, James Weldon [1871-1938]TCLC 3,
19; BLC 2; DAM MULT, POET
See also BW 1; CA 104; 125; CDALB 1917-
1929; CLR 32; DLB 51; MTCW; SATA 31
Johnson, Joyce [1935-] .... CLC 58
See also CA 125; 129
Johnson, Lionel (Pigot) [1867-1902]TCLC 19
See also CA 117; DLB 19
Johnson, Mel
See Malzberg, Barry N(athaniel)
Johnson, Pamela Hansford [1912-1981]C L C
1, 7, 27
See also CA 1-4R; 104; CANR 2, 28; DLB 15;
MTCW
Johnson, Robert [1911(?)-1938] ..... TCLC 69
Johnson, Samuel [1709-1784] .... LC 15; DA;
DAB; DAC; DAM MST; WLC
See also CDBLB 1660-1789; DLB 39, 95, 104,
142
Johnson, Uwe [1934-1984] CLC 5, 10, 15, 40
See also CA 1-4R; 112; CANR 1, 39; DLB 75;
MTCW
Johnston, George (Benson) [1913-] .. CLC 51
See also CA 1-4R; CANR 5, 20; DLB 88
Johnston, Jennifer [1930-] .... CLC 7
See also CA 85-88; DLB 14
Jolley, (Monica) Elizabeth [1923-] . CLC 46;
SSC 19
See also CA 127; CAAS 13; CANR 59
Jones, Arthur Llewellyn [1863-1947]
See Machen, Arthur
See also CA 104
Jones, D(ouglas) G(ordon) [1929-] ... CLC 10
See also CA 29-32R; CANR 13; DLB 53
Jones, David (Michael) [1895-1974]CLC 2, 4,
7, 13, 42
See also CA 9-12R; 53-56; CANR 28; CDBLB
1945-1960; DLB 20, 100; MTCW

Jones, David Robert [1947-]
See Bowie, David
See also CA 103
Jones, Diana Wynne [1934-] .... CLC 26
See also AAYA 12; CA 49-52; CANR 4, 26,
56; CLR 23; DLB 161; JRDA; MAICYA;
SAAS 7; SATA 9, 70
Jones, Edward P. [1950-] .... CLC 76
See also BW 2; CA 142
Jones, Gayl [1949-] .CLC 6, 9; BLC 2; DAM
MULT
See also BW 2; CA 77-80; CANR 27, 66; DLB
33; MTCW
Jones, James [1921-1977] ... CLC 1, 3, 10, 39
See also AITN 1, 2; CA 1-4R; 69-72; CANR 6;
DLB 2, 143; MTCW
Jones, John J.
See Lovecraft, H(oward) P(hillips)
Jones, LeRoi .... CLC 1, 2, 3, 5, 10, 14
See also Baraka, Amiri
Jones, Louis B. .... CLC 65
See also CA 141
Jones, Madison (Percy, Jr.) [1925-] .... CLC 4
See also CA 13-16R; CAAS 11; CANR 7, 54;
DLB 152
Jones, Mervyn [1922-] .... CLC 10, 52
See also CA 45-48; CAAS 5; CANR 1; MTCW
Jones, Mick [1956(?)-] .... CLC 30
Jones, Nettie (Pearl) [1941-] .... CLC 34
See also BW 2; CA 137; CAAS 20
Jones, Preston [1936-1979] .... CLC 10
See also CA 73-76; 89-92; DLB 7
Jones, Robert F(rancis) [1934-] .... CLC 7
See also CA 49-52; CANR 2, 61
Jones, Rod [1953-] .... CLC 50
See also CA 128
Jones, Terence Graham Parry [1942-]CLC 21
See also Jones, Terry; Monty Python
See also CA 112; 116; CANR 35; INT 116
Jones, Terry
See Jones, Terence Graham Parry
See also SATA 67; SATA-Brief 51
Jones, Thom [1945(?)-] .... CLC 81
See also CA 157
Jong, Erica [1942-]CLC 4, 6, 8, 18, 83; DAM
NOV, POP
See also AITN 1; BEST 90:2; CA 73-76; CANR
26, 52; DLB 2, 5, 28, 152; INT CANR-26;
MTCW
Jonson, Ben(jamin) [1572(?)-1637] LC 6, 33;
DA; DAB; DAC; DAM DRAM, MST,
POET; DC 4; PC 17; WLC
See also CDBLB Before 1660; DLB 62, 121
Jordan, June [1936-] . CLC 5, 11, 23; BLCS;
DAM MULT, POET
See also AAYA 2; BW 2; CA 33-36R; CANR
25; CLR 10; DLB 38; MAICYA; MTCW;
SATA 4
Jordan, Neil (Patrick) [1950-] .... CLC 110
See also CA 124; 130; CANR 54; INT 130
Jordan, Pat(rick M.) [1941-] .... CLC 37
See also CA 33-36R
Jorgensen, Ivar
See Ellison, Harlan (Jay)
Jorgenson, Ivar
See Silverberg, Robert
Josephus, Flavius [c. 37-100] .... CMLC 13
Josipovici, Gabriel [1940-] .... CLC 6, 43
See also CA 37-40R; CAAS 8; CANR 47; DLB
14
Joubert, Joseph [1754-1824] .... NCLC 9
Jouve, Pierre Jean [1887-1976] .... CLC 47
See also CA 65-68
Jovine, Francesco [1902-1950] .... TCLC 79
Joyce, James (Augustine Aloysius) [1882-1941]
TCLC 3, 8, 16, 35, 52; DA; DAB; DAC;
DAM MST, NOV, POET; PC 22; SSC 3,

26; WLC
See also CA 104; 126; CDBLB 1914-1945;
DLB 10, 19, 36, 162; MTCW
Jozsef, Attila [1905-1937] .... TCLC 22
See also CA 116
Juana Ines de la Cruz [1651(?)-1695] ... LC 5
Judd, Cyril
See Kornbluth, C(yril) M.; Pohl, Frederik
Julian of Norwich [1342(?)-1416(?)] ..... LC 6
See also DLB 146
Junger, Sebastian [1962-] .... CLC 109
See also CA 165
Juniper, Alex
See Hospital, Janette Turner
Junius
See Luxemburg, Rosa
Just, Ward (Swift) [1935-] .... CLC 4, 27
See also CA 25-28R; CANR 32; INT CANR-
32
Justice, Donald (Rodney) [1925-] CLC 6, 19,
102; DAM POET
See also CA 5-8R; CANR 26, 54; DLBY 83;
INT CANR-26
Juvenal [c. 55-c. 127] .... CMLC 8
Juvenis
See Bourne, Randolph S(illiman)
Kacew, Romain [1914-1980]
See Gary, Romain
See also CA 108; 102
Kadare, Ismail [1936-] .... CLC 52
See also CA 161
Kadohata, Cynthia .... CLC 59
See also CA 140
Kafka, Franz [1883-1924]TCLC 2, 6, 13, 29,
47, 53; DA; DAB; DAC; DAM MST, NOV;
SSC 5, 29; WLC
See also CA 105; 126; DLB 81; MTCW
Kahanovitsch, Pinkhes
See Der Nister
Kahn, Roger [1927-] .... CLC 30
See also CA 25-28R; CANR 44, 69; DLB 171;
SATA 37
Kain, Saul
See Sassoon, Siegfried (Lorraine)
Kaiser, Georg [1878-1945] .... TCLC 9
See also CA 106; DLB 124
Kaletski, Alexander [1946-] .... CLC 39
See also CA 118; 143
Kalidasa [fl. c. 400-] .... CMLC 9; PC 22
Kallman, Chester (Simon) [1921-1975]CLC 2
See also CA 45-48; 53-56; CANR 3
Kaminsky, Melvin [1926-]
See Brooks, Mel
See also CA 65-68; CANR 16
Kaminsky, Stuart M(elvin) [1934-] .. CLC 59
See also CA 73-76; CANR 29, 53
Kane, Francis
See Robbins, Harold
Kane, Paul
See Simon, Paul (Frederick)
Kane, Wilson
See Bloch, Robert (Albert)
Kanin, Garson [1912-] .... CLC 22
See also AITN 1; CA 5-8R; CANR 7; DLB 7
Kaniuk, Yoram [1930-] .... CLC 19
See also CA 134
Kant, Immanuel [1724-1804] ...NCLC 27, 67
See also DLB 94
Kantor, MacKinlay [1904-1977] .... CLC 7
See also CA 61-64; 73-76; CANR 60, 63; DLB
9, 102
Kaplan, David Michael [1946-] .... CLC 50
Kaplan, James [1951-] .... CLC 59
See also CA 135
Karageorge, Michael
See Anderson, Poul (William)
Karamzin, Nikolai Mikhailovich [1766-1826]

Krumb
See Crumb, R(obert)

Krumgold, Joseph (Quincy) [1908-1980]**CLC 12**
See also CA 9-12R; 101; CANR 7; MAICYA; SATA 1, 48; SATA-Obit 23

Krumwitz
See Crumb, R(obert)

Krutch, Joseph Wood [1893-1970] ... **CLC 24**
See also CA 1-4R; 25-28R; CANR 4; DLB 63

Krutzch, Gus
See Eliot, T(homas) S(tearns)

Krylov, Ivan Andreevich [1768(?)-1844] **NCLC 1**
See also DLB 150

Kubin, Alfred (Leopold Isidor) [1877-1959] **TCLC 23**
See also CA 112; 149; DLB 81

Kubrick, Stanley [1928-] .... **CLC 16**
See also CA 81-84; CANR 33; DLB 26

Kumin, Maxine (Winokur) [1925-]**CLC 5, 13, 28; DAM POET; PC 15**
See also AITN 2; CA 1-4R; CAAS 8; CANR 1, 21, 69; DLB 5; MTCW; SATA 12

Kundera, Milan [1929-]**CLC 4, 9, 19, 32, 68; DAM NOV; SSC 24**
See also AAYA 2; CA 85-88; CANR 19, 52; MTCW

Kunene, Mazisi (Raymond) [1930-] . **CLC 85**
See also BW 1; CA 125; DLB 117

Kunitz, Stanley (Jasspon) [1905-] **CLC 6, 11, 14; PC 19**
See also CA 41-44R; CANR 26, 57; DLB 48; INT CANR-26; MTCW

Kunze, Reiner [1933-] .... **CLC 10**
See also CA 93-96; DLB 75

Kuprin, Aleksandr Ivanovich [1870-1938] **TCLC 5**
See also CA 104

Kureishi, Hanif [1954(?)-] .... **CLC 64**
See also CA 139; DLB 194

Kurosawa, Akira [1910-] .... **CLC 16; DAM MULT**
See also AAYA 11; CA 101; CANR 46

Kushner, Tony [1957(?)-] .... **CLC 81; DAM DRAM**
See also CA 144

Kuttner, Henry [1915-1958] .... **TCLC 10**
See Vance, Jack
See also CA 107; 157; DLB 8

Kuzma, Greg [1944-]........................... **CLC 7**
See also CA 33-36R

Kuzmin, Mikhail [1872(?)-1936] ... **TCLC 40**

Kyd, Thomas [1558-1594] .... **LC 22; DAM DRAM; DC 3**
See also DLB 62

Kyprianos, Iossif
See Samarakis, Antonis

La Bruyere, Jean de [1645-1696] .... **LC 17**

Lacan, Jacques (Marie Emile) [1901-1981] **CLC 75**
See also CA 121; 104

Laclos, Pierre Ambroise Francois Choderlos de [1741-1803] .... **NCLC 4**

La Colere, Francois
See Aragon, Louis

Lacolere, Francois
See Aragon, Louis

La Deshabilleuse
See Simenon, Georges (Jacques Christian)

Lady Gregory
See Gregory, Isabella Augusta (Persse)

Lady of Quality, A
See Bagnold, Enid

La Fayette, Marie (Madelaine Pioche de la Vergne Comtes [1634-1693] .... **LC 2**

Lafayette, Rene
See Hubbard, L(afayette) Ron(ald)

Laforgue, Jules [1860-1887]**NCLC 5, 53; PC 14; SSC 20**

Lagerkvist, Paer (Fabian) [1891-1974]**CLC 7, 10, 13, 54; DAM DRAM, NOV**
See also Lagerkvist, Par
See also CA 85-88; 49-52; MTCW

Lagerkvist, Par .... **SSC 12**
See also Lagerkvist, Paer (Fabian)

Lagerloef, Selma (Ottiliana Lovisa) [1858-1940] ....
TCLC 4, 36
See also Lagerlof, Selma (Ottiliana Lovisa)
See also CA 108; SATA 15

Lagerlof, Selma (Ottiliana Lovisa)
See Lagerloef, Selma (Ottiliana Lovisa)
See also CLR 7; SATA 15

La Guma, (Justin) Alex(ander) [1925-1985] **CLC 19; BLCS; DAM NOV**
See also BW 1; CA 49-52; 118; CANR 25; DLB 117; MTCW

Laidlaw, A. K.
See Grieve, C(hristopher) M(urray)

Lainez, Manuel Mujica
See Mujica Lainez, Manuel
See also HW

Laing, R(onald) D(avid) [1927-1989]**CLC 95**
See also CA 107; 129; CANR 34; MTCW

Lamartine, Alphonse (Marie Louis Prat) de [1790-1869]**NCLC 11; DAM POET; PC 16**

Lamb, Charles [1775-1834] .. **NCLC 10; DA; DAB; DAC; DAM MST; WLC**
See also CDBLB 1789-1832; DLB 93, 107, 163; SATA 17

Lamb, Lady Caroline [1785-1828] **NCLC 38**
See also DLB 116

Lamming, George (William) [1927-]**CLC 2, 4, 66; BLC 2; DAM MULT**
See also BW 2; CA 85-88; CANR 26; DLB 125; MTCW

L'Amour, Louis (Dearborn) [1908-1988]**CLC 25, 55; DAM NOV, POP**
See also AAYA 16; AITN 2; BEST 89:2; CA 1-4R; 125; CANR 3, 25, 40; DLBY 80; MTCW

Lampedusa, Giuseppe (Tomasi) di [1896-1957] **TCLC 13**
See also Tomasi di Lampedusa, Giuseppe
See also CA 164; DLB 177

Lampman, Archibald [1861-1899] **NCLC 25**
See also DLB 92

Lancaster, Bruce [1896-1963] .... **CLC 36**
See also CA 9-10; CAP 1; SATA 9

Lanchester, John .... **CLC 99**

Landau, Mark Alexandrovich
See Aldanov, Mark (Alexandrovich)

Landau-Aldanov, Mark Alexandrovich
See Aldanov, Mark (Alexandrovich)

Landis, Jerry
See Simon, Paul (Frederick)

Landis, John [1950-] .... **CLC 26**
See also CA 112; 122

Landolfi, Tommaso [1908-1979] . **CLC 11, 49**
See also CA 127; 117; DLB 177

Landon, Letitia Elizabeth [1802-1838]**NCLC 15**
See also DLB 96

Landor, Walter Savage [1775-1864]**NCLC 14**
See also DLB 93, 107

Landwirth, Heinz [1927-]
See Lind, Jakov
See also CA 9-12R; CANR 7

Lane, Patrick [1939-] **CLC 25; DAM POET**
See also CA 97-100; CANR 54; DLB 53; INT 97-100

Lang, Andrew [1844-1912] .... **TCLC 16**
See also CA 114; 137; DLB 98, 141, 184; MAICYA; SATA 16

Lang, Fritz [1890-1976] .... **CLC 20, 103**
See also CA 77-80; 69-72; CANR 30

Lange, John
See Crichton, (John) Michael

Langer, Elinor [1939-] .... **CLC 34**
See also CA 121

Langland, William [1330(?)-1400(?)] **LC 19; DA; DAB; DAC; DAM MST, POET**
See also DLB 146

Langstaff, Launcelot
See Irving, Washington

Lanier, Sidney [1842-1881] ..**NCLC 6; DAM POET**
See also DLB 64; DLBD 13; MAICYA; SATA 18

Lanyer, Aemilia [1569-1645] .... **LC 10, 30**
See also DLB 121

Lao Tzu .... **CMLC 7**

Lapine, James (Elliot) [1949-] .... **CLC 39**
See also CA 123; 130; CANR 54; INT 130

Larbaud, Valery (Nicolas) [1881-1957]**TCLC 9**
See also CA 106; 152

Lardner, Ring
See Lardner, Ring(gold) W(ilmer)

Lardner, Ring W., Jr.
See Lardner, Ring(gold) W(ilmer)

Lardner, Ring(gold) W(ilmer) [1885-1933] **TCLC 2, 14**
See also CA 104; 131; CDALB 1917-1929; DLB 11, 25, 86; DLBD 16; MTCW

Laredo, Betty
See Codrescu, Andrei

Larkin, Maia
See Wojciechowska, Maia (Teresa)

Larkin, Philip (Arthur) [1922-1985]**CLC 3, 5, 8, 9, 13, 18, 33, 39, 64; DAB; DAM MST, POET; PC 21**
See also CA 5-8R; 117; CANR 24, 62; CDBLB 1960 to Present; DLB 27; MTCW

Larra (y Sanchez de Castro), Mariano Jose de [1809-1837] .... **NCLC 17**

Larsen, Eric [1941-] .... **CLC 55**
See also CA 132

Larsen, Nella [1891-1964] . **CLC 37; BLC 2; DAM MULT**
See also BW 1; CA 125; DLB 51

Larson, Charles R(aymond) [1938-] **CLC 31**
See also CA 53-56; CANR 4

Larson, Jonathan [1961-1996] .... **CLC 99**
See also CA 156

Las Casas, Bartolome de [1474-1566] **LC 31**

Lasch, Christopher [1932-1994] ..... **CLC 102**
See also CA 73-76; 144; CANR 25; MTCW

Lasker-Schueler, Else [1869-1945] **TCLC 57**
See also DLB 66, 124

Laski, Harold [1893-1950].............. **TCLC 79**

Latham, Jean Lee [1902-1995] .... **CLC 12**
See also AITN 1; CA 5-8R; CANR 7; CLR 50; MAICYA; SATA 2, 68

Latham, Mavis
See Clark, Mavis Thorpe

Lathen, Emma .... **CLC 2**
See also Hennissart, Martha; Latsis, Mary J(ane)

Lathrop, Francis
See Leiber, Fritz (Reuter, Jr.)

Latsis, Mary J(ane) [1927(?)-1997]
See Lathen, Emma
See also CA 85-88; 162

Lattimore, Richmond (Alexander) [1906-1984] **CLC 3**
See also CA 1-4R; 112; CANR 1

Laughlin, James [1914-1997] .... **CLC 49**
See also CA 21-24R; 162; CAAS 22; CANR 9, 47; DLB 48; DLBY 96, 97

Laurence, (Jean) Margaret (Wemyss) [1926-1987] **CLC 3, 6, 13, 50, 62; DAC; DAM**

Macdonald, Ross .... **CLC 1, 2, 3, 14, 34, 41**
  See also Millar, Kenneth
  See also DLBD 6
MacDougal, John
  See Blish, James (Benjamin)
MacEwen, Gwendolyn (Margaret) [1941-1987]
    CLC 13, 55
  See also CA 9-12R; 124; CANR 7, 22; DLB
  53; SATA 50; SATA-Obit 55
Macha, Karel Hynek [1810-1846] . **NCLC 46**
Machado (y Ruiz), Antonio [1875-1939]
    TCLC 3
  See also CA 104; DLB 108
Machado de Assis, Joaquim Maria [1839-1908]
    TCLC 10; BLC 2; SSC 24
  See also CA 107; 153
Machen, Arthur .... **TCLC 4; SSC 20**
  See also Jones, Arthur Llewellyn
  See also DLB 36, 156, 178
Machiavelli, Niccolo [1469-1527] .. **LC 8, 36;**
    DA; DAB; DAC; DAM MST; WLCS
MacInnes, Colin [1914-1976] .... **CLC 4, 23**
  See also CA 69-72; 65-68; CANR 21; DLB 14;
  MTCW
MacInnes, Helen (Clark) [1907-1985]**CLC 27,**
    39; DAM POP
  See also CA 1-4R; 117; CANR 1, 28, 58; DLB
  87; MTCW; SATA 22; SATA-Obit 44
Mackay, Mary [1855-1924]
  See Corelli, Marie
  See also CA 118
Mackenzie, Compton (Edward Montague)
  [1883-1972] ....
CLC 18
  See also CA 21-22; 37-40R; CAP 2; DLB 34,
  100
Mackenzie, Henry [1745-1831] ...... **NCLC 41**
  See also DLB 39
Mackintosh, Elizabeth [1896(?)-1952]
  See Tey, Josephine
  See also CA 110
MacLaren, James
  See Grieve, C(hristopher) M(urray)
Mac Laverty, Bernard [1942-] .... **CLC 31**
  See also CA 116; 118; CANR 43; INT 118
MacLean, Alistair (Stuart) [1922(?)-1987]
    CLC 3, 13, 50, 63; DAM POP
  See also CA 57-60; 121; CANR 28, 61; MTCW;
  SATA 23; SATA-Obit 50
Maclean, Norman (Fitzroy) [1902-1990]**C L C
  78; DAM POP; SSC 13**
  See also CA 102; 132; CANR 49
MacLeish, Archibald [1892-1982] . **CLC 3, 8,
  14, 68; DAM POET**
  See also CA 9-12R; 106; CANR 33, 63; DLB
  4, 7, 45; DLBY 82; MTCW
MacLennan, (John) Hugh [1907-1990]**CLC 2,
  14, 92; DAC; DAM MST**
  See also CA 5-8R; 142; CANR 33; DLB 68;
  MTCW
MacLeod, Alistair [1936-] .... **CLC 56; DAC;
  DAM MST**
  See also CA 123; DLB 60
Macleod, Fiona
  See Sharp, William
MacNeice, (Frederick) Louis [1907-1963]
    CLC 1, 4, 10, 53; DAB; DAM POET
  See also CA 85-88; CANR 61; DLB 10, 20;
  MTCW
MacNeill, Dand
  See Fraser, George MacDonald
Macpherson, James [1736-1796] .... **LC 29**
  See also Ossian
  See also DLB 109
Macpherson, (Jean) Jay [1931-] .... **CLC 14**
  See also CA 5-8R; DLB 53
MacShane, Frank [1927-] .... **CLC 39**

  See also CA 9-12R; CANR 3, 33; DLB 111
Macumber, Mari
  See Sandoz, Mari(e Susette)
Madach, Imre [1823-1864] .... **NCLC 19**
Madden, (Jerry) David [1933-] ..... **CLC 5, 15**
  See also CA 1-4R; CAAS 3; CANR 4, 45; DLB
  6; MTCW
Maddern, Al(an)
  See Ellison, Harlan (Jay)
Madhubuti, Haki R. [1942-]**CLC 6, 73; BLC
  2; DAM MULT, POET; PC 5**
  See also Lee, Don L.
  See also BW 2; CA 73-76; CANR 24, 51; DLB
  5, 41; DLBD 8
Maepenn, Hugh
  See Kuttner, Henry
Maepenn, K. H.
  See Kuttner, Henry
Maeterlinck, Maurice [1862-1949] . **TCLC 3;
  DAM DRAM**
  See also CA 104; 136; DLB 192; SATA 66
Maginn, William [1794-1842] .... **NCLC 8**
  See also DLB 110, 159
Mahapatra, Jayanta [1928-] . **CLC 33; DAM
  MULT**
  See also CA 73-76; CAAS 9; CANR 15, 33, 66
Mahfouz, Naguib (Abdel Aziz Al-Sabilgi)
  [1911(?)-]
  See Mahfuz, Najib
  See also BEST 89:2; CA 128; CANR 55; DAM
  NOV; MTCW
Mahfuz, Najib .... **CLC 52, 55**
  See also Mahfouz, Naguib (Abdel Aziz Al-
  Sabilgi)
  See also DLBY 88
Mahon, Derek [1941-] .... **CLC 27**
  See also CA 113; 128; DLB 40
Mailer, Norman [1923-]**CLC 1, 2, 3, 4, 5, 8, 11,
  14, 28, 39, 74, 111; DA; DAB; DAC; DAM
  MST, NOV, POP**
  See also AITN 2; CA 9-12R; CABS 1; CANR
  28; CDALB 1968-1988; DLB 2, 16, 28, 185;
  DLBD 3; DLBY 80, 83; MTCW
Maillet, Antonine [1929-] .... **CLC 54; DAC**
  See also CA 115; 120; CANR 46; DLB 60; INT
  120
Mais, Roger [1905-1955] .... **TCLC 8**
  See also BW 1; CA 105; 124; DLB 125; MTCW
Maistre, Joseph de [1753-1821] ..... **NCLC 37**
Maitland, Frederic [1850-1906] ...... **TCLC 65**
Maitland, Sara (Louise) [1950-] .... **CLC 49**
  See also CA 69-72; CANR 13, 59
Major, Clarence [1936-]**CLC 3, 19, 48; BLC 2;
  DAM MULT**
  See also BW 2; CA 21-24R; CAAS 6; CANR
  13, 25, 53; DLB 33
Major, Kevin (Gerald) [1949-]**CLC 26; DAC**
  See also AAYA 16; CA 97-100; CANR 21, 38;
  CLR 11; DLB 60; INT CANR-21; JRDA;
  MAICYA; SATA 32, 82
Maki, James
  See Ozu, Yasujiro
Malabaila, Damiano
  See Levi, Primo
Malamud, Bernard [1914-1986]**CLC 1, 2, 3, 5,
  8, 9, 11, 18, 27, 44, 78, 85; DA; DAB; DAC;
  DAM MST, NOV, POP; SSC 15; WLC**
  See also AAYA 16; CA 5-8R; 118; CABS 1;
  CANR 28, 62; CDALB 1941-1968; DLB 2,
  28, 152; DLBY 80, 86; MTCW
Malan, Herman
  See Bosman, Herman Charles; Bosman, Herman
  Charles
Malaparte, Curzio [1898-1957] ..... **TCLC 52**
Malcolm, Dan
  See Silverberg, Robert
Malcolm X .... **CLC 82; BLC 2; WLCS**

  See also Little, Malcolm
Malherbe, Francois de [1555-1628] ...... **LC 5**
Mallarme, Stephane [1842-1898]**NCLC 4, 41;
  DAM POET; PC 4**
Mallet-Joris, Francoise [1930-] .... **CLC 11**
  See also CA 65-68; CANR 17; DLB 83
Malley, Ern
  See McAuley, James Phillip
Mallowan, Agatha Christie
  See Christie, Agatha (Mary Clarissa)
Maloff, Saul [1922-] .... **CLC 5**
  See also CA 33-36R
Malone, Louis
  See MacNeice, (Frederick) Louis
Malone, Michael (Christopher) [1942-] **C L C
  43**
  See also CA 77-80; CANR 14, 32, 57
Malory, (Sir) Thomas [1410(?)-1471(?)] .. **L C
  11; DA; DAB; DAC; DAM MST; WLCS**
  See also CDBLB Before 1660; DLB 146; SATA
  59; SATA-Brief 33
Malouf, (George Joseph) David [1934-] **C L C
  28, 86**
  See also CA 124; CANR 50
Malraux, (Georges-)Andre [1901-1976] **C L C
  1, 4, 9, 13, 15, 57; DAM NOV**
  See also CA 21-22; 69-72; CANR 34, 58; CAP
  2; DLB 72; MTCW
Malzberg, Barry N(athaniel) [1939-] . **CLC 7**
  See also CA 61-64; CAAS 4; CANR 16; DLB
  8
Mamet, David (Alan) [1947-] **CLC 9, 15, 34,
  46, 91; DAM DRAM; DC 4**
  See also AAYA 3; CA 81-84; CABS 3; CANR
  15, 41, 67; DLB 7; MTCW
Mamoulian, Rouben (Zachary) [1897-1987]
    CLC 16
  See also CA 25-28R; 124
Mandelstam, Osip (Emilievich) [1891(?)-
  1938(?)] ....
TCLC 2, 6; PC 14
  See also CA 104; 150
Mander, (Mary) Jane [1877-1949] **TCLC 31**
  See also CA 162
Mandeville, John [fl. 1350-] .... **CMLC 19**
  See also DLB 146
Mandiargues, Andre Pieyre de .... **CLC 41**
  See also Pieyre de Mandiargues, Andre
  See also DLB 83
Mandrake, Ethel Belle
  See Thurman, Wallace (Henry)
Mangan, James Clarence [1803-1849]**N C L C
  27**
Maniere, J.-E.
  See Giraudoux, (Hippolyte) Jean
Manley, (Mary) Delariviere [1672(?)-1724]
    LC 1
  See also DLB 39, 80
Mann, Abel
  See Creasey, John
Mann, Emily [1952-] .... **DC 7**
  See also CA 130; CANR 55
Mann, (Luiz) Heinrich [1871-1950] **TCLC 9**
  See also CA 106; 164; DLB 66
Mann, (Paul) Thomas [1875-1955]**TCLC 2, 8,
  14, 21, 35, 44, 60; DA; DAB; DAC; DAM
  MST, NOV; SSC 5; WLC**
  See also CA 104; 128; DLB 66; MTCW
Mannheim, Karl [1893-1947] .... **TCLC 65**
Manning, David
  See Faust, Frederick (Schiller)
Manning, Frederic [1887(?)-1935] **TCLC 25**
  See also CA 124
Manning, Olivia [1915-1980] .... **CLC 5, 19**
  See also CA 5-8R; 101; CANR 29; MTCW
Mano, D. Keith [1942-] .... **CLC 2, 10**
  See also CA 25-28R; CAAS 6; CANR 26, 57;

DLB 6

Mansfield, Katherine TCLC 2, 8, 39; DAB; SSC 9, 23; WLC
See also Beauchamp, Kathleen Mansfield
See also DLB 162

Manso, Peter [1940-] .... CLC 39
See also CA 29-32R; CANR 44

Mantecon, Juan Jimenez
See Jimenez (Mantecon), Juan Ramon

Manton, Peter
See Creasey, John

Man Without a Spleen, A
See Chekhov, Anton (Pavlovich)

Manzoni, Alessandro [1785-1873]. NCLC 29

Mapu, Abraham (ben Jekutiel) [1808-1867] NCLC 18

Mara, Sally
See Queneau, Raymond

Marat, Jean Paul [1743-1793] .... LC 10

Marcel, Gabriel Honore [1889-1973]CLC 15
See also CA 102; 45-48; MTCW

Marchbanks, Samuel
See Davies, (William) Robertson

Marchi, Giacomo
See Bassani, Giorgio

Margulies, Donald .... CLC 76

Marie de France [c. 12th cent. -]CMLC 8; PC 22

Marie de l'Incarnation [1599-1672].... LC 10

Marier, Captain Victor
See Griffith, D(avid Lewelyn) W(ark)

Mariner, Scott
See Pohl, Frederik

Marinetti, Filippo Tommaso [1876-1944] TCLC 10
See also CA 107; DLB 114

Marivaux, Pierre Carlet de Chamblain de [1688-1763] .... LC 4; DC 7

Markandaya, Kamala .... CLC 8, 38
See also Taylor, Kamala (Purnaiya)

Markfield, Wallace [1926-] .... CLC 8
See also CA 69-72; CAAS 3; DLB 2, 28

Markham, Edwin [1852-1940] .... TCLC 47
See also CA 160; DLB 54, 186

Markham, Robert
See Amis, Kingsley (William)

Marks, J
See Highwater, Jamake (Mamake)

Marks-Highwater, J
See Highwater, Jamake (Mamake)

Markson, David M(errill) [1927-] .... CLC 67
See also CA 49-52; CANR 1

Marley, Bob .... CLC 17
See also Marley, Robert Nesta

Marley, Robert Nesta [1945-1981]
See Marley, Bob
See also CA 107; 103

Marlowe, Christopher [1564-1593] ... LC 22; DA; DAB; DAC; DAM DRAM, MST; DC 1; WLC
See also CDBLB Before 1660; DLB 62

Marlowe, Stephen [1928-]
See Queen, Ellery
See also CA 13-16R; CANR 6, 55

Marmontel, Jean-Francois [1723-1799]LC 2

Marquand, John P(hillips) [1893-1960] C L C 2, 10
See also CA 85-88; DLB 9, 102

Marques, Rene [1919-1979] ..CLC 96; DAM MULT; HLC
See also CA 97-100; 85-88; DLB 113; HW

Marquez, Gabriel (Jose) Garcia
See Garcia Marquez, Gabriel (Jose)

Marquis, Don(ald Robert Perry) [1878-1937] TCLC 7
See also CA 104; 166; DLB 11, 25

Marric, J. J.

See Creasey, John

Marryat, Frederick [1792-1848] ...... NCLC 3
See also DLB 21, 163

Marsden, James
See Creasey, John

Marsh, (Edith) Ngaio [1899-1982]CLC 7, 53; DAM POP
See also CA 9-12R; CANR 6, 58; DLB 77; MTCW

Marshall, Garry [1934-] .... CLC 17
See also AAYA 3; CA 111; SATA 60

Marshall, Paule [1929-] CLC 27, 72; BLC 3; DAM MULT; SSC 3
See also BW 2; CA 77-80; CANR 25; DLB 157; MTCW

Marsten, Richard
See Hunter, Evan

Marston, John [1576-1634] ......LC 33; DAM DRAM
See also DLB 58, 172

Martha, Henry
See Harris, Mark

Marti, Jose [1853-1895] ...... NCLC 63; DAM MULT; HLC
See also HW

Martial [c. 40-c. 104] .... PC 10

Martin, Ken
See Hubbard, L(afayette) Ron(ald)

Martin, Richard
See Creasey, John

Martin, Steve [1945-] .... CLC 30
See also CA 97-100; CANR 30; MTCW

Martin, Valerie [1948-] .... CLC 89
See also BEST 90:2; CA 85-88; CANR 49

Martin, Violet Florence [1862-1915]TCLC 51

Martin, Webber
See Silverberg, Robert

Martindale, Patrick Victor
See White, Patrick (Victor Martindale)

Martin du Gard, Roger [1881-1958]TCLC 24
See also CA 118; DLB 65

Martineau, Harriet [1802-1876] .... NCLC 26
See also DLB 21, 55, 159, 163, 166, 190; YABC 2

Martines, Julia
See O'Faolain, Julia

Martinez, Enrique Gonzalez
See Gonzalez Martinez, Enrique

Martinez, Jacinto Benavente y
See Benavente (y Martinez), Jacinto

Martinez Ruiz, Jose [1873-1967]
See Azorin; Ruiz, Jose Martinez
See also CA 93-96; HW

Martinez Sierra, Gregorio [1881-1947]TCLC 6
See also CA 115

Martinez Sierra, Maria (de la O'LeJarraga) [1874-1974] .... TCLC 6
See also CA 115

Martinsen, Martin
See Follett, Ken(neth Martin)

Martinson, Harry (Edmund) [1904-1978] CLC 14
See also CA 77-80; CANR 34

Marut, Ret
See Traven, B.

Marut, Robert
See Traven, B.

Marvell, Andrew [1621-1678] LC 4, 43; DA; DAB; DAC; DAM MST, POET; PC 10; WLC
See also CDBLB 1660-1789; DLB 131

Marx, Karl (Heinrich) [1818-1883]NCLC 17
See also DLB 129

Masaoka Shiki .... TCLC 18
See also Masaoka Tsunenori

Masaoka Tsunenori [1867-1902]
See Masaoka Shiki

See also CA 117

Masefield, John (Edward) [1878-1967] C L C 11, 47; DAM POET
See also CA 19-20; 25-28R; CANR 33; CAP 2; CDBLB 1890-1914; DLB 10, 19, 153, 160; MTCW; SATA 19

Maso, Carole [19(?)-] .... CLC 44

Mason, Bobbie Ann [1940-] CLC 28, 43, 82; SSC 4
See also AAYA 5; CA 53-56; CANR 11, 31, 58; DLB 173; DLBY 87; INT CANR-31; MTCW

Mason, Ernst
See Pohl, Frederik

Mason, Lee W.
See Malzberg, Barry N(athaniel)

Mason, Nick [1945-] .... CLC 35

Mason, Tally
See Derleth, August (William)

Mass, William
See Gibson, William

Masters, Edgar Lee [1868-1950]TCLC 2, 25; DA; DAC; DAM MST, POET; PC 1; WLCS
See also CA 104; 133; CDALB 1865-1917; DLB 54; MTCW

Masters, Hilary [1928-]..................... CLC 48
See also CA 25-28R; CANR 13, 47

Mastrosimone, William [19(?)-] .... CLC 36

Mathe, Albert
See Camus, Albert

Mather, Cotton [1663-1728] .... LC 38
See also CDALB 1640-1865; DLB 24, 30, 140

Mather, Increase [1639-1723] .... LC 38
See also DLB 24

Matheson, Richard Burton [1926-] ..CLC 37
See also CA 97-100; DLB 8, 44; INT 97-100

Mathews, Harry [1930-] .... CLC 6, 52
See also CA 21-24R; CAAS 6; CANR 18, 40

Mathews, John Joseph [1894-1979] CLC 84; DAM MULT
See also CA 19-20; 142; CANR 45; CAP 2; DLB 175; NNAL

Mathias, Roland (Glyn) [1915-]........CLC 45
See also CA 97-100; CANR 19, 41; DLB 27

Matsuo Basho [1644-1694] .... PC 3
See also DAM POET

Mattheson, Rodney
See Creasey, John

Matthews, Greg [1949-] .... CLC 45
See also CA 135

Matthews, William (Procter, III) [1942-1997] CLC 40
See also CA 29-32R; 162; CAAS 18; CANR 12, 57; DLB 5

Matthias, John (Edward) [1941-] .... CLC 9
See also CA 33-36R; CANR 56

Matthiessen, Peter [1927-]CLC 5, 7, 11, 32, 64; DAM NOV
See also AAYA 6; BEST 90:4; CA 9-12R; CANR 21, 50; DLB 6, 173; MTCW; SATA 27

Maturin, Charles Robert [1780(?)-1824] NCLC 6
See also DLB 178

Matute (Ausejo), Ana Maria [1925-] CLC 11
See also CA 89-92; MTCW

Maugham, W. S.
See Maugham, W(illiam) Somerset

Maugham, W(illiam) Somerset [1874-1965] CLC 1, 11, 15, 67, 93; DA; DAB; DAC; DAM DRAM, MST, NOV; SSC 8; WLC
See also CA 5-8R; 25-28R; CANR 40; CDBLB 1914-1945; DLB 10, 36, 77, 100, 162, 195; MTCW; SATA 54

Maugham, William Somerset
See Maugham, W(illiam) Somerset

Maupassant, (Henri Rene Albert) Guy de [1850-1893] ....
NCLC 1, 42; DA; DAB; DAC; DAM MST; SSC 1; WLC
See also DLB 123

Maupin, Armistead [1944-] ... CLC 95; DAM POP
See also CA 125; 130; CANR 58; INT 130

Maurhut, Richard
See Traven, B.

Mauriac, Claude [1914-1996] .... CLC 9
See also CA 89-92; 152; DLB 83

Mauriac, Francois (Charles) [1885-1970]
CLC 4, 9, 56; SSC 24
See also CA 25-28; CAP 2; DLB 65; MTCW

Mavor, Osborne Henry [1888-1951]
See Bridie, James
See also CA 104

Maxwell, William (Keepers, Jr.) [1908-]C L C 19
See also CA 93-96; CANR 54; DLBY 80; INT 93-96

May, Elaine [1932-] .... CLC 16
See also CA 124; 142; DLB 44

Mayakovski, Vladimir (Vladimirovich) [1893-1930] ....
TCLC 4, 18
See also CA 104; 158

Mayhew, Henry [1812-1887] .... NCLC 31
See also DLB 18, 55, 190

Mayle, Peter [1939(?)-] .... CLC 89
See also CA 139; CANR 64

Maynard, Joyce [1953-] .... CLC 23
See also CA 111; 129; CANR 64

Mayne, William (James Carter) [1928-]C L C 12
See also AAYA 20; CA 9-12R; CANR 37; CLR 25; JRDA; MAICYA; SAAS 11; SATA 6, 68

Mayo, Jim
See L'Amour, Louis (Dearborn)

Maysles, Albert [1926-] .... CLC 16
See also CA 29-32R

Maysles, David [1932-] .... CLC 16

Mazer, Norma Fox [1931-] .... CLC 26
See also AAYA 5; CA 69-72; CANR 12, 32, 66; CLR 23; JRDA; MAICYA; SAAS 1; SATA 24, 67

Mazzini, Guiseppe [1805-1872] ..... NCLC 34

McAuley, James Phillip [1917-1976] CLC 45
See also CA 97-100

McBain, Ed
See Hunter, Evan

McBrien, William Augustine [1930-]CLC 44
See also CA 107

McCaffrey, Anne (Inez) [1926-]CLC 17; DAM NOV, POP
See also AAYA 6; AITN 2; BEST 89:2; CA 25-28R; CANR 15, 35, 55; CLR 49; DLB 8; JRDA; MAICYA; MTCW; SAAS 11; SATA 8, 70

McCall, Nathan [1955(?)-] .... CLC 86
See also CA 146

McCann, Arthur
See Campbell, John W(ood, Jr.)

McCann, Edson
See Pohl, Frederik

McCarthy, Charles, Jr. [1933-]
See McCarthy, Cormac
See also CANR 42, 69; DAM POP

McCarthy, Cormac [1933-]CLC 4, 57, 59, 101
See also McCarthy, Charles, Jr.
See also DLB 6, 143

McCarthy, Mary (Therese) [1912-1989]C L C 1, 3, 5, 14, 24, 39, 59; SSC 24
See also CA 5-8R; 129; CANR 16, 50, 64; DLB 2; DLBY 81; INT CANR-16; MTCW

McCartney, (James) Paul [1942-]CLC 12, 35

See also CA 146

McCauley, Stephen (D.) [1955-] .... CLC 50
See also CA 141

McClure, Michael (Thomas) [1932-].CLC 6, 10
See also CA 21-24R; CANR 17, 46; DLB 16

McCorkle, Jill (Collins) [1958-] .... CLC 51
See also CA 121; DLBY 87

McCourt, Frank [1930-] .... CLC 109
See also CA 157

McCourt, James [1941-] .... CLC 5
See also CA 57-60

McCoy, Horace (Stanley) [1897-1955]T C L C 28
See also CA 108; 155; DLB 9

McCrae, John [1872-1918] .... TCLC 12
See also CA 109; DLB 92

McCreigh, James
See Pohl, Frederik

McCullers, (Lula) Carson (Smith) [1917-1967]
CLC 1, 4, 10, 12, 48, 100; DA; DAB; DAC; DAM MST, NOV; SSC 9, 24; WLC
See also AAYA 21; CA 5-8R; 25-28R; CABS 1, 3; CANR 18; CDALB 1941-1968; DLB 2, 7, 173; MTCW; SATA 27

McCulloch, John Tyler
See Burroughs, Edgar Rice

McCullough, Colleen [1938(?)-]CLC 27, 107; DAM NOV, POP
See also CA 81-84; CANR 17, 46, 67; MTCW

McDermott, Alice [1953-] .... CLC 90
See also CA 109; CANR 40

McElroy, Joseph [1930-] .... CLC 5, 47
See also CA 17-20R

McEwan, Ian (Russell) [1948-] . CLC 13, 66; DAM NOV
See also BEST 90:4; CA 61-64; CANR 14, 41, 69; DLB 14, 194; MTCW

McFadden, David [1940-] .... CLC 48
See also CA 104; DLB 60; INT 104

McFarland, Dennis [1950-] .... CLC 65
See also CA 165

McGahern, John [1934-]CLC 5, 9, 48; SSC 17
See also CA 17-20R; CANR 29, 68; DLB 14; MTCW

McGinley, Patrick (Anthony) [1937-]CLC 41
See also CA 120; 127; CANR 56; INT 127

McGinley, Phyllis [1905-1978] .... CLC 14
See also CA 9-12R; 77-80; CANR 19; DLB 11, 48; SATA 2, 44; SATA-Obit 24

McGinniss, Joe [1942-] .... CLC 32
See also AITN 2; BEST 89:2; CA 25-28R; CANR 26; DLB 185; INT CANR-26

McGivern, Maureen Daly
See Daly, Maureen

McGrath, Patrick [1950-] .... CLC 55
See also CA 136; CANR 65

McGrath, Thomas (Matthew) [1916-1990]
CLC 28, 59; DAM POET
See also CA 9-12R; 132; CANR 6, 33; MTCW; SATA 41; SATA-Obit 66

McGuane, Thomas (Francis III) [1939-]C L C 3, 7, 18, 45
See also AITN 2; CA 49-52; CANR 5, 24, 49; DLB 2; DLBY 80; INT CANR-24; MTCW

McGuckian, Medbh [1950-] ..CLC 48; DAM POET
See also CA 143; DLB 40

McHale, Tom [1942(?)-1982] .... CLC 3, 5
See also AITN 1; CA 77-80; 106

McIlvanney, William [1936-] .... CLC 42
See also CA 25-28R; CANR 61; DLB 14

McIlwraith, Maureen Mollie Hunter
See Hunter, Mollie
See also SATA 2

McInerney, Jay [1955-] . CLC 34, 112; DAM POP

See also AAYA 18; CA 116; 123; CANR 45, 68; INT 123

McIntyre, Vonda N(eel) [1948-] .... CLC 18
See also CA 81-84; CANR 17, 34, 69; MTCW

McKay, ClaudeTCLC 7, 41; BLC 3; DAB; PC 2
See also McKay, Festus Claudius
See also DLB 4, 45, 51, 117

McKay, Festus Claudius [1889-1948]
See McKay, Claude
See also BW 1; CA 104; 124; DA; DAC; DAM MST, MULT, NOV, POET; MTCW; WLC

McKuen, Rod [1933-] .... CLC 1, 3
See also AITN 1; CA 41-44R; CANR 40

McLoughlin, R. B.
See Mencken, H(enry) L(ouis)

McLuhan, (Herbert) Marshall [1911-1980]
CLC 37, 83
See also CA 9-12R; 102; CANR 12, 34, 61; DLB 88; INT CANR-12; MTCW

McMillan, Terry (L.) [1951-]CLC 50, 61, 112; BLCS; DAM MULT, NOV, POP
See also AAYA 21; BW 2; CA 140; CANR 60

McMurtry, Larry (Jeff) [1936-] CLC 2, 3, 7, 11, 27, 44; DAM NOV, POP
See also AAYA 15; AITN 2; BEST 89:2; CA 5-8R; CANR 19, 43, 64; CDALB 1968-1988; DLB 2, 143; DLBY 80, 87; MTCW

McNally, T. M. [1961-] .... CLC 82

McNally, Terrence [1939-].CLC 4, 7, 41, 91; DAM DRAM
See also CA 45-48; CANR 2, 56; DLB 7

McNamer, Deirdre [1950-] .... CLC 70

McNeile, Herman Cyril [1888-1937]
See Sapper
See also DLB 77

McNickle, (William) D'Arcy [1904-1977]CLC 89; DAM MULT
See also CA 9-12R; 85-88; CANR 5, 45; DLB 175; NNAL; SATA-Obit 22

McPhee, John (Angus) [1931-] .... CLC 36
See also BEST 90:1; CA 65-68; CANR 20, 46, 64, 69; DLB 185; MTCW

McPherson, James Alan [1943-]CLC 19, 77; BLCS
See also BW 1; CA 25-28R; CAAS 17; CANR 24; DLB 38; MTCW

McPherson, William (Alexander) [1933-]CLC 34
See also CA 69-72; CANR 28; INT CANR-28

Mead, Margaret [1901-1978] .... CLC 37
See also AITN 1; CA 1-4R; 81-84; CANR 4; MTCW; SATA-Obit 20

Meaker, Marijane (Agnes) [1927-]
See Kerr, M. E.
See also CA 107; CANR 37, 63; INT 107; JRDA; MAICYA; MTCW; SATA 20, 61

Medoff, Mark (Howard) [1940-] CLC 6, 23; DAM DRAM
See also AITN 1; CA 53-56; CANR 5; DLB 7; INT CANR-5

Medvedev, P. N.
See Bakhtin, Mikhail Mikhailovich

Meged, Aharon
See Megged, Aharon

Meged, Aron
See Megged, Aharon

Megged, Aharon [1920-] .... CLC 9
See also CA 49-52; CAAS 13; CANR 1

Mehta, Ved (Parkash) [1934-] .... CLC 37
See also CA 1-4R; CANR 2, 23, 69; MTCW

Melanter
See Blackmore, R(ichard) D(oddridge)

Melies, Georges [1861-1938] .... TCLC 81

Melikow, Loris
See Hofmannsthal, Hugo von

Melmoth, Sebastian

Miyamoto, Yuriko [1899-1951] ...... **TCLC 37**
  See also DLB 180
Miyazawa, Kenji [1896-1933] .... **TCLC 76**
  See also CA 157
Mizoguchi, Kenji [1898-1956] .... **TCLC 72**
Mo, Timothy (Peter) [1950(?)-] .... **CLC 46**
  See also CA 117; DLB 194; MTCW
Modarressi, Taghi (M.) [1931-] .... **CLC 44**
  See also CA 121; 134; INT 134
Modiano, Patrick (Jean) [1945-] ...... **CLC 18**
  See also CA 85-88; CANR 17, 40; DLB 83
Moerck, Paal
  See Roelvaag, O(le) E(dvart)
Mofolo, Thomas (Mokopu) [1875(?)-1948]
  TCLC 22; BLC 3; DAM MULT
  See also CA 121; 153
Mohr, Nicholasa [1938-] .... **CLC 12; DAM
  MULT; HLC**
  See also AAYA 8; CA 49-52; CANR 1, 32, 64;
  CLR 22; DLB 145; HW; JRDA; SAAS 8;
  SATA 8, 97
Mojtabai, A(nn) G(race) [1938-]**CLC 5, 9, 15,
  29**
  See also CA 85-88
Moliere [1622-1673]**LC 28; DA; DAB; DAC;
  DAM DRAM, MST; WLC**
Molin, Charles
  See Mayne, William (James Carter)
Molnar, Ferenc [1878-1952]**TCLC 20; DAM
  DRAM**
  See also CA 109; 153
Momaday, N(avarre) Scott [1934-]**CLC 2, 19,
  85, 95; DA; DAB; DAC; DAM MST,
  MULT, NOV, POP; WLCS**
  See also AAYA 11; CA 25-28R; CANR 14, 34,
  68; DLB 143, 175; INT CANR-14; MTCW;
  NNAL; SATA 48; SATA-Brief 30
Monette, Paul [1945-1995] .... **CLC 82**
  See also CA 139; 147
Monroe, Harriet [1860-1936] .... **TCLC 12**
  See also CA 109; DLB 54, 91
Monroe, Lyle
  See Heinlein, Robert A(nson)
Montagu, Elizabeth [1917-] .... **NCLC 7**
  See also CA 9-12R
Montagu, Mary (Pierrepont) Wortley [1689-
  1762] .... **LC 9; PC 16**
  See also DLB 95, 101
Montagu, W. H.
  See Coleridge, Samuel Taylor
Montague, John (Patrick) [1929-]**CLC 13, 46**
  See also CA 9-12R; CANR 9, 69; DLB 40;
  MTCW
Montaigne, Michel (Eyquem) de [1533-1592]
  LC 8; DA; DAB; DAC; DAM MST; WLC
Montale, Eugenio [1896-1981] **CLC 7, 9, 18;
  PC 13**
  See also CA 17-20R; 104; CANR 30; DLB 114;
  MTCW
Montesquieu, Charles-Louis de Secondat
  [1689-1755] .... **LC 7**
Montgomery, (Robert) Bruce [1921-1978]
  See Crispin, Edmund
  See also CA 104
Montgomery, L(ucy) M(aud) [1874-1942]
  TCLC 51; DAC; DAM MST
  See also AAYA 12; CA 108; 137; CLR 8; DLB
  92; DLBD 14; JRDA; MAICYA; YABC 1
Montgomery, Marion H., Jr. [1925-] . **CLC 7**
  See also AITN 1; CA 1-4R; CANR 3, 48; DLB
  6
Montgomery, Max
  See Davenport, Guy (Mattison, Jr.)
Montherlant, Henry (Milon) de [1896-1972]
  CLC 8, 19; DAM DRAM
  See also CA 85-88; 37-40R; DLB 72; MTCW
Monty Python

  See Chapman, Graham; Cleese, John
  (Marwood); Gilliam, Terry (Vance); Idle,
  Eric; Jones, Terence Graham Parry; Palin,
  Michael (Edward)
  See also AAYA 7
Moodie, Susanna (Strickland) [1803-1885]
  NCLC 14
  See also DLB 99
Mooney, Edward [1951-]
  See Mooney, Ted
  See also CA 130
Mooney, Ted .... **CLC 25**
  See also Mooney, Edward
Moorcock, Michael (John) [1939-]**CLC 5, 27,
  58**
  See also CA 45-48; CAAS 5; CANR 2, 17, 38,
  64; DLB 14; MTCW; SATA 93
Moore, Brian [1921-]**CLC 1, 3, 5, 7, 8, 19, 32,
  90; DAB; DAC; DAM MST**
  See also CA 1-4R; CANR 1, 25, 42, 63; MTCW
Moore, Edward
  See Muir, Edwin
Moore, George Augustus [1852-1933] **T C L C
  7; SSC 19**
  See also CA 104; DLB 10, 18, 57, 135
Moore, Lorrie .... **CLC 39, 45, 68**
  See also Moore, Marie Lorena
Moore, Marianne (Craig) [1887-1972]**CLC 1,
  2, 4, 8, 10, 13, 19, 47; DA; DAB; DAC;
  DAM MST, POET; PC 4; WLCS**
  See also CA 1-4R; 33-36R; CANR 3, 61;
  CDALB 1929-1941; DLB 45; DLBD 7;
  MTCW; SATA 20
Moore, Marie Lorena [1957-]
  See Moore, Lorrie
  See also CA 116; CANR 39
Moore, Thomas [1779-1852] .... **NCLC 6**
  See also DLB 96, 144
Morand, Paul [1888-1976] . **CLC 41; SSC 22**
  See also CA 69-72; DLB 65
Morante, Elsa [1918-1985] .... **CLC 8, 47**
  See also CA 85-88; 117; CANR 35; DLB 177;
  MTCW
Moravia, Alberto [1907-1990]**CLC 2, 7, 11, 27,
  46; SSC 26**
  See also Pincherle, Alberto
  See also DLB 177
More, Hannah [1745-1833] .... **NCLC 27**
  See also DLB 107, 109, 116, 158
More, Henry [1614-1687] .... **LC 9**
  See also DLB 126
More, Sir Thomas [1478-1535] ..... **LC 10, 32**
Moreas, Jean .... **TCLC 18**
  See also Papadiamantopoulos, Johannes
Morgan, Berry [1919-] .... **CLC 6**
  See also CA 49-52; DLB 6
Morgan, Claire
  See Highsmith, (Mary) Patricia
Morgan, Edwin (George) [1920-] ..... **CLC 31**
  See also CA 5-8R; CANR 3, 43; DLB 27
Morgan, (George) Frederick [1922-] **CLC 23**
  See also CA 17-20R; CANR 21
Morgan, Harriet
  See Mencken, H(enry) L(ouis)
Morgan, Jane
  See Cooper, James Fenimore
Morgan, Janet [1945-] .... **CLC 39**
  See also CA 65-68
Morgan, Lady [1776(?)-1859] .... **NCLC 29**
  See also DLB 116, 158
Morgan, Robin (Evonne) [1941-] .... **CLC 2**
  See also CA 69-72; CANR 29, 68; MTCW;
  SATA 80
Morgan, Scott
  See Kuttner, Henry
Morgan, Seth [1949(?)-1990] .... **CLC 65**
  See also CA 132

Morgenstern, Christian [1871-1914]**TCLC 8**
  See also CA 105
Morgenstern, S.
  See Goldman, William (W.)
Moricz, Zsigmond [1879-1942] ...... **TCLC 33**
  See also CA 165
Morike, Eduard (Friedrich) [1804-1875]
  NCLC 10
  See also DLB 133
Moritz, Karl Philipp [1756-1793] .... **LC 2**
  See also DLB 94
Morland, Peter Henry
  See Faust, Frederick (Schiller)
Morren, Theophil
  See Hofmannsthal, Hugo von
Morris, Bill [1952-] .... **CLC 76**
Morris, Julian
  See West, Morris L(anglo)
Morris, Steveland Judkins [1950(?)-]
  See Wonder, Stevie
  See also CA 111
Morris, William [1834-1896] .... **NCLC 4**
  See also CDBLB 1832-1890; DLB 18, 35, 57,
  156, 178, 184
Morris, Wright [1910-] ... **CLC 1, 3, 7, 18, 37**
  See also CA 9-12R; CANR 21; DLB 2; DLBY
  81; MTCW
Morrison, Arthur [1863-1945] .... **TCLC 72**
  See also CA 120; 157; DLB 70, 135, 197
Morrison, Chloe Anthony Wofford
  See Morrison, Toni
Morrison, James Douglas [1943-1971]
  See Morrison, Jim
  See also CA 73-76; CANR 40
Morrison, Jim .... **CLC 17**
  See also Morrison, James Douglas
Morrison, Toni [1931-]**CLC 4, 10, 22, 55, 81,
  87; BLC 3; DA; DAB; DAC; DAM MST,
  MULT, NOV, POP**
  See also AAYA 1, 22; BW 2; CA 29-32R;
  CANR 27, 42, 67; CDALB 1968-1988; DLB
  6, 33, 143; DLBY 81; MTCW; SATA 57
Morrison, Van [1945-] .... **CLC 21**
  See also CA 116
Morrissy, Mary [1958-] .... **CLC 99**
Mortimer, John (Clifford) [1923-]**CLC 28, 43;
  DAM DRAM, POP**
  See also CA 13-16R; CANR 21, 69; CDBLB
  1960 to Present; DLB 13; INT CANR-21;
  MTCW
Mortimer, Penelope (Ruth) [1918-] .... **CLC 5**
  See also CA 57-60; CANR 45
Morton, Anthony
  See Creasey, John
Mosca, Gaetano [1858-1941] .... **TCLC 75**
Mosher, Howard Frank [1943-] .... **CLC 62**
  See also CA 139; CANR 65
Mosley, Nicholas [1923-] .... **CLC 43, 70**
  See also CA 69-72; CANR 41, 60; DLB 14
Mosley, Walter [1952-]**CLC 97; BLCS; DAM
  MULT, POP**
  See also AAYA 17; BW 2; CA 142; CANR 57
Moss, Howard [1922-1987]**CLC 7, 14, 45, 50;
  DAM POET**
  See also CA 1-4R; 123; CANR 1, 44; DLB 5
Mossgiel, Rab
  See Burns, Robert
Motion, Andrew (Peter) [1952-] .... **CLC 47**
  See also CA 146; DLB 40
Motley, Willard (Francis) [1909-1965]**CLC 18**
  See also BW 1; CA 117; 106; DLB 76, 143
Motoori, Norinaga [1730-1801] ..... **NCLC 45**
Mott, Michael (Charles Alston) [1930-] **C L C
  15, 34**
  See also CA 5-8R; CAAS 7; CANR 7, 29
Mountain Wolf Woman [1884-1960] **CLC 92**
  See also CA 144; NNAL

See also CA 41-44R; CANR 14; JRDA; SATA 5, 77

Nexo, Martin Andersen [1869-1954]**TCLC 43**

Nezval, Vitezslav [1900-1958] .... **TCLC 44**
See also CA 123

Ng, Fae Myenne [1957(?)-] .... **CLC 81**
See also CA 146

Ngema, Mbongeni [1955-] .... **CLC 57**
See also BW 2; CA 143

Ngugi, James T(hiong'o) .... **CLC 3, 7, 13**
See also Ngugi wa Thiong'o

Ngugi wa Thiong'o [1938-] **CLC 36; BLC 3; DAM MULT, NOV**
See also Ngugi, James T(hiong'o)
See also BW 2; CA 81-84; CANR 27, 58; DLB 125; MTCW

Nichol, B(arrie) P(hillip) [1944-1988]**CLC 18**
See also CA 53-56; DLB 53; SATA 66

Nichols, John (Treadwell) [1940-] .... **CLC 38**
See also CA 9-12R; CAAS 2; CANR 6; DLBY 82

Nichols, Leigh
See Koontz, Dean R(ay)

Nichols, Peter (Richard) [1927-]**CLC 5, 36, 65**
See also CA 104; CANR 33; DLB 13; MTCW

Nicolas, F. R. E.
See Freeling, Nicolas

Niedecker, Lorine [1903-1970] .. **CLC 10, 42; DAM POET**
See also CA 25-28; CAP 2; DLB 48

Nietzsche, Friedrich (Wilhelm) [1844-1900] **TCLC 10, 18, 55**
See also CA 107; 121; DLB 129

Nievo, Ippolito [1831-1861] .... **NCLC 22**

Nightingale, Anne Redmon [1943-]
See Redmon, Anne
See also CA 103

Nik. T. O.
See Annensky, Innokenty (Fyodorovich)

Nin, Anais [1903-1977]**CLC 1, 4, 8, 11, 14, 60; DAM NOV, POP; SSC 10**
See also AITN 2; CA 13-16R; 69-72; CANR 22, 53; DLB 2, 4, 152; MTCW

Nishida, Kitaro [1870-1945] .... **TCLC 83**

Nishiwaki, Junzaburo [1894-1982] ..... **PC 15**
See also CA 107

Nissenson, Hugh [1933-] .... **CLC 4, 9**
See also CA 17-20R; CANR 27; DLB 28

Niven, Larry .... **CLC 8**
See also Niven, Laurence Van Cott
See also DLB 8

Niven, Laurence Van Cott [1938-]
See Niven, Larry
See also CA 21-24R; CAAS 12; CANR 14, 44, 66; DAM POP; MTCW; SATA 95

Nixon, Agnes Eckhardt [1927-] .... **CLC 21**
See also CA 110

Nizan, Paul [1905-1940] .... **TCLC 40**
See also CA 161; DLB 72

Nkosi, Lewis [1936-] . **CLC 45; BLC 3; DAM MULT**
See also BW 1; CA 65-68; CANR 27; DLB 157

Nodier, (Jean) Charles (Emmanuel) [1780-1844] .... **NCLC 19**
See also DLB 119

Noguchi, Yone [1875-1947] .... **TCLC 80**

Nolan, Christopher [1965-] .... **CLC 58**
See also CA 111

Noon, Jeff [1957-] .... **CLC 91**
See also CA 148

Norden, Charles
See Durrell, Lawrence (George)

Nordhoff, Charles (Bernard) [1887-1947] **TCLC 23**
See also CA 108; DLB 9; SATA 23

Norfolk, Lawrence [1963-] .... **CLC 76**
See also CA 144

Norman, Marsha [1947-] .... **CLC 28; DAM DRAM; DC 8**
See also CA 105; CABS 3; CANR 41; DLBY 84

Normyx
See Douglas, (George) Norman

Norris, Frank [1870-1902] .... **SSC 28**
See also Norris, (Benjamin) Frank(lin, Jr.)
See also CDALB 1865-1917; DLB 12, 71, 186

Norris, (Benjamin) Frank(lin, Jr.) [1870-1902] **TCLC 24**
See also Norris, Frank
See also CA 110; 160

Norris, Leslie [1921-] .... **CLC 14**
See also CA 11-12; CANR 14; CAP 1; DLB 27

North, Andrew
See Norton, Andre

North, Anthony
See Koontz, Dean R(ay)

North, Captain George
See Stevenson, Robert Louis (Balfour)

North, Milou
See Erdrich, Louise

Northrup, B. A.
See Hubbard, L(afayette) Ron(ald)

North Staffs
See Hulme, T(homas) E(rnest)

Norton, Alice Mary
See Norton, Andre
See also MAICYA; SATA 1, 43

Norton, Andre [1912-] .... **CLC 12**
See also Norton, Alice Mary
See also AAYA 14; CA 1-4R; CANR 68; CLR 50; DLB 8, 52; JRDA; MTCW; SATA 91

Norton, Caroline [1808-1877] .... **NCLC 47**
See also DLB 21, 159, 199

Norway, Nevil Shute [1899-1960]
See Shute, Nevil
See also CA 102; 93-96

Norwid, Cyprian Kamil [1821-1883]**NCLC 17**

Nosille, Nabrah
See Ellison, Harlan (Jay)

Nossack, Hans Erich [1901-1978] .... **CLC 6**
See also CA 93-96; 85-88; DLB 69

Nostradamus [1503-1566] .... **LC 27**

Nosu, Chuji
See Ozu, Yasujiro

Notenburg, Eleanora (Genrikhovna) von
See Guro, Elena

Nova, Craig [1945-] .... **CLC 7, 31**
See also CA 45-48; CANR 2, 53

Novak, Joseph
See Kosinski, Jerzy (Nikodem)

Novalis [1772-1801] .... **NCLC 13**
See also DLB 90

Novis, Emile
See Weil, Simone (Adolphine)

Nowlan, Alden (Albert) [1933-1983]**CLC 15; DAC; DAM MST**
See also CA 9-12R; CANR 5; DLB 53

Noyes, Alfred [1880-1958] .... **TCLC 7**
See also CA 104; DLB 20

Nunn, Kem .... **CLC 34**
See also CA 159

Nye, Robert [1939-] **CLC 13, 42; DAM NOV**
See also CA 33-36R; CANR 29, 67; DLB 14; MTCW; SATA 6

Nyro, Laura [1947-] .... **CLC 17**

Oates, Joyce Carol [1938-]**CLC 1, 2, 3, 6, 9, 11, 15, 19, 33, 52, 108; DA; DAB; DAC; DAM MST, NOV, POP; SSC 6; WLC**
See also AAYA 15; AITN 1; BEST 89:2; CA 5-8R; CANR 25, 45; CDALB 1968-1988; DLB 2, 5, 130; DLBY 81; INT CANR-25; MTCW

O'Brien, Darcy [1939-] .... **CLC 11**
See also CA 21-24R; CANR 8, 59

O'Brien, E. G.

See Clarke, Arthur C(harles)

O'Brien, Edna [1936-]**CLC 3, 5, 8, 13, 36, 65; DAM NOV; SSC 10**
See also CA 1-4R; CANR 6, 41, 65; CDBLB 1960 to Present; DLB 14; MTCW

O'Brien, Fitz-James [1828-1862] ..**NCLC 21**
See also DLB 74

O'Brien, Flann .... **CLC 1, 4, 5, 7, 10, 47**
See also O Nuallain, Brian

O'Brien, Richard [1942-] .... **CLC 17**
See also CA 124

O'Brien, (William) Tim(othy) [1946-]**CLC 7, 19, 40, 103; DAM POP**
See also AAYA 16; CA 85-88; CANR 40, 58; DLB 152; DLBD 9; DLBY 80

Obstfelder, Sigbjoern [1866-1900] **TCLC 23**
See also CA 123

O'Casey, Sean [1880-1964]**CLC 1, 5, 9, 11, 15, 88; DAB; DAC; DAM DRAM, MST; WLCS**
See also CA 89-92; CANR 62; CDBLB 1914-1945; DLB 10; MTCW

O'Cathasaigh, Sean
See O'Casey, Sean

Ochs, Phil [1940-1976] .... **CLC 17**
See also CA 65-68

O'Connor, Edwin (Greene) [1918-1968]**C L C 14**
See also CA 93-96; 25-28R

O'Connor, (Mary) Flannery [1925-1964]**CLC 1, 2, 3, 6, 10, 13, 15, 21, 66, 104; DA; DAB; DAC; DAM MST, NOV; SSC 1, 23; WLC**
See also AAYA 7; CA 1-4R; CANR 3, 41; CDALB 1941-1968; DLB 2, 152; DLBD 12; DLBY 80; MTCW

O'Connor, Frank .... **CLC 23; SSC 5**
See also O'Donovan, Michael John
See also DLB 162

O'Dell, Scott [1898-1989] .... **CLC 30**
See also AAYA 3; CA 61-64; 129; CANR 12, 30; CLR 1, 16; DLB 52; JRDA; MAICYA; SATA 12, 60

Odets, Clifford [1906-1963] .. **CLC 2, 28, 98; DAM DRAM; DC 6**
See also CA 85-88; CANR 62; DLB 7, 26; MTCW

O'Doherty, Brian [1934-] .... **CLC 76**
See also CA 105

O'Donnell, K. M.
See Malzberg, Barry N(athaniel)

O'Donnell, Lawrence
See Kuttner, Henry

O'Donovan, Michael John [1903-1966] **C L C 14**
See also O'Connor, Frank
See also CA 93-96

Oe, Kenzaburo [1935-]**CLC 10, 36, 86; DAM NOV; SSC 20**
See also CA 97-100; CANR 36, 50; DLB 182; DLBY 94; MTCW

O'Faolain, Julia [1932-] . **CLC 6, 19, 47, 108**
See also CA 81-84; CAAS 2; CANR 12, 61; DLB 14; MTCW

O'Faolain, Sean [1900-1991]**CLC 1, 7, 14, 32, 70; SSC 13**
See also CA 61-64; 134; CANR 12, 66; DLB 15, 162; MTCW

O'Flaherty, Liam [1896-1984]**CLC 5, 34; SSC 6**
See also CA 101; 113; CANR 35; DLB 36, 162; DLBY 84; MTCW

Ogilvy, Gavin
See Barrie, J(ames) M(atthew)

O'Grady, Standish (James) [1846-1928] **TCLC 5**
See also CA 104; 157

O'Grady, Timothy [1951-]................ **CLC 59**

See Codrescu, Andrei

Parini, Jay (Lee) [1948-] .... **CLC 54**
See also CA 97-100; CAAS 16; CANR 32

Park, Jordan
See Kornbluth, C(yril) M.; Pohl, Frederik

Park, Robert E(zra) [1864-1944] ... **TCLC 73**
See also CA 122; 165

Parker, Bert
See Ellison, Harlan (Jay)

Parker, Dorothy (Rothschild) [1893-1967]
CLC 15, 68; DAM POET; SSC 2
See also CA 19-20; 25-28R; CAP 2; DLB 11, 45, 86; MTCW

Parker, Robert B(rown) [1932-]**CLC 27; DAM NOV, POP**
See also BEST 89:4; CA 49-52; CANR 1, 26, 52; INT CANR-26; MTCW

Parkin, Frank [1940-] .... **CLC 43**
See also CA 147

Parkman, Francis, Jr. [1823-1893] **NCLC 12**
See also DLB 1, 30, 186

Parks, Gordon (Alexander Buchanan) [1912-]
CLC 1, 16; BLC 3; DAM MULT
See also AITN 2; BW 2; CA 41-44R; CANR 26, 66; DLB 33; SATA 8

Parmenides [c. 515B.C.-c. 450B.C.]**CMLC 22**
See also DLB 176

Parnell, Thomas [1679-1718] .... **LC 3**
See also DLB 94

Parra, Nicanor [1914-] .... **CLC 2, 102; DAM MULT; HLC**
See also CA 85-88; CANR 32; HW; MTCW

Parrish, Mary Frances
See Fisher, M(ary) F(rances) K(ennedy)

Parson
See Coleridge, Samuel Taylor

Parson Lot
See Kingsley, Charles

Partridge, Anthony
See Oppenheim, E(dward) Phillips

Pascal, Blaise [1623-1662] .... **LC 35**

Pascoli, Giovanni [1855-1912] .... **TCLC 45**

Pasolini, Pier Paolo [1922-1975] **CLC 20, 37, 106; PC 17**
See also CA 93-96; 61-64; CANR 63; DLB 128, 177; MTCW

Pasquini
See Silone, Ignazio

Pastan, Linda (Olenik) [1932-]**CLC 27; DAM POET**
See also CA 61-64; CANR 18, 40, 61; DLB 5

Pasternak, Boris (Leonidovich) [1890-1960]
CLC 7, 10, 18, 63; DA; DAB; DAC; DAM MST, NOV, POET; PC 6; SSC 31; WLC
See also CA 127; 116; MTCW

Patchen, Kenneth [1911-1972] **CLC 1, 2, 18; DAM POET**
See also CA 1-4R; 33-36R; CANR 3, 35; DLB 16, 48; MTCW

Pater, Walter (Horatio) [1839-1894]**NCLC 7**
See also CDBLB 1832-1890; DLB 57, 156

Paterson, A(ndrew) B(arton) [1864-1941]
TCLC 32
See also CA 155; SATA 97

Paterson, Katherine (Womeldorf) [1932-]
CLC 12, 30
See also AAYA 1; CA 21-24R; CANR 28, 59; CLR 7, 50; DLB 52; JRDA; MAICYA; MTCW; SATA 13, 53, 92

Patmore, Coventry Kersey Dighton [1823-1896] .... **NCLC 9**
See also DLB 35, 98

Paton, Alan (Stewart) [1903-1988]**CLC 4, 10, 25, 55, 106; DA; DAB; DAC; DAM MST, NOV; WLC**
See also CA 13-16; 125; CANR 22; CAP 1; MTCW; SATA 11; SATA-Obit 56

Paton Walsh, Gillian [1937-]
See Walsh, Jill Paton
See also CANR 38; JRDA; MAICYA; SAAS 3; SATA 4, 72

Patton, George S. [1885-1945] .... **TCLC 79**

Paulding, James Kirke [1778-1860] **NCLC 2**
See also DLB 3, 59, 74

Paulin, Thomas Neilson [1949-]
See Paulin, Tom
See also CA 123; 128

Paulin, Tom .... **CLC 37**
See also Paulin, Thomas Neilson
See also DLB 40

Paustovsky, Konstantin (Georgievich) [1892-1968] ....
CLC 40
See also CA 93-96; 25-28R

Pavese, Cesare [1908-1950] **TCLC 3; PC 13; SSC 19**
See also CA 104; DLB 128, 177

Pavic, Milorad [1929-] .... **CLC 60**
See also CA 136; DLB 181

Payne, Alan
See Jakes, John (William)

Paz, Gil
See Lugones, Leopoldo

Paz, Octavio [1914-1998]**CLC 3, 4, 6, 10, 19, 51, 65; DA; DAB; DAC; DAM MST, MULT, POET; HLC; PC 1; WLC**
See also CA 73-76; 165; CANR 32, 65; DLBY 90; HW; MTCW

p'Bitek, Okot [1931-1982] . **CLC 96; BLC 3; DAM MULT**
See also BW 2; CA 124; 107; DLB 125; MTCW

Peacock, Molly [1947-] .... **CLC 60**
See also CA 103; CAAS 21; CANR 52; DLB 120

Peacock, Thomas Love [1785-1866]**NCLC 22**
See also DLB 96, 116

Peake, Mervyn [1911-1968] .... **CLC 7, 54**
See also CA 5-8R; 25-28R; CANR 3; DLB 15, 160; MTCW; SATA 23

Pearce, Philippa .... **CLC 21**
See also Christie, (Ann) Philippa
See also CLR 9; DLB 161; MAICYA; SATA 1, 67

Pearl, Eric
See Elman, Richard (Martin)

Pearson, T(homas) R(eid) [1956-] .... **CLC 39**
See also CA 120; 130; INT 130

Peck, Dale [1967-] .... **CLC 81**
See also CA 146

Peck, John [1941-] .... **CLC 3**
See also CA 49-52; CANR 3

Peck, Richard (Wayne) [1934-] .... **CLC 21**
See also AAYA 1, 24; CA 85-88; CANR 19, 38; CLR 15; INT CANR-19; JRDA; MAICYA; SAAS 2; SATA 18, 55, 97

Peck, Robert Newton [1928-] .. **CLC 17; DA; DAC; DAM MST**
See also AAYA 3; CA 81-84; CANR 31, 63; CLR 45; JRDA; MAICYA; SAAS 1; SATA 21, 62

Peckinpah, (David) Sam(uel) [1925-1984]
CLC 20
See also CA 109; 114

Pedersen, Knut [1859-1952]
See Hamsun, Knut
See also CA 104; 119; CANR 63; MTCW

Peeslake, Gaffer
See Durrell, Lawrence (George)

Peguy, Charles Pierre [1873-1914] **TCLC 10**
See also CA 107

Peirce, Charles Sanders [1839-1914]**TCLC 81**

Pena, Ramon del Valle y
See Valle-Inclan, Ramon (Maria) del

Pendennis, Arthur Esquir

See Thackeray, William Makepeace

Penn, William [1644-1718] .... **LC 25**
See also DLB 24

PEPECE
See Prado (Calvo), Pedro

Pepys, Samuel [1633-1703]**LC 11; DA; DAB; DAC; DAM MST; WLC**
See also CDBLB 1660-1789; DLB 101

Percy, Walker [1916-1990]**CLC 2, 3, 6, 8, 14, 18, 47, 65; DAM NOV, POP**
See also CA 1-4R; 131; CANR 1, 23, 64; DLB 2; DLBY 80, 90; MTCW

Perec, Georges [1936-1982] .... **CLC 56**
See also CA 141; DLB 83

Pereda (y Sanchez de Porrua), Jose Maria de [1833-1906] .... **TCLC 16**
See also CA 117

Pereda y Porrua, Jose Maria de
See Pereda (y Sanchez de Porrua), Jose Maria de

Peregoy, George Weems
See Mencken, H(enry) L(ouis)

Perelman, S(idney) J(oseph) [1904-1979]**CLC 3, 5, 9, 15, 23, 44, 49; DAM DRAM**
See also AITN 1, 2; CA 73-76; 89-92; CANR 18; DLB 11, 44; MTCW

Peret, Benjamin [1899-1959] .... **TCLC 20**
See also CA 117

Peretz, Isaac Loeb [1851(?)-1915] **TCLC 16; SSC 26**
See also CA 109

Peretz, Yitzkhok Leibush
See Peretz, Isaac Loeb

Perez Galdos, Benito [1843-1920] . **TCLC 27**
See also CA 125; 153; HW

Perrault, Charles [1628-1703] .... **LC 2**
See also MAICYA; SATA 25

Perry, Brighton
See Sherwood, Robert E(mmet)

Perse, St.-John
See Leger, (Marie-Rene Auguste) Alexis Saint-Leger

Perutz, Leo [1882-1957] .... **TCLC 60**
See also DLB 81

Peseenz, Tulio F.
See Lopez y Fuentes, Gregorio

Pesetsky, Bette [1932-] .... **CLC 28**
See also CA 133; DLB 130

Peshkov, Alexei Maximovich [1868-1936]
See Gorky, Maxim
See also CA 105; 141; DA; DAC; DAM DRAM, MST, NOV

Pessoa, Fernando (Antonio Nogueira) [1898-1935] ....
TCLC 27; HLC; PC 20
See also CA 125

Peterkin, Julia Mood [1880-1961] .... **CLC 31**
See also CA 102; DLB 9

Peters, Joan K(aren) [1945-] .... **CLC 39**
See also CA 158

Peters, Robert L(ouis) [1924-] .... **CLC 7**
See also CA 13-16R; CAAS 8; DLB 105

Petofi, Sandor [1823-1849] .... **NCLC 21**

Petrakis, Harry Mark [1923-] .... **CLC 3**
See also CA 9-12R; CANR 4, 30

Petrarch [1304-1374]**CMLC 20; DAM POET; PC 8**

Petrov, Evgeny .... **TCLC 21**
See also Kataev, Evgeny Petrovich

Petry, Ann (Lane) [1908-1997] **CLC 1, 7, 18**
See also BW 1; CA 5-8R; 157; CAAS 6; CANR 4, 46; CLR 12; DLB 76; JRDA; MAICYA; MTCW; SATA 5; SATA-Obit 94

Petursson, Halligrimur [1614-1674] ..... **LC 8**

Phaedrus [18(?)B.C.-55(?)] .... **CMLC 25**

Philips, Katherine [1632-1664] .... **LC 30**
See also DLB 131

Philipson, Morris H. [1926-] .... **CLC 53**
See also CA 1-4R; CANR 4
Phillips, Caryl [1958-]**CLC 96; BLCS; DAM MULT**
See also BW 2; CA 141; CANR 63; DLB 157
Phillips, David Graham [1867-1911]**TCLC 44**
See also CA 108; DLB 9, 12
Phillips, Jack
See Sandburg, Carl (August)
Phillips, Jayne Anne [1952-]**CLC 15, 33; SSC 16**
See also CA 101; CANR 24, 50; DLBY 80; INT CANR-24; MTCW
Phillips, Richard
See Dick, Philip K(indred)
Phillips, Robert (Schaeffer) [1938-] . **CLC 28**
See also CA 17-20R; CAAS 13; CANR 8; DLB 105
Phillips, Ward
See Lovecraft, H(oward) P(hillips)
Piccolo, Lucio [1901-1969] .... **CLC 13**
See also CA 97-100; DLB 114
Pickthall, Marjorie L(owry) C(hristie) [1883-1922] ....
TCLC 21
See also CA 107; DLB 92
Pico della Mirandola, Giovanni [1463-1494]
LC 15
Piercy, Marge [1936-]**CLC 3, 6, 14, 18, 27, 62**
See also CA 21-24R; CAAS 1; CANR 13, 43, 66; DLB 120; MTCW
Piers, Robert
See Anthony, Piers
Pieyre de Mandiargues, Andre [1909-1991]
See Mandiargues, Andre Pieyre de
See also CA 103; 136; CANR 22
Pilnyak, Boris .... **TCLC 23**
See also Vogau, Boris Andreyevich
Pincherle, Alberto [1907-1990]. **CLC 11, 18; DAM NOV**
See Moravia, Alberto
See also CA 25-28R; 132; CANR 33, 63; MTCW
Pinckney, Darryl [1953-] .... **CLC 76**
See also BW 2; CA 143
Pindar [518B.C.-446B.C.] . **CMLC 12; PC 19**
See also DLB 176
Pineda, Cecile [1942-] .... **CLC 39**
See also CA 118
Pinero, Arthur Wing [1855-1934] **TCLC 32; DAM DRAM**
See also CA 110; 153; DLB 10
Pinero, Miguel (Antonio Gomez) [1946-1988]
CLC 4, 55
See also CA 61-64; 125; CANR 29; HW
Pinget, Robert [1919-1997] .... **CLC 7, 13, 37**
See also CA 85-88; 160; DLB 83
Pink Floyd
See Barrett, (Roger) Syd; Gilmour, David; Mason, Nick; Waters, Roger; Wright, Rick
Pinkney, Edward [1802-1828] .... **NCLC 31**
Pinkwater, Daniel Manus [1941-] ..... **CLC 35**
See also Pinkwater, Manus
See also AAYA 1; CA 29-32R; CANR 12, 38; CLR 4; JRDA; MAICYA; SAAS 3; SATA 46, 76
Pinkwater, Manus
See Pinkwater, Daniel Manus
See also SATA 8
Pinsky, Robert [1940-]**CLC 9, 19, 38, 94; DAM POET**
See also CA 29-32R; CAAS 4; CANR 58; DLBY 82
Pinta, Harold
See Pinter, Harold
Pinter, Harold [1930-]**CLC 1, 3, 6, 9, 11, 15, 27, 58, 73; DA; DAB; DAC; DAM DRAM,**

MST; WLC
See also CA 5-8R; CANR 33, 65; CDBLB 1960 to Present; DLB 13; MTCW
Piozzi, Hester Lynch (Thrale) [1741-1821]
NCLC 57
See also DLB 104, 142
Pirandello, Luigi [1867-1936] .. **TCLC 4, 29; DA; DAB; DAC; DAM DRAM, MST; DC 5; SSC 22; WLC**
See also CA 104; 153
Pirsig, Robert M(aynard) [1928-] .**CLC 4, 6, 73; DAM POP**
See also CA 53-56; CANR 42; MTCW; SATA 39
Pisarev, Dmitry Ivanovich [1840-1868]**NCLC 25**
Pix, Mary (Griffith) [1666-1709] .... **LC 8**
See also DLB 80
Pixerecourt, (Rene Charles) Guilbert de [1773-1844] ....
NCLC 39
See also DLB 192
Plaatje, Sol(omon) T(shekisho) [1876-1932]
TCLC 73; BLCS
See also BW 2; CA 141
Plaidy, Jean
See Hibbert, Eleanor Alice Burford
Planche, James Robinson [1796-1880]**N C L C 42**
Plant, Robert [1948-] .... **CLC 12**
Plante, David (Robert) [1940-]**CLC 7, 23, 38; DAM NOV**
See also CA 37-40R; CANR 12, 36, 58; DLBY 83; INT CANR-12; MTCW
Plath, Sylvia [1932-1963]**CLC 1, 2, 3, 5, 9, 11, 14, 17, 50, 51, 62, 111; DA; DAB; DAC; DAM MST, POET; PC 1; WLC**
See also AAYA 13; CA 19-20; CANR 34; CAP 2; CDALB 1941-1968; DLB 5, 6, 152; MTCW; SATA 96
Plato [428(?)B.C.-348(?)B.C.] **CMLC 8; DA; DAB; DAC; DAM MST; WLCS**
See also DLB 176
Platonov, Andrei .... **TCLC 14**
See also Klimentov, Andrei Platonovich
Platt, Kin [1911-] .... **CLC 26**
See also AAYA 11; CA 17-20R; CANR 11; JRDA; SAAS 17; SATA 21, 86
Plautus [c. 251B.C.-184B.C.]**CMLC 24; DC 6**
Plick et Plock
See Simenon, Georges (Jacques Christian)
Plimpton, George (Ames) [1927-] ..... **CLC 36**
See also AITN 1; CA 21-24R; CANR 32; DLB 185; MTCW; SATA 10
Pliny the Elder [c. 23-79] .... **CMLC 23**
Plomer, William Charles Franklin [1903-1973]
CLC 4, 8
See also CA 21-22; CANR 34; CAP 2; DLB 20, 162, 191; MTCW; SATA 24
Plowman, Piers
See Kavanagh, Patrick (Joseph)
Plum, J.
See Wodehouse, P(elham) G(renville)
Plumly, Stanley (Ross) [1939-] .... **CLC 33**
See also CA 108; 110; DLB 5, 193; INT 110
Plumpe, Friedrich Wilhelm [1888-1931]
TCLC 53
See also CA 112
Po Chu-i [772-846] .... **CMLC 24**
Poe, Edgar Allan [1809-1849]**NCLC 1, 16, 55; DA; DAB; DAC; DAM MST, POET; PC 1; SSC 1, 22; WLC**
See also AAYA 14; CDALB 1640-1865; DLB 3, 59, 73, 74; SATA 23
Poet of Titchfield Street, The
See Pound, Ezra (Weston Loomis)
Pohl, Frederik [1919-] .... **CLC 18; SSC 25**

See also AAYA 24; CA 61-64; CAAS 1; CANR 11, 37; DLB 8; INT CANR-11; MTCW; SATA 24
Poirier, Louis [1910-]
See Gracq, Julien
See also CA 122; 126
Poitier, Sidney [1927-] .... **CLC 26**
See also BW 1; CA 117
Polanski, Roman [1933-] .... **CLC 16**
See also CA 77-80
Poliakoff, Stephen [1952-] .... **CLC 38**
See also CA 106; DLB 13
Police, The
See Copeland, Stewart (Armstrong); Summers, Andrew James; Sumner, Gordon Matthew
Polidori, John William [1795-1821]**NCLC 51**
See also DLB 116
Pollitt, Katha [1949-] .... **CLC 28**
See also CA 120; 122; CANR 66; MTCW
Pollock, (Mary) Sharon [1936-]**CLC 50; DAC; DAM DRAM, MST**
See also CA 141; DLB 60
Polo, Marco [1254-1324] .... **CMLC 15**
Polonsky, Abraham (Lincoln) [1910-]**CLC 92**
See also CA 104; DLB 26; INT 104
Polybius [c. 200B.C.-c. 118B.C.] ... **CMLC 17**
See also DLB 176
Pomerance, Bernard [1940-] . **CLC 13; DAM DRAM**
See also CA 101; CANR 49
Ponge, Francis (Jean Gaston Alfred) [1899-1988] ....
CLC 6, 18; DAM POET
See also CA 85-88; 126; CANR 40
Pontoppidan, Henrik [1857-1943] . **TCLC 29**
Poole, Josephine .... **CLC 17**
See also Helyar, Jane Penelope Josephine
See also SAAS 2; SATA 5
Popa, Vasko [1922-1991] .... **CLC 19**
See also CA 112; 148; DLB 181
Pope, Alexander [1688-1744]**LC 3; DA; DAB; DAC; DAM MST, POET; WLC**
See also CDBLB 1660-1789; DLB 95, 101
Porter, Connie (Rose) [1959(?)-] .... **CLC 70**
See also BW 2; CA 142; SATA 81
Porter, Gene(va Grace) Stratton [1863(?)-1924]
TCLC 21
See also CA 112
Porter, Katherine Anne [1890-1980]**CLC 1, 3, 7, 10, 13, 15, 27, 101; DA; DAB; DAC; DAM MST, NOV; SSC 4, 31**
See also AITN 2; CA 1-4R; 101; CANR 1, 65; DLB 4, 9, 102; DLBD 12; DLBY 80; MTCW; SATA 39; SATA-Obit 23
Porter, Peter (Neville Frederick) [1929-]**C L C 5, 13, 33**
See also CA 85-88; DLB 40
Porter, William Sydney [1862-1910]
See Henry, O.
See also CA 104; 131; CDALB 1865-1917; DA; DAB; DAC; DAM MST; DLB 12, 78, 79; MTCW; YABC 2
Portillo (y Pacheco), Jose Lopez
See Lopez Portillo (y Pacheco), Jose
Post, Melville Davisson [1869-1930]**TCLC 39**
See also CA 110
Potok, Chaim [1929-] **CLC 2, 7, 14, 26, 112; DAM NOV**
See also AAYA 15; AITN 1, 2; CA 17-20R; CANR 19, 35, 64; DLB 28, 152; INT CANR-19; MTCW; SATA 33
Potter, (Helen) Beatrix [1866-1943]
See Webb, (Martha) Beatrice (Potter)
See also MAICYA
Potter, Dennis (Christopher George) [1935-1994] ....
CLC 58, 86

See also CA 89-92

Schnitzler, Arthur [1862-1931]**TCLC 4; SSC 15**
See also CA 104; DLB 81, 118

Schoenberg, Arnold [1874-1951] ... **TCLC 75**
See also CA 109

Schonberg, Arnold
See Schoenberg, Arnold

Schopenhauer, Arthur [1788-1860]**NCLC 51**
See also DLB 90

Schor, Sandra (M.) [1932(?)-1990] ... **CLC 65**
See also CA 132

Schorer, Mark [1908-1977] .... **CLC 9**
See also CA 5-8R; 73-76; CANR 7; DLB 103

Schrader, Paul (Joseph) [1946-] .... **CLC 26**
See also CA 37-40R; CANR 41; DLB 44

Schreiner, Olive (Emilie Albertina) [1855-1920]
TCLC 9
See also CA 105; 154; DLB 18, 156, 190

Schulberg, Budd (Wilson) [1914-] **CLC 7, 48**
See also CA 25-28R; CANR 19; DLB 6, 26, 28; DLBY 81

Schulz, Bruno [1892-1942] **TCLC 5, 51; SSC 13**
See also CA 115; 123

Schulz, Charles M(onroe) [1922-] .... **CLC 12**
See also CA 9-12R; CANR 6; INT CANR-6; SATA 10

Schumacher, E(rnst) F(riedrich) [1911-1977]
CLC 80
See also CA 81-84; 73-76; CANR 34

Schuyler, James Marcus [1923-1991] **CLC 5, 23; DAM POET**
See also CA 101; 134; DLB 5, 169; INT 101

Schwartz, Delmore (David) [1913-1966]**C L C 2, 4, 10, 45, 87; PC 8**
See also CA 17-18; 25-28R; CANR 35; CAP 2; DLB 28, 48; MTCW

Schwartz, Ernst
See Ozu, Yasujiro

Schwartz, John Burnham [1965-] .... **CLC 59**
See also CA 132

Schwartz, Lynne Sharon [1939-] ...... **CLC 31**
See also CA 103; CANR 44

Schwartz, Muriel A.
See Eliot, T(homas) S(tearns)

Schwarz-Bart, Andre [1928-] .... **CLC 2, 4**
See also CA 89-92

Schwarz-Bart, Simone [1938-]**CLC 7; BLCS**
See also BW 2; CA 97-100

Schwob, (Mayer Andre) Marcel [1867-1905]
TCLC 20
See also CA 117; DLB 123

Sciascia, Leonardo [1921-1989]**CLC 8, 9, 41**
See also CA 85-88; 130; CANR 35; DLB 177; MTCW

Scoppettone, Sandra [1936-] .... **CLC 26**
See also AAYA 11; CA 5-8R; CANR 41; SATA 9, 92

Scorsese, Martin [1942-] .... **CLC 20, 89**
See also CA 110; 114; CANR 46

Scotland, Jay
See Jakes, John (William)

Scott, Duncan Campbell [1862-1947]**TCLC 6; DAC**
See also CA 104; 153; DLB 92

Scott, Evelyn [1893-1963] .... **CLC 43**
See also CA 104; 112; CANR 64; DLB 9, 48

Scott, F(rancis) R(eginald) [1899-1985] **C L C 22**
See also CA 101; 114; DLB 88; INT 101

Scott, Frank
See Scott, F(rancis) R(eginald)

Scott, Joanna [1960-] .... **CLC 50**
See also CA 126; CANR 53

Scott, Paul (Mark) [1920-1978] .... **CLC 9, 60**

See also CA 81-84; 77-80; CANR 33; DLB 14; MTCW

Scott, Sarah [1723-1795] .... **LC 44**
See also DLB 39

Scott, Walter [1771-1832]**NCLC 15, 69; DA; DAB; DAC; DAM MST, NOV, POET; PC 13; WLC**
See also AAYA 22; CDBLB 1789-1832; DLB 93, 107, 116, 144, 159; YABC 2

Scribe, (Augustin) Eugene [1791-1861]**NCLC 16; DAM DRAM; DC 5**
See also DLB 192

Scrum, R.
See Crumb, R(obert)

Scudery, Madeleine de [1607-1701] ...... **LC 2**

Scum
See Crumb, R(obert)

Scumbag, Little Bobby
See Crumb, R(obert)

Seabrook, John
See Hubbard, L(afayette) Ron(ald)

Sealy, I. Allan [1951-] .... **CLC 55**

Search, Alexander
See Pessoa, Fernando (Antonio Nogueira)

Sebastian, Lee
See Silverberg, Robert

Sebastian Owl
See Thompson, Hunter S(tockton)

Sebestyen, Ouida [1924-] .... **CLC 30**
See also AAYA 8; CA 107; CANR 40; CLR 17; JRDA; MAICYA; SAAS 10; SATA 39

Secundus, H. Scriblerus
See Fielding, Henry

Sedges, John
See Buck, Pearl S(ydenstricker)

Sedgwick, Catharine Maria [1789-1867]
NCLC 19
See also DLB 1, 74

Seelye, John [1931-] .... **CLC 7**

Seferiades, Giorgos Stylianou [1900-1971]
See Seferis, George
See also CA 5-8R; 33-36R; CANR 5, 36; MTCW

Seferis, George .... **CLC 5, 11**
See also Seferiades, Giorgos Stylianou

Segal, Erich (Wolf) [1937-]**CLC 3, 10; DAM POP**
See also BEST 89:1; CA 25-28R; CANR 20, 36, 65; DLBY 86; INT CANR-20; MTCW

Seger, Bob [1945-] .... **CLC 35**

Seghers, Anna .... **CLC 7**
See also Radvanyi, Netty
See also DLB 69

Seidel, Frederick (Lewis) [1936-] ..... **CLC 18**
See also CA 13-16R; CANR 8; DLBY 84

Seifert, Jaroslav [1901-1986] **CLC 34, 44, 93**
See also CA 127; MTCW

Sei Shonagon [c. 966-1017(?)] .... **CMLC 6**

Selby, Hubert, Jr. [1928-]**CLC 1, 2, 4, 8; SSC 20**
See also CA 13-16R; CANR 33; DLB 2

Selzer, Richard [1928-] .... **CLC 74**
See also CA 65-68; CANR 14

Sembene, Ousmane
See Ousmane, Sembene

Senancour, Etienne Pivert de [1770-1846]
NCLC 16
See also DLB 119

Sender, Ramon (Jose) [1902-1982] ... **CLC 8; DAM MULT; HLC**
See also CA 5-8R; 105; CANR 8; HW; MTCW

Seneca, Lucius Annaeus [4B.C.-65]**CMLC 6; DAM DRAM; DC 5**

Senghor, Leopold Sedar [1906-]**CLC 54; BLC 3; DAM MULT, POET**
See also BW 2; CA 116; 125; CANR 47; MTCW

Serling, (Edward) Rod(man) [1924-1975]

CLC 30
See also AAYA 14; AITN 1; CA 162; 57-60; DLB 26

Serna, Ramon Gomez de la
See Gomez de la Serna, Ramon

Serpieres
See Guillevic, (Eugene)

Service, Robert
See Service, Robert W(illiam)
See also DAB; DLB 92

Service, Robert W(illiam) [1874(?)-1958]
TCLC 15; DA; DAC; DAM MST, POET; WLC
See also Service, Robert
See also CA 115; 140; SATA 20

Seth, Vikram [1952-]**CLC 43, 90; DAM MULT**
See also CA 121; 127; CANR 50; DLB 120; INT 127

Seton, Cynthia Propper [1926-1982] **CLC 27**
See also CA 5-8R; 108; CANR 7

Seton, Ernest (Evan) Thompson [1860-1946]
TCLC 31
See also CA 109; DLB 92; DLBD 13; JRDA; SATA 18

Seton-Thompson, Ernest
See Seton, Ernest (Evan) Thompson

Settle, Mary Lee [1918-] .... **CLC 19, 61**
See also CA 89-92; CAAS 1; CANR 44; DLB 6; INT 89-92

Seuphor, Michel
See Arp, Jean

Sevigne, Marie (de Rabutin-Chantal) Marquise de [1626-1696] .... **LC 11**

Sewall, Samuel [1652-1730] .... **LC 38**
See also DLB 24

Sexton, Anne (Harvey) [1928-1974]**CLC 2, 4, 6, 8, 10, 15, 53; DA; DAB; DAC; DAM MST, POET; PC 2; WLC**
See also CA 1-4R; 53-56; CABS 2; CANR 3, 36; CDALB 1941-1968; DLB 5, 169; MTCW; SATA 10

Shaara, Michael (Joseph, Jr.) [1929-1988]
CLC 15; DAM POP
See also AITN 1; CA 102; 125; CANR 52; DLBY 83

Shackleton, C. C.
See Aldiss, Brian W(ilson)

Shacochis, Bob .... **CLC 39**
See also Shacochis, Robert G.

Shacochis, Robert G. [1951-]
See Shacochis, Bob
See also CA 119; 124; INT 124

Shaffer, Anthony (Joshua) [1926-] . **CLC 19; DAM DRAM**
See also CA 110; 116; DLB 13

Shaffer, Peter (Levin) [1926-] **CLC 5, 14, 18, 37, 60; DAB; DAM DRAM, MST; DC 7**
See also CA 25-28R; CANR 25, 47; CDBLB 1960 to Present; DLB 13; MTCW

Shakey, Bernard
See Young, Neil

Shalamov, Varlam (Tikhonovich) [1907(?)-1982] .... **CLC 18**
See also CA 129; 105

Shamlu, Ahmad [1925-] .... **CLC 10**

Shammas, Anton [1951-] .... **CLC 55**

Shange, Ntozake [1948-] .. **CLC 8, 25, 38, 74; BLC 3; DAM DRAM, MULT; DC 3**
See also AAYA 9; BW 2; CA 85-88; CABS 3; CANR 27, 48; DLB 38; MTCW

Shanley, John Patrick [1950-] .... **CLC 75**
See also CA 128; 133

Shapcott, Thomas W(illiam) [1935-] **CLC 38**
See also CA 69-72; CANR 49

Shapiro, Jane .... **CLC 76**

Shapiro, Karl (Jay) [1913-] **CLC 4, 8, 15, 53**
See also CA 1-4R; CAAS 6; CANR 1, 36, 66;

29
See also CA 13-16R; DLB 13
Sinclair, Andrew (Annandale) [1935-]**CLC 2, 14**
See also CA 9-12R; CAAS 5; CANR 14, 38; DLB 14; MTCW
Sinclair, Emil
See Hesse, Hermann
Sinclair, Iain [1943-]............................ **CLC 76**
See also CA 132
Sinclair, Iain MacGregor
See Sinclair, Iain
Sinclair, Irene
See Griffith, D(avid Lewelyn) W(ark)
Sinclair, Mary Amelia St. Clair [1865(?)-1946]
See Sinclair, May
See also CA 104
Sinclair, May [1863-1946] .... **TCLC 3, 11**
See also Sinclair, Mary Amelia St. Clair
See also CA 166; DLB 36, 135
Sinclair, Roy
See Griffith, D(avid Lewelyn) W(ark)
Sinclair, Upton (Beall) [1878-1968]**CLC 1, 11, 15, 63; DA; DAB; DAC; DAM MST, NOV; WLC**
See also CA 5-8R; 25-28R; CANR 7; CDALB 1929-1941; DLB 9; INT CANR-7; MTCW; SATA 9
Singer, Isaac
See Singer, Isaac Bashevis
Singer, Isaac Bashevis [1904-1991]**CLC 1, 3, 6, 9, 11, 15, 23, 38, 69, 111; DA; DAB; DAC; DAM MST, NOV; SSC 3; WLC**
See also AITN 1, 2; CA 1-4R; 134; CANR 1, 39; CDALB 1941-1968; CLR 1; DLB 6, 28, 52; DLBY 91; JRDA; MAICYA; MTCW; SATA 3, 27; SATA-Obit 68
Singer, Israel Joshua [1893-1944] . **TCLC 33**
Singh, Khushwant [1915-] .... **CLC 11**
See also CA 9-12R; CAAS 9; CANR 6
Singleton, Ann
See Benedict, Ruth (Fulton)
Sinjohn, John
See Galsworthy, John
Sinyavsky, Andrei (Donatevich) [1925-1997] **CLC 8**
See also CA 85-88; 159
Sirin, V.
See Nabokov, Vladimir (Vladimirovich)
Sissman, L(ouis) E(dward) [1928-1976] **C L C 9, 18**
See also CA 21-24R; 65-68; CANR 13; DLB 5
Sisson, C(harles) H(ubert) [1914-] ..... **CLC 8**
See also CA 1-4R; CAAS 3; CANR 3, 48; DLB 27
Sitwell, Dame Edith [1887-1964]**CLC 2, 9, 67; DAM POET; PC 3**
See also CA 9-12R; CANR 35; CDBLB 1945-1960; DLB 20; MTCW
Siwaarmill, H. P.
See Sharp, William
Sjoewall, Maj [1935-] .... **CLC 7**
See also CA 65-68
Sjowall, Maj
See Sjoewall, Maj
Skelton, Robin [1925-1997] .... **CLC 13**
See also AITN 2; CA 5-8R; 160; CAAS 5; CANR 28; DLB 27, 53
Skolimowski, Jerzy [1938-] .... **CLC 20**
See also CA 128
Skram, Amalie (Bertha) [1847-1905]**TCLC 25**
See also CA 165
Skvorecky, Josef (Vaclav) [1924-]**CLC 15, 39, 69; DAC; DAM NOV**
See also CA 61-64; CAAS 1; CANR 10, 34, 63; MTCW
Slade, Bernard .... **CLC 11, 46**

See also Newbound, Bernard Slade
See also CAAS 9; DLB 53
Slaughter, Carolyn [1946-] .... **CLC 56**
See also CA 85-88
Slaughter, Frank G(ill) [1908-] .... **CLC 29**
See also AITN 2; CA 5-8R; CANR 5; INT CANR-5
Slavitt, David R(ytman) [1935-] ...**CLC 5, 14**
See also CA 21-24R; CAAS 3; CANR 41; DLB 5, 6
Slesinger, Tess [1905-1945] .... **TCLC 10**
See also CA 107; DLB 102
Slessor, Kenneth [1901-1971] .... **CLC 14**
See also CA 102; 89-92
Slowacki, Juliusz [1809-1849] .... **NCLC 15**
Smart, Christopher [1722-1771] **LC 3; DAM POET; PC 13**
See also DLB 109
Smart, Elizabeth [1913-1986] .... **CLC 54**
See also CA 81-84; 118; DLB 88
Smiley, Jane (Graves) [1949-] ... **CLC 53, 76; DAM POP**
See also CA 104; CANR 30, 50; INT CANR-30
Smith, A(rthur) J(ames) M(arshall) [1902-1980] .... **CLC 15; DAC**
See also CA 1-4R; 102; CANR 4; DLB 88
Smith, Adam [1723-1790] .... **LC 36**
See also DLB 104
Smith, Alexander [1829-1867] .... **NCLC 59**
See also DLB 32, 55
Smith, Anna Deavere [1950-] .... **CLC 86**
See also CA 133
Smith, Betty (Wehner) [1896-1972] . **CLC 19**
See also CA 5-8R; 33-36R; DLBY 82; SATA 6
Smith, Charlotte (Turner) [1749-1806]**N C L C 23**
See also DLB 39, 109
Smith, Clark Ashton [1893-1961] ..... **CLC 43**
See also CA 143
Smith, Dave .... **CLC 22, 42**
See also Smith, David (Jeddie)
See also CAAS 7; DLB 5
Smith, David (Jeddie) [1942-]
See Smith, Dave
See also CA 49-52; CANR 1, 59; DAM POET
Smith, Florence Margaret [1902-1971]
See Smith, Stevie
See also CA 17-18; 29-32R; CANR 35; CAP 2; DAM POET; MTCW
Smith, Iain Crichton [1928-] .... **CLC 64**
See also CA 21-24R; DLB 40, 139
Smith, John [1580(?)-1631] .... **LC 9**
See also DLB 24, 30
Smith, Johnston
See Crane, Stephen (Townley)
Smith, Joseph, Jr. [1805-1844] .... **NCLC 53**
Smith, Lee [1944-] .... **CLC 25, 73**
See also CA 114; 119; CANR 46; DLB 143; DLBY 83; INT 119
Smith, Martin
See Smith, Martin Cruz
Smith, Martin Cruz [1942-] ..**CLC 25; DAM MULT, POP**
See also BEST 89:4; CA 85-88; CANR 6, 23, 43, 65; INT CANR-23; NNAL
Smith, Mary-Ann Tirone [1944-] ..... **CLC 39**
See also CA 118; 136
Smith, Patti [1946-] .... **CLC 12**
See also CA 93-96; CANR 63
Smith, Pauline (Urmson) [1882-1959] **T C L C 25**
Smith, Rosamond
See Oates, Joyce Carol
Smith, Sheila Kaye
See Kaye-Smith, Sheila
Smith, Stevie .... **CLC 3, 8, 25, 44; PC 12**

See also Smith, Florence Margaret
See also DLB 20
Smith, Wilbur (Addison) [1933-] ...... **CLC 33**
See also CA 13-16R; CANR 7, 46, 66; MTCW
Smith, William Jay [1918-] .... **CLC 6**
See also CA 5-8R; CANR 44; DLB 5; MAICYA; SAAS 22; SATA 2, 68
Smith, Woodrow Wilson
See Kuttner, Henry
Smolenskin, Peretz [1842-1885] ..... **NCLC 30**
Smollett, Tobias (George) [1721-1771] . **LC 2**
See also CDBLB 1660-1789; DLB 39, 104
Snodgrass, W(illiam) D(e Witt) [1926-]**CLC 2, 6, 10, 18, 68; DAM POET**
See also CA 1-4R; CANR 6, 36, 65; DLB 5; MTCW
Snow, C(harles) P(ercy) [1905-1980]**CLC 1, 4, 6, 9, 13, 19; DAM NOV**
See also CA 5-8R; 101; CANR 28; CDBLB 1945-1960; DLB 15, 77; MTCW
Snow, Frances Compton
See Adams, Henry (Brooks)
Snyder, Gary (Sherman) [1930-]**CLC 1, 2, 5, 9, 32; DAM POET; PC 21**
See also CA 17-20R; CANR 30, 60; DLB 5, 16, 165
Snyder, Zilpha Keatley [1927-] .... **CLC 17**
See also AAYA 15; CA 9-12R; CANR 38; CLR 31; JRDA; MAICYA; SAAS 2; SATA 1, 28, 75
Soares, Bernardo
See Pessoa, Fernando (Antonio Nogueira)
Sobh, A.
See Shamlu, Ahmad
Sobol, Joshua .... **CLC 60**
Socrates [469B.C.-399B.C.] .... **CMLC 27**
Soderberg, Hjalmar [1869-1941]... **TCLC 39**
Soderberg, Edith (Irene)
See Soedergran, Edith (Irene)
Soedergran, Edith (Irene) [1892-1923]**T C L C 31**
Softly, Edgar
See Lovecraft, H(oward) P(hillips)
Softly, Edward
See Lovecraft, H(oward) P(hillips)
Sokolov, Raymond [1941-] .... **CLC 7**
See also CA 85-88
Solo, Jay
See Ellison, Harlan (Jay)
Sologub, Fyodor .... **TCLC 9**
See also Teternikov, Fyodor Kuzmich
Solomons, Ikey Esquir
See Thackeray, William Makepeace
Solomos, Dionysios [1798-1857] .... **NCLC 15**
Solwoska, Mara
See French, Marilyn
Solzhenitsyn, Aleksandr I(sayevich) [1918-] **CLC 1, 2, 4, 7, 9, 10, 18, 26, 34, 78; DA; DAB; DAC; DAM MST, NOV; WLC**
See also AITN 1; CA 69-72; CANR 40, 65; MTCW
Somers, Jane
See Lessing, Doris (May)
Somerville, Edith [1858-1949] .... **TCLC 51**
See also DLB 135
Somerville & Ross
See Martin, Violet Florence; Somerville, Edith
Sommer, Scott [1951-] .... **CLC 25**
See also CA 106
Sondheim, Stephen (Joshua) [1930-]**CLC 30, 39; DAM DRAM**
See also AAYA 11; CA 103; CANR 47, 68
Song, Cathy [1955-] .... **PC 21**
See also CA 154; DLB 169
Sontag, Susan [1933-]**CLC 1, 2, 10, 13, 31, 105; DAM POP**
See also CA 17-20R; CANR 25, 51; DLB 2,

Swift, Jonathan [1667-1745]**LC 1; DA; DAB; DAC; DAM MST, NOV, POET; PC 9; WLC**
    See also CDBLB 1660-1789; DLB 39, 95, 101; SATA 19
Swinburne, Algernon Charles [1837-1909] **TCLC 8, 36; DA; DAB; DAC; DAM MST, POET; WLC**
    See also CA 105; 140; CDBLB 1832-1890; DLB 35, 57
Swinfen, Ann .... **CLC 34**
Swinnerton, Frank Arthur [1884-1982] **C L C 31**
    See also CA 108; DLB 34
Swithen, John
    See King, Stephen (Edwin)
Sylvia
    See Ashton-Warner, Sylvia (Constance)
Symmes, Robert Edward
    See Duncan, Robert (Edward)
Symonds, John Addington [1840-1893]**NCLC 34**
    See also DLB 57, 144
Symons, Arthur [1865-1945] .... **TCLC 11**
    See also CA 107; DLB 19, 57, 149
Symons, Julian (Gustave) [1912-1994]**CLC 2, 14, 32**
    See also CA 49-52; 147; CAAS 3; CANR 3, 33, 59; DLB 87, 155; DLBY 92; MTCW
Synge, (Edmund) J(ohn) M(illington) [1871-1909] ....
TCLC 6, 37; DAM DRAM; DC 2
    See also CA 104; 141; CDBLB 1890-1914; DLB 10, 19
Syruc, J.
    See Milosz, Czeslaw
Szirtes, George [1948-] .... **CLC 46**
    See also CA 109; CANR 27, 61
Szymborska, Wislawa [1923-] .... **CLC 99**
    See also CA 154; DLBY 96
T. O., Nik
    See Annensky, Innokenty (Fyodorovich)
Tabori, George [1914-]....................... **CLC 19**
    See also CA 49-52; CANR 4, 69
Tagore, Rabindranath [1861-1941] **TCLC 3, 53; DAM DRAM, POET; PC 8**
    See also CA 104; 120; MTCW
Taine, Hippolyte Adolphe [1828-1893]**N C L C 15**
Talese, Gay [1932-] .... **CLC 37**
    See also AITN 1; CA 1-4R; CANR 9, 58; DLB 185; INT CANR-9; MTCW
Tallent, Elizabeth (Ann) [1954-] .... **CLC 45**
    See also CA 117; DLB 130
Tally, Ted [1952-] .... **CLC 42**
    See also CA 120; 124; INT 124
Tamayo y Baus, Manuel [1829-1898]**NCLC 1**
Tammsaare, A(nton) H(ansen) [1878-1940] **TCLC 27**
    See also CA 164
Tam'si, Tchicaya U
    See Tchicaya, Gerald Felix
Tan, Amy (Ruth) [1952-]........ **CLC 59; DAM MULT, NOV, POP**
    See also AAYA 9; BEST 89:3; CA 136; CANR 54; DLB 173; SATA 75
Tandem, Felix
    See Spitteler, Carl (Friedrich Georg)
Tanizaki, Jun'ichiro [1886-1965] **CLC 8, 14, 28; SSC 21**
    See also CA 93-96; 25-28R; DLB 180
Tanner, William
    See Amis, Kingsley (William)
Tao Lao
    See Storni, Alfonsina
Tarassoff, Lev
    See Troyat, Henri

Tarbell, Ida M(inerva) [1857-1944]**TCLC 40**
    See also CA 122; DLB 47
Tarkington, (Newton) Booth [1869-1946] **TCLC 9**
    See also CA 110; 143; DLB 9, 102; SATA 17
Tarkovsky, Andrei (Arsenyevich) [1932-1986] **CLC 75**
    See also CA 127
Tartt, Donna [1964(?)-] .... **CLC 76**
    See also CA 142
Tasso, Torquato [1544-1595] .... **LC 5**
Tate, (John Orley) Allen [1899-1979]**CLC 2, 4, 6, 9, 11, 14, 24**
    See also CA 5-8R; 85-88; CANR 32; DLB 4, 45, 63; MTCW
Tate, Ellalice
    See Hibbert, Eleanor Alice Burford
Tate, James (Vincent) [1943-] .. **CLC 2, 6, 25**
    See also CA 21-24R; CANR 29, 57; DLB 5, 169
Tavel, Ronald [1940-] .... **CLC 6**
    See also CA 21-24R; CANR 33
Taylor, C(ecil) P(hilip) [1929-1981] .. **CLC 27**
    See also CA 25-28R; 105; CANR 47
Taylor, Edward [1642(?)-1729] .. **LC 11; DA; DAB; DAC; DAM MST, POET**
    See also DLB 24
Taylor, Eleanor Ross [1920-] .... **CLC 5**
    See also CA 81-84
Taylor, Elizabeth [1912-1975] .. **CLC 2, 4, 29**
    See also CA 13-16R; CANR 9; DLB 139; MTCW; SATA 13
Taylor, Frederick Winslow [1856-1915]**TCLC 76**
Taylor, Henry (Splawn) [1942-] .... **CLC 44**
    See also CA 33-36R; CAAS 7; CANR 31; DLB 5
Taylor, Kamala (Purnaiya) [1924-]
    See Markandaya, Kamala
    See also CA 77-80
Taylor, Mildred D. .... **CLC 21**
    See also AAYA 10; BW 1; CA 85-88; CANR 25; CLR 9; DLB 52; JRDA; MAICYA; SAAS 5; SATA 15, 70
Taylor, Peter (Hillsman) [1917-1994] **CLC 1, 4, 18, 37, 44, 50, 71; SSC 10**
    See also CA 13-16R; 147; CANR 9, 50; DLBY 81, 94; INT CANR-9; MTCW
Taylor, Robert Lewis [1912-] .... **CLC 14**
    See also CA 1-4R; CANR 3, 64; SATA 10
Tchekhov, Anton
    See Chekhov, Anton (Pavlovich)
Tchicaya, Gerald Felix [1931-1988]**CLC 101**
    See also CA 129; 125
Tchicaya U Tam'si
    See Tchicaya, Gerald Felix
Teasdale, Sara [1884-1933] .... **TCLC 4**
    See also CA 104; 163; DLB 45; SATA 32
Tegner, Esaias [1782-1846] .... **NCLC 2**
Teilhard de Chardin, (Marie Joseph) Pierre [1881-1955] .... **TCLC 9**
    See also CA 105
Temple, Ann
    See Mortimer, Penelope (Ruth)
Tennant, Emma (Christina) [1937-] **CLC 13, 52**
    See also CA 65-68; CAAS 9; CANR 10, 38, 59; DLB 14
Tenneshaw, S. M.
    See Silverberg, Robert
Tennyson, Alfred [1809-1892] **NCLC 30, 65; DA; DAB; DAC; DAM MST, POET; PC 6; WLC**
    See also CDBLB 1832-1890; DLB 32
Teran, Lisa St. Aubin de .... **CLC 36**
    See also St. Aubin de Teran, Lisa
Terence [195(?)B.C.-159B.C.]**CMLC 14; DC 7**

Teresa de Jesus, St. [1515-1582] .... **LC 18**
Terkel, Louis [1912-]
    See Terkel, Studs
    See also CA 57-60; CANR 18, 45, 67; MTCW
Terkel, Studs .... **CLC 38**
    See also Terkel, Louis
    See also AITN 1
Terry, C. V.
    See Slaughter, Frank G(ill)
Terry, Megan [1932-] .... **CLC 19**
    See also CA 77-80; CABS 3; CANR 43; DLB 7
Tertullian [c. 155-c. 245] .... **CMLC 29**
Tertz, Abram
    See Sinyavsky, Andrei (Donatevich)
Tesich, Steve [1943(?)-1996] .... **CLC 40, 69**
    See also CA 105; 152; DLBY 83
Teternikov, Fyodor Kuzmich [1863-1927]
    See Sologub, Fyodor
    See also CA 104
Tevis, Walter [1928-1984] .... **CLC 42**
    See also CA 113
Tey, Josephine .... **TCLC 14**
    See also Mackintosh, Elizabeth
    See also DLB 77
Thackeray, William Makepeace [1811-1863] **NCLC 5, 14, 22, 43; DA; DAB; DAC; DAM MST, NOV; WLC**
    See also CDBLB 1832-1890; DLB 21, 55, 159, 163; SATA 23
Thakura, Ravindranatha
    See Tagore, Rabindranath
Tharoor, Shashi [1956-] .... **CLC 70**
    See also CA 141
Thelwell, Michael Miles [1939-] .... **CLC 22**
    See also BW 2; CA 101
Theobald, Lewis, Jr.
    See Lovecraft, H(oward) P(hillips)
Theodorescu, Ion N. [1880-1967]
    See Arghezi, Tudor
    See also CA 116
Theriault, Yves [1915-1983] . **CLC 79; DAC; DAM MST**
    See also CA 102; DLB 88
Theroux, Alexander (Louis) [1939-]**CLC 2, 25**
    See also CA 85-88; CANR 20, 63
Theroux, Paul (Edward) [1941-]**CLC 5, 8, 11, 15, 28, 46; DAM POP**
    See also BEST 89:4; CA 33-36R; CANR 20, 45; DLB 2; MTCW; SATA 44
Thesen, Sharon [1946-] .... **CLC 56**
    See also CA 163
Thevenin, Denis
    See Duhamel, Georges
Thibault, Jacques Anatole Francois [1844-1924]
    See France, Anatole
    See also CA 106; 127; DAM NOV; MTCW
Thiele, Colin (Milton) [1920-] .... **CLC 17**
    See also CA 29-32R; CANR 12, 28, 53; CLR 27; MAICYA; SAAS 2; SATA 14, 72
Thomas, Audrey (Callahan) [1935-] . **CLC 7, 13, 37, 107; SSC 20**
    See also AITN 2; CA 21-24R; CAAS 19; CANR 36, 58; DLB 60; MTCW
Thomas, D(onald) M(ichael) [1935-]**CLC 13, 22, 31**
    See also CA 61-64; CAAS 11; CANR 17, 45; CDBLB 1960 to Present; DLB 40; INT CANR-17; MTCW
Thomas, Dylan (Marlais) [1914-1953] **T C L C 1, 8, 45; DA; DAB; DAC; DAM DRAM, MST, POET; PC 2; SSC 3; WLC**
    See also CA 104; 120; CANR 65; CDBLB 1945-1960; DLB 13, 20, 139; MTCW; SATA 60
Thomas, (Philip) Edward [1878-1917]**T C L C 10; DAM POET**

Truffaut, Francois [1932-1984] **CLC 20, 101**
See also CA 81-84; 113; CANR 34

Trumbo, Dalton [1905-1976] .... **CLC 19**
See also CA 21-24R; 69-72; CANR 10; DLB 26

Trumbull, John [1750-1831] .... **NCLC 30**
See also DLB 31

Trundlett, Helen B.
See Eliot, T(homas) S(tearns)

Tryon, Thomas [1926-1991]**CLC 3, 11; DAM POP**
See also AITN 1; CA 29-32R; 135; CANR 32; MTCW

Tryon, Tom
See Tryon, Thomas

Ts'ao Hsueh-ch'in [1715(?)-1763].......... **LC 1**

Tsushima, Shuji [1909-1948]
See Dazai Osamu
See also CA 107

Tsvetaeva (Efron), Marina (Ivanovna) [1892-1941] ....
TCLC 7, 35; PC 14
See also CA 104; 128; MTCW

Tuck, Lily [1938-] .... **CLC 70**
See also CA 139

Tu Fu [712-770] .... **PC 9**
See also DAM MULT

Tunis, John R(oberts) [1889-1975] ... **CLC 12**
See also CA 61-64; CANR 62; DLB 22, 171; JRDA; MAICYA; SATA 37; SATA-Brief 30

Tuohy, Frank .... **CLC 37**
See also Tuohy, John Francis
See also DLB 14, 139

Tuohy, John Francis [1925-]
See Tuohy, Frank
See also CA 5-8R; CANR 3, 47

Turco, Lewis (Putnam) [1934-] ... **CLC 11, 63**
See also CA 13-16R; CAAS 22; CANR 24, 51; DLBY 84

Turgenev, Ivan [1818-1883] .. **NCLC 21; DA; DAB; DAC; DAM MST, NOV; DC 7; SSC 7; WLC**

Turgot, Anne-Robert-Jacques [1727-1781]**LC 26**

Turner, Frederick [1943-] .... **CLC 48**
See also CA 73-76; CAAS 10; CANR 12, 30, 56; DLB 40

Tutu, Desmond M(pilo) [1931-]**CLC 80; BLC 3; DAM MULT**
See also BW 1; CA 125; CANR 67

Tutuola, Amos [1920-1997] ... **CLC 5, 14, 29; BLC 3; DAM MULT**
See also BW 2; CA 9-12R; 159; CANR 27, 66; DLB 125; MTCW

Twain, MarkTCLC **6, 12, 19, 36, 48, 59; SSC 6, 26; WLC**
See also Clemens, Samuel Langhorne
See also AAYA 20; DLB 11, 12, 23, 64, 74

Tyler, Anne [1941-]**CLC 7, 11, 18, 28, 44, 59, 103; DAM NOV, POP**
See also AAYA 18; BEST 89:1; CA 9-12R; CANR 11, 33, 53; DLB 6, 143; DLBY 82; MTCW; SATA 7, 90

Tyler, Royall [1757-1826] .... **NCLC 3**
See also DLB 37

Tynan, Katharine [1861-1931] .... **TCLC 3**
See also CA 104; DLB 153

Tyutchev, Fyodor [1803-1873] .... **NCLC 34**

Tzara, Tristan [1896-1963].... **CLC 47; DAM POET**
See also CA 153; 89-92

Uhry, Alfred [1936-] **CLC 55; DAM DRAM, POP**
See also CA 127; 133; INT 133

Ulf, Haerved
See Strindberg, (Johan) August

Ulf, Harved

See Strindberg, (Johan) August

Ulibarri, Sabine R(eyes) [1919-] ..... **CLC 83; DAM MULT**
See also CA 131; DLB 82; HW

Unamuno (y Jugo), Miguel de [1864-1936]
TCLC 2, 9; DAM MULT, NOV; HLC; SSC 11
See also CA 104; 131; DLB 108; HW; MTCW

Undercliffe, Errol
See Campbell, (John) Ramsey

Underwood, Miles
See Glassco, John

Undset, Sigrid [1882-1949] ..... **TCLC 3; DA; DAB; DAC; DAM MST, NOV; WLC**
See also CA 104; 129; MTCW

Ungaretti, Giuseppe [1888-1970]**CLC 7, 11, 15**
See also CA 19-20; 25-28R; CAP 2; DLB 114

Unger, Douglas [1952-] .... **CLC 34**
See also CA 130

Unsworth, Barry (Forster) [1930-] ..**CLC 76**
See also CA 25-28R; CANR 30, 54; DLB 194

Updike, John (Hoyer) [1932-]**CLC 1, 2, 3, 5, 7, 9, 13, 15, 23, 34, 43, 70; DA; DAB; DAC; DAM MST, NOV, POET, POP; SSC 13, 27; WLC**
See also CA 1-4R; CABS 1; CANR 4, 33, 51; CDALB 1968-1988; DLB 2, 5, 143; DLBD 3; DLBY 80, 82, 97; MTCW

Upshaw, Margaret Mitchell
See Mitchell, Margaret (Munnerlyn)

Upton, Mark
See Sanders, Lawrence

Urdang, Constance (Henriette) [1922-] **C L C 47**
See also CA 21-24R; CANR 9, 24

Uriel, Henry
See Faust, Frederick (Schiller)

Uris, Leon (Marcus) [1924-]**CLC 7, 32; DAM NOV, POP**
See also AITN 1, 2; BEST 89:2; CA 1-4R; CANR 1, 40, 65; MTCW; SATA 49

Urmuz
See Codrescu, Andrei

Urquhart, Jane [1949-] .... **CLC 90; DAC**
See also CA 113; CANR 32, 68

Ustinov, Peter (Alexander) [1921-] ..... **CLC 1**
See also AITN 1; CA 13-16R; CANR 25, 51; DLB 13

U Tam'si, Gerald Felix Tchicaya
See Tchicaya, Gerald Felix

U Tam'si, Tchicaya
See Tchicaya, Gerald Felix

Vachss, Andrew (Henry) [1942-] .... **CLC 106**
See also CA 118; CANR 44

Vachss, Andrew H.
See Vachss, Andrew (Henry)

Vaculik, Ludvik [1926-] .... **CLC 7**
See also CA 53-56

Vaihinger, Hans [1852-1933] .... **TCLC 71**
See also CA 116; 166

Valdez, Luis (Miguel) [1940-] **CLC 84; DAM MULT; HLC**
See also CA 101; CANR 32; DLB 122; HW

Valenzuela, Luisa [1938-]**CLC 31, 104; DAM MULT; SSC 14**
See also CA 101; CANR 32, 65; DLB 113; HW

Valera y Alcala-Galiano, Juan [1824-1905]
TCLC 10
See also CA 106

Valery, (Ambroise) Paul (Toussaint Jules) [1871-1945]**TCLC 4, 15; DAM POET; PC 9**
See also CA 104; 122; MTCW

Valle-Inclan, Ramon (Maria) del [1866-1936]
TCLC 5; DAM MULT; HLC
See also CA 106; 153; DLB 134

Vallejo, Antonio Buero

See Buero Vallejo, Antonio

Vallejo, Cesar (Abraham) [1892-1938]**T C L C 3, 56; DAM MULT; HLC**
See also CA 105; 153; HW

Vallette, Marguerite Eymery
See Rachilde

Valle Y Pena, Ramon del
See Valle-Inclan, Ramon (Maria) del

Van Ash, Cay [1918-] .... **CLC 34**

Vanbrugh, Sir John [1664-1726]**LC 21; DAM DRAM**
See also DLB 80

Van Campen, Karl
See Campbell, John W(ood, Jr.)

Vance, Gerald
See Silverberg, Robert

Vance, Jack .... **CLC 35**
See also Kuttner, Henry; Vance, John Holbrook
See also DLB 8

Vance, John Holbrook [1916-]
See Queen, Ellery; Vance, Jack
See also CA 29-32R; CANR 17, 65; MTCW

Van Den Bogarde, Derek Jules Gaspard Ulric Niven [1921-]
See Bogarde, Dirk
See also CA 77-80

Vandenburgh, Jane .... **CLC 59**

Vanderhaeghe, Guy [1951-] .... **CLC 41**
See also CA 113

van der Post, Laurens (Jan) [1906-1996]**CLC 5**
See also CA 5-8R; 155; CANR 35

van de Wetering, Janwillem [1931-] **CLC 47**
See also CA 49-52; CANR 4, 62

Van Dine, S. S. .... **TCLC 23**
See also Wright, Willard Huntington

Van Doren, Carl (Clinton) [1885-1950]**TCLC 18**
See also CA 111

Van Doren, Mark [1894-1972] ...... **CLC 6, 10**
See also CA 1-4R; 37-40R; CANR 3; DLB 45; MTCW

Van Druten, John (William) [1901-1957]
TCLC 2
See also CA 104; 161; DLB 10

Van Duyn, Mona (Jane) [1921-]**CLC 3, 7, 63; DAM POET**
See also CA 9-12R; CANR 7, 38, 60; DLB 5

Van Dyne, Edith
See Baum, L(yman) Frank

van Itallie, Jean-Claude [1936-] .... **CLC 3**
See also CA 45-48; CAAS 2; CANR 1, 48; DLB 7

van Ostaijen, Paul [1896-1928] ...... **TCLC 33**
See also CA 163

Van Peebles, Melvin [1932-]**CLC 2, 20; DAM MULT**
See also BW 2; CA 85-88; CANR 27, 67

Vansittart, Peter [1920-] .... **CLC 42**
See also CA 1-4R; CANR 3, 49

Van Vechten, Carl [1880-1964] .... **CLC 33**
See also CA 89-92; DLB 4, 9, 51

Van Vogt, A(lfred) E(lton) [1912-] ...... **CLC 1**
See also CA 21-24R; CANR 28; DLB 8; SATA 14

Varda, Agnes [1928-] .... **CLC 16**
See also CA 116; 122

Vargas Llosa, (Jorge) Mario (Pedro) [1936-]
CLC 3, 6, 9, 10, 15, 31, 42, 85; DA; DAB; DAC; DAM MST, MULT, NOV; HLC
See also CA 73-76; CANR 18, 32, 42, 67; DLB 145; HW; MTCW

Vasiliu, Gheorghe [1881-1957]
See Bacovia, George
See also CA 123

Vassa, Gustavus
See Equiano, Olaudah

NOV, POP
See also AITN 1; CA 1-4R; 132; CAAS 1; CANR 1, 27; INT CANR-27; MTCW
Wallant, Edward Lewis [1926-1962] **CLC 5, 10**
See also CA 1-4R; CANR 22; DLB 2, 28, 143; MTCW
Walley, Byron
See Card, Orson Scott
Walpole, Horace [1717-1797] .... **LC 2**
See also DLB 39, 104
Walpole, Hugh (Seymour) [1884-1941] **TCLC 5**
See also CA 104; 165; DLB 34
Walser, Martin [1927-] .... **CLC 27**
See also CA 57-60; CANR 8, 46; DLB 75, 124
Walser, Robert [1878-1956] **TCLC 18; SSC 20**
See also CA 118; 165; DLB 66
Walsh, Jill Paton .... **CLC 35**
See Paton Walsh, Gillian
See also AAYA 11; CLR 2; DLB 161; SAAS 3
Walter, Villiam Christian
See Andersen, Hans Christian
Wambaugh, Joseph (Aloysius, Jr.) [1937-] **CLC 3, 18; DAM NOV, POP**
See also AITN 1; BEST 89:3; CA 33-36R; CANR 42, 65; DLB 6; DLBY 83; MTCW
Wang Wei [699(?)-761(?)] .... **PC 18**
Ward, Arthur Henry Sarsfield [1883-1959]
See Rohmer, Sax
See also CA 108
Ward, Douglas Turner [1930-] .... **CLC 19**
See also BW 1; CA 81-84; CANR 27; DLB 7, 38
Ward, Mary Augusta
See Ward, Mrs. Humphry
Ward, Mrs. Humphry [1851-1920] **TCLC 55**
See also DLB 18
Ward, Peter
See Faust, Frederick (Schiller)
Warhol, Andy [1928(?)-1987] .... **CLC 20**
See also AAYA 12; BEST 89:4; CA 89-92; 121; CANR 34
Warner, Francis (Robert le Plastrier) [1937-] **CLC 14**
See also CA 53-56; CANR 11
Warner, Marina [1946-] .... **CLC 59**
See also CA 65-68; CANR 21, 55; DLB 194
Warner, Rex (Ernest) [1905-1986] ... **CLC 45**
See also CA 89-92; 119; DLB 15
Warner, Susan (Bogert) [1819-1885] **NCLC 31**
See also DLB 3, 42
Warner, Sylvia (Constance) Ashton
See Ashton-Warner, Sylvia (Constance)
Warner, Sylvia Townsend [1893-1978] **CLC 7, 19; SSC 23**
See also CA 61-64; 77-80; CANR 16, 60; DLB 34, 139; MTCW
Warren, Mercy Otis [1728-1814] ... **NCLC 13**
See also DLB 31, 200
Warren, Robert Penn [1905-1989] **CLC 1, 4, 6, 8, 10, 13, 18, 39, 53, 59; DA; DAB; DAC; DAM MST, NOV, POET; SSC 4; WLC**
See also AITN 1; CA 13-16R; 129; CANR 10, 47; CDALB 1968-1988; DLB 2, 48, 152; DLBY 80, 89; INT CANR-10; MTCW; SATA 46; SATA-Obit 63
Warshofsky, Isaac
See Singer, Isaac Bashevis
Warton, Thomas [1728-1790] .. **LC 15; DAM POET**
See also DLB 104, 109
Waruk, Kona
See Harris, (Theodore) Wilson
Warung, Price [1855-1911] .... **TCLC 45**
Warwick, Jarvis
See Garner, Hugh

Washington, Alex
See Harris, Mark
Washington, Booker T(aliaferro) [1856-1915] **TCLC 10; BLC 3; DAM MULT**
See also BW 1; CA 114; 125; SATA 28
Washington, George [1732-1799] .... **LC 25**
See also DLB 31
Wassermann, (Karl) Jakob [1873-1934] **TCLC 6**
See also CA 104; DLB 66
Wasserstein, Wendy [1950-] **CLC 32, 59, 90; DAM DRAM; DC 4**
See also CA 121; 129; CABS 3; CANR 53; INT 129; SATA 94
Waterhouse, Keith (Spencer) [1929-] **CLC 47**
See also CA 5-8R; CANR 38, 67; DLB 13, 15; MTCW
Waters, Frank (Joseph) [1902-1995] **CLC 88**
See also CA 5-8R; 149; CAAS 13; CANR 3, 18, 63; DLBY 86
Waters, Roger [1944-] .... **CLC 35**
Watkins, Frances Ellen
See Harper, Frances Ellen Watkins
Watkins, Gerrold
See Malzberg, Barry N(athaniel)
Watkins, Gloria [1955(?)-]
See hooks, bell
See also BW 2; CA 143
Watkins, Paul [1964-] .... **CLC 55**
See also CA 132; CANR 62
Watkins, Vernon Phillips [1906-1967] **CLC 43**
See also CA 9-10; 25-28R; CAP 1; DLB 20
Watson, Irving S.
See Mencken, H(enry) L(ouis)
Watson, John H.
See Farmer, Philip Jose
Watson, Richard F.
See Silverberg, Robert
Waugh, Auberon (Alexander) [1939-] **CLC 7**
See also CA 45-48; CANR 6, 22; DLB 14, 194
Waugh, Evelyn (Arthur St. John) [1903-1966] **CLC 1, 3, 8, 13, 19, 27, 44, 107; DA; DAB; DAC; DAM MST, NOV, POP; WLC**
See also CA 85-88; 25-28R; CANR 22; CDBLB 1914-1945; DLB 15, 162, 195; MTCW
Waugh, Harriet [1944-] .... **CLC 6**
See also CA 85-88; CANR 22
Ways, C. R.
See Blount, Roy (Alton), Jr.
Waystaff, Simon
See Swift, Jonathan
Webb, (Martha) Beatrice (Potter) [1858-1943] **TCLC 22**
See also Potter, (Helen) Beatrix
See also CA 117
Webb, Charles (Richard) [1939-] .... **CLC 7**
See also CA 25-28R
Webb, James H(enry), Jr. [1946-] .... **CLC 22**
See also CA 81-84
Webb, Mary (Gladys Meredith) [1881-1927] **TCLC 24**
See also CA 123; DLB 34
Webb, Mrs. Sidney
See Webb, (Martha) Beatrice (Potter)
Webb, Phyllis [1927-] .... **CLC 18**
See also CA 104; CANR 23; DLB 53
Webb, Sidney (James) [1859-1947] **TCLC 22**
See also CA 117; 163; DLB 190
Webber, Andrew Lloyd .... **CLC 21**
See also Lloyd Webber, Andrew
Weber, Lenora Mattingly [1895-1971] **CLC 12**
See also CA 19-20; 29-32R; CAP 1; SATA 2; SATA-Obit 26
Weber, Max [1864-1920] .... **TCLC 69**
See also CA 109
Webster, John [1579(?)-1634(?)] **LC 33; DA; DAB; DAC; DAM DRAM, MST; DC 2;**

WLC
See also CDBLB Before 1660; DLB 58
Webster, Noah [1758-1843] .... **NCLC 30**
Wedekind, (Benjamin) Frank(lin) [1864-1918] **TCLC 7; DAM DRAM**
See also CA 104; 153; DLB 118
Weidman, Jerome [1913-] .... **CLC 7**
See also AITN 2; CA 1-4R; CANR 1; DLB 28
Weil, Simone (Adolphine) [1909-1943] **TCLC 23**
See also CA 117; 159
Weinstein, Nathan
See West, Nathanael
Weinstein, Nathan von Wallenstein
See West, Nathanael
Weir, Peter (Lindsay) [1944-] .... **CLC 20**
See also CA 113; 123
Weiss, Peter (Ulrich) [1916-1982] **CLC 3, 15, 51; DAM DRAM**
See also CA 45-48; 106; CANR 3; DLB 69, 124
Weiss, Theodore (Russell) [1916-] **CLC 3, 8, 14**
See also CA 9-12R; CAAS 2; CANR 46; DLB 5
Welch, (Maurice) Denton [1915-1948] **TCLC 22**
See also CA 121; 148
Welch, James [1940-] .. **CLC 6, 14, 52; DAM MULT, POP**
See also CA 85-88; CANR 42, 66; DLB 175; NNAL
Weldon, Fay [1931-] **CLC 6, 9, 11, 19, 36, 59; DAM POP**
See also CA 21-24R; CANR 16, 46, 63; CDBLB 1960 to Present; DLB 14, 194; INT CANR-16; MTCW
Wellek, Rene [1903-1995] .... **CLC 28**
See also CA 5-8R; 150; CAAS 7; CANR 8; DLB 63; INT CANR-8
Weller, Michael [1942-] .... **CLC 10, 53**
See also CA 85-88
Weller, Paul [1958-] .... **CLC 26**
Wellershoff, Dieter [1925-] .... **CLC 46**
See also CA 89-92; CANR 16, 37
Welles, (George) Orson [1915-1985] **CLC 20, 80**
See also CA 93-96; 117
Wellman, John McDowell [1945-]
See Wellman, Mac
See also CA 166
Wellman, Mac [1945-] .... **CLC 65**
See also Wellman, John McDowell; Wellman, John McDowell
Wellman, Manly Wade [1903-1986] . **CLC 49**
See also CA 1-4R; 118; CANR 6, 16, 44; SATA 6; SATA-Obit 47
Wells, Carolyn [1869(?)-1942] .... **TCLC 35**
See also CA 113; DLB 11
Wells, H(erbert) G(eorge) [1866-1946] **TCLC 6, 12, 19; DA; DAB; DAC; DAM MST, NOV; SSC 6; WLC**
See also AAYA 18; CA 110; 121; CDBLB 1914-1945; DLB 34, 70, 156, 178; MTCW; SATA 20
Wells, Rosemary [1943-] .... **CLC 12**
See also AAYA 13; CA 85-88; CANR 48; CLR 16; MAICYA; SAAS 1; SATA 18, 69
Welty, Eudora [1909-] **CLC 1, 2, 5, 14, 22, 33, 105; DA; DAB; DAC; DAM MST, NOV; SSC 1, 27; WLC**
See also CA 9-12R; CABS 1; CANR 32, 65; CDALB 1941-1968; DLB 2, 102, 143; DLBD 12; DLBY 87; MTCW
Wen I-to [1899-1946] .... **TCLC 28**
Wentworth, Robert
See Hamilton, Edmond
Werfel, Franz (Viktor) [1890-1945] **TCLC 8**
See also CA 104; 161; DLB 81, 124

See also AITN 2; CA 49-52; 97-100; CANR 4, 34, 64; DLB 5, 169; MTCW

Wright, Judith (Arandell) [1915-]CLC 11, 53; PC 14
See also CA 13-16R; CANR 31; MTCW; SATA 14

Wright, L(aurali) R. [1939-] .... CLC 44
See also CA 138

Wright, Richard (Nathaniel) [1908-1960] CLC 1, 3, 4, 9, 14, 21, 48, 74; BLC 3; DA; DAB; DAC; DAM MST, MULT, NOV; SSC 2; WLC
See also AAYA 5; BW 1; CA 108; CANR 64; CDALB 1929-1941; DLB 76, 102; DLBD 2; MTCW

Wright, Richard B(ruce) [1937-] .... CLC 6
See also CA 85-88; DLB 53

Wright, Rick [1945-] .... CLC 35

Wright, Rowland
See Wells, Carolyn

Wright, Stephen [1946-] .... CLC 33

Wright, Willard Huntington [1888-1939]
See Van Dine, S. S.
See also CA 115; DLBD 16

Wright, William [1930-]..................... CLC 44
See also CA 53-56; CANR 7, 23

Wroth, LadyMary [1587-1653(?)] .... LC 30
See also DLB 121

Wu Ch'eng-en [1500(?)-1582(?)] .... LC 7

Wu Ching-tzu [1701-1754] .... LC 2

Wurlitzer, Rudolph [1938(?)-].. CLC 2, 4, 15
See also CA 85-88; DLB 173

Wycherley, William [1641-1715] ... LC 8, 21; DAM DRAM
See also CDBLB 1660-1789; DLB 80

Wylie, Elinor (Morton Hoyt) [1885-1928] TCLC 8; PC 23
See also CA 105; 162; DLB 9, 45

Wylie, Philip (Gordon) [1902-1971]. CLC 43
See also CA 21-22; 33-36R; CAP 2; DLB 9

Wyndham, John .... CLC 19
See also Harris, John (Wyndham Parkes Lucas) Beynon

Wyss, Johann David Von [1743-1818] N C L C 10
See also JRDA; MAICYA; SATA 29; SATA-Brief 27

Xenophon [c. 430B.C.-c. 354B.C.] CMLC 17
See also DLB 176

Yakumo Koizumi
See Hearn, (Patricio) Lafcadio (Tessima Carlos)

Yanez, Jose Donoso
See Donoso (Yanez), Jose

Yanovsky, Basile S.
See Yanovsky, V(assily) S(emenovich)

Yanovsky, V(assily) S(emenovich) [1906-1989] CLC 2, 18
See also CA 97-100; 129

Yates, Richard [1926-1992] ...... CLC 7, 8, 23
See also CA 5-8R; 139; CANR 10, 43; DLB 2; DLBY 81, 92; INT CANR-10

Yeats, W. B.
See Yeats, William Butler

Yeats, William Butler [1865-1939]TCLC 1, 11, 18, 31; DA; DAB; DAC; DAM DRAM, MST, POET; PC 20; WLC
See also CA 104; 127; CANR 45; CDBLB 1890-1914; DLB 10, 19, 98, 156; MTCW

Yehoshua, A(braham) B. [1936-] CLC 13, 31
See also CA 33-36R; CANR 43

Yep, Laurence Michael [1948-] .... CLC 35
See also AAYA 5; CA 49-52; CANR 1, 46; CLR 3, 17; DLB 52; JRDA; MAICYA; SATA 7, 69

Yerby, Frank G(arvin) [1916-1991]CLC 1, 7, 22; BLC 3; DAM MULT
See also BW 1; CA 9-12R; 136; CANR 16, 52;

DLB 76; INT CANR-16; MTCW

Yesenin, Sergei Alexandrovich
See Esenin, Sergei (Alexandrovich)

Yevtushenko, Yevgeny (Alexandrovich) [1933-] .... CLC 1, 3, 13, 26, 51; DAM POET
See also CA 81-84; CANR 33, 54; MTCW

Yezierska, Anzia [1885(?)-1970] .... CLC 46
See also CA 126; 89-92; DLB 28; MTCW

Yglesias, Helen [1915-] .... CLC 7, 22
See also CA 37-40R; CAAS 20; CANR 15, 65; INT CANR-15; MTCW

Yokomitsu Riichi [1898-1947] .... TCLC 47

Yonge, Charlotte (Mary) [1823-1901] T C L C 48
See also CA 109; 163; DLB 18, 163; SATA 17

York, Jeremy
See Creasey, John

York, Simon
See Heinlein, Robert A(nson)

Yorke, Henry Vincent [1905-1974] ... CLC 13
See also Green, Henry
See also CA 85-88; 49-52

Yosano Akiko [1878-1942] . TCLC 59; PC 11
See also CA 161

Yoshimoto, Banana .... CLC 84
See also Yoshimoto, Mahoko

Yoshimoto, Mahoko [1964-]
See Yoshimoto, Banana
See also CA 144

Young, Al(bert James) [1939-] CLC 19; BLC 3; DAM MULT
See also BW 2; CA 29-32R; CANR 26, 65; DLB 33

Young, Andrew (John) [1885-1971] ... CLC 5
See also CA 5-8R; CANR 7, 29

Young, Collier
See Bloch, Robert (Albert)

Young, Edward [1683-1765]............ LC 3, 40
See also DLB 95

Young, Marguerite (Vivian) [1909-1995]C L C 82
See also CA 13-16; 150; CAP 1

Young, Neil [1945-] .... CLC 17
See also CA 110

Young Bear, Ray A. [1950-] ... CLC 94; DAM MULT
See also CA 146; DLB 175; NNAL

Yourcenar, Marguerite [1903-1987] CLC 19, 38, 50, 87; DAM NOV
See also CA 69-72; CANR 23, 60; DLB 72; DLBY 88; MTCW

Yurick, Sol [1925-] .... CLC 6
See also CA 13-16R; CANR 25

Zabolotsky, Nikolai Alekseevich [1903-1958] TCLC 52
See also CA 116; 164

Zamiatin, Yevgenii
See Zamyatin, Evgeny Ivanovich

Zamora, Bernice (B. Ortiz) [1938-] CLC 89; DAM MULT; HLC
See also CA 151; DLB 82; HW

Zamyatin, Evgeny Ivanovich [1884-1937] TCLC 8, 37
See also CA 105; 166

Zangwill, Israel [1864-1926] .... TCLC 16
See also CA 109; DLB 10, 135, 197

Zappa, Francis Vincent, Jr. [1940-1993]
See Zappa, Frank
See also CA 108; 143; CANR 57

Zappa, Frank .... CLC 17
See also Zappa, Francis Vincent, Jr.

Zaturenska, Marya [1902-1982] ... CLC 6, 11
See also CA 13-16R; 105; CANR 22

Zeami [1363-1443] .... DC 7

Zelazny, Roger (Joseph) [1937-1995]CLC 21
See also AAYA 7; CA 21-24R; 148; CANR 26, 60; DLB 8; MTCW; SATA 57; SATA-Brief

39

Zhdanov, Andrei A(lexandrovich) [1896-1948] TCLC 18
See also CA 117

Zhukovsky, Vasily [1783-1852] ...... NCLC 35

Ziegenhagen, Eric .... CLC 55

Zimmer, Jill Schary
See Robinson, Jill

Zimmerman, Robert
See Dylan, Bob

Zindel, Paul [1936-] ... CLC 6, 26; DA; DAB; DAC; DAM DRAM, MST, NOV; DC 5
See also AAYA 2; CA 73-76; CANR 31, 65; CLR 3, 45; DLB 7, 52; JRDA; MAICYA; MTCW; SATA 16, 58

Zinov'Ev, A. A.
See Zinoviev, Alexander (Aleksandrovich)

Zinoviev, Alexander (Aleksandrovich) [1922-] CLC 19
See also CA 116; 133; CAAS 10

Zoilus
See Lovecraft, H(oward) P(hillips)

Zola, Emile (Edouard Charles Antoine) [1840-1902] ......
TCLC 1, 6, 21, 41; DA; DAB; DAC; DAM MST, NOV; WLC
See also CA 104; 138; DLB 123

Zoline, Pamela [1941-] .... CLC 62
See also CA 161

Zorrilla y Moral, Jose [1817-1893] . NCLC 6

Zoshchenko, Mikhail (Mikhailovich) [1895-1958] .... TCLC 15; SSC 15
See also CA 115; 160

Zuckmayer, Carl [1896-1977] .... CLC 18
See also CA 69-72; DLB 56, 124

Zuk, Georges
See Skelton, Robin

Zukofsky, Louis [1904-1978]CLC 1, 2, 4, 7, 11, 18; DAM POET; PC 11
See also CA 9-12R; 77-80; CANR 39; DLB 5, 165; MTCW

Zweig, Paul [1935-1984] .... CLC 34, 42
See also CA 85-88; 113

Zweig, Stefan [1881-1942] .... TCLC 17
See also CA 112; DLB 81, 118

Zwingli, Huldreich [1484-1531] .... LC 37
See also DLB 179

Literary Criticism Series
Cumulative Topic Index

This index lists all topic entries in Gale's *Classical and Medieval Literature Criticism, Contemporary Literary Criticism, Literature Criticism from 1400 to 1800, Nineteenth-Century Literature Criticism,* and *Twentieth-Century Literary Criticism.*

Topic Index

Topic Index

Topic Index

Topic Index

Twentieth-Century Literary Criticism
Cumulative Nationality Index